D0132443

Our Sexuality

SEVENTH EDITION

Our Sexuality

SEVENTH EDITION

ROBERT CROOKS

KARLA BAUR

Brooks/Cole Publishing Company

I(T)P® An International Thomson Publishing Company

Pacific Grove • Albany • Belmont • Bonn • Boston • Cincinnati • Detroit • Johannesburg • London • Madrid
Melbourne • Mexico City • New York • Paris • Singapore • Tokyo • Toronto • Washington

Sponsoring Editor: *Marianne Taflinger*
Project Development Editor: *Jim Strandberg*
Marketing Manager: *Michael Campbell*
Editorial Assistants: *Scott Brearton, Rachael Bruckman*
Advertising Communications: *Jean Thompson*
Production Coordinator: *Kirk Bomont*
Project Management: *Greg Hubit*
Manuscript Editor: *Linda Purrington*
Permissions Editor: *Mary Kay Hancharick*
Interior and Cover Design: *Roy R. Neuhaus*
Illustrations: *Rolin Graphics*
Cover Photograph: *Digital Vision, PhotoDisc*
Art Editor: *Lisa Torri*
Photo Researcher: *Roberta Spieckerman*
Composition and Prepress: *GTS Graphics, Inc.*
Printing and Binding: *R. R. Donnelley, Roanoke*

For more information, contact:

BROOKS/COLE PUBLISHING COMPANY
511 Forest Lodge Road
Pacific Grove, CA 93950
USA

International Thomson Publishing Europe
Berkshire House 168-173
High Holborn
London, WC1V 7AA
England

Thomas Nelson Australia
102 Dodds Street
South Melbourne, 3205
Victoria, Australia

Nelson Canada
1120 Birchmount Road
Scarborough, Ontario
Canada M1K 5G4

International Thomson Editores
Seneca 53
Col. Polanco
11560 México, D. F., México

International Thomson Publishing GmbH
Königswinterer Strasse 418
53227 Bonn
Germany

International Thomson Publishing Asia
60 Albert Street
#15-01 Albert Complex
Singapore 189969

International Thomson Publishing Japan
Hirakawacho Kyowa Building, 3F
2-2-1 Hirakawacho
Chiyoda-ku, Tokyo 102
Japan

Printed in the United States of America

10 9 8 7 6 5 4

Library of Congress Cataloging-in-Publication Data

Crooks, Robert
Our sexuality / Robert Crooks, Karla Baur. — 7th ed.
p. cm.
Includes bibliographical references (p. 633) and indexes.
ISBN 0-534-35467-X
1. Sex 2. Sex customs—United States. I. Baur, Karla.
II. Title.
HQ21.C698 1999
306.7—dc21 98-26371

For our loving spouses,
Sami Tucker and Jim Hicks

About the Authors

The integration of psychological, social, and biological components of human sexuality in this text is facilitated by the blending of the authors' academic and professional backgrounds. Robert Crooks has a Ph.D. in psychology. His graduate training stressed clinical and physiological psychology. In addition, he has considerable background in sociology, which served as his minor throughout his graduate training. His involvement with teaching human sexuality classes at the university and college level spans two decades.

Karla Baur has a master's degree in social work; her advanced academic work stressed clinical training. She is a licensed clinical social worker with a specialty in sex therapy. Karla has been certified as a sex educator, therapist, and sex therapy supervisor by the American Association of Sex Educators, Counselors, and Therapists. She has instructed sexuality classes at several colleges and universities and provides training for other mental health professionals.

The authors have a combined total of 51 years of teaching, counseling, and research in the field of human sexuality. Together they taught sexuality courses at Portland Community College for a number of years. They present workshops and guest lectures to a wide variety of professional and community groups, and they counsel individuals, couples, and families on sexual concerns. Their combined teaching, clinical, and research experiences, together with their graduate training, have provided them with an appreciation and sensitive understanding of the highly complex and personal nature of human sexuality.

It is the authors' belief that a truly sensitive understanding of our sexuality must be grounded in *both* the female and the male perspectives and experiences. In this sense, their courses, their students, and this text have benefited from a well-balanced perception and a deep appreciation of human sexual behavior.

Brief Contents

Contents

Chapter 5 Male Sexual Anatomy and Physiology 115

Chapter 6 Sexual Arousal and Response 141

PART THREE SEXUAL BEHAVIOR 179

Chapter 7 Love and the Development of Sexual Relationships 179

Chapter 8 Communication in Sexual Behavior 211

Chapter 9 Sexual Behaviors 241

Chapter 10 Sexual Orientations 269

PART THREE SEXUALITY AND THE LIFE CYCLE 301

Chapter 11 Contraception 301

Chapter 12 Conceiving Children: Process and Choice 339

Chapter 13 Sexuality During Childhood and Adolescence 379

Chapter 14 Sexuality and the Adult Years 409

PART SIX SOCIAL ISSUES 543

Chapter 18 Atypical Sexual Behavior 543

Chapter 19 Sexual Victimization 567

Preface

Our Sexuality, now in its seventh edition, offers a comprehensive and academically sound introduction to the biological, psychosocial, behavioral, and cultural aspects of sexuality in a personally meaningful way. The warm and enthusiastic response to the earlier editions has been gratifying and has inspired us to provide you with an even more effective learning tool for you and your students.

A Bolder, Brighter Seventh Edition

- **On the Edge** boxes, a feature new to this edition, address challenging and controversial questions concerning sexuality at the turn of the twenty-first century. Topics include: Should sex reassignment surgery be permitted for teenagers? Should prostate cancer be treated? Is an affair in cyberspace a real affair? Should gay marriage be legalized? Nearly every chapter of the seventh edition includes an On the Edge box, and these will provide stimulating reading as well as excellent starters for class discussion.

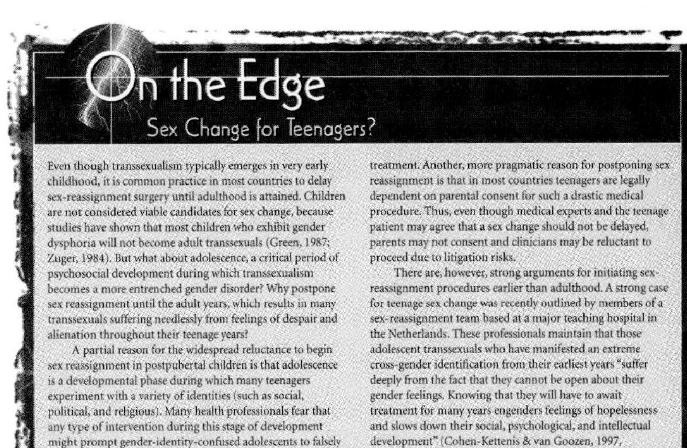

On the Edge

Sex Change for Teenagers?

Even though transsexualism typically emerges in very early childhood, it is common practice in most countries to delay sex-reassignment surgery until adulthood is attained. Children are not considered viable candidates for sex change, because studies have shown that most children who exhibit gender dysphoria will not become adult transsexuals (Green, 1987; Zuger, 1984). But what about adolescence, a critical period of psychosocial development during which transsexualism becomes a more entrenched gender disorder? Why postpone sex reassignment until the adult years, which results in many transsexuals suffering needlessly from feelings of despair and alienation throughout their teenage years?

A partial reason for the widespread reluctance to begin sex reassignment in postpubertal children is that adolescence is a developmental phase during which many teenagers experiment with a variety of identities (such as social, political, and religious). Many health professionals fear that any type of intervention during this stage of development might prompt gender-identity-confused adolescents to falsely conclude they are transsexuals and thus wrongly seek medical treatment. Another, more pragmatic reason for postponing sex reassignment is that in most countries teenagers are legally dependent on parental consent for such a drastic medical procedure. Thus, even though medical experts and the teenage patient may agree that a sex change should not be delayed, parents may not consent and clinicians may be reluctant to proceed due to litigation risks.

There are, however, strong arguments for initiating sex-reassignment procedures earlier than adulthood. A strong case for teenage sex change was recently outlined by members of a sex-reassignment team based at a major teaching hospital in the Netherlands. These professionals maintain that those adolescent transsexuals who have manifested an extreme cross-gender identification from their earliest years "suffer deeply from the fact that they cannot be open about their gender feelings. Knowing that they will have to await treatment for many years engenders feelings of hopelessness and slows down their social, psychological, and intellectual development" (Cohen-Kettenis & van Goozen, 1997, p. 264).

- **Let's Talk About It** boxes, also new to this edition, extend the applicability of the well-regarded Communication in Sexual Behavior chapter by supplying practical advice throughout the text on how to communicate effectively about sensitive sexual and relationship issues. Among the topics covered in these boxes: Coping with jealousy in Chapter 7, "coming out" to friends and family in Chapter 10, and a "Lovetalk" exercise on sexual turn-ons and -offs in Chapter 16.
- **Sexual Health,** broadly defined, continues to be an important focus of ***Our Sexuality.*** Margin icons are again used to call attention to coverage of sexual health matters throughout the text, and Chapters 4 and 5 on female and male anatomy and physiology have been reorganized to devote separate sections in each to sexual health coverage. Your Sexual Health boxes

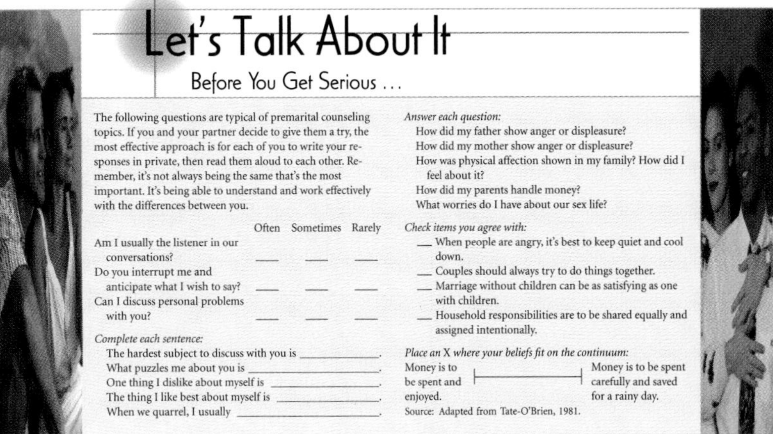

Let's Talk About It

Before You Get Serious . . .

The following questions are typical of premarital counseling topics. If you and your partner decide to give them a try, the most effective approach is for each of you to write your responses in private, then read them aloud to each other. Remember, it's not always being the same that's the most important. It's being able to understand and work effectively with the differences between you.

	Often	Sometimes	Rarely
Am I usually the listener in our conversations?	___	___	___
Do you interrupt me and anticipate what I wish to say?	___	___	___
Can I discuss personal problems with you?	___	___	___

Complete each sentence:

The hardest subject to discuss with you is __________.
What puzzles me about you is __________.
One thing I dislike about myself is __________.
The thing I like best about myself is __________.
When we quarrel, I usually __________.

Answer each question:

How did my father show anger or displeasure?
How did my mother show anger or displeasure?
How was physical affection shown in my family? How did I feel about it?
How did my parents handle money?
What worries do I have about our sex life?

Check items you agree with:

__ When people are angry, it's best to keep quiet and cool down.
__ Couples should always try to do things together.
__ Marriage without children can be as satisfying as one with children.
__ Household responsibilities are to be shared equally and assigned intentionally.

Place an X where your beliefs fit on the continuum:

Money is to be spent and enjoyed. |————| Money is to be spent carefully and saved for a rainy day.

Source: Adapted from Tate-O'Brien, 1981.

have also been added to the text, including one on medications that reduce oral contraceptive effectiveness in Chapter 11, and a self-assessment on the Index of Sexual Satisfaction in Chapter 15.

WORLD WIDE WEB

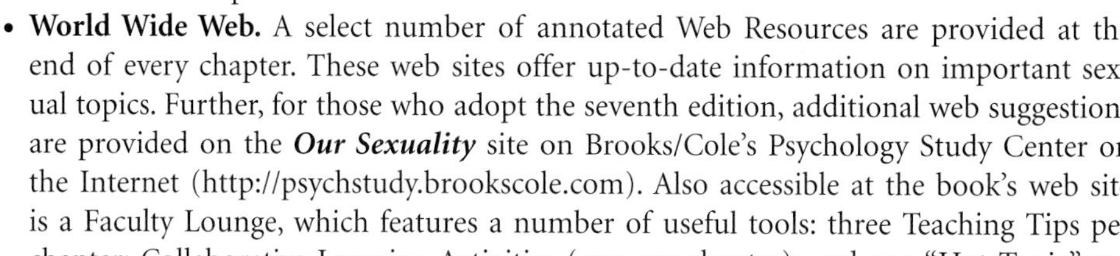

- **World Wide Web.** A select number of annotated Web Resources are provided at the end of every chapter. These web sites offer up-to-date information on important sexual topics. Further, for those who adopt the seventh edition, additional web suggestions are provided on the ***Our Sexuality*** site on Brooks/Cole's Psychology Study Center on the Internet (http://psychstudy.brookscole.com). Also accessible at the book's web site is a Faculty Lounge, which features a number of useful tools: three Teaching Tips per chapter; Collaborative Learning Activities (one per chapter); and one "Hot Topic" per chapter, an extension of the new On the Edge feature. Within the web site's Research and Teaching Showcase, ten updates per year will be provided to highlight significant new journal articles or guest lectures by specialists. Finally, students will appreciate this site's Test Yourself feature, with Interactive Quizzes of 10 to 15 questions per chapter.

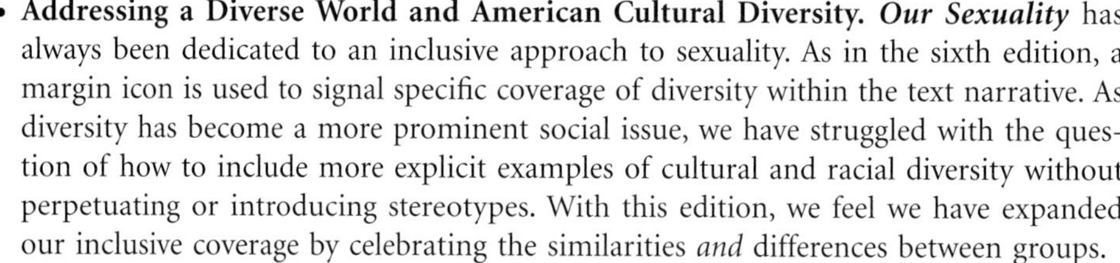

DIVERSITY

- **Addressing a Diverse World and American Cultural Diversity. *Our Sexuality*** has always been dedicated to an inclusive approach to sexuality. As in the sixth edition, a margin icon is used to signal specific coverage of diversity within the text narrative. As diversity has become a more prominent social issue, we have struggled with the question of how to include more explicit examples of cultural and racial diversity without perpetuating or introducing stereotypes. With this edition, we feel we have expanded our inclusive coverage by celebrating the similarities *and* differences between groups.
- **Sexuality and Diversity** boxes, many new to this edition, provide focused attention to issues of sexual diversity, whether cross-cultural or multicultural. In Chapter 9, we show how oral sex preferences among men and women are more a product of class than of race, while in Chapter 7, a Sexuality and Diversity box emphasizes the continuing importance of race/ethnicity in partner choice for many. But our attention to diversity is not limited to these boxes; it is also integrated throughout the text. For example, in Chapter 2, we present an extended discussion of how the National Health and Social Life Survey was comprehensive in surveying white European Americans, African Americans, and Hispanic Americans, but was admittedly underrepresentative of Asian Americans and Native Americans.

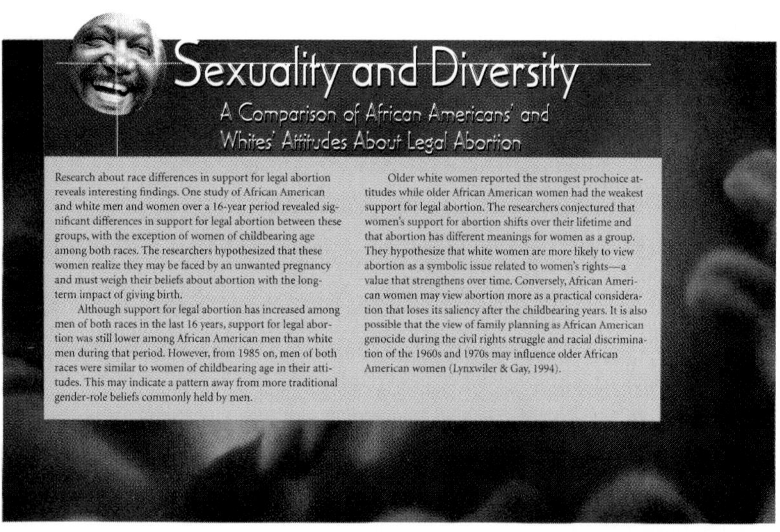

Sexuality and Diversity

A Comparison of African Americans' and Whites' Attitudes About Legal Abortion

Research about race differences in support for legal abortion reveals interesting findings. One study of African American and white men and women over a 16-year period revealed significant differences in support for legal abortion between these groups, with the exception of women of childbearing age among both races. The researchers hypothesized that these women realize they may be faced by an unwanted pregnancy and must weigh their beliefs about abortion with the long-term impact of giving birth.

Although support for legal abortion has increased among men of both races in the last 16 years, support for legal abortion was still lower among African American men than white men during that period. However, from 1985 on, men of both races were similar to women of childbearing age in their attitudes. This may indicate a pattern away from more traditional gender-role beliefs commonly held by men.

Older white women reported the strongest prochoice attitudes while older African American women had the weakest support for legal abortion. The researchers conjectured that women's support for abortion shifts over their lifetime and that abortion has different meanings for women as a group. They hypothesize that white women are more likely to view abortion as a symbolic issue related to women's rights—a value that strengthens over time. Conversely, African American women may view abortion more as a practical consideration that loses its saliency after the childbearing years. It is also possible that the view of family planning as African American genocide during the civil rights struggle and racial discrimination of the 1960s and 1970s may influence older African American women (Lynxwiler & Gay, 1994).

- **Sexual Orientations: Integrated Coverage Plus an In-Depth Chapter.** Sexual orientation issues have always received thoughtful coverage in ***Our Sexuality,*** and we have long used a language of inclusiveness in this text (for example, using the generic term "partner" rather than references to "man" or "woman" whenever appropriate). For the seventh edition, we have more fully integrated gays, lesbians, and bisexuals throughout the text. We note the growing acceptance of gays and lesbians in the mainstream media in Chapter 1 (a point developed in greater depth in Chapter 10), and cover gay and lesbian issues in specific sections of Chapters 7, 13, and 14. Also, the discussion of sexual expression of gay males and lesbians has now been moved to Chapter 9 on Sexual Behaviors.

  In addition, we have retained a separate chapter on Sexual Orientations (Chapter 10) in our book. We feel this is necessary in order to focus more fully, in one discrete chapter, on such topics as what determines sexual orientation (including a critique of Daryl Bem's "exotic-becomes-erotic" theory), societal attitudes, gay lifestyles (including the process of "coming out"), and the gay rights movement.

- **Impact of Media on Sexuality.** Since media pervades our lives, we devote more attention in this edition to the role of television, magazines, newspapers, and the Internet in reflecting and shaping societal and personal attitudes toward human sexuality. For example, the appearance of the breast cancer story line in "Murphy Brown" and the "coming out" episode of "Ellen" reflect an expanded public willingness to engage in such issues, even as they stake new ground. However, we also challenge how commercial television programming—and even "Sesame Street" on public television—play on stereotypes about sexuality and gender roles. The role of the Internet as a means of sexual communication—for good or for ill—is explored in many chapters, in On the Edge boxes or the text narrative itself.
- **Cutting-Edge Research.** Reviewers of this text have given us consistently high marks for the remarkable currency of the cited research. Users of the seventh edition will not be disappointed in this regard! We have included several hundred new reference citations from 1996, 1997, and 1998.
- **Streamlined Coverage.** In this revision, the number of chapters was reduced from 22 to 20. The coverage of sexuality and aging has been incorporated into Chapters 4, 5, 6, and 14 of this edition. What was a separate chapter on chronic illness, disability, and sexual adjustment has been streamlined and placed in Chapter 15, The Nature and Origin of Sexual Difficulties.
- **A Bold New Design.** For the seventh edition, a striking visual design was developed to give the book a more contemporary look. We believe the result is an inviting, colorful, and appealing text for students and professors.
- **New Anatomical Art Throughout the Book.** Beautiful new renderings of most of the anatomical art was commissioned for this edition. The result is a new, improved look that provides students with crisp, modern drawings that complement the new design.

Continuing Features

- **A Personal Approach.** Users of the text have responded favorably to our attempts to make the subject human and personal, and in the seventh edition we have retained and strengthened the elements that contribute to this approach.
- **Authors' Files.** One of the most popular features of ***Our Sexuality*** is the voices of real people woven into the text through the use of Authors' files. These quotations, taken from the experiences and observations of students, clients, and colleagues, have been given fresh infusion for this edition thanks to feedback from students enrolled in college courses on human sexuality in the United States and Canada. Moreover, each chapter now opens with an Authors' files quote, dramatizing an important concept pertinent to that chapter.
- **Nonjudgmental Perspective.** Consistent with our personal focus, we have avoided a prescriptive stance on most issues introduced in the text. We have attempted to provide information in a sensitive, nonsexist, inclusive, nonjudgmental manner that assumes the reader is best qualified to determine what is most valid and applicable in her or his life.
- **Psychosocial Orientation.** We focus on the roles of psychological and social factors in human sexual expression, reflecting our belief that human sexuality is governed more by psychosocial factors than by biological factors. At the same time, we provide the reader with a solid basis in the anatomy and physiology of human sexuality, and explore new research pertaining to the interplay of biology, psychology, and social learning.
- **Critical Thinking Questions.** These questions, integrated into the text and marked by an icon in the margin, are designed to encourage students to apply their knowledge and experience in developing their own outlook on the topic under discussion. Each question encourages students to stop and think about what they are reading in an attempt to facilitate higher-order processing of information and learning.

CRITICAL THINKING

- **Pedagogy.** Individuals learn in different ways. We therefore provide a variety of pedagogical aids to be used as the student chooses. Each chapter opens with an **outline** of major topic headings, complete with **chapter opening questions** that focus attention on important topics. **Key words** are boldfaced within the text, and selected key words are followed by a **pronunciation guide.** A **running glossary** in the text margin provides a helpful learning tool. The chapters also contain **Critical Thinking questions,** set off in italics, with an icon in the margin. Each chapter concludes with a **summary** in outline form for student reference, followed by several **Thought Provokers**—questions designed to stimulate thought and discussion—annotated **suggested readings,** and a new feature, **Web Resources.** A complete **glossary,** as well as a complete **bibliography,** are provided at the end of the book.

Organization

The organization of this book has been designed to reflect a logical progression of topics. We begin, in **Part One—Introduction,** with the social and cultural legacy of sexuality in our society. We then describe how sex research is conducted and discuss the difficulties of gathering information in this sensitive area of human behavior. We conclude the opening unit with a detailed exploration of a variety of gender issues.

The three chapters of **Part Two—Biological Basis** present the biological foundations of sexuality, with separate chapters on male and female sexual anatomy, followed by coverage of sexual arousal and sexual response patterns integrated into one chapter. In **Part Three—Sexual Behavior,** a variety of relationship issues and sexual behaviors are discussed.

In **Part Four—Sexuality and the Life Cycle,** we discuss contraception, pregnancy, and issues pertaining to sexuality throughout the life cycle. Sexual problems and their treatment and a detailed chapter on sexually transmitted diseases constitute the three chapters of **Part Five—Sexual Problems.**

The final section, **Part Six—Social Issues,** includes discussions of atypical sexuality, sexual victimization, pornography, and prostitution.

Integrated Teaching and Learning Aids

Instructor's Manual (ISBN 0-534-36020-3), *by Wendy Hunter of Mira Costa College:* Includes teaching suggestions for delivering dynamic lectures, evaluating students, exploring new teaching techniques, helping students develop intercultural awareness, using the Internet, and using the student Study Guide. For each chapter of the text, the manual includes learning objectives; lecture notes in outline format; handouts; and suggestions for guest speakers, videos and films, small group projects, field research, and field trips.

Printed Test Items (ISBN 0-534-36021-1), *by Lauren Kuhn of Portland Community College:* Includes approximately 3000 test items in multiple-choice, true/false, short-answer, and essay format, all page-referenced and keyed to learning objectives; also contains about 150 questions available on the Internet and questions from the student Study Guide.

Thomson World Class Testing Tools (Windows ISBN 0-534-35989-2, Macintosh ISBN 0-534-35990-6): This fully integrated suite of test creation, delivery, and classroom management tools includes World Class Test, Test Online, and World Class Management software. World Class Testing Tools allow professors to deliver tests via print, floppy, hard drive, LAN, or the Internet. With these tools, professors can create cross-platform exam files from publisher files or existing WESTest 3.2 test banks, create and edit questions, and provide their own feedback to objective test questions, enabling the system to work as a tutorial or an examination. In addition, professors can generate questions algorithmically, creating tests that include multiple-choice, true/false, and matching questions.

Professors can also track the progress of an entire class or an individual student. Testing and tutorial results can be integrated into the class management tool, which offers scoring, gradebook, and reporting capabilities.

Transparency Acetates (ISBN 0-534-35991-4): Approximately 75 four-color acetates based on text figures and illustrations and outside sources illustrate male and female anatomy and physiology, hormonal interactions, childbirth, and sexual behavior patterns.

Electronic Transparencies (ISBN 0-534-35992-2): Four-color images are also available for presentation through Adobe Acrobat. Instructors can zoom in on a particular aspect of the figure and size it larger. They can search by key word, queue up slides, and print out figures.

***Our Sexuality*'s Exclusive Video Library:** Offers a list of videotapes for professors to use, covering such topic areas as Homosexuality, Date Rape and Violence, Pregnancy and Child Birth, Sexual Harassment, AIDS and other Sexually Transmitted Diseases, Safe Sex and Contraceptives, Communicating About Relationships, and Intimate Relationships.

Study Guide (ISBN 0-534-35988-4), *by Lauren Kuhn of Portland Community College:* Includes review of key terms and concepts, chapter overviews with fill-ins, matching exercises, short-answer and multiple-choice questions, and critical thinking/personal reflection questions and exercises.

World Wide Web: A select number of annotated Web Resources are provided at the end of every chapter. These web sites offer up-to-date information on important sexual topics. Additional web suggestions are provided on the ***Our Sexuality*** site on Brooks/Cole's Psychology Study Center on the Internet (http://psychstudy.brookscole.com).

InfoTrac: A fully searchable online university library for students that offers full articles from more than 600 scholarly and popular publications, including such periodicals as the *American Journal of Psychology.* Access to InfoTrac College Edition is available on a password-protected web site that is updated daily.

Acknowledgments

The quality and longevity of ***Our Sexuality*** are due to talents and insights that extend beyond those of the authors. We are especially indebted to the staff of Brooks/Cole, the reviewers, and our students, who have added immeasurably to the merit of our book.

We owe special gratitude to reviewers and contributors to the seventh edition. Instructors who lent their expertise at various stages of the revision process of this and previous editions are listed on the following pages. Several instructors enlisted their students' reactions and insights to add fresh perspective to many of the Authors' files in the seventh edition. For this assistance, our sincere thanks go to Thomas Johns and Loren Smith of American River College, Vera Konig of Nassau Community College, Pearl Hawe and Satya Krishnan of New Mexico State University, Christine Harris of Cosumnes River College, Kris Hammar of Diablo College, Barbara Schnelker of Palomar College, Judy Hendricks of Cuesta College, Eric Krenz of California State University–Fresno, Jerry Strouse of Central Michigan University, Gary Lesniak of Portland Community College, Sue McKenzie of Dawson College, and Anne Kolath of Allan Hancock College. A special thank-you in this regard to Lauren Kuhn of Portland Community College for forwarding some especially insightful comments from students in her human sexuality classes.

Our greatest debt for the seventh edition is to senior developmental editor Jim Strandberg. His creative ideas and consistent enthusiasm were a sustaining support to us from beginning to end of the revision process. Jim's visionary efforts, many of which went beyond the requirements of his job, contributed much to the excellence of this edition. Marianne Taflinger, acquisitions editor, got the revision off and rolling, and her editorial skills are revealed in the quality of this revision. Editorial assistants Scott Brearton and Rachael Bruckman competently took care of a myriad of details.

Senior designer Roy Neuhaus managed in exemplary fashion the demanding job of designing and implementing the new and exciting design elements of this edition. Lisa Torri oversaw the re-rendering of much of the art program, thus complementing the improved design in this edition with crisper, more appealing anatomical drawings. Kirk Bomont, production coordinator, managed the complicated production efforts. Faith Stoddard, senior assistant editor, supervised the development of the supplements package.

Several talented freelance professionals added their talents. Research assistant Sami Tucker performed her usual exhaustive search of the recent journal literature so essential to the extensive updates implemented in the seventh edition. Greg Hubit, production editor, skillfully kept the production process rolling. Linda Purrington provided attentive and precise copyediting. Photo researcher Roberta Spieckerman added vitality to the images incorporated in this edition. Linda Turner, reference librarian at Eastern Carolina University, researched the Web Resources for each chapter.

Finally, we wish to thank our family and friends (What?! Another revision? Didn't you just finish one?) for keeping life moving positively while we were buried (and sometimes a little grumpy). They have been remarkably patient and resilient, for which we are grateful.

Robert Crooks
Karla Baur

REVIEWERS

Seventh Edition

Sylvester Allred
Northern Arizona University

Betsy Bergen
Kansas State University

Thomas E. Billimek
San Antonio College

Rosemary Cogan
Texas Tech University

David W. Gallagher
Pima Community College

Kenneth George
University of Pennsylvania

David A. Gershaw
Arizona Western College

Mike Godsey
College of Marin

Pearl A. Hawe
New Mexico State University

Barbara Iliardi
University of Rochester

Sally Klein
Dutchess Community College

Peggy Kleinplatz
University of Ottawa

Robin Kowalski
Western Carolina University

Eric Krenz
California State University–Fresno

Vickie Krenz
California State University–Fresno

Lauren Kuhn
Portland Community College

Laura Madson
New Mexico State University

Jerald J. Marshall
University of Central Florida

Susanne McKenzie
Dawson College

Gilbert Meyer
Illinois Valley Community College

Kay Murphy
Oklahoma State University

Jean L. Nash
Family Nurse Practitioner, Portland, Oregon

Roberta Ogletree
Southern Illinois University, Carbondale

Barbara Rienzo
University of Florida

Jaye F. Van Kirk
San Diego Mesa College

Laurie Volm
Lake Grove Women's Clinic, Tualatin, Oregon

Mary Ann Watson
Metropolitan State College of Denver

Paul Weikert
Grand Valley State University

William Yarber
Indiana University

First Through Sixth Editions

Daniel Adame
Emory University

Linda Anderson
University of North Carolina

Veanne Anderson
Indiana State University

Wayne Anderson
University of Missouri, Columbia

Betty Sue Benison
Texas Christian University

M. Betsy Bergen
Kansas State University

Jane Blackwell
Washington State University

John Blakemore
Monterey Peninsula College

Marvin J. Branstrom
Cañada College

Tom Britton, M.D.
Planned Parenthood, Portland, Oregon

Charles Carroll
Ball State University

Joan Cirone
California Polytechnic State University

Bruce Clear
The First Unitarian Church, Portland

David R. Cleveland
Honolulu Community College

Jeff Cornelius
New Mexico State University

Joseph Darden
Kean College

Brenda M. DeVellis
University of North Carolina

Lewis Diana
Virginia Commonwealth University

Beverly Drinnin
Des Moines Area Community College

Judy Drolet
Southern Illinois University, Carbondale

Andrea Parrot Eggleston
Cornell University

John P. Elia
San Francisco State University

Carol Ellison
Clinical Psychologist

Catherine Fichten
Dawson College

Karen Lee Fontaine
Purdue University, Calumet

Lin S. Fox
Kean College of New Jersey

Gene Fulton
University of Toledo

Glen G. Gilbert
Portland State University

Brian A. Gladue
University of Cincinnati

Stephen Harmon
University of Utah

Claudette Hastie-Beahrs
Clinical Social Worker

Thomas Johns
American River College

David Johnson
Portland State University

James Johnson
Sam Houston State University

Richard A. Kaye
Kingsborough Community College

Patricia B. Koch
Pennsylvania State University

Virginia Kreisworth
San Diego State University

Miriam LeGare
California State University, Sacramento

Sandra Leiblum
University of Medicine and Dentistry/
Robert Wood Johnson Medical School

Frank Ling
University of Tennessee

Roger W. Little
University of Illinois, Chicago

Sanford Lopater
Christopher Newport University

Joseph LoPiccolo
University of Missouri

Peter Maneno
Normandale College

Christel J. Manning
Hollins College

Leslie McBride
Portland State University

Deborah McDonald
New Mexico State University

Sue McKenzie
Dawson College

Brian McNaught
Gloucester, Massachusetts

Deborah Miller
College of Charleston

John Money
Johns Hopkins University

Denis Moore
Honolulu Metropolitan Community Church

Charlene Muehlenhard
University of Kansas

Louis Munch
Ithaca College

Ronald Murdoff
San Joaquin Delta College

James Nash
California Polytechnic State University

Teri Nicoll-Johnson
Modesto Junior College

Al Ono, M.D.
Obstetrician/Gynecologist

Bruce Palmer
Washington State University

Monroe Pasternak
Diablo Valley College

Calvin D. Payne
University of Arizona

J. Mark Perrin
University of Wisconsin, River Falls

John W. Petras
Central Michigan University

Valerie Pinhas
Nassau Community College

Ollie Pocs
Illinois State University

Robert Pollack
University of Georgia

Patty Reagan
University of Utah

Deborah Richardson
University of Georgia

Barbara Safriet
Lewis and Clark Law School

Nancy Salisbury, M.D.
Portland, Oregon

Marga Sarriugarte
Portland Rape Victim Advocate Project

Dan Schrinsky, M.D.
Portland, Oregon

Cynthia Schuetz
San Francisco State University

Lois Shofer
Essex Community College

Sherman K. Sowby
California State University, Fresno

Wendy Stock
Texas A&M University

Diana Taylor
Oregon Health Sciences University

Perry Treadwell
Decatur, Georgia

Thomas Tutko
San Jose State University

James E. Urban
Kansas State University

Peter Vennewitz
Portland Planned Parenthood

Margaret Vernallis
California State University, Northridge

John P. Vincent
University of Houston

Marianne Whatley
University of Wisconsin-Madison

David Winchester, M.D.
Urologist

Deborah R. Winters
New Mexico State University

1

Perspectives on Sexuality

The Authors' Perspectives

Why do the authors emphasize a psychosocial perspective in Our Sexuality*?*

Which two themes in our cultural legacy do the authors question?

Our Media Culture

How has media treatment of homosexuality changed in recent years?

The Sex-for-Reproduction Legacy

How did this legacy develop through Western history, and is it shared by Eastern cultures?

What major scientific development has helped separate sexual pleasure from reproduction?

The Gender-Role Legacy

What two opposing images of women developed during the Middle Ages?

What practice, spanning over 200 years, represented the peak of antagonism toward women?

A Cross-Cultural Perspective: Social Norms and Sexual Diversity

Does cross-cultural evidence point toward any universal rules for sexual behavior?

What factors contribute to diversity and similarity of sexual attitudes and behaviors within the United States?

Sexuality: Personal or Public Domain?

What have been some of the factors in shaping contemporary sexual choices and issues?

What are some potential benefits and drawbacks of exploring one's sexuality in cyberspace?

I wish I had had this course and read this book when I was younger. It would have helped me feel less confused about sexuality and more confident in making decisions that were in my best interest. It could have saved me some unnecessary grief. (Authors' files)

Most students take this course, at least in part, to enhance their personal understanding and development. We offer this book as a tool for exploring your perspectives on human sexuality. We will present a wide array of information about attitudes, ideas, and behaviors. However, the final expert on your sexuality is *you,* and we encourage you to evaluate all the information we present within the framework of your own convictions and experience.

We welcome you to this book and your human sexuality class.

The Authors' Perspectives

It is safe to assume that any controversial topic will elicit a wide range of responses. Few topics generate as much attention and evoke so much pleasure and distress as the many possibilities of the expression and control of human sexuality. In any beginning sexuality class—or in almost any other group, for that matter—attitudes toward sexuality will likely range from very liberal to extremely conservative. Students in sexuality classes represent a diversity of ages, ethnic and religious backgrounds, and sexual and life experiences. Some have had sexual encounters with one or many partners; some have had long-term marriages or other partnerships; others have not been sexually involved with another person. Many people relate sexually only with members of the other sex;* some seek sexual contact with members of the same sex; still others have sexual relationships with either sex. There are virtually no universals in sexual attitudes, experiences, or preferences.

With this in mind, we have attempted to bring an inclusive philosophy to our book. We hope something in the following pages will speak to the diversity of *all* our readers. At the same time, we do have a distinct point of view. It is appropriate to tell you about our perspective—our orientation and our biases—so you can recognize and evaluate it for yourself as you read the text.

A Psychosocial Orientation

Psychosocial
Refers to a combination of psychological and social factors.

This book has a **psychosocial** orientation, reflecting our view that human sexuality is governed more by psychological factors (motivational, emotional, attitudinal) and by social conditioning (the process by which we learn our social groups' expectations and norms) than by the effects of biological factors such as hormones and instincts. The psychological and social factors are so intertwined that it is often difficult to distinguish clearly between the two.

We may not always be aware of it, but our sexual attitudes and behaviors are strongly shaped by our society in general and by the social groups, in particular, to which we belong (Laumann et al., 1994). The subtle ways in which we learn society's expectations regarding sexuality often lead us to assume that our behaviors or feelings are biologically innate, or natural. However, an examination of sexuality in other societies (or even in different ethnic, socioeconomic, and age groups within our own society) and in other historical periods reveals a broad range of acceptable behavior. What we regard as natural is clearly relative. Understanding the impact of culture and individual experience can

*We use the term *other sex* instead of *opposite sex* to emphasize that men and women are similar or alike in more ways than they are opposite.

make it easier to make decisions about our own sexuality. Therefore, our major emphasis will be on the psychosocial aspects of human sexuality.

It is also clear that the biology of sex plays an important role in human sexuality, and throughout this text we will be looking in some detail at the biological foundations of sexual behavior. We discuss the role of hormones, the nervous system, and genetic variables as we examine the "nature vs. nurture" debate concerning human sexuality.

A controversial theory about the impact of biology on our sexuality is called *sociobiology* (Wilson, 1975). Sociobiology theory proposes that behavior patterns that increase "reproductive success" have a genetic basis that has been passed along through thousands of years of human existence. Our interest in the attractiveness of a partner—physical fitness, body build, lustrous hair—could stem from the genetically coded desire for a healthy reproductive partner. Dating and courtship are opportunities to assess the best mate for reproductive vigor. Male and female differences related to their biological investment in parenting account for divergence between the sexes in numbers and selectivity of sexual partners. In essence, the more women a man has sex with, the greater the chances that his genes will carry on to the next generations, so he is inclined to pursue multiple sexual partners. In contrast, the woman has fewer opportunities to pass on her genes—each pregnancy requires significant time and biological investment. Each successful pregnancy also requires greater material resources to ensure the continued life and health of her child. Therefore, male ambition and material success increase the males' "attractiveness" to females, who have a genetic predisposition to spend their reproductive resources wisely. Although science currently lacks a way to prove this and similar theories, the ideas fuel provocative debate.

Our Cultural Legacy: Questioning Two Themes

Along with a psychosocial orientation, we have biases about two themes pertaining to sexuality, both of which are of long standing in most Western cultures. The first is related to the idea that reproduction is the only legitimate reason for sexual activity. In North America one of the most prominent expressions of this theme is the notion that sex equals intercourse. Certainly penile–vaginal intercourse can be a very fulfilling part of sexual expression, but excessive emphasis on intercourse often has negative consequences. For one, it perpetuates the notion that sexual response and orgasm are supposed to occur during penetration. Such a narrow focus places tremendous performance pressures on both women and men and can create unrealistic expectations of coitus itself.

The sex-for-reproduction view also may result in devaluing other forms of sexual behavior. Some activities—for instance, kissing, body caresses, and manual or oral stimulation of the genitals—are often relegated to the secondary status of *foreplay* (usually considered to be any activity before intercourse), implying that they are to be followed by the "real sex" of coitus. Sexual activity between members of the same sex also does not fit the model of sex for reproduction. These and other noncoital sexual behaviors—such as masturbation, sexual fantasy, and anal intercourse—have been defined at various times in our own and other cultures as immoral, sinful, perverted, or illegal. We present them in this text as viable sexual options for those who choose them.

The other theme we oppose is the rigid distinction between male and female roles. This legacy is based on far more than the physiological differences between the sexes. Research does show certain sex differences in some areas. However, socialization shapes and exaggerates our biological tendencies, and rigid gender-role conditioning can limit each person's full range of human potential and produce a negative impact on our sexuality. For example, teaching "appropriate" behavior for men and women may contribute to the notion that the man must always initiate sexual activity while the woman must comply, placing tremendous responsibility on the male and severely limiting the woman's likelihood of discovering her own needs.

Our psychosocial orientation and our biases—our opposition to the sex-for-reproduction theme and our belief that rigid gender roles are limiting—will appear throughout this text. In this chapter, we want to explore these ideas more thoroughly from a historical and a cross-cultural perspective. First let's take a look at our media culture, which is both a reflection of and an influence on contemporary sexuality.

Our Media Culture

First let us take a look at what the media say about sexuality. Mass media as we now know them have existed for a very short time in human history. Printed books, magazines and newspapers, radio and movies existed before the first black-and-white televisions of the late 1940s. The continued explosion of media technology since then—color and big-screen TV, movie videos, cable, satellite, and, of course, computer technology and the Internet—bombards us with vivid media exposure, as discussed further in the "On the Edge" box. The emergence of virtual reality may be the next frontier.

Concurrent with huge technological advances have come greater sexualization of the media. Fifty years ago a Hollywood movie would not be released to the public unless husband and wife were seen in separate beds (Lapham, 1997). Today, during a trip to the grocery store for a late night snack, we can pick up magazines such as *Playboy* with nude photos that take bikini wax to new extremes or perhaps this year's swimsuit edition of *Sports Illustrated.* Men's magazines such as *Details, Maxim,* and *Men's Health* have gone beyond sex-object photography to sexual and relationship how-to articles. Examples include "Be Better Than Her Last Lover," "In Bed with the Sex Experts," "Can I Have Multiple Orgasms?", or a horror story about penis enlargement, "An Inch Too Far" (Dobosz, 1997). Women's magazines contain articles about sex such as "The Secret, Sexual You. Turn Her Loose," "His Sexual Fantasies—Your Worst Nightmare," or "The Sex Workout." Magazines for teenage girls, such as *Seventeen* and *YM* each have nearly two million subscribers who read about how to make themselves prettier, skinnier, and sexier with "Boy Magnet Beauty" and "Mega Makeovers: Go from So-So to Supersexy" (Higgenbotham, 1996). Romance novels with their studly bare-chested men on their covers and euphemistic sexual scenes are common (Aronson, 1998). At the checkstand the front

On the Edge
The Impact of Cyberspace on Sexuality in the Twenty-First Century

The largest and best research study about sexuality to date in the United States concludes that attitudes and behaviors are dramatically influenced by ongoing interactions with those in our social groups (Laumann et al., 1994). This research was conducted before the 1990s explosion in cyberspace communication. People in disparate social groups—different ages, races, religions, ethnic groups, economic groups—are now able to discuss whatever they choose, in complete anonymity. What will be the effects of the free-for-all sexual communication available on the Internet, where the only limitation on who talks to whom is access to a computer with a modem? Will the Internet be an electronic melting pot of differing sexual attitudes and information, or will people be more inclined to pursue like-minded electronic conversations?

Some college human sexuality courses are now being taught via the Internet. Hundreds of colleges and universities currently offer virtual degrees where students log on to the Internet for homework assignments, listen to audio stream lectures, and chat on Web sites with fellow classmates from China to Saudi Arabia (Hamilton & Miller, 1997). For your term paper on marriage, you could talk to a student from India who was anticipating her arranged marriage or engage in a debate about the pros and cons of male circumcision with students of different faiths for your class journal. The possibilities are endless, and the impact of this communi-

pages of the tabloids titillate us with topics such as "Cops Probe Daddy's Secret Porn Life" and the latest speculation about Michael Jackson's sexuality. News media—TV, radio, and newspapers—often give precedence to the sexual misadventures of politicians and media figures over critical local, national, and international issues and events (Dowd, 1997).

Or we can stop by the video store to rent films of varying degrees of sexual explicitness, to watch in the privacy of our own homes. On our way home we pass the latest daring Calvin Klein billboard advertisement. We often hear explicit sexual messages on the radio and can listen to the sexual ruminations of Howard Stern's radio show.

The possibilities for confronting more sex in the media at home are endless. Enjoying some couch-potato time we see sexual images in most advertising, whether for coffee or cars, proving that sex sells when packaged in young, hard-body wrapping. Standard network programming is rife with sexual innuendo. If we want to join the 30 million adults in the United States who admit to watching soap operas, we can see vivid examples of sexual intrigue based on infidelity, dishonesty, revenge, and exploitation (Greenberg & Busselle, 1996). Talk shows often cover sexual topics such as "Pregnant Exotic Dancers," "Cousins in Love," or "Immortalized on Video in Compromising Positions." Of course, options for sexual explicitness on cable and satellite TV are extensive. MTV music videos emphasize erotic and sexually suggestive imagery. *Playboy* has its own channel, and other channels play hard-core pornographic videos.

The media simultaneously reflect society as they influence it. Television in particular has played a role in breaking down cultural taboos on sensitive sexual topics. Programs and made-for-television shows on incest, rape, and abortion have helped reduce the stigma of such topics. Murphy Brown's diagnosis of breast cancer in her 1997 TV

On the Edge

cation revolution on sexual attitudes and behaviors is potentially epic.

Whether or not your college course is taught on the Internet, sexuality in a myriad of forms has made its presence known in cyberspace. By 1998 there were 62 million users of the Internet. It offers a dynamic source of self-help information from Web sites for breast cancer, to message boards posting wig care tips for transsexuals, to up-to-the-minute findings in AIDS research. Some people chat on line to explore their sexuality by comparing experiences and opinions. Others hunt for Web sites offering the most explicit sexual images. The net has become a huge dating service, an interactive personal ad opportunity where people can have on-line conversations to see if they may want to meet face to face (Francis, 1997). Some are also using cyberspace to have on-line extramarital affairs, while others use chat rooms to talk about their wildest fantasies in the safety of complete anonymity. Users can go into a fantasy hot tub with others and describe in graphic detail what they are doing or would like to do. Participants can represent themselves by any name, gender, physical characteristics, and personal profile they wish.

Cyberspace is an interactive adult book store: Sexual commerce is plentiful with "cyberstrippers" and interactive sexual talk, pictures, and live-action video conferencing where subscribers can tell the strippers what they want them to do. In five to ten years, Internet users will be able to hook up sensory devices to themselves to stimulate the sensations they are imagining on line, creating new dimensions to virtual reality (Maxwell, 1996).

The constructive and destructive possibilities of cyberspace on sexuality appear as unlimited as those potentials in human nature. What might be the most helpful and the most harmful consequences of this far-reaching communication technology? What role, if any, do you think our government should take in controlling communication on the Internet?

Mixed Media, © 1997 Tribune Media Services, Inc. All rights reserved.

show season promoted open discussion of that topic, as have shows about menopause, impotence, and artificial insemination. Perhaps the most dramatic example of television's educational possibilities related to sexuality has been the mainstreaming of gays and lesbians into programming. Beginning in the mid-1990s gay and lesbian characters have been developed on shows such as *Roseanne, Melrose Place, Friends,* and *NYPD Blue.* An episode of the family show *Dr. Quinn, Medicine Woman* dealt with the town's homophobic reactions when poet Walt Whitman visited. And, of course, Ellen Degeneres's coming out show on *Ellen* was an event of the season in 1997 (Marin & Miller, 1997).

Throughout the text we will discuss media images and their impact in various areas of our sexual lives.

The Sex-for-Reproduction Legacy

We have noted that a prevailing belief in Western culture is that the purpose of sexual activity should be procreation. Where did this idea come from, and how relevant is it to us today?

The concept of sex for reproduction is associated with both Judaic and Christian traditions. Childbearing was tremendously important to the ancient Hebrews. Their history of slavery and persecution made them determined to preserve their people—to "be fruitful, and multiply, and replenish the earth" (Genesis 1:28). Yet to "know" a partner sexually, within marriage, was also recognized as a profound physical and emotional experience (Carswell, 1969; Haffner, 1997). The Song of Solomon in the Bible contains very sensuous love poetry. The bridegroom speaks:

How fair is thy love, . . . my spouse!
how much better is thy love than wine!
and the smell of thine ointments than all spices!
Thy lips, oh my spouse, drop as the honeycomb,
honey and milk are under thy tongue (Solomon 4:10–11).

And the bride:

I am my beloved's and his desire is toward me.
Come, my husband, let us go forth into the field;
Let us lodge in the villages . . .
There will I give thee my loves (7:10–13).

The joyful appreciation of sexuality displayed in these lines was a part of the Judaic tradition. This view was overshadowed, however, by teachings of the Christian church. To understand why this happened, it is necessary to remember that Christianity developed during the later years of the Roman Empire. This was a period of social instability when many exotic cults were imported from Greece, Persia, and other parts of the empire to provide sexual entertainment and amusement. Early Christians separated themselves from these practices by associating sex with sin.

Interpretations of Adam and Eve's transgressions in the Garden of Eden have influenced values about sexuality.

We know very little about Jesus' views on sexuality. Paul of Tarsus, however, had a crucial influence on the early church (he died in A.D. 66, and many of his writings were incorporated into the New Testament). Paul emphasized the importance of overcoming "desires of the flesh"—including anger, selfishness, hatred, and nonmarital sex—to inherit the Kingdom of God. He associated spirituality with sexual abstinence and saw **celibacy** (SEL-a-ba-sē), the state of being unmarried and therefore abstaining from sexual intercourse, as superior to marriage. Later church fathers expanded on the theme of sex as sin. Augustine (354–430) declared that lust was the original sin of Adam and Eve; his writings formalized the notion that intercourse could take place only within marriage for the purpose of procreation.

Celibacy
Historically defined as the state of being unmarried; currently defined as not engaging in sexual behavior.

The belief that sex is sinful persisted throughout the Middle Ages (the period from the fall of the Western Roman Empire in A.D. 476 to the beginning of the Renaissance, about 1400), and Thomas Aquinas (1225–1274) further refined this idea in a small section of his *Summa Theologica.* Aquinas maintained that human sexual organs were designed for procreation and that any other use—as in homosexual acts, oral–genital sex, anal intercourse, or sex with animals—was against God's will and therefore heretical. From Aquinas's time on, homosexuals were to find neither refuge nor tolerance anywhere in the Western world (Boswell, 1980).

The view of nonreproductive sex as sinful was modified by Protestant reformers of the sixteenth century. Both Martin Luther (1483–1546) and John Calvin (1509–1564) recognized the value of sex in marriage. According to Calvin, marital sex was permissible if it stemmed "from a desire for children, or to avoid fornication, or to lighten and ease the cares and sadnesses of household affairs, or to endear each other" (Taylor, 1971, p. 62). The Puritans, often maligned for having rigid views about sex, also shared an appreciation of sexual expression within marriage (D'Emilio & Freedman, 1988). One man was expelled from Boston when, among other offenses, "he denyed . . . conjugal . . . fellowship unto his wife for the space of 2 years . . ." (Morgan, 1978, p. 364).

Although we have been discussing Western traditions linking sex with procreation, the same guidelines did not necessarily apply throughout the world. In ancient China, for instance, Taoism (dating from around the second century B.C.) actively promoted sexual activity not only for procreation but also to achieve spiritual growth and harmony. Indeed, the earliest known sex manuals were produced in China sometime around 200 B.C. Although men were encouraged not to waste semen through masturbation, practices such as anal intercourse and oral–genital stimulation were accepted. (These liberal Taoist attitudes were replaced by a much stricter sexual propriety that emerged during a renaissance of Confucianism around A.D. 1000, and Chinese sexual expression remains quite conservative today [Ruan, 1991].) The Hindu culture of ancient India also celebrated sexual pleasure as one means of reaching spiritual fulfillment. As in ancient China, Hindus were guided by a sex manual, the *Kama Sutra,* dating from about the third to fifth century A.D.

Seventeenth-century bronze from Tibet showing the supreme Buddha Kalacakra consummating love with Visvamata, mother of all.

A third major non-Western religion, Islam, has also placed a high value on sexual behavior within marriage, and not just for procreation. The prophet Muhammad (c. A.D. 570–632) prohibited celibacy, valuing intercourse within marriage as the highest good in human life but opposing intercourse before marriage. Within classical Islamic faith, however, both *polygyny* (one man having multiple wives at the same time) and concubinage are permitted.

One other influence should be mentioned in any discussion of the sex-for-procreation legacy. The availability of modern contraception today permits intercourse without procreation more reliably than do older methods. Contraceptive devices have been used for centuries (McLaren, 1990). Condoms made from goat bladders were used by men in ancient times. In Rome during the first century B.C., women used amulets, magic, or inserted soft wool pads to block the cervix—a precursor to the modern diaphragm, which was developed in Europe in the 1870s.

With the possible exception of the diaphragm, none of these methods was as reliable as the oral contraceptive pill, introduced in the late 1950s and early 1960s, soon to be followed by the intrauterine device (IUD), "morning-after pills," and spermicides. The widespread acceptance of these contraceptives and the availability of legal abortion has permitted sexuality to be separated from procreation as never before in the Western cultures. The world has changed, too, so that today many people are concerned with the ecological and economic costs of bearing children, costs that were not as relevant in the preindustrial world. Despite these changes, however, the legacies of the Hebrew and Christian Bibles, of Augustine and Thomas Aquinas, and of the Reformation are still very much with us. Thus, the sex-for-reproduction issue in the twentieth-century Western world represents a complex conflict among the values of personal pleasure, practicality, and tradition.

The Gender-Role Legacy

A second issue about which we have a bias is the legacy of gender roles. Roles of women and men are changing in modern Western society, but each change, going as it does against tradition, has been difficult to achieve.

How far back do we have to look to find the roots of this legacy? As the "When God Was a Woman" box suggests, gender roles among early human groups who revered great goddesses might have been quite different from what we now regard as traditional. By the time Hebraic culture was established, however, these gender roles were highly specialized. The Book of Proverbs lists the duties of a good wife: She must instruct servants, care for her family, and keep household accounts. Bearing children (especially sons) was essential; so was obedience to her husband.

Christianity reaffirmed Judaism's traditional gender roles. Paul of Tarsus used man's creation before woman's and Eve's disobedience to God to explain why women should be submissive:

> I permit no woman to teach or to have authority over men. . . . For Adam was formed first, then Eve; and Adam was not deceived, but the woman was deceived and became a transgressor (I Timothy 2:11–15).

The view that women should be subservient to men prevailed throughout the Middle Ages. During this period, however, two contradictory images of women evolved, gaining strength so that each had its own impact on women's place in society. The first was the image of the Virgin Mary; the second, the image of Eve as an evil temptress.

The cult of the Virgin was imported to the West by Crusaders returning from Constantinople. Previously a figure of secondary importance in the Western church, Mary now was transformed into a gracious, compassionate protector and an exalted focus of religious devotion. The practice of *courtly love,* which evolved at about this time, reflected a compatible image of woman as pure and above reproach. Ideally, a young knight would fall in love with a married woman of higher rank. After a lengthy pursuit, he would find favor, but his love would remain unconsummated because her marriage vows ultimately proved inviolable. This paradigm caught the medieval imagination, and troubadours performed ballads of courtly love throughout the courts of Europe.

The other medieval image provides a counterpoint to the unattainable, compassionate Madonna: Eve as the evil temptress of the Garden of Eden. This image, promoted by the church, reflected an increasing emphasis on Eve's sin and an antagonism toward women. This antagonism reached its climax in the witch-hunts that began in the late fifteenth century—after the Renaissance was well under way—and lasted for close to

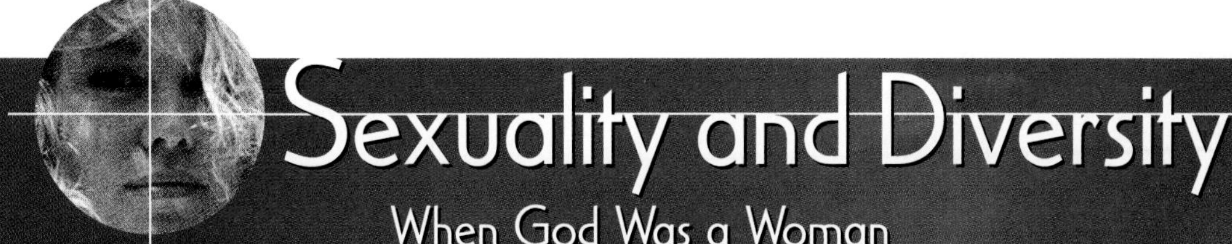

Sexuality and Diversity
When God Was a Woman

Accurate knowledge of sexuality and gender roles in early human history is virtually impossible. Available information is sparse and subject to distorted interpretation by historians influenced by their own cultural biases. The following paragraphs summarize the provocative historical thesis of art historian Merlin Stone (1976).

In prehistoric and early historic periods of human development (about 7000 B.C.–A.D. 599), religions existed in which people revered great goddesses who had life-giving and important roles. In nearly all areas of the world, female deities were extolled as healers. Some were powerful, courageous warriors and leaders in battle. The Greek goddess Demeter and the Egyptian goddess Isis were both invoked as lawgivers and dispensers of wisdom and justice. In the ancient Middle East, where some of the earliest evidence of agricultural development has been found, the goddess Ninlil was revered for having provided her people with an understanding of planting and harvesting.

As the role of the male in reproduction came to be understood and male kinship lines became important, religions headed by female deities were persecuted and suppressed by the newer religions, which held male gods supreme.

Through the imposition and eventual acceptance of the male-centered religions, women came to be regarded as inferior creatures, divinely intended for the production of children and the pleasure of men. In their new role as passive and obedient vessels, women were far removed from the status of the ancient goddesses.

The Egyptian goddess Isis on the bow of a boat, leading a procession.

Antagonism toward women reached a climax during the witch-hunts of the fifteenth century.

200 years (Hitchcock, 1995). Ironically, while Queen Elizabeth I (1533–1603) helped elevate women's status and brought England to new heights, an estimated 100,000 women were executed as witches in both Europe and America during her reign (Barstow, 1994).

Witch-hunting had ended by the time of the eighteenth-century Enlightenment, which was partly an outgrowth of the new scientific rationalism: Ideas were now based on facts that could be objectively observed, rather than on subjective beliefs. Women were to enjoy increased respect, at least for a short time. Some women, such as Mary Wollstonecraft of England, were famous for their intelligence, wit, and vivacity. Wollstonecraft's book *The Vindication of the Rights of Women* (1792) attacked the prevailing practice of giving young girls dolls rather than schoolbooks. Wollstonecraft also asserted that sexual satisfaction was as important to women as to men, and that premarital and extramarital sex were not sinful.

Unfortunately, these progressive views did not prevail. The Victorian era, which took its name from the queen who ascended the British throne in 1837 and ruled for over 60 years, brought a sharp turnaround. The sexes had highly defined roles. Upper- and middle-class Victorian women were valued for their delicacy and ladylike manners—and consequently constrained by such restrictive devices as corsets, hoops, and bustles, which prevented them from freely moving their bodies. Popular opinion of female sexuality was reflected by the widely quoted physician William Acton, who wrote, "The majority of women are not very much troubled with sexual feelings of any kind" (Degler, 1980, p. 250). Women's duties centered around fulfilling their families' spiritual needs and providing a comfortable home for their husbands to retreat to after working all day. The world of women was clearly separated from that of men. Intensely passionate friendships sometimes developed between women, providing the support and comfort that were often absent in marriage.

Victorian men were expected to conform to the strict propriety of the age, but (alas!) they were often forced to lay aside morality in the pursuit of business and political interests. They also sometimes laid aside morality in the pursuit of sexual companionship, because the separation of the worlds of husbands and wives created an emotional (and physical) distance in many Victorian marriages. Ironically, prostitution flourished at this time, right alongside propriety and sexual repression. Victorian men could smoke, drink, and joke with the women who had turned to prostitution out of economic necessity.

Perhaps more than any age, nineteenth-century Western culture was full of sexual contradictions. Women's sexuality was polarized between the opposing images of Madonna and whore. Men were trapped between the ideal of purity and the frank pleasures of physical expression.

The twentieth century changed this precarious dichotomy. The women's suffrage movement, which began in the late nineteenth century with the goal of giving women the right to vote, grew out of several related developments such as the temperance movement to eliminate liquor consumption, the abolition of slavery, and the demand that women be permitted to attend universities and hold property. The passage in 1920 of the Nineteenth Amendment to the U.S. Constitution, which guaranteed women the right to vote, did not usher in a new era of equality. But World War II created an environment for increased equality and further expansion and flexibility of gender roles, as thousands of women left the traditional homemaker role and took paying jobs for the first time. Not until the 1960s, however, after the flurry of postwar marriages, the baby boom, and widespread disappointment in the resulting domesticity of women, did a new movement for gender-role equality begin. Yet we still carry the legacy of Victorianism and earlier traditions in the gender roles we all learn as children, and this legacy limits both men and women. In Chapter 3, we will discuss the impact of gender roles on contemporary American women and men.

In the Victorian era, the marriageable woman possessed morals that were as tightly laced as her corset. Ironically, prostitution flourished at this time.

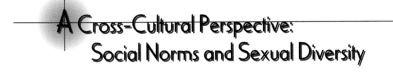

A Cross-Cultural Perspective: Social Norms and Sexual Diversity

What constitutes normal sexual behavior? Many of us have our own ideas about what is normal and what is not, but often the meaning of a given act (sexual or otherwise) can be fully understood only by looking at the cultural and historical context within which it occurs. There is such cultural diversity among the peoples of the world that even the idea of what is sexually arousing varies greatly. For example, female breasts often trigger sexual arousal in Western males, but they create no erotic interest for the men of New Guinea. Furthermore, the meaning and importance of sexual activity varies enormously from one culture to another. In some societies, such as the Mangaian society of Polynesia, sex is highly valued. Other societies, such as the Manus society of New Guinea, view almost any sexual act as undesirable and shameful.

Do you think any rules governing sexual behavior apply to all cultures? If so, what might these rules be? Take a moment to consider the answers to these questions before reading on.

The diversity of sexual expression throughout the world tends to mask a fundamental generalization that can be applied without exception to all social orders: All societies

All cultures practice marriage in one form or another. Shown here: (left) a Cambodian wedding ceremony; (right) a Jewish wedding ceremony.

have rules regulating the conduct of sexual behavior. Although exact regulations vary from one society to the next, no social order has seen fit to allow sexuality to remain totally unregulated. "Every society shapes, structures and constrains the development and expression of sexuality in all of its members" (Beach, 1978, p. 116).

Diversity Around the World

To illustrate the range of sexual attitudes, behaviors, and relationships around the world, we will highlight three different societies: China, the Islamic Middle East, and Sweden. We will examine various aspects of sexuality that you will find discussed in various chapters of this text.

China

Although China has a rich history of erotic literature and art, the Communist government has purposefully eliminated "decadent" Western sexual behaviors. Following the Communist victory in 1949, pornography was outlawed, and government soldiers shut down brothels. The country all but eradicated sexually transmitted diseases. Sex outside of marriage was considered to be a bourgeois transgression and sex more than once a week a counterproductive diversion of energy (Wehrfritz, 1996).

China's insulation from the Western world is observable by its late involvement in the sexual sciences. Its first national conference on sexology was held in 1992. A lack of books and written information was a common concern among the presenters interested in sex education for Chinese citizens. Physicians maintain that inadequate sexual knowledge is the main cause of sexual disorders, most commonly seen in wives. Many men do not know that a woman has a clitoris. Most married women see procreation as the reason for sex, and once they have their children, are no longer interested. Marital sex is seen by most women as a service to their husbands rather than something pleasurable for themselves (Livingston, 1997).

Unlike your college or university, no sex education is provided in Chinese higher education, and little exists in schools. Only 50% of rural and 35% of urban teenage girls had accurate knowledge about menstruation. Adolescents and young adults are less sexually active than in the United States. Compared to much higher North American statistics, 23% of men and 12% of women Chinese college students report having experienced intercourse. In addition, only half of those use birth control. Although 8% of university students report being gay, homosexuals are very closeted (Livingston, 1997).

Changes in sexual attitudes and behavior in China are appearing. More sexual content is found in film, television, and advertising. Divorce rates, particularly in urban areas, are increasing. The divorce rate rose from less than 5% in 1981 to 12% in 1996. Rates of

Traditionally garbed Muslim women share the sidewalk with students in Western dress coming home from school.

sexually transmitted diseases, and of premarital and extramarital sex, are greater than before. At Beijing's airport vibrators and specialty condoms are for sale at the snack counter. The increase in sexually transmitted diseases is especially problematic because few doctors have been trained to treat them (Cowley et al., 1996).

The Islamic Middle East

Islam is the world's fastest growing religion and predominates in the Middle East. Its followers are called Muslims and adhere to the teachings of the Prophet Muhammad (662 A.D.). Muhammad believed that sex was to be enjoyed by man and woman alike in marriage and encouraged husbands to be "slow and delaying." Women are believed to be inherently sexual: Muhammad's son-in-law proclaimed "Almighty God created sexual desire in ten parts: then he gave nine parts to women and one to men." The custom of women wearing veils, female circumcision, and segregation of the sexes until marriage are deemed necessary to contain the power of female sexuality (Brooks, 1995; Schmetzer, 1997). Wearing a veil is the law in some countries (Power, 1998).

Arranged marriages are common, and producing a male heir is important. A vicious Arab curse is "May your womb shrivel up." Sex outside of marriage is a serious transgression, and ghastly penalties are imposed, particularly for adultery. Tradition sanctions "honor killings" for wives who have dishonored their husbands by having sex outside their marriage. Being stoned or burned to death is common punishment. Male homosexuals suffer the same fate (Brooks, 1995).

Sweden

Swedish family law and public health services have been intentional and instrumental in promoting open, relaxed attitudes toward sexuality and equality for men and women in family life. By the 1930s family planning services were offered by the government. Sex education became a compulsory subject in schools in 1954—the same era in which June and Ward Cleaver of "Leave It to Beaver" TV fame were sleeping in single beds. The government combined free contraceptive services and sex education aimed at preventing unwanted pregnancies with the legalization of abortion in 1974. The rate of teen pregnancies has declined since then. By the 1960s couples living together without being married had become widely accepted. Currently, about 20% of couples living together are unmarried. Swedish family law promotes equal responsibility between men and women for caring for children. The government sponsors fathers' training groups and offers equal—and extensive—parental leave for both parents (Swedish Institute, 1997).

Diversity Within the United States

Considerable diversity exists within our borders. This was true even before Europeans began arriving in North America, as we see in the box on Native American sexual diversity. Since that time, individuals of many ethnic and religious groups have made their homes in the United States, resulting in a wide range of sexual values and behaviors.

Throughout this text, we will come across many examples of the diversity that exists between different subcultures within our society. For example, Asian Americans—*on the whole*—are less likely to engage in premarital intercourse than are Latinos, African Americans, or Americans of European extraction (Cochran et al., 1991). Again, Latino culture—*on the whole*—often endorses sexual exploration for males but places a high value on chastity before marriage for women (Comas-Diaz, 1987). Some Latino women may be chaperoned throughout their courtship to help protect their virginity until marriage (Comas-Diaz & Greene, 1994). Another group-related difference is in oral–genital sex, which tends to be most common among young, college-educated whites and least common among African Americans and individuals with less education (Michael et al., 1994).

It should be stressed that such differences are generalities, not universal truths—for within subgroups, great diversity exists. For example, Asian Americans include the descen-

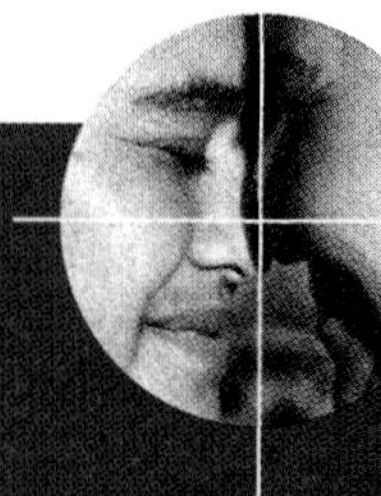

Sexuality and Diversity

Our Legacy of Intolerance of Native American Sexual Diversity

Most European settlers were shocked at the sexual lives of the Native Americans and tried to convert them to their Christian mores. Native American sexual customs varied widely from region to region, each tribe had its own culture, language, religion, and customs (Brown, 1997), but the fundamental differences between Indian and European sexual customs provided one basis for the Europeans to justify their self-proclaimed superiority over the Indians. Viewing Native Americans as "savages" helped Europeans rationalize the massacres and disenfranchisement of the native populations.

Native Americans did have different sexual customs from the Europeans. They did not associate nudity, sexual intercourse, or reproductive functions with sin. In fact, many aspects of sexuality and reproduction had spiritual meanings that were reflected in puberty rites and ritual festivals and dances. Many Native American tribes accepted premarital sexual intercourse and polygyny (the marriage of one male to more than one woman). Among tribes such as the Sioux (of the Dakotas), polygyny helped maintain family structure despite wartime losses of men. The practice also gave women the benefit of sharing domestic labor with other women.

In many tribes, women had considerable choice in their selection of sexual partners, and severe marital discord was resolved by separating without stigma or penalty. Among the Zuni of New Mexico, for instance, a woman could divorce her husband simply by collecting his belongings and placing them outside the door. Since no one "owned" another person's sexuality, prostitution did not exist prior to the arrival of Europeans, and rape was extremely rare. Even during the colonial-era Indian wars, Native American men did not sexually assault captured white women.

Children in some tribes grew up with few restrictions on sexual experimentation, ranging from masturbation to sexual play with other children. Children were seen as members of the entire tribe, rather than as belonging primarily to a European-style nuclear family; hence monogamy was not dants of Chinese laborers brought to the United States in the nineteenth century to build the first railroads. They also include refugees from the Vietnam and Korean wars, as well as individuals who came from Hong Kong, Japan, the Pacific Islands, and many other Asian countries to study, start businesses, or stay for other reasons. The Latino population is also composed of many groups that consider themselves culturally distinct (Zamora-Hernandez & Patterson, 1996). Furthermore, a significant proportion of the U.S. population is *multiracial,* having predecessors from two or more racial groups (Fong et al., 1995). Race and ethnicity are rarely simplistic, nonoverlapping classifications (Smith, 1995).

The degree of *acculturation*—that is, replacing traditional beliefs and behavior patterns with those of the dominant culture—also creates differences within subcultures. Many ethnic groups that have lived in North America for several generations are well assimilated (Barkley & Mosher, 1995). Some of these groups, such as Hawaiians, African Americans, and Native Americans, are undergoing a process of ethnic revival, attempting to recapture aspects of their cultures (Williams & Ellison, 1996).

Within the same ethnic group, socioeconomic status and education are crucial in influencing sexual attitudes and behaviors. Low-income and middle-income people often differ; the same is often true of people at different educational levels. For instance, people with more education masturbate more often than do less-educated people (Kinsey, 1948; Michael et al., 1994).

Sexual attitudes and behaviors also vary widely within specific religious groups. Thus, although Pope John Paul II espouses the traditional Roman Catholic view condemning all sexual activity that does not potentially lead to procreation, the views of American Catholics run the gamut on issues such as contraception, abortion, and homosexuality. Similarly, Orthodox Jews have much more conservative and traditional views regarding sexuality than do Reform Jews; and fundamentalist Protestant Christians often see things very differently from Christians who do not interpret the Bible literally.

Sexuality and Diversity

significant in assuring that children would be nurtured. As a Montagnais Indian responded to a Jesuit missionary who was describing the merits of monogamy, "You French people love only your children, but we all love all the children of our tribe" (D'Emilio & Freedman, 1988, p. 8).

Another practice that horrified Europeans was the recognition among some Native American groups, including the Zuni, Navajo, and also the Crow of the Great Plains, of a virtual "third gender," known to Native Americans as "Two Spirit" people. Two Spirit people have been documented in 150 Native American societies. They were men and women who pursued the traditional roles of the other sex—crafts and domestic work for men and warfare and hunting for women. They usually were spiritual leaders and enjoyed social and economic prestige within their tribes. Children with Two Spirit tendencies were given special care and encouragement, and adults whose interests and abilities went beyond customary sex-role behaviors usually demonstrated exceptional productivity and talent that the whole community respected (Roscoe, 1994).

In some cases, Two Spirit people always dressed like the other sex; others cross-dressed only when performing a cross-gendered activity. Sexual patterns varied as well and could involve heterosexual, bisexual, or homosexual relationships, including same-sex marriages (Roscoe, 1994). The community acceptance of cross-dressing and homosexual behavior evoked particularly strong censure from Europeans who were eager to convert Native Americans to Christianity and monogamy.

We-Wah, a Zuni "Two Spirit" man, adopted a lifelong role of a woman.

Sexuality: Personal or Public Domain?

The historical, cross-cultural, and intracultural perspectives we have examined in this chapter may help us appreciate the unique position in which we currently find ourselves. Men and women in our society today have new freedoms and responsibilities. To a far greater degree than was possible for the ancient Hebrews, the early Christians, the Europeans of the Middle Ages, or the Victorian Europeans and North Americans of a century ago—and to a far greater degree than is possible for many non-Western societies, such as many Arab cultures, today—we can define our own sexuality on the basis of personal choices.

This responsibility has been hard won, and it is largely a result of psychological, scientific, and social advances that have taken place primarily in the twentieth century. Psychological advances came with the work of such people as Sigmund Freud (1856–1939) and Havelock Ellis (1859–1939), who recognized sexuality in both women and men as natural and recognized that different individuals have differing sexual needs; and Theodore Van de Velde (1873–1937), who emphasized the importance of sexual pleasure and satisfaction. As these ideas became accepted by more people, a growing tolerance for a wider variety of behaviors resulted.

Findings of sex researchers such as Alfred Kinsey provided scientific data that brought further acceptance of masturbation, homosexuality, and nonmarital intercourse as normal expressions of sexuality. Research such as that done by William Masters and Virginia Johnson broadened public understanding of the sexual response cycle. In Chapter 2 we will look at the work of these and other pioneering sex researchers. This new awareness of sexual interests and individual variations also contributed to a greater tolerance and respect for the individual's right to make sexual decisions.

In the early 1960s, the invention of the oral contraceptive pill and the increased availability of other reliable contraceptive devices helped bring sexual decisions even more firmly into the personal domain. By the end of that decade, contraception had become accepted as a matter of personal decision. Moreover, in 1973 the U.S. Supreme Court ruled in a landmark decision that abortion is a woman's choice, one that government cannot prohibit. In the increasingly tolerant atmosphere of the late 1960s and 1970s, attitudes began to change about another traditional taboo, homosexuality. Homosexual men and women began to openly declare their sexual orientation—and to demand that such a personal matter should not affect their rights and responsibilities as citizens. The popular stigma surrounding homosexuality had begun to dissipate when the AIDS crisis, which arose in the 1980s, dramatically increased the visibility of homosexual individuals and amplified both positive and negative public sentiments toward homosexuality.

These many changes have come rapidly, and our society is still in a state of flux. One result has been a sense of uncertainty about personal and social values. For example, although young women and men have had more access to information, contraception, and medical care, there has been an epidemic of sexually transmitted diseases, unwanted pregnancies, and widespread confusion about personal values. However, the risk of contracting a terminal disease—AIDS—has led many individuals to be more conservative and cautious in their sexual behavior. In addition, we now face controversies about ethical and legal policies in almost every area related to human sexuality, from surrogate parenthood to what is censored on the Internet.

Some people believe personal choice should be the foundation for decisions related to sexuality; others are dedicated to limiting personal control and bringing many choices about sexuality back into the public domain. For example, antiabortion groups continue to attempt to make abortion illegal. Other groups oppose certain types of contraception, rights for homosexuals, pornography, and sex education, and they are attempting to enact social policy to support their views. Such conflicts between personal decisions and social control of various aspects of sexuality will undoubtedly continue into the twenty-first century.

Summary

THE AUTHORS' PERSPECTIVES

Because the authors have a psychosocial orientation, this book stresses the role of psychological factors and social conditioning in shaping human sexuality.

The book critically explores the effects of two pervasive themes related to sexuality: sex limited to reproduction and inflexible gender roles. The authors' biases predispose them against these legacies of Western culture.

OUR MEDIA CULTURE

Mass media as we know them have existed a short time relative to the greater human experience. Their impact on society, and sexuality in particular, is significant.

The media's mainstreaming of gay men and lesbians has been a major change in the late 1990s.

THE SEX-FOR-REPRODUCTION LEGACY

A prominent belief in Western culture is that sex is for reproduction only. This idea has deep historical roots.

The ancient Hebrews stressed the importance of childbearing but also had an appreciation of sexuality within marriage.

Christian writers such as Paul of Tarsus, Augustine, and Thomas Aquinas contributed to the view of sex as sinful, justifiable only in marriage for the purpose of procreation.

Leaders of the Reformation of the sixteenth century challenged the requirement that clergy remain celibate and recognized sexual expression as an important aspect of marriage.

Other religious traditions, including Taoism, Hinduism, and Islam, have not emphasized sex for reproduction to the exclusion of other reasons for sexual expression.

Technical advances in contraception in the twentieth century have permitted people to separate sexuality from procreation to a degree not previously possible.

THE GENDER-ROLE LEGACY

A second prominent belief in our culture is that women and men should conform to rigid gender roles. This idea, also, goes far back in Western history.

Gender-role differences between men and women were well established in ancient Hebraic culture. Women's most important roles were to manage the household and bear children, especially sons.

The New Testament writings of Paul emphasized the subservience of women.

Two contradictory images of women developed in the Middle Ages: the pure and unattainable woman-on-a-pedestal, manifest in the cult of the Virgin Mary and in courtly love; and the evil temptress represented by Eve and by the women persecuted as witches.

Women were viewed as asexual in the Victorian era, and the lives of "proper" Victorian men and women were largely separate. Men often employed prostitutes for companionship as well as sexual relations.

A CROSS-CULTURAL PERSPECTIVE: SOCIAL NORMS AND SEXUAL DIVERSITY

To appreciate the importance of social conditioning, we must look at sexual attitudes and behaviors in other cultures.

Communist China's government has attempted to isolate its people from "decadent" Western sexual attitudes and practices. Little sex education occurs in schools, and lack of sexual knowledge affects married couples. The sexual conservatism has also resulted in low rates of sexually transmitted diseases.

In the Islamic Middle East, veils, female circumcision, and segregation of the sexes until marriage are considered necessary to contain female sexuality.

Swedish family law and public health services promote open attitudes about sex outside of marriage in conjunction with preventing unwanted pregnancies, while promoting equal parenting responsibility for men and women.

Variations in acculturation, religious orthodoxy, and socioeconomic status create diversity within ethnic groups of the United States.

SEXUALITY: PERSONAL OR PUBLIC DOMAIN?

Greater knowledge, more reliable contraceptives, and legal decisions have increased the contemporary individual's ability to make personal decisions regarding sexuality. Our society is changing, resulting in some uncertainty about personal decisions. Social policies and laws can either restrict or expand personal options.

Thought Provokers

1. If you could design and implement your ideal sexual norms within a society, what would these be?
2. In what ways do restrictive sexual norms contribute beneficially to a society?
3. How do you think the two contradictory images of women—the Virgin Mary and the temptress Eve—are manifest in contemporary attitudes and media images?
4. How does someone like the singer and actress Madonna affect traditional images of women, and to what extent?

Suggested Readings

Barstow, Anne (1994). *Witchcraze.* San Francisco: Pandora. A compelling, comprehensive legacy of the witch-hunts and gender-based violence.

Boswell, John (1980). *Christianity, Social Tolerance, and Homosexuality.* Chicago: University of Chicago Press. A comprehensive study of Western beliefs concerning homosexuality from ancient Greece to the fourteenth century.

Degler, Carl (1980). *At Odds: Women and the Family in America from the Revolution to the Present.* Oxford: Oxford University Press. A historical survey of American women and their families.

D'Emilio, John; and Freedman, Estelle (1988). *Intimate Matters.* New York: Harper & Row. A full-length examination of the history of sexuality and how the meaning and place of sexuality in the United States have changed.

Sasson, Jean (1992). *Princess.* New York: Avon. A true story of women's lives behind the veil in Saudi Arabia.

Suggs, Robert; and Miracle, Andrew (Eds.) (1993). *Culture and Human Sexuality.* Pacific Grove, CA: Brooks/Cole. A superb collection of articles that details the sexual attitudes, behaviors, and mores of societies around the world.

Web Resources

Human Sexuality Web
www.umkc.edu/sites/hsw/index.html
Designed, maintained, and updated by graduate students at the University of Missouri-Kansas City, this site contains information concerning sex education, sexual counseling, sexual health issues, and other sexual topics.

SIECUS
www.siecus.org
SIECUS is a well-respected, nonprofit organization specializing in sex education and sexuality. Its Web site provides current and reliable information.

Ask NOAH About Sexuality
noah.cuny.edu/sexuality/sexuality.html
NOAH (New York Online Access to Health) offers detailed and relevant resources on sexual issues in both English and Spanish on its Web site.

2

Sex Research: Methods and Problems

The Goals of Sexology

What are the major goals of sexology? How do they compare with those of other scientific disciplines?

Is applying research findings to control or modify behavior a legitimate aim of sex research?

Nonexperimental Research Methods

What are the advantages and disadvantages of each of the three nonexperimental research methods used to study sexuality?

Which of the nonexperimental research methods has provided the most data about human sexuality?

The Experimental Method

How do researchers study sexual behavior in laboratory investigations of human sexuality?

What are the advantages and limitations of experimental studies of human sexuality?

Feminist Theory and Sex Research

What are the limitations of traditional sex research, from the perspective of feminist theory?

How might these limitations be corrected according to feminist scholars?

The Popular Media and Sex Research

How reliable is information about sexual behavior provided by popular media sources?

What methodology problems flaw magazine sex surveys?

Evaluating Research: Some Questions to Ask

To what degree can we rely on the findings of sex research?

What important questions should be asked when evaluating a particular example of sex research?

I am always skeptical of sex studies reported in newspapers, magazines, and books. How can you accurately study something so private? (Authors' files)

> A number of social observers have suggested that men who are active consumers of sexually violent films, magazines, and other pornography are likely to adopt abusive attitudes toward women. As a result, they show an increased tendency to commit rape and other abusive acts toward women.

> Many people believe that a few drinks make sex more enjoyable. After imbibing a little alcohol, they say that their inhibitions relax; they feel more sensual and also more friendly toward the person they are with.

> Early in this century, Sigmund Freud asserted that women's orgasms resulting from vaginal penetration are more "mature" than those resulting from clitoral stimulation alone. A common assumption today is that "vaginal" orgasms are superior to clitoral orgasms.

You have probably heard each of these three assertions before, and you may agree with one or even all of them. But if you were called on to prove that they were true or untrue, how would you go about compiling evidence or, as the author of the quote at the top of this page asks, how do you study sex?

Sexology
The study of sexuality.

The role of **sexology,** the study of sexuality, is to test such assumptions in a scientific way, to find out whether they are true or false and to document what underlying relationships, if any, they reveal. This task is not easy. Although intrinsically interesting to most of us, human sexual behavior is also inherently difficult to study, for it occupies an intensely private area in our lives that few of us are willing to reveal to others. In addition, the subject matter of sexology abounds with myth, exaggeration, secrecy, and value judgments.

Despite these problems, sex researchers have accumulated a growing body of knowledge about human sexual behaviors and attitudes—including the three assumptions with which we began this chapter: Does violent pornography lead to abusive behaviors such as rape? Does alcohol increase sexual pleasure? What are the differences between vaginal and clitoral orgasms? We will revisit these and other questions in this chapter as we discuss the methods used to study sexuality, the kinds of questions appropriate to each method, and also the problems inherent in each method. In the process, we will also learn something about evaluating published research.

We hope that in the following pages you may begin to appreciate what we know and do not know and how confident we can be about the available knowledge. You may also begin to sense the directions we can take to further expand our scientific knowledge of sexual behavior. Perhaps at some future time, you will contribute to our understanding of this important area of human experience. We invite you to do so.

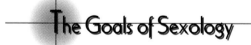

The Goals of Sexology

People who study human sexuality share certain goals with scientists in other disciplines. These include the goals of *understanding, predicting,* and *controlling* or influencing the events that are the subject matter of their respective fields.

The first two scientific goals—understanding and predicting behavior—are not difficult to comprehend. A pharmacologist, for example, who knows how blood pressure medications interfere with sexual functioning, might be able to use this knowledge to predict what dosage of a drug could be tolerated by a patient with a particular health condition without experiencing impaired sexual functioning. Similarly, a psychologist who knows something about the way certain behavior patterns influence the quality of couples' interactions may be able to help a couple predict whether they will have a happy marriage.

The third goal, using scientifically acquired knowledge to control behavior, is a more difficult concept to comprehend.

Can the application of scientific knowledge to control people's behavior be considered a legitimate goal of sexology?

Understandably, many people express concern about the legitimacy of applying scientific knowledge to control people's behavior. A certain amount of skepticism in this area is probably healthy, and it would be inaccurate to suggest that all knowledge acquired through research leads directly to behavior control. Nevertheless, sexologists have been able to influence, to one degree or another, a large body of phenomena. For example, understanding how adolescents make decisions about contraceptive use has resulted in the development of school-based sex-education programs, many of which are linked to family planning clinic services. These innovative programs have often resulted in positive behavioral changes such as increased contraceptive use among teenagers. Similarly, knowledge about the psychobiological causes of certain sexual problems, such as premature ejaculation and lack of vaginal lubrication, has enabled specialists to develop various therapies aimed at controlling such disruptive symptoms, as we will see in Chapter 16.

Most of us would not object to the goal of controlling or influencing events in the examples just described. However, like other scientists, sexologists must also contend with situations where the application of this goal raises important questions. For instance, is it appropriate for fertility specialists to use their knowledge to help a couple conceive a child of their desired biological sex, or for a sex therapist to subject imprisoned sex offenders to aversive stimuli (such as putrid odors) in an effort to control deviant sexual urges? Clearly, the goal of controlling or influencing human behavior should be carefully evaluated within a framework of ethical consideration.

Compared with many other disciplines, the field of sexology is an infant science, having originated largely within the twentieth century. The pioneering work of Alfred Kinsey, who was the first to conduct an extensive general survey of American sexual behaviors, took place only in the late 1940s and early 1950s. Many questions remain unanswered. However, a considerable body of knowledge is accumulating, including information from diverse cultures (see the boxed discussion "Sex Research in Other Countries"). In the remainder of this chapter, we will examine some of the research methods that have been used to explore human sexuality.

Sexuality and Diversity

Sex Research in Other Countries

Most of the available data about human sexual attitudes and behavior come from investigations within our own North American society. However, sexual expression in other societies has captured the interest of a small number of ethnographers, whose findings provide us with some intriguing if sketchy glimpses into sexual mores and behaviors in other cultures. Throughout this book we will encounter examples of the diversity of sexual expression around the world. Whether we are learning about the sex lives of people who live on the plains of Tanzania, in the rain forests of New Guinea, or on an island in Polynesia, we can expect not only to acquire an increased awareness of the diversity of human sexual expression throughout the world but also to improve our understanding of our own society's sexual standards and values.

While discussions throughout our book draw on numerous studies, a few sources are particularly noteworthy. One is the monumental work by anthropologist Clellan Ford and psychologist Frank Beach, who surveyed human sexuality in 190 societies throughout the world. Although their classic book, *Patterns of Sexual Behavior* (1951), was published over four decades ago, the work of Ford and Beach remains one of our best sources on cultural variations in human sexual expression. A more recent source is an excellent reader, *Culture and Human Sexuality* (1993), edited by David Suggs and Andrew Miracle. It contains essays about sexual expression in several diverse societies.

Although ethnographers have played a central role in cross-cultural sex research, in recent years scientists from other fields (psychology, sociology, medicine, etc.) have taken a more active role in gathering data in other countries. For example, the World Health Organization (WHO), motivated by a pressing need to better understand the varied ways in which

(continued on next page)

Nonexperimental Research Methods

We began this chapter with three common notions about human sexual behavior: that exposure to violent pornography can increase a man's tolerance of and willingness to commit sexually violent acts such as rape; that alcohol can enhance sexual responsiveness; and that vaginal orgasms are superior to clitoral orgasms. How do researchers go about investigating hypotheses such as these? In this section we look at three nonexperimental methods: the case study, the survey, and direct observation. Later in the chapter, we will learn about a fourth method, experimental research. Table 2.1 summarizes these four major methods of studying sexual behavior. As we will see, not every research method is appropriate to every type of research question.

Case Study

Case study
Examines either a single subject or a small group of subjects, each studied individually and in depth.

A **case study** examines either a single subject or a small group of subjects, each of whom is studied individually and in depth. Data are gathered using a variety of means that may include direct observation, questionnaires, testing, and even experimentation.

People often become subjects for case studies because they behave in an atypical way or have a physical or emotional disorder. Thus a large portion of our information about sexual response difficulties (for instance, erectile inhibition in men and lack of orgasmic response in women) comes from case studies of individuals seeking treatment for these problems. Also, much of what we know about sex offenders, transsexuals, incest victims, and the like has been learned from case studies.

Not surprisingly, a number of case studies have investigated the relationship between sexually violent media and rape. In many of these studies, rapists report high levels of

Sexuality and Diversity

the AIDS virus may be spread, began conducting extensive investigations of sexual behavior in a host of countries in the late 1980s (Booth, 1989). This research continues in the 1990s (see Chapter 17 for more details).

The worldwide AIDS crisis provided impetus for two major survey investigations recently completed in France and England. In the French study, conducted in 1991 and 1992, potential subjects were notified by mail that they had been identified by France's Health Ministry to be part of a representative national sample to be surveyed. A remarkably high participation rate of 76.5% yielded a sample of 20,055 men and women, ages 18 to 69, who were interviewed by telephone. Among findings especially relevant to the AIDS crisis was evidence that many of the youthful respondents do not use condoms during coitus because they are too expensive in France. Furthermore, 13% of men and 6% of women had multiple sex partners in the previous year and thus were at increased risk of being infected by the AIDS virus. In contrast, rates of extramarital sexual involvements were found to be declining, a positive finding relative to AIDS prevention (ACSF Investigators, 1992). A similar national study was conducted by British researchers who surveyed 18,876 men and women, ages 16 to 59, living in England, Scotland, and Wales. This investigation revealed that 14% of men and 7% of women, respectively, had multiple sex partners in the previous 12 months, figures quite comparable to those obtained in the French study (Johnson et al., 1992).

One of the most intriguing examples of sex research in another country recently emerged with the publication of a national sex survey of 23,000 Chinese conducted by sociologist Liu Dalin. Among other things, this survey found that approximately 50% of young people engage in premarital intercourse, almost 70% of respondents expressed approval of extramarital sex, most Chinese couples engage in little or no foreplay prior to initiating intercourse, and women are more likely than men to initiate divorce proceedings (Southerland, 1990).

A legitimate goal of sex research is to understand the universalities as well as the diversities in human sexual behavior. What better way is there to accomplish this than through a search for behavior patterns that are shared across cultural boundaries?

Table 2.1 A Summary of Research Methods

Method	*Brief Description*	*Advantages*	*Disadvantages*
Case study	Examines a single subject or a small group of subjects, each of whom is studied individually and in depth	Flexibility of data-gathering procedures In-depth explorations of behaviors, thoughts, and feelings	Limited generalizability of findings Accuracy of data limited by fallibility of human memory Not suitable for many kinds of research questions
Survey	Data pertaining to sexual attitudes and behaviors derived from relatively large groups of people via questionnaires or interviews	Relatively cheap and quick method for obtaining large amounts of data Can obtain data from more people than it is practical to study in the laboratory or via case studies	Problems of: Nonresponse Demographic bias Inaccurate information
Direct observation	Researchers observe and record responses of participating subjects	Virtually eliminates the possibility of data falsification Behavioral record can be kept indefinitely on videotapes or films	Subjects' behavior may be influenced by presence of observer(s) or the artificial nature of the environment where observations are made
Experimental method	Subjects presented with certain events (stimuli) under managed conditions that allow for reliable measurement of their reactions	Provides a controlled environment for managing relevant variables Suited to discovering causal relationships between variables	Artificiality of laboratory settings may adversely influence or bias subjects' responses

exposure to sexually violent films, magazines, and books (Marshall, 1988). For example, Kenneth Bianchi, the infamous Los Angeles "Hillside Strangler" who raped and killed several women, was shown to have "collected magazines and films that featured violent pornography . . ." (Norris, 1988, p. 197).

Because case-study evidence shows that rapists often report high exposure to sexually violent pornography, can we conclude that a cause-and-effect relationship exists between this exposure and rape?

It is unclear whether violent attitudes toward women and behaviors such as rape result directly from exposure to sexually violent media. The mere fact that rapists seem more inclined than nonrapists to consume pornography does not necessarily imply a cause-and-effect relationship. Perhaps there are other plausible explanations. For example, the types of environments that tend to socialize men to be violent toward women might also be characterized by easy access to violent pornography. Thus, while the case-study method shows that this media exposure is often associated with rape, it cannot tell us the exact nature of the relationship.

The case-study method has also been used to investigate the common assertion that alcohol enhances sexual responsiveness and pleasure. In fact, evidence from some of these studies suggests just the reverse, at least among chronic alcoholics. Case studies of alcoholic subjects have shown decreased arousability as well as lowered sexual interest, although it is possible that this effect is due to the general physical deterioration that accompanies heavy, long-term alcohol use.

The case-study approach offers some advantages to researchers, one of which is the flexibility of data-gathering procedures. Although it offers little opportunity for investigative control, the open-ended format of the case study often provides opportunities to acquire insight into specific behaviors. The highly personal, subjective information about what individuals actually think and feel about their behavior represents an important step beyond simply recording activities. This method sacrifices some control, but it offers opportunities to explore specific behaviors, thoughts, and feelings in depth, and can add considerable dimension to our information.

There are some limitations to the case-study method, however. Because case studies typically focus on individuals or small samples of especially interesting or atypical cases, it is often difficult to generalize findings accurately to broader populations. A second limitation of case studies is that a person's past history, especially as it pertains to the years of childhood and adolescence, usually does not become a target of research until he or she manifests some unusual behavior later in life, as an adult. Human memory is fallible: Is it possible for a researcher to accurately reconstruct a subject's earlier life from accounts provided by the subject? Even if family members and friends are also questioned, there are no guarantees, for people often have trouble accurately remembering events from years ago. Furthermore, memory may also be subject to intentional efforts to distort or repress facts.

A third limitation of the case study is that it is not suitable for many kinds of research questions. For instance, the case study might not be the best method for testing the third assumption on this chapter's opening page—that vaginal orgasms are superior to clitoral orgasms. And because personal accounts may be influenced by factors such as emotions, values, and the vagaries of memory, the reliability of this method might also be in doubt. As we will see shortly, this type of research problem is better suited to another method, direct observation.

All these cautions about limitations of the case study method can be applied to the cases we cite in our Authors' Files selections throughout this book. Nevertheless, we believe that each of these cases presents relevant personal reflections of experiences, thoughts, and feelings, and we include them so that you may draw perspective, not conclusions, from them.

Survey

Survey
A research method in which a sample of people are questioned about their behaviors and/or attitudes.

Most of our information about human sexuality has been obtained from a second important research method, the **survey,** in which people are asked about their sexual experiences or attitudes. The survey method enables researchers to collect data from a large number of people, usually more than can be studied in a clinical setting or in the laboratory. Surveys may be conducted orally, through face-to-face or telephone interviews, or through paper-and-pencil questionnaires. Recently, computerized interviews have been used to gather information about sexual behaviors and other sensitive topics. The boxed discussion "Computerized Assessment of Sexual Behavior" describes this innovative interview technique.

Although the methods of conducting written and oral surveys are somewhat different, their intent is the same. Each tries to use a relatively small group, called the *survey sample,* to draw inferences or conclusions about a much larger group with a particular characteristic (called a *target population*). Examples of target populations might be married adults or high school adolescents.

Choosing the Sample

The questions asked by sexologists often apply to populations that are too large to study in their entirety. For example, if you wanted to obtain information about the sexual practices of American married couples in their later years, your population would include all married couples in the United States over a given age, say 65. Clearly, it would be impos-

Most information about human sexual behavior has been obtained through questionnaire or interview surveys.

sible to question everyone in this group. Sex researchers resolve this problem by obtaining data from a relatively small sample of the target population. The confidence with which we can draw conclusions about the larger population depends on the technique used to select this sample.

Typically, researchers strive to select a **representative sample,** that is, a sample in which various subgroups are represented proportionately to their incidence in the target population. Target populations can be subdivided into smaller subgroups by criteria such as age, economic status, geographic locale, religious affiliation, and so on. In a representative sample, every individual in the larger, target population has a chance of being included.

Representative sample
A type of limited research sample that provides an accurate representation of a larger target population of interest.

What procedures would you use to select a representative sample that could be surveyed to assess the sexual practices of older American married couples? How would you ensure the representativeness of your selected sample?

A good beginning would be to obtain U.S. Census Bureau statistics on the number of married couples, both partners age 65 and older, who reside in major geographic regions of the United States (East, South, and so forth). Next, you would select subgroups for your sample according to the actual distribution of the larger population. Thus, if 25% of older married couples live in the East, 25% of your sample would be drawn from this region. Similarly, if 15% of older married couples in the East fall in an upper socioeconomic status category, 15% of those subjects selected from the East would be drawn from this group.

Once you had systematically compiled your lists of potential subjects, your final step would be to select your actual subjects from these lists. To ensure that all members of each subgroup had an equal chance of being included, you might use a table of random numbers to generate random selections from your lists. If these procedures were correctly applied, and your final sample was large enough, you could be reasonably confident that your findings could be generalized to all married American couples, age 65 or older.

Another kind of sample, the **random sample,** is selected from a larger population using randomization procedures. A random sample may or may not be the same as a representative sample. For example, let's assume that you are a social scientist on the faculty of a very large urban university whose faculty, graduate students, and undergraduate students are inclined to hold liberal political and social views. You wish to conduct a survey that will provide an update on "swinging" (a form of consensual extramarital sex

Random sample
A randomly chosen subset of a population.

practiced by married couples). It is convenient to draw your subjects from married couples affiliated with your university. You obtain a roster of all married students and faculty at your university (which number several thousand), and you randomly select your survey sample from this group.

You design an excellent, anonymously administered questionnaire, with clear, concise questions, and are gratified that a substantial majority of your sample respond to your survey. Can you now be relatively confident that your results reflect the general attitude of married couples toward swinging, if not in the greater U.S. population, at least in your geographical region? Unfortunately, you cannot, because you have selected subjects from a sample that is not necessarily representative of the broader community. Your university population is characterized by liberal political and social views, traits that probably render them atypical of the broader population of married couples. (Indeed, surveys have shown that most swingers tend to be middle- to upper-middle-class whites with relatively conservative to moderate political and social views [Gilmartin, 1977; Karlen, 1988].)

Thus, even though randomization is often a valid selection tool, a study sample will not be truly representative unless it reflects all the important subgroups in the target population.

All things considered, representative samples generally allow for more accurate generalizations to the entire target population than do random samples. However, random samples are often quite adequate and thus are used widely.

On the Edge

Computerized Assessment of Sexual Behavior

We have learned that sex research is especially difficult, because most of us are uncomfortable revealing information about such a private area of our lives. When children or adolescents are being asked sensitive questions, the problems of obtaining reliable answers are greatly magnified, since young people are notoriously reticent to divulge sexual information to adults, regardless of their professional status (Paperny, 1997; Romer et al., 1997). This reluctance to divulge information or to seek professional advice on sexual matters has undoubtedly contributed to the epidemic proportions of sex abuse of children, teenage pregnancies, and the escalating incidence of sexually transmitted diseases among America's youth. Health officials have tried many approaches in their efforts to identify high-risk children and adolescents and to develop effective modes of intervention to prevent health-damaging sexual behaviors. Unfortunately, most attempts have met with only limited success, hindered largely by information barriers imposed by the nature of the issues being addressed (Paperny, 1997). However, the recent advent of computers as tools for interviewing children and adolescents holds great promise for overcoming the barriers researchers and clinicians face when conducting interviews on sensitive topics with youthful respondents.

A number of studies have shown that computers are an effective way to take medical and behavioral histories (Grossman, 1971; Space, 1981; Stout, 1981). Adolescents have demonstrated a willingness to readily reveal sensitive information to a computer (Millstein & Irvin, 1983). One recent study of several hundred adolescents found that computers were more effective and accurate than written questionnaires for obtaining information about sensitive issues (Paperny et al., 1990).

David Paperny (1997), M.D. and professor of pediatrics and adolescent medicine at the University of Hawaii School of Medicine, recently reported on a decade of research using computerized adolescent health assessment. Paperny and his colleagues developed an interactive multimedia computer program titled "Youth Health Provider." This program provides an anonymous and nonjudgmental device for obtaining a comprehensive social and behavioral health history that also has the capability of dispensing important information about health-maintaining practices. The entire program is self-administered, requires no supervision, and is completed in strictly enforced privacy. Questions are presented both orally and by on-screen print and are answered by pressing a button or touching the monitor screen. The Youth Health Provider is an interactive, branching program that takes a directed history based on specific screening questions and previous answers. It proceeds in a logical manner similar to how a clinician might proceed in a face-to-face interview. Depending on individual

Questionnaires and Interviews

Once selected, subjects within a sample may be surveyed either by a written questionnaire or by an interview. Both procedures involve asking the participants a set of questions that may range from a few to over 1000. These may be multiple-choice, true–false, or discussion questions; subjects may respond alone, in the privacy of their homes, or in the presence of a researcher.

Sex researchers who use surveys take into consideration the relative benefits and shortcomings of questionnaires versus interviews. Before reading on, take a minute to list what you consider to be some pluses and minuses of each approach.

Each survey method has advantages and disadvantages. Questionnaires tend to be quicker and cheaper to administer than interview surveys. In addition, because there is greater anonymity in filling out a form than in facing an interviewer, subjects may be considerably more likely to answer questions honestly, with minimal distortion. Sexual behavior is highly personal, and, in interviews, subjects may be tempted to describe their behaviors or attitudes in a more favorable light. Finally, because most written questionnaires can be evaluated objectively, their data are less subject to researcher bias than are interviews.

On the other hand, interviews have some advantages that questionnaires do not share. First, the format of an interview is more flexible. If a particular question is

On the Edge

The effectiveness of "Youth Health Provider," developed by David Paperny, suggests that teenagers are more willing to share sensitive information on sexual behavior with a computer.

responses, a teenage respondent may be asked up to 350 questions. The program internally validates certain responses for consistency and an opportunity to clarify answers is offered if responses are inconsistent.

Assessment of data obtained from over 5000 computer interviews with adolescents strongly indicates that this method provides valid and accurate response data on sensitive issues in a manner that teenagers clearly prefer over questionnaires or personal interviews. Paperny reports that exceptional enthusiasm for the program has been consistently expressed by both the adolescent participants and the various clinicians and educators who work with these young subjects. In addition to providing thorough, accurate behavioral and health histories, this program also offers a way to identify problem areas and health needs, provides problem-specific health advice and local referrals, and dispenses printed take-home materials relevant to a particular respondent's circumstances. In summary, this thorough, accurate, painless, and enthusiastically received computerized health assessment program with educational multimedia "may be one of the most promising interventions for adolescent health promotion" (p. 69).

The use of computers to obtain information about sexual behaviors has also been shown to be valuable when the subjects are children. A recent study of several hundred African-American children found that interviews conducted by a talking computer elicited more information about sexual experiences than did face-to-face interviews (Romer et al., 1997). The results of this study, together with David Paperny's findings with adolescents, strongly suggest that a computerized interview is an innovative, time-saving, accurate, enthusiastically received, and highly feasible method to study the sexual behavior of children, adolescents, and—as time will undoubtedly reveal—adults as well.

confusing to the subject, the interviewer can clarify it. In addition, interviewers have the option of varying the sequence of questions if it seems appropriate for a particular respondent. And finally, skillful interviewers may establish excellent rapport with subjects, and the resulting sense of trust may produce more revealing responses than is possible with paper-and-pencil questionnaires.

Problems of Sex Survey Research: Nonresponse, Demographic Bias, and Inaccuracy

Regardless of the survey strategy employed, sex researchers find that it is very difficult to secure a representative sample. This is because many people do not want to participate in studies of this nature. For instance, assuming that you used proper sampling procedures to choose your sample of older married couples in the example discussed earlier, what proportion of your representative sample would actually be willing to answer your questions? **Nonresponse,** the refusal to participate in a research study, is a common problem that consistently plagues sex survey research.

Nonresponse
The refusal to participate in a research study.

No one has ever conducted a major sex survey in which 100% of the selected subjects voluntarily participated. In fact, some studies include results obtained from samples in which only a small minority responded.

Are people who agree to take part in sex surveys any different from those who refuse?

Perhaps volunteer subjects in sex research are a representative cross section of the population, but we have no theoretical or statistical basis for that conclusion. As a matter of fact, the opposite might well be true. People who volunteer to participate may be the ones who are the most eager to share their experiences, who have explored a wide range of activities, or who feel most comfortable with their sexuality. (Or it may be that the most experienced people are those who are least willing to respond because they feel their behaviors are atypical or extreme.) A preponderance of experienced, inexperienced, liberal, or conservative individuals might bias any sample.

Self-selection
The bias introduced into research study results due to participants' willingness to respond.

Research suggests that **self-selection,** or "volunteer bias," is an important concern for sex researchers (Clement, 1990). A number of studies strongly suggest that volunteers for

In recent years researchers have begun to explore the relationship between ethnicity and sexual behavior in the United States. These efforts, although so far quite limited, seek to provide information about an aspect of American sexual behavior largely overlooked in earlier studies. Throughout our text we will describe results from several studies as we discuss ethnicity in relation to a variety of topics. In this box we limit our observations to a few pertinent findings from a contemporary study that represents the best sex survey ever conducted in the United States. The National Health and Social Life Survey (NHSLS) used a representative research sample of 3432 American adults, approximately 75% of which were white, 12% African Americans, 8% Hispanic Americans, and the balance drawn from other ethnic/racial groups, notably Asian Americans and Native Americans (Laumann et al., 1994). This ethnic distribution in the research population reflects U.S. demographics, wherein African Americans represent the largest ethnic minority, followed in frequency by Hispanic Americans. The following information provides a brief preview of some important ethnicity findings of this study, to be discussed in more detail later in our text.

This investigation revealed the impact of ethnicity on several sexual behaviors including, but not limited to, (1) numbers of sexual partners, (2) likelihood of choosing sex partners from the same ethnic group, (3) oral sex, (4) anal sex, (5) masturbation, and (6) experience with coercive sex. A larger percentage of African Americans (27.1%) reported having more than one sex partner in the past year than both Hispanic Americans (19.9%) and whites (15.1%). However, ethnic differences in number of sex partners are less pronounced when assessed over a longer time frame. The relevant statistics for a five-year span are 48.0% for African Americans, 36.6% for Hispanic Americans, and 37.2% for whites.

sex research tend to be more sexually experienced and to hold more positive attitudes toward sexuality and sex research than do nonvolunteers (Bogaert, 1996; Clement, 1990; Morokoff, 1986; Wiederman, 1993). In addition, research indicates that women may be less likely than men to volunteer for sex research (Wiederman et al., 1994), a finding that suggests female sex research samples are more highly selected than male samples.

Another kind of problem that affects sex surveys is **demographic bias.** Most of the data available from sex research in the United States have come from samples weighted heavily toward white, middle-class volunteers. Typically, college students and educated white-collar workers are disproportionately represented.

Demographic bias
A kind of sampling bias in which certain segments of society (such as Caucasian, middle-class, white-collar workers) are disproportionately represented in a study population.

How much effect do nonresponse and demographic bias have on sex research findings? We cannot say for sure. But as long as elements of society, including the less educated and ethnic and racial minorities, are underrepresented, we must be cautious in generalizing findings to the population at large. The informational deficit pertaining to sexual behaviors of American racial/ethnic minorities is beginning to lessen with the recent emergence of several studies that have included members of various ethnic minority groups in the United States (see the boxed discussion "Research on American Ethnicity and Sexuality").

A third type of problem inherent in sex survey research has to do with the accuracy of subjects' responses. Most data about human sexual behavior are obtained from respondents' own reports of their experiences. How closely does actual behavior correspond to these subjective, after-the-fact reports?

As we saw in the discussion of case studies, people's actual behavior may be quite different from what they report (Newcomer & Udry, 1988). In the survey method as well, human memory is one potential problem (Catania et al., 1990). How many people accurately remember when they first masturbated and with what frequency or at what age they first experienced orgasm? Some people may also consciously or unconsciously conceal certain facts about their sexual histories because they view them as abnormal, foolish, or painful to remember. People may feel pressure to deny or minimize their experiences regarding behaviors such as incest, homosexuality, and masturbation where strong taboos exist. In other cases, people may purposely inflate their experience, perhaps out of a desire to appear more liberal, experienced, or proficient.

Sexuality and Diversity

One finding of interest was that the percentage of noncohabitational sexual partnerships from the same ethnic group was very high, exceeding 90%, for both African Americans and whites. In marked contrast, Hispanic American respondents reported that only about 50% of their noncohabitational sexual partnerships were with members of their ethnic group.

The following table outlines several other notable ethnic variations in sexuality. Two of the most pronounced differences are in the area of oral sex and masturbation. African Americans report markedly lower rates of involvement in both these sexual practices than either whites or Hispanic Americans.

Ethnicity and Sexual Practices

	White		*African Americans*		*Hispanic Americans*	
	Men	*Women*	*Men*	*Women*	*Men*	*Women*
Experience with giving oral sex (%)	81.4	75.3	50.5	34.4	70.7	59.7
Experience with receptive oral sex (%)	81.4	78.9	66.3	48.9	73.2	63.7
Experience with anal sex (%)	25.8	23.2	23.4	9.6	34.2	17.0
Did not masturbate at all in last year (%)	33.4	55.7	60.3	67.8	33.3	65.5
Masturbated at least once per week in last year (%)	28.3	7.3	16.9	10.7	24.4	4.7
Women ever sexually forced by a man (%)		23.0		19.0		14.0

Source: Laumann et al., 1994.

Alfred Kinsey, a pioneer sex researcher, conducted one of the most comprehensive surveys on human sexuality.

The Kinsey Reports

The studies of Alfred Kinsey are perhaps the best known and most widely cited example of survey research. With his associates, Kinsey published two large volumes in the decade following World War II: One, on male sexuality, was published in 1948; the follow-up report on female sexuality was published in 1953. These volumes contain the results of extensive survey interviews, the aim of which was to determine patterns of sexual behavior in American males and females.

The Kinsey sample consisted of 5300 white males and 5940 white females. Respondents came from both rural and urban areas in each state, and represented a range of ages, marital status, occupations, educational levels, and religions. However, the sample had a disproportionately greater number of better-educated, city-dwelling Protestants, whereas older people, rural dwellers, and those with less education were underrepresented. African Americans and other racial minorities were completely omitted from the sample. And finally, all subjects were volunteers. Thus, in no way can Kinsey's study population be viewed as a representative sample of the American population.

Although published four decades ago, many of Kinsey's data are relevant today (Reinisch & Beasley, 1990). The passage of time has not altered the validity of certain findings—for example, that sexual behavior is influenced by educational level, or that heterosexuality or homosexuality is often not an all-or-none proposition. However, certain other areas—such as coital rates among unmarried people—are more influenced by changing societal norms. Therefore, we might expect the Kinsey data to be less predictive of contemporary practices in these areas. Nevertheless, even here the data are still relevant in that they provide one possible basis for estimating the degree of behavioral change over the years.

The National Health and Social Life Survey

The outbreak of the devastating AIDS epidemic in the 1980s occurred at a time when the U.S. public health community was very ill-informed about the contemporary sexual practices of the citizenry. To fill this informational void with data that might be used to predict and prevent the spread of AIDS, in 1987 an agency within the U.S. Department of Health and Human Services called for proposals to study the sexual attitudes and practices of American adults. A team of distinguished researchers at the University of Chicago answered this call with a plan for a national survey to assess the prevalence of a broad array of sexual practices and attitudes and to place them in their social contexts within the U.S. population. The research team—Edward Laumann and his colleagues, John Gagnon, Robert Michael, and Stuart Michaels—was initially heartened by the acceptance of their proposal in 1988 and by provision of government funds adequate to support a survey of 20,000 people.

A sample size this large would have allowed the investigators to draw reliable conclusions about various subpopulations in America, such as diverse ethnic minorities and homosexuals. However, after more than two years of extensive planning, the research team's efforts were dealt a crushing blow when federal funding for their study was withdrawn. In 1991, conservative members of Congress, offended by the prospect of government funding of sex research, introduced legislation that effectively eliminated federal funding for such studies.

Undaunted by this setback, Laumann and his colleagues secured funding from several private foundations that enabled them to proceed with their project, but with a much smaller sample size. The research team, working with the National Opinion Research Center (NORC) at the University of Chicago, used sophisticated sampling techniques to select a representative sample of 4369 Americans, ages 18 to 59. An amazing 79% of the sample subjects agreed to participate, yielding a final study group of 3432 respondents. This high response rate dramatically demonstrated that a broad array of people will participate in a highly personal sex survey when they are assured that there are important societal benefits for such research and the confidentiality of their responses is guaranteed.

Furthermore, this unusually high participation rate, together with the fact that the study population closely approximated many known demographic characteristics of the general U.S. population, yielded data most social scientists believed to reliably indicate the sexual practices of most 18- to 59-year-old American adults.

Forced to limit their sample size, Laumann and his associates had to forgo sampling a broad range of subpopulations and instead oversampled African Americans and Hispanic Americans to secure valid information about these two largest ethnic minorities in America. Thus although the study population was representative of white Americans, black Americans, and Hispanic Americans, too few members of other racial/ethnic minorities (such as Jews, Asian Americans, and Native Americans) were included to provide useful information about these groups.

Laumann and his colleagues trained 220 professionals, with prior interview experience, to interview all 3432 respondents face-to-face. They designed the questionnaire to be easily understood and to flow naturally across various topics. Using trained and experienced interviewers ensured that respondents understood all questions posed. In addition, the questionnaire contained internal checks to measure consistency of answers, to validate the overall responses.

The NHSLS research team (left to right): Robert T. Michael, John H. Gagnon, Stuart Michaels, and Edward O. Laumann.

This excellent study, entitled the National Health and Social Life Survey (NHSLS), provided the most comprehensive information about adult sexual behavior in America since Kinsey's research. In fact, because Laumann and his associates used far better sampling techniques than did the Kinsey group, this study stands alone as the single best sex survey ever conducted within the United States and one that reliably reflects the sexual practices of the general U.S. adult population in the 1990s. An analysis of the NHSLS findings was published in two books, one a detailed and scholarly text titled *The Social Organization of Sexuality: Sexual Practices in the United States,* by Laumann, Gagnon, Michael, and Michaels (1994). Michael, Gagnon, Laumann, and Gina Kolata—a respected *New York Times* science author—wrote a less technical companion volume for the general public titled *Sex in America: A Definitive Study.* This book, also published in 1994, emerged as a very popular trade book.

Like all sex research, the NHSLS has its share of detractors. However, most sexologists, including the authors of this text, are impressed with the excellent methodology and scope of the study and generally accept its findings as representing the best data currently available. Not surprisingly, publication of the two descriptive books created a storm of media attention. This was especially true because the NHSLS findings contradicted conventional wisdom—promulgated by magazine surveys and mass media images—that envisioned a "sex crazy" American populace madly pursuing excessive indulgence in all kinds of conventional and unconventional sexual practices. In reality, results of this survey reflect an American people who are more content with their erotic lives, less sexually active, and more sexually conservative than was widely believed. These findings are especially ironic in view of the judgmental opposition by conservative legislators to the Laumann study, out of fear it would provide a mandate for excessive sexual expression. In later chapters we will examine the various findings of this important study in some detail.

Survey Findings Regarding Two Issues: Violent Pornography and Alcohol Use

How might the survey method be used to clarify the three assertions with which we began this chapter? The first assertion, concerning violent media and men's likelihood to develop abusive attitudes and behaviors toward women, has been the subject of a number of surveys in the last decade or so.

One of the more notable studies involved 222 male nonoffender college students who were administered a questionnaire regarding their use of pornography as well as their self-reported likelihood of committing rape or using sexual force. Of these men, 81% had used nonviolent pornography during the previous year, whereas 35% had used sexually violent pornography. Of the subjects who used sexually violent pornography, many more indicated a likelihood of raping or using sexual force against a woman than did subjects who used only nonviolent pornography (Démare et al., 1988). Other surveys of different populations of men (including some imprisoned rapists) have provided further indications that exposure to sexually violent media may lead to increased tolerance for sexually aggressive behavior, greater acceptance of the myth that women want to be raped, reduced sensitivity to rape victims, desensitization to violence against women, and, in some cases, to an increased probability of committing a rape (Donnerstein & Linz, 1984; Rosen & Beck, 1988).

The second assertion, concerning the effect of alcohol on sexual responsiveness, has also been the subject of survey research. One study conducted in the 1970s asked 20,000 middle- and upper-middle-class Americans whether drinking enhanced their sexual pleasure (Athanasiou et al., 1970). Most respondents answered yes—60% stated that alcohol helped put them "in the mood" for sex, with a significantly higher proportion of women providing this response. This finding should be interpreted with some caution, however, for as we have seen, people's memories of events may differ considerably from their actual behaviors. For the third assertion, regarding the superiority of vaginal orgasms, any survey results would also need to be interpreted with caution, for the same reasons. A more appropriate method for studying this question is direct observation, to which we turn next.

Direct Observation

Direct observation
A method of research in which subjects are observed as they go about their activities.

A third method for studying human sexual behavior is **direct observation.** Here, researchers observe and record responses of participating subjects. Although observational research is quite common in social sciences such as anthropology, sociology, and psychology, little research of this nature occurs in sexology because of the highly personal and private nature of human sexual expression. (It is not surprising, therefore, that no one has employed direct observation to study the link between violent pornography and rape or between alcohol use and sexual arousal.)

The most famous example of direct observational research is the widely acclaimed work of William Masters and Virginia Johnson. Along with the Kinsey research, Masters and Johnson's study of human sexual response is probably the most often mentioned sex research, and it is cited frequently in this text. These investigators used direct observation in a laboratory setting to learn about physiological changes during sexual arousal. (Their study remains the only major piece of research to have done this.) The result, *Human Sexual Response* (1966), was based on laboratory observations of 10,000 completed sexual response cycles. Results of these observations are presented in Chapter 6. The Masters and Johnson research sample consisted of sexually responsive volunteers, 382 women and 312 men, drawn largely from

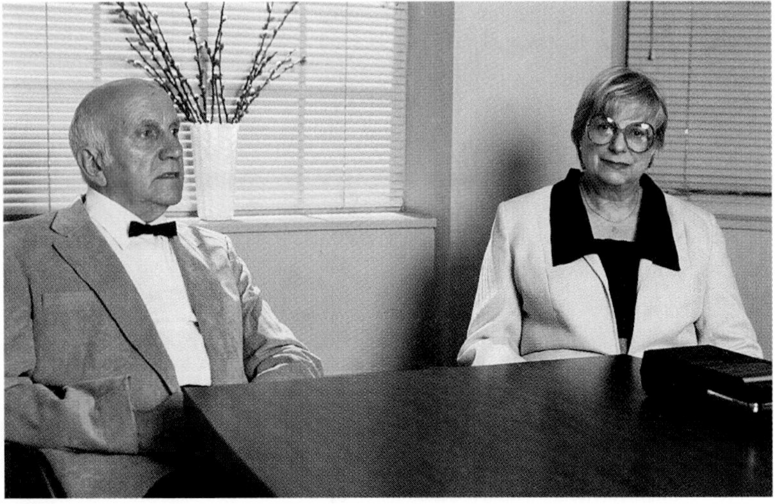

William Masters and Virginia Johnson used direct observation to study the physiological sexual responses of women and men.

an academic community, of above-average intelligence and socioeconomic background—obviously not a representative sample of the entire U.S. population. However, the physical signs of sexual arousal, the subject of their study, appear to be rather stable across a wide range of people with diverse backgrounds.

Masters and Johnson used a number of techniques to record physiological sexual responses. These included the use of photographic equipment and instruments to measure and record muscular and vascular changes throughout the body. They also used direct observation, as well as ingenious measurement devices, to record changes in sex organs, as described in the boxed discussion, "Technology for Sex Research." Masters and Johnson recorded responses in a variety of stimulus situations in their laboratory: masturbation, coitus with a partner, artificial coition, and stimulation of the breasts alone. As a follow-up to all recorded observations, each participant was extensively interviewed.

Our Sexuality

Technology for Sex Research

Experimental research and direct observation studies of human sexual responses often employ measures of sexual arousal. Until recently, researchers had to rely largely on subjective reports of these responses. However, advances in technology have produced several devices for measuring sexual arousal.

The penile strain gauge is a flexible loop that looks something like a rubber band with a wire attached. It is actually a thin rubber tube filled with a fine strand of mercury. A tiny electrical current from the attached wire flows through the mercury continuously. The gauge is placed around the base of the penis; as an erection occurs, the rubber tube stretches, and the strand of mercury becomes thinner, changing the flow of the current. These changes are registered by a recording device called a polygraph. The penile strain gauge can measure even the slightest changes in penis size and, in fact, is so sensitive that it can record every pulse of blood into the penis. In the interests of privacy, a subject can attach the gauge to his own penis. Researchers may also measure male sexual arousal with the penile plethysmograph or the metal-band gauge, devices that also fit around the penis and reflect small changes in its circumference.

When a woman is sexually aroused, her vaginal walls fill with blood in a manner comparable to the engorgement of a man's penis. The vaginal photoplethysmograph is a device designed to measure this increased vaginal blood volume. It consists of an acrylic cylinder about the size and shape of a tampon, which is inserted into the vagina. The cylinder contains a light that is reflected off the vaginal walls, and a photocell that is sensitive to the reflected light. When the vaginal walls fill with blood during sexual arousal, less light is reflected to the photocell. These changes in light intensity, continuously recorded by a polygraph, provide a measure of sexual arousal comparable to that provided by the penile strain gauge. Like the male device, the vaginal photoplethysmograph can be inserted in privacy by the research subject. In addition to the vaginal photoplethysmograph, two other devices are currently being used to measure female sexual response. The vaginal myograph and rectal myograph are implements inserted into the vagina or rectum that measure muscular activity in the pelvic area.

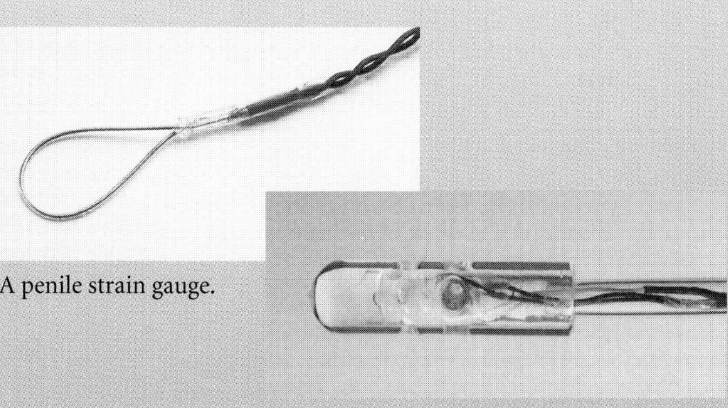

A penile strain gauge.

A vaginal photoplethysmograph.

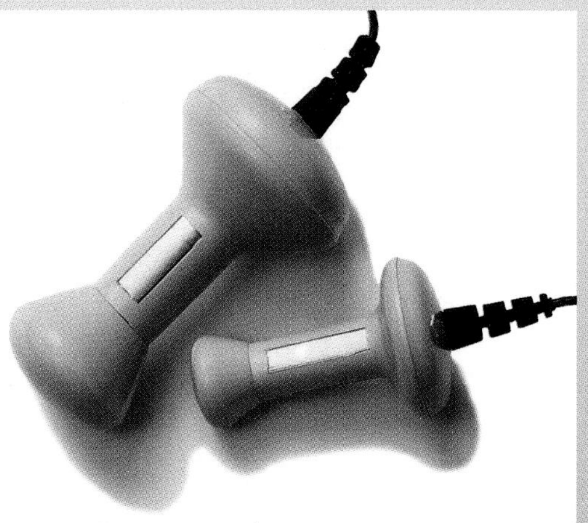

Vaginal and rectal myographs.

Masters and Johnson's observational approach provided a wealth of information about the manner in which women and men respond physiologically to sexual stimulation. Among other findings, they observed no biological difference between women's orgasms resulting from clitoral and vaginal stimulation. This observation (as well as some contradictory findings by other researchers) will be discussed at greater length in Chapter 6.

When it is well conducted, as was Masters and Johnson's study, direct observation has clear advantages as a research method. For studying sexual response patterns, seeing and measuring sexual behavior firsthand is clearly superior to relying on subjective reports of past experiences. Direct observation virtually eliminates the possibility of data falsification through memory deficits, boastful inflation, or guilt-induced repression. Furthermore, records of such behaviors can be kept indefinitely on videotapes or films.

But this approach also has disadvantages. A major problem lies in the often unanswerable question of just how much a subject's behavior is influenced by the presence of even the most discreet observer. This question has been asked often since the publication of Masters and Johnson's research. Researchers using direct observation attempt to minimize this potential complication by being as unobtrusive as possible, remaining in a fringe location, observing through one-way glass, or perhaps using remotely activated videocameras. But the subject is still aware that he or she is being observed.

Although there is merit to criticisms of the direct observation method, Masters and Johnson's research has demonstrated that it can withstand the test of time. Their findings are still applied in many areas—including infertility counseling, conception control, sex therapy, and sex education—with beneficial results.

The Experimental Method

Experimental research Research conducted in precisely controlled laboratory conditions so subjects' reactions can be reliably measured.

A fourth method, **experimental research,** is being used with increasing frequency to investigate human sexual behavior. This method involves presenting subjects with certain events (stimuli) under managed conditions that allow for reliable measurement of their reactions. Sex research must follow strict ethical guidelines, as outlined in the accompanying boxed discussion.

As typically conducted in a laboratory environment, experimental research has a major advantage over other methods in that it provides a controlled environment in which all possible influences on subjects' responses, other than the factors that are being investigated, may be ruled out. A researcher employing this method manipulates a particular set of conditions, or variables, and observes the impact of this manipulation on subjects' behavior. The experimental method is particularly suited to discovering causal relationships between variables.

Independent variable In an experimental research design, a condition or component that is under the control of the researcher who manipulates or determines its value.

Dependent variable In an experimental research design, the outcome or resulting behavior that the experimenter observes and records but does not control.

There are two types of *variables* (behaviors or conditions that may have varied values) in any experimental research design: independent and dependent. An **independent variable** is a condition or component of the experiment that is under the control of the researcher who manipulates or determines its value. Conversely, the **dependent variable** is the outcome or resulting behavior that the experimenter observes and records but does not control.

With this brief summary of the experimental method in mind, let us consider how this technique might clarify the relationship between sexually violent media and rape attitudes and behavior. A number of research studies have provided compelling evidence that sexually violent media may cause attitudes to shift toward greater tolerance of sexually aggressive behavior and may actually contribute to some rapists' assaultive behaviors. We will consider three experiments, the first involving college men and the other two employing convicted rapists as subjects.

The first study was conducted with 271 college men who were divided into two groups. Subjects in the first group were exposed to movies with nonviolent sexual themes, while subjects in the second group saw R-rated films in which men were portrayed committing sexual violence against women (who eventually experienced a transformation from victim to willing partner). A few days after viewing the movies, all subjects completed an attitude questionnaire. The results demonstrated that the men who viewed the violent films were generally much more accepting of sexual violence toward women than those subjects who were exposed to movies with consensual, nonviolent erotic themes (Malamuth & Check, 1981).

What were the independent and dependent variables in this study?

The independent variable in this experiment was the degree of violence in the movies observed by the participants. The dependent variable was the subjects' responses to the questionnaire administered days after the film-viewing sessions.

Two other research studies, each with comparable research designs, compared the erectile responses (dependent variable) of matched groups of rapists and nonrapists to two different taped descriptions of sexual activity (the independent variable), one involving rape and the other mutually consenting sexual activity (Abel et al., 1977; Barbaree et al., 1979). While subjects listened to tapes, penile tumescence (engorgement) was measured with a penile strain gauge, described earlier in the boxed discussion. In both experiments, rapists experienced erections while listening to violent descriptions of rape, whereas their nonrapist counterparts did not. Descriptions of consenting sexual activity produced similar levels of arousal in both groups of men.

These findings, as well as others we will consider in a later chapter, suggest that repetitive exposure to sexually violent media not only encourages attitudes of violence toward women but also influences at least some men who rape, to "sexualize" violence.

The experimental method has also been used to study the relationship between alcohol use and sexual responsiveness (although it has not been used to study vaginal orgasms). In one study of 48 male college students, a penile strain gauge was used to measure engorgement as subjects watched a sexually explicit film, first while not under

Ethical/Legal Issues

Ethical Guidelines for Human Sex Research

Researchers in a range of investigative fields, including sexology, share a common commitment to maintain the welfare, dignity, rights, well-being, and safety of their human subjects. In the last two decades, detailed lists of ethical guidelines have been prepared by a number of professional organizations, including the American Psychological Association (1990), the American Medical Association (AMA), and the Society for the Scientific Study of Sex (SSSS).

These codes, or ethical guidelines, require, among other things, that no pressure or coercion be applied to ensure the participation of volunteers in research, and that researchers avoid procedures that might cause serious physical or psychological harm to human subjects. If an experiment involves even the slightest risk of harm or discomfort, investigators are required to obtain informed consent from their subjects. Researchers must also respect a subject's right to refuse to participate at any time during the course of a study. In addition, special steps must be taken to protect the confidentiality of the data and maintain participants' anonymity unless they agree to be identified.

The issue of deception in research remains controversial. Some studies would lose their effectiveness if participating subjects knew in advance exactly what the experimenter was studying. The ethical guideline generally applied to this issue is that if deception must be used, a postexperiment debriefing must thoroughly explain to participants why it was necessary. At such time, subjects must be allowed to request that their data be removed from the study and destroyed.

Sometimes it is hard for researchers to weigh objectively the potential benefits of a study against the possibility of harming its subjects. Recognizing this difficulty, virtually every institution conducting research in the United States has established ethics committees that review all proposed studies. If they perceive that the subjects' (human or otherwise) welfare is insufficiently safeguarded, the proposal must be modified or the research cannot be conducted. In addition, federal funding for research is denied to any institution that fails to conduct an adequate ethics committee review before collecting data.

the influence of alcohol and then several days later after consuming controlled amounts of alcohol. Findings showed that sexual arousal was reduced by drinking alcohol, and that the more alcohol was consumed, the greater was the reduction (Briddell & Wilson, 1976). A similar experiment tested the relationship between arousal and alcohol intake in women, with consistent results (Wilson & Lawson, 1976).

These studies illustrate one of the primary advantages of the experimental method. Because they can control variables precisely, researchers are able to draw conclusions about causal relationships to a degree not possible with other research methods. However, this method also has disadvantages. One of the most important limitations has to do with the artificiality of laboratory settings, which may adversely influence or bias subjects' responses. As in direct observation research, the very fact that people know they are in an experiment can alter their responses from those that might occur outside the laboratory.

Before concluding this chapter we turn our attention to two additional areas of concern regarding how we acquire information about sexual practices. The first area we consider pertains to feminist theory and scholarship as applied to contemporary sex research. The second area of interest deals with an element of the popular media that seeks to provide information and/or advice pertaining to sexual behavior.

Feminist Theory and Sex Research

Feminist theory emerged as an important influence on research in sexology and other areas of the social sciences in the 1970s and 1980s. Although there is no single feminist perspective on research, several common threads are worth noting in reference to sex research. One widely held view is that research in sexology has been largely dominated by white middle-class men, who develop research strategies based on a model of male sexuality that also promotes heterosexuality as the norm (Irvine, 1990; Jackson, 1984). Feminist scholars believe that this emphasis on male sexuality consistently promotes a narrow view of sexual activity as centered on a penis in a vagina (see our discussion "Sex for Reproduction" in Chapter 1). Such a limiting perspective often results in sex researchers de-emphasizing and devaluing the female experience of sex (MacKinnon, 1986; Pollis, 1988). This inevitably creates a dearth of scientific knowledge about important aspects of female sexuality, such as the female orgasm and the importance to women of nonintercourse activities such as shared touching and kissing.

This lack of attention to women has been especially evident in studies of homosexuals, where until recently almost all scientific research focused on gay men, essentially ignoring lesbian women. Women have also been largely forgotten and marginalized in much of the research conducted in the medical and health care systems of the United States, according to a book by Sue Rosser titled *Women's Health—Missing from U.S. Medicine* (1994). Rosser presents a persuasive case that this minimalization of women has influenced health policies in many adverse ways. She powerfully documents the fact that resources and attention are often devoted to women's health issues only when those problems are related to men's interest in controlling reproduction. Another wrenching example described by Rosser is the limited research on AIDS in women. Even though this disease epidemic has increasingly involved women as victims, most of the drug trials have included only men—a potentially serious oversight in that females may respond differently to drug therapy. Although there have been some improvements on both of these fronts in the last few years, Rosser's book remains a compelling indictment of contemporary research practices.

Feminist scholars also believe that the scope of sex research, with its primary emphasis on quantitative data collection, should be expanded to include more detailed exploration of the subjective and qualitative experience and meaning of sexuality for both women and men (Peplau & Conrad, 1989). Examples of this type of research include such studies as those conducted by Francine Klagsbrun (1985) and Ruthellen Josselson (1992), both of whom conducted in-depth interviews with married couples in which they explored the meaning, impact, and relationship value of a range of intimate experiences.

Feminist scholars do not seek to replace traditional empirical sex research. Rather, they are committed to correcting some of the limitations that stem from this perspective while adding a rich body of data, particularly that of a qualitative nature, to enhance our understanding of how women and men experience their sexuality.

The Popular Media and Sex Research

Most of us are bombarded daily with a barrage of mass media information allegedly designed to inform us about our sexuality. These popular media sources—which include magazine sex surveys, pop psychology books, and sex-advice columnists—are a main source of knowledge about sex for many people. Clearly sex sells, especially the informational variety, which fills an apparent collective longing of the public for meaningful knowledge about sexuality. But how reliable is this information? This question may be best addressed by briefly considering popular magazine sex surveys.

Magazine Sex Surveys

A number of popular magazines have conducted large-scale surveys of their readers' sexual attitudes and behaviors. Some of the most widely quoted of these surveys have evolved from questionnaires printed in *Redbook* (Levin & Levin, 1975; Tavris & Sadd, 1977), *McCall's* (Gittleson, 1980), *Psychology Today* (Athanasiou et al., 1970), and *Consumer Reports* (Brecher, 1984). Sample sizes in these surveys have been prodigious, ranging from 20,000 to over 100,000 respondents.

At first glance, these enormous sample sizes would appear to add credibility to magazine surveys. However, as in other aspects of life, bigger is not necessarily better, and a well-selected representative sample of several hundred to a few thousand subjects is a much more valuable source of information than a highly selective sample of 20,000. Furthermore, keep in mind that each magazine sample represents, at best, only the readership of that magazine and therefore cannot be viewed as representative of the larger population. We cannot even conclude that people who respond to a magazine questionnaire are similar to the greater numbers of readers who elect not to respond. Thus, when you read the results of a magazine survey, remember to use caution when generalizing beyond that small, select segment of society who first reads a particular magazine, and then decides to respond to an enclosed sex questionnaire.

Let us consider a typical example of a magazine sex survey. The October 1974 issue of *Redbook* included a 60-item multiple-choice questionnaire on female sexual attitudes and behavior. Over 100,000 women returned the questionnaire, and analysis of the results provided the basis for two subsequent articles in the September and October 1975 issues of the magazine. The complete results of this survey were eventually published in a book titled *The Redbook Report on Female Sexuality* (Tavris & Sadd, 1977). Despite its prodigious size, the *Redbook* respondent sample cannot be viewed as representative of the general population of American women. Segments of the larger population who were underrepresented included all those who were not likely to read the magazine—namely, women who had not finished high school, women over 50 years of age, nonwhite women, and unmarried women. Beyond the obvious bias created by the magazine's limited audience, the problem of self-selection or volunteer bias likely had some effect, too. Only about 2% of the magazine's readers actually returned the survey questionnaire.

Despite the clearly flawed research methodology inherent in biased samples, the *Redbook* survey is noteworthy because of its huge sample size. Sexologists are not often presented with such quantities of data, and thus pay cautious attention to such information in spite of its qualitative flaws. Some of the noteworthy findings of this survey include the following: The majority of married women reported that they were active sex partners (initiating sexual encounters and being active during relations); oral–genital sex was almost universally experienced; 7 out of 10 respondents reported sex with their husbands to be "good" or "very good"; the more religious a woman was, the more satisfied she seemed to be with her marital sexual relations; one-third had experienced extramarital intercourse; and finally, 4% had had a sexual experience with another woman by the age of 40.

We could describe other examples of magazine surveys, but this seems unnecessary in that the general limitations about this kind of pseudoresearch should be apparent by now and would not be altered by further descriptions. Magazine surveys fail to employ scientific methodology, and they use inherently biased samples. This is not to say that all the information they yield is completely worthless, as some critics have asserted (see Laumann et al., 1994, p. 45). Rather, as long as we remember the primary reason such studies are undertaken (to entertain and sell product), and remain skeptical about the unscientific methods employed, we may acquire some insights into how certain select samples of people experience their sexuality.

Evaluating Research: Some Questions to Ask

We hope that the material presented here and elsewhere in our book will help differentiate legitimate, scientific sex research from the many frivolous, nonscientific polls and opinion surveys that are widespread in the contemporary media. Even when you are exposed to the results of serious investigations, it is wise to maintain a critical eye and to avoid the understandable tendency to accept something as factual just because it is presented as being "scientific." The following list of questions may prove useful as you evaluate the legitimacy of any research, sex or otherwise, that you are exposed to.

1. What are the researchers' credentials? Are they professionally trained? Are they affiliated with reputable institutions (research centers, academic institutions, etc.)? Are they associated with any special interest groups that may favor a particular research finding or conclusion?
2. In what type of media were the results published: reputable scientific journals, scholarly textbooks, popular magazines, newspapers?
3. What approach or type of research method was employed, and were proper scientific procedures adhered to?
4. Were a sufficient number of subjects employed, and is there any reason to suspect bias in their selection method?
5. Is it reasonable to apply the research findings to a larger population beyond the sample group, and to what extent can legitimate generalizations be made?
6. Is there any reason to believe that the research methodology may have biased the findings? (Did the presence of an interviewer encourage false responses? Did the cameras place limitations on the response potentials?)
7. Are there any other published research findings that support or refute the study in question?

Summary

THE GOALS OF SEXOLOGY

The goals of sexology include understanding, predicting, and controlling behavior.

Pursuit of the goal of controlling behavior is often modified or tempered by ethical issues.

NONEXPERIMENTAL RESEARCH METHODS

Nonexperimental methods for studying sexuality include case studies, surveys, and direct observation.

Case studies typically produce a great deal of information about one or a few individuals. They have two advantages:

flexibility and the opportunity to explore specific behaviors and feelings in depth. Disadvantages include lack of investigative control, possible subjective bias on the researcher's part, and poor sampling techniques that often limit the possibility of making generalizations to broad populations.

Most information about human sexual behavior has been obtained through questionnaire or interview surveys of relatively large populations of respondents. Questionnaires have the advantage of being anonymous, inexpensive, and quickly administered. Interviews are more flexible and allow for more rapport between researcher and subject.

Sex researchers who use surveys share certain problems. These include the following:

- The virtual impossibility of getting 100% participation of randomly selected subjects makes it difficult to obtain a representative sample. Self-selection of samples, or "volunteer bias," is a common problem.
- Biases created by nonresponse: Do volunteer participants have significantly different attitudes and behaviors from nonparticipants?
- Demographic biases: Most samples are heavily weighted toward white, middle-class, better-educated participants.
- The problem of accuracy: Respondents' self-reports may be less than accurate because of limitations of memory, boastfulness, guilt, or simple misunderstandings.

The Kinsey surveys were broad-scale studies of human sexual behavior that were somewhat limited by sampling techniques that overrepresented young, educated, city-dwelling people.

The National Health and Social Life Survey stands alone as the single best and most representative sex survey ever conducted within the United States. It has provided a reliable view of the sexual practices of the general U.S. adult population in the 1990s.

There is very little direct-observation sex research due to the highly personal nature of sexual expression. When it can be done, observation significantly reduces the possibility of data falsification. However, subjects' behavior may be altered by the presence of an observer. Furthermore, the reliability of recorded observations may sometimes be compromised by preexisting researcher biases.

THE EXPERIMENTAL METHOD

In experimental research, subjects are presented with events (stimuli) under managed conditions that allow for reliable measurement of their reactions.

The purpose of the experimental method is to discover causal relationships among independent and dependent variables.

An independent variable is a condition or component of the experiment that is controlled or manipulated by the experimenter. The dependent variable is the outcome or resulting behavior that the experimenter observes and records but does not control.

Experimental research offers two advantages: control over the relevant variables and direct analysis of possible causal factors. However, the artificial nature of the experimental laboratory setting may alter subject responses from those that might occur in a natural setting.

FEMINIST THEORY AND SEX RESEARCH

Feminist scholars believe that sex researchers place too great an emphasis on males, a perspective that often results in the de-emphasis and devaluing of the female experience of sex. Feminist scholars also believe that the scope of sex research, with its primary emphasis on quantitive data, should be expanded to include more detailed exploration of the subjective and qualitative experience and meaning of sexuality for both sexes.

THE POPULAR MEDIA AND SEX RESEARCH

Popular media sources, such as magazine sex surveys, are a main source of knowledge about sex for many people. However, despite the use of very large sample sizes, reported findings must be cautiously interpreted since such surveys generally employ flawed research methodology and utilize inherently biased samples.

EVALUATING RESEARCH: SOME QUESTIONS TO ASK

In evaluating any study of sexual behavior, it is helpful to consider who conducted the research, examine the methods and sampling techniques, and compare the results with those of other reputable studies.

Thought Provokers

1. Of the four research techniques discussed in this chapter—clinical case studies, surveys, direct observation, and experimental laboratory studies—survey research has provided the most data about human sexuality. Why do you think this is so? Which method do you think is best for learning about our sexuality? Why?
2. A radio talk-show host informs his listening audience that women enjoy sex more in the morning than in the evening. When pressed by a questioner, he says he knows this to be true from personal experience. How would you go about determining the validity of this assertion? Which of the four methodologies discussed in this chapter could be effectively used to test this hypothesis? Why? Might you gain valuable information by applying more than one of these techniques?

Suggested Readings

Abramson, Paul (1990). "Sexual Science: Emerging Discipline or Oxymoron?" *Journal of Sex Research,* 27, 147–165. An excellent article that discusses some of the methodological problems that sex researchers encounter, while making a strong case for the importance of scientific rigor in this area of research.

Bullough, Vern (1994). *Science in the Bedroom: A History of Sex Research.* New York: Basic Books. A scholarly, highly readable, and enlightening discussion of the history of sex research from the early nineteenth century to the present.

Byrne, Donn; and Kelley, Kathryn (Eds.) (1986). *Alternative Approaches to the Study of Sexual Behavior.* Hillsdale, NJ: Erlbaum. This informative book provides in-depth discussions of the investigative methods employed by contemporary sex researchers.

Journal of Sex Research, February 1986, Volume 22. A special issue of this journal devoted entirely to issues related to methodology in sex research. The many excellent articles in this volume address such topics as sampling bias, the interaction of volunteer bias with different forms of sex research techniques, the relationship between objective and subjective measures of sexual responsiveness, and a critical analysis of sex research methodology.

Kimmel, Allan (1988). *Ethics and Values in Applied Social Research.* Beverly Hills, CA: Sage. This book provides an illuminating and thought-provoking analysis of the ethical issues that often confront researchers in the social sciences.

Laumann, Edward; Gagnon, John; Michael, Robert; and Michaels, Stuart (1994). *The Social Organization of Sexuality.* Chicago: University of Chicago Press. An informative report on the most comprehensive and representative survey to date of sexual practices and attitudes in the American population.

Pomeroy, Wardell (1972). *Dr. Kinsey and the Institute for Sex Research.* New York: Harper & Row. An informed and entertaining look at Kinsey and his research, as seen through the "insider" eyes of one of his original research colleagues.

Web Resources

Kinsey Institute for Research in Sex, Gender, and Reproduction
www.indiana.edu/~kinsey/index.html
The Kinsey Institute, founded by the pioneer sexologist Alfred Kinsey, sponsors a site dedicated to supporting interdisciplinary research in the study of human sexuality. The Research and Publications section on its Web site describes the center's newest published research in human sexuality.

Center for Sex Research
www.csun.edu/~sr2022/
California State University at Northridge houses the Center for Sex Research, and its faculty members maintain this Web site. With updates on current topics and links to other organizations, this Web site is another good resource for those seeking reliable and up-to-date information.

Sexology NetLine
home.netinc.ca/~sexorg/
Maintained by a professional organization of sexologists from the Institute for Advanced Study of Human Sexuality, this Web site contains frank information for those with questions about human sexuality.

3

Gender Issues

Male and Female, Masculine and Feminine

What is the difference between sex and gender?

What is the relationship between gender identity and gender role?

Gender-Identity Formation

Is our sense of being male or female based more on biological factors or on social learning?

What causes transsexualism?

Gender Roles

What are the relative influences of parents, peers, schools, textbooks, television, and religion as agents in the socialization of gender roles?

How do gender-role expectations affect our sexuality?

I was taught early on what appropriate gender behavior was. I remember thinking how unfair it was that I had to do weekly cleaning duties while all my brother had to do was take out the garbage. When I asked my mom why, she said, "Because he is a boy and that is man's work and you are a girl and you do woman's work." (Authors' files)

My father worked all his life as a laborer and he was strong, macho, and clearly the one who was in charge in my home. My mother, who took care of all the children and home duties, expected me to be feminine and ladylike so I could become a good wife and mother, just like her, I suppose. (Authors' files)

Examine the following sentence and fill in the blanks: In this particular society, "the _______ is the dominant, impersonal, managing partner, while the _______ is the less responsible, emotionally dependent person."

If you assumed that the word *man* belongs in the first space and *woman* belongs in the second, you are mistaken—for within the society in question, the Tchambuli of New Guinea, traditional masculine and feminine behavior patterns are complete opposites of stereotypical American patterns (Mead, 1963). (The opening anecdotal accounts illustrate common American gender-role stereotypes.) The sharp difference between Tchambuli expectations for men and women and those that predominate in American culture raises certain fundamental questions: What constitutes maleness and femaleness? How can the expectations and assumptions for each sex differ so greatly from one society to another? If some gender-related behaviors are learned, do any of the behavioral differences between men and women have a biological basis? How do gender-role expectations affect sexual interactions? These are questions that we address in this chapter.

Male and Female, Masculine and Feminine

Through the ages people have held to the belief that we are born males or females and just naturally grow up doing what men or women do. The only explanation required has been a simple allusion to "nature taking its course." This viewpoint has a simplicity that helps make the world seem an orderly place. However, closer examination reveals a much greater complexity in the process by which our maleness and femaleness are determined, and in the way our behavior, sexual and otherwise, is influenced by this aspect of our identity. This fascinating complexity is our focus in the pages that follow. But first it will be helpful to clarify a few important terms.

Sex and Gender

Sex
Biological maleness and femaleness.

Gender
The psychological and sociocultural characteristics associated with our sex.

Many writers use the terms *sex* and *gender* interchangeably. However, each word has a specific meaning. **Sex** refers to our biological femaleness or maleness. There are two aspects of biological sex: *genetic sex,* which is determined by our sex chromosomes, and *anatomical sex,* the obvious physical differences between males and females. **Gender** is a concept that encompasses the special psychosocial meanings added to biological maleness or femaleness. Thus, while our sex is linked to various physical attributes (chromosomes, penis, vulva, and so forth), our gender refers to the psychological and sociocultural characteristics associated with our sex—or in other words, our femininity or masculinity. In this chapter, we use the terms *masculine* and *feminine* to characterize the behaviors that are typically attributed to males and females. One undesirable aspect of these labels is that they may limit the range of behaviors that people are comfortable expressing (Sheinberg & Penn, 1991). For example, a man might hesitate to be nurturing lest he be labeled feminine, and a woman might be reticent to act assertively for fear of being considered masculine. It is not our intention to perpetuate the stereotypes often associated with these labels. However, we find it necessary to use these terms when discussing gender issues.

When we meet people for the first time, most of us quickly note their sex and make assumptions based on their maleness or femaleness about how they are likely to behave: These are **gender assumptions.** For most people, gender assumptions are an important part of routine social interaction. We identify people as being either the same sex as ourselves or the other sex. (We have avoided using the term *opposite sex* because we believe it overstates the differences between males and females.) Many of us may find it hard to interact with a person whose gender is ambiguous. When we are unsure of our identification of someone's gender, we may become confused and uncomfortable.

Gender assumptions Assumptions about how people are likely to behave based on their maleness or femaleness.

Gender Identity and Gender Role

Gender identity refers to each individual's subjective sense of being male or female. Most of us realize that we are either male or female in the first few years of life. However, there is no guarantee that a person's gender identity will be consistent with his or her biological sex, and some people experience considerable confusion in their efforts to identify their own maleness or femaleness. We will look into this area in more detail later in this chapter.

Gender identity How one psychologically perceives oneself as either male or female.

Gender role (sometimes called *sex role*) refers to a collection of attitudes and behaviors that are considered normal and appropriate in a specific culture for people of a particular sex. Gender roles establish sex-related behavioral expectations that people are expected to fulfill. Behavior thought to be socially appropriate for a male is called masculine, for a female, feminine. When we use the terms *masculine* and *feminine* in subsequent discussions, we are referring to these socialized notions.

Gender role A collection of attitudes and behaviors that are considered normal and appropriate in a specific culture for people of a particular sex.

Gender-role expectations are culturally defined and vary from society to society. For example, Tchambuli society considers emotionally expressive behavior appropriate for males. American society takes a somewhat different view. A kiss on the cheek is considered a feminine act and therefore inappropriate between men in American society. In contrast, such behavior is consistent with masculine role expectations in many European and Middle Eastern societies.

Beside being culturally based, our notions of masculinity and femininity are also dependent on the era in which they occur. For instance, if an American father in the 1950s had stayed home to care for his preschool children while his wife traveled on business, his behavior would probably have raised eyebrows, if not engendered ridicule. Today, young couples are more likely to divide household labor according to practical needs rather than preconceived notions of how men and women "should" behave. More than any other time in our history, the present era is marked by redefinition of male and female roles. Many of us who have grown up subjected to strong gender-role conditioning are now exploring how these roles have shaped our lives and are seeking to break away from their limiting influences. Being part of this change can be both exciting and confusing. We will consider the impact of traditional and changing gender roles later in this chapter (and also throughout our text). But first let us turn our attention to the processes whereby we acquire our gender identity.

Gender-Identity Formation

Like the knowledge that we have a particular color hair or eyes, gender is an aspect of our identity that most people take for granted. Certainly gender identity usually—but not always—"comes with the territory" of having certain biological parts. But there is

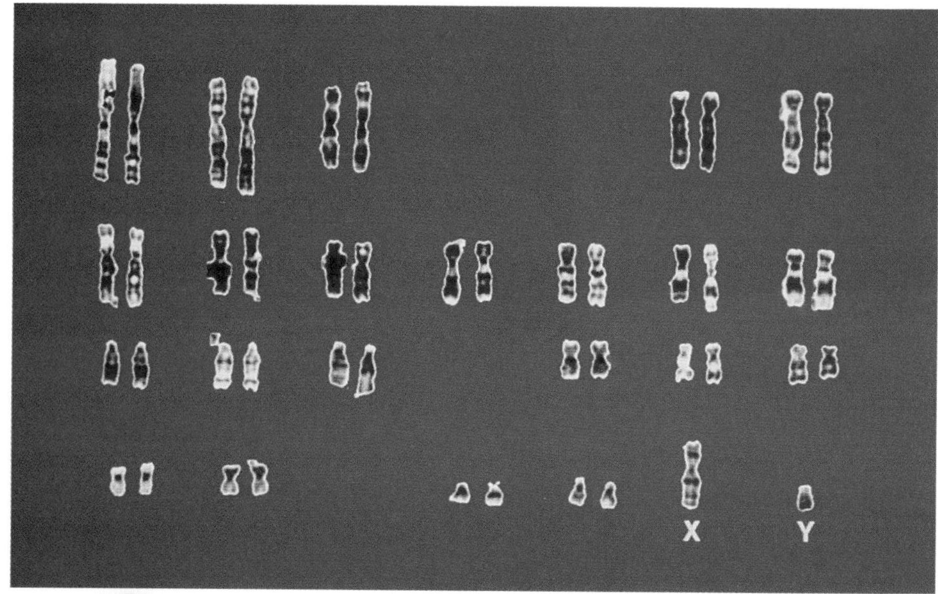

Figure 3.1

Human cells contain 22 pairs of matched autosomes and one pair of sex chromosomes. A normal female has two X chromosomes, and a normal male has an X and a Y chromosome.

more to it than simply looking like a female or a male. As we will see in the following paragraphs, the question of how we come to think of ourselves as either male or female has two answers. The first explanation centers on biological processes that begin shortly after conception and are completed before birth. But a second important explanation has to do with social-learning theory, which looks to cultural influences during early childhood to explain both the nuances of gender identity and the personal significance of being either male or female. We explore first the biological processes involved in gender-identity formation.

Gender Identity as a Biological Process: Normal Prenatal Differentiation

From the moment of conception, many biological factors contribute to the differentiation of male or female sex. In the following paragraphs, we will explore how biological sex differentiation occurs during prenatal development. Our discussion follows a chronological sequence: We begin at conception, looking at chromosomal differences between male and female, then continue with the development of gonads, production of hormones, the development of internal and external reproductive structures, and finally sex differentiation of the brain.

Sperm
The male reproductive cell.

Ovum
The female reproductive cell.

Autosomes
The 22 pairs of human chromosomes that do not significantly influence sex differentiation.

Sex chromosomes
A single set of chromosomes that influences biological sex determination.

Chromosomal Sex

Our biological sex is determined at conception by the chromosomal makeup of the **sperm** (male reproductive cell) that fertilizes an **ovum** or egg (female reproductive cell). With the exception of the reproductive cells, human body cells contain a total of 46 chromosomes, arranged as 23 pairs (see Figure 3.1). Twenty-two of these pairs are matched; that is, the two chromosomes of each pair look almost identical. These matched sets, called **autosomes** (AW-tuh-somes), are the same in males and females and do not significantly influence sex differentiation. One chromosome pair, however—the **sex chromosomes**—

differs in females and males. Females have two similar chromosomes, labeled XX, whereas males have dissimilar chromosomes, labeled XY.

As noted above, the reproductive cells are an exception to the 23-pair rule. As a result of a biological process known as *meiosis,* mature reproductive cells contain only half the usual complement of chromosomes—one member of each pair. (This process is necessary to avoid doubling the chromosome total when sex cells merge at conception.) A normal female ovum (or egg) contains 22 autosomes plus an X chromosome. A normal male sperm cell contains 22 autosomes plus either an X or Y chromosome. If the ovum is fertilized by a sperm carrying a Y chromosome, the resulting XY combination will produce a male child. In contrast, if an X-bearing sperm fertilizes the ovum, the result will be an XX combination and a female child. Two X chromosomes are necessary for internal and external female structures to develop completely. But if one Y chromosome is present, male sexual and reproductive organs will develop (Harley et al., 1992; Page et al., 1987).

Why is the Y chromosome essential for male development?

Researchers have recently located a single gene on the short arm of the human Y chromosome that seems to be responsible for initiating the sequence of events that leads to the development of the male gonads, or **testes.** (As we will see shortly, the testes in turn release hormones that stimulate the development of other male structures.) The maleness (testis-determining) gene is called *SRY* (Eicher, 1994; Swain et al., 1998).

Testes
Male gonads inside the scrotum that produce sperm and sex hormones.

At present it is unclear what SRY gene product (or substance produced via a genetic trigger) induces the development of testes. Nor are most researchers convinced that a single SRY gene and gene product are the sole determinants of male gonadal sex. Rather, it is anticipated that further research will uncover a battery of genes that interact to unleash the gene product or products that shape gonadal differentiation (Cherfas, 1991; Eicher, 1994; Mittwoch & Burgess, 1991).

Findings from a recent study conducted by scientists from Italy and the United States suggest that there also may be a gene or genes for femaleness. These researchers studied four cases of male-to-female sex reversal in individuals with XY chromosomes and a working SRY (maleness) gene. Three of the four exhibited clearly identifiable female external genitals; the fourth had ambiguous genitals. If the maleness gene were the dominant determinant of biological sex, these reversals would not have occurred. What was the cause? Examination of these individuals' DNA revealed that a tiny bit of genetic material on the short arm of their X chromosome had been duplicated. As a result, each of these subjects had a double dose of a gene designated as DSS. This condition resulted in feminization of an otherwise chromosomally normal male fetus (Bardoni et al., 1994).

These findings suggest that a gene (or genes) on the X chromosome helps push the undifferentiated gonads in a female direction just as the SRY gene helps to start construction of male sex structures. Such observations contradict the long-held belief that the human fetus is inherently female and that, unlike male prenatal differentiation, no gene triggers are necessary for female differentiation. As one leading investigator recently stated, "I don't think there is any question that the development of the ovaries will prove to be an extremely active process. . . . We've only just begun to understand the details of sex determination" (Page, in Angier, 1994, p. 7).

Gonadal Sex

In the first weeks after conception, the structures that will become the reproductive organs, or **gonads,** are the same in males and females (see Figure 3.2a). Differentiation begins about 6 weeks after conception. Genetic signals determine whether the mass of undifferentiated sexual tissue develops into male or female gonads (Clarnette et al., 1997; Crews, 1994). At this time, a SRY gene product (or products) in a male fetus triggers the transformation of embryonic gonads into testes. In the absence of SRY, and perhaps under the influence of a DSS or other femaleness gene, the undifferentiated gonadal tissue develops into **ovaries** (see Figure 3.2b).

Gonads
The male and female sex glands—ovaries and testes.

Ovaries
Female gonads that produce ova and sex hormones.

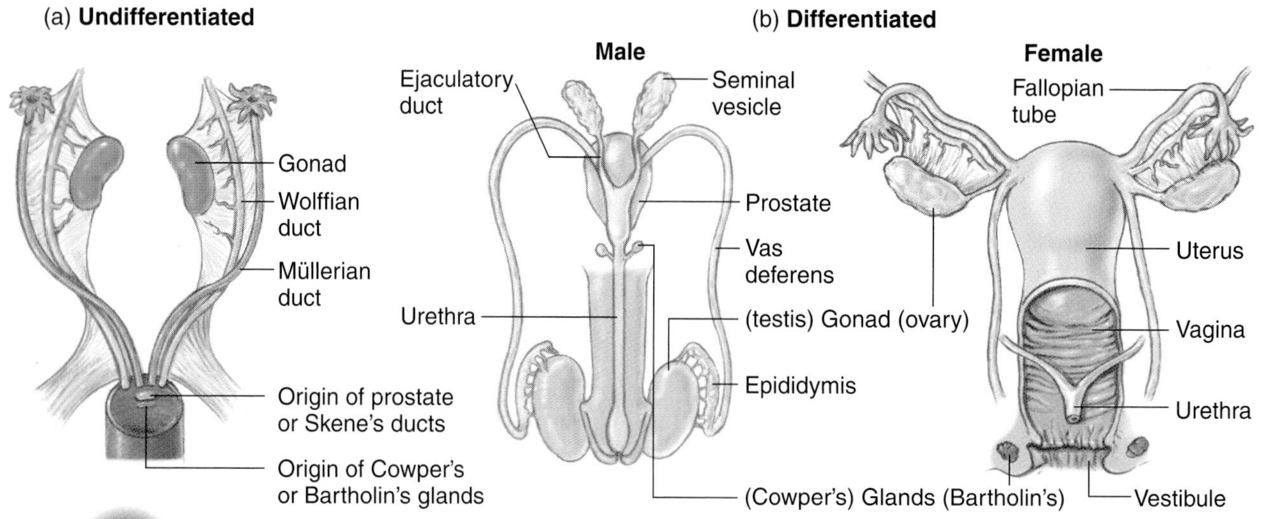

(a) **Undifferentiated** (b) **Differentiated**

Gonad
Wolffian duct
Müllerian duct
Origin of prostate or Skene's ducts
Origin of Cowper's or Bartholin's glands

Male **Female**
Ejaculatory duct
Seminal vesicle
Prostate
Vas deferens
Urethra
(testis) Gonad (ovary)
Epididymis
(Cowper's) Glands (Bartholin's)
Fallopian tube
Uterus
Vagina
Urethra
Vestibule

Figure 3.2

Prenatal development of male and female internal duct systems from undifferentiated (before sixth week) to differentiated.

Once the testes or ovaries develop, these gonads begin releasing their own sex hormones. As we will see next, these hormones become the critical factor in further sex differentiation, and genetic influence ceases.

Hormonal Sex

Like other glands in the *endocrine system* (a system of ductless glands that includes the pituitary, thyroid, parathyroids, adrenals, and pancreas), the gonads produce hormones and secrete them directly into the bloodstream. Ovaries produce two classes of hormones: **estrogens** (ES-trō-jens) and **progestational compounds.** Estrogens, the most important of which is *estradiol,* influence the development of female physical sex characteristics and help regulate the menstrual cycle. Of the progestational compounds, only *progesterone* is known to be physiologically important. Its function is to help regulate the menstrual cycle and stimulate development of the uterine lining in preparation for pregnancy. The primary hormone products of the testes are **androgens** (AN-drō-jens). The most important androgen is *testosterone,* which influences both the development of male physical sex characteristics and sexual motivation. In both sexes the adrenal glands also secrete sex hormones, including small amounts of estrogen and greater quantities of androgen.

Estrogens
A class of hormones that produce female secondary sex characteristics and affect the menstrual cycle.

Progestational compounds
A class of hormones, including progesterone, that are produced by the ovaries.

Androgens
A class of hormones that promote the development of male genitals and secondary sex characteristics and influence sexual motivation in both sexes. These hormones are produced by the adrenal glands in males and females and by the testes in males.

Sex of the Internal Reproductive Structures

By about eight weeks after conception, the sex hormones begin to play an important role in sex differentiation as the two duct systems shown in Figure 3.2a—the *Wolffian ducts* and the *Müllerian ducts*—begin to differentiate into those internal structures shown in Figure 3.2b. In a male fetus, androgens secreted by the testes stimulate the Wolffian ducts to develop into the vas deferens, seminal vesicles, and ejaculatory ducts. Another substance released by the testes is known as *Müllerian-inhibiting substance (MIS).* MIS causes the Müllerian duct system to shrink and disappear in males (Clarnette et al., 1997; Lee et al., 1997). In the absence of androgens, the fetus develops female structures (Clarnette et al., 1997). The Müllerian ducts develop into the fallopian tubes, uterus, and the inner third of the vagina, and the Wolffian duct system degenerates.

Sex of the External Genitals

The external genitals develop according to a similar pattern. Until the gonads begin releasing hormones during the sixth week, the external genital tissues of male and female fetuses are undifferentiated (see Figure 3.3). These tissues will develop into either male

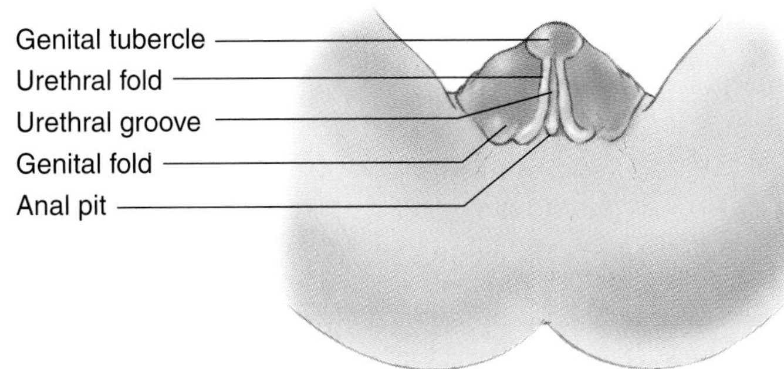

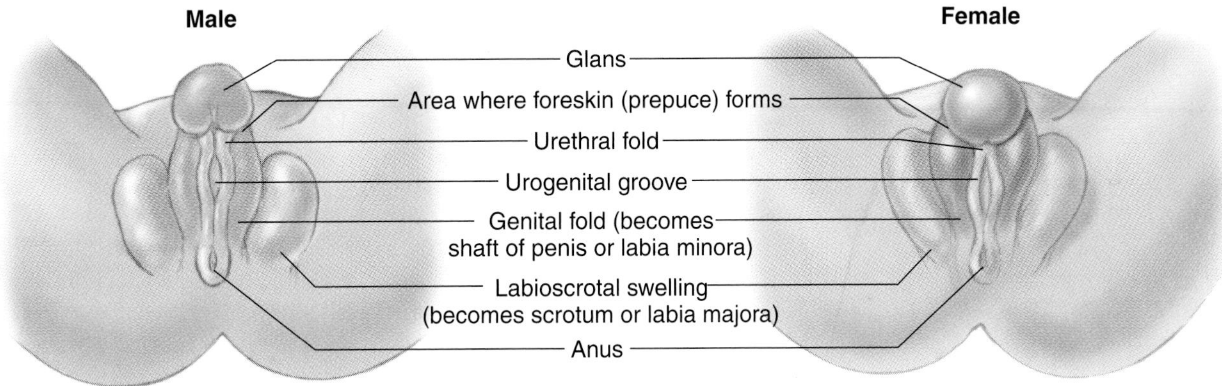

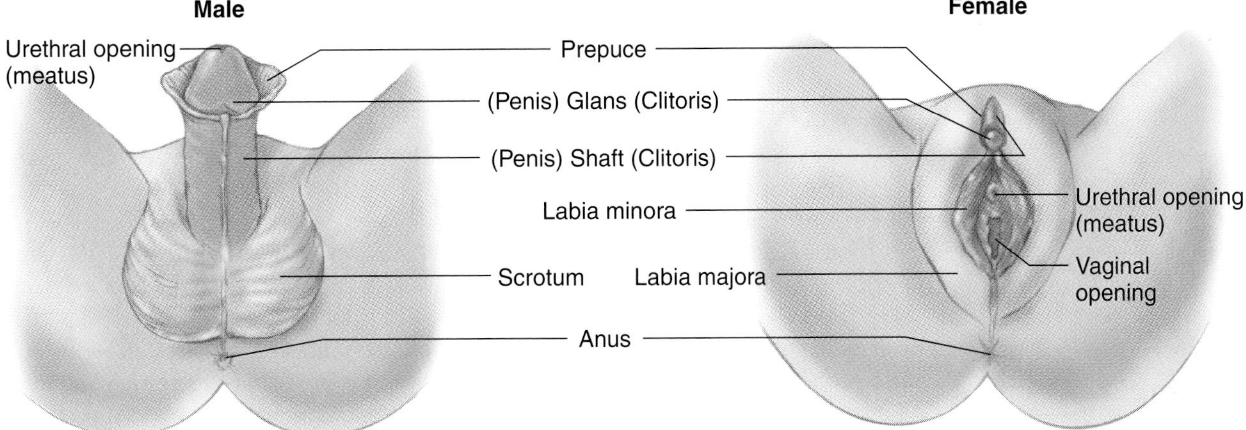

Figure 3.3

Prenatal development of male and female external genitals from undifferentiated to fully differentiated.

or female external genitals depending on the presence or absence of a testosterone product released in males, known as *dihydrotestosterone (DHT)*. DHT stimulates the *labioscrotal swelling* to become the scrotum, and the *genital tubercle* and *genital folds* to differentiate into the glans and shaft of the penis, respectively. The genital folds fuse around the urethra to form the shaft of the penis, and the two sides of the labioscrotal swelling fuse to form the scrotum; these fusions do not occur in females. In the absence of testosterone (and possibly under the influence of a substance(s) triggered by the DSS or femaleness gene), the genital tubercle becomes the clitoris, the genital folds become the inner vaginal lips (labia minora), and the two sides of the labioscrotal swelling differentiate into the outer vaginal lips (labia majora). By the twelfth week, the differentiation process is complete: The penis and scrotum are recognizable in males; the clitoris and labia can be identified in females.

Because the external genitals, gonads, and some internal structures of males and females originate from the same embryonic tissues, it is not surprising that they have corresponding, or homologous, parts. Table 3.1 summarizes these female and male counterparts. We will look at the form and function of human sex organs in more detail in Chapters 4 and 5.

Table 3.1 Homologous Sex Organs

Female	*Male*
Clitoris	Glans of penis
Hood of clitoris	Foreskin of penis
Labia minora	Shaft of penis
Labia majora	Scrotal sac
Ovaries	Testes
Skene's ducts	Prostate gland
Bartholin's glands	Cowper's glands

Sex Differentiation of the Brain

Research suggests that certain important functional and structural differences exist in the brains of human females and males that result, at least in part, from prenatal sex-differentiation processes (Gur et al., 1995; Reiner, 1997; Witelson, 1991). These differences appear to involve at least two major brain areas: the *hypothalamus* (hy-poh-THAL-ah-mus) and the left and right *cerebral hemispheres* (see Figure 3.4).

A number of studies link marked differences between the male and female hypothalamus to the presence or absence of circulating testosterone during prenatal differentiation (Reiner, 1997; Reinisch et al., 1991; Zhou et al., 1995). In the absence of circulating testosterone, the female hypothalamus develops specialized receptor cells that are extremely sensitive to estrogen in the bloodstream. In fetal males, the presence of testosterone prevents these cells from developing sensitivity to estrogen. This prenatal differentiation is critical for events that take place later on. During puberty, the estrogen-sensitive female hypothalamus directs the pituitary to release hormones in cyclic fashion, initiating the menstrual cycle. In males, the estrogen-insensitive hypothalamus directs a relatively steady production of sex hormones.

Research has uncovered several intriguing findings pertaining to sex differences in one tiny hypothalamic region called the *bed nucleus of the stria terminalis (BST)*. The BST has been shown to contain estrogen and androgen receptors and to play an essential role in the sexual behavior of nonhuman animals (Allen & Gorski, 1990; Breedlove, 1995). A recent study reported that a central subdivision of the BST (BSTc) is 44% larger in heterosexual men than in heterosexual women (Zhou et al., 1995). These researchers theorized that differences in the adult size of the BSTc is determined during prenatal development as a function of the organizing action of sex hormones. Another study found that a particular caudal or posterior part of the BST (BNST-dspm) is 2.5 times larger in men than women (Allen & Gorski, 1990). These demonstrations of sex differences in these two locations within the BST suggest that this hypothalamic region may influence human sex differences as well as affect human sexual functioning.

Researchers have also reported sex differences in an anterior region of the hypothalamus called the *preoptic area (POA)*. Two studies found one specific region within this area, named the *sexually dimorphic nucleus of the preoptic area* (SDN-POA), to be significantly larger in adult men than in adult women (Allen et al., 1989; Swaab & Fliers, 1985). Investigators theorized that this difference was also induced prenatally by the action of sex hormones.

These and other studies, too numerous to mention, clearly demonstrate that certain important sex differences exist in the human hypothalamus. These findings provide strong support for the notion that there is a biological substrate for sex differences in human sexual behavior (Diamond & Sigmundson, 1997). However, a clear understanding of the exact nature and mechanisms of these differences must await clarification by further research, and we must exercise caution in attributing behavioral sex differences to biological causes. Nevertheless, the mounting evidence about the influence of prena-

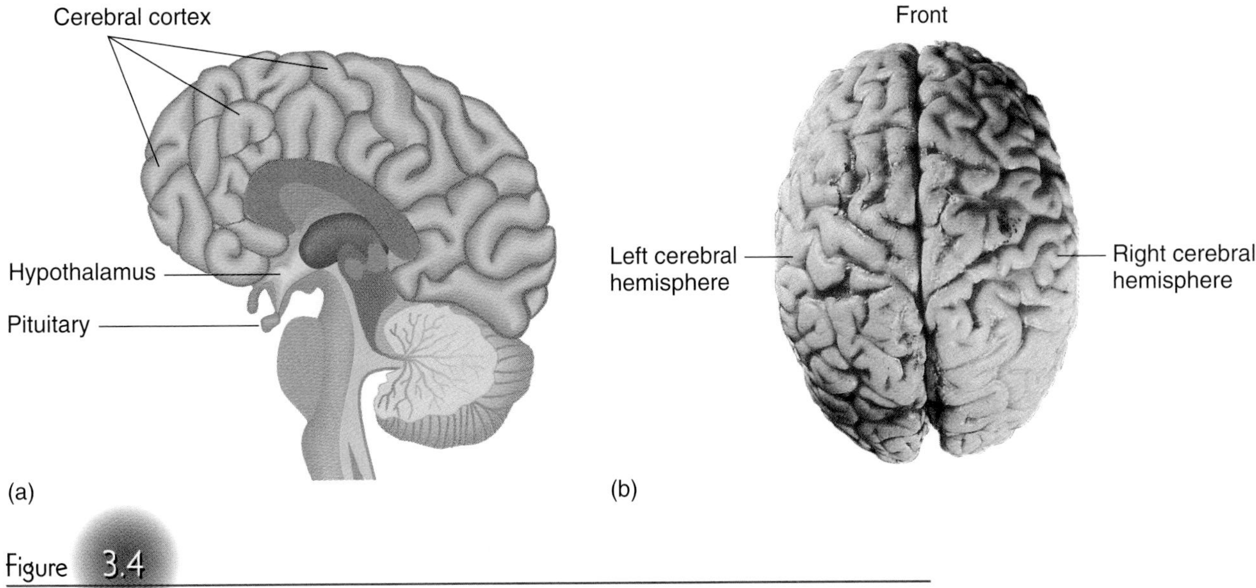

Figure 3.4

Parts of the brain: (a) cross section of the human brain showing the hypothalamus; (b) top view showing the left and right cerebral hemispheres.

tal sex hormones on the developing fetal brain has led some theorists to speculate that gender-biased behavior in children and adults may result, at least in part, from a generalized sex-hormone-induced masculinization or feminization of the brain during prenatal development (Collaer & Hines, 1995; Durden-Smith & de Simone, 1995). From this perspective, it may be that "the organ that appears to be critical to psychosexual development and adaptation is not the external genitalia, but the brain" (Reiner, 1997, p. 225).

Sex differences have also been demonstrated in the structure of the cerebral hemispheres and in the degree of hemispheric specialization for verbal and spatial cognitive skills (Diamond, 1991; Shaywitz et al., 1995). Females often score somewhat higher than males on tests of verbal skills, whereas the reverse is often true for spatial tests (Halpern, 1992; Voyer et al., 1995). Some researchers suggest that differences in hemispheric structure indicate a possible biological basis for such sex differences (Geschwind & Behan, 1984; Witelson, 1988 & 1991).

However, many theorists argue that reported sex differences in cognitive skills are largely due to psychosocial factors (Geary, 1989; Hyde, 1996). They cite substantial evidence that such differences have declined sharply in recent years (Hyde & Plant, 1995; Voyer et al., 1995). And some writers argue that biological explanations for gender differences in cognitive (and behavioral) traits, far from being based on solid scientific evidence, are merely unsubstantiated justifications for supporting traditional gender roles. (See, for example, *Myths of Gender: Biological Theories About Women and Men,* a book written by developmental geneticist Anne Fausto-Sterling [1985].) Clearly, until such time as additional data are obtained, we cannot conclude that there is a biological basis for alleged sex differences in cognitive skills.

Abnormal Prenatal Differentiation

Thus far we have considered only normal prenatal differentiation. However, much of what is known about the impact of biological sex differentiation on the development of gender identities comes from studies of abnormal differentiation.

We have seen that the differentiation of internal and external sex structures occurs under the influence of biological cues. When these signals deviate from normal patterns, the result can be ambiguous biological sex. People with ambiguous or contradictory sex characteristics are sometimes called *hermaphrodites* (her-MAF-roh-dites), a term derived from the mythical Greek deity Hermaphroditus, who was thought to possess attributes of both sexes.

True hermaphrodites Exceedingly rare individuals who have both ovarian and testicular tissue in their bodies; their external genitals are often a mixture of male and female structures.

Pseudohermaphrodites Individuals whose gonads match their chromosomal sex, but whose internal and external reproductive anatomy has a mixture of male and female structures or structures that are incompletely male or female.

We can distinguish between **true hermaphrodites** and **pseudohermaphrodites.** True hermaphrodites, who have both ovarian and testicular tissue in their bodies, are exceedingly rare (Parker, 1998; Unlu et al., 1997). Their external genitals are often a mixture of female and male structures. Pseudohermaphrodites are much more common. They also possess ambiguous internal and external reproductive anatomy, but unlike true hermaphrodites, pseudohermaphrodites are born with gonads that match their chromosomal sex. Studies of pseudohermaphrodites have helped to clarify the relative roles of biology and social learning in the formation of gender identity. This condition may occur because of an abnormal combination of sex chromosomes or as a result of prenatal hormonal abnormalities. In this section we consider evidence from five varieties of pseudohermaphrodites, summarized in Table 3.2.

Sex-Chromosome Disorders

Errors occasionally occur at the first level of biological sex determination, and individuals are born with one or more extra sex chromosomes or missing one sex chromosome. Over 70 abnormalities of the sex chromosomes have been identified (Levitan & Montagu, 1977). These irregularities may be associated with various physical, health, and behavioral effects. We will consider two of the most widely researched of these abnormalities.

Turner's syndrome A relatively rare condition, characterized by the presence of one unmatched X chromosome (XO), in which affected individuals have normal female external genitals, but their internal reproductive structures do not develop fully.

TURNER'S SYNDROME **Turner's syndrome** is a relatively rare condition characterized by the presence of only one sex chromosome, an X. This condition, estimated to occur in about one in every 2000 live female births (Gravholt et al., 1998), results when an atypical ovum containing 22 autosomes and no sex chromosomes is fertilized by an X-bearing sperm. (The same ovum fertilized by a Y-bearing sperm does not survive.) The resulting chromosome number in the fertilized egg is 45 rather than the normal 46; the sex chromosome combination is designated XO. People with this combination develop normal external female genitals and consequently are classified as females. However, their internal reproductive structures do not develop fully—ovaries are absent or represented only by fibrous streaks of tissue. Turner's syndrome females do not develop breasts at puberty (unless given hormone treatment), do not menstruate, and, of course, are sterile. As adults, women with this condition tend to be unusually short (Gravholt et al., 1998).

Because the gonads are absent or poorly developed and hormones are consequently deficient, Turner's syndrome permits gender identity to be formed in the absence of gonadal and hormonal influences (the second and third levels of biological sex determination). Turner's syndrome individuals identify themselves as female, and as a group they are not distinguishable from biologically normal females in their interests and behavior (Money & Ehrhardt, 1972). This characteristic strongly suggests that a feminine gender identity can be established in the absence of ovaries and their products.

Klinefelter's syndrome A condition, characterized by the presence of two X chromosomes and one Y (XXY), in which affected individuals have undersized external male genitals.

KLINEFELTER'S SYNDROME A much more common sex chromosome error in humans is **Klinefelter's syndrome.** This condition, estimated to occur once in about every 500 live male births (Kruse et al., 1998), results when an atypical ovum containing 22 autosomes and two X chromosomes is fertilized by a Y-bearing sperm, creating an XXY individual. Despite the presence of both the XY combination characteristic of normal males and the XX pattern of normal females, Klinefelter's syndrome individuals are anatomically male. This condition supports the view that the presence of a Y chromosome triggers the formation of male structures. However, the presence of an extra female sex chromosome impedes the continued development of these structures, and Klinefelter's syndrome males typically are sterile and have undersized penises and testicles. Their interest in sexual activity is often weak or absent (Money, 1968; Rabock et al., 1979).

Table 3.2 Summary of Some Examples of Abnormal Prenatal Sex Differentiation

Syndrome	*Chromosomal Sex*	*Gonadal Sex*	*Reproductive Internal Structures*	*External Genitals*	*Fertility*	*Secondary Sex Characteristics*	*Gender Identity*
Turner's syndrome	45, XO	Fibrous streaks of ovarian tissue	Uterus and fallopian tubes	Normal female	Sterile	Undeveloped; no breasts	Female
Klinefelter's syndrome	47, XXY	Small testes	Normal male	Undersized penis and testicles	Sterile	Some feminization of secondary characteristics; may have breast development and rounded body contours	Usually male, although higher than usual incidence of gender identity confusion
Androgen insensitivity syndrome	46, XY	Undescended testes	Lacks a normal set of either male or female internal structures	Normal female genitals and a shallow vagina	Sterile	At puberty, breast development and other signs of normal female sexual maturation appear, but menstruation does not occur	Female
Fetally androgenized females	46, XX	Ovaries	Normal female	Ambiguous (typically more male than female)	Fertile	Normal female (individuals with adrenal malfunction must be treated with cortisone to avoid masculinization)	Female, but significant level of dissatisfaction with female gender identity; very oriented toward traditional male activities
DHT-deficient males	46, XY	Undescended testes at birth; testes descend at puberty	Vas deferens, seminal vesicles, and ejaculatory ducts, but no prostate; partially formed vagina	Ambiguous at birth (more female than male); at puberty, genitals are masculinized	Produce viable sperm but unable to inseminate	Female before puberty; become masculinized at puberty	Prepuberty gender identity difficult to ascertain (lack of data); approximately 90% have assumed traditional male gender role at puberty

Presumably, this low sex drive is related, at least in part, to deficient production of hormones from the testes.

Klinefelter's syndrome males tend to be tall and are often somewhat feminized in their physical characteristics; they may exhibit breast development and rounded body contours. They also tend to be passive and to lack ambition, and they frequently show some intellectual impairment. Testosterone treatments during adolescence and adulthood can enhance the development of male secondary sexual characteristics and may increase sexual interest (Kolodny et al., 1979). These individuals usually identify themselves as male; however, they manifest a higher-than-expected degree of gender-identity confusion (Mandoki et al., 1991).

Disorders Affecting Prenatal Hormonal Processes

The ambiguous sex characteristics associated with pseudohermaphroditism can also result from genetically induced biological errors that produce deviations in prenatal hormonal processes. We consider three examples of hermaphroditism caused by hormonal errors.

Androgen insensitivity syndrome (AIS)
A condition resulting from a genetic defect that causes chromosomally normal males to be insensitive to the action of testosterone and other androgens. These individuals develop female external genitals of normal appearance.

ANDROGEN INSENSITIVITY SYNDROME A rare genetic defect causes a condition known as **androgen insensitivity syndrome (AIS),** also called *testicular feminization syndrome,* in which the body cells of a chromosomally normal male fetus are insensitive to androgens (Clarnette et al., 1997). The result is feminization of prenatal development, so that the baby is born with normal-looking female genitals and a shallow vagina. Not surprisingly, AIS babies are identified as female and reared accordingly. The anomaly is often discovered only in late adolescence, when a physician is consulted to find out why menstruation has not commenced. A study of 10 AIS individuals revealed that all but one—a child reared in a dysfunctional environment—had acquired a clear female gender identity and behaved accordingly (Money et al., 1968). These findings seem to support the importance of social learning in shaping gender-identity formation.

Fetally androgenized female
Chromosomally normal (XX) female who, as a result of excessive exposure to androgens during prenatal sex differentiation, develops external genitalia resembling those of a male.

FETALLY ANDROGENIZED FEMALES In a second type of abnormal sex differentiation, chromosomally normal females are prenatally masculinized by exposure to excessive androgens, either from a genetically induced malfunctioning of their own adrenal glands (*adrenogenital syndrome*) or from androgenlike substances ingested by their mothers during pregnancy (Clarnette et al., 1997). (In the 1950s, some pregnant women were given androgenlike drugs to reduce the risk of miscarriage.) As a result, such babies are born with masculine-looking external genitals: An enlarged clitoris may look like a penis, and fused labia may resemble a scrotum (see Figure 3.5). These babies are usually identified as female by medical tests, treated with minor surgery or hormone therapy to eliminate their genital ambiguity, and reared as girls. Nevertheless, one noteworthy study reported that 20 out of 25 **fetally androgenized females** identified themselves as "tomboys," engaged in traditionally male activities, and rejected behaviors and attitudes commonly associated with a female gender identity (Money & Ehrhardt, 1972). These findings, which appear to reflect the significant impact of biological factors in gender-identity formation, contrast markedly with the AIS study described earlier.

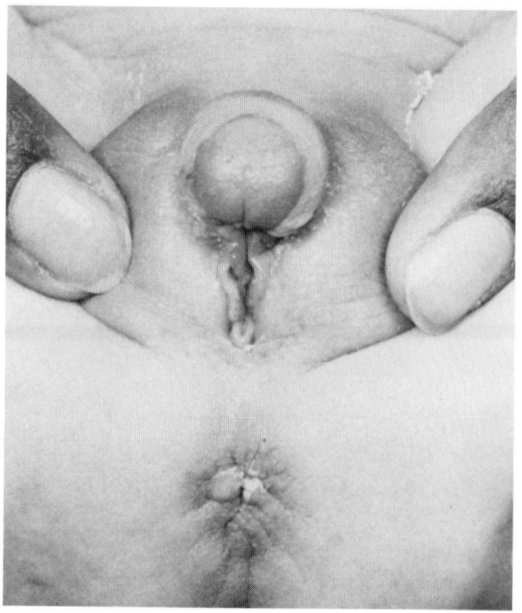

Figure 3.5

Masculinized external genitals of a fetally androgenized female baby.

DHT-DEFICIENT MALES A third variety of abnormal prenatal differentiation is caused by a genetic defect that prevents conversion of testosterone into the hormone dihydrotestosterone (DHT), which is essential for normal development of external genitals in a male fetus. In males with this disorder, the testes do not descend before birth, the penis and scrotum remain undeveloped so that they resemble a clitoris and labia, and a shallow vagina is partially formed. Because their genitals look more female than male, these **DHT-deficient males** are typically identified as female and reared as girls. (Males who experience this abnormal sex-differentiation pattern are also sometimes described as exhibiting *5-alpha reductase syndrome.*) However, because their testes are still functional, an amazing change occurs at puberty as accelerated testosterone production reverses the DHT deficiency. This causes their testes to descend and their clitorislike organs to enlarge into penises. In short, these DHT-deficient males undergo rapid transformation, from apparently female to male! How do they respond?

DHT-deficient male
Chromosomally normal (XY) male who develops external genitalia resembling those of a female as a result of a genetic defect that prevents the prenatal conversion of testosterone into DHT.

In one study, a team of Cornell University researchers investigated 18 DHT-deficient males who had been reared as female in rural communities in the Dominican Republic (Imperato-McGinley et al., 1979). When their bodies changed at puberty, 16 responded to this transformation by embracing traditional male gender roles mandated by their culture. These findings challenge the widely held belief that once gender identity is formed in the first few years of life it may not be changed without severe emotional trauma. To the contrary, they suggest that gender identity may be malleable even as late as adolescence.

Some important questions have been raised about this study, however. First, the culture of this Caribbean nation is very male oriented, which may have influenced these youths to switch gender identity more readily. Indeed, some were exposed to extreme social pressure in the form of ridicule, as locals called them *quevote,* which means "penis at 12" or *machihembra,* "first woman, then man." And second, the research was conducted retrospectively, after the subjects were adults. Because people's recollections are not always reliable, it cannot be determined with certainty whether all these youths had experienced unambiguous female gender socialization as children.

These three examples of abnormal sex differentiation appear to provide contradictory evidence. In the first example of AIS males, chromosomal males insensitive to their own androgens acquired a female gender identity consistent with the way in which they were reared. In the second instance, prenatally masculinized chromosomal females behaved in a typically masculine manner even though they were reared female. Finally, in the third instance, chromosomal males whose biological maleness was not apparent until puberty were able to successfully switch their gender identity to male, despite early socialization as girls. Are these results at odds with one another, or is there a plausible explanation for their seeming inconsistencies?

As described earlier, some data suggest that prenatal androgens influence sex differentiation of the brain just as they trigger masculinization of the sex structures. The same gene defect that prevents masculinization of the genitals of AIS males in the first example may also block masculinization of their brains, thus influencing the development of a female gender identity. Similarly, the masculinizing influence of prenatal androgens on the brain might also account for the tomboyish behaviors of fetally androgenized females in the second example. But what about DHT-deficient males who appear to make a relatively smooth transition from a female to male gender identity? Perhaps these boys' brains were prenatally programmed along male lines. Presumably, they had normal levels of androgens and, with the exception of genital development, were able to respond appropriately to these hormones at critical stages of prenatal development. We cannot state with certainty that prenatal androgens masculinize the brain. However, this interpretation offers a plausible explanation for how DHT individuals, already hormonally predisposed toward a male gender identity despite being identified as female, are able to change to a male identity at adolescence in response to changes in their bodies.

These fascinating studies underscore the complexity of biological sex determination. We have seen that many steps, each susceptible to errors, are involved in sex differentiation prior to birth. These investigations also raise a fundamental question: Just what makes us female or male? To further amplify this question, we now turn to the role of social-learning factors in influencing gender-identity formation *after* birth.

Social-Learning Influences on Gender Identity

Thus far we have considered only the biological factors involved in the determination of gender identity. Our sense of femaleness or maleness is not based exclusively on biological conditions, however. Social-learning theory suggests that our identification with either masculine or feminine roles or a combination thereof (androgyny) results primarily from the social and cultural models and influences that we are exposed to during our early development. (Lips, 1997; Lorber, 1995).

What do you consider to be some of the important social and cultural influences that shape our gender identities?

Even before their baby is born, parents (and other adults involved in childrearing) have preconceived notions about how boys and girls differ. And through a multitude of subtle and not-so-subtle means, they communicate these ideas to their children (Witt, 1997). Gender-role expectations influence the environments in which children are raised, from the choice of room color to the selection of toys. They also influence the way parents think of their children. For example, in one study parents were asked to describe their newborn infants. Parents of boys described them as "strong," "active," and "robust," while parents of daughters used words such as "soft" and "delicate"—even though all their babies were of similar size and muscle tone (Rubin et al., 1974). Not surprisingly, gender-role expectations also influence the way parents respond to their children: A boy may be encouraged to suppress his tears if he scrapes a knee and to show other "manly" qualities such as independence and aggressiveness, whereas girls may be encouraged to be nurturing and cooperative (Hyde, 1996; Mosher & Tomkins, 1988; Siegal, 1987).

By about 18 months, most children have developed a firm gender identity. From this point, gender-identity reinforcement typically becomes somewhat self-perpetuating, as most children actively seek to behave in ways that they are taught are appropriate to their own sex (Kohlberg, 1966; Sedney, 1987). It is not unusual for little girls to go through a period of insisting that they wear fancy dresses or practice baking in the kitchen—sometimes to the dismay of their own mothers, who have themselves adopted more practical wardrobes and have abandoned the kitchen for a career! Likewise, young boys may develop a fascination for superheroes, policemen, and other cultural role models, and try to adopt behaviors appropriate to these roles.

Anthropological studies of other cultures also lend support to the social-learning interpretation of gender-identity formation. In several societies, the differences between males and females that we often assume to be innate are simply not evident. In fact, Margaret Mead's classic book *Sex and Temperament in Three Primitive Societies* (1963) reveals that other societies may have very different views about what is considered feminine or masculine. In this widely quoted report of her fieldwork in New Guinea, Mead discusses two societies that minimize differences between the sexes. She notes that among the Mundugumor, both sexes exhibit aggressive, insensitive, uncooperative, and nonnurturing behaviors that would be considered masculine by our society's norms. In contrast, among the Arapesh, both males and females exhibit gentleness, sensitivity, cooperation, nurturing, and nonaggressive behaviors that would be judged feminine in our society. And among the Tchambuli, as we saw in this chapter's opening paragraphs, masculine and feminine gender roles are actually reversed from what Americans view as typical. Because there is no evidence that people in these societies are biologically different from Americans, their often diametrically different interpretations of what is masculine and what is feminine seem to result from different processes of social learning.

Finally, proponents of the social-learning interpretation of gender-identity formation refer to various studies of children born with ambiguous external genitals who are assigned a particular sex and reared accordingly. Much of the early work in this area was performed at Johns Hopkins University Hospital by a team headed by John Money. At the time these treatment approaches were being implemented, Money and his colleagues believed that a person is psychosexually neutral or undifferentiated at birth, and that

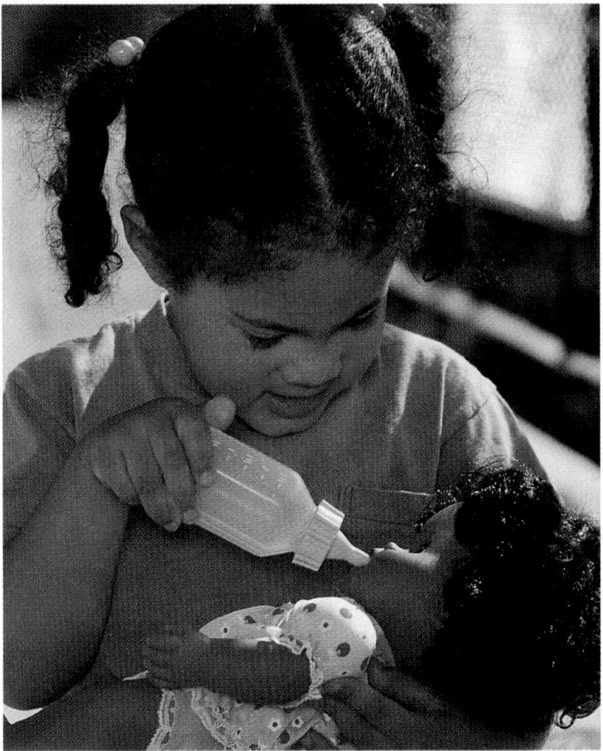

Although parents are becoming more sensitive to the kinds of toys children play with, many still choose different toys and play activities for boys and girls.

social-learning experiences are the essential determinants of gender identity and gender-role behavior (Money et al., 1955; Money, 1961 & 1963; Money & Ehrhardt, 1972). Therefore, little attention was paid to matching external genitals with sex chromosomes. Rather, because the guiding principle was how natural the genitals could be made to look, many of these pseudohermaphroditic infants were assigned to the female sex, in that surgical reconstruction of ambiguous genitalia to those of a female form is mechanically easier and esthetically and functionally superior to constructing a penis (Diamond & Sigmundson, 1997).

Money and his colleagues followed these surgically altered children over a period of years and found that, in most cases they evaluated, children whose assigned sex did not match their chromosomal sex developed a gender identity consistent with the manner in which they were reared (Money, 1965; Money & Ehrhardt, 1972). One interesting example involved two children treated at Johns Hopkins, both of whom were chromosomally XX females who had been prenatally masculinized by exposure to excessive androgens. This problem was correctly diagnosed in one child at the age of two, and her masculinized external genitals were surgically altered to a female appearance. This child demonstrated childhood tomboyism (a common trait for girls) but was quite feminine in appearance, had a female gender identity, dated boys, and fantasized about getting married to a man. The second child was incorrectly identified as a male with a stunted penis. This mistaken diagnosis was not discovered until the age of 3½, at which time the child had a firm male gender identity. Consequently, a decision was reached to further masculinize his genitals via surgery, and later on he was given hormone treatments at puberty. As an adolescent he closely associated with other males and was sexually attracted to females. In conclusion, even though both these children were chromosomally female and had internal female sex structures, they were treated and reared differently and each acquired a gender identity consistent with their assigned sex. Such findings appear to strongly endorse the role played by social learning in shaping the formation of gender identity.

One particularly unusual study of two identical twin boys (Money, 1975) has frequently been cited in support of the social-learning interpretation. At the age of eight

cathy® **by Cathy Guisewite**

months, a circumcision accident destroyed most of the penile tissue of one of the boys. Because no amount of plastic surgery could adequately reconstruct the severely damaged penis, it was recommended that the child be raised as a female and receive appropriate sex-change surgery. A few months later the parents decided to begin raising him as a girl. Shortly thereafter, castration and initial genital surgery was performed to facilitate feminization. Further surgery to fashion a full vagina was to wait until the child was older. Follow-up analyses of these twins during their early childhood years revealed that, despite possessing identical genetic materials, they responded to their separate social-learning experiences by developing opposite gender identities. Furthermore, the child reassigned to the female gender was described as developing into a normally functioning girl child.

If the story of these twins ended here, we would have strong evidence of the dominant role of social learning in gender-identity formation. However, in 1979 the psychiatrist following this case revealed that the assigned female member of the pair was experiencing considerable difficulty in making her adjustment as a female (Williams & Smith, 1979). A more recent follow-up (Diamond & Sigmundson, 1997) found that, beginning at age 14 years, and still unaware of the XY chromosome status, and against the recommendations of family and treating clinicians, this person decided to no longer live as a female. This adamant rejection of living as a female, together with a much improved emotional state when living as a male, convinced therapists of the appropriateness of sexual reassignment. His postsurgical adjustment was excellent and, aided by testosterone treatments, he "emerged" as an attractive young man. At the age of 25 he married a woman and adopted her children and continues to live comfortably in his role as father and husband.

This case illustrates the critical importance of long-term, longitudinal studies of children who have been sex reassigned. The early childhood phase of the follow-up of this child was widely reported in the press and the academic and medical community as providing clear evidence that gender identity is psychologically neutral at birth as yet unwritten upon by social-learning experiences. Now, after many years during which this viewpoint remained predominant, we find out how wrong this interpretation may be. Even John Money, formerly a major proponent of this perspective, no longer holds such an extreme view (see Money, 1994a).

Now, as the twentieth century draws to a close, several eminent researcher-theorists argue that until such time as we have more data, we must assume that conclusions about sex reassignment of children may be erroneous because of the conspicuous lack of critically needed long-term studies. In fact, evidence is increasing that despite great care in rearing chromosomal males sex-reassigned as females, some or perhaps even many of them, manifest strong male tendencies in their developmental years and may even change their assigned sex after they reach puberty (Diamond & Sigmundson, 1997; Reiner, 1997). One leading authority, William Reiner of the Johns Hopkins University Hospital, recently stated that "anatomical (genital) relatedness and appearance may be less dynamic than the prenatal hormonally differentiated brain" (1997, p. 224).

The Interactional Model

Scientists have argued for decades about the relative importance of nature (biological determinants) versus nurture (social learning and the environment) in shaping human development. Today it seems clear that gender identity is a product of both biological factors and social learning. The evidence is simply too overwhelming to conclude that normal infants are psychosexually neutral at birth. We have seen that human infants possess a complex and yet to be fully understood biological substrate that predisposes them to interact with their social environment in either a masculine or feminine mode. However, few contemporary researchers believe that human gender identity has an exclusively biological basis. There is simply too much evidence supporting the important role of life experiences in shaping the way we think about ourselves—not only as masculine or feminine, but in all aspects of how we relate to those around us. Consequently, most theorists and researchers support an *interactional model,* which acknowledges both biology and experience in the development of gender identity (Golombok & Fivush, 1995). Hopefully, as we acquire more data from further research, especially from long-term, longitudinal analyses, we will gain a clearer understanding of the relative impact of these two powerful forces on gender-identity formation and gender-role behavior.

A Special Case of Gender-Identity Difficulty: Transsexualism

A **transsexual** is a person whose gender identity is opposite to his or her biological sex (Cole et al., 1997; Pauly, 1990). He or she feels trapped in a body of the wrong sex, a condition known as **gender dysphoria** (dis-FOR-ē-a) (Blanchard et al., 1987a). Thus, an anatomically male transsexual feels that he is a woman betrayed by some quirk of fate that provided him with male genitals. He wishes to be socially identified as the woman he sincerely believes himself to be. Rather than experiencing sexual excitement when cross-dressing, as is the case with transvestism, he experiences a sense of comfort with himself. (We will discuss transvestism in Chapter 18.)

Transsexual
A person whose gender identity is opposite to his or her biological sex.

Gender dysphoria
See Transsexual.

In the 1960s and early 1970s, when medical procedures for altering sex were first being developed in this country, approximately three out of every four people requesting a sex change were men who wished to be women (Green, 1974). Although most health professionals believe that males seeking sex reassignment still outnumber females, there is evidence that the ratio has narrowed appreciably in recent years (Landen et al., 1998; Pauly, 1990).

A vast accumulation of clinical literature has focused on the characteristics, causes, and treatment of transsexualism. Certain factors are well established: We know that most transsexuals are biologically normal individuals with healthy sex organs, intact internal reproductive structures, and the proper complement of XX or XY chromosomes. Furthermore, transsexualism is usually an isolated condition and not part of any general psychopathology such as schizophrenia or major depression. One recent study found that less than 10% of a sample of 137 transsexuals evidenced symptoms associated with mental illness (Cole et al., 1997). What is less understood is why these individuals reject their anatomies. A leading scholar in this area, Leslie Lothstein (1984), published a critical review of 30 years of psychological evaluation of transsexuals, in which he concluded that no clear understanding of the nature and etiology of transsexualism has yet emerged. Considerable controversy also exists regarding the most appropriate clinical strategies for dealing with this condition. Keeping this continued debate in mind, we will summarize our current tenuous state of knowledge about this highly unusual gender-identity difficulty.

Many transsexuals develop a sense of being at odds with their genital anatomy in very early childhood; some recall identifying strongly with characteristics of the other sex as early as five, six, or seven years of age. In some cases, these children's discomfort is partially relieved by imagining themselves to be members of the other sex, but many of them eventually progress beyond mere imagining to actual cross-dressing. Less commonly, a strong identity with the other sex may not emerge until adolescence or adulthood.

What do you think causes transsexualism?

Many theories have attempted to explain transsexualism, but current evidence is inconclusive (Money, 1994b). Some writers maintain that biological factors may play a decisive role. One theory suggests that prenatal exposure to inappropriate amounts of hormones of the other sex might cause improper brain differentiation (Pauly, 1974). Some support for this theory was provided by a recent study in which a female-sized BSTc was found in six male-to-female transsexuals (Zhou et al., 1995). You will recall from our earlier discussion of brain differentiation that the BSTc is an area of the hypothalamus that is normally almost 50% larger in heterosexual men than in heterosexual women. According to this study's authors, the unusually small, femalelike BSTc in these six biological males with a female gender identity "cannot be explained by differences in adult sex hormones" (p. 70). Although we must wait for additional research to confirm this intriguing finding, this discovery does suggest that gender-identity formation may be drastically transformed by altered patterns of interaction between the developing brain and prenatal sex hormones.

It has also been suggested that transsexualism may be induced by abnormal levels of adult sex hormones. However, this explanation is contradicted by numerous indications that sex hormone levels are normal in adult transsexuals (Meyer et al., 1986; Zhou et al., 1995).

Another theory pertaining to the causes of transsexualism, which has some supporting evidence, holds that social-learning experiences contribute significantly to the development of this condition. A child may be exposed to a variety of conditioning experiences that support behaving in a manner traditionally attributed to the other sex (Green, 1974; Money & Primrose, 1968). The child may develop a close, identifying relationship with the parent of the other sex, and this identification may be strongly reinforced by the adult's reaction. The little boy may play at being a girl, and the girl may be "Daddy's little man." Such cross-gender behaviors may be so exclusively rewarded that it may be difficult or impossible for the individual to develop the appropriate gender identity.

Several studies have reported unusual attachments between male-to-female transsexuals and their mothers, whereas the presence of cold, rejecting mothers and unusual identification with their fathers have been found in the early development of female-to-male transsexuals (Pauly, 1974; Stoller, 1968 & 1972). One study of transsexuals who were aware of their cross-gender identification as youths revealed a high incidence of early traumatic experiences in a disturbed family environment (Meyer & Dupkin, 1985).

Difficult as it is to determine the causes of transsexualism, it is perhaps even more challenging to resolve the problem of reversed gender identity. Most transsexuals follow a heterosexual script and prefer to have sexual relations with a member of the other sex. The fact that the "other sex" happens to have the same genitals as they do makes it difficult to find a partner. Most transsexuals want to interact with heterosexuals: A male transsexual wants to be desired as a woman by a heterosexual man, and most transsexual women are not satisfied with a lesbian relationship. These sexual needs are often hard to meet. Heterosexuals and homosexuals can generally find willing sex partners who match their orientations, but transsexuals' most desired partners are likely to reject them for making such advances.

Psychotherapy, without accompanying biological alterations, has generally been reported to be unsuccessful in helping transsexuals adjust to their bodies (Roberto, 1983; Tollison & Adams, 1979). It would seem then that the best course of action might be for them to change their bodies to match their minds, through surgical and hormonal alteration of genital anatomy and body physiology. Beneficial as it may be, however, the process of medical alteration is not a simple solution, for it is both time-consuming and costly. One leading authority on the treatment of transsexualism suggested that all possible alternatives, including psychotherapy, be explored before considering irreversible sex-change surgery (Pauly, 1990).

Sex-Reassignment Procedures

The initial step of a sex change involves extensive screening interviews, during which the person's motivations for undergoing the change are thoroughly evaluated. Those with real conflicts and confusion about their gender identity (that is, who are not really sure which sex they are) or those seeking the operation on a whim are not considered for surgical alteration. Individuals with an apparently genuine incongruence between their gender identity and biological sex are then instructed to adopt a lifestyle consistent with their gender identity (i.e., dress style and behavior patterns). If, after several months to a year or longer, it appears that the individual has successfully adjusted to that lifestyle, the next step is hormone therapy, a process designed to accentuate latent traits of the desired sex. Thus, males wishing to be females are given drugs that inhibit testosterone production, together with doses of estrogen that induce some breast growth, soften the skin, reduce facial and body hair, and help to feminize body contours. Muscle strength also diminishes, as does sexual interest, but there is no alteration of vocal pitch. Transsexual women who want to become male are treated with testosterone, which helps to increase growth of body and facial hair and produces a deepening of the voice and a slight reduction in breast size. Testosterone also suppresses menstruation. Most health professionals providing the sex-change procedures require that a candidate live for one year or more as a member of the other sex, while undergoing hormone therapy, before taking the final, drastic step of surgery. At any time during this phase, the process can be successfully reversed, although few transsexuals choose this option.

The final step of a sex change is surgery (see Figure 3.6). Surgical procedures are most effective for men wishing to be women. The scrotum and penis are removed, and a vagina is created through reconstruction of pelvic tissue (see Figure 3.6a). During this surgical procedure, great care is taken to maintain the sensory nerves that serve the skin of the penis, and this sensitive skin tissue is relocated to the inside of the newly fashioned vagina. Intercourse is possible, although use of a lubricant may be necessary, and many male-to-female transsexuals report postsurgical capacity to experience sexual arousal and orgasm (Blanchard et al., 1987; Lief & Hubschman, 1993; Money & Walker, 1977). Hormone treatments may produce sufficient breast development, but some individuals also

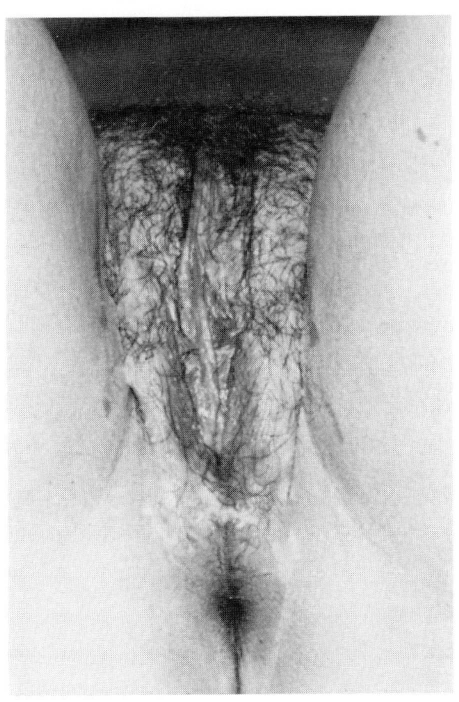

(a)

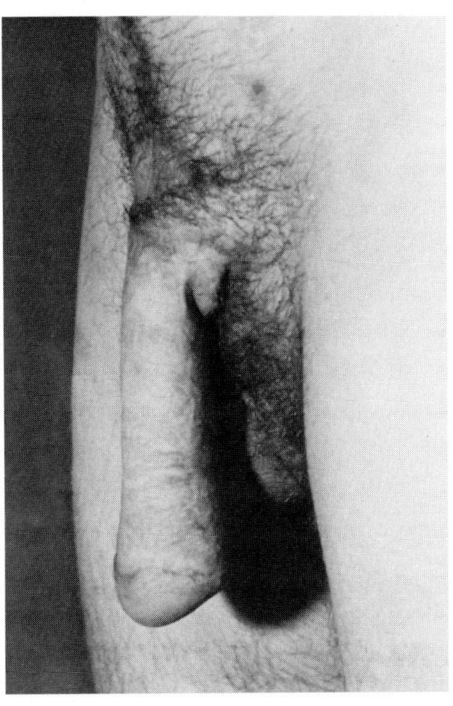

(b)

Figure 3.6

The genitals following sex change surgery: (a) Male-to-female sex-change surgery is generally more effective than (b) female-to-male sex-change surgery.

receive implants. Body and facial hair, which has been reduced by hormone treatments, may be further removed by electrolysis.

Biological females who desire to be male generally have their breasts, uteri, and ovaries surgically removed and their vaginas sealed off. The process of constructing a penis is much more difficult than that of fashioning a vagina. Generally, the penis is fashioned from abdominal skin or from tissue from the labia and perineum (see Figure 3.6b). This constructed organ is not capable of natural erection in response to sexual arousal. However, several artificial devices are available for providing a rigid penis for purposes of intercourse. One involves fashioning a small, hollow skin tube on the underside of the penile shaft into which a rigid silicone rod can be inserted. Another alternative is to use an implanted inflatable device, which will be described in Chapter 16. If erotically sensitive tissue from the clitoris is left embedded at the base of the surgically constructed penis, erotic feelings and orgasm are sometimes possible. In fact, one recent study of 25 surgically altered transsexuals found that although 90% of the total group reported satisfaction with surgical results and with postoperative sexual activity, orgasmic capacity actually increased in the female-to-male group, whereas it declined somewhat in the male-to-female subjects (Lief & Hubschman, 1993).

Outcomes of Sex Reassignment

Several reports provide some basis for optimism about the potential success of sex-reassignment surgery. One important publication drew conclusions from three worldwide literature reviews on the outcome of sex-change surgery (Lundstrom et al., 1984). It reported that approximately nine out of ten transsexuals undergoing hormonal and surgical sex-reassignment procedures experienced a satisfactory result. This high incidence of positive outcomes appears to be equally likely for male-to-female and female-to-male

On the Edge
Sex Change for Teenagers?

Even though transsexualism typically emerges in very early childhood, it is common practice in most countries to delay sex-reassignment surgery until adulthood is attained. Children are not considered viable candidates for sex change, because studies have shown that most children who exhibit gender dysphoria will not become adult transsexuals (Green, 1987; Zuger, 1984). But what about adolescence, a critical period of psychosocial development during which transsexualism becomes a more entrenched gender disorder? Why postpone sex reassignment until the adult years, which results in many transsexuals suffering needlessly from feelings of despair and alienation throughout their teenage years?

A partial reason for the widespread reluctance to begin sex reassignment in postpubertal children is that adolescence is a developmental phase during which many teenagers experiment with a variety of identities (such as social, political, and religious). Many health professionals fear that any type of intervention during this stage of development might prompt gender-identity-confused adolescents to falsely conclude they are transsexuals and thus wrongly seek medical treatment. Another, more pragmatic reason for postponing sex reassignment is that in most countries teenagers are legally dependent on parental consent for such a drastic medical procedure. Thus, even though medical experts and the teenage patient may agree that a sex change should not be delayed, parents may not consent and clinicians may be reluctant to proceed due to litigation risks.

There are, however, strong arguments for initiating sex-reassignment procedures earlier than adulthood. A strong case for teenage sex change was recently outlined by members of a sex-reassignment team based at a major teaching hospital in the Netherlands. These professionals maintain that those adolescent transsexuals who have manifested an extreme cross-gender identification from their earliest years "suffer deeply from the fact that they cannot be open about their gender feelings. Knowing that they will have to await treatment for many years engenders feelings of hopelessness and slows down their social, psychological, and intellectual development" (Cohen-Kettenis & van Goozen, 1997, p. 264).

transsexuals. Another study, which used a large sample of both groups, reported that 94% would have the surgery again if they had it to do over (Blanchard et al., 1985). Still other, more recent reports have revealed that transsexuals who underwent surgery were satisfied with the outcome and demonstrated markedly better social adjustment than those who had not been surgically altered (Lief & Hubschman, 1993; Rakic et al., 1996; Shroder & Carroll, 1996).

Finally, in terms of postsurgical sexual orientation, almost all female-to-male transsexuals desire female sexual partners. However, male-to-female transsexuals may be sexually oriented to either sex after surgery, with most preferring male sex partners (Blanchard et al., 1987b; Zhou et al., 1995).

All the research we have discussed describes results for transsexuals who underwent sex change surgery after reaching adulthood. In most countries, including the United States, it is common practice to delay beginning sex-reassignment procedures until the transsexual individual is at least 18 years of age and usually over 21 (Cohen-Kettenis & van Goozen, 1997). However, in recent years adolescents in the Netherlands have undergone sex reassignment. The results of this controversial program are discussed in the boxed discussion "Sex Change for Teenagers."

At the time of this writing, controversy continues in the scientific community over the relative benefits of sex-change surgery. Clearly, we do not have the complete picture at the present time, and there is a vital need for continued research. However, many health professionals support sex-reassignment surgery as an option for some individuals who experience great distress as a result of a strong identification with the other sex. These professionals stress the importance of careful diagnostic screening as well as good surgical procedures to yield an aesthetically pleasing result. Perhaps, as one writer suggests, we may eventually come to view such procedures as "sex confirmation" rather than sex reassignment (Edgerton, 1984).

On the Edge

Another persuasive argument for commencing sex-change procedures on adolescent transsexuals is that the physical appearance outcomes are much better as compared to starting later in adulthood. This is especially true for male-to-female transsexuals who, instead of having to deal with a deep voice and facial scarring from hair removal procedures, are able to pass easily as female. Clearly, this is a profound and lifelong advantage. Finally, a number of studies have revealed that unfavorable postoperative outcomes are often related to a later rather than an early start of sex-reassignment procedures (Green & Fleming, 1990; Leavitt & Berger, 1990).

Adolescent transsexuals at the Netherlands center are subjected to an intensive two-phase diagnostic process similar to that employed with adult transsexuals seeking a sex change. This involves extensive interviews and testing, followed by assuming a lifestyle consistent with their gender identity and partial hormone treatments. Throughout this process the adolescent's family is involved and their support for a sex change is achieved. Adolescents who successfully pass through these diagnostic procedures are referred for surgery.

The Netherlands researchers recently reported a follow-up study of 22 transsexuals (15 female-to-male and 7 male-to-female) who had undergone sex reassignment while still adolescents. All subjects had experienced their last surgical procedure at least one year and as long as five years prior to the start of the study. Data pertaining to the posttreatment adjustment of each subject were compared with his or her pretreatment data. Postoperatively, gender dysphoria was absent in all subjects, and all scored within a normal range on a number of psychological tests. All 22 exhibited healthy social functioning in their daily lives, and none expressed regret for having undergone sex reassignment. Most were also reportedly satisfied with their posttreatment physical appearance. This was especially true of the male-to-female subjects.

The appropriateness of sex reassignment for adolescents remains a topic of widespread debate within the health community. However, the pioneering efforts of the Netherlands sex-change team demonstrates that, at least for some transsexuals, "starting the sex reassignment procedure before adulthood results in favorable postoperative functioning, provided that careful diagnosis takes place in a specialized gender team and that the criteria for starting the procedure early are stringent" (Cohen-Kettenis & van Goozen, 1997, p. 263).

Gender Roles

We have seen that social learning is an important influence in the formation of gender identity early in life, so that even by the age of two years, most children have no doubt about whether they are boys or girls. This influence continues throughout our lives, as we are influenced by *gender roles* (or *sex roles*)—that is, behaviors that are considered appropriate and normal for men and women in a society.

The ascribing of gender roles leads naturally to certain assumptions about how people will behave. For example, men in North American society are expected to be independent and aggressive, whereas women are supposed to be dependent and submissive. Once these expectations are widely accepted, they may begin to function as stereotypes. A **stereotype** is a generalized notion of what a person is like based only on that person's sex, race, religion, ethnic background, or similar category. Stereotypes do not take individuality into account.

Stereotype
A generalized notion of what a person is like that is based only on that person's sex, race, religion, ethnic background, or similar criterion.

Many common gender-based stereotypes are widely accepted in our society. Some of the prevailing notions about men maintain that they are aggressive (or at least assertive), logical, unemotional, independent, dominant, competitive, objective, athletic, active, and above all, competent. Conversely, women are frequently viewed as passive, nonassertive, illogical, emotional, dependent, subordinate, warm, and nurturing.

Not all people hold these gender-role stereotypes, and in recent years we have seen a trend away from strict adherence to gender-typed behavior. Research suggests that women may be less entrenched than men in rigid gender-role stereotypes and are perhaps more inclined to embrace positions of equality in relation to men (Larsen & Long, 1988). However, many men also feel constrained by traditional roles.

Despite the potentially limiting impact of stereotypic gender roles on our lives, they still pervade our society (Doyle & Paludi, 1991; Hyde, 1996). Indeed, many individuals are comfortable fulfilling a traditional masculine or feminine role, and we do not wish to demean or question the validity of their lifestyles. Rather, we are concerned with finding out why gender roles are so prevalent in society. We turn next to this question.

How Do We Learn Gender Roles?

You have probably heard the argument that behavioral differences between men and women are biologically determined, at least to some degree. Men cannot bear children, nor can they nurse them. Likewise, biological differences in hormones, muscle mass, and brain structure and function may influence some aspects of behavior. However, most theorists, including ourselves, explain gender roles as largely a product of **socialization**—that is, the process by which individuals learn, and adopt, society's expectations for behavior. As is shown in the boxed discussion "Ethnic Variations in Gender Roles," different cultural and ethnic groups within a society have varying expectations for men's and women's behaviors. How does society convey these expectations? In the following sections, we look at five agents of socialization: parents, peers, school, television, and religion.

Socialization
The process whereby our society conveys behavioral expectations to the individual.

Take a few moments to think about the respective roles of these agents of socialization in your own life. In what way did each of these influences shape your gender-role expectations? Were some of these agents more influential than others? Can you think of any additional influences?

Parents as Shapers of Gender Roles

Many social scientists view parents as influential agents of gender-role socialization (Hardesty et al., 1995; Leaper et al., 1998; Witt, 1997). A child's earliest exposure to what it means to be female or male is typically provided by parents (Witt, 1997). And, as we saw earlier in the discussion of gender-identity formation, parents often have different expectations for girls and boys, and they demonstrate these expectations in their interactions. Baby girls often receive more attention than baby boys (Jacklin et al., 1984), and parents are more likely to treat them as if they were fragile—for instance, hesitating to bounce them up and down (Doyle & Paludi, 1991). Likewise, a girl may be cuddled when she cries out of pain or frustration, whereas a boy may be admonished that "boys don't cry." In general, parents tend to be more protective and restrictive of girl babies while providing less intervention and more freedom for boys (Skolnick, 1992).

Although more and more parents today try to avoid teaching their children sex stereotypes, many still encourage their children to engage in sex-typed play activities and household chores (Lytton & Romney, 1991; McHale et al., 1990). And even when parents make a conscious effort not to teach gender roles, some behaviors may seem so "natural" that they occur unconsciously. Thus a boy's father may invite him to play catch, change the oil in the family car, or mow the lawn together, whereas a girl may receive more frequent reminders to keep her room tidy or invitations to help prepare meals. This differential treatment has the effect of guiding children toward specific and different adult roles (Fisher-Thompson, 1990). Research suggests that fathers are more likely to convey gender-role expectations than are mothers (Lamb, 1981; Power, 1985).

Although parents undoubtedly are involved in shaping gender roles, there is some question about the strength of their influence. One study analyzed data from 172 separate investigations of the role of parents as agents of gender-role socialization and found that parents treat boys and girls in remarkably similar ways, with the one exception that parents tend to encourage sex-typed activities (Lytton & Romney, 1991). These findings

Sexuality and Diversity

Ethnic Variations in Gender Roles

Throughout this text we have focused primarily on gender assumptions that are prevalent among the traditional mainstream—white Americans of European origin. Here we look briefly at gender roles among three different American ethnic groups: Hispanic Americans, African Americans, and Asian Americans.

Traditional Hispanic American gender roles are epitomized in the cultural stereotypes of *marianismo* and *machismo.* Marianismo derives from the Roman Catholic notion that women should be pure and self-giving—like the Virgin Mary. It ascribes to women the primary role of mothers who are faithful, virtuous, passive, and subordinate to their husbands, while at the same time acting as the primary preserver of the family and tradition (Bryjak & Soroka, 1994; Espin, 1992; Sanchez-Ayendez, 1988). Not surprisingly, this emphasis often places considerable stress on Hispanic American women. Although entering the workplace in increasing numbers, they are still expected to care for their children, perform household chores, and serve their husbands' needs.

The concept of machismo projects an image of the Hispanic American male as strong, virile, and dominant—the head of household and major decision maker in the family (Bryjak & Soroka, 1994; Espin, 1992; Sanchez-Ayendez, 1988; Torres, 1998). Machismo also embodies the notion that it is acceptable to be sexually aggressive and to seek conquests outside the marriage. Thus Hispanic culture is often expressive of a double standard in which wives are to remain faithful to one man while husbands may have outside affairs (Espin, 1992). Machismo has another side, for it is also characterized by generosity, respect for others, the use of fair and just authority, courage, and responsibility for the safety and honor of one's family (Sanchez-Ayendez, 1988; Torres, 1998; Vasquez, 1994).

Of course, marianismo and machismo are just stereotypes, and many Hispanic Americans do not embrace these gender-role assumptions (Vasquez, 1994). Furthermore, assimilation, urbanization, and upward mobility of Hispanic Americans are combining to diminish the impact of these cultural stereotypes as they reduce gender-role inequities (Schaefer, 1990).

Among a second ethnic group, African Americans, women play a central role in families that tend to differ from the traditional nuclear family model of mother, father, and children (Bulcroft et al., 1996; Greene, 1994; Reid & Comas-Diaz, 1990). African American women have traditionally been a bulwark of strength in their communities since the days of slavery. Because females were not economically dependent on males under the system of slavery, African American men did not typically assume the dominant role in the family. This accounts, in part, for why relationships between African American women and men have tended more toward egalitarianism

(continued on next page)

The establishment of stereotypic masculine or feminine roles may be influenced by traditional childrearing practices.

Sexuality and Diversity

and economic parity than has been true of other cultural groups, including the dominant white culture (Blee & Tickamyer, 1995; Bulcroft et al., 1996; Greene, 1994). This historical absence of economic dependence also helps explain why so many African American households are headed by women who define their own status.

Another factor is the high unemployment rate among African American males—almost three times that for whites (U.S. Department of Labor, 1990). The realities of unemployment undoubtedly contribute to some African American men's avoidance of marriage and absenteeism from the home. Consequently, African American women often assume gender-role behaviors that reflect a reversal of gender patterns that are traditional among white Americans.

Although African Americans may not adhere as strongly as other cultural groups to the concept of the nuclear family, certain characteristics contribute to stability and cohesion in both family and community. These include (1) intense kinship bonds among a variety of households; (2) strong work, achievement, and education ethics; (3) unusually high levels of adaptability and flexibility in family and gender roles; and (4) commitment to religious values and participation in church activities (Ho, 1987; Reid & Comas-Diaz, 1990; Schaefer, 1990).

A third minority group, Asian Americans, represent great diversity both in heritage and countries of origin (China, the Philippines, Japan, India, Korea, Vietnam, Cambodia, Thailand, and others). Asian Americans tend to place more value on family, group solidarity, and interdependence than do white Americans (Bradshaw, 1994). Like her Latina counterparts, the Asian American woman's family obligations are expected to take higher priority than her own individual aspirations. Thus, although more Asian American women work outside the home than do women in any other American ethnic group, many spend their lives supporting others and subordinating their needs to the family (Bradshaw, 1994; Cole, 1992). As a result, achievement-oriented Asian women are often caught in a double bind, torn between contemporary American values of individuality and independence and the traditional gender roles of Asian culture.

While there is no "typical" pattern, the diverse Asian cultures still perpetuate the gender-role assumption of male dominance (Bradshaw, 1994; Lai, 1992). In Chinese American families, for instance, even though husband and wife occupy equal breadwinning roles, the wife usually assumes the role of helper to her husband rather than equal partner (Wong, 1988). Similarly, in many Vietnamese American families where both spouses work full time, the wife often has sole responsibility for household chores and childcare. However, there is a movement toward more parity in family life among younger Vietnamese American couples (Tran, 1988); and the same is true among third-generation Japanese Americans (Kitano, 1988).

As these accounts illustrate, social learning and cultural traditions influence gender-role behaviors within American society.

suggest that parental impact on gender-role socialization may not be as powerful an influence as commonly believed.

The Peer Group

A second important influence in the socialization of gender roles is the peer group. One element of peer-group influence that begins early in life is a voluntary segregation of the sexes from one another (Maccoby, 1988 & 1990; Powlishta et al., 1993). This begins during the preschool years, and by first grade, children select members of their own sex as playmates about 95% of the time (Maccoby & Jacklin, 1987). Segregation of the sexes, which continues into the school years, contributes to sex typing in play activities that help prepare children for adult gender roles (Moller et al., 1992). Girls often play together with dolls and tea sets, and boys frequently engage in athletic competitions and play with toy guns. Such peer influences contribute to the socialization of women who are inclined to be nurturing and nonassertive and men who are comfortable being competitive and assertive.

By late childhood and adolescence, the influence of peers becomes even more important (Doyle & Paludi, 1991; Hyde, 1996). Children of this age tend to view conformity as very important, and adhering to traditional gender roles promotes social acceptance by their peers (Absi-Semaan et al., 1993; Martin, 1990; Moller et al., 1992). Most individuals who do not behave in ways appropriate to their own sex are subjected to pressure in the form of ostracism or ridicule. And evidence indicates that children of the current generation continue to respond to their peers in gender-stereotyped ways despite important changes in our society in recent years (McAninch et al., 1996).

Gender-typed images can impose significant limitations on an individual. One particularly negative aspect of adolescent gender typing is the notion that one cannot be both feminine and an achiever. The potential impact of this limiting assumption is revealed in the following account:

> I like high school, and I am a good student. In fact, I could be an outstanding student. But I am afraid of what others might think of me if I do too well. My boyfriend is into sports and not schoolwork. We take some classes together. Many times I purposely score below my ability on tests so as not to show him up. What would he think about his girlfriend being a brain? (Authors' files)

Schools, Textbooks, and Gender Roles

A recent study sponsored by the American Association of University Women found that girls and boys receive quite different treatment in the classroom. Among other findings, this study reported that teachers call on and encourage boys more than girls; that boys who call out answers without being recognized are generally not penalized, whereas girls tend to be reprimanded for the same behavior; and that boys are more likely to receive praise for the content of their work, whereas girls receive praise for its neatness (Kantrowitz, 1992). Other research has had similar findings. Two major studies found that teachers are more tolerant of bad behavior among elementary school boys than girls and that boys are more likely than girls to receive attention, remedial help, praise, and criticism from their instructors (AAUW, 1992; Sadker & Sadker, 1985). Still another study found that although teachers pay more attention to girls who act dependent, they are more likely to respond to boys who behave in independent or aggressive ways (Serbin, 1980).

One aspect of peer-group structure among American children that helps to perpetuate traditional gender roles is the tendency to select same-sex playmates most of the time.

As these findings illustrate, schools are still another important influence in gender-role socialization. Teachers are often guided by their own gender stereotypes in their interaction with students (Rodgers, 1987; Sadker & Sadker, 1990, 1994). Thus instructors may expect boys to excel in subjects such as math and science, while assuming that girls will do better in English and literature. As a result, boys and girls may receive differential encouragement. This can have a restrictive influence on students, who may not try as hard in fields in which they receive little encouragement (AAUW, 1992; Eccles & Midgley, 1990).

School textbooks have also tended to perpetuate gender-role stereotypes. In the early 1970s, two major studies of children's textbooks found that girls were typically portrayed as dependent, unambitious, and not very successful or clever, while boys were shown to have just the opposite characteristics (Saario et al., 1973; Women on Words and Images, 1972). In the early 1980s, men played the dominant roles in about two out of every three stories in American reading texts—an improvement from four out of every five stories in the early 1970s (Britton & Lumpkin, 1984). Textbook publishers in the 1990s have improved markedly in their efforts to avoid gender stereotypes. However, like the culture they represent, textbooks are still not completely free of stereotyped gender roles. An analysis of 62 children's schoolbooks found that although girls were attributed a wider range of behaviors than in the past, females were still less likely to appear as principal characters than were males, and they were portrayed in a narrower range of occupations (Purcell & Stewart, 1990). Another study of children's books from public libraries found that while female characters were featured almost as frequently as males, they were still more likely to demonstrate passive, dependent, and nurturing behaviors (Kortenhaus & Demarest, 1993).

Television and Gender-Role Stereotypes

Another powerful agent of gender-role socialization is television. Depictions of men and women on the TV screen are often blatantly stereotypic (Larson, 1996; Media Report to Women, 1993a; Ward & Wyatt, 1994; Wood, 1994). Whereas men most often appear as active, intelligent, adventurous, and in charge, women are more likely to play passive, less competent characters who are better at domestic tasks than at thinking for themselves. In commercials and even on the television news, men appear as the authoritative sources on most topics (Bellizzi & Milner, 1991; Bretl & Cantor, 1988; Lovdal, 1989). It is safe to assume that these depictions have some impact as agents of socialization, considering that most American children spend hours in front of the TV each day. As on adult television, children's programs are also not adverse to portraying gender-role stereotypes. For example, even *Sesame Street*—public television's immensely popular and long-running children's show—is guilty of sexism in its programming. During 1992, 84% of the characters featured on the show were male compared to 76% in 1987 (Media Report to Women, 1993b). However, on a more positive note, we have recently seen the emergence of several new series that center on teenage women who are capable and self-assured, such as *Buffy the Vampire Slayer, Daria, Sabrina the Teenage Witch, The Secret World of Alex Mack,* and *Moesha.*

A recent analysis of advertisements on children's shows revealed that boys were featured more than girls and that the content of most advertisements portrayed traditional stereotypes for male/female roles (Smith, 1994). Another study found that commercials on MTV are strongly gender stereotyped and that women are generally portrayed as having value primarily via their physical appearance (Signorielli et al., 1994). Similar findings were obtained in a more recent study of children's selection of favorite television characters in which girl subjects, ages 7 to 12, valued female television personalities primarily for their attractive physical appearance rather than for their capabilities and competencies (Hoffner, 1996).

A 1995 Louis Harris poll of girls and young women, grades 3 through 12, supports what feminist groups have been saying for years—that American television fails to realistically portray females of all ages. Many of the survey respondents were resentful of how they are portrayed on television shows that too often insult and devalue young girls and women. According to one successful woman in television, the blame for the continued devaluation of women can be placed directly on network executives. Marta Kauffman, cocreator and coproducer of *Friends,* a hit NBC sitcom, recently stated "It's a very sexist industry. There aren't enough women in power at the networks. And there are certain ways that networks believe women should be perceived" (in Schulberg, 1995, p. 10).

As in the case of schoolbooks, there has been progress on this front in recent years as the television industry becomes increasingly aware of gender biases in its programming. Today, the lead roles played by women in prime-time television shows more often allow them to behave in assertive and competent ways—as in programs such as *Chicago Hope, ER, Homicide: Life on the Street, Profiler, The X-Files,* and *Ellen.* However, even popular television shows that feature strong women often have a disproportionate number of male characters in lead roles (e.g., *Chicago Hope* and *Homicide: Life on the Street*). Furthermore, the increased presence of powerful women on television shows may have more to do with product marketing than with deliberate efforts to erase long-time gender stereotypes. Women are more likely than men to purchase the products advertised in commercials (Waters & Huck, 1989).

Even the process of watching television reflects gender roles, according to recent research that found that men in heterosexual couples use and control the remote control device more than women. According to this study's author, these results "confirm that couples create and strengthen stereotypical notions of gender through the exercise of power, even in the mundane, joint, leisure activity of watching television" (Walker, 1996, p. 813).

Religion and Gender Roles

Organized religion plays an important role in the lives of many Americans. Despite differences in doctrines, a common trend runs through most religions relative to views about gender roles (Eitzen & Zinn, 1994). As one writer recently noted, any child who receives religious instruction is likely to be socialized to accept certain gender stereotypes (Basow, 1992). In Jewish, Christian, and Islamic traditions, these stereotypes commonly embrace an emphasis on male supremacy, with God presented as male through language such as "Father," "He," or "King." The biblical conceptualization of Eve as created from Adam's rib provides a clear endorsement of the gender assumption that females are meant to be secondary to males. And the Christian New Testament generally continues the tradition of male preeminence by placing greater emphasis on Jesus as the son of a male God rather than of Mary, the virgin mother (Eitzen & Zinn, 1994).

The composition of the leadership of most religious organizations in the United States provides additional evidence of male dominance and of the circumscription of female gender roles. Until 1970, no women were ordained as clergy in any American Protestant denomination. There were no female rabbis until 1972, and the Roman Catholic church still does not allow female priests.

Currently, there are movements to change the traditional patriarchal nature of organized religion in America. Female enrollment in seminaries and divinity schools increased from 10% in 1972 to almost 30% in 1989 (Renzetti & Curan, 1992). The number of ordained women in Protestant ministries has more than doubled in the last decade, and the number of female rabbis has also increased significantly (Eitzen & Zinn, 1994, Ribadeneira, 1998).

Efforts are also under way to reduce sexist language in church proceedings and religious writings. In 1983, the National Council of Churches published guidelines for a more "inclusive language" designed to eliminate exclusively male metaphors for God and to replace other terms such as "Son of God," "God the Father," "mankind," and "fellowship" with more gender-neutral terms such as "child of God," "Creator," "humanity," and "community." Some religious groups, such as Reform Judaism, are very vocal in their support for equal rights and treatment of women. We can expect these new trends toward gender-role parity eventually to reduce or minimize organized religion's reinforcement of traditional gender-role stereotypes.

In recent years there has been a dramatic increase in the number of women ordained as clergy.

We see then that family and friends, schools and textbooks, television (as well as other media such as movies, magazines, and popular music), and religion frequently help develop and reinforce traditional gender-role assumptions and behaviors in our lives. We are all affected by gender-role conditioning to some degree, and we might discuss at great length how this process discourages development of each person's full range of human potential. However, this text deals with our sexuality, so it is the impact of gender-role conditioning on this aspect of our lives that we examine in the following section.

What are some ways in which gender-role expectations and stereotypes have influenced your views of sexuality and the manner in which you relate intimately to others?

Gender-Role Expectations: Their Impact on Our Sexuality

Gender-role expectations exert a profound impact on our sexuality. Our beliefs about males and females, together with our assumptions about what constitute appropriate behaviors for each, may affect many aspects of sexual experience. Our assessment of ourselves as sexual beings, the expectations we have for intimate relationships, our perception of the quality of such experiences, and the responses of others to our sexuality may all be significantly influenced by our identification as male or female.

In the following pages, we examine some of our gender-role assumptions and their potential effects on relations between the sexes. We do not mean to imply that only heterosexual couples are limited by these assumptions. Gender-role stereotypes may influence people regardless of their sexual orientation, although homosexual couples may be affected somewhat differently by them.

Women as Undersexed, Men as Oversexed

A long-standing assumption in many Western societies is the mistaken belief that women are inherently less sexually inclined than men. Such gender stereotypes may result in women being subjected to years of negative socialization during which they are taught to suppress or deny their natural sexual feelings. Legions of women have been told by parents, peers, and books that sex is something a woman engages in to please a man, preferably her husband. A related gender assumption that is pervasive in our society is the view that "normal women" do not enjoy sex as much as men.

Although these stereotypes are beginning to fade as people strive to throw off some of the behavior constraints of generations of socialization, many women are still influenced by such views. How can a woman express interest in being sexual or actively seek her own pleasure if she believes that women are not supposed to have sexual needs? Some women, believing that it is not appropriate to be easily aroused sexually, may direct their energies to blocking or hiding these normal responses. Some people who adhere to these stereotypes believe that any woman who openly expresses sexual interest or responds sexually is "easy," "sleazy," or a "slut." However, men who manifest similar behavior may be characterized as "studs," "Casanovas," or "playboys," terms that are often meant to be ego enhancing rather than demeaning.

Males may be harmed by being stereotyped as supersexual. A man who is not instantly aroused by a person he perceives as attractive and/or available may feel somehow inadequate. After all, are not all men supposed to be instantly eager when confronted with a sexual opportunity? We believe that such an assumption is demeaning and reduces men to insensitive machines that respond instantly when the correct button is pushed. Male students in our classes frequently express their frustration and ambivalence over this issue. The following account is typical of these observations:

> When I take a woman out for the first time, I am often confused over how the sex issue should be handled. I feel pressured to make a move, even when I am not all that inclined to hop into the sack. Isn't this what women expect? If I don't even try, they may think there is something wrong with me. I almost feel like I would have to explain myself if I acted uninterested in having sex. Usually it's just easier to make the move and let them decide what they want to do with it. (Authors' files)

Clearly, this man believes he is expected to pursue sex, even when he doesn't want to, as part of his masculine role. This stereotypical view of men as the initiators of sex in developing relationships can be distressing for both sexes, as we see in the next section.

Men as Initiators, Women as Recipients

In our society, men traditionally initiate intimate relationships, from the opening invitation for an evening out to the first overture toward sexual activity. As the following comments reveal, this can make men feel burdened and pressured:

> Women should experience how anxiety-provoking it can be. I get tired of always being the one to make the suggestion, since there's always the potential of being turned down. (Authors' files)

> I feel that every woman I date expects me to put the move on her. (Authors' files)

> During lovemaking, my wife usually expects me to make all the initial moves. Sometimes I wish I could just lie back and be taken over sexually instead of being the one who must orchestrate the whole thing. (Authors' files)

This last comment reflects a concern voiced by many of our male students and clients. Even in established relationships, men are frequently expected to initiate each sexual encounter. This may result in sex becoming more of a duty than a pleasure. Yet men who grow up being socialized to be active, assertive, and even aggressive are usually accustomed to being in control in most situations. It may be very difficult to relinquish this role in the bedroom. Thus, even though a man may fantasize about being taken over sexually, actually having such an experience may be stressful.

A woman who feels compelled to accept a passive female role may have a very difficult time initiating sex. It could be even harder for her to assume an active role during sexual activity. Many women are frustrated, regretful, and understandably angry that such cultural expectations are so deeply ingrained within our society. The following comments, expressed by women talking together, reflect some of these thoughts:

> It has been my experience that men may say they want women to be more assertive, but when we take the initiative they frequently act shocked, put off, or threatened. (Authors' files)

> I like to ask men out, and have often done so. But it's frustrating when many of the men I ask out automatically assume that I want to jump in bed with them just because I take the initiative to make a date. (Authors' files)

> It is hard for me to let my man know what I like during lovemaking. After all, he is supposed to know, isn't he? If I tell him, it's like I am usurping his role as the all-knowing one. (Authors' files)

The last comment relates to another common gender myth about sexual functioning—the notion that men are more knowledgeable and better able than women to direct a sexual encounter.

Men as "Sexperts"

Considering that gender-role socialization conditions males to be competent leaders and females to be passive followers, is it any wonder that men are expected to act as experts in sexual matters? Men are not the only ones who see themselves as "sexperts"; women, in fact, may coerce men into playing the expert role by subscribing to this mistaken notion. Some men enjoy being cast as "teacher" or "mentor." However, others may feel quite burdened by the need to play the expert and thus, by implication, to be responsible for the outcome of sexual sharing. As one man states,

> Sometimes sex is more like work than fun. I have to make all the decisions—when and where we are going to have sex and what we are going to do together. It's my responsibility to make sure it works out good for both of us. This can put a lot of pressure on me and it gets real tiring always having to run the show. It would be nice to have someone else call the shots for a change. Only it has been my experience that women are real reluctant to take the lead. (Authors' files)

Fortunately, some of these destructive patterns are showing signs of eroding. Many of our male students speak with a sense of delight and relief about their sexual encounters with women who initiate sex, play an active role during lovemaking, and assume responsibility for their own pleasure. In recent years, women too have seemed more inclined to view men as sexual equals rather than all-knowing experts.

Women as Controllers, Men as Movers

Many women grow up believing that men always have sex on their minds. For such a woman, it may be a logical next step to become the controller of what takes place during sexual interaction. By this we do not mean actively initiating certain activities, which she sees as the prerogative of men, the movers. Rather, a woman may see her role as controlling her male partner's rampant lust by making certain he does not coerce her into unacceptable activities. Thus, instead of enjoying how good it feels to have her breasts caressed, she may concentrate her attention on how to keep his hand off her genitals. This concern with control may be particularly pronounced during the adolescent dating years. It is not surprising that a woman who spends a great deal of time and energy regulating sexual intimacy to preserve her "honor" (something else she learns from gender-role conditioning) may have difficulty experiencing sexual feelings when she finally allows herself to relinquish her controlling role.

Conversely, men are often conditioned to see women as sexual challenges and to go as far as they can during sexual encounters. They too may have difficulty appreciating the good feelings of being close to and touching someone when all they are thinking about is what they will do next. Men who routinely experience this pattern may have a hard time relinquishing the mover role and being receptive rather than active during sexual interaction. They may be confused or even threatened by a woman who switches roles from controller to active initiator.

Men as Unemotional and Strong, Women as Nurturing and Supportive

Perhaps one of the most undesirable of all gender-role stereotypes is the notion that being emotionally expressive, tender, and nurturing is appropriate only for women. We have already seen that men are often socialized to be unemotional (Mosher & Tomkins, 1988). A man who is trying to appear strong may find it difficult to express vulnerability, deep feelings, and doubts. This conditioning can make it exceedingly difficult for a man to develop emotionally satisfying intimate relationships.

For example, a man who accepts the assumption of nonemotionality may approach sex as a purely physical act during which expressions of feelings have no place. This results in a limited kind of experience that can leave both parties feeling dissatisfied. Women often have a negative reaction when they encounter this characteristic in men because women tend to place great importance on openness and willingness to express feelings in a relationship. However, we need to remember that many men must struggle against a lifetime of "macho" conditioning when they try to express long-suppressed emotions. Women, on the other hand, may grow tired of their role as nurturers, particularly when their efforts are greeted with little or no reciprocity.

We have discussed how strict adherence to traditional gender roles may limit and restrict the ways we express our sexuality. These cultural legacies may often be expressed more subtly today than in the past, but rigid gender-role expectations linger on, inhibiting our growth as multidimensional people and our capacity to be fully ourselves with others. Although many people are breaking away from stereotyped gender roles and learning to accept and express themselves more fully, we cannot underestimate the extent of gender-role learning that still occurs in our society.

There is growing evidence, however, that many people are now striving to integrate both masculine and feminine behaviors into their lifestyles. This trend, often referred to as androgyny, is the focus of the final section in this chapter.

Transcending Gender Roles: Androgyny

Androgyny
A blending of typical male and female behaviors in one individual.

The word **androgyny** (an-DRAW-jin-ē), meaning "having characteristics of both sexes," is derived from the Greek roots *andr,* meaning man, and *gynē,* meaning woman. The term is used to describe flexibility in gender role. Androgynous individuals are those who have integrated aspects of masculinity and femininity into their personalities and behavior. Androgyny offers the option of expressing whatever behavior seems appropriate in a given situation instead of limiting responses to those considered gender appropriate. Thus, androgynous men and women might be assertive on the job but nurturing with friends, family members, and lovers. Many men and women possess characteristics that are consistent with traditional gender assumptions but also have interests and behavioral tendencies typically ascribed to the other sex. Actually, people may range from being very masculine or feminine to being *both* masculine and feminine—that is, androgynous.

A social psychologist, Sandra Bem (1974), developed a paper-and-pencil inventory for measuring the degree to which individuals are identified with masculine or feminine behaviors or a combination thereof. Other similar devices have been developed since Bem's pioneering work (Spence & Helmreich, 1978). Armed with these devices for measuring androgyny, a number of researchers have investigated how androgynous individuals compare with strongly gender-typed people.

A number of studies indicate that androgynous people are more flexible in their behaviors, less limited by rigid gender-role assumptions, have higher levels of self-esteem, make better decisions in group settings, and exhibit more social competence and motivation to achieve than do people who are strongly gender-typed or those who score low in both areas (Katz & Ksansnak, 1994; Kirchmeyer, 1996; Rose & Montemayor, 1994; Vonk & Ashmore, 1993). Research also demonstrates that masculine and androgynous people of both sexes are more independent and less likely to have their opinions swayed than are individuals who are strongly identified with the feminine role (Bem, 1975). In fact, both androgyny and high masculinity appear to be adaptive for both sexes at all ages (Sinnott, 1986). However, feminine and androgynous people of both sexes appear to be significantly more nurturing than are those who adhere to the masculine role (Bem et al., 1976; Coleman & Ganong, 1985).

We need to be cautious about concluding that androgyny is an ideal state, free of potential problems (Sampson, 1985). One study found that masculine-typed males demonstrated better overall emotional adjustment than did androgynous males (Jones et al., 1978). Another study, of college professors in their early careers, found that androgynous individuals exhibited greater personal satisfaction but more job-related stress than those who were strongly gender typed (Rotheram & Weiner, 1983). In a large sample of college students, masculine personality characteristics were also more closely associated with being versatile and adaptable than was the trait of androgyny (Lee & Scheurer, 1983). Other studies have also indicated that it may be masculinity, and not femininity or androgyny, that is more closely associated with successful adjustment and positive self-esteem (Basoff & Glass, 1983; Taylor & Hall, 1982; Unger & Crawford, 1992). This may be "because masculine attributes are viewed more positively and consequently lead to greater social rewards" (Burn et al., 1996, p. 420). Thus, although androgyny is often associated with emotional, social, and behavioral competence, more information is necessary for a complete picture of the impact of androgyny on personal adjustment and satisfaction.

What are the implications of androgyny for sexual behavior?

There is evidence that androgynous individuals, both male and female, have more positive attitudes toward sexuality and are more aware of and expressive of feelings of love than are those who are traditionally gender-typed (Ganong & Coleman, 1987; Walfish & Myerson, 1980). Androgynous people also appear to be more tolerant and less likely to judge or criticize the sexual behaviors of others (Garcia, 1982). Studies have found that androgynous women are more orgasmic and experience more sexual satisfaction than do feminine-typed women (Kimlicka et al., 1983; Radlove, 1983). However, two separate investigations revealed that masculine males were significantly more comfortable with sex than were androgynous females, indicating that biological sex may still exert a stronger effect than gender typing (Allgeier, 1981; Walfish & Myerson, 1980).

Our own guess is that androgynous people tend to be flexible and comfortable in their sexuality. We would expect such people, whether men or women, to have great capacity to enjoy both the emotional and the physical aspects of sexual intimacy. Androgynous lovers are probably comfortable both initiating and responding to invitations for sexual sharing, and they are probably not significantly limited by preconceived notions of who must do what—and how—during their lovemaking. These observations are supported by research indicating that androgynous couples experience more emotional and sexual satisfaction and personal commitment in their relationships than do gender-typed couples (Rosenzweig & Daily, 1989; Stephen & Harrison, 1985).

Research on androgyny continues, and we certainly have good reasons to be cautious about an unequivocally enthusiastic endorsement of this behavioral style. Nevertheless, most of the evidence collected thus far suggests that people who are able to transcend traditional gender roles may be able to function more comfortably and effectively in a wider range of situations. Androgynous individuals can select from a broad repertoire of feminine and masculine behaviors. They may choose to be independent, assertive, nurturing, or tender, based not on gender-role norms but rather on what provides them and others optimum personal satisfaction in a given situation.

Summary

MALE AND FEMALE, MASCULINE AND FEMININE

The processes whereby our maleness and femaleness are determined and the manner in which they influence our behavior, sexual and otherwise, are highly complex.

Sex refers to our biological maleness or femaleness as reflected in various physical attributes (chromosomes, reproductive organs, genitals, and so forth).

Gender encompasses the special psychosocial meanings added to biological maleness or femaleness or, in other words, our masculinity or femininity. Our ideas of masculinity and femininity involve gender assumptions about behavior based on a person's sex.

Gender identity refers to each individual's subjective sense of being male or female.

Gender role refers to a collection of attitudes and behaviors considered normal and appropriate in a specific culture for people of a particular sex.

Gender roles establish sex-related behavioral expectations, which are culturally defined and therefore vary from society to society and era to era.

GENDER-IDENTITY FORMATION

Research efforts to isolate the many biological factors that influence a person's gender identity have resulted in the identification of six biological categories, or levels: chromosomal sex, gonadal sex, hormonal sex, sex of the internal reproductive structures, sex of the external genitals, and sex differentiation of the brain.

Under normal conditions, these biological variables interact harmoniously to determine our biological sex. However, errors may occur at any of the six levels. The resulting abnormalities in the development of a person's biological sex may seriously complicate acquisition of a gender identity.

The social-learning interpretation of gender-identity formation suggests that our identification with either masculine or feminine roles results primarily from the social and cultural models and influences to which we are exposed.

Most contemporary theorists embrace an interactional model in which gender identity is seen as a result of a complex interplay of biological and social-learning factors.

Transsexualism is a special case of gender-identity complexity in which a person's gender identity is different from his or her biological sex. The scientific community has not reached a consensus about the causes and best treatment of this condition. However, some transsexuals have changed their bodies to match their identities by means of hormone treatments and surgery.

GENDER ROLES

Widely accepted gender-role assumptions may begin to function as stereotypes, which are notions about what people are like based not on their individuality but on their inclusion in a general category such as age or sex.

There are many common gender-based stereotypes in our society that may encourage us to prejudge others and restrict our opportunities.

Socialization is the process whereby society conveys its behavioral expectations to us. Parents, peers, schools, textbooks, television, and religion all act as agents in the socialization of gender roles.

Gender-role expectations exert a profound impact on our sexuality. Our assessment of ourselves as sexual beings, the expectations we have for intimate relationships, our perception of the quality of such experiences, and the responses of others to our sexuality may all be significantly influenced by our own perceptions of our gender roles.

Androgynous individuals are people who have moved beyond traditional gender roles by integrating aspects associated with both masculinity and femininity into their lifestyles.

Thought Provokers

1. We have seen that gender-identity formation is influenced by both biological and social-learning factors. Do you think the evidence more strongly supports one or the other as the major contributor to gender-identity formation? Why or why not?
2. In exploring the origins of your own gender identity, do you believe that you were socialized to be strongly gender-typed, or were you raised in a manner supporting androgynous behavior? Do you believe these socialization experiences have had any impact on how you feel about masculinity and femininity and on your sexual attitudes and behaviors?
3. Which gender-role assumptions have had the least impact on your sexuality? The greatest impact? Have you ever had a relationship in which any of these assumptions became a significant issue?

Suggested Readings

Cook, Ellen (1985). *Psychological Androgyny*. New York: Pergamon Press. An excellent review of the pertinent androgyny research literature. Also provides relevant practical information about androgynous lifestyles.

Hyde, Janet (1996). *Half the Human Experience: The Psychology of Women* (4th ed.). Boston: Houghton Mifflin. An excellent summary of theories and research dealing with the psychology of women and gender roles.

Levant, Ronald; and Pollack, William (Eds.) (1995). *A New Psychology of Men*. New York: Basic Books. This excellent collection of articles provides an informative overview of an emerging field. Topics covered include men's changing roles, male development and psychological functioning, and men's health and gender-role stress.

Lips, Hillary (1997). *Sex and Gender* (3rd ed.). Mountain View, CA: Mayfield. This informative text provides a thorough review of the professional literature pertaining to sex differences in social behavior and experiences. The author presents information suggesting that gender differences are relatively small and, when present, stem largely from the socialization of gender-role expectations.

Mead, Margaret (1963). *Sex and Temperament in Three Primitive Societies*. New York: Morrow. An eminent anthropologist's analysis of three societies in which male and female gender roles differ from those of North American society.

Money, John (1994). *Sex Errors of the Body and Related Syndromes: A Guide to Counseling Children, Adolescents, and Their Families* (2nd ed.). Baltimore: Brooks. A thorough discussion of a broad range of conditions that result from developmental errors. Money discusses developmental implications of these conditions and offers insights and advice pertaining to appropriate medical and psychological intervention.

Money, John; and Ehrhardt, Anke (1972). *Man and Woman, Boy and Girl*. Baltimore: Johns Hopkins University Press. An in-depth analysis of the psychosocial and biological factors that influence the development of gender identity. Essential reading for anyone desiring a more thorough understanding of the processes of gender identity and gender role.

Morris, Jan (1974). *Conundrum*. New York: New American Library. A widely acclaimed personal account of the transsexual experience.

Web Resources

WWW.

Androgyny and Gender Dialectics
www.math.uio.no/~thomas/gnd/androgyny.html
A Web site devoted to challenging conventional notions of gender, with numerous links to controversial research studies, theories on androgyny, and opinions.

Ingersoll Gender Center
www.ingersollcenter.org/
The Ingersoll Center is a nonprofit agency for the transsexual, transvestite, and transgender community. Among the highlights of its Web site are a catalog of publications, opinion pieces, and a host of links to related organizations

4

Female Sexual Anatomy and Physiology

I had three children and was 45 years old before I ever really looked at my genitals. I was amazed at the delicate shapes and subtle colors. I'm sorry it took me so long to do this because I now feel more sure of myself sexually after becoming more acquainted with me. (Authors' files)

Many women are as unacquainted with their genitals as this woman was. However, gaining knowledge and understanding of her body can be an important aspect of a woman's sexual well-being. This chapter presents a detailed description of all female genital structures, external and internal. It is intended to be easy to use for reference, and we encourage women readers to do a self-exam as part of reading it. We begin with a discussion of the genital self-exam and the external structures, then discuss the underlying structures and the internal organs. The chapter continues with information about the breasts and menstruation, and closes with women's health information.

Genital Self-Exam

We are born with curiosity about our bodies. In fact, physical self-awareness and exploration are important steps in a child's development. Unfortunately, many of us receive negative conditioning about the sexual parts of our bodies from earliest childhood. We learn to think of our genitals as "privates," "down there," not to be looked at, touched, or enjoyed. It is common for people to react with discomfort to the suggestion of a genital self-exam.

This self-exploration exercise can help you become more aware of your genitals. Like many other exercises and information throughout this text that are aimed to help you improve your own self-knowledge or sexual health, this exercise is highlighted with a "To Your Sexual Health" icon. Some readers may choose to read about this exercise but not do it. Others may wish to try some or all of the steps. If you choose to do the exploration, you may experience a variety of feelings. Some people feel selfish for spending time on themselves. You may find it difficult to remain focused on the experience instead of thinking about daily concerns. The exercise may be enjoyable for some people and not for others. Primarily, it provides an opportunity to learn about yourself—your body and your feelings.

To begin the examination, use a hand mirror, perhaps in combination with a full-length mirror, to look at your genitals from different angles and postures—standing, sitting, lying down (see Figure 4.1). As you are looking, try to become aware of whatever feelings you have about your genital anatomy. You may find it helpful to draw a picture of your genitals and label the parts (identified in Figure 4.2). All women have the same parts, but the shades of color, shapes, and textures vary from woman to woman.

Women have different kinds of reactions to looking at their genitals:

I don't find it to be an attractive part of my body. I wouldn't go as far as to call it ugly. I think it would be easier to accept if it was something you weren't taught to hide and think was dirty, but I've never been able to understand why men find the vulva so intriguing. (Authors' files)

I think it looks very sensuous; the tissues look soft and tender. I was told by a previous partner that my vulva was very beautiful. His comment made me feel good about my body. (Authors' files)

Besides examining yourself visually, use your fingers to explore the various surfaces of your genitals. Focus on the sensations produced by the different kinds of touching. Note which areas are most sensitive and how the nature of stimulation may vary from place to place. The primary purpose of doing this exercise is to explore, not to become

Figure 4.1

Routine self-examination is an aspect of preventive health care.

sexually aroused. However, if you do become sexually excited during this self-exploration, you may be able to notice changes in the sensitivity of different skin areas that occur with arousal.

The genital self-exam serves another purpose beside helping us feel more comfortable with our anatomy and sexuality. Periodic self-examinations, particularly of the genitals, can augment routine medical care. For self-examinations to be most effective, do them regularly at least once a month: People who know what is normal for their own bodies can often detect small changes and seek medical attention promptly. Problems usually require less extensive treatment when they are detected early. If you discover any changes, consult a health practitioner immediately. **Gynecology** (gī-na-KOL-ō-jē) is the medical specialty for female sexual and reproductive anatomy.

Gynecology
The medical practice specializing in women's health and in diseases of the female reproductive and sexual organs.

The Vulva

The **vulva** encompasses all female external genital structures—the hair, the folds of skin, and the urinary and vaginal openings. *Vulva* is the term we use most frequently in this text to refer to the external genitals of the female. For reference, see Figure 4.2.

Vulva
The external genitals of the female, including the mons veneris, labia majora, labia minora, clitoris, and urinary and vaginal openings.

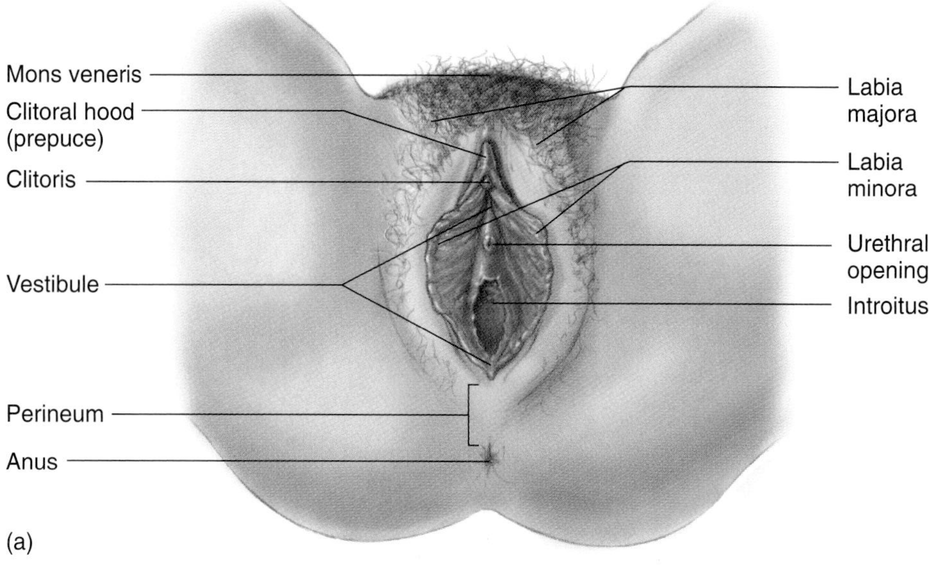

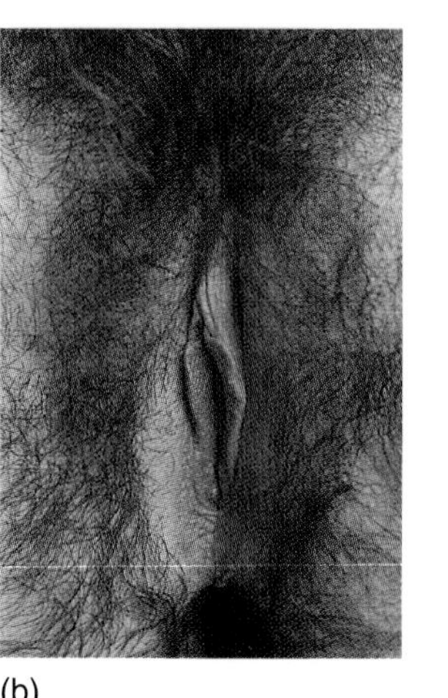

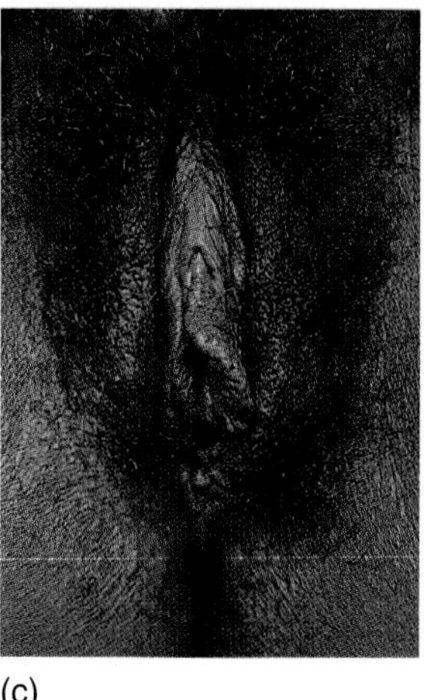

Figure 4.2

The structures and variations of the vulva: (a) external structures and (b)–(d) different colors and shapes. There are many common variations of external female genitals.

The appearance of the vulva, which varies from person to person (Gardner, 1992), has been likened to that of certain flowers, seashells, and other forms found in nature. Transformed vulvalike shapes have been used in artwork, including *The Dinner Party* by Judy Chicago. This work consists of 39 ceramic plates symbolizing significant women in history.

The Mons Veneris

Mons veneris
A triangular mound over the pubic bone above the vulva.

Translated from Latin, **mons veneris** means "the mound of Venus." Venus was the Roman goddess of love and beauty. The mons veneris, or *mons,* is the area covering the pubic bone. It consists of pads of fatty tissue between the bone and the skin. Touch and pressure on the mons can be sexually pleasurable, due to the presence of numerous nerve endings.

At puberty the mons becomes covered with hair that varies in color, texture, and thickness from woman to woman. Sometimes women are concerned about these differences:

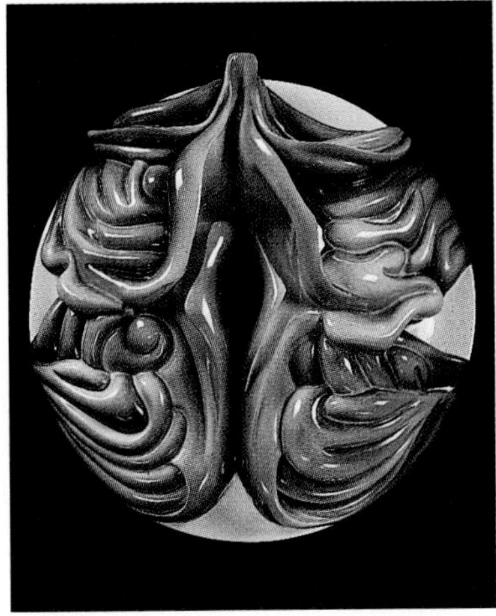

Two examples of the plates in Judy Chicago's *The Dinner Party,* an exhibit symbolizing women in history. On the left is the Georgia O'Keeffe plate and on the right, the Emily Dickinson plate.

I always felt uncomfortable in college physical education classes because I had very thick, dark pubic hair, more so than most other women. One day my best friend and I were talking and she mentioned that she felt self-conscious in the showers after P.E. class because her pubic hair was light-colored and sparse. I told her my concerns. We laughed and both decided to stop worrying about it. (Authors' files)

During sexual arousal the scent that accompanies vaginal secretions is held by the pubic hair and can add to sensory erotic pleasure.

The Labia Majora

The **labia majora** (LĀ-bē-a ma-JŌ-ra), or outer lips, extend downward from the mons on each side of the vulva. They begin next to the thigh and extend inward, surrounding the labia minora and the urethral and vaginal openings. Next to the thigh, the outer lips are covered with pubic hair; their inner parts, next to the labia minora, are hairless. The skin of the labia majora is usually darker than the skin of the thighs. The nerve endings and underlying fatty tissue are similar to those in the mons.

The Labia Minora

The **labia minora** (LĀ-bē-a min-ŌR-a), or inner lips, are located within the outer lips and often protrude between them. The inner lips are hairless folds of skin that join at the **prepuce** (PRĒ-pyoos), or clitoral hood, and extend downward past the urinary and vaginal openings. They contain sweat and oil glands, extensive blood vessels, and nerve endings. They also vary considerably in size, shape, length, and color from woman to woman, as Figure 4.2 shows. During pregnancy, the inner lips become darker in color.

In the Hottentot culture of Africa, pendulous labia are considered a sign of beauty, and women start pulling on them early in childhood in an effort to increase their size.

The Clitoris

The **clitoris** (KLIT-o-ris) comprises the external **shaft** and **glans** and the internal **crura** (KROO-ra), or roots, which project inward from each side of the clitoral shaft. The shaft and glans are located just below the mons area, where the inner lips converge. They are covered by the clitoral hood, or prepuce. Genital secretions, skin cells, and bacteria combine to form **smegma,** which may accumulate under the hood and occasionally form

Labia majora
The outer lips of the vulva.

Labia minora
The inner lips of the vulva, one on each side of the vaginal opening.

Prepuce
The foreskin or fold of skin over the clitoris.

Clitoris
A highly sensitive structure of the female external genitals the only function of which is sexual pleasure.

Shaft
The length of the clitoris between the glans and the body.

Glans
The head of the clitoris; richly endowed with nerve endings.

Crura
The innermost tips of the cavernous bodies that connect to the pubic bones.

Smegma
A cheesy substance of glandular secretions and skin cells that sometimes accumulates under the hood of the clitoris.

lumps and cause pain during sexual arousal or activity. Smegma can be prevented from collecting in this area by drawing back the hood when washing the vulva. If the smegma is already formed, a health care practitioner can remove it.

If you look at Figure 4.3, which shows the clitoris with the hood removed, you can see that the glans is supported by the shaft. The shaft itself cannot be seen, but it can be felt and its shape seen through the hood. It contains two small spongy structures called the **cavernous bodies,** which engorge with blood during sexual arousal. These become the crura (internal leglike stalks) as they connect to the pubic bones in the pelvic cavity. The glans is often not visible under the clitoral hood, but it can be seen if a woman gently parts the labia minora and retracts the hood. The glans looks smooth, rounded, and slightly translucent.

Cavernous bodies
The structures in the shaft of the clitoris that engorge with blood during sexual arousal.

How important is the clitoris in sexual arousal? Take a few moments to consider what you already know about the role of the clitoris in sexual arousal. Think about what you have read, heard, and experienced personally. See how your ideas match the information that follows.

Initially, it may be easier for a woman to locate her clitoris by touch rather than sight because of its sensitive nerve endings and small size. The external part of the clitoris, although tiny, has about the same number of nerve endings as the head of the penis. The clitoral glans in particular is highly sensitive, and women usually stimulate this area with the hood covering it to avoid direct stimulation, which may be too intense. Research into female masturbation patterns has produced findings in keeping with the physiological data about the location and concentrations of nerve endings. Clitoral stimulation, not vaginal insertion, is the most common way women achieve arousal and orgasm when masturbating.

Although other sexual organs have additional functions in reproduction or waste elimination, the only purpose of the clitoris is sexual arousal. In part for this reason, the clitoris is often removed during the controversial practice of female genital mutilation that occurs in some parts of the world. (See the boxed discussion, "Female Genital Mutilation: Torture or Tradition?")

A good deal of controversy has surrounded the role of the clitoris in sexual arousal and orgasm. Despite long-existing scientific knowledge about the highly concentrated nerve endings in the clitoris, the erroneous belief has persisted that vaginal rather than clitoral stimulation is—or should be—exclusively responsible for female sexual arousal and orgasm. However, there are relatively few nerve endings in the vagina as compared with the clitoris, and the clitoris is more sensitive to touch than the vagina. Some nerve endings respond to light touch in the outer third of the vagina, but almost none is present in the inner two-thirds. (This is why women do not feel tampons or diaphragms when they are correctly in place.) Nevertheless, many women experience erotic feelings in the vagina and find the internal pressure and stretching sensations during manual stimulation or intercourse highly pleasurable. Some experience more intense arousal from

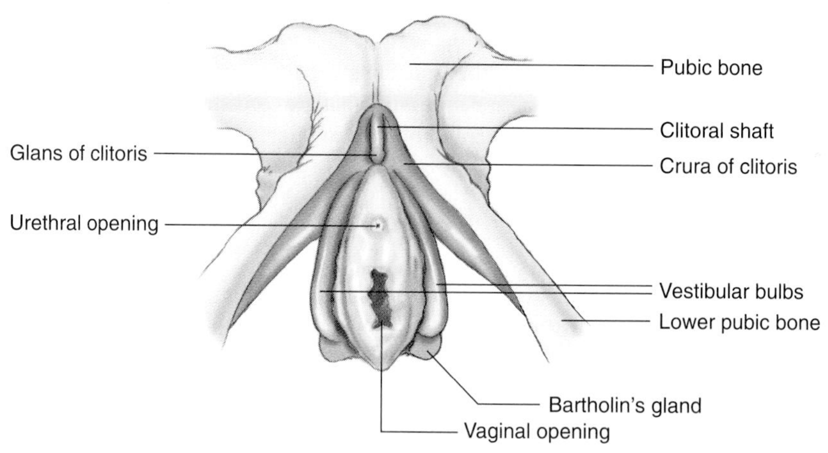

Figure 4.3
The underlying structures of the vulva.

vaginal than from clitoral stimulation. As more and more scientific research is done, a wider range of individual variation becomes apparent. The size, shape, and position of the clitoris vary from woman to woman. These normal differences have no known relation to sexual arousal and functioning.

The Vestibule

The **vestibule** (VES-ti-byool) is the area of the vulva inside the labia minora. It is rich in blood vessels and nerve endings, and its tissues are sensitive to touch. (In architectural terminology, the word *vestibule* refers to the entryway of a house.) Both the urinary and the vaginal openings are located within the vestibule.

Vestibule
The area of the vulva inside the labia minora.

The Urethral Opening

Urine collected in the bladder passes out of a woman's body through the urethral opening. The **urethra** (yoo-RĒ-thra) is the short tube connecting the bladder to the urinary opening, located between the clitoris and the vaginal opening.

Urethra
The tube through which urine passes from the bladder to outside the body.

The Introitus and the Hymen

The opening of the vagina, called the **introitus** (in-TRŌ-i-tus), is located between the urinary opening and the anus. Partially covering the introitus is a fold of tissue called the

Introitus
The opening to the vagina.

Sexuality and Diversity
Female Genital Mutilation: Torture or Tradition?

Some form of female genital mutilation has been practiced at some time in almost all parts of the world, including the United States from 1890 through the late 1930s to "cure" masturbation (Gillespie, 1977). It still occurs today in the United States when girls are born with a larger than normal clitoris—a topic of increasing controversy. It also occurs in over 30 countries in Africa, the Middle East, and Asia (Odoi et al., 1996). Females, from infants to adults, in these parts of the world undergo several types of genital mutilation. The village midwife performs the procedures, which are usually arranged by the girl's mother (McConville, 1998). The simplest procedure, *circumcision,* consists of cutting off the clitoral hood. Another common practice is the removal of the clitoris itself, called *clitoridectomy.* In the most extreme practice, *genital infibulation,* the clitoris is entirely removed and the labia cut off (Stewart, 1997). Then both sides of the vulva are scraped raw and stitched up (sometimes with thorns) while the girl is held down. Razor blades or broken glass are used to cut the tissue, and the procedure is done without anesthetics, disinfectants, or sterile instruments (Abusharaf, 1998). The tissue grows together, leaving only a small opening for urine and menstrual flow to pass through (Woolard & Edwards, 1997).

The main objective of genital mutilation is to ensure virginity before marriage (Omer-Hashi, 1997). Young girls are considered unmarriageable if they do not have the prescribed excision. Because marriage is usually the only role for a woman in these cultures, her future and her family's pride depend on upholding this tradition (Ebong, 1997). In addition, an Egyptian religious leader stated, "Girls who are not circumcised when young have a sharp temperament and bad habits."

Serious gynecological and obstetrical complications often arise from genital infibulation. Bleeding and pain can lead to shock and death, prolonged bleeding can lead to anemia, and infection can cause delayed healing, tetanus, and gangrene. Fetal death sometimes occurs because of difficult birth due to extensive vaginal scarring (Ortiz, 1998).

It is estimated that 80 million women and girls now living have undergone one of these mutilating "surgeries" (Bishop, 1997). A study of married Egyptian women found that 97% of them had been genitally mutilated (El Hadi, 1997). African and Arab physicians and health workers report

(continued on next page)

Hymen
Tissue that partially covers the vaginal opening.

hymen (HĪ-men), which is typically present at birth and usually remains intact until initial coitus. Occasionally, this tissue may be too thick to break easily during intercourse; it may then require a minor incision by a medical practitioner. In rare cases, an *imperforate hymen* completely covers the vaginal opening and causes menstrual flow to collect inside the vagina. When this condition is discovered, a medical practitioner can open the hymen with an incision. Usually, however, the vaginal opening is partially open and flexible enough to insert tampons before the hymen has been broken (Pokorny, 1997).

Although it is rare, it is possible for a woman to become pregnant even if her hymen is still intact and she has not experienced penile penetration. If semen is placed on the labia minora, the sperm can swim from outside to inside the vagina and fertilize an ovum. Unless pregnancy is desired, sexual play rubbing the penis and vulva together should be avoided unless contraception is used.

Although the hymen may serve to protect the vaginal tissues early in life, it has no other known function. Nevertheless, many societies, including our own, have placed great significance on its presence or absence. Euphemisms such as "cherry" or "maidenhead" described the hymen. In our society and many others, people have long believed that a woman's virginity can be proved by the pain and bleeding that may occur with initial coitus, or "deflowering." At different times in various cultures, bloodstained wedding night bedsheets were seen as proof that the groom had wed "intact goods" and that the marriage had been consummated. Although pain or bleeding sometimes occurs, the hymen can be partial, flexible, or thin enough for there to be no discomfort or bleeding; it may even remain intact after intercourse. One study found that 25% of women reported no pain with first intercourse, 40% reported moderate pain, and 33% severe pain. Women who experienced pain during first intercourse were younger than women who did not, had more conservative sexual values, more often had negative feelings about their partner and about intercourse with him, and more often had expected no pain (Weis, 1983).

Sexuality and Diversity

widespread sexual problems among women who have had clitoridectomies and infibulations. One physician reported that 80% of infibulated women that he had examined over the years said they had never experienced any sexual pleasure (McClearly, 1994).

In recent years the outcry over female genital mutilation pushed the United Nations to suspend its policy of nonintervention in the cultural practices of individual nations. In 1980, the World Health Organization (WHO) and the United Nations Children's Fund (UNICEF) jointly adopted a plan to encourage leaders of nations where such practices occur to use their influence to bring them to an end. In 1990, the Organization of African Unity condemned traditional practices that are harmful to children. The United Nations Fourth World Conference on Women in 1995 also condemned female genital mutilation. In 1996 the Minister of Health in Egypt prohibited physicians from performing female genital mutilation in private or public health facilities, and Egypt's highest court upheld the ban in 1997 (Ghalwich, 1997). The most recent ruling is a defeat for Islamic fundamentalists who believe that female genital mutilation protects women from the consequences of excessive sexual desire (Lancaster, 1997). Unfortunately, the strength of cultural tradition in many societies remains difficult to overcome (Thomas, 1998).

Complex legal issues are arising from this conflict (Shapiro, 1998). For example, a Nigerian-born woman living in the United States with her six- and four-year-old daughters, both U.S. citizens, was granted a suspension of deportation on the grounds that her family back in Nigeria would force her daughters to be circumcised (Baker, 1994). Canada was the first nation to recognize female genital mutilation as a basis for granting refugee status. In 1996 the highest U.S. immigration court granted asylum to a West African teenager for protection against female genital mutilation (Supervile, 1996). What policies do you think the United States should have about female genital excisions?

"Stop excision"—the emblem of the National Committee for Struggle Against the Practice of Excision, Burkina Faso

If a woman manually stretches her hymen before initial intercourse, she may be able to minimize the discomfort that sometimes occurs. To do this, first insert a lubricated finger (using saliva or a water-soluble sterile lubricant) into the vaginal opening and press downward toward the anus until you feel some stretching. After a few seconds, release the pressure and relax. Repeat this step several times. Next, insert two fingers into the vagina and stretch the sides of the vagina by *opening* the fingers. Repeat the downward stretching with two fingers as well.

The Perineum

The **perineum** (per´-a-NĒ-am) is the area of smooth skin between the vaginal opening and the anus (the sphincter through which bowel movements pass). The perineal tissue is endowed with nerve endings and is sensitive to touch.

Perineum
The area between the vagina and anus of the female and the scrotum and anus of the male.

During childbirth, an incision called an *episiotomy* is sometimes made in the perineum to prevent the ragged tearing of tissues that may happen as the newborn passes through the birth canal. Many medical practitioners believe this incision is essential, but other health care specialists disagree. We will consider this issue in more detail in Chapter 12.

Underlying Structures

If the hair, skin, and fatty pads were removed from the vulva, several underlying structures could be seen (see Figure 4.3). The shaft of the clitoris would be visible, no longer concealed by the hood, as would be the crura. These bodies are part of the vast network of bulbs and vessels that engorge with blood during sexual arousal. The **vestibular** (ves-TIB-yoo-ler) **bulbs** alongside the vagina also fill with blood during sexual excitement, causing the vagina to increase in length and the vulvar area to become swollen. These bulbs are similar in structure and function to the spongy tissue in the penis that engorges during arousal and causes erection.

Vestibular bulbs
Two bulbs, one on each side of the vaginal opening, that engorge with blood during sexual arousal.

Bartholin's glands on each side of the vaginal opening were once believed to be the source of vaginal lubrication during sexual arousal; however, they typically produce only a drop or two of fluid just prior to orgasm. The glands are usually not noticeable, but sometimes the duct from a Bartholin's gland becomes clogged, and the fluid that is normally secreted remains inside and causes enlargement. If this occurs and the swelling does not subside within a few days, it is best to see a health care practitioner.

Bartholin's glands
Two small glands slightly inside the vaginal opening that secrete a few drops of fluid during sexual arousal.

Besides the glands and network of vessels, a complex musculature underlies the genital area (see Figure 4.4). The *pelvic floor muscles* have a multidirectional design that allows the vaginal opening to expand greatly during childbirth and to contract afterward.

Internal Structures

Internal female sexual anatomy consists of the vagina, cervix, uterus, and ovaries. These are discussed in the following sections. Refer to Figure 4.5 for cross-section and front views of the female pelvis.

The Vagina

The **vagina** is a canal that opens between the labia minora and extends into the body, angling upward toward the small of the back to the cervix and uterus. Women who are unfamiliar with their anatomy may have a difficult time when they first try inserting tampons into the vagina:

Vagina
A stretchable canal in the female that opens at the vulva and extends about four inches into the pelvis.

Figure 4.4

The underlying muscles of the vulva. These muscles can be strengthened using the Kegel exercises described in the box below.

Mucosa
Collective term for the mucous membranes; moist tissue that lines certain body areas such as the penile urethra, vagina, and mouth.

Kegel exercises
A series of exercises that strengthen the muscles underlying the external female or male genitals.

No matter how hard I tried, I couldn't get a tampon in until I inserted a finger and realized that my vagina slanted backward. I had been pushing straight up onto the upper wall. (Authors' files)

The unaroused vagina is approximately 3 to 5 inches long. The walls form a flat tube. The analogy of a glove is often used to illustrate the vagina as a potential rather than actual space, with its walls able to expand enough to serve as a birth passage. In addition, the vagina changes in size and shape during sexual arousal, as we will discuss in Chapter 6.

The vagina contains three layers of tissue: mucous, muscle, and fibrous tissue. All these layers are richly endowed with blood vessels. The **mucosa** (myoo-KŌ-sa) is the layer

Your Sexual Health

Kegel Exercises

The pelvic floor muscles squeeze involuntarily at orgasm; they also can be trained to contract voluntarily, through a series of exercises known as **Kegel** (KEG-al) **exercises** (Yalsin, 1998). These exercises were developed by Arnold Kegel in 1952 to help women regain urinary control after childbirth. (Not uncommonly, women who have recently given birth lose urine when they cough or sneeze, due to excessive stretching and tearing of perineal muscles during childbirth.)

Kegel exercises have been shown to have other effects besides restoring muscle tone. After about six weeks of regular exercise, many women report increased sensation during intercourse as well as a general increase in genital sensitivity. This seems to be associated with their increased awareness of their sex organs as well as their improved muscle tone.

The steps for the Kegel exercises are as follows:

1. Locate the muscles surrounding the vagina. This can be done by stopping the flow of urine to feel which muscles contract. An even more effective way of contracting the pelvic floor muscles is to contract the anal sphincter as if to hold back gas.
2. Insert a finger into the opening of your vagina and contract the muscles you located in step 1. Feel them squeeze your finger.
3. Squeeze the same muscles for 10 seconds. Relax. Repeat 10 times.
4. Squeeze and release as rapidly as possible, 10 to 25 times. Repeat.
5. Imagine trying to suck something into your vagina. Hold for 3 seconds.
6. This exercise series should be done three times a day. (Ono, 1994)

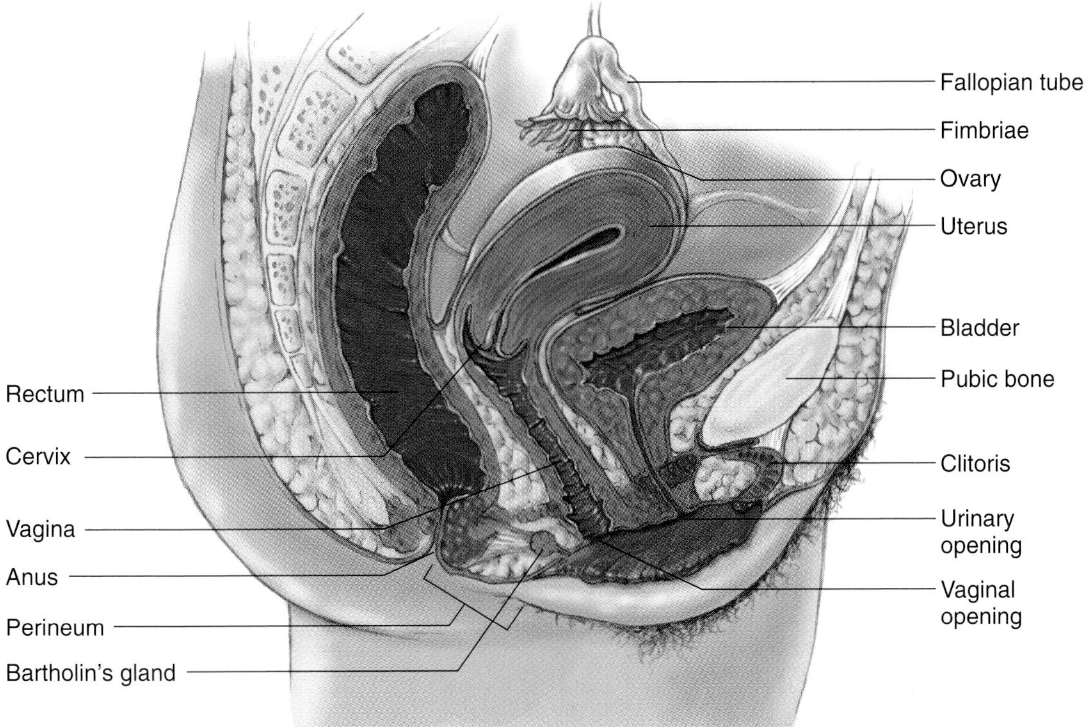

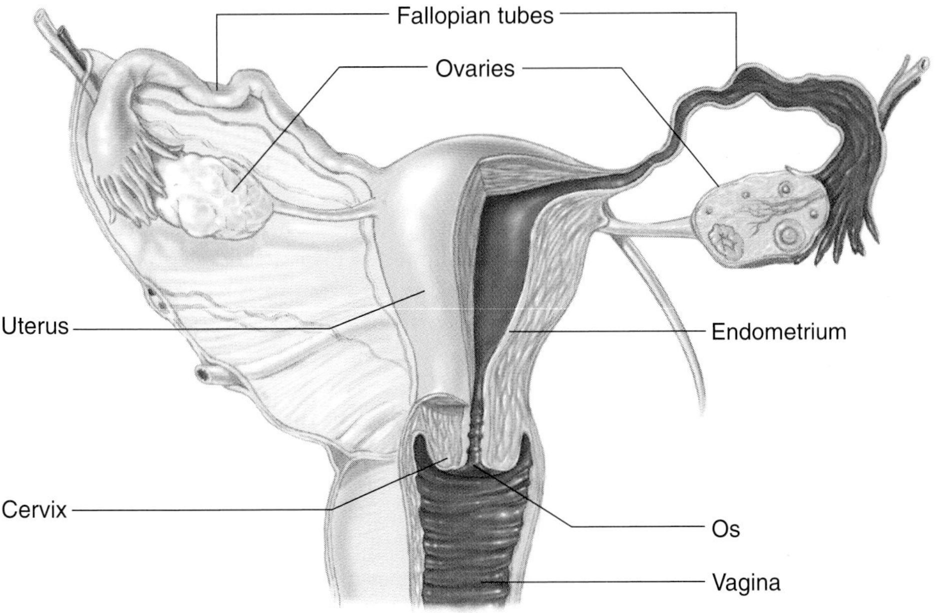

Figure 4.5

Internal female sexual anatomy: (a) cross-section side view of female internal structures; (b) front view of the internal organs. Parts of the ovaries, uterus, and vagina are shown cut away.

of mucous membrane that a woman feels when she inserts a finger inside her vagina. The folded walls, or **rugae** (ROO-jē), feel soft, moist, and warm, resembling the inside of one's mouth. The walls normally produce secretions that help maintain the chemical balance of the vagina. During sexual arousal, a lubricating substance exudes through the mucosa.

Rugae
The folds of tissue in the vagina.

Most of the second layer, composed of muscle tissue, is concentrated around the vaginal opening. Because of the concentration of musculature in the outer one-third and the expansive ability of the inner two-thirds of the vagina, a situation often develops that can be at best funny and at worst embarrassing. During headstands and certain yoga or coital positions with the pelvis elevated, gravity causes the inner two-thirds to expand and draw air into the vagina. The outer muscles tighten, and the trapped air is forced back out through the tightened muscles, creating a sound we usually associate with a different orifice. One student has suggested calling this phenomenon "varting," because the sound is similar to that of a fart (fortunately, there is no unpleasant smell).

Surrounding the muscular layer is the innermost vaginal layer, composed of fibrous tissue. This layer aids in vaginal contraction and expansion and acts as connective tissue to other structures in the pelvic cavity.

Arousal and Vaginal Lubrication

So far in this chapter, we have described the parts of the female sexual anatomy, but we have said relatively little about how these structures function. Because lubrication is a unique feature of the vagina, the process is explained here. Other physiological aspects of female arousal will be discussed in Chapter 6.

Vasocongestion
The engorgement of blood vessels in particular body parts in response to sexual arousal.

During sexual arousal, a clear, slippery fluid begins to appear on the vaginal mucosa within 10 to 30 seconds after effective physical or psychological stimulation begins. By inserting a clear, phallus-shaped camera into the vagina, Masters and Johnson determined that this lubrication is a result of **vasocongestion,** the pooling of blood in the pelvic area. During vasocongestion, the extensive network of blood vessels in the tissues surrounding the vagina engorge with blood. Clear fluid seeps from the congested tissues to the inside of the vaginal walls to form the characteristic slippery coating of the sexually aroused vagina.

Nature has designed the lubrication response of the human female to sexual arousal. What advantages does this physiological process provide?

Vaginal lubrication serves two functions. First, it enhances the possibility of conception by helping to alkalinize the normally acidic vaginal chemical balance. Sperm travel faster and survive longer in an alkaline environment than in an acidic one. (The seminal fluid of the male also helps alkalinize the vagina.) Second, vaginal lubrication can increase sexual enjoyment. During manual–genital stimulation, the slippery wetness can increase the sensuousness and pleasure of touching. During oral–genital sex, some women's partners enjoy the erotic scent and taste of the vaginal lubrication. During intercourse, vaginal lubrication makes the walls of the vagina slippery, which facilitates entry of the penis into the vagina. Lubrication also helps make the thrusting of intercourse pleasurable. Without adequate lubrication, entry of the penis and subsequent thrusting can be very uncomfortable for the woman—and often for the man. Irritation and small tears of the vaginal tissue can result.

Women vary in the amount of vaginal lubrication that occurs during sexual arousal. In addition, vaginal lubrication can be inhibited by conditions such as anxiety, the use of some drugs, and changes in hormone balance. Some women who take birth control pills find that vaginal lubrication is reduced. Many women experience a decrease in lubrication due to the hormonal changes after childbirth and following menopause. We will discuss each of these situations in more detail in later sections of the text.

You can remedy insufficient vaginal lubrication in several ways, depending on the source of the difficulty. Changing the anxiety-producing circumstances and engaging in effective stimulation are important. Saliva, lubricated condoms, or a nonirritating, water-soluble lotion can be used to provide additional lubrication. Occasionally hormone treatment is necessary.

Grafenberg spot
Glands and ducts located in the anterior wall of the vagina. Some women may experience sexual pleasure, arousal, orgasm, and an ejaculation of fluids from stimulation of the Grafenberg spot.

The Grafenberg Spot

The **Grafenberg spot** is an area located within the anterior (or front) wall of the vagina, about one centimeter from the surface and one-third to one-half the way in from the vaginal opening. It consists of a system of glands (Skene's glands) and ducts that surround the urethra. This area is believed to be the female counterpart to the male prostate gland, developed from the same embryonic tissue (Heath, 1984).

The Grafenberg spot has generated considerable interest because of reports that some women experience sexual arousal, orgasm, and perhaps even an ejaculation of fluid when stimulated there (Darling et al., 1990), although many women do not have such an area of increased sensation. We will further discuss the role of the Grafenberg spot in female sexual response in Chapter 6.

Vaginal Secretions and Chemical Balance of the Vagina

Both the vaginal walls and the cervix produce secretions that are white or yellowish in color. These secretions are normal and are a sign of vaginal health. They vary in appearance according to hormone-level changes during the menstrual cycle. (Keeping track of these variations is the basis for one method of birth control, discussed in Chapter 11.) The taste and scent of vaginal secretions may also vary with the time of a woman's cycle and her level of arousal.

The vagina's natural chemical and bacterial balance helps promote healthy mucosa. The chemical balance is normally rather acid (pH 4.0 to 5.0).* A variety of factors can alter this balance and result in vaginal problems. Among these are too-frequent **douching** (rinsing out the inside of the vagina) and using feminine-hygiene sprays. Advertising has played on our cultural negativity about female sexual organs, turning misguided attempts to eradicate normal secretions and scents into an extremely profitable business. Women grow up hearing slogans such as "Unfortunately, the trickiest deodorant problem a girl has isn't under her pretty little arms," and "Our product eliminates the moist, uncomfortable feeling most women normally have just because they're women." However, douching is definitely *not* necessary for routine hygiene; and frequent douching can alter the natural chemical balance of the vagina, thereby increasing susceptibility to infections (Baird et al., 1996). This unnecessary practice can also make it more difficult (but not impossible!) to become pregnant (Baird et al., 1996). Feminine-hygiene sprays can cause irritation, allergic reactions, burns, infections, dermatitis of the thighs, and numerous other problems. In fact, genital deodorant sprays and body powders have been associated with increased risk of ovarian cancer (Cook et al., 1997). Deodorant tampons are another example of a product that women do not need: Menstrual fluid has virtually no odor until it is outside the body. Regular bathing with a mild soap and washing between the folds of the vulva are all that are necessary for proper hygiene.

Douching
Rinsing out the vagina with plain water or a variety of solutions. It is usually unnecessary for hygiene, and too-frequent douching can result in vaginal irritation.

The Cervix

The **cervix** (SER-viks), located at the back of the vagina, is the small end of the pear-shaped uterus (see Figure 4.5). The cervix contains mucus-secreting glands. Sperm pass through the vagina into the uterus through the **os,** the opening in the center of the cervix.

A woman can see her own cervix if she learns to insert a **speculum** into her vagina. She can also ask for a mirror when she has her pelvic exam. A woman can feel her own cervix by inserting one or two fingers into the vagina and reaching to the end of the canal. (Sometimes squatting and bearing down brings the cervix closer to the vaginal entrance.) The cervix feels somewhat like the end of a nose, firm and round in contrast to the soft vaginal walls.

Cervix
The small end of the uterus, located at the back of the vagina.

Os
The opening in the cervix that leads to the interior of the uterus.

Speculum
An instrument with two blades used to open the vaginal walls during a gynecological exam.

The Uterus

The **uterus** (YOO-te-rus), or womb, is a hollow, thick, pear-shaped organ, approximately 3 inches long and 2 inches wide in a woman who has never had a child. (It is somewhat

Uterus
A pear-shaped organ inside the female pelvis, within which the fetus develops.

*pH is a measure of acidity or alkalinity. A neutral substance (neither acid nor alkaline) has a pH of 7. A lower number means a substance is more acid; a higher number means more alkaline.

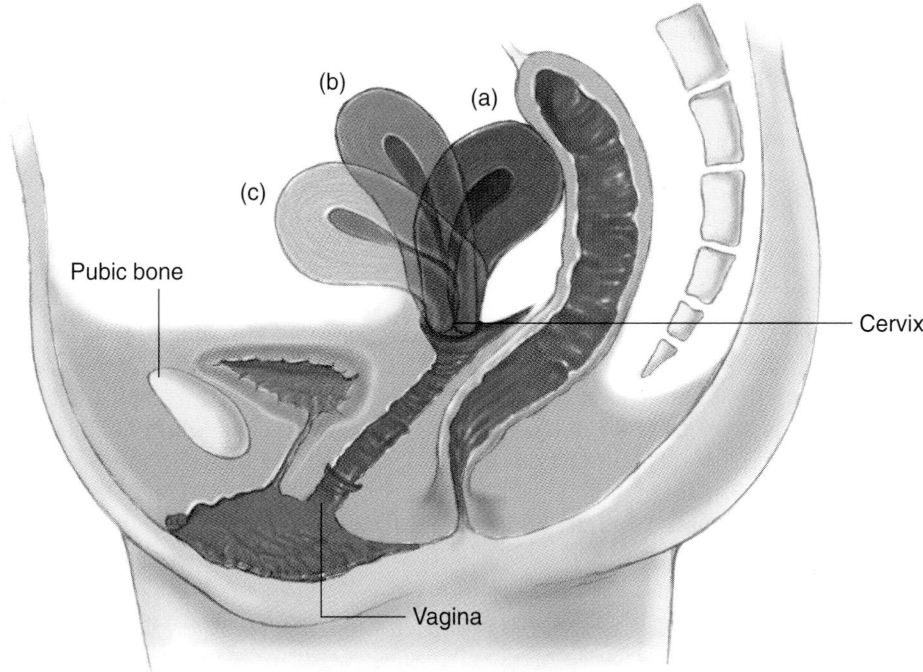

Figure 4.6

Various positions of the uterus in the pelvic cavity: (a) retroflexed, (b) midline, and (c) anteflexed.

larger after pregnancy.) The uterus is suspended in the pelvic cavity by ligaments; in different women its position may vary from *anteflexed* (tipped forward toward the abdomen) to *retroflexed* (tipped back toward the spine), as shown in Figure 4.6. Women with retroflexed uteri may be more likely to experience menstrual discomfort or have difficulty inserting a diaphragm. Although it was once thought that this condition interfered with conception, it does not impair fertility.

The walls of the uterus consist of three layers. The external layer is a thin membrane called the **perimetrium** (per-i-MĒ-trē-um). The middle layer, or **myometrium** (mī′-o-MĒ-trē-um), is made of longitudinal and circular muscle fibers that interweave like the fibers of a basket, enabling the uterus to stretch during pregnancy and contract during labor and orgasm. At the top of the uterus, an area called the *fundus,* the uterine walls are especially thick. The inner lining of the uterus is called the **endometrium** (en′-dō-MĒ-trē-um). Rich in blood vessels, the endometrium nourishes the *zygote* (united sperm and egg), which travels down to the uterus from the fallopian tubes after fertilization takes place. In preparation for this event, it thickens in response to hormone changes during the monthly menstrual cycle, discussed later in this chapter. The endometrium is also a source of hormone production.

Perimetrium
The thin membrane covering the outside of the uterus.

Myometrium
The smooth muscle layer of the uterine wall.

Endometrium
The tissue that lines the inside of the uterine walls.

Fallopian tubes
Two tubes in which the egg and sperm travel, extending from the sides of the uterus.

Fimbriae
Fringelike ends of the fallopian tubes into which the released ovum enters.

Ovaries
Female gonads that produce ova and sex hormones.

Ovulation
The release of a mature ovum from the ovary.

The Fallopian Tubes

Each of the two 4-inch **fallopian** (fa-LŌ-pē-an) **tubes** extends from the uterus toward the ovary, at the left or the right side of the pelvic cavity (see Figure 4.5). The outside end of each tube is shaped like a funnel, with fringelike projections called **fimbriae** (FIM-brē-a) that cover the ovary. When the egg leaves the ovary, it is drawn into the tube by the fimbriae.

Once the egg is inside the tube, the movements of tiny, hairlike *cilia* and the contractions of the tube walls move it along at a rate of approximately 1 inch every 24 hours. The egg remains viable for fertilization for about 24 to 48 hours. Therefore, fertilization occurs while the egg is still close to the ovary. After fertilization, the zygote begins developing as it continues traveling down the tube to the uterus.

The Ovaries

The two **ovaries,** about the size and shape of almonds, are located at the ends of the fallopian tubes, one on each side of the uterus. They are connected to the pelvic wall and the uterus by ligaments. The ovaries are endocrine glands that produce two classes of sex hormones. The estrogens, as mentioned in Chapter 3, influence development of female physical sex characteristics and help regulate the menstrual cycle. The progestational compounds also help regulate the menstrual cycle and promote maturity of the uterine lining in preparation for pregnancy. Around the onset of puberty, the female sex hormones play a critical role in initiating maturation of the uterus, ovaries, and vagina, and in the development of the *secondary sex characteristics,* such as pubic hair and breasts.

The ovaries contain 40,000 to 400,000 immature ova, which are present at birth. During the years between puberty and menopause, one or the other ovary typically releases an egg during each cycle. An average woman will release approximately 450 eggs in her lifetime. **Ovulation** (ō-vyoo-LĀ-shun), or egg maturation and release, occurs as the result of the complex chain of events we know as the menstrual cycle, discussed at the end of this chapter.

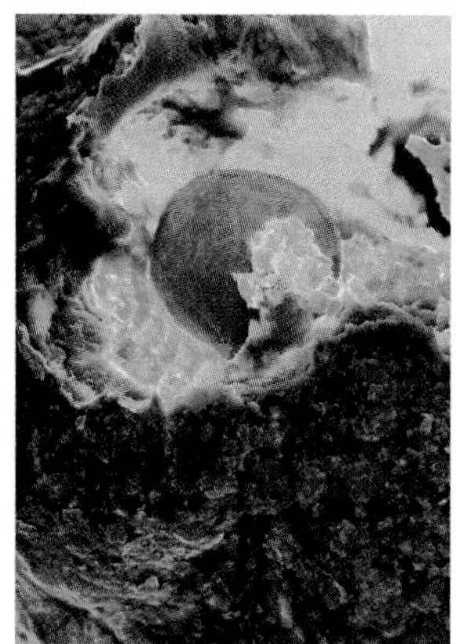

Colored electron micrograph of ovulation. The egg (orange) has ruptured the surface of the ovary. Cells (light green) and fluid (yellow) formerly provided nutrients and protection to the egg in the ovary.

Gynecological Health Concerns

Gynecological health problems range from minor infections to cancer. This section provides information and self-help information on several topics.

Urinary Tract Infections

Women often develop infections of the urinary tract, the organ system that includes the urethra, bladder, and kidneys. If the infection progresses all the way to the kidneys, severe illness can result (Service, 1997). About one out of every five women will have a urinary tract infection in her lifetime; many have more than one (Leiner, 1997).

The symptoms of urinary tract infections are usually uncomfortable and may include a frequent need to urinate, a burning sensation when urinating, blood or pus in the urine, and sometimes lower pelvic pain (D'Epiro, 1997a). A conclusive diagnosis of a urinary tract infection requires laboratory analysis of a urine sample. Such an infection generally responds to short-term antibiotic treatment. Vaccines for women who have recurrent infections are being developed (Uehling at al., 1997).

Urinary tract infections are usually caused by bacteria from the rectum or vagina, or infectious agents from a partner's sexual organs, that enter the urethral opening. Coitus is the most frequent means by which bacteria enter the urinary tract: These organisms can be massaged into the urethra by the thrusting motions of intercourse. Bladder infections often occur during periods of frequent intercourse. Poor hygiene or wiping the genitals from back to front after defecation can also introduce bacteria into the urethra. Using a diaphragm and spermicide increases the risk of urinary tract infections (Hooton, 1996). Repeatedly stretching the bladder muscle beyond its normal capacity (which is reached with the first urge to urinate) weakens the muscle so that it cannot expel all the urine; thus some urine remains in the bladder, increasing the risk of infection. Other factors linked to infections include urinary tract abnormalities, diabetes, pregnancy, and a history of childhood urinary tract infections.

Observing a few routine precautions may help prevent urinary tract infections. Careful wiping from front to back after both urination and bowel movements helps keep bacteria away from the urethra. Washing the genital and rectal areas thoroughly each day, and urinating as soon as you feel the urge will also reduce the likelihood of infection. For those who have frequent problems with such infections, washing before and after intercourse may help. A woman's sexual partner can also help by washing his or her hands and genitals before sexual contact; intercourse positions that cause less friction against the urethra may also help. Women can also use sterile, water-soluble lubricating jelly (not petroleum jelly) when vaginal lubrication is insufficient, because irritated tissue is more susceptible to infection. Urinating immediately after intercourse helps wash out bacteria (Leiner, 1997). Having your health care practitioner recheck the fit of your diaphragm is a good idea. It also can be helpful to drink plenty of liquids, especially cranberry juice, and to avoid substances such as coffee, tea, and alcohol, which have an irritating effect on the bladder (Greenwood, 1989).

Vaginal Infections

Vaginitis
Inflammation of the vaginal walls caused by a variety of vaginal infections.

When the natural balance of the vagina is disturbed or a nonnative organism introduced, a vaginal infection, or **vaginitis** (vaj′-a-NĪ-tis), can result. Usually the woman herself first notices symptoms of vaginitis: irritation or itching of the vagina and vulva, unusual discharge, and sometimes a disagreeable odor. (An unpleasant odor can also be due to a forgotten tampon or diaphragm.) Some of the different types of vaginal infections are yeast infections, bacterial infections, and trichomoniasis, discussed further in Chapter 17.

A number of factors increase a woman's susceptibility to vaginitis: having diabetes (Saunders, 1998), the use of antibiotics, emotional stress, a diet high in carbohydrates, hormonal changes caused by pregnancy or birth control pills, chemical irritants, coitus without adequate lubrication, and heat and moisture retained by nylon underwear and panty hose. One study found that women who wear panty hose had three times more yeast infections than those who did not (Heidrich et al., 1984). Menstrual flow increases the alkalinity of the vagina, which promotes yeast growth in some women.

It is important for vaginitis to be treated and cured. Chronic irritation resulting from long-term infections may play a part in predisposing a woman to cervical cell changes that can lead to cancer. Over-the-counter treatments for yeast infections are now available. Some health care practitioners provide suggestions for nondrug treatment of vaginitis. The following suggestions may help prevent vaginitis from occurring in the first place (Solomini, 1991):

1. Eat a well-balanced diet low in sugar and refined carbohydrates.
2. Maintain general good health with adequate sleep, exercise, and emotional release.
3. Use good hygiene, including the following:
   a. Bathe regularly with mild soap.
   b. After urinating and having bowel movements, wipe from front to back, vulva to anus.
   c. Wear clean cotton underpants (nylon holds in heat and moisture that encourages bacterial growth).
   d. Avoid using feminine-hygiene sprays, colored toilet paper, bubble bath, and other people's washcloths or towels to wash or wipe your genitals.
   e. Ensure that your sexual partner's hands and genitals are clean before beginning sexual activity.
4. Be sure you have adequate lubrication before coitus: natural lubrication or a sterile, water-soluble lubricant. Do not use petroleum-based lubricants (such as Vaseline), because they are not water soluble and are likely to remain in the vagina and harbor bacteria. Petroleum-based lubricants can also weaken and will eventually degrade latex condoms or diaphragms.
5. Use condoms if you or your partner are nonmonogamous.
6. Women who are prone to yeast infections after menstruation may find it helpful to douche with two tablespoons of white vinegar in a quart of warm water once the flow ceases. However, too-frequent douching can alter the vagina's chemical balance and increase susceptibility to infection. Research has shown douching to be correlated to pregnancy occurring in the fallopian tubes (Kendrick et al., 1997).

Self-Exams and Vaginal Health Care

A self-exam can sometimes help detect vaginal infection. The skin of the genital area may turn red instead of its usual pink, and this, along with irritation, is a sign that treatment may be necessary. Many health care practitioners use a mirror to show a woman the inside of her vagina during her regular exam, and some will teach her how to use the speculum, the instrument that holds the vaginal walls open. They may also give the woman a plastic speculum that she can use during vaginal self-exams at home.

The Pap Smear

Pap smear
A screening test for cancer of cells from the cervix.

The **Pap smear,** a screening test for cervical cancer, is taken from the cervix. The vaginal walls are held open with a speculum, and a few cells are removed with a cervical brush or a small wooden spatula; these cells are put on a slide and sent to a lab to be examined. The cells for a Pap smear are taken from the *transition zone,* the part of the cervix where long, column-shaped cells called *columnar cells* meet flat-shaped cells called *squamous cells* (Jones, 1992). A Pap smear is not painful, because there are so few nerve endings on the cervix. A vaginal Pap smear is done when the woman's cervix has been removed (Volm, 1997).

The Pap smear is an essential part of every woman's routine preventive health care including sexually active adolescents (Mangan et al., 1997). Since the widespread use of Pap smears began in the 1950s, the death rate from cervical cancer has decreased dramatically (O'Leary et al., 1998). Nevertheless, it remains the eighth most common cause of cancer death in young women in the United States (Austin & McLendon, 1997) and the leading cause of cancer death in young women worldwide (Munger, 1995). Based on a health care provider's recommendation, a woman may have this test once every two years, every year, twice a year, or even more frequently. Pap tests are 80% to 90% accurate in detecting cervical cancer, and regular tests increase the likelihood of discovering cancer (Austin & McLendon, 1997).

Some subgroups of women are less likely than others to have routine Pap smears. For example, lesbians get Pap smears less often than heterosexuals (Moran, 1996). This may be due to their lack of need for routine contraceptive visits to a gynecologist or to medical professionals' lack of knowledge or discomfort with homosexuality. Socioeconomic level can also affect the rate of Pap test screening. Unlike the general rate of decline in mortality from cervical cancer, the death rate has increased in recent years among Native American women. The main cause seems to be the inefficient and unskilled health care system available to Native Americans, which uses temporary physicians who work with administrators who have inadequate training and experience in health care management (Mahmoodian, 1997).

When the results of a Pap smear indicate abnormal cells, further tests are necessary before a conclusive diagnosis can be made. A *colposcopy* (an exam using a special microscope) and a tissue *biopsy* (surgical removal of a small piece of cervical tissue, which is then examined under a microscope) are two of the additional tests that can be done (Massad et al., 1997).

Abnormal cell changes occur up to 15 years before cancer develops (Higgins, 1997). Several simple, highly effective, lifesaving treatments are used for cervical abnormalities. *Cryosurgery* (freezing of tissues) is one method of removing small numbers of abnormal cells from the surface of the cervix. Elimination of tissue by means of a biopsy is also often effective (Soutter et al., 1997). In more severe cases, a woman may need a complete hysterectomy.

An increased risk of developing cervical cancer has been linked to a number of factors. Women at greater risk of developing this cancer include those who have had genital warts; those who have had several male sexual partners; women whose first coital experience came at an early age (Stack, 1997); and those whose husbands are at increased risk due to occupational contact with toxic materials (Robinson, 1993). Women who smoke cigarettes or are exposed to the cigarette smoke of others also have increased rates of cervical cancer (Gram et al., 1992). In addition, the general incidence of cervical cancer increased during the 1990s in women under the age of 35, including adolescents (Campion, 1992).

Surgical Removal of the Uterus and Ovaries

Sometimes a woman needs to have a hysterectomy (his´-te-REK-to-ME), surgical removal of the uterus, or an oophorectomy (o-of-o-REK-to-mE), surgical removal of the ovaries, or both. These procedures are necessitated by various medical problems, including bleeding disorders; cervical, uterine, or ovarian cancer (Pogrebin, 1998); the presence of benign (noncancerous) tumors (Maher, 1997; Shurpin, 1997); and severe pelvic infections. The potential physical complications of these operations are similar to those of any major surgery.

An estimated 33% of women have a hysterectomy by age 65, making it the most frequently performed major operation for women in the United States (Wilcox et al., 1994). In some situations, the reasons for a hysterectomy are discretionary: A woman can often be treated successfully with other medical options, including laser treatments or medications for bleeding disorders (Bernhard, 1994). Before consenting to undergo a hysterectomy or similar surgery, it is important for a woman to obtain a second opinion; to fully inform herself of the benefits, risks, and alternatives to surgery; and to arrange for thorough preoperative and postoperative information and counseling.

The effects of this type of surgery on a woman's sexuality vary. Some women find that the elimination of medical problems and painful intercourse, assured protection from unwanted pregnancy, and lack of menstruation may enhance their sexual functioning. Research indicates that these women have intercourse as frequently after recovering from a hysterectomy as before the surgery (Kilkku, 1983). However, other women may experience an alteration or decrease in their sexual response after removal of the uterus. Sensations from uterine vasocongestion and elevation during arousal, as well as uterine contractions during orgasm, will be absent and may change the physical experience of sexual response. Some changes may result from damage to the nerves of the vagina and cervix. Scar tissue or alterations to the vagina may also have an effect. When ovaries are removed, symptoms common to menopause will occur without hormone-replacement therapy. Often the crucial variable in postsurgical sexual adjustment is the quality of the partner relationship and how the woman and her partner perceive the surgery (Helstrom et al., 1995). Sometimes general physical or emotional problems may interfere with sexual functioning.

The Breasts

Secondary sex characteristics
The physical characteristics other than genitals that indicate sexual maturity, such as body hair, breasts, and deepened voice.

Mammary glands
Milk glands in the female breast.

Breasts are not a part of the internal or external female genitalia. Instead, they are **secondary sex characteristics** (physical characteristics other than genitals that distinguish male from female). In a physically mature woman, the breasts are composed internally of fatty tissue and **mammary** (MAM-ar-ē), or milk, **glands** (see Figure 4.7). There is little variation from woman to woman in the amount of glandular tissue present in the breast, despite differences in size. This is why the amount of milk produced after childbirth does not correlate to the size of the breasts. Variation in breast size is due primarily to the amount of fatty tissue distributed around the glands. It is common for one breast to be slightly larger than the other.

Breast size is a source of considerable preoccupation for many women and men in our society. Large breasts are often considered to be linked with "sexiness." Surgeries to enlarge or reduce breast size reflect the dissatisfaction many women feel because their breasts do not fit the cultural ideal. (Prior to the January 1992 restrictions on implants,

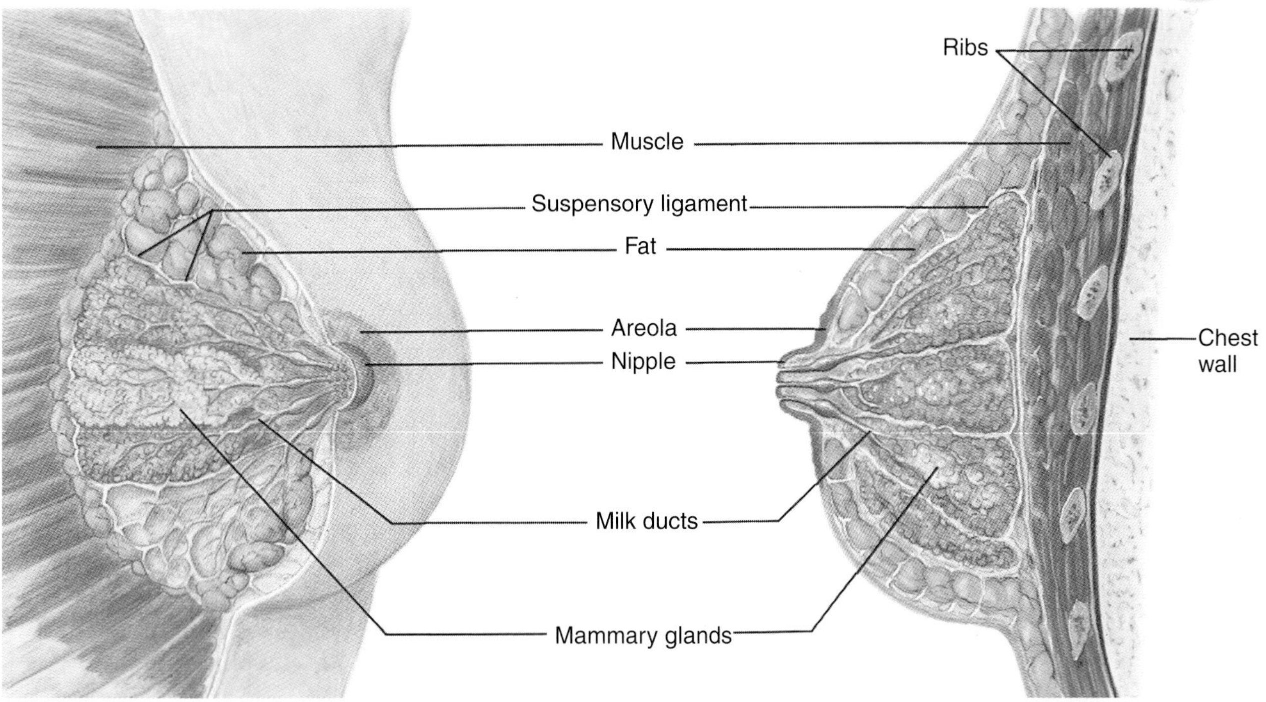

Figure 4.7

Cross-section front and side views of the female breast.

150,000 women a year received implants [Schwartz & Kaplan, 1992]). Research has not yet confirmed the safety or risks of implants, yet thousands of women report unusual and debilitating symptoms and illnesses after receiving implants (Begley, 1996).

Many women believe that their breasts are too small, too big, or not the right shape:

In talking with my friends about how we feel about our breasts, I discovered that not one of us feels really comfortable about how she looks. I've always been envious of women with large breasts because mine are small. But my friends with large breasts talk about feeling self-conscious about their breasts too. (Authors' files)

The glandular tissue in the breast responds to sex hormones. During adolescence, both the fatty and the glandular tissue develop markedly. Breasts show some size variations at different phases of the menstrual cycle and when influenced by pregnancy, nursing, or birth control pills.

The **nipple** is in the center of the **areola** (a-RĒ-ō-la), the darker area of the external breast. The areola contains sebaceous (oil-producing) glands that help lubricate the nipples during breast-feeding. The openings of the mammary glands are in the nipples. Some nipples point outward from the breast, others are flush with the breast, and still others sink into the breast. The nipples become erect when small muscles at the base of the nipple contract in response to sexual arousal, tactile stimulation, or cold.

Breast and nipple stimulation is an important source of pleasure and arousal during masturbation or sexual interaction for many women. Some find it helps build the sexual intensity that leads to orgasm, others enjoy it for its own sake. In contrast, other women find breast and nipple touching unpleasant.

Nipple
The central pigmented area of the breast, which contains numerous nerve endings and milk ducts.

Areola
The darkened circular area surrounding the nipple of the breast.

Breast Self-Exam

A monthly breast examination is an important part of self-health care for women. This exam can help a woman know what is normal for her own breasts. She can do the breast exam herself and can also teach her partner to do it. The steps of a breast exam are

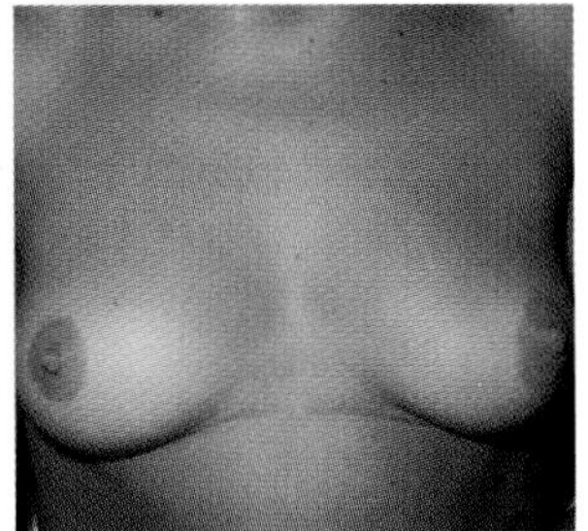
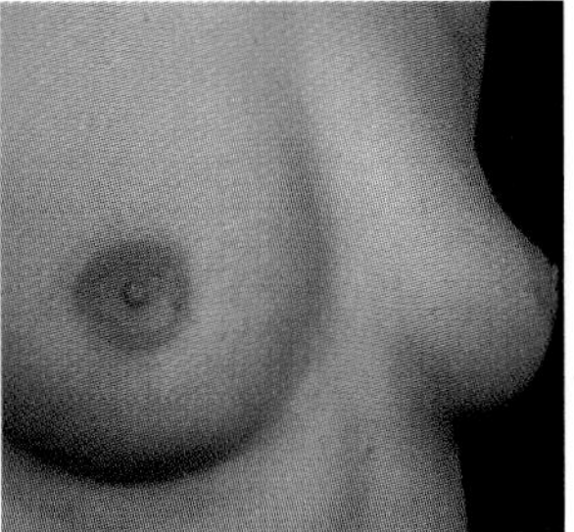
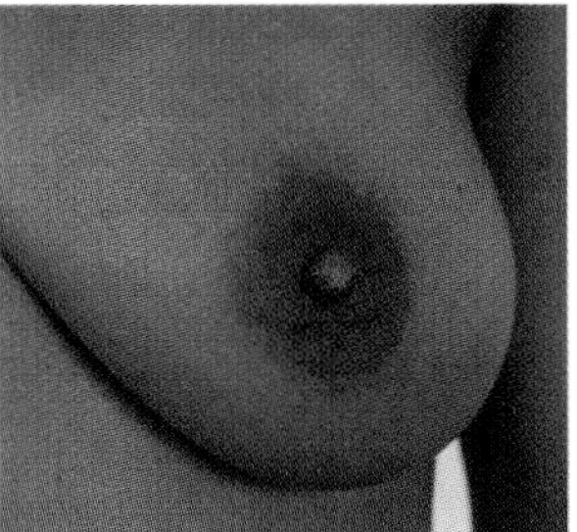
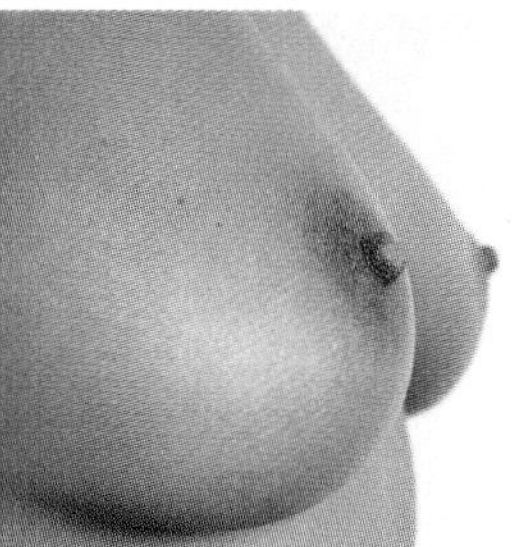

Breast size and shape vary from woman to woman.

illustrated in the box, "How to Examine Your Breasts." Because of cyclic changes in the breast tissue, the best time to do the routine exam is following menstruation. For a woman who is not menstruating (during pregnancy, or after menopause or a hysterectomy), doing the exam at the same time each month is best. Many breasts normally feel lumpy. Once a woman becomes familiar with her own breasts, she can notice any changes. If there is a change, she should consult a physician, who may recommend further diagnostic testing. Ninety percent of breast lumps, most of which are not malignant, are found by women themselves. It is helpful to fill out a chart, like the one shown in Figure 4.8, to keep track of lumps in the breasts. Most breast cancer is found by self-examination (Schifeling & Hamblin, 1991).

Breast Cancer Screening

Mammography
A highly sensitive X-ray test for the detection of breast cancer.

Breast self-exam and routine breast exams by your health care provider are important screening tools. In addition, **mammography** (mam-OG-ra-fē) is a highly sensitive X-ray screening test to help detect cancerous breast lumps. It uses low levels of radiation to create an image of the breast, called a *mammogram,* on film or paper. Mammography can often detect a breast lump up to several years before it can be felt manually; it can also sometimes find cancerous cell changes that occur even before a lump develops. With earlier detection of breast cancer, an increase in breast-conserving treatments may be possible.

There has been considerable disagreement among medical professionals about the routine use of mammography in women 40 to 49 years old. It is less effective for detecting breast cancer in women under 50 years of age than in those over 50, mainly due to the greater density of the breast tissue that makes it more difficult for the mammogram to find potential problem areas (D'Epiro, 1997b). However, almost 6000 women in their forties are killed each year by breast cancer, and the American Medical Association, the American Cancer Society, and the National Cancer Advisory Board recommend routine mammograms for this age group because regular mammograms significantly improve women's breast cancer survival rate (Muldoon, 1997a; Taub, 1997). In response to these recommendations, President Clinton, whose mother died of breast cancer, took steps to budget funds for mammograms for low-income women and to encourage health insurance coverage for mammograms (Muldoon, 1997).

Although mammography is a highly effective screening test, it may miss a significant number of tumors (Begley & Springen, 1997). Research is exploring better breast-screening technology (Cowley, 1997). The best method for early detection of breast cancer is a combination of monthly manual self-exams, routine exams by a health care practitioner, and mammography as recommended.

It is especially important for lesbians to be conscientious about scheduling regular exams and mammograms; they tend to be screened less often than heterosexual women because they do not have birth control medical appointments. Lesbians may also avoid health care services rather than confront insensitivity and ignorance of medical practitioners (Gallagher, 1997b). Many lesbians report that past negative experiences have made them less likely to seek services when they have a problem (Rankow, 1997).

In 5% to 10% of women, breast cancer may develop from flaws in a gene (Burke et al., 1997). Women with this gene flaw have up to an 85% chance of developing breast cancer. Women now have the opportunity to decide whether or not to have a preventive mastectomy (Schrag et al., 1997; Watson et al., 1998). At the least, women with this gene flaw could be followed more closely (Lynch & Casey, 1997).

Breakthrough research in 1998 found that tamoxifen, an anti-estrogen medication used to treat breast cancer, is also effective in preventing breast cancer. The study subjects were women at high risk for breast cancer. The group who took tamoxifen instead of the placebo had 45% fewer cases of breast cancer. Significant side effects are possible (Koglin, 1998).

Breast Lumps

Three types of lumps can occur in the breasts. The two most common are *cysts,* which are fluid-filled sacs, and *fibroadenomas,* which are solid, rounded tumors. Both are benign (not cancerous or harmful) tumors, and together they account for approximately 80% of breast lumps. In some women the lumps create breast tenderness ranging from mild to

Your Sexual Health

How to Examine Your Breasts

1. **In the shower**
   Examine your breasts during a bath or shower; hands glide more easily over wet skin. With fingers flat, move your hands gently over every part of each breast. Use your right hand to examine your left breast, left hand for your right breast. Check for any lump, hard knot, or thickening.

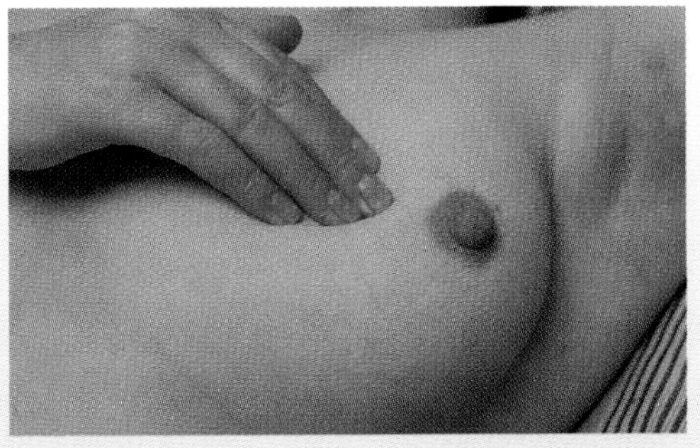

2. **Before a mirror**
   Inspect your breasts with arms at your sides. Next, raise your arms high overhead. Look for any changes in the contour of each breast: a swelling, dimpling of the skin, or changes in the nipple.

   Then rest your palms on your hips and press down firmly to flex your chest muscles. Left and right breasts will not match exactly—few women's breasts do.
3. **Lying down**
   To examine your right breast, put a pillow or folded towel under your right shoulder. Place your right hand behind your head—this distributes breast tissue more evenly on the chest. With your left hand, fingers flat, press gently in small circular motions around an imaginary clock face. Begin at the outermost top of your right breast for 12 o'clock, then move to one o'clock, and so on around the circle back to 12. A ridge of firm tissue in the lower curve of each breast is normal. Then move in an inch, toward the nipple, and keep circling to examine *every part of your breast,* including the nipple. This requires at least three more circles. Now slowly repeat this procedure on your left breast.

   Finally, squeeze the nipple of each breast gently between thumb and index finger. Any discharge, clear or bloody, should be reported to your doctor immediately—as should the discovery of any unusual lump, swelling, or thickening anywhere in the breast.

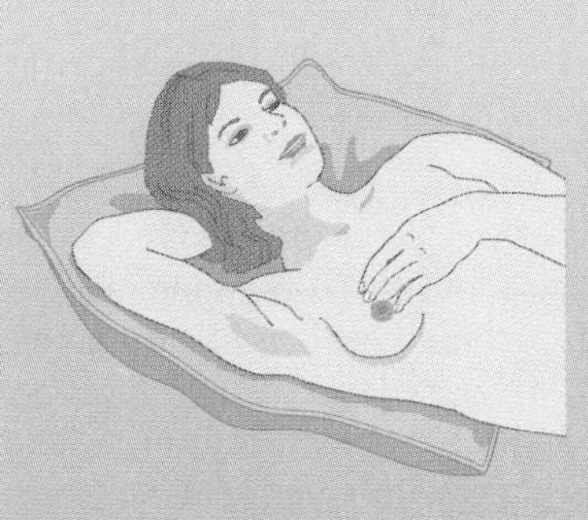

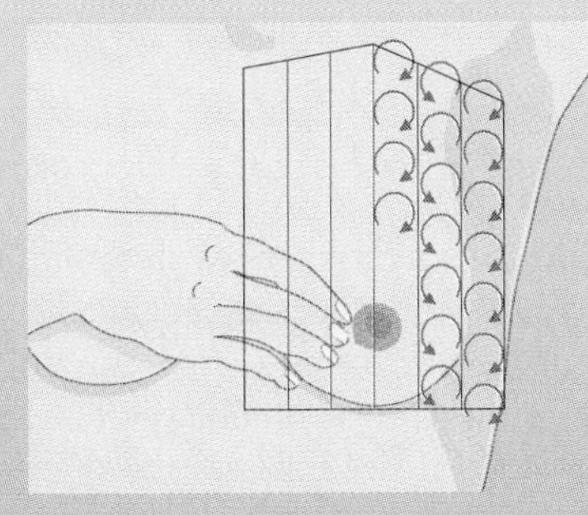

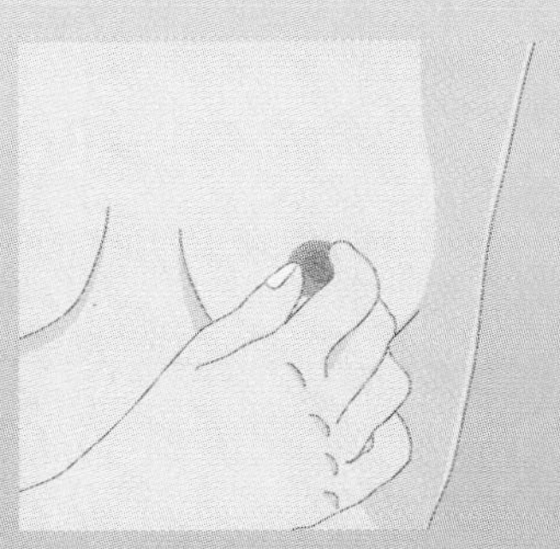

Fill out a chart, like the one shown here, each month when you examine your breasts. Record the date of the examination and the date your last period started. For any lump you find, mark

1. its location
2. its size (BB, pea, raisin, grape)
3. its shape (rounded or elongated)

Compare each month's record with the last one, and consult your health practitioner regarding any changes. A new or changing lump should be checked as soon as possible. Most such lumps will prove to be benign.

Today's date _______________

Last period started __________

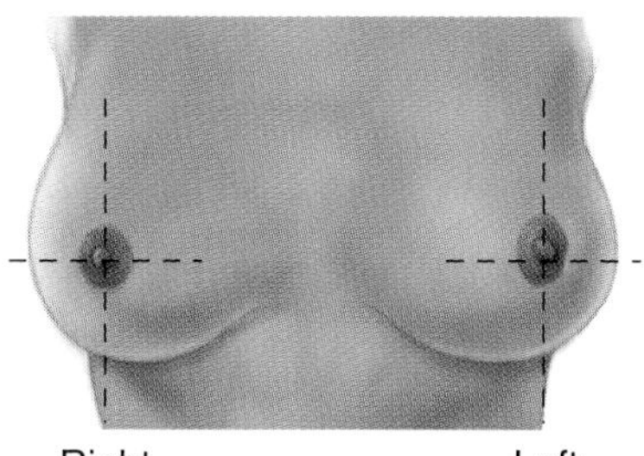

Figure 4.8

It is helpful to use a chart similar to this one to keep track of lumps in the breasts.

severe discomfort, which is called *fibrocystic disease* (Deckers & Ricci, 1992). The causes of fibrocystic disease are unknown but believed to be hormonally related. Caffeine in coffee, tea, cola drinks, and chocolate may contribute to the development of benign breast lumps. Dietary changes that have helped some women reduce their symptoms include a diet high in fish, chicken, and grains, and low in red meat, salt, and fats. Vitamin supplements of 600 units of vitamin E and vitamin-B complex in 110-mg daily doses have also helped some women (Sloane, 1985).

The third kind of breast lump is a *malignant tumor* (a tumor made up of cancer cells). Breast cancer affects approximately one in nine North American women; 180,000 cases are diagnosed each year, and breast cancer kills about 44,000 women a year (Josephson, 1998). The risk of breast cancer rises with age (Thomas et al., 1996). The good news is that mortality from breast cancer is at its lowest since 1950 (Chu et al., 1996). However, breast cancer mortality has declined among white women, whereas death rates have remained constant for black women (Chevarley & White, 1997). Certain risk factors increase or decrease a woman's chances of developing breast cancer including exposure to pesticides, radiation, and environmental pollution (Landsberg, 1997). Other factors are outlined in Table 4.1. However, about 80% of women with breast cancer do not have any of the known risk factors (Duda, 1995).

If a lump is found, further diagnostic testing is necessary. *Needle aspiration* involves inserting a fine needle into the lump to determine if there is fluid inside. If so, it is usually a cyst and can be drained. A biopsy of the tissue of any lump can be analyzed for cancer cells (Cowley & Rosenberg, 1992).

Breast Cancer

Once breast cancer has been diagnosed, several forms of treatment may be used. Radiation therapy, chemotherapy (Basade & Gulati, 1998), hormone therapy, immunotherapy, *lumpectomy* (only the lump and small amounts of surrounding tissue are removed), **mastectomy** (surgical removal of all or part of the breast), or a combination of these procedures may be performed. With mastectomy, the amount of the breast and surrounding tissue that is removed by surgery varies from *radical mastectomy* (the entire breast, under-

Mastectomy
Surgical removal of the breast(s).

Table 4.1 Risk Factors for Breast Cancer

Higher Risk	*Lower Risk*
Older than age 50	Younger than age 50
Family history of breast cancer	No family history of breast cancer
No pregnancies	Having given birth to twins (Westall, 1997)
More than 14 alcoholic drinks a week	Less than 14 alcoholic drinks a week
First child after age 30	First child before age 30
Never breast-fed a child	Having breast-fed a child (Furberg et al., 1997)
Menstruation onset before age 12	Menstruation onset after age 12
Consistent menstrual cycle length of less than 26 days or more than 34	
Menopause after age 50	Early menopause
Obesity	Slenderness
Cancer in one breast	No cancer
Sedentary lifestyle	Regular exercise (Thune et al., 1997)
	Both ovaries removed early in life

Note: Abortion does not increase the risk of breast cancer (Wise, 1997). Eighty percent of women who develop breast cancer have *no* known risk factors (Heck & Pamuk, 1997; Pritchard, 1997).

lying muscle, and lymph nodes are removed) to *simple mastectomy* (breast tissue, the nipple and areola, and a sample of lymph nodes are removed) to lumpectomy. If the cancer is small, localized, and in an early stage, a lumpectomy with chemotherapy or radiation may provide as good a chance of cure as a mastectomy (Love, 1997; Pritchard, 1997).

Breast cancer and its treatments may adversely affect a woman's sexuality. Beyond the physical recuperation from surgery and side effects of other treatments, the loss of one or both breasts almost certainly is significant to a woman and her present or future partners. In our culture, a woman's breasts are often considered a symbol of femininity and are therefore a vital part of her body image. The stimulation of a woman's breasts during lovemaking, by massaging, licking, or sucking—and the stimulation her partner receives from doing these things and from simply looking at her breasts—are often important components of sexual arousal, for both the woman and her partner; consequently, surgical removal of one or both breasts may create problems in sexual adjustment for the couple (Polinsky, 1995). Research indicates that sexual adjustment is better following partial rather than radical mastectomy (Steinberg et al., 1985).

A mastectomy presents unique problems for a woman who is not in a long-term relationship. She may have difficulty deciding when to tell someone she is dating about her surgery. Her own feelings of acceptance and comfort and her judgment about timing are important. Also, she needs to understand that her partner will require some time to adjust to the information about her mastectomy. Still, it may help her to keep in mind that a loving relationship is based on more than physical characteristics.

The American Cancer Society's Reach to Recovery program provides a very important service to women with breast cancer. Volunteers in the program, who have all had one or both breasts removed, meet with a woman who has recently undergone a mastectomy and offer her emotional support and encouragement. They also provide positive models of women who have made a successful adjustment to the results of their surgery.

Table 4.2 Five-Year Survival Rate for U.S. Women by Stage of Cancer at Diagnosis

Stage of Cancer	*Survival Rate at 5 Years*	*% of Cancer Diagnosed at This Stage*
Local (confined to breast)	96.8%	60%
Regional (spread to lymph nodes)	75.9%	31%
Distant (spread to other organs)	20.6%	6%

In North America one woman dies of breast cancer approximately *every 12 minutes.*

Source: Smith, 1997.

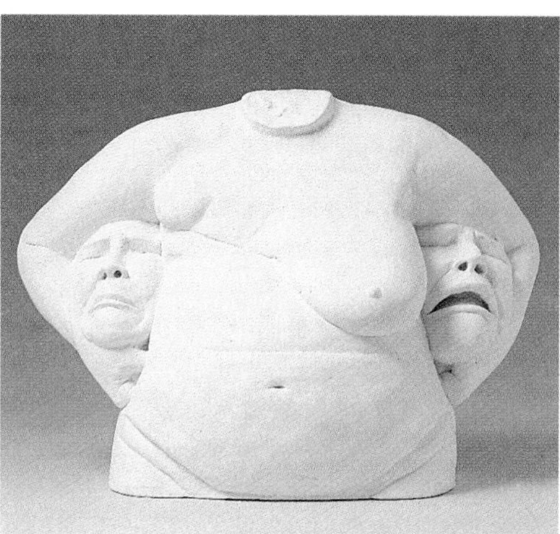
The artist, Nancy Fried, created "Portrait of Grief" following her own mastectomy

Reconstructive breast surgery may enhance a woman's general and sexual adjustment following a mastectomy. In many cases, a new breast can be made from a silicone pouch containing saline water and placed under the woman's own skin and chest muscle. To improve the possibilities for breast reconstruction, it is helpful to have presurgical discussions with both the surgeon removing the tissue and the plastic surgeon doing the reconstruction (Becker & Maraist, 1987). Silicone implants had been widely available for 30 years—and over 2 million women in the United States had received them (Skolnick, 1992)—before the FDA began clinical trials testing the safety of silicone breast implants in early 1992. Implants continue to be available for mastectomy patients while the FDA studies potential problems. The "Breast Implants—Safe or Not?" box discusses this controversy further.

On the Edge

Breast Implants—Safe or Not?

All women who currently have breast implants, or women who would like to get them, hope they cause no harm. Unfortunately, at this time, the verdict on the health-damaging impact of silicone breast implants is still out. The most intense controversy has to do with whether or not the silicone gel in the implants causes unusual and debilitating autoimmune reactions.

The first silicone implants were put on the market in 1963. Previously, silicone fluid was injected directly into breasts. Problems with it migrating to form lumps at other places in the body, massive infections, collapsed lungs, and pneumonia led to emergency legislation to make silicone injections illegal. Instead of injection, a silicone bag filled with silicone gel was developed. The implant was considered a medical product, not a drug, so no Food and Drug Administration (FDA) testing was required, and none was conducted. Implants did not have to meet any government safety standards (Byrne, 1996).

A known problem with implants is capsular contraction: Scar tissue hardens around the implant and presses it into a hard disc instead of a soft capsule. It is the most common reason women who have implants for cosmetic reasons later have them removed. The capsular contraction can be painful and disfiguring, but is not as serious as when silicone gel is released into the body by leakage through the semipermeable shells or rupture. A 43-year-old woman with severe symptoms who received her implants in 1983 describes the symptoms she believes to be caused from silicone leakage: "I developed a hard capsule over a couple of years. Then the next thing was crippling fatigue. I had chronic cystitis . . . and joint pain. My skin became so sensitive, I got sunburns through my clothes. . . . By 1991, my lungs were actually burning. . . . I stopped working in 1995 because of loss of function" (Jamison, 1996, p. 48). More than 100,000 women out of the one million in the United States who have implants are currently ill with different kinds of inflammatory reaction (Washburne, 1996). Silicone implants were taken off the market, except for reconstructive use with mastectomy patients, in 1992 for testing. Prior to this, women spent $4.5 million a year on implants (Stott-Kendall, 1997).

Two studies in the mid-1990s reported that women with silicone breast implants were no more likely than other women to have autoimmune diseases. Unfortunately, these studies do not provide the final word about the safety of silicone implants and have been criticized on several fronts. First, both studies have been charged with conflict of interest due to research funds coming from implant manufacturers. Neither study looked at enough women who had had implants for at least 10 years (the average latency period for symptoms to appear seems to be 8 to 10 years). This would be comparable to determining whether or not smoking causes lung cancer by testing only people in their 30s. One study only reviewed med-

Because cancer spreads, it is especially important to remember to do regular breast exams and screenings. Early detection can lead to a higher survival rate, less drastic surgery, and easier and more successful breast reconstruction (Salazar et al., 1994).

Menstruation

Menstruation (men′-stroo-Ā-shun), the sloughing off of uterine lining that takes place if conception has not occurred, is a sign of normal physical functioning. Negative attitudes about it, however, persist in contemporary American society (Koff et al., 1990).

Menstruation
The sloughing off of the built-up uterine lining that takes place if conception has not occurred.

Attitudes About Menstruation

American folklore reveals many interesting ideas about menstruation. It has been thought that a woman should not bathe or wash her hair during her menstrual period because she would become ill or stop menstruating. In the 1920s, women commonly believed that a permanent wave given during menstruation would not curl their hair. Other myths include the belief that it is harmful for a woman to be physically active during menstruation, that a corsage worn by a menstruating woman will wilt, and that a tooth filling

On the Edge

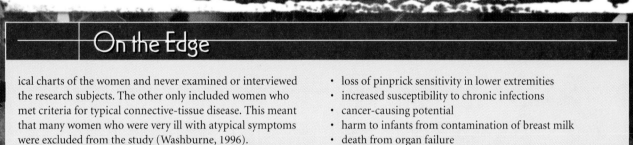

ical charts of the women and never examined or interviewed the research subjects. The other only included women who met criteria for typical connective-tissue disease. This meant that many women who were very ill with atypical symptoms were excluded from the study (Washburne, 1996).

A review of research and case examples paints a more pessimistic picture. There is some evidence that silicone may provoke immune response, chronic inflammation, neurological damage, and toxic reaction. The consequences appear most serious when the implant ruptures and the gel migrates into the circulatory system, lymph system, organs (including the brain), and glands and creates inflammatory reactions. Some other potential consequences include (Stott-Kendall, 1997):

- tissue damage of organs where silicone migrates
- chronic fatigue syndrome
- inflammatory immune diseases
- short-term memory loss
- loss of pinprick sensitivity in lower extremities
- increased susceptibility to chronic infections
- cancer-causing potential
- harm to infants from contamination of breast milk
- death from organ failure

Research is essential in helping women make informed decisions about implants. We hope further research will answer important questions about their safety or danger. The National Institutes of Health are currently conducting a study, and Harvard's new Women's Health Cohort Study (funded by an implant manufacturer) is in process. Research results will also affect the viability of lawsuits women have against companies that manufacture silicone implants. However, legal maneuvering by manufacturers may prevent women with debilitating illnesses from recovering settlements even if silicone implants are clearly shown to cause autoimmune illnesses (Springen & Hager, 1995).

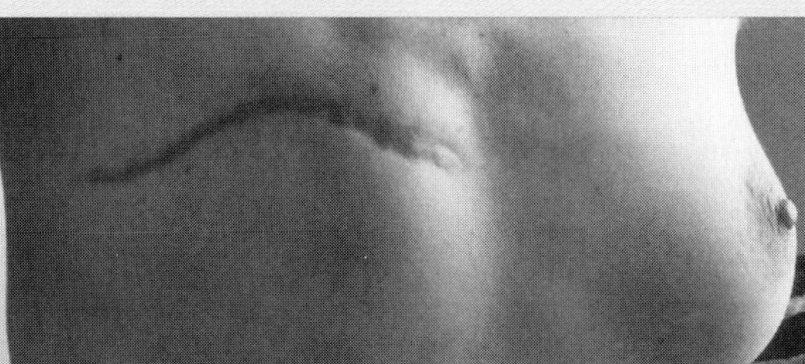

Mastectomy without reconstructive surgery

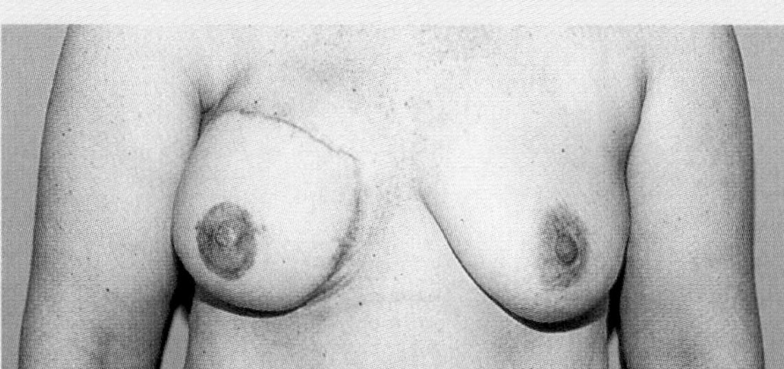

Reconstructive surgery following mastectomy

done during menstruation will fall out (Milow, 1983). The boxed discussion, "Menstruation: Curse or Blessing?" describes further controversy surrounding this event.

Despite these myths and negative societal attitudes toward menstruation, most women associate regular menstrual cycles with healthy functioning and femininity (Woods et al., 1987). Some women and families are redefining it more positively. For example, some may have a celebration or give a gift to a young woman when she starts her first menstrual period. One aspect of the menstrual cycle that people often see as positive is its cyclic pattern, typical of many natural phenomena.

The poet May Sarton describes the analogy of the menstrual cycle and nature in this 1937 poem:

There were seeds
within her
that burst at intervals
and for a little while
she would come back
to heaviness,
and then before a surging miracle
of blood,
relax,
and re-identify herself,
each time more closely
with the heart of life.
'I am the beginning,
the never-ending,
the perfect tree.'
And she would lean
again as one
on the great curve of the earth,
part of its turning,
as distinctly part
of the universe as a star—
as unresistant,
as completely rhythmical.

Controversy exists about the meaning of menstrual rituals in various cultures. Menstrual customs may provide women a means of solidarity, influence, and autonomy. The meanings are often ambiguous, and little is actually known about the significance of menstrual taboos in many cultures. In some societies a menstruating woman is isolated from the community and remains in a "menstrual hut." Researchers have rarely asked about the meaning of and experiences in the menstrual huts. Do women feel resentful and diminished or honored and pleased by the break from normal labor? Scattered reports suggest considerable variability, with positive meanings being fairly common. For example, in some Native American traditions, women were believed to be at their most powerful during menstruation. They would retreat to a "moonlodge" to be free of mundane daily chores. Blood flow was believed to purify women and to enable them to gather spiritual wisdom to benefit the entire tribe. Most Native American tribes also had celebrations for girls' first menstruation (Owen, 1993).

In a few cultures, menstruation is described in lyrical words and positive images. The Japanese expression for a girl's first menstruation is "the year of the cleavage of the melon," and one East Indian description of menstruation is the "flower growing in the house of the god of love" (Delaney et al., 1976).

Another possibility is that the taboos are meant to constrain women and reinforce their lower social status. A Roman historian wrote that bees will leave their hive, boiling linen will turn black, and razors will become blunt if touched by a menstruating woman. The Old Testament states, "And if a woman have an issue and her issue in her flesh be blood, she shall be apart seven days: and whosoever toucheth her shall be unclean until the even" (Leviticus 15:19). Contemporary Orthodox Judaism follows this teaching: Women are not to engage in sexual activity until they have attended a ceremonial cleansing bath following menstruation (Rothbaum & Jackson, 1990). One intention of this abstinence during menstruation is to keep the couple's desire for each other as fresh as in early married life.

Native American women retreated to special huts during menstruation.

Menarche

The menstrual cycle usually begins in the early teens, between the ages of 11 and 15, although some girls begin earlier or later. The average age of first menstruation in the United States is 12 years of age (Herman-Giddens et al., 1997). The first menstrual bleeding is called the **menarche** (me-NAR-kē). The timing of the menarche appears to be related to heredity, general health, and altitude (average menarche is earlier in lower altitudes) and occurs during a time of other changes in body size and development (Forbes, 1992). Menstrual cycles end at menopause, which in most women occurs between the ages of 45 and 55. Differences in the age of menarche are often a concern for young women, especially those who begin earlier or later than the norm.

Menarche
The initial onset of menstrual periods in a young woman.

Although many people believe menstruation should be kept private, accurate information about this significant physiological development in young women is important to both boys and girls. Do you think most parents provide their children with sufficient information on menstruation? Why or why not?

Many young women are not adequately informed about the developments and changes that accompany the onset of menstruation. One study found that 43% of women reported feeling confused, frightened, panicky, or ill when they started their first period, and one-third of the women surveyed did not know about menstruation before they began to menstruate (Research Forecasts, 1981). The information that girls do receive may be scanty, confusing, or frightening.

Young men are probably even less likely to receive information about menstruation. One study found that men are most likely to learn about menstruation from friends (31%), school (21%), and mothers (20%). Ninety-one percent of both men and women thought that information about menstruation should be provided in schools (Research Forecasts, 1981).

Menstrual Physiology

During the menstrual cycle, the uterine lining is prepared for the implantation of a fertilized ovum. If conception does not occur, the lining sloughs off and is discharged as menstrual flow. The length of the menstrual cycle is usually measured from the beginning of the first day of flow to the day before the next flow begins. The menstrual period itself typically lasts 2 to 6 days (Johnson, 1991). It is normal for the volume of the menstrual flow (usually 6 to 8 ounces) to vary. The cycle length varies from woman to woman; it can be anywhere from 24 to 42 days (Belsey & Pinol, 1997). These time differences occur in the phase before ovulation. Fourteen days, plus or minus 2 days, is the interval between ovulation and the onset of menstruation, even when there is several weeks' difference in the total length of the cycle. Life changes and stress can affect cycle length

(Harlow & Matanoski, 1991). If a woman experiences a dramatic change in her usual pattern, she should seek medical attention.

Menstrual synchrony Simultaneous menstrual cycles that sometimes occur among women who live in close proximity.

Menstrual Synchrony

An interesting phenomenon known as **menstrual synchrony** sometimes occurs among women who live together and have considerable contact with one another: They develop similar menstrual cycles (Weller & Weller, 1997). The function of the uniform cycles is unknown, but the trigger is believed to be related to the sense of smell.

How might researchers test the hypothesis that menstrual synchrony is related to the sense of smell? Think of a possible research design before reading on.

To test this hypothesis, researchers had subjects with normal menstrual cycles swab their upper lips with either perspiration extract from another woman or with plain alcohol. Within three menstrual cycles, 80% of the subjects who had received the perspiration extract were menstruating in sync with their perspiration donors. The control group showed no menstrual cycle changes (Cutler et al., 1986).

The Menstrual Cycle

The menstrual cycle is regulated by intricate relationships among the hypothalamus and various endocrine glands, including the pituitary gland (located in the brain), the adrenal glands, and the ovaries and uterus (see Figure 4.9). The hypothalamus monitors hormone levels in the bloodstream throughout the cycle, releasing chemicals that stimulate the pituitary to produce two hormones that affect the ovaries: **follicle-stimulating hormone (FSH)** and **luteinizing** (LOO-te-nīz-ing) **hormone (LH).** FSH stimulates the ovaries to produce estrogen and also causes ova to mature in follicles (small sacs) within the ovaries. LH causes the ovary to release a mature ovum. LH also stimulates the development of the **corpus luteum** (the portion of the follicle that remains after the matured egg has been released), which produces the hormone progesterone.

The menstrual cycle is a self-regulating and dynamic process. Each hormone is secreted until the organ it acts on is stimulated; at that point the organ releases a substance that circulates back through the system to reduce hormonal activity in the initiating gland. This *negative-feedback mechanism* provides an internal control that regulates hormone fluctuation during the three phases of the menstrual cycle: the menstrual phase, the proliferative phase, and the secretory phase. These phases, described in the following paragraphs, are illustrated in Figure 4.10.

Follicle-stimulating hormone (FSH) A pituitary hormone. Secreted by a female during the secretory phase of the menstrual cycle, FSH stimulates the development of ovarian follicles. In males, it stimulates sperm production.

Luteinizing hormone (LH) The hormone secreted by the pituitary gland that stimulates ovulation in the female. In males it is called interstitial cell hormone (ISCH) and stimulates production of androgens by the testes.

Corpus luteum A yellowish body that forms on the ovary at the site of the ruptured follicle and secretes progesterone.

Menstrual phase The phase of the menstrual cycle when menstruation occurs.

Proliferative phase The phase of the menstrual cycle in which the ovarian follicles mature.

Menstrual Phase

During the **menstrual phase,** the uterus sheds the thickened inner layer of the endometrium, which is discharged through the cervix and vagina as menstrual flow. Menstrual flow typically consists of blood, mucus, and endometrial tissue.

The shedding of the endometrium is triggered by reduced progesterone and estrogen levels in the bloodstream. As these hormone levels fall, the hypothalamus stimulates the pituitary gland to release FSH. This action initiates the second, proliferative, phase of the menstrual cycle.

Proliferative Phase

During the **proliferative phase,** the pituitary gland increases production of FSH, which stimulates the developing follicles to mature and to produce several types of estrogen. Estrogen in turn causes the endometrium to thicken. Although several follicles begin to mature, usually only one reaches maturity; the other follicles degenerate. When the level of ovarian estrogen circulating in the bloodstream reaches a peak, the pituitary gland depresses the release of FSH and stimulates LH production.

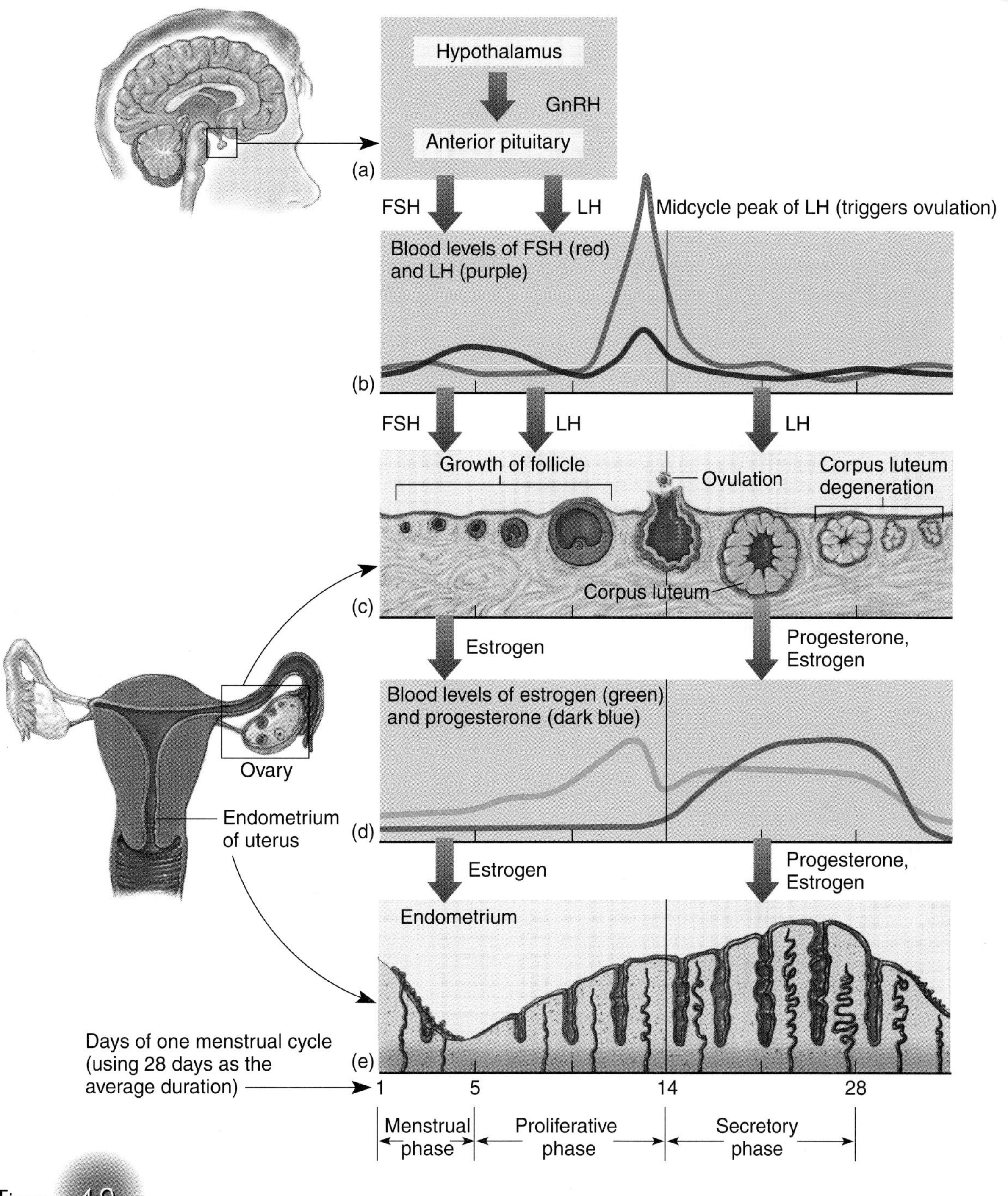

Figure 4.9

Changes in the ovary and uterus, correlated with changing hormone levels during menstrual cycle. *Green* arrows indicate which hormones dominate the cycle's first phase (when the follicle matures), then the second phase (when the corpus luteum forms). (a,b) FSH and LH cause changes in ovarian structure and function. (c,d) Estrogen and progesterone from the ovary cause changes in the endometrium. (Starr & McMillan, 1997, p. 298)

At approximately 14 days *before* the onset of the *next* menstrual period, ovulation occurs. In response to the spurt of LH secreted by the pituitary gland, the mature follicle ruptures, and the ovum is released. Some women experience a twinge, cramp, or pressure in the lower abdomen, called *Mittelschmerz* (German for *middle pain*), at ovulation.

(a) **Proliferative phase**

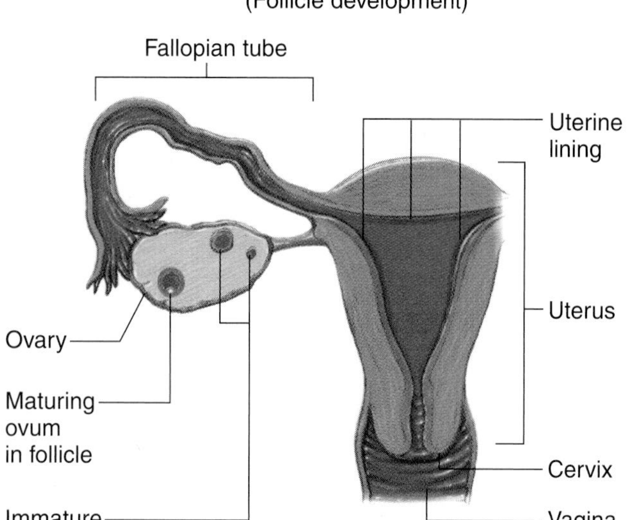

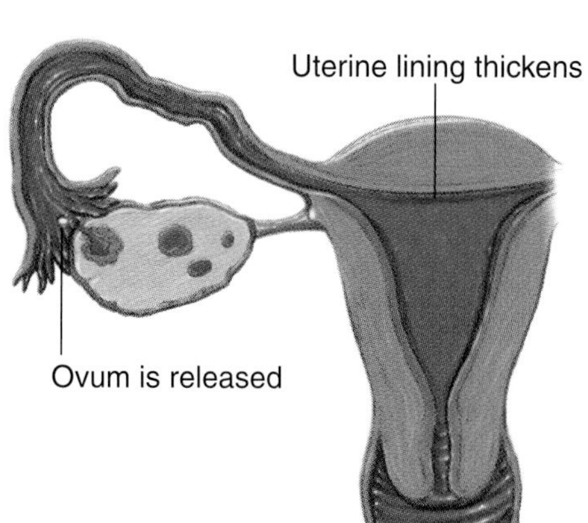

(b) **Secretory phase**

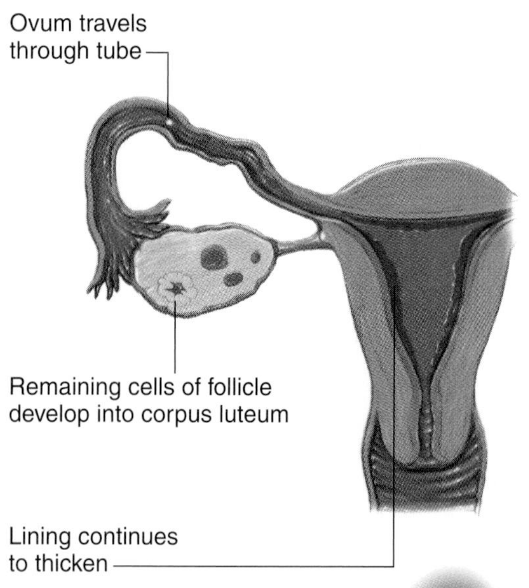

(c) **Menstrual phase**

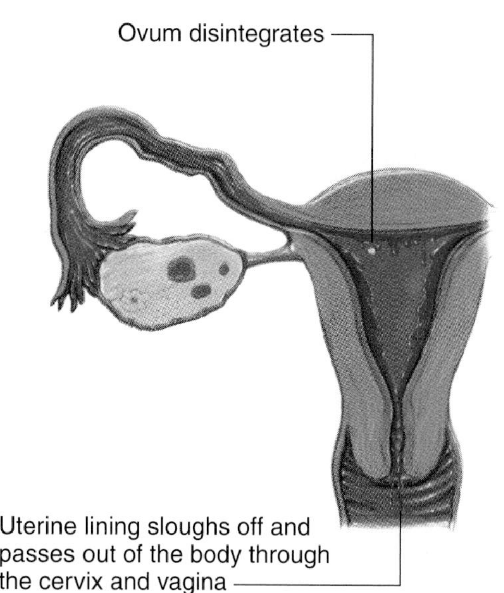

Figure 4.10

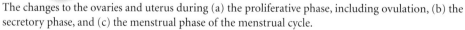

The changes to the ovaries and uterus during (a) the proliferative phase, including ovulation, (b) the secretory phase, and (c) the menstrual phase of the menstrual cycle.

Mittelschmerz is caused by the swelling and bursting of the follicle or by a little fluid or blood from the ruptured follicle irritating the sensitive abdominal lining. The released ovum then travels to the fallopian tube. Occasionally, more than one ovum is released. If two ova are fertilized, nonidentical twins will develop. When one egg is fertilized and then divides into two separate zygotes, identical twins result.

Around the time of ovulation, cervical mucus secretions increase due to increased levels of estrogen. The mucus also changes, becoming clear, slippery, and stretchy. The pH of this mucus is more alkaline; as noted earlier, a more alkaline vaginal environment contributes to sperm motility and longevity. This is the time in the cycle when a woman can most easily become pregnant.

Secretory Phase

During the **secretory phase,** continued pituitary secretions of LH cause the cells of the ruptured follicle to develop into a yellowish bump called the corpus luteum. The corpus luteum secretes progesterone, which inhibits the production of the cervical mucus during ovulation. Together with estrogen produced by the ovaries, progesterone causes the endometrium to thicken and engorge with blood in preparation for implantation of a fertilized egg. If implantation does not occur, the pituitary gland responds to high estrogen and progesterone levels in the bloodstream by shutting down production of LH and FSH. This causes the corpus luteum to degenerate, and estrogen and progesterone production decreases. This reduction of hormone levels triggers the sloughing off of the endometrium, initiating the menstrual phase once again.

Secretory phase
The phase of the menstrual cycle in which the corpus luteum develops and secretes progesterone.

Sexual Activity and the Menstrual Cycle

A number of studies have attempted to determine whether sexual behavior is related to the menstrual cycle, with varied findings. Some studies show little variation in sexual arousal at different points in the menstrual cycle (Meuwissen & Over, 1992). Others suggest that sexual feelings and behavior increase during ovulation (Dennerstein et al., 1994) and also during menstruation and the preceding few days (Friedman et al., 1980). In an attempt to control for external variables such as contraceptive use, fear of pregnancy, and male influence, one study examined the relationship between cycle phase and sexual response and activity in a sample of lesbians. In this sample, partner- and self-initiated sexual activity increased in frequency at midcycle, as did orgasm, but sexual thoughts and fantasies peaked in the first 3 days following the onset of menstruation (Matteo & Rissman, 1984). Great individual variation exists; we encourage women readers and their partners to notice their own patterns.

Intercourse during menstruation is often avoided (Barnhart et al., 1995; Chrisler et al., 1994). One phone interview survey found that 51% of men and 56% of women believed that women should abstain from intercourse during menstruation (Research Forecasts, 1981). Another study found that both men and women initiated substantially fewer sexual activities during menstruation than at any other time during the cycle (Harvey, 1987). Although from a medical point of view there are no health reasons to avoid intercourse during menstruation (except in the case of excessive bleeding or other menstrual problems), many couples do so.

Reasons for avoiding sex during a woman's period vary. Uncomfortable physical symptoms of menstruation can reduce sexual desire or pleasure, and the messiness can inhibit sexual playfulness. Religious beliefs can also be a factor. Some women and men avoid sexual activity because of culturally induced shame about menstruation.

If people do prefer to abstain from coitus during menstruation, the remaining repertoire of sexual activities is still available:

> When I'm on my period, I leave my tampon inside and push the string in, too. My husband and I have manual and oral stimulation, and a great time! (Authors' files)

Some women use a diaphragm to hold back the menstrual flow during coitus. Orgasm by any means of stimulation can be beneficial to a menstruating woman. The uterine contractions and release of vasocongestion often reduce backache, feelings of pelvic fullness, and cramping. As the boxed discussion "Lovemaking and Menstruation" points out, it is helpful for couples to communicate their feelings about sexual activity during menstruation.

Menstrual Cycle Problems

Most women undergo some physical or mood changes, or both, during their menstrual cycles (McFarlane & Williams, 1994). In many cases the changes are minor. In some cases women experience heightened pleasant moods during ovulation or menstruation (McFarlane et al., 1988). At times, problems with the menstrual cycle occur. Negative attitudes about menstruation appear to be related to disruptive and painful menstrual cycle symptoms; women who have problem symptoms have more negative attitudes about menstruation than do women with mild or no symptoms (Woods, 1986). Adolescent females report more acute menstrual distress than do adult females. The relatively unstable hormone shifts during adolescence may predispose them to more menstrual cycle problems (Wilson et al., 1991).

Premenstrual syndrome (PMS)
Symptoms of physical discomfort and emotional irritability, also called premenstrual tension, that occur 2 to 12 days prior to menstruation.

Premenstrual Syndrome

Premenstrual syndrome (PMS) is the term used to identify a myriad of physical and psychological symptoms that occur before each menstrual period and are severe enough to interfere with some aspects of life (Mortola, 1998). It is important to identify the cyclic manifestation of the symptoms in order to differentiate PMS from other physical or psychological problems. Random, community-based studies indicate that 10% to 20% of

Let's Talk About It

Lovemaking and Menstruation

Women who make love regularly have to deal in some way with menstruation, and so do their partners. Caring about a woman's experience during her period may help avoid misunderstanding and build intimacy. For lesbian couples, women are often more naturally attuned to their female partners' menstrual cycles because of their own familiarity with the experience.

A woman's partner might ask her if she gets cramps and, if so, how they feel. Pain is not the only consideration. The bloated feeling caused by water retention may not hurt, but it can be fairly uncomfortable. In some women with pronounced menstrual water retention, it can feel like the flu.

Partners can do several things to help women deal with painful menstruation. They might make a cup of soothing herbal tea—chamomile and mint herb teas may be especially effective—or massage the lower back or abdomen.

Partners can also try to discuss with their lovers how they feel about making love premenstrually or during menstruation. Some women prefer not to; discomfort can interfere with the undivided attention lovemaking deserves. On the other hand, some women say lovemaking right before or during menstruation helps alleviate cramps. During orgasm the uterus contracts, and the cervix opens. This helps speed menstrual flow and can reduce the duration of cramps. Partners should bear in mind, however, that this is not an experience shared by all women. They might also inquire about breast tenderness and keep it in mind during sensual explorations.

Different cultures and religions have different perspectives on lovemaking during a woman's period. As a result, many people—both men and women—have deep feelings about it. It is important to listen carefully to a lover's feelings about making love during menstruation and to try to respect them.

For couples who do make love during a woman's period, there are several things to remember. Menstruation may change a woman's natural vaginal lubrication. Menstrual fluid irritates some penises, but a man can use a condom if this is a problem. Intercourse with a tampon in place is not recommended, but a woman can use a diaphragm or cervical cap to catch the flow. Even if a barrier method is not your primary or preferred form of contraception, you may want to use one at this time.

If a couple would rather not have genital intercourse during a woman's period, there are other satisfying ways to make love (though some couples may prefer to avoid cunnilingus during menstruation).

Whatever an individual or couple prefers, the important thing is to try to communicate as openly as possible about the issues menstruation raises—and to decide together what the most comfortable responses will be. (Adapted from Michael Castleman, 1981)

women experience severe symptoms, and 30% to 50% experience mild or moderate symptoms (Woods et al., 1987). The causes of PMS are unknown, but fluctuations in sex hormones and their effects on various organ systems are believed to be involved (Redei & Freeman, 1995; Schmidt et al., 1998). Some women with PMS symptoms experience stresses and negative life events as more troubling during the premenstrual phase than other times of the month (Berger, 1998; Fontana & Badawy, 1997).

Reported PMS symptoms include negative emotions such as anxiety, irritability, depression, anger, insomnia, confusion, tearfulness, social withdrawal, and uncomfortable physical symptoms such as fluid retention, breast tenderness, weight gain, headaches, dizziness, nausea, increased appetite, and craving for sweets (Fontaine & Seal, 1997; Ginsburg, 1995). These symptoms may vary from mild to severe, and most women experience several of them.

Some PMS symptoms can be disruptive to close relationships. One survey found that partners of women with PMS symptoms reported disruption from increased conflict and withdrawal (Brown & Zimmer, 1986).

Simple measures that improve overall well-being may reduce PMS symptoms (Aganoff & Boyle, 1994; Hatcher et al., 1994; Parker, 1994):

1. Eat a well-balanced diet that is
   a. high in complex carbohydrates with regular, small meals throughout the day
   b. moderate in protein with a minimum of red meat
   c. low in refined sugar and salt
   d. low in tea, coffee, caffeine-containing beverages, chocolate, and alcohol
2. Eliminate smoking.
3. Exercise aerobically at least 30 minutes, three to four times weekly.
4. Practice a relaxation technique twice daily for 15 minutes.

Medications, including antidepressants, may also be helpful (Ginsburg, 1995).

Popular culture, as reflected by the media, tends to put forth negative and distorted perspectives about the menstrual cycle, particularly PMS. An analysis of 78 magazine articles perpetuated the stereotype of the maladjusted woman, listing 131 different symptoms of PMS. Titles include "The Taming of the Shrew Inside of You" and "Premenstrual Frenzy" (Chrisler & Levy, 1990). Most scientific research about menstruation has focused on negative effects. However, one study compared women's responses to a "Menstrual Joy Questionnaire" with those of a commonly used research tool, the "Menstrual Distress Questionnaire." The MJQ's questions about such positive qualities as increased sexual desire, high spirits, feelings of affection, and self-confidence did result in subjects later reporting more positive attitudes and fewer negative symptoms about menstruation. The researchers concluded that the way menstruation is portrayed by research and popular culture affects how women think about their menstrual cycles (Chrisler et al., 1994).

Dysmenorrhea

Painful menstruation is called **dysmenorrhea** (dis´-men-o-RĒ-a). *Primary dysmenorrhea* occurs during menstruation and is usually caused by the overproduction of **prostaglandins,** chemicals that cause the muscles of the uterus to contract. Most uterine contractions are not even noticed, but strong ones are painful. Problems with primary dysmenorrhea usually appear with the onset of menstruation at adolescence. The symptoms are generally most noticeable during the first few days of a woman's period and include abdominal aching and/or cramping (Kennedy, 1997). Some women may also experience nausea, vomiting, diarrhea, headache, dizziness, fatigue, irritability, or nervousness (Hatcher et al., 1994).

Dysmenorrhea
Pain or discomfort before or during menstruation.

Prostaglandins
Hormones that induce uterine contractions.

Secondary dysmenorrhea occurs prior to or during menstruation and is characterized by constant and often spasmodic lower abdominal pain that typically extends to the back and thighs. The symptoms are often similar to those of primary dysmenorrhea and are caused by factors other than prostaglandin production; possible causes include the presence of an intrauterine device (IUD), pelvic inflammatory disease (chronic infection of the reproductive organs), benign uterine tumors, obstruction of the cervical opening, and **endometriosis** (en′-do-MĒ-trē-Ō-sis). This condition, which affects up to 15% of premenopausal women, occurs when endometrial-like tissue implants in the abdominal cavity. The implanted tissue often adheres to other tissue in the pelvic cavity, reducing mobility of the internal structures and engorging with blood during the proliferative phase (Thomas, 1995). The engorged tissues and adhesions can cause painful menstruation, lower backache, and pain from pressure and movement during intercourse (Biley, 1995). Following a diagnosis of the cause of secondary dysmenorrhea, appropriate treatment can be implemented.

Endometriosis
A condition in which uterine tissue grows on various parts of the abdominal cavity.

Amenorrhea

Amenorrhea
The absence of menstruation.

Besides discomfort or pain, another fairly common menstrual difficulty is **amenorrhea** (a-men′-o-RĒ-a), the absence of menstruation. There are two types of amenorrhea—primary and secondary. *Primary amenorrhea* is the failure to begin to menstruate at puberty. It may be caused by problems with the reproductive organs, hormonal imbalances, poor health, or an imperforate hymen. *Secondary amenorrhea* involves the disruption of an established menstrual cycle, with the absence of menstruation for 3 months or more. This is a normal condition during pregnancy and breast-feeding. It is also common in women who have just begun menstruating and women approaching menopause. Sometimes poor health and emotional distress are the causes (Xiao & Ferin, 1997).

Rigorous athletic training can interfere with ovulation. Amenorrhea is more common among athletes than among the general population (Odden & Daniel, 1998). It is not known whether the disruption of normal menstrual cycles in athletes is caused by intensive exercise, low body fat, the physical or emotional stress of training and competing, or a combination of all of these (McGee, 1997).

Recent research indicates that women who experience athletic amenorrhea also experience decreased estrogen levels. This reduction in estrogen may place them at increased risk for developing serious health problems such as decreased bone mineral density with a resultant increased incidence of bone fractures, and atrophy of the genital tissues. Athletic amenorrhea may be reversed by improving diet, gaining weight, or in some cases, decreasing training intensity. If these modifications in lifestyle are unacceptable or ineffective, estrogen therapy may be indicated (Epp, 1997).

Medical or hormonal problems can produce amenorrhea (Hagan & Knott, 1998). Women with *anorexia nervosa,* an eating disorder that often results in extreme weight loss, frequently stop menstruating due to hormonal changes that accompany emaciation (Schweiger, 1991). Women who discontinue the birth control pill occasionally do not resume menstruation for several months, but this situation is usually temporary and resolves spontaneously. It is a good idea for a woman who does not have a period within a week of when expected to consult a health care practitioner (Schachter & Shoham, 1994).

Self-Help for Menstrual Problems

Women may be able to alleviate some of the unpleasant symptoms accompanying menstruation by their own actions. Moderate exercise throughout the month, as well as proper diet, can contribute to improvement of menstrual-related difficulties. For example, an increase in fluids and fiber helps with the constipation that sometimes occurs before and during menstruation. Decreasing salt intake and avoiding food high in salt (salad dressing, potato chips, bacon, pickles, to name a few) can help reduce swelling and bloating caused by water retention. Food supplements such as calcium, magnesium, and B vitamins may also help relieve cramps and bloating. For PMS symptoms such as anxiety and irritability, the suggestions on page 107 may be helpful.

A woman who experiences menstrual-related pain may find it useful to keep a diary to track symptoms, stresses, and daily habits such as exercise, diet, and sleep. She may be able to note a relationship between symptoms and habits and modify her activities accordingly. The information may also be helpful for specific diagnosis if she consults a health care practitioner.

Toxic Shock Syndrome

In May 1980, the Centers for Disease Control (CDC) published the first report of **toxic shock syndrome (TSS)** in menstruating women. Symptoms of TSS, which is caused by toxins produced by the bacterium *Staphylococcus aureus,* include fever, sore throat, nausea, vomiting, diarrhea, red skin flush, dizziness, and low blood pressure (Hanrahan, 1994). Because TSS progresses rapidly and can cause death, a person with several of the symptoms of TSS should consult a physician immediately.

Toxic shock syndrome (TSS) A disease that may cause a person to go into shock, occurring most commonly in menstruating women.

TSS is a rare disease and the number of TSS cases reported has fallen sharply since the peak in 1980, due likely to the removal of highly absorbent tampons from the market (Petitti & Reingold, 1988). Some guidelines have been developed that may help prevent toxic shock. One suggestion has been to use sanitary napkins instead of tampons. For women who want to continue using tampons, it is advisable to use regular instead of super-absorbent tampons, to change them three to four times during the day, and to use napkins for some time during each 24 hours of menstrual flow. A woman should consult her health care practitioner for further up-to-date suggestions pertaining to prevention and detection of TSS.

Menopause

The term **climacteric** (klī-MAK-ter-ik) refers to the physiological changes that occur during the transition period from fertility to infertility in both sexes. In women around 40 years of age, the ovaries begin to slow the production of estrogen. The period prior to complete cessation of menstruation is called *perimenopause.* Menstruation continues, but cycles may become irregular, with erratic and absent or heavy bleeding as menopause approaches. Up to 90% of women may experience a change in menstrual patterns and sexual response prior to menopause (Mansfield et al., 1995). **Menopause,** one of the events of the female climacteric, refers to the permanent cessation of menstruation. Menopause occurs as a result of certain physiological changes and takes place at a mean age of 51. Research indicates that women who experience earlier menopause began their periods by age 11, had shorter cycle lengths, had fewer pregnancies, and had less time of oral contraceptive use than women who experienced menopause later. In essence, many women who have early menopause have a history of more ovulatory cycles (Cramer et al., 1995).

Climacteric Physiological changes that occur during the transition period from fertility to infertility in both sexes.

Menopause Cessation of menstruation due to the aging process or surgical removal of the ovaries.

The general public and the medical community have begun to focus more on menopause because of the great increase in the number of women who live many years after menopause. In 1900 in the United States the average life expectancy of a woman was 51 years. Today the average life expectancy for women is 82 years. Currently, 40 million women in the United States are postmenopausal (Begley & Springen, 1997). By the year 2020, there will be 60 million postmenopausal women. In practical terms, this means that most women experience the second half of their adult life following menopause; menopause can be seen as the gateway to a second adulthood (Sheehy, 1993). There are already signs that the "baby boom" generation will encourage the health care system to deal with menopause more thoroughly than before (Andrews, 1995).

During menopause, the pituitary continues to secrete follicle-stimulating hormone (FSH); however, the ovaries cease production of mature ova. Ovarian estrogen output also slows, although the adrenals, liver, and adipose (fat) tissue continue to produce some estrogen after menopause. After menopause, the ovaries and the adrenal glands continue to produce androgens (Hughes et al., 1991).

Menopause is often surrounded by confusion. The experience varies greatly from woman to woman. Some women may experience few physical symptoms other than cessation of menstruation. For these women, menopause is surprisingly uneventful:

After hearing comments for years about how menopause was so traumatic, I was ready for the worst. I was sure surprised when I realized I had hardly noticed it happening. (Authors' files)

In addition, most women feel relieved that they no longer need to be concerned about pregnancy, contraception, and menstruation. They may experience an increased sense of freedom in sexual intimacy as a result.

However, for many women, menopause brings a range of symptoms that can vary from mild to severe. These symptoms are caused by the decline in estrogen. The most acute menopausal symptoms occur in the two years prior and two years following the last menstrual period. A woman in her 40s may first notice changes in her menstrual flow and sleep patterns. "Hot flashes" and night sweats are also common difficulties. Hot flashes can range from a mild feeling of warmth to a feeling of intense heat and profuse perspiration, especially around the chest, neck, and face. A severe hot flash can soak clothing or sheets in perspiration. The flashes usually last for three to six minutes, though they may last up to an hour. Hot flashes occur because hormones influence the nerves that control the blood vessels. As hormone levels fluctuate, the diameter of the blood vessels changes. Rapid dilation of the vessels causes a woman to experience a momentary rush of heat. The sensation can be quite disconcerting. Hot flashes can occur several times a day and during sleep; they usually cease within two years. About 75% of women will experience hot flashes (Shaw, 1997). Women smokers experience hot flashes more frequently than nonsmokers (Staropoli et al., 1997). Some women report a decrease in frequency of intercourse during the period in which they are experiencing hot flashes (McCoy et al., 1985).

Other symptoms arising from the decrease in estrogen can significantly affect a woman's daily life. Sleep disturbance may increase during menopause. A typical example is a woman who can readily fall asleep but wakes one or more times during the night feeling agitated and has difficulty falling back to sleep. This pattern can easily result in fatigue and irritability during the day. Menopausal symptoms can also include dizziness, difficulty with balance, diminished pleasure from touch, itchy or burning skin, sensitivity to clothing or touch, and numbness or tingling in hands and feet. In addition, estrogen deficiency can cause severe headaches, short-term memory loss, difficulty concentrating, depression, and increased anxiety (Pearce et al., 1997; Yaffe et al., 1998).

Hormone-Replacement Therapy

Hormone-replacement therapy (HRT)
The use of supplemental hormones during and after menopause.

Hormone-replacement therapy (HRT) involves taking supplemental estrogen, progesterone, and possibly testosterone to compensate for the decrease in natural hormone production that occurs during the female climacteric. About 25% of postmenopausal women use some form of HRT (Ginsburg et al., 1996). HRT may alleviate some of the problems resulting from the significant reduction in estrogen after menopause.

Given what you have learned about menopause, what difficulties do you think HRT could ameliorate or resolve?

The estrogen in HRT can contribute to a woman's general sense of well-being by reducing hot flashes as well as the depression, sleep disturbances, and anxiety caused by estrogen deficiency (Karlberg et al., 1995). In addition to these benefits, HRT can provide some very real health benefits. It significantly increases a woman's protection against life-threatening *osteoporosis* (abnormal bone loss) and resultant fractures, particularly of the hip (Hart & Magos, 1998). Estrogen also provides strong protection from cardiovascular disease (Brinton & Schainer, 1997). Its use reduces the incidence of Alzheimer's disease

(Hardee, 1997; Chen et al., 1998). It can help maintain the urethral and vaginal tissues, vaginal lubrication, clitoral sensitivity, orgasmic response, and sexual interest (Barlow et al., 1997; Smith, 1998), all of which may be affected in some women at around the age of menopause. Including testosterone in the hormone replacement may be particularly helpful in maintaining sexual desires (Crenshaw, 1996), as discussed further in Chapter 6.

A significant increase in the incidence of endometrial cancer has been associated with the exclusive and continuous use of estrogen (Rabin, 1998). Now, however, it is common practice to combine progestin with estrogen for about 10 days out of a 30-day cycle. The addition of progestin has reduced, but not eliminated, the risk of endometrial cancer with HRT (Beresford et al., 1997; McGonigle, 1997). The progestin causes the uterine lining to shed each month, and a monthly flow results. When this occurs, it is less likely that the lining will develop cancer from estrogen stimulation. Women who have had a hysterectomy do not need to take progestin, because they have no risk of uterine cancer (von Schoultz, 1997).

Progestins may reduce the beneficial effect of estrogen in protecting against heart disease by unfavorably altering the type of fats in the bloodstream. The risks of heart disease are significantly increased in smokers, diabetics, the very obese, women who do not exercise, and women with high blood pressure and high cholesterol levels.

Women who have endometrial cancer or estrogen-dependent breast cancer cannot receive HRT because it can accelerate the rate of growth of these cancers. HRT does not cause these cancers; in fact, taking low-dose estrogen combined with progesterone reduces the chances of developing breast cancer. Women who need to be most cautious about HRT are those who have benign breast tumors or a strong family history of mothers or sisters with estrogen-dependent breast cancer (Kenemans et al., 1997). (Breast cancer that occurs after menopause is usually non-estrogen-dependent.)

Current research suggests that a menopausal woman should weigh the potential benefits and risks of hormone-replacement therapy against the symptoms of hormone deficiency (Grodstein, 1997). For many women, the benefits far outweigh the potential risks (Hartmann & Huber, 1997; Kenemans, 1997). We recommend thorough discussion of the matter with a physician specializing in menopause and HRT.

A new option in hormone replacement therapy to address the risks of breast and uterine cancer became available in 1998. Pharmaceutical companies are developing new forms of estrogen they hope will bring all the benefits but none of the risks of estrogen. Called SERMS, selective estrogen receptor modulators, they mimic estrogen in some sites in the body and interfere with estrogen at others. This allows the medication to provide the beneficial effects of estrogen on heart disease, cholesterol, and bone loss while acting like a protective antiestrogen for breast and uterine cancer. Research results appear positive, but many questions remain to be answered fully (Begley & Springen, 1997; Mestel, 1997).

There are also some alternatives to HRT. Continued frequent sexual activity helps maintain vaginal lubrication during sexual arousal. Research has found that vaginal changes due to aging are less pronounced in women who are sexually active through intercourse or masturbation than in sexually inactive women. Vaginal lubricants and moisturizers can also be used to help with vaginal lubrication. Physical exercise, good nutrition, and food supplements can sometimes alleviate some menopausal symptoms (Slaven & Lee, 1997). For example, the American Heart Association reports that soy protein, such as found in tofu, can reduce the intensity of hot flashes and night sweats in some women (Barile, 1997).

Summary

GENITAL SELF-EXAM

Genital self-exploration is a good way for a woman to learn about her own body and to notice any changes that may require medical attention.

THE VULVA

The female external genitals, also called the vulva, are composed of the mons veneris, labia majora, labia minora, clitoris, and urethral and vaginal openings. Each woman's vulva is unique in shape, color, and texture.

The mons veneris and labia majora have underlying pads of fatty tissue and are covered by pubic hair beginning at adolescence.

The labia minora are folds of sensitive skin that begin at the hood over the clitoris and extend downward to below the vaginal opening, or introitus. The area between them is called the vestibule.

The clitoris is composed of the external glans and shaft and the internal crura. The glans contains densely concentrated nerve endings. The only function of the clitoris is sexual pleasure.

The urethral opening is located between the clitoris and vaginal introitus.

Many cultures have placed great importance on the hymen as proof of virginity. However, there are various sizes, shapes, and thicknesses of hymens, and many women can have initial intercourse without pain or bleeding. Also, women who have decided to have coitus can learn how to stretch their hymens to help make their first experience comfortable.

UNDERLYING STRUCTURES

Below the surface of the vulva are the vestibular bulbs and the pelvic floor muscles.

INTERNAL STRUCTURES

The vagina, with its three layers of tissue, extends about 3 to 5 inches into the pelvic cavity. It is a potential rather than an actual space and increases in size during sexual arousal, coitus, and childbirth. The other internal reproductive structures are the cervix, uterus, fallopian tubes, and ovaries.

Vaginal lubrication, the secretion of alkaline fluid through the vaginal walls during arousal, is important both in enhancing the longevity and motility of sperm cells and in increasing the pleasure and comfort of intercourse.

The Grafenberg spot is located about 1 centimeter from the surface of the top wall of the vagina. Many women report erotic sensitivity to pressure in some area of their vaginas.

The vaginal walls and cervix produce normal secretions.

GYNECOLOGICAL HEALTH CONCERNS

About one out of every five women will experience a urinary tract infection caused by bacteria that enter the urethra.

Occasionally, a vaginal infection occurs that results in irritation, unusual discharge, or a disagreeable odor.

The Pap smear has reduced deaths from cervical cancer significantly.

There is considerable medical controversy about the appropriate use of hysterectomy. A hysterectomy or oophorectomy may, in some cases, have an effect—either positive or negative—on a woman's sexuality.

THE BREASTS

The breasts are composed of fatty tissue and milk-producing glands. A monthly self-exam of the breasts is an important part of health care.

Three types of lumps can appear in the breasts: cysts, fibroadenomas, and malignant tumors. Careful diagnosis of a breast lump is important. Mammography and other tests can help detect and diagnose breast cancer. Less radical surgeries for breast cancer are often as effective as more severe procedures.

MENSTRUATION

The menstrual cycle results from a complex interplay of hormones. The cycle is divided into the proliferative, the secretory, and the menstrual phases. Although negative social attitudes have been historically attached to menstruation, some people are currently redefining it in a more positive fashion.

There are usually no medical reasons to abstain from intercourse during menstruation. However, many people do limit their sexual activity during this time.

Some women have difficulties with premenstrual syndrome (PMS) or primary or secondary dysmenorrhea. Knowledge about the physiological factors that contribute to these problems is increasing, and some of the problems can be treated.

Amenorrhea occurs normally during pregnancy, while breastfeeding, and after menopause. It can also be due to medical problems or poor health.

Toxic shock syndrome (TSS) is a rare condition that occurs most often in menstruating women. Its symptoms include fever, sore throat, nausea, red skin flush, dizziness, and low blood pressure. If untreated, it can be fatal.

MENOPAUSE

Menopause is the cessation of menstruation and signals the end of female fertility. Fifty-one is the average age of menopause. Due to increases in life expectancy, women can expect to live half of their adult lives following menopause.

Most women experience few uncomfortable symptoms during the aging process and maintain sexual interest and response. Others experience symptoms such as hot flashes, sleep disturbance, depression or anxiety, headaches, and sensitivity to touch due to declining estrogen levels.

Hormone-replacement therapy (HRT) is a medical treatment for menopausal symptoms and helps protect against osteoporosis and heart disease. Potential side effects necessitate careful use of such therapy. Continued sexual activity also helps maintain sexual functioning.

Thought Provokers

1. What factors have influenced your positive and negative feelings about your body and your vulva?
2. If a good friend of yours were told she needed a hysterectomy, how would you advise her?
3. What do you observe in the media and in others' comments and reactions that indicate positive and negative attitudes about menstruation and menopause?

Suggested Readings

Crawford, Amanda (1996). *The Herbal Menopause Book.* Freedom, CA: Crossing Press. A practical guide for herbal, nutrition, and mind–body techniques for helping with menopause.

Bouris, Karen (1993). *The First Time.* Berkeley, CA: Conari Press. A collection of personal stories about "losing virginity" as a pivotal female experience.

LaTour, Kathy (1993). *The Breast Cancer Companion.* New York: Morrow. A comprehensive book about breast care and concerns, including diverse personal accounts.

Love, Susan (1997). *Dr. Susan Love's Hormone Book.* New York: Random House. Provides information on coping with menopause and making informed choices.

Malesky, Gale; and Inlander, Charles (1991). *Take This Book to the Gynecologist with You.* Reading, MA: Addison-Wesley. A comprehensive guide to women's health care.

Meshorer, Marc; and Meshorer, Judith (1986). *Ultimate Pleasure: The Secrets of Easily Orgasmic Women.* New York: St. Martin's Press. Based on in-depth interviews with easily orgasmic women, this book describes how women take an active role in creating, building, and experiencing arousal.

Murcia, Andy; and Stewart, Bob (1989). *Man to Man: When the Woman You Love Has Breast Cancer.* New York: St. Martin's Press. Personal stories and practical information for men confronted with their partners' diagnosis of breast cancer.

Northrup, Christiane (1994). *Women's Bodies, Women's Wisdom.* New York: Bantam. A book about women's health issues, with a holistic health perspective.

Our Gift of Love (1996.) Salt Lake City: Gibbs Smith. Personal stories of breast cancer courage. Women and family members write their poignant experiences with breast cancer from diagnosis to reconstruction.

Steinem, Gloria (1978). "If Men Could Menstruate." *Ms.,* October. A humorous yet provocative "political fantasy" about how menstruation would be treated in our society if men, instead of women, menstruated.

Resources

1. The National Alliance of Breast Cancer Organizations (NABCO). 1-888-80-NABCO (1-888-806-2226) www.nabco.org. Leading information resource on breast cancer and network of breast cancer organizations. Provides assistance and referral about breast cancer, and voices the interests of survivors and women at risk. The quarterly *NABCO News* updates professionals and the public about research, programs, and policy. Annual list compiles books, brochures, hotlines, and video resources useful to patients and professionals.
2. American Cancer Society
   1-800-ACS-2345 (1-800-227-2345)
   www.cancer.org
3. Breast Cancer Resource Committee
   (202) 463-8020
4. Cancer Care, Inc.
   1-800-813-HOPE (1-800-813-4673)
   www.cancercareinc.org
5. Hadassah (the leading Jewish women's organization)
   (212) 303-8094
   www.hadassah.org

Web Resources

www.

Gyn101
www.gyn101.com/
A visit to this Web site walks you through a first visit to a gynecologist. How to choose a gynecologist, what to expect in a gynecological exam, a glossary, suggested readings, and questions to ask your health care provider are among the resources available.

OBGYN.net Women and Patients
www.obgyn.net/women/women.htm
This site includes valuable reference information on gynecological health, as well as columns from contributors, selected articles from the journal *The Female Patient,* a weekly chat schedule on women's health topics, and an extensive array of Web links to related sites.

North American Menopause Society
www.menopause.org/home.htm
The resources available at this Web site include basic facts about menopause, frequently asked questions (FAQs), and educational materials available both to consumers and health care providers.

5

Male Sexual Anatomy and Physiology

Sexual Anatomy

What are the major external and internal male sex structures, and what functions do they serve?

Why is it important to conduct regular genital self-exams, and what should a man look for?

Male Sexual Functions

What physiological processes cause an erection? How do psychological and physiological factors interact to influence erections?

How does ejaculation occur?

Some Concerns About Sexual Functioning

How does penis size affect sexual interaction?

Why are most males circumcised shortly after birth? What is the current medical evidence regarding the value and risks of circumcision?

Male Genital Health Concerns

What kinds of diseases and injuries affect the male genital and reproductive structures, and how are these conditions treated?

Why is it important for men to be aware of the importance of routine examinations of the prostate gland?

Who needs a lecture on male anatomy? Certainly not the men in this class. It's hanging out there all our lives. We handle and look at it each time we pee or bathe. So what's the mystery? Now the female body—that's a different story. That's why I'm in the class. Let's learn something that isn't so obvious. (Authors' files)

This quote, from a student in a sexuality class, illustrates two common assumptions. The first is that male sexual anatomy is simple. All you need to know is "hanging out there." The second, perhaps more subtle, implication is that female genital structures are considerably more complicated and mysterious than are men's.

These assumptions call for some rethinking, for a few reasons. One is that there is more than meets the eye. In the sexual anatomy of men as well as women, there is complexity as well as wide variation from one individual to another. Another reason is that knowing about our own sexual anatomy and functioning, although it does not guarantee sexual satisfaction, at least provides a degree of comfort with our bodies and perhaps a greater ability to communicate with a partner. Equally important, an understanding of our own bodies provides an important basis for detecting potential health problems. This chapter provides information that every man should know regarding self-exams and health care. (For further information on this important topic, see the list of Suggested Readings at the end of this chapter.)

More than one teacher of human sexuality has noted that students "think they know everything" about their own anatomy . . . until their first exam. For this reason, we begin this chapter by issuing a challenge: Do you know the answers to the following questions?

- What is the content of semen, and where is semen produced?
- Are male orgasm and ejaculation one and the same process?
- Do circumcised men have greater erotic sensation than uncircumcised men?
- Does testicular cancer generally produce soreness and discomfort?

As you read the answers in the following pages, note that health-related information is marked with a special icon. As in Chapter 4, we encourage readers to use the pages that follow as a reference for their own self-knowledge and improved health.

Sexual Anatomy

We begin with discussions of the various structures of the male sexual anatomy. Descriptive accounts are organized according to parts of the genital system, for easy reference. Later in this chapter (and in Chapter 6), we will look more closely at the way the entire system functions during sexual arousal.

Penis
A male sexual organ consisting of the internal root and external shaft and glans.

Root
The portion of the penis that extends internally into the pelvic cavity.

Shaft
The length of the penis between the glans and the body.

Glans
The head of the penis; richly endowed with nerve endings.

Cavernous bodies
The structures in the shaft of the penis that engorge with blood during sexual arousal.

The Penis

The **penis** consists of nerves, blood vessels, fibrous tissue, and three parallel cylinders of spongy tissue. It does not contain a bone, nor an abundance of muscular tissue, contrary to some people's beliefs. However, an extensive network of muscles are present at the base of the penis. These muscles help eject both semen and urine through the urethra.

A portion of the penis extends internally into the pelvic cavity. This part, including its attachment to the pubic bones, is referred to as the **root.** When a man's penis is erect, he can feel this inward projection by pressing a finger up between his anus and scrotum. The external, pendulous portion of the penis, excluding the head, is known as the **shaft.** The smooth, acorn-shaped head is called the **glans.**

Running the entire length of the penis are the three chambers referred to earlier. The two larger ones, the **cavernous bodies** *(corpora cavernosa),* lie side by side above the

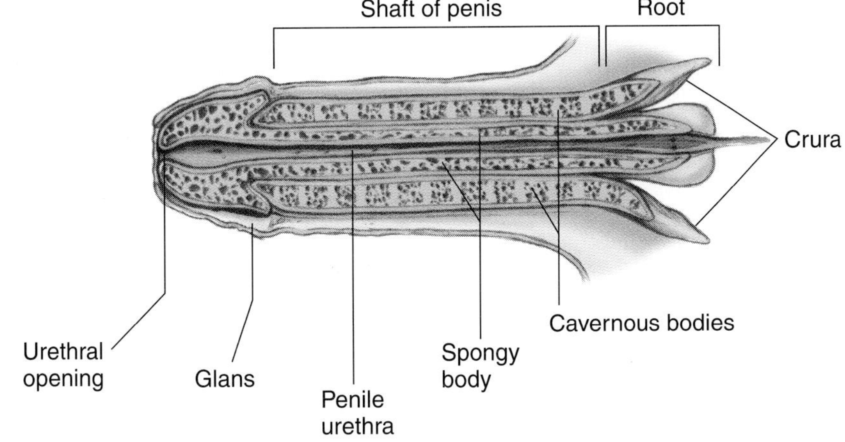

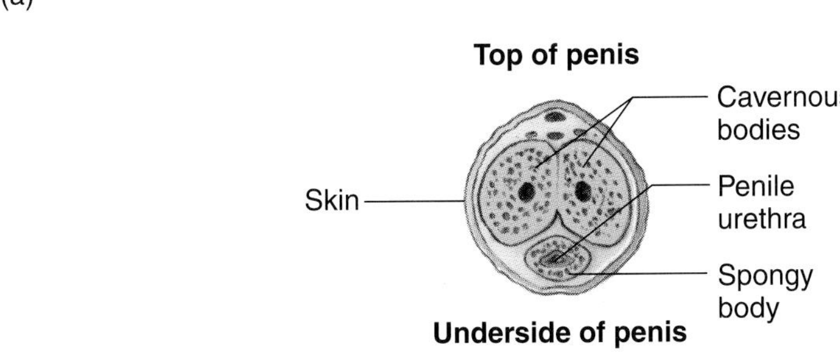

Figure 5.1

Interior structure of the penis: (a) side view and (b) cross section of the penis.

smaller third cylinder, the **spongy body** *(corpus spongiosum).* At the root of the penis, the innermost tips of the cavernous bodies, or *crura,* are connected to the pubic bones. At the head of the penis, the spongy body expands to form the glans. These structures are shown in Figure 5.1.

Spongy body
A chamber that forms a bulb at the base of the penis, extends up into the penile shaft, and forms the penile glans.

All these chambers are similar in structure. As the terms *cavernous* and *spongy* imply, they are made of spongelike irregular spaces and cavities. Each chamber is also richly supplied with blood vessels. When a male is sexually excited, the chambers become engorged with blood, resulting in penile erection. During sexual arousal, the spongy body may stand out as a distinct ridge along the underside of the penis.

The skin covering the penile shaft is usually hairless and quite loose, which allows for expansion when the penis becomes erect. Although the skin is connected to the shaft at the neck (the portion just behind the glans), some of it folds over and forms a cuff, or hood, over the glans. This loose covering is called the **foreskin,** or *prepuce.* In some males it covers the entire head, whereas in others only a portion is covered. Typically, the foreskin can be retracted (drawn back from the glans) quite easily. *Circumcision* involves the surgical removal of this sleeve of skin. Although familiar in our culture, circumcision is only one of many procedures for altering male genitalia that are practiced around the world (see the boxed discussion, "Male Genital Modification and Mutilation: Some Cultural Beliefs and Practices"). Circumcision is also discussed at greater length later in this chapter.

Foreskin
A covering of skin over the penile glans.

The entire penis is sensitive to touch, but the greatest concentration of nerve endings is found in the glans. Although the entire glans area is extremely sensitive, there are two specific locations that many men find particularly responsive to stimulation. One is the rim, or crown, that marks the area where the glans rises abruptly from the shaft. This distinct ridge is called the **corona** (ko-RŌ-na). The other is the **frenulum** (FREN-yoo-lum), a thin strip of skin connecting the glans to the shaft on the underside of the penis. The location of these two areas is shown in Figure 5.2.

Corona
The rim of the penile glans.

Frenulum
A highly sensitive, thin strip of skin that connects the glans to the shaft on the underside of the penis.

Most men enjoy having the glans stimulated, particularly the two areas just mentioned, but individuals vary in their preferences. Some may occasionally or routinely prefer being stimulated in genital areas other than the glans of the penis. The mode of stimulation, either manual (by self or partner) or oral, may influence the choice of preferred sites. Some of these variations and individual preferences are noted in the following accounts:

When I masturbate I frequently avoid the head of my penis, concentrating instead on stroking the shaft. The stimulation is not so intense, which allows a longer time for buildup to orgasm. The result is that the climax is generally more intense than if I focus only on the glans. (Authors' files)

During oral sex with my girlfriend, I sometimes have to put my hand around my penis, leaving just the head sticking out, so she will get the idea what part feels best. Otherwise, she spends a lot of time running her tongue up and down the shaft, which just doesn't do it for me. (Authors' files)

Strengthening Musculature Around the Penis

As previously mentioned, the internal extension of the penis is surrounded by an elaborate network of muscles. This musculature is comparable to that in the female body, and strengthening these muscles by doing Kegel exercises may produce benefits for men similar to those experienced by women. In most men these muscles are quite weak because they are usually only contracted during ejaculation. The following is a brief out-

Sexuality and Diversity

Male Genital Modification and Mutilation: Some Cultural Beliefs and Practices

Throughout the world, people hold strong beliefs about the importance and implications of altering male genitals using a variety of procedures. These rituals and customs have been chronicled through the ages. (Female genital mutilation is also widespread, as was discussed in Chapter 4.)

The most common genital alteration is *circumcision,* the surgical removal of the foreskin. Circumcision is practiced in many societies for religious, ritual, or hygienic reasons. Historically, this is a very old practice. Examinations of Egyptian mummies have revealed evidence of circumcision as far back as 6000 B.C., and Egyptian records at least 5000 years old depict circumcised men.

For thousands of years, Jews have practiced circumcision according to scripture (Genesis 17:9–27) as a religious rite. The ceremony, called a *bris,* takes place on the eighth day after birth. Similarly, the followers of Islam also have a long-standing tradition of circumcision. Although circumcision is widespread among Middle Eastern and African societies, it is relatively uncommon in Europe today.

A variation of circumcision, called *superincision* (in which the foreskin, instead of being removed, is split lengthwise and folded back) is practiced among certain South Pacific cultures as a kind of rite of passage or initiation ritual into sexual maturity. Mangaia and the Marquesan Islands are two societies where this procedure is performed when a boy reaches adolescence (Marshall, 1971; Suggs, 1962).

Castration, removal of the testes, represents a more extreme male genital mutilation that also has its roots in antiquity. This practice has been justified for a variety of reasons: to prevent sexual activity between harem guards (eunuchs) and their charges; to render war captives docile; to preserve the soprano voices of European choirboys during the Middle Ages; and as part of religious ceremonies (in ancient Egypt, hundreds of young boys were castrated in a single ceremony). In the United States, castration was sometimes performed during the mid-nineteenth century as a purported "cure" for the evils of masturbation. During this same time period, American medical journals also reported that castration was often a successful treatment for "insanity."

In more modern times, castrations have occasionally been performed for legal reasons, either as a method of eugenic selection (for example, to prevent a mentally disabled person from having offspring), or as an alleged deterrent to sex offenders (see Chapter 6). The ethical basis of these operations is highly controversial. Finally, castration is sometimes performed as medical treatment for diseases such as prostate cancer and genital tuberculosis (Albertsen et al., 1997; Silver et al., 1991).

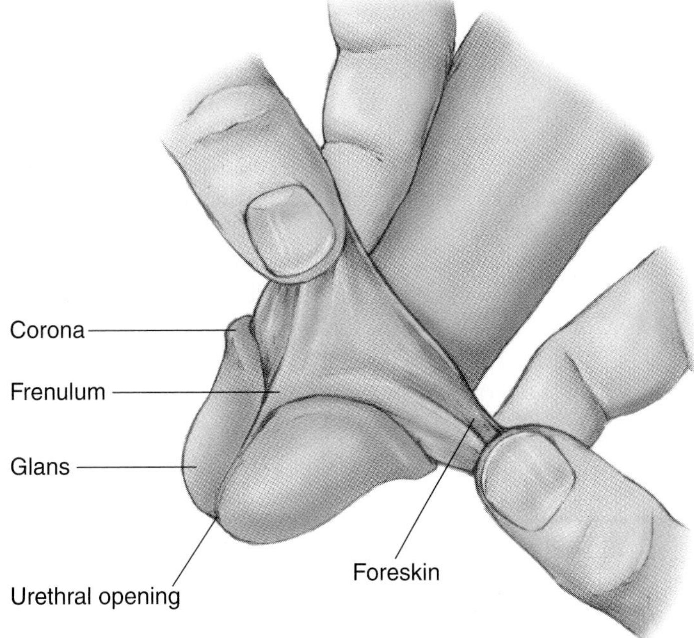

Figure 5.2

This figure, a view of the underside of the penis, shows the location of the corona and frenulum—two areas on the penis that harbor a high concentration of sensitive nerve endings.

line of how these muscles may be located and strengthened, adapted from *Male Sexuality* (Zilbergeld, 1978, p. 109):

1. Locate the muscles by stopping the flow of urine several times while urinating. The muscles you squeeze to accomplish this are the ones on which you will concentrate. If you do a correct Kegel while not urinating, you will notice your penis move slightly. Kegels done when you have an erection will cause your penis to move up and down.
2. Begin the exercise program by squeezing and relaxing the muscles 15 times, twice daily. Do not hold the contraction at this stage. (These are called "short Kegels.")
3. Gradually increase the number of Kegels until you can comfortably do 60 at a time, twice daily.
4. Now practice "long Kegels" by holding each contraction for a count of three.
5. Combine the short and long Kegels in each daily exercise routine, doing a set of 60 of each, once or twice a day.
6. Continue with the Kegel exercises for at least several weeks. You may not notice results until a month or more has passed. By this time the exercises will probably have become automatic, requiring no particular effort.

Some of the positive changes men have reported after doing the male Kegels include stronger and more pleasurable orgasms, better ejaculatory control, and increased pelvic sensation during sexual arousal.

The Scrotum

The **scrotum** (SKRŌ-tum), or scrotal sac, is a loose pouch of skin that is an outpocket of the abdominal wall in the groin area directly underneath the penis (see Figure 5.3). Normally, it hangs loosely from the body wall, although influences such as cold temperatures or sexual stimulation may cause it to move closer to the body.

Scrotum
The pouch of skin of the external male genitals that encloses the testicles.

The scrotal sac consists of two layers. The outermost is a covering of thin skin that is darker in color than other body skin. It typically becomes sparsely covered with hair at adolescence. The second layer, known as the *tunica dartos,* is composed of smooth muscle fibers and fibrous connective tissue.

Within the scrotal sac are two separate compartments, each of which houses a single **testis** (plural *testes*), or *testicle.* (For a diagram of the testis within the scrotal sac, see

Testis
Male gonad inside the scrotum that produces sperm and sex hormones.

Spermatic cord
A cord attached to the testicle that contains the vas deferens, blood vessels, nerves, and cremasteric muscle fibers.

Figure 5.4.) Each testis is suspended within its compartment by the **spermatic** (sper-MAT-ik) **cord.** The spermatic cord contains the sperm-carrying tube, or *vas deferens,* as well as blood vessels, nerves, and *cremasteric muscle* fibers that influence the position of the testicle in the scrotal sac. These muscles can be voluntarily contracted, causing the testicles to move upward. Most males find they can produce this effect with practice; this exercise is one way for a man to become more familiar with his body. As shown in Figure 5.3, you can locate the spermatic cord by palpating the scrotal sac above either testicle with thumb and forefinger. The cord is a firm, rubbery tube that is generally quite pronounced.

The scrotum is very sensitive to any temperature change, and numerous sensory receptors in its skin provide information that prevents the testicles from becoming either too warm or too cold. When the scrotum is cooled, the tunica dartos contracts, wrinkling the outer skin layer and pulling the testicles up closer to the warmth of the body. This process is involuntary, and the reaction sometimes has amusing ramifications:

When I took swimming classes in high school, the trip back to the locker room was always a bit traumatic. After peeling off my swimsuit, it seemed like I had to search around for my balls. The other guys seemed to have the same problem, since they were also frantically tugging and pulling to get everything back in place. (Authors' files)

Are you aware of any types of stimulation, other than cold, that influence the position of the scrotum?

Figure 5.3

The scrotum and the testes. The spermatic cord can be located by palpating the scrotal sac above either testicle with thumb and forefinger.

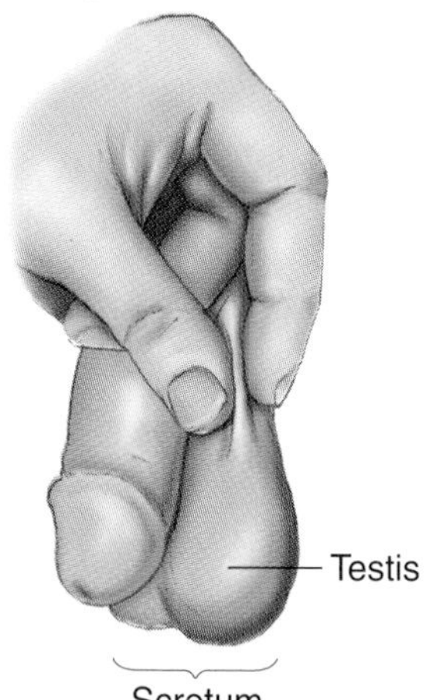

Another kind of stimulation that causes the scrotum to draw closer to the body is sexual arousal. One of the clearest external indications of impending male orgasm is the drawing up of the testicles to a position of maximum elevation. The major scrotal muscle involved in this response is the cremasteric muscle, mentioned earlier. Sudden fear may also cause strong contractions of this muscle, and it is also possible to initiate contractions by stroking the inner thighs. This response is known as the *cremasteric reflex.*

The movements of the testes and scrotal sac are influenced by factors other than temperature change, sexual arousal, and strong emotion. These structures have the rather amazing property of virtually constant movement, a result of the continuous contraction–relaxation cycles of the cremasteric musculature.

The Testes

The testes, or testicles, have two major functions: the secretion of male sex hormones and the production of sperm. The testes form inside the abdominal cavity, and late in fetal development they migrate through the *inguinal canal* from the abdomen to the scrotum (Clarnette et al., 1997).

Cryptorchidism
A condition in which the testicles fail to descend from the abdominal cavity to the scrotal sac.

At birth the testes are normally in the scrotum, but in some cases one or both fail to descend. This condition, known as **cryptorchidism** (krip-TOR-ki-dizm) (meaning "hidden testis"), affects 3% to 4% of newborn boys (McClure, 1988). Undescended testicles often move into place spontaneously sometime after birth, usually in the first year or two, and no treatment is needed.

There are reasons why it is important for new parents to watch out for undescended testes, especially when both testicles are affected. For one, sperm production is affected by temperature. Average scrotal temperature is approximately 3.1°C (5.6°F) lower than body temperature (Tessler & Krahn, 1966), and sperm production appears to be optimal at this lower temperature. Undescended testicles remain at internal body temperature, which is too high to permit sperm production, and infertility may result (Parrott, 1989). In addition to being a factor in infertility, cryptorchidism is also associated with an increased risk for developing a hernia or testicular cancer (Rao et al., 1991; Walbrecker, 1995). Surgical or hormonal treatment may be necessary to allow the testicles to descend (Elder, 1988; Moul & Belman, 1988). However, surgical repair does not always correct infertility. That is because associated abnormalities may also exist in another structure, the *epididymis* (discussed shortly). These abnormalities can interfere with the production

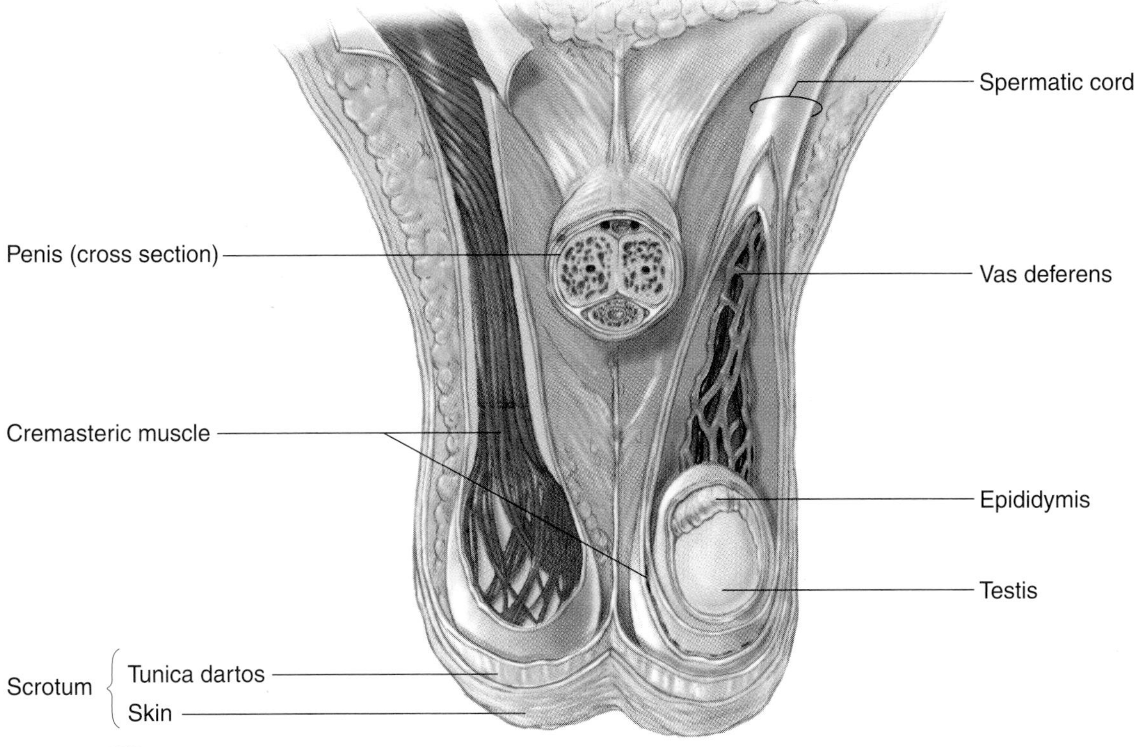

Figure 5.4

Underlying structures of the scrotum. This illustration shows portions of the scrotum cut away to reveal the cremasteric muscle, spermatic cord, vas deferens, and a testis within the scrotal sac.

and/or transportation of sperm even after the position of the testes has been corrected (Koff & Scaletscky, 1990).

Because sperm production is inhibited by heat, can soaking in a hot tub or visiting a sauna be effective methods of birth control?

It has long been known that sperm production is impaired by increased heat, although we are not sure exactly how and why. As a result, both early and contemporary writers have suggested that hot baths may be an effective method of male contraception. This notion has been supported by some evidence. For example, it has been reported that a 30-minute exposure to heat within a tolerable temperature range can arrest sperm production for as long as several weeks (Dickinson, 1949). Even so, sitting in the health spa sauna or a hot tub is not a recommended method of birth control. Considering the wide range of variables—including temperature, frequency, and time of exposure—it would be reckless to rely on this procedure for protection against conception.

In most men, the testicles are asymmetrical. Note that in Figure 5.3 the left testicle hangs lower than the right. This is usually the case, as the left spermatic cord is generally longer than the right. Although this difference has often been attributed to excessive masturbation, there is no truth to this assertion. It is no more unusual than a woman having one breast that is larger than the other. Our bodies simply are not perfectly symmetrical.

It is important for men to become familiar with their testicles and to examine them regularly. The testicles can be affected by a variety of diseases, including cancer, sexually transmitted diseases, and an assortment of infections. (Diseases of the male sex organs are discussed at the end of this chapter and in Chapter 17.) Most of these conditions have observable symptoms, and early detection allows for rapid treatment; it may also prevent far more serious complications.

Unfortunately, most men do not regularly examine their testicles. Research suggests that among high-school-age males the percentage is extremely low, perhaps 2% or less. Even among male college students, the rate is very small, probably fewer than 10% (Best & Davis, 1997; Best et al., 1996; Cromer et al., 1992). Furthermore, one recent study indicated that instruction about testicular self-examination in high school health classes is also relatively uncommon (Wohl & Kane, 1997). Yet this simple, painless, and potentially lifesaving process, which only takes a few minutes, is an excellent method for detecting early signs of disease. This procedure is described and illustrated in the boxed discussion "Male Genital Self-Examination."

The Seminiferous Tubules

Seminiferous tubules
Thin, coiled structures in the testicles in which sperm are produced.

Within and adjacent to the testes are two separate areas involved in the production and storage of sperm. The first of these, the **seminiferous** (sem´-i-NI-fer-us) **tubules** (sperm-bearing tubules), are thin, highly coiled structures located in the approximately 250 cone-

Your Sexual Health

Male Genital Self-Examination

You may conduct a self-examination of your genitals standing, reclining against a backrest, or in a sitting position (see photo). A good time is after a hot shower or bath, because heat causes the scrotal skin to relax and the testes to descend. This relaxed, accessible state of your testes may make detecting any unusual condition easier.

First, notice the cremasteric cycle of contraction and relaxation, and experiment with initiating the cremasteric reflex. Then explore the testicles one at a time. Place the thumbs of both hands on top of a testicle and the index and middle fingers on the underside. Then apply a small amount of pressure and roll the testicle beneath your fingertips. The surface should be fairly smooth and firm in consistency. There are individual variations in the contour and texture of male testicles, and it is important to know your own anatomy so that you can note changes. Having two testicles allows for direct comparison, which is helpful in spotting abnormalities (although it is common for the two testicles to vary slightly in size). Areas that appear swollen or are painful to the touch may indicate the presence of an infection. The epididymis, which lies along the back of each testicle, occasionally becomes infected, sometimes causing an irregular area to become tender to the touch.

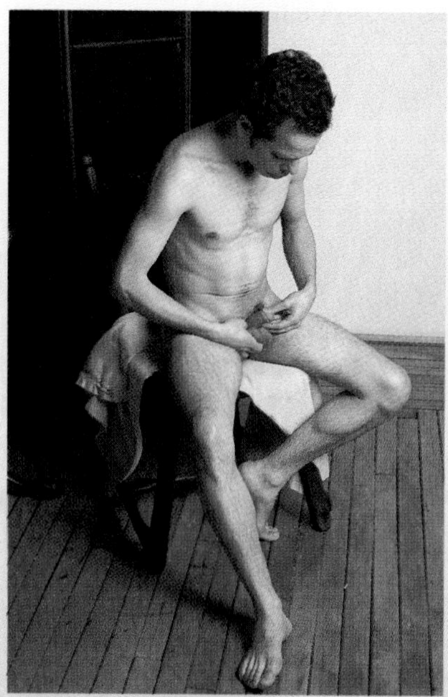

Self-examination can increase a man's familiarity with his genitals. Any irregularity, such as a lump or tender area in the scrotum, should be examined immediately by a physician.

Also, be aware of any mass within the testicle that feels hard or irregular to the fingertips and can be painless to touch. This mass, which may be no larger than a BB shot or small pea, could be an indication of early stage testicular cancer. This cancer, although relatively rare, may progress rapidly. Early detection and prompt treatment is essential to successful recovery. Testicular cancer will be discussed further at the end of this chapter.

While examining your genitals, also be aware of any unusual changes in your penis, A sore or unusual growth anywhere on its surface may be a symptom of an infection, sexually transmitted disease, or in rare cases, penile cancer. Although cancer of the penis is among the rarest of cancers, it is also one of the most traumatic and, unless diagnosed and treated early, very deadly (Gordon et al., 1997). Penile cancer usually begins as a small, painless sore on the glans or, in the case of uncircumcised men, the foreskin. The sore may remain the same for weeks, months, or even years until it changes into a cauliflower-like mass that is chronically inflamed and tender. Clearly, the time to first seek medical attention is immediately after first noticing the sore, when the prospect for a cure remains good. We will have more to say about cancer of the penis later in this chapter.

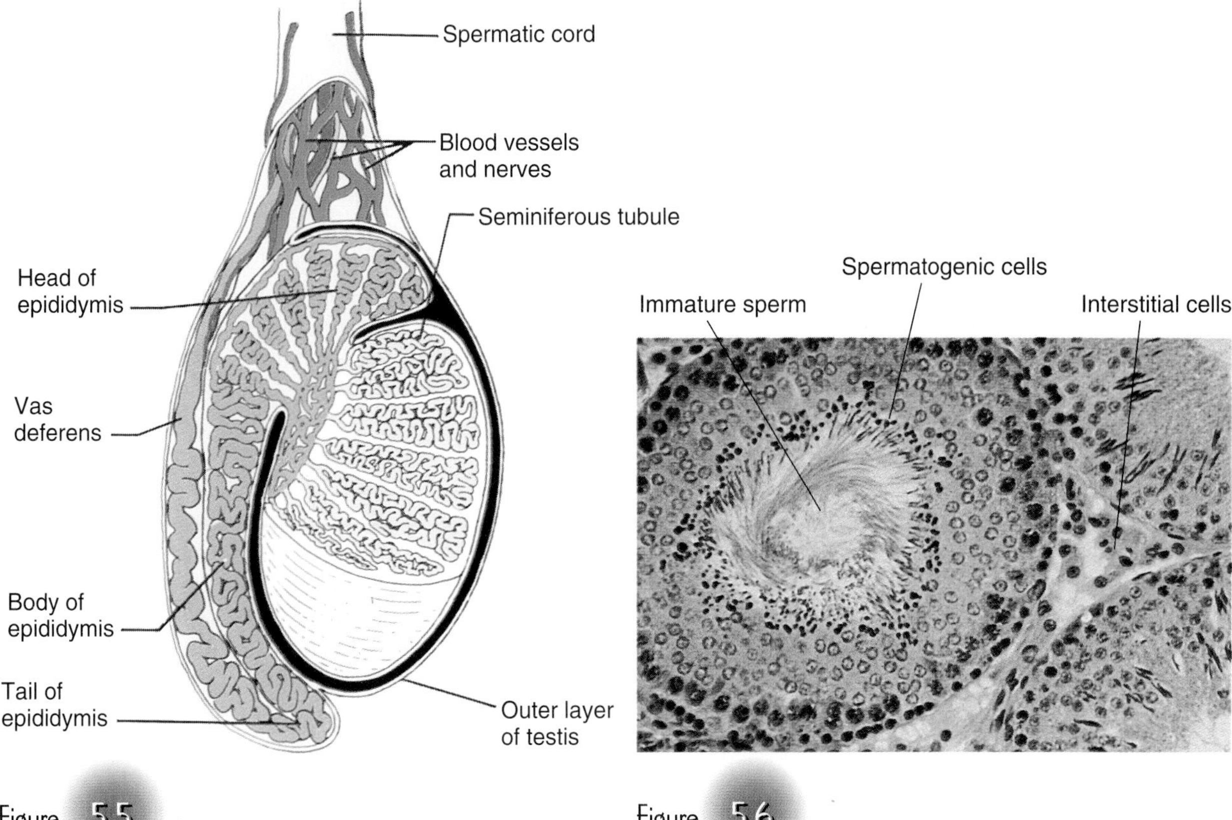

Figure 5.5

Internal structure of a testis. Sperm are produced in the seminiferous tubules and transported to the epididymis, which serves as a storage chamber.

Figure 5.6

This cross-section view of the seminiferous tubules shows spermatogenic (sperm-making) cells and the interstitial cells.

shaped lobes that make up the interior of each testicle (see Figures 5.5 and 5.6). Sperm production takes place within these tubules, usually beginning sometime after the onset of puberty. Men continue to produce viable sperm well into their old age, often until death, although the production rate diminishes with aging. The **interstitial** (in′-ter-STISH-al) **cells,** or *Leydig's cells,* are located between the seminiferous tubules. These cells are the major source of androgen, and their close proximity to blood vessels allows for direct secretion of their hormone products into the bloodstream. (We will discuss the role of hormones in sexual behavior in Chapter 6.)

Interstitial cells
Cells located between the seminiferous tubules that are the major source of androgen in males.

The Epididymis

The second important area for sperm processing is the **epididymis** (ep′-i-DID-i-mus) (literally, "over the testes"). Sperm produced in the seminiferous tubules move through a maze of tiny ducts into this C-shaped structure that adheres to the back and upper surface of each testis (see Figure 5.5). Evidence suggests that the epididymis serves primarily as a storage chamber where sperm cells undergo additional maturing, or ripening, for a period of several weeks. During this time they are completely inactive. Researchers theorize that a selection process also occurs in the epididymis, in which abnormal sperm cells are eliminated by the body's waste removal system.

Epididymis
The structure along the back of each testicle, in which sperm maturation occurs.

The Vas Deferens

Vas deferens
A sperm-carrying tube that begins at the testicle and ends at the urethra.

Sperm held in the epididymis eventually drain into the **vas deferens** (vas DEH-fur-renz), a long, thin duct that travels up through the scrotum inside the spermatic cord. The vas

Vasectomy
Male sterilization procedure that involves removing a section from each vas deferens.

deferens is close to the surface of the scrotum along this route, which makes the common male sterilization procedure, **vasectomy** (va-SEK-tō-mē), relatively simple. (Vasectomy will be described in Chapter 11.)

The spermatic cord exits the scrotal sac through the inguinal canal, an opening that leads directly into the abdominal cavity. From this point the vas deferens continues its upward journey along the top of the bladder and loops around the ureter, as shown in Figure 5.7. (This pathway is essentially the reverse of the route taken by the testis during its prenatal descent.) Turning downward, the vas deferens reaches the base of the bladder, where it is joined by the excretory duct of the seminal vesicle, forming the **ejaculatory duct.** The two ejaculatory ducts (one from each side) are very short, running their entire course within the prostate gland. At their termination, they open into the prostatic portion of the **urethra** (yoo-RĒ-thra), the tube through which urine passes from the bladder.

Ejaculatory ducts
Two short ducts located within the prostate gland.

Urethra
The tube through which urine passes from the bladder to outside the body.

The Seminal Vesicles

Seminal vesicles
Small glands adjacent to the terminals of the vas deferens that secrete an alkaline fluid (conducive to sperm motility) that constitutes the greatest portion of the volume of seminal fluid released during ejaculation.

The **seminal vesicles** (SEM-i-nal VES-i-kuls) are two small glands adjacent to the terminals of the vas deferens (see Figure 5.7). Their role in sexual physiology is not completely understood. It was once assumed that they functioned primarily as storage centers for sperm. However, it is now known that they secrete an alkaline fluid that is very rich in fructose sugar. This secretion constitutes a major portion of the seminal fluid, perhaps as much as 70%, and its sugar component seems to contribute to sperm nutrition and motility (Spring-Mills & Hafez, 1980). Up to this point in its journey from the testicle, a sperm cell is transmitted through the elaborate system of ducts by the continuous movement of *cilia,* tiny hairlike structures that line the inner walls of these tubes. Once stimulated by energy-giving secretions of the seminal vesicles, however, sperm propel themselves by the whiplike action of their own tails.

The Prostate Gland

Prostate gland
A gland located at the base of the bladder that produces about 30% of the seminal fluid released during ejaculation.

The **prostate** (PROS-tāt) **gland** is a structure about the size and shape of a walnut, located at the base of the bladder (see Figure 5.7). As described earlier, both ejaculatory ducts and the urethra pass through this organ. The prostate is made up of smooth muscle fibers and glandular tissue, whose secretions account for about 30% of the seminal fluid released during ejaculation.

Although the prostate is continually active in a mature male, it accelerates its output during sexual arousal. Its secretions flow into the urethra through a system of sievelike ducts, and here they combine with sperm and the seminal vesicle secretions to form the seminal fluid. The prostatic secretions are thin, milky, and alkaline in nature. This alkalinity helps counteract the unfavorable acidity of the male urethra and the female vaginal tract, making a more hospitable environment for sperm. We will discuss some prostate gland health concerns at the end of this chapter.

The Cowper's Glands

Cowper's glands
Two pea-sized glands located alongside the base of the urethra in the male that secrete an alkaline fluid during sexual arousal.

The **Cowper's glands,** or *bulbourethral glands,* are two small structures, each about the size of a pea, located one on each side of the urethra just below where it emerges from the prostate gland (see Figure 5.7). Tiny ducts connect both glands directly to the urethra. When a man is sexually aroused, these organs often secrete a slippery, mucuslike substance that appears in droplet form at the tip of the penis. Like the prostate's secretions, this fluid is alkaline and helps buffer the acidity of the urethra; it is also thought to lubricate the flow of seminal fluid through the urethra. Contrary to some reports, though, it has virtually no function as a vaginal lubricant during coitus. In many men

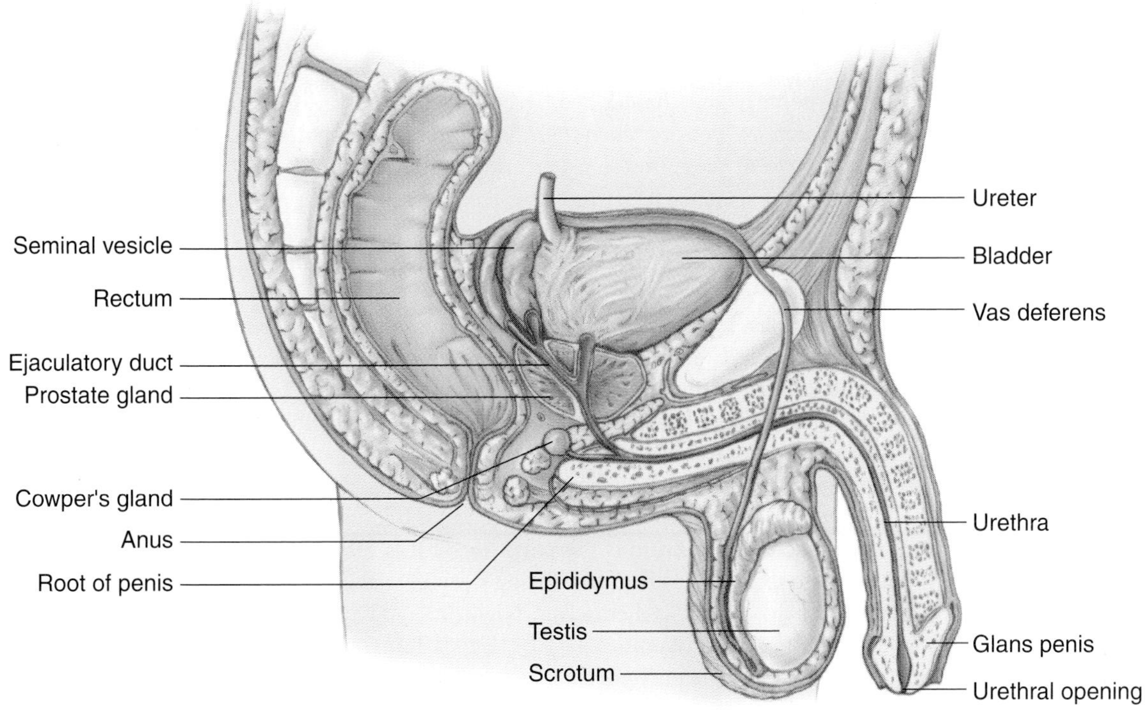

Figure 5.7

Male sexual anatomy: A cross-section side view of the male reproductive organs.

this secretion does not appear until well after the beginning of arousal, often just prior to orgasm. Other men report that it occurs immediately after they get an erection, and still others rarely or never produce these preejaculatory droplets. All these experiences are normal variations of male sexual functioning.

The fluid from the Cowper's glands should not be confused with semen; however, it does occasionally contain active, healthy sperm. This is one reason among many why the withdrawal method of birth control is not highly effective. (Withdrawal and other methods of birth control are discussed in Chapter 11.)

Semen
A viscous fluid ejaculated through the penis that contains sperm and fluids from the prostate, seminal vesicles, and Cowper's glands.

Semen

As we have seen, the **semen** or **seminal fluid** ejaculated through the opening of the penis comes from a variety of sources. Fluids are supplied by the seminal vesicles, prostate, and Cowper's glands, with the seminal vesicles providing the greatest portion (Eliasson & Lindholmer, 1976; Spring-Mills & Hafez, 1980). The amount of seminal fluid a man ejaculates—roughly one teaspoonful on the average—is influenced by a number of factors, including the length of time since the last ejaculation, the duration of arousal before ejaculation, and age (older men tend to produce less fluid). The semen of a single ejaculation typically contains between 200 and 500 million sperm, which account for only about 1% of its total volume. Chemical analysis shows that semen is also made up of acids (ascorbic and citric), water, enzymes, fructose sugar, bases (phosphate and bicarbonate buffers), and a variety of other substances. None of these materials is harmful if swallowed during oral sex. However, semen of an HIV-infected man can provide a vehicle for transmission of the virus through open sores or bleeding gums in the mouth of the recipient (see Chapter 17).

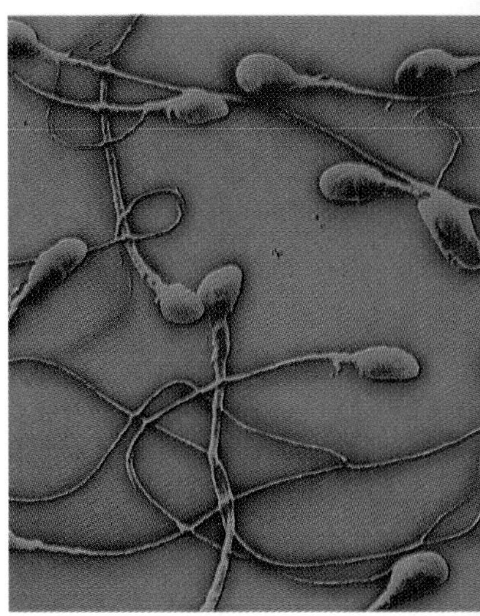

Sperm, as seen under a microscope.

Male Sexual Functions

Up to this point in the chapter, we have looked at the various *parts* of the male sexual system, but we have not described their *functioning* in much detail. In the following pages, we examine two of these functions, erection and ejaculation.

Erection

Erection
The process whereby the penis or clitoris engorges with blood and increases in size.

An **erection** is a process coordinated by the autonomic nervous system. When a male becomes sexually excited, the nervous system sends out messages that cause expansion of the arteries leading to the three erectile chambers in the penis. As a result, the rate of blood flow into these parallel cylinders increases rapidly. Because blood flowing out of the penis through veins cannot keep up with the inflow, it accumulates in the spongelike tissues of the three erectile chambers, causing erection (tumescence). The penis remains erect until the messages from the nervous system stop and the inflow of blood returns to normal.

The capacity for erection is present at birth. It is very common and quite natural for infant boys to experience erections during sleep or diapering, from stimulation by clothing, and later by touching themselves. Nighttime erections occur during the rapid-eye-movement (REM), or dreaming, stage of sleep (Chung & Choi, 1990). Erotic dreams may play a role, but the primary mechanism seems to be physiological, and erections often occur even when the dream content is clearly not sexual. Often a man awakens in the morning just after completing a REM cycle. This explains the phenomenon of "morning erections," which was once erroneously attributed to a full bladder.

Although an erection is basically a physiological response, it also involves psychological components. In fact, some writers distinguish between psychogenic (from the mind) and physiogenic (from the body) erections—although in most cases of sexual arousal there are simultaneous inputs from both thoughts and physical stimulation.

How great an influence does the mind have on erections? We know that it can inhibit the response: When a man becomes troubled by erection difficulties, the problem may be of psychological origin, as we will discuss in Chapter 16. There is also extensive evidence that men are able to enhance their erection (as reflected in increased penile tumescence) by forming vivid mental images or fantasies of sexual activity (Dekker et al., 1985; Smith & Over, 1987).

What kinds of nonsexual triggers might induce erectile responses?

Logically, one might expect erection to occur only in response to obvious sexual stimuli. That this is not always the case can be embarrassing, perplexing, amusing, or anxiety-arousing. Nearly every man can recall scenes of unwanted erections during adolescent school days—the teacher saying "Bob, come up here and do the math problem on the board," when math was the farthest thing from Bob's mind; the trips down school halls with a notebook held in a strategic location; the delayed exit from the swimming pool after playful frolicking.

Erections also happen in situations that seem entirely nonsexual, such as riding a bike, lifting heavy weights, or straining during defecation (particularly in little boys).

Ejaculation

Ejaculation
The process whereby semen is expelled from the body through the penis.

The second basic male sexual function is **ejaculation**—the process whereby the semen is expelled through the penis to the outside of the body. Many writers equate male orgasm with ejaculation. However, these two processes do not always take place simultaneously (Dunsmuir & Emberton, 1997). Prior to puberty a boy may experience hundreds of "dry orgasms"—orgasms without any ejaculation of fluid. Occasionally, a man may have more than one orgasm in a given sexual encounter, with the second or third producing little

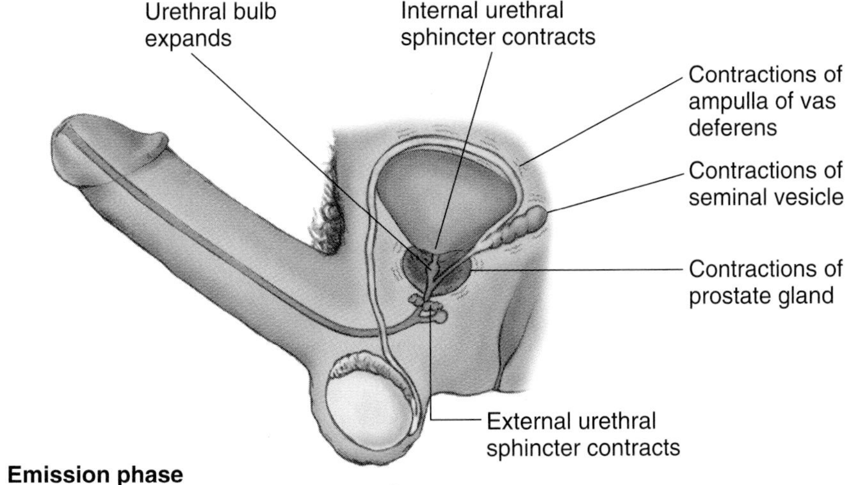

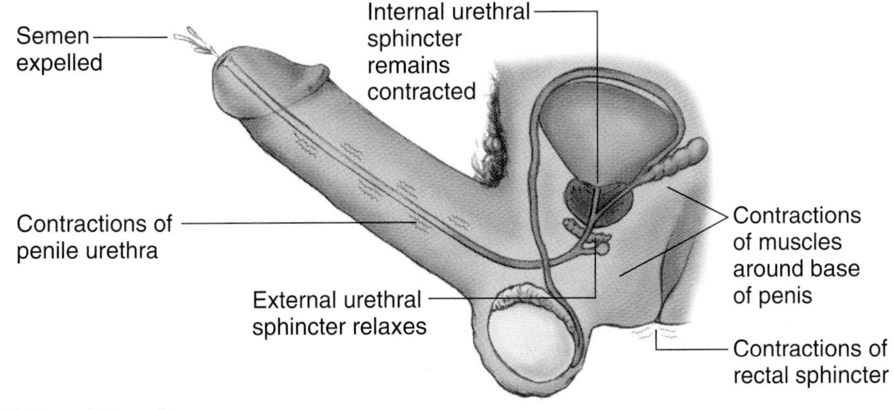

Figure 5.8

Male sexual anatomy during ejaculation: (a) the emission phase and (b) the expulsion phase.

or no expelled semen. Conversely, research reveals that some men may experience a series of nonejaculatory orgasms culminating in a final orgasm accompanied by expulsion of semen (Dunn & Trost, 1989; Hartman & Fithian, 1984; Robbins & Jensen, 1978). Thus, although male orgasm is generally associated with ejaculation, these two processes are not one and the same and do not necessarily occur together.

From a neurophysiological point of view, ejaculation—like erection—is basically a spinal reflex. Effective sexual stimulation of the penis (manual, oral, or coital) results in the buildup of neural excitation to a critical level. When a threshold is reached, this triggers several internal physical events.

The actual ejaculation occurs in two stages (see Figure 5.8). During the first stage, sometimes called the **emission phase,** the prostate, seminal vesicles, and *ampulla* (upper portions of the vas deferens) undergo contractions. This forces their various secretions down into the ejaculatory ducts and prostatic urethra. At the same time, both internal and external *urethral sphincters* (two muscles, one located where the urethra exits the bladder and the other below the prostate) close, trapping seminal fluid in the *urethral bulb* (the prostatic portion of the urethra, between these two muscles). The urethral bulb expands like a balloon. A man typically experiences this first stage as a subjective sense that orgasm is inevitable, the "point of no return" or "ejaculatory inevitability."

Emission phase
The first stage of male orgasm, in which the seminal fluid is gathered in the urethral bulb.

In the second stage, sometimes called the **expulsion phase,** the collected semen is expelled out of the penis by strong, rhythmic contractions of muscles that surround the urethral bulb and root of the penis. In addition, there are contractions along the entire urethral route. The external urethral sphincter relaxes, allowing fluid to pass through, while the internal sphincter remains contracted to prevent the escape of urine. The first two or three muscle contractions around the base of the penis are quite strong and occur

Expulsion phase
The second stage of male orgasm, during which the semen is expelled from the penis by muscular contractions.

at close intervals. Most of the seminal fluid is expelled in spurts corresponding to these contractions. Several more muscle responses typically occur, with a gradual diminishing of intensity and lengthening of time intervals between contractions. The entire expulsion stage usually occurs in three to ten seconds.

Retrograde ejaculation Process by which semen is expelled into the bladder instead of out of the penis.

Nocturnal emission Involuntary ejaculation during sleep, also known as a "wet dream."

Some men have an experience known as **retrograde ejaculation,** in which semen is expelled into the bladder rather than through the penis. This results from a reversed functioning of the two urethral sphincters (the internal sphincter relaxes, while the external contracts). The condition sometimes occurs in men who have undergone prostate surgery. In addition, illness, congenital anomaly, and certain drugs, most notably tranquilizers, can induce this reaction. Retrograde ejaculation itself is not harmful (the seminal fluid is later eliminated with the urine). However, a man who consistently experiences this response would be wise to seek medical attention, not only because its effective result is sterility but also because it may be a sign of an underlying health problem.

Sometimes a man experiences orgasm without direct genital stimulation. The most familiar of these occurrences are **nocturnal emissions,** which are commonly known as "wet dreams." The exact mechanism that produces this response is not fully understood. (Women may also experience orgasm during sleep.) The possibility of a man using fantasy alone to reach orgasm in a waking state is exceedingly remote, and we have never heard a firsthand account of this phenomenon. Kinsey and his associates (1948) stated that only three or four of the males in their sample of over 5000 reported this experience. In contrast, significantly greater numbers of women in his sample (roughly 2%) reported orgasms from fantasy alone (Kinsey et al., 1953). Another kind of nongenitally induced ejaculation that men sometimes report is reaching orgasm during sex play (activities such as mutual kissing or manual or oral stimulation of their partner) when there is no penile stimulation.

Some Concerns About Sexual Functioning

Men frequently voice a variety of concerns about sexual functioning. Several of these will be addressed throughout our text. At this point we will discuss two areas that receive considerable attention—the significance of penis size and the necessity and impact of circumcision. Claims are frequently made that one or both of these physical characteristics may influence the sexual pleasure of a man or his partner. In the following sections, we examine the available evidence.

Penis Size

When I was a kid, my friends were unmerciful in their comments about my small size. They would say things like, "I have a penis, John has a penis, but you have a pee-pee." Needless to say, I grew up with a very poor self-image in this area. Later it was translated into anxiety-ridden sexual encounters where I would insist that the room be completely dark before I would undress. Even now, when I realize that size is irrelevant in giving sexual pleasure, I still worry that new partners will comment unfavorably about my natural endowment. (Authors' files)

All my life I have been distressed about the size of my penis. I have always avoided places such as community showers where I would be exposed to others. When my penis is hard it is about five inches long; but when it is flaccid, it is rarely longer than an inch or inch and a half, and thin as well. I don't like to be nude in front of the girls I sleep with, and that feeling of uneasiness is often reflected during sex. (Authors' files)

These men are not alone in their discomfort. Their feelings are echoed in more accounts than we can remember. Penis size has occupied the attention of most men and many women at one time or another. Generally, it is more than idle curiosity that stimulates interest in this topic. For many it is a matter of real concern, perhaps even cause for apprehension or anguish.

It does not take much imagination to understand why penis size often seems so important. As a society, we tend to be overly impressed with size and quantity. Bigger cars are better than compacts, the bigger the house the better it is, and by implication, big penises provide more pleasure than smaller ones. Certainly, the various art forms, such as literature, painting, sculpture, and movies, do much to perpetuate this obsession with big penises.

The modern Western world is not alone in its preoccupation with penis size, as the photograph on this page illustrates. Even the fascinating Indian sex manuals, the *Ananga Ranga* and the *Kama Sutra,* classify men according to three categories: the hare-man, whose erect penis measures 6 finger-widths; the bull-man (9 finger-widths long); and the horse-man (12 or more finger-widths long). In ancient Greek mythology, preoccupation with penis size found a focal point in Priapus, son of the goddess Aphrodite and the god Dionysus, who was usually portrayed as a lasciviously grinning little man with a greatly oversized penis.

The result of all this attention to penis size is that men often come to view size in and of itself as an important attribute in defining their masculinity or their worth as lovers. Such a concept of virility can contribute to a poor self-image. Furthermore, if either a man or his partner views his penis as being smaller than it should be, this can decrease sexual satisfaction for one or both of them—not because of physical limitations, but rather as a self-fulfilling prophecy.

What are your perspectives on the issue of penis size and sexual intimacy? Do you believe that a man's penis size influences his partner's pleasure during intercourse? How might you relate the information acquired in Chapter 4 to this issue?

As we learned in Chapter 4, the greatest sensitivity in the vaginal canal is concentrated in its outer portion. (We focus here on heterosexual penile–vaginal intercourse because concerns about penis size often relate to this kind of sexual activity.) Although some women do find pressure and stretching deep within the vagina to be pleasurable, this is not usually requisite for female sexual gratification. In fact, some women may even find deep penetration painful, particularly if it is quite vigorous:

You asked if size was important to my pleasure. Yes, but not in the way you might imagine. If a man is quite large, I worry that he might hurt me. Actually, I prefer that he be average or even to the smaller side. (Authors' files)

Preoccupation with penis size is evident in a variety of cultures and art forms.

There is a physiological explanation for the pain or discomfort some women feel during deep penetration. Because the female ovaries and male testicles originate from the same embryonic tissue source, they share some of the same sensitivity. If the penis bangs into the cervix and causes the uterus to be slightly displaced, this may in turn jar an ovary. The resulting sensation is somewhat like a male's experience of getting hit in the testicles. Fast stretching of the uterine ligaments has also been implicated in deep-penetration pain. However, some women find slow stretching of these same ligaments to be pleasurable.

These observations indicate the importance of being gentle and considerate during intercourse. If one or both partners want deeper or more vigorous thrusting, they can experiment by gradually adding these components to their coital movements. It may also be helpful for the woman to be in an intercourse position other than female supine (see Figure 9.8), so she has more control over the depth and vigor of penetration.

Most textbooks on human sexuality report average dimensions of penises. We will not do this because such information seems unimportant. Figure 5.9 shows several flaccid (nonerect) penises of different sizes, all well within the normal range. It is worth noting that penis size is not related to body shape, height, length of fingers, race, or anything else (Money et al., 1984). It should also be mentioned that small flaccid penises tend to increase more in size during erection than do penises that are larger in the flaccid state

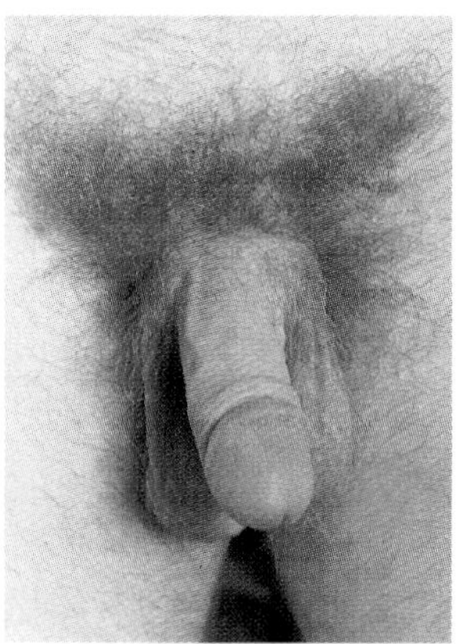
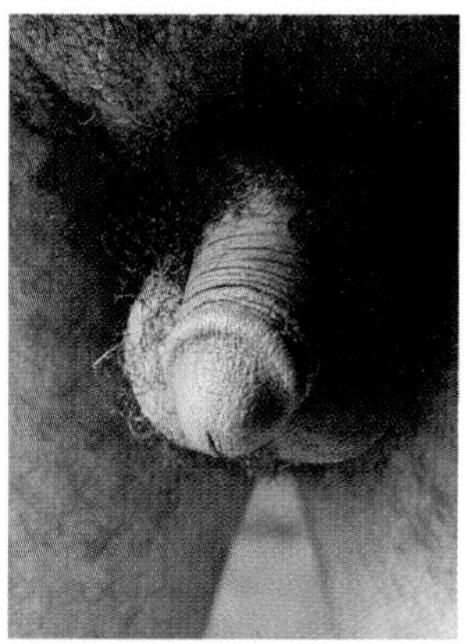
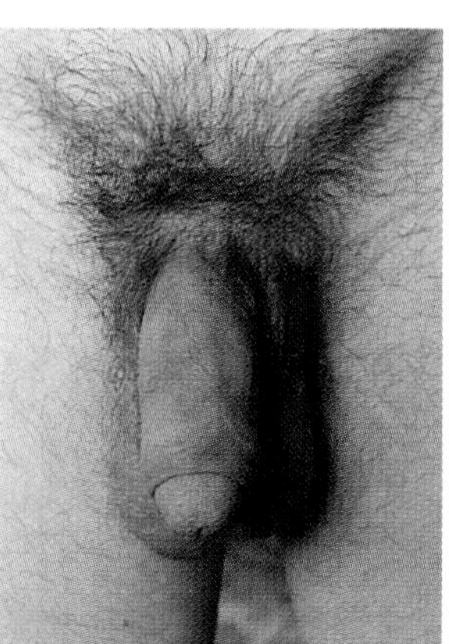

Figure 5.9

There are many variations in the shape and size of the male genitals. The penis in the right photo is uncircumcised.

(Jamison & Gebhard, 1988; Masters & Johnson, 1966). These collective facts are reflected in the comment offered by an extremely tall, husky male:

I think most people just naturally assumed, judging from my large stature, that I would have a big penis. In fact, when I'm flaccid it looks like all I have is testicles and a glans. My shaft is practically invisible. However, when I get hard I know my penis is quite adequate in size. When I was a teenager, the problem was how to let my buddies know this when it's not really cool to walk around with a hard-on. What I did was simply avoid taking showers with others if at all possible. Now I feel okay about my body, but for a while there I was really self-conscious. (Authors' files)

As we close this section, it is important to note that even though physiological evidence indicates that large penises are not a necessary prerequisite for female sexual pleasure during coitus, some women do have subjective preferences regarding penis size and shape, just as some men have such preferences about breasts. It is noteworthy, however, that research indicates women are no more sexually aroused by depictions of large penises than by portrayals of medium or small penises (Fisher et al., 1983).

Circumcision

A characteristic that many people associate with differences in male sensitivity—and also differences in hygiene—is the presence or absence of the foreskin.

Circumcision
Surgical removal of the foreskin of the penis.

Circumcision (ser´-kum-SIZH-un) is the surgical removal of the foreskin, shown in Figure 5.10. As previously described in the Sexuality and Diversity box, circumcision is widely practiced throughout the world for religious, ritual, or hygienic reasons. In the United States, this operation is performed on the majority of male infants (with parental consent), generally on the second day after birth.

The routine practice of circumcision in this country has reflected concern by the medical profession about hygiene. If not routinely cleaned, the area under the foreskin of an uncircumcised male can harbor a variety of infection-causing organisms. Indeed, many people assume that circumcision is important for hygiene. How do such assumptions affect a person's self-image and sexual relations? Consider the following account provided by a surgeon:

When I was serving as ship's surgeon on a large carrier during the Vietnam conflict, I had a very interesting experience. A young sailor came to me requesting circumcision. When I asked him why he wanted to undergo such an operation, he stated that his wife refused to engage in oral sex because she viewed him as unclean. After I performed the simple operation, an amazing thing happened. Many more men came with the same request. Apparently the word had circulated rapidly. Their reasons were essentially the same as the first seaman's. They either felt unclean themselves or were viewed in this way by partners. (Authors' files)

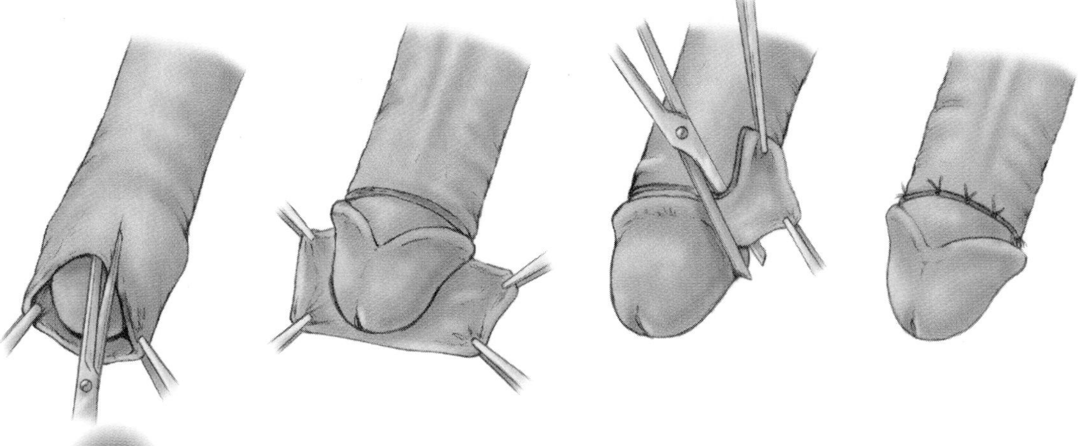

Figure 5.10

Circumcision, the surgical removal of the foreskin, is practiced throughout the world.

Such accounts are echoed in numerous other reports, including those of students in our own classes.

Does medical evidence support the view that circumcision is necessary for good hygiene?

Numerous studies have looked into the question, with mixed results. In support of circumcision, research has shown that uncircumcised males are more at risk for penile cancer than are circumcised males (Gordon et al., 1997; Williamson, 1997; Wiswell, 1997). In addition, organisms harbored under the foreskin can cause vaginal infections in women who have sexual relations with uncircumcised men. Some investigators have also suggested that the female partners of uncircumcised men are at increased risk of cervical cancer (Snyder, 1991; Wiswell, 1997). One recent study of 2776 men attending a sexually transmitted disease clinic found that uncircumcised subjects were more likely to have gonorrhea and syphilis than were circumcised subjects (Cook et al., 1994). However, analysis of data obtained from 1410 men included in the NHSLS study (see Chapter 2) found no significant differences between circumcised and uncircumcised men in their likelihood of contracting sexually transmitted diseases (Laumann et al., 1997). Nevertheless, there are strong indications that uncircumcised men may be more likely to become infected with the AIDS virus (HIV) via heterosexual intercourse than their circumcised counterparts (Caldwell et al., 1997; Urassa et al., 1997; Wiswell, 1997). Various studies have found the prevalence of HIV infection to be 1.7 to 8.2 times as high in men with foreskins as in circumcised men (Royce et al., 1997).

There are several arguments against routine circumcision, many of which have been raised with greater frequency in recent years. First, the foreskin may serve some important function yet to be determined. Second, some have expressed concern that sexual function may be altered by excising the foreskin; we will consider this question shortly. Finally, some think performing this procedure on a newborn is unnecessarily traumatic and an invitation to possible surgical complications. Because the use of general anesthesia and narcotic analgesia is contraindicated for infants, circumcision is often performed without anesthesia (Herschel et al., 1998; Taddio et al., 1997a). However, infants undergoing circumcision without anesthesia feel and respond to pain (Williamson, 1997; Wiswell, 1997). Furthermore, research indicates that the pain experienced by infants during circumcision may have long-lasting effects on future infant behavior. For example, in one study infants who were circumcised without anesthesia demonstrated a stronger pain response to subsequent routine vaccination than uncircumcised infants (Taddio et al., 1997b). In response to such findings, an increasing number of physicians who perform infant circumcision are either applying a topical analgesic or injecting a local anesthetic agent directly into the penis to reduce or eliminate pain associated with this operation (Taddio et al., 1997a; Williamson, 1997; Wiswell, 1997). Some of the health risks of circumcision include hemorrhage, infections, mutilation, shock, psychological trauma, and even death in extremely rare cases (Gluckman et al., 1995; Hanukoglu et al., 1995; Wiswell, 1997).

Because circumcision is an issue with so many pros and cons, it is not surprising that the medical profession in the United States has historically gone back and forth on the matter. In the 1960s and 1970s, circumcision underwent serious reconsideration as a preventive medical practice. The 1975 policy statement of the American Academy of Pediatrics (AAP) concluded that there was no medical indication for circumcision and recommended against its routine practice. Many American hospitals followed this lead by establishing the policy of performing circumcision only at parents' request or as elective surgery. However, most parents continued to ask for the procedure, in part due to social concerns such as appearance and perceived future ridicule by peers. Circumcision remains the most common surgery performed on infants in the United States and at least 1.2 million to 1.8 million newborn boys (60% to 90%) are circumcised annually (Wiswell, 1997).

In the late 1980s, several studies reported markedly higher rates of urinary tract infections among uncircumcised boys as compared with their circumcised counterparts (Fergusson et al., 1988; Herzog, 1989). The AAP abandoned its former position that there are no valid medical indications for circumcising male infants and in March 1989 announced a neutral stance, suggesting that circumcision has both medical advantages and some risks. In its task force report, it recommended that "the benefits and risks . . . be explained to the parents and informed consent obtained" (Shoen et al., 1989, p. 390).

To put this new evidence and the altered stance of the AAP into perspective, one might ask how harmful urinary tract infections are in otherwise healthy male children. In reality, the risks associated with this kind of infection are quite low, and it is by no means clear that an increased likelihood of a urinary tract infection in uncircumcised male children is a good medical reason for routine circumcision (Snyder, 1991; Van Howe, 1998). Furthermore, many of the studies designed to assess the relationship between circumcision and disease are marred by methodological problems such as failure to control for variations in personal hygiene practices. For example, newborns from lower socioeconomic groups are more likely to be uncircumcised and perhaps also less likely to experience good genital hygiene. Data not corrected for these factors may be suspect (Thompson, 1990).

Beyond the issue of hygiene, another question has often been raised about circumcision: Do circumcised men enjoy any erotic or functional advantages over uncircumcised men (or vice versa)?

Phimosis
A condition characterized by an extremely tight penile foreskin.

Some people assume that circumcised men respond more quickly during penile–vaginal intercourse because of the fully exposed glans. However, except when there is a condition known as **phimosis** (an extremely tight prepuce), there is no difference in contact during intercourse. The foreskin of an uncircumcised man is retracted during coitus, so the glans is fully exposed. It might be assumed, in fact, that the glans of a circumcised man is less sensitive, due to the toughening effect of constant exposure to chafing surfaces. Masters and Johnson (1966) investigated both of these questions and found no evidence of differences in responsiveness. However, the Masters and Johnson data fail to include the all-important dimension of subjective assessment by men who have experienced both conditions after achieving sexual maturity. Occasionally we have encountered men in our classes who have been circumcised during their adult years. Some of these men have reported experiencing physiological differences in sexual arousal—such as a decrease in the sensitivity of the glans—following circumcision. But these reactions have not been consistent. Other men afforded this unique comparative opportunity have found no perceivable differences in sexual excitability. It would seem that there are still unanswered questions about the relationship between circumcision and male sexual arousal, and "little consensus exists regarding the role of the foreskin in sexual performance and satisfaction" (Laumann et al., 1997, p. 1052).

Male Genital Health Concerns

The male genital and internal reproductive structures may be adversely affected by a variety of injuries and diseases. We will describe some of these health concerns in the following pages. Should you become affected by any of these conditions, we urge immediate consultation with a physician. **Urology** (yoo-ROL-O-je) is the medical specialty that focuses on the male reproductive structures.

Urology
The medical specialty dealing with reproductive health and genital diseases of the male and urinary tract diseases in both sexes.

The Penis: Health-Care Issues

Caring for the penis is an important aspect of sexual self-health. Washing the penis regularly with soap and water, at least once a day, is an excellent self-health practice. (There is also evidence, discussed in Chapter 17, that washing the genitals before and after sex may reduce the chances of exchanging infectious organisms with your partner.) If you are uncircumcised, pay particular attention to drawing the foreskin back from the glans and washing all surfaces, especially the underside of the foreskin. A number of small glands located in the foreskin secrete an oily, lubricating substance. If these secretions are allowed to accumulate under the foreskin, they combine with sloughed-off dead skin cells to form a cheesy substance called **smegma.** When it builds up over time, smegma generally develops an unpleasant odor, becomes grainy and irritating, and can serve as a breeding ground for infection-causing organisms. Sometimes the glans or shaft of the penis may develop an eczemalike reaction—"weepy" and sore—that may result from an allergic reaction to the vaginal secretions of your partner. Wearing a condom may help alleviate this condition, but it is important that you consult a physician to clarify its origin and treatment.

Smegma
A cheesy substance of glandular secretions and skin cells that sometimes accumulates under the foreskin of the penis or hood of the clitoris.

It is wise to protect your penis by avoiding putting it in potentially harmful places such as partners' mouths that have herpes blisters or vaginas with unusual sores, growths, odors, or discharges. Some sexual gadgets may also be quite hazardous to penile health. For example, never use a "cock ring" (a tight-fitting ring that encircles the base of the penis). Although this device may be successful in accomplishing its intended purpose of sustaining erections, it may also destroy penile tissue by cutting off the blood supply. In recent years sexually oriented magazines such as *Penthouse* have published testimonials attesting to the pleasure of masturbating with a vacuum cleaner. This is not a good idea! Research suggests that severe penile injuries (including decapitation of the glans) resulting from masturbating with vacuum cleaners and electric brooms may be much more common than reported (Benson, 1985; Grisell, 1988).

On rare occasions, the penis may be fractured (Adducci & Ross, 1991; Hargreaves & Plail, 1994). This injury involves a rupture of the cavernous bodies when the penis is in an erect state. This injury most commonly occurs during coitus. Recently, a student reported his encounter with this painful injury:

> I was having intercourse with my girlfriend in a sitting position. She was straddling my legs using the arms of the chair and her legs to move her body up and down on my penis. In the heat of passion, she raised up a little too far, and I slipped out. She sat back down hard, expecting me to repenetrate her. Unfortunately, I was off target and all of her weight came down on my penis. I heard a cracking sound and experienced excruciating pain. I bled quite a bit inside my penis, and I was real sore for quite a long time. (Authors' files)

This account suggests that it is wise to take some precautions during coitus. This injury usually happens "in the heat of passion" and often involves putting too much weight on the penis when attempting to gain or regain vaginal penetration. When the woman is on top, the risk increases. Communicating the need to go slow at these times can avert a painful injury. Treatment of penile fractures varies from splinting and ice packs to surgery. Most men injured in this fashion regain normal sexual function, and surgical treatment generally provides the best results (Kalash & Young, 1984).

Penile Cancer

As stated earlier in this chapter, men may be afflicted with penile cancer, a rare malignancy that can be deadly if not diagnosed and treated in its earliest stages. Of the approximately 1300 men in the United States who develop penile cancer in a given year, only half will be alive five years later. However, if the cancer is caught early, and it has not spread to lymph nodes, the five-year survival rate is about 90% (Gordon et al., 1997). Such startling figures argue eloquently for the critical importance of seeking medical attention for any sore on the penis (see the boxed discussion "Male Genital Self-Examination" earlier in this chapter for a description of early symptoms of penile cancer). Risk factors associated with penile cancer include being over age 50; a history of multiple sexual partners and sexually transmitted diseases, especially genital herpes; poor genital hygiene, which contributes to smegma-induced inflammation of the glans; being uncircumcised (see earlier discussion of circumcision); and a long history of tobacco use, which increases a man's lifetime chance of developing penile cancer from 1 in 100,000 to 1 in 600 (Fair et al., 1993; Gordon et al., 1997). Penile cancer left untreated will ultimately destroy the entire penis and spread to lymph nodes and beyond.

Testicular Cancer

Testicular cancer accounts for only about 1% of all cancers that occur in males; however, it is one of the most common of the malignancies that occur in young men ages 15 to 34 (Wohl & Kane, 1997). During the early stages of testicular cancer, there are usually no symptoms beyond a mass within the testicle, The mass feels hard or irregular to the fingertips and is distinguishable from surrounding healthy tissue. It may be painless to touch, but some men do report tenderness in the area of the growth. Occasionally other symptoms are reported; these may include fever, tender breasts and nipples, and painful accumulation of fluid or swelling in the scrotum. Some types of testicular cancers tend to grow more rapidly than do any other tumors that have been studied. Therefore, for successful treatment, it is important to detect the mass as soon as possible and to seek medical attention immediately. Improved therapeutic procedures have consistently yielded a survival rate better than 90% among men treated for early detected testicular cancer (Walbrecker, 1995; Wohl & Kane, 1997). Some men may procrastinate in seeking medical treatment because they are afraid such procedures may create erectile problems or reduce their capacity to enjoy sexual pleasure. In fact, this occurs only rarely.

Diseases of the Prostate

As you will recall from our earlier discussion, the prostate gland is a walnut-sized structure at the base of the bladder that contributes secretions to the seminal fluid. The prostate is a focal point of some of the more common "male problems" that range from inflammation and enlargement to cancer.

Prostatitis

One of the most frequent disorders of the prostate gland, *prostatitis,* occurs when the prostate becomes enlarged and inflamed, often as a result of an infectious agent such as the gonococcus bacterium (responsible for gonorrhea) or the protozoan *Trichomonas.* (These agents are discussed in Chapter 17.) Prostatitis may occur in a man of any age. Its symptoms include any or all of the following: pain in the pelvic area or base of the penis, lower abdominal ache, backache, aching testicles, the urgent need to urinate frequently, burning sensation while urinating, a cloudy discharge from the penis, and difficulties with sexual functions such as painful erections or ejaculations and reduced sexual interest. Prostatitis can be effectively treated by a variety of prescription drugs, most commonly antibiotics (Roberts et al., 1997).

Benign Prostatic Hyperplasia

As men grow older, the prostate gland tends to increase in size, a condition known as *benign prostatic hyperplasia.* About 50% of men between ages 50 and 60 experience this problem (Van Rooyen, 1997). The enlarged gland tends to put pressure on the urethra, thus decreasing urine flow. If this problem is severe, surgery or medications can help (Crowley et al., 1995; Nickel, 1998; Van Rooyen, 1997).

Prostate Cancer

Some men also develop benign or malignant tumors of the prostate, and the potential for this becomes greater with increasing age. American Cancer Society statistics indicate that each year more than 300,000 American men are diagnosed with prostate cancer, over 40,000 deaths occur as a result of this disease, and that 10% of men in the United States will develop prostate cancer in their lifetimes (Goolsby, 1998; Coley et al., 1997a). Cancer of the prostate is the most frequently diagnosed cancer (other than that of the skin) in American males and is currently the second leading cause of cancer death among men in the United States, after lung cancer (Goolsby, 1998; Rodriguez et al., 1997a). Factors known to be associated with the development of prostate cancer include old age, family history of prostate cancer, black race, smoking, a prior history of sexually transmitted disease(s), and a diet high in saturated fats (Gambert, 1997; Goolsby, 1998; Rodriguez et al., 1997). The incidence of this cancer among African American men is the highest in the world and, for unknown reasons, these men have a poorer survival rate than white men for comparable stages of prostate cancer (Pienta et al., 1995; Rodriguez et al., 1997a).

Many of the men who die each year from cancer of the prostate would have benefited from early diagnosis and treatment (Coley et al., 1997a; Pinkowish, 1997). Consequently, it is very important for men to be aware of the early symptoms of this disease, which may include many of those previously listed for prostatitis (particularly pain in the pelvis and lower back and urinary complications). However, prostate cancer often lacks easily detectable symptoms in its early stages, and an early diagnosis may be accomplished by a physical examination.

A physician examines the prostate by inserting a finger into the rectum, a procedure called a digital rectal examination. Under normal conditions, this is only mildly uncomfortable. In recent years transrectal ultrasound, which uses sound waves to reflect the prostate on a TV screen, has also been employed to detect prostate cancer (Brawer, 1997; Smith et al., 1997; Thompson, 1997). Initially clinicians believed that this new procedure provided the best possible diagnostic tool for determining the extent or possible spread of the cancer beyond the boundaries of the prostate. However, enthusiasm for transrectal ultrasound has recently been tempered by recognition that this procedure often fails to detect microscopic extensions of tumor beyond the prostate. In fact, one recent study revealed that transrectal ultrasound and digital rectal examinations were essentially equal in their capacity to determine the extent of prostatic cancer (Smith et al., 1997).

The discovery of a marker for prostate cancer—*prostate-specific antigen (PSA)*—detectable by a blood test, has added another key tool for physicians to employ in diagnosing early prostate cancer (Coley et al., 1997a; Nash & Oesterling, 1997). However, the use of PSA to detect prostate cancer is not yet clinically precise, because both benign and malignant tumors can cause elevations in PSA (Woodrum et al., 1998). Furthermore, a recent study found that ejaculation can cause a significant increase in PSA levels that may persist for up to 48 hours. The authors of this investigation recommend that men avoid ejaculating for at least 48 hours prior to having a PSA test (Tchetgen et al., 1996). A normal PSA is usually considered to be any level below 4 nanograms per milliliter of blood (Goolsby, 1998; Uno et al., 1998).

The various diagnostic procedures for prostate cancer may also uncover signs of cancer in the colon or rectum. Women too develop cancers of the rectum and colon; about 50,000 men and women die of these diseases each year. The American Cancer Society therefore recommends an annual rectal examination for men and women age 40 and older, and a rectal exam plus a PSA test for men 50 and older (Coley et al., 1997b; Frizzell, 1998). The Cancer Society also recommends a combination of a rectal examination (digital or ultrasound) and a PSA test beginning at age 40 for men with a family history of prostate cancer and for African American men. The use of only a PSA test, without an accompanying rectal examination, is not advisable in that rectal examinations sometimes detect cancer that would be missed by PSA measurement (Coley et al., 1997a).

What might be some reasons why men are often reluctant to have a rectal prostate examination?

Many men are hesitant to have rectal examinations. They may be uncomfortable about homosexual associations when the examining physician is male, or they may fear what the examination might reveal. Many men believe that prostate surgery will inevitably interfere with sexual functioning. Although it can interfere, men treated for prostate cancer commonly experience continued sexual functioning.

On the Edge

To Treat or Not to Treat: Health Risks and Benefits of Prostate Cancer Treatment versus "Watchful Waiting"

Medical experts differ widely on the question of whether treatment should be immediate or deferred after a diagnosis of prostate cancer. A growing volume of articles in the medical literature reveal that this a controversy without simple answers and one that is likely to endure for some time. Arguments for immediate surgical, radiation, or antiandrogen treatments, especially for younger men, include prolongation of survival time, more vitality, significantly less bodily pain, prevention of bladder obstruction, and prevention of cancer spread to other areas (notably the spinal cord) (Albertsen et al., 1997; Lange, 1995; Medical Research Council, 1997). Support for deferred treatment ("watchful waiting") is provided by studies indicating that surgical, radiation, or hormonal treatments may result in a variety of problems including incontinence, retrograde ejaculation (semen expelled into the bladder rather than out of the penis), difficulty achieving erections, and inability to experience orgasm (Coley et al., 1997b; Dunsmuir & Emberton, 1997; Goluboff et al., 1998). However, in some cases postsurgical erection problems that occur after a radical prostatectomy may be averted by surgical techniques that avoid cutting a small group of nerves involved in facilitating erection (Fleming et al., 1993; Middleton, 1997). In addition, orgasm without erection is possible for many men, and treatment options described in Chapter 16 can be helpful for men who do experience erectile difficulties.

A factor complicating the "to treat or not to treat" issue is that many men, especially those afflicted after age 70, die from unrelated causes before developing health-impairing symptoms of this often slow-to-progress disease (Medical Research Council, 1997). In two major studies of large research populations, 59% and 33%, respectively, of patients in the deferred treatment category died from other causes before manifesting prostate cancer symptoms (Byar, 1973; Medical Research Council, 1997). This substantial possibility of dying before developing any serious complications from untreated prostate cancer provides cause for thoughtful pause before subjecting men to medical treatment that may yield a variety of problems. In light of these findings, it may be desirable to defer treatment of men over 70 who have asymptomatic prostate cancer that has not spread to other areas of the body. In contrast, most men diagnosed prior to age 70 develop indicators for treatment sometime during their postdiagnosis lifetimes, a finding that lends considerable support for the benefits of immediate treatment in younger men (Medical Research Council, 1997). Nevertheless, for some men, the well-defined potential adverse consequences of early treatment of prostate cancer "will appear to overwhelm even the

Once prostate cancer has been diagnosed, it may be treated in a number of ways. The treatments of choice for younger men are generally surgery, radiation therapy, or hormonal therapy (Goolsby, 1998). Among surgical options are radical prostatectomy (removal of the entire prostate gland), partial prostatectomy in which cancerous portions of the prostate are removed via the urethra, and cryoprostatectomy wherein the cancerous cells are destroyed via freezing (Medical Research Council, 1997; Menon, 1997). Because growth of prostatic cancer tumors is stimulated by androgen (Medical Research Council, 1997; Uno et al., 1998), another treatment option is either *orchidectomy* (surgical removal of the testes) or application of androgen-blocking hormones (Albertsen et al., 1997; Menon, 1997). Finally, because the danger or complications of surgery, radiation, or hormone therapy in older men may outweigh potential benefits, an approach called expectant management that involves "watchful waiting" with deferred treatment may be deemed most appropriate (Coley et al., 1997b; Medical Research Council, 1997; Menon, 1997). Expectant management is currently the most favored strategy for dealing with diagnosed prostate cancer outside of the United States (Coley et al., 1997b).

At the time of this writing there is considerable controversy about what is the optimal approach to treating early detected prostatic cancer. Furthermore, a debate rages over whether or not the benefits outweigh the health risks of treatment. These timely issues are discussed in the box "To Treat or Not to Treat: Health Risks and Benefits of Prostatic Cancer Therapy versus "Watchful Waiting."

On the Edge

maximum benefits presented, especially because risks are faced immediately whereas potential benefits are usually delayed for years" (Coley et al., 1997b, p. 477). Furthermore, even aggressive treatment of prostate cancer does not preclude the need for further cancer treatment at some future time. In one recent study of 3173 men who underwent radical prostatectomy within three months of prostate cancer diagnosis, 35% received radiation or hormone injections or had an orchidectomy within five years of the original surgery (Lu-Yao et al., 1996).

Because of the current lack of sufficient information from well-controlled, long-term studies of treatment outcomes, clinicians who treat prostate cancer must struggle to decide which prostate tumors are relatively insignificant and which warrant aggressive treatment. Researchers are presently attempting to remedy this problem by seeking to discover biological markers that will indicate what types of prostate tumors are likely to develop relatively rapidly into serious life-eroding or life-threatening cancers (Coetzee et al., 1997; Gburek et al., 1997; Stattin et al., 1997). A study just released indicates that a new type of PSA test may offer a powerful tool for both detecting the presence of prostate cancer and estimating its growth rate. The standard or traditional PSA test measures the amount of PSA protein that is chemically bound to another substance. The new test measures the amount of chemically free PSA. Researchers have found that when 25% or less of circulating PSA was chemically free, cancer was found to be present 95% of the time. Furthermore, the lower the percentage of free PSA, the more aggressive the cancer (Catalona et al., 1998). Prostate cancer kills, but not everyone, and the race is now on to identify the "bad actors." Until such time as clearer indicators are forthcoming (we hope before our youthful male readers reach middle age), the trend will be to carefully evaluate, on a case-by-case basis, the pros and cons of immediate versus deferred treatment of prostate cancer.

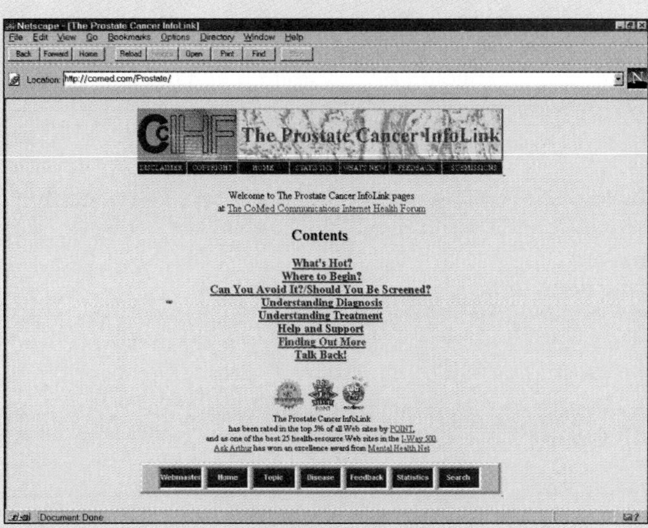

The Prostate Cancer InfoLink (http://comed.com/Prostate)

Summary

SEXUAL ANATOMY

The penis consists of an internal root within the body cavity; an external, pendulous portion known as its body, or shaft; and the smooth, acorn-shaped head, called the glans. Running the length of the penis are three internal chambers filled with spongelike tissue that becomes engorged with blood during sexual arousal.

The scrotum is a loose outpocket of the lower abdominal wall, consisting of an outer skin layer and an inner muscle layer. Housed within the scrotum are the two testes, or testicles, each suspended within its respective compartment by the spermatic cord.

Human testes have two major functions: sperm production and secretion of sex hormones.

Sperm development requires a scrotal temperature slightly lower than normal body temperature.

The interior of each testicle is divided into a large number of chambers that contain the thin, highly coiled seminiferous tubules in which sperm production occurs.

Adhering to the back and upper surface of each testicle is a C-shaped structure, the epididymis, within which sperm maturation occurs.

Sperm travel from the epididymis of each testicle through a long, thin tube, the vas deferens, which eventually terminates at the base of the bladder, where it is joined by the ejaculatory duct of the seminal vesicle.

The seminal vesicles are two small glands, each near the terminal of a vas deferens. They secrete an alkaline fluid that constitutes about 70% of the semen and appears to nourish and stimulate sperm cells.

The prostate gland, located at the base of the bladder and traversed by the urethra, provides about 30% of the seminal fluid released during ejaculation.

Two pea-sized structures, the Cowper's glands, are connected by tiny ducts to the urethra just below the prostate gland. During sexual arousal, they often produce a few drops of slippery, alkaline fluid, which appear at the tip of the penis.

Semen consists of sperm cells and secretions from the prostate, seminal vesicles, and Cowper's glands. The sperm component is only a tiny portion of the total fluid expelled during ejaculation.

MALE SEXUAL FUNCTIONS

Penile erection is an involuntary process that results from adequate sexual stimulation—physiological, psychological, or both.

Ejaculation is the process by which semen is transported out through the penis. It occurs in two stages: the emission phase, when seminal fluid is collected in the urethral bulb, and the expulsion phase, when strong muscle contractions expel the semen. In retrograde ejaculation, semen is expelled into the bladder.

SOME CONCERNS ABOUT SEXUAL FUNCTIONING

Penis size does not significantly influence the ability to give or receive pleasure during penile–vaginal intercourse. Neither is it correlated with other physical variables such as body shape or height.

Circumcision, the surgical removal of the foreskin, is widely practiced in this country. Medical evidence supporting its hygienic benefits is inconclusive, as are data concerning its effect on erotic or functional elements of sexual expression.

MALE GENITAL HEALTH CONCERNS

The male genital and internal reproductive structures may be adversely affected by a variety of diseases and injuries.

Injuries to the penis may be avoided by not using various sexual gadgets and by taking precautions during coitus.

Penile cancer is a rare malignancy that can be deadly if not diagnosed and treated in its earliest stage. Testicular cancer is more common than penile cancer, especially in young men. If detected in its early stages, testicular cancer is also highly curable.

The prostate gland is a focal point of some of the more common male problems, including prostatitis, benign prostatic hyperplasia, and prostate cancer. A variety of drugs and/or surgical procedures are used to treat these conditions. Considerable controversy exists about what constitutes the best treatment strategy for diagnosed prostate cancer.

Thought Provokers

1. If you had a newborn son, would you have him circumcised? When? Why or why not?
2. Do you believe that penis size is an important factor in a woman's coital satisfaction? What effect, if any, has the "bigger-is-better" view of penis size had on your own sexual functioning?
3. What are some of the possible negative or positive effects of nocturnal emissions in an adolescent male? What can be done to minimize any adverse consequences of this natural occurrence?

Suggested Readings

Blank, Joani (1975). *The Playbook: For Men/About Sex.* Burlingame, CA: Down There Press. This is an informally written self-awareness workbook for men. It includes topics such as body image, genital awareness, masturbation, sexual response, relationships, and fantasy.

Garnick, Marc (1996). *The Patient's Guide to Prostate Cancer: An Expert's Successful Treatment Strategies and Options.* New York: NAL-Dutton. This excellent, accessible book, written by one of the top physician experts on prostate cancer, provides potentially lifesaving information about all aspects of prostate cancer including risk factors, diagnostic procedures, impact of the disease on sexual functioning, and treatment strategies.

Gilbaugh, James (1993). *Men's Private Parts.* New York: Crown Publishers. A urologist provides practical advice about male sexual anatomy and physiology in an easy-to-read and sometimes humorous format.

Kinsey, Alfred C.; Pomeroy, Wardell B.; and Martin, Clyde E. (1948). *Sexual Behavior in the Human Male.* Philadelphia: Saunders. Besides extensive data on male sexual behaviors, this volume contains an abundance of details about a male's sexual anatomy and the manner in which he responds physiologically to sexual stimulation.

Silverstein, Judith (1986). *Sexual Enhancement for Men.* New York: Vantage Press. This book offers both a thoughtful and sensitive discussion of concerns and issues pertaining to male sexuality and some excellent suggestions for enhancing sexual functioning and for overcoming a range of sexual problems. Silverstein also puts into perspective many of the sexual myths and pressures that often erode the quality of male sexual functioning.

Zilbergeld, Bernie (1992). *The New Male Sexuality: A Guide to Sexual Fulfillment.* New York: Bantam. An exceptionally well-written and informative treatment of male sexuality, including such topics as sexual functioning, self-awareness, and overcoming difficulties.

Web Resources

Male Health Center
www.malehealthcenter.com/
An array of information is provided at this site, much of it related to male genital health, birth control from the male perspective, and sexual functioning.

Circumcision Information and Resource Pages
www.cirp.org/CIRP
While providing general information about the pros and cons of circumcision, and articles written from opposing viewpoints, this site takes the point of view that other than for religious or cultural reasons, in most cases male circumcision is an unnecessary surgery.

Prostate Cancer Dot Com
www.prostatecancer.com/pcdc.html
This Web site is devoted to providing current information on prostate cancer and its treatment. The numerous resources available here include journal abstracts, discussion forums, and descriptions of various treatment strategies.

6

Sexual Arousal and Response

Sexual Arousal

What is the role of hormones in human sexual arousal?
In what ways does the brain influence arousal?
How do the senses of touch, vision, smell, taste, and hearing contribute to erotic arousal?

Sexual Response

What common physiological changes accompany each stage of the sexual response cycle?
How are the sexual responses of men and women similar? How are they different?

There was never any heat or passion in my five-year relationship with Doug. He was a nice man, but I could never bridge the gap between us, which was due, in large part, to his unwillingness or inability to let go and express his feelings and vulnerability. Our love-making was like that too—kind of mechanical, as though he was there physically but not emotionally. I seldom felt any sexual desire for Doug, and sometimes my body barely responded during sex. How different it is with Matt, my current and, hopefully, lifetime partner. There was an almost instant closeness and intimacy at the beginning of our relationship. The first time we made love I felt like I was on fire. It was like we were melded together, both physically and emotionally. Sometimes just hearing his voice or the slightest touch arouses me intensely. (Authors' files)

Sexual arousal and response in humans are influenced by many factors: hormones, our brain's capacity to create images and fantasies, our emotions, various sensory processes, the level of intimacy between two people, and a host of other influences. We begin this chapter by discussing some of the things that influence sexual arousal. We then turn our attention to the ways in which our bodies respond to sexual stimulation. We concentrate primarily on biological factors and events associated with human sexual arousal and response, but this focus on physiology is not meant to minimize the importance of psychological and cultural influences. In fact, psychosocial factors probably play a greater role than do biological ones in the extremely varied patterns of human sexual response, as we will discover in later chapters.

Sexual Arousal

In this section, we single out a number of factors as we explore the complexity of human sexual arousal: the role of hormonal influences; the impact of brain functions; sensory input and the individual ways we interpret it; and, finally, the reputed effects of certain foods and drugs.

The Role of Hormones

For years sex researchers have held differing opinions about the relative importance of hormones in human sexual arousal and behavior. These differences exist for several good reasons. For one, it is extremely difficult to distinguish between the effects of physiological processes, especially hormone production, and those of psychosocial processes such as early socialization, peer-group learning, and emotional development. Furthermore, until recently much of the data relating sexuality and hormones were derived from poorly controlled studies of limited research populations. However, in recent years a number of well-designed, carefully implemented investigations have given us a better understanding of the complex relationship between hormones and sexual activity.

Which hormones are important in human sexuality? Have different hormones been linked with male versus female sexual functions?

No doubt you have heard the common descriptive expressions "male" sex hormones and "female" sex hormones. As we shall see, linking specific hormones to one or the other sex is somewhat misleading in that *both* sexes produce so-called male sex hormones and female sex hormones. As we learned in Chapter 3, the general term for male sex hormones is *androgens.* In males, about 95% of total androgens are produced by the testes. Most of the remaining 5% is produced by the outer portions of the adrenal glands (called the adrenal cortex). A woman's ovaries and adrenals also produce androgens in approximately equal amounts (Rako, 1996). The dominant androgen in both males and females is testosterone. Men's bodies typically produce 20 to 40 times as much testosterone as women (Crenshaw, 1996; Rako, 1996). Female sex hormones, estrogens, are produced predominantly by the ovaries in females. Male testes also produce estrogens but in much smaller quantities than occur in female's bodies. In the following sections we will consider the evidence linking testosterone to sexual functioning in both sexes as well as examine the role of estrogens in female sexuality.

Hormones in Male Sexual Behavior

A number of lines of research have linked testosterone with male sexuality (Crenshaw, 1996; Everitt & Bancroft, 1991). This research indicates that testosterone generally has a greater impact on male sexual desire (libido) than on sexual functioning (Crenshaw, 1996). Thus a man with a low testosterone level may have little interest in sexual activity but, nevertheless, be fully capable of erection and orgasms. However, testosterone does influence sensitivity of the genitals, and thus a deficiency of this hormone may decrease sexual pleasure (Crenshaw, 1996; Rako, 1996). Furthermore, some men may experience erectile difficulties that are associated with testosterone deficiency.

One source of information about testosterone's impact on male sexual function is studies of men who have undergone **castration.** This operation, called **orchidectomy** in medical language, involves removal of the testes and is sometimes performed as medical treatment for such diseases as genital tuberculosis and prostate cancer (Albertsen et al., 1997; Greenstein et al., 1995; Menon, 1997). Two European studies reported that surgically castrated male subjects experienced significantly reduced sexual interest and activity within the first year after undergoing this operation (Bremer, 1959; Heim, 1981). Other researchers have recorded incidences of continued sexual desire and functioning for as long as 30 years following castration, without supplementary testosterone treatment (Ford & Beach, 1951; Greenstein et al., 1995). However, even in those instances when sexual behavior persists following castration, the levels of sexual interest and activity generally diminish, often markedly. The fact that this reduction occurs so frequently indicates that testosterone is a very important biological instigator of sexual desire.

Castration
Surgical removal of the testes.

Orchidectomy
The surgical procedure for removing the testes.

A second line of research investigating links between hormones and male sexual functioning involves androgen-blocking drugs. In recent years, a class of drugs known as *antiandrogens* has been used in Europe and America to treat sex offenders as well as certain medical conditions such as advanced prostate cancer. Antiandrogens drastically reduce the amount of testosterone circulating in the bloodstream (Bradford & Pawlak, 1993a & 1993b; Crenshaw, 1996; Crenshaw & Goldberg, 1996). One of these drugs, *medroxyprogesterone acetate* (*MPA,* also known by its trade name, *Depo-Provera*), has received a great deal of media attention in the United States in the last few years. A number of studies have found that Depo-Provera and other antiandrogens are often effective in reducing both sexual interest and sexual activity in human males (and females) (Crenshaw, 1996; Crenshaw & Goldberg, 1996; Bradford & Pawlak, 1993a & 1993b). However, altering testosterone levels is not a 100% effective treatment for sex offenders, especially in cases where sexual assaults stem from nonsexual motives such as anger or the wish to exert power and control over another person.

A third source of evidence linking testosterone to sexual motivation in males is research on **hypogonadism,** a state of testosterone deficiency that results from certain diseases of the endocrine system. If this condition occurs before puberty, maturation of the primary and secondary sex characteristics is retarded, and the individual may never develop an active sexual interest. The results are more variable if testosterone deficiency occurs in adulthood. Extensive studies of hypogonadal men conducted by a number of researchers provide strong evidence that testosterone plays an important role in male

Hypogonadism
Impaired hormone production in the testes that results in testosterone deficiency.

sexual desire (Davidson & Rosen, 1992; Morales et al., 1997; Zini et al., 1990). For example, it has been shown that when hypogonadal men receive hormone treatments to replace testosterone, they often experience a return of normal sexual interest and activity. If the treatments are temporarily suspended, sexual desire and activity decline within two to three weeks (Cunningham et al., 1989; Findlay et al., 1989).

Do you think that estrogens are as important in women's sexuality as androgens are in men's?

Hormones in Female Sexual Behavior

Although it is known that estrogens help maintain the elasticity of the vaginal lining and also contribute to vaginal lubrication (Crenshaw, 1996; Hutchinson, 1995), the role of estrogens in female sexual motivation is still unclear. Some researchers who have studied postmenopausal women (menopause is associated with marked reduction in estrogen production), or women who have had their ovaries removed for medical reasons, have reported that when these women receive estrogen-replacement therapy (ERT), they experience not only heightened vaginal lubrication but also somewhat increased sexual desire, pleasure, and orgasmic capacity (Dennerstein et al., 1980; Dow et al., 1983). Theresa Crenshaw (1996), a renowned specialist in sexual medicine, maintains that the sexual benefits that often result from ERT in women occur because estrogen provides "mood-mellowing" benefits and thus creates an emotional atmosphere receptive to sexual involvement with another. However, other investigators have found ERT to have no discernible impact on sexual desire and activity (Furuhjelm et al., 1984; Myers et al., 1990). In view of these contradictory findings, the role of estrogens in female sexual motivation and functioning remains unclear.

Far less ambiguity exists regarding the role of testosterone in female sexuality. In recent years an accumulation of evidence from many sources leaves little doubt that testosterone plays an important role as the major libido hormone in females (Crenshaw, 1996; Hutchinson, 1995; Rako, 1996). Numerous experimental evaluations of the effects of testosterone on female sexuality have yielded evidence of a positive correlation between levels of circulating testosterone and frequency of sexual activity (Bancroft et al., 1991; Bellerose & Binik, 1993; Hulter & Lundberg, 1994). For instance, two investigations revealed that women who received testosterone after their ovaries were surgically removed reported markedly greater levels of sexual desire, sexual arousal, and sexual fantasies than subjects who received estrogen alone or a *placebo* (a pharmacologically inert substance) (Sherwin & Gelfand, 1987; Sherwin et al., 1985). Another study of women who had their ovaries removed found that subjects who were provided with a combination of testosterone plus estrogen supplements reported higher levels of sexual desire and arousal than women who received estrogen only or no hormone replacement (Bellerose & Binik, 1993). The results of studies such as these, together with her own extensive clinical and research experience, has led Theresa Crenshaw (1996) to conclude "that testosterone plays a powerful role in female sexuality, and that when a woman's testosterone dwindles, so does her sex life" (p. 146). Susan Rako (1996), another noted physician authority on testosterone and female sexuality, recently authored *The Hormone of Desire.* This book emerged from Rako's search for answers to her own medical dilemma associated with adverse symptoms of menopausally induced testosterone deficiency. Her exhaustive investigation led her to conclude that "testosterone is the hormone responsible for the experience of sexual desire not only for men but also for women" (p. 25).

How Much Testosterone Is Necessary for Normal Sexual Functioning?

Now that we have learned that testosterone plays a critical role in maintaining sexual desire in both sexes, we may ask, "How much is necessary to ensure normal sexual arousability?" The answer to this question is complex and influenced by several factors, outlined as follows:

Testosterone in the bodies of both sexes comes in two forms: attached (bound) and unattached (free). About 95% of the testosterone circulating in a man's blood is testosterone bound on a protein molecule (either albumin or globulin), where it is inactive or metabolically ineffective. The remaining 5% is the unbound or free version of testosterone, which is metabolically active and influences male libido (Crenshaw, 1996). Comparable figures for women are 97% to 99% bound testosterone and only 1% to 3% free to produce effects on bodily tissues (Rako, 1996). The sum of free and bound testosterone in both sexes is total testosterone. The normal range of total testosterone in the blood of a man varies between 250 and 1200 ng/dl (nanograms per deciliter) and the normal range of free testosterone in men is 1.0 to 5.0 ng/dl. In women, the normal range of total testosterone is 20 to 50 ng/dl, and free testosterone typically ranges from 0.1 to 0.5 ng/dl (Crenshaw, 1996; Rako, 1996). In reference to these normal range statistics, it is important to add that the essential amount, or "critical mass," of testosterone necessary for adequate functioning varies from person to person within both sexes (Crenshaw, 1996; Rako, 1996).

The fact that women normally have much smaller amounts of testosterone than men does not mean they have lower or weaker sex drives. Rather, it appears that women's body cells are more sensitive to testosterone than men's are. Therefore, for females a little testosterone is all that is necessary to stimulate libido (Bancroft, 1984; Crenshaw, 1996).

Raising the level of testosterone above a normal range is unlikely to stimulate a further increase in sexual energy or motivation (Crenshaw, 1996; Rako, 1996). Furthermore, too much testosterone can have adverse effects on both sexes. Excess testosterone supplements in men may cause a variety of problems including disruption of natural hormone cycles, salt retention, fluid retention, and hair loss. Furthermore, although there is no evidence that testosterone can cause cancer of the prostate, it can stimulate growth of preexisting cancer of this gland (Crenshaw, 1996; Rako, 1996). In women, excess testosterone can stimulate significant growth of facial and body hair, increased muscle mass, reduction in breast size, and enlargement of the clitoris. However, "only the use of irresponsibly high doses of testosterone over a sustained period of time can produce undesirable effects" (Rako, 1996, p. 25). Furthermore, as we have seen, supplementary testosterone can help restore sexual desire to men and women with deficient levels of this libido hormone.

A normal level of total testosterone in either sex does not necessarily rule out a biological basis for a flagging sex drive, because the key hormonal component in libido—free testosterone—may be abnormally low even though total testosterone levels, male or female, are within normal limits. Consequently, should you find yourself experiencing testosterone deficiency (see next section), it is important that, as an informed consumer of health care, you request to have your free testosterone levels assessed in addition to total testosterone. Until recently, most physicians only ordered testing of total testosterone. Even today, this improper and incomplete testing procedure is still followed by some medical practitioners (Crenshaw, 1996). Details pertaining to proper methods for measuring testosterone levels in women and men are described in Rako's book and Crenshaw's critically acclaimed text, *The Alchemy of Love and Lust* (1996).

Finally, there are marked sex differences in the rate at which testosterone production diminishes with aging. When a woman's ovaries begin to shut down at menopause, there is often a rather rapid reduction in her total body testosterone levels that can take place over a matter of months. For other women, the onset of testosterone deficiency may be more gradual, taking place over a period of several years. (Women who have their ovaries surgically removed are more likely to experience an abrupt or precipitous loss of testosterone.) Even though a women's adrenals continue to produce testosterone, their output also diminishes when her ovaries are no longer producing normal levels of testosterone (Rako, 1996).

In contrast, in men the decline in total body testosterone with aging is usually much less rapid or precipitous. Although it is true that testosterone production in both the testes and adrenals diminish with aging, the changes over time are generally gradual rather than abrupt and typically take place over an extended number of years. This is probably due, in large part, to the continued functioning of the testes, which, unlike ovaries, do not undergo a fairly rapid shutdown in the middle of life.

What Are the Signs of Testosterone Deficiency?

The general signs of testosterone deficiency are similar in both sexes, even though they may have a more rapid onset in women than men for reasons previously described. The most obvious symptoms of testosterone deficiency, as described by Rako (1996) and Crenshaw (1996), are

1. Decrease in one's customary level of sexual desire.
2. Reduced sensitivity of the genitals and the nipples to sexual stimulation.
3. Overall reduction in general levels of sexual arousability, possibly accompanied by decreased orgasmic capacity and/or less intense orgasms.
4. Diminished energy levels. Research has shown that testosterone and other androgens have some biological impact on virtually all bodily tissues, and are essential for promoting efficient cellular functioning, nourishment for growth and tissue maintenance, and healthy muscles and bones (Yen & Jaffe, 1991). Without enough effective testosterone, our bodies regress into what biologists call a "catabolic state" in which we are likely to experience a loss of muscle tone and vital energy (Rako, 1996).
5. And, for some women only, thinning and loss of pubic hair.

Testosterone-Replacement Therapy

If you find yourself experiencing some of these symptoms, it may be appropriate to seek medical advice regarding possible testosterone-replacement therapy (TRT). At the present time men generally find it much easier than women to secure medical advice about TRT. The use of testosterone supplements to treat male sexual difficulties is relatively common. In marked contrast, there is widespread reluctance on the part of the medical community to prescribe supplementary testosterone for women who manifest symptoms of deficiency (Crenshaw, 1996; Rako, 1996). Too often physicians adhere rigidly to the notion that "testosterone for women is unnatural" (Rako, 1996, p. 36). This misinformed position completely overlooks the obvious fact that testosterone is a sex hormone that occurs naturally in females as well as males. Two medical authorities on gynecology and menopause, Wulf Utian of Case Western Reserve University and Isaac Schiff of Harvard Medical School, recently observed that American physicians typically lack knowledge about the role of testosterone in maintaining women's general vitality and sexual health (Utian & Schiff, 1994). These physician experts stress the need for educating physicians as well as consumers of health care, especially postmenopausal women, about the use of supplementary testosterone.

Where can a woman find a physician who knows about the adverse impact of testosterone deficiency in women and is comfortable with and informed about the proper application of TRT? Rako addresses this in her book. In 1993, approximately half of the physicians attending the annual meeting of the North American Menopause Society indicated they were currently prescribing testosterone for women. These medical practitioners represent perhaps the best source of informed specialists on TRT that a woman is likely to find. The North American Menopause Society will provide, on request, a referral list of member physicians, grouped by state. The address of this professional organization is listed at the end of this chapter.

Before describing some of the actual TRT methods, it is important to stress that testosterone supplementation is not necessary or appropriate for every woman whose ovaries either reduce hormonal outputs at menopause or are surgically removed. Based on her extensive experience practicing sexual medicine, Theresa Crenshaw (1996) concludes that estrogen supplementation alone "is often enough to maintain normal female well-being, including sexual desire and activity" (p. 255). However, Crenshaw further observes that testosterone often needs to be added to estrogen-replacement therapy to "ensure robust, dependable sexual desire and response" (p. 255). Susan Rako (1996) also observes that some women have the genetic predisposition to maintain testosterone production that will keep them sexually vital, without TRT, for decades following menopause.

Because of the highly individualized manner in which people, men and women, respond to hormones, there is no clear-cut right or wrong approach to TRT. Rather, what is of critical importance is for the informed consumer to take adequate time to find a physician who will work with him or her to find the best dosage level and method of administration to effectively alleviate the symptoms of testosterone deficiency.

Testosterone supplements can be administered to men or women orally (swallowing), sublingually (under the tongue tablets), by injection, or by implantation of a pellet. A scrotal skin patch is also used in men and is likely to be available to women in the near future. Testosterone may also be applied to women via vaginal creams. Rako, Crenshaw, and other experts on TRT caution against taking too much testosterone. Taking a dosage greater than necessary to eliminate deprivation symptoms is not likely to improve libido and general energy level, and may result in one or more adverse side effects previously described.

The Brain

From our experience, we know that the brain plays an important role in our sexuality. Our thoughts, emotions, and memories are all mediated through its complex mechanisms. Sexual arousal can occur without any sensory stimulation; it can be produced by the process of *fantasy* (in this case, thinking of erotic images or sexual interludes), and some individuals may even reach orgasm during a fantasy experience without any physical stimulation (Kinsey et al., 1948 & 1953; Whipple et al., 1992).

We know that specific events can cause us to become aroused. Less apparent is the role of individual experience and cultural influence, both of which are mediated by our

Sexuality and Diversity

Cultural Variations in Sexual Arousal

Although the biological mechanisms underlying human sexual arousal and response are essentially universal, the particular sexual stimuli and/or behaviors that people find arousing are greatly influenced by cultural conditioning. For example, in Western societies, where the emphasis during sexual activity tends to be heavily weighted toward achieving orgasm, genitally focused activities are frequently defined as optimally arousing. In contrast, devotees to Eastern Tantric traditions (where spirituality is interwoven with sexuality) often achieve optimal pleasure by emphasizing the sensual and spiritual aspects of shared intimacy rather than orgasmic release (Devi, 1977). In the following paragraphs, we will provide brief examples of some other facets of cultural diversity in human sexual arousal.

Kissing on the mouth, a universal source of sexual arousal in Western society, may be rare or absent in many other parts of the world. Certain North American Eskimo people and inhabitants of the Trobriand Islands would rather rub noses than lips, and among the Thonga of South Africa, kissing is viewed as odious behavior. The Hindu people of India are also disinclined to kiss because they believe such contact symbolically contaminates the act of sexual intercourse. In their survey of 190 societies, Clellan Ford and Frank Beach (1951) found that mouth kissing was acknowledged in only 21 societies and practiced as a prelude or accompaniment to coitus in only 13.

Oral sex (both cunnilingus and fellatio) is a common source of sexual arousal among island societies of the South Pacific, in industrialized nations of Asia, and in much of the Western world. In contrast, in Africa (with the exception of northern regions), such practices are likely to be viewed as unnatural or disgusting behavior.

Foreplay in general, whether it be oral sex, sensual touching, or passionate kissing, is subject to wide cultural variation. In some societies, most notably those with Eastern traditions, couples may strive to prolong intense states of sexual arousal for several hours (Devi, 1977). Although varied patterns of foreplay are common in Western cultures, these activities often are of short duration as lovers move rapidly toward the "main event" of coitus. In still other societies, foreplay is either sharply curtailed or absent altogether. For example, the Lepcha farmers of the southeastern Himalayas limit foreplay to men

(continued on next page)

brains. Clearly, we do not all respond similarly to the same stimuli. Some people may be highly aroused if their partners use explicit sexual language; others may find such words to be threatening or a sexual turnoff. Cultural influences also play an important role, as we see in the boxed discussion, "Cultural Variations in Human Sexual Arousal." Thus the smell of genital secretions may be more arousing to many Europeans than to members of our own deodorant-conscious society. The brain is the storehouse of our memories and cultural values, and consequently its influence over our sexual arousability is profound.

Strictly mental events such as fantasies are the product of the ***cerebral cortex,*** *the "thinking center" of the brain that controls functions like reasoning, language, and imagination. Do you think that any other brain centers are involved in sexual arousal? If so, which areas?*

Cerebral cortex
The thin outer layer of the brain's cerebrum that controls higher mental processes.

Limbic system
A subcortical brain system composed of several interrelated structures that influences the sexual behavior of humans and other animals.

The cortex represents only one level of functioning at which the brain influences human sexual arousal and response. At a subcortical level, the **limbic system** seems to play an important part in determining sexual behavior, both in humans and in other animals (Everitt, 1990; Kimble, 1996).

Figure 6.1 shows some key structures in the limbic system. These include the *cingulate gyrus,* the *amygdala,* the *hippocampus,* and parts of the *hypothalamus,* which plays a regulating role. Research links various sites in this system with sexual behavior. For instance, several animal studies have implicated the hypothalamus in sexual functioning. Researchers have reported increased sexual activity in rats, including erections and ejaculations, triggered by stimulation in both anterior and posterior regions of the hypothalamus (Caggiula & Hoebel, 1966; Van Dis & Larsson, 1971; Vaughn & Fisher, 1962). When certain parts of the hypothalamus are surgically destroyed, there may be a dramatic reduction in the sexual behavior of both males and females of several species (Hitt et al., 1970; Sawyer, 1960).

Sexuality and Diversity

briefly caressing their partners' breasts, and among the Irish inhabitants of Inis Beag, precoital sexual activity is reported to be limited to mouth kissing and rough fondling of the woman's lower body by her partner (Messenger, 1971).

Another indicator of cultural diversity is the wide variety in standards of attractiveness. Although physical qualities exert a profound influence on human sexual arousal in virtually every culture, standards of attractiveness vary widely, as can be seen in the accompanying photos of women and men from around the world who are considered to be attractive in their own cultures. What may be attractive or a source of erotic arousal in one culture may seem strange or unattractive in others. For instance, although some island societies attach erotic significance to the shape and textures of female genitals, most Western societies do not. To cite a final example, in many societies bare female breasts are not generally viewed as erotic stimuli, as they are in America. In fact, aside from general indicators of good health (healthy skin, hair, teeth, etc.), there is little agreement among the world's diverse cultures about what makes a potential sexual partner attractive (Gray & Wolfe, 1992).

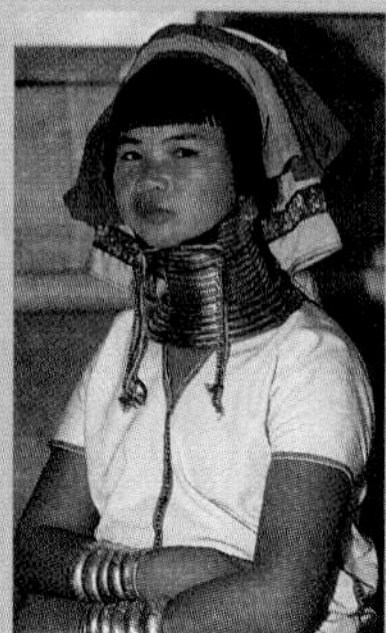
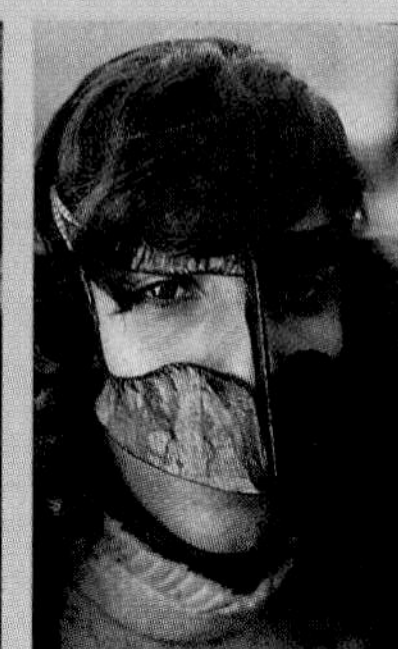

Our standards of physical attractiveness vary widely, as can be seen in these six photos of women and men from around the world who are considered in their cultures to be attractive.

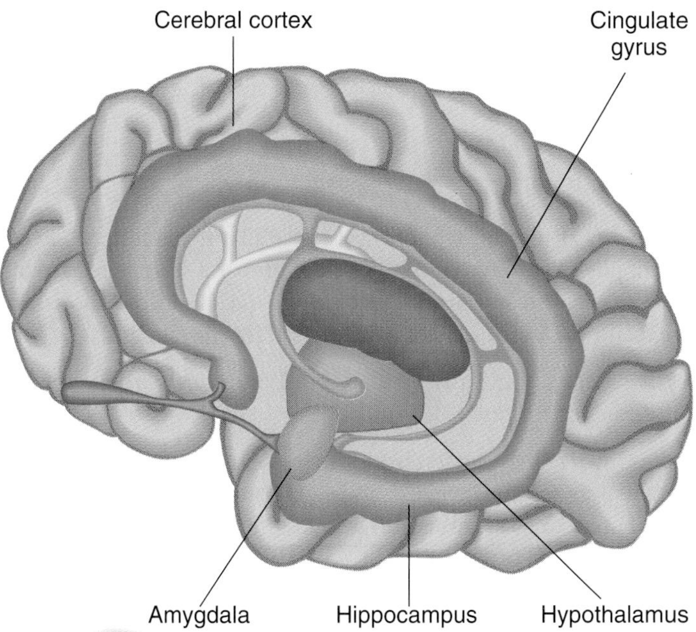

Figure 6.1

The limbic system, a region of the brain associated with emotion and motivation, is important in human sexual function. Key structures, shaded in color, include the cingulate gyrus, portions of the hypothalamus, amygdala, and the hippocampus.

Some of the most striking findings come from the research of James Olds, who in the 1950s conducted a series of experiments involving limbic system stimulation of rats. Olds designed a system that enabled the rats to self-stimulate their brains: He implanted tiny electrodes in several regions of the limbic system (within the hypothalamus and septal area) and connected these electrodes to a special apparatus with a lever. The results? The rats responded by pressing the lever over and over again, to the point of exhaustion—as frequently as several thousand times per hour. This response, and the intense pleasure that the rats seemed to be experiencing, led Olds to call these limbic system regions "pleasure centers" (Olds, 1956). Olds's rats were unable to tell him whether the pleasure they were experiencing was sexual in nature. Subsequent research with humans is more enlightening.

For ethical reasons, few experiments have studied the effects of brain stimulation on humans. However, there is some evidence that electrical stimulation of the hypothalamus in human subjects produces sexual arousal, sometimes culminating in orgasm (Sem-Jacobsen, 1968). Furthermore, there are recorded cases in which electrical and chemical brain stimulation of humans, done for therapeutic purposes, has had similar impact.

Medical researcher Robert Heath (1972) experimented with limbic system stimulation in patients suffering from various disorders. He theorized that stimulation-induced pleasure would prove to have some therapeutic value. One patient, a man with an emotional disorder, was provided with a self-stimulation device that he used up to 1500 times per hour to administer stimulation to his septal area. He described the stimulation as producing intense sexual pleasure, protesting each time the unit was taken away from him. Another patient, a woman with an epileptic disorder, reported intense sexual pleasure and experienced multiple orgasmic responses as a direct result of brain stimulation.

It is doubtful that researchers will ever find one specific "sex center" in the brain. However, it is clear that both the cerebral cortex and the limbic system play important roles in initiating, organizing, and controlling human sexual arousal and response. In addition, the brain interprets a variety of sensory inputs that often exert a profound influence on sexual arousal. We examine this topic in the next section.

The Senses

It has been said that the brain is the most important sense organ for human sexual arousal. This observation implies that any sensory event, if properly interpreted by the brain, can serve as an effective sexual stimulus. The resulting variety in the sources of erotic stimulation helps explain the tremendous sexual complexity of humans.

In your opinion, which of the major senses (touch, vision, smell, taste, or hearing) typically has the greatest impact on sexual interaction?

Of the major senses, touch tends to predominate during sexual intimacy. However, all the senses have the potential to become involved, and sights, smells, sounds, and tastes all may be important contributors to erotic arousal. There are no blueprints for the what and how of sensory stimulation. Each of us is unique; we have our own individual triggers of arousal.

Sensual touching is one of the most frequent sources of erotic stimulation.

Touch

Stimulation of the various skin surfaces is probably a more frequent source of human sexual arousal than any other type of sensory stimulus. The nerve endings that respond to touch are distributed unevenly throughout the body, which explains why certain areas are more sensitive than others. Those locations that are most responsive to tactile pleasuring are commonly referred to as the **erogenous zones.** A distinction is often made between primary erogenous zones—those areas that contain dense concentrations of nerve endings—and secondary erogenous zones, which include other areas of the body that have become endowed with erotic significance through sexual conditioning.

A list of **primary erogenous zones** generally includes the genitals, buttocks, anus, perineum, breasts (particularly the nipples), inner surfaces of the thighs, armpits, navel, neck, ears (especially the lobes), and the mouth (lips, tongue, and the entire oral cavity). It is important to remember, however, that just because a given area qualifies as a primary erogenous zone, there is no guarantee that stimulating it will produce arousal in a sexual partner. What is intensely arousing for one person may produce no reaction—or even irritation—in another.

The **secondary erogenous zones** include virtually all other regions of the body. For example, if your lover tenderly kissed and stroked your upper back during each sexual interlude, this area could be transformed into an erogenous zone. These secondary locations become eroticized because they are touched within the context of sexual intimacies. A man describes how touch enhances his sexual experiences:

> I love being touched all over, particularly on my back. Each touch helps to develop trust and a sense of security. (Authors' files)

Erogenous zones
Areas of the body that are particularly responsive to sexual stimulation.

Primary erogenous zones
Areas of the body that contain dense concentrations of nerve endings.

Secondary erogenous zones
Areas of the body that have become erotically sensitive through learning and experience.

Vision

In our society, visual stimuli appear to be of great importance. Prime evidence is the emphasis we often place on physical appearance, including such activities as personal grooming, wearing the right clothes, and the extensive use of cosmetics. Therefore, it is not surprising that vision is second only to touch in the hierarchy of stimuli that most people view as sexually arousing.

Do you think that there are sex differences in how males and females respond to visual erotica?

The popularity of sexually explicit men's magazines in our society suggests that the human male is more aroused by visual stimuli than is the female. Early research seemed to support this conclusion. Kinsey found that more men than women reported being sexually excited by visual stimuli such as pinup erotica and stag shows (Kinsey et al., 1948 & 1953). However, this finding reflects several social influences, including the greater cultural inhibitions attached to such behavior in women at the time of his research and the simple fact that men had been provided far more opportunities to develop an appetite for such stimuli. This latter interpretation is supported by later research that used physiological recording devices (see Chapter 2) to measure sexual arousal under controlled laboratory conditions. These studies have demonstrated strong similarities in the physical responses of males and females to visual erotica (Fisher, 1983; Rubinsky et al., 1987). Recent research findings suggest that when sexual arousal is measured by self-reports rather than physiological devices, women are less inclined than men to report being sexually aroused by visual erotica (Koukounas & McCabe, 1997; Mosher & MacIan, 1994). This finding may reflect the persistence of cultural influences that make women reluctant to acknowledge being aroused by filmed erotica, or it may indicate that females have greater difficulty than males identifying signs of sexual arousal in their bodies, or it may be due to a combination of these factors.

Smell

A person's sexual history and cultural conditioning often influence what smells he or she finds arousing. We typically learn through experience to view certain odors as erotic and others as offensive. From this perspective, there may be nothing intrinsic to the fragrance of genital secretions that might cause them to be perceived as either arousing or distasteful. We might also argue the contrary—that the smell of genital secretions would be universally exciting to humans were it not that some people learn to view them as offensive. This latter interpretation is supported by the fact that some societies openly recognize the value of genital smells as a sexual stimulant. For example, in areas of Europe where the deodorant industry is less pervasive, some women use the natural bouquet of their genital secretions, strategically placed behind an ear or in the nape of the neck, to arouse their sexual partners.

Two women, followed by two men, describe the impact of smell on their sexuality:

> Smell is very erotic because it is the essence of love for me: It's a natural invitation to explore.

> Sometimes my partner exudes a sex smell that makes me instantly aroused.

> I enjoy associating a body scent or perfume with lovemaking, because when the smell comes around again I find it to be very arousing.

> There is really something stimulating about the scent of a woman and I enjoy both the smell and taste of a woman's skin. (Authors' files)

Among other animals, smells are often more important than visual stimuli in eliciting sexual response. The females of many species secrete certain substances, called **pheromones** (FARE-oh-mones), during their fertile periods (Crenshaw, 1996; Rasmussen et al., 1996; Roelofs, 1995). If you have ever had a female dog in heat and observed male dogs coming from miles around to scratch at your door, you will not doubt for a moment the importance of smell in sexual arousal. The relationship of sexual arousal to pheromones has been likened to that between salivation and the smell of food. Actually, these responses are quite different. The noses of dogs and other animals contain two channels of sensory input, "each with its own organ, nerves and bumps in the brain" (Moran in Blakeslee, 1993, p. 11). One of these channels, the *olfactory system,* responds to conventional smells, such as the odor of fresh meat. A second system, called the *vomeronasal system,* is comprised of two tiny pitlike organs (vomeronasal organs or VNO)

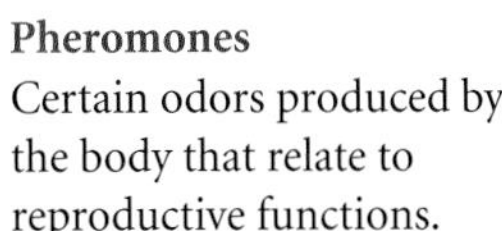

Pheromones
Certain odors produced by the body that relate to reproductive functions.

whose exclusive task is detecting pheromones. This system appears to be distinct and separate from odor-sensing olfactory organs (Weller, 1998).

Research on nonhuman animals has isolated a variety of pheromones, most of them associated with reproduction (Eggert & Muller, 1989; Rasmussen et al., 1996; Roelofs, 1995). For instance, in the early 1970s, researchers isolated fatty acids called *copulins* from vaginal secretions of female rhesus monkeys; these pheromones are a potent sexual attractant (Michael et al., 1971). Some years later, it was discovered that sexually aroused human females secrete a vaginal substance similar to this rhesus monkey pheromone (Cowley & Brooksbank, 1991; Michael et al., 1974; Morris & Udry, 1978). Another substance that has commanded attention in the search for erotic odors in humans is a powerful pheromone called *alpha androstenal,* secreted by pigs. This substance has also been found in some human secretions, including perspiration (Gower & Ruparelia, 1993). One study revealed that men and women who wore surgical masks sprayed with alpha androstenal rated women in photographs as more attractive than did subjects in a control group who wore untreated masks (Kirk-Smith et al., 1978).

Despite these suggestive results, many researchers have maintained that there is no convincing evidence that any odors are natural sexual attractants for humans (Hassett, 1978; Rogel, 1978; White, 1981). However, this viewpoint may be changing. The findings of two recent studies support the contention that humans possess a vomeronasal system that may be activated by pheromones (Stern & McClintock, 1998; Takami et al., 1993). And new evidence gathered by David Berliner, a former professor of anatomy who now heads a private biotechnology company, may forever alter how we think about human pheromones. Berliner claims to have isolated a number of pheromones from human skin cells that act as sex attractants through their impact on the human vomeronasal system (Berliner et al., 1996; Monti-Bloch et al., 1994; Blakeslee, 1993). Other researchers have also reported evidence supporting the existence of human pheromones (Cohn, 1994; Dranov, 1995; Stern & McClintock, 1998). A number of companies have moved aggressively to capitalize on this emerging human pheromones research by marketing perfumes containing substances that reportedly act as sexual attractants. The box titled "Perfumes and Sex" discusses attempts to commercialize these alleged human pheromones.

Perfumes and Sex

Until recently, commercially available perfumes have not capitalized on the use of pheromones to influence people. However, in recent years a number of American and international corporations have expended large cash outlays on the commercial development and marketing of perfumes that allegedly contain substances that possess human pheromone properties. A company founded by David Berliner, Erox, markets two lines of pheromone perfumes under the brand name *Realm,* one for women and one for men. Berliner and Erox claim that Realm contains a pheromone with the capacity to elicit both a sexual arousal response and a favorable emotional reaction in the other sex. The composition of the woman's version of this perfume is different from that of the man's. Unfortunately, to date Berliner has not made a full disclosure of the identity and structure of these alleged his-and-her perfume pheromones. Until such time as this information is made available, and noncommercial laboratories have an opportunity to test the sexual attractant properties in the Erox perfumes, we cannot be certain that these love potion perfumes are genuine and effective.

Bottles of Realm perfume by Erox, a pheromone-based perfume.

Other commercial enterprises are also pursuing the development and marketing of sexual fragrances based on pheromones, both

Significant changes are now occurring in the somewhat esoteric field of pheromone research. As stated by one researcher, "Five years ago, most of us did not believe pheromones existed in humans. But now, the field is coming to life" (Beauchamp in Blakeslee, 1993, p. 10). Nevertheless, until supportive findings are provided by many laboratories, the question of whether pheromones play a significant role in human sexual behavior is still open.

The near obsession of many people in our society with masking natural body odors makes it very difficult to study the effects of these smells. Any natural odors that might trigger arousal tend to be well disguised with armpit and genital sprays. Nevertheless, each person's unique experiences may allow certain smells to acquire erotic significance, as the following anecdotes reveal:

I love the smells after making love. They trigger little flashes of erotic memories and often keep my arousal level in high gear, inducing me to go on to additional sexual activities. (Authors' files)

During oral sex the faint odor of musk from my lover's vulva drives me wild with passion. I guess it is all the memories of special pleasures associated with these smells that produces the turn-on. (Authors' files)

In a society that is often concerned about natural odors, it is nice to see that some people appreciate scents associated with sexual intimacy and their lovers' bodies.

Taste

Taste seems to play a relatively minor role in human sexual arousal. This is no doubt influenced, at least in part, by an industry that promotes breath mints and flavored vaginal douches. Besides making many individuals extremely self-conscious about how they taste or smell, such commercial products may mask any natural tastes that relate to sexual activity. Nevertheless, some people are still able to detect and appreciate certain tastes they learn to associate with sexual intimacy:

On the Edge

human and nonhuman. For example, the International Foundation of Fragrances and Flavors "has invested a fortune in hopes of bottling human sexual pheromones as a perfume" (Crenshaw, 1996, p. 69). Some companies have manufactured expensive perfumes that contain known animal pheromones such as muscone (a pheromone produced by deer), civetone (from civet cats), or castoreum (from beavers). A major perfume manufacturer began in the 1980s to market a women's cologne and men's aftershave containing alpha androstenal (the aftershave lotion is called *Jovan*). The company that manufacturers these fragrances obviously believes they will work for humans as well as pigs. If you are inclined to test out this claim by using an alpha androstenal containing perfume or aftershave, do not expect miracles because the effect of pig pheromones on humans, if it exists at all, is probably quite weak. Also, because alpha androstenal is a powerful pheromone for pigs, it would be a good idea to stay away from pig farms!

We know that in nonhuman animals, whose sense of smell is paramount, pheromones play a major role as sexual attractants. Only time will tell if pheromones in perfumes, colognes, and aftershave lotions will prove to be genuine sexual attractants for humans. It is unlikely that such products, even if eventually proven to have a true pheromone effect, will ever produce irresistible sexual compulsions in humans comparable to those exhibited by animals influenced by sexual scents. Rather, it seems more likely that fragrances containing human pheromones will be shown to influence sensuality rather than sexuality, creating a sense of well-being and intimacy with another rather than raw lust (Crenshaw, 1996).

When I am sucking my man, I can taste the salty little drops that come out of his penis just before he comes. I get real excited about that time, because I know he is about to take that sweet ride home. (Authors' files)

Hearing

Whether people make sounds during sexual activity is highly variable, as is a partner's response. Some people find words, intimate/erotic conversation, moans, and orgasmic cries to be highly arousing; others prefer that their lovers keep silent during sex play. Some people, out of fear or embarrassment, may make a conscious effort to suppress spontaneous noises during sexual interaction. Because of the silent, stoical image accepted by many males, it may be exceedingly difficult for men in particular to talk, cry out, or groan during arousal. Yet in one research study, many women reported that their male partners' silence hindered their own sexual arousal (DeMartino, 1970). Female reluctance to emit sounds during sex play may be influenced by the notion that "nice" women are not supposed to be so passionate that they make noises.

Besides being sexually arousing, talking to each other during a sexual interlude can be informative and helpful ("I like it when you touch me that way," "A little softer," and so on). If you happen to be a person who enjoys noisemaking and verbalizations during sex, your partner may respond this way if you discuss the matter beforehand. We will talk about discussing sexual preferences in Chapter 8.

A man and a woman describe how sounds affect their lovemaking:

It is very important for me to hear that my partner is enjoying the experience. A woman who doesn't mind moaning is a pleasure to be with. It is good to be with someone who does not mind opening up and letting you know she is enjoying you. If my partner doesn't provide enough voice communication with sex, forget it. (Authors' files)

I like to hear our bodies slapping together as we make love and to hear him moan and groan for more. I also like to hear my name being called and I like to say his. (Authors' files)

Foods and Chemicals

Up to this point, we have considered the impact of hormones, brain processes, and sensory input on human sexual arousal. Several other factors also may affect a person's arousability in a particular situation. Some of these directly affect the physiology of arousal; others can have a strong impact on a person's sexuality through the power of belief. In the pages that follow, we examine the effects of a number of products that people use to attempt to heighten or reduce sexual arousal.

Aphrodisiacs: Do They Work?

Aphrodisiac
A substance that allegedly arouses sexual desire and increases the capacity for sexual activity.

An **aphrodisiac** (af-ruh-DĒZ-ē-ak) (named after Aphrodite, the Greek goddess of love and beauty) is a substance that supposedly arouses sexual desire or increases a person's capacity for sexual activities. Almost from the beginning of time, people have searched for magic potions and other agents to revive flagging erotic interest or produce Olympian sexual performances. That many have reported finding such sexual stimulants bears testimony, once again, to the powerful role of the mind in human sexual activity. We first consider a variety of foods that have been held to possess aphrodisiac qualities, then turn our attention to other alleged sexual stimulants, including alcohol and an assortment of chemical substances.

Do you believe that any food or chemical substances ingested by humans have genuine aphrodisiac properties?

Almost any food that resembles the male external genitals has at one time or another been viewed as an aphrodisiac (Eskeland et al., 1997). Many of us have heard the jokes about oysters, although for some a belief in the special properties of this particular shellfish is no joking matter. One wonders to what extent the oyster industry profits from this pervasive myth. Other foods sometimes considered aphrodisiacs include bananas, celery, cucumbers, tomatoes, ginseng root, and potatoes. Particularly in Asian countries, there is a widespread belief that the ground-up horns of animals such as rhinoceros and reindeer are powerful sexual stimulants. (Have you ever used the term *horny* to describe a sexual state? Now you know its origin.) Unfortunately, the rhinoceros population in Africa has dwindled to the point of near extinction, due largely to the erroneous belief that rhinoceros horn is an effective aphrodisiac (Tudge, 1991).

A number of drugs are also commonly thought to have aphrodisiac properties. Of these drugs, perhaps more has been written about the supposed stimulant properties of alcohol than about any other presumed aphrodisiac substance. In our culture, there is widespread belief in the erotic enhancement properties of alcoholic beverages:

I am a great believer in the sexual benefits of drinking wine. After a couple glasses I become a real "hound in bed." I can always tell my wife is in the mood when she brings out a bottle of chilled rosé. (Authors' files)

Far from being a stimulant, alcohol has a depressing effect on higher brain centers, thus reducing cortical inhibitions such as fear and guilt that often block sexual expression (Cocores & Gold, 1989). Alcohol may also stimulate sexual activity by providing a convenient rationalization for behavior that might normally conflict with one's values ("I just couldn't help myself with my mind fogged by booze").

Consumption of significant amounts of alcohol, however, can have serious negative effects on sexual functioning (Cocores & Gold, 1989; Geller, 1991; Rosen, 1991). As we saw in Chapter 2, research has demonstrated that with increasing levels of intoxication, both men and women experience reduced sexual arousal (as measured physiologically), decreased pleasurability and intensity of orgasm, and increased difficulty in attaining orgasm (Briddell & Wilson, 1976; Heaton & Varrin, 1991; Rosen & Ashton, 1993; Wilson & Lawson, 1976). Heavy alcohol use may also result in general physical deterioration, a process that commonly reduces a person's interest in and capacity for sexual activity.

Alcohol use may have even more serious potential consequences in conjunction with sexual activity. Research has demonstrated a strong association between the use of alcohol and an inclination to participate in sexual practices that have a high risk for contracting a life-threatening disease such as AIDS (Avins et al., 1994; Centers for Disease Control, 1996; Sieving et al., 1997). (Other mind-altering drugs, such as marijuana, have also been implicated in high-risk sexual behavior.)

In addition to alcohol, several other drugs have also been ascribed aphrodisiac qualities. Some of the substances included in this category are amphetamines, barbiturates, cantharides (also known as "Spanish fly"), cocaine, LSD and other psychedelic drugs, marijuana, amyl nitrite (a drug used to treat heart pain, also known as "poppers"), and L-dopa (a medication used in the treatment of Parkinson's disease). As you will see in the summary provided in Table 6.1, not one of these drugs possesses attributes that qualify it as a true sexual stimulant.

Researchers are currently studying one drug that may eventually be shown to have aphrodisiac qualities for at least some people. Since the 1920s, there have been reports of the aphrodisiac properties of *yohimbine hydrochloride*, or yohimbine, a crystalline alkaloid derived from the sap of the tropical evergreen yohimbe tree that grows in West Africa. Experiments conducted by Stanford researchers with male rats have found that injections of yohimbine induce intense sexual arousal and performance in these animals (Clark et al., 1984). The data suggest that this drug may be a true aphrodisiac, at least for rats. Several recent studies with male humans suggest that yohimbine treatment has the capacity to positively affect sexual desire or performance, at least in men with erectile disorders (Mann et al., 1996; Rowland et al., 1997a). A recent meta-analysis that used computerized literature searches found that yohimbine is superior to placebos in the treatment of male erectile disorder (Ernst & Pittler, 1998). However, these findings are still inconclusive, for more than half of all human subjects administered yohimbine have experienced little or no sexual benefit (Rosen, 1991; Rosen & Ashton, 1993). For example, in one recent study, 8 of 11 male subjects with erectile disorder reported moderate to strong positive effects of yohimbine on sexual functioning. However, no enhancing effects of yohimbine on sexual performance were reported by any of the 15 sexually functional men also included in this study (Rowland et al., 1997a). It is hoped that further research will clarify whether yohimbine is a genuine aphrodisiac for humans.

In view of the widespread inclination of humans to seek out substances with aphrodisiac qualities, and in light of escalating advances in the realm of sexual medicine, it seems likely that genuine aphrodisiacs will be introduced in the near future. In fact, one may already be available in European markets, as indicated in the box titled "European Research Suggests Discovery of a Genuine Aphrodisiac." However, at the present time, people continue to use the various substances previously described despite clear-cut evidence they lack true aphrodisiac qualities. Why do so many people around the world swear by the effects of a little powdered rhino horn, that special meal of oysters and banana salad, or the marijuana cigarette before an evening's dalliance? The answer lies in

Table 6.1 Some Alleged Aphrodisiacs and Their Effects

Name (and Street Name)	*Reputed Effect*	*Actual Effect*
Alcohol	Enhances arousal; stimulates sexual activity	Can reduce inhibitions to make sexual behaviors less stressful. It is actually a depressant and in quantity can impair erection ability, arousal, and orgasm.
Amphetamines ("speed," "uppers")	Elevate mood; enhance sexual experience and abilities	Central nervous system stimulants; they reduce inhibitions. High doses or long-term use can cause erectile disorder, delayed ejaculation, inhibition of orgasm in both sexes, and can reduce vaginal lubrication in women.
Amyl nitrite ("snappers," "poppers")	Intensifies orgasms and arousal	Dilates arteries to brain and also to genital area; produces time distortion, warmth in pelvic area. It can decrease sexual arousal, inhibit or block erection, delay orgasm, and produce dizziness, headaches, and fainting.
Barbiturates ("barbs," "downers")	Enhance arousal; stimulate sexual activity	Reduce inhibitions in similar fashion to alcohol, and may decrease sexual desire, impair erection, and inhibit ejaculation. They are physically addictive, and overdose may produce severe depression and even death due to respiratory failure.
Cantharides ("Spanish fly")	Stimulates genital area, causing person to desire coitus	Not effective as a sexual stimulant. It acts as a powerful irritant that can cause inflammation to lining of bladder and urethra; can result in permanent tissue damage and even death.
Cocaine ("coke")	Increases frequency and intensity of orgasm; heightens arousal	Central nervous system stimulant; it loosens inhibitions and enhances sense of well-being; may impair erection or cause spontaneous or delayed ejaculation. Regular use can induce depression and anxiety. Chronic sniffing can produce lesions and perforations of nasal passage.
LSD and other psychedelic drugs (including mescaline, psilocybin)	Enhance sexual response	No direct physiological enhancement of sexual response. May produce altered perception of sexual activity; frequently associated with unsatisfactory erotic experiences.
L-dopa	Sexually rejuvenates older males	No documented benefits to sexual ability. It occasionally produces a painful condition known as priapism (constant, unwanted erection).
Marijuana	Elevates mood and arousal; stimulates sexual activity	Enhances mood and reduces inhibitions in a way similar to alcohol. It may distort the time sense, with the resulting illusion of prolonged arousal and orgasm.
Yohimbine	Induces sexual arousal and enhances sexual performance	Appears to have genuine aphrodisiac effect on rats. Recent evidence suggests it may enhance sexual desire or performance in some humans.

Sources: Crenshaw, 1996; Crenshaw & Goldberg, 1996; Eisner et al., 1990; Finger et al., 1997; Rosen & Ashton, 1993; Rowland et al., 1997a; Yates & Wolman, 1991.

faith and suggestion; these are the ingredients frequently present when aphrodisiac claims are made. If a person believes something will improve his or her sex life, this faith is often translated into the subjective enhancement of sexual pleasure. From this perspective, literally anything has the potential of serving as a sexual stimulant. Consistent with this perspective is Theresa Crenshaw's (1996) cogent observation that "love, however you define it, seems to be the best aphrodisiac of all" (p. 89).

Anaphrodisiacs

Several drugs are known to inhibit sexual behavior. Substances that have this effect are called **anaphrodisiacs** (an-af-ruh-DĒZ-ē-aks). Common drugs with anaphrodisiac potential include opiates, tranquilizers, antihypertensives (blood pressure medicine), antidepressants, antipsychotics, nicotine, birth control pills, sedatives, ulcer drugs, appetite suppressants, steroids, anticonvulsants used for treating epilepsy, over-the-counter allergy medicines that cause drowsiness, and drugs for treating cancer, heart disease, fluid retention, and fungus infections (Crenshaw, 1996; Crenshaw & Goldberg, 1996; Finger et al., 1997).

Anaphrodisiac
A substance that inhibits sexual desire and behavior.

A great deal of evidence indicates that regular use of *opiates,* such as heroin, morphine, and methadone, often produces a significant—and sometimes a dramatic—decrease in sexual interest and activity in both sexes (Ackerman et al., 1994; Finger et al., 1997). Serious impairment of sexual functioning associated with opiate use may include erectile problems and inhibited ejaculation in males and reduced capacity to experience orgasm in females.

Tranquilizers, used widely in the treatment of a variety of emotional disorders, have been shown sometimes to reduce sexual motivation, impair erection, and delay or inhibit orgasm in both sexes (Crenshaw & Goldberg, 1996; Olivera, 1994).

Many *antihypertensives,* drugs used for treating high blood pressure, have been experimentally demonstrated to seriously inhibit erection and ejaculation, reduce the intensity of orgasm in male subjects, and reduce sexual interest in both sexes (Finger et al., 1997; Prisant et al., 1994).

On the Edge

European Research Suggests Discovery of a Genuine Aphrodisiac

Norwegian researchers recently reported experimental investigations of a commercial product, *Libido* (Libid, Libbido, Erosom, and Ardorare, names used in different markets), which may prove to be a genuine aphrodisiac for humans (Eskeland et al., 1997). The Libido product is derived primarily from protein fractions extracted from fertilized, partly incubated, chicken eggs. This material is made into a powder and ingested orally after being dissolved in juice or water. Over the course of three experiments, these researchers demonstrated the following effects of Libido:

- A dramatic increase in sexual desire among 16 healthy men, ages 47–60, who did not report problems with sexual desire prior to their participation in this research
- An enhanced sex drive in over half of 31 otherwise healthy men with reported low sexual desire, ages 38–65
- Increased sexual desire in 84% of 31 men, ages 57–74, who reported almost complete lack of sexual desire prior to their participation

None of the participants in any of these three studies reported any side effects from Libido ingestion. Clearly, it is too soon to conclude that Libido is a genuine aphrodisiac substance. More studies need to be conducted by other investigators to verify the findings of the Norwegian research team. This is especially essential in light of the admitted interest these researchers have in the commercial potential of this product. Furthermore, long-term studies should be conducted to ascertain the possible occurrence of adverse side effects that may surface when Libido is consumed for extended periods of time. Finally, as acknowledged by the Norwegian researchers in the closing comments of their published article, future studies need to investigate the possible effect of Libido in women.

Another class of commonly prescribed psychiatric medications, *antidepressants,* almost without exception cause adverse changes in sexual response that include erectile disorder in men and delayed or absent orgasmic response in both sexes (Finger et al., 1997).

Antipsychotic drugs are also very likely to disrupt sexual response. Potential adverse reactions include erectile disorder and delay of ejaculation in men and orgasm difficulties and reduced sexual desire in both sexes (Finger et al., 1997).

Many people are surprised to hear that birth control pills are also commonly associated with reduced sexual desire. The majority of oral contraceptives contain the hormone progesterone or a synthetic version of progesterone. (*Progestin* is a term used to describe a large group of synthetic drugs that have a progesterone-like effect.) Progesterone is so potent in inhibiting desire that injections of the progesterone compound, Depo-Provera (see earlier discussion), are sometimes used to "chemically castrate" sex offenders (Crenshaw & Goldberg, 1996). Among the three categories of oral contraceptives, the progestin-only pill (sometimes called the minipill), is the strongest inhibitor of sexual motivation (see Chapter 11 for a more detailed discussion of birth control pills). In addition, synthetic progesterone is the major ingredient in the widely used Norplant implant birth control device.

Perhaps the most widely used and least recognized anaphrodisiac is *nicotine.* There is evidence that smoking can significantly retard sexual motivation and function by constricting the blood vessels (thereby retarding vasocongestive response of the body to sexual stimulation) and by reducing testosterone levels in the blood (Hirschkowitz et al., 1992; Mannino et al., 1994; Rosen, 1991).

Paradoxically, the most widely known substance used as an anaphrodisiac, *potassium nitrate,* or saltpeter, is completely ineffective as a sexual deterrent. Many of us have heard the joke about the newlyweds being dosed with saltpeter on their wedding night. In reality, there is no physiological basis for this kind of tale, unless the need for frequent urination can be viewed as a sexual deterrent (potassium nitrate increases urine flow through diuretic action).

Sexual Response

Human sexual response is a highly individual physical, emotional, and mental process. Nevertheless, there are a number of common physiological changes that allow us to outline some general patterns of the sexual response cycle. Masters and Johnson (1966) and Helen Singer Kaplan (1979), noted sex therapist and author, have described these patterns. We briefly outline Kaplan's ideas before turning to a detailed analysis of Masters and Johnson's work.

Kaplan's Three-Stage Model

Kaplan's model of sexual response, an outgrowth of her extensive experience as a sex therapist, contains three stages: *desire, excitement,* and *orgasm* (see Figure 6.2). She suggests that sexual difficulties tend to fall into one of these three categories, and that it is possible for a person to have difficulty in one while continuing to function normally in the other two.

One of the most distinctive features of Kaplan's model is that it includes desire as a distinct stage of the sexual response cycle. Many other writers, including Masters and Johnson, do not discuss aspects of sexual response that are separate from genital changes. Kaplan's description of desire as a prelude to physical sexual response stands as a welcome addition to the literature. However, not all sexual expression is preceded by desire. For example, a couple may agree to engage in sexual activity even though they may not be feeling sexually inclined at the time. Frequently, they may find that their bodies begin to respond sexually to the ensuing activity, despite their lack of initial desire.

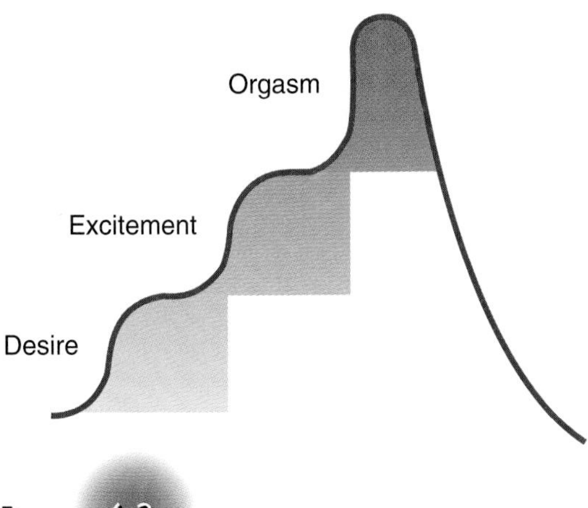

Figure 6.2

Kaplan's three-stage model of the sexual response cycle. This model is distinguished by its identification of desire as a prelude to sexual response. Source: Kaplan, 1979.

Masters and Johnson's Four-Phase Model

Masters and Johnson distinguish four phases in the sexual response patterns of both men and women: *excitement, plateau, orgasm,* and *resolution*. In addition, they include a *refractory period* (a recovery stage in which there is a temporary inability to reach orgasm) in the male resolution phase. Figures 6.3 and 6.4 illustrate these four phases of sexual response in women and men. These charts provide basic "maps" of common patterns, but a few cautions to the reader are in order.

First, the simplified nature of these diagrams can easily obscure the richness of individual variation that can and does occur. Masters and Johnson were charting only the physiological responses to sexual stimulation. Biological reactions may follow a relatively predictable course, but there is tremendous variability in individual subjective responses to sexual arousal. These personal differences are suggested in the several individual reports of arousal, orgasm, and resolution included later in this chapter.

The second caution has to do with a too literal interpretation of the so-called plateau stage of sexual response. In the behavioral sciences, the term *plateau* is typically used to

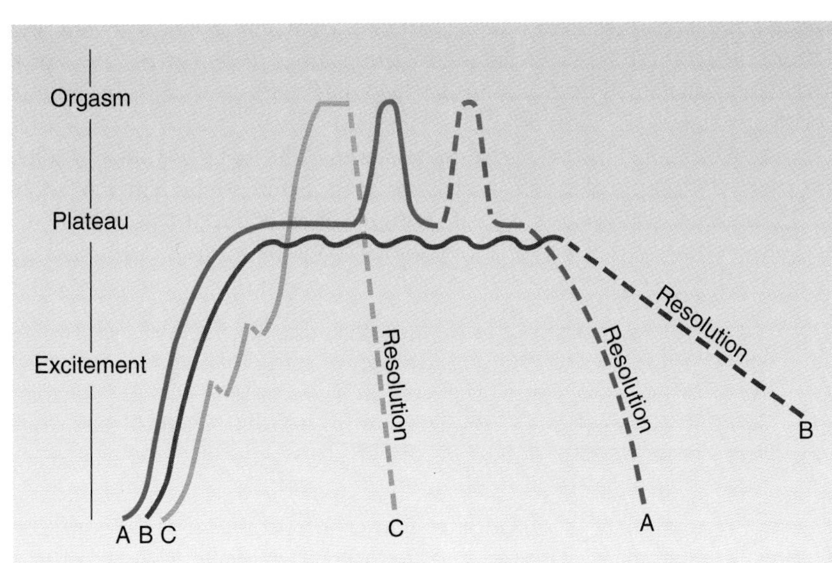

Figure 6.3

Female sexual response cycle. Masters and Johnson identified three basic patterns in female sexual response. Pattern A most closely resembles the male pattern, except that a woman can have one or more orgasms without dropping below the plateau level of sexual arousal. Variations of this response include an extended plateau with no orgasm (pattern B) and a rapid rise to orgasm with no definitive plateau and a very quick resolution (pattern C). Source: Masters & Johnson, 1966.

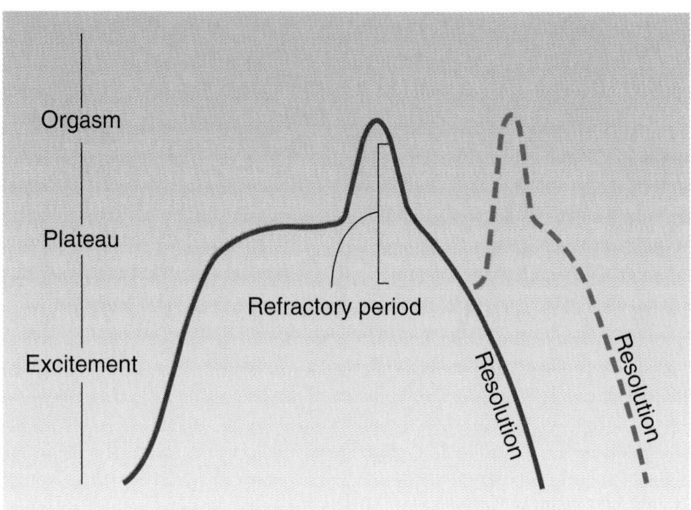

Figure 6.4

Male sexual response cycle. Only one male response pattern was identified by Masters and Johnson. However, men do report considerable variation in their response pattern. Note the refractory period: Males do not have a second orgasm immediately after the first. Source: Masters & Johnson, 1966.

describe a leveling-off period where no observable changes in behavior can be detected. For example, it might refer to a flat spot in a learning curve where no new behaviors occur for a certain period of time. It has been diagrammed in just this manner in the male chart and in pattern A of the female chart. Actually, the plateau level of sexual arousal involves a powerful surge of sexual tensions that are definitely measurable (for example, as increased heart and breathing rates). Thus it is far from an unchanging state.

Our third caution is a warning against a tendency to use such charts as personal checklists. Although we encourage self-references throughout this book, this is one area where a too enthusiastic self-checking can lead to potential problems in the form of "spectatoring." The following quote illustrates this point:

After learning about the four stages of sexual response in class, I found myself "standing back" and watching my own reactions, wondering if I had passed from excitement into plateau. Also, I began to monitor the responses of my partner, looking for the telltale signs that would tell me at what point he was. Suddenly I found myself doing clinical observations rather than allowing myself to fully experience the good feelings. It was a real put-off, and I had to force myself to stop being the observer and become more of a participant. (Authors' files)

The descriptions in the following pages should not be viewed as standards for analyzing or intellectualizing your feelings or for evaluating how "normal" your reactions are. We stress that there are many natural variations from these patterns. Perhaps familiarity with these generalized descriptions may help illuminate some of the complexity of your own responses.

In much of the discussion that follows, we will be looking at the physiological reactions and subjective reports of women and men. Before we become too involved in the several specific processes of sexual response, it is important to note that the basic responses of men and women are very similar—a point Masters and Johnson stressed in their research:

> Certainly there are reactions to sexual stimulation that are confined by normal anatomic variation to a single sex. There also are differences in established reactive patterns to sexual stimuli—for example, duration and intensity of response—that usually are sex-linked in character. However, parallels in reactive potential between the two sexes must be underlined. Similarities rather than differences of response have been emphasized by this investigation. (Masters & Johnson, 1966, p. 273)

Two fundamental physiological responses to effective sexual stimulation occur in both women and men. These are *vasocongestion* and *myotonia*. These two basic reactions are the primary underlying sources for almost all biological responses that take place during sexual arousal.

Vasocongestion is the engorgement with blood of body tissues that respond to sexual excitation. Usually the blood flow into organs and tissues through the arteries is balanced by an equal outflow through the veins. During sexual arousal, however, the arteries dilate, increasing the inflow beyond the capacity of the veins to carry blood away. This results in widespread vasocongestion in both superficial and deep tissues. The visible congested areas may feel warm and appear swollen and red, due to increased blood content. The most obvious manifestations of this vasocongestive response are the erection of the penis in men and lubrication of the vagina in women. In addition, other body areas may become engorged—the labia, testicles, clitoris, nipples, and even the earlobes.

Vasocongestion
The engorgement of blood vessels in particular body parts in response to sexual arousal.

The second basic physiological response is **myotonia** (mī-ō-TŌ-nē-a), the increased muscle tension that occurs throughout the body during sexual arousal. Myotonia is evident in both voluntary flexing and involuntary contractions. Its most dramatic manifestations are facial grimaces, spasmodic contractions of the hands and feet, and the muscular spasms that occur during orgasm.

Myotonia
Muscle tension.

The phases of the response cycle follow the same general patterns regardless of the method of stimulation. Masturbation, manual stimulation by one's partner, oral pleasuring, penile–vaginal intercourse, dreaming, fantasy, and, in some women, breast stimulation can all result in completion of the response cycle. Often the intensity and rapidity of response vary according to the kind of stimulation.

In the next several pages, we outline the major physiological reactions to sexual stimulation that occur during each of the four phases of the sexual response cycle. Subjective reports of several individuals are included. For each stage, we list reactions common to both sexes and those unique to just one. You will note the strong similarities in the sexual response patterns of men and women. We will discuss some important differences in greater detail at the conclusion of this chapter.

Excitement phase
Masters and Johnson's term for the first phase of the sexual response cycle, in which engorgement of sexual organs and increases in muscle tension, heart rate, and blood pressure occur.

Excitement

The first phase of the sexual response cycle, the **excitement phase,** is characterized by a number of responses common to men and women, including muscle tension and some increase in the heart rate and blood pressure. In both sexes, several areas of the sexual anatomy become engorged. For example, the clitoris, labia minora, vagina, nipples, penis, and testes all increase in size, and most of them deepen in color. Some responses, such as the appearance of a **sex flush** (a pink or red rash on the chest or breasts), occur in both sexes but are more common in women. Still other responses, specific to just one sex, are illustrated in Figures 6.5–6.8, which show changes in the sexual anatomy of women and men throughout the phases of the cycle.

Sex flush
A pink or red rash that may appear on the chest or breasts during sexual arousal.

The excitement phase may vary in duration from less than a minute to several hours. Both males and females may show considerable variation in the degree of their arousal during this phase. For example, a man's penis may vary from flaccid to semierect to fully erect. Similarly, vaginal lubrication in women may vary from minimal to copious.

Although the physiological characteristics outlined in the figures represent general patterns, different people experience these changes in differing ways. The following two reports give some indication of the subjective variations in how women describe their own feelings during sexual arousal:

> Sexual arousal for me is something I look forward to when I realize my husband and I will have sex. His touching, kissing, and loving me in this way brings me to a height of excitement that is incredible. At first I felt selfish about him giving me so much satisfaction through stimulation, but he enjoys it so much, it's a wonderful time. Often we don't have intercourse because we are caught up in the "foreplay" of lovemaking. (Authors' files)

> When I am aroused, I get warm all over, and I like a lot of holding and massaging of other areas of my body besides my genitals. After time passes with that particular stimulation, I prefer more direct manual stroking if I want orgasm. (Authors' files)

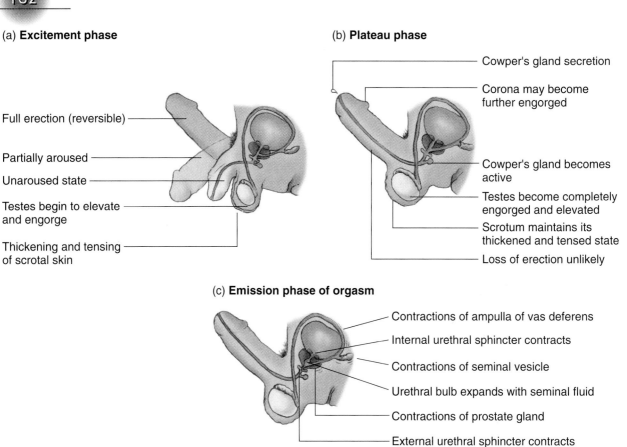

(a) **Excitement phase**

Full erection (reversible)
Partially aroused
Unaroused state
Testes begin to elevate and engorge
Thickening and tensing of scrotal skin

(b) **Plateau phase**

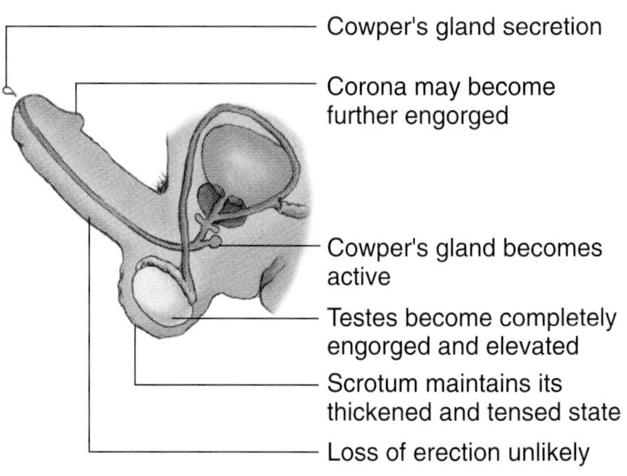

(c) **Emission phase of orgasm**

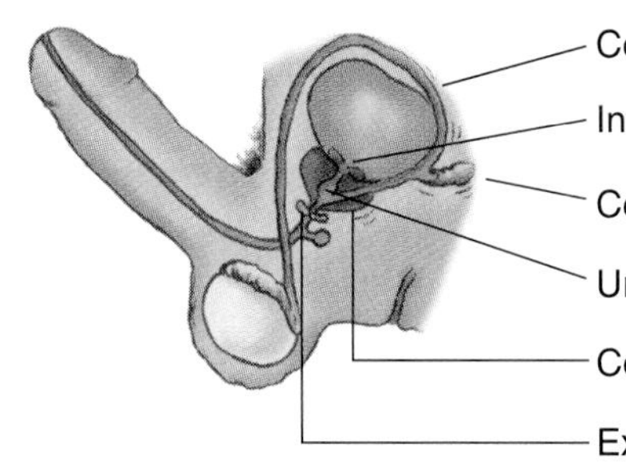

(d) **Expulsion phase of orgasm**

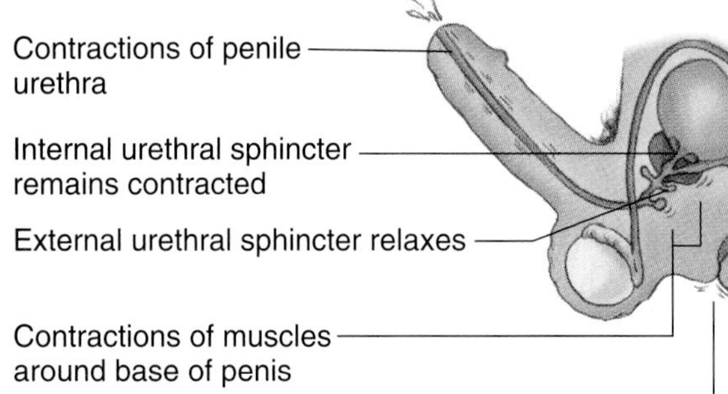

(e) **Resolution phase**

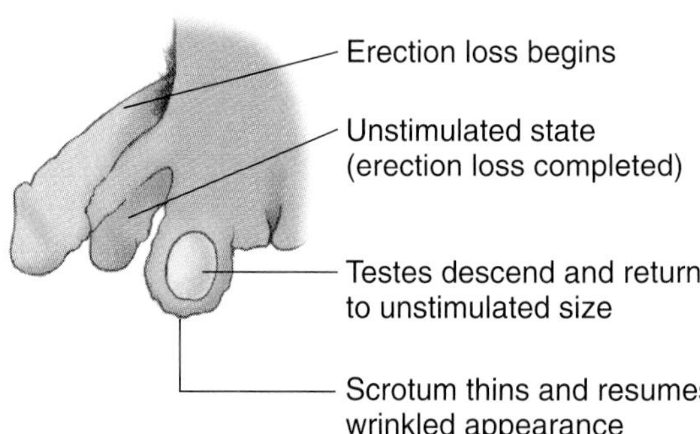

Figure 6.5

Major changes in external and internal male sexual anatomy during the sexual response cycle.

Two men provide their descriptions of sexual arousal in the following accounts:

When I am sexually aroused, my whole body feels energized. Sometimes my mouth gets dry, and I may feel a little lightheaded. I want to have all of my body touched and stroked, not just my genitals. I particularly like the sensation of feeling that orgasm is just around the corner, waiting and tantalizing me to begin the final journey. Sometimes a quick rush to climax is nice, but usually I prefer making the arousal period last as long as I can stand it, until my penis feels like it is dying for the final strokes of ecstasy. (Authors' files)

When aroused, I feel very excited, and I fantasize a lot. Then all of a sudden, a warm feeling comes over me, and it feels like a thousand pleasure pins are being stuck into my loins all at the same time. (Authors' files)

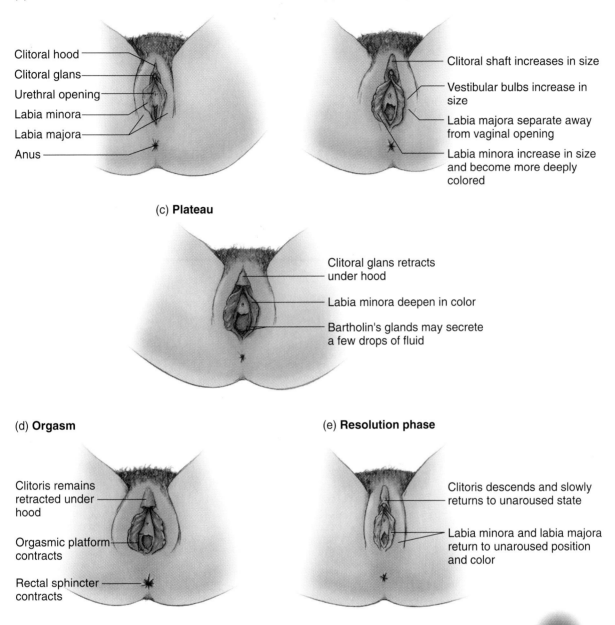

(a) **Unaroused state**

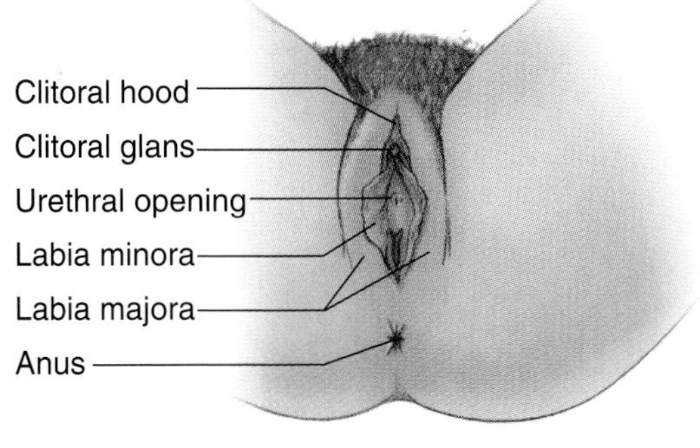

(b) **Excitement phase**

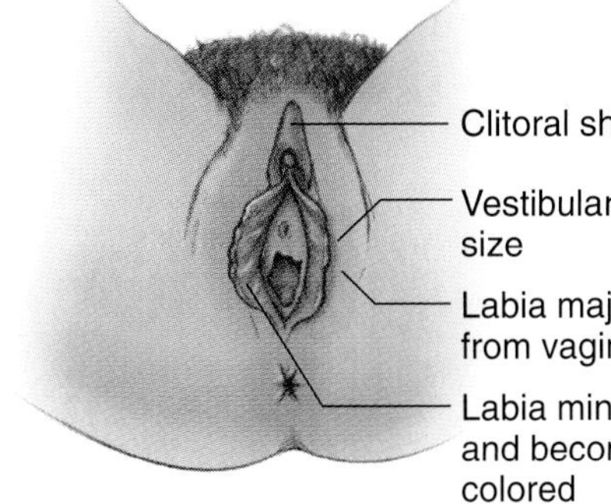

(c) **Plateau**

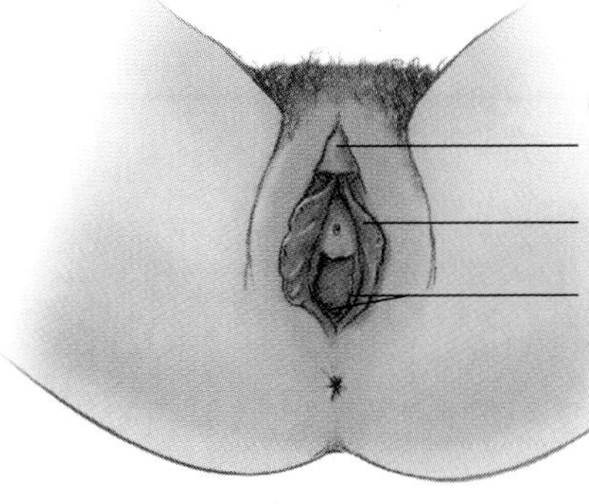

(d) **Orgasm**

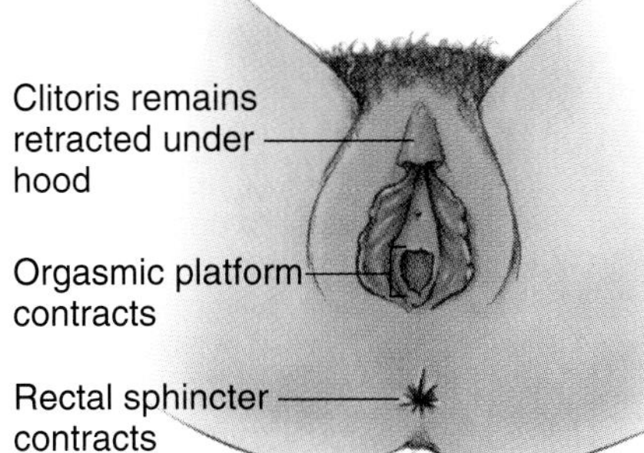

(e) **Resolution phase**

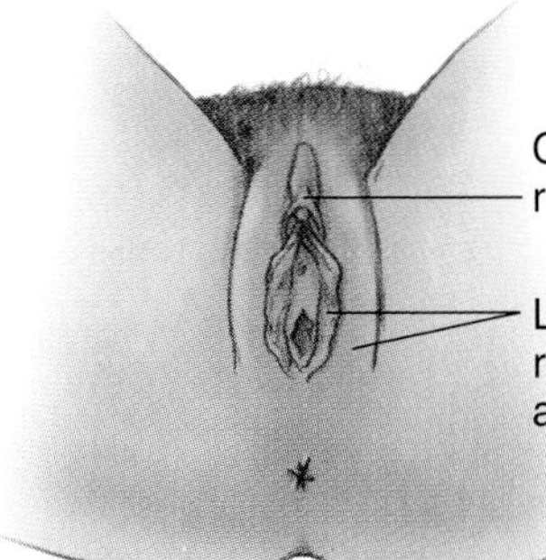

Figure 6.6

Major changes in the external female genitals during the sexual response cycle.

Plateau

During the **plateau phase,** sexual tension continues to mount until it reaches the peak that leads to orgasm. It is difficult to define clearly the point at which a sexually responding individual makes the transition to this phase. Unlike the excitement phase, the plateau phase has no clear external sign such as lubrication or erection to mark its onset. Instead, several of these signs become more pronounced as they accelerate toward the peaks reached in the next phase. Both heart rate and blood pressure continue to rise; breathing grows faster; sex flushes and coloration of the genitals become more noticeable. Muscle tension continues to build up, and the face, neck, hands, and feet may undergo involuntary contractions and spasms in both the plateau and orgasm phases. Among women, the plateau phase is also distinguished by development of the *orgasmic platform,* a term

Plateau phase
Masters and Johnson's term for the second phase of the sexual response cycle, in which muscle tension, heart rate, blood pressure, and vasocongestion increase.

(a) **Unaroused state**

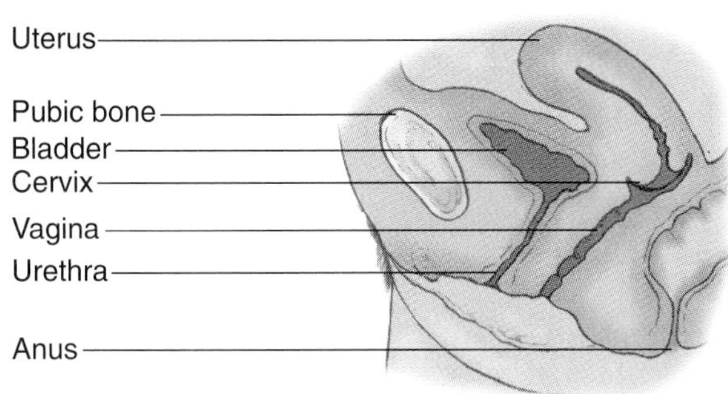

(b) **Excitement phase**

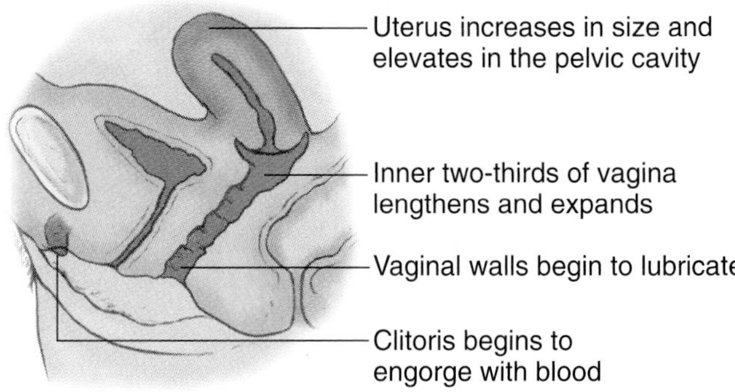

(c) **Plateau phase**

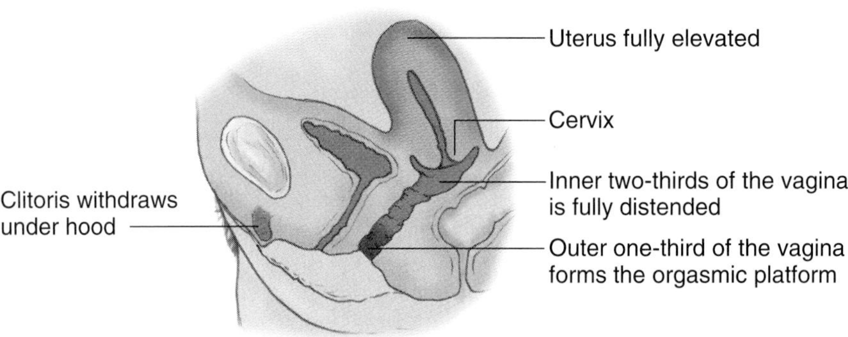

(d) **Orgasm**

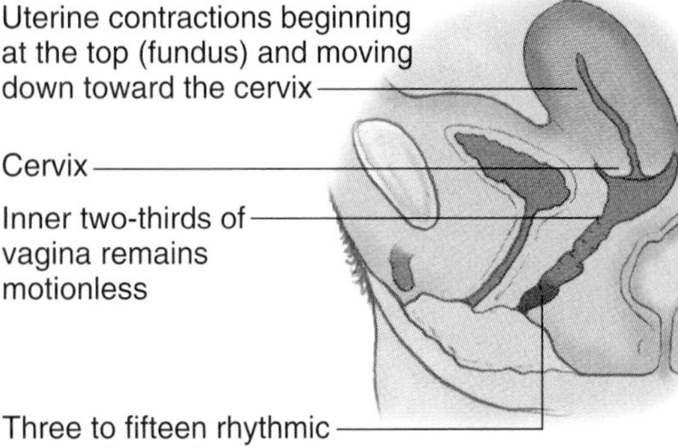

(e) **Resolution phase**

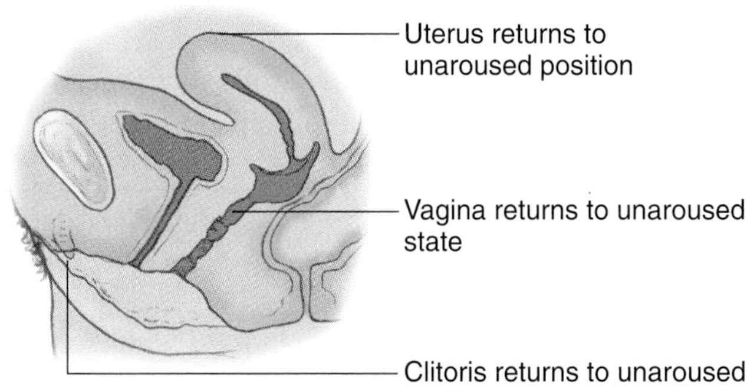

Figure 6.7

Major changes in the internal female genitals during the sexual response cycle.

used by Masters and Johnson to describe the markedly increased engorgement of the outer third of the vagina.

The plateau phase is often very brief, typically lasting a few seconds to several minutes. However, many people find that prolonging sexual tensions at this high level produces greater arousal and ultimately more intense orgasms. This is reported in the following subjective accounts:

When I get up there, almost on the verge of coming, I try to hang in as long as possible. If my partner cooperates, stopping or slowing when necessary, I can stay right on the edge for several minutes, sometimes even longer. I know that all it would take is one more stroke and I'm over the top. Sometimes my whole body gets to shaking and quivering, and I can feel incredible sensations shooting through me like electric charges. The longer I can make this supercharged period last, the better the orgasm. (Authors' files)

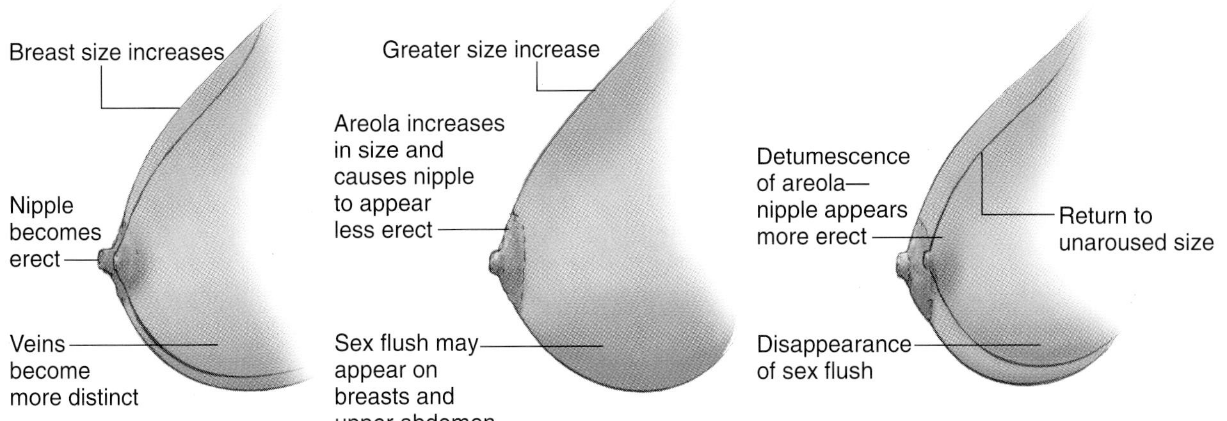

Figure 6.8

Changes in the breasts during the sexual response cycle.

When I masturbate, I like to take myself almost to the point of climaxing and then back off. I can tell when orgasm is about to happen because my vagina tightens up around the opening, and sometimes I can feel the muscles contract. I love the sensations of balancing myself on the brink, part of me wanting to come and the other part holding out for more. The longer I maintain this delicate balance, the more shattering the climax. Sometimes the pleasure is almost beyond bearing. (Authors' files)

Orgasm

As effective stimulation continues, many people move from plateau to **orgasm.** This is particularly true for men, who almost always experience orgasm after reaching the plateau level. (However, as described in Chapter 5, orgasm is not always accompanied by ejaculation.) When ejaculation occurs, it takes place in two phases. During the first or *emission phase* the seminal fluid is gathered in the urethral bulb, a process accompanied by a subjective sense that orgasm is inevitable. In the second or *expulsion phase* semen is expelled out of the penis by muscular contractions.

Orgasm
A series of muscular contractions of the pelvic floor muscles occurring at the peak of sexual arousal.

In contrast to men, women may obtain plateau levels of arousal without the release of sexual climax. This is often the case during penile–vaginal intercourse when the man reaches orgasm first, or when effective manual or oral stimulation is replaced with penetration as the female approaches orgasm. More will be said about this later.

Orgasm is the shortest phase of the sexual response cycle, typically lasting only a few seconds. Female orgasms often last slightly longer than do male orgasms. Figures 6.5–6.8 summarize the primary physiological responses during orgasm.

Do you think that men and women experience orgasm in significantly different ways?

For both sexes, the experience of orgasm can be an intense mixture of highly pleasurable sensations—but whether that experience differs from male to female has been the subject of considerable debate. This question was evaluated in two separate experimental analyses of orgasm descriptions provided by college students (Wiest, 1977; Wiest et al., 1995). When compared using a standard psychological rating scale, women's and men's subjective descriptions of orgasm were found to be indistinguishable in both investigations. Similar results were obtained in an earlier study, in which a group of 70 expert judges were unable to distinguish reliably between the written orgasm reports of men and women (Proctor et al., 1974).

Beyond the question of sex differences in orgasmic experiences, it is clear that there is great individual variation in how people, both men and women, describe orgasms. In the box entitled "Subjective Descriptions of Orgasm," some accounts selected from our files illustrate the diversity of these descriptions. The first one is by a woman and the second by a man. The final three—labeled Reports A, B, and C—contain no specific references that identify the sex of the describer. Perhaps you would like to try to determine whether they were reported by a man or a woman. The answers follow the summary at the end of the chapter.

Although the physiology of female orgasmic response can be clearly outlined, some past and present issues about its nature need to be discussed. Misinformation about female orgasm has been prevalent in our culture. We saw in Chapter 2 that Freud's theory of the "vaginal" versus the "clitoral" orgasm has had a great, if misguided, impact on people's thinking about female sexual response. Freud viewed the vaginal orgasm as more mature than the clitoral orgasm, and thus preferable. The physiological basis for this theory was the assumption that the clitoris is a stunted penis. This led to the conclusion that erotic sensations, arousal, and orgasm resulting from direct stimulation of the clitoris were all expressions of "masculine" rather than "feminine" sexuality—and therefore undesirable (Sherfey, 1972). At adolescence, a woman was supposed to transfer her erotic center from the clitoris to the vagina. If she was not able to make this transition, psychotherapy was sometimes used to attempt to help her attain "vaginal" orgasms. Unfortunately, this theory led many women to believe incorrectly that they were sexually maladjusted.

Our modern knowledge of embryology has established the falseness of the theory that the clitoris is a masculine organ, as we have seen in our discussion of the genital differentiation process in Chapter 3. In one researcher's words, "to reduce clitoral eroticism to the level of psychopathology because the clitoris is an innately masculine organ . . . must now be considered a travesty of the facts" (Sherfey, 1972, p. 47). Travesty of facts or not, during Freud's time, this sexual-center transfer theory was taken so seriously that surgical removal of the clitoris was recommended for little girls who masturbated, to help them later attain "vaginal" orgasms.

Surgical clitoridectomies are no longer performed in our culture. Yet social conditioning, which can be as effective as a scalpel, continues: Freud's operational definition of female sexual health is still with us in many respects. For example, a woman's reluc-

Sexuality and Diversity

Subjective Descriptions of Orgasm*

Female: When I'm about to reach orgasm, my face feels very hot. I close my eyes and open my mouth. It centers in my clitoris, and it feels like electric wires igniting from there and radiating up my torso and down my legs to my feet. I sometimes feel like I need to urinate. My vagina contracts anywhere from 5 to 12 times. My vulva area feels heavy and swollen. There isn't another feeling like it—it's fantastic!

Male: Orgasm for me draws all my energy in toward a core in my body. Then, all of a sudden, there is a release of this energy out through my penis. My body becomes warm and numb before orgasm; after, it gradually relaxes and I feel extremely serene.

Report A: It's like an Almond Joy, "indescribably delicious." The feeling runs from the top of my head to the tips of my toes as I feel a powerful surge of pleasure. It raises me beyond my physical self into another level of consciousness, and yet the feeling seems purely physical. What a paradox! It strokes all over, inside and out. I love it simply because it's mine and mine alone.

Report B: An orgasm to me is like heaven. All my tensions and anxieties are released. You get to the point of no return, and it's like an uncontrollable desire that makes things start happening. I think that sex and orgasm are one of the greatest phenomena that we have today. It's a great sharing experience for me.

Report C: Having an orgasm is like the ultimate time I have for myself. I am not excluding my partner, but it's like I can't hear anything, and all I feel is a spectacular release accompanied with more pleasure than I've ever felt doing anything else. (Authors' files)

*For Reports A, B, and C, try to determine if the subject was male or female. To find the answers, turn to the summary at the end of this chapter.

tance to ask her partner to stimulate her clitoris manually during coitus (or to do it herself) typifies the learned belief that she "should" experience orgasm from vaginal stimulation alone. However, cultural conditioning can work two ways. With knowledge and support, a woman can change her attitude about her sexual feelings and behaviors.

Contrary to Freud's theory, the research of Masters and Johnson suggests that there is only one kind of orgasm in females, physiologically speaking, regardless of the method of stimulation. The intensity of orgasms, however, often varies with the type of stimulation.

Masters and Johnson's view that there is no physiological basis for defining different types of female orgasms has been contested by Josephine and Irving Singer (1972). These authors contend that, besides noting observable physiological variations, it is important to take emotional satisfaction into consideration in accounting for differences in female orgasmic response. With this in mind, the Singers have described three types of female orgasm—vulval, uterine, and blended. They suggest that a *vulval orgasm* corresponds to the type of orgasmic response described by Masters and Johnson and that it may be induced by either coital or manual stimulation. The vulval orgasm is accompanied by contractions of the orgasmic platform and typically is not followed by a refractory period. A *uterine orgasm,* in contrast, occurs only as a result of vaginal penetration and is characterized by a woman involuntarily holding her breath as orgasm approaches and explosively exhaling at climax. The Singers suggest that this type of orgasm often induces a profound sense of relaxation and sexual satiation and is typically followed by a refractory period. Finally, they describe a *blended orgasm* that is a combination of the first two types, characterized by both contractions of the orgasmic platform and breath-holding.

When the Singers' conceptualization of female orgasm was first published, many professionals in the field of sexuality assigned it little credibility. The apparent similarity of the Singers' "uterine orgasms" and Freud's "vaginal orgasms" may have caused some to fear a revival of the old theory of superior vaginal versus inferior clitoral orgasms. However, the Singers did not claim that one type of orgasm was superior to another. One of the major problems for any theory suggesting vaginal erotic response has been the widespread belief that the vagina is largely insensitive to sexual stimulation. However, this idea has been challenged by evidence indicating erotic sensitivity within the vagina (Ladas, 1989). In one study, for example, examiners used their fingers to apply moderate to strong rhythmic pressure to all areas of the vaginal walls of 48 subjects. Over 90% of the women stimulated in this fashion reported considerable erotic sensitivity of the vagina, most commonly on the anterior (front) wall. Some reported sensitivity in more than one area. Many of the women experienced orgasm from this manual stimulation of their vaginas (Alzate & Londono, 1984).

The Grafenberg Spot

A number of studies have reported that some women are capable of experiencing orgasm, and perhaps ejaculation, when an area along the anterior wall of the vagina is vigorously stimulated (Davidson et al., 1989; Whipple & Komisaruk, 1988; Zaviacic & Whipple, 1993). This area of erotic sensitivity, briefly mentioned in Chapter 4, has been named the *Grafenberg spot* (or *G spot*) in honor of Ernest Grafenberg (1950), a gynecologist who first noted the erotic significance of this location within the vagina almost 50 years ago. However, the presence of glandular structures in this area was noted in the medical literature over 100 years ago (Skene, 1880). It has been suggested that the Grafenberg spot is not a point that can be touched by the tip of one finger but, rather, is a fairly large area composed of the lower anterior wall of the vagina and the underlying urethra and surrounding glands (Heath, 1984).

The Grafenberg spot may be located by "systematic palpation of the entire anterior wall of the vagina between the posterior side of the pubic bone and the cervix. Two fingers are usually employed, and it is often necessary to press deeply into the tissue to reach the spot" (Perry & Whipple, 1981, p. 29). This exploration may be conducted by a woman's partner, as shown in Figure 6.9. Some women are able to locate their Grafenberg spots through self-exploration.

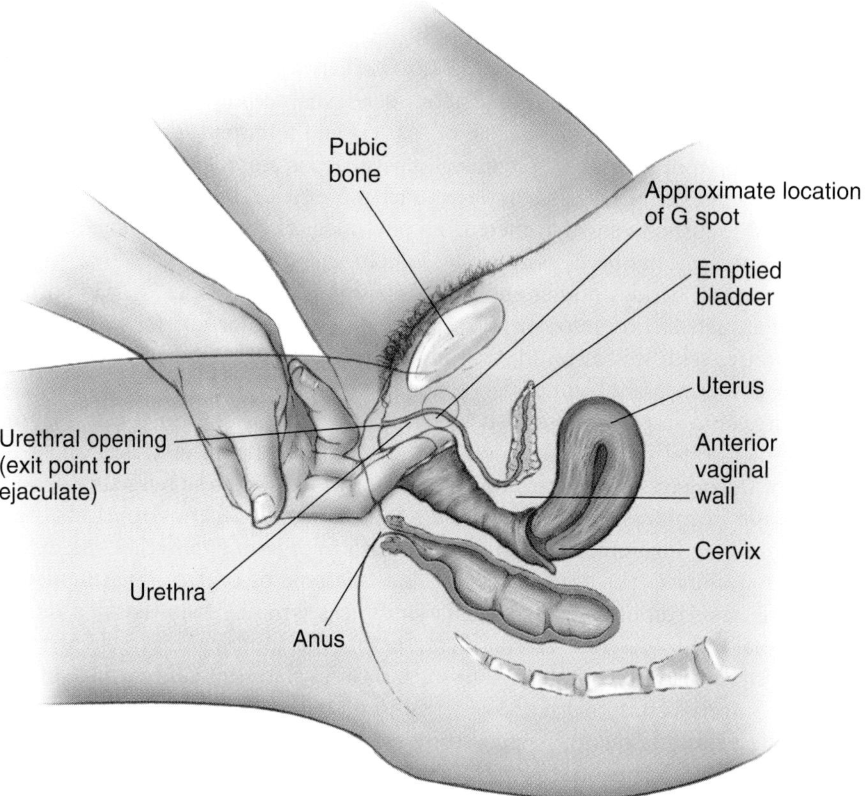

Figure 6.9

Locating the Grafenberg spot. Usually two fingers are used, and it is often necessary to press deeply into the anterior wall of the vagina to reach the spot.

During initial searching for the sometimes elusive Grafenberg spot, a woman or her partner must rely on the sensations produced by manual stimulation. When the area is located, women report a variety of initial sensations, including a slight feeling of discomfort, a brief sensation of needing to urinate, or a pleasurable feeling. After a minute or more of stroking, the sensations usually become more pleasurable, and the area may begin to swell discernibly. Continued stimulation of the area may result in an orgasm that is often quite intense. The following account describes a 19-year-old college student's first-time orgasm, experienced as a result of Grafenberg spot stimulation.

I had never had an orgasm before, probably because I was taught that masturbation was a sin. After hearing about the G-spot in class I decided to try and locate it in my body. I turned on my favorite music and sat in front of a mirror on my door. I had never really looked at my genitals before. I sat and inspected them and found how each part felt to be touched. After this experimentation, I tried to find my G-spot. The sensation was strange at first, like I urgently had to pee. After awhile it felt like a huge force was building inside me, and then an intense release. I was so surprised and excited. I had thought something was wrong with me. (Authors' files)

Perhaps the most amazing thing about Grafenberg spot orgasms is that they are sometimes accompanied by the ejaculation of fluid from the urethral opening. Research indicates that the source of this fluid is the "female prostate" discussed in Chapter 4. The ducts from this system empty directly into the urethra. In some women, Grafenberg orgasms result in fluid being forced through these ducts and out the urethra. In view of the homologous nature of Grafenberg spot tissue and the male prostate, we might speculate that the female ejaculate is similar to the prostatic component of male seminal fluid (Zaviacic & Whipple, 1993). This notion has been supported by research in which specimens of female ejaculate were chemically analyzed and found to contain high levels of an enzyme, prostatic acid phosphatase (PAP), characteristic of the prostatic component of semen (Addiego et al., 1981; Belzer et al., 1984). Many women report that the fluid has a mild semenlike scent. One study found concentrations of fructose in the female ejaculate (Zaviacic et al., 1988). (You will recall from Chapter 5 that fructose is also a component of male ejaculate.) The fructose level in the orgasmic expulsions of women is considerably higher than that found in their urine, a finding that "suggests that the female ejaculate cannot be simply regarded as urine" (Zaviacic et al., 1988, p. 323).

Although the existence of Grafenberg spot orgasms, sometimes accompanied by ejaculation, has been reported with some degree of reliability, our understanding of this phenomenon is far from complete. For example, how common are these responses? (A survey of 2350 U.S. and Canadian professional women revealed that 40% of the respondents reported that sometimes they experienced a fluid release ejaculation at the moment of orgasm [Darling et al., 1990].) Is there a connection between Grafenberg spot stimulation and the uterine orgasm described by the Singers? Is the female Grafenberg area a genuine homologue of the male prostate? Clearly, considerably more research is necessary before conclusive answers can be obtained for these and other questions. In the meantime, we encourage women and their partners who want to explore this intriguing information in relation to their own sexual response and activities to do so. However, it may be self-defeating to treat Grafenberg spot orgasm as a new sexual achievement to be relentlessly pursued. It would be unfortunate if the reexamination of some of our beliefs about female orgasm were to lead to a reemergence of attributing emotional or physiological superiority to any one orgasmic pattern.

Resolution

During the final phase of the sexual response cycle, **resolution,** the sexual systems return to their nonexcited state. If no additional stimulation occurs, the resolution begins immediately after orgasm. Some of the changes back to a nonexcited state take place rapidly, whereas others occur more slowly. Figures 6.5–6.8 summarize the major physiological changes associated with resolution.

Resolution phase
The fourth phase of the sexual response cycle as outlined by Masters and Johnson, in which the sexual systems return to their nonexcited state.

The self-reports that follow provide some indication of how people vary in their feelings after orgasm. The first two are by females, the third by a male.

> After a satisfying experience with my husband, I want to be held, as if to finalize and complete our union. Sometimes I like to talk and sometimes I just like to be able to touch him and be touched by his whole body. (Authors' files)

> After orgasm I feel very relaxed. My moods do vary—sometimes I'm ready to start all over; other times I can jump up and really get busy; and at other times I just want to sleep. (Authors' files)

> After orgasm I feel relaxed and usually very content. Sometimes I feel like sleeping, and other times I feel like I want to touch my partner if she is willing. I like to hold her and just be there. (Authors' files)

These subjective reports sound very similar. But there is one significant difference in the responses of women and men during this phase—their physiological readiness for further sexual stimulation. After orgasm, the male typically enters a **refractory period**—a time when no amount of additional stimulation will result in orgasm. The length of this period ranges from minutes to days, depending on a variety of factors such as age, frequency of previous sexual activity, and the degree of the man's emotional closeness to and sexual desire for his partner. In contrast to men, women generally experience no comparable refractory period: They are physiologically capable of returning to another orgasmic peak from anywhere in the resolution phase. However, a woman may or may not want to do so. In the last two sections of this chapter we discuss the impact of aging on sexual arousal and response and then consider some differences between men's and women's patterns of sexual response.

Refractory period
The period of time following orgasm in the male during which he cannot experience another orgasm.

Aging and the Sexual Response Cycle

As people grow older, they will notice changes in sexual arousal and response patterns. In this section we briefly summarize some of the more common variations that occur in the sexual response cycles of women and men.

The Sexual Response Cycle of Older Women

In general, all phases of the response cycle continue to occur for older women, but with somewhat decreased intensity (Masters & Johnson, 1966).

EXCITEMENT PHASE The first physiological response to sexual arousal, vaginal lubrication, typically begins more slowly in an older woman. Instead of 10–30 seconds, it may take several minutes or longer before vaginal lubrication is observed. In most cases, the amount of lubrication is reduced. Research using the vaginal photoplethysmograph found that postmenopausal women's vaginal blood-volume increase during sexual arousal is smaller than in premenopausal women. However, women in both groups reported similar levels of sexual activity and enjoyment, indicating that the somewhat lowered vasocongestion response is within the range necessary for normal function (Morrell et al., 1984).

The decrease in circulating estrogen also changes urethral and vaginal tissues. Urethral tissue can lose tone and become dry, often leading to urinary tract infections and urinary incontinence when sneezing, coughing, exercising, or engaging in sexual activity (Capewell et al., 1992). Vaginal mucosa become thinner and change to a lighter pinkish color. Both the length and the width of the vagina decrease, and these changes contribute to the diminished expansive ability of the inner vagina during sexual arousal.

When there is considerably diminished lubrication and vaginal expansion during sexual response, uncomfortable or painful intercourse can result. In addition, some women report decreased sexual desire and sensitivity of the clitoris, both of which interfere with sexual excitement. Hormone-replacement therapy and vaginal lubricants can often help these symptoms.

PLATEAU PHASE During the plateau phase, the vaginal orgasmic platform develops, and the uterus elevates. In a postmenopausal woman, these changes occur to a somewhat lesser degree than before menopause (Masters & Johnson, 1966).

ORGASM PHASE Contractions of the orgasmic platform and the uterus continue to occur at orgasm, although the number of these contractions is typically reduced in an older woman. In some postmenopausal women, uterine contractions that take place at orgasm can be painful. Several women in Masters and Johnson's study continued to experience multiple orgasmic response. However, one-third of the women in another study reported significantly reduced capacity or inability to experience orgasm (Sarrel, 1988).

Orgasm appears to be an important aspect of sexual activity to older women. One survey (Starr & Weiner, 1981) found that 69% of women ages 60–91 listed "orgasm" first in response to the question "What do you consider a good sexual experience?" Only 17% of the women answered "intercourse" to this same question. In addition, "orgasm" was the most frequent response to the question "What in the sex act is most important to you?" Sixty-five percent of the women reported that their frequency of orgasm was the same as when they were younger.

RESOLUTION PHASE The resolution phase typically occurs more rapidly in postmenopausal women. Labia color change, vaginal expansion, orgasmic platform formation, and clitoral retraction all disappear soon after orgasm. This is most likely due to the overall reduced amount of pelvic vasocongestion during arousal.

In summary, the effects of aging on female sexuality vary considerably. Most women experience minor changes, and some others find their sexual interest, excitement, and orgasm seriously affected. An active sex life helps maintain vaginal health, and a functional and interested partner and good couple communication contribute to gratifying sexual relations for the older woman. Hormone-replacement therapy, as we saw in the preceding discussion, can also resolve many of the problems that interfere with enjoyable sexual response.

The Sexual Response Cycle of Older Men

Most changes in the sexual response cycle of older men involve alterations in the intensity and duration of response (Masters & Johnson, 1966).

EXCITEMENT PHASE During youth, many males can experience an erection in a few seconds. This ability is typically altered with the aging process. Instead of 8–10 seconds, a man may now require several minutes of effective stimulation to develop an erect penis. More direct physical stimulation, such as hand caressing or oral stimulation, may also be desirable or necessary. This slowed rate of erectile response may cause alarm, stimulating a fear of impotence in some men:

> I guess it was the little things adding up that finally made me realize it was taking me longer to get a hard-on—the fact that I could go to bed with an extremely desirable woman and still be flaccid; that kissing and hugging often wasn't enough to get me started. At first I was shaken up at this discovery, thinking that maybe I would lose my potency. However, I received some good advice from my physician, who assured me that while things may slow down a bit, they continue to remain functional. (Authors' files)

Fortunately, this man received good advice. Most men retain their erectile capacities throughout their lifetimes. When a man and his partner understand that a slowed rate of obtaining an erection is normal, the altered pattern has little or no effect on their enjoyment of sexual expression.

However, some men who are fearful that they will ultimately lose their erectile function may develop such anxiety that their fears become reality. A preoccupation with erection leads some men to stop being sexually active (Friedan, 1993). Other very real complications may have to do with health problems: Heart disease, high blood pressure, diabetes, and associated medications can also interfere with erection (Feldman et al., 1994).

PLATEAU PHASE Older men do not typically experience as much *myotonia* (muscle tension) during the plateau phase as when they were younger. Testes may not elevate as close to the perineum. Complete penile erection is frequently not obtained until late in the plateau phase, just prior to orgasm. One result of these changes is that the older man is often able to sustain the plateau phase much longer than he did when he was younger, which may significantly enhance his pleasure. Many men and their partners appreciate this prolonged opportunity to enjoy other sensations of sexual response besides ejaculation. When a man engages in intercourse, his partner also may appreciate his greater ejaculatory control.

ORGASM PHASE Most aging males continue to experience considerable pleasure from their orgasmic responses. In fact, about 73% of older men in one study reported that orgasm was "very important" in their sexual experiences (Starr & Weiner, 1981). However, they may note a decline in intensity. Frequently absent are the sensations of ejaculatory inevitability that correspond with the emission phase of ejaculation. The number of muscular contractions occurring during the expulsion phase are typically reduced, and so is the force of ejaculation. The seminal fluid is usually less copious and somewhat thinner in consistency.

RESOLUTION PHASE Resolution typically occurs more rapidly in older men. Loss of erection is usually quite rapid, especially compared to younger men. Testicles generally descend immediately after ejaculation.

Although resolution becomes faster with aging, the refractory period between orgasm and the next excitement phase gradually lengthens. Men may begin to notice this as early as their 30s or 40s. Often, by age 60, the refractory period may last for several hours, even days in some cases.

Some Differences Between the Sexes

More and more, writers are emphasizing the basic similarities of sexual response in men and women. We see this as a positive trend away from the once-popular notion that great differences exist between the sexes—an opinion that undoubtedly helped create a big market for many "love manuals" designed to inform readers about the mysteries and complexities of the "opposite sex." Now we know that much can be learned about our partners by carefully observing our own sexual patterns. Nevertheless, there are some real and important primary differences. In the following pages, we outline and discuss some of them.

What do you think are some of the significant differences between the sexes in sexual response patterns?

Greater Variability in Female Response

One major difference between the sexes is the range of variations in the sexual response cycle. Although the graphs in Figures 6.3 and 6.4 do not reflect individual differences, they do demonstrate a wider range in the female response. One pattern is outlined for the male and three for the female.

In the female chart, the sexual response pattern represented by line A is most similar to the male pattern. It differs in an important way, however, in its potential for additional orgasms without dropping below the plateau level. Line B represents quite a different female pattern: a smooth advance through excitement to the level of plateau, where the responding woman may remain for some time without experiencing orgasm. The consequent resolution phase is more drawn out. Line C portrays a rapid rise in excitement, followed by one intense orgasm and a quick resolution.

Although it appears that women often have more variable sexual response patterns than men, this does not imply that all males experience the response cycle in exactly the same way. Men report considerable variation from the Masters and Johnson standard, including several mild orgasmic peaks followed by ejaculation, prolonged pelvic contractions after the expulsion of semen, and extended periods of intense excitement prior to ejaculation that feel like one long orgasm (Zilbergeld, 1978). In other words, there is no single pattern of sexual response, nor is there one "correct way." All patterns and variations—including one person's different reactions to sexual stimuli at different times or in different situations—are completely normal.

The Male Refractory Period

The presence of a refractory period in the male cycle is certainly one of the most significant differences in sexual responses between the sexes. Men typically find that a certain minimum time must elapse after an orgasm before they can experience another climax. Most women have no such physiologically imposed "shutdown phase."

Why do you think the refractory period exists? Why do only men experience this phenomenon?

There is considerable speculation about why only men have a refractory period. It seems plausible that some kind of short-term neurological inhibitory mechanism is triggered by ejaculation. This notion is supported by some fascinating research conducted by three British scientists (Barfield et al., 1975). These researchers speculated that certain chemical pathways between the midbrain and the hypothalamus—pathways known to be involved in regulating sleep—might have something to do with postorgasm inhibition in males. To test their hypothesis, the researchers destroyed a specific site, the *ventral medial lemniscus,* along these pathways in rats. For comparative purposes, they surgically eliminated three other areas in hypothalamic and midbrain locations in different rats. Later observations of sexual behavior revealed that the elimination of the ventral medial lemniscus had a dramatic effect on refractory periods, cutting their duration in half.

Other research with rats has provided further evidence implicating the brain in the male refractory period. In two studies, large lesions made in an area below the hypothalamus resulted in greatly increased ejaculatory behavior (Heimer & Larsson, 1964; Lisk, 1966). Another investigation revealed that electrical stimulation of the posterior hypothalamus can produce dramatic declines in the intervals between a male rat's copulatory activities (Caggiula, 1970).

Some people believe that the answer to the riddle of refractory periods is somehow connected with the loss of seminal fluid during orgasm. Most researchers have been skeptical of this idea because there is no known substance in the expelled semen to account for an energy drain, marked hormone reduction, or any of the other implied biochemical explanations.

Still another explanation suggests that there may be an evolutionary advantage in male refractory periods—that is, that the ultimate goal of survival of the species is served best if men experience a shutdown after orgasm and women do not. According to this theory, it is advantageous for women to be able to continue copulatory activity with more than one male because this practice increases the number of sperm in the reproductive tract, thus increasing the possibility of impregnation. The presence of additional sperm might also allow for increased natural selection of the fittest (the fastest swimmers, the longest living, and so forth). The evidence for this theory is tenuous at best, but it is nevertheless a provocative thesis. Whatever the reason for it, the refractory period is common not just to human males but to males of virtually all other species for which data exist, including rats, dogs, and chimpanzees.

Multiple Orgasms

Differences between the sexes occur in still a third area of sexual response patterns: the ability to experience **multiple orgasms.** Technically speaking, the term *multiple orgasms* refers to having more than one orgasmic experience within a short time interval.

Multiple orgasms
More than one orgasm experienced within a short time period.

Although researchers differ in their views of what constitutes a multiple orgasmic experience, for our own purposes we can say that if a man or woman has two or more sexual climaxes within a short period, that person has experienced multiple orgasms. There is, however, a distinction between males and females that is often obscured by such a definition. It is not uncommon for a woman to have several sequential orgasms, separated in time by the briefest of intervals (perhaps only seconds). In contrast, the spacing of male orgasms is typically more protracted.

How many women experience multiple orgasms? Kinsey (1953) reported that about 14% of his female sample regularly had multiple orgasms. In 1970 a survey of *Psychology Today* readers revealed a 16% figure (Athanasiou et al., 1970). Surveys of our own student population over the years have produced a similar percentage of women who regularly experience more than one orgasm during a single sexual encounter.

On the surface, it might seem that the capacity for multiple orgasms is limited to a minority of women. However, the research of Masters and Johnson showed this assumption to be false:

> If a female who is capable of having regular orgasms is properly stimulated within a short period after her first climax, she will in most instances be capable of having a second, third, fourth, and even a fifth and a sixth orgasm before she is fully satiated. As contrasted with the male's usual inability to have more than one orgasm in a short period, many females, especially when clitorally stimulated, can regularly have five or six full orgasms within a matter of minutes. (1961, p. 792)

Thus, we find that most women have the capacity for multiple orgasms, but apparently only a small portion of the female population experiences them. Why is there a large gap between capacity and experience? The answer may lie in the source of stimulation. The Kinsey report, the *Psychology Today* survey, and our own student surveys mentioned earlier are all based on orgasm rates during penile–vaginal intercourse. For a variety of reasons—not the least of which is the male's tendency to stop after his orgasm—women are not likely to continue coitus beyond their initial orgasm. In sharp contrast, several researchers have demonstrated that women who masturbate and those who relate sexually to other women are considerably more likely both to reach initial orgasm and to continue to additional orgasms (Athanasiou et al., 1970; Masters & Johnson, 1966).

We do not mean to imply by this discussion that all women should be experiencing multiple orgasms. On the contrary, many women may prefer sexual experiences during which they have a single orgasm, or perhaps no orgasm at all. The data on multiple orgasmic capacities of women are not meant to be interpreted as the way women "should" respond. This could lead to a new kind of arbitrary sexual standard. The following quotes illustrate the tendency to set such standards:

When I was growing up, people considered any young, unmarried woman who enjoyed and sought active sexual involvements to be disturbed or promiscuous. Now I am told that I must have several orgasms each time I make love in order to be considered "normal." What a switch in our definitions of normal or healthy—from the straightlaced, noninvolved person to this incredible creature who is supposed to get it off multiply at the drop of a hat. (Authors' files)

Sometimes men ask me why I don't come more than once. It is as though they want me to perform for them. The truth is, one orgasm is all I typically need to be satisfied. Sometimes it is nice not even to worry about having a climax. All this emphasis on producing multiple orgasms is a real put-off to me. (Authors' files)

As suggested earlier, multiple orgasms are considerably less common among males. They are most often reported by very young men, their frequency declining with age. Even at college age, it is unusual to find men who routinely experience more than one orgasm during a single sexual encounter. However, we agree with Alex Comfort (1972), who asserts that most men are probably more capable of multiple orgasms than they realize. Many have been conditioned by years of masturbation to get it over as quickly as possible to avoid detection. Such a mental set hardly encourages an adolescent to continue experimenting after the initial orgasm. Through later experimentation, though, many men make discoveries similar to the one described in the following personal reflection of a middle-aged man:

Somehow it never occurred to me that I might continue making love after experiencing orgasm. For 30 years of my life, this always signaled endpoint for me. I guess I responded this way for all the reasons you stated in class and a few more you didn't cover. My wife was with me the night you discussed refractory periods. We talked about it all the way home, and the next day gave it a try. Man, am I mad at myself now for missing out on something really nice all of these years. I discovered that I could have more than one orgasm in one session, and while it may take me a long time to come again, the getting there is a very nice part. My wife likes it, too! (Authors' files)

There is evidence to suggest that some men may actually be capable of experiencing a series of orgasms in a very short time period. In one study, 13 men reported that they had the capacity to experience a series of preejaculatory orgasms culminating in a final orgasm with ejaculation. Most of these men related having three to ten orgasms per sexual encounter. Unfortunately, only one of these 13 individuals was studied in the laboratory, where his claim was substantiated with physiological data. Apparently, the key to these multiple responses was the men's ability to withhold ejaculation because the final orgasm in the series, accompanied by ejaculation, triggered a refractory period (Robbins & Jensen, 1978).

More recently, Marian Dunn and Jan Trost reported their findings from interviews with 21 men, ages 25 to 69, all of whom stated that they were usually but not always multiply orgasmic. For the purpose of their investigation, these researchers defined male multiple orgasms as "two or more orgasms with or without ejaculation and without, or with only very limited, detumesence [loss of erection] during one and the same sexual encounter" (1989, p. 379). Their patterns varied, with some experiencing ejaculation with the first orgasm, followed by more "dry" orgasms. Others reported having several orgasms without ejaculation followed by a final ejaculatory orgasm. Still others reported variations on these two themes.

The results of these studies, although largely unsubstantiated by corroborative laboratory investigations, do provide mounting evidence that some men do experience multiple orgasms. If these findings are ultimately verified, and if more men become aware of the possibility of experiencing multiple orgasms, future surveys may reveal that the percentage of men experiencing more than one orgasm during one sex session may be closer to that of their female counterparts than presently believed.

It is not necessary for lovemaking always to end with ejaculation. Many men may find it pleasurable to continue sexual activity after a climax:

> One of the best parts of sex for me is having intercourse again shortly after my first orgasm. I find it is relatively easy to get another erection, even though I seldom experience another climax during the same session. The second time round I can concentrate fully on my partner's reactions without being distracted by my own building excitement. The pace is generally mellow and relaxed, and it is a real high for me psychologically. (Authors' files)

Thus multiple orgasms can be seen not as an ultimate goal to be sought above all else but rather as a possible area to explore. A relaxed approach to this possibility may give interested women and men an opportunity to experience more of the full range of their sexual potentials.

Summary

SEXUAL AROUSAL: THE ROLE OF HORMONES

Both sexes produce so-called male sex hormones and female sex hormones. In men, the testes produce about 95% of total androgens and some estrogens. A woman's ovaries and adrenals produce androgens in roughly equal amounts, and estrogens are produced predominantly by her ovaries.

The dominant androgen in both sexes is testosterone. Men's bodies typically produce 20 to 40 times as much testosterone as women but women's body cells are more sensitive to testosterone than men's are.

Although it is difficult to distinguish the effects of sex hormones and those of psychological processes on sexual arousal, research strongly indicates that testosterone plays a critical role in maintaining sexual desire in both sexes.

A major symptom of testosterone deficiency in both sexes—a decrease in one's customary level of sexual desire—may be eliminated by testosterone-replacement therapy. However, raising the level of testosterone above a normal range is unlikely to stimulate a further increase in sexual motivation and may have adverse effects on both sexes.

SEXUAL AROUSAL: THE BRAIN

The brain plays an important role in human sexual arousal by mediating our thoughts, emotions, memories, and fantasies.

There is evidence linking stimulation and surgical alteration of various brain sites with sexual arousal in humans and other animals.

The limbic system, particularly the hypothalamus, plays an important part in sexual function.

SEXUAL AROUSAL: THE SENSES

Touch tends to predominate among the senses that stimulate human sexual arousal. Locations on the body that are highly responsive to tactile pleasuring are called erogenous zones. Primary erogenous zones are areas with dense concentrations of nerve endings; secondary erogenous zones are other areas of the body that become endowed with erotic significance as the result of sexual conditioning.

Vision is second only to touch in providing stimuli that most people find sexually arousing. Recent evidence suggests that women respond as much as men to visual erotica.

Research has yet to clearly demonstrate whether or not smell and taste play a biologically determined role in human sexual arousal, but our own unique individual experiences may allow certain smells and tastes to acquire erotic significance. However, our culture's obsession with "personal hygiene" tends to mask natural smells or tastes that relate to sexual activity.

Research on nonhuman animals has isolated a variety of pheromones (sexual odors) that are strongly associated with reproductive sexual activities.

Recent studies have also provided tentative but not conclusive evidence that humans may also produce pheromones that act as sexual attractants.

Some individuals find sounds during lovemaking to be highly arousing, whereas others prefer that their lovers be silent during love play. Besides being sexually stimulating to some, communication during a sexual interlude can also be very informative.

SEXUAL AROUSAL: FOODS AND CHEMICALS

At this point there is no clear evidence that any substance that we eat, drink, or inject has genuine aphrodisiac qualities. Faith and suggestion account for the apparent successes of a variety of alleged aphrodisiacs.

Certain substances are known to have an inhibitory effect on sexual behavior. These anaphrodisiacs include drugs such as opiates, tranquilizers, antihypertensives, antidepressants, antipsychotics, nicotine, birth control pills, and sedatives.

SEXUAL RESPONSE: KAPLAN'S THREE-STAGE MODEL

Kaplan's model of sexual response contains three stages: desire, excitement, and orgasm.

This model is distinguished by its inclusion of desire as a distinct stage of the sexual response cycle separate from genital changes.

SEXUAL RESPONSE: MASTERS AND JOHNSON'S FOUR-PHASE MODEL

Masters and Johnson describe four phases in the sexual response patterns of both women and men: excitement, plateau, orgasm, and resolution.

During excitement, both sexes experience increased myotonia (muscle tension), heart rate, and blood pressure. Sex flush and nipple erection often occur, especially among women. Female responses include engorgement of the clitoris, the labia, and the vagina (with vaginal lubrication), elevation and enlargement of the uterus, and breast enlargement. Males experience penile erection, enlargement and elevation of the testes, and sometimes Cowper's gland secretions.

The plateau phase is marked by dramatic accelerations of myotonia, hyperventilation, heart rate, and blood pressure. In females, the clitoris withdraws under its hood, the labia minora deepen in color, the orgasmic platform forms in the vagina, the uterus is fully elevated, and the areolas become swollen. In males, the corona becomes fully engorged, the testicles continue both elevation and enlargement, and Cowper's glands are active.

Orgasm is marked by involuntary muscle spasms throughout the body. Blood pressure, heart rate, and respiration rate peak. Orgasm is slightly longer in duration in females. Male orgasm typically occurs in two stages, emission and expulsion. It is difficult to distinguish subjective descriptions of female and male orgasms.

Masters and Johnson suggest that there is only one kind of physiological orgasm in females, regardless of the method of stimulation. Josephine and Irving Singer counter with the contention that women may experience three different kinds of orgasms.

Some women are capable of experiencing orgasm and perhaps ejaculation when the Grafenberg spot, an area along the anterior wall of the vagina, is vigorously stimulated.

During resolution, sexual systems return to their nonexcited state, a process that may take several hours, depending on a number of factors. Erection loss occurs in two stages, the first very rapid and the second more protracted.

AGING AND THE SEXUAL RESPONSE CYCLE

As women and men grow older, they notice changes in their sexual arousal and response patterns. For both sexes, all phases of the response cycle generally continue to occur, but with somewhat decreased intensity.

An older woman typically requires more time to achieve vaginal lubrication. The sexual response cycle of the older woman is also characterized by less vaginal expansion, diminished orgasmic intensity, and a more rapid resolution.

Less commonly, women may experience a decrease in sexual desire, clitoral sensitivity, and/or the capacity for orgasm.

Older men typically require longer periods of time to achieve erection and reach orgasm. Greater ejaculatory control may be beneficial to sexual pleasure for both their partners and themselves.

The sexual response cycle of the aging male is also characterized by less myotonia, reduced orgasmic intensity, more rapid resolution, and longer refractory periods.

SEXUAL RESPONSE: SOME DIFFERENCES BETWEEN THE SEXES

Many writers now emphasize the fundamental similarities in the sexual responses of men and women. However, there are certain important primary differences between the sexes.

As a group, females demonstrate a wider variability in their sexual response patterns than do men.

The presence of a refractory period in the male is one of the most significant differences in the response cycles of the two sexes. No cause for this period has been clearly demonstrated, but there is some evidence that neurological inhibitory mechanisms are activated by ejaculation.

Multiple orgasms occur more often in females than in males. Women are more likely to experience multiple orgasms while masturbating than during coitus. Recent evidence suggests that some men may also be capable of experiencing a series of orgasms in a very short time period.

ANSWERS TO SEXUALITY & DIVERSITY BOX QUIZ

Report A = Male

Report B = Female

Report C = Female

Thought Provokers

1. Assume that research eventually reveals that yohimbine or some other substance has genuine aphrodisiac qualities. What possible benefits might be associated with its use? What possible abuses might arise? Would you consider using an aphrodisiac? If so, under what conditions?
2. It has traditionally been assumed that men have more capacity and desire for sexual expression than do women. Do you believe this is a valid assumption? Why has this viewpoint been so pervasive across most Western cultures?
3. It has been said that women enjoy hugging and touching more than genital sex, whereas men have little interest in the "preliminaries," preferring to "get down to the real thing." Do you believe this statement reflects a genuine difference between the sexes? Are there sex differences in patterns of sexual turn-ons and turn-offs? If so, are they learned or biologically determined?
4. Women collectively appear to have a greater capacity for orgasm, to experience orgasm from a wider range of stimulation, and to have more problems experiencing orgasm than men. To what factors do you attribute this greater variation in female orgasmic response patterns?

Suggested Readings

Brecher, Ruth; and Brecher, Edward (1966). *An Analysis of Human Sexual Response.* New York: New American Library. A simplified, accurate reporting of the Masters and Johnson (1966) research findings.

Crenshaw, Theresa (1996). *The Alchemy of Love and Lust.* New York: Putnam. A superbly informative and entertaining book by one of America's leading authorities on sexual medicine. In addition to providing current data on the impact of testosterone and estrogens on our sexuality, Crenshaw also provides compelling information about such diverse topics as love, attraction, the senses, aging, and longevity.

Crenshaw, Theresa; and Goldberg, James (1996). *Sexual Pharmacology: Drugs That Inhibit Sexual Function.* New York: Norton. A must-read for anyone wishing to expand his or her knowledge about a broad array of prescription medications that have adverse sexual side effects.

Kaplan, Helen Singer (1979). *Disorders of Sexual Desire.* New York: Brunner/Mazel. The book deals primarily with the treatment of sexual difficulties, particularly problems of desire. It contains excellent information about the effects of a variety of drugs on sexuality.

Masters, William; and Johnson, Virginia (1966). *Human Sexual Response.* Boston: Little, Brown. This highly technical book outlines the authors' major contributions to the understanding of the physiology of human sexual response. It is a good source for those readers who would like more detailed information about physiological responses to sexual stimulation.

Rako, Susan (1996). *The Hormone of Desire.* New York: Harmony Books. A moving, often profound gem of a book that began as one woman physician's search for answers to her own personal and sexual discomfort associated with menopausal-induced testosterone deficiency. Meticulously researched and packed with valuable facts, this book is an excellent source of information about testosterone-replacement therapy.

Resource

North American Menopause Society, P.O. Box 94527, Cleveland, Ohio 44101

Web Resources

Biological Bases of Behavior
salmon.psy.plym.ac.uk/year1/bbb.htm
This site is provided as lecture support for classes taught by Professor Paul Kenyon at the University of Plymouth in Devon, U.K. Two especially useful pages on this site are those on Hormones and Sexual Behavior and Psychosexual Differentiation. Both pages offer research information and references.

Sex Response Cycle
www.sexualitydata.com/topics/sex_response_cycle.html
This Web site provides information about the sexual response cycle as described by Masters and Johnson. In addition, the sexuality database included with this site allows users to perform key word searches of such topics as orgasms, G spots, and erogenous zones.

7

Love and the Development of Sexual Relationships

What Is Love?

Can love be defined? Can it be meaningfully measured?

Types of Love

Do successful relationships begin with passionate love and later evolve into companionate love?

What are the theoretical frameworks for conceptualizing what people experience when they report being in love?

Falling in Love: Why and with Whom?

What are the most important factors influencing our choice of a mate? Do women and men tend to select the same qualities in a mate?

The Development of Intimacy

How do intimate relationships differ from friendships? What qualities do they share?

Issues in Loving Relationships

Does sexual intimacy deepen a relationship?

Are feelings of jealousy a sign of love?

Maintaining Relationship Satisfaction

What ingredients do most lasting, satisfying love relationships have in common?

For me, the potential for falling in love begins with a physical attraction. But looks only count for so much. I need an intimate friendship and closeness in order to possibly fall in love. Trust is another important part of a relationship that can lead to love. A prospective partner would also need to share some of my interests, and I would need to share some of his. Finally, and perhaps most important, good communication in a relationship is essential for me to be truly in love. (Authors' files)

Love, intimacy, and sexual relationships are important and complex aspects of people's lives. In this chapter we look at these interactions from various perspectives and examine some of the research dealing with them. We consider a number of questions: What is love? What kinds of love are there? What determines why we fall in love with one person and not another? How does sex fit into relationships? How does love relate to jealousy? And finally, what factors influence the development of intimacy in a relationship, and what qualities or behaviors help in maintaining intimacy over many years?

What Is Love?

O Love is the crooked thing,
There is nobody wise enough
To find out all that is in it
For he would be thinking of love
Till the stars had run away
And the shadows eaten the moon.
(Yeats, "The Brown Penney")

Love has intrigued people throughout history. Its joys and sorrows have inspired artists and poets, novelists, filmmakers, and other students of human interaction. Indeed, love is one of the most pervasive themes in the art and literature of many cultures. Each of our own lives has been influenced in significant ways by love, beginning with the love we received as infants and children. Our best and worst moments in life may be tied to a love relationship.

Love has been the inspiration for some of our greatest works of literature, art, and music.

Love is a special kind of attitude with strong emotional and behavioral components. It is also a phenomenon that eludes easy definition or explanation. As the following definitions suggest, love can mean very different things to different people:

> Love is patient and kind; love is not jealous or boastful; it is not arrogant or rude. Love does not insist on its own way; it is not irritable or resentful; it does not rejoice at wrong, but rejoices in the right. Love bears all things, believes all things, hopes all things, endures all things. (New Testament, I Corinthians 13:4–7)

> Love is a temporary insanity curable by marriage or by removal of the patient from the influences under which he incurred the disorder. (Bierce, 1943, p. 202)

> Love is that condition in which the happiness of another person is essential to your own. (Heinlein, 1961, p. 345)

As difficult as love is to define, can it be meaningfully measured? Some social scientists have attempted to do so, with varied results (Davis & Latty-Mann, 1987; Hatfield & Sprecher, 1986a; Pam et al., 1975; Rubin, 1970). Perhaps the most ambitious attempt to measure love was undertaken some years ago by psychologist

Zick Rubin (1970 & 1973). Using responses to a questionnaire administered to several hundred dating couples at the University of Michigan, Rubin developed a 13-item measurement device that he called a love scale. On this scale people are asked to indicate whether a particular statement accurately reflects their feelings about another person, usually someone they are interested in romantically.

As measured by Rubin's scale, love has three components: attachment, caring, and intimacy. *Attachment* is a person's desire for the physical presence and emotional support of the other person. *Caring* is an individual's concern for the other's well-being. *Intimacy* is the desire for close, confidential communication with the other.

Some people may argue that it is simply not possible to measure an emotion such as love, particularly with a paper-and-pencil measurement device such as the love scale. Nevertheless, Rubin did obtain some evidence supporting the validity of his scale. For example, the scale was used to investigate the popular belief that lovers spend a great deal of time looking into one another's eyes (Rubin, 1970). Couples were observed through a one-way mirror while they waited to participate in a psychological experiment. The findings revealed that weak lovers (couples who scored below average on the love scale) made significantly less eye contact than did strong lovers (those with above-average scores).

Perhaps in the years ahead we will have access to a variety of new perspectives on the question "What is love?" largely because there has been a marked increase in the number of scientists who have begun to study love. What accounts for this rise in interest in love studies? A recent interview with a leading social scientist, psychologist Elaine Hatfield (author of *Love, Sex, and Intimacy* [1993]), provided one plausible explanation: The ranks of women scientists are swelling, and women may be more willing than men to consider love a legitimate topic for serious research (Gray, 1993).

Types of Love

Love takes many forms. Love exists between parent and child and other family members. Love between friends, known to the ancient Greeks as *philia,* involves concern for the other's well-being. Lovers may experience two additional types of love: passionate love and companionate love. In this section we look more closely at these two widely discussed types of love, then present two contemporary models or theories of love.

Passionate Love

Passionate love, also known as romantic love or infatuation, is a state of extreme absorption with and desire for another. It is characterized by intense feelings of tenderness, elation, anxiety, sexual desire, and ecstasy. Generalized physiological arousal, including increased heartbeat, perspiration, blushing, and stomach churning, along with a feeling of great excitement, often accompanies this form of love. Statements or thoughts typical of this state of mind include the following: "My emotions have been on a roller coaster," "Sometimes I feel I can't control my thoughts; they are obsessively on ________," "I yearn to touch and be touched," "I get extremely depressed when things don't go right in my relationship," and "No one else could love ________ like I do" (Hatfield & Rapson, 1987). Strong sexual desire is typically a major component.

Passionate love
State of extreme absorption in another person. Also known as romantic love.

Intense passionate love typically occurs early in a relationship. It sometimes seems as if the less one knows the other person, the more intense the passionate love. In passionate love, people often overlook faults and avoid conflicts. Logic and reasoned consideration are swept away by the excitement. One may perceive the object of one's passionate love as providing complete personal fulfillment.

Not surprisingly, passionate love is often short-lived. Love that is based on ignorance of a person's full character is bound to change with increased familiarity. Many couples choose to make some kind of commitment to each other (becoming engaged, moving in

According to Rubin's love scale, love consists of three components: attachment, caring, and intimacy.

together, getting married, and so forth) while still fired by the fuel of passionate love—only to feel disillusioned later. When ecstasy gives way to routine, and the annoyances and conflicts typical of ongoing relationships surface, lovers may begin to have some doubts about their partners.

The first weeks and months of my relationship with Bob were incredible. I felt like I had found the perfect partner, someone who filled all that was missing in my life. Then, suddenly, he started to get on my nerves, and we started fighting every time we saw each other. It took a while to realize that we were finally seeing each other as real people instead of dream companions. (Authors' files)

Some couples are able to work through this period to ultimately find a solid basis on which to build a lasting relationship of mutual love. Others discover, often to their dismay, that the only thing they ever really shared was passion. Unfortunately, many people who experience diminishing passion believe that this is the end of love, rather than a possible transition into a different kind of love.

On the other hand, some people look forward to a different kind of relationship. Erich Fromm once commented, "Romantic love is a delicious art form but not a durable one. In the end, its most persistent practitioners confess that they would like to escape from its patterned illusion into the next more realistically satisfying stage of an enduring relationship" (1965, p. 252).

Companionate Love

Companionate love
A type of love characterized by friendly affection and deep attachment based on extensive familiarity with the loved one.

Companionate love is a less intense emotion than passionate love. It is characterized by friendly affection and a deep attachment that is based on extensive familiarity with the loved one. It involves a thoughtful appreciation of one's partner. Companionate love often encompasses a tolerance for another's shortcomings along with a desire to overcome difficulties and conflicts in a relationship. This kind of love is committed to ongoing nurturing of a partnership. In short, companionate love is often enduring, while passionate love is almost always transitory.

Sex in a companionate relationship typically reflects feelings associated with familiarity, especially the security of knowing what pleases the other. This foundation of knowledge and sexual trust can encourage experimentation and subtle communication. Sexual pleasure strengthens the overall bond of a companionate relationship. Although sex is usually less exciting than in passionate love, it is often experienced as richer, more meaningful, and deeply satisfying, as the following statement reveals:

Between my first and second marriages, I really enjoyed the excitement of new sexual relationships, especially after so much sexual frustration in my first marriage. Even though I sometimes miss the excitement of those times, I would never trade it for the easy comfort, pleasure, and depth of sexual intimacy I now experience in my 17-year marriage. (Authors' files)

Although most relationships begin with a period of passionate love and only later evolve into companionate love, some have the opposite history. Companionate love may develop first in a situation where two people know each other for an extended period as acquaintances, friends, or coworkers. Often an initial sexual attraction is not present or is de-emphasized because of circumstances. In these relationships, passionate love is based on familiarity with the other person, rather than on the excitement of the unknown. One woman describes her experience:

My boyfriend Victor and I had been good friends for around one year. Our families are very close. We spend all of the holidays together. Victor and I started out as really close friends. I considered him to be my best friend. I never really saw him as my type, and I am definitely not his type. I do not know when everything changed, but somewhere during our friendship, we fell in love. It is the most wonderful relationship I have ever experienced. We are so open and honest with each other. Not too long ago, we made love to each other for the first time. It was enormously incredible. I think it was exceptional because we communicate totally with each other. I can tell him what I like and dislike without being ashamed for talking about sex, and vice versa. I know the reason we are so in love is because we began our relationship as friends. They say you and your mate should be best friends, and that is exactly what we are, friends and lovers. (Authors' files)

Sexuality and Diversity

Romantic Love: A Human Universal?

Is romantic love merely an invention of Western culture? Until recently, this viewpoint was widespread among anthropologists. To these social scientists, romance seemed to be an emotion a bit too complex for less sophisticated cultures whose members do not have ready access to romance-inducing amenities such as leisure time, a certain refinement in the arts, and material comforts. However, not all anthropologists endorsed this opinion. One noteworthy exception is Helen Fisher, author of *Anatomy of Love: The Natural History of Monogamy, Adultery and Divorce* (1992), a book widely read by both scientists and the general public. "I've never *not* thought that love was a very primitive, basic human emotion," states Fisher, "as basic as fear, anger or joy. It is so evident. I guess anthropologists have just been busy doing other things" (in Gray, 1993, p. 49).

Two anthropologists that have not been too busy doing other things to take a look at romantic love in other cultures are William Jankowiak and Edward Fischer. These scientists recently conducted far-ranging research to determine whether romantic love is common throughout the world. For the purpose of their investigation, they defined romantic love as "any intense attraction that involves the idealization of the other, within an erotic context, with the expectation of enduring for some time in the future" (1992, p. 150). Jankowiak and Fischer used five indicators, listed below, as they searched for evidence of romantic love:

1. accounts depicting personal anguish and longing
2. the use of love songs or folklore that highlight the motivations behind romantic involvement
3. elopement due to mutual affection
4. native accounts affirming the existence of passionate love
5. the investigating ethnographer's affirmation that romantic love is present

The presence of one or more of these indicators was considered evidence of romantic love. Using these criteria, Jankowiak and Fischer documented the existence of romantic love in 147 out of the 166 societies studied. Furthermore, they suggested that its absence in the other 19 societies was probably due to a deficiency in their study methods rather than a reflection of a truly "love absent" society.

Jankowiak and Fischer's findings contrast sharply with the notion that romantic love is primarily limited to Western culture. Indeed, their study suggests "that romantic love constitutes a human universal, or at the least a near-universal" (1992, p. 154).

Sternberg's Triangular Theory of Love

The distinction between passionate and companionate love has been further refined by psychologist Robert Sternberg (1986 & 1988), who has proposed an interesting theoretical framework for conceptualizing what people experience when they report being in love. According to Sternberg, love has three faces: passion, intimacy, and commitment (see Figure 7.1):

Passion
The motivational component of Steinberg's triangular love theory.

Intimacy
The emotional component of Steinberg's triangular love theory.

Commitment
The thinking component of Steinberg's triangular love theory.

- **Passion** is the motivational component that fuels romantic feelings, physical attraction, and desire for sexual interaction. Passion instills a deep desire to be united with the loved one. In a sense passion is like an addiction, because its capacity to provide intense stimulation and pleasure can exert a powerful craving in a person.
- **Intimacy** is the emotional component of love that encompasses the sense of being bonded with another person. It includes feelings of warmth, sharing, and emotional closeness. Intimacy also embraces a willingness to help the other and an openness to sharing private thoughts and feelings with the beloved.
- **Commitment** is the thinking or cognitive aspect of love. It refers to the conscious decision to love another and to maintain a relationship over time in spite of difficulties that may arise.

Sternberg maintains that passion tends to develop rapidly and intensely in the early stages of a love relationship and then declines as the relationship progresses. In contrast, intimacy and commitment continue to build gradually over time, although at different rates (see Figure 7.2).

All three of the components just described are important dimensions of a loving relationship, but they typically exist in different patterns and to varying degrees in different relationships. Moreover, they often change over time within the same relationship. Sternberg suggests that such variations yield different kinds of love, or at least differences in how people experience love. For instance, the absence of all three components yields what Sternberg calls *nonlove* (what most of us feel for casual acquaintances). When only intimacy is present, the experience is one of *friendship* or liking. If only passion exists, with-

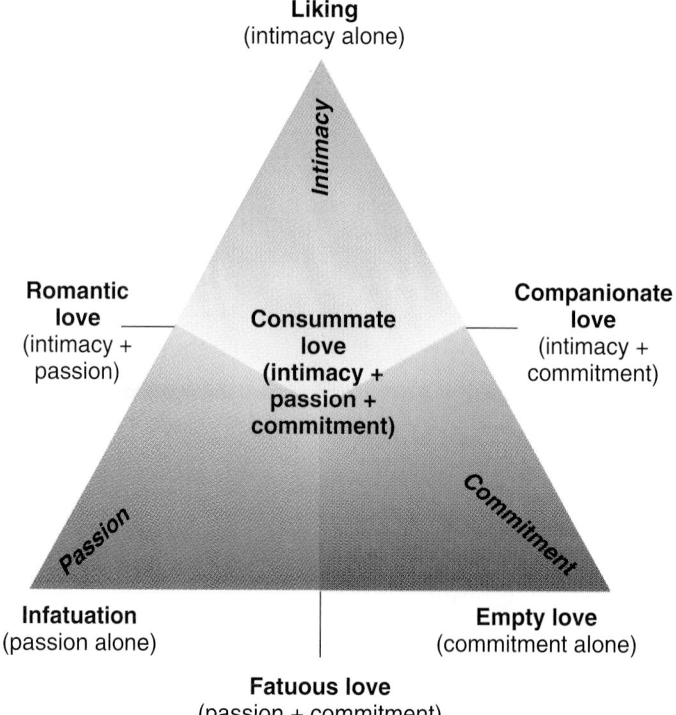

Figure 7.1

Sternberg's love triangle: (a) the three components of love, and (b) the various kinds of love as reflected in different combinations of the three components. *Note:* Nonlove is the absence of all three components.

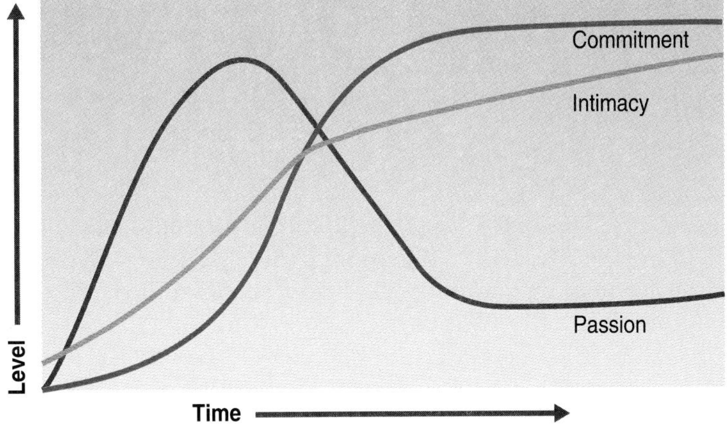

Figure 7.2

Sternberg theorizes that the passion component of love peaks early in a relationship and then declines, whereas the other two components, intimacy and commitment, continue to build gradually over time.

out intimacy or commitment, one experiences *infatuation.* The presence of commitment without passion and intimacy yields *empty love* (such as might be experienced in a long-term, static relationship). If intimacy and commitment exist without passion, one experiences *companionate love* (often characteristic of happy couples who have shared many years together). When passion and commitment are present but without intimacy, the experience is *fatuous love,* a kind of foolish involvement characteristic of whirlwind courtships or situations in which one worships and longs for another person from afar. Love characterized by passion and intimacy but no commitment is described by Sternberg as *romantic love.* Finally, when all three components are present, the experience is *consummate love,* the fullest kind of love that people often strive for but find difficult to achieve and/or sustain. Table 7.1 summarizes these eight kinds of love.

Empirical research on love models—including Sternberg's—is generally limited to only a few studies. One study of dating couples reported that the presence of two of Sternberg's love components—intimacy and commitment—was predictive of relationship stability and longevity (Hendrick et al., 1988). Another investigation found that married people demonstrated higher levels of commitment to their relationships than did unmarried people, a finding consistent with Sternberg's model (Acker & Davis, 1992). This same study found that although intimacy did not decline in longer relationships, passion declined for women but not for men. A more recent investigation of Sternberg's triangular theory found that lovers' definition and communication of the three components of love remained relatively stable over time (Reeder, 1996).

Table 7.1 Sternberg's Eight Varieties of Love and Their Different Patterns of Passion, Intimacy, and Commitment

Variety of Love	*Passion*	*Intimacy*	*Commitment*
1. Nonlove	○	○	○
2. Friendship	○	●	○
3. Infatuation	●	○	○
4. Empty love	○	○	●
5. Romantic love	●	●	○
6. Fatuous love	●	○	●
7. Companionate love	○	●	●
8. Consummate love	●	●	●

Source: Adapted from Sternberg, 1986.

Lee's Styles of Loving

Instead of attempting to describe different patterns or *types* of love, John Allan Lee (1974 & 1988) has proposed a theory that describes six different *styles of loving* that characterize intimate human relationships. According to Lee, people with a

- **Romantic** love style (*eros*) tend to place their emphasis on physical beauty as they search for ideal mates. Romantic, erotic lovers delight in the visual beauty and tactile/sensual pleasures provided by their lovers' bodies.

- **Game-playing** love style (*ludus*) like to play the field and acquire many sexual "conquests" with little or no commitment. Love is for fun, the act of seduction is to be enjoyed, and relationships are to remain casual and transitory.
- **Possessive** love style (*mania*) are inclined to seek obsessive love relationships that are often characterized by turmoil and jealousy. These people live a roller-coaster style of love where each display of affection from the lover brings ecstasy, whereas the mildest slight produces painful agitation.
- **Companionate** love style (*storge*) are slow to develop affection and commitment but tend to experience relationships that endure. This style is love without fever or turmoil, a peaceful and quiet kind of relating that usually begins as friendship and develops over time into affection and love.
- **Altruistic** love style (*agape*) are characterized by selflessness and a caring, compassionate desire to give to another without expectation of reciprocity. Such love is patient and never demanding or jealous.
- **Pragmatic** love style (*pragma*) are inclined to select lovers based on rational, practical criteria (such as shared interests) that are likely to lead to mutual satisfaction. These individuals approach love in a businesslike fashion by trying to get the best "romantic deal" by seeking partners with social, educational, religious, and interest patterns that are compatible with their own.

What happens when two different people in a relationship are naturally inclined toward different styles of loving?

For Lee, this is a critical question. He suggests that loving relationships frequently fail to thrive over time because "too often people are speaking different languages when they speak of love" (1974, p. 44). Even though both partners may try to build a lasting involvement, their efforts may be undermined by a losing struggle to integrate incompatible loving styles. In contrast, satisfaction and success in loving relationships often depend on finding a mate who "shares the same approach to loving, the same definition of love" (p. 44).

An inventory called the Love Attitude Scale has been developed to measure Lee's six loving styles (Hendrick & Hendrick, 1986), and this research tool has generated some empirical studies of his theory. One interesting study that employed this scale provided some support for Lee's hypothesis that relationship success is influenced by compatibility in styles of loving (Hendrick et al., 1988). A more recent study used the Love Attitude Scale to investigate the relationship between styles of loving and relationship satisfaction at different stages of life. The study sample included 250 adults in four groups: college-age single youth, young childless married adults, married adults with children living at home, and married adults whose grown-up children had left home. Two loving styles, *eros* and *agape*, were positively associated with relationship satisfaction for all life stages. Predictably, *ludus* was negatively associated with satisfaction for all three groups of married adults. *Storge* was significantly related to relationship satisfaction only for the married couples with children at home. *Mania* and, surprisingly, *pragma* were not significantly related to relationship satisfaction for any life-stage group (Montgomery & Sorell, 1997).

Falling in Love: Why and with Whom?

What determines why people fall in love and with whom they fall in love? These questions are exceedingly complex. Some writers believe that people fall in love to overcome a sense of aloneness and separateness. Psychoanalyst Erich Fromm (1965) suggested that union with another person is the deepest need of humans. Another psychoanalyst and writer, Rollo May, author of *Love and Will* (1969), also believes that as people experience their own solitariness, they long for the refuge of union with another through love. Some other observers see loneliness as a by-product of our individualistic and highly mobile society rather than as an inherent part of the human condition. This view emphasizes the con-

People who fall in love often share common interests.

nectedness that we all have with the people around us—through all our social relationships, language, and culture. According to this view, love relationships are one aspect of a person's social network, rather than a cure for the "disease" of loneliness (Solomon, 1981).

We have seen that love is a complex human emotion that can be explained, at least in part, by various psychosocial interpretations of its origins. However, the answer to why we fall in love may also encompass, to some degree, complex neurochemical processes that occur in our brains when we are attracted to another. We discuss some findings about the chemistry of love in the next section.

The Chemistry of Love

People caught up in the intense passion of blooming love often report feeling as though they are being swept away or that they are experiencing a kind of natural high. Such reactions may have a basis, at least in part, in brain chemistry, according to researchers Michael Liebowitz, author of *The Chemistry of Love* (1983), and Anthony Walsh, author of *The Science of Love: Understanding Love and Its Effects on Mind and Body* (1991). These authors contend that the initial elation and the energizing "high" of excitement, giddiness, and euphoria characteristic of passionate love are a result of surging levels of three key brain chemicals, called *neurotransmitters,* that allow brain cells to communicate with each other. These neurotransmitters, which include norepinephrine, dopamine, and especially *phenylethylamine* (PEA), are chemically similar to amphetamine drugs—and thus they produce amphetamine-like effects such as euphoria, giddiness, and elation. As Walsh notes, "When we meet someone who is attractive to us, the whistle blows at the PEA factory" (in Toufexis, 1993, p. 50).

Unfortunately, particularly from the perspective of "love junkies," the amphetamine-like highs associated with new love typically do not last—perhaps in part because the body eventually develops a tolerance for PEA and related neurotransmitters just as it does for amphetamines. With time, our brains may simply be unable to keep up with the demand for more and more PEA to produce love's special kick. Thus the "highs" we feel at the beginning of a relationship eventually diminish. This observation provides a plausible biological explanation for why passionate or romantic love is short-lived.

Liebowitz points out another parallel to amphetamine use. He notes that the anxiety, despair, and pain that follow the loss—or even potential loss—of a romantic love relationship are similar to what a person addicted to amphetamines experiences during drug withdrawal. In both cases, the loss of mood-lifting chemicals results in a sometimes protracted period of emotional pain.

Are there other brain chemicals that may help to explain why some relationships endure beyond the initial highs of passionate love? According to both Walsh and Liebowitz, the answer is yes. The continued progression from infatuation into the deep attachment characteristic of long-term loving relationships may result from the brain gradually stepping up production of another set of neurotransmitters called *endorphins.* These morphinelike chemicals are soothing substances that help produce a sense of security, tranquility, and peace. This may be another reason why abandoned lovers feel so terrible after their loss—they are deprived of their daily dose of feel-good chemicals.

What leads a person to fall in love with a particular individual? 

Just as we know little about why people fall in love, we have no simple explanation for why they fall in love with one particular person instead of another. A number of factors are often important: proximity, similarity, reciprocity, and physical attractiveness.

Proximity

Proximity
The geographical nearness of one person to another, which is an important factor in interpersonal attraction.

Although people often overlook **proximity,** or geographical nearness, in listing factors that attracted them to a particular person, it is one of the most important variables. We often develop close relationships with people whom we see frequently in our neighborhoods, in school, at work, or at church or synagogue.

Perhaps the most often quoted study of the effect of proximity on attraction was conducted by respected social psychologist Leon Festinger and his colleagues (1950) who evaluated friendship patterns among students living in a housing development consisting of 17 two-story buildings with five apartments per floor. All the residents were asked to name their three best friends among residents of the housing community. These friends almost invariably lived in the same building, with next-door neighbors being the most likely to be named as a friend and the next most likely living two doors away.

Why is proximity such a powerful factor in interpersonal attraction? Social psychologists have offered a number of plausible explanations. One is simply that familiarity breeds liking or loving. Research has shown that when we are repeatedly exposed to novel stimuli—whether they be unfamiliar musical selections, works of art, or human faces—our liking for such stimuli increases (Brooks & Watkins, 1989; Moreland & Zajonc, 1982; Nuttin, 1987). This phenomenon, called the **mere exposure effect,** explains in part why we are attracted to people in close proximity to us.

Mere exposure effect
The phenomenon by which repeated exposure to novel stimuli tends to increase an individual's liking for such stimuli.

The mere exposure effect even seems to influence our view of ourselves. Many of us are seldom satisfied with photographs of ourselves; our faces do not look quite right. One possible reason may be that the face we see in the photo is not the one we see staring back at us in the mirror. Because left and right are reversed in mirror images, the face we see looking back at us is always slightly different from what others see (see Figure 7.3). Thus we prefer the mirror image of our faces, whereas others will prefer the natural version. This was demonstrated by a study in which women subjects were shown two photos of themselves—one a normal photo and the other a mirror-image photo—and asked to indicate which they preferred. A close friend of each subject also indicated photo preferences. The results: Although most subjects preferred the mirror-image photographs, most of their friends preferred the normal photos (Mita et al., 1977).

Another likely reason why proximity influences with whom we fall in love is the fact that the more we see of others, the more familiar we become with their ways and thus the better able we are to predict their behavior. If you have a good idea of how someone is likely to behave in any given situation, you will probably be more comfortable with this person. It is also possible that when we know we will be seeing a lot of a person, we may be more motivated to see his or her good traits and to keep our interactions as positive as possible.

Figure 7.3 The Mere Exposure Effect

Which of these images do you prefer? Chances are you picked the left photo, since this is the Bill Cosby you are accustomed to seeing. However, Cosby would probably be inclined to express preference for the right photo, since this is the image he sees every day in the mirror. Most of us are seldom satisfied with photographs of ourselves because our faces do not look quite right. We are accustomed to seeing reflected images of ourselves in which left and right are reversed. Others are more likely to prefer the natural, non-reversed image of our faces.

Similarity

Similarity
Similarity of beliefs, interests, and values is a factor attracting people to one another.

Contrary to the old adage that opposites attract, people who fall in love often share common beliefs, values, attitudes, interests, and intellectual abilities (Capella & Palmer, 1990; Douglass & Douglass, 1993; Hatfield & Rapson, 1993; Sherman & Jones, 1994).

The recent NHSLS study (see Chapter 2) also revealed that people are generally inclined to form partnerships with people of similar attributes as reflected by race and ethnicity. The box discussion "Partner Choice and Race" describes this dimension of attraction.

Why are we drawn to people who are like us? For one thing, people with similar attitudes and interests are often inclined to participate in the same kinds of leisure activities.

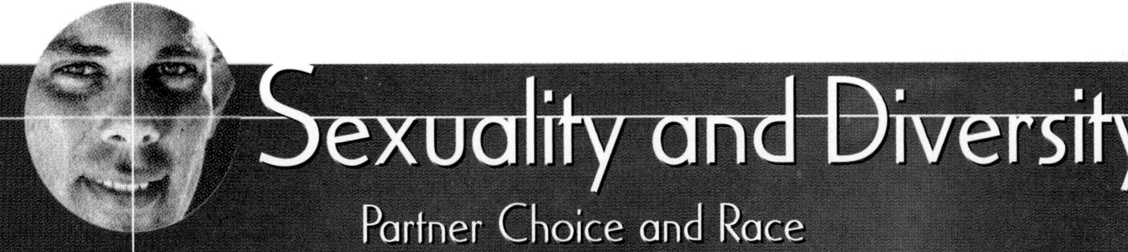

Sexuality and Diversity

Partner Choice and Race

The excellent NHSLS study, a nationwide survey of a representative sample of adults in the United States, provided data about the extent to which people form intimate relationships with members of the same race. As described in Chapter 2, a lack of funds forced Edward Laumann and his associates (1994) to include adequate numbers of only the two largest racial minorities in America. Consequently, the table included in this box contains data pertaining to only white Americans, African Americans, and Hispanic Americans. Furthermore, these data summarize a sample of almost 2000 nonmarital, noncohabitational heterosexual partnerships.

As you can see by examining the figures in this table, the percentages of same-race noncohabitational partnerships are very high for both sexes among whites and African Americans. In fact, an average of 91% of all noncohabitational partnerships reported by African American and white respondents involved relationships with members of the same race.

In contrast to this high percentage of racial group in-choice of partners among whites and African Americans, the percentage of racial group in-choice is considerably lower among Hispanic American respondents, ranging from 54% to 65% for men and women, respectively. Thus it would appear that "Hispanics as a group are less exclusive with respect to sexual partnering than are whites or blacks" (Laumann et al., 1994, p. 246).

Noncohabitational Sexual Partnerships by Race and Sex

	Percentage of Racial Group In-Choice	
Race	*Men*	*Women*
White	92%	87%
African American	82	97
Hispanic American	54	65

Source: Laumann et al., 1994.

Even more important, we are more likely to communicate well with people whose ideas and opinions are similar to ours, and communication is a very important aspect of enduring relationships. It is also reassuring to be with similar people, for they confirm our view of the world, validate our own experiences, and support our opinions and beliefs (Byrne et al., 1986; Sanders, 1982).

Reciprocity

Reciprocity
The principle that when we are recipients of expressions of liking or loving, we tend to respond in kind.

Still another factor drawing us to a particular individual is our perception that that person is interested in us. People tend to react positively to flattery, compliments, and other expressions of liking and affection. In the study of interpersonal attraction, this concept is reflected in the principle of **reciprocity,** which holds that when we are the recipients of expressions of liking or loving, we tend to respond in kind (Byrne & Murnen, 1988). Reciprocal responses can in turn set in motion a further escalation of the relationship: By responding warmly to people we believe feel positively toward us, we often induce them to like us even more (Curtis & Miller, 1988).

Physical Attractiveness

Physical attractiveness
Physical beauty is a powerful factor in attracting lovers to each other.

As you might expect, **physical attractiveness** often plays a dominant role in drawing lovers together. Despite the saying that beauty is only skin deep, it has been experimentally demonstrated that physically attractive people are more likely to be sought as friends and lovers and to be perceived as more likable, interesting, sensitive, poised, happy, sexy, competent, and socially skilled than people of average or unattractive appearance (Dion & Dion, 1987; Feingold, 1992; Hatfield & Rapson, 1993; Hatfield & Sprecher, 1986b).

Why is physical beauty such a powerful factor in attracting us to others? One answer has to do with aesthetics. We all enjoy looking at something or someone whom we consider to be beautiful. Another factor is that many people apparently believe that beautiful people have more to offer in terms of desirable personal qualities than those of us who are less attractive. We may also be attracted to beautiful people because they offer us the possibility of status by association. And perhaps beautiful people, by virtue of having been treated very well by others over the course of their lives, may be very secure and comfortable with themselves, a fact that may translate into especially satisfying relationships with others.

Whatever the reason, good looks seem to attract people even in some cases in which we would normally discount beauty as a factor. Some fascinating research by Judith Langlois and her colleagues strongly suggests that even infants exhibit a preference for beauty long before they are exposed to cultural standards of attractiveness and beauty. In one study infants from two to eight months old demonstrated marked preferences for attractive faces. When they were shown pairs of color slides of the faces of adult women previously rated by other adults for attractiveness, the infants demonstrated a strong inclination to look longer at the most attractive face in the pair (Langlois et al., 1987). In another study, 12-month-old infants demonstrated positive emotional and play responses when interacting with an adult stranger who wore a professionally constructed, lifelike, and very attractive latex theater mask. In contrast, when the stranger wore a mask portraying an unattractive face, the infants demonstrated more negative emotions and less play involvement (Langlois et al., 1990). In still another experiment, year-old infants played significantly longer with attractive dolls than with unattractive dolls (Langlois et al., 1990).

Do you think that both sexes are equally influenced by physical attractiveness in forming impressions of people they meet? Would both men and women be likely to rate good looks as a major factor in mate selection?

One study found that male college students placed significantly greater emphasis on physical appearance in selecting a partner for a sexual or long-term relationship than did female students. In contrast, college women placed greater emphasis on interpersonal warmth and personality characteristics (Nevid, 1984). Other studies have also found that American men place a greater emphasis on physical attractiveness than do American women (Bailey et al., 1994; Townsend & Levy, 1990; Wiederman & Allgeier, 1992). Do you think that this difference is typical of men and women in other cultures as well? The answer is provided in the boxed discussion, "Men's and Women's Preferences in Mate Selection: Are There Cross-Cultural Universals?"

Physical attractiveness seems to play the most important role in the early stages of a relationship. As researchers Elton McNeil and Zick Rubin conclude, "It seems likely that as the relationship progresses the impact of physical attractiveness tends to recede in importance. And we often perceive people whom we love as being beautiful, regardless of what anyone else might think" (1977, p. 581).

If physical attractiveness becomes less important as a relationship develops, what other changes take place over time? We turn to this question next as we investigate how intimacy develops in relationships.

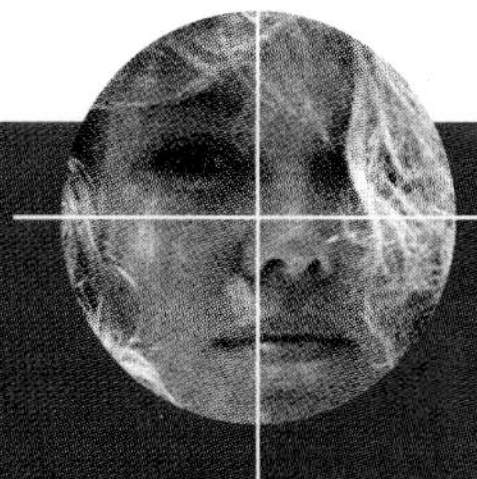

Sexuality and Diversity

Men's and Women's Preferences in Mate Selection: Are There Cross-Cultural Universals?

A recent cross-cultural study of sex differences in heterosexual mate preferences provided strong evidence that men worldwide place greater value than women on mates who are both young and physically attractive. In this study, conducted by psychologist David Buss (1994), subjects from 37 samples drawn from Africa, Asia, Europe, North and South America, Australia, and New Zealand were asked to rate the importance of a wide range of personal attributes in potential mates. These characteristics included dependability, good looks, age, good financial prospects, intelligence, sociability, and chastity.

Without exception, men in all of the surveyed cultures placed greater emphasis on a potential mate's youth and attractiveness than did women. This focus on youth was reflected in data demonstrating that at the time of marriage, men in these cultures were two to five years older than their spouses, on average.

In contrast to men's emphasis on youth and beauty, women placed greater value on potential mates who were somewhat older, had good financial prospects, and were dependable and industrious. This is not to say that physical attractiveness was unimportant to women of these varied cultures. In fact, many women considered physical attractiveness to be important—although less so than financial responsibility and dependability.

What accounts for the apparent consistency across so many cultures in what appeals to men and to women in a potential mate? And what accounts for the differences between men and women? Buss provides a *sociobiological* explanation—that is, he explains a species' behavior in terms of its evolutionary needs. According to Buss, evolution has biased mate preferences in humans as it has in other animals. Males are attracted to younger, physically attractive females because these characteristics are good predictors of reproductive success. Simply put, a younger woman has more reproductive years remaining than does an older woman. Furthermore, characteristics such as smooth unblemished skin, good muscle tone, lustrous hair, and similar features of physical attractiveness are indicative of good health—and thus are strong cues to reproductive value. On the other hand, women tend to find older, established men more attractive because characteristics such as wealth, a desirable environment, or high rank are the best predictors of security for their offspring. Youth and physical attractiveness are less important to females, because male fertility is less related to age than it is for females.

The Development of Intimacy

Students and others often want to know how to acquire and maintain intimacy, satisfaction, and sexual enjoyment in a relationship. Although opinions abound, there is no conclusive answer. This is probably because each of us is unique: What is secure and fulfilling to you may not be right for your partner. In effect, each of us must reinvent the wheel and discover for her- or himself how to initiate and maintain satisfactory relationships.

There is, however, a general progression that many intimate relationships follow as they develop over time. In the next paragraphs we look briefly at this very general sequence. But first, we look at a quality that is probably the most important foundation for building a satisfying relationship with another person. Paradoxically, that quality is self-love.

Self-Love

Satisfying intimacy within a relationship begins with self-love. How can this be? As we use the term, *self-love* does not mean conceit, selfishness, or lack of consideration of others; in fact, these qualities are usually indications of personal insecurities. By self-love we mean a genuine interest, concern, and respect for ourselves—the ability to look in the mirror and appreciate the person we see and to feel excited about that person's potential.

One very famous scholar of human development, Erik Erikson (1965), believed that positive self-feelings are a prerequisite to a satisfying relationship. As people feel secure in their own worth and identity, they are able to establish intimacy with others, both in friendship and eventually in a mutually satisfying sexual relationship based on love.

The Phases of a Relationship

One way of understanding the development of a relationship is to examine different aspects or phases of its growth; this may also give us some guidelines for maintaining a good relationship. As we discuss the various phases, it is important to remember that they are simply a convenient scheme; in reality, relationships are fluid, dynamic, and frequently unpredictable. We mean to give a framework for thinking about a relationship rather than a prescription for intimacy. (Note that in this discussion, sex is considered as only one part of the total context of a relationship.)

Inclusion

Inclusion is the first step one person takes in meeting another: It is simply an invitation to relate. Inclusion may take the form of one person making eye contact with another, or smiling at someone, or saying a friendly "hello." Many "how-to-pick-up-dates" books specialize in tips for initial inclusion.

Inclusion continues throughout a relationship, and the nature of inclusion behaviors provides the backbone of a positive relationship. A good morning kiss, a smile and hug after a day apart, a sincere "Tell me about your day," a compliment, or an expression of appreciation are some of the kinds of inclusions that can nourish an ongoing relationship.

Response

The way in which we respond to a gesture of inclusion may determine whether a relationship even begins. Quickly glancing away from someone's initial eye contact, or ignor-

When people feel secure in their own worth and identity, they are able to establish intimacy with others.

ing a smile or a "hello," may well deter any further friendly overtures. However, responding in kind—and perhaps going a step farther with a smile and a greeting—is likely to encourage the other person to initiate further contact. This relates back to the principle of reciprocity discussed earlier in this chapter. Continued gestures of inclusion, as well as warm responses, help to build positive feelings as interaction progresses.

Certain kinds of responses typically enhance a relationship's growth. These include listening to the other person and understanding her or his point of view, following through with agreements or plans, or showing enthusiasm about seeing the other person. Positive and consistent inclusions and responses are the foundation for the next important phases—care, trust, affection, and playfulness. These phases often develop simultaneously and build on each other.

Care

Care implies a genuine concern for another's welfare. Care motivates us to consider another person's desires and interests; it creates a desire to please and contribute to that individual's happiness.

Trust

Trust is essential to both the ongoing development of a relationship and its satisfactory continuance. It contributes to the belief that each partner will act consistently in ways that promote the relationship's growth and stability and that affirm each partner. Partners trust each other and themselves to be positive and constructive in their inclusions and responses.

Affection

Affection is characterized by feelings of warmth and attachment. It evokes a desire to be physically close to another and is often expressed by touching, holding hands, sitting close, hugging, and caressing. Affection can be signaled nonverbally by smiles, winks, and tender looks, and verbally by expressions of appreciation, liking, or loving.

Playfulness

This is the phase in the development of an intimate relationship in which each person exhibits delight and pleasure in the other. Exhilaration, abandon, and expansive laughter often accompany playfulness, whether it is a parent playing peek-a-boo with a child or lovers having a pillow fight.

Genitality

The final phase extends the relationship to include genital contact. There may have been varying degrees of sexual feeling and expression in previous phases, but in this phase a person has decided to express feelings through genital sex.

As you may have noted, the first six phases could characterize a variety of relationships, including a good friendship, a parent–child or sibling relationship, or a close mentor–student relationship. Close nonsexual friendships with members of our own and the other sex can be a very important part of our personal lives. One study found that characteristics of close friendships include enjoying one another's company; mutual trust that each will act in the other's best interest; respecting, assisting, supporting, and understanding one another; confiding experiences and feelings to each other; and being spontaneous in the relationship. This study also found that lover and spouse relationships had these general friendship qualities plus higher levels of passion, exclusiveness, self-sacrifice, and enjoyment of being together (Davis, 1985). With the foundation of the other phases, genital contact can be the culmination of deep intimacy and emotional closeness. Fromm (1965) stated that the use of the body for the purpose of seeking and expressing satisfaction with one another is what sex truly is and what gives it its most deeply felt meaning. According to Fromm, sex is important both in its role in initial attraction and in its cementing of a relationship through the fulfillment and pleasure it offers.

Issues in Loving Relationships

Loving sexual relationships in many ways build on and amplify the positive features of friendly relationships, but they also pose more complications than do friendships. Sexual relationships tend to have less acceptance than nonsexual friendships; they are also characterized by more criticism, conflict, ambivalence, and discussions about the relationship and its problems.

Why is this so? In the following paragraphs we explore some of the dynamics that cause complications in intimate relationships, focusing on three questions in particular. What is the relationship between love and sex? How can we make the very personal decision about whether to become sexually involved in a relationship? (And what is the best way of saying "no" to sexual involvement?) How does jealousy relate to love, and what can be done about jealousy in relationships? We turn next to these issues in intimate relationships.

What Is the Relationship Between Love and Sex?

Although we tend to associate sex with love, the connection is not always clear. It is certainly true that some couples, unmarried and married, engage in sexual relations without being in love. Conversely, love may exist independently of any sexual attraction or expression.

Despite these exceptions, the feelings of being in love with and sexually attracted to another person are frequently intertwined. The complex interplay between love and sex gives rise to many questions. Does sexual intimacy deepen a love relationship? Do men and women have different views of the relationship between sex and love? And is sex without love appropriate? Here, we attempt to shed some light on these and related questions.

Does Sexual Intimacy Deepen a Love Relationship?

I had known Chris for some time and thought I was ready to be sexual with him. So, after an evening out together, I asked him if I could stay at his place, and he said yes. I felt really aroused as we got in bed. I really enjoyed exploring the shapes and textures of his body. As we started to touch each other's genitals, though, I felt uncomfortable. If we proceeded in the direction we were headed, we would be going beyond the level of emotional intimacy I felt. It seemed that I would have to shut out the closeness I felt in order to go further. I had to choose between intimacy and genital contact. Our closeness was more important to me, and I told him that I wanted us to know each other more before going further sexually. (Authors' files)

The woman just quoted made the decision to postpone further sexual involvement until she became more comfortable in her relationship. Many individuals take an alternate course, moving quickly to sexual intimacy. In some cases, this may deepen a relationship. However, this result is certainly not assured. In fact, when a relationship becomes sexual without going through the phases described in the preceding section, the individuals involved may actually experience a reduction in feelings of emotional closeness.

It is reasonable to suspect that some people have attempted to justify their sexual behavior by deciding they are in love. As we will see shortly, this tendency is more common among women than men. Indeed, it is likely that some couples enter into premature commitments such as going steady, moving in together, becoming engaged, or even getting married to convince themselves of the depth of their love and thus the legitimacy of their sexual involvement.

Do Men and Women Have Different Views of Sex and Love?

In general, men and women tend to have somewhat different views concerning the relationship between sex and love (Hendrick & Hendrick, 1993; Leigh, 1989; Quadagno & Sprague, 1991). In our own sexuality classes, women have consistently associated love with sex to a greater extent than have men. In one survey of several hundred students, for instance, roughly 36% of women indicated that love is a necessary component of sexual relationships, compared with only 12% of men. Other studies have reported similar findings, indicating that it is easier for men than for women to have sexual intercourse for pleasure and physical release, without an emotional commitment (Chara & Kuennen, 1994; Clark & Hatfield, 1989; Townsend, 1995).

Despite these apparent differences, both men and women value love and affection in sexual relationships. Furthermore, two nationwide surveys of large representative samples of American men and women, conducted by *Parade* magazine in 1984 and 1994, reveal a trend toward convergence of male and female attitudes about the relationship between love and sex. In the earlier study 59% of men and 86% of women reported that it was difficult to have sex without love (Ubell, 1984). However, 10 years later 71% of the men now indicated it was difficult to relate sexually to someone without love, whereas the percentage of women expressing this viewpoint remained the same: 86% (Clements, 1994).

Do Heterosexuals, Gay Men, and Lesbians Have Different Views of Love and Sex?

I would not consider myself to be biased against homosexuals. However, I do feel some degree of disapproval of the gay lifestyle, which often seems to involve casual affairs based more on sex than genuine caring. Some gay men I know have had more partners in the last couple of years than I have had in a lifetime. (Authors' files)

This opinion, expressed by an acquaintance of one of the authors, reflects a belief widespread among heterosexuals that gay men and lesbians form sexual liaisons with same-sex lovers that are based primarily on sexual interaction and are often devoid of genuine attachment, love, commitment, and overall satisfaction. For example, in a study of several hundred American college students, different subgroups of subjects were provided with the same identical information about a paired couple, but with different sexual orientation status identifications: heterosexual, gay, and lesbian. Subjects were asked to rank the perceived level of love and satisfaction reflected in the descriptions. When the couple was identified as being heterosexual, the relationship received an average overall high ranking on both the love and satisfaction dimensions. In contrast, students who were told the description referred to a gay or lesbian couple assigned significantly lower scores for both love and satisfaction (Testa et al., 1987). This study clearly demonstrates a strong negative bias in respondents' perceptions of gay and lesbian relationships, because the described couple varied only on the dimension of sexual orientation.

A number of researchers have revealed the essential fallacy of this thinking by demonstrating that homosexuals, like heterosexuals, generally seek out loving, trusting, caring relationships that embrace many dimensions of sharing in addition to sexual intimacy (Adler et al., 1989; Blumstein & Schwartz, 1990; Kurdek, 1988 & 1995; Zak & McDonald, 1997). Lesbians and gay men differ in the degree to which they associate emotional closeness or love with sex, consistent with overall sex differences in views of sex and love. Whereas men in general are more likely than women to separate sex and love, as previously noted, gay men have shown a particularly strong inclination to make this separation. Some gay men, especially prior to the AIDS epidemic, have engaged in frequent casual sexual encounters without love or caring attachment (Bell & Weinberg, 1978). Rather than indicating that gay men do not value love, this finding merely reveals that some gay men value sex as an end itself. In contrast, most lesbians postpone sexual involvement until they have developed emotional intimacy with a partner (Leigh, 1989; Zak & McDonald, 1997). A number of researchers suggest that these differences between gay men and lesbians result from patterns of gender-role socialization that give more permission for casual sex for males than females. Furthermore, they argue that heterosexual men would be as likely as gay men to occasionally engage in loveless, casual sex if women were equally interested and were it not for the fact that most heterosexual couples assume that their relationship is exclusive (Foa et al., 1987; Leigh, 1989; Peplau, 1981).

Finally, love plays a very prominent role in the lives of homosexuals as a nexus for establishing a self-imposed identity as either a lesbian or a gay man. Many heterosexually oriented people have had sexual contact with same-sex partners. This is especially true during the late childhood years and adolescence, when same-sex contact can be either experimental and transitory or an expression of a lifelong orientation (see Chapter 13). These same-sex sexual activities are not sufficient, in and of themselves, for establishing an identity as a homosexually oriented person. Rather, it is falling in love with a same-sex person that often supplies the key element necessary to establish a gay or lesbian identity. Eminent sexologist John Money (1980) maintains that loving someone of the same sex, rather than simply having sex with her or him, is the essential ingredient that distinguishes being homosexual from heterosexual. It has also been suggested that loving a same-sex person unifies the emotional and physical aspects of a shared relationship, thereby solidifying commitment to being gay or lesbian (Troiden, 1988).

Sex and Relationships on Your Terms

Sexual expression can have many different meanings. It can be a validation of deep intimacy within a relationship. On the other hand, people can choose to be sexual as a part of a friendship or as a way of getting to know someone. For some, reproduction may be the primary purpose. For others, reducing sexual tension may be the motivation. Sex can be used as a way of experiencing new feelings, excitement, and risk. It can even be a kind of recreational pastime. People can use sex to try to alleviate feelings of insecurity—to prove their "manhood" or "womanhood" or to please someone or persuade that person to care. People can also use sex to experience the power to attract others or to avenge earlier rejections by enticing partners and then turning them down.

Each of us has the task of deciding how to express sexuality—but this task is complicated by the fact that many of the old rules that have governed sexual relationships are changing. Consider the comments of a recently divorced woman:

When I was dating 25 years ago in college, a kiss at the door on a first date was considered to mean I really liked the guy. And I was determined to be a virgin until I got married. These guidelines were held by most of my friends, and I felt a lot of security in them. Now I don't know how to behave. There really don't seem to be any standard rules. It's exciting and frightening to know I can make decisions because I want to. It is also confusing at times, and I sometimes wish I could still rely on the old standards. (Authors' files)

Some people base their decisions about sexuality on clear, preexisting rules expressed by their family, religion, or peer group. Many others do not have such specific guidelines, or they may disagree with the values they have been taught. These people need to understand their own personal values and develop their own guidelines. The following section discusses some options for making decisions about sexual expression.

Know What You Want

The first step in integrating sex into your life in a meaningful way is to consider what you value in life and relationships before becoming sexually involved. This is a variation on the "Know thyself" theme. Consider the following:

Often when I meet a man for the first time, I end up being swept off my feet and into bed. At the time it seems like the thing to do, but afterward I'm often left confused and a bit empty inside. It's not that I don't like sex. I'm just not sure about what role it should play in my life. (Authors' files)

This woman might be able to reduce the confusion and discomfort she experiences by evaluating her own expectations and needs. An important question for each of us to ask is "What role do I want relationships and sex to occupy in my life at this time?" The answer to this question often changes over time as a person faces new life situations.

As a part of this self-inventory, it might be helpful to consider the following questions:

- How comfortable am I with some of the contemporary approaches to sex and relationships?
- Which of the more traditional norms do I value?
- What are my values regarding sexual relationships, and where do they come from (family, church, friends, media)?
- What will I do to protect myself and a partner from sexually transmitted diseases or unwanted pregnancy?

You can further clarify your values in relation to a specific decision about sexual activity by asking another question: "Will a decision to engage in a sexual relationship—with this person and at this time—enhance my positive feelings about myself and the other person?" The answer to this question can help you act in a way that is consistent with your value system. It can also help prevent exploitative sexual encounters in which people do not consider each other's feelings.

What if the answer to the previous question is no? Then it may be appropriate to think about what kind of relationship, if any, might enhance positive feelings. Perhaps a sexual relationship is not right, but a nonsexual friendship would be. Or perhaps you do

Nonsexual friendships can offer companionship and enjoyment.

not feel ready for a sexual relationship yet, but want to leave open that possibility. At this point, communication and negotiation are important.

One risk of understanding and acting on your own feelings, desires, and values is that someone else may not see things the same way. Many people take such differences to mean that either they are wrong or the other person is wrong. However, more often than not, differences simply indicate that two people do not want the same thing at the same time. Occasionally a relationship cannot be established without compromising one person's situation or values. When this occurs, one option is to end the relationship, thereby allowing each individual to seek someone else with similar perspectives.

On other occasions, strategies such as clarification, negotiation, and compromise may establish a common foundation for a relationship. However, direct communication may sound easier than it is. The following sections illustrate some options for dealing with several specific relationship situations. Chapter 8 provides additional information on communication in sexual relationships.

Friendships Without Sex

Some people find it very difficult to communicate a desire for friendship without sex, especially when it appears that the other person wants a sexual relationship. Often they are concerned that the other person will feel bad or decide to end the relationship. However, most people would probably prefer to be told the truth directly rather than have to decipher vague, confusing responses. The following comment is fairly typical of our students:

> I hate it when I find myself in a relationship, and all I get is the runaround. I eventually get the picture when someone else doesn't reciprocate my feelings, but what a waste of time and energy. Why can't they just come out and say what they are feeling? At least I would know where I stand and could act accordingly. (Authors' files)

This person's feeling of frustration is understandable. However, one can attempt to resolve some of the uncertainty by asking the other person about his or her feelings. The following illustrates how one student did this:

> Jake and I had gone out several times, and at first he acted like he was attracted to me. But then he began to treat me more like a friend. He continued to ask me out but made no sexual gestures. I finally told him I was confused about how he felt about me. He seemed very concerned about my feelings as he told me that he wanted a friendship with me instead of a romantic relationship. I felt disappointed, and it was a little tough on my ego to not be desired sexually, but I decided that a friendship with him would be nice. And several years later, we are still friends. (Authors' files)

Saying "Not Yet" to a Sexual Relationship

One of the benefits of less rigid rules about "proper" sexual behavior is that they can make it easier for people to set their own pace in sexual relationships. It is common for a person to feel sexual attraction and to want a sexual relationship with someone—but not yet. The ability to delay sexual involvement until both people feel ready can do much to enhance the initial experience. Waiting until familiarity and trust are established and making sure that personal values are consistent can enhance not only a relationship but also positive feelings about oneself. Also, as discussed in Chapter 17, the possibility of contracting AIDS or other serious sexually transmitted diseases may be reduced by taking some time to assess the risk status of a prospective partner before beginning sexual relations.

When sexual attraction exists within a relationship, sex is not necessarily an "either/or" situation. There are progressive stages of intimacy, from holding hands to genital contact, and some people move slowly through these stages to savor and grow comfortable with the increasingly intimate contact. Gratification may be greater when the progression toward intimacy is gradual rather than when it is rushed:

I felt sexually attracted to Mike the first time I met him, but somehow, almost by mutual instinct, we moved very slowly sexually. We both agreed that was how we wanted it for this relationship. We spent several extremely enjoyable months kissing, touching, holding each other, and even sleeping together before we had intercourse. The entire experience has given new light to the expression "haste makes waste." (Authors' files)

Social expectations of "instant sex" can present a challenge to those who want to move gradually into a sexual relationship. What can you do to let another person know that you are not yet ready for sex, or that you want the relationship to progress slowly? It is often helpful to begin by indicating that you find the person attractive. You can acknowledge your desire for greater sexual intimacy, yet be definite about not being ready. Finally, you can let a partner know what kind of physical contact you want at a given point in the relationship; this can help avoid misunderstandings and reassure the other person.

Ending a Relationship

Over the years, our sexuality classes have included many lively discussions of the question "How do you prefer to be informed when someone does not wish to continue a relationship with you?" Although students have many different opinions and experiences, the large majority want to be told in a clear, unmistakable manner that their desire for a relationship is not reciprocated. A simple statement such as "I appreciate your interest in me, but I'm not attracted to you enough to want to develop a relationship with you" is the kind of ending that most of our students have indicated they would prefer.

Do you think it would be easier to tell someone that you want to end a relationship, or to be on the receiving end of this news?

Most of our students report that it is more difficult to break the news that they want to end a relationship. This finding has been supported by a recent survey of college students. Respondents who had decided to call off a relationship reported greater feelings of guilt, uncertainty, discomfort, and awkwardness than did those who had been rejected (Baumeister et al., 1993). There is rarely an easy way to end a relationship when one person is interested in maintaining it. This situation requires communication that is both effective and compassionate.

Managing Rejection

Fear of rejection can often inhibit people from initiating a relationship or expressing their desires within one. One man expresses his concern as follows:

I find it extremely stressful to ask a woman out for the first time. I just can't deal with the prospect of being turned down. I know it's irrational, but when someone says no, I feel lousy. (Authors' files)

To many people, a "no" affects their feelings of self-worth (Baumeister et al., 1993). A person who is rejected may feel unattractive, boring, unsexy, unintelligent, or inherently unlovable. But all of us experience rejection at some time, because our traits cannot match every person's preferences. The very characteristics that one person finds undesirable may well appeal to another, and the right to choose not to become involved with someone is certainly a right that most people want.

Although rejection can still be a painful experience, a few strategies may be helpful in dealing with being turned down. It is important to remember that each of us has worth, regardless of whether all people approve of us. Also, defending yourself to someone who has said no is not likely to be helpful, because being turned down is usually not a criticism but simply an expression of individual preference. Finally, even though rejection may make us want to give up on continued attempts to form close relationships, we can avoid rejection completely only if we isolate ourselves from most kinds of social interaction.

It is not always easy to maintain such a positive attitude in response to rejection. Indeed, especially when individuals have become close to one another, feelings may become quite intense. We look next at one response to real or imagined rejection—jealousy—and explore how it affects relationships and what can be done, if anything, to keep feelings of jealousy under control.

Jealousy in Relationships

Jealousy has been defined as an aversive emotional reaction evoked by a real or imagined relationship involving one's partner and a third person (Buunk & Bringle, 1987). Many people think that jealousy is a measure of devotion, and that the absence of jealous feelings implies a lack of love. However, some writers believe that jealousy is related more to injured pride, or to people's fear of losing what they want to control or possess, than to love. For example, a person who finds that a spouse enjoys someone else's company may feel inadequate and therefore jealous. Intense emotions of jealousy are often due to our imagining and fearing being abandoned by one's partner for someone else (Sharpsteen & Kirkpatrick, 1997). Jealous feelings may be further heightened by envy of certain characteristics of the rival, for we are more likely to be jealous of individuals who have qualities that we desire. In general, traits for which women show the most envy are attractiveness and popularity, whereas men are more envious of wealth and fame (Barker, 1987; Salovey & Rodin, 1985).

Some people are more prone to feel jealousy than are others. Individuals who have a low opinion of themselves, reflected in feelings of insecurity and inadequacy, are more likely to feel jealousy in a relationship (Buss, 1994; Fisher, 1992; Wiederman & Allgeier, 1993). This relates back to a point we have already made—that a healthy self-esteem is the foundation for building intimate relationships. Second, people who see a large discrepancy between who they are and who they would like to be are also prone to jealousy. Not surprisingly, such individuals also are likely to have low self-esteem. And third, people who place a high value on traits such as wealth, fame, popularity, and physical attractiveness may be more likely to feel jealousy in a relationship (Salovey & Rodin, 1985).

Jealousy is frequently a factor in precipitating violence in marriages (Adams, 1990; Buunk et al., 1996; Buss, 1994; Fisher, 1992) and dating relationships (Burcky et al., 1988; Himelein et al., 1994; Stets & Pirog-Good, 1987). Research demonstrates that jealousy-precipitated violence is most commonly directed toward one's partner/lover rather than against a third-party rival (Mathes & Verstraete, 1993; Paul & Galloway, 1994).

Jealousy is an uncomfortable feeling that can stifle the development of a relationship and also the pleasure associated with being together. For both men and women, the emotions and thoughts associated with jealousy are negative, including feeling anxious, depressed, or angry and having a sense of being less valued by and attractive to one's partner (Bush et al., 1988). Jealousy also has a paradoxical effect, for although the jealous person desires to maintain both the relationship and his or her own self-image, both of these are likely to be damaged when jealous feelings are expressed (Buunk & Bringle, 1987).

Although it is clear that jealousy has many negative effects, it is not always clear how jealous feelings should be handled when they occur in a relationship. The box "Coping with the Green-Eyed Monster" offers some suggestions to people who want to decrease feelings of jealousy, either in themselves or in their partners.

Do you think men and women respond differently to their feelings of jealousy?

Sex Differences in Jealousy

Not everyone responds to jealousy in the same way, and a number of studies have found some differences between how women and men react. In general, women are more likely to acknowledge jealous feelings and men more likely to deny them (Barker, 1987; Clanton & Smith, 1977). Furthermore, a jealous woman is more inclined to focus on and become

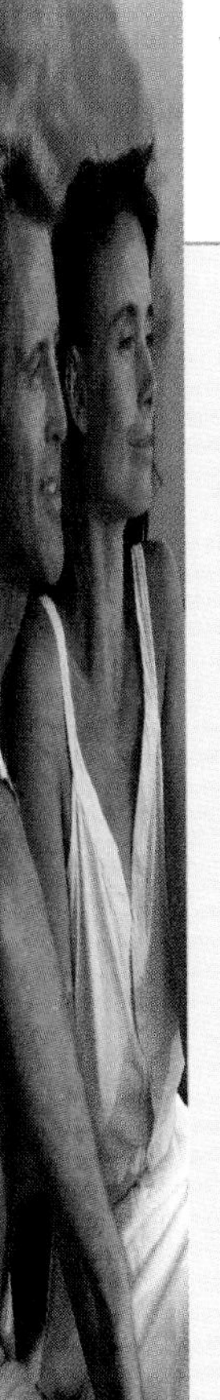

Let's Talk About It

Coping with the Green-Eyed Monster

In American culture, with its emphasis on possessiveness and exclusivity in relationships, it is common for the green-eyed monster, jealousy, to raise its ugly head at least sometime during the course of a relationship. Dealing with jealousy can be very difficult because such feelings often stem from a deep sense of inadequacy that resides within the jealous individual rather than within the relationship. A person threatened by insecurity-induced feelings of jealousy often withdraws from his or her partner or goes on the attack with accusations and/or threats. These ineffective coping behaviors often provoke a similar reaction in the nonjealous partner—withdrawal or counterattack. A more effective approach, from the perspective of the jealous person, is to acknowledge one's own feelings of jealousy and to clarify their source. Thus a jealous person might initiate discussion by saying something like "Mary, I am afraid for us, and a little bit crazy over all the time you spend working late with your coworkers, especially with that guy Bill!" Such an open acknowledgment of feelings without threats or accusations might prompt Mary to respond with reassurances, and a positive dialogue might ensue.

Jealousy is an uncomfortable feeling that often harms a relationship and stifles the pleasure associated with being together.

In many situations the jealous person will not acknowledge the existence of a problem and express a desire to work on it. If this is the case, the essential first step toward successful coping is to instill the motivation to begin working to eliminate the painful jealousy feelings and the destructive behaviors these feelings often induce. Robert Barker (1987), a marital therapist, provides valuable guidelines for how to accomplish this in his book *The Green-Eyed Marriage: Surviving Jealous Relationships.* Barker maintains that a jealous person is most likely to become motivated to work on the problem and to permit help from others when he or she

- *Is confident there is no danger of losing the valued partner.* Direct reassurance that the relationship is not in danger

(continued on next page)

distressed over the emotional involvement of her partner with another person, whereas a jealous man is more likely to be upset about the sexual relationship his lover has with another (Buss et al., 1992 & 1996; Buunk et al., 1996; Harris & Christenfeld, 1996). These sex differences in sexual jealousy appear to be consistent across other cultures, according to a recent study that reported finding them in Germany and the Netherlands in addition to the United States (Buunk et al., 1996).

David Buss and his colleagues (1992 & 1996) have suggested that these sex differences in the instigators of jealousy have emerged in the evolutionary history of humans. According to this viewpoint, which emphasizes the consequences of infidelity for the primary relationship, men are especially concerned about sexual infidelity because of uncertainty about their biological parentage of offspring and because they do not want to expend their resources on other men's children. Women, who need male investment in their offspring, have evolved to be more concerned about their partner's emotional infidelity or falling in love with others that might result in abandoning the primary relationship.

In still another sex difference in jealousy patterns, women often blame themselves when a conflict over jealousy arises, whereas men typically attribute their jealousy to a third party or to their partner's behavior (Barker, 1987; Daly et al., 1982; Clanton & Smith, 1977). Women have also been shown to be more inclined than men to deliberately provoke jealousy in their partners (White, 1981; White & Helbick, 1988). This latter sex difference in jealousy patterns may stem from the fact that women experiencing jealousy often suffer simultaneously from feelings of inadequacy and worthlessness. Consequently,

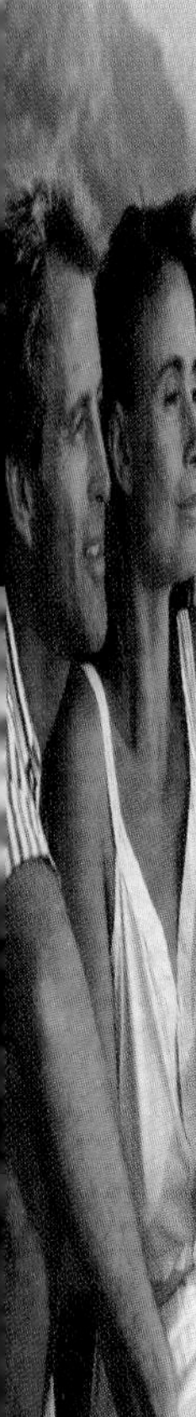

Let's Talk About It

is often ineffective and sometimes may even be counterproductive. A more effective strategy is to make references, at varied times, to being together in the future. Consequently, a nonjealous partner planning to initiate a discussion about jealousy at some future point might first pick a few opportune times to say such things as "It will be great when the children are all grown and we have more time just for us."

- *Is assured that the problem comes from the relationship rather than defects in one's character.* A jealous person is much more likely to pursue a coping process when both partners acknowledge that jealousy is a shared problem. The nonjealous partner can move thinking in this direction by stating, "This is a problem we share, and we both have to work equally to overcome it."
- *Is confident about being genuinely loved and respected.* Because jealousy often stems from feelings of inadequacy and insecurity, the nonjealous partner can help minimize these negative emotions and bolster self-esteem and confidence by "regularly reaffirming affection for the jealous person verbally, emotionally, and physically" (p. 100).
- *Is not provoked into feeling shame or guilt.* Understandably, many people who are undeservedly targets of jealousy become angry and inclined to strike back with sarcasm, ridicule, or put-downs in an effort to make their jealous partners feel so much guilt that they will be too ashamed to persist in their unfounded accusations. Unfortunately, these negative counterattacks are likely to have the opposite effect by promoting more anger and defensiveness. Worse yet, the jealous person may be even less willing to acknowledge a need for change.
- *Is able to empathize with the person who has been hurt by the jealous behavior.* When jealous people are able to understand and empathize with the pain their behavior has created in their partners, the incentive to change may be increased. The challenge for the nonjealous partner is to facilitate the development of empathy rather than guilt. This may be accomplished by verbalizing the hurt and pain, but not attributing its cause to the jealous partner. Thus, Mary might say to her jealous partner, "I really love you, Mike, and I feel really bad when I have to work late and I know you are at home wishing we could be together. It is really painful to think that my work situation sometimes appears to be more important than our relationship."

Once the motivation for change is established, and a couple begins a dialogue aimed at coping with jealousy, several of the communication strategies outlined in Chapter 8 may facilitate this process. Some of the suggestions for self-disclosure, listening, feedback, and asking questions may help to clearly establish what each partner wants and expects of the relation-

efforts to arouse jealousy in a partner may actually be an attempt to bolster self-worth by eliciting increased attention from a partner concerned about her actions. Men also often attach feelings of inadequacy to jealousy. However, the relationship is frequently reversed in men, with awareness of jealousy occurring first, followed by feeling inadequate (White & Helbick, 1988).

One interesting recent investigation assessed the relationship between perceived parenthood quality and jealousy. Women respondents in this study were more likely to become jealous over infidelity if their partner was perceived as potentially bad parent material because an inadequate father who abandons a relationship would be less likely than a good father to contribute to continued support of his children. In sharp contrast, male respondents were more likely to become jealous if their mates were perceived as potentially good parents because they might lose an ideal partner for producing and caring for their children (Sharpsteen, 1995).

Finally, men whose jealousy is aroused by real or imagined threats are more likely than women to confront a third-party rival and/or their own partner with demands, ultimatums, anger, and even violence (Barker, 1987; Stump, 1985). Women, on the other hand, are more inclined to avoid such confrontations and to "cling to their partners with greater tenacity" (Barker, 1987, p. 25). Consistent with this sex difference, women often respond to jealousy by increasing their efforts to be attractive to their primary partner, whereas not uncommonly men may seek revenge/retribution by pursuing extrarelationship involvements (Wiederman & Allgeier, 1993).

Let's Talk About It

ship. For example, after disclosing his fears, Mike might communicate to Mary that it would help reduce his concerns if she would spend less time working with Bill after hours, or maybe just include others from the office at these times.

When engaged in dialogue about jealousy issues, it is especially important to express one's views in a nonconfrontational way so that the jealous partner does not feel attacked or threatened. For example, imagine your partner saying to you, "The way you were hanging all over Steve (or Susan) last night at the party looked to everyone like you were ready to hop into the sack." Such a comment would probably put you on the defensive, prompting either withdrawal, denial, or a caustic counterattack. A far more effective way for expressing one's feelings, and for stimulating further helpful discussion, might be to say, "I felt alone and a little abandoned last night at the party when you spent so much time talking with Steve (or Susan)."

We end our discussion with a few additional suggestions for the person whose partner is being unreasonably jealous.

- *Make an effort to avoid provoking jealous behavior.* In spite of the fact that jealousy is generally instigated by feelings within an individual, and not by the actions of another person, it can be helpful to be attuned to whatever behaviors might be involved in activating jealous behavior. Thus, Mary might be wise to avoid working late with Bill while she and Mike are working to overcome the negative impact of jealousy on their relationship.
- *Do not submit to the third degree.* A jealous partner may try to grill you with questions about your imagined unfaithfulness. Instead of trying to answer all these unreasonable questions, focus on how the questions make you feel and stay with the simple truth (Forward & Buck, 1992).
- *Do not accept the status quo out of pity for your partner.* You may feel compassion and pity for your jealous partner because you understand why your lover is so jealous. For example, you may know that he or she was unloved and emotionally abandoned as a child and therefore feels desperately insecure in a relationship. Your awareness may prompt pity that may induce you to justify your partner's accusations. But that acceptance will not encourage your companion to work toward a solution to the jealousy that is eroding your relationship.
- *Be open to seeking outside help from a professional therapist.* Some couples may find it very difficult to cope with this problem because of the intensity associated with jealous feelings and behaviors. In such cases, successful resolution may require talking with a professional therapist. Guidelines for selecting a therapist are included in Chapter 16.

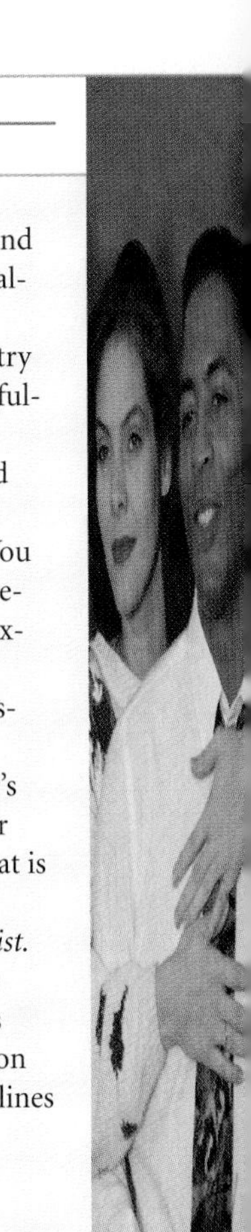

Maintaining Relationship Satisfaction

Human relationships present many challenges. To begin, there is the challenge of building positive feelings about oneself, as described in the section on self-love. There is the added task of establishing satisfying and enjoyable relationships with family, peers, teachers, coworkers, employers, and other people within our social network. A third challenge involves developing special, intimate relationships with friends and, when we want them, sexual relationships. Finally, many people confront the challenge of maintaining satisfaction and love within an ongoing, committed relationship. Commitment in a relationship is often demonstrated by the decision to marry. However, many couples have long-term committed relationships, either heterosexual or homosexual, that do not involve marriage. This section presents some of the factors that may contribute to ongoing satisfaction in relationships. We also discuss the value of sexual variety within a relationship.

Ingredients in a Lasting Love Relationship

Ingredients in a lasting love relationship include self-acceptance, appreciation of one another, commitment, good communication, realistic expectations, shared interests, and the ability to face conflict effectively. These characteristics are not static; they evolve and change and influence one another over time. Often they need to be deliberately cultivated. The efforts that partners make toward preservation are probably more important to relationship stability today than in the past when marriage as an institution was sustained more strongly by culture, religion, law, and the extended family.

In one study of 300 happily married couples, the most frequently named reason for an enduring and happy marriage was seeing one's partner as one's best friend. Qualities that individuals especially appreciated in a partner were caring, giving, integrity, and a sense of humor. These couples were aware of flaws in their mates, but they believed that the likable qualities were more important. Many said that their mates had become more interesting to them over time. They preferred shared rather than separate activities, which appeared to reflect the richness in the relationship. Another key was their belief in marriage as a long-term commitment and a sacred institution. Most couples were generally satisfied with their sex lives, and for some the sexual passion had become more intense over time. As one wife said, "The passion hasn't died. In fact, it has gotten more intense. The only thing that has died is the element of doubt or uncertainty that one experiences while dating or in the beginning of a marriage." However, fewer than 10% thought that good sexual relations kept their marriage together (Lauer & Lauer, 1985).

Maintaining frequent positive interactions is crucial to continued satisfaction in a relationship, as we saw in the earlier discussions of inclusion and response. The saying "It's the little things that count" is especially meaningful here. When one partner says to the other, "You do not love me anymore," that often means "You are not doing as many of the things you used to do that I interpret as meaning you love me." These behaviors are often so small that one may not really notice them. However, when couples do fewer things to make one another feel loved (or when

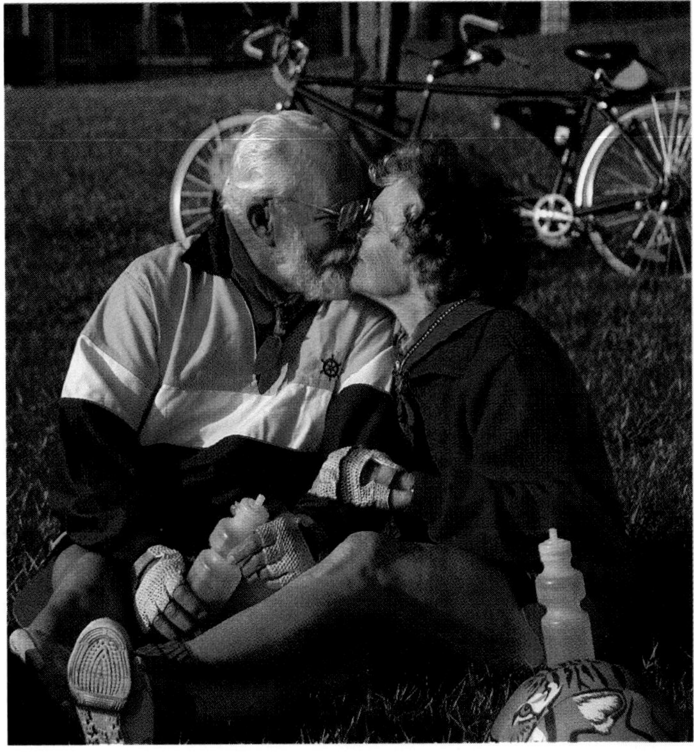

An older couple's intimacy and affection develop from years of shared experiences.

they stop doing them entirely), the deficit is often experienced as a lack of love. Continuing affectionate and considerate interaction helps maintain a feeling of love. One person writes,

> The kinds of things that enhance my feeling that my partner still loves me may seem quite inconsequential, but to me they aren't. When he gets up to greet me when I come home, when he takes my arm crossing the street, when he asks, "Can I help you with that," when he tells me I look great, when he holds me in the middle of the night, when he thanks me for doing a routine chore—I feel loved by him. Those little things—all added up—make a tremendous difference to me. (Authors' files)

You may also find that it is useful to talk with your partner, to communicate what is especially enjoyable to you, or to suggest new ideas. The golden rule ("Do unto others as you would have them do unto you") is not always applicable in relationships, because people's preferences are often quite different. Your partner may not know what you want unless you express yourself.

Enjoyment with and appreciation of one another in nonsexual areas typically enhance sexual interest and interactions. Often couples report a lack of desire for sexual intimacy when they are not feeling emotionally intimate.

Individual and Relationship Growth

Growth and change are important in maintaining vitality in a relationship. Each person's growth can provide an opportunity for the other partner to develop. Partners can draw on emotional, artistic, intellectual, spiritual, and physical dimensions for growth, to enrich each other's mutual enjoyment. At times, this dynamic of growth and change occurs without deliberate effort; at other times, it requires direct attention. Couples who maintain satisfactory levels of growth typically do not let love diminish by choosing to withdraw their energy from the relationship at the first sign of strain or boredom. Rather, they confront the difficulties and attempt to overcome them. For example,

My husband and I found it increasingly difficult to have time together because of our busy schedules. And then when we were together, we felt a little like strangers. So we decided to structure some time together learning something new. The dancing lessons we took even rekindled some romantic feelings. (Authors' files)

Each person brings her or his strengths and weaknesses into relationships, and a relationship itself has its own combination of strengths and weaknesses. A couple is rarely fully prepared for the myriad issues that arise from this combination. It is often helpful to view problems and dissatisfactions as challenges to overcome or differences to accept, rather than as sure signs that the relationship is about to fail. Couples need to be prepared to negotiate and renegotiate what they want out of life and out of their relationship, knowing that the arrangement they work out one day may become untenable the next. At the same time, partners in a committed relationship often recognize that their love for each other means accepting one another as unique human beings. These attitudes give a couple options for shaping a relationship uniquely suited to their individual and collective wants and needs.

Being in a committed relationship can itself be a source of growth. Such a relationship can make urgent demands on individuals so that they mature in directions and with a rapidity that would not otherwise occur. The "beneficial trauma" of confronting oneself intensely and learning to accept another deeply, as sometimes occurs within an intimate relationship, can facilitate individual growth. As Erich Fromm wrote, "Married lovers grow within love; they develop into better human beings" (1965, p. 288).

Sexual Variety: An Important Ingredient

There is a special little restaurant with great steaks and a cozy, intimate atmosphere that I love to visit once every few months. Good companionship, a favorite bottle of wine, a tasty dinner, and I am living. Let a friend invite me back the next day, and it is still good, but not quite so stimulating. Given an invitation for a third trip in as many days, and I might just as soon stop off for a McDonald's quarter-pounder. (Authors' files)

Many people have a strong desire to seek variety in life's experiences. They may acquire an assortment of friends, each providing a unique enrichment to their lives. Likewise, they read different kinds of books, pursue a variety of recreational activities, eat a variety of foods, and take a mixture of classes. Yet many of these same people settle for routine in their sex lives.

Unfortunately, many people enter into a committed relationship thinking that intense sexual excitement will always follow naturally when two people are in love. But, as we have seen in this chapter, the initial excitement must eventually be replaced by realistic and committed efforts to maintain the vitality and rewards of a working relationship. Once a person is committed to a primary partner, the variety offered by a succession of relationships is no longer available. For some individuals it may be necessary to seek variety in other ways.

Not every couple feels the need for sexual variety. Many people may feel quite comfortable with established routines and have no desire to change them. However, if you prefer to develop more variety in your sexual relationship, the following paragraphs may be helpful.

Can you think of any strategies or approaches to sexual intimacy that could add variety and zest to a couple's lovemaking in a long-term love relationship?

Communication is critical. Talk to your partner about your needs and feelings. Share with him or her your desire to try something different. Perhaps some of the guidelines in Chapter 8 will facilitate making requests and exchanging information.

Avoid routine times and places. Make love in places other than the bed (on the laundry room floor, in the shower, alongside a mountain trail) and at various times ("bird song in the morning," a "nooner," or in the middle of the night when you wake up feeling sexually aroused).

Some of the most exciting sexual experiences may be those that take place on the spur of the moment with little or no planning. It is easy to see how these encounters might occur frequently during courtship. It is also true that they may become distant memories after couples settle into the demanding daily schedules of living together. Nevertheless, you may find that striving to maintain this spontaneity will stand you in good stead as your relationship is nurtured over months or years together.

On the other hand, planning for intimate time—sexual and nonsexual—can also help maintain closeness. Make "dates" with one another and consciously continue the romantic gestures that came naturally early in the relationship. Make a commitment to place your energy and time toward your sexual relationship.

Do not let questions of what is "normal" get in the way of an enriched and varied erotic life. Too often, people refrain from experiencing something new because they feel that different activities are "abnormal." In reality, only you can judge what is normal for you. Contemporary writers in the field of sexology concur that any sexual activity is normal, as long as it gives pleasure and does not cause emotional or physical discomfort or harm to either partner. Emotional comfort is an important variable because "discomfort and conflict rather than intimacy and satisfaction can result if behaviors are tried which are too divergent from personal values and attitudes" (Barbach, 1982, p. 282).

Related to concerns about what is normal are concerns about frequency. Forget the magazine article that said that couples in your age category are having sex 2.7 times per week. The only right standard for you is to have sex as often as you and your partner desire.

Finally, partners sometimes find that books dealing with sexual techniques may benefit their erotic lives. We recommend that you read them together rather than separately. Discussing a particular written suggestion can often open up new possibilities of sexual sharing. Such books sometimes provide the necessary information and support for trying something new.

We do not mean to imply that all people must have active, varied sex lives to be truly happy; this is not the case. As we have already seen, some partners may find comfort and contentment in repeating familiar patterns of sexual interaction. Others may consider sex relatively unimportant compared with other aspects of their lives and may choose not to exert special efforts in pursuing its pleasures. However, if your sexuality is an important source of pleasure in your life, perhaps these suggestions and others in this text will be valuable to you.

Summary

WHAT IS LOVE?

Zick Rubin's love scale is a subjective rating scale that measures what he defines as the three components of love: attachment, caring, and intimacy. Studies of eye contact and physical proximity give some support to the validity of the scale.

TYPES OF LOVE

Passionate love is characterized by intense, vibrant feelings that tend to be relatively short-lived.

Companionate love is characterized by deep affection and attachment.

Sternberg's triangular theory maintains that love has three dimensions: passion and intimacy, which are the motivational and emotional components, respectively, and commitment, the cognitive component. Variations in the combinations in which these three components exist yield eight different kinds of love.

Lee has proposed a theory that describes six different styles of loving: romantic, game playing, possessive, companionate, altruistic, and pragmatic.

FALLING IN LOVE: WHY AND WITH WHOM?

Falling in love has been explained as resulting from the need to overcome a sense of aloneness, from the desire to justify sexual involvement, or as a consequence of sexual attraction.

The intense feelings of being passionately in love may have a basis in surging levels of the brain chemicals norepinephrine, dopamine, and especially phenylethylamine (PEA). The progression from passion to deep attraction may result from the gradual increase of endorphins in the brain.

Factors known to contribute strongly to interpersonal attraction and falling in love with another include proximity, similarity, reciprocity, and physical attractiveness. We often develop loving relationships with people whom we see frequently, who share similar beliefs, who seem to like us, and whom we perceive as physically attractive.

THE DEVELOPMENT OF INTIMACY

Self-love, meaning positive and accepting feelings toward oneself, is an important foundation for intimacy with others.

The phases of an intimate relationship are inclusion, response, care, trust, affection, playfulness, and genitality. Care, trust, affection, and playfulness usually develop concurrently and reinforce one another.

ISSUES IN LOVING RELATIONSHIPS

There are various perspectives on the connections between love and sex. Most students in our surveys report that love enriches sexual relations but is not necessary for enjoyment of sex.

Women consistently link love with sexual behavior more than do men, but research indicates men and women are becoming more similar on this issue.

Gay men and lesbian women, like heterosexuals, generally seek out loving, trusting, caring relationships that embrace many dimensions of sharing in addition to sexual intimacy.

Deciding one's own values in relation to sexual experiences is especially important today, in a time of changing expectations. Asking yourself, "Will a decision to engage in a sexual relationship—with this person at this time—enhance my positive feelings about myself and the other person?" can help you act in a way that is consistent with your value system.

There are many types of intimate relationships, including friendships without sex and love relationships in which the sexual component progresses gradually.

You can develop strategies for minimizing the pain of rejection, particularly if you remember that rejection usually occurs because your traits do not match another's subjective preferences, not because you are unworthy.

Some people consider jealousy a sign of love, but it may actually reflect fear of losing possession or control of another.

Jealousy is frequently a factor in precipitating violence in marriages and dating relationships.

Research indicates that men and women react differently to jealousy.

MAINTAINING RELATIONSHIP SATISFACTION

Individual and relationship growth can provide challenges and stimulation to the relationship, helping to maintain its vitality.

Sexual variety is often an important ingredient of enjoyable sex in a long-term relationship. For some, however, the security of routine is most satisfying.

Thought Provokers

1. Is sex without love appropriate? Why or why not? Do your male friends and female friends differ in their response to this question?
2. The section on jealousy discussed research findings that women were more envious of attractiveness and popularity, whereas men were more likely to be envious of wealth and fame. What do you think accounts for this difference?
3. Assume that you are the parent of a teenager who asks, "How do I know when I should have sex?" What would you answer?
4. What do you think are the key differences between companionate and passionate love? How do these characteristics fit into the list of things that make a marriage successful?

Suggested Readings

Ackerman, Diane (1994). *A Natural History of Love.* New York: Random House. This highly praised book provides a readable, entertaining, and informative exploration of the historical, cultural, and biological roots of love.

Barker, Robert (1987). *The Green-Eyed Marriage: Surviving Jealous Relationships.* An excellent book by a marriage and family therapist that covers the causes and effects of jealousy and strategies for overcoming its negative impact on relationships.

Beck, Aaron (1988). *Love Is Never Enough.* New York: Harper & Row. This book describes specific approaches couples may use to overcome misunderstandings, resolve conflicts, and solve relationship problems.

Fromm, Erich (1963). *The Art of Loving.* New York: Bantam Books. This is a classic on the topic of love. Fromm elucidates the power of love to develop human potential within oneself and within a relationship.

Hatfield, Elaine; and Rapson, Richard (1993). *Love, Sex, and Intimacy: Their Psychology, Biology, and History.* New York: HarperCollins College. An excellent text that describes the current status of research and theorizing in the area of loving relationships.

Hendrick, Susan; and Hendrick, Clyde (1992). *Liking, Loving, and Relating* (2nd ed.). Pacific Grove, CA: Brooks/Cole. In this text the authors provide an informative overview of research on the related topics of attraction, love, and relationships (both development and maintenance of).

Hendrix, Harville (1990). *Getting the Love You Want: A Guide for Couples.* New York: Perennial Library. A best-selling book by an educator and couples therapist that provides a wealth of practical information for couples who wish to heal conflicts and develop a lasting and mature love relationship.

Lerner, Harriet (1989). *The Dance of Intimacy.* New York: Harper & Row. This book provides a framework for understanding how intimate relationships can thrive or heal.

Weber, Ann; and Harvey, John (Eds.) (1994). *Perspectives on Close Relationships.* Boston: Allyn & Bacon. A collection of scholarly articles that deal with a variety of relationship issues, including attraction, attachment, love, sexual intimacy, and jealousy.

Web Resources

WWW.

Love and Relationships
www.topchoice.com/~psyche/love/
This site provides brief explanations of the results of various research studies about love, and also expresses opinions about related topics such as courtship strategies, love and lust, communication, and Internet relationships.

Jealousy Test
www.queendom.com/jealousy.html
Three forms of an online jealousy test are available at this Web site: for heterosexual females, for heterosexual males, and for gay men and lesbians. This type of test might be used as a way of exploring jealousy issues with your partner.

8

Communication in Sexual Behavior

The Importance of Communication

What is the basis for effective sexual communication and why do many couples find it difficult to talk about sexual needs?

Talking: Getting Started

What kinds of strategies can make it easier to begin communication about sex?

Listening and Feedback

What are some key traits of good listeners?

Discovering Your Partner's Needs

What are some effective ways of learning about your partner's wants and needs?

Learning to Make Requests

What principles can help us effectively express our own sexual needs?

Giving and Receiving Criticism

What strategies can be helpful in constructively criticizing a partner and responding to criticism?

Saying No

What are some potentially useful ways to say no to intimate involvements?

Nonverbal Sexual Communication

What aspects of nonverbal communication have particular significance for our sexuality?

Impasses

When communication results in a standoff, what options are available to couples?

I want to talk with my girlfriend about our sex life. So many times I have made up my mind to do this, but I can't seem to come up with *how* I should do this. How can I tell her about my body and its needs? What words do I use? Do I say, "I like it best when you caress along the entire length of my penis" or should I say, "It feels good when you touch all of my cock"? The first word sounds too clinical, but I am afraid the term *cock* might shock her and put her off. Just what words do lovers use? (Authors' files)

This is a chapter about sexual communication: the ways people express their feelings and convey their needs and desires to sexual partners. We consider the reasons why such attempts are sometimes unsuccessful; we also explore some ways to enhance this important aspect of our sexual lives.

The Importance of Communication

Sexual communication can contribute greatly to the satisfaction of an intimate relationship. We do not mean that extensive verbal dialogue is essential to all sexual sharing; there are times when spoken communication may be more disruptive than constructive. Nevertheless, partners who never talk about the sexual aspects of their relationship may be denying themselves an opportunity to increase their closeness and pleasure through learning about each other's needs and desires.

Central to this chapter is our belief that the basis for effective sexual communication is **mutual empathy**—the underlying knowledge that each partner in a relationship cares for the other and knows that the care is reciprocated. With this perspective in mind, we discuss various approaches to sexual communication that have proved helpful in the lives of many people. We do not claim to have the final word on the many nuances of human communication, nor do we suggest that the ideas offered here will work for everyone. Communication strategies often need to be individually modified; and sometimes the differences between two people are so profound that even the best communication cannot ensure a mutually satisfying relationship. We hope, though, that some of these shared experiences and suggestions can be helpful in your own life.

Mutual empathy
The underlying knowledge that each partner in a relationship cares for the other and knows that the care is reciprocated.

Some Reasons Why Sexual Communication Is Difficult

Why do so many people find it difficult to talk candidly with their partners about sexual needs? What do you consider to be the major stumbling blocks in this area?

Some of the most important reasons why sexual communication is difficult lie in our socialization, the language available for talking about sex, and the fears many people have about self-expression.

Socialization and Sexual Communication

The way we were reared as children often contributes to later difficulties in talking about sexual needs. Learning to cover our genitals, to think that eliminative functions are "dirty," or to hide self-pleasuring for fear of adverse reactions all may contribute to a sense of shame and discomfort with the sexual areas and functions of our bodies. The development of sexual attitudes during childhood and adolescence is discussed in Chapter 13.

The lack of communication about sexual matters in many American homes is detrimental in a number of ways. Not talking about sex at home deprives a young child of one valuable source of a vocabulary for talking about sex later in life. This lack of communication may also convey the implicit message that sex is not an acceptable topic for conversation. Furthermore, children acquire communication skills most effectively when they are provided with models of verbal interaction followed by the opportunity to express their own thoughts in an accepting atmosphere. None of these elements is typically available in a home where people simply do not talk about sex.

Lack of positive models frequently extends beyond the home. Few people have access to classroom or textbook sources that portray how couples talk about sex. Neither peer groups nor the popular media fill the gap by providing realistic or positive information.

Language and Sexual Communication

Another obstacle to effective communication is the lack of a suitable language of sex. By the time we are grown up and eager to communicate sexual needs and feelings, many of us do not know how to go about doing it. The very words we have learned to describe sex may have become associated with negative rather than positive emotions. Many of us have learned to snicker over taboo sex words or to use them in an angry, aggressive, or insulting manner. Consequently, it can be very uncomfortable to use those same words to describe an activity with someone for whom we really care.

Thus, when we want to begin engaging in sexual communication, we may find ourselves struggling to find the right language for this most intimate kind of dialogue. The range of words commonly used to describe genital anatomy gives some indication of our society's mixed messages about sexuality. Two extremes tend to predominate: street language at one end and the clinical terminology at the other.

The chapter opening anecdote revealed one man's consternation over trying to figure out what words to use for his own genitals. As this man discovered, our language lacks a comfortable sexual vocabulary. Many of us are not at ease with the words commonly available. We may find them to be too clinical, too harsh, or too juvenile to use in a caring way. Words such as *penis* and *vagina* often seem too technical or medical; but *cock, prick, cunt,* and *snatch* may sound too aggressive or insulting. And the terms available to describe sexual activity may produce similar problems. Invitations such as "Let's fuck" may be lovingly delivered, and excitedly received, by some, but may seem too cold, graphic, or aggressive to others. But a more scientific description, such as "Let's have sexual intercourse," may seem clumsy and impersonal.

Indeed, as authors of this textbook we face the same limitations of language. What is the best word or phrase to describe how two people interact together in explicitly sexual ways? Some of the more common street terms tend to sound crude and can objectify the participants, diminishing their interaction to the purely physical level. More formal terms such as *coitus* and *sexual intercourse* tend to put too much emphasis on heterosexual genital contact. We do not want our language to exclude homosexual interactions, nor do we want it to exclude a whole range of nongenital interactions—including touching, talking, and communicating through facial expressions. When the context of our discussion focuses more on the physical aspects of sexual interactions, we use the terms *sexual activity* and *sexual play,* which we consider both broad and neutral. When the focus is more on the emotional and spiritual aspects of sexual interactions, we use the terms *sexual intimacy, sexual sharing,* and *lovemaking* to emphasize the larger emotional and intellectual relationship between the participants. We recognize, though, that even these terms have different connotations—both good and bad—for different people. What terms are you most comfortable with, and why?

Within the context of our culture, it is very natural—or at least common—to feel shy or embarrassed when talking about sexuality with friends and lovers. Furthermore, ethnic variations in communication styles can significantly affect talking about sex (see the boxed discussion "Ethnic Variations in Intimate Communication"). However, this awkwardness can often be avoided or overcome, and people certainly find ways of learning to live with the vocabulary. For example, the context and tone in which sexual terms are used may create totally different meanings and reactions, as this woman's comment shows:

I have very different feelings about words depending on how they are used. My lover saying "I love your sweet cunt" is very different from hearing "You stupid cunt." (Authors' files)

Also, some people give their own or their partners' genitals nicknames, such as Fuzzylove, Slurpy, Artesia, Pokey, Peter, or Moby, in an attempt to avoid negative associations with much of the existing terminology.

Later in this book (Chapter 16), we explore some of the benefits and joys associated with talking to our lovers while we touch their bodies. We will see that this is a wonderful time to develop intimacy while learning about each other's needs and preferences. It is a particularly good way to discover what words are mutually acceptable.

Gender-Based Communication Styles

Still another factor that can hinder communication between heterosexual partners is the difference in women's and men's styles of relating to other people. According to Deborah Tannen (1990), a professor of linguistics at Georgetown University, men and women have different communication goals. Men use language to convey information, to achieve status in a group, to challenge others, and to prevent being pushed around. Men often enter into conversations concerned about who is one-up and who is one-down. From this perspective, communication becomes something of a contest to avoid being put in a one-down position. A man operating within this framework might be expected to be overly sensitive about asking for advice or for suggestions about how to respond in a particular situation (sexual or otherwise), being told to do something, or engaging in any other behavior that even remotely resembles being in a one-down or pushed-around position.

In contrast, Tannen maintains that women use language to achieve and share intimacy, to promote closeness, and to prevent others from pushing them away. Women are not typically socialized to use language as a defensive weapon to avoid being dominated

Sexuality and Diversity
Ethnic Variations in Intimate Communication

Textbooks, lectures, and general media sources that portray how couples can effectively communicate about intimate matters, especially sex, are not overly plentiful. Thus, it will come as no surprise that research data pertaining to ethnic variations in intimate communication are very limited. In the following paragraphs we draw on a sparse data base to offer a few generalizations about variations in styles of communicating about sexual intimacy that occur among white Americans, African Americans, Hispanic Americans, and Asian Americans.

The belief that good communication is the heart and soul of healthy intimate relationships is rather common among white Americans (especially white women) and, to a lesser extent, African Americans; however, among Hispanic Americans and Asian American couples there is generally much less emphasis on "working on" communication competence (Chang & Holt, 1991; Hecht et al., 1993; Ting-Toomey & Korzenny, 1991). Thus, although white Americans and African Americans may openly discuss sex with a partner, there is a general assumption among Hispanic American couples that they will not discuss their sexual relationship (Guerrero Pavich, 1986). Asian American couples are also less inclined to discuss sex, consistent with a general tendency to value nonverbal, indirect, and intuitive communication over explicit verbal interaction (Bradshaw, 1994; Del Carmen, 1990).

White Americans, and to a lesser extent African Americans, tend to be more self-oriented in intimate relationships than either Hispanic Americans or Asian Americans (Gudykunst et al., 1996; Hecht et al., 1990 & 1993; Trafimow et al., 1991). This stress on *individualism*—an ideology that places greater emphasis on the individual than the couple or group—is perhaps best reflected by the statement "I'm doing something with you and I will get my needs met (and you might as well)" (Hecht et al., 1993, p. 155). In contrast, Hispanic Americans and Asian Americans are more likely to stress *collectivism*—an ideology that focuses on the couple or group or controlled. Rather, their concern is often to use dialogue as a way to get close to another person—and as a way to judge how close to or distant from a valued partner they are.

A woman's goal in talking about her concerns is often to foster a sense of sharing and rapport and to achieve the feeling that "I am not alone." She wants a response that says, "I understand: I have been there too"—a reaction that puts both communicators on equal footing, allowing intimacy to be built around equality. Whereas a woman may only be looking for understanding or a willingness to talk openly about a concern, her male partner is often likely to respond with advice or solutions. This response on the part of the man frames him "as more knowledgeable, more reasonable, more in control—in a word, one-up. And this contributes to the distancing effect" (Tannen, 1990, p. 53). Women may minimize this relationship-eroding influence by clearly telling their male partners that, when dealing with intimacy or emotional troubles, they do not want to hear quickly offered solutions. Instead, they would prefer that their partner listen to their concerns and be willing to openly discuss and share viewpoints about problems on an equal footing.

Communication between heterosexual partners can be hindered by the difference in women's and men's styles of relating to other people.

Tannen stresses that the first step in improving communication is understanding and accepting that there are gender differences in communication styles; it is not a question of one style being more right or wrong than the other. As Tannen reports, many people have indicated that once they came to understand these differences in how the sexes use language, they were better able to put their problems of communication with the other sex in a manageable context—and often to arrive at solutions to difficult or seemingly unresolvable problems or predicaments.

Sexuality and Diversity

rather than on the individual. This perspective on intimate relationships is reflected by the statement "We are doing something together that we are both getting something out of" (Hecht et al., 1993, p. 155).

Perhaps because of the emphasis on individualism in white American relationships, overt conflict is considered natural and something to be dealt with and resolved. African American couples are less comfortable dealing with conflict, and Hispanic American couples tend to view conflicts as a negative indicator that a relationship is disharmonious or unbalanced (Collier, 1991; Ting-Toomey & Korzenny, 1991). Because harmonious relationships, and the collective good of the group, are valued over individualism and rewards for one's self, Asian Americans are also strongly inclined to avoid conflicts that may involve direct confrontation with a primary partner (Del Carmen, 1990).

In light of these general differences among ethnic groups in America, it follows that although Asian and Hispanic American couples may not necessarily encounter more relational sexual problems than white or African Americans, they are certainly less inclined to acknowledge or discuss such concerns. Furthermore, it is unlikely that either of these ethnic groups, Asian or Hispanic, would be inclined to seek professional help for relationship problems, especially those of a sexual nature.

Ethnic variations also exist in the area of nonverbal sexual communication. Hispanic Americans rely heavily on nonverbal communication to reveal sexual information, and they place particular emphasis on the use of touching to convey love, a desire for intimacy, or sexual intent (Hecht et al., 1990). Touching also plays a major role among African Americans, who touch more than white Americans; Asian Americans touch even less (Butts, 1981; Hecht et al., 1990; Henley, 1977).

Interpersonal distance—another important aspect of nonverbal sexual communication discussed later in this chapter—is much more contracted among Hispanic Americans than among white Americans, a fact that can lead to misunderstandings when members of these two ethnic groups interact. Thus a white American may misinterpret a close-standing Hispanic person as issuing an invitation for intimacy when, in actuality, the close proximity to another is typical of Hispanic culture (Bryjak & Soroka, 1994; Sluzki, 1982). African Americans also tend to establish smaller interpersonal distances than white Americans (Halberstadt, 1985).

Anxieties About Sexual Communication

Beyond the handicaps imposed by socialization and language limitations, difficulties in sexual communication for some people may also be rooted in anxieties about exposing themselves. Any sexual communication involves a certain amount of risk: By talking, people place themselves in a position vulnerable to judgment, criticism, and even rejection. The willingness to take risks may be related to the amount of trust that exists within a relationship. Some couples lack this mutual trust, and for them the risks of openly expressing sexual needs are too great to overcome. Others have a high degree of reciprocal caring and trust: For them the first hesitant steps into sexual dialogue may be considerably easier.

Even when a climate of goodwill prevails, however, it still may be difficult to establish a satisfying pattern of sexual dialogue. In such circumstances, a couple may be frustrated in their efforts to resolve their communication problems strictly on their own. Instead, they should probably seek professional counseling. (Chapter 16 provides some guidelines for seeking professional assistance.)

We have outlined some reasons why many people find it difficult to engage in meaningful and effective sexual communication. Despite these difficulties, communication is an important part of sexual sharing, just as it is an important part of many other aspects of a relationship. The potential rewards are enhanced sexual experiences and enriched relationships.

Talking: Getting Started

How does one begin communicating about sex? Apply your own experiences as you consider this question.

There are many ways of breaking the ice, and we explore a few of them here. These suggestions may be useful, not just at the beginning of a relationship, but throughout its course.

Talking About Talking

When people feel uneasy about a topic, often the best place to start is by talking about talking. Discussing *why* it is hard to talk about sex can be a good place to begin. Each partner has individual reasons, and understanding those reasons can help set a relationship on a solid foundation. Perhaps you can share experiences about earlier efforts to discuss sex with parents, teachers, physicians, friends, or lovers. It may be helpful to move gradually into the arena of sexual communication by directing your initial discussions to nonthreatening, less personal topics (such as new birth control methods, pornography laws, and so forth). Later, as your mutual comfort increases, you may be able to talk about more personal feelings and concerns.

Reading and Discussing

Because many people find it easier to read about sex than to talk about it, articles and books dealing with the subject may provide the stimulus for personal conversations. Partners can read the material separately, then discuss it together; or a couple can read it jointly and discuss their individual reactions. Often it is easier to make the transition from a book or article to personal feelings than to begin by talking about highly personal concerns.

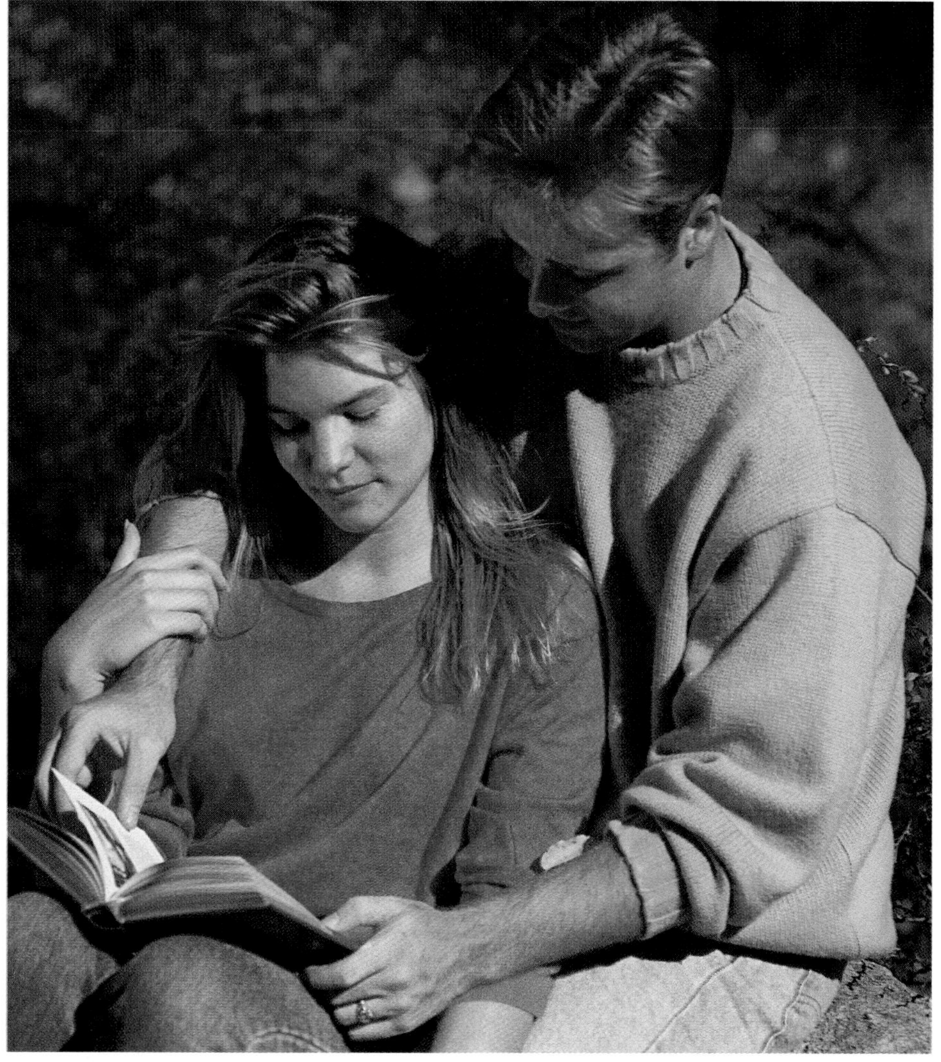

Reading together about sensitive matters facilitates discussion.

Sharing Sexual Histories

Another way to start talking is to share sexual histories. There may be many questions that you would feel comfortable discussing with your partner. For instance: How was sex education handled in your home or at school? How did your parents relate to each other—were you aware of any sexuality in their relationship? When did you first learn about sex, and what were your reactions? Many other items could be added to this brief list; the questions depend on the feelings and needs of each individual.

Listening and Feedback

Communication, sexual or otherwise, is most successful when it is two-sided, involving both an effective communicator and an active listener. In this section, we focus on the listening side of this process.

Have you ever wondered why certain people seem to draw others to themselves like metal to a magnet? With some thought you will probably conclude that, among other things, these individuals are often very good listeners. What special skills do they possess that make us feel they really care about what we have to say? Next time you are with such a person, observe closely. Make a study of his or her listening habits. Perhaps your list of good listening traits will include several of the following.

Be an Active Listener

Some people are *passive* listeners. They may stare blankly into space as their companion talks, perhaps grunting "uh-huh" now and then. Such responses may make us think that the person is indifferent, even when this is not the case, and we may soon grow tired of trying to share important thoughts with someone who does not seem to be receptive:

When I talk to my husband about anything really important, he just stares at me with a blank expression. It is like I am talking to a piece of stone. I think he hears the message, at least sometimes, but he rarely shows any response. Sometimes I feel like shaking him and screaming, "Are you still alive?" Needless to say, I don't try communicating with him very much anymore. (Authors' files)

Being an *active* listener means actively communicating that you are both listening to and genuinely interested in what your partner is saying. You may communicate this through attentive body language, appropriate and sympathetic facial expressions, nodding your head, asking questions ("Could you give me an example?"), or making brief comments ("I see your point"). Sometimes it may be helpful to reciprocate in the conversation. For example, as your partner relates a feeling or incident, you may be reminded of something in your own life, related to the point expressed by your partner. Making these associations and candidly expressing them—provided that you don't sidetrack the conversation to your own needs—can encourage your partner to continue voicing important concerns.

Maintain Eye Contact

Maintaining eye contact is one of the most vital aspects of good face-to-face communication. Our eyes are wondrously expressive of feelings. When people maintain eye contact when we are sharing important thoughts or feelings with them, the message is clear: They care about what we have to say. When we fail to maintain eye contact, we deny our partners valuable feedback about how we are perceiving their messages.

Provide Feedback

The purpose of communication is to provide a message that has some impact on the listener. However, a message's impact may not always be the same as its intent, for communications can be (and often are) misunderstood. This is particularly true with a topic such as sexuality, where language is often roundabout or awkward. Therefore, giving your partner some *feedback,* or reaction to her or his message, *in words* can be very helpful. Besides clarifying how you have perceived your partner's comments, such verbal feedback reinforces that you are actively listening.

We may also benefit by asking our partners to provide some response to a message we think is important. A comment such as "What are your thoughts about what I have just said?" may encourage feedback that can help you determine the impact of your message on your partner.

Support Your Partner's Communication Efforts

Many of us can feel quite vulnerable when communicating important messages to our partners. Support for our efforts can help alleviate our fears and anxieties and can encourage us to continue building the communication skills so important for a viable relationship.

Think how good it can feel, after struggling to voice an important concern, to have a partner say, "I'm glad you told me how you really feel," or "Thanks for caring enough to tell me what was on your mind." Such supportive comments can help foster mutual empathy, while ensuring that we will continue to communicate our thoughts and feelings candidly.

Express Unconditional Positive Regard

The concept of unconditional positive regard is borrowed from the immensely popular *Client-Centered Therapy,* authored by Carl Rogers (1951). In personal relationships, it means conveying to our partners the sense that we will continue to value and care for them regardless of what they do or say. Unconditional positive regard may encourage a person to talk about even the most embarrassing or painful concerns. The following anecdote reveals one person's response to this valued attribute:

I know that my wife will continue to love me no matter what I say or reveal. In an earlier marriage, I could never express any serious concerns without my wife getting defensive or just plain mean. As a consequence, I quit talking about the things that really mattered. What a relief it is to be with someone who I can tell what is on my mind without worrying about the consequences. (Authors' files)

Use Paraphrasing

One way to increase the probability that you and your partner will listen more effectively to each other is to use a technique called **paraphrasing.** This involves a listener summarizing, in his or her own words, the speaker's message.

Paraphrasing
A listener summarizing the speaker's message in his or her own words.

HE: It would be nice if you could be a little gentler. Do you know what I mean?
SHE: I think so—you want me to be less aggressive.
HE: That's not quite what I mean. I mean that when we make love, I would like you to touch me very lightly. I am so sensitive right before I come that anything more feels too rough.
SHE: Oh. I always thought you liked it when I'm sort of rough. I'm sorry I misunderstood. I'll try to be more gentle.

If the paraphrase is not satisfactory, the speaker can try to express the message again in different words. Then the listener can try to paraphrase again. Several attempts may be necessary to clear away discrepancies between the speaker's intent and the listener's interpretation. As time goes by, a couple typically finds that the need to use this approach diminishes as listening skills improve.

Discovering Your Partner's Needs

Discovering what is pleasurable to your partner is an important part of sexual intimacy. Many couples want to know each other's preferences but are uncertain how to find out. In this section, we look at some effective ways of learning about our partners' wants and needs.

Asking Questions

One of the best ways to discover your partner's needs is simply to ask. However, there are several ways of asking: Some can be helpful, whereas others may be ineffective or even counterproductive. We review a few of the most common ways of asking questions and the effect each is likely to have.

What do you think are the most effective ways of finding out what a partner wants? What ways do you think are ineffective?

Yes-or-No Questions

Imagine being asked one or more of the following questions in the context of a sexual interlude with your partner:

1. Was it good for you?
2. Do you like oral sex?
3. Was I gentle enough?
4. Did you come?
5. Do you like it when I stimulate you this way?
6. Do you like being on the bottom?
7. Is it okay if we don't make love tonight?
8. Am I a good lover?

Yes-or-no question
A question that asks for a one-word answer and thus provides little opportunity for discussing an issue.

Open-ended question
A question that allows a respondent to share any feelings or information she or he thinks is relevant.

At first glance, these questions may seem reasonably worded. However, they all share one characteristic that may reduce their effectiveness: They are **yes-or-no questions.** Each asks for a one-word answer, even though people's thoughts and feelings are rarely so simple.

For example, consider question 2, "Do you like oral sex?" Either answer—"Yes, I do," or "No, I don't"—gives the couple little opportunity to discuss the issue. Certainly, the potential for discussion exists. Nevertheless, in a world where sexual communication is often difficult under the best of circumstances, the asker may get no more than the specific information requested. In some situations, of course, a brief yes or no is all that is necessary. But the person responding may have mixed feelings about oral sex (for example), and the phrasing of the question leads to oversimplification. **Open-ended questions,** or questions that allow the respondent to state a preference, can make it easier for your partner to give accurate replies.

Open-Ended Questions

Some people find that asking open-ended questions is a particularly helpful way to discover their partners' desires. This approach places virtually no restrictions on possible answers; in a sense, it is like responding to a general essay question on an exam. ("What are some of the important aspects of human sexuality that you have learned thus far this term?") The following list gives some examples of open-ended questions:

1. What gives you the most pleasure when we make love?
2. What things about our sexual relationship would you most like us to change?
3. Where do you like to be touched?
4. What sexual positions do you like?
5. What is the easiest or most enjoyable way for you to reach orgasm?
6. What are your feelings about oral sex?

A primary advantage of open-ended questions is that they allow your partner freedom to share any feelings or information she or he thinks is relevant. With no limitations or restrictions attached, you may learn much more than a simple yes-or-no answer could provide.

One possible drawback of the open-ended approach is that your partner may not know where to begin when asked such general questions. Consider being asked something like "What aspects of our lovemaking do you like best?" Some people might welcome the unstructured nature of this question, but others might find it difficult to respond to such a broad query, particularly if they are not accustomed to openly discussing sex. If this is the case, a more structured approach may have a better chance of encouraging talk. There are several ways of structuring your approach; one is the use of either/or questions.

Either/Or Questions

The following list gives some examples of **either/or questions:**

1. Would you like the light on when we make love, or should we turn it off?
2. Am I being gentle enough, or am I being too gentle?
3. Is this the way you want to be touched, or should we experiment with a different kind of caress?
4. Would you like to try something different, or should we stop and just hold each other?
5. Would you like to talk now, or would you prefer we wait for another time?

Discovering what is pleasurable to your partner is an important part of sexual intimacy.

Either/or question
A question that allows statement of a preference.

Either/or questions offer more structure than do open-ended questions, and they also encourage more participation than simple yes-or-no queries. People often appreciate the opportunity to consider a few alternatives. The either/or question also shows your concern about your partner's pleasure. Thus, this kind of question may encourage a response at a time when a more open-ended question might be overwhelming. However, either/or questions can still be somewhat restrictive. There is always the possibility that your partner will not like either of the choices you offer. In this case, he or she can state another alternative that is preferable.

Beside asking questions, there are other ways of discovering the sexual needs of your partner. We discuss three other communication techniques here: self-disclosure, comparing notes, and giving permission.

Self-Disclosure

Direct questions often put people on the spot. Whether you have been asked, "Do you enjoy oral sex?" or "How do you feel about oral sex?" it may be quite difficult to respond candidly, simply because you do not know your partner's feelings on the subject. If the topic has strong emotional overtones, it may be very difficult to reply—no matter how thoughtfully the question has been phrased. It is the content, not the communication technique, that causes the problem.

With potentially loaded topics, a way to broach the subject may be to start with a self-disclosure:

For the longest time, I avoided the topic of oral sex with my lover. We did just about everything else, but this was one thing we had not tried—and hadn't even talked about. I personally was both excited and repelled by the prospect of this kind of sex. I didn't have the slightest idea what she felt about it. I was afraid to bring it up for fear she would think I was some kind of pervert. Eventually I could no longer tolerate not knowing her feelings. I brought it up by first talking about my mixed emotions, like feeling that maybe it wasn't natural but at the same time really wanting to try it out. As it turned out, she had similar feelings but was afraid to bring them up. Afterward we laughed about how we had both been afraid to break the ice. Once we could talk freely, it was easy to add this form of stimulation to our sex life. (Authors' files)

Personal disclosures require some give-and-take. It is much easier to share feelings about strongly emotional topics when a partner is willing to make similar disclosures.

Admittedly, such an approach may have risks, and occasionally one can feel vulnerable sharing personal thoughts and feelings. It may be especially difficult for men to discuss their feelings, as described in the boxed discussion "Men Who Cannot Communicate About Their Emotions." Nevertheless, the increased possibility for open, honest dialogue may be worth the discomfort a person may feel about making the first disclosure. In addition, research indicates that when one partner openly discusses his or her own feelings, the other is likely to do the same (DerLego et al., 1993; Hendrick & Hendrick, 1992).

A form of self-disclosure that some people find exciting and informative involves telling their partners about personal fantasies, as revealed in the following anecdote:

> I had this sexual fantasy that kept going through my mind. I would imagine coming home after a long, hard day of classes and being met by my partner, who would proceed to take me into the bedroom and remove all my clothes. Then he would pick me up and carry me into the bathroom, where the tub was full of hot water and bubbles. The fantasy would end with us making passionate love in the bathtub, with bubbles popping off around us. Finally, I shared my fantasy with him. Guess what happened when I came home after the next long day? It was even better than I had imagined! (Authors' files)

Understandably, many people might be concerned about the potentially negative effects of revealing such highly personal thoughts. Certain precautions can help reduce the possibility of an unpleasant outcome.

On the Edge

Men Who Cannot Communicate About Their Emotions

The inability to put one's feelings or emotions into words, or even to be aware of them—a condition labeled *alexithymia* in the psychological literature—was first described in people suffering from severe psychological dysfunctions such as post-traumatic stress disorder (Krystal, 1982). In the late 1990s a new perspective on alexithymia has emerged with the work of Ronald Levant (1997), a respected author, Harvard Medical School professor, and founder of a counseling center that specializes in treating men. Levant's extensive clinical experiences have led him to conclude that mild to moderate alexithymia is so widespread among men that it can be properly labeled **normative male alexithymia.**

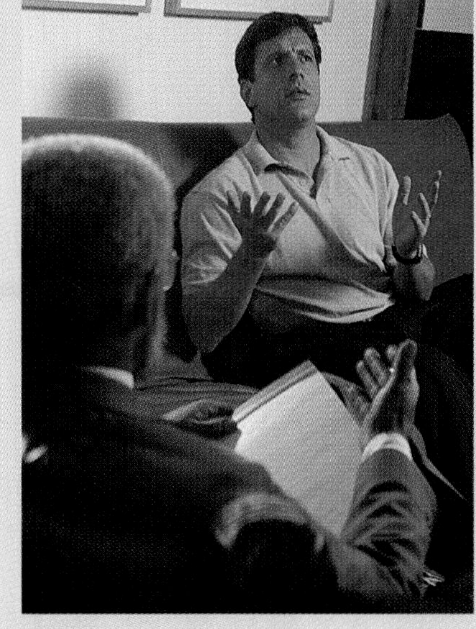

This pervasive condition has its origins in male gender-role socialization processes in the home and peer group. As you may recall from our discussion in Chapter 3, many parents communicate to their male children, by words and actions, the messages that "boys do not cry" and that "real men" are strong, unemotional, and silent. Many men were raised (and continue to be raised) to believe that they should be emotionally stoical. Evidence indicates that both parents contribute to the suppression of emotions in their male children.

Mothers express less emotion to their sons than to their daughters (Dunn et al., 1987; Malatesta et al., 1989). Fathers' communication with their sons is more likely to be expressed as verbal bantering, joking, and kidding around, whereas their conversations with daughters tend to focus more on emotions (Levant, 1997). The expression of vulnerable emotions, such as sadness, fear, and hurt, as well as the caring/connection emotions, such as fondness or affection, is actively encouraged in girls and discouraged in boys (Dunn et al., 1987; Siegal, 1987). In contrast, the expression of anger, although discouraged in girls, is the one emotion that is commonly allowed or encouraged in boys (Levant, 1997).

This decidedly negative aspect of male socialization is further ingrained by the peer group. Boys engage in play activities that often focus on dominance and aggression, where

Sharing fantasies like this is usually most successful when it is mutual rather than one-way. If your partner is unwilling to engage in such a conversation, at least for the present, it would be wise to respect this wish. Sometimes starting out with very mild fantasies can help desensitize fears and embarrassment and allow you to gauge the impact of such sharing on your partner and yourself. If you sense that your companion is feeling uncomfortable, it may be best not to press. It is probably advisable to avoid altogether any fantasies that you anticipate will be shocking to your companion; fantasies that involve other lovers may be particularly threatening.

Comparing Notes

While planning an evening out, many couples consider it natural to discuss each other's preferences: "Would you like to go to a concert, or would you rather go to the movies?" "How close do you like to sit?" "Do you prefer vegetarian, Italian, or meat and potatoes?" Afterward they may candidly evaluate the evening's events: "The drummer was great," "I think we should sit further from the speakers next time," "Boy, I wouldn't order the scampi again." Yet many of the same couples never think of sharing thoughts about mutual sexual enjoyment.

On the Edge

toughness and emotional stoicism is the proper operating style. These male patterns of recreation are typically devoid of the elements of play for girls that promote emotional self-awareness and empathy such as expressing and responding to each others' emotions, resolving conflicts, and maintaining harmony (Levant, 1997; Maccoby, 1990).

According to Levant, this "normative" aspect of conventional masculinity, so strongly ingrained in many men by early socialization, "has such broad and negative consequences that, at least in the context of modern life, it must be considered dysfunctional" (1997, p. 10). Men who are conditioned to live detached from their emotions as well as those of significant others have great difficulty in both communicating their intimate feelings and experiencing true intimacy. When men are unable to discuss or express tender, caring, and vulnerable emotions, they may be left with aggression and sexuality as the sole channels for emotional release. Because anger is one of the few emotions allowed under traditional male rearing, boys and then men often learn to channel vulnerable feelings such as sadness, fear, and shame into anger-induced aggression. In similar fashion, caring emotions are frequently channeled into sexuality. For many men, sexual sharing may be the only acceptable context in which to display and express affection and love.

Levant has created a treatment strategy to help his male clients develop "emotional intelligence." The major emphasis is on "psychoeducation," wherein various exercises are used to awaken a man's ability to empathize with others and to connect his emotional experience to thoughts about it. The first step in treatment is to expand a client's working vocabulary for emotions. An impoverished emotional vocabulary is typical of men with normative male alexithymia. The next step involves helping the client to become more aware of and able to identify the emotions of others. Levant has found that it is often less threatening to start with the feelings of others rather than one's own. In the third phase of treatment, the client begins to keep an "emotional log" in which he describes the context in which an emotion occurs (social situation, event, etc.) and identifies the emotion he is experiencing. The final phase involves continued practice in fostering the development of these new emotional skills. In group therapy sessions men may engage in role playing followed by feedback. Videotaping may also be employed, which allows men to observe and discuss the manner in which they express emotions. In individual therapy sessions, clients are encouraged to continue practicing by raising such questions as "How did you feel?" or "How do you think your partner felt?"

Levant has found that his clients' lives provide the most effective feedback and reinforcement for these new emotional skills. Men are energized and gratified by the often profound changes that are taking place in their lives. One of his clients said that "he felt like he had been living in a black-and-white television that had suddenly turned into a color set" (Levant, 1997, p. 23). Such changes become highly motivational as men discover that their emerging emotional empathy and increased ability to communicate intimate feelings reduce personal pain and conflicts, increase harmony in their relationships, and allow them to better integrate love and affection with sexuality.

Admittedly, it may be a big step from discussing an evening out to discussing sexual preferences and evaluating specific sexual encounters. Nevertheless, people do engage in this type of sexual dialogue. Some people feel comfortable discussing sexual preferences with a new lover before progressing to lovemaking. They may talk about what areas of their bodies are most responsive, how they like to be touched, what intercourse positions are particularly desirable, the easiest or most satisfying way to reach orgasm, time and location preferences, special turn-ons and turn-offs, and a variety of other likes and dislikes.

The appeal of this open, frank approach is that it allows a couple to focus on particularly pleasurable activities rather than discovering them by slow trial-and-error. However, some people may feel that such dialogues are far too clinical, perhaps even robbing the sexual experience of the excitement of experimentation and mutual discovery. Furthermore, what a person finds desirable may be different with different partners, so it may be difficult to assess one's own preferences in advance.

Couples may also find it helpful to discuss their feelings after having sex. They may offer reactions about what was good and what could be better. They may use this time to reinforce the things they found particularly satisfying in their partner's lovemaking ("I loved the way you touched me on the insides of my thighs"). A mutual feedback session can be extremely informative; it can also contribute to a deeper intimacy between two people.

Giving Permission

Giving permission Providing reassurance to one's partner that it is okay to talk about certain specific feelings or needs.

Discovering your partner's needs can be made immeasurably easier by the practice we call **giving permission.** Basically, this means providing encouragement and reassurance. One partner tells the other that it is okay to talk about certain specific feelings or needs—in fact, that he or she wants very much to know how the other feels about the subject.

HE: I'm not sure how you like me to touch you when we make love.
SHE: Any way you want to is good.
HE: Well, I want to know what you like best, and you can help me by saying what feels good while I touch you.

Many of us have had experiences where we have felt rebuffed in our efforts to communicate our needs to others. It is no wonder people often remain silent even when they want to share personal feelings. Giving and receiving permission to express needs freely can contribute to the exchange of valuable information.

Learning to Make Requests

People are not mind readers. Nevertheless, many lovers seem to assume that their partners know (perhaps by intuition?) just what they need. People who approach sex with this attitude are not taking full responsibility for their own pleasure. If sexual encounters are not satisfactory, it may be convenient to blame a partner—"You don't care about my needs"—when one's own reluctance to express needs may be the problem. Expecting partners to somehow know what is wanted without telling them places a heavy burden on them. Many people think that they "shouldn't have to ask." But in fact, asking a partner to do something can be an affirmative, responsible action that is helpful to both people.

Taking Responsibility for Our Own Pleasure

When two people are really in harmony with each other, you don't have to talk about your sexual wants. You each sense and respond to the other's desires. Talking just tends to spoil these magical moments. (Authors' files)

The situation this person describes seems to exist more in the fantasyland of idealized sex than in the real world. As we just noted, people are not mind readers, and intuition leaves much to be desired as a substitute for genuine communication. A person who expects another to know his or her needs by intuition is saying, "It's not my business to let you know my needs, but it is yours to know what they are"; and by inference, "If my needs are not fulfilled, it is your fault, not mine." Needless to say, this is a potentially destructive approach that may lead to blaming, misunderstandings, and unsatisfying sex.

In a similar vein, some people may take too much responsibility for their partners' sexual pleasure. Such a person says, in effect, "It is my job to satisfy you sexually. I will make all the decisions and assume responsibility for your pleasure." A person so intent on figuring out and fulfilling a partner's needs may find that his or her own needs are largely overlooked. Furthermore, such a take-charge attitude undermines a partner's inclination to assume responsibility for her or his own satisfaction.

In summary, the best way to get our needs met is to speak up. Two individuals willing to communicate their desires and take responsibility for their own pleasure create an excellent framework for effective, fulfilling sexual intimacy.

One woman stated her experience with assuming responsibility for her own pleasure:

> For much of my life, sex has been a hit-or-miss proposition, with the miss part predominating. Only recently have I discovered how to change this pattern. I know what I need sexually to be satisfied. I am very good at giving myself pleasure. Finally it occurred to me how futile it was to hope that my partners would somehow automatically know what I want, when it took me years to discover this for myself. I decided that the better I could express myself about my sexual needs, the greater the likelihood they would be fulfilled. Assuming this responsibility for my own pleasure was a big step, and I took it with a great deal of hesitancy and anxiety. But I have been pleasantly surprised. Most of my subsequent lovers have been relieved to have the guesswork taken out of our sexual experiences. One man praised me for being so open, and confided that I had relieved him of one of his greatest concerns, namely, not knowing what his partner desired from him during sex. (Authors' files)

Deciding to assume responsibility for our own satisfaction is an important step. Just as important are the methods we select for expressing our needs. The way a request is made has a decided effect on the reaction it draws. Some suggestions are listed in the next two sections.

Making Requests Specific

The more specific a request, the more likely it is to be understood and heeded. Although this principle is frequently noted by social psychologists and communication specialists, many of us neglect to apply it to our sexual dialogues. Lovers often ask for changes in the sexual aspects of their relationships in the vaguest language. It can be quite uncomfortable, even anxiety provoking, to be on the receiving end of an ill-defined request. Just how does one respond? Probably by doing very little, if anything.

The key to preventing unnecessary stress for both partners lies in delivering requests in as clear and concise a manner as possible. Thus, an alternative to the vague request "I'd like you to try touching me differently" might be something like "I would like you to touch me gently around my clitoris but not directly on it." Other examples of specific requests include the following:

1. I would like you to spend more time touching and caressing me all over before we have intercourse.
2. I want to be on top this time. It feels really good to me, and I love being able to watch you respond.
3. I like it when you lick the underside of the head of my penis. Not too hard, though—I'll tell you if I want it harder or softer.
4. I really enjoy it when you keep on kissing and caressing me after you're inside me.
5. I would like you to stroke my penis with your hand.

Using "I" Language

Many counselors encourage their clients to use "I" language when stating their needs to others. This forthright approach brings the desired response more often than does a general statement. For example, saying, "I would like to be on top," is considerably more likely to produce that result than "What would you think about changing positions?"

Many people find it difficult to ask for what they want in such clear, unequivocal language. Saying, "I want . . . ," may seem selfish, as the following two anecdotes illustrate:

I have trouble expressing my needs to my partner. Sometimes I think that all the energy I put out to please him distracts me from focusing on what feels good to my body. But it would be selfish for me to say so, so I don't. (Authors' files)

My main problem in talking about sex is asking for gratification for myself. I am always trying to please my partner, and often I do not receive sexual fulfillment. I find it difficult to ask her for certain forms of sexual expression. It is just not my nature to ask for anything. (Authors' files)

There is, however, a difference between being self-centered and recognizing that "I am as important as others in my life, and my needs are worthy of being met." Individuals whose own needs have been satisfied are often able to give much of themselves to others. Conversely, the philosophy of "never put myself first" may ultimately produce so much frustration and resentment that a person is left with few positive feelings to share.

Expressing requests directly may not always be effective. Some people may want to make all the decisions, and they may not take kindly to requests from their partners during lovemaking. A partner's assertiveness may be offensive to them. You may want to determine if this is your partner's attitude before a sexual encounter, for doing so may help you avoid an awkward situation. One way to do this is to ask the open-ended question "How do you feel about asking for things during lovemaking?" Or you may choose to wait and find out during sex play. At any rate, if a person appears closed to direct requests, you may wish to reevaluate your strategy. Perhaps making your needs known at some time other than during sexual interaction may give your partner a more relaxed opportunity to consider your desires. Nevertheless, we strongly encourage you to use "I" language in whatever context you make your requests. It may help you avoid the type of awkward scenario illustrated in the "without 'I' language" segment that follows (compare the results to the "with 'I' language" segment):

WITHOUT "I" LANGUAGE

SHE: What do you think about oral sex?
HE: Oh, I'm not sure. What do you think?
SHE: Well, I'm wondering if it is something we might enjoy.
HE: I'm not sure. I guess it's something that we could consider.

(This conversation might continue for quite some time without resolving anything, since both partners seem hesitant to do anything more than talk around the topic.)

WITH "I" LANGUAGE

SHE: I have been thinking about oral sex and I would very much like to try it when we make love.
HE: Well, I was thinking about it too, but I was nervous about bringing it up.
SHE: I think I would enjoy it. Would you be comfortable experimenting a little?
HE: Sure. I am glad you suggested it.

Giving and Receiving Criticism

Contrary to the popular romantic image, no two people can fill all of each other's needs all of the time. It seems inevitable in an intimate relationship that people will sometimes need to register complaints and request changes. This is not an easy process for caring individuals whose involvement is characterized by mutual empathy. When the criticism pertains to the emotionally intense area of sexual intimacy, it may be doubly difficult. Partners will want to think carefully about appropriate strategies and potential obstacles to accomplishing this delicate task.

Constructive Criticism Strategies

Perhaps the best way to begin, before verbalizing a complaint to your partner, is to examine the motivations underlying your need to criticize.

Be Aware of Your Motivation

The way criticism is offered may depend largely on the critic's motive. Consider the following two anecdotes:

My husband is a lousy lover. He doesn't know the first thing about how to turn me on, and when I tell him I don't get any pleasure out of our sex life he just clams up. I don't know what's the matter with him, but it sure burns me up. (Authors' files)

A couple of years ago I found out that my wife was involved in an affair with a man she works with. She claimed he was kind and gentle and that she couldn't help being attracted to him. Faced with my ultimatum, she changed jobs and stopped seeing him (I think). Since that time our sex life has been a real bust. She seems to lack enthusiasm, and we engage in sex much less frequently. Sometimes I think her having sex with the other guy has ruined our sex life. Maybe she thinks he was better than me. When I confront her about my dissatisfaction with her lack of enthusiasm she gets upset, and we usually end up having a fight. (Authors' files)

It seems clear that these people's motivations for criticizing are not based on a caring desire to make their relationships better. If the aim is to hurt, humiliate, blame, ridicule, or get even, it is likely that criticizing a partner will prove to be far more destructive than constructive. Being aware of your motives for criticizing your partner can help avoid this pitfall.

In this book we are concerned with constructive criticism that is prompted by a genuine desire for necessary change. It is not always easy to criticize effectively while maintaining mutual empathy and a sense of togetherness. However, certain strategies can help maintain empathy in a confrontational situation. One important consideration is picking the right time and place.

Choose the Right Time and Place

Whenever my lover brings up something that is bothering her about our sex life, it inevitably is just after we have made love. Here I am, relaxed, holding her in my arms, thinking good thoughts, and she destroys the mood with some criticism. It's not that I don't want her to express her concerns, but her timing is terrible. The last thing I want to hear after lovemaking is that it could have been better. (Authors' files)

This man's dismay is obvious. His partner's decision to voice her concerns during the afterglow of lovemaking works against her purpose. He may feel vulnerable, and he clearly resents having his good mood following sex broken by the prospect of potentially difficult conversation. Of course, other couples may find this to be a time when they are exceedingly close to each other and, thus, a good atmosphere in which to air concerns.

Many people, like the woman in the previous example, do not choose the best time to confront their lovers. Rather, the time chooses them: They jump right in when the problem is uppermost in their minds. Although there are some benefits to dealing with an issue immediately, it is not always the best strategy. You may be feeling disappointed, resentful, or angry, and these negative emotions, when running full tide, can easily get in the way of constructive interaction. Avoid registering complaints when anger is at its peak.

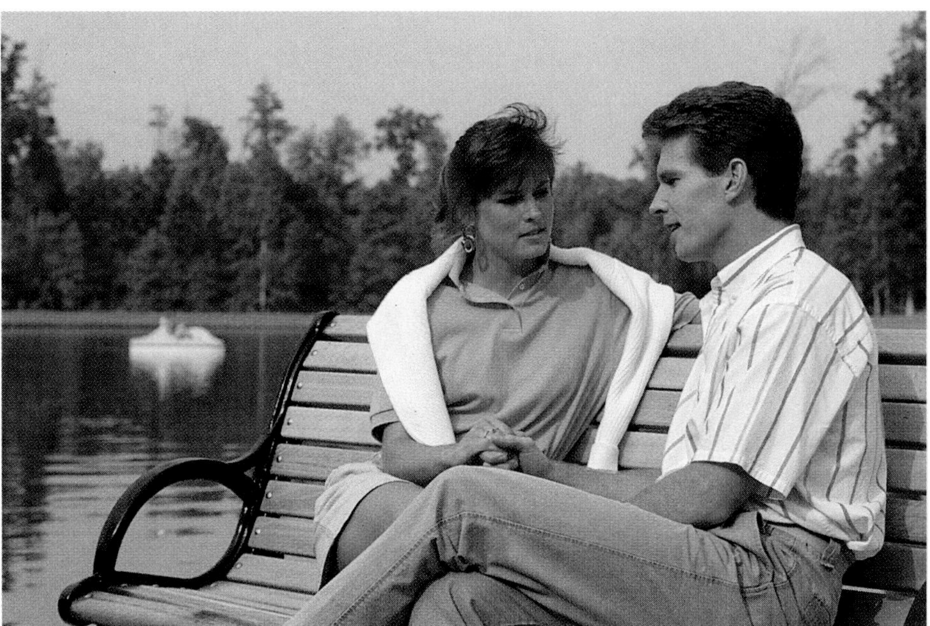

Choosing the right time and place to express sexual concerns can facilitate communication.

Although you may have every intention of making your criticism constructive, anger has a way of disrupting a search for solutions. Sometimes, however, it may be necessary to express anger; we consider how to do so appropriately at the end of this section.

In most cases, it is unwise to tackle a problem when either you or your partner has limited time or is tired, stressed, preoccupied, or under the influence of drugs or alcohol. Rather, try to select an interval when you have plenty of time and are both relaxed and feeling close to each other.

A pragmatic approach to timing is to simply ask your lover, "I really value our sexual relationship, but there are some concerns I would like to talk over with you. Is this a good time, or would you rather we talk later?" Be prepared for some anxiety-induced stalling. If your partner is hesitant to talk now, support his or her right to pick another time or place. However, it is important to agree on a time, particularly if you sense your partner might prefer to let the matter go.

Choosing the right place for expressing sexual concerns can be as important as timing. Some people may find that sitting around the kitchen table while sharing a pot of coffee is a more comfortable setting than the place where they make love, whereas others might prefer the familiarity of their bed. A walk through a park or a quiet drive in the country, far removed from the potential interferences of a busy lifestyle, may prove best for you. Try to sense your partner's needs. When and where is she or he most likely to be receptive to your requests for change?

Picking the right time and place to deliver criticism does not ensure a harmonious outcome, but it certainly improves the prospects of your partner responding favorably to your message. Using some other constructive strategies can also increase the likelihood of beneficial interaction. One of these is to combine criticism with praise.

Temper Criticism with Praise

The strategy of tempering criticism with praise is based largely on common sense. All of us tend to respond well to compliments, whereas harsh criticism alone is difficult to accept. The gentler approach of combining the two is a good way to reduce the negative impact of a complaint. It also gives your partner a broader perspective from which to evaluate the criticism, reducing the likelihood that he or she will respond in a defensive or angry manner. Consider how you might react differently to the following criticisms depending on whether or not they are accompanied by praise:

CRITICISM ALONE	CRITICISM WITH PRAISE
1. When we make love, you seem so inhibited.	1. I like it when you respond to me while we make love. I think it could be even better if you would take the initiative sometimes. Does this seem like a reasonable request?
2. I am really getting tired of your turning off the lights every time we make love.	2. I enjoy hearing and feeling you react when we make love. I also want to watch you respond. How would you feel about leaving the lights on sometimes?
3. I think our lovemaking is much too infrequent. It almost seems like sex is not as important to you as it is to me.	3. I love having sex with you, and it has been bothering me that we don't seem to have as much time for it recently. What do you think about this?

Sadly, just about all of us have been on the receiving end of criticisms such as those in the left column. Common reactions are anger, humiliation, anxiety, and resentment. Although some people may respond to such harsh complaints with a resolve to make things better, it is more likely that this will not occur. On the other hand, affirmative criticism, such as the examples in the right column, is more likely to encourage efforts to change.

There is a good deal of wisdom in the saying "People are usually more motivated to make a good thing better than to make a bad thing good." This applies as much to sexual activity as to any other area of human interaction. One of us was once approached by a woman who complained that her husband was often too rough with her during love play. She was reluctant to discuss her concern with him, however, for fear that he would feel put down or angered. She also had mixed feelings about her husband's roughness—it was part of the unbridled enthusiasm with which he related to her sexually, a zestiness she very much enjoyed. On those rare occasions when he did take the time to be gentle with her, she was very pleased. Now, the problem: How could she tell him she didn't like his roughness, while at the same time assuring that he would maintain his enthusiasm and not feel angry or inept?

What she finally told him was essentially what she had expressed in seeking advice. Sometimes it was terrific when he was gentle. She loved being pursued with enthusiasm and vigor. It could be even better if he would include more gentleness in their lovemaking. Although he was somewhat surprised and dismayed that he had not been able to detect her needs without being told, her husband's response was quite positive. What do you suppose his reaction might have been had she coldly complained, "Do you have to be so rough when we make love?"

It is also a good idea to ask for feedback when delivering criticisms. Regardless of how much warmth and goodwill we put into this difficult process, there is always the possibility that our partners may become silent or change the subject. Asking them how they feel about our requests for change helps to reduce these prospects. (Note that in the previous list, all "Criticism with Praise" examples end with requests for feedback.)

Nurture Small Steps Toward Change

Complete behavioral changes rarely occur immediately following criticism—no matter how positively the criticism is stated. Rather, they must be patiently nurtured, with each small step along the way properly acknowledged with words of appreciation. In the example of the woman wanting more gentleness from her husband, it would have been unreasonable for her to assume that once she expressed her criticism, her partner would completely change his ways. In fact, what occurred was a noticeable but minimal effort to be less vigorous in the next sexual encounter. Soon the old patterns ingrained over many years took over again.

Backsliding is natural and predictable, and, as with other unwanted behaviors, responding to it requires tact. Have you ever heard the words "I see you didn't pay a bit of attention to what I said"? Such a negative reaction could easily cool your desire to follow through with change. It is far more encouraging and reassuring to be on the receiving end of a message such as the one delivered by the wife to her "trying to be more gentle" husband: "I really appreciate the time you took to be gentle when we made love. It means a great deal that you care about my needs." With such a caring and supportive reaction, few people are likely to stick to old, undesirable behaviors.

Avoid "Why" Questions

People frequently use "why" questions as thinly veiled efforts to criticize or attack their partners while avoiding full responsibility for what is said. Have you ever asked or been asked any of the following?

1. Why don't you make love to me more frequently?
2. Why don't you show more interest in me?
3. Why don't you get turned on by me anymore?
4. Why can't you be more loving toward me?
5. Why are you so lazy?

Such queries have no place in a loving relationship: They are hurtful and destructive. Rather than representing simple requests for information, they are typically used to convey hidden messages of anger that people are unwilling to communicate honestly. These are hit-and-run tactics that cause defensiveness and seldom induce positive changes.

Express Anger Appropriately

Earlier in this chapter, we noted that it is wise to avoid confronting our partners when anger is riding high. However, there will probably be times when you feel compelled to express angry feelings. If so, certain guiding principles may help defuse a potentially explosive situation.

Avoid focusing your anger on the character of your partner ("You are an insensitive person"). Instead, try directing your anger toward his or her behaviors ("When you don't listen to my concerns, I think they are unimportant to you and I feel angry"). At the same time, express appreciation for your partner as a person ("You are very important to me, and I don't like feeling this way"). This acknowledges that we can be angered by our partners' behaviors yet still feel loving toward them—an often overlooked but important truth.

Anger is probably best expressed with clear, honest "I" statements rather than with accusatory and potentially inflammatory "you" statements. Consider the following:

"YOU" STATEMENTS	"I" STATEMENTS
1. You don't give a damn about me.	1. I feel ignored.
2. You always blame me for our problems.	2. I don't like being blamed.
3. You make me upset.	3. I am upset.
4. You make me angry.	4. I am angry.
5. You don't love me.	5. I feel unloved.

"I" statements are self-revelations that express how we feel without placing blame or attacking our partners' character. In contrast, "you" statements frequently are interpreted as attacks on the other person's character or attempts to fix blame.

Limit Criticism to One Complaint per Discussion

Many of us are inclined to avoid confrontations with our partners. This understandable reluctance to deal with negative issues can result in an accumulation of unspoken complaints. Consequently, when we finally reach the point where we need to "say something or bust," it may be difficult to avoid unleashing a barrage of criticisms that includes everything on our current list of grievances. Such a response, though understandable, may only serve to magnify rather than resolve conflicts between lovers, as reflected in the following account:

My wife lets things eat on her without letting me know when I do something that she disapproves of. She remembers every imagined shortcoming and blows it way out of proportion. But I never learn about it until she has accumulated a long list of complaints. Then she hits me with all of them at once, dredging them up like weapons in her arsenal, all designed to make me feel like an insensitive creep. I sometimes hear about things that happened years ago. She wonders why I don't have anything to say when she is done haranguing me. But what do you say when somebody has just given you 10 or 20 reasons why your relationship with her is lousy? Which one do you respond to? And how can you avoid being angry when somebody rubs your face in all your shortcomings, real or imagined? (Authors' files)

You can reduce the likelihood of creating such a counterproductive situation in your own relationships by limiting your criticisms to one complaint per discussion. Even if you have a half-dozen complaints you want to talk about, it will probably serve your relationship better to pick one and relegate the remaining concerns to later conversations.

Receiving Criticism

Delivering complaints to a partner is difficult; likewise, receiving criticisms from someone you love can also be an emotionally rending experience. However, as we have already said, people involved in an intimate, loving relationship inevitably experience the need to register complaints on occasion. How you respond to such criticism may have a significant impact not only on your partner's inclination to openly share concerns in the future but also on the probability that the complaint will be resolved in a manner that strengthens rather than erodes the relationship.

Can you think of some strategies for responding to criticism? What strategies have been helpful in your own experience?

When your partner delivers a criticism, take a few moments to gather your thoughts. A few deep breaths is probably a much better initial response than blurting out, "Yeah, well what about the time that you . . . !" Ask yourself, "Is this person trying to give me some information that may be helpful?" In a loving relationship where mutual empathy prevails, perhaps you will be able to see some potential for positive consequences, even though you have just received a painful message. There are several ways you can respond to such a communication. We hope one or more of the following suggestions provides helpful guidelines in these circumstances.

Empathize with Your Partner and Paraphrase the Criticism

Many of us have had the experience of expressing concerns to people we care about, only to have them come back with a criticism of their own. Such a response will likely result in increased defensiveness, which may precipitate withdrawal or antagonistic confrontation. Furthermore, when people match criticism with a countercomplaint, it appears that they are not trying to understand and empathize with the concern. In contrast, paraphrasing your partner's criticism suggests that you are making an effort to understand and appreciate what he or she is experiencing. For example, saying to your partner, "It sounds like you have been frustrated with our lovemaking," will probably have a much more beneficial effect than a comment such as "Well, you're not such a hot lover either!"

Paraphrasing a partner's criticism does not mean that you agree with it. Rather, you are simply saying, "This is what I am hearing—do I understand correctly?" We can

Responding appropriately to criticism can help strengthen a relationship.

empathize with our lovers' concerns even if we have different thoughts and feelings about them. This type of positive response increases the likelihood that your partner will voice important concerns in the future.

Acknowledge a Criticism and Find Something to Agree With

Perhaps if you allow yourself to be open to a criticism, you will see that there is some basis for it. For example, suppose your partner feels angry about your busy schedule and criticizes you for not devoting more time to the relationship. Maybe you think he or she is overreacting or forgetting all the time you have spent together. However, you also know that there is some basis for this concern. It can be helpful to acknowledge this by saying something like "I can understand how you might feel neglected because I have been so preoccupied with my new job." Such constructive acknowledgment can occur even if you think the criticism is largely unjustified. By reacting in an accepting and supportive manner, you are conveying the message that you hear, understand, and appreciate the basis for your partner's concern.

Ask Clarifying Questions

In some cases, your partner may deliver a criticism in such a vague manner that further clarification is needed. If this happens, ask questions. For example, suppose your partner complains that you do not take enough time in your lovemaking. You might respond by asking, "Do you mean that we should spend more time touching before we have intercourse, or that I should wait longer before coming, or that you want me to hold you for a longer time after we have sex?"

Express Your Feelings

It can be helpful to talk about your feelings in regard to the criticism rather than letting these emotions dictate your response. For instance, your partner's criticism may cause you to feel angry, hurt, or dejected. It is probably better to verbalize these emotional reactions by expressing feeling statements rather than by acting them out. Responses such as yelling, stomping out of the room, crying, or retreating into a shell of despair are unlikely to lead to productive dialogue. Instead, it may help to tell your partner, "That was really hard to hear, and I am hurt," or "Right now I feel angry, so I need to stop and take a few breaths and figure out what I am thinking and feeling."

Focus on Future Changes You Can Make

An excellent closure to receiving criticism is to focus on what the two of you can do to make things better. Perhaps this is the time to say, "My new job is really important to me, but our relationship is much more important. Maybe we can set aside some specific times each week where we both agree not to let outside concerns intrude on our time together." Sometimes people agree to make things better but neglect to discuss concrete changes that will resolve the issue that triggered the complaint. Taking the time to identify and agree on specific future changes is a crucial step in resolving the basis for the complaint.

Saying No

Many of us have difficulty saying no to others. Our discomfort in communicating this direct message is perhaps most pronounced when it applies to intimate areas of relationships. This is reflected in the following anecdotes:

> Sometimes my partner wants to be sexual when I only want to be close. The trouble is, I can't say no. I am afraid she would be hurt or angry. Unfortunately, I am the one who ends up angry at myself for not being able to express my true feelings. Under these circumstances, sex isn't very good. (Authors' files)

> It is so hard to say no to a man who suggests having sex at the end of a date. This is especially true if we have had a good time together. You never know if they are going to get that hangdog hurt look or become belligerent and angry. (Authors' files)

These accounts reveal some of the common concerns that may inhibit us from saying no. We may believe that a rejection will hurt the other person or perhaps cause him or her to become angry or even combative. Laboring under such fears, it may seem less stressful to simply comply. Unfortunately, this reluctant acquiescence can create such negative feelings that the resulting shared activity may be less than pleasurable for both ourselves and our partners.

Many of us have not learned that it is okay to say no. Perhaps more important, we may not have learned strategies for doing so. In the following section, we consider some potentially useful ways to say no.

A Three-Step Approach to Saying No

Many people have found it helpful to have a definite plan or strategy in mind for saying no to invitations for intimate involvements. This can help prevent being caught off guard and not knowing how to handle a potentially unpleasant interaction with tact. One approach that you may find helpful involves three distinct steps, or phases, outlined as follows:

1. Express appreciation for the invitation ("Thanks for thinking of me," "It's nice to know that you like me enough to invite me," and so forth). Perhaps you may also wish to validate the other person ("You are a good person").
2. Say no in a clear, unequivocal fashion ("I would prefer not to make love, go dancing, get involved in a dating relationship," and so forth).
3. Offer an alternative, if applicable ("However, I would like to have lunch sometime, give you a back rub," and so forth).

The positive aspects of this approach are readily apparent. We first indicate our appreciation for the expressed interest in us. At the same time, we clearly state our wish not to comply with the request. Finally, we end the exchange on a positive note by offering an alternative. Of course, this last step will not always be an option (for example, when turning down a request from someone with whom we wish to have no further social contact). Between lovers, however, there is often a mutually acceptable alternative.

Avoid Sending Mixed Messages

Saying no in clear, unmistakable language is essential to the success of the strategy just outlined. Nevertheless, many of us are probably guilty, at least sometimes, of sending mixed messages about our sexual and other intimate needs. Consider, for example, someone who responds positively to a partner's request for sexual intimacy but then spends an inordinate amount of time soaking in the bathtub while a patiently waiting partner falls asleep, or the person who expresses a desire to have sex but instead becomes engrossed in a late-night talk show. Both of these people are sending mixed messages that may reflect some of their own ambivalence about engaging in sexual relations.

The effect of such mixed messages is usually less than desirable. The recipient is often confused about the other person's intent. He or she may feel uncertain or even inadequate ("Why can't I figure out what you really want?"), and these feelings may evolve into anger ("Why do I have to guess?") or withdrawal. These reactions are understandable in such circumstances. Faced with contradictory messages, most of us are unsure what to do—act on the first message or on the second one? Consider the following:

> It really bothers me when my partner says we will make love when I get home from night school and then she is too busy studying to take a break. Even though it was her suggestion, sometimes I wonder if she had any intention to make love. (Authors' files)

All of us may benefit from taking stock from time to time to see if we send mixed messages. Try looking for inconsistencies between your verbal messages and your subsequent actions. Does your partner seem confused or uncertain when interacting with you? If you do spot yourself sending a double message, decide which one you really mean, then state it in unmistakable language. It may also be helpful to consider why you sent contradictory messages.

If you are on the receiving end of such contradictory messages, it may help to discuss your confusion and ask your partner which one of the two messages you should act on. Perhaps your partner will recognize your dilemma and act to resolve it. If she or he seems unwilling to acknowledge the inconsistency, it may help to express your feelings of discomfort and confusion as the recipient of the two conflicting messages.

Nonverbal Sexual Communication

Sexual communication is not confined exclusively to words. Sometimes a touch or smile may convey a great deal of information. Tone of voice, gestures, facial expression, and changes in breathing may also be important elements of the communication process:

> I can usually tell when my sweetheart is in the mood for some loving. There is a certain softness about her face and a huskiness that comes into her voice. She touches me more with her hands, and it almost seems like she presents her body as more open and vulnerable. There is some truth to all this stuff about body language. She rarely needs to verbalize her desire for sex because I usually get the message. (Authors' files)

> Sometimes when I want my lover to touch me in a certain place, I move that portion of my body closer to his hands or just shift my position to make the area more accessible. Occasionally, I will guide his hand with mine to show him just what kind of stimulation I want. (Authors' files)

These examples reveal some of the varieties of nonverbal communication that may have particular significance for our sexuality. In this section, we direct our attention to four important components of nonverbal sexual communication: facial expression, interpersonal distance, touching, and sounds.

Facial expressions of emotion are often a powerful component of nonverbal communication.

Facial Expression

Facial expressions often communicate the feelings a person is experiencing. Although there is certainly variation in people's expressions, most of us have learned to identify particular emotions from facial expressions with a high degree of accuracy. The rapport and intimacy between lovers may further increase the reliability of this yardstick.

Looking at our lovers' faces during sexual activity often gives us a quick reading of their level of pleasure. If we see a look of complete rapture, we are likely to continue providing the same type of stimulation. However, if the look conveys something less than ecstasy, we may decide to try something different or perhaps encourage our partners to provide some verbal direction.

Facial expressions can also provide helpful cues when talking over sexual concerns with a partner. If a lover's face reflects anger, anxiety, or some other disruptive emotion, it might be wise to deal with this emotion immediately ("I can tell you are angry. Can we talk about it?"). Conversely, a face that shows interest, enthusiasm, or appreciation can encourage us to continue expressing a particular feeling or concern. It is also a good idea to be aware of the nonverbal messages you are giving when your partner is sharing thoughts or feelings with you. Sometimes we may inadvertently shut down potentially helpful dialogue by tightening our jaws or frowning at an inappropriate time.

Interpersonal Distance

Social psychologists and communication specialists have much to say about *personal space*. In essence, this idea suggests that we tend to maintain differing degrees of interpersonal distance between ourselves and the people we have contact with, depending on the nature of our relationships (actual or desired). The intimate space to which we admit close friends and lovers restricts contact much less than the distance we maintain between ourselves and people we do not know or like.

It is instructive to watch what takes place between people meeting each other at places like singles bars and parties. Consider the following:

> When I meet people I am attracted to, I pay close attention to body language. If they seem uneasy or retreat when I move closer, it is a pretty good indication that my interest is not reciprocated. (Authors' files)

Decreased interpersonal space often indicates attraction and perhaps a desire for more intimate contact.

When someone attempts to decrease interpersonal distance, it is generally interpreted as a nonverbal sign that she or he is attracted to the other person or would like more intimate contact. Conversely, if someone withdraws when another person moves close, this action can usually be interpreted as a lack of interest or a gentle kind of rejection.

Lovers, whose interpersonal distance is generally at a minimum, can use these cues to signal desire for intimacy. When your lover moves in close, making his or her body available for your touches or caresses, the message of wanting physical intimacy (not necessarily sex) is quite apparent. Similarly, when he or she curls up on the other side of the bed, it may be a way of saying, "Please don't come too close tonight."

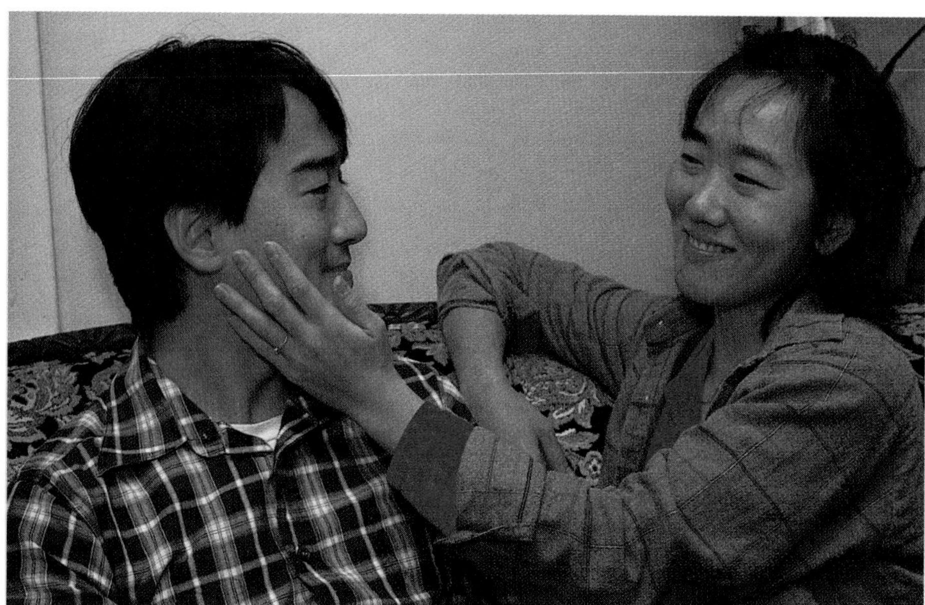

Touch is a powerful vehicle for nonverbal sexual communication.

Touching

Touch is a powerful vehicle for nonverbal sexual communication between lovers. Hands can convey special messages. For example, increasing or decreasing the tempo with which you rub your lover's back may signal a desire for more or less intense reciprocated stimulation. Reaching out and drawing your partner closer can indicate your readiness for more intimate contact. In the early stages of a developing relationship, touch can also be used to express a desire to become closer.

When I meet a man and find myself attracted to him, I use touch to convey my feelings. Touching him on the arm to emphasize a point or letting my fingers lightly graze across his hand on the table generally lets my feelings be known. (Authors' files)

Touch can also defuse anger and heal rifts between temporarily alienated lovers. As one man states,

I have found that a gentle touch, lovingly administered to my partner, does wonders in bringing us back together after we have exchanged angry words. Touching her is my way of reestablishing connection. (Authors' files)

Sounds

Many people, though by no means all, like making and hearing sounds during sexual activity. Some individuals find increased breathing, moans, groans, and orgasmic cries to be extremely arousing. Also, such sounds can be helpful indicators of how a partner is responding to lovemaking. Some people find the absence of sounds to be quite frustrating:

My man rarely makes any sounds when we make love. I find this to be very disturbing. In fact, it is a real turn-off. Sometimes I can't even tell if he has come or not. If he wasn't moving, I'd think I was making love to a corpse. (Authors' files)

Some people make a conscious effort to suppress spontaneous noises during sex play. In doing so, they deprive themselves of a potentially powerful and enjoyable form of nonverbal sexual communication. Not uncommonly, their deliberate silence also hinders their partners' sexual arousal, as the foregoing example illustrates.

In this section, we have acknowledged that not everything has to be spoken between lovers. However, facial expression, interpersonal distance, touching, and sounds cannot convey all of our complex needs and emotions in a close relationship; words are needed, too. One writer observes, "As a supplement to verbal communication, acts and gestures are fine. As a substitute, they don't quite make it" (Zilbergeld, 1978, p. 158).

Impasses

Candid communication between caring, supportive partners often leads to changes that are mutually gratifying. However, even an ample supply of openness, candor, support, and understanding cannot assure a meeting of the minds on all issues: Couples may reach impasses. Your partner may simply not want to try a new coital position. Or your suggestion to incorporate a vibrator into shared sex play may be just a bit too threatening. Perhaps the two of you cannot agree on the question of other relationships.

What can you do when communication results in a standoff? Continued discussion may be helpful. However, it is self-deceiving to assume that talk, even the most open and compassionate, will always lead to desired changes.

Sometimes it is useful to try to put yourself in your partner's shoes. Try to see things from the other person's perspective. If you have some difficulty with this, ask your partner for help ("I am having some trouble seeing this from your point of view—can you help me out?"). If you can understand his or her concern, by all means say so. Acknowledging the reasonableness of the other's viewpoint is a process called **validating** (Gottman et al., 1976). Validating does not mean that you give up your own position. You are not saying, "I am wrong and you are right." You are simply admitting that another point of view may make sense, given some assumptions that you may not share with your partner. Sometimes this process of trying to see the validity of another viewpoint may lead to new perspectives that can help end the deadlock. However, if you continue to disagree after this effort, it may be easier to accept the idea that you can have legitimate but different opinions.

Validating
The process of indicating that a partner's point of view is reasonable, given some assumptions that one may not share with one's partner.

At a time of impasse, it may also be beneficial for a couple to take a break from each other for a while. Sometimes forced continuation of a discussion, particularly when emotions are strong, is counterproductive. Scheduling another time to talk can be a good tactic. Perhaps in the future, after each partner has had the opportunity to privately consider the other's feelings, it may be possible to readdress the issue more successfully.

Sometimes people cannot or will not change, often for justifiable reasons. Certainly, all of us cherish our right to refuse to do something we consider objectionable. Granting the same right to someone close to us is an important ingredient in a relationship characterized by mutual respect.

Failure to reach a solution to an impasse is not necessarily cause for despair. At least the couple has openly discussed a sensitive issue. Possibly, they have also increased their understanding of each other and the level of intimacy between them. In the event that unresolved impasses threaten to erode a relationship, professional counseling may be desirable. (Chapter 16 includes guidelines for selecting a counselor.)

Summary

THE IMPORTANCE OF COMMUNICATION

Sexual communication often contributes positively to the contentment and enjoyment of a sexual relationship; infrequent or ineffective sexual communication is a common reason for people feeling dissatisfied with their sex lives.

An excellent basis for effective sexual communication is mutual empathy—the underlying knowledge that each partner in a relationship cares for the other and knows that care is reciprocated.

Childhood training, which often creates a sense of discomfort with sexual matters, may contribute to later difficulties in engaging in sexual communication.

Our language is characterized by a conspicuous absence of an effective, comfortable sexual vocabulary.

Differences in women's and men's styles of relating to other people can hinder communication. Men often use language to convey advice and information and to maintain a one-up status. In contrast, women typically use language to promote closeness and to achieve and share intimacy.

Some people object to sexual communication on the grounds that it disrupts spontaneity or that it may place one in a position of increased vulnerability to judgment, criticism, or rejection.

TALKING: GETTING STARTED

It is often difficult to start talking about sex. Some suggestions for doing this include talking about talking; reading about sex and discussing the material; and sharing sexual histories.

LISTENING AND FEEDBACK

Communication is most successful with an active listener and an effective communicator.

The listener may facilitate communication by maintaining eye contact with the speaker; providing some feedback or reaction to the message; expressing appreciation for communication efforts; maintaining an attitude of unconditional positive regard; and using paraphrasing effectively.

DISCOVERING YOUR PARTNER'S NEEDS

Efforts to communicate with sexual partners are often hindered by yes-or-no questions, which encourage limited replies. Effective alternatives include open-ended and either/or questions.

Self-disclosure may make it easier for a partner to communicate her or his own needs. Sharing fantasies, beginning with mild desires, may be a particularly valuable kind of exchange.

Comparing notes about sexual needs, preferences, and reactions, either before or after a sexual encounter, may be beneficial.

Giving permission encourages partners to share feelings freely.

LEARNING TO MAKE REQUESTS

Making requests is facilitated by (a) taking responsibility for one's own pleasure, (b) making sure requests are specific, and (c) using "I" language.

GIVING AND RECEIVING CRITICISM

Be aware of your motives for criticizing. Criticism that aims to hurt or blame a partner is likely to be destructive.

It is important to select the right time and place for expressing sexual concerns. Avoid registering complaints when anger is at its peak.

Criticism is generally most effective when tempered with praise. People are usually more motivated to make changes when they are praised for their strengths as well as criticized for things that need improvement.

It is beneficial to reward each small step in the process of changing undesirable behavior.

"Why" questions that blame a partner do not further the process of registering constructive criticisms.

It is wise to direct anger toward behavior rather than toward a person's character. Anger is probably best expressed with clear, honest "I" statements, rather than accusatory "you" statements.

Relationships are better served when criticisms are limited to one complaint per discussion.

Paraphrasing a partner's criticisms and acknowledging an understanding of the basis for his or her concerns can help establish a sense of empathy and lead to constructive dialogue.

It can be helpful to ask clarifying questions when criticisms are vague. Calmly verbalizing the feelings that are aroused when one is criticized often avoids nonproductive, heated exchanges.

An excellent closure to receiving criticism is to focus on what can be done to rectify the problematic issue in a relationship.

SAYING NO

One three-step strategy for saying no to invitations for intimate involvements includes expressing appreciation for the invitation; saying no in a clear, unequivocal fashion; and offering an alternative, if applicable.

To avoid sending mixed messages, occasionally check for inconsistencies between verbal messages and subsequent actions. Recipients of mixed messages might find it helpful to express their confusion and to ask which of the conflicting messages they are expected to act on.

NONVERBAL SEXUAL COMMUNICATION

Sexual communication is not confined to words alone. Facial expressions, interpersonal distance, touching, and sounds also convey a great deal of information.

The value of nonverbal communication lies primarily in its ability to supplement—not to replace—verbal exchanges.

IMPASSES

Sexual communication does not always lead to solutions. Seeing things from a partner's perspective may help when deadlocks occur, and it may also be helpful to suspend the discussion temporarily so that each person can privately consider the other's point of view. An unresolved impasse does not necessarily threaten a relationship; if it does, counseling may be desirable.

Thought Provokers

1. Assume that you are in the early stages of a developing relationship and anticipate making love the next time you are with your new companion. In your opinion, which technique(s) described in this chapter might be most helpful in contributing to satisfying sexual relations? Which suggestion(s) would be the most difficult for you to implement? Explain.
2. Some people think that combining praise with criticism is a manipulative technique, designed to coerce behavior changes by tempering requests with insincere praise. Do you agree with this view? Why or why not?
3. What do you think about sharing sexual fantasies as a way for intimate partners to discover each other's needs?

Suggested Readings

Brenton, Myron (1973). *Sex Talk.* Greenwich, CT: Fawcett Publications. This book provides some good ideas for improving sexual communication between partners and between parents and children.

Goodman, Gerald; and Esterly, Glenn (1988). *The Talk Book: The Intimate Science of Communication in Close Relationships.* Emmaus, PA: Rodale Press. An excellent resource for individuals seeking realistic and practical guidelines for strengthening relationships by learning to communicate more effectively.

Gottman, John (1994). *Why Marriages Succeed or Fail.* New York: Simon & Schuster. This informative book, based on 20 years of research on communication within relationships, provides excellent suggestions for enhancing couple communication.

McKay, Matthew; Davis, Martha; and Fanning, Patrick (1983). *Messages: The Communication Book.* Oakland, CA: New Harbinger Publications. This practical, skills-oriented book addresses such topics as sexual communication, conflict resolution, and family communication.

Tannen, Deborah (1990). *You Just Don't Understand: Women and Men in Conversation.* New York: Morrow. (Also available in paperback from Ballantine, 1991.) This highly readable, best-selling book uses vivid examples to outline the distinctly different conversational styles of males and females, the origins of these differing styles, and how such divergent communication modes lead to difficulties between the sexes. Throughout this gem of a book, the reader will discover much to help improve his or her communication with the other sex.

Web Resources

WWW.

Sexual Communication
ub-counseling.buffalo.edu/Relationships/Communication/sexcom.html
This site features a short, helpful pamphlet concerning sexual communication, produced by the Counseling Center at SUNY-Buffalo.

Psychological Self-Help
www.cmhc.com/psyhelp/
An online self-help book by Clayton Tucker-Ladd is available at this Web site. Chapter 10 deals with Dating, Love, Marriage, and Sex, and offers interesting analysis and strategies.

The Human Awareness Institute
www.hai.org/
The Human Awareness Institute offers a variety of workshops to help couples communicate more effectively and improve relationships. Information on these workshops is available at this site.

9

Sexual Behaviors

Celibacy

What are some of the benefits and disadvantages of celibacy?

Erotic Dreams and Fantasy

What are some of the functions of sexual fantasy?

How do male and female sexual fantasies differ?

Masturbation

How have attitudes about masturbation changed from the 1800s?

Sexual Expression: The Importance of Context and Meaning

What characteristics of sexual behavior lead it in positive or negative directions?

Kissing and Touching

Why is touching important?

Oral–Genital Stimulation

What are the technical terms for oral stimulation of a woman and of a man?

How common is oral–genital stimulation?

Anal Stimulation

How common is anal intercourse, and what are important precautions regarding its practice?

Gay and Lesbian Sexual Expression

Do you think gay male, lesbian, or heterosexual couples have sex more frequently?

Coitus and Coital Positions

What are some of the different intercourse positions?

What is an important element of Tantric sex?

My sexuality has had many different dimensions during my life. My childhood masturbation was a secret desire and guilt that I never did admit to the priest in the confessional. "Playing doctor" was intriguing and exciting in its "naughtiness." The discovery of my sexual self in the hours of hot kissing and petting of teenage and early college years was made meaningful in the arms of a young soul-mate love. My first intercourse experience was a profound physical and emotional experience; thirty years later the memory still brings me deep pleasure. As a young adult in the 1960s and 1970s my sexual expression alternated between periods of experimental, recreational sex and celibacy. The emergence of feminist thought brought the meaning of my sexuality beyond the personal to the political. Within marriage the comforts and challenges of commitment, combining sex with an intense desire to become pregnant, the primal experience of pregnancy, childbirth, and nursing greatly expanded the parameters of my sexuality. Now, balancing family, career, personal interests, and regular hair appointments, my sexuality is a quiet hum in the background. I'm looking forward to retirement and time for more than coffee and a kiss in the morning. (Authors' files)

People express their sexuality in many ways. The emotions and meanings that they attach to sexual behavior also vary widely. In this chapter, we define and explain some varieties of sexual expression, looking first at individuals and then explore meaning and context in sexual behavior before discussing couples' sexual behavior. We begin with a discussion of celibacy.

Celibacy

A physically mature person who does not engage in sexual behavior is said to be *celibate.* Celibacy, or abstinence, can be a viable option until the context for a sexual relationship is appropriate and positive for a given individual. Celibacy may not commonly be thought of as a form of sexual expression. However, when it represents a conscious decision not to engage in sexual behavior, this decision in itself is an expression of one's sexuality. There are two degrees of celibacy. In **complete celibacy,** a person neither masturbates nor has sexual contact with another person. In **partial celibacy,** the individual engages in masturbation but does not have interpersonal sexual contact.

Complete celibacy
Engaging neither in masturbation nor in interpersonal sexual contact.

Partial celibacy
Not engaging in interpersonal sexual contact but continuing to engage in masturbation.

Celibacy is most commonly thought of in connection with religious devotion: Joining a religious order or becoming a priest or nun often includes a vow of celibacy. The ideal of religious celibacy is to transform sexual energy into service to humanity. Mother Teresa of Calcutta and Mahatma Gandhi of India exemplified this ideal and are admired for their moral leadership (Sipe, 1990).

Individuals choose celibacy for a variety of reasons other than religious devotion. What do you think some of these reasons might be?

Celibacy, especially in the form of abstinence until marriage, has received more public attention in the 1990s. The media reflected this shift with characters on *Beverly Hills 90210, Step by Step,* and the character Cher in *Clueless,* who proudly proclaim their virginity. Abstinence has been promoted by school and church sex-education programs, community organizations, and groups such as Athletes for Abstinence (Eisenman, 1994).

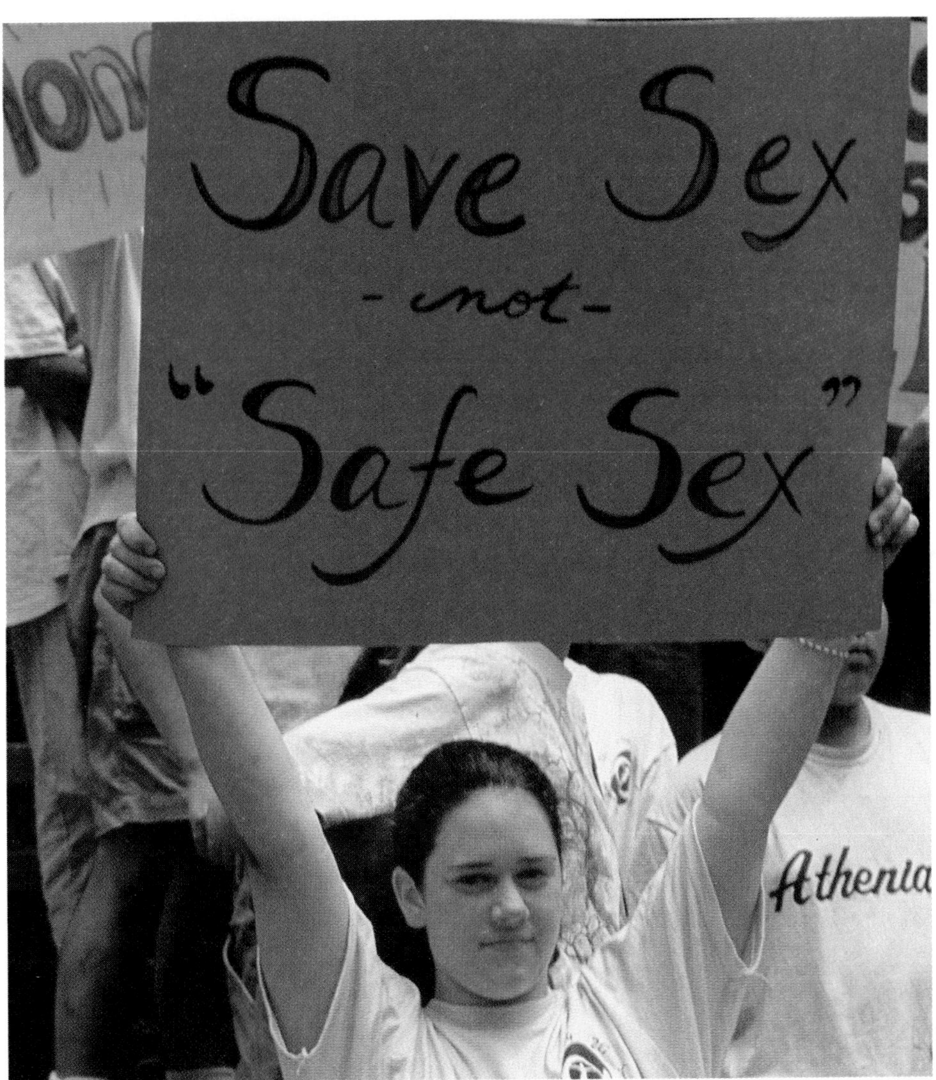

Young adults who pledged to wait until marriage to have intercourse marched together in Washington, D.C.

The founder of Athletes for Abstinence, former L.A. Laker basketball star A. C. Green, wanted to give teens the message to be proud of being virgins and of protecting their health and their future by abstaining from intercourse. In 1993 the Southern Baptist convention began the "True Love Waits" campaign. Participating teens sign a pledge of chastity until marriage. Other denominations and churches across the United States have joined the campaign (Werner, 1997).

Many factors may lead a person to be celibate. Some people choose to be celibate until marriage because of religious or moral beliefs. Others maintain celibacy until their personal criteria for a good sexual relationship have been met. Some may choose celibacy because they have experienced confusion or disappointment in past sexual relationships, and they want to spend some time establishing new relationships without the complicating factor of sexual interaction (Elliott & Brantley, 1997). As a 28-year-old man explains,

> There was a period not too long ago in my life where I had been abstinent for about four years. Part of the reason for me was that it was my preferred method of birth control. I had been on both sides of the cheating fence and began to realize that sex wasn't just something that I wanted to take, or could take, lightly. The feelings that can be created out of a physical relationship are simply too powerful to toy around with. I was terribly afraid of being hurt again, or of perhaps hurting someone else, so I chose not to get close to anyone. (Authors' files)

At times a person can be so caught up in other aspects of life that sex is simply not a priority. Health considerations such as concerns about pregnancy or sexually transmitted diseases also may prompt a decision not to have sexual intercourse.

Celibacy can also be an important aspect of treatment for individuals who are newly recovering from alcohol or drug dependency. Substance abusers often use drugs or alcohol in the effort to decrease their feelings of anxiety, and the anxiety created by involvement in sexual relationships can precipitate a return to drug or alcohol abuse. A period of celibacy affords individuals an opportunity to learn about their sexual feelings and desires without acting on them. Celibacy during recovery also lets people develop the skills to handle the anxiety involved in sexual relationships without turning to alcohol or drugs (Pinhas, 1989).

Some people find that a period of celibacy can be quite rewarding. There is often a refocusing on oneself during such a period: exploring self-pleasuring; learning to value one's aloneness, autonomy, and privacy; or giving priority to work and nonsexual relationship commitments. Friendships may gain new dimensions and fulfillment.

Many people do not choose to be celibate, however, for despite its rewards for some individuals, celibacy also has a number of disadvantages. These can include lack of physical affection and loneliness for sexual intimacy. Coming out of a period of celibacy may be difficult, too, for reestablishing sexual relationships can be awkward and frightening. It is interesting that of the many options for sexual expression, celibacy is one alternative that people sometimes have considerable trouble understanding. However, celibacy can be a personally valuable choice.

Erotic Dreams and Fantasy

Some forms of sexual experience occur within a person's mind, with or without accompanying sexual behavior. These are erotic dreams and fantasies—mental experiences that may arise from our imagination or life experience or may be stimulated by books, drawings, photographs, or movies.

Erotic Dreams

Erotic dreams and occasionally orgasm may occur during sleep without a person's conscious direction. Like other dreams, the content of erotic dreams can be logical or quite nonsensical. Explicit sexual expression in dreams varies widely, from common sexual activities to behaviors considered to be taboo. Both erotic dreams and waking fantasy can be ways to express and explore dimensions of experiences, feelings, and desires.

Nocturnal orgasm Involuntary orgasm during sleep.

Almost all the males and two-thirds of the females in Kinsey's research populations reported experiencing erotic dreams. A person may waken during such a dream and notice signs of sexual arousal: erection, vaginal lubrication, or pelvic movements. Orgasm can also occur during sleep and is called **nocturnal orgasm.** When orgasm occurs, males usually notice the ejaculate—hence the term "wet dream." Women also experience orgasm during sleep (Renshaw, 1991), but female orgasm may be more difficult to determine, due to the absence of such visible evidence. In one study of college women, 30% reported having experienced nocturnal orgasm. Another 30% had never heard of nocturnal orgasm. Women who had a higher frequency of intercourse and of orgasm with masturbation were more likely to experience and be aware of orgasms during sleep (Wells, 1983).

Erotic Fantasy

Erotic waking fantasies commonly occur during daydreams, masturbation, or sexual encounters with a partner. A review of the research found that about 95% of men and women reported having had sexual fantasies (Leitenberg & Henning, 1995). Greater sexual experience may contribute to increased sexual fantasizing. College students with more sexual experience report more frequent use of sexual fantasies than do those with less experience, and students with liberal sexual attitudes had longer, more explicit fantasies (Gold & Chick, 1988).

The content of sexual fantasies varies greatly and can range from vague, romantic images to graphic representations of imagined or actual past experiences. Fantasy content of homosexuals and heterosexuals is more similar than different, except for the sex of the imagined partner (Leitenberg & Henning, 1995). Research on fantasy content reveals this diversity, as shown in Tables 9.1 and 9.2. The tables provide an idea of the range of content and suggest some male and female differences, which we discuss later in this section.

Table 9.1 Male and Female Sexual Fantasies During Masturbation

Fantasy Content	*Men (%)*	*Women (%)*
Intercourse with loved one	75	70
Intercourse with strangers	47	21
Sex with more than one person of the other sex	33	18
Sexual activities that would not be done in reality	19	28
Forcing someone to have sex	13	3
Being forced to have sex	10	19
Homosexual activity	7	11

Source: Hunt, 1974.

Table 9.2 Stated Purpose of Fantasies During Intercourse

Purpose	*Men (%)*	*Women (%)*
To facilitate sexual arousal	38	46
To imagine activities that my partner and I do not engage in	18	13
To increase my partner's attractiveness	30	22
To relieve boredom	3	5
Uncertain	10	15

Source: Sue, 1979.

An in-depth study of women, age 19 to 66, found six common categories of roles women played in their private fantasies. The "Pretty Maiden" is the passive woman of another's desire. She is so powerfully attractive, she is irresistible, a plot commonly found in romance novels. The "Victim" is the object of sexual humiliation or violence and can indulge her curiosity about dangerous sex without actual danger. The "Wild Woman" is the pursuer and initiator of sexual pleasure on her terms. She imagines daring situations such as multiple partners or public places, to flaunt sexual convention. Singer/actress Madonna's earlier blatant sexual strutting is a good example. The "Dominatrix" gets her arousal from imposing power over another, unlike the "Beloved," who fantasizes intimacy with a cherished soul-mate partner of equal power and status. In the first five roles, the women are part of the action, whereas the "Voyeur" finds arousal in imagining watching others engage in sex. Erotic tension is heightened if her fantasy includes the risk of being caught watching (Maltz & Boss, 1996).

Functions of Fantasy

Erotic fantasies serve many functions, some of which are listed in Table 9.2. First, they can be a source of pleasure and arousal. Erotic thoughts typically serve to enhance sexual arousal during masturbation or partner sexual activities. Both male and female college students reported that the most common purpose of their fantasies during intercourse was to facilitate sexual arousal (Sue, 1979). The following two accounts, the first by a woman and the second by a man, show how fantasy can amplify pleasurable physical and emotional feelings:

> When my partner and I make love, I let my mind leave all other thoughts behind and totally experience and feel what is happening. All aromas become much more noticeable and pleasurable. The warmth increases, and I imagine my lover and me suspended in mist upon a bed of clouds. Our bodies come close together in my mind as arousal increases, and at the moment of orgasm it is as if we were mentally and physically one. I caress my lover's body, but it is as if it were part of my own. (Authors' files)

The fantasy that recurs most when I am making love is a visualization of being on an isolated tropical beach. The warm sun is baking our bodies golden brown. The rhythmic pounding of the waves eliminates all tension and worries. My partner and I are one. (Authors' files)

Sexual fantasies may also help overcome anxiety and facilitate sexual functioning or compensate for a somewhat negative sexual situation. Fantasies can be another way to mentally rehearse and anticipate new sexual experiences. Imagining seductive glances, that first kiss, or a novel intercourse position may help a person more comfortably implement these activities (Leitenberg & Henning, 1995).

Some sexual fantasies allow for tolerable expression of "forbidden wishes." The fact that a sexual activity in a fantasy is "forbidden" may make it more exciting. People in sexually exclusive relationships can fantasize about past lovers or others to whom they feel attracted, even though they are committed to a single sexual partner. In a fantasy, a person can experience lustful group sex, cross-orientation sexual liaisons, brief sexual encounters with strangers, erotic relations with friends and acquaintances, incestuous experiences, sex with animals, or any other sexual activity they can imagine, without actually engaging in them. The following are examples of the variety of "forbidden wishes" fantasies. A woman's masturbation fantasy:

I fantasize about being seduced by another woman. Although I've never had an affair with another woman, it really makes me sexually excited to think of oral sex being performed on me or vice versa. (Authors' files)

A man's masturbation fantasy reflects one study's findings that one in three men have same-sex fantasies (Ellis et al., 1987):

I usually think of some woman (no one that I know), blond, beautiful, lowering herself onto me, letting me eat her out in a "69." Oftentimes, a strong and bearded man is involved and gives me oral stimulation at the same time that the woman is kissing me or letting me eat her. (Authors' files)

Another function of erotic fantasy can be to provide relief from gender-role expectations (Pinhas, 1985). In fact, in women a degree of gender-role reversal may contribute to increased fantasizing. One study found that college women with more traditional feminine attitudes report fewer sexual fantasies than women who are more independent and hold more liberal views of women's roles (Brown & Hart, 1977). Women's fantasies of being the sexual aggressor and men's fantasies of being forced to have sex can offer alternatives to stereotypical roles. Three percent of women in Hunt's (1974) study and 16% in Sue's (1979) study reported fantasizing about forcing others to have sex. For women, this may be an unaccustomed role of feeling powerful. Conversely, 10% of men in Hunt's study and 21% in Sue's study reported fantasizing about being forced to have sex. In her first book about male sexual fantasy, Nancy Friday reported that one of the major themes is men's abdication of control in favor of passivity:

> It may seem lusty and dashing always to be the one who chooses the woman, who decides when, where, and how the bedroom scene will be played. But isn't her role safer? The man is like someone who has suggested a new restaurant to friends. What if it doesn't live up to expectations he has aroused? The macho stance makes the male the star performer. The hidden cost is that it puts the woman in the role of critic. (1980, p. 274)

Although fantasies of being forced to have sex provide an alternative to gender-role expectations for men, the same type of fantasy typically means something different to women. For women, who often learn to have mixed feelings about being sexual, this type of fantasy offers sexual adventures free from the responsibility and guilt of personal choice.

Male–Female Similarities and Differences in Sexual Fantasy

Men's and women's fantasy lives include some common aspects. First, the frequency of fantasy is similar for both sexes during sexual activity with a partner (Leitenberg & Henning, 1995). Second, both men and women indicate a wide range of fantasy content, as seen in Tables 9.2 and 9.3. A research summary of male–female content of sexual fantasy (Leitenberg & Henning, 1995) found notable differences.

- Men's fantasies are more active and focus more on the woman's body and on what he wants to do to it, whereas women's fantasies are more passive and focus more on men's interest in their bodies.
- Men's sexual fantasies focus more on explicit sexual acts, nude bodies, and physical gratification, whereas women use more emotional context and romance in their sexual fantasies.
- Men are more likely to fantasize about multiple partners and group sex than are women.
- Men are more likely to have dominance fantasies, whereas women are more likely to have submission fantasies.

Table 9.3 Male and Female Sexual Fantasies During Intercourse

Fantasy Content	*Men (%)*	*Women (%)*
Sex with a former lover	43	41
Sex with an imaginary lover	44	24
Oral–genital sex	61	51
Group sex	19	14
Being forced into a sexual relationship	21	36
Being observed engaging in sexual intercourse	15	20
Being found sexually irresistible by others	55	53
Being rejected or sexually abused	11	13
Forcing others to have sexual relations with you	24	16
Having others give in to you after resisting	37	24
Observing others engaging in sex	18	13
Sex with a member of the same sex	3	9
Sex with animals	1	4

Source: Sue, 1979.

The frequency of fantasies of being forced or forcing someone to have sex differs significantly between males and females. Although, as we have mentioned, such fantasies may take the form of gender-role reversal, they usually reflect an exaggeration of stereotypical gender roles of the male as active and the female as receptive. Research indicates that almost twice as many women as men fantasize about being forced to have sex (Knafo & Jaffe, 1984). It is important to note, however, that enjoyment of forced-sex fantasies does not mean women really want to be raped (Gold et al., 1991). A woman is in charge of her fantasies, but as a victim of sexual aggression, she is not in control.

Fantasies: Help or Hindrance?

Erotic fantasies are generally considered a healthy and helpful aspect of sexuality. Most people report that their sexual fantasies are pleasurable and arousing (Leitenberg & Henning, 1995). Many sex therapists encourage their clients to use sexual fantasy as a source of stimulation to help them increase interest and arousal. Sexual fantasies help many women experience arousal and orgasm during sexual activity, and a deficit of erotic fantasy is often present with problems of low sexual desire and arousal (Maltz & Boss, 1997). Research has also indicated that people who experience more guilt about sex feel less arousal to sexual fantasies than subjects who do not feel so guilty about sex (Follingstad & Kimbrell, 1986). Another study found that people who feel less guilt about sexual fantasy during intercourse reported more sexual fantasies and higher levels of sexual satisfaction and functioning than did those who felt more guilt (Cado & Leitenberg, 1990).

Although most of the available research supports erotic imagining as helpful, sexual fantasy has also been considered symptomatic of poor heterosexual relations or other problems (Shainess & Greenwald, 1971). Private fantasies during sex with a partner may erode the trust and intimacy in a relationship (Apfelbaum, 1980). Individuals who have experienced sexual abuse as children may use particular sexual fantasies to attempt to master their past trauma but find that these fantasies actually re-create and reinforce the original abuse. Some individuals, particularly women who have experienced sexual abuse, are troubled by intrusive, unwanted sexual fantasies that emerge when they become sexually aroused. Developing new fantasies based on self-acceptance and loving relationships can be a part of the healing process for these abused individuals (Maltz & Boss, 1997). Like most other aspects of sexuality, what determines whether fantasizing is helpful or disturbing to a relationship is its meaning and purpose for the individuals concerned.

Some people may decide to incorporate a particular fantasy into their actual sexual behavior. Acting out a fantasy can be pleasurable; however, if a fantasy is counter to one's value system or has possible negative consequences, one should consider the advantages and disadvantages of doing so. For some people, fantasies are more exciting when they remain imaginary, and are a disappointment in actual practice. Acting on fantasies developed in cyberspace relationships is very unpredictable, as described in "The Sexual Fantasy Frontier in Cyberspace" box.

Most people draw a distinct boundary between their fantasy world and the real world. For example, a woman who enjoys fantasizing about having intercourse with her partner's best friend might never really consider doing so. However, some people feel guilty about fantasizing; almost 20% of college men and women felt uneasy or ashamed about their fantasies during intercourse (Sue, 1979). For people who experience guilt over their fantasies, it is important to remember that thoughts and feelings are not the same

On the Edge
The Sexual Fantasy Frontier in Cyberspace

Cyberspace brings new possibilities and potential problems to people expressing their sexual fantasies on the Internet. Internet chat rooms let people who want to engage in explicit, verbal, sexual talk, link up with on-line relationships. In user-created private chat rooms, anything goes. Cybersex has been called a "highbrow" form of anonymous sex (Brown, 1997a). On the Internet people can assume any name, gender, race, or personality they want to pretend to be, and often disguise themselves as radically different from who they are in real life (Treadway, 1997). One survey found that 12% of male and 10% of female college students had participated in on-line sex (Elliott & Brantley, 1997). These numbers will likely increase rapidly over the next few years as more people venture into cyberspace.

Some people, women in particular, find cybersex a kind of sexual revolution where they can act out their wildest fantasies in complete safety, unlike in real life (Michals, 1997). One magazine writer decided to research personally the sexual possibilities on the Internet, using the screen name Pirategrrl, whose hobbies were swordplay and spanking. She thought this would be the right sort of character to cruise the infamous chat rooms. She was deluged with men and women eager to discuss Pirategrrl's interests. The writer found her alter ego Pirategrrl to be far bolder and funnier than her day-to-day self, and her wild stories became a delicious high for her.

She began an ongoing chat relationship with "Ravager," who described his hobbies as "training errant women, discipline as warranted." She teased him with unabashed questions about his sexual adventures. He sent Pirategrrl submission and domination scenarios. Exploring a topic that had always intrigued her, but that she had never discussed with anyone else, gave her a feeling of powerful intimacy with him. He asked for a picture of her, and she sent him one. He asked to meet in person, and she agreed. They met in a park and talked in a coffee shop as she interviewed him about life in "the scene." At one point he grabbed her hands and tied her wrists together. He then brought out a nipple clamp and screwed it to her finger until it hurt. She felt both afraid and aroused, but as they talked and the real 48-year-old engineer with a thin, lined face who'd had a bad day at the office emerged, the eroticism of Ravager faded away. He said goodbye in time to catch his train home (Darling, 1997).

Taking the cybersex Internet relationship off-line into real life is unpredictable, and the media are reporting more situations gone awry. At best, sexual fantasizing that stays strictly on-line remains untarnished by the realities and risks of daily life and living beings. This may be the main reason why so many people are chatting away their evenings.

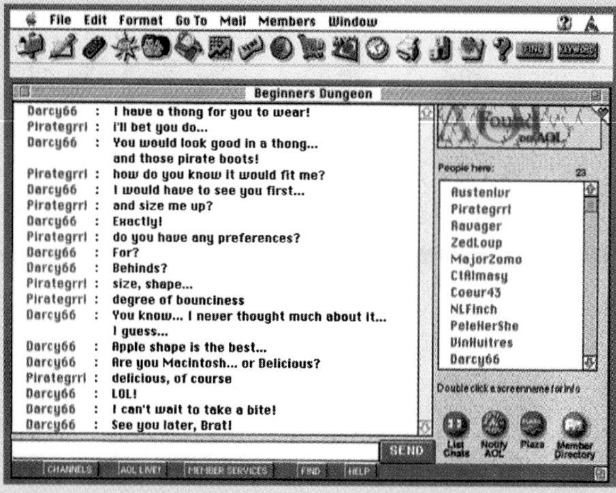

Pirategrrl's chat room conversation in "Beginners Dungeon."

MOMMA by Mell Lazarus. Courtesy of Mell Lazarus and News America.

as actions. As long as people feel able to refrain from acting out a fantasy that would hurt themselves or others, they probably do not need to be concerned.

In some cases, fantasy may contribute to a person acting in a way that is harmful to others. This is of particular concern with people who may sexually assault children or adults. A person who thinks that he or she is in danger of committing such an act should seek professional psychological assistance. Chapter 19 provides further information about fantasy and sexual offenders.

Masturbation

In this text, the word **masturbation** is used to describe self-stimulation of one's genitals for sexual pleasure. *Autoeroticism* is another term used for masturbation. We discuss some perspectives on and purposes of masturbation and specific techniques used in masturbation.

Masturbation Stimulation of one's own genitals to create sexual pleasure.

Perspectives on Masturbation

Masturbation has been a source of social concern and censure throughout Judeo–Christian history. This state of affairs has resulted in both misinformation and considerable personal shame and fear. Many of the negative attitudes toward masturbation are rooted in early Jewish and Christian views that procreation was the only legitimate purpose of sexual behavior. Because masturbation obviously could not result in conception, it was condemned. The "evils" of masturbation received a great deal of publicity in the name of science during the mid-eighteenth century, due largely to the writings of a European physician named Tissot. He wrote vividly about the mind- and body-damaging effects of "self-abuse." Tissot believed that semen was made from blood and that the loss of semen was debilitating to health. This view of masturbation influenced social and medical attitudes in Europe and North America for generations, as reflected by an "encyclopedia" of health published in 1918, which describes the following "symptoms" of masturbation:

> The health soon becomes noticeably impaired; there will be general debility, a slowness of growth, weakness in the lower limbs, nervousness and unsteadiness of the hands, loss of memory, and inability to study or learn, restless disposition, weak eyes and loss of sight, headache

and inability to sleep or wakefulness. Next come sore eyes, blindness, stupidity, consumption, spinal affection, emaciation, involuntary seminal emissions, loss of all energy or spirit, insanity and idiocy—the hopeless ruin of both body and mind. (Wood & Ruddock, 1918, p. 812)

In the 1800s, sexual abstinence, simple foods, and fitness were lauded as crucial to health. The Reverend Sylvester Graham, who promoted the use of whole-grain flours and whose name is still attached to graham crackers, wrote that ejaculation reduced precious "vital fluids." He beseeched men to abstain from masturbation and even marital intercourse to avoid moral and physical degeneracy. John Harvey Kellogg, M.D., carried Graham's work further and developed the cornflake to help prevent masturbation and sexual desire (Money, 1983). Other techniques to control masturbation included bandaging the genitals, tying one's hands at night, applying carbolic acid to the clitoris, and suturing foreskins shut, as well as mechanical devices (Michael et al., 1994).

Freud and most other early psychoanalysts recognized that masturbation does not harm physical health, and they saw it as normal during childhood. However, they believed that masturbation in adulthood could result in "immature" sexual development and the inability to form good sexual relationships. Current research indicates that masturbation is neither beneficial nor harmful to sexual adjustment in young adulthood (Leitenberg, 1993).

Contemporary views reflect conflicting beliefs about masturbation, and much of the traditional condemnation still exists. In 1976, the Vatican issued a "Declaration on Certain Questions Concerning Sexual Ethics," which described masturbation as an "intrinsically and seriously disordered act." This perspective was maintained again in 1993 by Pope John Paul II's condemnation of masturbation as morally unacceptable. Some individuals abstain from masturbation because of their religious beliefs.

I don't masturbate, because I've learned from my church and my parents that sexual love in marriage is an expression of God's love. Any other kind of sex diminishes the meaning I will find with my wife. (Authors' files)

In contrast, many view masturbation as a healthy and positive aspect of sexuality. For example, Betty Dodson, author of *Liberating Masturbation,* writes,

Masturbation, of course, is our first natural sexual activity. It's the way we discover our eroticism, the way we learn to respond sexually, the way we learn to love ourselves and build self-esteem. Sexual skill and the ability to respond are not "natural" in our society. Doing what "comes naturally" for us is to be sexually inhibited. Sex is like any other skill—it has to be learned and practiced. (1974, p. 13)

Purposes of Masturbation

People masturbate for a variety of reasons, not the least of which is the pleasure of arousal and orgasm. The most commonly reported reason is to relieve sexual tension (Michael et al., 1994). At certain times, the satisfaction from an autoerotic session may be more rewarding than an interpersonal sexual encounter, as the following quote illustrates:

I had always assumed that masturbation was a second-best sexual expression. One time, after reflecting back on the previous day's activities of a really enjoyable morning masturbatory experience and an unsatisfying experience that evening with a partner, I realized that first- and second-rate were very relative. (Authors' files)

Some people find that the independent sexual release available through masturbation can help them make better decisions about relating sexually with other people. Within a relationship, too, masturbation can help even out the effects of dissimilar sexual interest. Masturbation can be a shared experience:

When I am feeling sexual and my partner is not, he holds me and kisses me while I masturbate. Also, sometimes after making love I like to touch myself while he embraces me. It is so much better than sneaking off to the bathroom alone. (Authors' files)

In addition, some people find masturbation valuable as a means of self-exploration. Sex educator Eleanor Hamilton recommends masturbation to adolescents as a way to release tension and to become "pleasantly at home with your own sexual organs" (1978, p. 33). Indeed, people can learn a great deal about their sexual responses from masturbation. Self-stimulation is often helpful for women learning to experience orgasms and for men experimenting with their response patterns to increase ejaculatory control. (Masturbation as a tool for increasing sexual satisfaction is discussed in Chapter 16.) Finally, some people find that masturbation helps them get to sleep at night, for the same generalized feelings of relaxation that often follow a sexual encounter can also accompany self-pleasuring.

A common concern about masturbation is "doing it too much." Even in writings where masturbation is said to be "normal," masturbating "to excess" is often presented as unhealthy. A definition of excess rarely follows. If a person were masturbating so much that it significantly interfered with any aspect of his or her life, there might be cause for concern. However, in that case masturbation would be a symptom or manifestation of some underlying problem rather than the problem itself. For example, someone who is experiencing intense emotional anxiety may employ masturbation as an attempt to relieve anxiety or as a form of self-comforting. The problem in this case is the intense emotional anxiety—not the masturbation.

Table 9.4 Two Thousand College Students Answer "How Often Do You Masturbate?" (Percentages given only for far ends of the continuum)

	Men	*Women*
Two or more times a week	50%	16%
Never	12%	40%

Source: Elliott & Brantley, 1997.

How do you think masturbation patterns change during adulthood, especially following marriage?

Most men and women, both married and unmarried, masturbate on occasion. Women tend to masturbate more after they reach their twenties than they did in their teens. Kinsey hypothesized that this was due to increased erotic responsiveness, opportunities for learning about the possibility of self-stimulation through sex play with a partner, and a reduction in sexual inhibitions.

It is common for people to continue masturbation when married. In fact, individuals with higher frequency of partnered sexual activity also masturbate more often (Laumann et al., 1994). Masturbation is often considered inappropriate when a person has a sexual partner, however. Some people believe that they should not engage in a sexual activity that excludes their partners, or that their experiencing sexual pleasure by masturbation deprives their partners of pleasure. Others mistakenly interpret their partners' desire to masturbate as a sign that there is something wrong with their relationship. But unless it interferes with mutually enjoyable sexual intimacy in the relationship, masturbation can be considered a normal part of each partner's sexual repertoire. Moreover, one study found that married women who masturbated to orgasm had greater marital and sexual satisfaction than women who did not masturbate (Hurlbert & Whittaker, 1991).

Ethnicity and Masturbation

Adults who are most likely to masturbate, and to masturbate more frequently, have several characteristics in common. They have more liberal views and consider pleasure an important goal of sexuality. White men and women masturbate more than African American men and women. Hispanic women have the lowest rate of masturbation. In addition, the higher the education level, the more likely an individual is to masturbate. Contrary to expectation, people living with sexual partners are more likely to masturbate than those living alone. Given that white, college-educated people who are living with a partner are most likely to masturbate, it appears that this practice is strongly influenced by a person's social group (Laumann et al., 1994).

Self-Pleasuring Techniques

This section offers descriptions of self-pleasuring techniques. Self-exploration exercises can help a person become more aware of genital and whole-body sensations: Readers who would like to experiment with some or all of the steps are invited to do so. Readers who have moral objections to masturbation should follow their values and not do the techniques for self-pleasuring.

It is not unusual for someone first trying self-pleasuring to feel anxious. If this happens to you, two suggestions may be helpful. First, focus for a minute on physical relaxation: Take a few slow breaths, extending your belly outward as you inhale. Another way to relax yourself is to tense a body part, such as an arm and hand, for a few seconds, then release the tension. Second, try to clear your mind of thoughts related to the "rightness" or "wrongness" of self-pleasuring and allow yourself to concentrate instead on the positive physical sensations that can come from self-stimulation. Because the genitals are only one part of the body, we suggest involving your entire anatomy in the self-exam, to explore your sensuality as well as specific structures. Both men and women often report that their sexual feelings are enhanced by learning to be less genitally focused and more in touch with the sensual potentials that exist throughout their bodies.

Set aside a block of time (at least one hour for the entire exercise) when you will have privacy. Allow several minutes for your mind to quiet down from the noisy clatter of the day. A good way to begin is with a relaxing bath or shower. You can start the self-exploration while bathing, washing with soapy hands in an unhurried manner. Towel off leisurely and then explore all areas of your body with your fingertips, gently touching and stroking the skin of your face, arms, legs, stomach, and feet.

As you are touching yourself, focus on the various textures and shapes. Compare the sensations when you have your eyes open and closed. You may wish to experiment with using a body lotion, oil, or powder. After gentle stroking, try firmer, massaging pressures, paying extra attention to areas that are tense. You might like to allow yourself some pleasurable fantasies during this time. Notice whether your breathing is relaxed; let it be deep and slow. When you have completed this part, notice how you feel.

For the next step, continue the exploration with your genitals, experimenting with various kinds of pressure and stroking. Pay attention to what feels good. The following paragraphs offer descriptions of ways of touching that some people use during masturbation.

Specific techniques for masturbation vary. Males commonly grasp the penile shaft with one hand, as shown in Figure 9.1. Some men prefer to use lotion; others like the

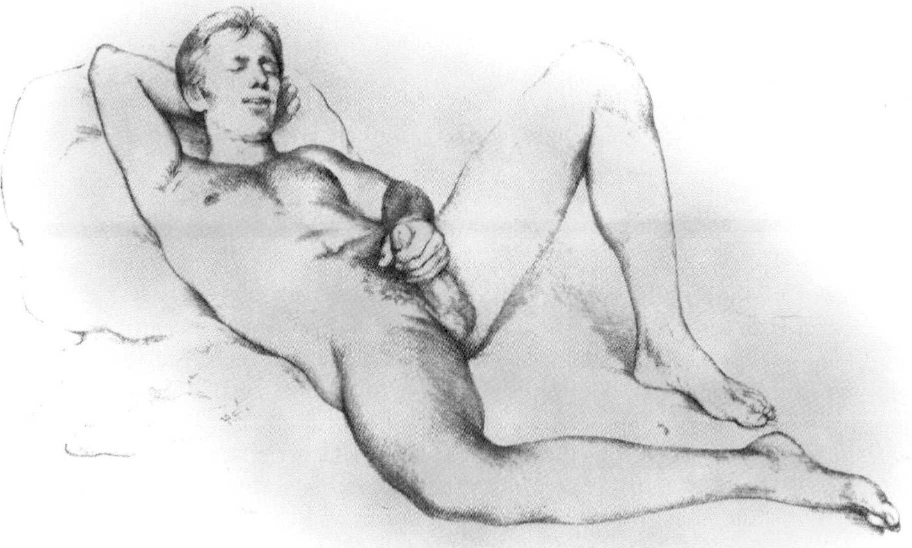

Figure 9.1

Male masturbation.

natural friction. Up-and-down motions of differing pressures and tempos provide stimulation. A man may also stroke the glans and frenulum or caress or tug the scrotum. Or, rather than using his hands, he may rub his penis against a mattress or pillow.

Women enjoy a variety of stimulation techniques. Typically, the hand provides circular, back-and-forth, or up-and-down movements against the mons and clitoral area (see Figure 9.2). The glans of the clitoris is rarely stimulated directly, though it may be stimulated indirectly when covered by the hood. Some women thrust the clitoral area against an object such as bedding or a pillow. Others masturbate by pressing their thighs together and tensing the pelvic floor muscles that underlie the vulva. Contrary to what is often portrayed in pornography, few women use vaginal insertion to reach orgasm during masturbation. Only 1.5% of women in Shere Hite's survey (1976) used vaginal insertion of a finger or penis-shaped object; over half of this small group had also used clitoral stimulation prior to insertion.

Some individuals and couples also use vibrators for added enjoyment or variation. Although some men enjoy using a vibrator on their genitals, women tend to be more enthusiastic about such devices. If you want to use a vibrator for sexual pleasure, experiment—both with the type of vibrator and with how it is used. By placing the vibrator on different areas of your body or genitals, you can find what is particularly arousing for you. Moving the pelvis or the vibrator may enhance your enjoyment.

Several different types of vibrators are available, and people's preferences vary. *The Good Vibrations Guide to Sex* by Cathy Winks and Anne Semans (1994) has a detailed discussion of vibrators. The penis-shaped, battery-operated ones usually provide less intense vibrations than do the others. These vibrators do not require an electrical outlet and are also the least expensive. Electric vibrators should never be used in or around water, as lethal electrical shock may result. Two basic kinds of handheld vibrators are the wand-shaped and the multiple-attachment types. Detachable, handheld pulsating shower

Figure 9.2

Female masturbation.

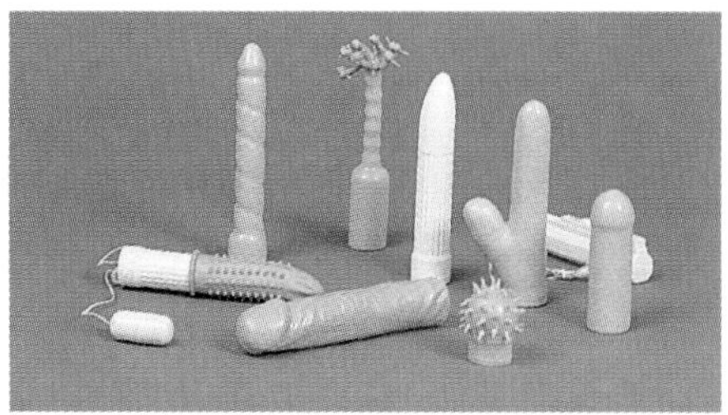

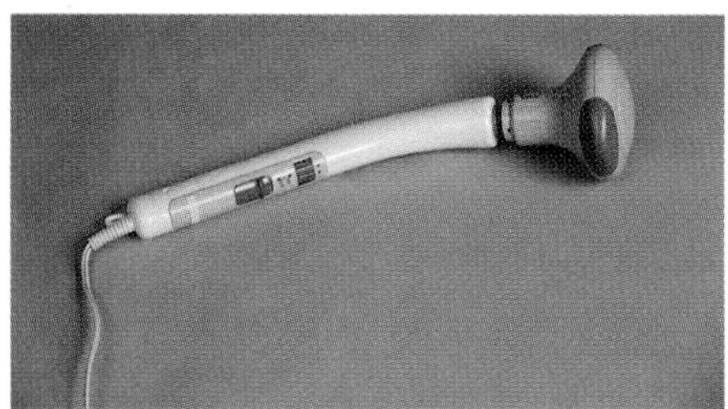

Two types of vibrators: (left) phallic shaped, (right) wand shaped.

heads are another alternative. Some women have long known that a stream of water coursing over their genitals can be very arousing.

Although masturbating is valuable for many people in varied situations, not everyone wants to do it. Sometimes, in our attempts to help people who would like to eradicate their negative feelings about self-stimulation, it may sound as if the message is that people *should* masturbate. This is not the case. Masturbation is an option for sexual expression—not a mandate.

Sexual Expression: The Importance of Context and Meaning

Up to this point in the chapter, we have been looking at ways that people express themselves sexually as individuals. However, many of the sexual behaviors with which we are concerned take place as interactions between people. In the sections that follow, we discuss some of the more common forms of shared sexual behavior. The sequence in which they are presented does not mean that such a progression is "best" in a particular sexual relationship or encounter; for example, a heterosexual couple may desire oral–genital stimulation *after* coitus rather than before. Nor is any one of these activities necessary in a given relationship or encounter: Complete sexual experience may consist of any or all of them. The discussions of shared sexual activities, with the exception of coitus and gay and lesbian sexual expression, are directed toward all individuals, regardless of their sexual orientation. In fact, because sex between same-sex partners does not duplicate the pervasive heterosexual model's emphasis on penile–vaginal intercourse, gay men and lesbians' sexual repertoire is often more expansive and creative than heterosexuals' (Nichols, 1989).

Aspects of Interactive Sexuality

Although the following sections include discussions of sexual techniques, a specific technique cannot stand on its own; it must exist or be used in the context of the relationship as a whole as described further in the following discussion of the Maltz hierarchy. Feelings, desires, and attitudes strongly influence choices about sexual activity. Sensitivity to your and your partner's sexual needs will help develop shared pleasure and arousal more effectively than any specific technique. Mutual consent is an important aspect of a sexual relationship, and sexual activities that both partners are willing to engage in are more likely to provide a couple with enjoyable sexual experiences.

There may be some male–female differences to consider in regard to feelings about various sexual activities. A research study asked college students about their preferences regarding foreplay, coitus, and "afterplay," and found that males were more likely to say they preferred coitus and females that they preferred foreplay and afterplay (none of the males said afterplay). Furthermore, females wanted to spend more time in foreplay and afterplay than did males (Denny et al., 1984). There is, of course, great individual variation in such preferences. Open communication can help couples establish their unique and changing attitudes and desires.

The Maltz Hierarchy

The context within which sexual behaviors occur is critically important for them to be self-affirming and relationship enhancing. Author and sex therapist Wendy Maltz has developed a model with levels of constructive or destructive expression of sexuality (Maltz, 1995). Maltz sees sexual energy as a neutral force; however, the intent and consequences of sexual behavior can lead in negative or positive directions. For example, marital intercourse may be intensely passionate; alternatively, it may be spousal rape.

The three positive levels of sexual interaction are built on mutual choice, caring, respect, and safety. As shown in Figure 9.3, *Level +1, Positive Role Fulfillment,* reflects well-defined gender roles established by social or religious custom where (in heterosexual relationships) the male is the initiator and the woman is receptive. Sexual interactions at this level are characterized by mutual respect and a lack of coercion and resentment; a strong sense of safety and predictability is present. Pregnancy and reduction of sexual tension are common goals for sex.

Level +2, Making Love, emphasizes mutual pleasure through individual sexual creativity and experimentation. Traditional gender-role behavior is set aside, and sex expands to an erotic recreational experience. Partners reveal themselves more deeply through sexual self-expression and communication that create greater intimacy.

Level +3, Authentic Sexual Intimacy, brings a shared sense of deep connection both to oneself and one's partner, with reverence toward the body in the erotic experience. The

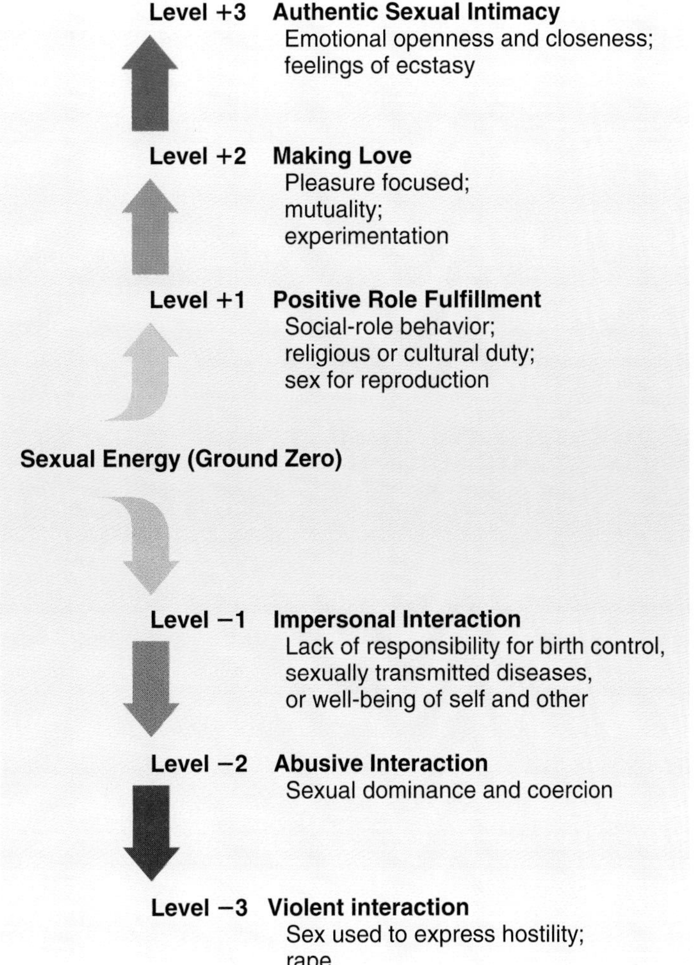

Figure 9.3

The Maltz hierarchy of sexual interactions (Maltz, 1995).

enjoyment of sensual pleasure includes a profound expression of love for one another. A 23-year-old college man describes this experience.

One night we just started kissing as we were laying in bed. It was the middle of the night, and we just started making love, very nice and slow and sensuous. I felt very connected with my girlfriend because it seemed like we were just melting into each other and focusing very intensely on each other.

Emotional honesty and openness are of paramount importance, and each partner gains a deeper sense of wholeness. Authentic sexual intimacy can be a momentary peak experience, or it may characterize an entire lovemaking experience.

Maltz points out that sexual interactions may also be upsetting or traumatic ordeals, often imposed on one person by another. On the negative side of her hierarchy, each level becomes increasingly destructive and abusive. *Level −1, Impersonal Interaction,* is marked by a lack of respect and responsibility toward oneself and the other person. Here, individuals disregard possible negative consequences to themselves or to their partners—including consequences such as unwanted pregnancy or exposure to sexually transmitted diseases such as AIDS. Enduring unpleasant sex or being dishonest about issues relevant to the partner (health status or meaning of the sexual experience) occurs at this level. These experiences result in uncomfortable, uneasy feelings.

Level −2, Abusive Interaction, involves one person's conscious domination of another by psychological coercion. Nonviolent acquaintance rape and incest are examples. Degrading coercive communication also is included. Through distortions in thinking, the exploitive person rationalizes or denies the harm he or she is inflicting on the other person. The experience usually damages the exploited person's self-esteem.

Level −3, Violent Interaction, occurs when sexual energy is used purposefully to express hostility. Sex organs are weapons and targets. Serial killers and rapists are the extreme example.

For sexual expression to be self-affirming and relationship enhancing, it needs to be experienced at one of the positive levels and to be congruent with the individual's value system.

Kissing and Touching

i like my body when it is with your
body. It is so quite new a thing.
Muscles better and nerves more.
i like your body. i like what it does,
i like its hows. i like to feel the spine
of your body and its bones, and the trembling
-firm-smooth ness and which i will
again and again and again
kiss, i like kissing this and that of you,
i like, slowly stroking the,shocking fuzz
of your electric fur,and what-is-it comes
over parting flesh. . . . And eyes big love-crumbs,

and possibly i like the thrill

*of under me you so quite new**

e. e. cummings

Kissing

Many of us can remember our first romantic kiss, most likely it was combined with feelings of awkwardness. Kissing can be an intense, erotic, profound experience, well suggested by the poet Tennyson: "Once he drew, with one long kiss, my whole soul through my lips."

The lips and mouth are generously endowed with sensitive, pleasure-producing nerve endings that make it feel good to kiss and to be kissed in infinite variations. Kissing with closed mouths tends to be more tender and affectionate, whereas open mouth, or deep, or "French kissing," is usually more sexually intense. Kissing can also include the gamut of oral activities such as licking, sucking, and mild biting. All places on the body are possibilities for kissing. Students describe some of their favorite kisses:

When my lover holds my face in her hands and tenderly kisses my eyelids, I melt.

I get so turned on when my husband thrusts his tongue into my mouth as his penis enters my vagina.

You haven't lived until you've had someone suck your toes.

In kissing my lover all over, I become intoxicated with his smell and taste. (Authors' files)

Touching

Touch is one of the first and most important senses that we experience when we emerge into this world. Infants who have been fed but deprived of this basic stimulation have died for lack of it. A classic animal study showed that when baby monkeys' and other primates' physical needs were met but they were denied their mothers' touch, they grew up to be extremely maladjusted (Harlow & Harlow, 1962). Touch forms the cornerstone of human sexuality shared with another. In Masters and Johnson's evaluation,

> Touch is an end in itself. It is a primary form of communication, a silent voice that avoids the pitfall of words while expressing the feelings of the moment. It bridges the physical separateness from which no human being is spared, literally establishing a sense of solidarity between two individuals. Touching is sensual pleasure, exploring the textures of skin, the suppleness of muscle, the contours of the body, with no further goal than enjoyment of tactile perceptions. (1976, p. 253)

Touch does not need to be directed to an erogenous area to be sexual. The entire body surface is a sensory organ, and touching—almost anywhere—can enhance intimacy and sexual arousal. Because different people may like different kinds of touching, it is helpful for couples to discuss their preferences openly.

Sensual touching can be pleasurable to both the giver and the receiver.

The entire body responds to touching, but some specific areas are, of course, more receptive to sexual feelings than others. Preferences vary from one person to another. Many men and women report breast stimulation (especially of the nipple) to be arousing. Others find it unpleasant. A few women reach orgasm from breast stimulation alone (Masters & Johnson, 1966). The size of the breasts is not related to how erotically sensitive they are. Some women's breasts become more sensitive, even tender, during certain times of their menstrual cycles. A woman may find that a firm touch that is highly arousing one week feels uncomfortable and harsh the next. Once again, ongoing communication between partners is important.

Genital stimulation is often highly pleasurable to women and men. Many people's first experience with manual–genital stimulation comes from masturbation, and this self-knowledge can form the basis of further learning with a partner. People who have not previously masturbated can explore and learn what is enjoyable with each other. One partner can touch the other, or they can explore each other's sensations simultaneously. Manual stimulation can provide pleasure or orgasm by itself, or it can be a prelude to other activities.

Manual Stimulation of the Female Genitals

There is great variation from one woman to another in the kind of genital touches that induce arousal. Even the same woman may vary in her preference from one moment to the next. Women may prefer gentle or firm movements on different areas of the vulva. Direct stimulation of the clitoris is uncomfortable for some women; touches above or along the sides may be preferable. Insertion of a finger into the vagina may enhance arousal. Anal stimulation or penetration is erotic to some women but not to others.

It is important not to touch the vulva or vagina with the same finger used for anal stimulation, because bacteria that are present in the rectum can cause infections if introduced into the vagina.

The vulval tissues are delicate and sensitive. If there is not enough lubrication to make the vulva slippery, it can become easily irritated. A lubricant such as K-Y jelly, a lotion without alcohol or perfume, or saliva can be used to moisten the fingers and vulva to make the touch more pleasurable.

Manual Stimulation of the Male Genitals

Men also have individual preferences for manual stimulation and, as with women, may desire a firmer or softer touch—and faster or slower strokes—as their arousal increases. Gentle or firm stroking of the penile shaft and glans and light touches or tugging on the scrotum may be desired. Some men experience uncomfortable sensitivity of the penile glans when it is touched immediately following orgasm. Some men find that lubrication with a lotion or saliva increases pleasure. (With heterosexual couples, if intercourse might follow, the lotion should be nonirritating to the woman's genital tissues.) Some men also enjoy manual stimulation or penetration of the anus.

Oral–Genital Stimulation

Both the mouth and genitals are primary biological erogenous zones, areas of the body generously endowed with sensory nerve endings. Therefore, couples who are psychologically comfortable with oral–genital stimulation often find both giving and receiving it to be highly pleasurable. Oral–genital contact can produce pleasure, arousal, or orgasm. As one woman states,

> I think that men put too much emphasis on a woman coming from "regular sex." A lot of women I know, including myself, have only experienced orgasm (aside from masturbation) through oral sex. I thoroughly enjoy getting and giving oral sex. I love the sounds, sights, smells, and tastes. (Authors' file)

Oral–genital stimulation can be done individually (by one partner to the other) or simultaneously. Some people prefer oral sex individually because they can focus on either giving or receiving. Others especially enjoy the mutuality of simultaneous oral–genital sex. Simultaneous stimulation is sometimes referred to as "69" because of the body positions suggested by that number (Figure 9.4). Besides the one illustrated, a variety of positions can be used; lying side by side and using a thigh for a pillow is another option. As

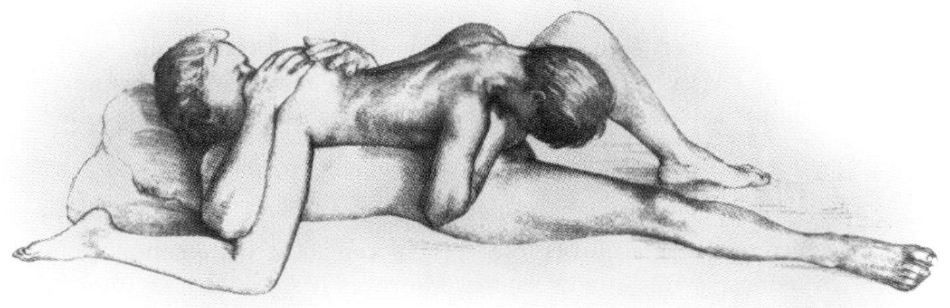

Figure 9.4

Simultaneous oral–genital stimulation in the "69" position.

arousal becomes intense during mutual oral–genital stimulation, partners need to be careful not to suck or bite too hard.

Different terminology is used to describe oral–genital stimulation of women and oral–genital stimulation of men. **Cunnilingus** (kun-i-LIN-gus) is oral stimulation of the vulva—the clitoris, labia minora, vestibule, and vaginal opening. Many women find the warmth, softness, and moistness of the partner's lips and tongue to be highly pleasurable and effective in producing sexual arousal or orgasm. Variations of stimulation include rapid or slow circular or back-and-forth tongue movement on the clitoral area, sucking the clitoris or labia minora, and thrusting the tongue into the vaginal opening. Some women are especially aroused by simultaneous manual stimulation of the vagina and oral stimulation of the clitoral area.

Cunnilingus
Oral stimulation of the vulva.

Fellatio (fel-Ā-shē-ō) is oral stimulation of the penis and scrotum. Both of Kinsey's studies found that, among heterosexual couples, women were less likely to stimulate their partners orally than the reverse. Options for oral stimulation of the male genitals include gently or vigorously licking and sucking the glans, the frenulum, and the penile shaft; and licking or enclosing a testicle in the mouth. Some men enjoy combined oral stimulation of the glans and manual stroking of the penile shaft, testicles, or anus.

Fellatio
Oral stimulation of the penis.

It is usually best for the partner performing fellatio to control the other's movements by grasping the penis manually below her or his lips to prevent it from going further into the mouth than is comfortable. This helps avoid a gagging reflex. Also, too vigorous thrusting could result in lacerations of the partner's lips as he or she attempts to protect the penis from his or her teeth.

Couples differ in their preference for including ejaculation into the mouth as a part of male oral–genital stimulation. Many find it acceptable, and some find it exciting; others do not. A couple can agree beforehand that the one who is being stimulated will indicate when he is close to orgasm and withdraw from his partner's mouth. For couples who are comfortable with ejaculating into the mouth, the ejaculate can be swallowed or not, according to one's preference.

Some people have psychological and/or moral qualms about oral–genital stimulation. As we have seen, sexual behaviors that do not have the potential of resulting in a pregnancy within marriage have historically been labeled immoral, and many people therefore believe that oral sex is wrong. Moreover, this belief has often been institutionalized into law. The term **sodomy** refers broadly to sexual behaviors other than coitus (including anal intercourse as well as oral–genital contact) that are still illegal in many states, with maximum jail sentences up to 20 years. In 1986, a heavily disputed U.S. Supreme Court decision upheld states' rights to have sodomy laws and to impose penalties (*Hardwick v. Bowers,* 106 S. Ct. 2841). Although rarely enforced, antisodomy laws remain on the statute books of many states.

Sodomy
An ill-defined legal category for noncoital genital contacts such as oral–genital and anal intercourse.

Other qualms arise from the belief that oral–genital stimulation is unsanitary or that the genitals are unattractive. It may be difficult for someone who has a negative image of his penis or her vulva to feel comfortable receiving oral stimulation. Many people also think that the genitals are "dirty" because they are close to the urinary opening and the anus. However, routine thorough washing of the genitals with soap and water is adequate for cleanliness.

Another reason that some heterosexual people object to oral sex stems from the belief that it is a homosexual act—even when experienced by heterosexual couples. Although many homosexuals engage in oral sex, the activity is not homosexual by nature. Rather, its homosexuality or heterosexuality depends on the sexes of the partners involved.

Given some of the concerns that people may have about oral sex, how common a practice do you think it is?

Despite these negative attitudes, oral–genital contact is quite common and has become even more so since Kinsey's studies. Moreover, it seems to have gained acceptance through a larger cross section of educational levels. Kinsey's research in the late 1940s and early 1950s revealed that 60% of college-educated couples, 20% of high-school-educated couples, and 10% of grade-school-educated couples had experienced oral–genital stimulation as part of marital sex. A 1980s study of 203 Canadian college women found that 61% had performed fellatio and 68% had experienced cunnilingus. Of those who had performed fellatio, 97% had also experienced cunnilingus (Herold & Way, 1983).

Within American society, however, differences in oral sex experience and attitudes still exist among population segments. In a 1990s survey, more African American men than white men (37% compared with 16%) reported never having performed or received oral sex (Billy et al., 1993). The boxed discussion, "Oral Sex Experiences Among American Men and Women," presents some further differences. Another study of American women found that career women are more likely than homemakers (65% to 43%) to consider oral sex a normal act (Janus & Janus, 1993).

Because oral–genital contact often involves an exchange of bodily fluids, there is a risk of transmitting or contracting the HIV virus (the virus that causes AIDS) (Baba et al., 1997). This virus can enter the bloodstream through small breaks in the skin of the mouth or genitals. Although the risk of transmitting the HIV virus through oral–genital contact is low, only monogamous partners who are both free from the virus are completely free from risk when engaging in such activities. (See Chapter 17 for a further discussion of precautions against transmitting the HIV virus.)

Anal Stimulation

Like oral–genital stimulation, anal stimulation may be thought by some to be a homosexual act. However, penile penetration of the anus is practiced regularly by about 10% of heterosexual couples (Voeller, 1991), and an estimated 25% of adults have experienced anal intercourse at least once (Seidman & Rieder, 1994). The anus has dense supplies of nerve endings that can respond erotically. Some women report orgasmic response from anal intercourse (Masters & Johnson, 1970), and heterosexual and homosexual men often experience orgasm from stimulation during penetration.

Individuals or couples may also use anal stimulation for arousal and variety during other sexual activities. Manually stroking the outside of the anal opening or inserting one or more fingers into the anus can be very pleasurable for some people during masturbation or partner sex.

Some important health risks are associated with anal intercourse. Anal intercourse is one of the riskiest of all sexual behaviors associated with transmission of the HIV virus, particularly for the receptive partner. For women, the risk of contracting this virus through unprotected anal intercourse is greater than the risk of contraction through unprotected vaginal intercourse (Silverman & Gross, 1997). Heterosexual and gay male couples who wish to reduce their risk of transmitting or contracting this deadly virus should refrain from anal intercourse or use a condom and practice withdrawal prior to ejaculation. Precautions against transmission of the HIV virus are discussed more fully in Chapter 17.

Because the anus contains delicate tissues, special care needs to be taken in anal stimulation. A nonirritating lubricant and gentle penetration are necessary to avoid discomfort or injury. It is helpful to use lubrication on both the anus and the penis or object being inserted. The partner receiving anal insertion can bear down (as for a bowel movement) to relax the sphincter. The partner inserting needs to go slowly and gently, keeping the penis or object tilted to follow the direction of the colon (Morin, 1981).

Heterosexual couples should never have vaginal intercourse directly following anal intercourse because bacteria that are present in the anus often cause vaginal infections. To prevent vaginal infections from this source, a couple should have vaginal intercourse before anal intercourse, or they should use a condom during anal intercourse and wash the man's genitals thoroughly with soap and water before moving on to penile–vaginal or penile–oral contact. Oral stimulation of the anus, known as *analingus* (or, in slang,

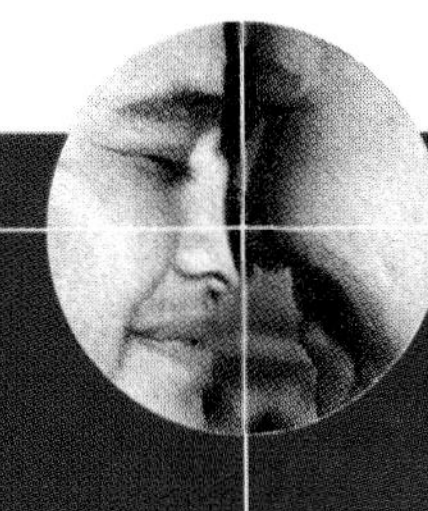

Sexuality and Diversity

Oral Sex Experiences Among American Men and Women

The recent National Health and Social Life survey (Laumann et al., 1994) questioned men and women of different racial, educational, and religious backgrounds to compare their experience of oral sex. The findings, summarized in the table, show significant differences related not only to racial group but also to educational level and religious affiliation. In general, whites (both men and women) have the highest level of experience with oral sex, followed by Hispanic Americans, with African Americans having the lowest rate of oral sex. People with more formal education are considerably more likely to have oral sex; this difference is even more significant for women than it is for men. Note that although this study found that men and women of all educational levels are today more likely to experience oral sex than were individuals in Kinsey's study (reported in the text discussion), the likelihood of this behavior is still positively associated with higher educational level. Another study comparing African American and white American men of matched socioeconomic status found similar rates of oral sex experience, indicating that socioeconomic status may be more important than race in sexual behavior (Samuels, 1997).

	*Performed Oral Sex (%)**		*Received Oral Sex (%)**	
Race	*Men*	*Women*	*Men*	*Women*
White	81	75	81	78
African American	51	34	66	49
Hispanic American	71	60	73	64
Education				
Less than high school	59	41	61	50
High school graduate	75	60	77	67
Any college	81	78	84	82
Religion				
Conservative Protestant	67	56	70	65
Other Protestant	82	74	83	77
Catholic	82	74	82	77
Other or none	79	78	83	83

*Rounded to nearest percent.

Source: Laumann et al., 1994, p. 141.

rimming), is very risky; various intestinal infections, hepatitis, and sexually transmitted diseases can be contracted or spread through oral–anal contact even with precautions of thorough washing and use of a dental dam.

Gay and Lesbian Sexual Expression

Homosexual individuals who are in sexual relationships engage in sexual behaviors similar to those of heterosexual persons, with the exception of penile–vaginal intercourse. Touching, kissing, body contact, manual–genital stimulation, oral–genital contact, and anal stimulation are techniques that are used during sexual interactions. Younger homosexual people are typically more likely to have experienced a greater variety of sexual behaviors than have older people (Bell & Weinberg, 1978), as is the case with the heterosexual population.

Lesbian Sexual Behaviors

Several misconceptions exist regarding lesbian sexual expression. One—the notion that sex between women is unsatisfactory because a penis is lacking—was contradicted by Kinsey's 1953 study. Indeed, Kinsey found that lesbian women had orgasms in a greater percentage of sexual encounters than did heterosexual married women. After five years of marriage, 55% of heterosexual women had orgasms in 60%–100% of sexual contacts. In contrast, 78% of homosexual women had orgasms in 60%–100% of their sexual encounters over a five-year period. Kinsey suggested that these results may be due to a better understanding of sexual and psychological response between members of the same sex than between those of different sexes. Shere Hite stated that greater sexual satisfaction between women may occur because "lesbian sexual relations tend to be longer and involve more all-over body sensuality" (1976, p. 413). Table 9.5 compares some sexual behaviors and responses of lesbian and heterosexual women.

Another mistaken belief is that dildos (penis-shaped devices) are used extensively among lesbians. In fact, only 2% of the homosexual women in Hunt's 1974 survey had ever used a dildo. Oral sex is very common (Laumann et al., 1994; Lever, 1994), and manual stimulation and rubbing genitals together or against the partner's body are included in lesbian sexual behaviors. Rubbing genitals against someone's body or genital area is

Figure 9.5

Lesbians often engage in prolonged sexual encounters.

Table 9.5 Comparison of Lesbian versus Heterosexual Womens' Last Sexual Experience

	Lesbian	*Heterosexual*
Percentage who		
Had more than one orgasm	32%	19%
Received oral sex	48%	20%
Lasted 15 minutes or less	4%	14%
Lasted more than one hour	39%	15%

Sources: Lesbian statistics from *Advocate* magazine survey (Lever, 1994); Heterosexual statistics from the National Health and Social Life Survey (Laumann et al., 1994).

called *tribadism*. Many lesbians like this form of sexual play because it involves all-over body contact and a generalized sensuality. Some women find the thrusting very exciting; others straddle a partner's leg and rub gently. Some rub the clitoris on the partner's pubic bone (Loulan, 1984).

It may be more difficult for lesbians to initiate a sexual relationship than for either heterosexual or male homosexual people. One explanation for this is that society conditions women to respond to sexual initiation rather than to take the lead. Each may wait for the other woman to take the first step.

A survey comparing heterosexual and homosexual patterns concluded that lesbian couples have sex less frequently than do heterosexual couples. The gap between the lovemaking frequency of lesbian and heterosexual couples widens dramatically as the relationships continue over time. In the first two years of the relationship, 76% of lesbians and 83% of heterosexual couples reported making love one or more times per week. After two years, 37% of lesbians and 73% of heterosexual couples reported that same frequency (Blumstein & Schwartz, 1983). One explanation for this may be that just as women are not socialized to initiate sexual relationships, they are not socialized to initiate individual sexual encounters within such a relationship.

Gay Male Sexual Behaviors

Contrary to the stereotype that sexual experiences between men are completely genitally focused, extragenital eroticism and affection are important aspects of sexual contact for many homosexual men:

> No doubt most people will always conceive of male sexuality in general, and male homosexuality in particular, in terms of phallic actions. . . . These and similar ideas have led to a widely held impression that homosexual practices lack precisely those kinds of affection which, in fact, are usually the main motives behind them. (Tripp, 1975, p. 102)

Hugging, kissing, snuggling, and total-body caressing are important. A survey of gay men found that 85% liked such interactions—more than any other category of sexual behavior (Lever, 1994), as seen in Figure 9.6 on the next page.

Although anal intercourse is often thought to be the most prevalent sexual behavior between homosexual men, research has shown that fellatio is in fact the most common mode of expression (Lever, 1994; Weinrich, 1991). Mutual masturbation is the next most common, and anal intercourse is least common. *Interfemoral intercourse,* when one man moves between the thighs of the other, is also a common part of gay lovemaking. Because HIV is spread through the exchange of bodily fluids, some gay men are changing their patterns of sexual activity by using condoms and avoiding any exchange of semen (Lafferty et al., 1997). (Chapter 17 includes a detailed discussion of AIDS prevention strategies.)

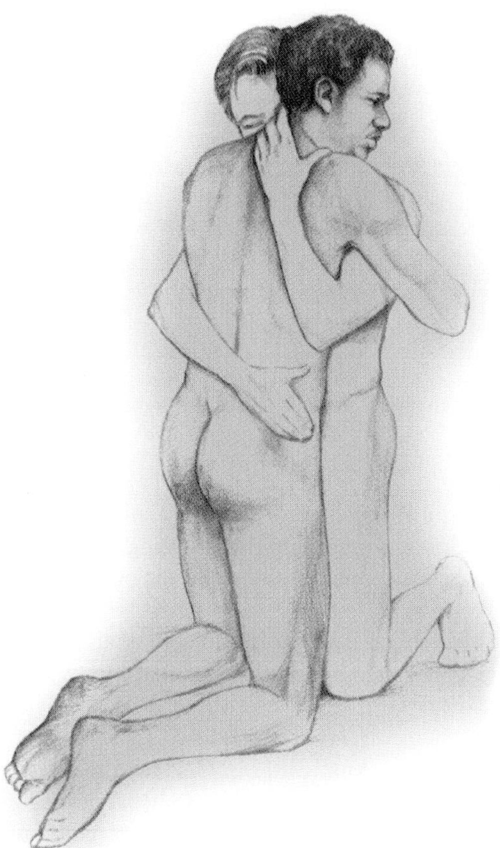

Figure 9.6

Gay men engage in a variety of sexual behaviors.

Coitus and Coital Positions

A couple may choose a wide range of positions for penile–vaginal intercourse, or coitus. Table 9.6 shows college students' three favorite positions. Many people may have a favored position, yet enjoy others as shown in Figures 9.7–9.10. A 30-year-old man states,

> Different intercourse positions usually express and evoke particular emotions for me. Being on top, I enjoy feeling aggressive; when on the bottom, I experience a special kind of receptive sensuality. In the side-by-side position, I easily feel gentle and intimate. I like sharing all these dimensions of myself with my lover. (Authors' files)

Each position provides varying opportunities for physical and emotional expression. The desirability of a particular position may change with one's mood at the moment. Alterations in health, age, weight, pregnancy, or partners may create different preferences. In some positions, one person will have greater freedom to initiate and control the tempo, angle, and style of movement to create arousing stimulation. In others, mutual control of the rhythm of thrusting works well. Some positions lend themselves to manual stimulation of the clitoris during intercourse, such as the woman above, sitting upright. Many couples like a position that allows them to have eye contact and to look at each other's bodies. The face-to-face, side-lying position can provide a particularly relaxed connection, with each partner having one hand free to caress the other's body. Rear entry can be a good position during pregnancy when pressure against the woman's abdomen is uncomfortable.

Table 9.6 College Students Answer "What's Your Favorite Intercourse Position?"

	Men	*Women*
Man on Top	25%	48%
Woman on Top	45%	33%
Doggie Style	25%	15%

Source: Elliott & Brantley, 1997.

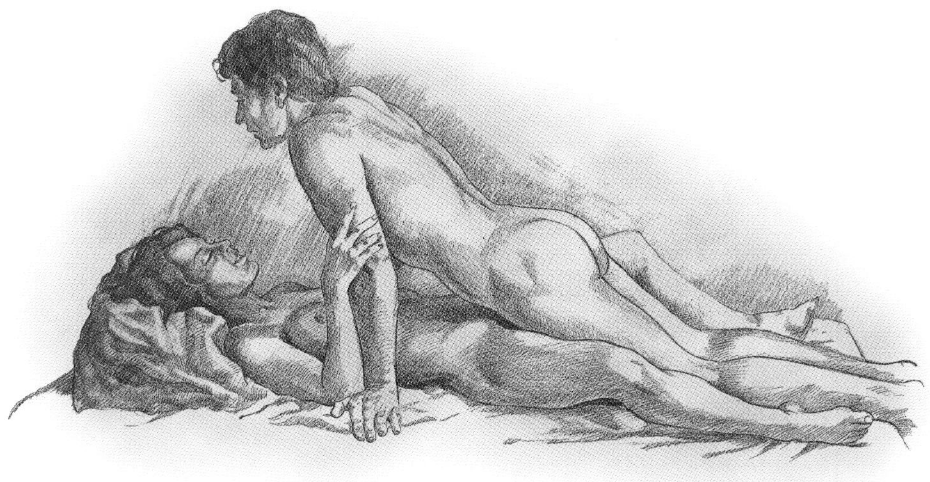

Figure 9.7

Man-above, face-to-face intercourse position.

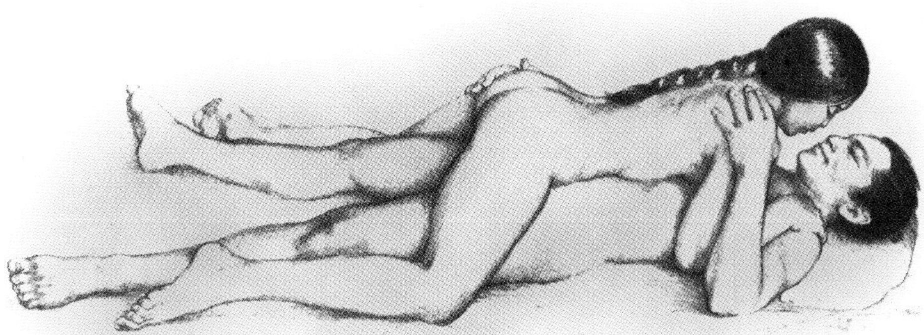

Figure 9.8

Two variations of the woman-above intercourse position.

Figure 9.9

Face-to-face, side-lying intercourse position.

A poem by Laura Kennedy (Maltz, 1996, p. 59) describes some of the intense feelings that can occur during intercourse.

I am in the most exquisite distress
astride you now,
sweating
feeling an impetuous volcano
strain at its peak
inside
wanting to explode
my sweetest self
all over you.

Intromission
Insertion of the penis into the vagina.

Beyond options for position, cooperation and consideration are important, particularly at **intromission** (entry of the penis into the vagina). Often the woman can best guide her partner's penis into her vagina by moving her body or using her hand. If the penis slips out of the vagina, which can occur fairly easily in some positions, a helping hand will most likely be welcome. Furthermore, both nonverbal and verbal communication about preferences of position, tempo, and movement can enhance the pleasure and arousal of both partners. Intercourse can occur with or without orgasm for one or both partners.

Frequency of Sexual Activity

The results of a 1998 survey of 10,000 people in the United States found that the national average of frequency of sexual activity is once a week, each episode lasting about half an hour (Robinson & Godbey, 1998). A confusing array of characteristics were correlated with a higher frequency of sex reported in this study. They included:

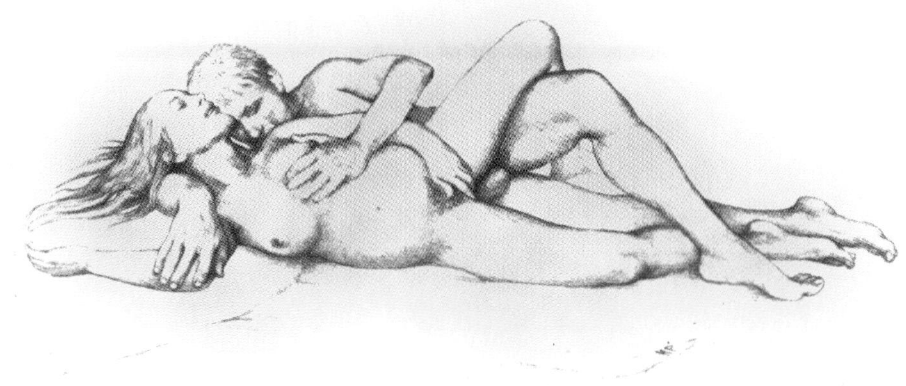

Figure 9.10

Rear-entry intercourse position, with pregnant woman simultaneously stimulating herself manually.

- having some college education (having attended graduate school correlated with less frequency, however)
- working 60 hours or more per week
- watching more TV, especially PBS
- loving jazz music
- being married
- defining oneself as "extreme liberal" or "extreme conservative"
- smoking and drinking

Some of these characteristics that go against conventional wisdom for having sex more often include a long work week, watching more TV, smoking and drinking, and not having a college degree (Sacks, 1998). The survey did not inquire about sexual satisfaction or specific sexual behaviors that occurred in the sexual experiences. Most other research has found that people with more formal education are more likely to engage in a wider variety of sexual activities during a sexual episode than are those with less formal education. However, what is meaningful and satisfying to a given individual and couple is most important.

Intercourse the Tantric Way

The concept of male orgasm as the ultimate and end point of heterosexual intercourse is alien to concepts and practices of Tantric sex. Margo Anand, in her book, *The Art of Sexual Ecstasy,* explains that Tantra was an ancient Eastern path of spiritual enlightenment, begun in India around 5000 B.C. Tantric thought holds that an erotic act of love between a god and a goddess created the world. Within this viewpoint, sexual expression can become a spiritual meditation.

In Tantric sex, the male learns to control and delay his own orgasm, and to redirect the sexual energy throughout his and his partner's body. Prior to intercourse, lovers usually slowly and erotically stimulate each other. When both partners are ready for intercourse, gentle, relaxed penetration is guided by the woman. The couple initially keeps thrusting to a minimum, generating energy by subtle, inner movements, such as contractions of the PC muscles. The couple harmonizes their breathing, finding a common rhythm of inhaling and exhaling, while visualizing the warmth, arousal, and energy in the genitals moving upward in their bodies. Movements can become active and playful, always slowing or stopping to relax before the man experiences orgasm. The couple welcomes feelings of profound intimacy, letting go, and ecstasy, often looking in each other's eyes, creating a "deep relaxation into the heart" (Anand, 1989).

Tantric Sex—the Infinite Cycle.

Summary

CELIBACY

Celibacy means not engaging in sexual activities. Celibacy can be complete (no masturbation or interpersonal sexual contact) or partial (the person masturbates). There are many circumstances in which celibacy is a positive way of expressing one's sexuality.

EROTIC DREAMS AND FANTASY

Erotic dreams often accompany sexual arousal and orgasm during sleep. Erotic fantasies serve many functions: They can enhance sexual arousal, help overcome anxiety or compensate for a negative situation, allow rehearsal of new sexual experiences, permit tolerable expression of "forbidden wishes," and provide relief from gender-role expectations.

MASTURBATION

Masturbation is self-stimulation of the genitals, intended to produce sexual pleasure.

Past attitudes toward masturbation have been highly condemnatory. However, the meaning and purposes of masturbation are currently being more positively reevaluated.

Masturbation is an activity that is continuous throughout adulthood although its frequency varies with age and sex.

SEXUAL EXPRESSION: THE IMPORTANCE OF CONTEXT AND MEANING

The meaning of sexual expression can vary from a profound sense of love for self and other to exploitation and abuse. The Maltz hierarchy delineates six levels.

KISSING AND TOUCHING

The entire body's surface is a sensory organ, and kissing and touch are basic forms of communication and shared intimacy.

Breast stimulation is arousing to most men and women, but some people find it unenjoyable.

Preferences as to the tempo, pressure, and location of manual genital stimulation vary from person to person. A lubricant, a nonirritating lotion, or saliva on the genitals may enhance pleasure.

ORAL–GENITAL STIMULATION

Oral–genital contact has become more common in recent years. Qualms about oral–genital stimulation usually stem from false ideas that it is unsanitary or solely a homosexual act, or from religious beliefs that it is immoral.

Cunnilingus is oral stimulation of the vulva; fellatio is oral stimulation of the male genitals.

ANAL STIMULATION

Couples may engage in anal stimulation for arousal, orgasm, and variety. Careful hygiene is necessary to avoid introducing anal bacteria into the vagina. To reduce the chances of transmitting the AIDS virus, couples should avoid anal intercourse or use a condom and practice withdrawal before ejaculation.

GAY AND LESBIAN SEXUAL EXPRESSION

Similar to heterosexuals, younger homosexuals have experienced a greater variety of sexual behaviors than have older gay men and women.

Oral sex is a common sexual behavior among homosexual men and women.

COITUS AND COITAL POSITIONS

The diversity of coital positions offers potential variety during intercourse. The man-above, woman-above, side-by-side, and rear-entry positions are common.

People who have sex more often have several characteristics in common that go against conventional wisdom.

Tantric sex emphasizes intense, prolonged sexual intimacy.

Thought Provokers

1. If your 10-year-old son asked you what you think about masturbation, what would you say? If your 10-year-old daughter asked?
2. What helpful functions, if any, do you think sexual fantasies serve? When do you think a person's fantasies indicate a problem?
3. Where do your sexual behaviors fall on the Maltz hierarchy?
4. Research indicates that heterosexual men prefer coitus whereas their female partners often prefer foreplay and "afterplay." Why do you think this is so?

Suggested Readings

Anand, Margo (1989). *The Art of Sexual Ecstasy.* Los Angeles: Tarcher. A comprehensive exploration of principles and practice of Tantric sex.

Dodson, Betty (1987). *Sex for One.* New York: Harmony Books. A lively, sometimes outrageous, book about masturbation.

Love, Patricia; and Robinson, Jo (1994). *Hot Monogamy.* New York: Dutton. This book describes a step-by-step program with exercises to extend knowledge of one's sexual self to enhance a sexual relationship.

Maltz, Wendy (1996). *Passionate Hearts.* Novato, CA: New World Library. A delightful and unique collection of poems that celebrate loving sexual intimacy.

Maltz, Wendy; and Boss, Suzie (1997). *In the Garden of Desire: The Intimate World of Women's Sexual Fantasies.* New York: Broadway Books. This book describes women's fantasy styles, the functions of fantasy, and steps to understand and overcome troubling fantasies.

Web Resources

The Celibate FAQ
mail.bris.ac.uk/~plmlp/celibate.html
Frequently asked questions (FAQs) and answers about choosing a celibate lifestyle are offered at this site. Examples include how to tell people you are celibate, and the advantages and disadvantages of celibacy.

10

Sexual Orientations

I've never been able to understand why some people get their shorts all bunched up over homosexuality. I grew up in the 1950s and was quite naive. I didn't learn about homosexuality until after I'd already experienced oral sex with my boyfriend. I loved doing it to him, but found it hard to believe he could enjoy licking and kissing me "down there." My first thought after I realized that homosexuals had oral sex with each other was "Wow, they must feel a lot more positive than I do about their own bodies to have oral sex with genitals like their own." With all the really awful problems in the world—child abuse, poverty, malnutrition, racial strife—why some people devote their time and energy into opposing homosexuality baffles me. (Authors' files)

Many people think of homosexuality as sexual contact between individuals of the same sex. However, this definition is not quite complete. It does not take into account two important dimensions—the context within which the sexual activity is experienced and the feelings and perceptions of the people involved. Nor does it encompass all the meanings of the word **homosexual,** which can refer to erotic attraction, sexual behavior, emotional attachment, and a definition of self (Eliason & Morgan, 1998). The following definition incorporates a broader spectrum of elements: A homosexual person is an individual "whose primary erotic, psychological, emotional, and social interest is in a member of the same sex, even though those interests may not be overtly expressed" (Martin & Lyon, 1972, p. 1).

Homosexual
A person whose primary erotic, psychological, emotional, and social orientation is toward members of the same sex.

A homosexual person's gender identity agrees with his or her biological sex. That is, a homosexual person perceives himself or herself as male or female, respectively, and feels attraction toward a same-sex person.

Gay
A homosexual, particularly a homosexual man.

Lesbian
A female homosexual.

A common synonym for homosexual is **gay.** *Gay* was initially used as a code word between homosexuals, and it has moved into popular usage to describe homosexual men and women, as well as social and political concerns related to homosexual orientation. Homosexual women are often referred to as **lesbians.** Pejorative words such as *faggot, fairy, homo, queer, lezzie,* and *dyke* have traditionally been used to demean homosexuality. However, within certain gay subcultures, some gay people use these terms with each other in positive or humorous ways (Bryant & Demian, 1998).

A Continuum of Sexual Orientations

Sexual orientation
Sexual attraction to one's own sex (homosexual) or the other sex (heterosexual).

Bisexuality
Attraction to both same- and other-sex partners.

Homosexuality, bisexuality, and *heterosexuality* are words that identify one's **sexual orientation**—that is, to which of the sexes one is attracted. Attraction to same-sex partners is a homosexual orientation, and attraction to other-sex partners is a heterosexual orientation. **Bisexuality** refers to attraction to both same- and other-sex partners. Because sexual orientation is only one aspect of a person's life, this text uses these three terms as descriptive adjectives rather than as nouns that label one's total identity.

In our society, we tend to make clear-cut distinctions between homosexuality and heterosexuality. Actually, the delineation is not so precise. A relatively small percentage of people consider themselves to be exclusively homosexual; over 90% think of themselves as exclusively heterosexual. These groups represent the opposite ends of a broad spectrum. Individuals between the ends of the spectrum exhibit varying mixtures of preference and/or experience, which may also change over time. Sexual orientation is best evaluated by observing patterns over a life span rather than at any given time (Fox, 1990).

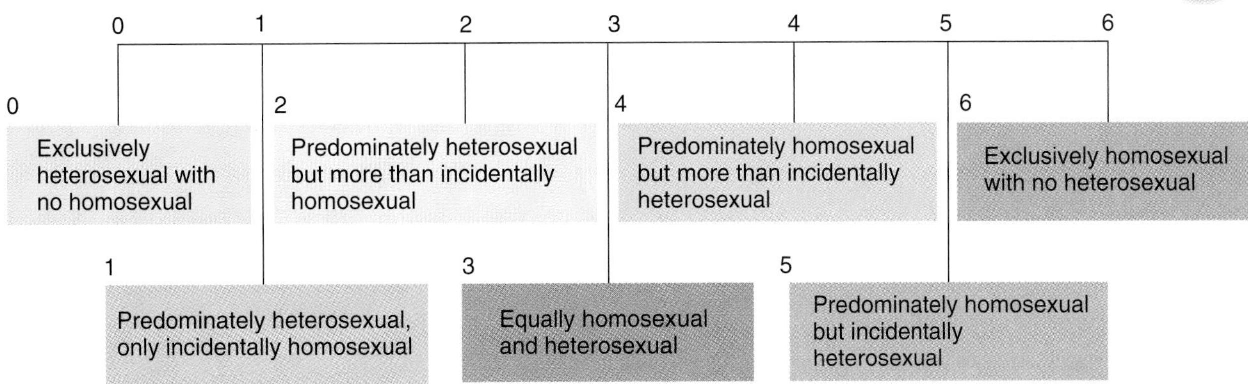

Figure 10.1

Kinsey's continuum of sexual orientation. (Adapted from Kinsey et al., 1948, p. 638.)

The Kinsey Scale

Figure 10.1 shows a seven-point continuum that Alfred Kinsey devised in his analysis of sexual orientations in American society (Kinsey et al., 1948). The scale ranges from 0 (exclusive contact with and erotic attraction to the other sex) to 6 (exclusive contact with and attraction to the same sex). In between are varying degrees of homosexual and heterosexual orientation; category 3 represents equal homosexual and heterosexual attraction and experience.

What proportion of people in our society fall into the exclusively homosexual category on the continuum?

According to the Kinsey data, the exclusively homosexual category comprised 2% of women and 4% of men. Kinsey's estimates were made some time ago, however, and they have been criticized. The more recent National Health and Social Life survey (see Table 10.1) found somewhat lower statistics of 1.4% of women and 2.8% of men who currently identify themselves as homosexual. However, two other questions elicited higher statistics. One asked subjects if they had had sex with another man or woman since age 18; about 5% of men and 4% of women had done so. A third question asked about feelings of sexual interest in same-sex partners. More respondents had felt sexual attraction to individuals of the same sex than had actually experienced a gay or lesbian sexual encounter; 5.5% of women and 6% of men said they were attracted to others of the same sex. The real answer to the question "How many people are homosexual?" is "It depends on how you ask the question" (Laumann et al., 1994).

Bisexuality

In interpreting the continuum shown in Figure 10.1, we want to caution against too broad a use of the word *bisexual.* There is a tendency to use behavior as the only criterion for sexual orientation and to use *bisexual* as a catchall to describe the considerable number of people who fall between exclusive heterosexuality and exclusive homosexuality. This grouping fails to take into account the context within which the sexual experiences occur and the feelings and thoughts of the individuals involved. It is the context, not the contact, that may be most significant. According to one definition, a bisexual person is one who can "enjoy and engage in sexual activity with members of both sexes, or recognizes a desire to do so" (MacDonald, 1981). The majority of bisexuals establish heterosexuality first in their lives and then, over time, include homosexual relationships. Most do not define themselves as bisexual until years after their initial dual attractions (Weinberg et al., 1994).

Table 10.1 Who's Straight, Gay, or Bi? How Do You Measure?

	Men	Women
Identify self as homosexual	2.8%	1.4%
Sex with a same-sex partner after age 18	5%	4%
Feelings of attraction toward someone of the same sex	6%	5.5%

Source: Laumann et al., 1994.

Kinsey's continuum of sexual orientation has been questioned, especially in regard to bisexuality. On Kinsey's scale, individuals lose degrees of one orientation as they move toward the opposite end of the scale; thus, bisexual individuals are seen as a compromise between the two extremes. In another model, a bisexual orientation is viewed as showing high rather than moderate degrees of both homosexuality and heterosexuality (Storms, 1980). This view is supported by the type and frequency of sexual fantasies reported by subjects in the various groups in a recent study. As might be expected, homosexual research participants reported more fantasy about the same sex than about the other sex, whereas heterosexual subjects reported the reverse. But contrary to what one might predict from the Kinsey scale, bisexual subjects reported as much same-sex fantasy as homosexual individuals and as much other-sex fantasy as heterosexual individuals. In other words, bisexual people seem to have a high degree of general erotic interest (Lever, 1997).

Types of Bisexuality

There are several different types of bisexuality: bisexuality as a real orientation, as a transitory orientation, as a transitional orientation, or as homosexual denial (Fox, 1990). Bisexuality as a real orientation means that some people are born with a natural attraction to both sexes, and this attraction continues into adulthood. An individual with this orientation might or might not be sexually active with more than one partner at a time but would continue to be capable of feelings of attraction to both sexes. Some research indicates that women move between straight, bisexual, and lesbian relationships more easily than men; men tend to be more fixed in their orientation (Burr, 1996).

Bisexual behavior can also be transitory—a temporary involvement by people who are actually heterosexual or homosexual. These individuals will return fully to their original orientation after a period of bisexual experimentation or experiences. Transitory homosexual behavior may occur in single-sex boarding schools and prisons, yet the people involved resume heterosexual relationships when the opportunities are again available. Some prostitutes or male hustlers may do business with either sex and yet be involved in only heterosexual or homosexual relationships in their personal lives.

Bisexuality can also be a transitional state in which a person is changing from one orientation to another. This person will remain in the new orientation, as illustrated in the following account:

> I had led a traditional life with a husband, two kids, and community activities. My best friend and I were very active in the PTA together. Much to our surprise, we fell in love. We were initially secretive about our sexual relationship and continued our marital lives, but then we both divorced our husbands and moved away to start a life together. The best way I can describe being with her is that life is now like a color TV, instead of a black-and-white. (Authors' files)

Finally, bisexuality may sometimes be an attempt to deny exclusive homosexual interests and to avoid the full stigma of homosexual identity (MacDonald, 1981). Gay men and lesbians sometimes view the bisexual person as someone who really is homosexual but lacks the courage to identify himself or herself as such. For example, a number of people marry to maintain a facade of heterosexuality but continue to have strong homosexual desires or secretive homosexual contacts. This type of bisexuality may be more likely to be expressed in Asian American culture. Asian culture traditionally values fulfilling family roles, respecting and obeying elders, having children, and continuing the family name. Within this context, an individual could feel particularly compelled to keep homosexual behavior hidden and private while meeting expected roles of marriage, family, and community to prevent bringing "shame" to the family (Matteson, 1997).

Bisexuals: Their Own Category

Sexual orientation is often viewed as an either/or situation—one is either heterosexual or homosexual. Many people are uncomfortable with shades of gray in sexual orientation. Western culture is dominated by dichotomous thinking and polarization, and the fluid sexuality of bisexuality defies black/white categorization (Firestein, 1996). Researchers have tended to categorize people who engage in sexual activity with both sexes as homosexual, when they would be more accurately understood as bisexual (Leland, 1995). Self-identified bisexual individuals may be met with ambivalence and suspicion and are often pressured by heterosexual or homosexual people to adhere to one orientation (Lever, 1995; Shernoff, 1998). Even without pressure, they may believe they must be "either/or." One study found that few bisexual men participated in the gay community (McKirnan et al., 1995). Bisexual individuals "who associate with the gay/lesbian community as well as with the heterosexual mainstream may find themselves shifting social identities: The attempt to bridge both worlds with a single identity can be a source of stress and discomfort in both social arenas" (Paul, 1984, p. 54). It can be uniquely challenging to develop an opposite-sex relationship after having had a gay or lesbian identity. For example, JoAnn Loulan, long-time lesbian activist and author of *Lesbian Sex*, received a great deal of negative reaction from other lesbians when she became involved with a man (Gideonse, 1997).

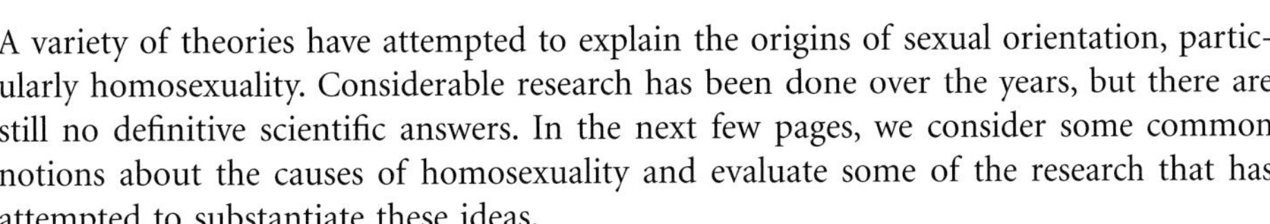

What Determines Sexual Orientation?

What determines sexual orientation? Do you think sexual orientation is caused by "nature" or "nurture"?

A variety of theories have attempted to explain the origins of sexual orientation, particularly homosexuality. Considerable research has been done over the years, but there are still no definitive scientific answers. In the next few pages, we consider some common notions about the causes of homosexuality and evaluate some of the research that has attempted to substantiate these ideas.

Bell and his colleagues (1981) have conducted the most comprehensive study to date about the development of sexual orientation. They used a sample of 979 homosexual men and women matched to a control group of 477 heterosexual people. All research subjects were asked questions about their childhood, adolescence, and sexual practices during four-hour, face-to-face interviews. The researchers then used sophisticated statistical techniques to analyze possible causal factors in the development of homosexuality or heterosexuality. This research is cited frequently throughout this section because of its excellent methodology.

Psychosocial Theories

Psychosocial explanations of the development of a homosexual orientation relate to life incidents, parenting patterns, or psychological attributes of the individual.

"By Default" Theory

Unhappy heterosexual experiences or the inability to attract partners of the other sex are sometimes believed to cause a person to become or choose to be homosexual. Stereotypes that homosexuals are less attractive than others are common. For example, in one study college students of both sexes were shown photographs of 22 women and asked to identify the half who were reputed to be homosexuals. The students tended to identify people they perceived as less attractive as the homosexuals (Dew, 1985). Statements such as "All a lesbian needs is a good lay" or "He just needs to meet the right woman" reflect the notion that homosexuality is a poor second choice for people who lack satisfactory heterosexual experiences. It is often assumed that lesbianism is due to resentment, dislike, fear, or distrust of men rather than attraction toward women. The illogic of this argument is clear if we turn it around and say that female heterosexuality is caused by a dislike and fear of women. Actually, research indicates that up to 70% of lesbians have had sexual experiences with men, and many report having enjoyed them. However, they prefer to be sexual with women (Klaich, 1974). Bell and his colleagues' analysis of their data indicated that "homosexual orientation among females reflects neither a lack of heterosexual experience nor a history of particularly unpleasant heterosexual experiences" (1981, p. 176).

Bell's research also found that homosexual and heterosexual groups did not differ in their frequency of dating during high school. This refutes the belief that lack of heterosexual opportunity causes homosexuality. The male and female homosexual subjects did tend, however, to feel differently about dating than did their heterosexual counterparts; fewer homosexual subjects reported that they enjoyed dating.

The Seduction Myth

Do you think homosexuality is "caught" or otherwise learned through seduction, or by exposure to an older homosexual person? Do you think it has origins in any earlier childhood experiences?

Another myth dispelled by the Bell study is that young men and women become homosexual because they have been seduced by older homosexuals. In contrast, most homosexual people have their first homosexual encounter with someone about their own age. Some people may believe that homosexuality can be "caught" from someone else, particularly a well-liked and respected homosexual teacher. However, a homosexual orientation appears to be established even before school age.

Freud's Theory

Another prevalent theory has to do with certain patterns in a person's family background. Psychoanalytic theory implicated both childhood experiences and relationships with parents: Sigmund Freud (1905) maintained that the relationship with one's father and mother was a critical factor. Freud believed that in "normal" development, we all pass through a "homoerotic" phase. He argued that boys could become fixated at this homosexual phase if they had a poor relationship with their father and an overly close relationship with their mother; the same thing might happen to a woman if she developed envy for the penis (Black, 1994). Later clinical research attempted to confirm this hypothesis (Bieber et al., 1962). Although these patterns were shown to exist in some cases (Saghir & Robins, 1973), it is also true that many homosexual individuals do not fit the mold—that is, their mothers are not dominant nor are their fathers emotionally detached. And at the same time, plenty of heterosexual people were reared in families where this pattern prevailed. Bell and his colleagues (1981) concluded that, although evidence suggests that male homosexuality may in some cases be related to poor father–son relationships, no particular phenomenon of family life could be singled out as "especially consequential for either homosexual or heterosexual development" (p. 190). Their findings were supported by another study of homosexual and heterosexual men who had never undergone therapy (Ross & Arrindell, 1988).

"The Exotic Becomes Erotic"

A psychologist, Daryl Bem (1995), has proposed a theory of development of sexual orientation based on the premise that the "exotic becomes erotic." This process involves a combination of psychosocial and biological factors. He proposes that genetic and biological factors influence childhood temperament in regards to aggression and activity level rather than sexual orientation per se. Most boys are more aggressive and active than girls and are attracted to activities distinct from those that appeal to girls. However, some children prefer gender-nonconforming play—boys who like to play dolls or girls who would rather play football are likely to have playmates of the other, rather than same, sex. Children will spend time with playmates and friends who enjoy similar kinds of activities. These like-minded children will feel familiar and comfortable, whereas children with opposite temperaments will seem dissimilar.

In essence, the theory proposes that as we move into adolescence, our erotic arousal is fueled by the anxiety we feel relating to someone who is different from us (exotic): the football-playing girl (or boy) with boyfriend buddies feels herself (himself) attracted to the girl she (he) never played with during her childhood. The exotic becomes erotic, and we find ourselves attracted to partners who differ from the preferred sex of our childhood playmates.

Bem's theory has been criticized on several fronts. First, research does not support Bem's supposition that gays and lesbians' childhood playmates are primarily of the other sex. Most children who grow up to be straight or gay had close same-sex friends, a significant proportion of friends of the same sex, and considerable contact with other-sex peers. Secondly, his theory is especially weak in regards to lesbians, who, in general, are particularly likely to form an erotic attraction rising out of an emotional attachment based on connectedness and familiarity. Multiple developmental pathways may be more salient than one model of development of sexual orientation (Peplau et al., 1998).

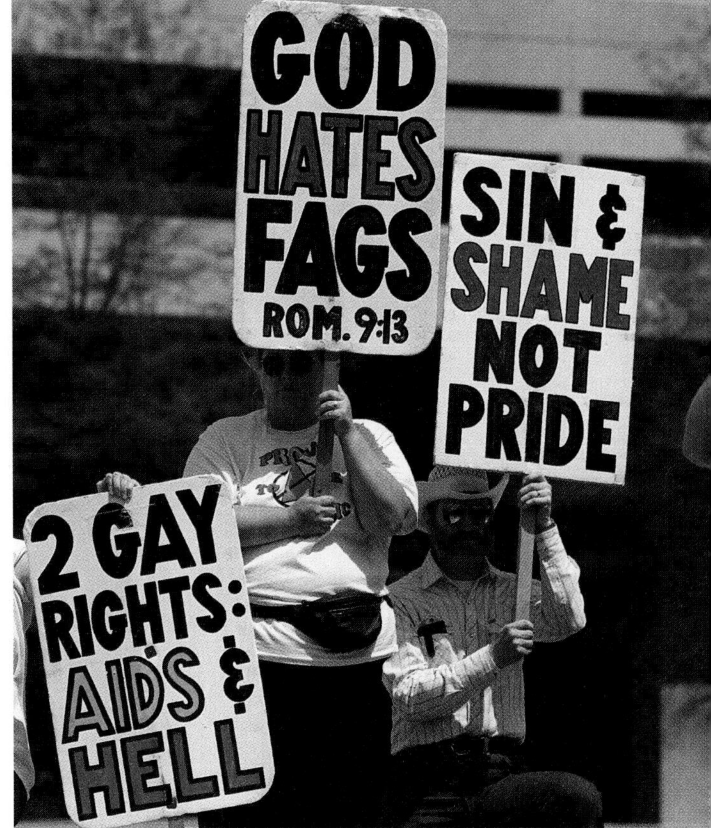

Gay men and lesbians are faced with the political action, hatred, and violence against homosexuality that is prevalent in the United States.

To Be Homosexual in a Heterosexual Society

In light of contemporary research on homosexuality—and taking into account that both the American Psychiatric and Psychological Associations no longer categorize homosexuality as a mental illness—most therapists and counselors have changed the focus of therapy. Rather than assuming that they must "cure" homosexual clients by changing their sexual orientation, therapists are trying instead to help them to love, live, and work in a society that harbors considerable hostility toward them (Moran, 1992). This change in therapeutic practice is significant in that it defines the problem as society's negativity toward homosexuality rather than homosexuality itself.

Biological Theories

Researchers have explored a number of areas in an effort to establish biological causes for sexual orientation.

Hormones

One line of investigation has been adult hormone levels, which some researchers have speculated may contribute to homosexuality. However, no well-controlled research has found a difference in the circulating levels of sex hormones in adult heterosexual and homosexual males (Money, 1988). And even if consistent differences could be identified, it would be difficult to tell whether they were a cause or result of sexual orientation. The stress and anxiety that many homosexual people experience as a result of societal oppression may itself influence hormone levels. Many researchers believe that adult hormone levels will prove irrelevant because sexual orientation is established well before adulthood (Money, 1988).

Another line of research has investigated prenatal hormone levels. As we saw in Chapter 3, these can alter the masculine and feminine development of the fetal brain. Some researchers believe that prenatal hormone levels can also contribute to homosexual orientation (Zuger, 1989). Laboratory research with animals has demonstrated that hormones given prenatally can masculinize fetal females and demasculinize fetal males. This results in other-sex social and mating behavior when the animals mature.

There is a critical period during human gestation in which the fetus is especially sensitive to levels of sex hormones. Prenatal hormonal imbalances during this period could contribute to homosexuality (Meyer-Bahlburg et al., 1995). It may also be possible for both prenatal masculinization and feminization to coexist to some degree, with a consequent bisexual orientation. Nutritional changes, medicine and drugs, and maternal stress alter maternal hormones in animals (Money, 1988). However, a 1991 study found no correlation between maternal stress during pregnancy and sexual orientation of the human offspring (Bailey & Pillard, 1991). Any conclusions drawn about humans from animal studies are uncertain, and it is obviously unethical to experiment on human fetuses.

The Brain

Research published in 1991 reported structural differences in the brains of homosexual and heterosexual men, lending plausibility to a biological basis for sexual orientation. Salk Institute scientist Simon LeVay (1991) studied the brains of 41 cadavers—19 homosexual men, 16 presumed heterosexual men, and 6 presumed heterosexual women. He found that the anterior hypothalamus, an area of the brain that influences sexual behavior, was half as large in homosexual men as in heterosexual men. LeVay cautioned that the difference he observed provides no direct evidence that it causes sexual orientation. However, his findings encourage further research in this direction (Nimmons, 1994).

Genetic Factors

A third line of research has suggested the possibility that genetic factors may contribute to homosexuality (Hamer et al., 1993; Turner, 1995). Researchers studied three all-male groups: identical twins, fraternal twins, and adoptive brothers. They found that when one brother was homosexual, so were 52% of the identical twins, 22% of the fraternal twins, and 11% of the adoptive brothers (Bailey & Pillard, 1991; Bailey et al., 1993). A similar study of women found the same pattern (Bailey & Pillard, 1994). These results may also be due in part to environmental factors, but the large differences between identical twins and the other two groups strongly indicate a genetic component to sexual orientation. Some researchers have hypothesized that genes affect the part of the brain that LeVay studied (Holden, 1992).

Gender Nonconformity

Gender nonconformity A lack of conformity to stereotypic masculine and feminine behaviors.

Other evidence for a biological predisposition toward homosexuality comes from the strong link that exists between adult homosexuality and **gender nonconformity** as a child. Gender nonconformity concerns the extent to which an individual conforms to stereotypic characteristics of masculinity or femininity during childhood; it is measured by asking respondents how traditionally masculine or feminine they were as children and how much they enjoyed conventional boys' or girls' activities.

Researchers have found that male and female homosexual adults are more likely to have experienced gender nonconformity during childhood than have heterosexual adults (Bailey & Zucker, 1995; Phillips & Over, 1995). One-half of homosexual males, but only one-quarter of heterosexual males, did not conform to a typical "masculine" identity pattern, whereas about four-fifths of homosexual females, but only two-thirds of heterosexual females, were not highly "feminine" during childhood (Bell et al., 1981).

Similar patterns have been documented cross-culturally. A comparative study of males in the United States, Guatemala, and Brazil indicated that gender nonconformity

Table 10.2 How the Belief That Homosexuals Are "Born That Way" Influences Attitudes About Homosexuality

Total Adults 1154		Those who say homosexuality . . . is a choice (%)	cannot be changed (%)
78%	Say homosexuals should have equal rights in terms of job opportunities	69	90
55%	Object to having a homosexual as a child's elementary schoolteacher	71	39
46%	Say homosexual relations between consenting adults should be legal	32	62
34%	Would permit their child to play at the home of a friend who lives with a homosexual parent	21	50
22%	Have a close friend or family member who is gay or lesbian	16	29

Source: Schmalz, 1993.

related to childhood toy and activity interests, as well as sexual interest in other boys, were behavioral indicators of adult homosexual orientation (Whitam, 1980).

Bell and his colleagues speculated that "if there is a biological basis for homosexuality, it probably accounts for gender nonconformity as well as for sexual orientation" (1981, p. 217). A 15-year longitudinal study that compared gender-role behavior in boys and later sexual orientation found similar results (Green, 1987). In addition, research on cognitive abilities in adults has found that cognitive patterns of homosexual men fall between the cognitive patterns of heterosexual men and heterosexual women in regard to spatial ability and verbal fluency, again suggesting brain differences (McCormick et al., 1990).

Implications if Biology Is Destiny

What do you think the impact would be if sexual orientation were absolutely proven to be biologically caused?

The evidence for biological causation of homosexuality raises some important issues. If homosexuality were found to be biologically based, the assumption that homosexuality is unnatural would be challenged because something biologically innate is natural for that person. Society might thus become more accepting of homosexuality (Stein, 1994). People who believe homosexuals were "born that way" have more positive, accepting attitudes about homosexuality than those who believed that homosexuals chose or learned to be homosexual (Gelman et al., 1993; Wolfe, 1998). Table 10.2 illustrates how this one belief shapes many other attitudes about homosexuality. Yet opinions are almost evenly divided on whether homosexuality is biologically caused. In one survey, 44% of respondents thought that homosexuality is a matter of choice, while 43% believed it is something that a person cannot change (Schmalz, 1993).

What additional changes might result if homosexuality were proven to be biologically caused? For one, parents who have blamed themselves or have been blamed by others for causing what they view as an aberration might be relieved of their guilt. Society's expectations for gender-role behaviors might become more flexible if gender nonconformity was accepted as based on biology. On the other hand, if homosexuality were shown to be biologically caused and homosexuals were labeled as biologically "defective," attempts to use abortion to eliminate homosexuality or biologic engineering to prevent or change homosexuality in utero might be implemented (Gideonse, 1997; Gore, 1998).

In Conclusion

In conclusion, research suggests that there is a biological predisposition to exclusive homosexuality. However, the causes of sexual orientation in general, and especially bisexuality, remain speculative and most likely rely on multiple developmental pathways. It seems most appropriate to think of the continuum of sexual orientation as influenced by an interaction of various psychosocial and biological factors, which may be unique for each person, than to think in terms of a single cause for sexual orientation (Kitzinger & Wilkinson, 1995).

Societal Attitudes

Around the world, societal attitudes toward homosexuality vary considerably. As we see in the boxed discussion, "Homosexuality in Cross-Cultural Perspective," most societies consider at least some homosexual practices socially acceptable.

Religious Attitudes Toward Homosexuality

Within the Judeo–Christian tradition that predominates in our own North American culture, homosexuality has been viewed negatively. Many religious scholars believe that the condemnation of homosexuality increased during a reformation movement beginning in the seventh century B.C., through which Jewish religious leaders wanted to develop a distinct, closed community that was different from others of the time. Homosexual activities were a part of the religious services of many groups of people in that era, and rejecting such religious rituals was one way of enhancing the uniqueness of their religion (Kosnik et al., 1977). Strong prohibitive biblical scriptures were written: "You shall not lie with a man as one lies with a female, it is an abomination" (Leviticus 18:22). We saw in Chapter 1 that the primary purpose of sexual interaction in the Judeo–Christian tradition is procreation, not pleasure. The pursuit of sexual pleasure outside of that purpose,

Sexuality and Diversity

Homosexuality in Cross-Cultural Perspective

Attitudes toward homosexuality have varied considerably. A number of studies of other cultures have revealed widespread acceptance of homosexual activities. One survey of 190 societies found that two-thirds of them considered homosexuality socially acceptable for certain individuals or on specific occasions (Ford & Beach, 1951). Homosexuality has been widely accepted in many earlier cultures. For example, over 50% of 225 Native American tribes accepted male homosexuality, and 17% accepted female homosexuality (Pomeroy, 1965). In ancient Greece, homosexual relationships between men were considered a superior intellectual and spiritual expression of love, whereas heterosexuality provided the more pragmatic benefits of children and a family unit.

Some societies *require* their members to engage in homosexual activities. For example, all male members of the Sambia society in the mountains of New Guinea engage in exclusively homosexual activities from approximately seven years of age until their late teens or early twenties, when they marry. Sambian men believe that a prepubertal boy becomes a strong warrior and hunter by drinking as much semen as possible from postpubertal boys' penises. Once a boy reaches puberty, he must no longer fellate other boys but can experience erotic pleasure from fellatio by boys who cannot yet ejaculate. From the start of their erotic lives and during the years of peak orgasmic capacity, young men engage in frequent, obligatory, and gratifying homoeroticism. During the same period, look-

whether practiced by homosexual or heterosexual individuals, has traditionally been viewed as immoral. However, in more recent years some theologians have modified their views. The boxed discussion, "Four Contemporary Christian Views on Homosexuality," summarizes the major theological positions on homosexuality within the Christian church today.

Laws against homosexual behaviors, which stem from biblical injunctions against same-sex contact, have historically been exceedingly punitive. People with homosexual orientations have been tortured and put to death throughout Western history. In the American colonies, homosexual people were condemned to death by drowning and burning. In the late 1770s, Thomas Jefferson was among the political leaders who suggested reducing the punishment from death to castration for men who committed homosexual acts (Katz, 1976).

From Sin to Sickness

In the early- to mid-1900s, there was a shift in societal attitudes toward homosexuality. The belief that homosexual people were sinners was replaced to some degree by the belief that they were "sick" (Esterberg, 1990). The medical and psychological professions have used drastic treatments in attempting to cure the "illness" of homosexuality. Surgical procedures such as castration were performed in the 1800s. As late as 1951, lobotomy (brain surgery that severs nerve fibers in the frontal lobe of the brain) was performed as a "cure" for homosexuality. Psychotherapy, drugs, hormones, hypnosis, shock treatments, and aversion therapy (pairing nausea-inducing drugs or electrical shock with homosexual stimuli) have all been used to the same end (Kaiser, 1994; Katz, 1976).

Actually, the research of several decades contradicts the notion that homosexual people are "sick." The first major research to compare the adjustment of nonpatient heterosexual and homosexual individuals found no significant differences between the two groups (Hooker, 1967). Further research has supported these findings (Isay, 1989; Mannion, 1981; Wilson, 1984). Alan Bell and Martin Weinberg summarized that "homosexual adults who have come to terms with their homosexuality, who do not regret their sexual orientation, and who can function effectively sexually and socially, are no more distressed psychologically than are heterosexual men and women" (1978, p. 216). In 1973

Sexuality and Diversity

ing at or touching females is taboo. Yet as they approach marriage, these youths create powerful erotic daydreams about women. During the first weeks of marriage, they experience only fellatio with their wives, but they then change to include intercourse as a part of their heterosexual activity. Following marriage, they stop homosexual activity, experience great sexual desire for women, and engage exclusively in heterosexual activity for the rest of their lives (Stoller & Herdt, 1985).

Recent events in Cuba demonstrate how a society can make rapid changes regarding homosexuality. During the 35 years of the Communist revolution, lesbians and gay men were seen as deviant anti-revolutionaries and were expelled from the Communist party and state and university jobs. Some were sent to labor camps. The persecution caused many, especially gay intellectuals, to leave Cuba in the early 1980s. In 1992, Castro blamed the previous homophobia on ingrained machismo attitudes. He expressed support for gay rights and described homosexuality as a natural human tendency that must be respected. This shift may be an attempt to stop the exodus of gay professionals or may be due to the national priority of the economic crisis. For whatever reason, gay men and lesbians now can walk down the street holding hands and join one of the several gay organizations without fear of reprisal (Otis, 1994).

However, violation of basic human rights for gays and lesbians is a common experience in many places around the globe. Amnesty International USA has increased its attention to these problems. This group has documented abuses ranging from the decapitation murder of a bisexual politician in Brazil, "social cleansing" death squads in Colombia, the death penalty for homosexual acts in Iran, exile to labor camps in China, to fabricated charges against gay and AIDS activists in many countries (Levy, 1994).

the American Psychiatric Association, after great internal conflict, removed homosexuality per se from its diagnostic categories of mental disorders. However, heterosexist bias remains a concern in mental health and family therapy research and treatment (Clark & Serovich, 1997; Tyler et al., 1997).

Homophobia

Homophobia
Irrational fears of homosexuality, the fear of the possibility of homosexuality in oneself, or self-loathing toward one's own homosexuality.

Some of society's antihomosexual attitudes stem from what Martin Weinberg (1973) labeled **homophobia.** Homophobia is defined as irrational fears of homosexuality in others, the fear of homosexual feelings within oneself, or self-loathing because of one's homosexuality. It stems from ignorance and popular myths that give rise to homosexual prejudice. Negative, hostile attitudes toward homosexuality have also been labeled "homohatred" (Kirk & Madsen, 1989). Beliefs that deny, denigrate, or stigmatize non-heterosexual behavior, identity, relationships, and communities are also defined as "heterosexism" (Berkman & Zinberg, 1997).

The recent recognition and discussion of homophobia represent a significant shift in views toward homosexuality: Although still very common, homophobic attitudes are more likely to be viewed as the problem, rather than homosexuality itself. However, some reactions to the AIDS crisis have reflected strong homophobic bias. Jerry Falwell, founder of the now-defunct fundamentalist political group Moral Majority, called the outbreak of AIDS a "form of judgment of God upon a society." Research findings show that negative attitudes toward homosexual persons correlate with negative attitudes toward people with AIDS (Bruce & Tarant, 1997; O'Hare et al., 1996).

Sexuality and Diversity
Four Contemporary Christian Views on Homosexuality

Current theological positions toward homosexuality demonstrate a great range of convictions within Christian churches. Different stances arise between denominations and also within the same denomination (Woodward & Underwood, 1997). For example, within the Episcopal Church an openly gay bishop works in California without problem, whereas a heterosexual bishop in New Jersey was nearly stripped of his title for ordaining a gay man (Dahir, 1997). In addition, the 1997 National Conference of Catholic Bishops directed parents to love their gay and lesbian children: "God does not love someone any less simply because he or she is homosexual." However, the Pope and church doctrine remain morally opposed to homosexuality (Briggs, 1997, p. A1).

Theologian James Nelson (1980) described four stances represented in contemporary Christianity. The first is a rejecting–punitive orientation, which unconditionally rejects homosexuality and bears a punitive attitude toward gay people. This position is the predominant one in Christian history. For many centuries, the church ostracized homosexual people from church and community life and gave its blessings to civil persecutions, including killing discovered homosexuals. The theology of this position rests on selective biblical literalism. The Greek Orthodox church's statement from the Biennial Clergy–Laity Congress of 1976 exemplifies this theological position:

> [T]he function of the sexual organs of a man and a woman . . . are ordained by nature to serve the procreation of human kind. Therefore, any and all uses of the human sex organs for purposes other than those ordained by creation, runs contrary to the nature of things as decreed by God. . . . The Orthodox Church believes that homosexuality should be treated by society as an immoral and dangerous perversion and by religion as a sinful failure. (Batchelor, 1980, p. 237)

The 1997 Southern Baptist boycott of the Disney corporation for "promotion of homosexuality" is an example of this thinking in action (Heitz, 1997). The church's resolution urges its 15 million members of the nation's largest Protestant denomination to protest what they judge to be Disney's "anti-Christian and anti-family direction." They object to Disney providing its employees domestic partnership benefits, per-

Homophobia can be exhibited in many ways, both subtle (even unconscious) and blatant. College students taking human sexuality classes report some examples of homophobia they have seen:

> The silence that follows when someone mentions that he or she is gay; queer jokes; calling them rude names like fag, queer, fairy, and treating them as if they had some disease; beating and harassing gays. (Authors' files)

Many psychologists believe that such aggression toward homosexuals is an attempt to deny or suppress homosexual feelings in oneself. Men tend to express more negative attitudes in general toward homosexual men than do women (Louderback & Whitley, 1997).

Gender-Role Threat

Any gender-role reversal can be perceived as threatening. Some people have viewed male homosexuals as "defective" because they are believed to share characteristics with women—the "inferior" sex (Lewes, 1988). Some men in their teens and twenties are particularly hostile toward gay men. Comments from students indicate particularly negative attitudes of young males about gay men.

> I hate gay men.

> When my friends are driving around town and spot a car with a rainbow flag bumper sticker, they get outraged and want to run the car off the road. (Authors' files)

Sexuality and Diversity

mitting "Gay Days" at its theme parks and allowing Disney-owned ABC to air *Ellen*'s coming-out show (Kopenec, 1997). The Christian men's group the Promise Keepers also appear to have this first orientation. Bill McCartney, the founder of the group, has said, "We see homosexuality as a sin," and participants in their 1997 Washington, D.C., rally screamed antilesbian epithets at members of the National Organization of Women who were protesting the event (*"The Advocate Report,"* November 11, 1997).

The rejecting–nonpunitive position maintains that homosexuality is inherently unnatural and must be condemned, but because of Christ's grace, the homosexual person must not be condemned. This position supports the civil liberties of gay people, recognizing the injustice and hypocrisy in their persecution. A reaction to the Baptist boycott of Disney exemplifies this position. "Unlike the Southern Baptist Convention, most people of faith recognize that they can disagree over whether or not homosexuality is right and still agree that discrimination against gay people is wrong" (Kopenec, 1997, p. A6). A pastor of a Baptist church in Texas, who believes homosexuality is a sin but opposes the boycott, also believes the right way to confront immorality is to learn what Jesus taught: Let him who is without sin cast the first stone (Morganthau, 1997).

The third position, qualified acceptance, maintains that homosexuality is a sin but acknowledges that homosexuality is largely unsusceptible to change by contemporary medical and psychological science. Therefore, homosexual people who cannot refrain from sexual interaction should maintain fully committed relationships.

The fourth major theological position is full acceptance. This perspective views sexuality as intrinsically important to the capacity for human love. It maintains that ethical sexual relationships include commitment to each other, trust, tenderness, and respect for the other regardless of the sex of the partners. Full acceptance includes providing a church blessing of the union of those who vow a lifelong commitment to each other. Although many churches' official policies do not allow church bonding ceremonies for gays and lesbians, some clergy support and perform bonding ceremonies for homosexual couples (Dotinga, 1998). As another aspect of complete acceptance, gay Christians are welcomed into every aspect of the life of the congregation, including ordination as ministers. (The first major American denomination to ordain an openly gay candidate was the United Church of Christ in 1972; it was followed four years later by an Episcopalian church.) Full acceptance also includes support for the civil rights of gays and lesbians. The advocates of full acceptance are still a minority. However, the support of churches is crucial for the civil rights movement for gay men and lesbians to be fully successful (Sullivan, 1997).

Homophobia may be related to traditional gender-role stereotypes: Individuals who hold more traditional gender-role stereotypes tend to have more negative feelings about homosexuality than do others (Louderback & Whitley, 1997; Kyes & Tumbelaka, 1994). Bell and his colleagues discussed the idea that homosexuality confronts people with their ability to tolerate diversity in gender roles:

> In a society such as ours a special loathing is reserved for any male who appears to have forfeited the privileges and responsibilities associated with upholding the conventional imagery of males. The spectre of a group of males living outside the strict confines of "masculinity" can appear as a threat to men who are not entirely certain about their own maleness and thus heighten whatever antagonisms are expressed toward those who do not follow male "rules." Similarly, to the degree that lesbianism is associated with the rejection of traditionally "feminine" roles and responsibilities, heterosexual women may feel threatened by those who do not join their ranks. (1981, p. 221)

In Latin American and East Asian societies gender role is a far more important variable than the sex of the partner. A critical distinction has been who penetrates whom in anal and oral sex. The male who is the insertive partner maintains his manhood and is considered heterosexual. However, the receptive partner is viewed as femalelike and, therefore, homosexual and inferior (Matteson, 1997).

Although heterosexual women and men hold similar attitudes toward lesbians and gay men, research finds that heterosexual men hold more negative attitudes toward gay men than they do toward lesbians. It appears that the erotic value straight men attribute to lesbians ameliorates the men's negative attitudes. Men's sexual interest in women being sexual together is exemplified in men's magazines and X-rated videos showing women together. The general tendency of men to view women in sexual terms may lead them to eroticize women having sex, resulting in more positive feelings than toward men having sex together, which threaten men's notions of masculinity (Louderback & Whitley, 1997). A female student states,

Many men I know are incredibly repulsed by male homosex, but actually sexually aroused by female homosex—the double standard really irks me. (Authors' files)

Homophobia's Impact on Heterosexuals

Another expression of homophobia may be the careful avoidance of any behavior that might be interpreted as homosexual. In this sense, homophobia can restrict the lives of heterosexual people. For example, during lovemaking, heterosexual men may be unable to enjoy having their nipples stimulated or may be reluctant to allow their female partners to take the lead, if they believe these behaviors demonstrate homosexual tendencies (Wells, 1991). Same-sex friends or family members may refrain from spontaneous embraces, people may shun "unfeminine" or "unmasculine" clothing, or a woman may decide not to identify herself as a feminist because she fears being called a lesbian. Homophobia may have an especially significant impact on the depth of intimacy in male friendships. Men's fear of same-sex attraction often keeps them from allowing themselves the emotional vulnerability required for deep friendship, thus limiting their relationships largely to competition and "buddyship" (Nelson, 1985).

Homophobic attitudes can change over time, with experience or deliberate effort. However, sex-role belief systems tend to be complex and difficult to change, yet are probably necessary to alter in order for heterosexuals, particularly men, to feel less negative toward homosexuality (Louderback & Whitley, 1997). Education can also play a role: Most students who take courses in human sexuality become more tolerant (Stevenson, 1990; Walters, 1994). One of our students described how this process occurred in his life:

My own reaction to learning that one of my fraternity brothers was gay was discomfort. I increasingly avoided him. I am sorry now that I didn't confront myself as to why I felt that way. I was homophobic. And because I didn't deal with that then, it kept me from developing a closeness with my other men friends. I lost something in those relationships because I was afraid that being physically and emotionally close to another male meant that I, too, was homosexual. I finally began to explore why I felt so uncomfortable touching or being touched by another man. Today I am no longer threatened or frightened by physical closeness from another man, even if I know his sexual preference is other men. I am secure enough to deal with that honestly. (Authors' files)

Homosexuality and the Media

Homosexuality has become more visible—and has been portrayed in a more positive light—in the 1990s media (Isherwood, 1997). The 1993 film *Philadelphia,* starring Tom Hanks, was the first major Hollywood feature to confront homophobia and AIDS and was a box-office success. Other prominent actors played homosexual roles in films, including Wesley Snipes and Patrick Swayze as flamboyant drag queens in *To Wong Foo Thanks for Everything Julie Newmar.* Robin Williams was a partner in a longtime gay relationship in *Birdcage,* a movie about two families with opposing social and sexual points of view. This popular film boldly proposed the acceptance of gays and was a box-office smash. These films showed the exotic or tragic side of homosexuality, which may be more acceptable to Hollywood than depicting gays as ordinary, reasonably complicated people who work or sit in class near you (Cortiss, 1998).

In the later 1990s more movies portrayed homosexuals in more ordinary roles. The financial success of earlier gay-themed films has created a new openness in Hollywood (Galvin, 1997). *The Incredibly True Adventure of Two Girls in Love* was a realistic story about two girls next door in a teenage lesbian relationship. In *My Best Friend's Wedding,* Rupert Everett plays Julia Roberts's charming, dynamic gay friend, who was the most likable person in the movie (Peyser, 1997). The film *In and Out,* with Kevin Klein and Tom Selleck, is a comedy about the outing of an Indiana farm town high school teacher and coach, and addresses the controversy about gay teachers (Stuart, 1997). Clint Eastwood directed *Midnight in the Garden of Good and Evil,* about a real-life gay murder in Georgia (Guthmann, 1997).

The pinnacle of portraying gays as regular folks was, of course, Ellen DeGeneres's coming out on her television show. Before her 1997 show, which drew a record 36.1 million viewers (DeCaro, 1997), there were at least two dozen gay characters on prime-time TV in supporting roles (Marin & Miller, 1997). The show *Roseanne* featured a number of lesbian and gay characters, *NYPD Blue*'s gay male receptionist had a boyfriend who is a policeman, on *Sisters* a lesbian character had had a baby by in vitro fertilization, and *Spin City, Beverly Hills 90210, Melrose Place,* and *Friends* featured homosexual characters as well. In *The Practice,* an attorney struggled with his homophobia when his 62-year-old mother asked his legal help to marry her lesbian partner. The soap opera *All My Children* had a gay teenager integrated into the story lines (Pela, 1998). Even *The Simpsons*' Homer met a gay character who, unlike himself, was intelligent. In-depth study of gay issues took place on television, including the PBS showing of *Pride Divide,* a documentary that explored the differences and conflicts between gay men and lesbians (Stockwell, 1997). However, *Ellen* was the first TV program with a gay person in the starring role and it continued to address gay issues until its end-of-season cancelation (Stockwell, 1998). The show drew strong support and condemnation, as reflected by letters to the editor in *Time* magazine (May 5, 1997) following an article about the episode. "Ellen's coming out will help everyone else see that gays are not freaks but are normal and sometimes even famous" versus "Your report was an affront to decency in general and the troubled family unit in particular." The show's overall acclaim was emphasized by DeGeneres winning an Emmy for best comedy writing for the coming out episode (Golden, 1998).

Ellen DeGeneres, lead actress on ABC's *Ellen* TV series, who made history in 1997 by coming out in real life and as a leading character on a comedy show, with her real-life partner Anne Heche.

Issues around homosexuality are frequent topics on television talk shows and news programs (Gideonse, 1998). On *20/20,* Olympic gold medalist Greg Louganis revealed he is gay and has AIDS, and on a *Barbara Walters Special* Elton John talked proudly about being gay and thanked his lover for his support when he received an Academy Award for his song in Disney's *The Lion King* (White, 1997). Rock star Melissa Etheridge and singer k. d. lang are out. Tennis great Martina Navratilova has been out since the early 1980s. After winning his second Mr. USA International title in 1997, Gene Kuffel, a middle-school teacher, announced he is gay. He will represent the United States in the Mr. International competition. Kuffel states, "I know there are kids out there . . . who need to be told and shown that it's OK to be who they are" (Lemon, 1997, p. 29). The teen character Lawrence in the popular newspaper comic strip *For Better or Worse* was the first mainstream comic to feature a gay person. These and similar developments may provide an opportunity for greater familiarity with and understanding of homosexuality as gays are more commonly known in mainstream media.

Lifestyles

We have seen in the preceding section that homosexual people cannot be clearly distinguished from heterosexual people on the basis of hormonal balance or mental health. This leads to another observation: Homosexual lifestyles are as varied as heterosexual lifestyles. All social classes, occupations, races, religions, and political persuasions are represented among homosexual people. The only characteristics that homosexual people necessarily have in common are their desire for emotional and sexual fulfillment with someone of the same sex and their shared experience of oppression from a hostile social environment.

Despite their many similarities to heterosexual people and the wide variety of their lifestyles, stereotypes about homosexual people exist (Hersch, 1991a). Many of these concern their physical appearance (Terry, 1990). It is true that some homosexual individuals dress and act according to commonly held stereotypes. Characteristics often associated with an identifiable homosexual man include exaggerated "feminine" gestures and tight and flashy clothing; in contrast, the image of a stereotypically recognizable lesbian includes such attributes as short hair and highly "masculine" clothing and gestures.

Although the incidence of people who fit such stereotypes is small, the stereotypes persist (Herek et al., 1991). This is in part because people who believe that homosexual individuals look a certain way notice and categorize (sometimes erroneously) those who seem to fit the image. The fact that most homosexual people may not fit the stereotype at all often goes unnoticed. One study found that neither heterosexual nor homosexual subjects could exceed chance levels of discriminating between videotaped interviews of homosexual and heterosexual men and women (Berger, 1990).

There are far more basic elements of a homosexual lifestyle than how a person dresses. We look briefly at some of these in the following sections.

Coming Out

The extent to which homosexual individuals decide to be secretive or open about their sexual orientation has a significant effect on their lifestyle. There are various degrees of being "in the closet," and several steps are involved in the process of **coming out**—acknowledging, accepting, and openly expressing one's homosexuality (Patterson, 1995). Although these decisions are unique to each individual and situation, there are often some common elements.

Coming out
The process of becoming aware of and disclosing one's homosexual identity.

Self-Acknowledgment

Individuals become aware of their homosexual feelings at different stages of life, as shown in Table 10.3. Very "closeted" homosexual men and women may attempt to suppress their sexual orientation even from their own awareness. These people may actively seek sexual encounters with members of the other sex, and it is not uncommon for them to marry in an attempt to convince themselves of their "normalcy." Some homosexual individuals who have previously been married (one-third of the women and one-fifth of the men in the Bell and Weinberg study) may have done so to avoid openly confronting their sexual orientation. As one man, now openly homosexual, said,

As I look back now, I can see that my playboy lifestyle was really an attempt to convince myself that the nagging attraction I felt for John was just a good friendship. It was as if I thought I could change my feelings by having sex with enough women. (Authors' files)

The initial step in coming out is usually a person's realization that she or he feels different from the heterosexual model (Herdt, 1992). Some people report knowing they were homosexual when they were small children. Many realize during adolescence (or not until college) that something is missing in their heterosexual involvements and that they find same-sex peers sexually attractive (Mallon, 1996). Once individuals recognize homosexual feelings, they must confront their own internalized homophobia as they deal with the reality that they are members of a stigmatized minority group (Katz, 1995; Wagner et al., 1994).

Table 10.3 When Did You Know? (When Gay or Bisexual College Students Say They Became Aware of Their Sexual Orientation)

	Female	*Male*
College	37%	13%
High school	46%	50%
Junior high	6%	20%
Grade school	11%	17%

Source: Elliott & Brantley, 1997.

Self-Acceptance

Accepting one's homosexuality is the next important step after realizing it. Self-acceptance is often difficult, for it involves overcoming the internalized negative and homophobic societal view of homosexuality:

> Initially a homosexual person often has difficulty from the pervasive condemnatory attitudes toward homosexuality. Like the prejudiced heterosexual, his early impressions about homosexuality came from the culture around him. As a child he heard the same nasty references to homosexuals. He has heard them called "queers," seen them portrayed as dissolute and sad, on stage and screen, in novels, in newspaper articles. His own attitude toward homosexuality has evolved out of a context almost wholly derogatory. His prejudice against himself is an almost exact parallel to the prejudice against homosexuals held in the larger culture. (Weinberg, 1973, p. 74)

When individuals realize that they belong to a socially stigmatized group, self-acceptance becomes a difficult but essential challenge (Hiratsuka, 1993). One study found that African American lesbians and gay men had greater incidence of depressive distress than whites, most likely due to the doubly stigmatized status of race and sexual orientation (Cochran & Mays, 1994).

Few public and private high schools have gay student organizations; most gay and lesbian adolescents experience confusion about their feelings and have few places to go for support and guidance (Rotello, 1996). They typically endorse the erroneous, negative stereotypes about homosexuality and may fail to recognize their homosexual feelings or may feel particularly bad about themselves for their feelings and for the intense unhappiness, persecution, and rejection that seem inevitable (Telljohann et al., 1995). They are also likely to believe that they are the only young persons to feel this way—and thus to feel acutely alone and separate from their peer group, which is so important at this stage of life (Nelson, 1997). Internet chat rooms and message boards can provide important connections to others with similar feelings and ease feelings of isolation. Some research has found that adolescents can cope effectively and develop an integrated and positive identity (Edwards, 1996).

Families that are very rigid, moralistic, and gender stereotyped contribute added stress to gay and lesbian adolescents (Hackenbruck, 1987). Some parents throw their gay children out of the house or stop support for schooling (Warren, 1997). Due to these difficulties, gay youths are seven times more likely than heterosexual male adolescents to attempt suicide. Lesbian teens are only slightly more likely to attempt suicide than straight girls (Remafedi, 1997). Isolation, low self-esteem, and physical and verbal abuse are frequently cited as the reasons for suicide attempts (Proctor & Groze, 1994). It can be helpful for gay and lesbian adolescents to find at least one supportive, nonjudgmental adult with whom to talk (Morrow, 1993); family support is particularly valuable (Anderson, 1998; Hershberger & D'Augelli, 1995). A 15-year-old boy found that support from Ann Landers when he wrote that he felt suicidal because "I have nobody to talk to. I am scared. I feel worthless." She wrote back saying that he was not alone and needed help to accept himself as he was. She encouraged him to write to the National Youth Advocacy Coalition and ended, "Good luck to you, dear." More support groups and gay teen organizations are developing to help them deal with the difficulties they face (Barrett, 1997).

Disclosure

Following acknowledgment and self-acceptance is the decision to be secretive or open. Being homosexual usually requires ongoing decisions about whether to be in or out of the closet, as new relationships and situations unfold (Kelly, 1998). The "Guidelines for

Let's Talk About It

Guidelines for Coming Out to Friends

The unexpected is to be expected when a gay or lesbian comes out to a friend. A friend who is "liberal" may have more difficulty with it than another more "conservative" person. It is essential to remember that their reactions say something about their own strengths and weaknesses, rather than anything about you. The following guidelines are meant to be a beginning in devising your own plan of disclosure. They are adapted from the book, *Outing Yourself* (1995) by Michelangelo Signorile.

1. *Support network.* You should have a support network of gays in place, especially those who have come out to lots of different people in their lives. Their experiences and support will give you a solid base from which to act.
2. *First choice.* Try to make your first disclosure to a heterosexual an easy one. You might not choose your best straight friend, because the stakes are so high. Pick someone whom you would expect to be accepting. The person also needs to be trustworthy and capable of keeping your news private for a while as you come out to others.
3. *Mental practice.* Practice imagining yourself coming out in realistic detail as you plan. Picture yourself in a familiar setting where you will both be comfortable. Envision feeling pleased with yourself for sharing something you feel good about (not something you have to apologize for). Practice saying, "There's something I want to tell you about myself, because our friendship is important to me. I trust you, and you're close to me. I am a lesbian/I am gay."
4. *Advance planning.* Plan the time—be sure to allow enough time to talk at length if things go well. Plan the place—somewhere you will both be comfortable. Arrange to have at least one of your gay friends available for support afterward and to debrief. Be prepared to calmly answer such questions as "How do you know you're gay? How long have you known? What caused it? Can you change? Do you have AIDS?"
5. *Rely on patience.* Remember that you are telling them something they have not had a chance to prepare for, whereas you have had a lot of time to prepare. Many people will be surprised, shocked, and confused and need some time to think or ask questions. An initial negative reaction does not necessarily mean the person will not accept it. If a friend reacts negatively, but shows respect, stay, and talk things over. Sympathize with his or her shock and confusion. "I can see this news upsets you."
6. *Control your anger.* If the person becomes hostile or insulting, politely end the meeting. "I'm sorry you aren't accepting my news well, and it's best for me to go now." Don't give your friend a real reason to be mad at you by being mean, rude, or flying off the handle.

As you come out to people, you will find that some are not capable or willing to maintain their friendship with you. With others, letting them know you more fully will allow the meaning and closeness in the relationship to grow. Over time, you will create a network of friends with whom you can enjoy the freedom of being your full self.

Coming Out to Friends" box offers some suggestions for coming out. Heterosexuals sometimes do not understand disclosure issues, as exemplified by the following comment:

I don't see any reason why they have to tell anyone. They can just lead their lives without making such a big deal out of it. (Authors' files)

The decision is usually not as easy as it may appear from an outsider's perspective. Deciding to remain in the closet may erode a person's self-respect, yet consequences from disclosure often encourage secrecy. Interpersonal relationships often remain distant:

> To avoid awkwardness or dishonesty, many of us just refrain from talking openly about our personal lives. Our co-workers and co-students see us as shy, withdrawn, reserved, snobbish—when actually we are trying to protect ourselves from *their homophobia!* (Loulan, 1984, p. 17)

Concealment can intensify social isolation and personal loneliness. It also inhibits participation in any gay rights activities (Sullivan, 1998). Whatever security is gained by concealment can also be jeopardized by discovery at any time. **Passing** is a term sometimes used for maintaining the false image of heterosexuality (Lynch, 1992). Passing as heterosexual is usually quite easy because most people assume that everyone is heterosexual. However, passing is unacceptable to many individuals.

Passing
Appearing to be heterosexual and avoiding presenting oneself as homosexual.

In some daily interactions, sexual orientation is irrelevant, but homosexuality and heterosexuality are strong undercurrents that touch many parts of life. As one gay man notes:

> . . . my life as a gay man isn't something that takes place only in the privacy of my bedroom. It affects who my friends are, whom I choose to share my life with, the work I do, the organizations I belong to, the magazines I read, where I vacation and what I talk about. (Marcus, 1993, p. 10)

Barbara Jordan, who died in 1996, kept her lesbianism a secret throughout her accomplished public life. She was the first black woman to be elected to the Texas state senate. She was elected to the U.S. House of Representatives and awarded the Presidential Medal of Freedom in 1994. She received national attention and respect when she served on the House Judiciary Committee during the nationally televised Nixon impeachment hearings. She and her lifetime companion, Nancy Earl, had built a house and lived together until Barbara's death. The first public acknowledgment of their relationship was in Barbara's obituary, where Nancy Earl was listed as Barbara's "longtime companion" (Moss, 1996).

Imagine being a closeted homosexual person and hearing a friend make a derogatory reference to "fags" or "dykes," being asked, "When are you going to settle down and get married?" or being invited to bring a date to an office party. In one writer's words, "Because of its devalued status, affirmation of homosexuality (or disclaiming it) becomes a more significant act than the same would be for a heterosexual, with significant consequences for a lifestyle" (Gagnon, 1977, p. 248).

Passing also can negatively affect the quality of gay and lesbian relationships:

> The daily act of having to live a double life—one that you show in public, one that you act in private—negatively influences our sexual expression. It is difficult to be sexual with someone you have denied all week at work. Switching gears from being "friends" outside your home to passionate lovers inside has a devastating effect on our ability to be sexually free. (Loulan, 1984, p. 23)

With some exceptions, the more within "the system" a person is or desires to be, the more risk there is in being open about one's sexual orientation. Jobs, social position, and friends may all be placed in jeopardy (Day & Schoenrade, 1997; Druzin et al., 1998). The conservativeness of the surrounding community may further affect one's decisions about whether or not to come out and to whom (Tafel, 1998). For example, a gay medical student may have been out in college, but goes back in the closet during medical school for fear of discrimination in his career path (Wallick, 1997). Many more homosexuals who live in cities are out than those who live in suburbs or small, rural towns. The greater ease of being open about one's homosexuality attracts people to urban life (Michael et al., 1994).

Coming out may be a particularly difficult issue for homosexual adults who are parents. In fact, some stay in marriages for this reason (Green & Clunis, 1989). Approximately 60% of homosexual men and women who have been married have at least one child (Bell & Weinberg, 1978). The difficulties that a gay parent faces in attempting to attain custody or visitation rights may be severe. It is not unusual for gay parents to lose these rights strictly on the basis of their sexual orientation, regardless of their fitness as parents (Schwartz, 1991). Yet some courts hold that homosexuality itself is not proof of unfitness. The pattern of court decisions at this time is arbitrary and uncertain.

Telling the Family

Disclosing one's homosexuality to family can be more difficult than disclosing it to others (Cain, 1991). Coming out to one's family is a particularly significant step, as the following account by a 35-year-old man illustrates:

> Most of my vacation at home went well, but the ending was indeed difficult. Gay people kept cropping up in conversation. My mother was very down on them (us), and I of course was disagreeing with her. Finally she asked me if I was "one of them." I said yes. It was very difficult for her to deal with. She asked a lot of questions, which I answered as calmly, honestly, and rationally as I could. We spent a rather strained day together. It was so painful for me to see her suffering so much heartache over this, and not even having a clue that the issue is the oppression of gay people. I just wish my mother didn't have to suffer so much from all this. (Authors' files)

Parents often do experience difficult feelings from the revelation that a child is homosexual (Savin-Williams & Dubé, 1998). They may react with anger or with guilt about what they "did wrong" (Woog, 1997). The organization Parents, Families, and Friends of Lesbians and Gays (PFLAG), which has over 400 chapters nationwide, helps parents and others develop understanding, acceptance, and support. Families may be very frightened about their gay sons and brothers being HIV positive. Because telling the family is so difficult, many homosexual people do not do so. Approximately half of the respondents in the Bell and Weinberg survey believed that their parents did not know about their homosexuality. Fathers were somewhat less likely to know than were mothers. Table 10.4 shows more recent data from readers of *The Advocate*, a gay newsmagazine.

In the past, each person usually decided if, when, and how to come out (except when his or her homosexuality was discovered by accident). Now, however, many homosexual men are compelled to come out when they test positive for HIV (the AIDS virus), which has been closely associated with homosexuality, or if they begin showing symptoms of this deadly disease. Other homosexual men and women—often celebrities or prominent business or political leaders—may find others abruptly opening the closet door for them. *Outing* is the term used when an individual or group publicizes the homosexual orientation of someone who would otherwise not be open about it. Some gay rights activists have outed others in recent years to try to combat homophobic attitudes and policies; it remains a highly controversial tactic (Rotello, 1995).

Table 10.4 Readers of the Newsmagazine *The Advocate* Answer the Question "Have You Come Out to Your Parents?"

Answer	*Percentage*
Yes, and they took the news well.	63%
Yes, and they rejected me.	11%
No.	26%

Source: *The Advocate*, January 20, 1998, p. 22.

DOONESBURY
by Garry Trudeau

GO DOONESBURY@http://www.doonesbury.com

The Double Minority: Homosexuality and Ethnicity

Gay ethnic minority individuals have to learn to live in three different communities—ethnic, gay, and the larger society. Each of these fails to support some aspect of the person's identity (Zamora-Hernandez & Patterson, 1996). With the exception of Native Americans, traditional attitudes and values within most ethnic groups in the United States create even more difficulty for gays and lesbians of color coming out than for whites. The more traditional and less acculturated the person and his or her family, the greater the negative attitudes about homosexuality and the less likely it is that the individual will be involved in the gay community. The cultural primacy of the heterosexual family may make it virtually impossible for parents to accept their child's homosexuality (Paradis, 1997), and lingering racism in the white gay community makes acceptance more difficult for ethnic gays (Gomez, 1997; Ryan et al., 1996).

The movement to reclaim traditional Native American spiritual beliefs has led to increased tolerance for homosexuality among this group. Pre-European Native American beliefs centered around the Great Spirit, who is believed to give each person a sacred life quest. The unique tolerance of individual differences, including gender role and sexual orientation, stems from the sacredness of an individual's personal mission as part of the great unknowable plan of the Great Spirit (Brown, 1997b). This positive value for individual differences has persisted despite the assaults on their culture, as indicated by the fact that the families of American Indian lesbians and gay men usually do not reject them (Epstein, 1997a).

When the ethnic group places high, or even exclusive importance on a woman's childbearing role and subservience to men, lesbianism is a direct threat to these values (Guerro-Pavich, 1986; Morales, 1992). This pattern commonly occurs in Hispanic and Asian cultures (Espin, 1987; Chan, 1995). In addition, when the traditional culture expects virginity for the unmarried woman and views "good women" as primarily nonsexual, being lesbian is an affront to both of these traditional beliefs (Trujillo, 1991).

The cultural emphasis on *machismo* in Hispanic cultures often results in gay Hispanics maintaining secrecy about their sexual orientation. The emphasis in the lower socioeconomic segment of the African American community on tough masculinity as the ideal gender norm creates particular difficulty for gender-nonconforming gays (Leard, 1996).

Asian cultures, in particular, place great significance on loyalty and conformity to one's family and little importance on individual needs and desires. The Asian is usually seen as a representative of his or her family, rather than as an individual, In addition, sexuality is not to be talked about and is to be kept private. Coming out publicly as gay, or even talking about sex in the family, is antithetical to values of traditional Asian Americans. Being openly homosexual is seen as shaming the family and threatening the family's future. Not marrying and creating heirs to carry on the family name is a failure for the whole extended family. However, secretly engaging in homosexual behavior while otherwise meeting family expectations may not create guilt (Matteson, 1997).

The African American community, in general, has stronger negative views of homosexuals than do whites (Poussaint, 1990; Ernst et al., 1991). Although black leaders such as Coretta King and Jesse Jackson support gay civil rights, the influence of strong fundamentalist Christian beliefs may contribute to the higher degree of intolerance (Gallagher, 1997; Monroe, 1997). This strong disapproval of homosexuality interfered with black leaders being active in the early fight against AIDS (Quimby & Friedman, 1989).

To a greater extent than white homosexuals, gays and lesbians from ethnic groups with traditional values are more likely to stay in the closet with their families and community than to be open and face alienation from their families and heritage. They are often forced to make a choice between their gay and ethnic identities and will most likely have to deal with prejudice toward homosexuality in their ethnic community and racism in the gay communities (Garcia, 1996). Gay and lesbian relationships between members of different ethnic groups often have difficult issues arise from cultural differences (Isensee, 1996). The experience of a biracial couple illustrates the difficulties:

> John, a white 33-year-old, well integrated in his gay identity, recently ended a six-month relationship with William, a 28-year-old black man in his first gay relationship. John had been "out" to his family since late adolescence. His mother and siblings were relatively accepting of his gay identity, but he had no contact with his father, who was rejecting toward his son. Recently, John had become politically active in several gay activist groups, which was alarming to William, who feared exposure to his own family, friends, and co-workers. Consequently, John felt stifled and controlled by William's desire that he be less public in his sexual identity.

> William would not acknowledge the nature of their relationship to his friends and family, a refusal that John experienced as invalidating and an expression of William's internalized homophobia. Compounding these difficulties were the expressions of racism that their relationship had evoked; cautious and even hostile reactions of some of his closest gay friends, and his mother's concern about John's "safety" and about the racism of "others" if he and William were to continue their relationship. (Paradis, 1997, p. 304)

Gay ethnic subcultures sometimes evolve as a way of managing these dilemmas (Longres, 1996). In the 1993 march on Washington, many marched in ethnic contingents. Gay ethnic self-help, social, and political organizations have been developed to enhance the sense of belonging (Zamora-Hernandez & Patterson, 1996).

Involvement in the Gay Community

The need to belong is a deeply felt human trait. For many homosexual individuals, a sense of community helps provide a sense of belonging and the affirmation and acceptance that are missing in the larger culture. Social and political involvement with other homosexual people is another step in the coming-out process. In larger cities, gay and lesbian bars and cafés cater to different groups or clientele. Like heterosexual bars, these gathering places range from low-key socializing spots to establishments with reputations for casual pickups. Particularly in years past, gay bars—as well as certain designated recreational areas, restaurants, and bathhouses—served an important function: Often they were the only places where homosexual patrons could drop the facade of heterosexuality. In recent years, this need has diminished to some extent. Gay people have helped found service organizations, educational centers, and professional organizations such as the Gay and Lesbian Medical Association (Lukes & Land, 1990). Religious organizations for gay people have been established, including the 40,000-member Metropolitan Community Church with 400 congregations in 19 countries and denominational groups such as Dignity for Roman Catholics and Integrity for Episcopalians. Homosexuals living outside large cities often have very limited options for involvement in the gay community (Gallagher, 1994; Michael et al., 1994).

The AIDS crisis has precipitated increased community involvement and coherence (Fineman, 1993). The gay and lesbian communities have mobilized educational efforts, developed innovative programs for caring for AIDS patients, created an impressive network of volunteers to provide needed support for persons with AIDS, and lobbied—often quite visibly—for increased AIDS awareness and medical research funding.

The Gay Internet Community

The Internet has provided a gay "virtual community" in ways never before possible. Regardless of where someone lives, if they are connected to the Internet, they have private access to other lesbians and gays for almost any reason (Bawer, 1998). As it does among heterosexuals, the Internet offers cybersex, sexual information, and services (Friess, 1998). More importantly, it provides access to resources that otherwise might not be readily available as well as avenues for closeted lesbians and gays to discuss their concerns with others. They can seek relationships through personal ads, do research on gay-friendly vacation destinations, contact teen suicide prevention lines, keep current on new AIDS treatments, participate in an ethnic minority support group, or do political networking (Weinrich, 1997).

Homosexual Relationships

Some people mistakenly think that homosexual partners always enact the stereotypically active "male" or passive "female" roles. This notion stems in part from the pervasive heterosexual model of relationships. Because this model of male–female role-playing has historically been the predominant one in our culture, both heterosexual and homosexual intimate relationships have been patterned after it. However, options for more egalitarian relationships have increased in recent years, and these are being followed by both heterosexual and homosexual couples. In this regard, a homosexual relationship may well be more flexible than a heterosexual one in our society.

Aspects of Gay and Lesbian Relationships

One study that compared characteristics of homosexual and heterosexual relationships found major differences: Heterosexual couples were likely to adhere more closely to traditional gender-role expectations than were homosexual couples. Most of the homosexual relationships studied resembled "best friendships" combined with romantic and erotic attraction. The researcher suggested that studies of homosexual couples can provide insights and models for heterosexual couples who are trying to establish more egalitarian relationships (Peplau, 1981). As a gay man states, "Whether lesbian, gay, or heterosexual, what validity does a relationship possess if its participants cannot find openness and honesty, fulfillment and freedom in it?" (Boyd, 1997).

The Peplau study found many similarities between homosexual and heterosexual relationships, and reported that most differences in relationships have more to do with whether the partners are men or women than with whether they are homosexual or heterosexual. Matched samples of homosexual females and males and heterosexual females and males all indicated that "being able to talk about my most intimate feelings" with a partner was most important in a love relationship. The research also found that partners in a love relationship, regardless of sexual orientation, must reconcile desires for togetherness and independence. For many individuals, these desires were not mutually exclusive; some people wanted both a secure love relationship and meaningful activities and friendships separate from the relationship. Responses from homosexual and heterosexual women were distinct in some ways from those of homosexual and heterosexual men. Women placed greater importance on emotional expressiveness within a relationship than did men. Women also gave higher ratings to the importance of having an egalitarian relationship and having similar attitudes and political beliefs.

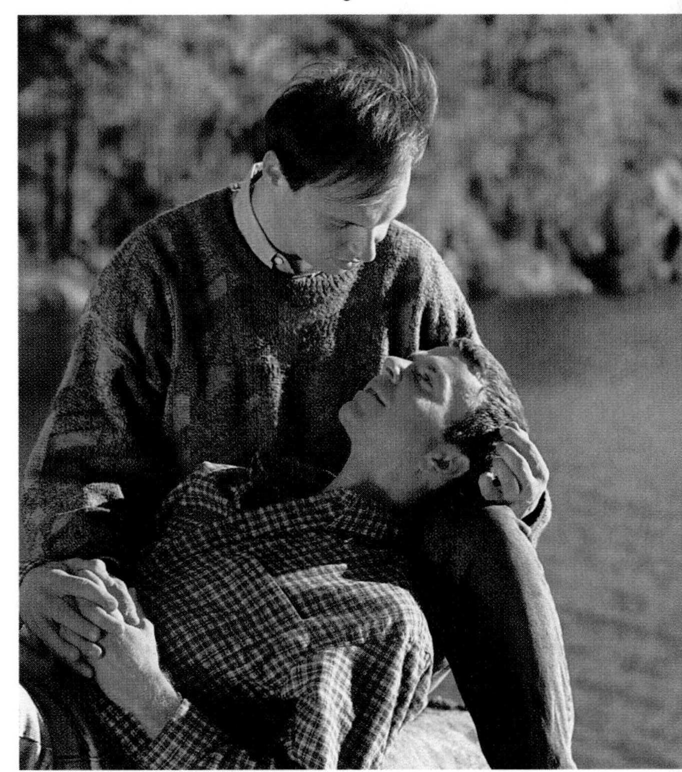

Like heterosexuals, homosexuals have relationships that vary from casual encounters to close, caring involvements.

Sexual Attitude and Behavior Differences of Gays and Lesbians

There are some differences between homosexual men and women in the number of their sexual partners. Lesbians are likely to have had far fewer sexual partners, and lesbian couples are much more likely than male couples to have monogamous relationships (Lever, 1997). A 1990 study found that 94% of gay men in relationships for more than 10 years had been sexual with someone other than their partner (Blumstein & Schwartz, 1990). Prior to the AIDS epidemic, some homosexual men had frequent casual sexual encounters—sometimes hundreds or more (Bell & Weinberg, 1978; Kinsey et al., 1948). These encounters were sometimes exceedingly brief, occurring in bathhouses, public restrooms, or in film booths in pornography shops. This type of brief, recreational sexual contact may be on the rise again as AIDS has become less of an issue for some men in the gay community (Peyser, 1997).

Homosexual women also differ from homosexual men in the extent to which they associate emotional closeness with sex—a finding consistent with the heterosexual patterns discussed in Chapter 7. In one study, most of the lesbians waited to have sex with a partner until they had developed emotional intimacy. Although 46% of gay men had become friends with

A gay couple following their holy union ceremony.

their partners before having sex, as a group they were more likely than lesbians to have had sexual experiences with casual acquaintances or people they had just met.

What explains the tendency toward less sexual exclusivity among gay men than among lesbians?

One researcher has suggested that gender-role socialization places more emphasis on and gives more permission for casual sex for males than for females. Men's and women's motivations for sexual involvement are different, regardless of the sex of their partners (Leigh, 1989). Heterosexual relationships are to some extent a compromise between male and female gender-role expectations and thus may include exclusiveness for both partners. However, with gay male relationships, this particular compromise is not typically as necessary, and casual sex outside an intimate relationship can occur more easily (Peplau, 1981).

However, sexual involvement with many partners is not universal among homosexual men (Isay, 1989; Kurdek, 1995). Many men feel no desire for multiple relationships, and others have decided that multiple relationships do not adequately meet their needs. Some men want to have a strong emotional relationship before becoming sexually involved. And for some men, being involved in an ongoing relationship eliminates sexual interest in other men. In some cases, the growing desire of homosexual men to modify the definition of masculinity has encouraged them to develop committed, multidimensional relationships rather than pursuing casual sexual encounters (Sullivan, 1998). A recent survey of readers of a gay magazine, *The Advocate,* found that 26% of men were in relationships that had lasted at least 10 years (Lever, 1997). Also, many gay men have reduced the numbers of their sexual partners or established monogamous relationships because of concerns about contracting AIDS (Kelaher et al., 1994).

Marriage between two people of the same sex is not legally recognized by any state, but is currently a significant gay rights issue, as discussed in the "Homosexual Marriage" box on pages 294–295. Many homosexual couples share significant one-to-one relationships. One-half of the lesbians and one-quarter of the homosexual men in Bell and Weinberg's study were in primary relationships. A survey by *Advocate* magazine found that 87% of women and 52% of men were in monogamous relationships (Lever, 1997). The Metropolitan Community Church, which primarily serves gay people, performs holy unions (this term is used because marriage is a legal contract) that provide the spiritual significance of marriage for homosexual couples. The Unitarians and Reform Judaism also bless gay unions. In Denmark, gay people can legally marry (McNaught, 1991).

Family Life

Traditionally, a family has been considered to consist of a heterosexual couple and their offspring, but many forms of family life exist in contemporary society: Homosexual individuals also form family units, either as single parents or as couples, with children included in the family through a variety of circumstances. Some homosexual individuals or couples become parents with adopted or foster children. Most laws about adoption by gay parents are ambiguous, and in many cases gays adopt as single individuals (Woog, 1998). In 1998 New Jersey became the first state in the nation to allow gay and lesbian couples to jointly adopt children (Padawer, 1998). Many have children who were born in previous heterosexual marriages (Kantrowitz, 1996). About one-third of lesbians are biological mothers from heterosexual relationships or by artificial insemination (Baker, 1990).

In 1998, Michael Galluccio and Jon Holden were the first openly gay couple in the United States to legally adopt a child.

Children may also be conceived by lesbians through artificial insemination or with a partner chosen solely for this purpose (Quimby, 1994). Semen can be obtained from a sperm bank or by individual arrangements with a selected donor. One woman who became pregnant through a donor she selected reports,

> A close male friend ejaculated in privacy and brought his semen to our bedroom. We put the sperm in a cervical cap and inserted it to ensure contact between the semen and the cervix. Now we have a beautiful baby boy. (Authors' files)

Another alternative for lesbian couples involves collecting ovum from one partner, fertilizing them in vitro, then placing them into the other woman's uterus to carry until birth. This process may help both women to be legally recognized as parents (O'Hanlan, 1995).

A homosexual man who wants to be a father may make a personal agreement with a woman who agrees to carry his child. When a man or woman selects a surrogate or donor known to him or her, it is important for the future biological and legal parents to discuss their respective rights and responsibilities; a legal document supporting the agreement is advisable. Many new concepts of family are emerging, and the desire for legal and social recognition of gay and lesbian families is increasing.

The custody of children in divorce proceedings is commonly biased toward the mother. However, if the mother is an acknowledged lesbian, this may jeopardize her claim to custody (Allen & Demo, 1995). A homosexual father attempting to gain custody has the double disadvantage in court of being a man and being homosexual (Schwartz, 1990). Some people have challenged the ability of homosexual parents to provide a positive family environment for children. However, research has found that children of lesbian mothers are essentially no different from other children in terms of self-esteem, gender-related problems, gender roles, sexual orientation, and general development (Green, 1992; McNeill et al., 1998). Another study of young adults found no differences in psychological well-being between those raised by lesbian or heterosexual mothers (Tasker & Golombok, 1995). Lesbian mothers have been found to be similar to heterosexual mothers in lifestyle, maternal interests, and parenting behavior (Gibbs, 1989). In addition, because most homosexuals have straight parents, it follows that most children with gay or lesbian parents grow up as heterosexual (Bailey et al., 1995; Golombok & Tasker, 1996).

Unfortunately, children with gay or lesbian parents are frequently confronted with other people's prejudices. They often have to learn to ignore name calling, friends' parents restricting visits to their homes, and others' ignorance. For example, when her sixth-grade teacher asked for examples of different kinds of families, a girl who lived with her mother and her female partner raised her hand and offered, "Lesbian." The teacher replied, "This is such a nice town. There wouldn't be any lesbians living here" (Kantrowitz, 1996, p. 53).

The growing gay rights movement, which began in the 1960s and is epitomized by the 1993 March on Washington, has provided support for many homosexual men and women. The following section describes some of the movement's activities.

The Gay Rights Movement

Forty years before World War II, the first organization promoting education about homosexuality and the abolition of antigay laws was founded in Germany. However, the Nazi rise to power ended the homosexual rights movement in Germany (Schoofs, 1997). It was not until the 1950s in the United States that some organizations for gay people were established despite the very conservative atmosphere of the times. The Mattachine Society had chapters in many cities, providing a national network for support and communication among homosexuals. The Daughters of Bilitis, an organization of lesbians, published a journal called *The Ladder,* which contained fiction, poetry, and political articles. The goals of both organizations were to educate homosexual and heterosexual people about homosexuality, increase understanding of homosexuality, and eliminate laws discriminatory toward homosexual individuals (Katz, 1976).

The Stonewall Incident and Beyond

During the 1960s, many people began to question traditional aspects of American life in all areas, including the sexual. In this atmosphere, more gay people began to respond to social and political changes and to question and challenge the social problems they faced.

On the Edge

Homosexual Marriage

"By the power vested in me, I now pronounce you husband and husband." In the last several years, legal gay marriage has been a hotly contested issue and the subject of a great deal of legislative action. In the mid-1990s it appeared possible that Hawaii might make same-sex marriages legal if it were decided that depriving gays of marrying violated the state constitution's provision for equal rights. Without legal marriage, gay couples do not have the same rights regarding inheritance, child custody, joint insurance policies for health, home, or auto, status as next of kin for hospital visits, or even to make funeral arrangements for a partner. In 1996 the U.S. Congress passed the Defense of Marriage Act, which gave states the right not to recognize same-sex marriages performed in other states, and many individual states followed with laws to prohibit legal recognition of same-sex marriages (Green, 1997). In 1997 Hawaii fell short of legalizing same-sex marriage, but did provide couples who register as "reciprocal beneficiaries" many of the benefits of marriage, including medical insurance and survivorship rights (Essoyan, 1997). In November 1998, voters in Hawaii will decide whether to allow the legislature to "reserve marriage to opposite-sex couples" (Gallagher, 1997). In general, the public is less supportive of family rights than of civil rights for lesbians and gays, as indicated in Table 10.5 on page 296. The debate will continue; the following are examples of the opposing points of view on the issue.

A proponent of gay marriage, Andrew Sullivan, formerly a senior editor of *The New Republic* and author of "Virtually Normal: An Argument about Homosexuality" states,

> What we seek is not some special place in America but merely to be a full and equal part of America . . . some of us are lucky enough to meet the person we truly love. And we want to commit to that person in front of our family and country for the rest of our lives. It's the most simple, the most natural, the most human instinct in the world. . . . We are only asking that when the government gives out civil marriage licenses, those of us who are gay should be treated like anybody else. It seeks to change no one else's rights or marriages in any way. It seeks merely to promote monogamy, fidelity, and the disciplines of

The symbolic birth of gay activism occurred in 1969 in New York City when police raided a gay bar, the Stonewall. Police raids on gay bars were common occurrences, but this time the bar's patrons resisted and fought back. A riot ensued and did not end until the following day. The Stonewall incident served as a catalyst for the formation of gay rights groups, and activities such as Gay Pride Week and parades are held in yearly commemoration of the Stonewall riot (Herrell, 1992). In 1994, over a million people gathered in New York to celebrate the 25th anniversary of Stonewall.

Over a million gays and lesbians marched in New York in 1994 to celebrate the 25th anniversary of Stonewall.

Since the early 1970s, groups have worked to end various kinds of discrimination against homosexual people. The National Gay Task Force was founded in 1973 to work with homosexual men and women around the country to help achieve legal rights. The gay rights movement has been primarily concerned with legislation related to consensual sex and civil rights. (By 1996, only Kansas, Oklahoma, Missouri, Arkansas, and Tennessee had explicit laws against sex between same sex partners [Kaplan & Klaidman, 1996].) Further modifications of consensual sex and civil rights laws are seen as essential to providing homosexual people with the same legal protection that heterosexual people enjoy (Foley, 1998). The movement's central philosophy is that private consensual sexual expression is not a matter of legal concern, nor is homosexuality adequate reason to deny or rescind housing or employment (Anez, 1997).

By the 1990s, several states had established laws prohibiting antigay discrimination (Bull, 1997). The majority of Americans believe that gays should have equal job opportunities. However, certain segments of the population are more likely to support gay rights than are others. According to Schmaltz (1993), people who are relatively well educated

On the Edge

> family life among people who have long been cast to the margins of society. Why indeed would any conservative seek to oppose those very family values for gay people that he or she supports for everybody else? (Sullivan, 1996, p. 26)

An opponent of gay marriage, William Bennett, editor of *The Book of Virtues,* and codirector of Empower America states,

> The legal union of same-sex couples would shatter the conventional definition of marriage, change the rules which govern behavior, endorse practices which are completely antithetical to the tenets of all of the world's religions, send conflicting signals about marriage and sexuality, particularly to the young, and obscure marriage's enormous consequential function—procreation and child-rearing. It is an honorable estate, instituted of God and built on moral, religious, sexual and human realities. Marriage is based on . . . the different, complementary nature of men and women—and how they refine, support, encourage and complete one another. It is the institution through which we propagate, nurture, educate and sustain our species." (Bennett, 1996, p. 27)

The cover of *Daddy's Wedding.* This book by Michael Willhoite and other books, such as *Heather Has Two Mommies* and *Daddy's Roommate,* are highly controversial.

Table 10.5 Attitudes About Family versus Civil Rights for Lesbians and Gays

A 1997 survey found that people are more likely to oppose legal marriage and adoption by homosexuals and more likely to be in favor of equal rights in housing and employment for homosexuals.

Answering Yes to:	*Percentage*
Do you oppose homosexuals' right to legal marriage?	56%
Do you oppose homosexuals' right to adopt children?	49%
Should homosexuals have equal rights in housing?	80%
Should homosexuals have equal rights in employment?	84%

Source: Morganthau, 1997.

and not particularly religious are more likely to support gay rights. In addition, women tend to be more supportive than men, and people under age 45 tend to support gay rights more than do older adults. In addition, Table 10.5 shows differences in support for employment and housing compared to marriage and adoption.

Goals of the Gay Rights Movement

"There is no room in American medicine or American life for discrimination against people because of their sexual orientation. Gays and lesbians are part of the American family."—Al Gore, in 1997 address to the AIDS Action Foundation

A major legislative goal of gay rights advocates is an amendment to the 1964 Civil Rights Act that would broaden it to include "affectional or sexual orientation" along with race, creed, color, and sex. This would make it illegal to discriminate in housing, employment, insurance, and public accommodations on the grounds of sexual orientation (Cohn, 1992). Courts of law and juries are becoming more likely to award settlements in anti-gay-bias cases (Gallagher & Moss, 1997). Many large private corporations and the Federal Civil Service Commission have established equal-opportunity employment in regard to homosexuality. This means that it is illegal for these employers to discriminate against anyone in hiring or firing on the basis of sexual orientation. In 1997 President Bill Clinton addressed a gay and lesbian civil rights organization—the first president ever to do so—pledging to push for legislation against job discrimination (Sobieraj, 1997). Some local governments have adopted laws prohibiting discrimination on the basis of sexual orientation. Some U.S. corporations, as seen in Table 10.6, have "domestic partnership" policies that grant gays a variety of spousal rights, such as insurance benefits and bereavement leave (Salholz, 1990). In 1994, Vermont became the first state to extend health benefits to domestic partners. Expansion of family rights, such as the formal recognition of gay and lesbian marriages or the legal right of a co-parent to raise a child upon the death of the birth mother, are further goals (Haffner & Portelli, 1998).

Following Bill Clinton's election in 1992, the status of gays and lesbians in the military became a hotly debated issue. In his first days in office Clinton moved to fulfill a campaign pledge to ban discrimination against gays and lesbians in the U.S. Armed Forces. In doing so, he was barraged by vocal opponents, a skeptical public, and nearly unanimous opposition by top military leaders. The "Don't ask, don't tell" policy evolved (Schmitt, 1994) as a compromise between homosexuals who demanded the right to serve without censure and military leaders who were uncomfortable with openly sanctioning the inclusion of avowed homosexuals. According to this policy, homosexuals were allowed to serve in the military with

Table 10.6 A Sample of U.S. Companies That Extend Domestic-Partner Benefits to Gays and Lesbians

U.S. West	Hewlett-Packard
American Express	IBM
Barnes and Noble	Microsoft
Coors Brewing	Time Warner
Disney	Xerox
Eastman Kodak	

the assurance that they would not be scrutinized for their sexual orientation provided that they keep their orientation secret. Unfortunately, the "Don't ask, don't tell" policy has had the reverse effect of its intent: More gays and lesbians have been forced out of the military than ever before (Vistica & Thomas, 1998). The debate has been fueled by the belief that the military would lessen its effectiveness if it officially opened its ranks to homosexual individuals. The reality is that gays have always served in the U.S. military—and have always met with hostility. Countless taxpayer dollars have been spent on investigating and discharging homosexual personnel (Caplan, 1994; Jones & Koshes, 1995; Shilts, 1993), money that could be better spent on combating sexual misbehavior and harassment—whether homosexual or heterosexual in nature.

Although discrimination against lesbians and gays has lessened in North America, homosexuals face extreme persecution and abuse in many other places in the world. The United States now grants political asylum for persecution based on sexual orientation. Prior to 1990 the Immigration and Naturalization Service deemed homosexuality legal grounds for exclusion to this country (Burr, 1996). Some of the people who have been granted asylum include

- a Russian lesbian who was repeatedly arrested, fired from jobs, and threatened with psychiatric institutionalization
- a gay Brazilian man who was raped at gunpoint by police and taken to jail, where the commanding officer encouraged criminals to gang-rape and brutalize him
- a lesbian activist who could face the death penalty for homosexuality in her native Iran (Landsberg, 1996)

In other places, discrimination is decreasing. In 1994 Japan had its first-ever gay pride parade. In 1996 the new constitution in South Africa provides some of the most comprehensive protection in the world for lesbians and gays (Buttenweiser, 1997).

Many gay men and lesbians have become involved in gay rights advocacy for the first time as a result of their concerns about AIDS (Clarke, 1985). Much recent gay activism has focused on funding for AIDS research, providing support for victims and their friends and families, public education about AIDS, and volunteer work. As traumatic and painful as the AIDS epidemic has been, the community response has strengthened the gay community.

Reaction Against Gay Rights

As the gay rights movement has made progress with improved political changes and greater acceptance, these gains have mobilized reactionary groups to attempt to pass discriminatory legislation on the basis of "no special rights" and by inflaming uneducated fears of child molestation (Jenny et al., 1994; Leland, 1994). In 1992, Colorado voters adopted a ballot measure that prohibited local governments from enacting laws to protect gay people from job and housing discrimination. (In 1994, the Colorado Supreme Court ruled the ballot measure unconstitutional.) Similar ballot measures have appeared in other state elections (Johnson, 1994). Table 10.7 shows changes in the laws since 1972.

Antigay sentiment can escalate to drastic proportions. Many cities are reporting an increase in the number and intensity of violent physical assaults on gays (Condon, 1997; Quinn, 1997). These events indicate a pathological fear and hatred of homosexuality. At the same time, they deepen the commitment of gays and others to eradicate the attitudes that contribute to such violence. The National Gay Task Force has started a major project to monitor and document violence against homosexuals. The data will be used as a tool for civil rights advocacy and to help reduce gay victimization. In 1990, President Bush signed into law the Hate Crimes Statistics Act, which provides resources to document hate crimes in the United

Table 10.7 Laws Prohibiting Antigay Discrimination

	1972	*1997*		*1972*	*1997*
Cities	1	161	*States*	0	11

Source: Dobosz, 1997.

States. In 1997 President Clinton decried the rise of hate crimes and said, "Hate crimes leave deep scars not only on the victims, but on our larger community" (*The Advocate*, July 22, 1997, p. 20). Gay rights advocates are attempting to pass antidiscriminatory legislation in various places throughout the country. It is our hope that the gay civil rights movement will prevail and that homosexual Americans will be freer to live, work, and contribute to society.

Summary

The word *homosexual* can be an objective or subjective appraisal of sexual behavior, emotional affiliation, and/or self-definition.

A CONTINUUM OF SEXUAL ORIENTATIONS

Kinsey's seven-point continuum ranges from exclusive heterosexuality to exclusive homosexuality. Kinsey based his ratings on a combination of overt sexual behaviors and erotic attractions.

According to estimates from the National Health and Social Life survey, approximately 2.8% of men and 1.4% of women identify themselves as homosexual.

Bisexuality can be characterized by overt behaviors and/or erotic responses to both males and females. As with heterosexuality and homosexuality, a clear-cut definition of bisexuality is difficult to establish.

Four types of bisexuality include bisexuality as a real orientation, a transitory orientation, a transitional orientation, or homosexual denial.

WHAT DETERMINES SEXUAL ORIENTATION?

A number of psychosocial and biological theories attempt to explain the development of homosexuality. Some of the psychosocial theories relate to parenting patterns, life experiences, or the psychological attributes of the person.

Theories of biological causation look to prenatal or adult hormone differences as well as genetic factors. A biological predisposition is suggested by findings of childhood gender nonconformity among many homosexual adults.

Daryl Bem's "exotic becomes erotic" theory suggests that a combination of psychological and biological factors determine sexual orientation.

Sexual orientation, regardless of where it falls on the continuum of heterosexuality and homosexuality, seems to be formed from a composite of factors that are unique to each individual.

SOCIETAL ATTITUDES

Cross-cultural attitudes toward homosexuality vary from condemnation to acceptance. Negative attitudes toward homosexuality still predominate in our society.

Current theological positions toward homosexuality include the rejecting–punitive, rejecting–nonpunitive, qualified-acceptance, and full-acceptance stances.

Homophobia is the irrational fear of homosexuality, the fear of homosexual feelings within oneself, or self-loathing because of one's own homosexuality. Young males often exhibit the most extreme homophobia.

Homosexuality has been portrayed in a more positive light in the 1990s media, a development that may help lead toward greater familiarity with and acceptance of homosexuality.

LIFESTYLES

Contrary to popular stereotypes, homosexual individuals exhibit a wide variety of lifestyles.

The choice of coming out or being "in the closet" often has a significant impact on a homosexual person's lifestyle. The steps of coming out involve recognizing one's homosexual orientation, deciding how to view oneself, and being open about one's homosexuality. Gays and lesbians who belong to traditional ethnic groups may have the most difficulty getting support for coming out.

As gender-role stereotyping has decreased, many homosexual and heterosexual couples have developed more egalitarian relationships. Some of the differences reported between homosexual men and homosexual women may be attributed to general gender-role differences between men and women.

THE GAY RIGHTS MOVEMENT

Gay rights activists have been promoting consenting adult and civil rights legislation and, more recently, campaigning for greater AIDS awareness and funding for medical research. These activities have met with opposition from various individuals and groups.

Thought Provokers

1. How would you react if you learned that your roommate didn't share your sexual orientation?
2. Should gays and lesbians be allowed legal marriages?
3. If homosexuality could be detected within the first three months of pregnancy, should elective abortion be permitted?

Suggested Readings

Cammermeyer, Margarethe (1994). *Serving in Silence.* New York: Viking. The story of a Vietnam veteran who received the Bronze Star and Nurse of the Year award and was discharged from the military for being homosexual after 26 years of distinguished service.

Clark, Don (1987). *The New Loving Someone Gay.* Millbrae, CA: Celestial Arts. This book is designed to increase understanding and communication between homosexual people and their friends and families.

Isensee, R. K. (1996). *Love Between Men: Enhancing Intimacy and Keeping Your Relationship Alive.* This book shows approaches to improve communication, solve everyday conflicts, and satisfy a partner's emotional and sexual needs.

Kaiser, Charles (1997). *The Gay Metropolis: 1940–1996.* Boston: Houghton Mifflin. A rich history of six decades of evolving transformation in the gay community.

Loulan, JoAnn (1984). *Lesbian Sex.* San Francisco: Spinsters/Aunt Lute. This is an excellent book about lesbian sexual activities, relationships, and lifestyles, with exercises designed to enhance self-awareness and sexual expression.

Martin, April (1993). *The Lesbian and Gay Parenting Handbook.* New York: HarperCollins. Drawing on interviews with families and experts, this book discusses different options for gays becoming parents, legal considerations, and special issues related to gay family life.

Signorile, Michelangelo (1995). *Outing Yourself: How to Come out as Lesbian or Gay to Your Family, Friends and Coworkers.* New York: Simon & Schuster. A 14-step program of guidance and advice about coming out.

Sullivan, Andrew (1995). *Virtually Normal.* New York: Knopf. A gay conservative deals with his gay sexual orientation and offers unique perspectives on other conservatives.

Van Gelder, Lindsay; and Brandt, Pamela (1996). *The Girls Next Door.* New York: Simon & Schuster. More than 100 interviews of lesbians around the country reflect how gay women think, love, and live.

Weinberg, Martin; Williams, C.; and Pryor, D. (1994). *Dual Attraction: Understanding Bisexuality.* New York: Oxford University Press. This book discusses research and issues about bisexuality.

Whitehead, Sally (1997). *The Truth Shall Set You Free: A Family's Passage from Fundamentalism to a New Understanding of Faith, Love, and Sexual Identity.* The memoirs of a 20-year marriage, the husband's disclosure that he is gay, and the resultant divorce with a continued family life.

Resources

The National Gay Task Force, 2320 17th Street NW, Washington, D.C. 20009; (202) 332-6483. This group provides information about social, political, and educational organizations in particular locales.

National Center for Lesbian Rights, 870 Market Street, Suite 570, San Francisco, CA 94102; (415) 392-6257. A legal resource center working to eradicate discrimination.

Parents and Friends of Lesbians and Gays (PFLAG), 1101 14th Street NW, Suite 1030, Washington, D.C. 20005; (202) 638-4200. This group provides support and counseling for parents and public education on gay rights.

Web Resources

WWW.

Sexual Orientation: Science, Education, and Policy
psychology.ucdavis.edu/rainbow/default.html
This site builds on the work of Dr. Gregory Herek at the University of California at Davis. Herek's research focuses on sexual orientation, anti-gay violence, homophobia, and other concerns of gay men and lesbians.

Human Rights Campaign
www.hrcusa.org/
The Human Rights Campaign is an organization dedicated to securing equal rights for lesbians and gay men. This Web site features updated information on issues related to gay rights, and suggests courses of action to change government policies.

The Other Queer Page
www.im1ru12.org/toqp/index.html
This site provides a variety of information and links, including a listing of gay, lesbian, bisexual and transgender resources—ranging from "coming out" to the fight for equal rights.

11

Contraception

It's a good thing that there are lots of birth control options, because I've used most of them at one time or another except for Norplant and the monthly injections. I was able to be on the pill before my boyfriend and I first started having intercourse in college. That was before AIDS, so I didn't need to use anything else "embarrassing." I tried the combination pill and the minipill, then used an IUD for a while. After I was first married, we used natural family planning and the diaphragm or cervical cap successfully. After our children were born, foam and condoms filled in for us until my husband got a vasectomy. I never had any particular problems with any of the methods, and I'm very grateful to never have had an unwanted pregnancy, but it sure is nice to be free of needing to use contraceptives. (Author's files)

Historical and Social Perspectives

People's concern with controlling conception goes back at least to the beginning of recorded history (McLaren, 1990). In ancient Egypt, women placed dried crocodile dung next to the cervix to prevent conception. In sixth-century Greece, eating the uterus, testicle, or hoof paring of a mule was recommended. In more recent historical times, the eighteenth-century Italian adventurer Giovanni Casanova was noted for his animal-membrane condoms tied with a ribbon at the base of the penis. In seventeenth-century western Europe, condoms, withdrawal of the penis from the vagina before ejaculation, and vaginal sponges soaked in a variety of solutions were used for contraception.

Contraception in the United States

Although we may take for granted the variety of contraceptive, or birth control, methods available in the United States today, this state of affairs is quite recent. Throughout American history, both the methods available for contraception and the laws concerning their use have been restrictive. In the 1870s Anthony Comstock, then secretary of the New York Society for the Suppression of Vice, succeeded in enacting national laws that prohibited disseminating contraceptive information through the U.S. mail on the grounds that such information was obscene (these were known as the Comstock Laws). At that time, the only legitimate form of birth control was abstinence, and reproduction was viewed as the only acceptable reason for sexual intercourse.

Margaret Sanger was the person most instrumental in promoting the changes in birth control legislation and availability in the United States. Sanger was horrified at the misery of women who had virtually no control over their fertility and bore child after child in desperate poverty. In 1915 she opened an illegal clinic where women could obtain and learn to use the diaphragms she had shipped from Europe. She also published birth control information in her newspaper *The Woman Rebel.* As a result, Sanger was arraigned for violating the Comstock Laws. She fled to Europe to avoid certain prosecution but later returned to promote research on birth control hormones, a project financed by her wealthy friend Katherine Dexter McCormack. These women wanted to develop a reliable method by which women could control their own fertility (Kalb, 1997). However, it was not until 1960 that the first birth control pills came on the U.S. market, after limited testing and research in Puerto Rico. Fertility control through contraception rather than abstinence was a profound shift that implied an acceptance of female sexual expression and broadened the roles that women might choose (D'Emilio & Freedman, 1988).

In 1965 the U.S. Supreme Court ruled in *Griswold* v. *Connecticut* that states could not prohibit the use of contraceptives by married people, basing the decision on the right to privacy of married couples (381 U.S. 479). In 1972 the Supreme Court case *Eisenstadt* v. *Baird* extended the right to privacy to unmarried individuals by decriminalizing the use of contraception by single people (405 U.S. 438).

During ensuing years, laws governing contraceptive availability continued to change. Most states have liberalized their laws to allow the dispensing of contraceptives to adolescents without parental consent and the displaying of condoms and spermicidal foam on open pharmacy shelves rather than behind the counter. But many people still oppose television ads for condoms, and controversy continues on the national level about whether to require parental notification when minors receive contraceptive services from government-funded organizations. The concern is, of course, that teens who would not otherwise choose to have intercourse would do so if contraception were easily available. However, research indicates that the rate of sexual activity does not increase even when condoms are available at no cost at school (Guttmacher et al., 1997). However, the availability and acceptability of contraception are still contested issues.

Margaret Sanger was dedicated to helping women and families have every child be a wanted child.

Contraception as a Contemporary Issue

In recent years the availability and use of reliable birth control have been seen as increasingly desirable for a variety of reasons. The typical heterosexual woman in the Western world is trying to become pregnant or is pregnant for only a small percentage of her reproductive life. For most of the other time she is trying to prevent pregnancy. There has been a growing emphasis on having planned and wanted children. Many couples who want children wait for some years to establish their relationship and financial stability before starting a family. Birth control also enables couples and individuals to limit the size of their families. In particular, women who want to combine a career and parenthood depend on birth control. Finally, men and women who choose *not* to be parents can avoid unwanted pregnancies more successfully with effective birth control methods.

The use of birth control can also contribute to the physical health of the mother. Pregnancy itself has health risks, and spacing pregnancies usually results in better health for mothers and their children, particularly when nutrition and health care are inadequate. In some cases, birth control is used to avoid the possibility of bearing children with hereditary diseases or birth defects.

Population growth is another concern that plays a part in some people's decision to limit their family size. Each day brings 250,000 more people into the world (Bond, 1997). Ninety-five percent of that growth is expected to occur in poorer, developing countries, where the population already exceeds the availability of bare necessities—housing, food, and fuel (Reifsnider, 1997). For example, 37% of people in India cannot buy enough food to nourish themselves. Furthermore, overpopulation is a dire threat to the earth's environment. Some environmentalists urge the world to cut the growth rate in half over the next decade, which translates to limiting family size to two children throughout the world (one child per family in some areas) (Toufexis, 1989). For these reasons, many people see birth control as necessary to combat world hunger and environmental devastation.

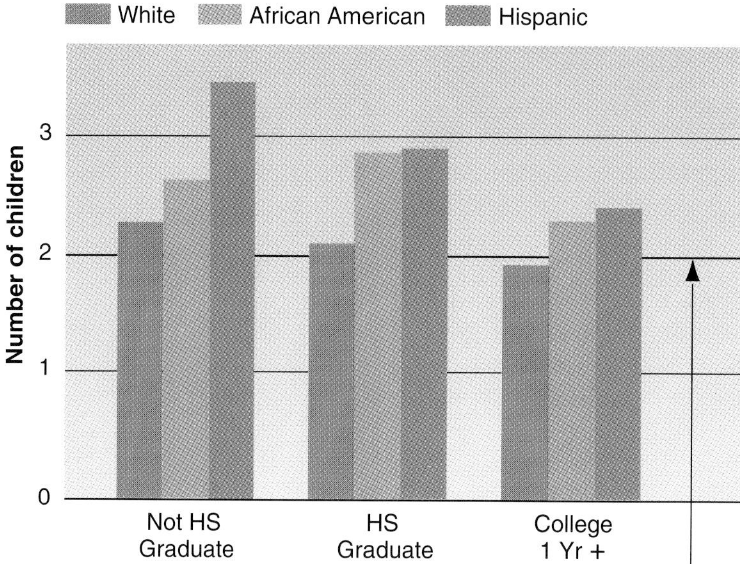

White
African American
Hispanic
Number of children
0
1
2
3
Not HS Graduate
HS Graduate
College 1 Yr +
As the education of women increases, the number of children they have decreases. Reproductive patterns among racial groups become more similiar the higher the education level (Grant, 1994).

Figure 11.1

Average number of children, by mother's education level and race/ethnicity in the United States.

The 1994 United Nations Conference on Population and Development attempted to address these concerns. An inherent factor in controlling population levels is expanding women's opportunity for education. Across the globe, women with higher levels of education have fewer children (Robey et al., 1992); and as Figure 11.1 illustrates, this pattern also holds across racial lines in the United States. The boxed discussion, "Birth Control by Bicycle," presents one creative solution being implemented in Zimbabwe in the effort to control high population growth rates.

Sexuality and Diversity

Birth Control by Bicycle

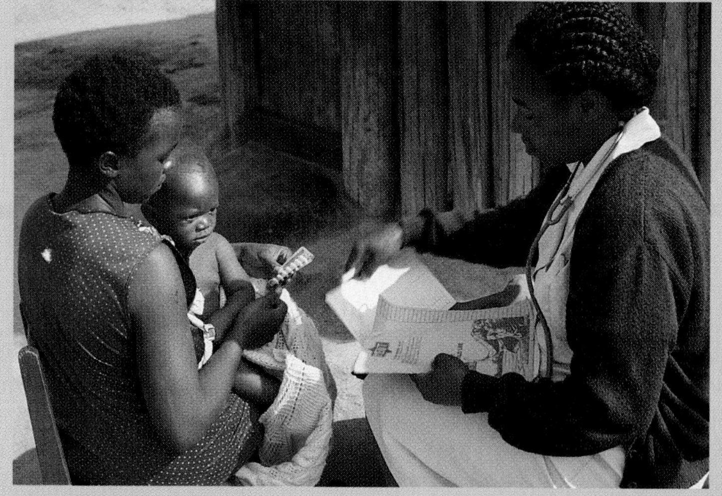

In a continent of exploding fertility rates, Zimbabwe's population growth has slowed. Despite opposition from the Roman Catholic Church, the government funds birth control programs. The woman in this photograph—paid a living wage of $58 a month—is one of the many health workers who travel by bicycle to rural areas, bringing free birth control pills and condoms to women who otherwise would not have those options. About 40% of women in Zimbabwe use contraceptives, compared with an average of 14% in sub-Saharan Africa (Keller, 1994).

Objections to contraception often stem from religious mandate, and some individuals and couples do not use birth control devices due to their religious beliefs or ethnocultural background (Robey et al., 1996). The official doctrine of the Roman Catholic Church (as well as some other religions, such as the fundamental Muslim faith) holds that contraceptive means other than abstinence and methods based on the menstrual cycle are immoral. In 1995 Pope John Paul II's "Evangelium Vitae"—"Gospel of Life"—reaffirmed that contraception and sterilization were morally unacceptable. However, many contemporary religions approve of and even favor the use of birth control. Moreover, there is a wide diversity of views even among leaders of the Catholic church. In fact, a poll of nuns and priests found that 44% did not believe that contraceptive use by married couples was a sin (Stammer, 1994).

Given that the official doctrine of the Catholic church prohibits the use of contraceptives, do you think Catholic women are less likely than non-Catholics to use birth control?

The discrepancy between doctrine and practice is wide: Most practicing Catholics in the United States use some kind of artificial contraception. In fact, the difference between Catholic and non-Catholic use of contraceptive devices is minimal. An investigation of birth control practices among a large sample of women of childbearing age found that 88.7% of Protestant women and 88.3% of Catholic women used artificial contraceptive devices (Bachrach, 1984).

Sharing Responsibility and Choosing a Birth Control Method

Each birth control method has its advantages and disadvantages. An individual or couple will find that one method will suit a certain situation best. Sharing the responsibility will enhance its use.

It Takes Two

In promoting contraception, Margaret Sanger wanted to give women control over their own fertility. However, control should not mean total responsibility by the woman. It is not wise for a man to assume that a woman has "taken care of herself." As a male student asks,

If you have sex with a girl and she tells you she's on the pill, how do you know if she's telling the truth? (Authors' files)

Many women do not regularly practice birth control, especially if they are not in a long-term relationship, and some use methods inconsistently or incorrectly (Kusseling et al., 1995). Dealing with an unwanted pregnancy is very difficult, and fear of unwanted pregnancy can negatively affect both partners' sexual experience. It is in the best interests of both partners to be actively involved in choosing and using contraception (Wang et al., 1998). No one wants to be "surprised" with an unexpected pregnancy, but the saying goes, "If you're not part of the solution, you're part of the problem."

Would you be more careful if it was you that got pregnant?
See your pharmacist for free information on family planning, venereal disease and other communicable diseases.
For the Clinic nearest you call your local Health Department or (800) 952-5250
Photography by DALE ALISON BARON
Sponsored by PPS Pharmacists Planning Service, Inc in conjunction with La Clinica De La Raza, Oakland, California
© PPSI 1986

Sharing the responsibility of contraception can enhance a relationship. Talking about birth control can be a good way to practice discussing personal and sexual topics. Failing to talk about birth control may cause women to resent men for putting the entire responsibility on them. One writer emphasized that taking care of business before couples get down to pleasure often enhances lovemaking by reducing stress and building trust

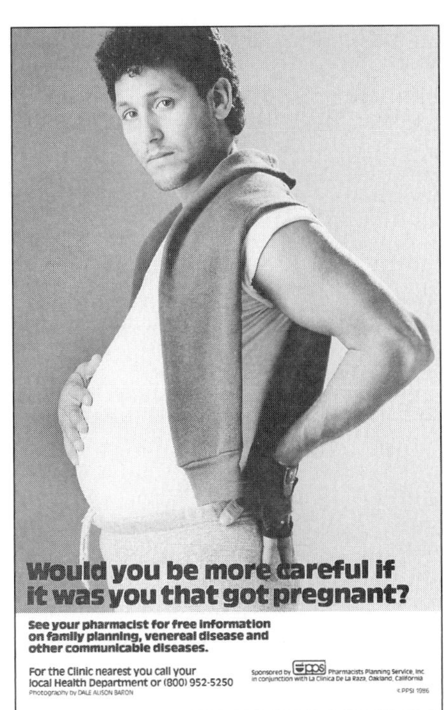

(Castleman, 1980). For these reasons, we recommend that women and men share the responsibility for birth control.

The first step in sharing contraceptive responsibility may simply be for either partner to ask the other about birth control before having intercourse the first time. In our experience talking with students and clients, this initial question is rarely asked. Research finds that both male and female college students need to develop skills to discuss contraception. Women need to become effective in obtaining contraceptives, and men need to learn to be assertive about refusing to engage in intercourse without effective contraception (Van den Bossche & Robinson, 1997). Openness on the part of the male partner to using condoms or engaging in noncoital sexual activities, whether as the contraceptive method of choice or as a backup or temporary method, is another way to share responsibility for birth control.

Reading about and discussing the various alternatives and their side effects and choosing the one that seems best are important ways for both partners to be involved. Most birth control clinics offer classes that are open to partners. The man can also participate by accompanying his partner when a medical exam is needed. Many physicians or nurse practitioners are comfortable with the woman's partner being present during such exams. The partner can be supportive about the cramping and discomfort some women experience from an IUD insertion, and can learn to check the string. Expenses for both the exam and the birth control method can also be shared. Male partners can learn to insert the diaphragm or cervical cap and foam, and to put on condoms. We

On the Edge

Infanticide

Infanticide, especially neonaticide (killing an infant within 24 hours after birth), has occurred in almost every culture throughout history. Infants were "exposed," leaving them outside for cold, starvation, or predators to kill. Moses and Oedipus are famous examples in history of infants who survived (Ehrenreich, 1998). Infanticide tragically filled the gap left by the lack of safe and effective birth control. The babies who had no one willing or able to care for them were left to die. This is also a contemporary concern. For example, human rights organizations have made allegations that parents and state-run orphanages in China deliberately let children die of starvation and neglect (Birchard, 1998; Bogert & Wehrfritz, 1996).

In the modern United States, contraceptives and abortion are legal and safe, and adoption is usually easy to arrange. However, each year in the United States over 50 newborn babies are killed by their mothers shortly after birth. As the graph indicates, the number of infant murders, even with population increases, decreased after oral contraceptives and abortion became legal. However, surrendering a child for adoption has always been available, but a young woman has to be able to ask for help for her and her baby.

The murders are usually committed by young, unmarried women, many of them typical middle-class girls (Ehrenreich, 1998). Women of all races and socioeconomic classes commit this crime, a majority of the babies are white, but a disproportionate number, compared to the percentage of general popu-

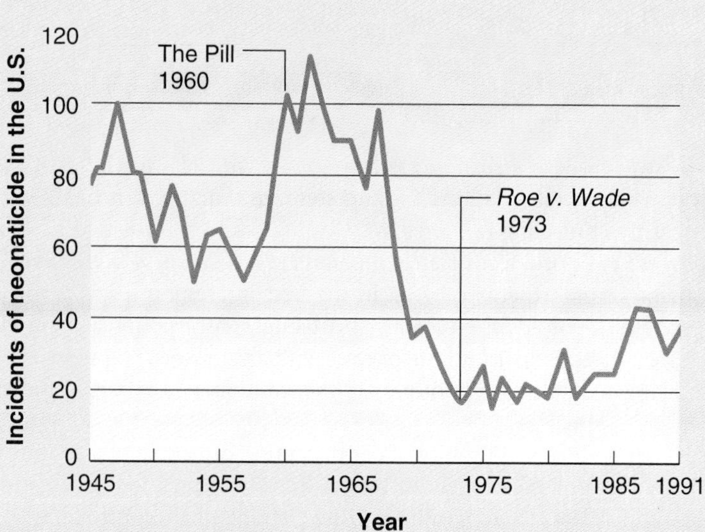

When oral contraception and abortion were legalized, the number of infant murders decreased. (Kantrowitz, 1997)

strongly believe that sharing the responsibility for birth control can help provide both better sexual relationships and improved contraceptive effectiveness.

Choosing a Birth Control Method

Many forms of birth control are available to couples. However, an ideal method—one that is 100% effective, completely safe with no side effects, reversible, separate from sexual activity, inexpensive, easy to obtain, usable by either sex and not dependent on the user's memory—is not available now or in the foreseeable future. Each of the methods currently available has advantages and disadvantages with regard to effectiveness, safety, cost, and convenience. It is a good idea to be familiar with the various methods available because most people will use several of them during their active sex lives.

Effectiveness

Several variables influence the effectiveness of birth control. Among the most important of these variables is human error, which is not taken into account in rating the theoretical effectiveness of a method. Human error on the part of the health care practitioner may result in an improperly inserted IUD or a poorly fitted diaphragm, as discussed later in this chapter. More frequently, it is the fault of the user. Poor or improper knowledge

On the Edge

lation, are black. Most had options available to them along the way—college health clinics, high school programs for pregnant teens and mothers, and Planned Parenthood services—but failed to use them.

Some of the cases include an 18-year-old New Jersey student who delivered her son in the bathroom during her senior prom, reportedly choking him to death before tossing him in the garbage. In Los Angeles a 19-year-old was charged with dumping her baby girl in a garbage can outside her middle-class suburban home. A 20-year-old business major at the University of Southern California secretly delivered a baby girl whom a USC maintenance worker found dead in a dumpster. Sometimes boyfriends are involved. An 18-year-old college freshman and her boyfriend were charged with putting their newborn son in a trash bin after killing him (Kantrowitz, 1997).

Experts in these rare homicides believe that the young women use elaborate, irrational psychological mechanisms to be able to convince themselves that they are not pregnant. They may be stereotypical "good girls" who feel overwhelmed by shame (Ehrenreich, 1998). The thought of family and friends finding out seems worse than killing or abandoning their baby. They wear baggy clothes and isolate themselves from detection by others. The self-delusion may continue until the moment of birth in a kind of "psychotic denial." Many of these women are so disconnected from reality they don't remember feeling any pain during the delivery. They do not see their babies as human, but as foreign bodies that have passed through them. Most of these young women have no prior mental illness; a few may be antisocial personalities who feel no concern about their child and kill because it's more convenient for them (Kantrowitz, 1997).

A sophomore business major at the University of Southern California went home for summer break in May. The day after her departure, a maintenance worker found the strangled body of a newborn girl at the bottom of a trash chute in her apartment building.

of the correct use of the method, negative beliefs about using a method, an uninvolved partner, forgetfulness, or deciding that "this one time won't matter" all greatly increase the chances of pregnancy (Jones & Forrest, 1992).

Are people who feel guilty about sex are more or less likely to use contraception effectively than people who have positive attitudes about sexuality? Why or why not?

Research indicates that men and women who do not use contraception or use it ineffectively or inconsistently have several characteristics in common. People who feel guilty about sex are likely to use contraception ineffectively (Strassberg & Mahoney, 1988). Negative attitudes toward sexuality often interfere with the ability to process information about sexuality and birth control, so that a person is more likely to choose less effective methods and to use them inconsistently. In addition, women who are uncomfortable with their sexuality are likely to take a passive role in contraceptive decision making, leaving

Table 11.1 Factors to Consider When Choosing a Birth Control Method

Method	*Failure Rate* If Used Correctly and Consistently*	*Typical Number* Who Become Pregnant Accidentally*	*Cost (in dollars per year for 100 occurrences of intercourse)*
"Outercourse"	0	0	0
Estrogen-progestin pills	0.1	3	$130–$260 ($10–$20 per cycle)
Progestin-only pills	0.5	3	$130–$260 ($10–$20 per cycle)
Norplant	0.09	0.09	$130–$170 if kept 5 years
Depo-Provera	0.3	0.3	$140 ($35 per injection)
Condoms (male)	3	12	$50 (50¢ each)
Condoms (female)	5	21	$250 ($2.50 each)
Diaphragm with spermicide	6	18	$155–$255 ($20 diaphragm, $50–$150 for fitting, $85 for spermicide)
Cervical cap			
Woman has been pregnant	26	36	Same as diaphragm
Woman never pregnant	9	18	
Spermicides	6	21	$85 (85¢ per application)
Progestasert T IUD	1.5	2	$160
Copper-T IUD	0.6	0.8	$160 1st year; less if kept more years
Tubal sterilization	0.4	0.4	$1,200–$2,500
Vasectomy	0.1	0.15	$250–$1,000
Fertility awareness: "rhythm," calendar, basal temperature, cervical mucus	1–9	20	0
Withdrawal	4	19	0
No method	85	85	0

*Number of women out of 100 who become pregnant by the end of the first year of using a particular method.

Source: Hatcher et al., 1994.

themselves vulnerable to their partners' contraceptive behavior (Gerrard, 1987). The box "Infanticide" describes an extreme response to guilt and denial.

Contraceptive effectiveness is best compared by looking at **failure rates** (the number of women out of 100 who become pregnant by the end of the first year of using a particular method). The first column of Table 11.1 shows the failure rate for a large number of women or men using the most common birth control methods correctly and consistently; the second column shows the rate of accidental pregnancies resulting from improper or inconsistent use. To reduce the potential rate of failure, many couples may choose to use backup methods.

Failure rate
The number of women out of 100 who become pregnant by the end of one year of using a particular contraceptive.

Backup methods
Using a second contraceptive method simultaneously with a first.

Using Backup Methods to Increase Contraceptive Effectiveness

Under various circumstances, a couple may need or want to use **backup methods**—that is, more than one method of contraception used simultaneously. Backup methods can

Table 11.1 continued

Advantages	*Disadvantages*
No medical side effects. Helps develop nonintercourse sexual intimacy	Risk of unplanned intercourse
Very effective; no interruption of sexual experience; reduced menstrual cramps and flow	Possible side effects; increased risk of pregnancy if forgotten
Very effective; no interruption of sexual experience; no estrogen-related side effects	Breakthrough bleeding
Very effective; no interruption of sexual experience; don't have to remember to take it; no estrogen-related side effects	Breakthrough bleeding; difficult removal
Very effective; no interruption of sexual experience; don't have to remember on daily basis; no estrogen-related side effects	Breakthrough bleeding side effects; clinic visit and injection every 3 months
Some protection from STDs; available without a prescription	Interruption of sexual experience; reduces sensation
Same as male condoms	Same as male condoms
No side effects; can be put in prior to sexual experience	Needs practice to use correctly
Same as diaphragm	Same as diaphragm
No prescription necessary. Some protection from STDs	Interruption of sexual experience, skin irritation for some
Very effective; no interruption of sexual activity; don't have to remember to use	Side effects; increased menstrual flow and cramps; may be expelled
Highly effective; permanent	Not easy to reverse for fertility
Easier procedure than tubal sterilization	Not easy to reverse for fertility
Acceptable to Catholic Church; no medical side effects	Uncertainty of "safe times"; periods of abstinence from intercourse or use of other methods
No medical side effects	Interruption of intercourse
Acceptable only if pregnancy desired	

help reduce the human element in failure rates. Some examples of these circumstances include the following:

- During the first cycle of the pill.
- For the remainder of the cycle after forgetting to take one or more birth control pills or after several days of diarrhea or vomiting while on the pill.
- The first month after changing to a new brand of pills.
- When taking medications, such as antibiotics, that reduce effectiveness of the pill.
- During the initial one to three months after IUD insertion.
- When first learning to use a new method of birth control.
- When the couple wants to increase the effectiveness of contraception. For instance, using foam and condoms together offers very effective protection.

Condoms, foam, or a diaphragm are possible backup methods that can be combined in many ways with other birth control methods for extra contraceptive protection.

Which Contraceptive Method Is Right for You?

Effectiveness is not the only important factor in choosing a method of birth control. Many additional factors—including cost, ease of use, and potential side effects—influence couples' decisions about whether to use a particular birth control method (Pasquale, 1994). Table 11.1 summarizes some of the most important factors, including comparative costs, advantages and disadvantages, and effectiveness of the most commonly used methods.

Beyond the variables listed in the table, the decision about which birth control method to use must take into account one more important factor—the individuals who will be using it. The survey presented in the boxed discussion "Which Contraceptive Method Is Best for You?" is designed to help you take into account your own concerns, circumstances, physical condition, and personal qualities as you make this very individual decision. As we discuss a number of commonly used methods in the paragraphs that follow, we present more specific information that may be helpful in making this choice.

Your Sexual Health

Which Contraceptive Method Is Best for You?

Answer yes or no to each statement as it applies to you and, if appropriate, your partner.

1. You have high blood pressure or cardiovascular disease.
2. You smoke cigarettes.
3. You have a new sexual partner.
4. An unwanted pregnancy would be devastating to you.
5. You have a good memory.
6. You or your partner have multiple sexual partners.
7. You prefer a method with little or no bother.
8. You have heavy, crampy periods.
9. You need protection against STDs.
10. You are concerned about endometrial and ovarian cancer.
11. You are forgetful.
12. You need a method right away.
13. You're comfortable touching your and your partner's genitals.
14. You have a cooperative partner.
15. You like a little extra vaginal lubrication.
16. You have sex at unpredictable times and places.
17. You are in a monogamous relationship and have at least one child.

Scoring:

Recommendations are based on yes answers to the following numbered statements:

The combination pill: 4, 5, 6, 8, 9, 16
The progestin-only pill: 1, 2, 5, 7, 16
Condoms: 1, 2, 3, 6, 9, 12, 13, 14
Norplant and Depo-Provera: 1, 2, 4, 7, 11, 16
Diaphragm or cervical cap: 1, 2, 13, 14
The IUD: 1, 2, 7, 11, 13, 16, 17
Spermicides: 1, 2, 12, 13, 14, 15

Source: Hales, 1994.

"Outercourse"

Throughout the remainder of this chapter, we will look at contraceptive methods designed to prevent pregnancy resulting from coitus. One important method deserves special mention because it involves a different fundamental decision at the point when a couple becomes intimate—the decision to be sexual without engaging in penile–vaginal intercourse.

Noncoital forms of sexual intimacy, called **outercourse,** can be a viable form of birth control (Hatcher, 1988). Outercourse includes all avenues of sexual intimacy other than penile–vaginal intercourse, including kissing, touching, petting, mutual masturbation, and oral and anal sex. The voluntary avoidance of coitus offers effective protection from pregnancy, providing the male does not ejaculate near the vaginal opening. Outercourse can be used as a primary or temporary means of preventing pregnancy, and it can also be used when it is inadvisable to have intercourse for other reasons—for example, following childbirth or abortion, or during a herpes outbreak. This method has no undesirable contraceptive side effects, but does not eliminate the chances of spreading sexually transmitted diseases.

Outercourse
Noncoital forms of sexual intimacy.

Hormone-Based Contraceptives

Many of the most common birth control methods used by women work by artificially altering hormone levels. Hormone-based contraceptives can have several effects, such as inhibiting ovulation, altering the mucous lining of the cervix so that it blocks the passage of sperm, or preventing the fertilized egg from implanting successfully in the uterus (see Chapter 12). This section looks at the most popular hormone-based birth control methods, including oral contraceptives, Norplant, Depo-Provera, and "morning-after pills."

Oral Contraceptives

Oral contraceptives are the reversible method of birth control most commonly used by women in the United States today, including college-age women (Peterson et al., 1998). Three basic types of oral contraceptives are currently on the market: the constant-dose combination pill, the multiphasic pill, and the progestin-only pill (currently called the minipill) (see Figure 11.2).

The Pill: Three Basic Types

The **constant-dose combination pill,** which has been available since the early 1960s and is the most commonly used oral contraceptive in the United States today, contains two hormones, synthetic estrogen and progestin (a progesterone-like substance). The dosage of these hormones remains constant throughout the menstrual cycle. There are more than 32 different varieties, containing varying amounts and ratios of these two hormones.

Constant-dose combination pills
Birth control pills that contain a constant daily dose of estrogen and progestin.

The **multiphasic pill,** which has been on the market since 1984, is another type of oral contraceptive. Unlike the constant-dose combination pill, the multiphasic pill provides fluctuations of estrogen and progesterone levels during the menstrual cycle. The multiphasic pill is designed to reduce the total hormone dosage and side effects while maintaining contraceptive effectiveness.

Multiphasic pills
Birth control pills that vary the dosages of estrogen and progestin during the cycle.

The **progestin-only pill,** which has been on the market since 1973, contains only 0.35 mg of progestin—about one-third the amount in an average-strength combination pill. The progestin-only pill contains no estrogen. Like the combination pill, the progestin-only pill has a constant-dose formula.

Progestin-only pills
Contraceptive pills that contain a small dose of progestin and no estrogen.

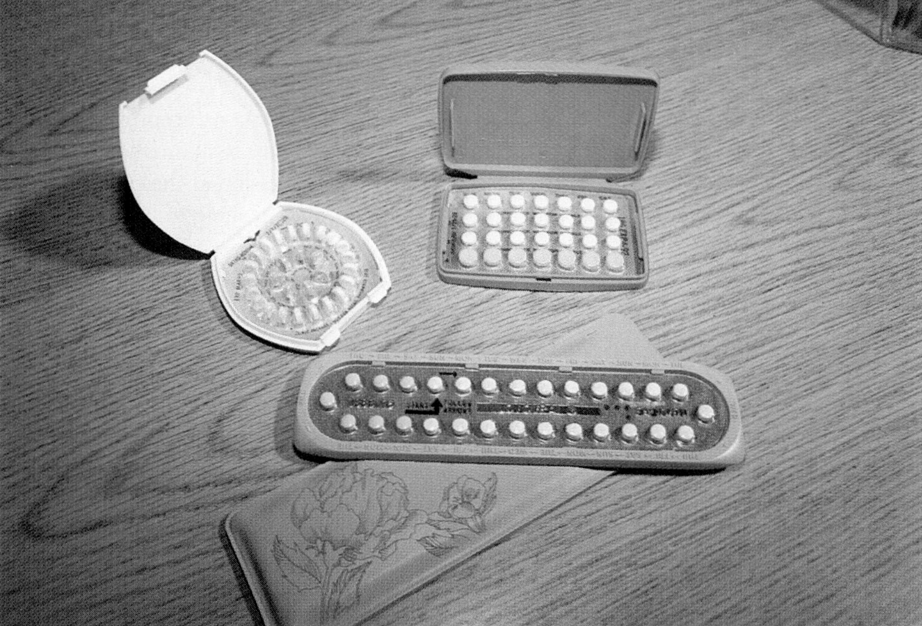

Figure 11.2

There are currently three basic types of pills: the combination pill, the multiphasic pill, and the progestin-only pill. Although most birth control pills come in packages of 28 pills, some types come in 21-day supplies.

How Oral Contraceptives Work

Both the combination pill and the multiphasic pill prevent conception primarily by inhibiting ovulation. The estrogen in these pills affects the hypothalamus, inhibiting the release of the pituitary hormones LH and FSH, which would otherwise begin the chain of events culminating in ovulation (see Chapter 4). The progestin in these pills provides secondary contraceptive protection by thickening and chemically altering the cervical mucus so that it hampers the passage of sperm into the uterus. Progestin also causes changes in the lining of the uterus, making it less receptive to implantation by a fertilized egg. In addition, progestin may inhibit ovulation by mildly disturbing hypothalamic, pituitary, and ovarian function.

The progestin-only pill works somewhat differently. Most women who take the progestin-only pill probably continue to ovulate at least occasionally. The primary effect of this pill is to alter the cervical mucus to a thick and tacky consistency that effectively blocks sperm. As with the combination pill, secondary contraceptive effects may be provided by alterations in the uterine lining that make it unreceptive to implantation.

How to Use Oral Contraceptives

There are several acceptable ways to begin taking oral contraceptives; a woman who does so should carefully follow the instructions of her health care practitioner.

Forgetting to take one or more pills sharply reduces the effectiveness of this method, as does taking the pill at a different time each day (Peterson et al., 1998). Pill users should take the pill at the same time every day; taking the pill at approximately the same time each day maximizes effectiveness. Because oral contraceptives maintain particular hormone levels in the body, missing one or more pills can lower hormone levels and allow ovulation to occur (Rosenberg et al., 1995). You must take a missed pill as soon as you remember; then take the next pill at the regular time. If you forget more than one pill, it is best to consult your health care practitioner. You should also use a backup method such as foam or condoms for the remainder of your cycle.

Advantages of Oral Contraceptives

Birth control pills have several advantages. They can be taken at a time separate from sexual activity, which many people believe helps maintain sexual spontaneity. In addition, the pill has the advantage of being reversible, so that a woman may easily stop using it if her needs change. If the combination pill is used correctly, it is a highly effective method, as Table 11.1 shows. The effectiveness is an important benefit. One student states,

I've used the pill for 11 years. It's not a very big responsibility to take a pill every day compared to the responsibility that comes with being a parent. (Authors' files)

The combination pill also often eliminates *Mittelschmerz* (pain at ovulation) and reduces menstrual cramps and the amount and duration of the flow. In addition, some women notice that taking oral contraceptives diminishes premenstrual tension symptoms. Oral contraceptives can help relieve endometriosis and may decrease the incidence of benign breast disease (Hatcher et al., 1994). Use of oral contraceptives reduces the risk of endometrial and ovarian cancer (Miracle-McMahill et al., 1977; Recer, 1997). Other potential advantages include breast enlargement and a decrease in acne in some women (Burkman, 1995). A woman who was pleased with this method explained,

I really like the pill I'm taking. My periods are light, and the bad cramps I used to have are gone. I hadn't been using anything before taking the pill. It's a tremendous relief to make love and not be afraid of getting pregnant. (Authors' files)

These advantages explain, in part, why the pill is more commonly used than any other reversible method of birth control. The progestin-only pill has the advantage that it eliminates any estrogen-related side effects and reduces the likelihood of progestin-related problems because of the low progestin dosage. Adverse reactions to the combination pill may be reduced by switching to the progestin-only pill (Hatcher et al., 1994).

Disadvantages of Oral Contraceptives

One of the biggest disadvantages of the pill is that it does not protect against AIDS and other STDs. Condoms should be used in conjunction with the pill when protection from these diseases is needed.

Because the hormones in birth control pills circulate in the bloodstream through the entire body, a variety of side effects may result from this form of contraception. However, it is important to note that most modern contraceptive pills contain less than 50 milligrams of estrogen, compared with 150 milligrams in the early birth control pills. The reduced amount of hormone greatly reduces the risk of side effects (Hansen & Lundvall, 1997). For most healthy women *who do not smoke,* the benefits of oral contraceptives outweigh the risks (Carr & Ory, 1997; Chasan-Taber & Stampfer, 1998).

Serious problems associated with the pill can be summarized by the acronym ACHES and are described in Table 11.2. We look first at some of the problems that have been associated with the estrogen–progestin pills, then examine possible side effects of the progestin-only pill.

Use of the pill may be related to emotional changes. Some women see a correlation between their moods and use of oral contraceptives. Studies have shown an increase in depression in women on the pill (Hatcher et al., 1994); because depression can affect all aspects of a woman's life, it is not to be taken lightly. A woman who suspects her depression may be pill-related can use another contraceptive method for a time and observe any changes in her moods.

Many women take the pill to increase the spontaneity and enjoyment of their sexual expression, and some do experience improvement in their sexual lives. However, a decrease in

Table 11.2 Remember "ACHES" for the Pill

Initial	*Symptoms*	*Possible Problem*
Symptoms of possible serious problems with the birth control pill, represented by their initials.		
A	Abdominal pain (severe)	Gallbladder disease, liver tumor, or blood clot
C	Chest pain (severe) or shortness of breath	Blood clot in lungs or heart attack
H	Headaches (severe)	Stroke, high blood pressure, or migraine headache
E	Eye problems: blurred vision, flashing lights, or blindness	Stroke, high blood pressure, or temporary vascular problems at many possible sites
S	Severe leg pain (calf or thigh)	Blood clot in legs

Source: Adapted from Hatcher et al., 1994.

sexual motivation or vaginal lubrication during arousal may also occur (Crenshaw & Goldberg, 1996). A change in type of pill may help. A small study of university students found that women using multiphasic pills experienced greater sexual interest and response than those using constant-dose pills (McCoy & Matyas, 1996).

Oral contraceptives interact with other medications and can diminish the therapeutic effect of the medication, or the medication can diminish the contraceptive effectiveness of the pill. Some medications that can interfere with oral contraceptive effectiveness are listed in the box below.

Although the reduced amount of hormones in the progestin-only pill causes fewer potential side effects, this pill too has some disadvantages. First, it must be taken consistently and regularly to be effective. Irregular and "breakthrough" bleeding (a light flow between menstrual periods) happens more frequently with the progestin-only pill than with the combination pill. However, the bleeding irregularities usually diminish in two or three months, as they do with the combination pill. Ectopic pregnancy, in which the zygote is implanted outside the uterus, is rare but more likely for users of progestin-only pills.

Additional Comments on Oral Contraceptives

Women vary in their responses to the particular hormone combinations of different oral contraceptives. Some side effects—such as nausea, fluid retention, increased appetite, acne, depression, or bleeding irregularities—can be eliminated by changing the type of pill. Generally, a woman will be given a type of pill that works well for her and that has the lowest practical hormonal potency, to reduce the possibility of side effects.

Women with a history of certain conditions, however, should use a different method of contraception; these conditions include blood clots, strokes, circulation problems, heart problems, jaundice, cancer of the breast or uterus, and undiagnosed genital bleeding. In addition, a woman who currently has a liver disease or who suspects or knows that she is pregnant should not take the pill. Women who have problems with migraine headaches, depression, high blood pressure, epilepsy, diabetes or prediabetes symptoms, asthma, or varicose veins should weigh the potential risks most carefully and use the pill only under close medical supervision.

Your Sexual Health

Medications That Reduce Oral Contraceptive Effectiveness

Some medications can reduce the effectiveness of birth control pills. Tell every physician who gives you medication that you are taking oral contraceptives. Use a backup method, such as foam or condoms, when you use

Barbiturates
Ampicillin
Tetracycline
Antihistimines
Tegretol
Dilantin
Rifampin (for tuberculosis)
Phenylbutazone (for arthritis)

Source: Stewart et al., 1987.

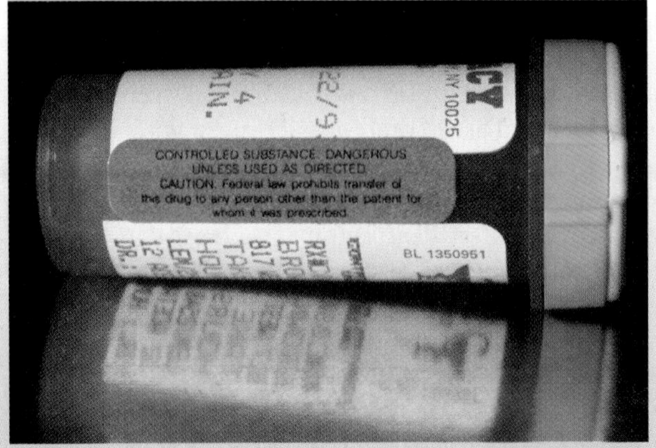

Norplant

Norplant consists of six thin, flexible capsules made of a soft, rubberlike material (called Silastic) filled with synthetic progestin. The capsules are implanted under the skin of a woman's upper arm, as shown in Figure 11.3. Norplant has been tested for 20 years in 46 countries, and became available in the United States in 1991. It was the first new contraceptive system approved in the United States in 30 years (Thomas & LeMelle, 1995). Two years after its approval, 500,000 women in the United States had received it (Kantrowitz & Wingert, 1993).

How Norplant Works

The implanted capsules release synthetic progestin gradually into the bloodstream over a five-year period to prevent conception in the same manner as the progestin-only pill (Wehrle, 1994). Norplant provides effective contraception within 24 hours of insertion (Monaghan, 1992).

How to Use Norplant

Norplant is inserted and removed by a health care practitioner. A local anesthetic is used to numb a small area; the capsules are then placed under the skin in a fan pattern through an incision about ⅛ inch long. Insertion usually takes 10 to 15 minutes. Once inserted, the capsules are not easily seen.

Figure 11.3

How Norplant works: Norplant capsules implanted in a woman's arm release progestin over a five-year period.

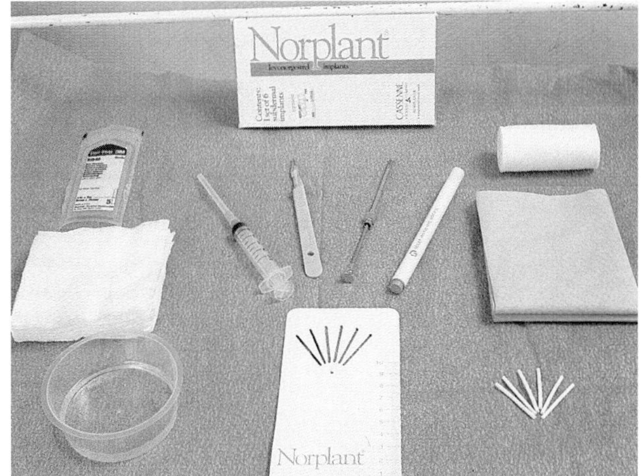

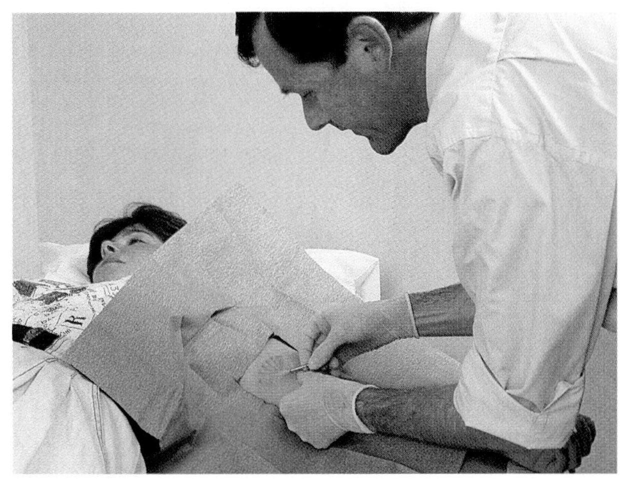

Advantages of Norplant

Once inserted, Norplant provides highly effective contraception for five years without the woman needing to remember to take a pill daily or use a barrier method when having sexual intercourse (Cromer & Harel, 1997). Adolescents who use Norplant are considerably less likely than pill users to become pregnant unintentionally (Berenson et al., 1997; Suman et al., 1998). Fertility is not compromised; a woman's ability to become pregnant returns within 24 hours following removal. Norplant releases about one-fifth the hormones that the pill does per day, yet it is more effective because the release is constant (Berenson & Wiemann, 1995).

Disadvantages of Norplant

The cost of using Norplant is high, approximately $650. (This is about the same as five years' worth of birth control pills.) Norplant offers no protection from STDs. Side effects and contraindications are the same as for oral contraceptives. The most common side effect is the same as for the minipill: menstrual irregularity (Barnhart et al., 1997). Menstrual irregularity decreases after the first year of use (Kaunitz & Jordan, 1997). Other reported side effects include cramps, headaches, weight gain, and nausea. In one study, more than one in ten women had the implant removed within one year because of side effects (Frank et al., 1993). Removal of Norplant has sometimes been difficult and painful, or has caused scarring and permanent nerve damage. To eliminate the need for removal, biodegradable implants are being studied (Singh et al., 1997).

Depo-Provera

Depo-Provera is an injectable contraceptive. It has been available worldwide for more than 20 years and was approved by the U.S. Food and Drug Administration in 1992 (Kaunitz, 1994).

How Depo-Provera Works

The active ingredient is *medroxyprogesterone acetate,* a progestin, which inhibits the secretion of gonadotropins and prevents follicular maturation and ovulation. This causes the endometrial lining of the uterus to thin, preventing implantation of a fertilized egg. Like Norplant, Depo-Provera is a progestin-only medication. It also alters the cervical mucus (Mastroianni & Robinson, 1995).

How to Use Depo-Provera

The shot needs to be given once every 12 weeks, ideally within five days of the beginning of menstruation.

Advantages of Depo-Provera

Because it contains only progestin, estrogen-related side effects do not occur. The main advantage of Depo-Provera is not needing to take a pill daily or use a barrier method at the time of intercourse, as one student states:

I am on Depo-Provera. I love it. It's really effective, and I can't mess it up. (Authors' files)

In some cultures or situations, Depo-Provera is advantageous for a woman who wishes to use contraception without anyone other than her health care practitioner knowing. Depo-Provera also may have a protective action against endometrial and ovarian cancer (Hatcher et al., 1994).

Disadvantages of Depo-Provera

The most common side effects are menstrual irregularities, particularly lack of menstruation. Some women report menstrual spotting, weight gain, headaches, breast tenderness, dizziness, and mood changes as other side effects (Earl & David, 1994). Depo-Provera provides no protection against STDs.

Barrier Methods

Hormone-based methods cause changes in a woman's body that inhibit conception and implantation. Another group of contraceptive devices work in a different way—by preventing healthy sperm from reaching an ovum. In this section, we look at several barrier methods, including condoms, diaphragms, and cervical caps. We also include vaginal spermicides in this section because their effect is also to prevent sperm from reaching an egg and also because spermicidal creams and jellies are frequently used in conjunction with other barrier methods.

Condoms

Condom
A sheath that fits over the penis and is used for protection against unwanted pregnancy and sexually transmitted diseases.

Condoms, also called prophylactics and rubbers, are currently the only temporary method of birth control available for men. A condom is a sheath that fits over the erect penis and is made of thin surgical latex or sheep membrane. A new type of condom made of polyurethane is thinner, stronger, and more heat sensitive and comfortable than latex.

Condoms have a long history. A penile sheath was used in Japan during the early 1500s, and in 1564 an Italian anatomist, Fallopius, described a penile sheath made of linen. Mass production of inexpensive modern condoms began after the development of vulcanized rubber in the 1840s (Vinson & Epperly, 1991). Condoms are one of the most popular contraceptive methods used in the United States and, next to the pill, the most commonly used by college-age adults (Piccinino & Mosher, 1998).

Condoms are available without prescription at pharmacies, from family planning clinics, by mail order, in vending machines, and in some areas in school-based condom availability programs (Guttmacher et al., 1997). Most condoms are packaged—rolled up and wrapped in foil or plastic—and come lubricated or nonlubricated, in various shapes, textures, and colors. There is less chance of the condom breaking if it is lubricated, and some men report less reduction of penile sensation during intercourse with lubricated condoms. Sheep membrane, natural-skin condoms are more expensive but often interfere less with sensation than do the latex ones. However, some sexually transmitted diseases, including the AIDS virus, can pass through natural-membrane condoms but not through latex or polyurethane condoms. The pores in natural-membrane condoms are larger than the HIV virus.

Some university health services distribute free condoms to students in hopes of reducing STDs and pregnancy rates.

Some condoms have a small nipple on the end, called a reservoir tip, and others have a contoured shape or textured surface (Figure 11.4). Some are made with a spermicide, *nonoxynol-9,* on their inner and outer surfaces. Spermicidal condoms are not as effective as the combination of a condom and a vaginal spermicide. Condoms have an average shelf life of about five years, although not all packages are dated. They should not be stored in hot places, such as the glove compartment of a car or a back pocket, because heat can deteriorate the latex.

How the Condom Works

When a man uses a condom properly, both the ejaculate and the fluid from Cowper's gland secretions, sometimes called "precum," are contained within the tip. The condom thus serves as a mechanical barrier, effectively preventing any sperm from entering the vagina.

How to Use the Condom

Most condoms are packaged rolled up. Correct use includes unrolling the condom over the erect penis before any contact between the penis and the vulva occurs. Sperm in the Cowper's gland secretions or in the ejaculate can travel from outside the labia to inside the vagina. For maximum comfort and sensation, an uncircumcised man can retract the foreskin before rolling the condom over the penis (Bolus, 1994). With plain-end condoms (without the reservoir tip), the end needs to be twisted before rolling the condom down over the penis, as shown in Figure 11.4b. This leaves some room at the end for the ejaculate and reduces the chances of the condom breaking. If a condom breaks or slips off during intercourse, contraceptive foam, cream, or jelly should be inserted into the vagina *immediately.*

A condom breaks more easily without vaginal lubrication, so if the condom is nonlubricated, some vaginal secretion, saliva, or water-based lubricant needs to be put on the vulva and outside of the condom before inserting the penis into the vagina. *Do* **not** *use*

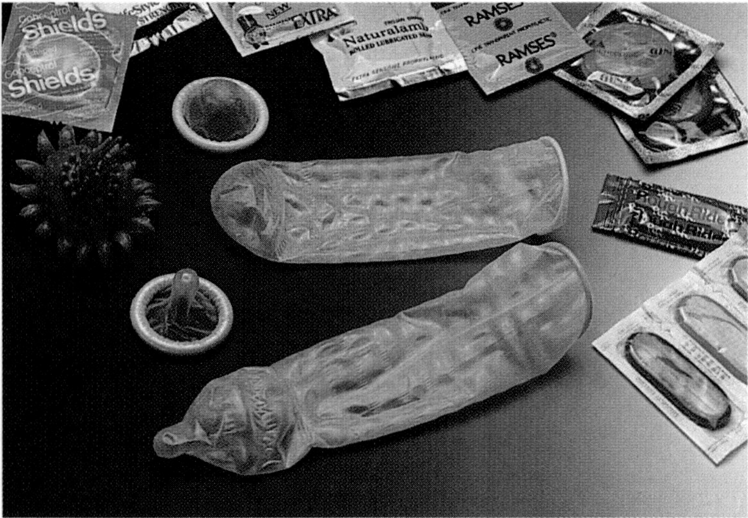

(a)

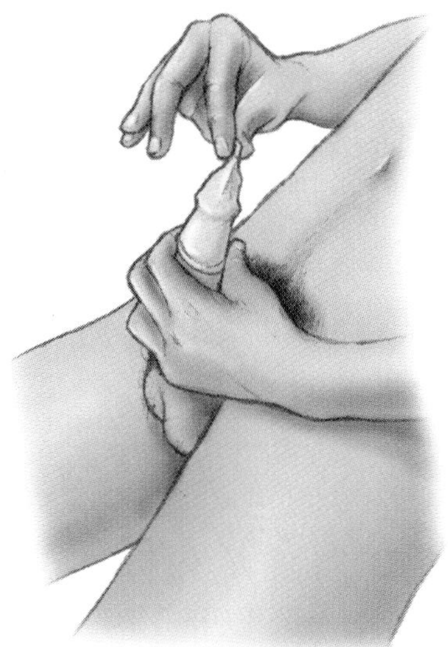

(b) The end of a plain-end condom needs to be twisted as it is rolled onto the penis in order to leave space at the tip.

Figure 11.4

(a) Unrolled condoms with plain and reservoir ends. (b) The correct method of using a plain-end condom.

oil-based lubricants such as baby oil, Vaseline, massage oil, vegetable oils, or hand lotions with mineral or other oils because they reduce the condom's integrity and increase the chances of breakage (Spruyt et al., 1998). Because the penis begins to lose its size and hardness soon after ejaculation, it is important to hold the condom at the base of the penis before withdrawing from the vagina. Otherwise the condom may slip off and spill semen inside the vagina:

The first time I used a rubber, I relaxed inside her after I came, holding her for a while. Then I withdrew, leaving the rubber behind. My first thought was, "Oh, no, it's dissolved." I reached inside her vagina and found the rubber. We used some foam right away but were nervous until her next period. (Authors' files)

Condoms are best disposed of in the garbage rather than the toilet, because they can clog plumbing.

Advantages of Condoms

Condoms have become more widely used in recent years (Piccinino & Mosher, 1998). Latex and polyurethane condoms provide the best protection from contracting and spreading sexually transmitted diseases (including AIDS) and vaginal infections. Condoms containing the spermicide nonoxynol-9 provide additional protection. For this reason, individuals who are not in a disease-free, monogamous relationship should use spermicidal condoms even if they are using other birth control methods as well (Critelli & Suire, 1998), as a student describes:

I use the birth control pill and condoms. The condom just makes me feel safer against STDs and adds extra prevention against pregnancy. (Authors' files)

Strategies to encourage partner use are discussed in the "Let's Talk About It" box.

Nonlubricated condoms can be used for protection from infection during fellatio (Hatcher et al., 1994). However, it is important to remember that while condoms greatly decrease the chances of contracting STDs, they do not totally eliminate this risk.

Condoms are available without prescription. No harmful side effects are associated with their use. If condoms are not used as the primary method of birth control, they are useful as a backup. Some men prefer the slightly diminished sensation they experience with condoms because it helps prolong the duration of intercourse before ejaculation.

Because the semen is contained inside the condom, some women appreciate the tidiness:

> I really like the juiciness of sex when I can bathe afterward, but when we go camping and don't have a stream or shower handy, my husband uses condoms so it's not as messy. (Authors' files)

Condom packaging aimed at teens attempts to promote the idea that condoms are sexy to use.

Disadvantages of Condoms

Unless putting on a condom is incorporated as a part of sexual interaction, it can interrupt spontaneity. Some men see reduced penile sensitivity as a disadvantage (Grady et al., 1993); others believe that condom use is antithetical to good sex and will not use them for that reason (Browne & Minichiello, 1994). In addition, some men find that they are unable to maintain an erection while putting on a condom. Occasionally, people are allergic to latex condoms.

Other disadvantages of condom use have to do with effectiveness. Condoms can have pinhole-size leaks, or they may break or slip off. For this reason, membrane condoms and old condoms should be avoided (if a condom is yellow or sticky, it should be discarded), and care should be taken to use condoms properly (Spruyt et al., 1998).

The Female Condom

In 1988 couples in several countries began testing a "woman's condom," which was approved for sale in the United States in 1992 (Connell, 1994). It resembles a regular condom (see Figure 11.5), but it is worn internally by the woman. A flexible plastic ring at

Let's Talk About It

Don't Go Inside Without Your Rubbers On

The percentage of unmarried women in the United States using condoms almost doubled between 1982 and 1987. Women's opinions of condoms have become more favorable, and women purchase 50% of condoms sold today. Eighty-eight percent of women polled said that they were likely to "insist" on using a condom with their next sexual partner.

These changes represent good "condom sense" because along with unwanted pregnancy, women have much more to lose than men when a couple does not use a condom: A woman is three times more likely to get a sexually transmitted disease (including AIDS) from one act of intercourse than is a man, and bacterial STDs do much more damage to a woman's reproductive tract than to a man's and can ruin her subsequent ability to have a baby.

One study found that refusing to have sex unless a partner used a condom was the most common approach used by college women to encourage condom use (De Bro et al., 1994).

The book, *Before You Hit the Pillow Talk* (Foley & Nechas, 1995), offers suggestions for communicating about condoms. Basically, be clear and assertive and don't get drawn into an argument. Deciding beforehand that you will not have intercourse without using a condom will give your position the strength it needs. Some examples of specific conversation follow.

PARTNER'S STATEMENT	YOUR RESPONSE
"I'm on the pill. You don't need to use a rubber."	"I'd like to use one anyway, then we'll be doubly protected."
"It doesn't feel as good with a condom."	"It will still feel better than nothing."
"It's not very romantic."	"Neither is pregnancy or disease."
"I wouldn't do anything to hurt you."	"Great. Let me help you put it on."
"I'd rather not have sex if we have to use a condom."	"OK. What would you like to do instead?"

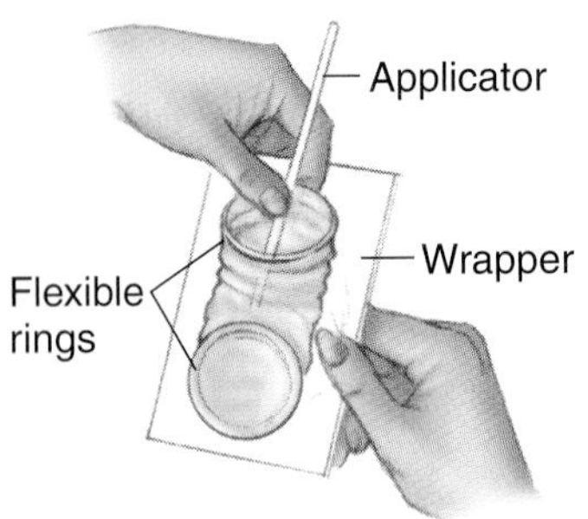

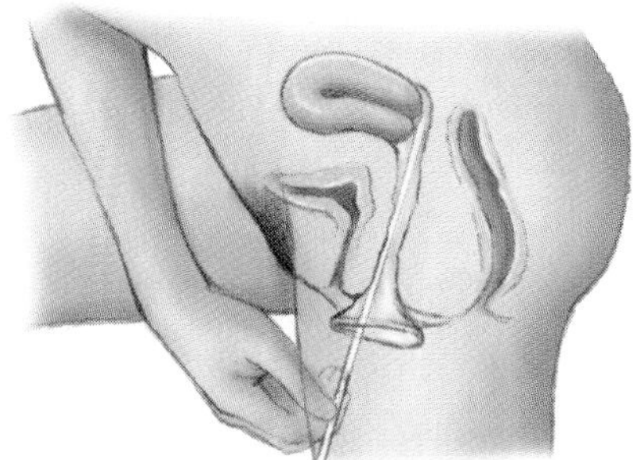

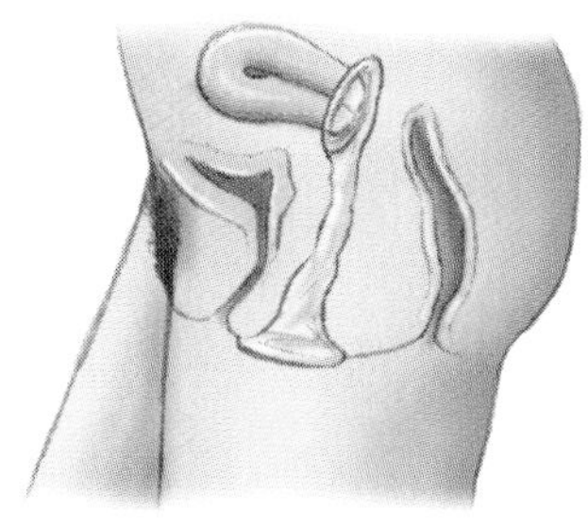

Figure 11.5

A female condom consists of two diaphragmlike flexible polyurethane rings and a soft, loose-fitting polyurethane sheath.

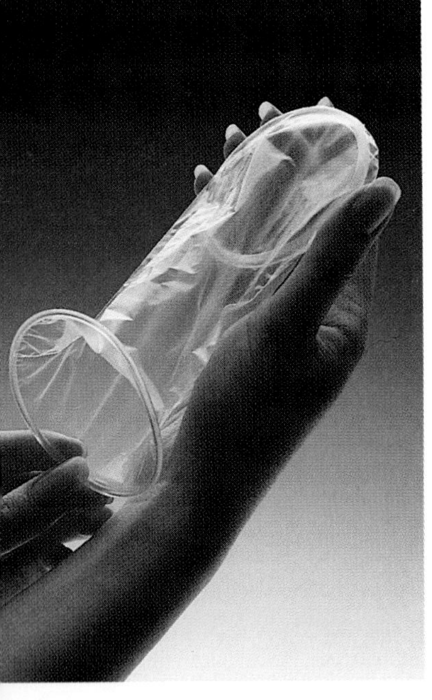

the closed end of the sheath fits loosely against the cervix, rather like a diaphragm (discussed in the following section). Another ring encircles the labial area. Although the female condom fits the contours of the vagina, the penis moves freely inside the sheath. The female condom covers some of the vulva and may provide more protection from sexually transmitted diseases than would traditional condoms (Trussell et al., 1994). However, it does not have spermicide on it. The female condom is made of polyurethane or latex.

Diaphragms

The **diaphragm,** shown in Figure 11.6a, is a round, soft latex dome with a thin, flexible spring around the rim. It is inserted into the vagina along with a spermicidal contraceptive cream or jelly. The diaphragm rim fits around the back of the cervix and underneath and behind the pubic bone, as shown in Figure 11.6b. Some women's cervixes are located farther back in the vagina, and others are closer to the opening. Therefore, diaphragms vary from two to four inches in diameter to fit each individual correctly. Diaphragms are also made with different kinds of springs: the coil spring, the flat spring, or the arcing spring. Some women find that one style is easier to insert and fits better than another. For example, the arcing spring may stay in place better than a coil spring for a woman with reduced vaginal muscle tone.

How the Diaphragm Works

When fitted and inserted properly, the diaphragm covers the cervix, thus providing a mechanical barrier to prevent sperm from entering the cervix and uterus. The spermicidal cream or jelly serves as a chemical barrier, effectively killing any sperm that might migrate around the rim of the diaphragm and toward the cervix.

How to Use the Diaphragm

The diaphragm must be fitted by a skilled practitioner. A size estimate is made during the pelvic exam; then different sizes and types are inserted until the best fit is found. It is very important for the examiner to instruct the woman thoroughly on how to insert and care for her diaphragm. Then the woman practices inserting it herself in the examination room until she is able to do so correctly. The examiner makes a final check to confirm that the woman has learned the proper insertion technique.

Figure 11.6b illustrates how the diaphragm is used. First, a teaspoon of spermicidal cream or jelly (available at pharmacies without a prescription) is put into the cup of the diaphragm. Some of the spermicide should also be spread around the inside of the rim. The sides of the rim are then squeezed together with one hand, while the other hand opens the inner lips of the vulva. Some women prefer to use a plastic diaphragm introducer, whereas others prefer manual insertion. The diaphragm is then pushed into the vagina, with the cream side facing up. The woman may be standing, lying, or squatting while she or her partner inserts the diaphragm.

Diaphragm
A birth control device consisting of a latex dome on a flexible spring rim. The diaphragm is inserted into the vagina with contraceptive cream or jelly and covers the cervix.

(a)

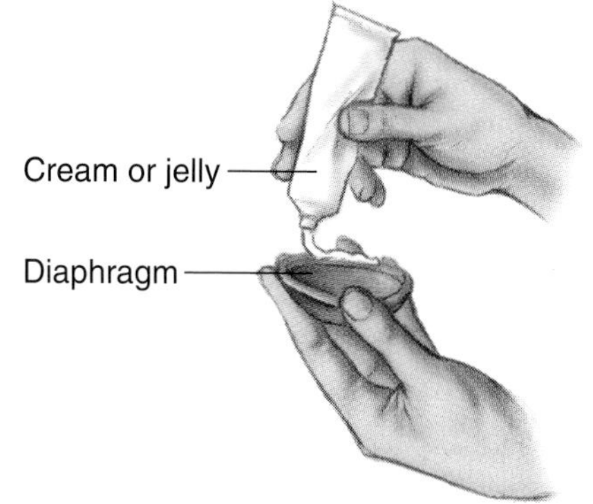

Squeeze spermicide into dome of diaphragm and around the rim.

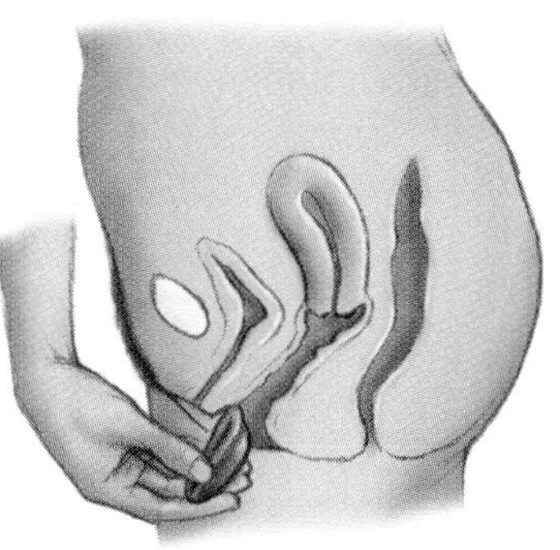
Squeeze rim together; insert jelly-side up.

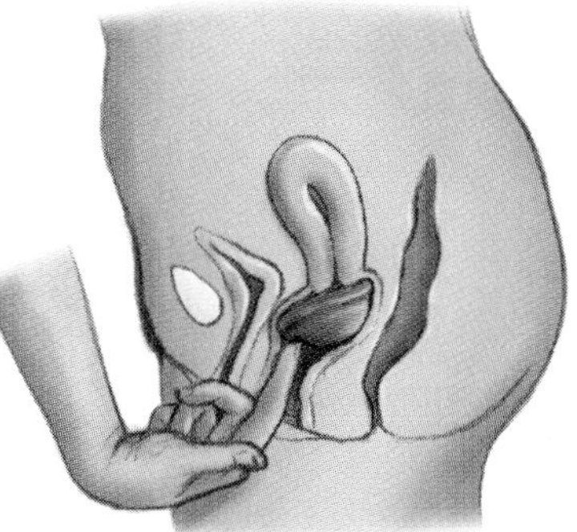
Check placement to make certain cervix is covered.

(b)

Figure 11.6

(a) The diaphragm is made of a soft latex dome on a coil and is used with contraceptive cream or jelly. (b) These figures illustrate the insertion and checking of a diaphragm.

After the diaphragm is inserted, it is important for the woman or her partner to feel it with the fingers to determine whether the dome covers the cervix. Occasionally, the back rim lodges in front of the cervix, so that the diaphragm offers no contraceptive protection. When the diaphragm is placed correctly, it rarely can be felt by the woman or her partner during intercourse.

Some sources state that the diaphragm can be inserted up to six hours prior to intercourse; others recommend that the diaphragm be inserted no more than two hours prior to intercourse without an additional application of spermicide. The shorter time span may afford better protection. The diaphragm can also be inserted just before intercourse. Some women prefer to insert the diaphragm ahead of time, in privacy, whereas others share the insertion with their partners. As one man explained:

> I have always hated "just-before" birth control devices like condoms and diaphragms. However, with my present partner, the diaphragm is part of our sexual excitement. We usually become quite stimulated before reaching for the jelly and diaphragm, and I often use manual clitoral stimulation while she inserts it. I have also learned to put it in while she continues to stimulate herself and me at the same time. Also, the leftover jelly is a good lubricant. The pause between being ready for intercourse and actually doing it seems to heighten the whole thing. (Authors' files)

The diaphragm should remain in the vagina for at least six hours following intercourse to assure that the spermicide has killed all sperm in the vaginal folds. It is important not to douche during this time. If intercourse occurs again before eight hours elapse, the diaphragm can be left in place, but additional spermicidal cream or jelly needs to be inserted with an applicator tube. Reusable plastic applicators can be purchased with the spermicide.

Several cases of toxic shock syndrome (TSS) have been reported in association with diaphragm use. Therefore, a diaphragm should not be left in the vagina for more than 24 hours (Hatcher et al., 1994). To remove it, insert a finger into the vagina under the front rim of the diaphragm. Squatting or bearing down may make it easier to find the rim. After a gentle pull with one finger to break the air seal, it is easier to grasp the rim with two fingers and pull the diaphragm out. After removal, wash the diaphragm with a mild soap and warm water. Carefully and thoroughly dry it, dust it with cornstarch, and return it to its case.

A well-cared-for diaphragm can last for several years. It should remain soft, flexible, and free of defects. To make certain of this, check it periodically. You can detect tiny leaks by placing water in the dome or by holding it up to the light, stretching it slightly and checking for defects. Bring along your diaphragm when you have your yearly Pap smear so that its fit and condition can be evaluated. A woman may need a different diaphragm after a pregnancy (including an aborted pregnancy) or a weight loss or gain of 10 pounds or more. *Do* **not** *use oil-based lubricants because they will deteriorate the latex.*

A most important point in the effective use of the diaphragm is to have it available and use it consistently. It simply will not do any good at home in a drawer when you are at the beach for the weekend. Depending on your lifestyle, the best place for it may be in your purse, bedroom, bathroom—wherever is most convenient. Some women prefer to own two diaphragms to assure availability.

Advantages of the Diaphragm

Through learning to use the diaphragm, a woman may become more knowledgeable and comfortable with her body. She may also find diaphragm use helpful in making decisions about relating sexually with others.

> Since I've been using the diaphragm, I've moved more slowly into sexual relations. I want to discuss my method with a new partner before we have intercourse. If I feel like I'm not comfortable enough to talk about birth control, then I know I'm not ready to have intercourse. (Authors' files)

Some people think that there may be some additional positive side effects to proper use of the diaphragm. Spermicidal jellies and creams may slightly decrease the incidence of vaginal infections as well as gonorrhea, pelvic inflammatory disease, and AIDS (Hatcher et al., 1994). In addition, the use of any barrier method may help reduce the risk of cervical cell changes that can lead to cancer (Coker et al., 1992).

Disadvantages of the Diaphragm

The diaphragm is not without disadvantages, its high failure rate being the most significant. Its use has decreased since the late 1980s, primarily because it does not prevent the transmission of HIV effectively (Piccinino & Mosher, 1998). Some people may find that it is inconvenient, that using it interrupts spontaneity, or that the spermicidal cream or jelly is messy. The spermicidal cream or jelly can also interfere with the couple's enjoyment of oral–genital sex. However, a couple can engage in oral–genital contact before inserting the diaphragm, or the woman's partner can focus stimulation on the clitoral rather than the vaginal area. Occasionally, women or their partners experience irritation from a particular spermicide. Sometimes switching to a different brand solves that difficulty. In rare instances, the woman or man is allergic to the latex of the diaphragm. Using a plastic diaphragm can eliminate this problem.

Poor diaphragm fit may occasionally cause problems. Because diaphragms are fitted when a woman is not sexually aroused, they may not fit as well during arousal due to the vaginal expansion that occurs. The penis may then slip between the diaphragm and cervix, compromising the diaphragm's effectiveness. This is most likely to happen during position changes, with reinsertion of the penis, and in the woman-above position. The spermicidal cream or jelly still provides some contraceptive protection if this occurs. If either partner feels the diaphragm during intercourse, she or he should check to see if it is correctly in place. A few women report bladder discomfort, urethral irritation, or recurrent cystitis from diaphragm use (Hooton et al., 1991). Using another diaphragm size or rim type may eliminate these difficulties. A few women with certain pelvic-structure problems, such as marked loss of vaginal muscle tone and support, cannot use the diaphragm effectively.

Cervical Caps

The **cervical cap** is a thimble-shaped cup made of rubber or plastic (see Figure 11.7). The cap is like a miniature diaphragm, but it fits only over the cervix and can be left in place longer. Like the diaphragm, the cap comes in different sizes. Health care practitioners usually recommend that it be used with a spermicide (Hatcher et al., 1994).

Cervical cap
A plastic or rubber cover for the cervix that provides a contraceptive barrier to sperm.

Different versions of the cervical cap have been used for centuries. European women melted beeswax into cervical disks. In eighteenth-century Europe, Casanova promoted the idea of using a squeezed-out lemon half to cover the cervix. The modern cervical cap was developed in 1838 by a German gynecologist, who took a wax impression of each patient's cervix and made custom cervical caps out of rubber (Seaman & Seaman, 1978). Cervical caps have been widely available in Europe for many years and were finally approved for sale in the United States in 1988.

How to Use the Cervical Cap

The cervical cap comes in different sizes and must be individually fitted by a skilled practitioner. When a woman uses the cap, she or her partner fills it one- to two-thirds full with spermicide. The cap is inserted by folding its edges together and sliding it into the vagina along the vaginal floor. The cap is then pressed onto the cervix. The woman or her partner then sweeps a finger around the cap to confirm that the cervix is covered, and depresses the dome of the cap to feel the cervix through the rubber. A woman can usually reach her cervix most easily if she is in a squatting or upright sitting position. The cap can be inserted up to six hours before intercourse. It should not be removed for at least six hours following intercourse, and douching should be avoided during this period. It can be left in place up to 24 hours but should be removed by that time to avoid

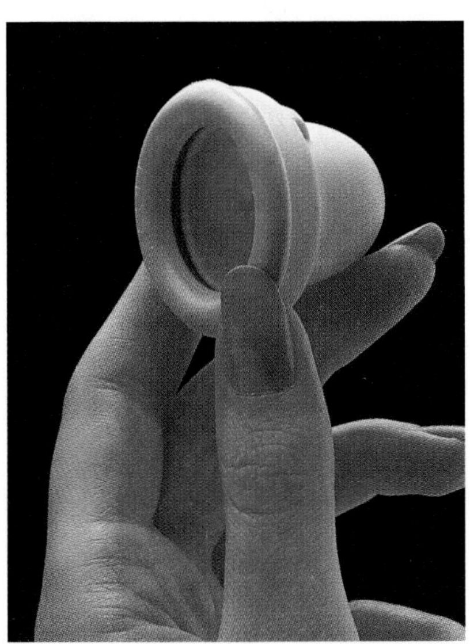

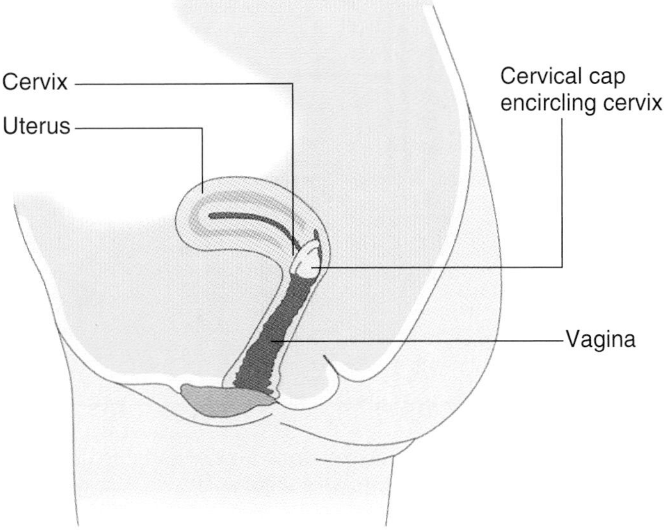

Figure 11.7

The cervical cap is smaller than the diaphragm and covers only the cervix.

risk of toxic shock syndrome (TSS). Pulling on one side of the rim breaks the suction to permit easy removal of the cap from the vagina. After removal, the cap should be washed with warm water and soap and dried. *Do* **not** *use oil-based lubricants, because they will deteriorate the latex* (Hatcher et al., 1994).

Advantages of the Cervical Cap

A major advantage of the cervical cap is the lack of side effects. Women who cannot use the diaphragm because of pelvic-structure problems or loss of vaginal muscle tone or support can often use this method. It is less expensive to use than the diaphragm because it requires less spermicide, but the cap itself is more expensive than the diaphragm, resulting in a similar overall cost. Unlike the diaphragm, the cervical cap does not require repeated applications of spermicide with additional intercourse (Weiss et al., 1991).

Disadvantages of the Cervical Cap

The high failure rate is an important disadvantage. A woman who has distortions of her cervix from cysts, lacerations, or pregnancy is usually an unsuitable candidate for cervical cap use. Caps do not successfully fit about 6% of women (Klitsch, 1988). Some women and their partners may have allergic reactions to the spermicide or rubber. The cap is usually more difficult to learn to use than the diaphragm, and for some women it is uncomfortable to wear. There is some concern that wearing the cap for prolonged periods may cause problems by damaging the cervix or interrupting the normal discharge of cervical secretions. Although there are no clear data on this matter, the Food and Drug Administration (FDA) recommends a Pap smear after three months of using the cervical cap (Klitsch, 1988). The cap may also become dislodged during intercourse, greatly reducing its contraceptive effectiveness.

Vaginal Spermicides

Vaginal spermicides Foam, cream, jelly, suppositories, and film that contain a chemical that kills sperm.

There are several types of **vaginal spermicides:** foam, suppositories, creams and jellies, and contraceptive film. *Foam* is a white substance resembling shaving cream. It comes in pressurized cans and has a plastic applicator. Foam is available in pharmacies without a prescription. (Feminine-hygiene products, although often displayed along with various brands of foam, are *not* contraceptives.) *Vaginal suppositories* have an oval shape and contain the same spermicidal chemical found in foam. Some *contraceptive creams and jellies* are made to be used without a diaphragm or cervical cap. However, they are not as effective as foam, and many health care practitioners recommend that they not be used without a diaphragm or cervical cap. *VCF,* a vaginal contraceptive film, is a paper-thin, 2-inch by 2-inch sheet that is laced with spermicide. It is packaged in a matchbooklike container with 10 to 12 sheets.

How Spermicidal Methods Work

Foam, suppositories, creams and jellies, and VCF all contain a *spermicide,* or chemical that kills sperm. When foam is inserted with the applicator, it rapidly covers the vaginal walls and the cervical os, or opening to the uterus (see Figure 11.8). Contraceptive vaginal suppositories take about 20 minutes to dissolve and cover the walls. One brand of suppositories, Encare, effervesces and creates a foam inside the vagina; other brands melt. Once VCF is inserted into the vagina, next to the cervix, it dissolves into a stay-in-place gel.

How to Use Vaginal Spermicides

Complete instructions for use come with each package of vaginal spermicide. It is important to use them as directed for maximum protection. As in the case of spermicides used with the diaphragm, another application of spermicide is necessary before each additional

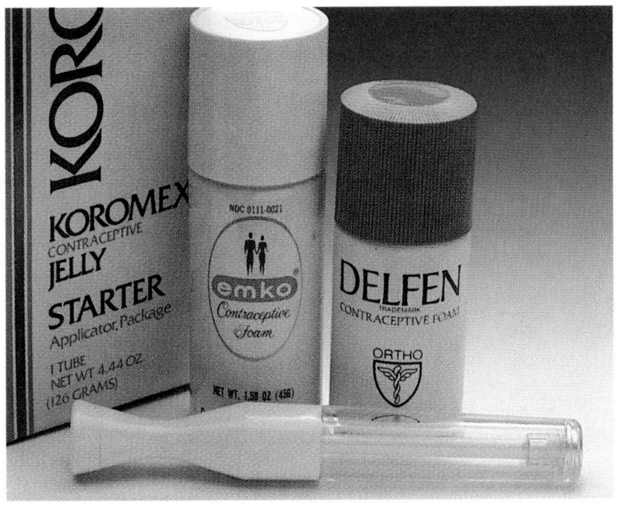

(a)

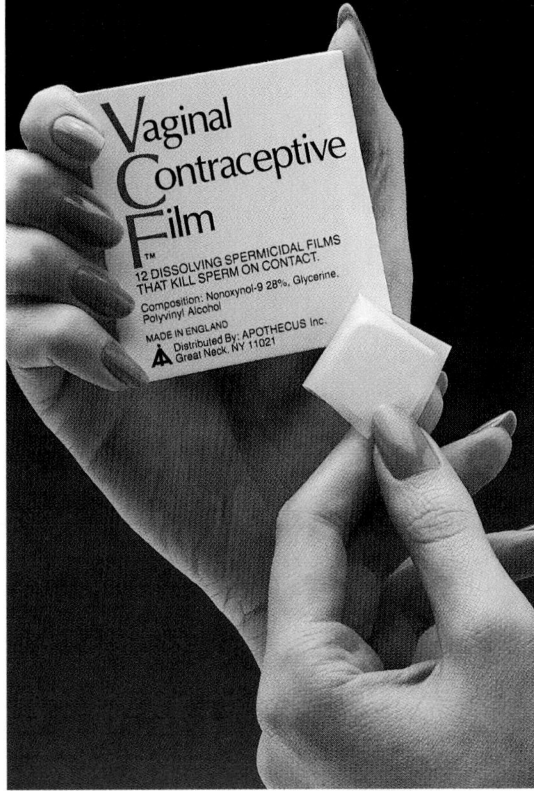

(c)

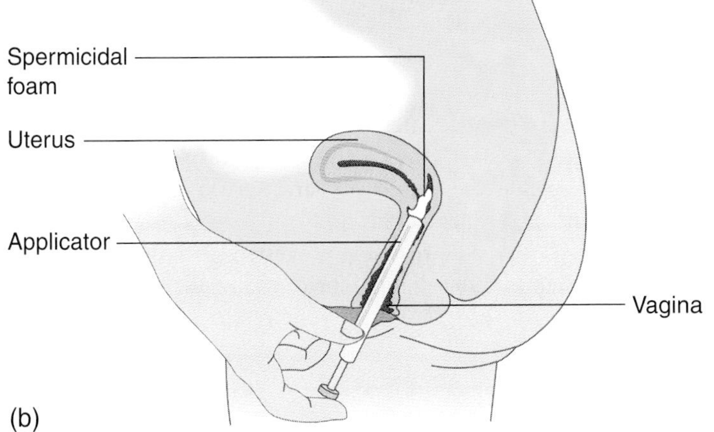

(b)

Figure 11.8

Vaginal spermicides are available in pharmacies without a prescription:
(a) Foam and applicator.
(b) The filled applicator is inserted into the vagina, and the foam is deposited in the back of the vaginal canal.
(c) Vaginal contraceptive film.

act of intercourse. A woman needs to wait eight hours after intercourse if she wants to douche to assure that the spermicide has killed the sperm. It is probably better to shower than to take a bath, to prevent the spermicide from being rinsed out of the vagina. For highly effective contraception, use vaginal spermicides and a condom together.

Advantages of Vaginal Spermicides

Because spermicides and VCF are sold over the counter in pharmacies, using them does not require a visit to a physician's office. They have no known dangerous side effects for women, and some couples welcome the additional lubrication that spermicides provide. Like the diaphragm, vaginal spermicides may give some protection against vaginal infections, sexually transmitted diseases (including AIDS), and pelvic inflammatory disease (PID) (Hatcher et al., 1994). The suppository has the advantage of being small and convenient to use. VCF can be used by people who are allergic to foams and jellies; also, unlike foams and jellies, VCF dissolves gradually and almost unnoticeably.

Disadvantages of Vaginal Spermicides

Occasionally, a woman or her partner may report irritation of genital tissues from foam or suppositories. Changing brands will often alleviate this difficulty, but in some cases any brand causes discomfort. Spermicides can increase the incidence of yeast infections (Hatcher et al., 1994) and urinary tract infections (Fihn et al., 1988). Some of the suppositories may not dissolve completely and therefore feel gritty. Some women or couples dislike the additional lubrication during intercourse or the postcoital discharge following intercourse. Because of the unpleasant taste, using vaginal spermicides may limit couples who like to engage in cunnilingus after intercourse (although they can still do so before inserting the foam or suppositories). These products may also have a soaplike scent that is disagreeable to some users. In addition, some people feel that insertion of spermicides interrupts spontaneity, even though the procedure takes only about 30 seconds.

Intrauterine Devices

Intrauterine device (IUD) A small, plastic device that is inserted into the uterus for contraception.

Intrauterine devices, commonly referred to as **IUDs,** are small plastic objects that are inserted into the uterus through the cervical os. Several types of IUDs were available in this country during the 1960s and 1970s, but many companies removed their IUDs from the market because of numerous lawsuits charging that the devices caused infections, infertility, or death from infection when pregnancy occurred with an IUD in place (Pollack & Girvin, 1992). Although the companies successfully defended most suits, the legal costs were prohibitively high and liability insurance became unavailable (Truman et al., 1995).

Types of IUDs

Two types of IUDs are currently available: the Copper-T (ParaGard), a plastic T with copper wire wrapped around its stem and copper sleeves on the side arms, and the Progestasert T (see Figure 11.9), a plastic T with slow-releasing progesterone in the plastic. Both have fine plastic threads attached, cut to hang slightly out of the cervix into the vagina.

How the IUD Works

Both the copper and the progesterone in IUDs are effective in preventing fertilization. The copper in Copper-T seems to affect the motility and/or viability of sperm, while the progesterone in the Progestasert T has effects similar to those of hormonal contraceptive methods such as the pill, Norplant, and Depo-Provera. In addition, the uterine lining may be slightly irritated and inflamed due to the presence of this foreign object, thus reduc-

Figure 11.9

The Progestasert T intrauterine device.

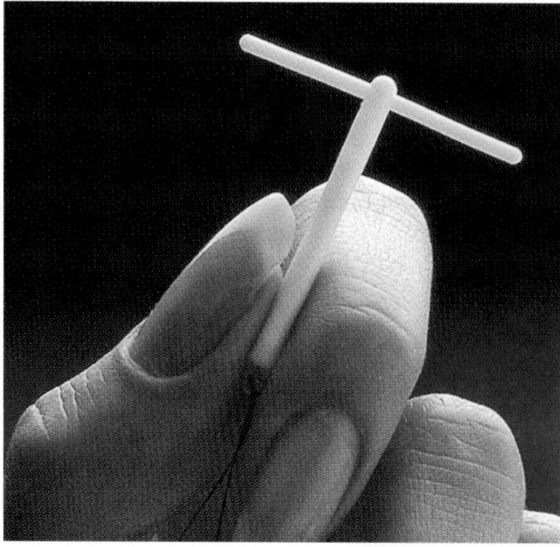
(a)

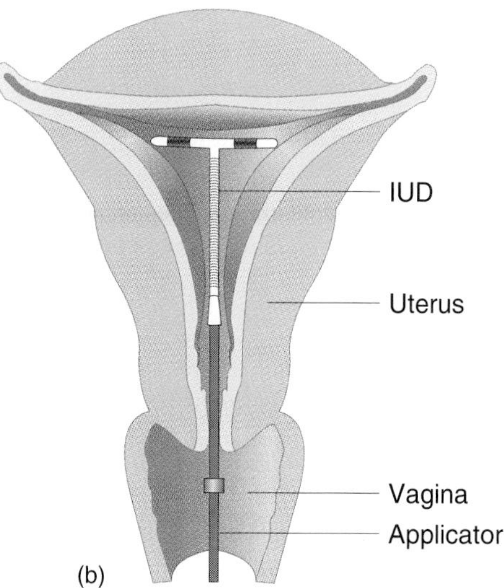

(b)

ing the likelihood that a fertilized ovum will implant (Spinnato, 1997). The IUD also alters the sensitive timing of the ovum as it passes through the fallopian tubes.

How to Use the IUD

The IUD is inserted by a health care professional using sterile instruments. Most IUDs come with an inserter. The inserter and IUD are introduced through the cervical os into the uterus; the inserter is then withdrawn, leaving the IUD in place. The Progestasert T needs to be replaced every year because the progesterone gradually loses its effectiveness. The copper IUD is replaced every 10 years (Volm, 1997). IUDs should be removed when a woman reaches menopause and stops menstruating (Hatcher et al., 1994).

IUDs should be used only by women in stable, monogamous relationships, with no history of sexually transmitted diseases or pelvic inflammatory disease, who have at least one child or have completed childbearing, are 25 years or older, and have ready access to medical facilities (Lee et al., 1988). A woman should be screened for gonorrhea and chlamydia before IUD insertion because the procedure may cause the bacteria associated with these STDs to be pushed farther into the uterus.

While a woman is using an IUD, she or her partner needs to check each month after her menstrual period to see that the string is the same length as when the device was inserted. To do this, one of them reaches into the vagina with a finger and finds the cervix. If the cervix is far back in the vagina and difficult to reach, the woman can squat or bear down to make it more accessible. The string should be felt in the middle of the cervix, protruding out of the small indentation in the center. Occasionally it curls up in the os and cannot be felt, but any time a woman or her partner cannot find it, she needs to check with her health care specialist. She should also seek attention if the string seems longer or the plastic protrudes out of the os; this probably means that her body is expelling the IUD.

Advantages of the IUD

The primary advantage of the IUD is that it provides a woman with highly effective contraceptive protection with little inconvenience beyond the monthly checking of the string. The IUD allows uninterrupted sexual interaction. Beyond the initial cost for the IUD and insertion, there are no further supplies to be purchased. Although an IUD is usually not inserted until two to three months after childbirth, it does not interfere with breast-feeding (as the pill does) once it is in place. Some women who experience initial discomfort after the insertion find that this diminishes in a month or two. Ninety-eight percent of IUD users say they are happy with this method (Hatcher et al., 1994).

Disadvantages of the IUD

Serious problems associated with the IUD can be summarized by the acronym PAINS (see Table 11.3). The most serious complication of IUD use is that it increases a woman's chances of pelvic inflammatory disease (PID). PID can occur if bacteria are introduced into the sterile environment of the uterus during insertion. An IUD is likely to aggravate a gonorrhea infection and make treatment more difficult. Most physicians recommend removal of an IUD when a woman is being treated for a uterine infection. Fallopian tube problems resulting from IUD use can also be a contributing factor in infertility. Increased

Table 11.3 Remember "PAINS" for the IUD

Initial	*Symptoms*
Symptoms of possible serious problems with the IUD, represented by their initials.	
P	Period late, no period
A	Abdominal pain
I	Increased temperature, fever, chills
N	Nasty discharge, foul discharge
S	Spotting, bleeding, heavy periods, clots

Source: Adapted from Hatcher et al., 1994.

risk of PID has been found almost exclusively in women involved in high-risk behaviors such as having multiple partners (Connell, 1991).

Discomfort, cramping, bleeding, or pain may occur during insertion. The discomfort or bleeding sometimes continues for a few days and occasionally much longer. The hormonal IUD results in less menstrual bleeding and cramping than the Copper-T (Datey et al., 1995).

From 2 to 20% of users expel their IUDs within the first year following insertion (Hatcher et al., 1994). This is most likely to occur during menstruation, so a woman needs to check her tampons or sanitary napkins before disposing of them. Also, her partner might feel the IUD protruding out of the cervix during intercourse.

In rare cases, the IUD breaks through the uterine wall. This perforation can partially extend through the wall, or the IUD can slip completely through the uterus into the abdominal cavity. If an IUD string seems to become shorter, this may be an indication that the IUD is perforating, and the woman should seek immediate medical attention.

If a woman becomes pregnant with an IUD in place, she has a 50% chance of a miscarriage (Hatcher et al., 1994). Because of some reports of deaths of pregnant IUD users in 1974, removal of the IUD when a woman becomes pregnant is now recommended. If an IUD is removed during the first three months of pregnancy, the risk of a subsequent miscarriage is only slightly higher than for nonusers of IUDs and less than if the woman kept the IUD in place (Britton, 1988).

Besides the IUD and hormonal and barrier methods, a number of other contraceptive options are available. We look at these in the paragraphs that follow after we discuss emergency contraception.

Emergency Contraception

Emergency contraception prevents pregnancy after unprotected intercourse (Trussell et al., 1997). A woman may need emergency contraception following a method failure—a condom breaking, a diaphragm slipping, or sexual assault or neglecting to use contraception (Gold et al., 1997). The risk of pregnancy from unprotected midcycle intercourse is 20–30% (Buttermore & Nolan, 1993). Awareness and use of postcoital contraception could prevent an estimated 2.3 million unintended pregnancies each year in the United States (Hanson, 1997). For contraception after intercourse, administration of birth control pills or insertion of a Copper-T IUD are the methods most commonly used.

Studies have shown that taking tablets of birth control pills (so-called "morning after" pills) within 72 hours following unprotected intercourse effectively prevents pregnancy. High doses of estrogens or progestins are also given as emergency contraceptives.

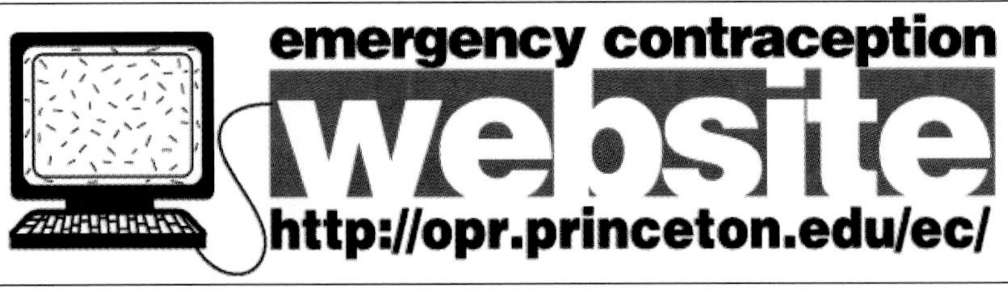

These hormone treatments are presumed to work by producing impenetrable cervical mucus, inhibiting ovulation, altering tubal transport time, and affecting the uterine lining so that the developing embryo cannot implant on it. Nausea or vomiting is a potential side effect of morning-after pills. Long-term health effects on the woman or the fetus are unknown; the possibility of cancer in children of women who take morning-after pills but continue the pregnancy has not been ruled out. If a woman uses any kind of morning-after pill, she should be aware of and watch for pill-related side effects (Hatcher et al., 1994).

Copper IUDs provide another option for emergency contraception. They may be inserted up to a week after unprotected intercourse. They can be left in place to provide ongoing contraception, if desired. A failure rate of less than 1% makes the copper IUD the most effective form of emergency contraception. Its use is limited to women who are at low risk of pelvic inflammatory disease and sexually transmitted diseases (Lindberg, 1997). It is usually not desirable for women who have not given birth or have a history of ectopic pregnancy to use the IUD for emergency contraception (Hanson, 1997).

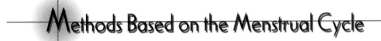

Methods Based on the Menstrual Cycle

The birth control methods that we have already discussed require the use of pills or devices. Some of these methods have side effects in some users, and there may be serious health risks in the use of oral contraceptives and the IUD. The barrier methods we have looked at—condoms, vaginal spermicides, and the diaphragm—have fewer side effects, but they require that the couple use them each time they have intercourse.

Many couples are interested in a birth control method that has no side effects, is inexpensive, and does not interrupt spontaneity during sexual interaction. In the next paragraphs, we look at some methods of birth control based on the menstrual cycle, which may answer some of these couples' needs. These methods are sometimes referred to as *natural family planning* or *fertility awareness* methods. They are based on the fact that a fertile woman's body reveals subtle and overt signs of cyclic fertility that can be used both to help prevent and to plan conception. The three fertility awareness methods—mucus, calendar, and basal body temperature—are most effective when used together. About 4% of women in the United States use natural family planning (Stanford et al., 1998).

The Mucus Method

The **mucus method,** also called the *ovulation method,* is based on the cyclic changes of cervical mucus. These natural changes, if carefully observed, reveal periods of fertility in a woman's cycle. To use this method, a woman learns to "read" the amounts and textures of vaginal secretions and to maintain a daily chart of the changes. A woman reads her mucus by wiping herself every time she goes to the toilet and observing the secretions on the tissue:

Mucus method
A birth control method based on determining the time of ovulation by means of the cyclical changes of the cervical mucus.

- After menstruation there are usually some "dry days" when there is no vaginal discharge on the vulva.
- When a yellow or white sticky discharge begins, unprotected coitus should be avoided.
- Several days later, the ovulatory mucus appears. It is clear, stringy, and stretchy in consistency, similar to egg white. A drop of this mucus will stretch between an open thumb and forefinger. A vaginal feeling of wetness and lubrication accompanies this discharge, which has a chemical balance and texture that facilitate the entry of sperm into the uterus.
- Approximately four days after the ovulatory mucus begins and 24 hours after a cloudy discharge resumes, it is considered safe to resume unprotected intercourse.

The fertile period usually totals 9 to 15 days out of each cycle. The temperature method, discussed later in this section, is often combined with the mucus method to better estimate the time of ovulation.

In many cities, classes in this method are offered at a hospital or clinic. Each woman's mucus patterns may vary, and a class is the best way to learn to interpret the changes.

Calendar method
A method of birth control based on abstinence from intercourse during calendar-estimated fertile days.

The Calendar Method

With the **calendar method,** also called the *rhythm method,* a woman estimates the calendar time during her cycle when she is ovulating and fertile. To use the calendar method, a woman keeps a chart, preferably for one year, of the length of her cycles. (She cannot be using oral contraceptives during this time because they impose a cycle that may not be the same as her own.)

- The first day of menstruation is counted as day 1. The woman counts the number of days of her cycle, the last day being the one before the onset of menstruation.
- To determine the high-risk days on which she should avoid unprotected coitus, she subtracts 18 from the number of days of her shortest cycle. For example, if her shortest cycle was 26 days, day 8 would be the first high-risk day.
- To estimate when unprotected coitus could resume, she subtracts 10 from the number of days in her longest cycle. For example, if her longest cycle is 32 days, she would be able to resume intercourse on day 22.

A woman using the rhythm method avoids coitus without birth control during her midcycle ovulation, either by abstaining from coitus or by using another method of contraception from days 8 through 22. Forms of lovemaking other than intercourse can continue during the high-risk days.

The Basal Body Temperature Method

Basal body temperature
A method of birth control based on body temperature changes before and after ovulation.

Another way of estimating high-fertility days is through temperature. Immediately prior to ovulation, the **basal body temperature** (**BBT,** the body temperature in the resting state on waking in the morning) drops slightly. After ovulation, the corpus luteum releases more progesterone, which causes the body temperature to rise slightly (0.2°F). Because these temperature changes (shown in Figure 11.10) are slight, a thermometer with easy-to-read gradations must be used. Special electronic thermometers have also been developed for measuring BBT and are effective in indicating fertile times in the cycle.

Advantages of Methods Based on Menstrual Cycle

Major advantages of methods based on the menstrual cycle are that there are no side effects and that they are free or very inexpensive. Some women and their partners report increased comfort and appreciation of their bodies' cycles and processes when they adopt these methods. Should they choose abstinence over penile–vaginal intercourse during the fertile days, this interval can provide time and motivation for noncoital sexual relating. Knowledge of cyclic changes can also help a couple plan a pregnancy. Also, these methods are acceptable to some religious groups that oppose other contraceptive methods.

Disadvantages of Methods Based on Menstrual Cycle

Methods based on the menstrual cycle restrict spontaneity of intercourse and ejaculation during fertile times. Furthermore, learning to accurately detect the mucus and temperature changes involves practice, and with all these methods, a couple must keep accurate records for several cycles before beginning to rely on them for contraception. Consider-

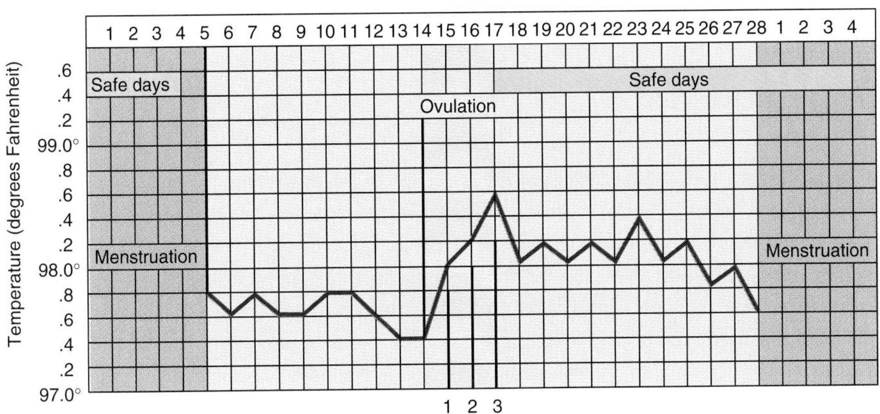

Figure 11.10

Charting basal body temperature during a model menstrual cycle.

able commitment is essential to maintain daily observation and charting. These methods are more difficult for women who have irregular cycles, and some women are unable to see mucus and temperature patterns clearly. Also, vaginal infections, semen, and contraceptive foams, jellies, and creams make it more difficult to accurately interpret mucus.

Although temperature changes are often good indicators of ovulation, this method is fallible. Slight temperature variations can result from many conditions—a low-grade infection or cold, unrestful sleep, and so forth. Also, because sperm can remain alive in the fallopian tubes for up to 72 hours, the preovulation temperature drop does not occur far enough ahead of time to safely avoid coitus. Although the temperature method is more effective in preventing an undesired pregnancy than no method, it is quite unreliable.

Even after careful arithmetic, the calendar method is very unreliable. Ovulation usually occurs about 14 days before the onset of menstruation; however, even with a woman who ordinarily has regular cycles, the timing of ovulation and menstruation may vary due to factors such as illness, fatigue, or emotional extremes. For a woman who routinely or periodically has irregular cycles, the calendar method is even less safe and requires longer abstention from coitus. Present research indicates that methods based on the menstrual cycle are considerably less effective than most others (Hatcher et al., 1994).

Sterilization

One other method of contraception has become common in recent years due to improved surgical techniques and increasing societal acceptance. *Sterilization* is the most effective method of birth control except abstinence from coitus, and its safety and permanence appeal to many who want no more children or prefer to remain childless. Sterilization is the leading method of birth control in the United States and around the world: Half of all female sterilizations throughout the world each year are done in China (Tang & Chung, 1997). Although some research is being conducted on ways of reversing sterilization, at present the reversal procedures involve complicated surgery, and their effectiveness is not guaranteed. Therefore, sterilization is recommended only to those who desire a permanent method of birth control.

Because sterilization is best considered permanent, a person should carefully explore his or her situation and feelings before deciding on the procedure. Questions to consider include:

- Are there any circumstances under which I would want (more) children (for example, if my child died, or if I began a new relationship)?
- Is my sense of masculinity or femininity tied to my fertility?
- What are my alternatives to sterilization?
- How does my partner feel about the decision?

In the following paragraphs, we look at the procedures for sterilization of females and males.

Female Sterilization

In recent years female sterilization has become a relatively safe, simple, and inexpensive procedure. Almost 30% of women in the United States choose sterilization. This percentage will likely increase as members of the baby boom generation complete their families (Miracle-McMahill et al., 1997). Sterilization can be accomplished by a variety of techniques that use small incisions and either local or general anesthesia.

Tubal sterilization Female sterilization accomplished by severing or tying the fallopian tubes.

Tubal sterilization can be done in several ways. A *minilaparotomy* involves a small abdominal incision. Each fallopian tube is gently pulled to this incision; then it is cut and tied, or clips or rings are applied. The tubes are then allowed to slip back into place within the abdomen. Another procedure, *laparoscopy*, is shown in Figure 11.11. One or two small incisions are made in the abdomen, usually at the navel and slightly below the pubic hairline. A narrow, lighted viewing instrument called a laparoscope is inserted into the abdomen to locate the fallopian tubes. The tubes are then tied off, cut, or cauterized to block passage of sperm and eggs. Other methods have also been developed to block the tubes. A band or a clip is sometimes applied to a tube instead of removing a segment. The ligated (tied) or cut tubes prevent the sperm and egg from meeting in the tube, thus preventing pregnancy. The incisions are generally so small that adhesive tape rather than stitches is used to close them after surgery. Sometimes the incision is made through the back of the vaginal wall, and the procedure is called a *culpotomy*.

Sterilization acts only as a roadblock in the tubes. It does not further affect a woman's reproductive and sexual system. Until menopause her ovaries continue to release their eggs. The released egg simply degenerates, as do millions of other cells daily. The woman's hormone levels and the timing of menopause are not altered. Her sexuality is not physiologically changed, but she may find that her interest and arousal increase because she no longer is concerned with pregnancy or birth control methods. Research indicates that sterilization does not have a detrimental effect on a woman's sexual satisfaction (Shain et al., 1991).

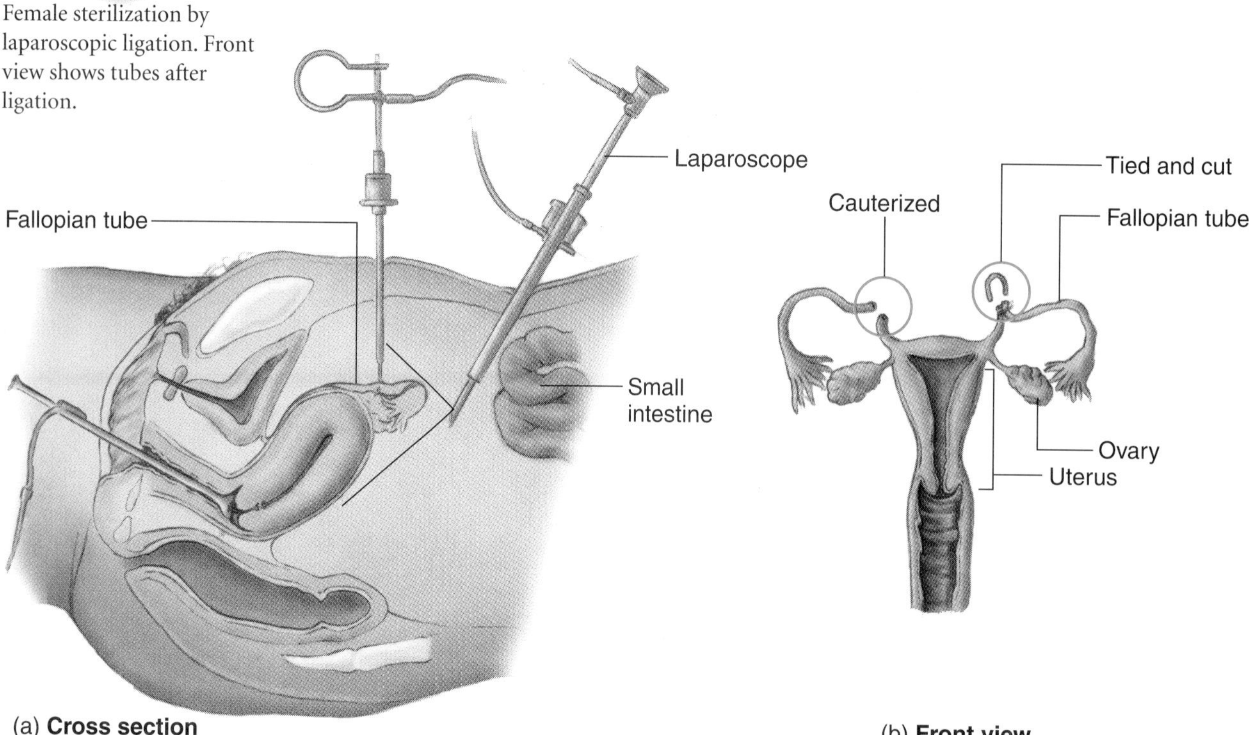

Figure 11.11

Female sterilization by laparoscopic ligation. Front view shows tubes after ligation.

Some pain or complications can result from female sterilization. The gas pains most women experience during recovery can be very painful (Volm, 1997). A woman may experience some pain at the site of the incision, and if the tubes are sealed by burning, other tissue in the pelvic cavity may be accidentally burned. Postsurgical bleeding is also a possible complication. In rare cases where the tubes have not been completely blocked, ectopic pregnancy has occurred (Peterson et al., 1997). To minimize the possibility of complications, it is important for a woman to choose a physician who is experienced in sterilization procedures.

Surgical reversal of female sterilization is sometimes successful. Rates of postsurgical pregnancy are about 75%. Microsurgical techniques (microscope-enhanced surgery) are usually most effective (Yoon et al., 1997).

Male Sterilization

In general, male sterilization is safer, has fewer complications following surgery, is considerably less expensive, and is as effective as female sterilization. However, vasectomy is used by only about 10% of married men in the United States, compared to 30% of women who have female sterilization (Piccinino & Mosher, 1998). **Vasectomy** is a minor surgical procedure that involves cutting and closing each vas deferens, the sperm-carrying duct (Figure 11.12). The operation is typically performed in a physician's office. Under a local anesthetic, a small incision is made in the scrotal sac, well above the testicle. The vas is lifted out and a small segment removed. The free ends are tied off, clipped, or cauterized to prevent rejoining. After the procedure is repeated on the opposite side, the incisions are closed and the operation is completed, usually in less than 20 minutes. A man can expect some short-term postoperative problems such as swelling, inflammation, or bruising in the region of the surgery that last from one day to two weeks. About 25% of men report some brief pain following vasectomy; a few from that group continued to experience discomfort for more than three months that required analgesics or medical attention (Rasheed et al., 1997).

Vasectomy
Male sterilization procedure that involves removing a section from each vas deferens.

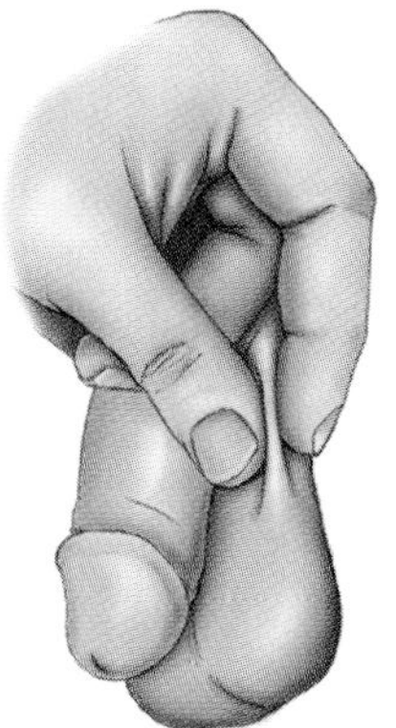

(1) The vas deferens is located.

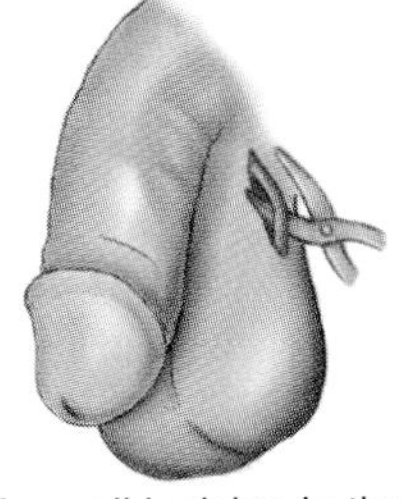

(2) A small incision in the scrotum exposes the vas.

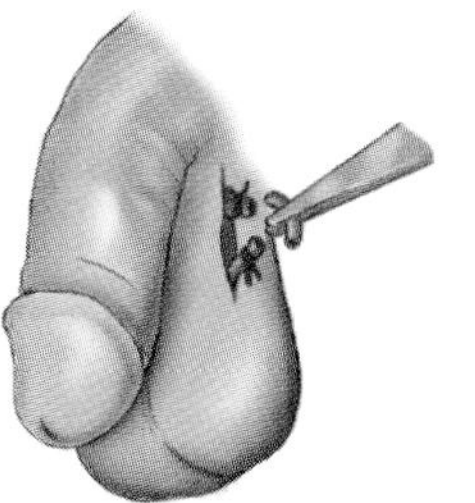
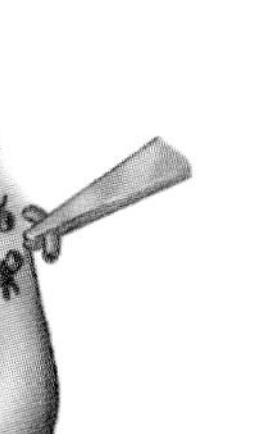

(3) A small section of the vas is removed, and the ends are cut and/or cauterized.

(4) The incision is closed.

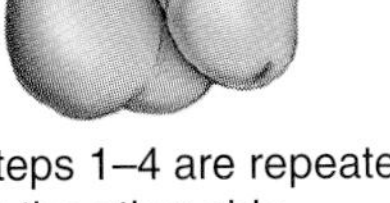

(5) Steps 1–4 are repeated on the other side.

Figure 11.12

Male sterilization by vasectomy.

A vasectomy procedure developed in China in 1974, known as no-scalpel vasectomy, substitutes small punctures for the conventional incision. The vas deferens is lifted out of the puncture opening and ligated. Side effects are reduced with no-scalpel vasectomy (Jow & Goldstein, 1994).

Vasectomy prevents sperm produced in the testes from entering the semen produced by the internal reproductive organs (see Chapter 5). However, because a significant number of sperm are stored beyond the site of the incision, a man remains fertile for some time after the operation. Sperm may be present in the first 10 to 20 postoperative ejaculations, or for up to several months. Therefore, effective alternative methods of birth control should be used until semen analysis reveals no sperm present in the seminal fluid. Many physicians recommend that a vasectomized man have two consecutive negative evaluations before engaging in unprotected intercourse. Generally, these checks occur 6 and 12 weeks after the operation (De Knijff et al., 1997). In rare cases, the two free ends of the severed vas grow back together (this is called *recanalization*) (Brahams, 1995).

Unlike castration, vasectomy does not alter testicular production of male sex hormones or absorption of the hormones into the bloodstream. A vasectomized man also continues to produce sperm that are absorbed and eliminated by his body. His ejaculations contain almost as much semen after the operation as before because sperm constitute less than 5% of the total ejaculate. The characteristic odor and consistency of the semen also remain the same.

Most men report that vasectomy does not affect their sexual functioning. Some report improvements, often due to greater spontaneity of sexual expression and less fear of impregnating their partners. A few report a reduction in sexual desire, which may be related to concerns about their continued masculinity.

Some research has found an association between vasectomy and an increase in prostate cancer (Giovannucci et al., 1993). However, the results are inconclusive as to whether or not vasectomy contributes to the development of a later cancer, and other studies have not found this correlation (Howards, 1994). Further research is needed to clarify this question (Howards & Peterson, 1993).

Vasovasostomy Surgical reconstruction of the vas deferens to reverse a vasectomy.

Some men request a **vasovasostomy,** a reversal of a vasectomy. Approximately 80% of vasovasostomies are done for men in a second marriage following divorce (Fallon et al., 1981). With selected patients and experienced microsurgeons, the chances of reconnecting the vas have increased (Fox, 1994). The shorter the interval between vasectomy and vasovasostomy, the better the outcome. However, the major problem complicating vasovasostomy is reduced fertility following reconnection of the vas (Jarow et al., 1994). After vasovasostomy, many men have low sperm counts, reduced sperm motility, or both. Another factor in reduced postvasovasostomy fertility may be the antisperm antibodies that develop in some vasectomized men. The best measure of vasovasostomy success is subsequent pregnancy; various studies report an average pregnancy rate of 50% using current vasovasostomy techniques (Matthews et al., 1997).

Less-Than-Effective Methods

There are other contraceptive methods that are far less effective and less commonly used than the ones we have been discussing. We mention some of them here, partly because they are used both as primary birth control methods and as backups for other methods and partly because people may have misconceptions about their effectiveness. We discuss nursing, withdrawal, and douching as methods of birth control.

Nursing

Nursing a baby delays a woman's return to fertility after childbirth; however, it is not a reliable method of birth control because there is no way of knowing when ovulation will resume. *Amenorrhea* (lack of menstruation) usually occurs during nursing, but it is not a reliable indication of inability to conceive. Nearly 80% of breast-feeding women ovulate before their first menstrual period. The longer a woman breast-feeds, the more likely it is that ovulation will occur (Hatcher et al., 1994).

Withdrawal

The practice of the man removing his penis from the vagina just before he ejaculates is known as *withdrawal.* Theoretically, withdrawal could be an effective method of birth control. However, this method is not very effective. It may be difficult for the man to judge exactly when he must withdraw. His likely tendency is to remain inside the vagina as long as possible, and this may be too long. Both partners may experience anxiety about whether he will withdraw in time, and this can have the effect of reducing the pleasure of sex. Furthermore, even withdrawing before ejaculation does not protect against pregnancy. The preejaculatory Cowper's gland secretions may carry sperm from a previous ejaculation that remain in the urethra, and these sperm can fertilize the egg. Also, sperm deposited on the labia after withdrawal can swim into the vagina.

Douching

Although some women use *douching* after intercourse as a method of birth control, it is very ineffective. After ejaculation some sperm reach the inside of the uterus in a matter of one or two minutes. And in fact, the movement of the water from douching may actually help sperm reach the opening of the cervix. Furthermore, frequent douching is not recommended because it can irritate vaginal tissues.

New Directions in Contraception

The spectrum of choices available for contraception widened markedly with the advent of the pill and the IUD. Currently with hormonal contraceptives, "less is better"; we now have lower-dose oral contraceptives, subcutaneous capsules, and injections. As we have seen in this chapter, however, there are still potential health hazards and inconveniences associated with available methods. Unwanted pregnancies occur each year because of contraceptive and user failure. Further research is needed to improve the safety, reliability, and convenience of birth control.

However, research requires funding. Most clinical trials for contraception occur in foreign countries with the financial help of the United States (Benagiano & Collingham, 1997). U.S. funds for international family planning programs to conduct clinical trials on contraception were cut for many years. The funds were made available again in July 1996, but at only 65% of previous levels. In addition, some pharmaceutical companies have dropped their contraceptive research programs because of the great expense of extensive clinical trials needed for product approval by the Food and Drug Administration and concern about product liability expenses. In fact, some companies have taken contraceptives off the market because liability insurance became unavailable or prohibitively expensive. The only new products likely to be available soon are contraceptive vaginal rings and some modified implant systems (Hanson, 1997). Given these limitations, we look at some future possibilities for both men and women.

New Directions for Men

Presently, male contraception is limited to condoms, vasectomy, and the withdrawal method. Research and development in male contraception by pharmaceutical companies are very limited. The expense of research and fear of lawsuits for side effects of new methods for both men and women are the main reasons for lack of investment in contraceptive research (Vines, 1994). However, some research efforts currently are under way that suggest other methods may be available in the future. These efforts have concentrated on inhibiting sperm production, motility, or maturation.

A gonadotropin-releasing hormone inhibitor (LHRH agonist) is currently under study as a male contraceptive. LHRH agonist has been shown to reduce the number and motility of sperm in men who received daily injections of the substance. Testosterone levels also dropped, and inability to achieve an erection occurred in more than half of the men in the study. This side effect disappeared after treatment stopped. However, testosterone combined with LHRH agonist is effective in maintaining sexual functioning while producing temporary infertility. Drugs that impair other phases of sperm production are being studied (Aldous, 1994).

Testosterone-derivative and progestin-related drugs that reduce sperm count to an acceptable level of protection are being researched. Although they currently require weekly injections, which are impractical, they may be developed into implants that are active for up to a year. A significant difficulty with developing a reversible male contraceptive is being able to reduce sperm level without interfering with sexual interest and function. Another possibility may be medications that inhibit ejaculation but not orgasm (Aldous, 1994).

A Brazilian pharmaceutical company is conducting a final clinical trial on a contraceptive pill for men they hope to market in 1999. Called NoFertil, it destroys male sperm without loss of erectile function. It is made from gossypol, a substance produced by the cotton plant. Gossypol was first tested in China in the 1970s, but caused irreversible infertility in 10–15% of the men who used it. Because of this, the company plans to market NoFertil to men who already have children. Meanwhile, Chinese scientists are testing a perennial plant, triptergium, known as Thunder God Vine. For centuries the powdered root of this vine has been used to repel insects and to treat fever, skin diseases, and rheumatoid arthritis. Chinese researchers found a significant reduction in sperm density and motility during use of this plant and complete restoration of fertility a month after stopping its use (Williams, 1996).

New Directions for Women

In contrast to the sparse picture of new developments for male contraception, an array of contraceptive methods for women is currently under experimentation. The widespread use of Norplant has set the stage for the development of other implants. Some of the implants under study have fewer capsules than Norplant. Others are biodegradable capsules or pellets that dissolve harmlessly in the body and do not require removal. Most of these innovations are expected to be on the market by the year 2000. Injectables using variations in hormones are under study (Bahamondes et al., 1997). A cream containing Progestin is rubbed on the skin and the hormone is slowly absorbed into the bloodstream. Vaginal rings that slowly release hormones that are absorbed into the blood through the vaginal mucosa are also being evaluated (Reifsnider, 1997).

Variations on diaphragms and cervical caps are in the experimental phase. One-size-fits-all diaphragms, disposable diaphragms, and a cervical caplike device, the Femcap, may be available by the end of the decade. IUDs of varying shapes and hormonal compounds also may be developed (Reifsnider, 1997).

An antiprogesterone substance, *RU-486*, has been approved by the FDA and is in use in the United States, Britain, France, and China. When given late in the menstrual cycle, RU-486 leads to menstruation by preventing implantation or causing the fertilized zygote to slough off of the uterine wall (Jouzaitis, 1994). When the drug is administered within 10 days of the expected onset of the missed menstrual period, most women experience menstruation. Antiabortion groups oppose the use of RU-486 because it can induce abortion, and they are campaigning to prevent it from being marketed in the United States

(Dipierri, 1994). Although it is controversial as a method of preventing implantation, RU-486 also shows promise in slowing or stopping the growth of some types of breast tumors, treating endometriosis, assisting in cervical dilation during labor, and treating Cushing syndrome, a serious endocrine disorder (Aguillaume & Tyrer, 1995).

Summary

HISTORICAL AND SOCIAL PERSPECTIVES

From the beginning of recorded history, humankind has been concerned with birth control.

Margaret Sanger opened the first birth control clinics in the United States at a time when it was illegal to provide birth control information and devices.

Objections to contraception stem from religious doctrine. However, most church members in the United States use some kind of artificial contraception.

SHARING RESPONSIBILITY AND CHOOSING A BIRTH CONTROL METHOD

The male partner can share contraceptive responsibility by being informed, asking a new partner about birth control, accompanying his partner to her exam, using condoms and/or coital abstinence if the couple chooses, and sharing the expense of the exam and method.

Comparison of relative convenience, safety, cost, and effectiveness may influence the choice of contraception.

People who feel guilty and have negative attitudes about sexuality are less likely to use contraception effectively than people who have positive attitudes about sexuality.

HORMONE-BASED CONTRACEPTIVES

Three types of oral contraceptives are currently available. The constant-dose combination pill contains steady doses of estrogen and progestin. The multiphasic pill provides fluctuations of estrogen and progesterone levels throughout the cycle. The progestin-only pill consists of low-dose progestin.

Advantages of oral contraceptives are high effectiveness and lack of interference with sexual activity. The birth control pills are also associated with lower incidences of cancer of the uterus and ovary, ovarian cysts, benign breast disease, and pelvic inflammatory disease. An additional advantage of the combination and multiphasic pills is reduction of menstrual flow and cramps. The advantage of the progestin-only pill is the reduced chance of harmful side effects.

Some of the disadvantages of the constant-dose combination and multiphasic pills are possible side effects such as blood clots, increased probability of heart attack, high blood pressure, more rapid growth of cancer of the breast and uterus, depression, and reduced sexual interest. Disadvantages of the progestin-only pill include irregular bleeding and the possibility of additional side effects. In general, the health risks of oral contraceptives are far lower than those from pregnancy and birth.

Norplant, made of Silastic rods filled with synthetic progestin, is an additional form of birth control, which became available in 1991. Its main advantages are ease of use and high effectiveness. Its main disadvantages are irregular bleeding and the potential of hormone-related side effects.

Depo-Provera is an injectable contraceptive that lasts for three months.

BARRIER METHODS

Condoms are available in a variety of styles, including some lubricated with nonoxynol-9. Advantages include protection from sexually transmitted diseases, improved ejaculatory control, and ready availability as a backup method. Disadvantages include interruption of sexual activity and reduced penile sensation. A female condom has also been developed.

Diaphragm use has decreased. Advantages include lack of side effects, high effectiveness with knowledgeable and consistent use, and possible promotion of vaginal health. Some disadvantages are interruption of sexual activity, potential irritation from the spermicidal cream or jelly, and possible misplacement during insertion or intercourse.

The cervical cap has similar advantages and disadvantages to the diaphragm. Some women who have problems fitting the diaphragm can use the cervical cap, but cervical caps will not fit all women.

Vaginal spermicides (including foam, vaginal suppositories, creams and jellies, and contraceptive film) are available without a prescription. Spermicides with nonoxynol-9 help protect against sexually transmitted diseases, including AIDS. Advantages of vaginal spermicides are lack of serious side effects and added lubrication. Disadvantages include possible irritation of genital tissues and interruption of sexual activity.

INTRAUTERINE DEVICES

The Copper-T and the Progestasert T are currently the only intrauterine devices (IUDs) on the U.S. market. Advantages of the IUD include uninterrupted sexual interaction and simplicity of use. Disadvantages include the possibility of increased cramping, spontaneous expulsion, uterine perforation, pelvic inflammatory disease, and pregnancy complications.

EMERGENCY CONTRACEPTION

Oral contraceptives and the IUD can be used for emergency contraception when a woman has had unprotected intercourse.

METHODS BASED ON THE MENSTRUAL CYCLE

Methods based on the menstrual cycle—including the mucus, calendar, and basal body–temperature methods—help in planning coital activity to avoid a woman's fertile period.

STERILIZATION

At this time, sterilization should be considered permanent. A decision to be sterilized should be carefully evaluated.

Tubal ligation is the sterilization procedure most commonly performed for women. It does not alter a woman's hormone levels, menstrual cycle, or the timing of menopause.

Vasectomy, the sterilization procedure for men, is not effective for birth control immediately after surgery because sperm remain in the vas deferens above the incision. Most men report that vasectomy does not affect their sexual functioning.

LESS-THAN-EFFECTIVE METHODS

Breast-feeding, douching, and the withdrawal method are not reliable methods for contraception.

NEW DIRECTIONS IN CONTRACEPTION

Possible contraceptive methods for men in the future include a hormone inhibitor that would reduce the number and motility of sperm.

Possible contraceptive methods for women in the future include variations of the IUD, Norplant, injections, or the hormone-releasing vaginal ring. RU-486, an antiprogesterone substance that induces menstruation when administered within 10 days of a missed menstrual cycle, is used in Great Britain, France, and China. But political controversy exists concerning its approval for sale in the United States.

Thought Provokers

1. What do you think are the positive and negative effects of modern contraception on relationships and sexuality?
2. If you could design an ideal contraceptive, what would it be like?
3. What criteria should a married couple who do not want more children use to decide which one of them should be sterilized?
4. Why do you think people don't use contraception when they don't want to have a pregnancy?

Suggested Readings

Hatcher, Robert et al. (1994). *Contraceptive Technology: 11th edition.* New York: Irvington. A comprehensive, up-to-date book about birth control—a must for anyone who wants the latest information about the technology and effects of contraception.

Kass-Annesse, Barbara; and Danzer, Hal (1986). *The Fertility Awareness Workbook.* Atlanta: Printed Matter. This book contains fertility awareness charts, step-by-step instructions on how to record fertility signs, and specific advice on how to prevent pregnancy using fertility awareness.

McLaren, Angus (1990). *A History of Contraception.* Oxford, England: Basil Blackwell. A scholarly and readable history of the uses and meaning of fertility control through the ages.

Web Resources

Margaret Sanger Papers Project
www.nyu.edu/projects/sanger/index.html
The life, writings, and work of the American birth control pioneer, Margaret Sanger, are highlighted on this site. It also includes an extensive list of links to related sites.

International Planned Parenthood Federation
http://www.ippf.org/index.htm
The well-known organization promoting family planning and contraception provides this Web site, with breaking news, press releases, journal articles, and other resources.

Successful Contraception
www.arhp.org/success/index.html
The Association of Reproductive Health Professionals provides this Web site. Along with excellent information about various methods of contraception, this site includes an interactive feature to help you choose the method of birth control most appropriate for you.

12

Conceiving Children: Process and Choice

Parenthood as an Option

What are the pros and cons of being parents or remaining child-free?

Becoming Pregnant

What are some of the causes of male and female infertility?

What treatments are available for infertility, and how do they work?

Spontaneous and Elective Abortion

How can a miscarriage affect a woman and couple emotionally?

What medical procedures are used for abortion?

The Experience of Pregnancy

How does pregnancy impact sexuality?

A Healthy Pregnancy

How does the fetus change in each trimester of pregnancy?

What factors can harm the fetus during pregnancy?

Childbirth

What options are available for childbirth in the United States today?

What occurs in each of the three stages of childbirth?

Postpartum

I've been an "expectant" father twice, but my role was drastically different the second time because of changes in obstetrical practices. During my first child's birth, it was the classic scene of Dad pacing the waiting room floor while my wife was in the delivery room. In my second marriage, the pregnancy was "our pregnancy" from the beginning. I went to doctor's appointments and saw our baby's ultrasound pictures. Seeing his heart beat so early in the pregnancy gave me a feeling of connection right from the start. We attended prepared childbirth classes together, and I was there from start to finish during labor and when she delivered our baby. I went with him to the nursery for all the weighing, measuring, and cleaning, then brought him back to his mother in the birthing suite. I wish I'd had those experiences with my first child's birth. (Authors' files)

One of the most important decisions you will probably make in your lifetime is whether or not to become a parent. In this chapter we address the pros and cons of parenthood. We also discuss the processes of conception, pregnancy, and birth and some of the emotions that accompany them, from the viewpoints of the parents. We encourage people who desire further information to seek more extensive references or to consult a health care practitioner. As a starting point, we look at the option of parenthood and some of the alternatives that are available for people who want to become parents.

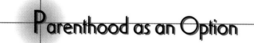

Parenthood as an Option

Remaining childless has many potential advantages. Individuals and couples have much more time for themselves, more financial resources, and more spontaneity in regard to their recreational, social, and work patterns. Nonparents can more fully pursue careers, leaving more opportunity for fulfillment in their professional lives. At the same time, there is usually more time and energy for companionship and intimacy in an adult relationship (Lavee et al., 1996). Not having to worry about providing for the physical and psychological needs of children can make a difference, for conflict about *who* does *what* for the children is a major source of disenchantment for many couples (Cowan & Cowan, 1992; Johnson & Huston, 1998). In general, childless marriages are less stressful; and some studies show that they are happier and more satisfying than marriages with children, especially in the years following a first child's birth (Crohan, 1996; Lavee et al., 1996). Note, however, that this discrepancy may be due in part to the fact that many unhappily married couples remain together because they have young children. Research indicates that having a baby does not help a troubled marriage. In fact, couples who had the most strain following the birth of their baby had the most marital problems prior to the pregnancy (Cowan & Cowan, 1992).

There are also many potential advantages to having children. Children give as well as receive love, and their presence may enhance the love between couples as they share in the experiences of raising their offspring. Successfully managing the challenges of parenthood can also build self-esteem and provide a sense of accomplishment. Parenthood is often an opportunity for discovering new and untapped dimensions of oneself that can give one's life greater meaning and satisfaction. Many parents say that they have experienced tremendous personal growth and have become better people through parenthood. Children offer ongoing stimulation and change as they develop through childhood, as one father experienced:

> His presence helped me to break out of my adult world in which everything was ordered and set, and allowed me to experience the world of childhood, where everything is free and spon-

> taneous. Past memories, long since forgotten, of earlier years and relationships with my own family would surface, effortlessly, to my awareness. (Greenburg, 1986, p. 7)

One-child families are mandated in most of today's China. Severe unemployment, food shortages, and the threat of widespread famine require drastic measures. In 1970 the average Chinese woman had six children; today the average is less than two (Bogert & Wehrfritz, 1996).

Adults may also want to raise children who are not biologically their own. Their desire to adopt a child or children may be partly motivated by a concern with overpopulation and a desire to give parentless children love and security. Another common reason that people seek to adopt is that they are unable to have children due to infertility. Currently in the United States, potential adoptive white parents outnumber the healthy white newborn infants available for adoption, and there is a long waiting period. However, adoption of nonwhite babies has become more common, and children or adolescents who are older or disabled are being placed more and more frequently in adoptive homes.

The potential rewards of either becoming parents or remaining childless may be romanticized or unrealistic for a given person or couple, and some people experience considerable ambivalence.

> I wish I could decide once and for all to have a baby, or even figure out whether I want one. Then I could plan the rest of my life. . . . One day I'm so absorbed by my career that I think I can't possibly have a child. Then the next day, I'm staring somewhat jealously at pregnant women. I see mothers and babies everywhere. It looks good to me. But I always scare myself away before I actually do anything about it. (Faux, 1984, p. 167)

There are no guarantees that the benefits of either children or child-free living will meet your own expectations. Still, it is important to consciously consider the options beforehand because parenthood is a permanent and major life decision and responsibility. And because we all change, your feelings about parenthood may very well change during your life. As one writer put it, having children changes your life—but so does not having them (Cole, 1987).

Becoming Pregnant

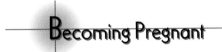

There are, of course, several options for becoming parents without actually experiencing pregnancy and childbirth. Most people who have children, however, are biological parents. In the remainder of this chapter, we look at some of the developments, experiences, and feelings involved in the physiological process of becoming parents, starting with becoming pregnant. This first step may be difficult for some couples.

Enhancing the Possibility of Conception

Picking the right time for intercourse is important in increasing the probability of conception. Conception is most likely to occur during a six-day period ending on the day of ovulation (Wilcox et al., 1995). It is difficult to predict the exact time of ovulation, but

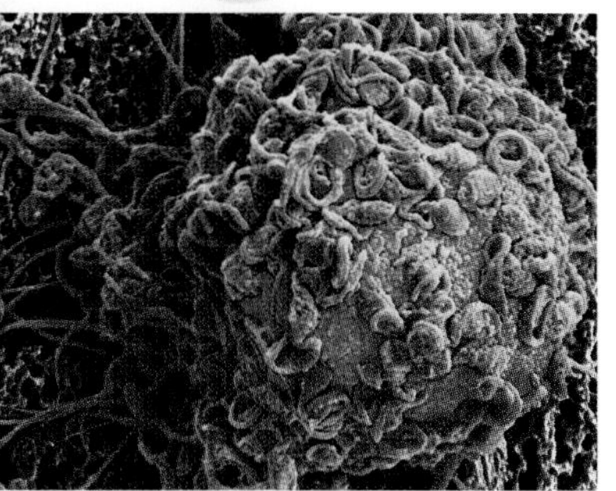
The very first stage of pregnancy—only one of the sperm surrounding this ovum will fertilize it.

several methods permit a reasonable approximation. One is the mucus method discussed in Chapter 11, in which coital activity is timed according to the fertile period in the woman's menstrual cycle. Body temperature and the principles of the calendar method may also be used in estimating ovulation time. Ovulation-predictor tests that measure the rise in LH in urine prior to ovulation can accurately identify the best time for conception and can be purchased over the counter.

Infertility

Sixty percent of couples become pregnant within three months, but if attempts at impregnation are unsuccessful after six months, a couple should consult a physician (Ono, 1994). It has been estimated that as many as one in six U.S. couples attempting pregnancy experiences fertility problems and seeks treatment for infertility each year (Pearson, 1992). Because approximately 50% of infertility cases involve male factors, it is important that both partners be evaluated (Sheynkin & Schlegel, 1997). We usually think of infertility as the inability to conceive any children, but secondary infertility—the inability to conceive a second child—is also common (Beck, 1989).

Given recent medical and scientific advances, do you think most infertility cases can be treated successfully?

Infertility is a complex and distressing problem. Its causes are sometimes difficult to determine, and remain unidentified in as many as 15% of cases (Nilsson et al., 1994). In addition, as many as half of couples seeking treatment for infertility are ultimately unsuccessful in their efforts to conceive, despite trying various avenues of treatment (Office of Technology Assessment, 1988). In this section we look briefly at some common causes of female and male infertility and at the impact that infertility can have on individuals and their sexuality.

Female Infertility

A woman may have difficulty conceiving or be unable to conceive for a number of reasons. Failure to ovulate at regular intervals is quite common. This may be caused by a variety of factors, including age (Chandra & Stephen, 1998) (as shown in Figure 12.1), hormone imbalances, severe vitamin deficiencies, metabolic disturbances, poor nutrition, genetic factors, emotional stress, or medical conditions. Ovulation and thus pregnancy can also be inhibited by a below-normal percentage of body fat, due to excessive dieting or exercise. Even 10–15% below normal weight is sufficient to inhibit ovulation (Frish, 1988). Women who smoke cigarettes are less fertile and take longer to become pregnant than nonsmokers (Curtis et al., 1997). Smokers are also more likely to experience ectopic pregnancy (Laurent et al., 1992). Alcohol and drug abuse reduces fertility in women, and environmental toxins can also impair female fertility. A variety of medications are sometimes used to stimulate ovulation. Although often successful and generally safe, these drugs may produce certain complications, including a greatly increased chance of multiple births.

If tests indicate that the woman is ovulating and that her partner's semen quality is satisfactory, the next step often is a postcoital test to see whether the sperm remain viable and motile in the cervical mucus. A woman's cervical mucus may contain antibodies against her partner's sperm, or it may form a plug that blocks their passage (Ginsberg et al., 1997). Intrauterine insemination, placing semen directly into the uterus, may be helpful in some cases (Haas, 1994). Douching also reduces fertility, so women desiring pregnancy should not douche (Baird et al., 1997).

Infections, as well as other abnormalities of the cervix, vagina, uterus, fallopian tubes, or ovaries, can destroy sperm or prevent them from reaching the egg. Problems with the fallopian tubes account for as many as 36% of cases of female infertility (Healy et al., 1994). Scar tissue from old infections—in the fallopian tubes or in or around the

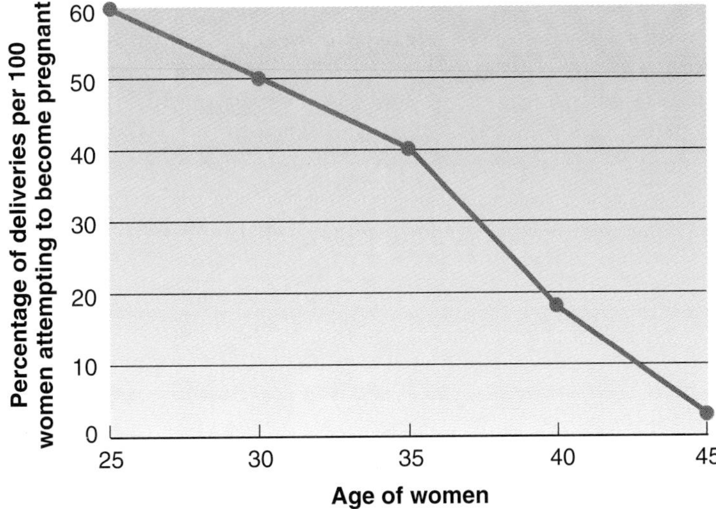

Figure 12.1

Increasing age = declining fertility. (Cohen, 1991, p. 16)

ovaries—can block the passage of sperm and eggs. Other major causes of female infertility are reproductive tract infections and tubal scarring from sexually transmitted diseases (STDs). Tubal problems can sometimes be resolved by surgery to remove scar tissue around the fallopian tubes and ovaries. A treatment that is demonstrating success involves inserting a balloon-type device into the fallopian tube and then inflating it to open the tube (Colino, 1991). Defects in the uterine cavity can prevent implantation of the fertilized egg, and endometriosis (growths of uterinelike tissue that develop in the pelvic cavity) can also result in infertility. As many as one in ten women of reproductive age may have endometriosis (Garner, 1997). Environmental exposure to dioxin, a chemical found in widely used herbicides and pesticides, may be contributing to a rise in rates of endometriosis (Begany, 1997).

Male Infertility

Most causes of male infertility are related to abnormalities in sperm number and/or motility (i.e., sperm cells that do not propel themselves with sufficient vigor). This can result from a number of causes. Infectious diseases of the male reproductive tract can alter sperm production, viability, and transport. For instance, mumps can affect the testes when it occurs during adulthood, lowering sperm output; or infection of the vas deferens can block the passage of sperm. A genital tract infection may produce an immune response that affects sperm; STD-caused infections are another major cause of infertility.

Environmental toxins such as chemicals, pollutants, and radiation may also produce low sperm counts and abnormal sperm cells (Paul, 1997a). Smoking, alcohol, and drug use and abuse reduce fertility as well (Curtis et al., 1997). Sperm absorb and metabolize environmental toxins more easily than do other body cells, which may result in birth defects (Tanenbaun, 1997).

Another major cause of infertility in men is a damaged or enlarged vein in the testis or vas deferens, called a **varicocele** (Schlegel, 1991). The varicocele causes blood to pool in the scrotum, which elevates temperature in the area, impairing sperm production. Varicoceles can usually be corrected surgically. Congenital abnormalities of the vas deferens, epididymus, and seminal vesicles can result in infertility (Vohra & Morgantaler, 1997).

Varicocele
A damaged or enlarged vein in the testis or vas deferens.

An unlikely cause of male sterility may be undescended testes. If this condition is not corrected before puberty, sperm will be less likely to mature because of the higher temperatures within the abdomen. Hormone deficiencies may also result in an inadequate number of sperm cells in the semen. This situation can sometimes be remedied by hormone therapy.

In cases where the sperm count is low, the optimal frequency of ejaculation during intercourse is usually every other day during the week the woman is ovulating, to increase the concentration of sperm (Speroff et al., 1989). In such circumstances, it is especially important for a couple to chart the woman's cycle so that they can reasonably predict her most fertile time. A man with a borderline sperm count might also want to avoid taking hot baths and wearing tight clothing and undershorts because these and similar environments subject the testicles to higher-than-normal temperatures.

Intracytoplasmic sperm injection (ICSI) Procedure in which a sperm is injected into an egg.

In cases of poor semen quality or quantity, two new reproductive technologies have made pregnancy possible in previously untreatable cases of male infertility (Ziebe et al., 1997). The first is the simple procedure of sperm retrieval from within the testes or epididymus using surgical biopsy or needle aspiration. The second step is **intracytoplasmic sperm injection (ICSI).** ICSI involves injecting each harvested egg with a single sperm (Turek et al., 1997). Fertilization rates are comparable to in vitro (in a laboratory dish) fertilization with sperm from normal ejaculation. Prior to the combination of these two technologies, the only options were donor insemination or adoption (Sheynkin & Shlegel, 1997).

A controversial use of ICSI is the retrieval and use of sperm from men who have just died. Although such requests are rare, doctors are receiving more requests from spouses or family members for postmortem sperm collection. The decision to comply with the request hinges on the doctor's personal feelings. Some will honor most requests, others will only do it if the man was married and wanted children. In this gray area of reproductive medicine, the question is whether or not it is ethical to take sperm without the consent of the donor (Kolata, 1997a).

Infertility and Sexuality

Most people grow up believing that they can conceive children when they decide to begin a family. Confronting infertility is an unanticipated shock and crisis. Women tend to express more emotional distress about infertility than do their partners, but both men and women experience increased anxiety, depression, and stress. The man is more likely to experience emotional distress when he is the cause of the infertility (Nachtigall et al., 1992). Problems with infertility can have profoundly negative effects on a couple's relationship and sexual functioning (Zoldbrod, 1993). When a couple is first informed of their infertility, they may deny it or downplay their desire to have children. As their infertility becomes more evident and undeniable, they may feel a great sense of isolation from others during social discussions of pregnancy, childbirth, and childrearing (Strickler, 1992). As one woman who has been unable to conceive stated:

> Coffee breaks at work are the worst times; everyone brings out their pictures of their kids and discusses their latest parental trials and tribulations. I can't help feeling like there's something wrong with me for not being able to get pregnant. When one of the women complains about having problems with something like child care, I just want to shout at her and tell her how lucky she is to be able to have such a "problem." (Authors' files)

Partners may also become isolated from each other and believe that the other does not really understand. Each may feel inadequate about his or her masculinity or femininity due to problems with conceiving. Each may feel anger and guilt and wonder, "Why me?" Finally, both may feel grief over life experiences they can never have: namely, pregnancy, birth, and conceiving and rearing their own biological children. Intercourse itself may evoke these uncomfortable feelings and become an emotionally painful rather than pleasurable experience. Studies have found that most infertile couples experience some sexual dissatisfaction or dysfunction at one point or another (Zoldbrod, 1993).

In addition, the medical procedures used in fertility diagnosis and treatment are often disruptive to the couple's sexual spontaneity. Sex can become very stressful and mechanical. Taking basal body temperature daily and timing intercourse according to ovulation can create tremendous performance anxiety that can interfere with sexual arousal and emotional closeness. Because of these psychological and sexual stresses, health care practitioners who work with infertility problems need to be sensitive to and skilled in helping affected couples (Pepe & Byrne, 1991).

Alternatives to Intercourse for Conception

Various alternatives have been developed to help couples overcome the problem of infertility. **Artificial insemination** is one option to be considered in certain instances. In this procedure, semen is mechanically introduced into the woman's vagina or cervix—or in some cases, after being specially prepared, directly into her uterus, a procedure called *intrauterine insemination.* Artificial insemination may also be used in cases where it is critical for a couple to preselect the sex of their baby, as described in the boxed discussion, "Preselecting the Baby's Sex: Technology and Cross-Cultural Issues." If the man is not producing adequate viable sperm or if a woman does not have a partner, artificial insemination with a donor's semen is another option.

Artificial insemination
A medical procedure whereby semen is placed in a woman's vagina, cervix, or uterus.

A **surrogate mother** is a woman who is willing to be artificially inseminated by the male partner of a childless couple, carry the pregnancy to term, deliver the child, and give it to the couple for adoption. This is done anonymously through an attorney or privately by arrangement between the woman and the couple. Surrogate mothers typically receive a fee of $10,000. The personal and legal issues of such arrangements remain complex and unresolved (Foote, 1998).

Surrogate mother
A woman who is artificially inseminated by the male partner in a childless couple, carries the pregnancy to term, delivers the child, and gives it to the couple for adoption.

Advances in reproductive technology have developed methods that can be used when infertility is due to blocked fallopian tubes, severe endometriosis, very low sperm count, inability of sperm to survive in the woman's cervix, and unexplained infertility of two or

Preselecting the Baby's Sex: Technology and Cross-Cultural Issues

The desire to have a child of a certain sex has existed since ancient times. Sex selection was done "after the fact." For example, in ancient Roman society infanticide was practiced against unwanted female babies (Faerman et al., 1997). Superstitions about determining the sex of the child during intercourse are part of Western folk tradition—for example, the belief that if a man wears a hat during intercourse he will father a male child or that hanging his trousers on the left bedpost will produce a girl.

Laboratory techniques to separate X- from Y-bearing sperm are now in widespread clinical use (Jancin, 1989). Once the laboratory separation process is complete, the desired X or Y fraction is introduced into the vagina by artificial insemination. Success rates of about 80% have been reported (Carson, 1988). However, the rather "unromantic" nature of semen collection and artificial insemination will probably limit the use of such sperm-separation techniques unless parents have compelling reasons to conceive a child of a particular sex (Office of Technology Assessment, 1988). Sex preselection offers benefits to couples at risk for passing on X-linked diseases to their children (Handyside et al., 1989). Additional technology for sex preselection is being developed.

In some countries in Asia—China, India, and South Korea—the preference for a son is particularly strong, and selective abortion of female fetuses is common. Prenatal ultrasound and amniocentesis make sex-selection abortion possible. Economic and cultural factors contribute to the importance of sons. For example, in India, daughters are a financial liability to the family. They will belong to the family into which they marry and require the expense of a dowry. However, sons provide for parents through their old age, offering security in the absence of governmental social support (Hwang & Saenz, 1997). In Hindu and Confucian religious traditions in Asia, only sons can pray for and release the souls of dead parents (McCauley et al., 1994). China's one-child policy has greatly reduced the birthrate—from 4.8 in 1970 to 1.8 children per family today—but parents' desire to have that one child be male has altered the natural birth ratio of 100 girls to 105 boys, to 100 girls to 114 boys (Schmetzer, 1995). Laws banning the use of prenatal testing for sex-selection abortion have been passed in these countries, but it still occurs illegally (Faison, 1997; Kumar, 1994).

In vitro fertilization (IVF) Procedure in which mature eggs are removed from a woman's ovary and fertilized by sperm in a laboratory dish.

Zygote intrafallopian transfer (ZIFT) Procedure in which the egg is fertilized in the laboratory and then placed in the fallopian tube.

Gamete intrafallopian transfer (GIFT) Procedure in which the sperm and ova are placed directly in the fallopian tube.

more years' duration. The world's first "test-tube baby," born in England in 1978, provided impetus to research in this area. In **in vitro fertilization (IVF),** the ovaries are stimulated by fertility drugs to produce multiple mature ova. Then mature eggs are removed from the woman's ovary and are fertilized in a laboratory dish by her partner's sperm. After two to three days, several fertilized eggs of two to eight cells each are then introduced into the woman's uterus. If this procedure is successful, at least one egg will implant and develop. Because more than one fertilized ovum is placed in the uterus, there is an increased chance of twins or triplets (Bollen et al., 1991). Studies indicate that babies conceived by IVF are as normal and healthy as those conceived naturally (Shoham et al., 1991).

Variations on in vitro fertilization involve transferring cells to the fallopian tube rather than the uterus. In a procedure known as **zygote intrafallopian transfer (ZIFT),** the egg is fertilized in the laboratory and then placed in the fallopian tube. Excess embryos are often frozen so that if the first implantation does not take place, the procedure can be repeated. In a more recently developed procedure, known as **gamete intrafallopian transfer (GIFT),** the sperm and ova are placed directly in the fallopian tube, where fertilization normally occurs.

Donated ova may be used for IVF in cases where the woman does not have ovaries, does not produce her own ova, or has an inheritable genetic disease. In a few controversial cases, donor eggs are used to help women give birth following menopause. Donation of ova is analogous to donor artificial insemination. Donors are usually women in their 20s undergoing IVF or a sister or friend of the infertile woman. When extra ova are retrieved, the women can anonymously donate them to another woman wanting the IVF procedure. More recently, advances in ova-retrieval techniques have made the procedures safe and easy enough for women who are not undergoing IVF ova retrieval themselves to donate ova (Hummel & Kettle, 1997). In certain cases where both partners are infertile, IVF may be done with both donated sperm and ova.

Problems with Assisted Reproductive Techniques

Assisted reproductive techniques are expensive and not usually successful, as shown in Table 12.1. One attempt at IVF costs between $6,000 and $10,000. Each subsequent attempt costs the same. After 20 years of scientific advances, 70–80% of couples who use the assisted reproductive techniques do not become parents (Begley, 1995).

Of pregnancies achieved by fertility treatments, 20–30% result in multiple births. The much publicized McCaughey septuplets born in 1997 highlighted this phenomenon (Cowley & Springer, 1997). Hormones that stimulate ovulation cause the release of multiple eggs, and often more than one is fertilized as shown in Figure 12.2. Multiple embryos

Table 12.1 Against the Odds: How the Methods Compare

Method	*Number of Procedures Done Each Year*	*Success Rate*	*Cost per Attempt*
Intrauterine Insemination	600,000	10%	$300
IVF	27,000	19%	$6,000–$10,000
GIFT	4,200	28%	$6,000–$10,000
ZIFT	1,500	24%	$8,000–$10,000
ICSI	1,000	24%	$10,000–$12,000

Source: Begley, 1995.

The Normal Ovary

During normal ovulation, one follicle matures, releasing its egg for fertilization in the fallopian tube.

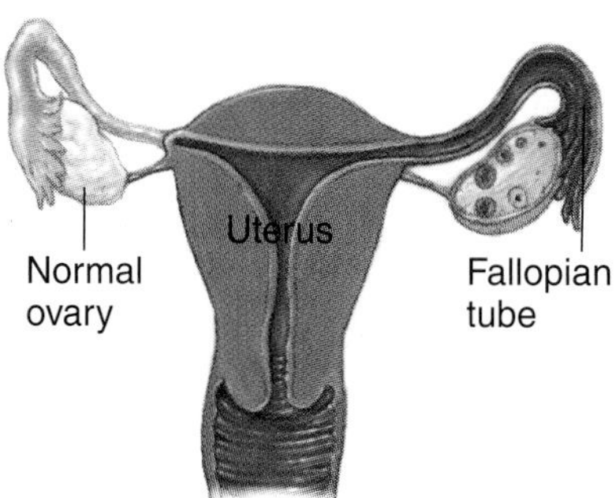

The Ovary on Drugs

Fertility drugs jump-start follicle development, increasing the likelihood that more than one follicle will release a fertile egg. Drug treatment can make the ovaries swell up to 10 times their normal volume—roughly the size of a grapefruit.

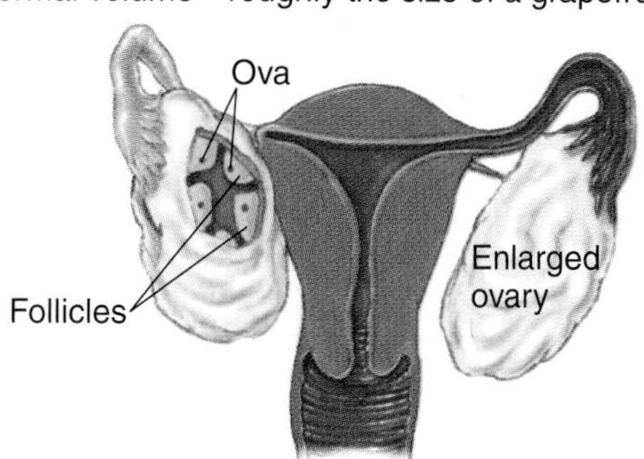

Multiple Birth

The human uterus isn't designed to hold numerous fetuses. When it is forced to, the crowding causes early delivery. The consequences for babies can range from brain damage to death.

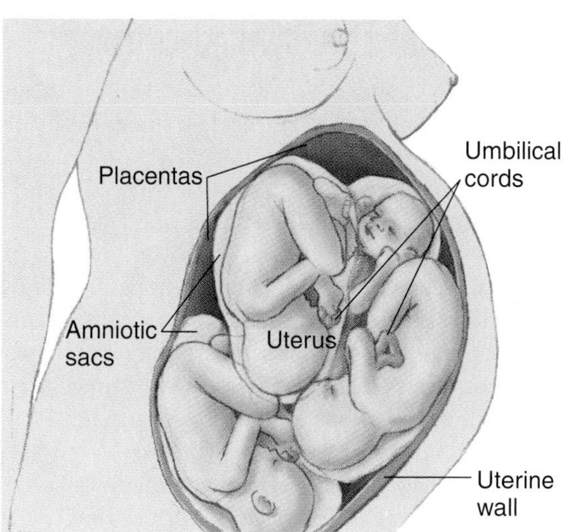

Figure 12.2

Women's hormonal rhythms normally ensure production of just one viable egg every month. By forcing the release of numerous eggs at once, fertility drugs raise the chance of multiple births. (Cowley & Springen, 1997)

At 2 pounds, 4 ounces, this baby was the largest of quadruplets born to a mother who gave birth 12 weeks early; she had taken fertility drugs. (Seligmann & Springen, 1996) Photo by Marty Katz

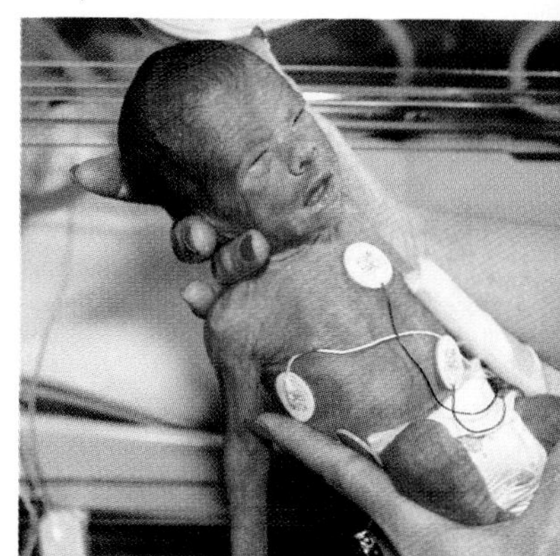

are implanted during IVF to increase the chances of conception. Any multiple birth increases the danger to babies, with greater incidence of prematurity, low birth weight, birth defects, and postnatal death. In some cases, one or more fetuses are aborted to increase the likelihood that at least one other will survive. For mothers, the risks of cesarean deliveries, high blood pressure, and other birth complications increase with multiple births (Seligmann & Springen, 1996). As a physician states, "The human uterus is not meant to carry litters" (Heyl, 1997, p. 66).

Controversy has arisen about whether or not ovulation-stimulating hormones in infertility treatment cause ovarian cancer. A review of the research on this topic concluded that the prevalent regimens of ovarian stimulation do not increase the risk of invasive cervical cancer (Mosgaard et al., 1997), but long-term studies are needed to more clearly assess potential risks (Unkila-Kallio et al., 1997).

Pregnancy Detection

The initial signs of pregnancy may provoke feelings from joy to dread, depending on the woman's desire to be pregnant and a variety of surrounding circumstances. Although some women may have either a light blood flow or "spotting" (irregular bleeding) after conception at the time of implantation, usually the first indications of pregnancy are fatigue and the absence of the menstrual period at the expected time. Breast tenderness, nausea, vomiting, or other nonspecific symptoms (such as extreme fatigue or change in appetite) may also accompany pregnancy in the first weeks or months.

Any or all of these clues may cause a woman to suspect she is pregnant. Medical techniques such as blood or urine tests and pelvic exams can make the determination with greater certainty. The blood, and hence urine, of a pregnant woman contains the hormone **human chorionic gonadotropin** (kō-rē-ON-ik gōn′-a-dō-TRŌ-pin) **(HCG),** secreted by the placenta. Sensitive blood tests for HCG have been developed that can detect pregnancy as early as 10 days after conception. Commercially available at-home pregnancy urine tests can detect pregnancy very shortly after a missed menstrual period.

Human chorionic gonadotropin (HCG)
A hormone that is detectable in the urine of a pregnant woman within one month after conception.

Because elective home pregnancy tests can yield both false positive and false negative results, they should always be confirmed by a health care practitioner (Salisbury, 1991). Around the sixth week after conception, an experienced practitioner can feel a subtle softening of the uterus during a pelvic exam.

Spontaneous and Elective Abortion

Not every pregnancy results in a birth. Many end by spontaneous or elective abortion.

Miscarriage

Even when pregnancy has been confirmed, complications may prevent full-term development of the fetus. Various genetic, medical, or hormonal problems may cause **spontaneous abortion, or miscarriage,** to occur, terminating the pregnancy. A miscarriage is a spontaneous abortion that occurs in the first 20 weeks of pregnancy.

Spontaneous abortion or miscarriage
The spontaneous expulsion of the fetus from the uterus early in pregnancy, before it can survive on its own.

About 10–20% of known pregnancies end in miscarriage (Paul, 1997). The majority of miscarriages occur within the first trimester (the first 13 weeks) of pregnancy; many occur before the woman knows she is pregnant. In many cases doctors are unable to determine the specific cause of the miscarriage (McBride, 1991).

Early miscarriages may appear as a heavier-than-usual menstrual flow; later ones may involve uncomfortable cramping and heavy bleeding (McKennett & Fullerton, 1995). Fortunately for women who desire a child, one miscarriage rarely means that a later pregnancy will be unsuccessful.

However, miscarriage can be a significant loss for the woman or couple. If the expectant parents strongly desired the pregnancy, have been trying to conceive for some time, or have miscarried before, the emotional impact may be particularly painful. Parents may experience grief, helplessness, guilt, and anger. As one woman explained:

> I had a miscarriage. I experienced it as the death of our child . . . and I am terrified of it happening again. . . . People minimize our loss when they say things like "You're young, you can have lots of babies," "It's God's will," or "It's for the best—there was probably something wrong with the baby." The truth is—as with any death—there is nothing one can say or do to fix it. . . . What helps me is to know that others view my child as real—for, like the Velveteen Rabbit, he was real to me. (Beck et al., 1988, p. 46)

Miscarriage can be a very lonely experience. Family and friends can help by acknowledging the loss and asking what the experience has been like for the person. Listening and allowing the parents to express their emotions and unique reactions to the miscarriage, without giving advice, can also be helpful (Cole, 1987). Couples may need to grieve the loss of this hoped-for pregnancy and baby for several months before pursuing another pregnancy (Salisbury, 1991). Some parents who lose an unborn child through miscarriage find it meaningful to name the baby or have a memorial service (Beck et al., 1988).

Elective Abortion

Elective abortion Medical procedure performed to terminate pregnancy.

In contrast to a spontaneous abortion, an **elective abortion** involves a decision to terminate a pregnancy by medical procedures. About 25% of all pregnancies in the United States end in elective abortion (Gober, 1997). Most women who have abortions are young: 20% are under 19, most are under 25. Young, white, unmarried women obtain the most abortions, but approximately 20% of abortions are for married women. Catholic women are as likely to obtain an abortion as other women, and about 18% of all abortions are obtained by born-again and evangelical Christians (Henshaw & Kost, 1996). Table 12.2 describes factors associated with higher and lower likelihood of abortion.

Procedures for Abortion

There are several different abortion procedures used at different stages of pregnancy. The most common are *suction curettage, D and E,* and *prostaglandin induction.* Orally administered drugs may be available in the United States for very early abortions (Grimes, 1997).

Suction curettage A procedure in which the cervical os is dilated by graduated metal dilators or by a laminaria; then a small plastic tube, attached to a vacuum aspirator, is inserted into the uterus, drawing the fetal tissue, placenta, and built-up uterine lining out of the uterus.

Suction curettage is usually done from 7 to 13 weeks after the last menstrual period. About 90% of abortions are done at or before 12 weeks (Hatcher et al., 1994). With suction curettage, the cervical os is usually dilated by graduated metal dilators or by a *laminaria,* a small cylinder of seaweed stem or artificial substance, inserted hours earlier. The laminaria slowly expands as it absorbs cervical moisture, gently opening the os. This gradual expansion reduces the chance of cervical trauma. During the abortion, a small plastic tube is inserted into the uterus. The tube is attached to a vacuum aspirator, which draws the fetal tissue, placenta, and built-up uterine lining out of the uterus. The suction curettage is performed by physicians at clinics or hospitals; the procedure takes about 10 minutes. However, admission, preparation, counseling, and recovery take longer. A local anesthetic may be used, and in some settings general anesthesia is available. Risks include uterine infection or perforation, hemorrhage, or incomplete removal of the uterine contents. If a pregnancy progresses past approximately 12 weeks, the suction curettage procedure is no longer as safe because the uterine walls have become thinner, making perforation and bleeding more likely.

Table 12.2 Factors Associated with Likelihood of Abortion

Characteristics of Women with Higher Likelihood of Abortion	*Characteristics of Women with Lower Likelihood of Abortion*
Age 18 to 24	Age 35 or older
Single	Married
Hispanic or black*	High income
Low income	Living in suburbs or rural areas
Covered by Medicaid	Born-again or evangelical Christian
Four or more children	

*Although white women obtain about 60% of all abortions, Hispanic and black women receive a higher proportion of abortions relative to the proportion of population size. A black woman is almost three times as likely as a white woman to have an abortion; a Hispanic woman is twice as likely as a non-Hispanic woman to experience an abortion.

Source: Henshaw & Kost, 1996.

Dilation and evacuation (D and E) An abortion procedure in which a curette and suction equipment are used.

Prostaglandins Hormones that are used to induce uterine contractions and fetal expulsion for second-trimester abortions.

For pregnancy termination between 13 and 21 weeks **D and E,** or **dilation and evacuation,** is the safest and most widely used technique (Schrinsky, 1988). A combination of suction equipment, special forceps, and a curette (a metal instrument used to scrape the walls of the uterus) is used. General anesthesia is usually required, and the cervix is dilated wider than with suction curettage. Second-trimester pregnancies may also be terminated by compounds such as **prostaglandins,** hormones that cause uterine contractions. The prostaglandin can be introduced into the vagina as a suppository or into the amniotic sac by inserting a needle through the abdominal wall; the fetus and placenta are usually expelled from the vagina within 24 hours. About 10% of all abortions in the United States are second-trimester (weeks 14–26) abortions. (See Figure 12.3.)

Using medications to induce abortions are referred to as *medical abortions.* Several medications are effective in inducing abortion in early pregnancy (Grimes, 1997). RU-486 has finished clinical trials in the United States, but a U.S. manufacturer or distributor may not arise because of threats of boycotts by antiabortion groups. However, other options using medications currently available have been researched and shown to be safe (Creinin et al., 1997). The anticancer drug, methotrexate, stops the division of malignant or fetal cells and has been used to end potentially fatal ectopic pregnancies as well as to treat cancer. An injection of methotrexate is given as early in the pregnancy as possible. Several days later, misoprostol, a common ulcer drug, is given as vaginal suppositories. The misoprostol induces contractions and expels the fetus as in a miscarriage (Schaff et al., 1997a). This medication treatment allows a woman to have an abortion as soon as she knows she is pregnant, rather than having to wait the six-week minimum for a surgical abortion (Schaff et al., 1997b).

Methotrexate and misoprostol are too valuable as cancer and ulcer treatments to be pressured off the market by antiabortion groups. The increased privacy for women and their physicians in using this method to end a pregnancy at an office visit rather than a clinic makes it more difficult for activists to identify and harass women and doctors using drug-induced abortion (Sanger, 1998). This approach has not, however, escaped their attention. After *The New England Journal of Medicine* published one of the first research papers on the high effectiveness of medical abortion, it received a fax from Randall Terry

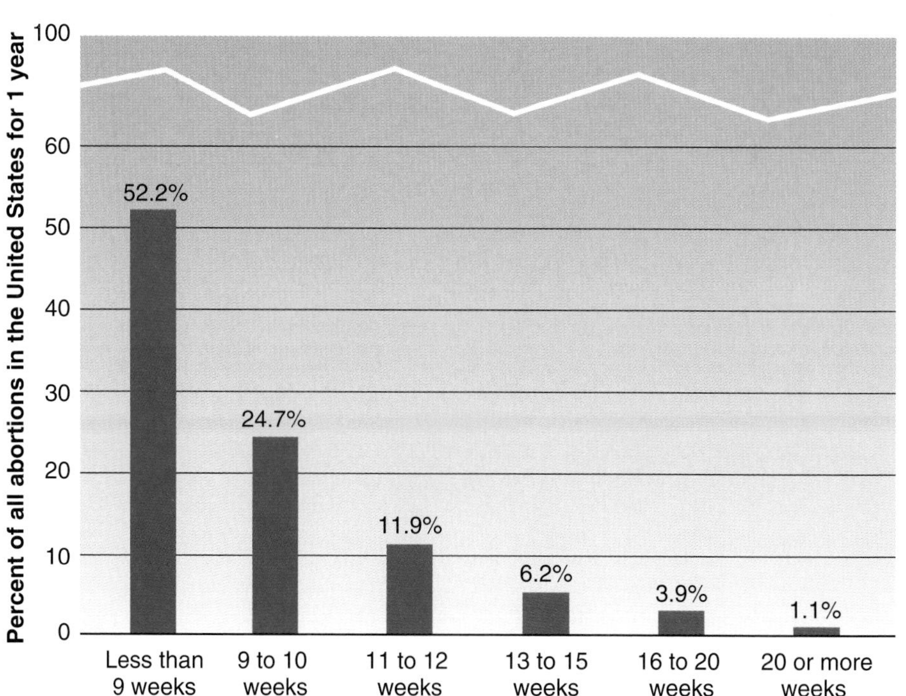

Figure 12.3

When abortions are performed. (Sontag, 1997, p. A8)

of the antiabortion group Operation Rescue, which stated, "Let . . . every chemical assassin . . . be forewarned: when abortion is made illegal again, you will be hunted down and tried for genocide" (Begley & Rosenberg, 1995, p. 76).

Complications from abortion procedures that induce labor contractions can include nausea, vomiting, and diarrhea; tearing of the cervix; excessive bleeding; and the possibility of shock and death. Research data have indicated that a first-trimester abortion has little effect on subsequent fertility or pregnancy (Frank et al., 1993); but research has also indicated that having two or more abortions may lead to a higher incidence of miscarriages or ectopic pregnancy in subsequent pregnancies (Madore et al., 1981; Tharaux-Deneux et al., 1998).

An abortion procedure done after 20 weeks gestation, called "intact dilation and evacuation" by medical professionals and "partial birth abortions" by opponents of abortion rights, was the subject of political controversy in the late 1990s (Rovner, 1998). Late abortions are rare. About 1% of abortions occur after 20 weeks. For the first time since *Roe* v. *Wade,* Congress considered banning an abortion procedure. The technique in question is done after 20 weeks of pregnancy and before viability at 24 weeks. It is reserved for seriously abnormal pregnancies; for young, indigent women who deny their pregnancies until the last minute; or for drug users whose lives are chaotic (Sontag, 1997). In this procedure, the cervix is dilated, sedation is given to the mother, and the fetus is pulled feet first out of the uterus.

Illegal Abortions

In countries where abortion is illegal, unsafe abortion procedures occur. Women attempt to self-induce abortion by enemas, laxatives, pills, herbs, soap, and various substances. Illegal abortionists typically insert a catheter or sharp instrument into the uterus to induce contractions (Jewkes et al., 1997). It is estimated that internationally 200 million unsafe abortions are performed yearly. Unsafe abortion is one of the leading causes of maternal death worldwide. For example, in Africa unsafe abortion practices account for 20–35% of maternal deaths (Rees et al., 1997).

Shared Responsibility

After a woman confirms that she is pregnant (assuming she was not trying to conceive), she must then decide whether to carry the pregnancy and keep the child, to give it up for adoption, or to have an abortion. There are several ways in which a couple can share responsibility for this decision and for the abortion itself if that choice is made. First, the man can help his partner clarify her feelings and can express his own regarding the unwanted pregnancy and how best to deal with it. One study of 1000 men interviewed in abortion clinics stressed the importance of men talking about their own feelings (Shostak et al., 1984). Important topics for a couple to discuss include each person's life situation at the time; their feelings about the pregnancy, possible choices, and each other; and their future plans as individuals and as a couple. If the man and woman disagree on what to do, the final decision rests with the woman: Male partners do not have a legal right to demand or deny abortion for the woman.

Once the woman has decided to have an abortion, the man can help pay medical expenses and accompany her to the clinic or hospital. According to several studies, about three-quarters of male partners of pregnant women agreed to the abortion decision and helped pay for the procedure (Shostak, 1979). The man can also be understanding about not having intercourse with the woman for at least a week following the abortion and can help in planning and implementing effective postabortion contraception. Because the abortion process is likely to evoke some difficult emotions, the couple may find it useful to continue to talk with each other about their reactions.

Choosing abortion is usually a difficult decision for a woman and her partner. It means weighing and examining highly personal values and priorities. When made, the decision is usually fraught with ambivalence. Even if the pregnancy was unwanted, both partners may feel loss and sadness. They may also feel regret, depression, anxiety, guilt, or anger about the abortion or why it was necessary.

Research indicates that legal abortion does not usually cause lasting emotional trauma. Women who have abortions usually experience some anxiety or depression, but these feelings resolve once the abortion is done (Rodman et al., 1987). Studies show that months or years following the abortion, most women express positive feelings about their choice (Dagg, 1991). However, women who have repeat abortions experience higher emotional distress in interpersonal relationships than do women having a first abortion (Freeman et al., 1980). Men often find themselves experiencing feelings of hurt, guilt, and anger following their partners' abortions (Shostak et al., 1984).

A great many factors can affect either partner's emotional response to the abortion. The reactions of close friends and family, the attitude of the medical staff and physician performing the abortion, the individuals' values about abortion, the voluntariness or pressure from others about the decision, and the nature and strength of the couple's relationship all can contribute to positive or negative reactions. One study found that support from partners, friends, and families was the most important variable in the degree of anxiety and depression women felt before and after abortion (Moseley et al., 1981). Another study found that women who became pregnant while using contraception tended to be more depressed after an abortion than were women who did not use contraception. The women who had used contraception believed that they would be unable to avoid future pregnancies, whereas those who blamed themselves for not using contraception said they planned to avoid future unwanted pregnancies by using birth control (Janoff-Bulman & Golden, 1984).

The timing of the abortion may also be important: Early abortions are medically, and usually emotionally, much easier than are later abortions. A woman having a legal abortion is also less likely to be as emotionally affected as she would be having an illegal, clandestine abortion.

Pregnancy Risk Taking and Abortion

In many cases, an unwanted pregnancy is clearly a matter of contraceptive failure. Approximately 58% of women who had an abortion were using contraception the month they became pregnant, condoms or the pill being the most common (Henshaw & Kost, 1996). Even though a woman and her partner used an effective birth control method correctly and consistently, the woman still became pregnant. For other women or couples seeking abortions, the pregnancy can be traced to contraceptive risk taking—that is, not using contraceptives consistently or reliably.

Why do you think some women risk an unwanted pregnancy by not using contraceptives reliably?

One researcher attempted to answer this question by surveying 500 women who had had abortions (Luker, 1975). Their answers are revealing. Several women said they had stopped using a method because they feared side effects. Others said they felt guilty obtaining contraceptives from a health care practitioner or pharmacy—an act that acknowledged their intent to engage in intercourse. Further research has found that young women with high degrees of guilt about sex are less likely to use contraception effectively than are women and men who do not feel guilty (Strassberg & Mahoney, 1988). Using drugs and alcohol also increases contraceptive risk taking, unless the woman is using the pill, Norplant, Depo-Provera, or an IUD.

Pregnancy prevention may interfere with romantic passion, and some women avoid contraception because they fear alienating a partner by asking for his cooperation in planning and using birth control. For some women who lack strong self-esteem, the loss of a relationship may be a more fearful consequence than the possibility of pregnancy. Unfortunately, such women are more likely to engage in intercourse with men who refuse to take precautions and who then walk away from responsibility if a pregnancy occurs (Malloy & Patterson, 1992).

One study found that about 11% of abortions were performed on women who had never used contraception, and that most of this group were teenagers (Henshaw & Kost, 1996). Actively seeking and using contraception is contrary to the traditional role of female passivity, a conflict that may especially affect younger women.

In some cases, lack of information about contraceptive methods results in risk taking. Some women take contraceptive risks believing they are unlikely to become pregnant. Couples who "get away with" risk taking once or twice are more likely to be careless in the future. For example, partners who forget to use the diaphragm a few times, without pregnancy resulting, are more likely to continue to "forget" more often.

Some women may take contraceptive risks because of the high social value placed on pregnancy. Pregnancy connotes fertility, womanhood, and adulthood in our society and is accordingly often considered a measure of a woman's worth. Pregnancy can also be a bargaining chip for marriage or can be used to test or coerce a man's commitment to a relationship or parenthood, or to try to prevent an impending breakup. Pregnancy can be a plea for help or an attempt to punish someone—usually the woman's parents. Life transitions may also affect risk taking. The mother who has just sent her last child off to school or the woman past 30 who has never been pregnant may become more careless in contraceptive use.

The Abortion Controversy

Elective abortion continues to be a highly controversial social and political issue in the United States and other countries (Reibstein, 1998). Beliefs regarding the beginning of life, the reproductive choices of women, the quality of life, and the role of law influence the stand one takes regarding elective termination of pregnancy. Women worldwide resort to abortion to prevent unwanted births. When abortion is illegal, many women have clandestine, unsafe procedures. Women who survive illegal abortion may suffer chronic health problems related to poor medical care (McCauley et al., 1994).

Abortion: A Historical Overview

Laws regulating abortion continue to change. Abortion early in pregnancy was legal in ancient China and Europe. In the thirteenth century, St. Thomas Aquinas delineated the Catholic Church's view that the fetus developed a soul 40 days after conception for males and 90 days for females. In the late 1860s, Pope Pius IX declared that human life begins at conception and is at any stage equally important to the mother's. The Roman Catholic Church still maintains this position. Pope John Paul II describes legal abortion as murder and a cause of grave moral decline. He also appeals to political leaders, particularly Catholics, to abolish prochoice abortion laws (O'Keefe, 1995).

Early American law, based on English common law, allowed abortion until the pregnant woman felt fetal movement, or *quickening* (usually during the fourth or fifth month). During the 1860s abortion became illegal in the United States, except when necessary to save the woman's life. Reasons for this change included the high mortality rate due to crude abortion procedures, the belief that population growth was important to the country's developing economy, and, perhaps, the male-dominated political system's response to the emerging movement of middle-class white women seeking independence and equality (Sheeran, 1987). The result was that women who were desperate to terminate unwanted pregnancies were forced to choose among terrifying options: illegal "backroom" abortions using unsafe, unskilled, and unsanitary procedures, or aborting themselves, sometimes using a wire coat hanger (Stubblefield & Grimes, 1994). If they had enough money, they might leave the country or persuade an American physician to perform an illegal abortion.

Roe v. *Wade* and Beyond

By the 1960s, advocacy groups of women and men were lobbying for change, and began to win a few battles on the state level. In 1973, based on the right to privacy, the U.S. Supreme Court in *Roe* v. *Wade* legalized a woman's right to decide to terminate her pregnancy before the fetus has reached the age of viability. *Viability* is defined as the fetus's ability to survive independently of the woman's body. This usually occurs by the sixth or seventh month of pregnancy, but most abortions are done before the third month. *Roe* v. *Wade* voided the existing state laws, which treated abortion as a criminal act for both the doctor performing the abortion and the woman undergoing the procedure. The Supreme Court ruling returned the abortion decision to the individual conscience.

However, the legalization of abortion in 1973 did not end the controversy. Legislation in the late 1970s greatly curtailed the availability of medically safe abortions to low-income women. In July 1977 the Hyde Amendment was passed, prohibiting federal Medicaid funds for abortions; it was later upheld by the Supreme Court. (Medicaid is a state and federal joint program to provide payment of medical services for low-income citizens.) The Court also established that states are not required to provide Medicaid funds for the purpose of elective pregnancy termination. (States may use their own funds to provide abortions for low-income women.) In 1993 the Hyde Amendment was modified to require states to fund abortions for rape and incest victims. However, some states refused to comply with this ruling (Kent, 1994).

Abortion supporters and opponents usually believe very strongly in their positions.

In 1988 the state of Missouri asked the U.S. Supreme Court to overturn *Roe* v. *Wade* and to uphold 1986 state restrictions on abortion that had been unconstitutional under *Roe* v. *Wade.* In July 1989 the Court ruled in favor of three state restrictions: Public employees are barred from performing or assisting in abortions not necessary to save the pregnant woman's life; public buildings cannot be used for performing abortions; and doctors must perform tests to determine whether the fetus is viable if they believe the woman may be at least 20 weeks pregnant. Although this ruling did not overturn the right to abortion, it does give other state legislatures the right to impose these limitations.

In June 1991 the Supreme Court, in *Rust* v. *Sullivan,* upheld legislation barring federally funded clinics from *discussing* the option of abortion with patients. This "gag rule" decision affected about 4000 clinics serving 4.5 million mostly low-income women. Critics of the "gag rule" viewed the prohibition on discussing abortion as a violation of the constitutional right of free speech (McBride, 1992). Further restrictions on abortion occurred in June 1992 when the Supreme Court ruled on *Planned Parenthood* v. *Casey.* States can now require a 24-hour waiting period before a woman can obtain an abortion, parental notification for women younger than 18, and detailed medical reports on each abortion performed. Although abortion remained legal, the cumulative restrictions limited the availability of abortion, particularly to young, rural, or low-income women, as shown in Figure 12.4 (Gober, 1997; Sanger, 1998).

The Clinton administration changed a number of laws related to abortion. It lifted the "gag rule" that had banned funds for family planning clinics providing abortion information and counseling. The Freedom of Access to Clinic Entrances Act was signed, prohibiting interference by protesters and providing criminal penalties for obstructing entrance to clinics. Military hospitals overseas were permitted to perform abortions, provided that women pay for them. And American policies cutting off aid to international

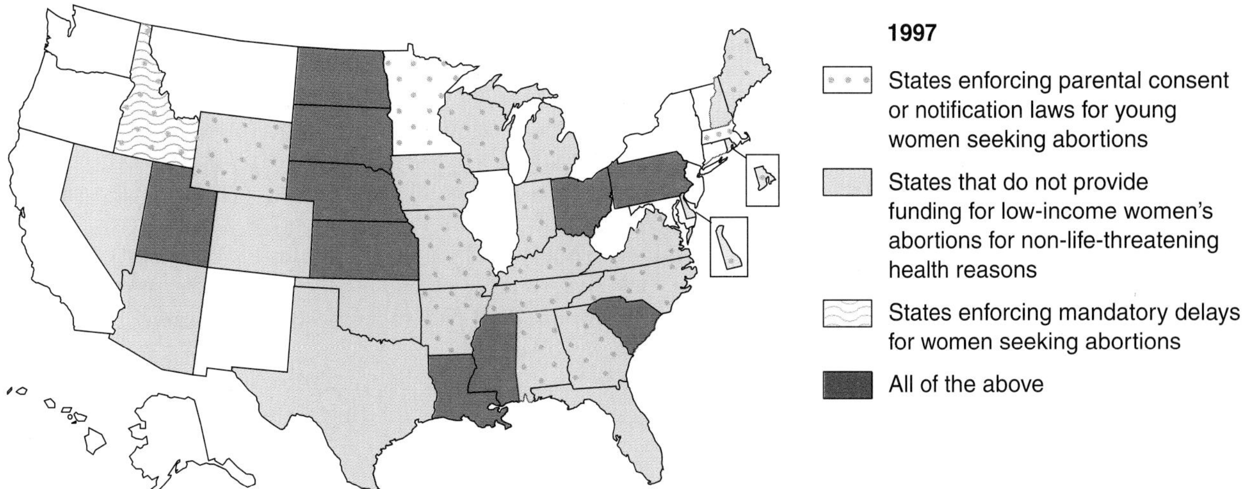

By 1997, 39 states had passed laws requiring consent or notification of one or both parents before a young woman could have an abortion.

- 17 states had passed legislation to ban "partial-birth" abortion methods since 1995, and bills to ban "partial-birth" abortion were under consideration in 5 other states.
- 19 states had passed mandatory delays before abortions.

Figure 12.4

Limitations on abortion (Dobosz et al., 1997).

family programs involved in abortion-related activities were reversed. However, access to abortion is less today than 10–15 years ago, particularly for women in rural areas and politically conservative states.

Abortion continues to be a major social and political issue in the United States, characterized by highly polarized opinions (Gorney, 1998). How future U.S. presidents and Congress will support or oppose abortion questions remains unknown.

The Current Debate

A 1992 survey, representative by sex, age, and income, found that 71% of respondents believe that abortion should remain legal (Clements, 1992). The boxed discussion, "A Comparison of African Americans' and Whites' Attitudes About Legal Abortion," looks at ethnic similarities and differences on this issue. The central concept in the abortion controversy is the moral debate between those arguing for the fetus's right to live and those arguing for the woman's right to choose to terminate her pregnancy. The antiabortion, or "prolife," advocates argue that life begins at conception and abortion is therefore immoral. One of their pamphlets states the following:

> At the moment of conception, all the elements that create a new human life are present. When the life-giving forces of the father and the mother unite, they form a unique human person. Life begins and from that moment, your formation has been purely a matter of development, growth and maturation.

Antiabortion groups want to reestablish national legislation, by constitutional amendment if necessary, to make abortion illegal and to establish the constitutional rights of the unborn fetus as an independent being (Epstein, 1997). Members of this minority are waging an active battle against legal and available abortion. A primary tactic has been to target prochoice incumbents in Congress to attempt to prevent their reelection. Antiabortion protesters also block clinic entrances and harass patients and staff (Greenhouse, 1994). Some extreme activists have burned or bombed abortion clinics or picketed at the homes of doctors who perform abortions.

Since 1993, prolife extremists have resorted to killing, believing that killing physicians is justified to save unborn babies. The following are some of the incidents:

- Dr. David Gunn, a physician who provided abortions in small towns in the South, was killed in March 1993 by three shots in the back by an abortion foe.
- A Florida physician, John Britton, and his security escort, retired Air Force officer James Barrett, were murdered in July 1994 by a prolife activist who had previously picketed clinics, carrying a sign, "Abortionists are murderers. Murderers should be executed."
- A gunman in Massachusetts shot and killed abortion clinic receptionists Shannon Lowney and Leanne Nichols and wounded several others in December 1994.
- Dr. Gary Romalis was gravely wounded in November 1994 as he sat eating breakfast in his home in Vancouver, British Columbia.
- In January 1998 a homemade bomb exploded in a health care clinic in Birmingham, Alabama, killing a security guard and seriously injuring a nurse.

In contrast, prochoice advocates see abortion as a social necessity, due to imperfect and sometimes unavailable birth control methods and lack of education. They want abortion to be an option for women faced with the dilemma of an unwanted pregnancy who decide that terminating it is their best alternative. Prochoice advocates support a woman's choice *not* to have an abortion, but they strongly oppose antiabortion legislation restricting others' choices. Many prestigious organizations have made public statements opposing antiabortion bills, including the National Academy of Sciences, the American Public Health Association, the American Medical Association, the American College of Obstetricians and Gynecologists, and many religious organizations.

Individuals who hold strong prochoice beliefs also have other beliefs that differ from those who oppose abortion. What other differences do you think distinguish the two groups?

Sexuality and Diversity

A Comparison of African Americans' and Whites' Attitudes About Legal Abortion

Research about race differences in support for legal abortion reveals interesting findings. One study of African American and white men and women over a 16-year period revealed significant differences in support for legal abortion between these groups, with the exception of women of childbearing age among both races. The researchers hypothesized that these women realize they may be faced by an unwanted pregnancy and must weigh their beliefs about abortion with the long-term impact of giving birth.

Although support for legal abortion has increased among men of both races in the last 16 years, support for legal abortion was still lower among African American men than white men during that period. However, from 1985 on, men of both races were similar to women of childbearing age in their attitudes. This may indicate a pattern away from more traditional gender-role beliefs commonly held by men.

Older white women reported the strongest prochoice attitudes while older African American women had the weakest support for legal abortion. The researchers conjectured that women's support for abortion shifts over their lifetime and that abortion has different meanings for women as a group. They hypothesize that white women are more likely to view abortion as a symbolic issue related to women's rights—a value that strengthens over time. Conversely, African American women may view abortion more as a practical consideration that loses its saliency after the childbearing years. It is also possible that the view of family planning as African American genocide during the civil rights struggle and racial discrimination of the 1960s and 1970s may influence older African American women (Lynxwiler & Gay, 1994).

One study of abortion attitudes found that people who approve of legally available abortions are more likely to support civil liberties and women's rights than are those who disapprove. People who disapprove of legal abortion are more likely than others to have strongly committed Catholic or fundamentalist Protestant affiliations (Granberg & Granberg, 1980); to have disapproving attitudes toward nonmarital sex, homosexuality, and government spending; to be politically conservative; and to have traditional attitudes about the female role (Deitch, 1983; Lynxwiler & Gay, 1994). Women who are prochoice activists tend to be college-educated, to have well-paid careers and few children, to have few ties to formal religion, and to have a strong vested interest in their work roles. Antiabortion activist women are more likely to be practicing Roman Catholics with large families, to have low-paying or no employment outside the home, and to base their self-esteem on their maternal roles. In addition, prochoice activists believe that intimacy is the most important purpose of sexuality, whereas antiabortion activists believe that procreation is the primary purpose of sexuality (Lynxwiler & Gay, 1994).

Research examining U.S. senators' and representatives' voting records demonstrates that many who are opposed to legal abortion tend to support capital punishment, oppose handgun control, and oppose legislation that promotes the health and well-being of families and their children—such as school lunch and milk programs. Voting records of prochoice legislative supporters have shown the opposite trends (Prescott, 1986). During the mid-1990s debate about reducing welfare expenses for women with children, increasing access to contraceptive services and abortion were rarely discussed as ways to help reduce the numbers needing welfare (Goodman, 1995).

How Women Decide

Research indicates that the political debate over the rights of the fetus or the woman are not the important questions women ask themselves when faced with an unwanted pregnancy. They rely on practical and emotional matters to make their decisions. Considerations such as the quality of her relationship with the father, her capacity to provide the child with a good life, the number of children she already has, and important life options that the pregnancy would impact are the real-life dilemmas each woman struggles with in deciding what to do. The following are examples of the conscientious questions women asked in their search for a decision:

> Did the woman love the man with whom she had become pregnant? Would he stay with her? Could she love the baby? Could she live with herself if she had a child and turned it over to strangers to raise? If she kept her child, could she care for it properly? Did she have marketable skills, an education, income? Would she ever acquire them if she went ahead with her pregnancy? Would the birth of another baby jeopardize the welfare of her existing children? Would the child be born with serious abnormalities? Would it suffer more than it would thrive? (Malloy & Patterson, 1992, p. 321)

It is likely that the abortion debate will remain passionate and bitter because of fundamental differences in life circumstances and values of people with strong commitments to one side or the other. However, most people experience considerable ambivalence about abortion (Connell, 1992). Many people who believe abortion is morally wrong also believe that any woman who wants an abortion should be able to obtain it legally (Stone & Waszak, 1992). As one woman stated:

> Part of my problem is that what I think and how I feel about this issue are two entirely different matters. . . . I cannot bring myself to say I am in favor of abortion. I don't want anyone to have one. I want people to use contraceptives and for those contraceptives to be foolproof. I want people to be responsible for their actions; mature in their decisions. I want children to be loved, wanted, well cared for. [At the same time,] I cannot bring myself to say I am against choice. I want women who are young, poor, single or all three to be able to direct the course of their lives. I want women who have had all the children they want or can afford or their

bodies can withstand to be able to decide their future. I want women who are in bad marriages or destructive relationships to avoid being trapped by pregnancy. . . . Even as I refuse to pass judgment on other women's lives, I weep for the children who might have been. (Smith, 1985, p. 16)

The Experience of Pregnancy

Pregnancy is a unique and significant experience for both the woman and her partner. In the following pages, we look at the experience and the impact it may have on the individuals and the couple. Many of the experiences will be encountered by heterosexual and lesbian couples alike. In this section, the heterosexual couple is used as a frame of reference; specific issues related to lesbians are addressed in Chapter 10.

The Woman's Experience

Each woman has different emotional and physical reactions to pregnancy, and the same woman may react differently to different pregnancies. Here are two reactions at the opposite ends of the continuum:

I loved being pregnant. My face glowed for nine months. I felt like a kindred spirit to all female mammals and discovered a new respect for my body and its ability to create life. The bigger I got, the better I liked it. (Authors' files)

If I could have babies without the pregnancy part, I'd do it. Looking fat and slowed down is a huge drag. (Authors' files)

Factors influencing a woman's emotional reactions can include how the decision for pregnancy was made, current and impending lifestyle changes, her relationship with others, her financial resources, her self-image, and hormonal changes. The woman's acquired attitudes and knowledge about childbearing and her hopes and fears about parenthood also contribute to her experience. Positive support and attention from her partner are very helpful in creating a happy pregnancy.

A woman's body changes dramatically throughout pregnancy, as seen at three, five, seven, and nine months, and with a newborn.

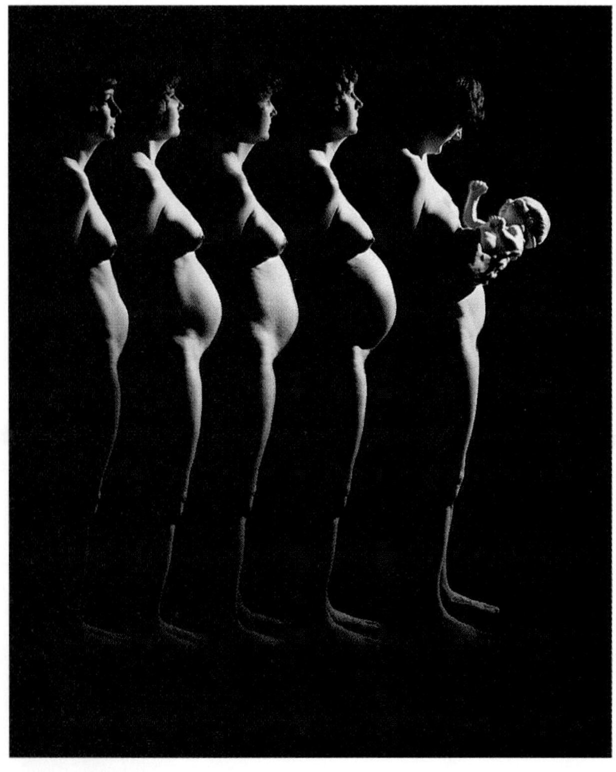

Women sometimes feel they should experience only positive emotions when they are pregnant. However, the physical, emotional, and situational aspects of a pregnancy often elicit an array of contradictory emotions including joy, depression, excitement, impatience, and fear. One study of 1000 women found a wide range of feelings about pregnancy. Thirty-five percent loved being pregnant, 8% hated it, 40% had mixed feelings about the pregnancy experience, and the remainder had varying experiences with different pregnancies. The researcher concluded that the emotional and physical experiences of pregnancy were very intertwined. The degree of physical discomfort influences a woman's feelings about the pregnancy and her life, and vice versa (Genevie & Margolies, 1987).

The marked changes that occur also have a significant effect on the experience of pregnancy. Several changes take place during the early stages of the first three months. Menstruation ceases. As the milk glands in the breasts develop, the breasts increase in size. The nipples and areola usually become darker in color. Nausea, sometimes called "morning sickness," may occur. Many women experience a marked increase in fatigue:

I'm ordinarily a very energetic woman, but during the first two months of my pregnancy, I couldn't get enough sleep. This meant a drastic change in my daily routine. (Authors' files)

Vaginal secretions may change or increase. Urination may be more frequent, and bowel movements less regular. However, there is little increase in the size of the woman's abdomen during these first three months.

More outward signs of pregnancy appear in the middle three months. The waistline thickens, and the abdomen begins to protrude. Fetal movements may be felt in the fourth or fifth month, which is usually very exciting and reassuring to the parents-to-be. Nausea and tiredness usually disappear by now, and a woman may experience heightened feelings of well-being. The breasts may begin to secrete a thin yellowish fluid called **colostrum** (ka-LOS-tram).

Colostrum
A thin fluid secreted by the breasts during later stages of pregnancy and the first few days following delivery.

During the last three months, the uterus and abdomen increase in size (see Figure 12.5). The muscles of the uterus occasionally contract painlessly. The enlarged uterus produces pressure on the woman's stomach, intestines, and bladder. This may cause discomfort, indigestion, and frequent urination. Fetal movements can be seen and felt from the outside of the abdomen.

Being an expectant father obviously does not involve the same physical experiences that a pregnant woman has (although occasionally a "pregnant father" may report psychosympathetic symptoms such as the nausea or tiredness his partner is experiencing). However, the experiences of pregnancy and birth are often profound for the father as well.

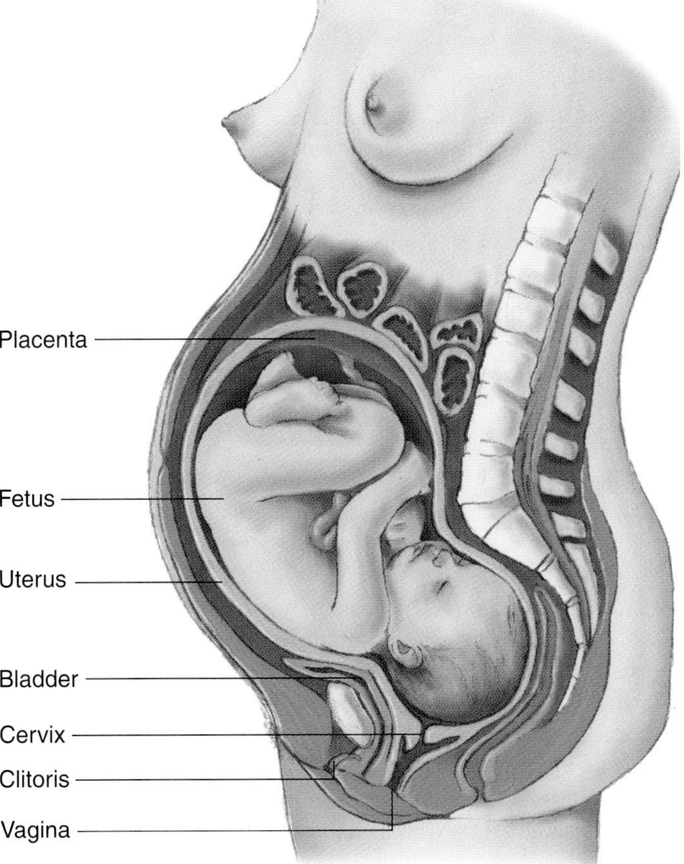

Figure 12.5

Pregnancy at the ninth month. The uterus and abdomen have increased in size to accommodate the fetus.

The Man's Experience

Significant changes have occurred in the last several decades in the role of the woman's partner during pregnancy, childbirth, and childrearing. Once seen as predominantly the woman's domain, pregnancy is now commonly viewed as a shared experience. With the advent of the prepared childbirth movement, described shortly, men frequently participate even in childbirth.

What exactly does the "male pregnancy" involve? Like the woman, her partner often reacts with a great deal of ambivalence. He may feel ecstatic, but he may also be fearful about the woman's and baby's well-being. Like many men, he may feel frightened about the impending birth and whether he will be able to "keep it together." He may feel especially tender toward his partner and become more solicitous. At the same time, he may feel a sense of separateness from the woman because of the physical changes only she is experiencing. However, fetal ultrasonography allows fathers to "see" the fetus in utero and can create greater feelings of involvement (Sandelowski, 1994). He may be proud at the prospect of becoming a father, but he may question his parenting ability. He may fear losing his wife's affection and attention to the pregnancy and baby (Brown, 1994). Most men feel concern over the impending increase in financial responsibility. In all, the expectant father has special needs, as does his partner, and it is important that the woman be aware of these needs and be willing to respond to them.

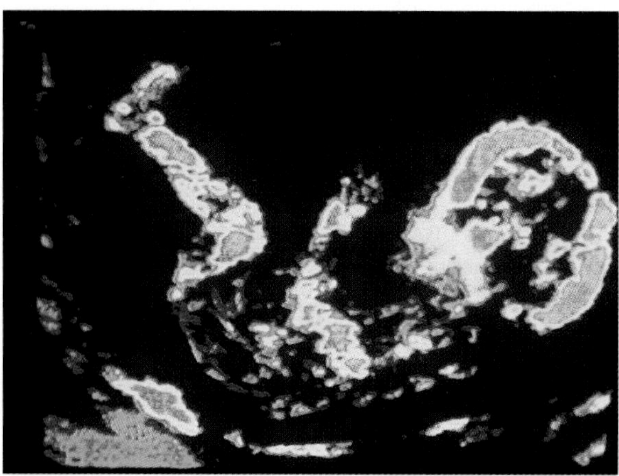

Ultrasound image of a fetus. Ultrasound monitoring is used in amniocentesis and chorionic villus sampling procedures.

Although men are encouraged to be active participants in the pregnancy and birth experience, they sometimes worry that their feelings of anxiety, anger, sadness, or fear might upset their partners and therefore are taboo (Chapman, 1992). It is important for the father-to-be to participate fully in the process of fatherhood by recognizing his own feelings and by receiving understanding from his partner, family, and health care providers. One study of expectant fathers found that when men did share their feelings with their partners, the relationships deepened (Shapiro, 1987). This mutual support can enhance the couple's level of sharing and closeness.

A man's active involvement throughout childbearing seems to initiate a positive interaction between the father and the newborn. Research supports the notion that fathers can be as nurturant of children as can mothers. Father–newborn interaction helps develop the paternal role, and programs in the hospital to increase father–newborn contact and to teach the father caregiving skills seem to facilitate this process (Sherwen, 1987).

Sexual Interaction During Pregnancy

A woman's sexual interest and responsiveness may change through the course of her pregnancy. Nausea, breast tenderness, and fatigue may inhibit sexual interest during the first three months. A resurgence of sexual desire and arousal may occur for some women in the second trimester (Masters & Johnson, 1966), but most research shows a progressive decline in sexual interest and activity over the nine months of pregnancy, with diminished sexual desire most common in the last three months (Bogren, 1991). Some of the most common reasons women give for decreasing sexual activity during pregnancy include physical discomfort, feelings of physical unattractiveness, and fear of injuring the unborn child (Colino, 1991). Women who have positive attitudes about sexuality tend to maintain more sexual interest, activity, and satisfaction during pregnancy than do women with negative attitudes about sexuality (Fisher & Gray, 1988). Also, a planned pregnancy results in fewer sexual problems than does an unplanned one, and women who experience more sexual arousal prior to pregnancy tend to lose interest in sex less than those who experience less sexual arousal. Many women also have increased desire for nonsexual affection as pregnancy progresses (Walbroehl, 1984). The key to sexuality and pregnancy is that feelings are highly individual: "Some feel sexier, more attractive and more easily aroused than ever before. . . . Others are completely turned off by the mere thought of sex" (Stern, 1987, p. 71).

For some women pregnancy can result in a heightened awareness of their bodies and an increased sensuality. Others feel intensely "womanly" and are less inhibited sexually. The increased vasocongestion of the genitals during pregnancy can heighten sexual desire and response for some women.

The partner's feelings also affect the sexual relationship during pregnancy. Reactions to the woman's changing body and to the need for adjustment in the couple's sexual repertoire may vary from increased excitement to inhibition for the partner. Especially late in pregnancy, awareness of the baby can make lovemaking seem like a crowded event:

> Sex during the third trimester requires a sense of humor. It doesn't seem to matter where you touch her anymore; the baby pops up everywhere. You can't escape the little kicks and jabs, and the thought of tiny feet and fists inches away (or closer) can be disconcerting. (Stern, 1987, p. 78)

Demi Moore's beautifully pregnant nude photo on the cover of *Vanity Fair* highlights the sensual richness of the pregnant woman's form.

For most couples, pregnancy is a time of significant emotional and physical changes. Open communication, accurate information, mutual support, and flexibility in sexual frequency and activities can help maintain and strengthen the bond between the couple.

It is now generally accepted that in pregnancies with no risk factors, sexual activity and orgasm may be continued as desired until the onset of labor. Women who are at risk for bleeding or premature labor will likely be advised differently (Schrinsky, 1988). Coitus or orgasm should not occur if spotting or vaginal or abdominal pain occurs or if the amniotic sac ("water bag") breaks. As with many other areas of sexual health care, a woman, her partner, and her health care practitioner can make an informed decision.

During pregnancy it may be necessary for a couple to modify intercourse positions. The side-by-side, woman-above, and rear-entry positions are generally more comfortable than the man-above position as pregnancy progresses. Oral and manual genital stimulation as well as total body touching and holding can continue as usual. In fact, pregnancy is a time when a couple may explore and develop these dimensions of lovemaking more fully; even if intercourse is not desired, intimacy, eroticism, and sexual satisfaction can continue.

A Healthy Pregnancy

Once a woman becomes pregnant, her own health habits and care play an important part in the development of a healthy fetus.

Fetal Development

The nine-month (40-week) span of pregnancy is customarily divided into three 13-week segments called *trimesters.* Characteristic changes occur in each trimester.

First-Trimester Development

Zygote
The single cell resulting from the union of sperm and egg cells.

Blastocyst
Multicellular descendant of the united sperm and ovum that implants on the wall of the uterus.

As with all mammals, a human begins as a **zygote** (ZĪ-gōt), a united sperm cell and ovum, which develops into the multicelled **blastocyst** (BLAS-tō-sist) that implants on the wall of the uterus about one week after fertilization (see Figure 12.6). Growth progresses steadily. By 9–10 weeks after a woman's last menstrual period, the fetal heartbeat can be heard with a special ultrasound stethoscope known as the *Doppler.* By the beginning of the second month from the time of conception, the fetus is ½ to 1 inch long, grayish, and

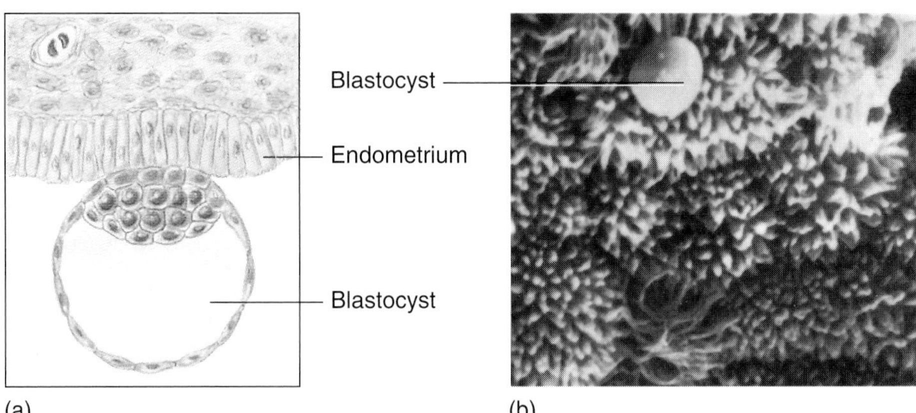

Figure 12.6

The blastocyst implanted on the uterine wall shown (a) in diagram and (b) in photo taken by scanning electron microscope.

crescent-shaped. During this same month, the spinal canal and rudimentary arms and legs form, as do the beginnings of recognizable eyes, fingers, and toes. During the third month, internal organs such as the liver, kidneys, intestines, and lungs begin limited functioning in the 3-inch fetus.

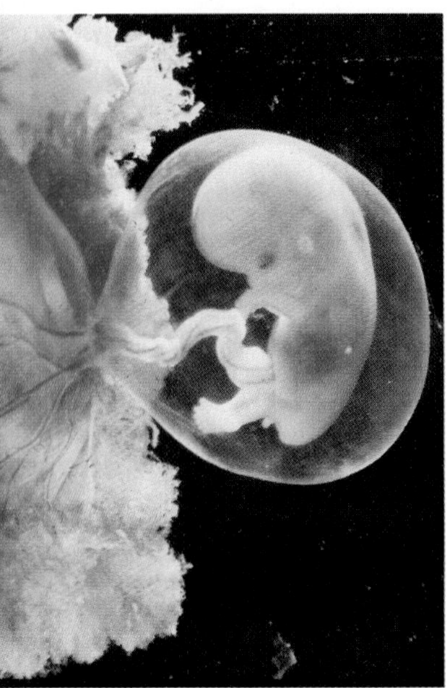

Fetal development at 9 weeks. The fetus (right) is connected to the placenta (left) by the umbilical cord.

Second-Trimester Development

The second trimester begins with the fourth month of pregnancy. By now the sex of the fetus can often be distinguished. External body parts including fingernails, eyebrows, and eyelashes are clearly formed. The fetus's skin is covered by fine, downlike hair. Future development primarily consists of growth in size and refinement of the features that already exist. Fetal movements, or quickening, can be felt by the end of the fourth month. By the end of the fifth month, the fetus's weight has increased to one pound. Head hair may appear at this time, and subcutaneous fat develops. By the end of the second trimester, the fetus has opened its eyes.

Third-Trimester Development

In the third trimester, the fetus continues to grow and to develop the size and strength it will need to live on its own, apart from the mother's warmth and sustenance. It increases in weight from 4 pounds in the seventh month to an average of over 7 pounds at birth. The downlike hair covering its body disappears, and head hair continues growing. The skin becomes smooth rather than wrinkled. It is covered with a protective creamy, waxy substance called the **vernix caseosa** (VER-niks kas′-Ē-Ō-sa).

Vernix caseosa
A waxy, protective substance on the fetus's skin.

Prenatal Care

The developments just described take place in most pregnancies. Occasionally, however, something may go wrong. The fetus may not develop normally, or the pregnancy may terminate early, as we discussed previously. The causes of these problems may be genetic and unpreventable, but the mother's own health and nutrition are also crucial in providing the best environment for fetal development. This is one reason why it is important for a woman to have a complete physical examination and health assessment before becoming pregnant. She should also have a test to determine her immunity to rubella (German measles), a disease that may cause severe fetal defects if the mother contracts it while she is pregnant. A prepregnancy HIV test should also be considered because the HIV virus can be transmitted to the developing fetus during pregnancy.

Thorough prenatal care is essential for promoting the health of both the mother and the fetus. Prenatal care can prevent about 50% of problems that babies can develop during pregnancy. Unfortunately, about 88 out of every 1000 babies are born without adequate prenatal care, a situation that increases the chances of problems including low birth weight, lung disorders, brain damage, and abnormal growth patterns (O'Neill, 1988).

Components of optimal prenatal care include good nutrition, general good health, adequate rest, routine health care, exercise, and childbirth education (Kolasa & Weismiller, 1997). Early in the pregnancy, the woman, her partner, and her health care practitioner should discuss the health needs of both the mother and the developing fetus; they can also begin to make plans for the birth. As women have increasingly taken up athletic activities, many have had questions about the effects of exercise on pregnancy. Moderate exercise is commonly recommended as important to a healthy pregnancy. See the boxed discussion, "Pregnancy: Latest Fitness Thinking," for current guidelines.

Risks to Fetal Development

The rapidly developing fetus is dependent on the mother for nutrients, oxygen, and waste elimination as substances pass through the **placenta** (a disk-shaped organ attached to the wall of the uterus, shown in Figure 12.7). The fetus is joined to the placenta by the umbilical cord. The fetal blood circulates independently within the closed system of the fetus and the inner part of the placenta. Maternal blood flows in the uterine walls and outer part of the placenta. Fetal and maternal blood do not normally intermingle. All exchanges between the fetal and maternal blood systems occur by passage of substances through the walls of the blood vessels. Nutrients and oxygen from the maternal blood pass into the fetal circulatory system; carbon dioxide and waste products from the fetus pass into the maternal blood vessels, to be removed by the maternal circulation.

Placenta
A disk-shaped organ attached to the uterine wall and connected to the fetus by the umbilical cord. Nutrients, oxygen, and waste products pass between mother and fetus through its cell walls.

The placenta prevents some kinds of bacteria and viruses from passing into the fetal blood system, but not all. Many do cross through the placenta, including the HIV virus. Furthermore, many substances ingested by the mother easily cross through the placenta

Your Sexual Health

Pregnancy: Latest Fitness Thinking

The American College of Obstetricians and Gynecologists has issued safety guidelines for women who wish to continue exercising during pregnancy. Consult your physician first. (Certain factors may be reasons to avoid exercise during pregnancy.)

Limit aerobic exercise to 15-minute sessions, and monitor your heart rate regularly. Keep it below 140 beats per minute. (Animal studies have indicated that increased body temperatures induced by too-vigorous exercise could have adverse effects on the fetus.) Walking is usually excellent exercise during pregnancy.

Avoid jerky stretches and exercises. The hormonal changes caused by pregnancy loosen the soft tissue that links bones within the joints, making a

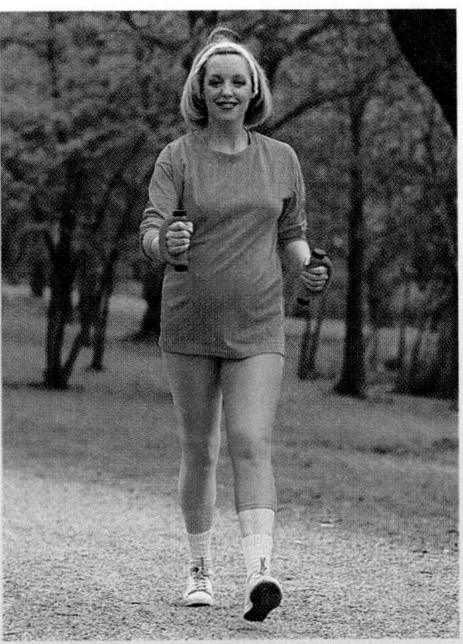

woman more susceptible to joint injury.

Drink fluids before and after exercise; stop immediately to drink if you become thirsty. Dehydration occurs much more rapidly than usual during pregnancy.

After the fourth month of pregnancy, don't do any exercises that are performed lying down on your back. The increased size of the uterus can interfere with the blood flow to a pregnant woman's heart and to the fetus. And finally, have reasonable expectations from exercise. Exercise can boost a pregnant woman's energy level; help her maintain muscle tone, strength, and endurance; and decrease the likelihood of back pain.

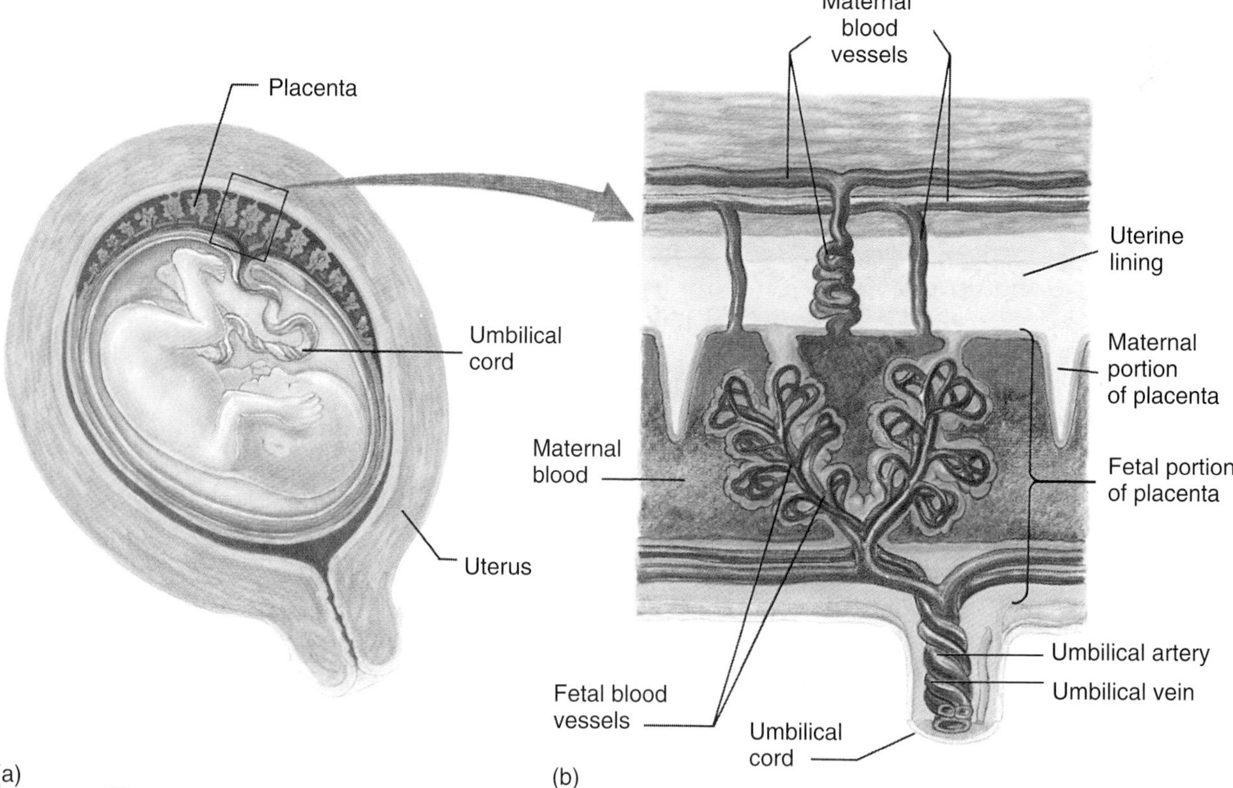

Figure 12.7

The placenta exchanges nutrients, oxygen, and waste products between the maternal and fetal circulatory systems. (a) The placenta attached to the uterine wall. (b) Close-up detail of placenta.

and can be damaging to the developing fetus. Certain medications, as well as recreational drugs, alcohol, and tobacco, are all dangerous, and in a number of tragic situations children have been damaged by medications taken by their mothers during pregnancy. As many as one in three infants may have been exposed to alcohol or other drugs in utero (Andrews & Patterson, 1995).

For example, the drug *thalidomide,* prescribed as a sedative to pregnant women in the early 1960s, was absorbed into the circulatory systems of fetuses, causing severe deformities to the extremities. A drug used to treat severe acne, Accutane, creates a risk of having a baby with a major malformation that is almost as high as that of thalidomide (Lammer et al., 1985). Some grown children of women who were given diethylstilbestrol (DES) while pregnant have developed genital tract abnormalities, including cancer. Tetracycline, a frequently used antibiotic, can damage an infant's teeth and cause stunted bone growth if it is taken after the fourteenth week of pregnancy. Antibiotics need to be prescribed selectively during pregnancy (Lynch et al., 1991). In animal studies, even nonprescription drugs such as aspirin have been implicated in fetal abnormalities. Toxic substances found in the polluted environment can also harm fetal development (Haney, 1994). Even caffeine—more than one cup of coffee a day—has been associated with lower birth weight (Vlajinac et al., 1997).

Some substances known to cause harm to the mother (see Table 12.3) also pose serious hazards to a developing fetus. Women who use illegal drugs may not report their use to their prenatal care health provider (Lindsay et al., 1997). The babies of mothers who regularly use addictive drugs such as amphetamines, heroin, cocaine, codeine, morphine, or opium during pregnancy are often born premature and with low birth weight and size (Sprauve et al., 1997). In addition, following birth these babies experience withdrawal from the drug: They have tremors, disturbed feeding and sleep patterns, and abnormal muscle tension and often require hospitalization in neonatal intensive care (Behnke et al., 1997). Approximately 100,000 cocaine-exposed infants are born each year. Children born to women who abuse cocaine have reduced head circumference and may experience permanent birth defects and damage to sensory, motor, and cognitive abilities (Eyler et al.,

1998; Jacobson et al., 1994). Mental and physical impairments in development can continue past infancy (Zambrana & Scrimshaw, 1997).

Another serious health hazard for the fetus is cigarette smoking (Källen, 1997). Approximately 29% of pregnant women in the United States smoke during their pregnancies. Passive smoking—exposure to cigarette smoke of others—affects the fetus as well (Ahluwalia et al., 1997). Exposure to cigarette smoke increases the chances of spontaneous abortion and of pregnancy complications that can result in fetal or infant death. Smoking reduces the amount of oxygen in the bloodstream, which can adversely affect the fetus by slowing its growth. Infants of mothers who smoked during pregnancy often weigh less and have increased breathing irregularities during sleep (Secker-Walker et al., 1997). In addition, children of mothers who smoked during their pregnancies have significantly lower developmental scores (Olds et al., 1994) and increased incidence of reading disorders compared with matched offspring of nonsmokers. Smoking also increases the incidence of serious and potentially lethal pregnancy and birth complications for the mother (McLaren & Neiburg, 1988). In addition, evidence suggests that maternal smoking increases the risk of childhood cancer (John et al., 1991). Children in nonsmoking families are less likely to get respiratory diseases such as bronchitis and pneumonia (Charlton, 1994). Most important, mothers who quit smoking in the first trimester had fewer preterm deliveries and low-birth-weight infants than those who continued smoking (Mainous & Hueston, 1994).

Table 12.3 Avoid During Pregnancy

- Alcohol
- Smoking
- Secondary smoke
- Illegal drugs
- Any over-the-counter and prescription medication not approved by your health care provider

Fetal alcohol syndrome (FAS) is the leading cause of developmental disabilities and birth defects in the United States. More than 8000 infants are born each year with FAS (Stutts et al., 1997). The numbers of women who reported drinking during pregnancy actually increased from 1991 to 1995; approximately 16% reported drinking in the previous month (Centers for Disease Control, 1997a). Heavy alcohol use can cause intrauterine death and spontaneous abortion, premature birth, congenital heart defects, damage to the brain and nervous system, and numerous physical malformations of the fetus. Any alcohol use can cause problems, and binge drinking (five or more drinks per occasion) is extremely toxic to the fetus (Nanson, 1997). Women who binge drink during pregnancy also often report using tobacco, cocaine, marijuana, and other illicit drugs (Gladstone et al., 1997). Most babies with FAS have below-normal IQs. Infants may be born addicted to alcohol and, consequently, experience alcohol withdrawal for several days following birth. The fetus is at risk of developing FAS if the mother has six or more drinks per day during her pregnancy. However, even one drink per day has also been associated with adverse birth effects. In 1981 the Food and Drug Administration advised women to abstain *completely* from alcohol use during pregnancy to avoid the risk of damage to their babies (Nanson, 1997). The effects of FAS persist through childhood; children with FAS continue to be small in size and developmentally delayed and to have behavior problems (Stutts et al., 1997).

Fetal alcohol syndrome (FAS)
Syndrome caused by heavy maternal prenatal alcohol use; characterized by congenital heart defects, damage to the brain and nervous system, numerous physical malformations of the fetus, and below-normal IQ.

Attempting to protect the fetus from harm, legal interventions with pregnant women who are abusing drugs and alcohol have occurred in recent years (Epstein, 1997b). State and local authorities have attempted to enforce involuntary drug testing, addictions treatment, or criminal prosecution and incarceration. In 1997 South Carolina's Supreme Court ruled that a viable fetus was protected under child-abuse laws and that a pregnant woman could be charged with doing harm to the fetus (Donnelly, 1997; Roan, 1998). These actions are usually discriminatory; they are rarely taken on upper-income white women whose drugs of choice tend to be alcohol or prescription drugs. Rather, most criminal prosecutors have pursued women who use illegal drugs. These tend to be low-income women of color served by public hospitals. Most of these criminal actions have been unsuccessful because the woman's confidentiality, privacy, and civil rights are protected by the Constitution. The U.S. Supreme Court has held that the basic human rights accorded to "persons" in the Constitution do not include fetuses (Andrews & Patterson, 1995).

Our knowledge about the effects of most of the drugs and other substances consumed by pregnant women is limited. What we do know now is that we are learning of more and more potential hazards. For this reason, no medications should be used during pregnancy unless they are absolutely necessary and are taken under close medical supervision.

Detection of Birth Defects

Amniocentesis
A procedure in which amniotic fluid is removed from the uterus and tested to determine if certain fetal birth defects exist.

Amniotic fluid
The fluid inside the amniotic sac surrounding the fetus during pregnancy.

Chorionic villus sampling (CVS)
A prenatal test that detects some birth defects.

If a woman and her physician have some reason to suspect that there may be fetal abnormalities, a reliable and accurate test known as **amniocentesis** (am′-nē-o-sen-TĒ-sis) can help establish whether certain problems exist (Wilson, 1998). The test is done during the fourteenth to sixteenth week of pregnancy. With the assistance of ultrasound guidance, a needle is inserted through the woman's abdominal wall and into the uterine cavity to draw out a sample of the **amniotic fluid** (fluid surrounding the fetus). Fetal cells from the fluid are cultured for chromosome analysis, and the fluid is tested in procedures that take two to three weeks to produce results (Whittle, 1998). A variety of potential birth defects can be detected by this means. However, many cannot be detected (Stranc et al., 1997).

Another technique for detection of birth defects is called **chorionic villus** (kō-rē-ON-ik VIL-us) **sampling,** or **CVS.** Chorionic villi are threadlike protrusions on a membrane surrounding the placenta. This test involves inserting a thin catheter with the assistance of ultrasound through the abdomen or vagina and cervix into the uterus, where a small sample of the chorionic villi is removed for analysis. This procedure has an advantage over amniocentesis: It can be done as early as the tenth week instead of the fourteenth (Ono, 1994).

Circumstances in which amniocentesis or CVS may be of benefit include maternal age over 35 years, a parent with a chromosomal defect, a previous child with defects such as *Down syndrome* (a chromosomal abnormality that results in impaired intellectual functioning and physical defects) or defects of the spine or spinal cord, or a familial background that suggests a significant risk of other disorders related to chromosomal abnormalities or metabolic defects. If the test results reveal a serious untreatable birth defect, the mother can have the pregnancy terminated. Amniocentesis and CVS involve the rare risks of damage to the fetus, induced miscarriage, and infection (Seligmann, 1992). Couples who have these procedures may also feel worried about harming the fetus, the possible diagnosis of abnormality, or having an abortion. For these reasons, the procedures are not recommended unless the potential risks are outweighed by the expected benefits.

In China, the 1995 "Law on Maternal Health Care" mandates premarital medical evaluations to determine if either partner has genetic, mental, or infectious diseases. These individuals must be cured or sterilized before being allowed to marry. In addition, doctors advise women whose fetuses have abnormalities to have an abortion. The goal is to prevent the transmission of genetic diseases in a country with 7% of the world's arable land and 22% of the world's population (Schmetzer, 1995).

Pregnancy After Age 35

Increasing numbers of women are deciding to have children after 35 years of age (Freda, 1994; Quimby, 1994). One out of every five women in the United States has her first baby after age 35 (Nachtigall, 1991), and first births among women older than 40 have increased 50% in the last 15 years (Muldoon, 1997b). Some couples are delaying childbearing for career, financial, or other reasons.

There are some increased risks to the fetus and mother with pregnancy at a later age. The rate of fetal defects due to chromosomal abnormalities (such as Down syndrome) rises with maternal age. The estimated risk of such fetal defects is 2.6 per thousand before age 30; it is 5.6 at age 35, 15.8 at age 40, and 53.7 at age 45 (Hook, 1981). However, healthy older women have no higher risk than younger women of having a child with birth defects *not* related to abnormal chromosomes (Baird et al., 1991).

Until recently it was thought that women age 35 and older were far more likely to experience serious complications of pregnancy and birth. However, many physicians have found that pregnancy after age 35 is both safe and not difficult to manage medically (Schrinsky, 1988). In fact, some research indicates that compared with first-time mothers in their mid-20s, women age 35 and older showed less anxiety and depression during pregnancy (Robinson et al., 1987). Women 35 and older may have higher rates of typical pregnancy and delivery complications, but have no increase in perinatal mortality

(Prysak et al., 1995). For women between ages 35 and 44, amniocentesis and elective abortion reduce the risk of bearing an infant with a severe birth defect to a level comparable with that for younger women (Catanzarite et al., 1995).

Another concern that women and their partners have when they consider postponing having a child until the woman is past her 20s is that her ability to become pregnant may be diminished. As women become older, their fertility decreases (Eisenberg & Schenker, 1997). However, for most women who want to postpone childbearing until they have completed their education and established themselves in a career, the risks are small compared with the benefits of waiting until they are ready.

Due to technological advances, women in their 40s, 50s, and even 60s can have babies begun by ovum donor IVF, as was first done in 1994 in Italy for a 59- and a 62-year-old woman. Donor eggs from young women eliminate the increased risk of genetic problems from an older woman's ovum. Screening for the mother's health also reduces risks of pregnancy-related health problems (Beck et al., 1994). Controversy about this practice is discussed in the box, "Assisted Reproductive Technology and Postmenopause Pregnancy."

Infant daughter, Cynthia, made her mother, at age 63, the oldest woman to give birth by assisted reproductive technology.

On the Edge

Assisted Reproductive Technology and Postmenopause Pregnancy

Circumstances lead some postmenopausal women to seek the help of assisted reproductive technology to become pregnant. A woman's child may have died, or she may not have had children and still wants to have a family. Reproductive technology has made it possible for women past the age of menopause to become pregnant, carry the pregnancy, and deliver their babies. The postmenopausal woman's own ova are not viable, but with hormonal assistance, her uterus can maintain a pregnancy. Ova are donated by a younger woman and fertilized with her husband's or donor sperm. The fertilized egg is inserted into the woman's uterus.

As of 1997, the oldest woman to give birth with the help of this technology was 63-year-old Arceli Keh. She and her husband had been married for 16 years and had no children, in spite of trying for a pregnancy since their marriage. She lied about her age to meet the infertility program's arbitrary guideline of 55 (Kolata, 1997b). After several failed embryo implantations, Arceli Keh became pregnant. The Kehs' daughter, Cynthia, weighed 6 lb., 4 oz., at birth and was very healthy. Her mother was able to breast-feed her. She and her husband are hoping to be able to have a second child (Glynn & Butterfield, 1997).

Also in 1997, actor Tony Randall became a first-time father at age 77, following in the footsteps of other men who became fathers in their sixties, seventies, and even eighties. Scientific and popular reactions to older men and women who have children are quite different. Little criticism is directed at the man who fathers late in life; in fact, paternity affirms his masculinity and virility. However, the older woman who becomes a mother is often judged negatively. Why do you think the typical reaction to a 60-year-old man versus a woman of similar age is so different?

Most of society agrees that assisted reproductive technology should be available to couples with infertility problems, but the general population is not supportive of using reproductive technologies to help older women have children (Eisenberg & Schenker, 1997). Doctors who provide this technological assistance to postmenopausal women have been accused of tampering with nature, acting irresponsibly, or playing God. Using assisted reproductive technology to treat infertility during the reproductive years when fertility is the norm is viewed as acceptable, but using it during menopause when infertility is the natural characteristic of that period is questioned (Ethics Committee of the American Society for Reproductive Medicine, 1997). Is it really ethical for women to be denied conception on the basis of age alone?

Life expectancy in the Western world is long enough to enable a healthy woman who has a child in her fifties or early sixties to raise the child into adulthood. Medical risks of pregnancy are greater for postmenopausal women (Kalb, 1997), but society does not prevent childbearing in younger women, even with life-threatening medical conditions.

Modern society protects the individual's right to privacy and reproductive choices. Modern society supports new reproductive choices due to the availability of assisted reproductive technologies. Younger women may have more physical energy for mothering, but an older woman deprived of parenthood for many years is highly motivated to focus her attention and resources to have a child. The wisdom and experience that accompany age are usually an advantage rather than a detriment to parenting. Older women who can afford to use reproductive technology are usually more financially secure and have more time to spend with their children than a younger woman (Eisenberg & Schenker, 1997). So what's the fuss about?

Childbirth

The full term of pregnancy usually lasts about 40 weeks from the last menstrual period, although there is some variation in length. Some women may have longer pregnancies; others may give birth to fully developed infants up to a few weeks before the nine-month term is over. The experience of childbirth also varies a good deal, depending on many factors: the woman's physiology, her emotional state, the baby's size and position, the kind of childbirth practices employed, and the kind of support she receives.

Contemporary Childbirth

Today's parents-to-be can expect to work as part of a team with their health care provider in preparing and planning for the physical and emotional aspects of childbirth. Most hospitals and health care providers are eager to help provide a safe and positive birth experience for the entire family. A cooperative effort involving all members of the team is most important. Each birth is different, and the variations are not predictable. Parents-to-be often participate in childbirth classes that provide thorough information about medical interventions and the process of labor and birth. The classes also provide training for the pregnant woman and her labor coach (either her partner or a friend) in breathing and relaxation exercises designed to cope with the pain of childbirth.

Approaches to contemporary childbirth began to develop when Grantly Dick-Read and Fernand Lamaze began presenting their ideas about childbirth in the late 1930s and early 1940s. They believed that certain attitudes and practices could help improve the experience of childbirth. Dick-Read believed that most of the pain during childbirth stemmed from the muscle tension caused by fear. To reduce anxiety, he advocated education about the birth process and relaxation with calm, consistent support during a woman's labor. The **Lamaze** philosophy is similar. This method consists of learning to voluntarily relax abdominal and perineal muscles and to use breathing exercises to dissociate the involuntary labor contractions from pain sensations. Although both of these methods are now incorporated into childbirth education classes throughout the United

Lamaze
A method of childbirth preparation using breathing and relaxation.

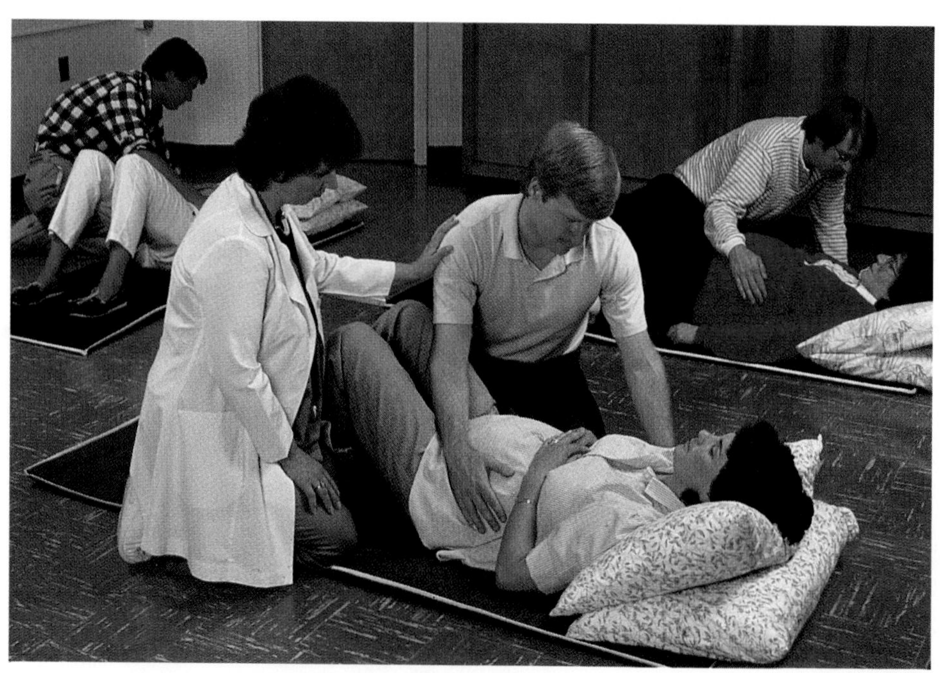

Prepared childbirth classes, such as this one, help prepare expectant mothers and fathers for childbirth.

States, women in the 1950s and 1960s who wanted to use these methods frequently had difficulty finding physicians willing to support them in the hospital. Because they questioned established obstetrical practice, these women were often seen as compromising the health of their infants. However, as feminists pursued women's rights in many areas, they stressed involvement in decision making about pregnancy and birth (Larimore, 1995). Their criticisms received extensive media coverage, and the public's concept of childbirth gradually changed, creating a demand for more flexible, family-centered birth experiences—which health care practitioners also began to support (Toussie-Weingarten & Jacobwitz, 1987).

Although they are sometimes referred to as "natural" childbirth methods, **prepared childbirth** is a more appropriate label for the Dick-Read, Lamaze, and other childbirth approaches. A woman and her partner are indeed preparing themselves when they participate in prepared-childbirth classes and rehearse these techniques during pregnancy. An additional benefit of prepared childbirth is the company and support of the labor coach, often the woman's partner. Contrary to the old image of the expectant father pacing in the waiting room, hospitals now permit labor coaches in the birthing or delivery room for uncomplicated vaginal—and in many cases, cesarean—births. Recent research found that women assisted by a trained birth attendant during labor had fewer cesarean sections, less pain medication, shorter length of labor, and greater satisfaction with the birth experience (McNiven et al., 1992).

Prepared childbirth
Birth following an education process that can involve information, exercises, breathing, and working with a labor coach.

Birthplace Alternatives

Along with more options for childbirth practices have come new options for places where childbirth occurs. Not many years ago, a husband, partner, family member, or labor coach could not be with the woman during labor and childbirth. The hospital setting was cold and impersonal, and the woman had little control over the medical procedures used during the birth process. But in recent years, as choices about labor and birth have increased, so have options for childbirth settings. Each birthplace is unique in terms of what it offers the parents and the infant.

Hospital Births

Hospitals have grown more receptive to individualized birth in recent years, and many now have *birthing rooms* with a homelike atmosphere. A birthing room offers families the opportunity for an emotionally supportive, homelike birth and yet has the medical backup services of the hospital. Participation of a partner, labor coach, and others; unmedicated childbirth; and immediate postbirth parent–infant contact are increasingly available. The following account describes a hospital birthing-room experience:

> My husband and I had a great deal of privacy during labor. We had consulted with our doctor prior to delivery. She agreed to use no medications unless I consented, and to let me try the sitting-up and holding-my-knees position during second-stage pushing. Our baby stayed with us awhile, and our parents could see the baby minutes after he was born. It really felt like *our* delivery rather than "being delivered." (Authors' files)

Regulations vary among physicians and hospitals, but most hospitals provide for experiences like this one. It is important to discuss and agree on childbirth plans with the practitioner before the time of birth.

An important aspect of the hospital setting is that it provides emergency medical care should birth complications arise. The hospital is the appropriate place for childbirth in any high-risk pregnancy. Conditions that raise the risk of complication include premature labor, the infant being in other than head-first

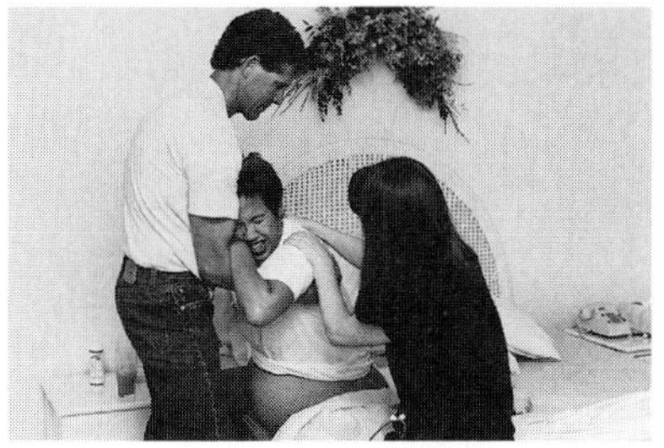

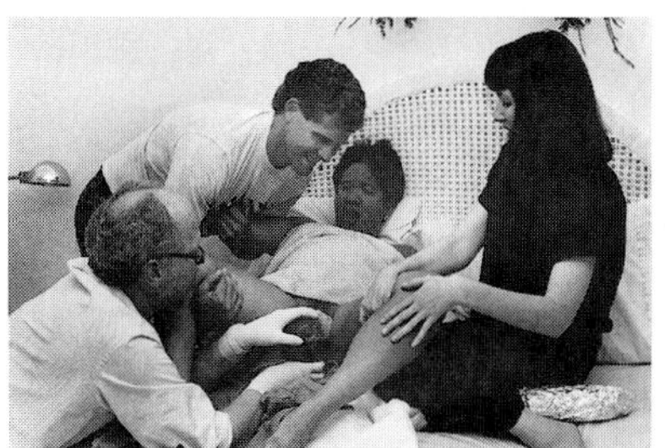

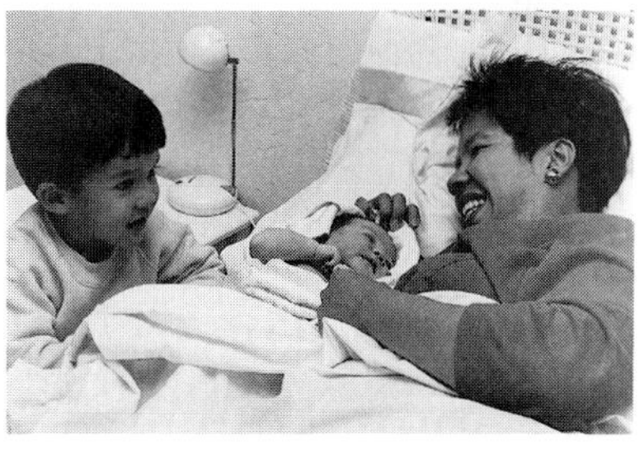

A birth in a birthing room.

Toxemia A dangerous condition during pregnancy in which high blood pressure occurs.

Placenta previa A birth complication in which the placenta is between the cervical opening and the infant.

presentation, blood incompatibility between mother and fetus, **toxemia** (toks-Ē-mē-a) (water retention and high blood pressure are early symptoms—the condition may result in convulsions if untreated), **placenta previa** (pla-SEN-ta PRĒ-vē-a) (the placenta positioned over the cervical opening), multiple births, five or more previous births, too small a pelvis, or maternal illness (Lieberman, 1987). Competent and thorough prenatal screening can detect most of these complications. However, even a birth that is expected to be low-risk can develop complications that require medical intervention.

Birthing Centers

Birthing centers, available in some areas, offer the homelike atmosphere of the birthing rooms in hospitals. Some are adjacent to hospitals, and others are separate, freestanding organizations. Limited emergency equipment is available at a birthing center. In the event of a serious complication, however, the woman would have to be transported to a hospital—for example, if an emergency cesarean birth were required. Only women with no foreseeable likelihood of birth complications should be accepted for care in a birthing center (Toussie-Weingarten & Jacobwitz, 1987).

Home Birth

Home birth became more common when families began seeking the family-centered birth experience that, in the past, hospitals did not provide. Proponents of home birth believe that with precautions—careful prenatal screening for complications, thorough preparations, a skilled attendant, and available emergency transportation—home birth can be relatively safe (Saunders, 1997). However, few physicians or certified nurse-midwives will assist with home births when hospitals are available because of both the medical risks and the possibility of malpractice suits from unfavorable birth outcomes (Toussie-Weingarten & Jacobwitz, 1987). The primary advantages of home birth are the familiar surroundings, the involvement of other family members or friends, and the reduced cost.

The greatest risks associated with home births are that lifesaving emergency equipment is not readily available and that emergencies are not always predictable. Opponents of home birth believe that having a baby at home presents an unnecessary risk to mother and infant. Controversy about home birth will continue due to the lack of research studies on its safety.

Stages of Childbirth

First-stage labor The initial stage of childbirth, in which regular contractions begin and the cervix dilates.

Effacement Flattening and thinning of the cervix that occurs before and during childbirth.

Second-stage labor The middle stage of labor, in which the infant descends through the vaginal canal.

Despite variations in childbirth, there are three generally recognizable stages in the process (see Figure 12.8). A woman can often tell that labor has begun when regular contractions of the uterus begin. Another indication of beginning **first-stage labor,** the gradual dilation of the cervix to 10 centimeters, may be the "bloody show" (discharge of the mucus plug from the cervix). The amniotic sac may rupture in the first stage of labor, an occurrence sometimes called "breaking the bag of waters." First-stage labor is shown in Figure 12.8a.

Before the first stage begins, the cervix usually has already **effaced** (flattened and thinned) and dilated slightly. It continues to dilate throughout the first stage, and it is the extent of dilation that defines the early, late, and "transition" phases of first-stage labor. The cervix is dilated up to 4 cm during the early phase, 4–8 cm in the active phase, and 8–10 cm during the final, or transition, phase of the first stage. Each phase becomes shorter, and the contractions become stronger; transition is usually the most intense. The first stage is the longest of the three stages, usually lasting 10–16 hours for the first childbirth and 4–8 hours in subsequent births.

Second-stage labor begins when the cervix is fully dilated and the infant descends farther into the vaginal birth canal. Usually the descent is head first, as shown in Figure

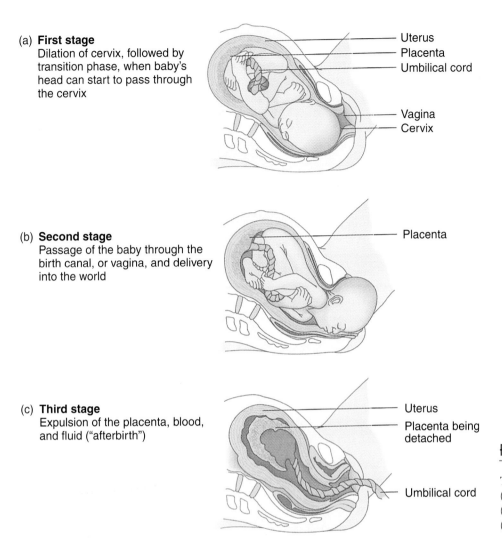

(a) **First stage**
Dilation of cervix, followed by transition phase, when baby's head can start to pass through the cervix

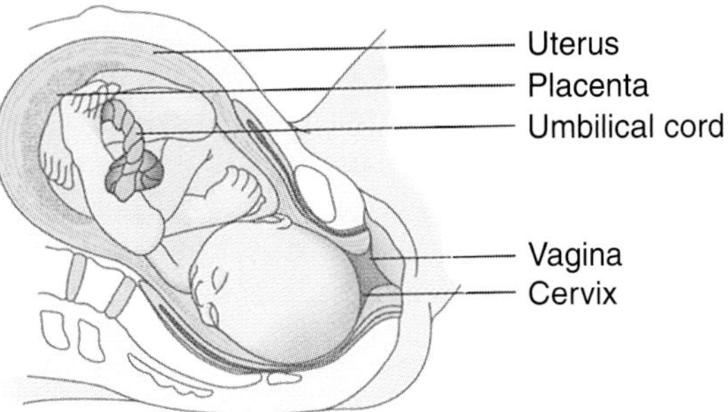

(b) **Second stage**
Passage of the baby through the birth canal, or vagina, and delivery into the world

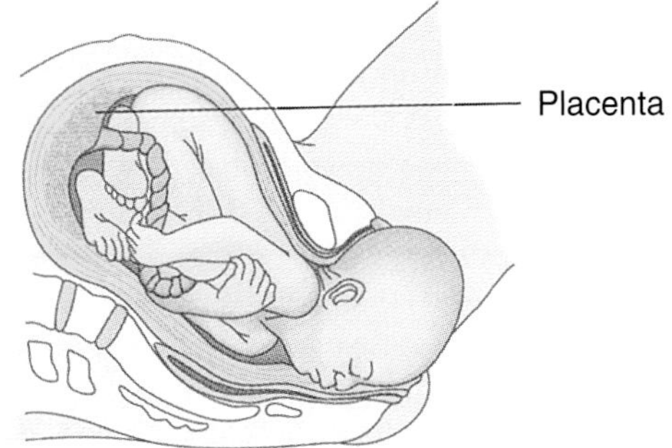

(c) **Third stage**
Expulsion of the placenta, blood, and fluid ("afterbirth")

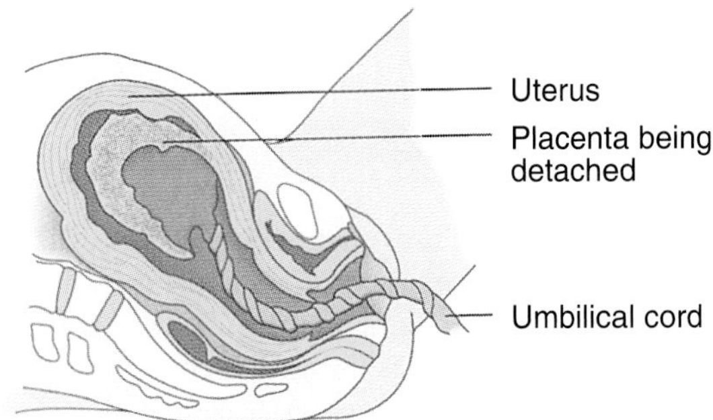

Figure 12.8

The three stages of childbirth: (a) first-stage labor, (b) second-stage labor, and (c) third-stage labor.

12.8b. The second stage often lasts from a half-hour to two hours—although it may be shorter or longer. During this time the woman can actively push to help the baby out, and many women report their active pushing to be the best part of labor:

> I knew what "labor" meant when I was finally ready to push. I have never worked so hard, so willingly. (Authors' files)

The second stage ends when the infant is born.

Third-stage labor lasts from the time of birth until the delivery of the placenta, shown in Figure 12.8c. With one or two more uterine contractions, the placenta usually separates from the uterine wall and comes out of the vagina, generally within a half-hour after the baby is born. The placenta is also called the **afterbirth.**

Third-stage labor
The last stage of childbirth, in which the placenta separates from the uterine wall and comes out of the vagina.

Afterbirth
The placenta and amniotic sac following their expulsion through the vagina after childbirth.

Medical Interventions: Pros and Cons

Women and their partners should be aware of the possible benefits and side effects of medical procedures used during childbirth (Saunders, 1997). Administering or using medications, fetal heart monitors, vacuum extraction and forceps, and performing an episiotomy or cesarean section are common medical interventions whose advantages and disadvantages need to be discussed with the health care provider before labor begins.

Medications

Local and regional anesthesia (such as spinal and epidural anesthesia) have negligible effects on the fetus and can greatly help the ease and comfort of labor (Volm, 1997). Medications containing narcotics affect the fetus as well as the mother. Research indicates that some medications can slow or stop labor, decrease blood pressure, and eliminate the ability to push during second-stage labor (Willson et al., 1983). The risks are small when medications are chosen and administered cautiously, and the woman can have a positive childbirth experience while being physically more comfortable during labor and childbirth (Schrinsky, 1988).

Episiotomy

Episiotomy
An incision in the perineum that is sometimes made during childbirth.

Performing an **episiotomy** (e-pis′-ē-OT-ō-me), or making an incision in the perineum from the vagina toward the anus, is sometimes done in hospital births (see Figure 12.9). The rationale for episiotomies is that they reduce the pressure on the infant's head and also help prevent vaginal tearing, which is more difficult to suture than a straight incision and often heals less well. Episiotomies also are thought to help preserve pelvic muscle tone and support. However, research shows that routine episiotomy during uncomplicated labor presents greater risks than benefits (Maier & Malony, 1997). Although the procedure is common in the United States, it is not considered necessary in most other countries (only 8% of birthing women in Holland, for example, have episiotomies). Relaxation, proper breathing and pushing, physician patience, manual stretching of the perineum, and freedom of leg movement can eliminate the need for many routine incisions.

The Use of Forceps

Forceps, a medical instrument shaped like salad tongs and designed to clasp the baby's head, are sometimes used to assist the infant out of the birth canal. Forceps are often used after analgesics and anesthetics have reduced the strength of uterine contractions. Careful use of forceps is justified in appropriate circumstances but not with routine, normal births. Vacuum extraction, placing a vacuum cup on the emerging baby's head, can also be used to help pull the infant through the birth canal (Paluska, 1997).

Delivery by Cesarean Section

Cesarean section
A childbirth procedure in which the infant is removed through an incision in the abdomen and uterus.

A **cesarean** (si-ZĀR-ē-an) **section,** in which the baby is removed through an incision made in the abdominal wall and uterus, can be lifesaving surgery for the mother and child. Cesarean birth may be recommended in a variety of situations, including when the fetal head is too large for the mother's pelvic structure, during maternal illness, or when there are indications of fetal distress during labor, or birth complications such as a breech presentation (feet or bottom coming out of the uterus first) (Hage et al., 1988). Mothers who experience cesarean birth often have a spinal or epidural anesthetic and are awake to greet their infants when the baby is born. In many hospitals, fathers remain with the woman during cesarean births.

Once a woman has given birth by cesarean section, do you think it is possible to have subsequent babies with vaginal deliveries?

A woman may have more than one baby by cesarean section. Also, most women can have subsequent vaginal births, depending on the circumstances of the earlier cesarean birth(s) and of the subsequent birth (Boyers & Gilbert, 1998; Roosmalen, 1997). Although many women who have cesarean births are less satisfied with their birth experiences than are women who have vaginal births, adjustment following childbirth is similar in the two groups (Padawer et al., 1988).

The percentage of cesarean sections performed in the United States increased dramatically after the mid-1960s and was the most common hospital surgical procedure in

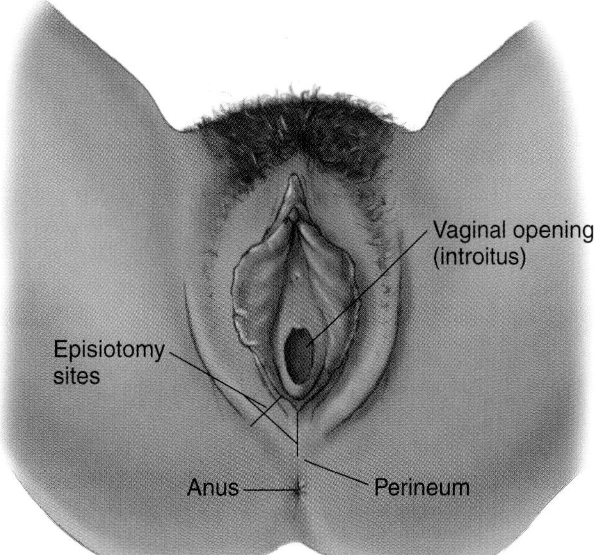

Figure 12.9

In an episiotomy, an incision is made in the perineum from the vagina toward the anus. Two possible incision sites are shown here.

the United States. Cesarean sections were done for 25% of live births (Gregory et al., 1994). This rate evoked controversy, and the rate has been reduced to 21% (Centers for Disease Control, 1997b). Some maintain that high rates reflect better use of medical technology, but others believe that cesarean sections are too readily used (Lagrew, 1996).

Postpartum

The first several weeks following birth are referred to as the **postpartum period.** This is a time of both physical and psychological adjustment for each family member and is likely to be a time of intensified emotional highs and lows. Understanding that these feelings are a common response to adjustments to the new baby may help new parents cope with the stresses involved. One woman described her feelings during this time as follows:

Postpartum period The first several weeks following childbirth.

> That calm, sure, unambivalent woman who moved through the pages of the manuals I read seemed as unlike me as an astronaut. Nothing, to be sure, had prepared me for the intensity of relationship already existing between me and a creature I had carried in my body and now held in my arms and fed from my breasts. Throughout pregnancy and nursing, women are urged to relax, to mime the serenity of madonnas. No one mentions the psychic crisis of bearing a first child, the excitation of long-buried feelings about one's own mother, the sense of confused power and powerlessness. . . . No one mentions the strangeness of attraction—which can be as single-minded and overwhelming as the early days of a love affair—to a being so tiny, so dependent, so folded-into itself—who is, and yet is not, part of oneself. (Rich, 1976, p. 36)

Combined with heightened excitement and happiness are often other feelings. The mother may cry easily without feeling fearful or sad (Zelkowitz & Milet, 1995). One new mother describes her "postpartum euphoria":

I would cry from happiness at almost anything. I was simply overflowing with joy and amazement and love. (Authors' files)

Postpartum depression has been reported for 10–15% of mothers (Wood et al., 1997). Such reactions may be partly due to the sudden emotional, physical, and hormonal changes following birth. Sleep deprivation from waking many times in the night to care for the newborn also is very stressful and diminishes emotional and physical reserves.

The new baby also affects the roles and interactions of all family members. The parents may experience an increased closeness to each other as well as some troublesome feelings. A partner may sometimes feel jealous of the close relationship between the mother and child. Both partners may want extra emotional support from the other, but each may have less than usual to give. A good support system for the new parents can be immensely helpful. The time and energy demands of caring for an infant can contribute to weariness and stress—feelings that may be compounded by the responsibility of having to care for this young being for the next 20 years: Conflict about the division of household and childcare labor can become problematic in the early months and years of the child's life, and both new mothers and fathers may experience anxiety and concern (Cowan & Cowan, 1992). Brothers and sisters may also be affected, as they often have some negative feelings about the attention given their new sibling. Some hospitals offer classes for expectant brothers and sisters to help them anticipate and cope with changes the new baby will bring.

Each of these feelings and concerns tends to diminish gradually as the family makes adjustments to new roles and expectations. Often, too, the adjustment is easier when family members have realistic expectations (or previous experience) to prepare them for the demands as well as the pleasure of the new arrival.

Breast-Feeding

For women who decide to nurse, breast-feeding is another opportunity for close physical contact with the baby.

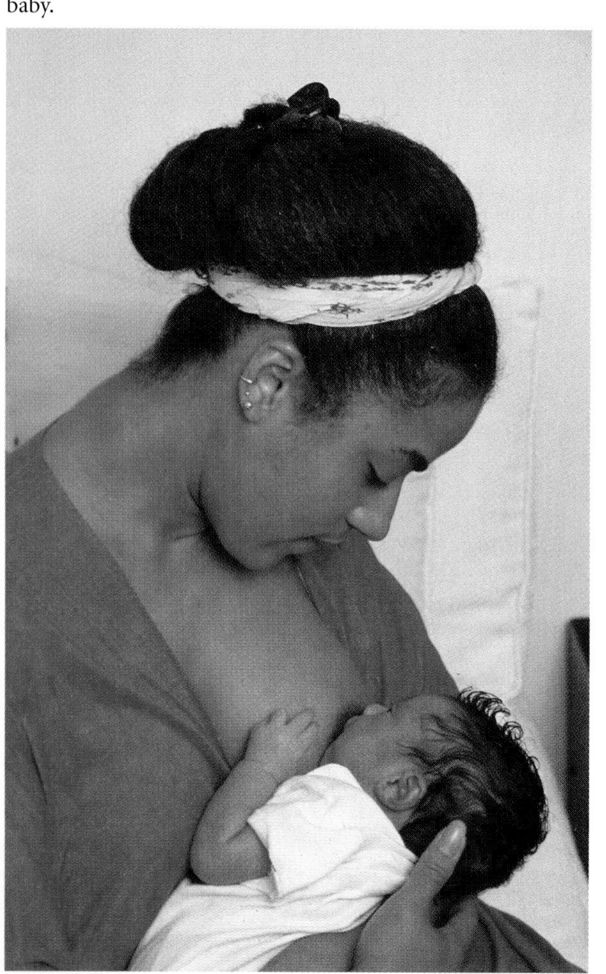

Right after birth, the breasts produce a yellowish liquid called colostrum, which contains antibodies and protein. Lactation, or milk production, begins about one to three days after birth. Pituitary hormones stimulate milk production in the breasts in response to the stimulation of the infant suckling the nipples. If a new mother does not begin or continue to nurse, milk production subsides within a matter of days.

Research shows that cigarette smoking reduces the amount of milk a nursing mother produces. Environmental, or secondary, smoke exposure from smokers around the mother also reduces the amount of milk she makes. Women who smoke or who inhale secondary smoke tend to nurse for shorter durations than mothers who do not smoke and are in smoke-free environments (Horta et al., 1997).

Nursing may temporarily inhibit ovulation, particularly for women who feed their babies only breast milk (Perez et al., 1992). However, as we saw in Chapter 11, nursing is not a reliable method of birth control. Estrogen-containing birth control pills should not be used during nursing because the hormones reduce the amount of milk and affect milk quality as well. However, progesterone-only pills can be used because progesterone affects neither milk supply nor quality (Salisbury, 1991). However, some couples prefer foam and condoms to avoid any extra hormones during nursing.

Breast-feeding has many practical and emotional advantages. Breast milk provides the infant with a digestible food filled with antibodies and other immunity-producing substances (Wold & Adlerberth, 1998). Nursing also induces uterine contractions that help speed the return of the uterus to its prepregnancy size. Breast-feeding can be a very positive emotional and sensual experience for the mother. For women who nurse, breast-feeding is another opportunity for close physical contact with the baby.

I love seeing the contentment spread over my baby's face as she fills her tummy with milk from my breasts. It's an awe-inspiring continuation of our physical connection during pregnancy to see her growing chubby-cheeked from nourishment my body provides her. (Authors' files)

Women with more positive attitudes toward sexuality in general are more likely to breast-feed and experience sexual interest and an earlier resumption of intercourse than are women with negative attitudes about sex (Fisher & Gray, 1988).

Nursing also has some short-term disadvantages. For one, nursing causes reduced levels of estrogen, which conditions and maintains vulvar tissue and promotes vaginal lubrication. As a result, the nursing mother's genitals may become sore from intercourse. The woman's breasts may also be tender and sore. Milk may be ejected involuntarily from her nipples during sexual stimulation—a source of potential amusement or embarrassment.

Some women may have negative feelings about breast-feeding. Many women feel ambivalent about this activity, perhaps partly because of our society's emphasis on breasts as sex symbols. Furthermore, some mothers' lives may be too demanding for the sole feeding responsibility of nursing, particularly if they return to work shortly after child-bearing (Ruben, 1992). It is often easier to share child-care responsibilities by bottle-feeding rather than nursing: The father can then play a greater role in holding and feeding the infant. However, a nursing mother can use a breast pump to extract her milk so that it is available to her partner or another caregiver for bottle-feeding the baby. Like other aspects of childcare, breast-feeding is a matter of exploration and personal preference.

Sexual Interaction After Childbirth

Lochia
A reddish uterine discharge that occurs following childbirth.

Couples are commonly advised that intercourse can resume after the flow of the reddish uterine discharge, called **lochia** (LŌ-kē-a), has stopped and after episiotomy incisions or vaginal tears have healed, usually about three to four weeks (Ono, 1994). However, most couples wait to resume intercourse after six to eight weeks following birth (Volm, 1997). An important factor to consider is when intercourse is physically comfortable for the woman. This depends on the type of birth, the size and presentation of the baby, the extent of episiotomy or lacerations, and the individual woman's rate of healing. The post-partum decrease in hormones, especially pronounced with breast-feeding, can cause discomfort during intercourse. After a cesarean birth, the couple needs to wait until the incision has healed enough for intercourse to occur without discomfort. Other sexual and affectionate relations can be shared while waiting.

Psychological readiness for sexual activity is another important factor. A new baby brings significant changes in daily life that can affect sexual intimacy. Desire for and frequency and satisfaction of sexual activity may decline during the first year following birth. An author of a book about pregnancy warns women to be prepared for their sex lives to be "downright crummy" for up to a year (Iovine, 1997b). "Mother Nature is using her entire arsenal of tricks, from hormones to humility, to keep you focused on your baby and not on getting pregnant again" (Iovine, 1997a, p. 158). Fatigue is a major factor. The demands on both the woman and her partner of caring for a new baby may mean that there is not much time or energy left for sexual expression. Fitting lovemaking into the baby's and parents' schedules can be quite a challenge. Concern about the baby can also interfere:

It seems that every time we start to make love, the baby cries. Even though I know he's been fed and is dry, I can't focus on my sexual feelings. And when he gets quiet, I worry that he's dead! My husband has the same reactions, so lots of times we don't get much going together. (Authors' files)

In addition, until the hormonal changes of pregnancy, birth, and breast-feeding have returned to the prepregnancy state, many women experience a decrease in sexual interest and response. It is important to note that men, as well as women, may not be particularly interested in sex in the first weeks or months following the birth of a baby (Gurian, 1988). Typically, women and men with more positive attitudes about sex in general show more sexual interest and earlier resumption of intercourse than do others with more negative attitudes about sexuality (Fisher & Gray, 1988).

Women and their partners whose sexual activity has been disrupted by pregnancy and birth may feel "out of practice" in their sexual relationship. It is often helpful to resume sexual activity in an unhurried, exploratory manner. Once intercourse is resumed, contraception is necessary if the woman wants to avoid another pregnancy.

Summary

PARENTHOOD AS AN OPTION

Increasing numbers of couples are choosing not to be parents. More women today choose careers over motherhood.

The realities of parenthood or child-free living are difficult to predict.

BECOMING PREGNANT

Timing intercourse to correspond to ovulation enhances the likelihood of conception.

Approximately one in six couples in the United States have problems with infertility, and a cause is not found in as many as 15% of infertile couples.

Failure to ovulate and blockage of the fallopian tubes are typical causes of female infertility. Low sperm count is the most common cause of male infertility.

Alcohol, drug use, cigarette smoking, and infections from sexually transmitted diseases reduce fertility in both women and men.

The emotional stress and the disruption of a couple's sexual relationship from infertility can result in sexual problems.

The legal and social issues related to artificial insemination, surrogate motherhood, and assisted reproductive technologies are complex and will continue to create controversy.

Artificial insemination is done with donor semen when the husband is infertile.

The first sign of a pregnancy is usually a missed menstrual period. Urine and blood tests and pelvic exams are used to determine pregnancy.

SPONTANEOUS AND ELECTIVE ABORTION

Spontaneous abortion, or miscarriage, occurs in approximately 10–20% of pregnancies. The majority of miscarriages occur within the first three months of pregnancy.

Elective abortion is a highly controversial social and political issue in the United States today. Suction curettage, D and E, prostaglandin induction, and medications are the medical techniques used to induce abortion.

Contraceptive method failure is a major contributor to women having repeat abortions.

Contraceptive risk taking sometimes precedes an unplanned pregnancy and consequent abortion.

In 1973 the U.S. Supreme Court legalized a woman's right to decide to terminate her pregnancy before the fetus reaches the age of viability. In 1977 the Hyde Amendment prohibited the use of federal Medicaid funds for abortion and limited low-income women's access to abortion. In the 1990s many state legislatures are imposing further limitations on the availability of abortion.

Prochoice and prolife advocates have fundamental differences in their beliefs about many aspects of life.

THE EXPERIENCE OF PREGNANCY

Some first-trimester physical changes include cessation of menstruation, fatigue, and breast tenderness. In the second trimester, the woman's abdomen begins to protrude, and she can feel fetal movements. By the third trimester, the abdomen is enlarged, and fetal movements are pronounced. Emotional reactions to pregnancy vary greatly.

Men have become increasingly involved in the prenatal, childbirth, and childrearing processes.

Although changes of position may be necessary, sensual and sexual interaction may continue as desired during pregnancy, except in occasional cases of medical complications.

A HEALTHY PREGNANCY

Pregnancy is divided into three trimesters, each of which is marked by fetal changes.

Nutrient, oxygen, and waste exchange between the woman and fetus occurs through the placenta. Substances harmful to the fetus can pass through the placenta from the mother's blood.

Smoking, alcohol and drug use, and certain medications can severely damage the developing fetus.

Amniocentesis and chorionic villus sampling are two tests that can be done during pregnancy to screen for certain birth defects.

More women are deciding to have children after age 35. These women have slightly decreased fertility and a somewhat higher risk of conceiving a fetus with chromosomal abnormalities. However, with careful monitoring of pregnancy and childbirth, their risks can be reduced to the level of those of younger women.

CHILDBIRTH

Prepared childbirth, popularized by Fernand Lamaze and Grantly Dick-Read, has changed childbirth practices. Most hospitals now support participation of the woman's partner and a team approach to decision making about the birth process.

Birthing clinics and home birth are additional alternatives to hospital birth, but neither has the advantage of the complete emergency medical backup sometimes necessary during birth.

Indications of first-stage labor are regular contractions of the uterus, discharge of the mucus plug, rupture of the amniotic sac, and cervical effacement and dilation of up to 10 cm.

Second-stage labor is the descent of the infant into the birth canal, ending with birth. The placenta is delivered in the third stage.

Medical interventions during birth (administering medications, using forceps, and performing episiotomies and cesarean sections) can be helpful in the birth process, but some people believe that these interventions and procedures are overused.

POSTPARTUM

There are many physical, emotional, and family adjustments to be made following the birth of a baby.

Breast-feeding has regained popularity in the United States. There are advantages and disadvantages to both breast- and bottle-feeding.

Intercourse after childbirth can usually resume once the flow of lochia has stopped and any vaginal tears or the episiotomy incision has healed. However, it may take longer for sexual interest and arousal to return to normal.

Thought Provokers

1. If you were in a position of deciding whether a large research grant would go toward developing a perfect contraceptive or a cure for infertility, what would you decide? Why?
2. If preconception sex selection became 100% accurate and inexpensive, what do you think the consequences would be?
3. What would you do if you or your partner were pregnant with sextuplets?
4. When you were born, what was your mother's birth experience like? Your father's?

Suggested Readings

Allen, Marie; and Marks, Shelly (1993). *Women Sharing from the Heart.* New York: Wiley. A book about women's experiences with miscarriage.

Cowan, Carolyn; and Cowan, Philip (1992). *When Partners Become Parents.* New York: Basic Books. This book describes the challenges facing couples with the arrival of a first child. It is based on a 10-year study of 100 couples.

Genevie, Louis; and Margolies, Eva (1987). *The Motherhood Report.* New York: Macmillan. An in-depth study of 1000 women addressing how they really feel about being mothers. It includes discussions of pregnancy, childbirth, and stages of childhood.

Gorney, Cynthia (1998). *Articles of Faith: A Frontline History of the Abortion Wars.* New York: Simon and Schuster. A thoughtful and balanced account of the battles over abortion.

Iovine, Vicki (1997). *The Girlfriends' Guide to Pregnancy.* New York: A Perigee Book. Warm and witty advice about pregnancy.

Louv, Richard (1993). *Fatherlove.* New York: Pocket Books. The fulfillment of fathering with one's children, bonding with one's father, grandchildren, and community are explored.

Nilsson, Lennart (1977). *A Child Is Born.* New York: Dell. A classic book of wonderful photographs of fetal development.

Reynolds, Karina (1997). *Pregnancy and Birth: Your Questions Answered.* New York: DK Publishing. Expert advice from a midwife and two obstetricians about every stage of pregnancy and birth. Excellent photos.

Rosenthal, Sara (1996). *The Fertility Sourcebook.* Los Angeles: Lowell House. A complete guide to planning conception, finding the right specialist, and evaluating fertility treatments.

Resources

International Childbirth Education Association, P.O. Box 20048, Minneapolis, MN 55420. Provides information and resources for childbirth education.

Resolve, Inc., 5 Water Street, Arlington, MA 02174-4814; (617) 643-2724. A national nonprofit organization that provides support groups, education, and publications for couples struggling with infertility.

Web Resources

www.

Alan Guttmacher Institute
www.agi-usa.org/
This nonprofit institute sponsors a great deal of useful research on issues relating to sexuality. Among the resources provided on its Web site: information on contraception, abortion, pregnancy, and birth.

National Abortion and Reproductive Rights Action League
www.naral.org/
A staunch advocacy group for abortion rights, the NARAL Web site provides a variety of information related to reproductive health.

InterNational Council on Infertility Information Dissemination (INCIID)
www.inciid.org/
For those who are in need of more information on infertility, this Web site offers fact sheets, recent news, geographical listings of health specialists in this field, and an opportunity to participate in chat discussions with experts.

13

Sexuality During Childhood and Adolescence

My earliest recollection of an experience that could be labeled as sexual in nature involved thrusting against the pillow in my crib and experiencing something that felt really good, which I now believe must have been an orgasm (actually, I remember doing this many times). I was probably around two at the time, give or take a few months. What is odd about these early experiences is that I distinctly remember sleeping in my parents' bedroom, but never being reprimanded for this "self-abuse" behavior. Either my parents were very heavy sleepers, or they were very avant garde in their view of sex. Knowing my parents, I presume the former is true. (Authors' files)

In many Western societies, including the United States, it was once common to view the period between birth and puberty as a time when sexuality remains unexpressed. However, as many of you can no doubt attest to from your own experiences, the early years of life are by no means a period of sexual dormancy. Perhaps you may even recall sensual/sexual experiences similar to the above account that may date from the early years of your life. In this chapter we will outline many of the common sexual experiences and behaviors that take place during the formative years from infancy through adolescence.

Sexual Behavior During Infancy and Childhood

Research over the last several decades has clearly demonstrated that a variety of behaviors and body functions, including sexual eroticism, develop during infancy and childhood. In some ways, sexuality may be especially important during this period because many experiences during these formative years may have great impact on the latter expression of adult sexuality. In the opening section of this chapter, we briefly outline some typical sexual and sensual behaviors that occur during infancy and childhood.

Infant Sexuality

In the first two years of life, a period generally referred to as infancy, many girls and boys discover the pleasures of genital stimulation (Lidster & Horsburgh, 1994). As reflected in the quote from the authors' files that opens this chapter, this activity often involves thrusting or rubbing the genital area against an object such as a doll or pillow. Pelvic thrusting and other signs of sexual arousal in infants, such as vaginal lubrication and penile erection, are often misinterpreted or unacknowledged. However, careful observers may note these indicators of sexuality in the very young (Calderone, 1983; Lively & Lively, 1991; Montauk & Clasen, 1989). In some cases, infants, both male and female, have been observed experiencing what appears to be an orgasm. The infant, of course, cannot offer spoken confirmation of the sexual nature of such reactions. However, the behavior is so remarkably similar to that exhibited by sexually responding adults that little doubt exists about its nature. The following quotation from Alfred Kinsey and his associates' book on female sexuality details the observations of a mother who had frequently observed her very young daughter engaging in unmistakably masturbatory activity:

> Lying face down on the bed, with her knees drawn up, she started rhythmic pelvic thrusts, about one second or less apart. The thrusts were primarily pelvic, with the legs tensed in a fixed position. The forward components of the thrusts were in a smooth and perfect rhythm which was unbroken except for momentary pauses during which the genitalia were readjusted against the doll on which they were pressed; the return from each thrust was convulsive, jerky. There were 44 thrusts in unbroken rhythm, a slight momentary pause, 87 thrusts followed by

> a slight momentary pause, concentration and intense breathing with abrupt jerks as orgasm approached. She was completely oblivious to everything during these later stages of the activity. Her eyes were glassy and fixed in a vacant stare. There was noticeable relief and relaxation after orgasm. (Kinsey et al., 1953, pp. 104–105)

Kinsey also detailed references to male infant sexuality:

> The orgasm in an infant or other young male is, except for lacking of ejaculation, a striking duplicate of orgasm in an older adult. The behavior involves a series of gradual physiologic changes, the development of rhythmic body movements with distinct penis throbs and pelvic thrusts, an obvious change in sensory capacities, a final tension of muscles, especially of the abdomen, hips, and back, a sudden release with convulsions, including rhythmic anal contractions—followed by the disappearance of all symptoms. A fretful babe quiets down under the initial sexual stimulation, is distracted from other activities, begins rhythmic pelvic thrusts, becomes tense as climax approaches, is thrown into convulsive action, often with violent arm and leg movements, sometimes with weeping at the moment of climax. (Kinsey et al., 1948, p. 177)

It is impossible to determine what such early sexual experiences mean to infants, but it is reasonably certain that these activities are gratifying. Many infants of both sexes engage quite naturally in self-pleasuring unless such behavior produces strong negative responses from parents or other caregivers.

Clearly, an infant is unable to differentiate sexual pleasure from other forms of sensual enjoyment. As reflected in the following quote, many of the natural, everyday activities involved in caring for an infant, such as breast-feeding and bathing, may involve pleasurable tactile stimulation that, although essentially sensual in nature, may stimulate a genital or sexual response (Frayser, 1994).

> Most activities associated with nurturing and hygienic care of babies is intimate and sensuous since it involves contact with sensitive organs—lips, mouth, anus, and genitals—that can produce in the infant a physiological response of a sensuous and sexual nature. These activities include (in addition to breast feeding) toilet training, bathing, cleaning, and diapering. (Martinson, 1994, p. 11)

Childhood Sexuality

People show considerable variation in their sexual development during childhood, and diverse influences are involved. Despite these differences, however, certain common features in the developmental sequence tend to emerge. As we outline some of these typical behaviors, keep in mind that each person's unique sexual history may differ in some respects from the described behaviors. It is also important to realize that most of what we know about childhood sexual behavior is based on recollections of adults who are asked to recall childhood experiences. As we noted in Chapter 2, it may be quite difficult to remember accurately experiences that occurred many years earlier.

A child may learn to express her or his affectionate and sensual feelings through activities such as kissing and hugging. The responses the child receives to these expressions of intimacy may have a strong influence on the manner in which he or she expresses sexuality in later years. The inclinations we have as adults toward giving and receiving affection seem to be related to our early opportunities for warm, pleasurable contact with significant others, particularly parents (Hatfield, 1994; Montauk & Clasen, 1989; Prescott, 1989). A number of researchers believe that children who are deprived of "contact comfort" (being touched and held) during the first months and years of life may have difficulty establishing intimate relationships later in their lives (Harlow & Harlow, 1962; Montagu & Matson, 1979; Prescott, 1989). Furthermore, other research suggests that affection and physical

Enjoying sexual intimacies as an adult may be related to childhood experiences of warm, pleasurable contact, particularly with parents.

violence are, to some extent, mutually exclusive. For example, a study of 49 separate societies found that in cultures where children are nurtured with physical affection there are few instances of adult violence. Conversely, high levels of adult violence are manifested in those cultures in which children are deprived of physical affection (Prescott, 1975).

Childhood Masturbation

Infants may fondle their genitals and masturbate by rubbing or thrusting their genital area against an object such as a pillow or doll, but the rhythmic manipulation of the genitals associated with adult masturbation generally does not occur until a child reaches the age of two and a half or three years (Martinson, 1994).

Masturbation is one of the most common sexual expressions during the childhood years. In various studies, approximately one-third of female respondents and two-thirds of males reported having masturbated prior to adolescence (Elias & Gebhard, 1969; Friedrich et al., 1991; Hunt, 1974). Most boys learn about masturbating from friends, and some may even receive instructions in the particulars of self-stimulation, as the following account indicates:

An older friend taught me about masturbation. One day in his basement, while we were changing from wet swim suits, he asked me if I had ever "jerked off." Well, I hadn't, and he proceeded to soap up his penis and demonstrate his technique. When I tried it, the sensations were very good but, unlike my friend, nothing came out of my penis. He told me to keep practicing, and I did. Several months later, I had my first ejaculation. (Authors' files)

In contrast to boys, most young girls do not discuss masturbation with friends. For them, discovery of this activity is usually a solitary and often an accidental event:

I discovered how to masturbate when I was about eight years old. My mother always encouraged me to thoroughly wash my "privates." One day in the tub, I decided to make them "squeaky clean." I slid my bottom under the faucet and directed a stream of warm water over my vulva. Wow! That was one kind of washing I really liked. In fact, I had my first orgasm, even though I didn't know what you called it. I soon improvised all kinds of ways to squirt water over my clitoris. (Authors' files)

It is clear that self-discovery and peer interactions are very important during childhood development of sexuality. These factors continue to be influential during the adolescent years, as we will discover later in this chapter. But first we turn our attention to the physical changes that accompany the onset of adolescence.

Parental reactions to self-pleasuring can be a very important influence on developing sexuality. In American society comments about masturbation that pass from parent to child are typically either nonexistent or often negative. Think back to your youth. Did your parents ever express to you that they accepted this activity? Or did you have an intuitive sense that your parents were comfortable with self-pleasuring in their children? Probably not. Most often, a verbal message to "stop doing that," a disapproving look, or a slap on the hand are the responses children receive to masturbation. These gestures may be noted even by a very young child who does not yet have developed language capabilities.

How can adults convey their acceptance of this very natural and normal form of self-exploration? One way to begin is by not reacting negatively to the genital fondling that is typical of infants and young children. Later, as we respond to children's questions about their bodies, it may be desirable to mention the potential for pleasure that exists in their genital anatomy ("It feels good when you touch it"). Respecting privacy—for example, knocking before entering a child's room—is another way to foster comfort with this very personal activity. Perhaps you may feel comfortable with making specific accepting responses to self-pleasuring activity in your children, as did the parent in the following account:

One day my seven-year-old son joined me on the couch to watch a football game. He was still in the process of toweling off from a shower. While he appeared to be engrossed in the activity on the screen, I noticed one hand was busy stroking his penis. Suddenly his eyes caught mine observing him. An uneasy grin crossed his face. I wasn't sure how to respond, so I simply stated, "It feels good, doesn't it?" He didn't say anything, nor did he continue touching himself, but his smile grew a little wider. I must admit I had some initial hesitancy in openly indicating my approval for such behavior. I was afraid he might begin openly masturbating in the presence of others. However, my fears were demonstrated to be groundless in that he continues to be quite private about such activity. It is gratifying to know that he can experience the pleasures of his body without the unpleasant guilt feelings that his father grew up with. (Authors' files)

Many parents are reluctant to openly express their acceptance of masturbation, afraid that their children, armed with this parental stamp of approval, will go off to some cloistered area and masturbate away the hours. Although this is an understandable concern, available evidence does not suggest that this response is likely. Children have many other activities to occupy their time.

Another concern, voiced in the previous anecdote, is that children will begin masturbating openly in front of others if they are aware that their parents accept such behavior. This also is a reasonable concern. Very few of us would be enthusiastic about needing to deal with Johnny or Suzy masturbating in front of Grandma. However, children are generally aware enough of social expectations to maintain a high degree of privacy in something as emotionally laden and personal as self-pleasuring. Most of them are much more capable of making important discriminations than parents sometimes acknowledge. In the event that children do masturbate in the presence of others, it would seem reasonable for parents to voice their concerns, taking care to label the choice of location and not the activity as inappropriate.

Many children masturbate. Telling them to stop this behavior rarely eliminates it, even if such requests are backed with threats of punishment or claims that masturbation causes mental or physical deterioration. Rather, these negative responses will most likely succeed only in greatly magnifying the guilt and anxiety associated with this behavior.

Childhood Sex Play

Besides self-stimulation, prepubertal children often engage in play that may be viewed as sexual in nature (Friedrich et al., 1991; Leitenberg et al., 1989; Martinson, 1994). Such play takes place with friends or siblings of the same or the other sex. It may occur as early as the age of two or three, but it is more likely to take place between the ages of four and seven. Alfred Kinsey (1948 & 1953) noted that 45% of the females and 57% of the males in his sample reported having these experiences by age 12. In another survey, parents of six- and seven-year-old children reported that 76% of their daughters and 83% of their sons had participated in some sex play with friends or siblings (Kolodny, 1980). More recently, 61% of a sample of college students reported engaging in one or more forms of sex play with another child before age 13 (Greenwald & Leitenberg, 1989). The activities may range from exhibition and inspection of the genitals, often under the guise of "playing doctor," to simulating intercourse by rubbing genital regions together. Although most adults, particularly parents, tend to react to the apparent sexual nature of this play, for many children the play aspects of the interaction may be far more significant than any sexual overtones:

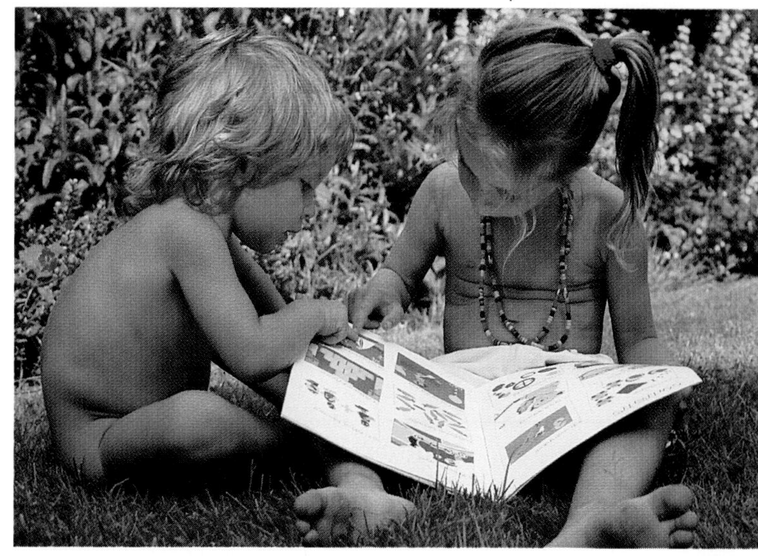

Many children find the play aspects of interactions such as this one more important than any sexual overtones.

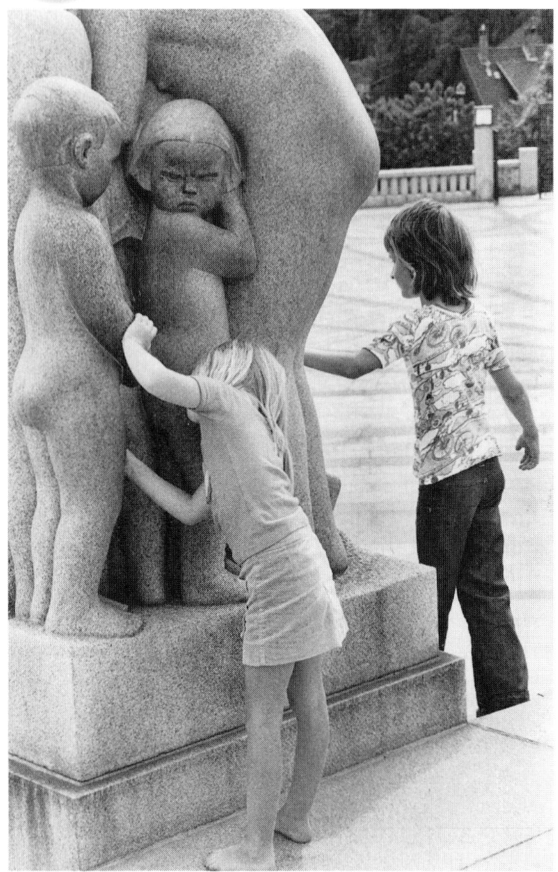

Childhood curiosity about sexuality takes many forms.

> When we think of preadolescent activities that look sexual—we, as adults, looking back on it, or as parents looking at it in our children—we respond to the sexual aspect; the sex is very important; the play is unimportant. To the child, however, the balance is exactly the opposite. The play is the major part; whatever sex might be in it, is mainly interesting because it is forbidden, like mommy's jewel box or daddy's tool chest. (Gagnon, 1977, p. 85)

As this quote suggests, curiosity about what is forbidden probably plays an important role in encouraging early sexual exploration. Curiosity about the sexual equipment of others, particularly the other sex, is quite normal (Calderone & Johnson, 1989). Many day-care centers and nursery schools now have bathrooms open to both sexes so that children can learn about sexual differences in a natural, everyday way.

Besides showing interest in sexual behaviors, many children in the five-to-seven age range begin to act in ways that mirror the predominant heterosexual marriage script in our society. This is apparent in the practice of "playing house," which is typical of children of this age. Some of the sex play described earlier occurs within the context of this activity.

By the time children reach the age of eight or nine, there is a pronounced tendency for boys and girls to begin to play separately, although romantic interest in the other sex may exist at the same time. Furthermore, despite an apparent decline in sex play with others, curiosity about sexual matters remains high. This is an age when many questions about reproduction and sexuality may be asked (Gordon & Gordon, 1989; Parsons, 1983).

Most 10- and 11-year-olds are keenly interested in body changes, particularly those involving the genitals and secondary sex characteristics such as underarm hair and breast development. They often wait in eager anticipation for these signs of approaching adolescence. Many prepubescent children may become extremely self-conscious about their bodies and may be quite reticent about exposing them to the view of others. Separation from the other sex is still the general rule, and children of this age often strongly protest any suggestions of romantic interest in the other sex (Goldman & Goldman, 1982).

Do you think that homosexual experiences are common or uncommon during childhood?

Sex play with friends of the same sex is common during the late childhood years (Leitenberg et al., 1989; Reinisch & Beasley, 1990). In fact, during this time when the separation of the sexes is particularly strong, same-sex activity is probably more common than heterosexual encounters (Martinson, 1994). These childhood same-sex encounters are a normal part of growing up, and in most instances they are transitory, soon replaced by the heterosexual courting of adolescence (Reinisch & Beasley, 1990; Thornburg & Aras, 1986; Van Wyk, 1984). We encourage parents who become aware of these behaviors to avoid responding in an overly negative fashion or labeling such activity as homosexual in the adult sense.

The Physical Changes of Adolescence

Adolescence is a time of dramatic physiological changes and social-role development. In Western societies it is the transition between childhood and adulthood that typically spans the period between ages 12 and 20. Most of the major physical changes of adolescence take place during the first few years of this period (Lerner et al., 1991; Wheeler, 1991).

However, important and often profound changes in behavior and role expectations occur throughout this phase of life. By cross-cultural standards, adolescence in our society is rather extended. In many cultures (and in Western society in preindustrial times), adult roles are assumed at a much earlier age. Rather than undergoing a protracted period of child–adult status, the child is often initiated into adulthood upon reaching puberty.

Puberty (Latin *pubescere,* to be covered with hair) is a term frequently used to describe the period of rapid physical changes in early adolescence. The onset of puberty is approximately two years earlier for girls than for boys (Lerner et al., 1991). The mechanisms that trigger the chain of developments are not fully understood. However, we do know that the hypothalamus plays a key role (Caufriez, 1997; Foster, 1992; Kulin, 1991). In general, when a child is between 8 and 14 years old, the hypothalamus increases secretions that cause the pituitary to release larger amounts of hormones known as **gonadotropins** into the bloodstream. These hormones stimulate activity in the gonads, and they are chemically identical in men and women. However, in males they cause the testes to increase testosterone production, whereas in females they act on the ovaries to produce elevated estrogen levels.

Puberty
A period of rapid physical changes in early adolescence during which the reproductive organs mature.

Gonadotropins
Pituitary hormones that stimulate activity in the gonads (testes and ovaries).

Secondary sex characteristics
The physical characteristics other than genitals that indicate sexual maturity, such as body hair, breasts, and deepened voice.

In response to higher levels of sex hormones, external signs of characteristic male and female sexual maturation begin to appear. The resulting developments—breasts; deepened voice; and facial, body, and pubic hair—are called **secondary sex characteristics.** Growth of pubic hair in both sexes and breast budding (slight protuberance under the nipple) in girls are usually the earliest signs of puberty. A growth spurt also follows, stimulated by an increase in sex hormones, growth hormone, and a third substance called insulinlike growth factor I (Caufriez, 1997). This spurt eventually terminates, again under the influence of sex hormones, which send signals to close the ends of the long bones. The growth spurt usually occurs approximately two years earlier in females than in males, and often results in girls being taller than boys during early adolescence (Malina, 1991; Middleman & Emans, 1995). External genitals also undergo enlargement; the penis and testes increase in size in the male, and the labia become enlarged in the female (see Figure 13.1).

Under the influence of hormone stimulation, the internal organs of both sexes undergo further development during puberty. In girls the vaginal walls become thicker, and the uterus becomes larger and more muscular. Vaginal pH changes from alkaline to acidic as vaginal and cervical secretions increase in response to the changing hormone status. Eventually, menstruation begins; the first menstrual period is called *menarche.*

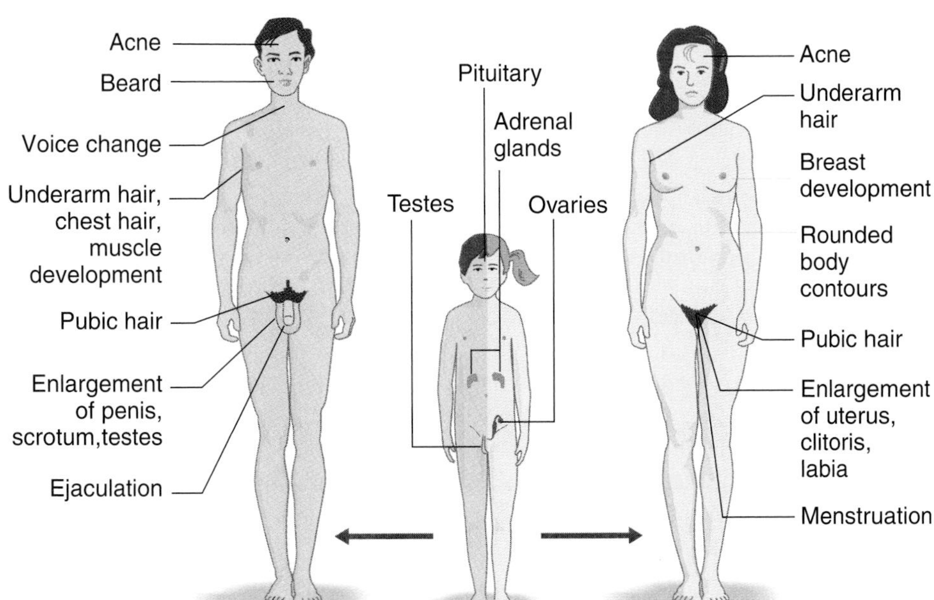

Figure 13.1

Hormonal changes during puberty, triggered by the influence of the hypothalamus over the pituitary gland, stimulate rapid growth and the development of secondary sex characteristics.

Initial menstrual periods may be irregular and occur without ovulation. Some adolescent girls may experience irregular menstrual cycles for several years before their periods become regular and predictable. Consequently, methods of birth control based on the menstrual cycle can be particularly unreliable for females in this age group. Most girls begin menstruating around the age of 12 or 13, but there is widespread variation in the age of menarche (Herman-Giddens et al., 1997; Wheeler, 1991). Research has suggested that menarche may be triggered when a certain minimum percentage of body fat is present (Frisch & McArthur, 1974). At the onset of puberty, the average ratio of lean to fatty tissue in females is five to one (that is, approximately one-sixth of the total body weight is fat), while at menarche it is about three to one (about one-fourth of body weight is fat). Other evidence supporting a connection between body fat and menarche comes from studies of female athletes and ballet dancers with prolonged and strenuous training schedules. These adolescents often experience delayed menarche or interrupted menstruation (Epp, 1997; Warren, 1982). Presumably, this results from having a low proportion of body fat.

A recent study of 17,077 girls, ages 3 through 12, from throughout the United States found that girls reach puberty earlier than suggested in standard pediatric textbooks (Herman-Giddens et al., 1997). Approximately 15% of the white girls in the study (about 90% of the study population) and nearly half of the African American subjects (10% of the study population) were found to have commenced development of secondary sex characteristics by age eight. The study authors raise the troubling question about whether the increased incidence of environmental estrogens—chemicals that mimic human estrogens—may be triggering this earlier onset of puberty. Common sources of environmental estrogens include certain plastics and insecticides that "degrade into substances that have estrogen-related physiological effects on living things" (p. 511).

The authors of this important study also suggest that perhaps the timing of sex education may need revising to include an earlier onset in school curriculums. The lead author of this study, Marcia Herman-Giddens, recently commented that "I don't think parents, teachers or society in general have been really thinking of children that young—second- and third-graders—having to deal with puberty" (in Coleman, 1997, p. A9). The boxed discussion "American Ethnicity and the Onset of Puberty" provides additional information about the significant differences in the onset of puberty in white and African American girls reported in this study.

In boys, the prostate gland and seminal vesicles increase noticeably in size during puberty. Although boys may experience orgasms throughout childhood, ejaculation is not possible until the prostate and seminal vesicles begin functioning under the influence of increasing testosterone levels. Typically, the first ejaculation occurs a year after the growth spurt has begun, usually around age 13, but as with menstruation, the timing is highly variable (Stein & Reiser, 1994). The initial appearance of sperm in the ejaculate typically occurs at about age 14 (Kulin et al., 1989; Wheeler, 1991). Kinsey (1948) reported that in two out of three boys, initial ejaculation occurred during masturbation. There appears to be a period of early adolescent infertility in many girls and boys following initial menstruation or ejaculation. However, this should not be depended on for birth control. In some males sperm production occurs in the early stages of puberty, and even the first ejaculation may contain viable sperm (Abrahams, 1982).

Voice changes caused by growth of the voice box (larynx) occur in both sexes, but they are more dramatic in boys, who often experience an awkward time when their speech alternates between low and high pitch. Facial hair in boys and axillary (underarm) hair in both sexes usually appears approximately two years after pubic hair does. Increased activity of oil-secreting glands in the skin can cause facial blemishes, or acne.

Many of these physical developments may be sources of concern or pride to the adolescent and his or her family and friends. Feeling self-conscious is a common reaction, and individuals who mature early or late often feel particularly self-conscious:

I was the first one to get hair on my chest. At first I would cut it off so I wasn't different from everyone else in the shower room. (Authors' files)

All my friends had started menstruating a long time before, and I still had not. I started wearing pads and a belt once a month so I wouldn't feel so out of it. (Authors' files)

The physical changes we have been describing are quite dramatic and rapid. Suddenly the body one has been living in for years undergoes mysterious changes that are often disconcerting:

I would never repeat my early teen years. My body was so unpredictable. At the most inopportune moments, my voice was cracking, my penis was erect, or a pimple was popping out on my face. Sometimes all these things would happen at the same time! (Authors' files)

Social changes also take place. Boy–girl friendships often change, and adolescents are likely to become—at least temporarily—more homosocial, relating socially primarily with members of the same sex. This phase does not last very long, however. The period of adolescence is marked not only by physical changes but also by important behavioral changes. In the following pages, we look at some important areas of adolescent sexual behavior.

Sexual Behavior During Adolescence

Adolescence is a period of exploration, when sexual behavior—both self-stimulation and partner-shared—generally increases. Although much of teenage sexuality represents a progression from childhood behaviors, a new significance is attached to sexual

Sexuality and Diversity

American Ethnicity and the Onset of Puberty

Of the 17,077 girls ages 3 to 12 included in the study by Marcia Herman-Giddens and her associates (1997), 1638 were African Americans (9.6%) and 15,439 were white (90.4%). As you can see from the table at right, the percentage of African American girls exhibiting secondary sex characteristics—such as breast development and/or pubic hair development—was proportionally greater for all ages. "At every age for each characteristic, African-American girls were more advanced than white girls" (p. 505). The average (mean) ages of onset of breast development for African American girls and white girls were 8.87 years and 9.96 years, respectively. For pubic hair development, the average age of onset was 8.78 years and 10.51 years for African American and white girls, respectively. The first menstrual period occurred at an average of 12.16 years in African-American girls and 12.88 years in white girls.

These findings suggest that there may be marked ethnic differences in both the onset of puberty and menarche, with African American girls entering puberty approximately 12 to 18 months earlier than white girls and beginning menstruation approximately 8.5 months earlier. The authors indicated that they had no explanation for these ethnic differences in the onset of pubertal changes in American girls. Perhaps future research will help to clarify the basis for this ethnic diversity.

Prevalence of Breast and/or Pubic Hair Development by Age and Ethnicity

Age	*White*	*African American*
3	1.0%	3.1%
4	0.9	7.6
5	1.9	5.7
6	3.7	14.3
7	6.7	27.2
8	14.7	48.3
9	38.2	77.4
10	67.9	94.6
11	88.0	98.4
12	96.6	100.0

Source: Herman-Giddens et al., 1997.

expression. We will look at some areas in which important developments occur during adolescence, including masturbation, petting, development of ongoing relationships, intercourse, and homosexuality. These changes are by no means restricted to our own culture. However, young people's sexual behaviors—and the way they are perceived by adults—vary greatly from one society to another (see the boxed discussion "Cultural Variations in Childhood and Adolescent Sexuality").

In our own culture, the male–female double standard prevails in most areas of adolescent sexuality: Feelings and behaviors that are considered acceptable for adolescent males are considered unacceptable or inappropriate for adolescent females. Some research suggests that the sexual double standard among American adolescents may be on the decline (Bolton & MacEachron, 1988; Sonenstein, 1986; Sprecher, 1989). We consider the sexual double standard before turning to specific behaviors.

The Double Standard

Although children have been learning gender-role stereotypes since infancy, the emphasis on gender-role differentiation often increases during adolescence. One way that gender-role expectations for males and females are revealed is through the double standard. As we will see in Chapter 15, the double standard has profound effects on both male and female sexuality throughout our lives. Sexually emerging teenagers receive the full brunt of this polarizing societal belief.

For males the focus of sexuality may be sexual conquest. Young men who are nonexploitative or inexperienced are often labeled with highly negative terms like "sissy." On

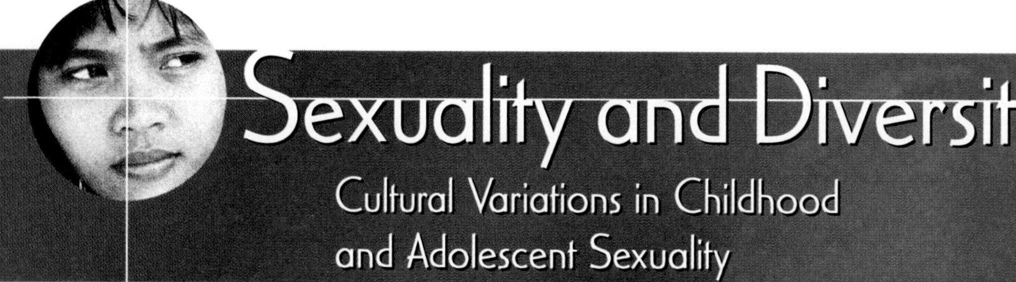

Sexuality and Diversity
Cultural Variations in Childhood and Adolescent Sexuality

Humans are capable of experiencing sexual arousal and pleasure in the very earliest stages of their lives. However, adult acceptance of youthful sexuality, as well as the actual expression of such activity, shows enormous variation from one society to another. A few examples provide some indication of cultural diversity in this area of sexual behavior. (Because the societies described here were studied in the 1950s, 1960s, 1970s, and 1980s, it is possible that some of their traditional practices may have changed.)

Many of the island societies of the South Pacific are very permissive about youthful sexual activity. Children of both sexes may engage in solo masturbation, group masturbation, and sex play with others, including manual manipulation, oral–genital contacts, and coitus. Children may receive extensive verbal instructions about sexual matters. In some areas they may be allowed to observe adult sexual activity.

Among the Mangaians of the South Pacific, children acquire a great deal of information about sexuality during their early years, as evidenced by their use of detailed vocabulary for describing sexual anatomy and function. (For example, they learn several different terms for the clitoris.) In the 1950s Donald Marshall (1971) noted that it was quite common for an entire Mangaian family of 5 to 15 members to sleep in one room. Because a good deal of sexual activity occurred at night in this room, Mangaian children had innumerable opportunities to see and hear sexual activities. One of us, Bob Crooks, visited Mangaia in 1982 and noted that in recent years many of the island inhabitants have moved into larger homes with multiple sleeping areas, a change that may reduce the exposure of young people to sexual activity.

Like the Mangaians, the children of the Marquesas Islands in French Polynesia develop remarkable sophistication about sex early in life. They also sleep with their parents and siblings in one room, with ample opportunity to observe sexual activity. Marquesan boys begin masturbating around age two or three and may engage in same-sex group activities involving genital fondling by age five or six. Boys may also engage in casual homosexual contacts during their youth. Marquesan girls also experience self-stimulation and homosexual contacts from an early age (Suggs, 1962).

Early childhood masturbation is common in other areas besides the South Pacific. Among the African Bala, children of both sexes are given free reign to masturbate from an early the other hand, peers often provide social reinforcement for stereotypically "masculine" attitudes and behaviors; for example, approval is given to aggressive and independent behaviors. For some young men, telling their peers about their sexual encounters is more important than the sexual act itself. As one young man recalls,

My own self-image was at stake. There I was—good-looking, humorous, athletic, liked to party—but still a virgin. Everybody just assumed that I was an expert at making love. I played this role and, without a doubt, always implied, "Yes, we did, and boy, was it fun." (Authors' files)

For females the message and the expectations are often very different. The following account illustrates one woman's view of both sides of the double standard:

It always seemed so strange, how society encouraged virginity in girls but it was okay for boys to lose theirs. I came from a large family, with my brother being the oldest child. I remember when word got around how much of a playboy my brother was (he was about 18). My parents were not upset, but rather seemed kind of proud. But when my sisters and I were ready to go out, our parents became suspicious. I can always remember how I felt and how if I ever became a parent I wouldn't allow such an inequality and emphasis on female virginity. (Authors' files)

Many girls face a dilemma. They may learn to appear "sexy" to attract males, yet they often experience ambivalence about overt sexual behavior. If she refuses to have sex, a young woman may worry that boyfriends will lose interest and stop dating her. But if she engages in sex, she may fear that she's gained a reputation for being "easy." The

Sexuality and Diversity

age. As in the Marquesas, Bala boys commonly engage in group masturbation.

Some permissive societies provide a rationale for prepubertal sexual activity. For example, the Chewa of Central Africa believe that sexual activity in children is essential to ensure adult fertility. The Lepcha of the southeastern Himalayas maintain that girls must be sexually active if they are to undergo normal growth as they develop into adulthood.

A few non-Western societies have strong prohibitions against self-stimulation similar to those of North American societies. For example, the African Ashanti forbid their children to masturbate. Little boys growing up in the Kwoma society of New Guinea live in fear of being caught with an erection. If they are, they may have their penises struck with a stick! Some Kwoma boys become so concerned about this possibility that they learn to urinate without touching their penises.

As with childhood sexual activity, an enormous cultural diversity exists in both attitudes toward and expression of adolescent coital activity. Some societies, more restrictive than our own, apply strong punishments to individuals caught indulging in such behavior. At the other extreme, some societies encourage coitus among unmarried young people. Representative of the latter group are the Romonum Islanders in the Truk group of the South Pacific. The Romonum consider premarital coital activity both natural and desirable for both sexes from early adolescence. Teenage males are often introduced to coitus by older women. Initiation into coitus by older adults is also common among the Lepcha of the Himalayas. However, in the Lepcha society, it is typically the young female who, by age 11 or 12, may be engaging in intercourse with adult males.

First coital experiences occur at an even younger age in the Trobriand Islanders society, located in a group of islands off the coast of New Guinea. Here, girls as young as 6 and boys of 10 or 11 years have their first coital experiences with other children under adult tutelage.

The Marquesans also openly encourage coitus throughout adolescence. This is generally accomplished through the practice known as night-crawling, where boys enter their chosen lover's house at night and have sexual relations while other family members are sleeping nearby. The practice of night-crawling also occurs on the island of Mangaia. However, it appears that night-crawling has lost some of its appeal in the years since Marshall studied Mangaian society. Several of Crooks's adult informants in 1982 stated that it is now uncommon, and some flatly denied it occurs. However, numerous young informants confirmed its continued existence, although in significantly altered form. It seems that parents have become less accepting of such behavior. An adolescent male caught in his lover's bedroom stands a good chance of being punished. Apparently, some Mangaian adolescents also disapprove of night-crawling. One 17-year-old woman adamantly stated to Crooks, "I'm a good girl—I'm not one of those."

double-standard dilemma often encompasses far more than sexual behavior. Girls may begin to define their worth by their boyfriends' accomplishments rather than their own. Wearing her boyfriend's letter jacket may bring a girl infinitely more status than earning one herself. Her abilities may even be seen as liabilities rather than assets. She may be concerned, for example, about getting better grades than her boyfriend.

Masturbation

Although a significant number of teenagers do not experience sexual intercourse by the age of 19, many masturbate. As we saw earlier in this chapter, masturbation is a common sexual expression during childhood. During adolescence the behavior tends to increase in frequency. A survey of teenage males revealed an average masturbation frequency of five times per week (LoPresto et al., 1985). Masturbation-frequency rates among females are notably lower for all age groups, including adolescents (Leitenberg et al., 1993; Walsh, 1989). By the time they have reached the end of adolescence, almost all males and approximately three out of four females have masturbated (Coles & Stokes, 1985; Janus & Janus, 1993; Kolodny, 1980).

Masturbation can serve as an important avenue for sexual expression during adolescence. Besides providing an always available outlet for sexual tension, self-stimulation is an excellent way to learn about one's body and its sexual potential (Weinstein & Rosen, 1991). Teenagers can experiment with different ways of pleasuring themselves, thereby increasing their self-knowledge. This information may later prove helpful during sexual interaction with a partner. In fact, many sex therapists believe that people who do not masturbate during adolescence may be missing an important element in their sexual development.

Petting

Petting
Physical contact including kissing, touching, and manual or oral–genital stimulation but excluding coitus.

Another form of noncoital sexual expression provides an important way for many couples to relate to one another, often as an alternative to intercourse. **Petting** refers to erotic physical contact that may include kissing, holding, touching, manual stimulation, or oral–genital stimulation—but not coitus. "Necking," "making out," and "messing around" are other expressions for petting. Perhaps one of the most noteworthy changes in the pattern of adolescent petting behaviors involves oral sex. A number of surveys have shown that the incidence of oral–genital stimulation among teenagers has risen dramatically, to a level two or three times higher than the rates reported in the Kinsey studies (Braverman & Strasburger, 1993a; Gagnon & Simon, 1987). Among teenagers of both sexes, cunnilingus is more frequently reported than fellatio.

"How far to go" in petting is often an issue. It can become a contest between the young man and woman, he trying to proceed as far as possible and she attempting to go only as far as is "respectable." Because "love" often motivates or justifies sexual behavior for girls, he may say "I love you" as a ploy to engage in further sexual behaviors.

However, petting is often not so narrowly goal oriented, and it may constitute a form of sexual expression that offers both members of a couple the highly valued combination of safety and enjoyment. Petting can be an opportunity for young people to experience sexual intimacy while technically remaining virgins. The steps from holding hands to genital stimulation can progress with increasing emotional intimacy. Through petting, adolescents begin to learn, within an interpersonal relationship, about their own and their partners' sexual responses. They can develop a repertoire of pleasurable sexual behaviors without the risk of pregnancy, as the following account shows:

> I had a great understanding with one boy I went out with in high school. We both knew we were not ready for intercourse. Because of this mutual decision—and our mutual affection—we felt very free to experiment together and spent most of our dates making out for hours. (Authors' files)

This account illustrates not just the function petting serves as a sexual outlet but also the importance of a partner relationship in adolescent sexual behavior.

Ongoing Sexual Relationships

Despite the lingering double standard, data indicate that early petting and intercourse experiences are now more likely to be shared within the context of an ongoing relationship than they were in Kinsey's time. It appears that contemporary adolescents are most likely to be sexually intimate with someone they love or to whom they feel emotionally attached (Laumann et al., 1994; Sprecher & McKinney, 1993). Furthermore, noteworthy changes in the attitudes and behaviors of both sexes are narrowing the gender gap. Teenage women seem to be more comfortable with having sex with someone for whom they feel affection rather than believing they must "save themselves" for a love relationship. At the same time, adolescent males are increasingly inclined to have sex within an affectionate or loving relationship, rather than engaging in sex with a casual acquaintance or stranger, which was once typical for adolescent males (Farber, 1992; Sorenson, 1973; Sprecher & McKinney, 1993).

Many adolescents form caring relationships with each other.

Sexual Intercourse

A frequently quoted statistic in sex research is the number of people in a given category who have engaged in "premarital sex." As a statistic in sex surveys, premarital sex is defined as penile–vaginal intercourse that takes place between a couple before they are married. Do you believe that this term may be misleading, and, if so, why?

There are two reasons why the term *premarital sex* may be misleading. First, as a measure that is frequently used to indicate the changing sexual or moral values of American youth, it excludes a broad array of noncoital heterosexual and homosexual activities. We have seen that petting can include extensive noncoital types of sexual contact, and that it often produces orgasm. For some people, maintaining virginity prior to marriage may not reflect a lack of sexual activity. Second, the term *premarital* has connotations that may seem highly inappropriate to some people:

> I really hate those survey questions that ask, "Have you engaged in premarital coitus?" What about those of us who plan to remain single? Does this mean we will be engaging in "premarital sex" all of our lives? I object to the connotation that marriage is the ultimate state that all are supposed to evolve into. (Authors' files)

Because of these limitations we avoid using the term *premarital sex* in subsequent discussions. We now turn to some of the available data on sexual intercourse during adolescence; then we look at two related areas, adolescent pregnancy and the use of contraceptives.

Incidence of Adolescent Coitus

Even though many contemporary teenagers have not experienced sexual intercourse, the results of eight nationwide surveys reveal a strong upward trend in adolescent coitus over the last several decades (see Table 13.1 on page 392). The more recent of these surveys suggests that this trend has leveled off somewhat over the last 10 years or so.

Do you think these trends in the rate of adolescent coitus over the past decades are roughly the same for all groups of teenage men and women? If not, how do the rates differ? Make an educated guess before reading on.

Table 13.1 Percentage of Adolescents Who Reported Experiencing Coitus by Age 19

	Females (%)	Males (%)
Kinsey (1948 & 1953)	20	45
Sorenson (1973)	45	59
Zelnick & Kantner (1977)	55	No males in survey
Zelnick & Kantner (1980)	69	77
Mott & Haurin (1988)	68	78
Forrest & Singh (1990)	74	No males in survey
Sonenstein et al. (1991)	No females in survey	79
Centers for Disease Control (1996)	66*	67*

*Percentages reporting having had intercourse by their senior year (usually ages 17 or 18).

Although coital rates for teenagers of both sexes have risen since Kinsey's time, there is some indication that the leveling-off trend in the past decade has not occurred among very young teenagers (Alan Guttmacher Institute, 1994; Centers for Disease Control, 1996; Miller et al., 1998). Furthermore, data from the NHSLS survey and other studies indicate that over the last several decades there has been a trend toward experiencing first coitus at an earlier age in both sexes that is consistent across a diverse range of ethnic groups (Laumann et al., 1994; Wiley et al., 1997). There are, however, variations among American ethnic groups in their experiences with adolescent sex that are described in the boxed discussion "American Ethnic Diversity in Adolescent Sex Experiences."

The increased incidence of adolescent coitus among both sexes, that has been particularly pronounced during the 1970s and 1980s, no doubt reflects marked changes in attitudes toward adolescent nonmarital coitus in the American population, especially among young people. Evidence of the shift in attitudes is shown in Table 13.2, which presents data obtained from three Gallup Polls conducted in 1969, 1978, and 1991.

Reasons for Engaging in Adolescent Coitus

A number of factors motivate teenagers to engage in sexual intercourse. An accelerated output of sex hormones, especially testosterone, increases sexual desire and arousability in both sexes. Some adolescents are motivated by curiosity and a sense of readiness to experience intercourse. About half of the men and a quarter of the women in the NHSLS study reported that their primary reason for engaging in their initial coital experience was curiosity and feeling ready for sex (Laumann et al., 1994). Many teenagers consider sexual intercourse to be a natural expression of affection or love (Sprecher & McKinney, 1993). Almost half of the women and a quarter of the men respondents in the NHSLS study reported that affection for partner was the primary reason for engaging in first intercourse (Laumann et al., 1994). Per pressure, pressure from dating partners, or a sense of obligation to a loyal partner, are other reasons that may influence adolescents to engage in premarital sex.

Table 13.2 Percentages of People Agreeing That Adolescent Nonmarital Intercourse Is Wrong

The following percentages reflect answers to the question "Do you think it is wrong for a man and a woman to have sex relations before marriage or not?"

	1969	1978	1991
Yes, it is wrong	68%	50%	40%
No, it is not wrong	21	41	54
Don't know	11	9	6

Source: Gallup Poll, 1969, 1978, 1991.

The NHSLS study provides the most comprehensive available data on reasons for having first intercourse. A relatively small percentage of the subjects included in this study had their first intercourse on their wedding night (about 7% of men and 21% of women). Most of the respondents who had experienced sexual intercourse during adolescence did so by age 19. As shown in Table 13.3, about 92% of the men surveyed said that their first coitus was something they wanted to happen. However, only 71% of the women reported that they wanted their first intercourse experience to happen when it did. Over 4% of the women reported being forced into first intercourse, compared to 0.3% of men.

As indicated in Table 13.4, curiosity/readiness for sex was the most common reason reported by men for having first intercourse followed by affection for partner. The rankings of these two primary motivations or reasons for first coitus were reversed for women.

Table 13.3 First Intercourse Wanted, Not Wanted, or Forced

First Intercourse	*Men*	*Women*
Wanted	92.1%	71.3%
Not wanted but not forced	7.6	24.5
Forced	0.3	4.2
N (number of subjects)	1,337	1,689

Source: Lauman et al., 1994.

The Effect of AIDS on Teenage Sexual Behavior

Many health professionals are concerned that American teens are particularly at risk for becoming infected with the HIV virus that causes AIDS (McGrath & Strasburger, 1995; Post & Botkin, 1995; Thomas et al., 1997). Various surveys have shown that most adolescents in the United States are familiar with the basic facts about AIDS and are aware that high-risk activities may lead to transmission of HIV.

Sexuality and Diversity

American Ethnic Diversity in Adolescent Sex Experiences

A variety of studies have consistently reported that African American teenagers are more likely to engage in adolescent coitus than either whites or Hispanic Americans (Centers for Disease Control, 1996; Kissinger et al., 1997; Michael et al., 1994). For example, a recent nationwide study reported that 73.4% of African American high school seniors had experienced sexual intercourse, compared to 57.6% of Hispanic Americans and 48.9% of whites (Centers for Disease Control, 1996). The results of this study, summarized in the table in this box, also revealed that African American youth tend to have their initial experiences with intercourse at an earlier age than either Hispanic Americans or whites. For example, 24.2% of African American respondents reported having initiated sexual intercourse before age 13 as compared to 8.8% of Hispanics and 5.7% of whites.

The NHSLS study also reported marked ethnic diversity in adolescent sex experiences. This nationwide survey revealed that approximately half of all African American male respondents reported having intercourse by the time they were 15, half of all Hispanic men had intercourse by about 16 and a half, and half of white men had coitus by the time they were 17. Figures for the other sex revealed that half of the African American women reported having intercourse by the time they were nearly 17, half of the white women had intercourse by about 17 and a half, and half of the Hispanic women had experienced coitus by the time they were almost 18 (Michael et al., 1994).

These ethnic differences in adolescent sexual experiences may be related more to economic status than race or ethnicity. Poverty is a strong predictor of sexual activity among adolescents (Brewster, 1994; Day, 1992; Kissinger et al., 1997). Teenagers from the least affluent segments of American society are more likely to engage in sexual activity than those from more affluent classes, and African Americans and Hispanic Americans are clearly less affluent than whites. Furthermore, recent studies indicate that African American adolescents raised in more affluent homes are significantly more likely to abstain from sexual intercourse than their poorer counterparts (Henley, 1993; Leadbeater & Way, 1995; Murry, 1996).

Ethnicity and Percentage of Adolescents Reporting Having Had Sexual Intercourse

Overall (males and females combined)	*Whites*	*Blacks*	*Hispanics*
By 12th grade	48.9	73.4	57.6
Before age 13	5.7	24.2	8.8

	Male			*Female*		
By Sex (male or female)	*Whites*	*Blacks*	*Hispanics*	*Whites*	*Blacks*	*Hispanics*
By 12th grade	48.9	81.0	62.0	49.0	67.0	53.3
Before age 13	7.6	41.4	12.9	3.6	10.4	5.0

Source: Centers for Disease Control, 1996.

Table 13.4 Reasons for Having First Intercourse

	First Coitus Wanted		First Coitus Not Wanted But Not Forced	
Attributed Reason	*Men*	*Women*	*Men*	*Women*
Affection for partner	24.9%	47.5%	9.9%	38.5%
Peer pressure	4.2	3.3	28.6	24.6
Curiosity/readiness for sex	50.6	24.3	50.5	24.9
Wanted to get pregnant	0.5	0.6	0.0	0.0
Physical pleasure	12.2	2.8	6.6	2.1
Under influence of alcohol or drugs	0.7	0.3	3.3	7.2
Wedding night	6.9	21.1	1.1	2.7
N	1,199	1,147	91	374

Source: Laumann et al., 1994.

Since most teenagers know the basic facts about the transmission and prevention of AIDS, do you think that adolescents today are altering their sexual behavior to reduce their own risk?

Unfortunately, even though most teens know the basic facts about AIDS, this knowledge has not resulted in behavior changes in many teenagers. Several recent studies of high school and college-age youths suggest that since most teenagers do not believe that they are at risk for contracting the virus that causes AIDS, most do not significantly alter their sexual behavior to avoid infection (Desiderato & Crawford, 1995; Clark et al., 1998; Sieving et al., 1997). Thus, knowledge of AIDS represents a necessary but apparently not sufficient condition for reduction of risky teenage sexual behavior.

"Many adolescents believe AIDS is a concern only for 'other' people. These teenagers believe that AIDS affects only homosexual men and intravenous drug abusers or that they are not at risk because their sexual activity is infrequent. They do not see the threat of AIDS; therefore they will not take precautions" (Tucker & Cho, 1991, pp. 51–52). It is hoped that public announcements such as that by the charismatic pro basketball star Earvin "Magic" Johnson that he is HIV-infected may help to alter the mistaken impression that AIDS happens only to "other" people.

The notion of the "personal fable" (Elkind, 1967) is relevant to a consideration of adolescent risk taking and sexual behavior. Adolescents are particularly susceptible to a kind of cognitive egocentrism, an illusionary belief pattern in which they view themselves as somehow invulnerable and immune to the consequences of dangerous and risky behavior (Braverman & Strasburger, 1994a; Hillis, 1994; Murstein & Mercy, 1994). Thus, large numbers of adolescents continue to engage in high-risk sexual behaviors, not because they are ignorant about AIDS and other sexually transmitted diseases (STDs), but rather because they falsely view themselves as being at very low (or no) risk of suffering negative consequences (Ku et al., 1993; Pleck et al., 1993).

Behaviors that put young people at risk for HIV infection include engaging in intercourse without condoms and spermicides; using alcohol, cocaine, and other drugs that impair judgment, reduce impulse control, and thus increase the likelihood of hazardous sexual activity; needle sharing among IV drug users; exposing themselves to multiple sexual partners; and choosing sex partners in a less discriminating manner (Centers for Disease Control, 1995a & 1996; Luster & Small, 1994; Sieving et al., 1997). The continuing trend toward a younger age of first intercourse is disturbing in that people who begin sexual activity by age 15 or younger tend to have significantly more lifetime sexual partners than those who begin having sexual intercourse at an older age (Genuis & Genuis,

1995; Seidman & Rieder, 1994). (Exposure to multiple sex partners is very high-risk sexual behavior—see Chapter 17.)

With the growing awareness that teenage women are at risk for HIV infection (and other STDs), most family clinic counselors now encourage clients, even those on the pill, to regularly use condoms and spermicides to protect themselves against STDs. Unfortunately, this advice is often unheeded for a variety of reasons. Many young women and their partners may be unwilling to deal with the minor inconvenience of condoms and spermicides when they believe they are already adequately protected from an unwanted pregnancy. Furthermore, some women may be pressured by partners who resist using condoms. This reluctance to add STD prevention to sexual activity was reflected in one study that found that of 308 teenage women who had received a prescription for oral contraceptives at a family planning clinic, only 16% used condoms consistently over a six-month period—even though 30% were judged to be at high risk for HIV infection because of multiple sex partners (Weisman et al., 1991).

Homosexuality

Various studies indicate that 6–11% of adolescent girls and 11–14% of boys report having experienced same-sex contact during their adolescent years (Haffner, 1993; Hass, 1979; Sorenson, 1973). The great majority of these contacts took place, not with older adults, but between peers. These data, or the behaviors they describe, do not entirely reflect later orientation. Same-sex contact with the intent of sexual arousal can be either experimental and transitory or an expression of a lifelong sexual orientation. As we saw in Chapter 10, many homosexual individuals do not act on their sexual feelings until adulthood, and many people with heterosexual orientations have one or more early homosexual experiences.

Some people, however, do define themselves as homosexual during adolescence. This identification may create severe problems for the young person (D'Augelli & Hershberger, 1993; Hersch, 1991; Nelson, 1997). It may begin with an awareness of having different feelings about sexual attractions than those commonly verbalized by peers; often a person will have a homosexual experience before she or he either applies a label of homosexuality to the behavior or understands its significance. Not being "part of the crowd" can be emotionally painful. Adolescents who are suspected of being homosexual are sometimes subjected to rejection or verbal and physical assault (Nelson, 1997; Van de Ven, 1995). Furthermore, adolescent gay men and lesbians also report experiencing high levels of antigay violence at the hands of family members (Hunter, 1990). In addition to being subjected to violent victimization, it may be very difficult for young people with a homosexual orientation to find confidants with whom they can share their concern or find guidance. Parents, ministers, physicians, and teachers often are unable to offer constructive help or support.

Most teenagers in America have little or no accurate information about homosexuality, and they may even be denied objective information about what it means to be gay or lesbian (Bidwell & Deisher, 1991; Dempsey, 1994). Furthermore, homosexual adolescents are often emotionally (if not physically) forsaken by their families and scorned by their peers (Dempsey, 1994; Hersch, 1991). We hope that in the future there will be an increased societal acceptance of homosexuality that will help make this time of life easier for adolescents with homosexual orientations.

Adolescent Pregnancy

Although recent years have brought greater availability of both contraceptive education and reproductive health care services to American adolescents, the alarmingly high rate of teenage pregnancies in the United States continues to be an urgent social concern. The

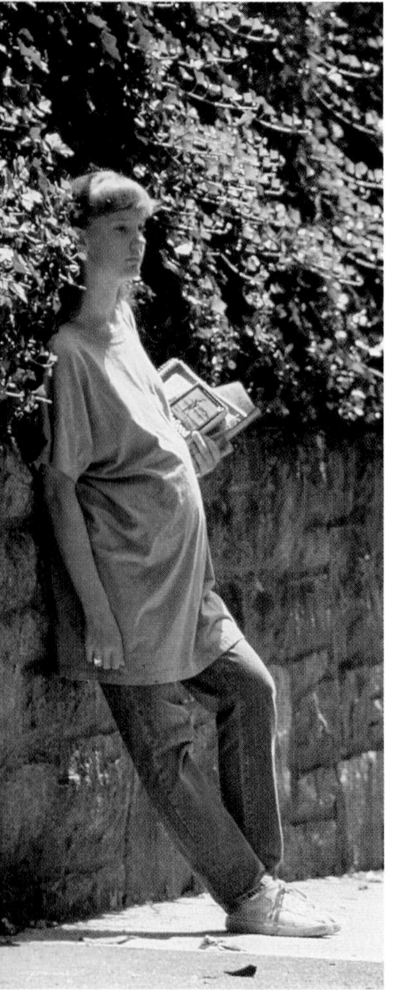

At least 1 out of every 11 unmarried American teenage women who are sexually active becomes pregnant each year. Many experience considerable hardship as a result of their pregnancy.

United States has the highest rate of teen pregnancy in the Western world (Alan Guttmacher Institute, 1996; Miller et al., 1998; Pistella & Bonati, 1998). Our best estimate suggests that of the approximately 11 million unmarried adolescent females who are sexually active, about 1 million become pregnant each year (Alan Guttmacher Institute, 1994; Roye & Balk, 1997; Pistella & Bonati, 1998; Wingert, 1998). Of these pregnancies, approximately 40% are aborted, 10% end in spontaneous abortions or stillbirths, and 50% result in live births (roughly one-fifth of all births annually in the United States) (Braverman & Strasburger, 1993a; Glasser et al., 1989; McGrew & Shore, 1991).

Negative Consequences of Teenage Pregnancy

These statistics represent a great deal of human suffering. A pregnant teenager is more likely to have complications than a woman in her 20s. These include toxemia, hemorrhage, miscarriages, and even maternal death (Hatcher et al., 1994; McGrew & Shore, 1991). Adolescent pregnancy is also associated with a prenatal and infant mortality rate that is markedly higher than among older pregnant women (Bright, 1987; Roye & Balk, 1997). Available data indicate that many of these negative health consequences are primarily due to inadequate prenatal care among pregnant teenagers rather than to biological immaturity; "pregnancy outcomes among adolescents who receive good prenatal care are no different from, or are better than, those of older women" (Trussell, 1988, p. 268).

A teenager's unintended pregnancy and the decision to keep her child often have a serious negative impact on her education as well as her financial resources (Braverman & Strasburger, 1993a; Fullerton, 1997; Roye & Balk, 1997). Approximately 95% of unmarried adolescent mothers who give birth choose to keep their babies (Stevens-Simon & White, 1991). It is now illegal to bar teenagers who are pregnant or already mothers from public school. Nevertheless, a large number of these young women, perhaps as many as 80%, drop out of school and many do not return (Stevens-Simon et al., 1996; White & DeBlassie, 1992). Faced with the burden of childcare duties and an inadequate education, teenage mothers are highly likely to be underemployed or unemployed and dependent on welfare services (McGrew & Shore, 1991; Roye & Balk, 1997; Stevens-Simon & White, 1991). Furthermore, low education levels and limited employment skills severely limit the efforts of these young mothers to obtain economic independence as they move beyond their teenage years.

The negative impact of adolescent pregnancy is further exhibited in the lives of the resulting children. Teenage mothers often provide parenting of a lower quality than that of adult mothers (Lamb et al., 1987; Stier et al., 1994). In comparison with older mothers, teenage mothers are more likely to abuse and/or neglect their children (Felsman et al., 1987).

It has been widely reported that the offspring of teenage mothers are at a greater risk of having physical, cognitive, and emotional problems than are children of adult mothers (Roye & Balk, 1997; Stevens-Simon & White, 1991). These children of young mothers are also more likely to demonstrate deficits in intellectual ability and school performance than children of older mothers (Kinard & Reinherz, 1987; Roye & Balk, 1997; Trussell, 1988).

Use of Contraceptives

Despite the economic, lifestyle, and emotional stress of pregnancy and parenthood, and despite the availability of birth control today, most sexually active American teenagers do not use contraceptives consistently or effectively (Orr et al., 1992; Seidman & Rieder, 1994). A number of studies have revealed that many teenagers do not use any contraception at all the first few times they have sexual intercourse, and only a minority consistently use a reliable method of birth control even after they have been sexually active for some time (Braverman & Strasburger, 1993b; Poppen, 1994). Data suggest that teenagers who use contraceptives often do so sporadically rather than consistently in each and every sexual encounter (Cates, 1991; Poppen, 1994). Studies have indicated that contraception is most likely to be used by adolescents who are in established relationships (Baker et al., 1988). However, even teenage couples involved in monogamous relationships in which contraception is discussed often use ineffective methods or are inconsistent in their use of more reliable techniques (Pleck et al., 1993; Polit-O'Hara & Kahn, 1985).

It is startling that although the United States has the highest teenage pregnancy rate in the industrialized world, the actual levels of sexual activity in this country are no higher than those reported in other nations (Braverman & Strasburger, 1993b; Jones et al., 1985). A number of factors contribute to this disconcerting distinction, many of which center around contraceptive use. The boxed discussion, "Adolescent Pregnancy in Six Nations," describes an in-depth comparative study of teenage pregnancy in several developed countries. This research demonstrates that we need more readily available contraception and improved sex education if we are to reduce the numbers of unwanted pregnancies.

Sexuality and Diversity

Adolescent Pregnancy in Six Nations

In the mid-1980s, a research team, led by Elise Jones, conducted an extensive comparative study of teenage pregnancy in a number of developed countries (Jones et al., 1985). Besides the United States, five nations were studied in depth: Canada, England, France, Sweden, and the Netherlands. All five of these countries were found to have lower adolescent pregnancy rates than the United States. The incidence of teenage pregnancy in England, the nation with the second highest rate among the six, is less than half that of the United States (Siecus Report, 1998). The two countries with the lowest incidence, Sweden and the Netherlands, have adolescent pregnancy rates less than one-fifth of America's. Yet the available evidence indicates that the proportions of adolescent females who have experienced sexual intercourse are similar in all of these countries with the exception of Sweden, which has higher proportions of sexually experienced teenagers at all ages (Trussell, 1988). What then accounts for the pronounced differences in pregnancy rates?

First, "teenagers are much less likely to get free or very low-cost contraception services in the United States than in the other five countries studied in detail" (Jones et al., 1985, p. 54). A major problem with the American family planning clinic system is that it was originally developed primarily as a service to the poor. Consequently, teenagers often avoid birth control clinics, regarding them as places that serve only people on welfare. In contrast, adolescents in countries like Sweden and the Netherlands have access to a dense network of clinics, many of which are directed largely toward meeting the special needs of youth. In 1975, just after Sweden liberalized its abortion laws, it also established a link between schools and contraceptive clinic services for adolescents. Many were concerned that increasing the availability of abortion might result in a marked rise in the number of teenage abortions—but in fact, the adolescent abortion rate in Sweden declined dramatically after 1975.

Second, the use of birth control pills is much less common among American teenagers than among the youth of the other five countries. This difference suggests that American adolescents use less effective birth control methods when they use anything at all.

Third, with the exception of Canada, school and community sex-education programs in the other five nations are much more extensive than in the United States. Sweden has established a compulsory sex-education curriculum in every school and for all grade levels. Sex education is enthusiastically supported by the vast majority of Swedish parents, most of whom had sex education while they were in school. The Netherlands' comprehensive sex-education program begins in primary school, and the government encourages teaching of contraception by subsidizing mobile educational teams (MacFarlane & McPherson, 1992). In addition, the Dutch media present extensive information about contraception and other aspects of sexuality. Surveys of Dutch teenagers have revealed a virtually universal knowledge of how to avoid pregnancy. In England and France, there is a national policy supporting the inclusion of sex education in the school curriculum. No such national policy exists in the United States or Canada.

A number of surveys have revealed that many American teenagers, perhaps the majority, lack knowledge about effective birth control. In addition, certain myths abound, such as the belief that a woman cannot get pregnant the first time she has intercourse or that infrequent coitus will not result in a pregnancy (Levinson, 1995; Trussell, 1988).

Inadequate knowledge is by no means the only reason for not using contraception. Another reason is that its use is an acknowledgment of premeditation (Braverman & Strasburger, 1993b). Some young people believe that the teenage woman who "does it" in the heat of the moment, without planning ahead, is more moral than the young woman who assumes responsibility for her sexual activity and uses birth control. This theme emerged when we asked high school students, "Why would a high-school-age woman who didn't want to become pregnant *not* use birth control?" Their answers: "She feels guilty. If she uses birth control, then she is admitting she is having sex." "Maybe people would think of her as a big sleaze if the word got out that she was on the pill or something." "She wants to consider it making love."

Strategies for Reducing the Teenage Pregnancy Rate

What can be done to reverse the trend of escalating teenage pregnancies in America? In your opinion, what strategies might prove helpful in accomplishing this aim?

Many authorities on adolescent sexuality agree that educational programs designed to increase teenagers' awareness of contraception and other aspects of sexuality will be much more effective if they treat sexuality as a positive aspect of our humanity rather than something that is wrong or shameful. Teenagers who have a positive and accepting attitude toward their sexuality are more likely to use contraceptives in an effective manner (Baker et al., 1988). In the European countries discussed in the box, sex is viewed as natural and healthy, and there is widespread acceptance of teenage sexual activity. This stands in sharp contrast to the United States, where sex is romanticized and flaunted but also portrayed as something sinful or dirty that should be hidden (Jones et al., 1985).

We offer a list of suggestions for reducing teenage pregnancy, gleaned from the writings and research of several eminent investigators of adolescent sexuality.

1. The American family planning clinic system needs to be upgraded to provide free or low-cost contraceptive services to all adolescents who want them. Schools and the media should become more involved in publicizing the fact that these services are not limited to the poor. Of equal importance is the need to publicize the fact that clinics maintain the confidentiality of their clients. Many teenagers are reticent about visiting a family planning clinic because they think the clinic staff might contact their parents (Braverman & Strasburger, 1993b).
2. The United States should follow the lead of several European nations, most notably Sweden, in establishing a compulsory national sex-education curriculum that is extended to all grade levels. Research clearly reveals that teenagers who have been exposed to sex education are considerably less likely to become pregnant than those who have had no such education, especially if exposure to sex education occurs before young people become sexually active (Allen et al., 1990; Firestone, 1994; Jones et al., 1985).
3. Efforts to educate teenagers to prevent unwanted pregnancies must recognize that male attitudes are important for the practice and effectiveness of birth control (Marsiglio, 1993; Meyer, 1991; Robinson & Frank, 1994). Adolescent boys often consider birth control to be their partners' responsibility (Braverman & Strasburger, 1993b; Pleck et al., 1988). Sex-education programs should stress that responsibility for contraception is shared. A survey of several thousand American teenagers revealed that respondents who believed responsibility for pregnancy prevention should be shared were more likely to have used effective contraception than those who felt the responsibility belonged to one partner or the other (Zabin et al., 1984).

4. Government agencies should continue a trend toward relaxing the restrictions on advertising and distributing nonprescription contraceptives, particularly the condom. Furthermore, condoms should be made readily available in high schools. A recent study assessed the rate of condom use and sexual activity among 7,119 students in New York City public high schools, where condoms are available in school, and compared these rates to those exhibited by 5,738 high school students in Chicago, where condoms are not made available in school. The results: The availability of condoms in schools significantly increased condom use by sexually active teenage subjects but did not contribute to an increase in rates of sexual activity (Guttmacher et al., 1997). These findings suggest that school-based condom availability can reduce teenage pregnancy and lower the risk of contracting sexually transmitted diseases, including HIV/AIDS. At the time of this writing, more than 400 schools in the United States have implemented such programs (Guttmacher et al., 1997).

In summary, we hope that in the years to come we will see widespread efforts to increase the acceptance and availability of contraception, as well as broadly focused sex-education programs that will help reduce teenage pregnancy rates in America.

In one final note on how teenage pregnancy may be reduced, there has been a very recent movement in many states to rigorously enforce statutory rape laws prohibiting sexual relations between adults and minors (Donovan, 1997). These efforts have been prompted in large part by studies that indicate that half or more of all babies born to adolescent women in the United States are fathered by adult men (Landry & Forrest, 1995; Males & Chew, 1996). For example, in 1993 alone, two-thirds of the babies born to adolescent mothers in California were fathered by adult men who, on average, were more than four years older than their underage female partner (Males & Chew, 1996). The new focus on prosecution under statutory rape laws has prompted considerable debate over the impact of this approach on adolescent pregnancies and births. This debate is described in the boxed discussion "Is Rigorous Enforcement of Statutory Rape Laws the Answer to Adolescent Pregnancy?"

On the Edge

Is Rigorous Enforcement of Statutory Rape Laws the Answer to Adolescent Pregnancy?

The title question above was recently posed in a thoughtful article by Patricia Donovan (1997) of the Alan Guttmacher Institute. Donovan observes that because adolescent mothers constitute a large portion of the dramatic increase in welfare caseloads over the last 25 years, together with the known fact that adult men father over half of babies born to teenagers, many states have acted to "more rigorously enforce statutory rape laws prohibiting sexual intercourse between adults and minors" (p. 30). The term *statutory rape* refers to intercourse with a person under the legal age of consent, which varies in different states but is typically 16 or 18.

In the last few years several states have taken steps to prosecute men who violate statutory rape laws. California has been especially committed to this strategy for reducing pregnancies and births among minors. In the fall of 1995, California's governor announced a plan known as the "Statutory Rape Vertical Prosecution Program" that allocated $2.4 million of the state's teenage pregnancy prevention funds to support prosecution of statutory rape cases. In addition to increasing criminal prosecution, California's legislators also enacted a statute in September of 1996 that allows civil penalties to be assessed against adult men convicted of statutory rape. Several other states, including Florida, Delaware, and Georgia, have also recently moved to identify and prosecute men who have sexual intercourse with minors.

Advocates of more rigorous enforcement of statutory rape laws argue that adult men will be deterred from engaging in sexual relations with underage women if they believe there is a good chance they will be prosecuted, a belief that can be established by a few highly publicized cases. Furthermore,

(continued on next page)

Sex Education

Many parents today want to provide some input into the sex education of their children. Societal values about sex are rapidly changing, and we all are exposed to contrasting opinions. How much should children see, or how much should they be told? Many parents—even some who are comfortable with their own sexuality—have difficulty judging the "best" way to act and react toward their children's sexuality.

Perhaps the information that we offer in the following paragraphs will help modify some of this uncertainty. We do not profess to have the last word on raising sexually healthy children, so we advise you to read this material with a critical eye. Along the way, however, you may acquire some new insights that will aid in your efforts to provide meaningful sex education for your children, either now or in the future.

Answering Children's Questions About Sex

We are often asked, "When should we start telling our children about sex?" One answer is "When the child begins to ask the questions." It seems typical for children to inquire about sex along with the myriad of other questions they ask about the world around them. Research has indicated that by about age four, most children begin asking questions about how babies are made (Martinson, 1980). What is more natural than to ask where you came from? Yet this curiosity is often stopped short by parental response. A flushed face and a few stammering words, a cursory "Wait till your mother (or father) comes home to ask that question," or "You're not old enough to learn about such things" are a few of the common ways communication in this vital area is blocked before it has a chance to begin. Putting questions off at this early age means that you may be con-

On the Edge

advocates maintain that diligent enforcement of statutory rape laws will, by itself, have an impact on adolescent pregnancy by removing from society many of these men who often are multiple offenders.

Even though it is too early to determine the effectiveness of programs such as California's vertical prosecution, it is clear that many law enforcement officials and state legislators see only benefits and no potential harm in implementing a strategy whose long-term impact is unknown. However, a number of reproductive health care providers and policymakers maintain that there are good reasons not to pursue this strategy.

These critics of the new push to enforce statutory rape laws suggest that this approach may create more problems than it would solve. Health professionals are especially worried that publicity about statutory rape prosecution "will discourage pregnant and sexually active adolescents from seeking medical care for fear of having to reveal the identity and age of their partners" (Donovan, 1997, p. 33). Furthermore, tougher statutory rape laws may jeopardize relationships between adolescent mothers and their adult male partners. Not all adult men who father babies with minor women are necessarily predators and irresponsible. Professionals who work with pregnant and parenting teenage women report that some adult men who father their children provide crucial support to the mothers and play an important role in the lives of their offspring. In such cases where the father is responsible, it would appear to be impractical and illogical to send him to jail. Finally, health professionals who design programs for encouraging fathers' involvement with their children and partners are understandably concerned that having to identify program participants who are adult men involved with minor mothers would clearly hinder their ability to enlist these men in their programs.

It is too early to determine if strict enforcement of statutory rape laws will have any significant impact, good or bad, on adolescent pregnancy and parenting. Donovan notes that at the present time, in spite of enthusiastic endorsement by many state officials, there is a widespread belief among health care professionals that this strategy will actually make matters worse while having no noticeable impact on adolescent pregnancy and birth rates.

fronted with the potentially awkward task of starting a dialogue on sexual matters at a later point in your children's development.

It can be helpful for parents to include information about sex (when appropriate) in everyday conversations that their children either observe or in which they participate. Accomplishing this with a sense of ease and naturalness may increase the comfort with which the children introduce their own questions or observations about sex.

If a child's questions either do not arise spontaneously or get sidetracked at an early age, there may be a point when you as a parent will feel it is important to begin to talk about sex. Perhaps a good starting point is to share your true feelings with your child—that possibly you are a bit uneasy about discussing sex or that maybe you are confused about some of your own feelings or beliefs. By expressing your own indecision or vulnerability, you may actually make yourself more accessible. During this initial effort, simply indicating your feelings and leaving the door open to future discussions may be all that is needed. An incubation period is often valuable, allowing a child to interpret your willingness to talk about sexuality. If no questions follow this first effort, it might be wise to select a specific area for discussion. Some suggested open-ended questions for a low-key beginning might be (1) How do you feel about the changes in your body? (2) What are some of the things that the kids at school say about sex? and (3) What are your feelings about birth control? Is it "proper"? Who should be responsible, male or female or both?

Understandably, parents sometimes tend to overload a child who expects a relatively brief, straightforward answer to his or her question. For example, five-year-olds who inquire, "Where did I come from?" probably are not asking for a detailed treatise on the physiology of sexual intercourse and conception. It may be more helpful to just briefly discuss the basics of sexual intercourse, perhaps including the idea of potential pleasure in such sharing. It is also a good idea to check to see if your child has understood your answer to his or her question. In addition, you might wish to ask if you have provided the information that was desired, and also to let the child know that you are open to more questions. When young children want more information, they will probably ask for it, provided an adult has been responsive to their initial questions.

Some parents may feel it is inappropriate to tell their children that sexual interaction is pleasurable. Others may conclude that there is value in discussing the joy of sex with their offspring, as revealed in the following account:

One evening, while I was sitting on my daughter's bed talking about the day's events, she expressed some concern over her next-door playmate's announcement that her father was going to purchase a stud horse. Apparently, she had been told to have me build a higher fence to protect her mare. Even though she knew all about horses mating, she asked why this was necessary. I explained the facts to her, and then she asked the real question on her mind: "Do you and Mom do that?" to which I replied, "Yes." "Do my uncle and aunt do that?" Again, "Yes," which produced the final pronouncement, "I don't think I'll get married." Clearly, she felt some strong ambivalence about what this sexual behavior meant to her. It seemed very important that I make one more statement—namely that not only did we do this but that it is a beautiful and pleasurable kind of sharing and lots of fun! (Authors' files)

Reluctance to express the message that sex can be enjoyable may stem from parents' concern that their children will rush right out to find out what kind of good times they have been missing. There is little evidence to support such apprehension. There are, however, many unhappy lovers striving to overcome early messages about the dirtiness and immorality of sex.

Initiating Conversations When Children Do Not Ask Questions

Some topics may never get discussed, at least not at the proper time, unless parents are willing to take the initiative. We are referring to certain aspects of sexual maturation that the child may not consider until he or she experiences them. These include menstruation, first ejaculation, and nocturnal (nighttime) orgasms. The desirability of preparing girls for their first period well in advance of the event has been well documented. Nevertheless, most women students in our classes have said that they knew little or nothing about menstruation until they were given sketchy accounts by peers or actually had their first period. It is also typical for males to be unprepared for or unaware of their potential for ejaculating when masturbating (Stein & Reiser, 1994). Experience with first menstruation or ejaculation can come as quite a shock to the unprepared, as revealed in the following two anecdotes:

I hadn't even heard of menstruation when I first started bleeding. No one was home. I was so frightened I called an ambulance. (Authors' files)

I remember the first time I ejaculated during masturbation. At first I couldn't believe it when something shot out of my penis. The only thing I could figure is that I had whipped up my urine. However, considering earlier lectures from my mother about the evils of "playing with yourself," I was afraid that God was punishing me for my sinful behavior. (Authors' files)

It is important that youngsters be aware of these physiological changes before they actually happen. Children's natural curiosity about sex may cause them to discuss these topics with friends, who are usually not the most reliable sources of information. It is certainly better for parents to provide a more accurate description of these natural events.

Some parents may find it relatively easy to discuss menstruation, but quite difficult to talk about nocturnal orgasms or first ejaculations because of their associations with sexual activity. However, discussing these events can also provide an opportunity to talk about self-pleasuring. Females as well as males may experience nocturnal orgasms. The fact that girls have no ejaculate to deal with does not eliminate possible confusion or guilt over the meaning of these occurrences.

When I was a little girl, I began to have these incredibly erotic dreams that sometimes produced indescribably good sensations. Looking back on it now, I realize these were my first experiences with nighttime orgasms. At the time I thought it was awful to have such good feelings connected with such wicked thoughts. I wish someone had told me then that it was normal. It certainly would have eliminated a lot of unnecessary anxiety. (Authors' files)

Most young people prefer that their parents be the primary source of sex information and that their mothers and fathers share equally in this responsibility (Braverman & Strasburger, 1994a; Sanders & Mullis, 1988). To the extent that parents do take an active role in the sex education of their children, mothers are far more likely than are fathers to fulfill this function (Coreil & Parcel, 1983; Thornburg, 1981). Unfortunately, most American parents do not provide adequate sex education to their children (Braverman & Strasburger, 1994a; Miller et al., 1998). Research has revealed that even where there is close and open communication between parents and children, sex often is not discussed (Fisher, 1987). Several studies have shown that friends are the principal source of information about sex for young people in the United States (Papini et al., 1988; Starr, 1997). Thus, the gap created by lack of information in the home is likely to be filled with incorrect information from peers and other sources. This can have serious consequences; for example, an adolescent may hear from friends that a girl will not get pregnant if she only has intercourse "now and then." Peers may also encourage traditional gender-role behavior, and they often put pressure on each other to become sexually active. Thus, the challenge for parents is whether they want to become actively involved in their children's sex education, minimizing some of the pitfalls faced by children and adolescents who turn to their peers for sex (mis)information.

Many people believe that sex education can itself cause problems, because the more children learn about sex, the more likely they are to experiment sexually. Do you think this assumption is valid? If so, do you believe it is a good reason not to teach children about sex?

Parents may hesitate to discuss sex with their children because they are concerned that such communication may encourage early sexual experimentation. However, there is no evidence that sex education leads to sexual activity. Moreover, there is ample evidence that adolescent children who talk openly with their parents about sexual matters, including contraception, are far more likely to use effective and consistent birth control than those teenagers who do not talk to their parents about sex (Baker et al., 1988; Milan & Kilmann, 1987). Furthermore, a recent national survey of over 12,000 adolescents in grades 7 through 12 found that teenagers who have developed strong emotional attachments to their parents, including feeling loved, understood, and paid attention to, are considerably less likely to become sexually active at an early age than other adolescents who lack this close emotional bonding with their parents (Resnick et al., 1997).

Parents may also hesitate to become involved in educating their children about sexuality because they are unsure of how and what to communicate about this important topic (Geasler et al., 1995). In response to this concern, educational programs for parents are now available in a number of U.S. cities. These programs can have a positive impact. One parent education program in San Antonio, Texas, was recently analyzed. After participating in four 2-hour sessions covering sexual anatomy, puberty, peer pressure, teenage sexual activity, contraception, and pregnancy, parents reported a significant increase in conversations with their children about sex. This finding prompted the investigators to conclude that "parent–child communication about sex can be facilitated by an educational program for parents" (Huston et al., 1990, p. 626).

School-Based Sex Education

In response to the frequent lack (or insufficiency) of information from the home and the inaccuracy of much of what children hear from peers, other social institutions are attempting to provide sex education. Some schools have included sex education as part of the curriculum, although the quality and extent of these programs vary considerably.

Various surveys reveal that, while most parents support the idea of sex education in schools, only a minority of American schools offer comprehensive sex-education courses (Horner et al., 1994; Kolasa et al., 1995; Whitehead, 1994). Public school sex-education programs are often hampered by pressures from well-organized and highly vocal minorities opposed to such education (Firestone, 1994). In response to these pressures, many school systems completely omit sex education from their curricula, and others attempt to avert controversy by allowing only discussions of "safe" topics such as reproduction and anatomy. As a consequence, some important areas for discussion, such as interpersonal aspects of sexuality and preventing pregnancy, may be entirely overlooked.

An argument sometimes expressed by those opposed to sex education in the schools is that such programs promote sexual experimentation. There are no data to support these claims. Quite the contrary, research has strongly suggested that while formal sex-education programs promote neither experimentation nor restraint, they do tend to improve knowledge, reduce high-risk sexual behavior, enhance communication with parents and partners, and contribute to more effective use of contraception (Braverman & Strasburger, 1994a; Cora-Bramble et al., 1992; Jacobs & Wolf, 1995).

Although opposition to sex education in the schools continues, a majority of parents support the idea.

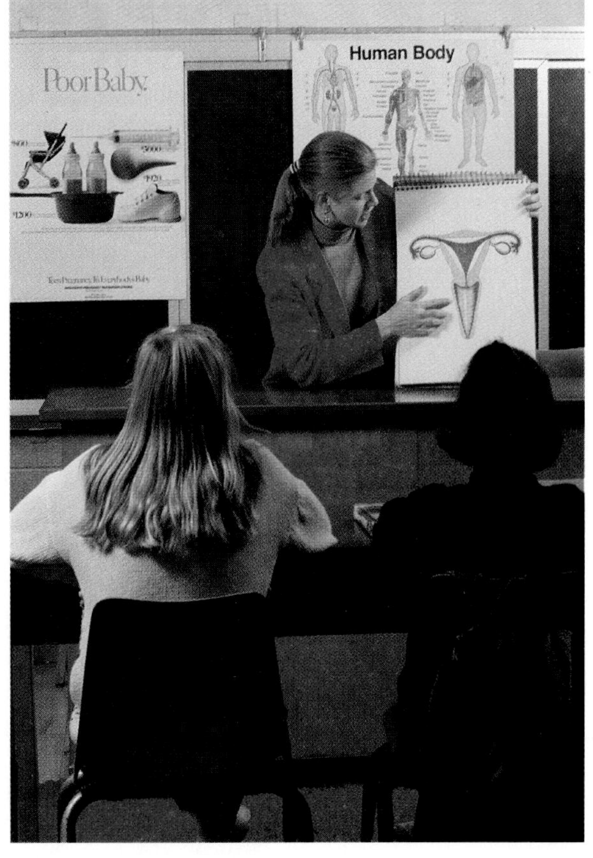

Androgynous Childrearing and Sexuality

The idea of rearing children in an androgynous fashion has much to offer to parents who want to minimize the limiting influence of gender-role expectations in the lives of their children. As discussed in Chapter 3, the term *androgyny* is used to describe flexibility in gender roles. In this sense, androgynous childrearing means raising a child in a way that encourages whatever feminine or masculine behaviors feel right, no matter what the child's sex.

In this text, we have often expressed our belief that rigid adherence to stereotypic gender roles may have a detrimental effect on sexual functioning. The examples are many, ranging from the man who is unable to express emotion and tenderness because it is not "masculine" to do so, to the woman who has great difficulty communicating her sexual needs because she has been conditioned to be passive. Numerous studies also have demonstrated that adherence to traditional gender-role behaviors is linked with an earlier age of sexual activity and with less effective contraceptive use (Scott-Jones & White, 1990; Ward & Wyatt, 1994). Many parents may wish to counteract these influences through the manner in which they rear their children. Perhaps such responses as reassuring little boys that it is okay to cry and reinforcing girls for appropriate expressions of assertiveness will help offset the impact of rigid gender roles.

Encouraging a child to develop as a human being first and a male or female second is a developmental goal that is receiving increasing support in our society. Those inclined to agree with the philosophy and intent of this evolving concept of androgyny may find the most fertile ground for its implementation in the home environment.

One of the truly striking aspects of a gender-role-dominated society is that boys and girls grow up playing primarily with same-sex peers. Little girls frequently get together to see who has the latest Barbie doll fashions, and boys often shoot each other with mock guns. Other than dating in adolescence, this same-sex pairing generally holds up throughout the developmental years. There may be many effects of this separation of the sexes, not the least of which are the awkwardness and lack of spontaneity that characterize many man–woman relationships. The separation of the sexes may often seem to be self-imposed—girls frequently do not want to play with boys and vice versa. However, a contributing factor may sometimes be adult approval of sex-specific play activities. Many now

People who do not conform to traditional gender-role stereotypes have more alternatives available to them.

believe that it is acceptable for boys to play with dolls and girls to push trucks through dirt piles. Would children play so consistently in same-sex groups if gender-neutral activities were encouraged more?

Besides encouraging or discouraging types of play, parental modeling is also an important influence in rearing children in an androgynous fashion (Weisner et al., 1994; Witt, 1997). Parents who feel comfortable sharing childcare and housework can provide models of androgynous behavior for their developing children. It may be particularly valuable to engage in behaviors that are markedly different from traditional gender-role stereotypes. For example, Dad may cook dinner or change diapers, while Mom works late at the office, changes the oil in the car, and so on. One recent study of 207 American families found that children whose parents modeled nontraditional gender-role behaviors displayed more non-gender-typed responses than children reared by parents who exhibited more traditional gender-role behaviors (Weisner et al., 1994).

We believe that people raised in an androgynous fashion may enjoy freedom to behave sensitively and sensibly, and that by lifting restrictive notions about "acting like a lady" or "being a man," adults can encourage their children to have a broader outlook. This potential is one of the possible benefits of this alternative approach to parenting.

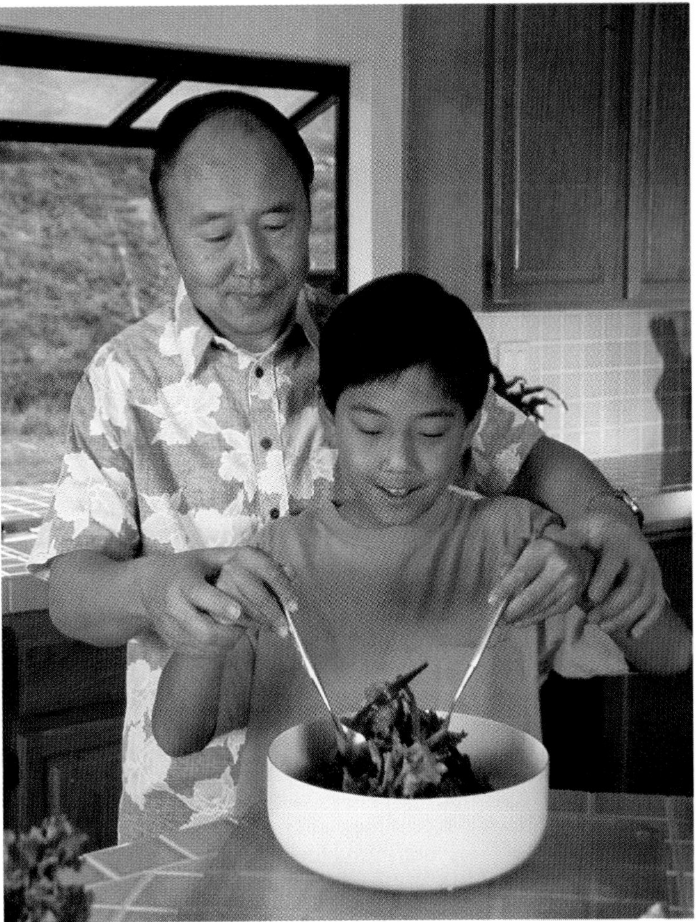

Parents can provide models of nonstereotypical behavior for their developing children.

Summary

The traditional view of infancy and childhood as a time when sexuality remains unexpressed is not supported by research findings.

SEXUAL BEHAVIOR DURING INFANCY AND CHILDHOOD

Infants of both sexes are born with the capacity for sexual pleasure and response, and some experience observable orgasm.

Self-administered genital stimulation is common among boys and girls during the first two years of life.

The inclinations we have as adults toward giving and receiving affection seem to be related to our early opportunities for pleasurable contact with others, especially parents.

Masturbation is one of the most common sexual expressions during the childhood years. Parental reactions can be a very important influence on developing sexuality.

Sex play with other children, which may occur as early as the age of two or three, increases in frequency during the five-to-seven age range.

Separation of the sexes becomes pronounced by the age of eight or nine. However, romantic interest in the other sex and curiosity about sexual matters are typically quite high during this stage of development.

The ages of 10 and 11 are marked by keen interest in body changes, continued separation of the sexes, and a substantial incidence of homosexual encounters.

THE PHYSICAL CHANGES OF ADOLESCENCE

Puberty encompasses the physical changes that occur in response to increased hormone levels. These physical developments include maturation of the reproductive organs and consequent menstruation in girls and ejaculation in boys.

SEXUAL BEHAVIOR DURING ADOLESCENCE

The sexual double standard often pressures males to view sex as a conquest and places females in a double bind about saying yes or no.

The number of adolescents who masturbate increases between the ages of 13 and 19.

Petting is a common sexual behavior among adolescents. One-half of adolescent girls and two-thirds of adolescent boys have engaged in petting to the point of orgasm.

Adolescent sexual expression is now more likely to take place within the context of an ongoing relationship than it was during Kinsey's time.

A significant increase in the number of both young men and young women who experience intercourse by age 19 has occurred over the last four decades. These increases have been considerably more pronounced among females.

Same-sex experiences during adolescence can be experimental or an expression of permanent sexual orientation.

ADOLESCENT PREGNANCY

One in eleven sexually active adolescent females becomes pregnant each year. Adolescent pregnancy is often associated with social, medical, educational, and financial difficulties.

The majority of adolescents who have intercourse do not regularly use contraceptives.

The low rate of contraceptive use among American adolescents seems to be related to a number of factors including inadequate availability of free or low-cost contraceptive services, minimal use of the most effective birth control methods, inadequate school sex-education programs, and an attitude among teenagers that assuming responsibility for birth control implies an immoral character.

Strategies for reducing the teenage pregnancy rate in America include upgrading the family planning clinic system, establishing a compulsory national sex-education curriculum, educating males about their contraceptive responsibility, and relaxing government restrictions on the distribution and advertising of nonprescription contraceptives, especially condoms.

SEX EDUCATION

One answer to the question of when to start discussing sex with our children is "When they start asking questions." If communication does not spontaneously occur, it may be helpful for parents to initiate dialogue, perhaps by simply sharing their feelings or asking nonstressful, open-ended questions.

Some important topics—particularly menstruation, first ejaculation, and nocturnal orgasms—are rarely discussed unless parents take the initiative.

Although the majority of adolescents prefer their parents to be the primary source of sex information, evidence indicates that peers are considerably more likely than parents to provide this information, often in a biased and inaccurate manner.

Research indicates that formal sex-education programs promote neither experimentation nor restraint, but they do tend to improve knowledge, enhance communication about sexual concerns, and aid in more effective use of contraception.

ANDROGYNOUS CHILDREARING AND SEXUALITY

Besides encouraging a child to develop her or his potential, androgynous childrearing practices help break down the stereotypical gender roles that often have a negative effect on sexual functioning.

Thought Provokers

1. Assume that you are a parent of a seven-year-old and that one day you find your child "playing doctor" with a playmate of the same age of the other sex. Both have lowered their pants, and they seem to be involved in visually exploring each other's body. How would you respond? Would you react differently according to the sex of your child?
2. Should parents provide birth control devices to their teenage children who are actively dating or going steady?
3. It has been suggested that rearing children in an androgynous fashion may foster uncertainty and lead to confusion over their proper roles in society. Do you agree with this assertion? Why or why not?
4. There is evidence that women who have had a history of masturbating to orgasm during their childhood or adolescence have an increased probability of experiencing satisfactory sexual relations as adults. In view of this finding, do you think parents should encourage their female children to engage in self-pleasuring?

Suggested Readings

Bass, Ellen; and Kaufman, Kate (1996). *Free Your Mind: The Book for Gay, Lesbian, and Bisexual Youth and Their Allies.* Scranton, PA: HarperCollins. This thoughtful and informative book provides young people with practical information about what it means to be homosexual and bisexual as well as offering validation, reassurance, and advice.

Calderone, Mary; and Johnson, Eric (1989). *The Family Book About Sexuality* (rev. ed.). New York: Harper & Row. This excellent book, helpful for both parents and children, offers practical advice and valuable insights into childhood sexuality.

Cassell, Carol (1987). *Straight from the Heart: How to Talk to Your Teenagers About Love and Sex.* New York: Simon & Schuster. A helpful book with lots of practical and sensible suggestions for parents who wish to communicate effectively with their teenage children about sex.

Harris, Robie; and Emberly, Michael (1996). *It's Perfectly Normal: Changing Bodies, Growing Up, Sex and Sexual Health.* Boston: Candlewick Press. A user-friendly book written for children age 10 and older that provides accessible information about puberty and sexuality. In addition to covering sexual anatomy and physiology, the book deals with important issues for young readers, including masturbation, coitus, contraception, abortion, sexual abuse, and sexually transmitted diseases.

Klein, Marty (1992). *Ask Me Anything.* New York: Simon & Schuster. A valuable resource book for any adult (parent, teacher, friend) who wishes to be prepared to provide factual and helpful advice to children who ask questions about sex.

Leight, Lynn (1990). *Raising Sexually Healthy Children.* New York: Avon. This well-written, insightful book provides a wealth of information to parents who wish to provide an atmosphere conducive to the development of positive sexual attitudes and healthy sexual behavior in their children.

Moglia, Ronald; and Knowles, Jan (Eds.). *All About Sex: A Family Resource on Sex and Sexuality* (1997). Westminster, MD: Random House. This helpful book provides valuable information about sexuality to family members, both child and adult, that may enhance family communication about sexual matters.

Pogrebin, Letty (1980). *Growing Up Free: Raising Your Child in the '80s.* New York: McGraw-Hill. An important source for parents who wish to rear their children in an androgynous fashion.

Web Resources

WWW.

All About Sex Discussion
www.allaboutsex.org/
Information on this site is divided into sections for teens, preteens, and parents. For the teens and preteens, frank but sensitive explanations of such topics as sex and sexuality, masturbation, sexual orientation, and virginity are provided.

National Campaign to Prevent Teen Pregnancy
www.teenpregnancy.org/
The focus of this Web site is to provide parents and teens with frank information to help reduce the number of teen pregnancies in the United States.

14

Sexuality and the Adult Years

Single Living

How have adult single living patterns changed in the United States?

In what ways do levels of sexual activity differ between single people and married couples?

Cohabitation

What explains the significant increase in the number of cohabiting couples in America?

What is the relationship between premarital cohabitation and subsequent marital happiness?

Marriage

Is it possible to successfully predict marital satisfaction?

What changes in sexual behaviors within marriage have occurred over the last few decades?

Extramarital Relationships

What are some of the reasons people engage in extramarital relationships?

What are the possible consequences of such behavior for the marriage and the individual?

Divorce

How have divorce rates changed over the last 10 to 15 years?

What are some of the causes of divorce?

Sexuality and Aging

What is the basis for the double standard in the sexuality of older men and women?

What are some psychological and lifestyle changes that occur in older individuals that can enhance their sexual lives?

Widowhood

Has the ratio of widows to widowers changed significantly during this century?

How is the postmarital adjustment of widowhood different from that of divorce?

I'm single again after my second divorce. In both marriages, sex became boring after about a year, and I love the exciting sex that comes with dating. (Authors' files)

After 44 years of marriage, with our kids in homes of their own, we can really enjoy ourselves. We often go out to dinner, come back home, dance to music from the 1940s, talk, kiss, massage each other and then maybe even have sexual intercourse. Our lovemaking can take several hours, and we're both completely satisfied. (Authors' files)

Intimate relationships of several forms occupy a position of considerable significance in many adults' lives. An adult's relationship status—as single, married, or living with someone—becomes an important social concern, as well as an important element in that person's self-identity. A person's relationship status may also have considerable influence on the sexual interactions he or she experiences during the adult years. This chapter examines several adult lifestyles and the influences of aging on intimate relationships.

Single Living

The number of single adults in the United States has increased from 10.9 million in 1970 to 25 million in 1997—25% of all U.S. households (U.S. Bureau of the Census, 1997). These figures represent a significant shift in adult living patterns, for in the past far fewer adults either divorced or remained unmarried (Marks, 1996). What explains this change? There are many reasons, including

- a tendency to marry at a later age
- a greater emphasis on advanced education
- an increase in numbers of people who choose not to marry at all
- an increase in couples living together outside of marriage
- the rising divorce rates
- more women placing career objectives ahead of marriage
- the increase in the number of women who do not depend on marriage for economic stability

The figures also reflect what may be a change in societal attitudes (Seccombe & Ishii-Kuntz, 1994). Until recently in the United States, a stigma was often attached to remaining single. This stigma applied particularly to women, as terms such as *old maid* and *spinster* indicate (Lewis & Moon, 1997). (Single men would most likely be referred to by the less-negative term *bachelor.*) Today these terms are heard less frequently, and it is quite possible that remaining single, either as an alternative to marriage or following divorce, will become an increasingly prominent lifestyle in American culture. If this happens, we may also see fewer people who marry primarily for convention's sake or to avoid the negative perception of the single state. Nevertheless, single life is still often seen as the period before, in between, or after marriage.

Single living encompasses a range of sexual lifestyles and differing levels of personal satisfaction. Levels of sexual activity among single people vary widely, just as they do among marrieds. Research suggests that married people experience higher levels of sexual activity and satisfaction than singles (Clements, 1994; Laumann et al., 1994). Some people who live alone remain celibate by choice or because of lack of available partners. Others may be involved in a long-term, sexually exclusive relationship with one partner. Some practice *serial monogamy,* moving through a succession of sexually exclusive relationships. Still others prefer concurrent sexual and emotional involvements with a number of different partners. Some single people develop a primary relationship with one partner and have occasional sex with others.

Single living is becoming more acceptable in our society and single people can enjoy the benefits of growth and independence (Lewis & Moon, 1997). However, most people still choose to enter into a long-term relationship with a partner. There are several kinds of long-term sexual relationships, and we examine these various options next.

Cohabitation

When I was a college student in the early 1960s, the possibility of living with someone dear to me, without the sanctity of marriage, simply never entered my mind. When I met a very special person and found myself wishing for the intimacy of sharing a home together, marriage was my only option. Although we had sex before we got married, we never even took a weekend trip together. The topic of unmarried people living together was never discussed, although I occasionally heard a hushed reference to someone "living in sin." (Authors' files)

This account reflects a once-prevalent societal attitude toward **cohabitation** (living together in a sexual relationship without being married) that has undergone considerable change in recent years. In the past few decades, there has been a significant increase in both the number of people choosing this living arrangement and societal acceptance of what was once an unconventional practice (Nock, 1995).

Cohabitation
Living together and having a sexual relationship without being married.

Domestic partnership
Unmarried couples living in the same household in committed relationships.

Living together is an available choice when marriage is not an option. People who are not technically divorced or those seeking child support may not wish to marry or they may want to avoid the financial costs of divorce. People in same-sex committed relationships cannot legally marry. **Domestic partnership** is becoming a more common term applied to heterosexual and homosexual couples who live in the same household in committed relationships but are not legally married, and businesses, cities, and states are establishing rights for access to benefits, such as health insurance, for couples in domestic partnerships. Census Bureau figures reveal that by 1997 unmarried couples living together in the United States numbered almost 4 million, compared to 1,589,000 in 1980 (U.S. Bureau of the Census, 1997).

Advantages of Cohabitation

A significant number of couples view their cohabitation not as a precursor to marriage but rather as an end in itself. Many couples prefer the relative informality of living together to the more official aspects of marriage. They appreciate the sense of being together because they want to, not as a result of the binding power of a legal contract, as the following account demonstrates:

I object to people constantly asking us when we are going to get married. We live together because it feels good and because it seems like a reasonable thing to do. Neither one of us has any intention of ever getting married, to each other or to anyone else. We have been together for over two years and plan to continue for a long time. One thing is certain. We are together because we want to be, not because we are in some kind of "training for marriage." (Authors' files)

The informality of living together may have other advantages. A couple may not feel as pressured to take on the new and demanding roles of wife and husband (Wineberg, 1994). As a result, the relationship is less likely to produce the sort of "identity crisis" that may follow when people try to live up to the social expectations attached to these roles. Another perceived advantage is that the stigma of breaking up is less than with a divorce.

Many cohabiting college students value the sharing of day-to-day activities.

Disadvantages of Cohabitation

Although living together offers some advantages to many couples, it also poses certain unique problems. Disapproval of parents and other family members can place considerable emotional strain on one or both partners. Some couples may also have difficulty renting or buying property together, although this problem is becoming less common. Owning property jointly does present other potential difficulties, however. Without a clear written contract, legal rights on dissolution of the relationship are less clear than with a divorce. Death of one or both partners can result in legal confusion in addition to the emotional trauma. Again, unless the couple has had the foresight to write a contract or to maintain up-to-date wills, there is no clearly established legal definition of partnership rights.

The Social Impact of Living Together

Many college students believe that cohabitation improves their chances for selecting partners with whom they will experience stable and happy marriages. In their view, living together allows two people to identify their own needs and expectations as well as those of their partner prior to making a long-term commitment.

Others argue just the opposite point—that living together will have an overall negative impact on the long-term stability of a possible future marriage. Faced with conflict, couples who live together may find it easier to break up than to work together to solve their problems. Once this pattern has been established, people may be more likely to respond to marital conflict in the same way.

What do you think research shows about the influence of living together on the success of a subsequent marriage?

Research studies indicate contradictory effects of living together before marriage. Some studies find that it has no significant effect on marital stability, sexual satisfaction, or likelihood of divorce (Newcomb & Bentler, 1980; Jacques & Chason, 1979; Watson & DeMeo, 1987). Other studies have found lower rates of satisfaction, happiness, and commitment and a greater likelihood of divorce within 10 years of marriage among couples who lived together (Booth & Johnson, 1988; Bumpass & Sweet; 1989; Nock, 1995). In summary, research does not indicate significant benefits in happiness and stability of marriage related to cohabitation before marriage. Living together permanently without marriage is also not common. About 90% of adults in the United States marry, many more than once. Marriage continues to enjoy widespread appeal as shown in Table 14.1. A closer look at the institution of marriage may provide some insight into its continuing allure.

Table 14.1 Marriage—More Popular Than Ever: Percentage of Adults in the United States Who Have Married in Their Lifetime

	Men	*Women*
1970	92.5%	92.3%
1995	95.8%	95.8%

Source: U.S. Bureau of the Census, 1997.

Marriage

Marriage is an institution found in virtually every society. It has traditionally served several functions, both personal and social. It typically provides societies with stable family units that serve as the primary conveyors of social norms. Most children acquire knowledge about their society's rules and mores through the teachings of their married parents or kinship groups. Marriage also structures an economic partnership that integrates childrearing, performance of household tasks, and earning into one family unit. Marriage also defines inheritance rights to family property. People have an understanding of these variables: Research finds that compatibility and a feeling of being "well matched" form a basis for a decision to commit to marriage (Surra & Hughes, 1997). However, a feeling of readiness for marriage is not just a result of finding someone compatible, but also from having factors outside the relationship in order. A person who is older, educationally and financially accomplished, and has support from friends and family for the chosen partner, is more likely to feel ready to get married than someone who is not in that situation (Holman & Daoli, 1997).

Marriage tends to regulate sexual behavior to help maintain the family line. It also frequently serves as a primary source of emotional and social support, the main reason most people marry. Marriage promises regular companionship, sexual gratification, a loving and enduring involvement, and parenting options, all within the security of a legitimized social institution. And on the whole, married people are generally happier and healthier, both physically and psychologically, than the unmarried (Horwitz et al., 1996).

Although marriage is integral to most cultures, it assumes many different forms (Gaylin, 1991; Mwamwenda & Mongooe, 1998). Western society has defined its own marriage ideal. Within this ideal, we can isolate a number of elements that many people take for granted—for instance, legality, permanence, heterosexuality, sexual exclusivity, emotional exclusivity, and monogamy (one man and one woman). But the elements that are traditional to marriage in most Western cultures are not necessarily the same in other societies. For example, some societies have marriages between one man and several women (polygyny), and a few recognize unions between one woman and several men (polyandry). Norms for marriage also change within a culture, as discussed in the box "Interracial Marriage."

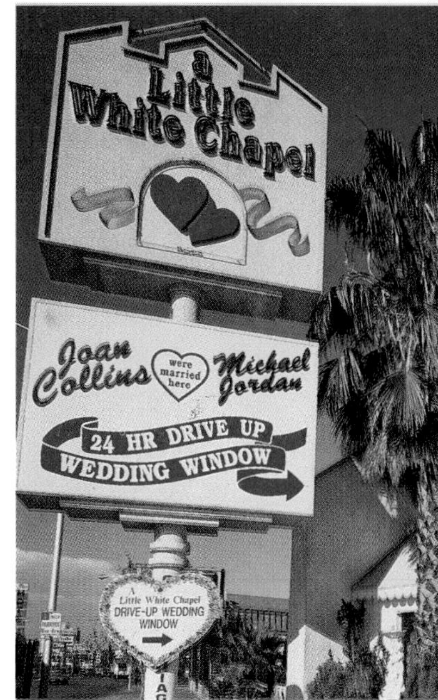

A Las Vegas marriage chapel offers a 24-hour drive-up window for a quickie wedding ceremony.

Sexuality and Diversity

Interracial Marriage

As recently as 1967, interracial marriage was banned in more than a dozen states. *Miscegenation*—sex between members of different races, whether or not the couple was married—was also illegal until the U.S. Supreme Court invalidated those laws. Since then, interracial marriage has increased dramatically: 2.2 percent of all marriages in the late 1990s are interracial, doubling the rate in 1980. Currently, 20% of married Asian Pacific Islanders have a non-Asian spouse, and 6% of married African Americans are wed to people outside their race. With over 2 million children under age 18 who are now of mixed race, the standard racial and ethnic census categories of "black," "white," "Asian," and "Hispanic" are simplistically out of step. Congress may decide to add a "mixed race" category to the census in the future (Leland & Beals, 1997).

Opinion polls have shown that about 30% of white Americans oppose black–white marriages. However, that attitude is less common among young adults, 60% of whom have dated someone of another race. Interracial marriage rates are higher in California than in any other state. In California, 10% of married couples are in mixed marriages (O'Connor, 1998).

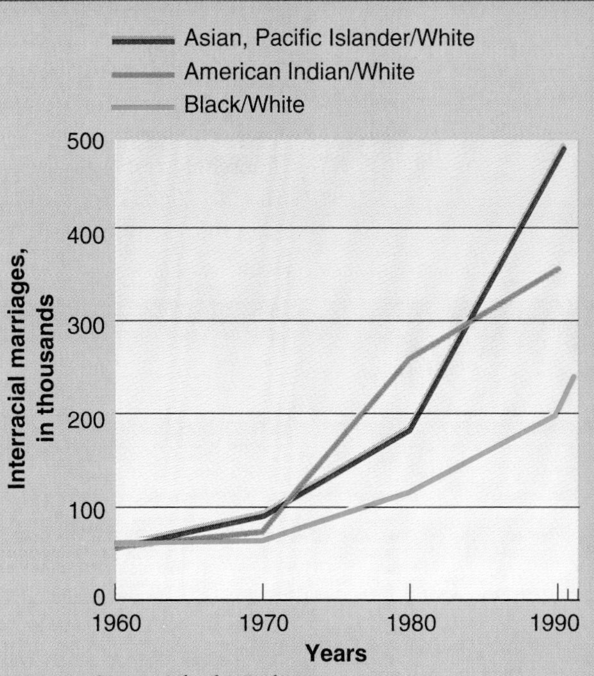

Source: Leland & Beals, 1997, p. 60.

Changing Expectations and Marital Patterns

The institution of marriage has been condemned and venerated in contemporary America. Currently, a large discrepancy exists between the American marriage ideal and actual marriage practices. Although, cohabitation, high divorce rates, and extramarital sexual involvement are all antithetical to the traditional ideal, they are widespread.

Some of the reasons for contradictions between ideal and actual marriage practices have to do with changes both in expectations for marriage and in its social framework. In previous eras, marriage fulfilled the primary function of providing an economically and socially stable environment in which to rear children. People who did not want to have children were frequently admonished not to marry (Ritter, 1919). "Romance" was often downplayed, and marriages in many societies, including some groups in America, were arranged through parental contracts. However, contemporary couples often expect their marriages to provide more than a stable unit for raising children. Most people today enter marriage with some hope or expectations for fulfilling their financial, social, sexual, emotional, and perhaps parental needs. Furthermore, many people hope that happiness is at least a likely if not automatic outcome of marriage. These high expectations are often difficult to fulfill.

Ironically, as people's expectations for marriage have expanded, there has been a corresponding decline in our society's marriage support networks. Extended families and small communities have become less prevalent; many married couples are isolated from their families and neighbors. This places further demands on the marriage to meet a variety of human needs, because couples are often hard pressed to find outside resources for help with household tasks, child-care assistance, financial aid, or emotional support. Furthermore, people now live much longer than they did in the past, a condition that raises the question of how marriages can keep pace with the ever-changing needs of each partner.

At a personal level, courtship experiences before marriage also contribute to the discrepancy between expectations and reality. Dating rarely offers a couple the kinds of experiences that would enable them to draw a realistic picture of the marriage relationship or learn the skills that may help resolve later difficulties. Both partners frequently present their more likable, sociable side and see only the positive aspects of the other's personality. Their time together is usually spent on pleasurable activities, with day-to-day problems kept separate from their interactions. Although the challenges of sharing everyday life after marriage can enrich and fulfill some couples, the lack of preparedness for meeting such challenges may disillusion others.

A couple can do many things to prepare for the experience of marriage. Some couples contemplating marriage make an effort to discuss such topics as finances and daily household responsibilities. They may plan the handling of finances for shared activities or a vacation. They may also decide to divide their living expenses equally or in proportion to their respective incomes.

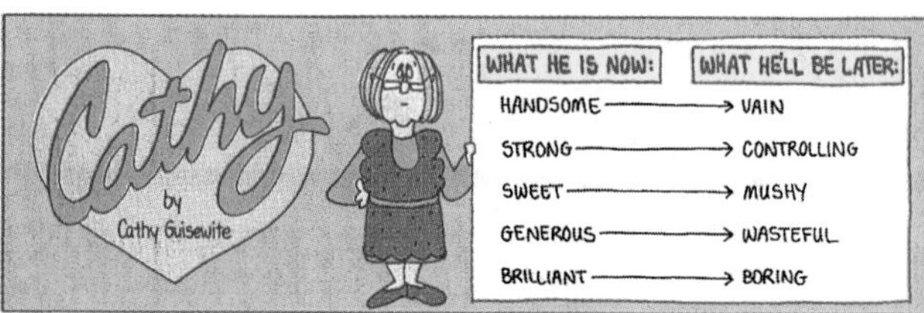

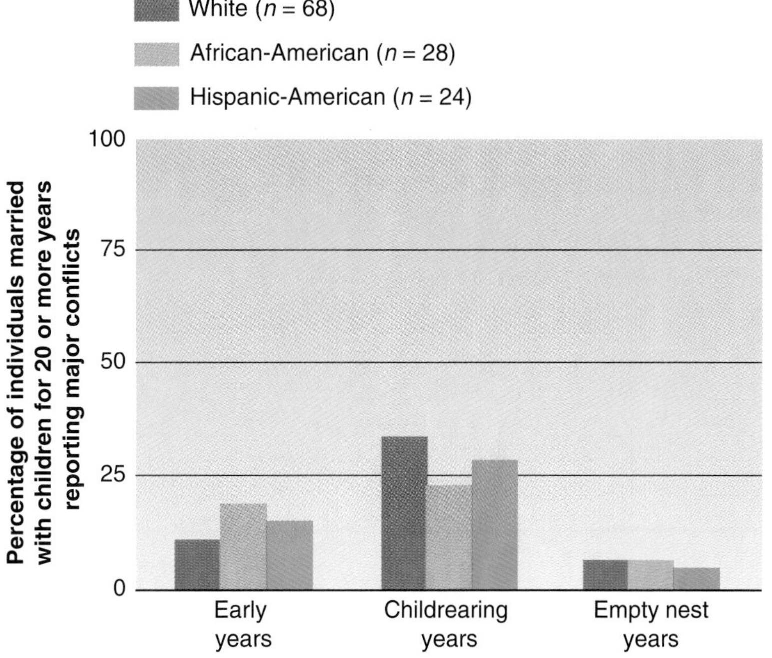

Figure 14.1

Percentage of married individuals with children reporting major conflict at different phases of marriage. (Mackey & O'Brien, 1998, p. 132).

Couples contemplating marriage also need to discuss their desires and decisions about children—whether they both want them, how many, and when. If neither partner has children at the time, they may want to make arrangements to share volunteer child care or baby-sitting for friends, to help assess and discuss their childrearing attitudes. They may also need to plan the logistics of caring for their own children. It is very important to be clear about aspirations and expectations concerning children, for married couples frequently disagree about childrearing practices. Couples experience more conflict during the childrearing years than in the early or empty-nest years of their marriages (see Figure 14.1).

Some couples may work on a cooperative household project or share homemaking activities. Building something together, organizing a party, trading workdays at each other's houses, or cooking meals for each other are activities that may help couples learn more about how well they can work together. The division of household labor is a common source of marital conflict throughout the Western world, and therefore worthy of thoughtful consideration (Kluwer et al., 1996; Mackey & O'Brien, 1998). A study of 141 married couples matched by age, race, and income found that couples in satisfying marriages have a high degree of closeness combined with a sense of individual independence that is supported by their spouse (Rankin-Esquer et al., 1997). These researchers conclude that an important task in marriage is to attend simultaneously to the closeness of the relationship and the individuality of each partner.

Problems that arise can make the couple aware of what differences they bring into the marriage. A "good marriage" is not necessarily a problem-free marriage but rather a relationship in which two people are committed to dealing with the problems that invariably arise.

Predicting Marital Satisfaction

Studies conducted by psychologist John Gottman and his colleagues have revealed surprisingly effective tools for predicting marital success. Their findings, described next, are summarized and discussed in his books: *Why Marriages Succeed or Fail* (1994a) and *What Predicts Divorce* (1993).

Gottman's team used a multimethod research model for collecting an extensive database drawn from 20 different studies of 2000 couples. Using videotapes of couples interacting as they discussed a problem area in their marriage, correlated with physiological measurements (such as heart rate, blood pressure, etc.), and backed up by questionnaires and interviews, Gottman and his associates identified a number of patterns that seemed to predict marital discord, unhappiness, and separation. Identifying such patterns has provided the basis for predicting with better than 90% accuracy whether a couple will separate within the first few years of marriage. These patterns included:

- facial expressions of disgust, fear, or misery
- high levels of heart rate
- defensive behaviors such as making excuses and denying responsibility for disagreement
- verbal expressions of contempt by the wife
- "stonewalling" by the husband (showing no response when his wife expresses her concerns)

Expressions of contempt can erode marital satisfaction and longevity.

The most important variable in predicting duration and happiness in marriage was found to be the number of positive compared to negative emotional interactions. Couples who were satisfied with their marriages demonstrated a ratio of five positive interactions to one negative interaction. Gottman summarizes: "It is the balance between positive and negative emotional interactions in a marriage that determines its well-being—whether the good moments of mutual pleasure, passion, humor, support, kindness and generosity outweigh the bad moments of complaining, criticism, anger, disgust, contempt, defensiveness and coldness" (1994a, p. 44).

The five-to-one ratio is more important than how much a couple fights or how compatible they are socially, financially, and sexually. When couples maintain this ratio, they can have long-lasting satisfying marriages regardless of their particular relationship style. Gottman found three different marriage styles: *validating, volatile,* and *conflict avoiding,* each with unique strengths and weaknesses. Validating couples discuss problems calmly, listen to each other's viewpoints, and work out solutions, compromising when necessary, yet are at risk of becoming passionless buddies. Volatile couples have intense emotional marriages characterized by frequent disagreements. They show respect for each other in their conflict and make up just as passionately as they argue. However, volatile couples can become too aggressive. Conflict avoidant couples cannot tolerate arguments or fighting and avoid disagreements with a "peace at any price" approach that interferes with facing problems that need to be resolved for the health of the relationship. Marriage longevity occurs equally in all three styles when the positive–negative emotional interaction ratio remains five to one.

Gottman's most recent research found further dimensions to patterns of newlyweds who wind up in stable and happy marriages (Gottman et al., 1998). These successful patterns are distinct for women and men. Research finds that women typically initiate discussions about concerns and problems in the marriage. To the extent that women use a "softened start-up," a calm, kind, diplomatic beginning to the discussion, they have stable and happy marriages. Conversely, men who accept influence from their wives end up in long-term good marriages. Husbands who reject their wives' requests and concerns, in essence, refuse to share their power with their wives, find themselves in unstable, unhappy marriages that are more likely to lead to divorce. A husband's ability to accept his wife's influence is unrelated to his age, income, occupation, or educational level. Although these patterns are unique for each sex, the positive interaction between them is evident: A wife would be more inclined to use a softened start-up if she knows her husband will be responsive to her, and a husband would be more likely to accept the influence of a wife who begins a conflict discussion in a diplomatic fashion.

Another intriguing area of research involves assessing the effectiveness of a premarital inventory called PREPARE in predicting marital satisfaction. PREPARE is a questionnaire containing 125 items designed to identify strengths and weaknesses in 11 relationship areas: (1) realistic expectations, (2) personality issues, (3) communication, (4) conflict resolution, (5) financial management, (6) leisure activities, (7) sexual relationship, (8) children and marriage, (9) family and friends, (10) egalitarian roles, and (11) religious orientation (Olson et al., 1987). In studies where couples took the inventory prior to marriage, and then were revisited three years after they married, the PREPARE inventory had over 80% accuracy in predicting which couples would divorce and which would have happy marriages (Murray, 1995).

What are the implications of these findings regarding effective methods for predicting marital happiness? How might such discoveries be applied to our own lives?

Given that current estimates suggest that 50% or more of all first marriages in the United States will end in separation or divorce (Centers for Disease Control and Prevention, 1998a), these findings strongly underscore the value of obtaining premarital counseling from professionals well versed in the use of predictive devices such as those used by Gottman and his associates and inventories such as PREPARE (Lebow, 1997). Currently, couples who choose to participate in premarital counseling have fewer risk factors for marital difficulties to begin with than couples who do not obtain premarital counseling. Therefore, the couples who need the most help are getting the least assistance to help improve their upcoming marriage (Sullivan & Bradbury, 1997). If areas of present or potential conflict are identified, a couple might then seek to resolve these difficulties through further counseling prior to taking their vows. In situations where conflict resolution efforts do not succeed, a couple might reconsider or at least postpone marriage. See the "Before You Get Serious" box for a sample of questions used in premarital counseling.

Let's Talk About It

Before You Get Serious . . .

The following questions are typical of premarital counseling topics. If you and your partner decide to give them a try, the most effective approach is for each of you to write your responses in private, then read them aloud to each other. Remember, it's not always being the same that's the most important. It's being able to understand and work effectively with the differences between you.

	Often	Sometimes	Rarely
Am I usually the listener in our conversations?	___	___	___
Do you interrupt me and anticipate what I wish to say?	___	___	___
Can I discuss personal problems with you?	___	___	___

Complete each sentence:

The hardest subject to discuss with you is ______________.
What puzzles me about you is ______________.
One thing I dislike about myself is ______________.
The thing I like best about myself is ______________.
When we quarrel, I usually ______________.

Answer each question:

How did my father show anger or displeasure?
How did my mother show anger or displeasure?
How was physical affection shown in my family? How did I feel about it?
How did my parents handle money?
What worries do I have about our sex life?

Check items you agree with:

___ When people are angry, it's best to keep quiet and cool down.
___ Couples should always try to do things together.
___ Marriage without children can be as satisfying as one with children.
___ Household responsibilities are to be shared equally and assigned intentionally.

Place an X where your beliefs fit on the continuum:

Money is to be spent and enjoyed. |——————| Money is to be spent carefully and saved for a rainy day.

Source: Adapted from Tate-O'Brien, 1981.

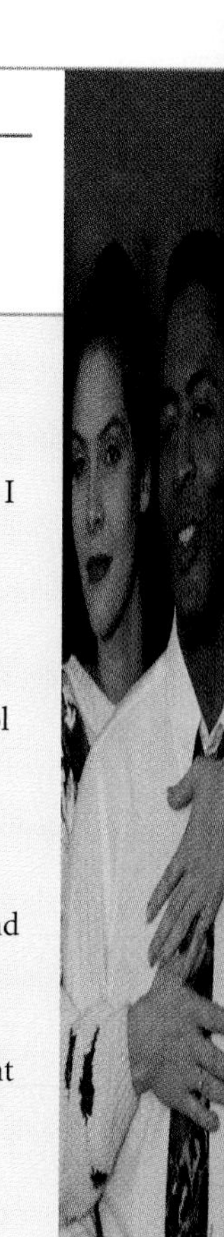

Sexual Behavior Within Marriage

We have seen that sexual behavior outside of marriage has changed considerably since Kinsey's time. How do you think sexual behavior within *marriage has changed?*

Contemporary developments in sexual mores and behavior are often discussed in the context of nonmarital or extramarital activities. However, the greatest impact of increased sexual liberalization may be on the marital relationship itself. As compared with Kinsey's research groups, contemporary married women and men in the United States appear to be engaging in sexual intercourse more often, experiencing a wider repertoire of sexual behaviors, and enjoying sexual interaction more. Several surveys have revealed significant changes in sexual activity among married couples in the years since Kinsey collected his data. The frequency and duration of precoital activity have increased, with more people focusing on these activities themselves rather than viewing them as preparation for coitus. Oral stimulation of the breasts and manual stimulation of the genitals have increased; so has oral–genital contact, both fellatio and cunnilingus (Clements, 1994; Laumann et al., 1994).

Married couples are engaging in a wider variety of sexual behaviors and enjoying sexual interaction more often.

Experiences with coitus also seem to have changed over the years. Today's married couples report using a wider variety of intercourse positions and increasing the duration of coitus beyond the two-minute average reported in Kinsey's 1948 study (Hunt, 1974; Petersen et al., 1983). The average frequency of marital coitus also appears to have increased to approximately two or three times per week for couples in their twenties and thirties, a frequency that gradually declines with increasing age (Blumstein & Schwartz, 1990; Patterson & Kim, 1991).

Evidence of Increasing Sexual Satisfaction in Marriage

One national survey of 7000 American couples found that the frequency of sexual interactions was strongly associated with sexual satisfaction in marriage (Blumstein & Schwartz, 1983). Of the married couples who were having sex three or more times a week, 90% reported satisfaction with their sex lives. In contrast, half of those who had sex one to four times a month—and only a third who had sex less than once a month—were satisfied. These researchers also found that sex is more exciting at the outset of marriage, and that in long-term relationships sex tends to be more "bread-and-butter" rather than "champagne-and-caviar."

A number of factors other than frequency of sexual interaction have also been linked to satisfaction with marital sex. Mutuality in initiating sex seems to contribute to the sexual satisfaction of both partners (Blumstein & Schwartz, 1983). Women who take an active role during lovemaking are more likely to be pleased with their sex lives than those who assume a more passive role (Tavris & Sadd, 1977). Research also suggests a positive correlation between marital happiness and female orgasm. In one survey of over 1000 women, those who had happy marriages reported considerably higher orgasm frequency than those who were unhappily married (Gebhard, 1966). There is evidence that orgasm frequency is increasing among married women (Peterson et al., 1983; Pietropinto & Simenauer, 1990), especially compared to unmarried women, as indicated in Table 14.2.

Good communication also seems important to sexual satisfaction within marriage. In one survey of 100,000 women, 88% of those who reported always discussing their sexual feelings with their partners described their sex lives as good or very good. In contrast, only 30% of those who never discussed sex with their partners described their sex lives as good or very good (Tavris & Sadd, 1977). A study of married couples found that participants who enjoyed a high-quality marital relationship also reported good sexual communication (Banmen & Vogel, 1985).

Table 14.2 Relationship Status and Orgasm Experience

Always or Usually Have an Orgasm with Partner

	Men	*Women*
Dating	94%	62%
Living together	95%	68%
Married	95%	75%

(How would you explain the difference in patterns for men and women?)

Source: Laumann et al., 1994.

Factors Limiting Sexual Satisfaction in Marriage

However, not all contemporary marriages reflect a trend toward increasing sexual satisfaction. Sexless unions are not at all uncommon, notes psychologist Ruthellen Josselson (1992). Josselson, who interviewed married people between the ages of 25 and 55, stated, "I was astonished at how many married couples said they hadn't had sex in years" (in Murray, 1992, p. 64). As we will see in Chapter 15, a lack of interest in sexual activity is the most frequent problem that brings people to seek sex therapy. It is important to note, however, that a lack of sexual interaction does not necessarily signify that platonic marriages are not satisfying and that they should be "fixed." For some couples sex is not, and perhaps never was, a high priority. And, as Josselson observes, "there are many forms of human connection. These couples are not willing to sacrifice a marriage that is working on other levels" (in Murray, 1992, p. 64).

A number of factors may interfere with marital sexual enjoyment. When people marry, their relationship often changes. They suddenly find themselves confronted with a new set of role expectations. They are no longer just friends and lovers but also husband and wife, and romance may be replaced by the stress of adjusting to the new identity. People often get caught up in a "rat race" lifestyle that can seriously erode the quality of marital sex. Holding down a job, doing laundry, fixing the lawn mower, socializing with two sets of relatives and friends, and countless other tasks can reduce the time a couple has for intimate sharing. Couples who become parents may discover that children can place unexpected strains on their relationship, in addition to interfering with their privacy and spontaneity (Emery & Tuer, 1993; Jouriles et al., 1991). They no longer have the independence of living separately, and day-to-day togetherness may erode their sense of individuality and autonomy. In addition, many people are less motivated to maintain personal attractiveness once they have secured a marriage partner; being overweight, out of shape, and poorly groomed may reduce sexual attractiveness and pleasure during sexual activity. Finally, boredom can be devitalizing. Sex may become routine and predictable. The discussion in Chapter 7 on maintaining relationship satisfaction may be helpful in enhancing sexual enjoyment in marriages and other long-term relationships.

The Good Marriage

A study of satisfying and long-lasting marriages (Wallerstein & Blakeslee, 1995) found that happiness in marriage occurred when couples liked and respected one another. Respect was based on the integrity of the partner's honesty, compassion, decency, fairness, and loyalty to the family. Happy couples found pleasure and comfort in each other's company and treated their marriages as needing continued attention. They understood that a good marriage is a process of ongoing change, dealing with each individual's needs and wishes pertaining to work, sex, parenting, friends, and health as they evolve during the life cycle. They believed that their marriages enhanced them as individuals and that the fit between their own needs and their partner's responses was unique and irreplaceable. They felt lucky to be with their spouse and did not take each other for granted.

These couples had successfully managed the challenges of the psychological tasks that create the foundation and framework of a happy marriage. The researchers identified each of these tasks:

- committing to the relationship and detaching emotionally from the families of childhood while building new connections with the extended families

- building intimacy and unity while maintaining room for autonomy
- expanding the relationship to include children, balancing parenthood while nurturing the couple relationship
- managing the unpredictable adversities of life—illness, death, natural disasters—in ways that enhanced the relationship
- finding ways to resolve differences, anger, and conflict without exploiting each other or giving away one's heart's desire
- establishing an imaginative and pleasurable sex life
- sharing laughter and keeping interest alive
- providing emotional nurturance and encouragement
- drawing sustenance and renewal from the memories of courtship and early marriage

Individuals in happy marriages demonstrated a capacity to be sensitive to their partner's inner state of mind and a willingness to reshape the marriage in response to new circumstances. Over the course of the marriage, they changed and developed personally and had a sense that they had experienced many different "marriages" within the evolution of their marriage. These happy couples exemplify how "neither the legal nor the religious cermony makes the marriage. *People* do, throughout their lives" (Wallerstain & Blakeslee, 1995, p. 331).

Extramarital Relationships

Extramarital relationship Sexual interaction by a married person with someone other than his or her spouse.

The term **extramarital relationship** is used to describe the sexual interaction of a married person with someone other than her or his spouse. The term is a general one that makes no distinction among the many ways in which extramarital sexual activity occurs. Such activity can be secret or based on an agreement between the married partners. The extramarital relationship may be casual or involve deep emotional attachment; it may last for a brief or extended time period. It may occur in cyberspace, as discussed in the box, "Are Extramarital Affairs in Cyberspace Real?" Sometimes it occurs within the context of an alternative lifestyle such as swinging. The following discussions examine extramarital relationships, both nonconsensual and consensual.

Nonconsensual Extramarital Relationships

Nonconsensual extramarital sex Engaging in an outside sexual relationship without the consent (or presumably the knowledge) of one's spouse.

In **nonconsensual extramarital sex,** the married person engages in an outside sexual relationship without the consent (or presumably the knowledge) of his or her spouse. This form of behavior has been given many labels, including "cheating," adultery, infidelity, having an affair, and "fooling around."

Why do people enter into nonconsensual extramarital relationships?

The reasons for nonconsensual extramarital sex are varied and complex (Atwood & Siefer, 1997). In many cases, the motive can be the person's attempt to reestablish his or her sense of individuality and autonomy, which has diminished within the context of a marriage (Schnarch, 1991). An individual may not be developed emotionally enough to maintain being true to oneself in the face of a partner's discomfort or disapproval, and then seeks a new, secret relationship to reestablish a sense of self (Shaw, 1997). For some, the motivation may be the need to confirm that they are still desirable to members of the other sex. In other cases people may be highly dissatisfied with their marriages. If emotional needs are not being met within the marriage, having an "illicit lover" may seem particularly inviting (Friedman, 1994). In some situations, affairs may also provide the impetus to end a marriage that is no longer satisfying (Brown, 1988). Occasionally the reason for outside involvements may be the unavailability of sex within the marriage. A lengthy separation, a debilitating illness, or a partner's inability or unwillingness to relate sexually may all influence a person to look elsewhere for sexual fulfillment. An affair may also be motivated by a desire for revenge (Sponaugle, 1989). In such instances the offending party may be quite indiscreet, to ensure that the "wronged" spouse will discover the infidelity. Sometimes nonconsensual extramarital relationships are motivated simply by a desire for excitement and variety: Although having no particular complaints about the marriage, some people want the adventure of extramarital affairs in their lives.

Particularly for people who are influenced by this last motivation, the secrecy of an illicit relationship sometimes adds to its appeal. Researchers have examined the allure of secrecy in relationships (Wegner et al., 1994). The researchers found that university alumni spent more time thinking about former lovers who were kept secret than those who were known to others. The researchers also set up a laboratory experiment involving male and female university students who had not met prior to the study. Subjects were seated in mixed-sex pairs for card games, and couples were asked to touch feet under the table while playing cards with another couple. Sometimes this game of footsie was secret; other times it was not. Couples in the "secret footsie" group reported greater attraction to each other after the game than did couples whose foot-touching was not secret. The researchers concluded that secrecy often creates attraction in relationships. Because most extramarital involvements are secret, it seems plausible that secrecy may be a motivating factor in these involvements.

How Common Are Extramarital Affairs?

Whatever the motivation, it is difficult to estimate the incidence of extramarital sexual involvements. Kinsey's surveys reported that approximately 50% of the men and 25% of the women in his samples had experienced extramarital sexual intercourse at least once

On the Edge

Are Extramarital Affairs in Cyberspace Real?

With access to the Internet burgeoning, the opportunity is now available to millions of people to connect, perhaps intimately, with others through their computers in the seemingly safe and private world of cyberspace.

Such access is celebrated as "better living through technology" by some, but it raises new problems as well. This relatively recent communication revolution offers the opportunity for an individual to explore intimate, secret connections outside one's marriage (or other committed relationship). While alone at home or at the office, under the guise of "working online" or "just surfing the Internet," a married individual might closet himself or herself away at the computer for hours at a time, or secretly communicate with an intimate partner via e-mail (Swartz, 1998).

The novelty of netsex might seem like a sexual paradise, where forbidden appetites can be freely indulged (Lieblum, 1997). For some, such on-line communications may help them to masturbate privately to a more interactive fantasy. But is such behavior harmful? After all, private masturbation by a married individual is not considered a problem.

Can cybersex be considered an extramarital affair if only words have been exchanged and the individuals have never met face to face? Does it require physical contact to be an affair? Some participants consider themselves still faithful if they have not met their on-line partner in person, regardless of how sexually explicit or intimate their chat is. A sex therapist addresses this question and concludes:

> Infidelity . . . consists of taking sexual energy of any sort—thoughts, feelings, and behaviors—outside of a committed sexual relationship in such a way that it damages the relationship, and then pretending that this drain of energy will affect neither partner nor the relationship, as long as it remains undiscovered. Hiding (these feelings) devitalizes the relationship, compromises integrity, and co-opts the other partner's choices to be responsible and responsive. (Shaw, 1997b, p. 29)

Some people use such secret cyber affairs as an outlet for aspects of their eroticism (for example, a desire to explore more aggressive sexual encounters or mild fetishes) that they are not willing to discuss with their partners in fear of discomfort or disapproval. Could such experimentation actually serve as a type of "practicing" that would help a spouse initiate a more expansive marital sex life? A sex and marital therapist thinks not: "A cyberrelationship may approximate a real relationship—but,

(continued on next page)

by age 40. More recent estimates vary widely. According to researchers at the Kinsey Institute in the late 1980s, roughly 40% of husbands and 30% of wives have experienced extramarital affairs (Reinisch et al., 1988). Statistics from a number of magazine surveys—including *Cosmopolitan*, *Playboy*, *Redbook*, and *New Woman*—claim higher rates, but magazine survey results are quite unreliable, as discussed in Chapter 2.

The National Health and Social Life Survey (NHSLS) of 3432 Americans, ages 18 to 59, provides more reliable rates of extramarital affairs. This survey reported extramarital involvement rates of 25% and 15%, respectively, among married men and women. Furthermore, 94% of the married subjects indicated that they had been monogamous in the past year (Laumann et al., 1994). Some writers suggest that these unexpectedly high rates of monogamy are due, at least in part, to fear of contracting AIDS or other sexually transmitted diseases through extramarital sexual involvements.

The Impact of Extramarital Sex on a Marriage

The effects of extramarital sex on a marriage vary. When secret involvements are discovered, the "betrayed" spouse may feel devastated. He or she may experience a variety of emotions, including feelings of inadequacy and rejection, extreme anger, resentment, shame, and jealousy. Jealousy may emerge from a sense of betrayal—the belief that the spouse is giving away something that belongs exclusively to the other partner. The fear that another person will usurp one's position of preeminence in the life of one's spouse may also be involved. Especially for men, part of sexual jealousy may stem from a sense of ownership. However, the discovery of infidelity does not inevitably erode the quality

On the Edge

then, so does sex with an inflatable doll. Neither one is likely to help people develop substantial capacity for an intimate relationship" (Schnarch, 1997, p. 19). Moreover, although such a secret liaison may make an individual feel more alive, the fantasies and illusions of virtual reality may make solving real-life issues all the more difficult. The secrecy and lying (even by omission) further erodes connection with the spouse and amplifies the attraction to the cyberrelationship (Shaw, 1997b).

Virtual affairs are becoming a common precipitating factor for couples seeking marital therapy, as the following situation illustrates. Jerry brought Beth to counseling because Beth was staying up all night and spending much of her day online. She claimed Jerry was preoccupied with his work and inattentive and overcontrolling of her. He had found a computer printout of a picture of a naked man and was convinced she had at least one online lover. She later traveled to meet a man she had fallen in love with online, although she later lost interest after she met him. Beth said she had not had sex with him, thereby remaining faithful to Jerry. She claimed that her current computer relationships were just good friends, but Jerry walked in when she was at the computer—nude, with her face flushed. The couple began to make some small positive changes in counseling, but failed to come to an appointment and were not heard from again. The treating therapist's concluding comments were "Virtual reality is no longer a game. Its impact is real and we, as consultants and experts on human relationships, may increasingly be asked to help our clients cope with their virtual lives" (Freedman, 1997, p. 71). The Internet did not "cause" the preexisting problems in Jerry and Beth's marriage, but it did allow her a unique forum to explore her sexuality in relative safety and privacy, enabling a dramatic acceleration of her distancing from Jerry (Treadway, 1997). However, if she did not have physical sexual contact with anyone, did she have an extramarital affair?

of a marriage. In some cases it may motivate a couple to search for and attempt to resolve sources of discord in their relationship—a process that may ultimately lead to an improved marriage.

Available data provide a hazy picture regarding the impact of extramarital sex on both the individual participant and the married couple. Blumstein and Schwartz's (1983) national survey of American couples revealed that the monogamous pairs in their sample had lower divorce rates than couples in which one or both had participated in extramarital relationships. This finding is consistent with the fact that extramarital relationships are often mentioned by divorced people as a cause of their marital breakup (Kelly, 1982). However, we cannot conclude that this apparent association necessarily reflects a cause-and-effect relationship. In at least some cases, extramarital sex may be a *symptom* of a disintegrating marriage rather than its cause. Involvement in an extramarital affair, whether or not it is discovered, may also have serious consequences for the participant—including loss of self-respect, severe guilt, betrayal of trust, stress associated with leading a secret life and not being able to talk about it with others, damage to reputation, loss of love, and complications of sexually transmitted diseases (Humphrey, 1987; Rubenstein, 1994).

Consensual Extramarital Relationships

Consensual extramarital relationships occur in marriages where both partners know about and agree to sexual involvements outside the marriage. A variety of arrangements fall under the category of consensual extramarital involvements, including unique perspectives of other societies, discussed in the "Attitudes Toward Extramarital Sexuality in Other Cultures" box. We briefly examine two: open marriage and swinging.

Consensual extramarital relationship
A sexual relationship that occurs outside the marriage bond with the consent of one's spouse.

Sexuality and Diversity
Attitudes Toward Extramarital Sexuality in Other Cultures

Marital coitus is the most common form of adult sexual activity in virtually all societies for which we have information.

Most societies have restrictive norms pertaining to extramarital sex. Nevertheless, many societies impose fewer restrictions on extramarital activity than does our own. Some societies even have formal rules allowing such behavior under special circumstances—during celebrations, as part of the marriage ceremony, or as a form of sexual hospitality (Frayser, 1985). With very few exceptions, men around the world are allowed greater access to extramarital coitus than are women. Some non-Western societies allow some form of extramarital coitus for wives (Gebhard, 1971). A few examples illustrate the diversity of this activity in other societies.

The aborigines of western Australia's Arnhem Land openly accept extramarital sexual relationships for both wives and husbands. They welcome the variety in experience and the break in monotony offered by extramarital involvements. Many also report increased appreciation of and attachment to the spouse as a result of such experiences. The Polynesian Marquesans, although not open advocates of extramarital affairs, nevertheless exhibit covert acceptance of such activity. A Marquesan wife often takes young boys or her husband's friends or relatives as lovers. Conversely, her husband may have relations with young unmarried girls or with his sisters-in-law. Marquesan culture openly endorses the practices of partner swapping and sexual hospitality, where unaccompanied visitors are offered sexual access to the host of the other sex. Sexual hospitality is also practiced by some Eskimo groups, where a married female host has intercourse with a male visitor. The Turu of central Tanzania regard marriage primarily as a cooperative, economic, and social bond. Affection between husband and wife is generally thought to be out of place; most members of this society believe that the marital relationship is endangered by the instability of love and affection. The Turu have evolved a system of romantic love, called Mbuya, that allows them to seek affection outside the home without threatening the stability of the primary marriage. Both husband and wife actively pursue these outside relationships.

Sexually Open Marriage

Open marriage
A marriage in which spouses, with each other's permission, have intimate relationships with other people as well as the marital partner.

The concept of **open marriage** received widespread public attention with the 1972 publication of George and Nena O'Neill's book *Open Marriage.* The essence of the O'Neills' thesis is that one relationship is unlikely to fulfill a person's total intimacy needs throughout the adult years. In an open marriage, people allow each other the freedom to have intimate emotional relationships with members of either sex without compromising their primary relationship. In a sexually open marriage, these intimacies include sexual sharing.

Those who support sexually open marriage believe that it is confining to limit sexual intimacy to only one person. Some have even argued that it is "essentially absurd to expect that all physical sexual expression for a fifty-year period will be confined to the marriage partner" (Roy & Roy, 1973, p. 144).

We have very limited information on the incidence of sexually open relationships in American society. Blumstein and Schwartz (1983) found that in 15% of 3574 married couples, both partners indicated having "an understanding that allows nonmonogamy under some circumstances." Nearly twice as many cohabitors (28%) had a similar understanding, while 29% of lesbian couples and 65% of male homosexual couples reported sexually open relationships.

Swinging

Swinging
The exchange of marital partners for sexual interaction.

Swinging, or comarital sex, refers to a form of consensual extramarital sex that a married couple shares (Atwood & Siefer, 1997). Husband and wife participate simultaneously and in the same location, sometimes at "conventions" with many couples, which distinguishes swinging from the extramarital sexual contact that might occur in an open marriage, where mutual participation is not usual. This activity was labeled "wife-swapping" in the past, but this term came into disrepute among swingers because it implies male ownership. Many participants believe it to be more morally acceptable than a secretive affair.

Swinging experienced its heyday in the 1970s and early 1980s, when most of the research on this social phenomenon was conducted. Since then, this form of consensual extramarital sex appears to be in decline. Available data suggest that fewer than 5% of American men and women have experienced swinging (Duckworth & Levitt, 1985; Tavris & Sadd, 1977).

Divorce

Current estimates suggest that half or more of all first marriages will end in divorce (Gottman, 1994b). These estimates are a common topic in the popular media, where the prevalence of divorce is often presented as a sign of societal rejection of the institution of marriage. This interpretation is not necessarily accurate. Available divorce statistics are not an entirely reliable indicator of the current state of American marriage.

Interpreting Divorce Statistics

Several factors have some bearing on how we interpret divorce statistics. A rise in divorce rates may reflect the increased ease of obtaining a legal marital dissolution more than a rise in dissatisfaction with marriage. Obtaining a legal divorce has become a simpler, less expensive process in recent years. Furthermore, a significant percentage of divorces involve people who have had more than one marriage and divorce. Therefore, a higher percentage of first marriages remain intact than a quick glance at the statistics indicates.

Do you think that dramatic increases in divorce rates have been steady since Kinsey's time?

Table 14.3 Marriage and Divorce Rates in the United States

(a) Number and Ratio of Divorces to Marriages, 1950, 1977, and 1996

	1950	*Ratio*	*1977*	*Ratio*	*1996*	*Ratio*
Number of divorces	385,000	1:4	1,097,000	1:2	1,150,000	1:2
Number of marriages	1,667,000		2,176,000		2,344,000	

(b) Number of Marriages and Divorces per 1000 U.S. Residents, 1970–1997

	'70	*'75*	*'80*	*'85*	*'90*	*'97**
Marriages	10.6	10.0	10.6	10.2	9.8	10.3
Divorces	3.5	4.8	5.2	5.0	4.7	4.3

*As of end of May 1997

Sources: (a) U.S. Bureau of the Census, 1978 & 1985. National Center for Health Statistics, 1982, 1985, 1989, 1992, 1995, 1997. (b) U.S. Bureau of the Census, 1985 & 1988. National Center for Health Statistics, 1989, 1992, 1995, 1997.

Research does confirm that the proportion of marriages ending in divorce has increased dramatically since the 1950s, as shown in Table 14.3. Table 14.3a shows that the ratio of divorce to marriage was one to four in 1950; by 1977 the ratio was one divorce to every two marriages. The ratio of divorces to marriages has shown a tendency to level off and has held relatively steady since 1977. In the last few years, another statistic, the *divorce rate* (number of divorces per 1000 residents), shown in Table 14.3b, has also shown a leveling off and even a slight decline. There were 3.5 divorces per 1000 U.S. residents in 1970, a rate that increased steadily until reaching a peak of 5.3 in 1981. Since then the divorce rate has slowly declined to 4.3 in 1997. It has been suggested that this leveling off of the divorce rate may reflect, in part, an increase in the number of cohabiting couples in America whose breakups are not included in divorce statistics.

Explaining High Divorce Rates

Several large-scale investigations have reported the demographic characteristics of divorced people, such as age, length of marriage, number of children, education level, profession, income, and so on. These studies have provided worthwhile data that can be used to predict probabilities of divorce for people sharing particular characteristics. However, they generally have relied on data provided by county, state, and federal bureaus, which almost never include reasons for divorce except for occasional reporting of legal grounds. In the absence of hard data, a number of writers have speculated on the factors responsible for the high divorce rates in America.

What do you consider to be some primary causes of divorce in America?

One frequently mentioned cause of divorce is the comparative ease of obtaining no-fault divorces since the liberalization of divorce laws during the 1970s. In an attempt to help marriages last and to counter the ease of divorce under "no fault" divorce laws, in 1997 Louisiana was the first state to offer the option of "covenant marriage" to couples applying for marriage licenses. Couples who choose covenant marriage agree to undergo premarital counseling and additional counseling if serious problems arise after marriage. The wait for the divorce to be final is extended from 180 days to two years, except in cases of a spouse committing domestic violence, child abuse, adultery, or a felony. At the least, the choice between standard marriage law and covenant marriage should promote meaningful conversations between couples contemplating marriage. Other states are considering implementing similar laws (Chapman, 1997; Etzioni, 1997).

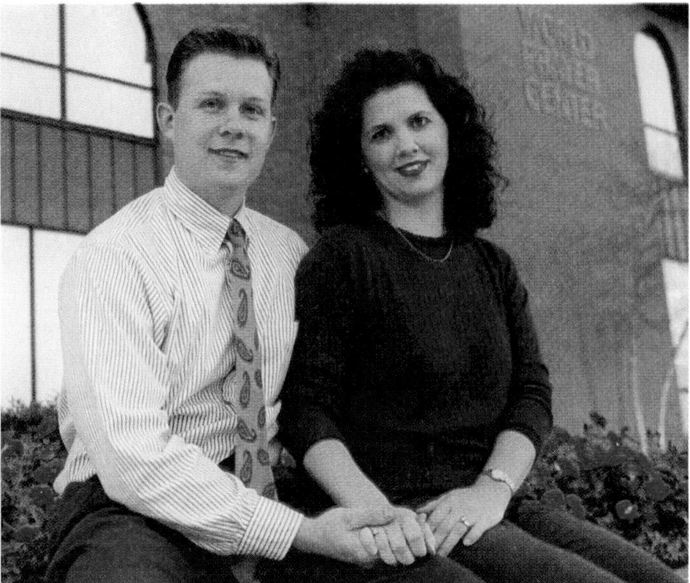

One of 400 couples who converted their marriages in 1998 to the new covenant marriage law in Louisiana.

Further reasons for the increase in divorce include a reduction in the social stigma attached to divorce (Holland, 1998). The marketing of greeting cards for divorce is an indication that the stigma of divorce is no longer so strong. Increasing expectations for marital and sexual fulfillment, which have caused people to become more disillusioned with and less willing to persist in unsatisfying marriages; the increased economic independence of women (Hiedemann et al., 1998); a greater abundance of wealth, which makes it easier for some people to maintain multiple families; and reduced influence of organized religion (Blackmun, 1996).

One study provided some much-needed empirical evidence of what divorced people perceived to be the cause(s) of their breakup (Cleek & Pearson, 1985). These researchers surveyed over 600 divorced men and women. The most frequently cited cause for divorce—by both sexes—was communication difficulties, followed by basic unhappiness and incompatibility.

Research has revealed two other variables—age at marriage and level of education—that may be associated with the decision to divorce. People who marry in their teen years are more than twice as likely to divorce than those who wed while in their 20s. Individuals who marry after age 30 have even lower divorce rates. Table 14.4 shows that men and women are waiting longer to marry. There also appears to be a demonstrable inverse relationship between level of education and divorce rates; that is, the lower the educational level, the higher the divorce rate. The one exception to this latter relationship is a disproportionately high divorce rate among women who have achieved postbaccalaureate degrees. Perhaps the increased economic and social independence of professional women with advanced degrees may contribute to this disparity in divorce rate trends (Martin & Bumpass, 1989; Norton & Moorman, 1987).

Table 14.4 Age at First Marriage

	Men	*Women*
1956	22	20
1994	26	24

Source: Blackmun, 1996a.

The correlation between age at marriage and divorce rates is of particular interest in light of a clear upward trend in the median age at first marriage. Prior to the turn of the century, most couples in the United States married while still in their teens. In 1950 the median marriage age was 22 and 20 for men and women, respectively, and by the 1990s these figures have risen to 26 for men and 24 for women. Perhaps the leveling off and even slight decline in the U.S. divorce rates in recent years may reflect, in part, the influence of a generalized rise in age at first marriage.

Helen Fisher, an anthropologist and author of *Anatomy of Love: The Natural History of Monogamy, Adultery, and Divorce* (1992), recently offered a provocative thesis about the course of relationships, from infatuation to divorce. Fisher contends that evolution has biologically programmed humans for serial pair-bonding characterized by a natural inclination to move on after four years, a pattern she calls the "four-year itch." To support this claim, Fisher cites divorce statistics from 62 cultures that reveal a peak in divorce rates around the fourth year of marriage. This "itch," she suggests, is a manifestation of ancestral patterns of pair-bonding in which early human couples needed to stay together just long enough for a child to be weaned from total dependence, a period of approximately four years. The birth of an additional child during this initial four-year period might then extend the union for about four more years. The idea that nature's design contributes to high divorce rates is a controversial theory that continues to be debated.

Adjusting to Divorce

Although the chain of events leading to marriage is unique for each individual, most people marry with the hope that the relationship will last. Divorce often represents loss of this hope and other losses as well: one's spouse, lifestyle, the security of familiarity, sometimes custody of one's children, and often part of one's identity (DeGarmo & Kitson, 1996). Many people who end nonmarital intimate relationships also experience these losses.

The loss a person feels in divorce is often comparable to the loss felt when a loved one dies (Napolitane, 1997). In both cases, the person undergoes a grieving process. There are important differences, however. When the grief is caused by death, rituals and social support may be helpful to the survivor. But no recognized grief rituals are provided by society to help the divorced person. Initially, a person may experience shock: "This cannot be happening to me." Disorganization may follow, a sense that one's entire world has turned upside down. Volatile emotions may unexpectedly surface. Feelings of guilt may become strong. Loneliness is common. Finally (usually not for several months or a year), a sense of relief and acceptance may come. If, after several months of separation, a person is not developing a sense of acceptance, she or he may need professional help.

The period after a divorce often involves many lifestyle changes and adjustments. However, the adjustment process can offer an opportunity for personal growth.

Although many of the feelings triggered by divorce are uncomfortable, even painful, they can be steps toward resolving the loss so that a person can reestablish intimate relationships. Grieving can lead to healing. And in fact, there is a potential for personal growth in the adjustment process that accompanies divorce. Many people experience a sense of autonomy for the first time in their lives. Others find that being single presents opportunities to experience more fully dimensions of themselves that had been submerged within the marriage. Learning to reach out to others for emotional support can help diminish feelings of aloneness. Divorce can offer an opportunity to reassess oneself and one's past, a process that may lead to the evolution of a new life.

Making the transition from marital to postmarital sexual relationships often presents a challenge to divorced individuals. The newly divorced person may experience considerable ambivalence about intimacy. Feelings of anger, rejection, or fear remaining from the trauma of the divorce may inhibit openness to intimate relationships. To protect themselves from emotional vulnerability, some people may withdraw from potential sexual relationships. Others may react by seeking many superficial sexual encounters.

Despite the problems newly single people often encounter in establishing nonmarital sexual expression, a majority of divorced individuals become sexually active within the first year following the breakup of their marriages (Stack & Gundlach, 1992). A survey of several hundred individuals also indicated that divorced people experience an overall increase in sexual activity following their divorces (Simenauer & Carroll, 1982). Even since widespread concern about AIDS, people continue to be sexually active after the breakup of their marriages. In one national survey, 74% of divorced and 80% of separated respondents reported being sexually active in the previous 12 months (Smith, 1991).

Approximately four out of five divorced persons remarry, most within three years of the divorce (Lown & Dolan, 1988). Although many remarried people report that their second marriage was better than the first, evidence indicates that second marriages are more likely to end in divorce than first marriages (Ganong & Coleman, 1989; Lown et al., 1989). Remarried people may be inclined to rate second marriages higher because they strive harder to achieve good communication, have fewer romantic illusions, and are more committed to effectively resolving conflicts. However, they are also inclined to monitor second marriages more closely than initial marriages, and may be less willing to stick around when things turn sour. Some researchers also believe that second marriages are more prone to fail because the trauma of divorce has been lessened somewhat by having gone through it once already (Blumstein & Schwartz, 1983). Furthermore, the financial stresses associated with remarriage (alimony and child support, high costs involved with establishing a new residence, and so forth) represent a major source of discord and divorce in remarried families.

The high divorce rate could also be seen as a vote of confidence for happy marriages. A writer explains, "Perhaps the divorce rate doesn't mean what it seems to mean. . . . Perhaps the divorce rate measures a sentimental hopefulness, a wistful pursuit of legalized happy-ever-after in which somehow, against all odds, we continue to believe. Unrealistic, maybe, but rather sweet. Besides, despite divorce being possible for under a hundred dollars and swiftly available in many locales, half of all our married folk stay together, for richer, for poorer, till death them do part. Perhaps things have never been better" (Holland, 1998, p. 93).

Sexuality and Aging

To a young adult, the altered sexual expression that accompanies aging may seem remote and unimportant. However, in the later years of life, most people begin to note certain changes taking place in their sexual response patterns. Some women and men who understand the nature of these variations may accept them with equanimity. Others may observe them with concern.

An important source of the confusion and frustration that many aging people feel is the prevailing notion that old age is a sexless time. However, sexuality can actually improve in later life. As a 76-year-old woman describes:

When I was married 47 years ago, my husband and I were both 29, and both virgins. I was taught that sex was for procreation only, so the adjustment to each other was not easy. The years of having babies, raising children, and, for my husband (a workaholic), getting established in his profession took much time and energy, and sex was an unimportant part of our lives. Now we are 76 years old and with the gift of time, good health, and financial security, our sex life is wonderful and very much a part of our fulfilling lives—truly, the best years of our lives. (Authors' files)

Why has aging in our society often been associated with sexlessness? There are a number of reasons. Part of the answer is that American culture is still influenced by the philosophy that equates sexuality with procreation. For people beyond their reproductive years, this viewpoint offers little beyond self-denial.

Moreover, American society focuses on youth. The media usually link love, sex, and romance with the young. There is also an often unspoken assumption in American society that it is not quite acceptable for older people to have sexual needs (Clements, 1996). With such widespread denial of the validity of sexual expression in the "golden years," it is not surprising that many people are confused about aging and sexuality. As the "sexual revolution" generation moves into senior citizenry, these ideas will be even more obsolete. In addition, as the percentage of seniors in the population increases, as shown in Table 14.5, Madison Avenue will target its advertising accordingly.

Table 14.5 Increases in Percentage of U.S. Population 65 or Older

Year	Percentage
1900	4%
1980	12%
2000	20%

Source: Segraves & Segraves, 1995.

The Double Standard and Aging

We have discussed the double standard as it relates to male and female sexual expression during adolescence and adulthood: Feelings and behaviors that are considered acceptable for males are often viewed as unacceptable or inappropriate for females. The assumptions and prejudices implicit in the sexual double standard continue into old age, imposing a particular burden on women.

Although a woman's sexual capabilities continue after menopause, it is not uncommon for her to be considered past her sexual prime relatively early in life (Kite et al., 1991). The cultural image of an erotically appealing woman is commonly one of youth. As a woman grows further away from this nubile image, she is usually considered less and less attractive (McQuaide, 1998). In our society, even young girls are sometimes advised not to frown ("You'll get wrinkles"); cosmetics, trendy clothing, and even surgery are often used to maintain a youthful appearance for as long as possible.

In contrast, the physical and sexual attractiveness of men is often considered to be enhanced by the aging process. Gray hair and facial wrinkles may be thought to look "distinguished" on men—signs of accumulated life experience and wisdom. Likewise, while the professional achievements of women may be perceived as threatening to a potential male partner, it is relatively common for a man's sexual attractiveness to be closely associated with his achievements and social status, both of which may increase with age.

The pairings of powerful, older men and young, beautiful women reflect the double standard of aging. The marriage of a 55-year-old man and a 25-year-old woman would probably generate a much smaller reaction than that of a 55-year-old woman and a 25-year-old man. And as you might expect, pairings of older men and younger women occur much more commonly than the reverse. However, the percentage of marriages of women older than their husbands has increased, and about 35% of women age 45 and older marry younger men (Gavzer, 1987).

Many contemporary older women find increased self-acceptance and self-expression in the years past 50.

What aspects of sexuality are most important to older men's and women's sense of well-being? Do you think these aspects are the same or different for older women and men?

One study (Stimson et al., 1981) suggested that the aspects of sexuality that contribute to a general feeling of well-being among the aged are different for men and women. For the older man, both sexual performance and attractiveness to the other sex appeared to be crucial to general feelings of well-being. For older women, the equation was somewhat different. Although sexual performance did not seem related to general feelings of well-being, feeling sexually attractive to the other sex was important; when the older woman no longer felt attractive, her general feelings of well-being decreased. Given that attractiveness in women is often equated with youthfulness, aging may affect a woman's sense of well-being more than a man's.

In response to the double standard of aging, the writer Susan Sontag has presented an alternative view:

> Women have another option. They can aspire to be wise, not merely nice; to be competent, not merely helpful; to be strong, not merely graceful; to be ambitious for themselves, not merely themselves in relation to men and children. They can let themselves age naturally and without embarrassment, actively protesting and disobeying the conventions that stem from this society's double standard about aging. Instead of being girls, girls as long as possible, who then age humiliatingly into middle-aged women and then obscenely into old women, they can become women much earlier—and remain active adults, enjoying the long, erotic career of which women are capable, for longer. Women should allow their faces to show the lives they have lived. (1972, p. 38)

Sexual Activity in Later Years

We have seen that our society tends to perceive the older years as a time when sexuality no longer has a place in people's lives (Adams et al., 1996). What does research show about the reality of sexuality among older people in our own society?

In fact, research findings indicate that in our society, sexual interest and activity continue to play a role in people's lives as a natural part of the aging process. In a survey of adults 65 and older, whose average age was 74, 40% reported being sexually active (Clements, 1996). It is true that a gradual pattern of decline often accompanies advancing age and that a number of variables may interfere with sexual activity, but many people remain sexually active well into their eighties and even later, adjusting successfully to the physical changes described in Chapter 6.

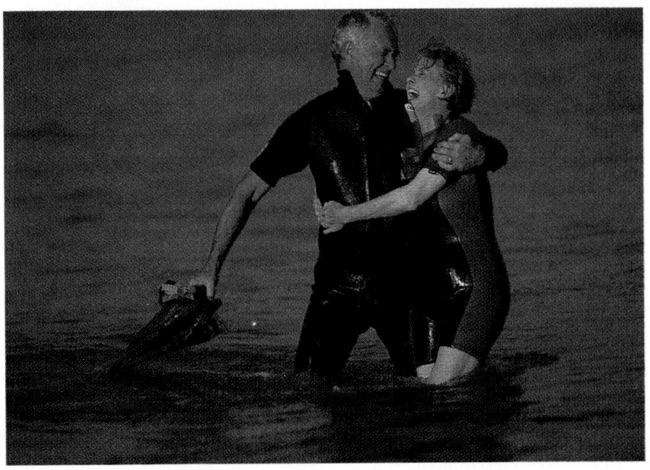

The need for affection and sexual intimacy extends into the older years, which can be a time of sharing and closeness.

Factors in Maintaining Sexual Activity

One factor determining sexual activity levels in later years is each person's individuality. If you enjoy reading mystery novels, talking on the phone, and eating chocolate ice cream as a young adult, you probably do not expect these preferences to change when you are 60 or 70 years old. Similarly, sexuality in the older years must be viewed along the continuum of each individual's personality. Kinsey's studies (1948 & 1953) revealed a close correlation between a person's sexual activity levels in early adulthood and his or her sexual activity in later years. Later supporting research has found that the differences among men and women in levels of sexual activity before middle age tended to be maintained as those individuals grew older (Bretschneider & McCoy, 1988; Leiblum & Bachmann, 1988). These findings do not necessarily demonstrate a cause-and-effect relationship between sexual activity in young adulthood and old age; it may simply be that those people who had the strongest interest in sex in their youth maintain that interest into old age.

Another factor in maintaining sexual activity in later years is, simply put, maintaining sexual activity. Masters and Johnson (1966) reported that regularity of sexual expression throughout the adult years (whether by masturbation or activity with a partner) was a crucial factor in maintaining satisfactory sexual functioning beyond youth and middle age. People who continue to be sexually active experience less decline in the ability to function sexually than those who stop having sex. One survey found that more older people approved of masturbation (62%) than engaged in it (Brecher, 1984). This study also found that the incidence of masturbation among both male and female respondents declined with age, and that a greater proportion of men than women—at all ages—reported masturbating (see Table 14.6).

A third factor influencing sexual activity in older adulthood is health. Poor health and illness have a greater impact on sexual functioning than age itself (Miller, 1995). With age, physical problems can interfere with many aspects of functioning, including sexuality; and in long-term relationships, the illness of one person is likely to affect not just that individual's sexual expression but also that of the partner (Segraves & Segraves, 1995). Besides contributing to general and sexual health, regular physical activity (walking, jogging, swimming, and so forth) and a healthy diet enhance sexual desire and erotic abilities (Clements, 1996).

Far from developing a total incapacity for recreational activities, older people may simply pursue them less often and at a more leisurely pace. The same can be true of one's sex life, particularly if misconceptions and anxieties are avoided or resolved.

An Emphasis on Quality over Frequency

Although older adulthood may bring some additional aches and pains and a general slowing down of physical functioning, for many people it also brings rewards. For couples

Table 14.6 Percentage of Older People Who Report That They Masturbate: Differences Between Men and Women

	Men (%)	*Women (%)*
Age 50–59	66	47
Age 60–69	50	37
Age 70 and above	43	33
Married	52	36
Unmarried	63	54

Source: Brecher, 1984.

who remain within a long-term relationship, the opportunities for sexual expression often increase. As pressures from work, children, and fulfilling life's goals wane, there is more time for sharing with a partner. Some people find their sex lives markedly improved by the greater opportunities to explore relaxed and prolonged lovemaking. Genital contact may become less frequent, but interest, pleasure, and frequency of nonintercourse activities such as caressing, embracing, and kissing may remain stable or increase.

Intimacy, a lifelong need, may find new and deeper dimensions with the personal maturity in later years (Shaw, 1994). As one man describes:

> I'm closer to my wife than I ever was. We've been together seventeen years, but I don't think we were ready before to be that close. Now I guess we're secure and comfortable enough in ourselves to accept the intensity of our intimacy. We have a deep, intimate, intense closeness now—the honesty of it, I never conceived of. We could be physically touching each other, close as in sex, but if you're not emotionally there, you don't really touch each other. Now everything has come together, and both of us are really involved in our marriage. (Friedan, 1994, p. 279)

With age, couples may increasingly emphasize quality rather than quantity of sexual experience. One study of heterosexual men found that, for younger men, the amount of sexual activity was important to their social confidence, whereas for older men it was the quality of their encounters that was crucial (Stimson et al., 1981). A small study of older gay men had similar findings. Most said they had sex less frequently than when they were younger, but half felt that it was more satisfying than before (Kimmel, 1978).

One survey of older adults found that, while sexual frequency declines, enjoyment of sex sometimes increases with age. Many respondents found new techniques for maintaining or enhancing their enjoyment of sex despite progressive physiological changes. For example, 43% of women and 56% of men provided oral stimulation to their partners. Some used fantasy or sexually explicit materials; others engaged in manual and oral stimulation of the breasts and genitals, anal stimulation, use of a vibrator, various coital positions, sex in the morning, or exclusive fondling and cuddling (Brecher, 1984).

Middle- and upper-middle-class older adults are more likely to include options beyond intercourse than are those in lower socio-

Sexual relationships may improve in later years when individuals redefine their sexual and affectional relationships.

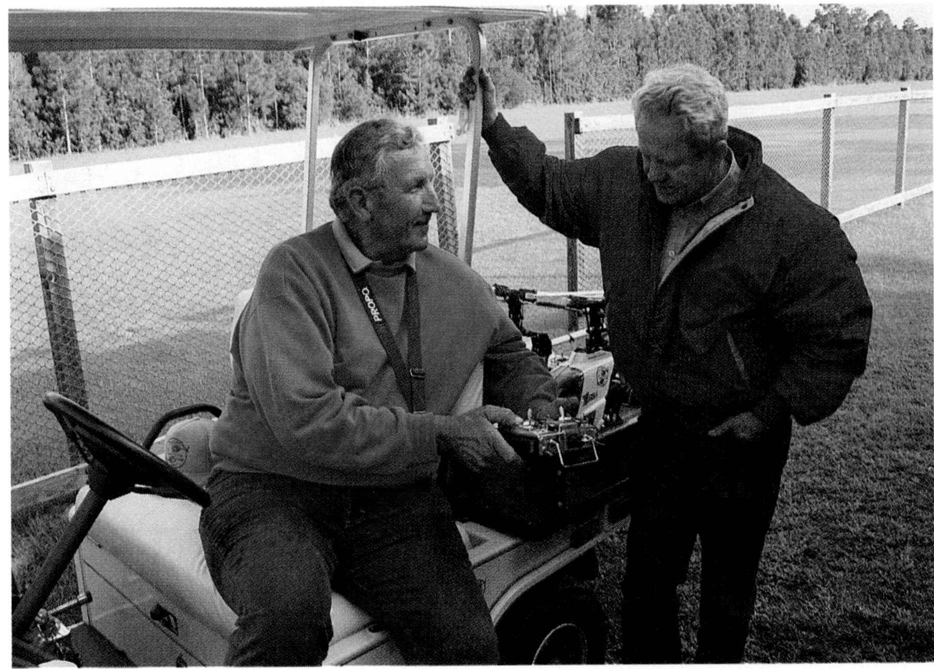

Nonsexual friendships often provide affection and closeness.

economic groups. In one study, most of the men in the lower socioeconomic group stopped all sexual activity when they were unable to have intercourse (Cogen & Steinman, 1990). These data support Kinsey's findings that the poor and working classes were strongly oriented toward intercourse, considering alternative expressions unacceptable. Openness to experimenting and developing new sexual strategies together with a supportive partner is instrumental in continuing sexual satisfaction (Bachmann, 1991). Some older individuals and couples participate in sex therapy to enhance their sexual lives (LoPiccolo, 1991).

Older people may also redefine their sexual and affectional relationships. Nonsexual friendships with either sex can offer affectionate physical contact, emotional closeness, intellectual stimulation, and opportunities for socializing. A supportive network of close friends helps to minimize loneliness and maintain enthusiasm for life, especially for the unmarried (Potts, 1997).

It is not uncommon for new sexual relationships to blossom in later adulthood. A 67-year-old woman explains:

> Eight years after my husband died, I met a widower on a tour of New Orleans. The physical attraction was intense for both of us. Neither of us had had sex for many years, but two days after discovering each other we were in bed with clothes strewn all over the floor. The sex (which neither of us was sure we'd be able to achieve) was sensational. We're very much in love but have decided not to marry because we both love our homes, need "space," and are financially independent. Our children accept our lifestyle and are very happy with our respective "significant other." (Authors' files)

Homosexual Relationships in Later Years

Most of the challenges and rewards of aging are experienced by adults, regardless of sexual orientation. Some unique aspects may be experienced by gay men and lesbians.

How do you think life satisfaction for older homosexual people compares with that for aging heterosexual adults?

The stereotypical view that homosexual people as a group face a lonely and unhappy old age is not supported by the limited research available. In fact, some gay men and lesbians may be better prepared for coping with the adjustments of aging than are many heterosexual men and women. Many homosexual individuals have planned for their own financial support and have consciously created a network of supportive friends (Kelly & Rice, 1986). Having successfully faced the adversities of belonging to a stigmatized group may also help them deal with the losses that come with aging.

One study found that older homosexual males match or exceed comparable groups in the general population on a measure of life satisfaction. The majority of these men reported that they socialized primarily with age peers. There was a change over time toward fewer sexual partners, but frequency of sexual activity remained quite stable, and 75% were satisfied with their current sex lives (Berger, 1982).

As a group, older lesbians may have some advantages over older heterosexual women. Because their partners are not statistically likely to die at a younger age, an older homosexual woman is less likely to be left alone than is a heterosexual woman—and if she is, she does not face a limited pool of potentially eligible partners. Furthermore, the double standard of aging is not usually an issue for lesbians: Research has revealed that most older lesbians prefer women of similar ages as partners (Raphael & Robinson, 1980).

Toward Androgyny in Later Life

Development toward androgyny in personal, interpersonal, and sexual styles occurs for many people in later life (Hyde et al., 1991). On a biological level, the hormonal differences between women and men tend to diminish. Estrogen levels in women decline rapidly following menopause, and androgen levels in men decline gradually from about age 30 on. The extent to which these hormonal changes contribute to increased androgyny is unknown.

On psychological and social levels, the gender-role differences between men and women also tend to diminish in later years. Expectations for gender-specific roles and responsibilities are more pronounced in younger adulthood, when the demands of supporting and rearing a family pressure men to focus on their jobs or careers and women to focus on taking care of the children. But with retirement approaching and children leaving home, such pressures tend to decline—thus freeing both women and men to develop more androgynous patterns.

One study found that older men and women developed other-sex characteristics by age 50 without relinquishing same-sex characteristics:

> Individuals who were the psychologically healthiest at age 50 showed increased androgyny over time. Women became more assertive and analytic while remaining nurturant and open to feelings. Men became more giving and expressive while they continued to be assertive and ambitious. (Livson, 1983, p. 112)

Some older men may give themselves more permission to show their feelings and personal selves more fully and to be more emotionally intimate (Friedan, 1994). One study found that men who were more emotionally expressive also experienced more sexual interest (Thomas, 1991). There is also often a shift in power within the marital relationship, with women being more likely to have increased power in later rather than in earlier life stages (Chiriboga & Thurnher, 1980).

These developments can help set the stage for a merging of sexual styles that may occur in later years. A more androgynous orientation allows individuals to expand their concepts of a sensuous man or woman (Rice & Kelly, 1987). Older males often become more similar to women in their sexual behavior, in that fantasy and ambience become more important and orgasm less so. Older adults may move away from the stereotypical focus of women on the relationship and men on genital sex. Over the lives of many of the subjects of one study, women developed a greater interest in genital sex and men in nongenital sexuality, thus realizing a more harmonious relationship (Bangs, 1985).

People who continue to grow in age can develop a wholeness of self that transcends the masculine–feminine split in women and men (Shaw, 1994). Intimacy then involves a sharing of that integrated, multidimensional self (Friedan, 1994). A sex and marital therapist further explains:

> The essence of sexual intimacy lies not in mastering specific sexual skills . . . but in the ability to allow oneself to deeply know and to be deeply known by one's partner. So simple to articulate, so difficult to achieve, this ability of couples to really see each other, to see inside each other during sex, requires the courage, integrity and maturity to face oneself and, even more frightening, convey that self—all that one is capable of feeling and expressing—to the partner. . . . Adult eroticism is more a function of emotional maturation than of physiological responsiveness. (Schnarch, 1993, p. 43)

This author believes that relatively few people reach their full potential for sexual intensity before their 50s or 60s. This strong sense of self that can create powerful sexual intimacy requires life experience and self-knowledge and acceptance to develop. The real treasure of the "last love" of partners who have experienced enough life to deeply know themselves and each other can make the "first love" of new partners pale by comparison (Schnarch, 1993). As a Turkish proverb comments, "Young love is from the earth, and late love is from heaven" (Koch-Straube, 1982).

Widowhood

Although a spouse can die during early or middle adult years, widowhood usually occurs later in life. In most cases, it is the man who dies first, a tendency that has become more pronounced during this century. The ratio of widows to widowers has more than doubled from the early 1900s to to the late 1990s (U.S. Bureau of the Census, 1997).

Men die an average of eight years earlier than women (Greene & Field, 1989). There are 4.5 widows for every one widower (U.S. Bureau of the Census, 1997). Women accustomed to expressing their sexuality exclusively within marriage find themselves suddenly alone. While older men without partners often seek younger female companions, we saw in the discussion of the double standard that older women are less likely to be involved with younger men. Thus for many older heterosexual women, the pool of potential new

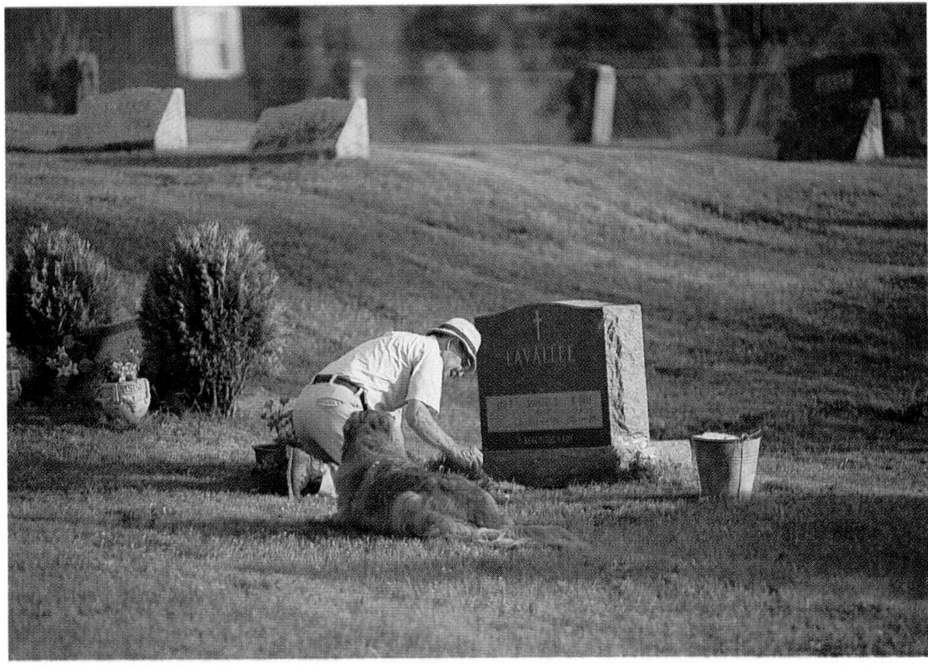

Widowerhood.

partners is limited. In addition, for older adults who live in nursing homes, the options for sexual expression may be severely curtailed by the attitudes and policies of the institution and its staff. The boxed discussion "Does Sexuality Have a Place in Nursing Homes?" looks at this unfortunate situation.

Many older adults remain interested in sexuality, however, even if partners are no longer available (Mulligan & Palguta, 1991). One survey of 200 healthy people ages 80–102 found that 88% of men and 72% of women fantasized about sex (Bretschneider & McCoy, 1988). For some older women and men, widowed or divorced, masturbation can become or continue to be a form of sexual release and expression. A study of 800 people between ages 60 and 91 reported that women are becoming more accepting of masturbation (Starr & Weiner, 1981). As a woman of 60 stated:

> I thought my life was over when my husband of 35 years died two years ago. I have learned so much in that time. I learned to masturbate. I had my first orgasm. I had an "affair." I have established intimate relationships with women for the first time in my life. (Authors' files)

The postmarital adjustment of widowhood is different in some ways from that of divorce. Widowed people typically do not have the sense of having failed at marriage. The grief may be more intense, and the quality of the emotional bond to the deceased mate is often quite high. For some people, this emotional tie remains so strong that other potential relationships appear dim by comparison. However, many people who have lost a spouse to death do remarry, about half of widowed men and a quarter of widowed women (Lown & Dolan, 1988).

Ethical/Legal Issues

Does Sexuality Have a Place in Nursing Homes?

The belief that sexual feelings and behaviors are inappropriate for older adults is so ingrained in our social traditions that until recently it has rarely been questioned. However, the treatment that older people have received in some nursing homes has come under increasing public scrutiny. Some nursing homes have been criticized for their insensitivity to the human rights of aged individuals (Pratt & Schmall, 1989). For instance, medications are sometimes prescribed without consideration of their effects on sexuality. Staff in nursing homes sometimes separate married couples who engage in sexual activities (Falk & Falk, 1980). Of the 5% of our population over age 65 who live in nursing homes at a given time, many are denied the adult rights of sexual opportunity and privacy (Richardson & Lazur, 1995).

These problems can be especially acute for older homosexual partners. Antihomosexual prejudice may make it extremely difficult for a gay person to express affection, much less have sexual contact with his or her lover or friend in hospitals or nursing homes (Kornblum, 1997). Even nursing homes that allow conjugal visits for their heterosexual residents are unlikely to do so for a homosexual couple.

Concerned individuals, progressive nursing home personnel, and organizations such as the Gray Panthers and Services to Ongoing Mature Aging are beginning to have some effect on restrictive nursing home practices (Fielo & Warren, 1997). As a result, staff education, programs on sexuality for residents, private lounges, and acceptance of the affectional and sexual needs and rights of elderly residents are being recognized as important elements of care. It is our hope that these policies and attitudes will gain wider acceptance, so that older adults who must reside in hospitals or nursing homes can still have opportunities for sexual expression and all the physical and emotional intimacy and joy that sexual activity can provide.

Summary

SINGLE LIVING

Although single living is often seen as a transition period before, in between, or after marriage, many people choose it as a long-term lifestyle.

The proportion of individuals who have never married has increased dramatically since 1970 for men and women in their 20s.

COHABITATION

Almost four million couples were cohabiting (living together without marriage) in 1997. Although cohabitors who later marry seem to have a higher risk of marital discord than couples who have not lived together prior to marriage, the exact nature of the relationship between cohabitation and marriage remains to be explained.

MARRIAGE

The primary element in the marriage ideal of our society is a permanent, sexually exclusive, and legal relationship between two heterosexual adults.

There are a variety of techniques for predicting, with a high degree of success, the probability that a couple will experience marital happiness. These assessment devices include questionnaires, videotapes of couple interaction, and physiological data reflective of arousal level.

Recent changes in sexual behaviors can be observed within the marital relationship. Married couples are engaging in a wider variety of sexual behaviors and experiencing coitus with greater frequency and duration than in the past.

EXTRAMARITAL RELATIONSHIPS

Nonconsensual extramarital relationships occur without the partner's consent.

Kinsey found that approximately 50% of married males and 25% of married females had experienced sexual intercourse outside marriage by age 40.

The results of magazine surveys suggest that the percentage of married American men and women who experience extramarital involvements may be significantly greater than reported in Kinsey's surveys, but data from the NHSLS found lower rates of extramarital sex than Kinsey did.

Consensual extramarital relationships occur with the spouse's knowledge and agreement. Examples of these involvements include sexually open marriage and swinging.

The sexually open-marriage concept can include emotional, social, and sexual components in the extramarital relationship.

Swinging, in which couples participate in sexual relations with others simultaneously and in the same location, experienced a popularity peak in the 1970s and is now in marked decline.

DIVORCE

The ratio of divorces to marriages has increased from one to four (1950) to one to two (1996).

In the last few years, the divorce rate (divorces per 1000 residents) has begun to level off and even decline somewhat.

Some of the causes of high divorce rates may include the liberalization of divorce laws, a reduction in the social stigma attached to divorce, unrealistic expectations for marital and sexual fulfillment, increased economic independence of women, reduced influence of organized religion.

One important study found that the most common reason given by men and women for their divorces was communication difficulty, followed by basic unhappiness and incompatibility.

Divorce typically involves many emotional, sexual, interpersonal, and lifestyle changes and adjustments.

SEXUALITY AND AGING

The options for sexual expression may change in the older years, as many individuals find themselves without a sexual partner. Masturbation may serve as one alternative.

Sexual relationships may improve during later years when individuals focus on intimacy and redefine their sexual and affectional relationships. Physical health and exercise can help maintain sexual functioning and satisfaction.

A blurring of stereotypic gender roles, an increase in androgyny, and a consequent merging of sexual styles often occur in later life.

It is unlikely that the physiosexual changes of aging alone will eliminate one's capacity to maintain a satisfying sex life.

WIDOWHOOD

The ratio of widows to widowers is now 4.5 to 1.

Thought Provokers

1. You and an intimate companion have decided to live together. What aspects of your cohabitation relationship would you want to discuss and reach agreement on first? What problems would you expect to face as a result of your changed relationship? Do you think that cohabitation might affect any future marriage you enter into?
2. Consider your married friends and relatives. Of those that have happy marriages, what seem to be the major factors that contribute to their satisfaction? What about those that are experiencing poor adjustment within their marriages? What appear to be the primary causes for their lack of happiness?
3. What images of aging and sexuality do you notice in the media? What effect do they create? Can you imagine yourself as a "sexy senior citizen"?
4. If you were getting married, would you opt for a covenant marriage or one that could be more easily terminated? Why?
5. Are there any advantages to old age that you are looking forward to? What do you think the potential advantages and disadvantages of the development in later years toward androgyny might be?

Suggested Readings

Anderson, Carol; and Stewart, Susan (1994). *Flying Solo: Single Women in Midlife.* New York: Norton. Interviews with 90 happily single women.

Blumstein, Philip; and Schwartz, Pepper (1983). *American Couples.* New York: Morrow. This highly acclaimed book provides a wealth of information about relationships among couples—married and cohabiting, heterosexual and homosexual.

Butler, Robert; and Lewis, Myrna (1993). *Love and Sex After Sixty.* New York: Harper & Row. This book provides extensive, down-to-earth health and living-adjustment information related to sexuality. Many useful suggestions are offered within a context of individual differences, with encouragement for personal and relationship growth.

Duff, Johnette; and Truitt, George (1991). *The Spousal Equivalent Handbook.* Houston: Sunny Beach. This highly readable handbook provides succinct and practical advice to unmarried people living together (other sex or same sex) regarding the legalities of partnership rights. Topics covered include cohabitation agreements, taxes, financial planning, durable and medical powers of attorney, and wills.

Friedan, Betty (1993). *The Fountain of Age.* New York: Simon & Schuster. This book explores the aging process as a time of exuberant discovery and development.

Schnarch, David (1997). *Passionate Marriage: Sex, Love, and Intimacy in Emotionally Committed Relationships.* New York: Norton. An engaging discussion showing how personal maturity and hot sex in marriage must be developed hand in hand.

Spring, Janis (1996). *After the Affair.* New York: HarperCollins. This book addresses recovery following an affair.

Wolf, Sharon (1997). *How to Stay Lovers for Life.* New York: Dutton. A marriage counselor describes how to diagnose and repair relationship problems and maximize passion.

Web Resources

WWW.

The Couples Place
www.couples-place.com/
Free information on building and improving relationships is accessible to public visitors of this site, and additional resources are available to those who sign up as members.

Divorce Source
www.divorcesource.com/
This Web site provides information on various aspects of divorce including child support and custody, alimony, and counseling. In addition, there is a divorce dictionary, access to related articles and publications, and live chat rooms.

Sexuality in Later Life
www.aoa.dhhs.gov/aoa/pages/agepages/sexualty.html
The National Institute on Aging and the Administration on Aging produce this Web page. Although brief, the information provided here reinforces the point that healthy sexuality can remain a vital aspect of life for the elderly.

15

The Nature and Origin of Sexual Difficulties

Origins of Sexual Difficulties
: *What kinds of illnesses and disabilities can interfere with sexual function?*
: *What relationship factors can create sexual problems?*

Desire-Phase Difficulties
: *What is the most common problem that brings people to sex therapists?*
: *What are the symptoms of sexual aversion?*

Excitement-Phase Difficulties
: *During what times in a woman's life is diminished lubrication normal?*
: *Why do the authors prefer the term* male erectile disorder *to* impotence?

Orgasm-Phase Difficulties
: *What percentage of women have never experienced orgasm? What percentage of men?*
: *How common is the problem of premature ejaculation?*

Dyspareunia
: *What conditions can cause painful intercourse in men?*
: *What conditions can cause painful intercourse in women?*

Over the years of our marriage, my sexual desire for my wife has diminished gradually to the point that it is presently almost nonexistent. There have been too many disputes over how we raise the children, too many insensitive comments, too many demands, not enough freedom to be my own person. When I look at her, I have to acknowledge that she is a remarkably beautiful woman, just as lovely as the day I was first attracted to her. I certainly feel no physical repulsion to her body. I guess it would be more accurate to say that I simply no longer have sexual feelings for her. One feeling I do have plenty of is hostility. I suspect it is this largely suppressed anger that has been the killer of my sexual interest. (Authors' files)

The next three chapters are concerned with some of the difficulties that can hinder sexual functioning and some ways of preventing or resolving these difficulties. This chapter looks at a number of relatively common sexual problems and the factors that frequently contribute to them. First we look at some common origins of problems—organic, cultural, individual, and interpersonal. We then discuss a number of specific problems related to sexual desire, arousal, and orgasm, and problems that cause painful intercourse. As throughout the text, relevant material pertains to individuals and couples regardless of sexual orientation. Chapter 16 outlines sex therapy approaches and ways of enhancing sexuality, even when no specific sexual problem exists. In Chapter 17 we turn our attention to understanding and preventing sexually transmitted diseases.

In reading this chapter, it is important to remember that sexual satisfaction is a subjective perception. A person or couple could experience some of the problems described in this chapter and yet be satisfied with their sex lives. For readers currently in a sexual relationship, the self-assessment inventory in the "Your Sexual Health" box will give you an indication of your level of satisfaction.

How common do you think sexual problems are? What percentage of people have sexual problems such as lack of desire, inability to experience an erection or orgasm, or rapid ejaculation?

Your Sexual Health

Self-Assessment

INDEX OF SEXUAL SATISFACTION

For readers who are sexually involved, this questionnaire is designed to measure the degree of satisfaction you have in the sexual relationship with your partner. It is not a test, so there are no right or wrong answers. Answer each item as carefully and accurately as you can by placing a number beside each one according to the following scale:

1 Rarely or none of the time
2 A little of the time
3 Some of the time
4 Good part of the time
5 Most or all of the time

1. I feel that my partner enjoys our sex life. _______
2. My sex life is very exciting. _______
3. Sex is fun for my partner and me. _______
4. I feel that my partner sees little in me except for the sex I can give. _______
5. I feel that sex is dirty and disgusting. _______
6. My sex life is monotonous. _______
7. When we have sex it is too rushed and hurriedly completed. _______
8. I feel that my sex life is lacking in quality. _______
9. My partner is sexually very exciting. _______
10. I enjoy the sex techniques that my partner likes or uses. _______
11. I feel that my partner wants too much sex from me. _______

Research indicates that sexual problems are quite common. The National Health and Social Life Survey found that sexual difficulties were prevalent in its sample, as shown in Table 15.1.

Origins of Sexual Difficulties

Determining the origins of sexual problems is often difficult and complex. There are several reasons for this. First, even when a sexual difficulty has been clearly identified, it is often hard to isolate the specific causes, because many varied influences and experiences contribute to sexual feelings and behavior. Second, it is usually difficult to identify a clear and consistent cause-and-effect relationship because the experiences that contribute to a specific sexual difficulty in one person may produce no such effects in another (LoPiccolo, 1989).

Table 15.1 Prevalence of Sexual Problems in a Nonclinical Sample

Percentage of adults in the general population who reported specific sexual problems in response to the question "In the last year, has there ever been a period of several months or more when you experienced . . . "

	Men	*Women*
Lack of sexual desire	16%	33%
Erection difficulties	10	—
Difficulty lubricating	—	19
Lack of orgasm	8	24
Premature orgasm	29	10
Pain during intercourse	3	14

Source: Laumann et al., 1994.

Your Sexual Health

12. I think sex is wonderful. ______
13. My partner dwells on sex too much. ______
14. I try to avoid sexual contact with my partner. ______
15. My partner is too rough or brutal when we have sex. ______
16. My partner is a wonderful sex mate. ______
17. I feel that sex is a normal function of our relationship. ______
18. My partner does not want sex when I do. ______
19. I feel that our sex life really adds a lot to our relationship. ______
20. My partner seems to avoid sexual contact with me. ______
21. It is easy for me to get sexually excited by my partner. ______
22. I feel that my partner is sexually pleased with me. ______
23. My partner is very sensitive to my sexual needs and desires. ______
24. My partner does not satisfy me sexually. ______
25. I feel that my sex life is boring. ______

Scoring Items 1, 2, 3, 9, 10, 12, 16, 17, 19, 21, 22, and 23 must be reverse-scored. (For example, if you answered 5 on the first item, you would change that score to 1.) After these positively worded items have been reverse-scored, if there are no omitted items, the score is computed by summing the item scores and subtracting 25. This assessment has been shown to be valid and reliable.

Interpretation Scores can range from 0 to 100, with a high score indicative of sexual dissatisfaction. A score of approximately 30 or above is indicative of dissatisfaction in one's sexual relationship.

Source: Adapted from Hudson et al., 1981.

The following paragraphs examine several factors that can interfere with a person's sexuality. Organic, cultural, individual, and relationship factors can all contribute to sexual difficulties. Significant interaction among these factors also occurs. Therefore, the separate categories we describe in the following pages are somewhat arbitrary. We hope that a clearer understanding of the events that shape sexuality will lead to increased satisfaction, communication, and pleasure.

Organic Factors

Physiological factors often play a role in sexual problems, so it is often desirable to have a general physical and a gynecological or urological exam to help rule out such causes (Gerdes, 1997; Knoll & Abrams, 1998). Sexual problems are frequently the result of a combination of physical and psychological factors rather than just one or the other (Levebvre, 1997; Martins & Reis, 1997). Any degree of physiological impairment can make a person's sexual response and functioning more vulnerable to disruption by negative emotions or situations. For example, a man with moderate diabetes may have no difficulty achieving an erection when he is rested and feeling comfortable with his partner but may be unable to do so when he is under stress—after a hard day at work or an argument with his partner. In fact, erectile disorders are the problems most likely to have an organic component.

Any disturbances in the vascular, endocrine, and neurological systems can contribute to sexual problems (Sipski & Alexander, 1997). Medications, surgeries, illnesses, disabilities, and "recreational" drugs can affect each of these systems, interfering with sexual interest and response as shown in Table 15.2.

Chronic Illness

Many of us will confront chronic illness in our own lives. The illness may impair the nerves, hormones, or blood flow essential to sexual functioning, and any accompanying pain and fatigue can distract from erotic thoughts and sensations or limit specific sexual activities (Burt, 1995). The following paragraphs describe the sexual impact of some specific illnesses.

DIABETES *Diabetes* is a disease that occurs when the pancreas fails to secrete adequate amounts of insulin. It affects 16 million people in the United States (Tilton, 1997). This disease of the endocrine system is a leading organic cause of erectile problems in men. Nerve damage or circulatory problems from diabetes can cause sexual problems (Hakim & Goldstein, 1996). Many diabetic men experience a reduction or loss of capacity for

Table 15.2 Sexual Effects of Some Abused and Illicit Drugs

Drugs	*Effects*
Alcohol	Chronic alcohol abuse causes hormonal alterations (reduces size of testes and suppresses hormonal function) and permanently damages the circulatory and nervous systems.
Marijuana	Reduces testosterone levels in men and decreases sexual desire.
Tobacco	Adversely affects small blood vessels in the penis and decreases the frequency and duration of erections (Mannino et al., 1994).
Cocaine	Causes erectile disorder and inhibits orgasm.
Amphetamines	High doses and chronic use result in inhibition of orgasm and decrease in erection and lubrication.
Barbiturates	Cause decreased desire, erectile disorders, and delayed orgasm.

Source: Finger et al., 1997.

erection, and a few diabetic men experience retrograde ejaculation (ejaculating into the bladder). Heavy alcohol use and poor blood sugar control increase the chances of erectile problems in diabetic men (McCulloch et al., 1984). Much less is known about the role of diabetes in women's sexual problems. Research has indicated that women who developed diabetes in adolescence report few sexual difficulties. However, women whose diabetes began in adulthood are likely to have problems with sexual desire, lubrication, and orgasm (Schreiner-Engle et al., 1987; Wincze et al., 1993).

ARTHRITIS *Arthritis* is a progressive, systemic disease that causes inflammation of the joints. Chronic inflammation can cause pain, destruction of the joint, or reduced joint mobility. Nerves and muscle tissues surrounding the affected joints are also often damaged. Arthritis does not directly impair sexual response, but body image problems, depression, chronic pain and fatigue, and medicines for the arthritis may diminish a person's interest in sex (Nadler, 1997). Pain or deformities in the hands may also make masturbation difficult or impossible without assistance. Arthritic impairment of hips, knees, arms, and hands may interfere with certain intercourse positions (Renshaw, 1995).

CANCER Cancer and its treatment can be particularly devastating to sexuality. The disease and its therapies can impair hormonal, vascular, and neurological functions necessary for normal sexual interest and response (Waldman & Eliasof, 1997). Pain can also greatly interfere with sexual interest and arousal. Chemotherapy and radiation therapy can cause hair loss, skin changes, nausea, and fatigue, all of which can negatively affect sexual feelings. Some cancer surgeries result in permanent scars, loss of body parts, or an ostomy (a surgically created opening for evacuation of body wastes after removal of the colon or bladder), all of which can result in a negative body image (Burt, 1995). Although all forms of cancer can affect sexual functioning, cancers of the reproductive organs can be especially devastating and therefore are of particular concern to many people (Anderson et al., 1989).

MULTIPLE SCLEROSIS *Multiple sclerosis (MS)* is a neurological disease of the brain and spinal cord in which damage occurs to the myelin sheath that covers nerve fibers; vision, sensation, and voluntary movement are affected. It is the most common disabling neurological condition for young adults in the United States (Schover et al., 1988). Studies have found that most MS patients experience changes in their sexual functioning and that at least half have sexual problems (Stenager et al., 1990). A person with MS may experience either a reduction or loss of sexual interest, genital sensation, arousal, or orgasm, as well as uncomfortable hypersensitivity to genital stimulation. Sexual arousal may not be possible by genital stimulation because of sensory losses (Smeltzer & Kelley, 1997). Vaginal dryness may affect women. These symptoms may vary and become worse over time.

CEREBROVASCULAR ACCIDENTS *Cerebrovascular accidents (CVA),* commonly called strokes, occur when brain tissue is destroyed due either to blockage of blood supply to the brain or to hemorrhage (breakage of a vessel, causing internal bleeding). Strokes often result in residual impairments of motor, sensory, emotional, and cognitive functioning that can have a negative effect on sexuality. Stroke survivors frequently report a decline in their frequency of interest, arousal, and sexual activity. Some factors that commonly influence the sexual behavior of people who have experienced a stroke include limited mobility, altered or lost sensation, impairment in verbal communication, and depression (Monga & Kerrigan, 1997).

Disabilities

Major disabilities such as spinal-cord injury, cerebral palsy, and blindness and deafness have widely varying effects on sexual responsiveness. Some people with these disabilities are able to maintain or restore satisfying sex lives; others find their sexual expression reduced or impaired by their difficulties (Welner, 1997). In the following sections, we look

Good communication and creative exploration can help individuals and couples minimize the sexual effects of disabilities and illnesses.

at some of these disabilities and discuss some of the sexual adjustments that people with these problems can make.

SPINAL-CORD INJURY People with *spinal-cord injuries (SCI)* have reduced motor control and sensation because the damage to the spinal cord obstructs the neural pathway between body and brain. The parts of the body that are paralyzed vary according to the location of the injury. A person can be *paraplegic* (a condition characterized by loss of feeling and voluntary muscle function of the trunk and legs) or *quadriplegic* (a condition characterized by loss of feeling and voluntary muscle function of the arms or hands, as well as of the trunk and legs). Injuries lower on the spine result in paraplegia, whereas higher spinal injuries cause quadriplegia.

Although the spinal-cord injury does not necessarily impair sexual desire and psychological arousal, a person with SCI may have impaired ability for arousal and orgasm; this varies according to the specific injury (Sipski, 1997). Some women and men with SCI are able to experience arousal or orgasm from psychological or physical stimulation; others are not (Kettl et al., 1991). Furthermore, a person with SCI may or may not be able to feel the arousal that he or she experiences. Some people with SCI report that the sensations they experience change or increase slightly over time. There is great individual variation in sexuality among those with spinal-cord injuries. Therefore, a person's sexual capacity cannot be predicted solely on the basis of the nature of the injury.

Overall, research indicates that 54–87% of men with SCI are able to experience erections. However, most such men are unable to ejaculate or experience orgasm (Alexander et al., 1994).

Much of the professional and personal sex education for individuals and couples faced with SCI consists of redefining and expanding sexual expression. Thus, although genital sensations may be very slight or nonexistent, heightened sexual responsiveness in other areas of the body may produce intense pleasure. Sensations in the inner arm, the breast, neck, or some other area that has retained some feeling may become an intensely satisfying substitute for lost genital sensitivity. In a technique known as *sensory amplification,* the individual concentrates on a physical stimulus to amplify its sensation—sometimes to the point of mental orgasm (Mooney et al., 1975).

Women with spinal-cord injuries usually lose sensations in the vulva (Berard, 1989), but other body areas above the level of the injury can become increasingly sensitive to erotic stimulation. Most women with SCI do not experience orgasm, but orgasmic-type sensations have been described from erotic stimulation, fantasy, or dreams. One woman described her experience:

> My head gets to a point where I don't think about what I am doing and it slides into the sensations . . . it feels good for a while and then subsides and I feel sort of satisfied. There is no peak at the end. (Becker, 1978, p. 194)

CEREBRAL PALSY *Cerebral palsy (CP)* is caused by damage to the brain that may occur before or during birth or during early childhood; it is characterized by mild to severe lack of muscular control. Involuntary muscle movements may disrupt speech, facial expressions, balance, and body movement. Involuntary, severe muscle contractions may cause limbs to jerk or assume awkward positions. A person's intelligence may or may not be affected. Unfortunately, it is often mistakenly assumed that people with CP are mentally disabled because of their physical difficulty in communicating.

Genital sensation is unaffected by CP. Spasticity and deformity of arms and hands may make masturbation difficult or impossible without assistance, and the same problems in the hips and knees may make certain intercourse positions painful or difficult (Joseph, 1991). For women with CP, chronic contraction of the muscles surrounding the vaginal opening may create pain during intercourse (Renshaw, 1987). Options that can be helpful to individuals with CP include trying different positions, propping legs up on pillows to help ease spasms, and exploring nongenital lovemaking. Partners can help with positions, and focusing on genital pleasure may help distract from pain.

The sexual adjustment of a person with CP depends not only on what is physically possible but also on environmental support for social contacts and privacy. People with CP and SCI may require the help of someone who can assist in preparation and positioning for sexual relations.

BLINDNESS AND DEAFNESS The sensory losses of blindness and deafness can affect a person's sexuality in several ways. A great deal of information and many attitudes and social interaction skills are acquired by seeing or hearing others, and visual or hearing deficits impair this learning process (Luey et al., 1995). In themselves, blindness and deafness do not appear to physically impair sexual interest or response. Other senses may play an important role, as a man who was born blind explains:

> During lovemaking, my other senses—touch, smell, hearing, and taste—serve as the primary way I become aroused. The caress of my partner, and the way she touches me, is tremendously exciting, perhaps even more so than for a sighted person. The feel of her breasts on my face, the hardness of her nipples pressing into my palms, the brush of her hair across my chest . . . these are just some of the ways I experience the incredible pleasures of sex. (Kroll & Klein, 1992, p. 136)

Coping and Enhancement Strategies

Individuals and couples can best cope with the sexual limitations of their illness or disability by accepting those limitations and developing the options that remain. For example, couples can minimize the effects of pain by planning sexual activity at optimal times of the day, using methods of pain control such as moist heat or pain medication, finding comfortable positions, and focusing on genital pleasure or arousing erotic images to distract from pain (Schover & Jensen, 1988). Expanding the definition of sexuality beyond genital arousal and intercourse to include dimensions such as erotic thoughts and sensual touch is also essential, as a 72-year-old man explains:

Sexual fulfillment after age 70 may take on a new richness. I had a prostatectomy a year and a half ago. I cannot muster more than a semierection (and that only by my wife's gentle caressing and body contact). Penetration is not possible, but by kissing, stroking gently, and by mutual masturbation, we come to wonderful mutual climax. I have no ejaculation, but a wonderfully satisfying "click." There is a lot of mutual sexuality—day to day—in looks, pats, hand holding, etc. Also, memory is a wonderful part of our lovemaking. (Authors' files)

Certainly, the limitations and special circumstances that illnesses and disabilities present are often a challenge for sexual adjustment (Hwang, 1997; Tepper, 1997). Good communication within relationships is especially important because the able-bodied partner is unlikely to know what the ill or disabled person can or cannot do or finds pleasing. Chronically ill and disabled people can greatly benefit from flexibility in sexual roles and innovation in sexual technique. As a woman with CP explained:

> My disability kind of makes things more interesting. We have to try harder and I think we get more out of it because we do. We both have to be very conscious of each other—we have to

> take time. That makes us less selfish and more considerate of each other, which helps the relationship in other areas beside sexuality. (Shaul et al., 1978, p. 5)

Exploration, experimentation, communication, and learning together are ways of relating that can contribute to pleasure and intimacy in the relationships of nondisabled couples too, as will be discussed further in the next chapter.

Medication Effects on Sexual Functioning

Several prescription and nonprescription medications have negative effects on sexuality in both sexes (Finger et al., 1997). The following is not a complete list; it just lists some of the more common ones. Heath care practitioners do not always remember to discuss potential sexual side effects of medications, so you may need to inquire about the possible effects on sexuality of any prescribed medicines. Often another medication can be substituted that will have fewer or milder negative effects on sexual interest, arousal, and orgasm. Therefore, individual consultation with a physician is crucial.

PSYCHIATRIC MEDICATIONS Antidepressants commonly cause changes in sexual response. Reduced sexual interest and arousal, and delayed or absent orgasm are commonly reported. Antipsychotic medications frequently result in lack of desire and erection, and delay or absence of ejaculation and orgasm. Tranquilizers such as Valium and Xanax can interfere with orgasmic response (Dunsmuir & Emberton, 1997).

ANTIHYPERTENSIVE MEDICATIONS Medications prescribed for high blood pressure can result in desire, arousal, and orgasm problems. Some hypertension medications are more likely than others to have negative sexual effects (Meston et al., 1997).

MISCELLANEOUS MEDICATIONS Prescription gastrointestinal and antihistamine medications can interfere with desire and arousal function. Methadone can cause decreased desire, arousal disorder, lack of orgasm, and delayed ejaculation. Anticancer drugs can cause gonadal damage and reduce hormone levels, resulting in loss of sexual desire both during and following treatments (Weiner & Rosen, 1997).

NONPRESCRIPTION MEDICATIONS Some over-the-counter antihistamines, motion sickness, and gastrointestinal medications have been associated with desire and erection problems.

Cultural Influences

Culture strongly influences both the way we feel about our sexuality and the way we express it. This section examines some influences in Western society—and particularly in the United States—that affect our sexuality and may contribute to sexual problems.

Negative Childhood Learning

We learn many of our basic, important attitudes about sexuality during childhood (Barone & Wiederman, 1998). Some people's views are strongly influenced by our cultural legacy that sex is sinful. It has been widely reported by a variety of therapist researchers that severe religious orthodoxy equating sex with sin is common to the backgrounds of many sexually troubled people. One researcher found that the more rigidly orthodox that married members of Jewish, Protestant, and Catholic churches were, the less sexual interest, response, frequency, and pleasure they reported in marital sex and the more sexual inhibitions, anxiety, guilt, shame, and disgust they experienced (Purcell, 1985). The 1994 National Health and Social Life survey, which interviewed a broad rep-

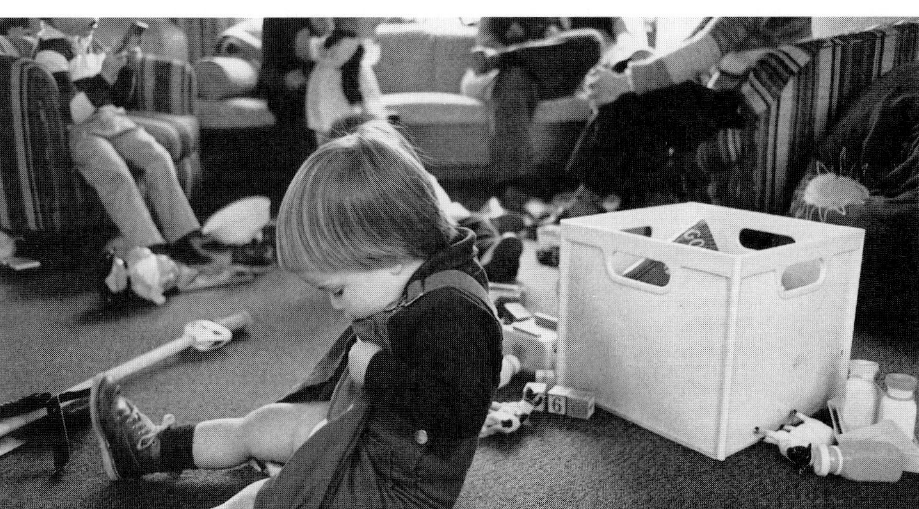

The way others react to childhood genital exploration may affect how children learn to feel about their sexual anatomy.

resentative sample cross section of 3432 Americans, found that the incidence of sexual problems decreases as educational level increases (see Table 15.2) (Laumann et al., 1994). The results from this survey are particularly significant because it is the most methodologically sound and comprehensive to date.

A child may or may not be told directly that sex is shameful or sinful, but this belief can be communicated in other ways. Sex therapist Helen Singer Kaplan described some aspects of childhood sexuality and the responses they often evoke in our society:

> Infants seem to crave erotic pleasure. Babies of both genders tend to touch their genitals and express joy when their genitals are stimulated in the course of diapering and bathing, and both little boys and girls stimulate their penis or clitoris as soon as they acquire the necessary motor coordination. At the same time, sexual expression is, in our society, systematically followed by disapproval and punishment and denial. (1974, p. 147)

The results are often guilt feelings about sexual pleasure from touching one's genitals. Conflict about erotic pleasure may thus be initiated early in a person's life. Kaplan summarized, "The interaction between the child's developing sexual urges and the experiences of growing up in our sexually alienating society probably produces some measure of sexual conflict in all of us" (p. 145).

While growing up, we learn important lessons about human relationships from our families. We observe and integrate the models we see around us. We notice how our parents use touch and how they feel about one another. For example, one researcher found that women with low sexual desire perceived their parents' attitudes toward sex and their affectionate interaction with each other to be significantly more negative than did those with normal sexual desire (Stuart et al., 1988).

The Sexual Double Standard

Although the rigidity of the sexual double standard appears to be diminishing somewhat, opposite sexual expectations for women and men are still quite prevalent in our society. Women are encouraged to be sexually cautious to avoid acquiring a reputation of being loose, but part of stereotypical masculine sexual success is "scoring" (Leitenberg & Henning, 1995). Masters and Johnson noted that "sociocultural influence more often than not places a woman in a position in which she must adapt, sublimate, inhibit or even distort her natural capacity to function sexually. . . . Herein lies a major source of woman's sexual dysfunction" (1970, p. 218).

The male side of the sexual double standard is also a function of cultural expectations. Men frequently learn that sexual conquest is a measure of "manliness."

> Erotic materials portray men as always wanting and always ready to have sex, the only problem being how to get enough of it. We have accepted this rule for ourselves and most of us believe that we should always be capable of responding sexually, regardless of the time and place, our feelings about ourselves and our partners, or any other factors. (Zilbergeld, 1978, p. 41)

As a result of these expectations, men tend to see sexual interaction as a "performance." These cultural expectations can produce discomfort, frustration, and resentment for men as well as for women (McCarthy, 1998).

A Narrow Definition of Sexuality

Besides early socialization experiences and continuing exposure to the sexual double standard, popular opinions about the appropriateness of sexual behaviors also influence our expressions of sexuality. Although attitudes about what is normal appear to have changed in recent years, certain assumptions still strongly affect sexual expression.

As we have seen repeatedly in this text, the notion that sex equals penile–vaginal intercourse is pervasive in our society. This assumption can significantly affect erotic behavior (McCarthy, 1994). Although coitus is certainly a viable option, it is just one alternative—not the only, most important, or best avenue for experiencing sexual pleasure. A strong inclination to view coitus as synonymous with sex can contribute to inadequate stimulation for women and place burdensome and anxiety-provoking expectations on intercourse. This view can also lead people to overlook other sensual enjoyments. In Bernie Zilbergeld's words, "Many men, when asked how it felt to touch their partners or be touched by them, have said that they didn't know because they were so busy thinking about getting to intercourse. In this way we [men] rob ourselves of pleasure and of fully experiencing the stimulation necessary for an enjoyable sexual response" (1978, p. 45).

Performance Anxiety

A wide variety of goals have been prescribed for sexuality throughout history. A common one has been procreation. Another is the man's physiological release, with the woman providing it as her duty. Once the woman's pleasure began to be considered a legitimate aspect of sexual contact, her orgasm and the ideal of the simultaneous orgasm became new goals to achieve. Now, as women's sexuality receives more attention, vaginal orgasms and multiple orgasms may be seen as essential to the sexual experience. The contemporary message about sexuality often appears to be "Sex is OK for both males and females, and you better be good at it" (LoPiccolo & Heiman, 1978, p. 56). What could and should be playful and pleasurable becomes work. "Performance anxiety" can block natural sexual arousal and release by diminishing the pleasurable sensations that would produce them—thus creating greater anxiety because "it's not working" (Rowland et al., 1996).

Arbitrary definitions of sexuality that impose external standards of success and failure reduce the opportunities for individuals and couples to determine what is satisfactory based on their own feelings. In addition, a transitory sexual problem such as an inability to achieve an orgasm or erection due to fatigue or just "not being in the mood" can produce such concern and anxiety that the problem develops into a pattern. One's own performance anxiety, a partner's response, or the combination of the two can turn a transitory difficulty into a serious problem. If a partner withdraws emotionally and physically, blames him- or herself, or feels insecure about the relationship as a result of the other's reduced response, the problem may be worse the next time due to anxiety about it recurring. Individuals or couples may also avoid sexual activity to protect themselves from either embarrassment or a sense of failure for not meeting arbitrary goals.

Individual Factors

Beyond the cultural setting and the influences it has on sexual feelings and expression, sexual difficulties may also stem from other physical, emotional, or psychological factors. Each of us is a unique, complex blend of biological, cultural, and emotional elements. Our sexuality is an expression of all these aspects of ourselves, which begin forming in childhood and continue to develop throughout our lives. Personal factors are important. Human reactions to life experiences are highly variable, so that two individuals may respond in totally different ways to the same situation.

Sexual Knowledge and Attitudes

Our knowledge and attitudes about sex have a direct influence on our sexual options. For example, if a woman knows about the function of her clitoris in sexual arousal and believes her own sexual gratification is important, she will most likely have experiences different from a woman who has neither this knowledge nor this belief. Even education and social class have an impact on sexual attitudes, behaviors, and problems, as shown in Table 15.3. We have seen in earlier chapters that the higher the educational and occupational level of a couple, the greater is their tendency to use a variety of noncoital stimulation methods and intercourse positions. In certain cases where difficulties are based on ignorance or misunderstanding, accurate information can sometimes alleviate sexual dissatisfaction.

Negative attitudes about sex also contribute to poor sexual responsiveness. Some people may unconsciously be so fearful of sexual pleasure that they prevent themselves from feeling sexual desire. These individuals may have developed a "turnoff" mechanism, described by Kaplan:

> Most of the patients I have studied tend to suppress their desire by evoking negative thoughts or by allowing spontaneously emerging negative thoughts to intrude when they have a sexual opportunity. They have learned to put themselves into negative emotional states.... In this

Table 15.3 Sexual Problems Correlated with Education Level*

Men	*Lack of Interest in Sex*	*Climax Too Early*	*Erectile Disorder*
Less than high school	22%	36%	15%
High school graduate	13	33	6
Finished college	16	26	9
Master's degree or above	13	24	9
Overall	16	20	10
Women	*Lack of Interest in Sex*	*Unable to Reach Orgasm*	*Pain During Sex*
Less than high school	43	30	16
High school graduate	35	28	17
Finished college	28	19	10
Master's degree or above	23	13	9
Overall	33	24	14

*Rounded to nearest percentage point.

Source: Laumann et al., 1994.

> manner they make themselves angry, fearful, or distracted, and so tap into the natural physiologic inhibitory mechanisms which suppress sexual desire. (1979, p. 83)

Kaplan noted that people were usually not aware of the active role they played in creating their inhibitions. Their lack of desire appeared to emerge automatically and involuntarily; they did not realize that they had control over the focus of their thoughts.

Self-Concept

The term *self-concept* refers to the feelings and beliefs we have about ourselves. For example, a woman who feels comfortable with her body, believes she is entitled to sexual pleasure, and takes an active role in attaining sexual fulfillment is likely to have a more satisfying sexual relationship than a woman who lacks those feelings about herself (Koppelman, 1988). Some studies have found that men and women with sexual problems are likely to have less self-confidence than people without sexual problems (Apt et al., 1994). A study of college undergraduates supports this finding: Students with high self-esteem were found to have higher sexual satisfaction (Hally & Pollack, 1993).

Emotional Difficulties

Personal emotional difficulties such as anxiety or depression are often related to poor self-concept. These difficulties can be a response to a current situation, or they may stem from unresolved past events. Whatever the source, emotional states have a strong impact on sexuality. Lack of sexual interest and response is a common symptom of depression (Dubovsky, 1991). Moreover, life problems such as a death in the family, divorce, or extreme family or work difficulties can create stress that results in lack of sexual interest. Severe stress and trauma as experienced by combat veterans also can result in sexual problems (Letourneau, 1997). Depression from multiple losses of friends and lovers due to the AIDS epidemic is, tragically, acute for many gay men. The fact that AIDS is a sexually transmitted disease further associates sex with feelings of depression.

Discomfort with certain emotions can also affect sexuality. Particularly important are a person's feelings about intimacy (Levine, 1992). Apprehension about intimacy can significantly influence sexual encounters. An individual who experiences intimacy as threatening may have considerable sexual difficulty (Kaplan, 1979). One study of individuals whose inhibited sexual desire did not improve with therapy found that they had negative feelings about closeness and intimacy in general (Chapman, 1984).

Sexual Abuse and Assault

Both childhood sexual abuse and adult sexual assault can greatly interfere with sexuality, as this quotation from the authors' files exemplifies:

> I had twelve years of Catholic schooling followed by three years of training in a Catholic hospital. My father died when I was seven years of age. My mother was full of rage because of her difficult childhood and abused me both physically and psychologically. I was sexually abused from the age of eight till about thirteen by a friend of my mother. So you see, I do have some cause for having no interest in sex. I wasn't able to tell anyone till I was about forty-five. I did go to counseling and it helped some, but I am far from healed. (Authors' files)

According to the National Health and Social Life Survey, 12% of men and 17% of women were sexually abused *before* adolescence. Adults who have experienced sexual abuse in childhood are more likely to report difficulties with sexuality (Laumann et al., 1994). Of any childhood experience, childhood sexual abuse has the greatest negative impact on adult sexual functioning.

The essential conditions for positive sexual interaction—consent, equality, respect, trust, and safety—are absent in sexual abuse. Boys and girls who are sexually abused experience sexual behavior and stimulation that are overwhelming for their level of physical and social development. They are robbed of the opportunity to explore and develop their sexuality at their own age-appropriate pace (Maltz, 1991). Due to the sexual abuse experiences, sexual activity becomes associated with emotional and often, physical pain. As one woman stated:

> In retrospect, I can see how the incest experiences of over 30 years ago still govern and pattern my sexuality. I have a very diminished sexual appetite, with little curiosity or interest. It is difficult for me to anticipate, enjoy, express, and receive love in a sexual, physical form. A wall of avoidance, fear, and dread has replaced any thrill or urge or anticipation. (Maltz & Holman, 1987, p. 75)

Research has shown that women with a history of childhood sexual abuse are two to four times more likely than other women to have chronic pelvic pain (Reiter & Milburn, 1994) and to experience depression, anxiety, and low self-esteem (Murrey et al., 1993). Incest survivors commonly report never having experienced orgasm (Becker et al., 1984).

In addition, sexual abuse survivors often experience specific aversion reactions to exactly what was done to them during the sexual assault (McNew & Abell, 1995). They may have "flashbacks," sudden images of the smells, sounds, sights, feelings, or other reminders of the sexual abuse that dramatically interrupt any positive feelings and sexual pleasure (Maltz, 1991). These symptoms and difficulties can also be very difficult for partners of survivors to understand and to cope with effectively (Chauncey, 1994).

Research has also indicated serious sexual consequences for survivors of adult sexual assault. One study of 372 female sexual assault survivors found that almost 59% were experiencing sexual problems following the assault—with about 70% of this group linking these problems to the assault. Fear of sex and lack of desire or arousal were the most frequently mentioned problems (Becker et al., 1986). And the effects of sexual assault can be long-lasting; 60% of rape victims had sexual problems for more than three years after the assault (Becker & Kaplan, 1991).

Relationship Factors

Besides personal feelings and attitudes, a variety of interpersonal factors can strongly influence the satisfaction or dissatisfaction two people experience in a sexual relationship. These factors often vary according to the couple and their particular circumstances. For example, one couple may find that an argument typically ends with passionate lovemaking, whereas another couple move to separate bedrooms for a week after a disagreement.

Unresolved Relationship Problems

Unresolved resentment, a lack of trust, inability to combine love and sexual desire, dislike of a partner, lack of attraction, poor sexual skills, boredom, or fear can easily lead to sexual dissatisfaction or disinterest. The dynamics of a whole relationship are highly significant in determining sexual satisfaction (Polonsky, 1998; Speckens et al., 1995). As we will see in Chapter 16, this is reflected in the strong emphasis in sex therapy on working with the couple rather than the individual. In many cases, a sexual difficulty is a symptom of a more general relationship problem.

For some couples, hostility or lack of trust or respect may inhibit sexual desire and response. It is usually difficult to feel desire for someone who arouses strong negative feelings. Often a person who experiences a lack of power and control in a relationship subconsciously loses sexual desire or response, thereby gaining some control in the sexual aspect of the relationship (LoPiccolo, 1992). Partners also need a balance of togetherness and separateness; sexual difficulties may occur when there is insufficient independence and overabundance of dependency and closeness within the relationship. Lesbian couples, in particular, experience lowered sexual desire from the loss of individuality within the intense closeness of the relationship (Nichols, 1989).

One partner may even use his or her lack of sexual interest, consciously or unconsciously, to hurt or punish the other. A person who is frequently pressured to engage in sex or who feels guilty about saying no may become less and less interested and feel increasingly diminished desire.

Ineffective Communication

Ineffective communication can contribute to and perpetuate sexual dissatisfaction. As we discussed in Chapter 8, talking is a basic tool for learning about needs and sharing desires. Without effective verbal communication, couples must base their sexual encounters on assumptions, past experiences, and wishful thinking—all of which may be inappropriate in the immediate situation. As one author notes:

> Men and women end up misunderstanding and making each other crazy. We are taught to be strangers in the night, talking different languages. We expect impossible things from one another, resent and blame each other for lack of fulfillment. (Keen, 1991, p. 79)

A frequent source of communication problems is stereotyped gender roles—in particular, the myth that "sex is exclusively the man's responsibility and that sexual assertiveness in a woman is 'unfeminine'" (Kaplan, 1974, p. 350). A woman who believes it is not her place to tell her partner that she is or is not in the mood to make love or that she would like another kind of stimulation (or any other sex-related desire) may find that the relationship becomes increasingly frustrating simply because her partner does not know what she wants. How could he? This is compounded by the popular myth that "If she/he really loved me, she/he could read my mind!" Difficulty communicating with a partner about the desire for direct clitoral stimulation is common in women who do not experience orgasm (Kelly et al., 1990).

For many reasons—limited communication skills, stereotyped gender roles, stereotyped images of romance, misplaced assumptions about the other person—couples sometimes operate under the belief that communication is unnecessary in a good sexual relationship. However, communicating sexual needs is often the first step in ensuring they are met. Communication is also the basis for the negotiations that are often necessary to reach compromises over individual differences.

Fears About Pregnancy or Sexually Transmitted Diseases

The fear of an unwanted pregnancy may interfere with coital enjoyment in a heterosexual relationship. Sometimes one partner is ambivalent about having a child but does not feel free to be direct about his or her reluctance. If a couple uses no birth control, this may result in intercourse being associated with thoughts such as "I sure hope I don't get pregnant." It is not easy to enjoy sex with that concern in the back of one's mind. Furthermore, a 100% effective temporary method of birth control is simply not available at this time. The reality is that, unless one of the partners is surgically sterilized or infertile, there is a risk of impregnation, however small, in all instances of heterosexual intercourse.

The relationship between pregnancy anxiety and arousal can sometimes be seen in women who are completely freed from the possibility of pregnancy through sterilization or menopause. It is not at all uncommon for a woman's sexual activity and desire to increase after she becomes infertile.

On the other hand, emotional reactions to infertility can also create sexual difficulties. Many couples who want to conceive and have difficulties doing so often find that their sexual relationship becomes anxiety ridden, especially if they have to modify and regulate the timing and pattern of sexual interaction to enhance the possibility of conception.

Anxiety about contracting a sexually transmitted disease, particularly AIDS, can interfere with sexual arousal in both homosexual and heterosexual relationships. For people who are not in a monogamous, disease-free relationship, some risk exists. Guidelines for safer sex are outlined in Chapter 17.

Sexual Orientation

Another reason that a woman or man may not experience sexual satisfaction in a heterosexual relationship can be a desire to be involved with individuals of the same sex (LoPiccolo & Friedman, 1988). It is understandable that a person with a homosexual orientation experiences sexual difficulty or a lack of satisfaction in heterosexual relations. Sexual difficulties with heterosexual partners are most likely to be considered problems by homosexual people who are attempting to conceal their orientation by relating sexually to partners of the other sex, or by bisexual or homosexual individuals who want to change their orientation to heterosexual. Although much progress has been made by gay rights groups, a homosexual orientation is still not generally accepted in our society. Following one's homosexual inclinations therefore involves facing significant societal disapproval, if not outright discrimination. To avoid these repercussions, many homosexual people attempt to relate heterosexually despite their lack of desire for such a relationship. Others have a commitment and a desire for the heterosexual relationship (often marriage) to continue and to be sexually fulfilling.

To this point in the chapter, we have looked at some of the broad factors that can underlie sexual problems. In the remainder of the chapter, we consider some of the specific problems that people encounter with the desire, excitement, and orgasm phases of sexual response. In reality, there is considerable overlap: Problems with desire and arousal also affect orgasm, and orgasm difficulties can easily affect a person's interest and ability to become aroused.

The sexual problems that we will discuss can vary in duration and focus from person to person. A specific difficulty can be of lifelong duration or be acquired at a specific time. A person may experience the problem in all situations with all partners (generalized type) or only in specific situations or with specific partners (situational type) (American Psychiatric Association, 1994). The categories and labels for the problems that we discuss come from the American Psychiatric Association's *Diagnostic and Statistical Manual (DSM IV)*. A few additions of our own are also included.

Desire-Phase Difficulties

Problems with sexual desire have received increased attention in recent years. This section discusses inhibited sexual desire, dissatisfaction with frequency of sexual activity, and sexual aversion. Therapies for desire-phase problems are considered in Chapter 16.

Hypoactive Sexual Desire Disorder (HSD)

Hypoactive sexual desire disorder (HSD) is a common sexual difficulty experienced by both men and women, although, as Table 15.1 points out, it is far more common among women. The most frequent problem that brings people to seek sex therapy, HSD is characterized by a lack of interest in sexual activity. Kaplan (1979) described it as a lack of "sexual appetite." HSD can be distinguished from excitement and orgasm difficulties. Some people with HSD do become aroused and experience orgasm when sexually stimulated, while others may react to physical and sexual contact with tension and anxiety instead of arousal. Others may experience HSD in a particular situation, such as with a spouse but not with a lover or when masturbating. Still others may derive pleasure from touching and physical closeness, but have no desire for erotic excitement.

Hypoactive sexual desire disorder (HSD)
Lack of interest in sexual activity.

Generalized, lifelong HSD is rare: People with this condition neither masturbate nor exhibit sexual fantasy, sexual activity, or the sexual aspects of a relationship. More commonly, people develop HSD at a specific point in their lives. In general, HSD is most commonly seen as a problem when it causes distress in a relationship.

Hypoactive sexual desire frequently reflects relationship problems.

HSD may originate from abusive personal experiences, as was illustrated in the authors' files on page 450. More commonly, it reflects unresolved relationship problems (Beck et al., 1991). One study found that women with HSD reported more dissatisfaction with relationship issues than women with other sexual problems such as painful intercourse or difficulty reaching orgasm (discussed later in this chapter). In this study, diminished desire was associated with a few specific relationship problems:

- The woman's partner did not behave affectionately except when intercourse was expected to follow.
- Communication and conflict resolution were unsatisfactory.
- The couple did not maintain love, romance, and emotional closeness.

This study also found that women with HSD often view intercourse as an obligation. In general, they were more likely to engage in intercourse to fulfill marital obligations and avoid hurting their spouses' feelings than were women without HSD (Stuart et al., 1988).

Lack of sexual desire can occur in homosexual men or women who have not fully accepted their sexual orientation. Internalized negative beliefs about homosexuality can interfere with joyful sexual expression, even in individuals who have accepted their homosexuality on many other levels (Nichols, 1989), as this woman explains:

It had been a 10-year struggle for me to accept myself as a lesbian. I tried dating men, but always found that a special, meaningful feeling was missing. I came out at work and to my Italian Catholic family, and became involved in gay rights activities. I had several relationships with women that didn't work out. Then I met Carol. I liked her, respected her, and was very attracted to her. I was looking for a long-term relationship, and the compatibilities and feelings were right. Sex was great until she told me she loved me. A switch went off and I stopped feeling interested. In therapy, I was able to realize that lingering feelings of my mother's disapproval had stopped me cold from allowing myself to be fully happy and complete in a "queer" relationship. I worked through those feelings and am now enjoying my sexuality in a loving, committed relationship for the first time in my life. (Authors' files)

Dissatisfaction with Frequency of Sexual Activity

Sexual partners usually have normal discrepancies in their preferences for amount, type, and timing of sexual activities. Sometimes the relationship can accommodate these individual differences. However, when sexual differences are a source of significant conflict or dissatisfaction, a couple can experience considerable discomfort.

Instead of moving toward some compromise, the couple may polarize in opposite directions. Feelings of resentment and power struggles may then develop. A common pattern that often emerges in these situations is that one partner feels constantly deprived and the other constantly pressured. Usually both feel unloved and guilty—one for asking too much and the other for not giving enough (Zilbergeld & Kilmann, 1984).

Sexual Aversion Disorder

Sexual aversion Extreme and irrational fear of sexual activity.

When low desire for sexual activity includes a fear of sex and a compelling desire to avoid sexual situations, this is considered **sexual aversion disorder.** Sexual aversion can range from feelings of discomfort, repulsion, and disgust to extreme, irrational fear of sexual activity. Even the thought of sexual contact can result in intense anxiety and panic. A person who experiences sexual aversion may exhibit physiological symptoms such as sweating, increased heart rate, nausea, dizziness, trembling, or diarrhea as a consequence of fear. Sexual aversion is often the result of sexual abuse or trauma.

Excitement-Phase Difficulties

Both men and women can experience difficulties in sexual arousal. Of course, most of us are not responsive sexually all of the time. Sometimes we may be too preoccupied with another aspect of our lives, too fatigued, or feeling somewhat distant from our partners. However, when physiological arousal, erotic sensations, or the subjective feeling of being "turned on" are chronically diminished or absent, inhibited sexual excitement exists. Among women excitement-phase difficulties most commonly take the form of lack of vaginal lubrication, whereas in men the most common problem is an inability to achieve or maintain erection.

Female Sexual Arousal Disorder

As we saw in Chapters 4 and 6, vaginal lubrication is a woman's first physiological response to sexual arousal. The persistent inability to attain or maintain the lubrication–swelling response can indicate female sexual arousal disorder. Biological factors, including low estrogen levels, can be a factor in lack of lubrication. (Diminished lubrication is normal while breast-feeding and following menopause). Feelings of apathy, anger, or fear may also inhibit arousal and lubrication.

Lack of lubrication in a particular situation does not necessarily mean something is wrong. Vaginal lubrication frequently decreases during prolonged coitus. This may be due to a long plateau phase (during the plateau phase, lubrication typically decreases). Or, it may be the result of exclusive coital stimulation that may not be adequate to induce continued lubrication. In the latter case, if continued sexual contact is desired, simultaneous manual stimulation of the clitoris or other parts of the body or changing to noncoital activities may increase lubrication. Increasing communication about arousing techniques and using vaginal lubricants can be helpful in some situations.

Male Erectile Disorder

The term often applied to male erection difficulty is *impotence*. The origin of this word suggests the primary reason for our opposition to its use: It comes from Latin and literally means "without power." The implication is that a man is powerless as a lover without an erection. It is likely that a man who cannot achieve or maintain an erection is deeply concerned (Willke et al., 1997). The implication that he is without value as a lover only contributes to this distress. As the following account indicates, however, this interpretation can be far from reality:

> I met a man once whose erectile capacity was completely destroyed by a spinal-cord injury in the precise region of the lower spine where erectile function is controlled. Although he couldn't get it up, he certainly had no trouble getting it on! I've often wondered if his acquired status of highly desired lover had something to do with his discovery that erections are not essential to meaningful sexual interaction. (Authors' files)

Instead of the term *impotence, DSM IV* uses the more neutral term **male erectile disorder,** which adequately describes this major male difficulty without the negative connotations just mentioned. *Erectile dysfunction* is another term commonly used in professional literature (Levine & Althof, 1991).

Male erectile disorder Persistent lack of erection sufficiently rigid for penetrative intercourse.

Erectile disorder is a common problem among men who seek sex therapy. An estimated 15% of men in the United States have erectile disorder (Clark, 1997), and one study found that 50% of men over age 40 had experienced the problem to some degree

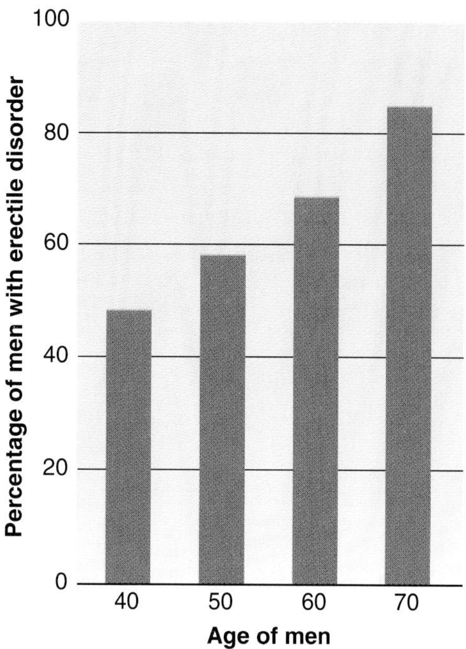

Figure 15.1

The incidence of erectile disorder related to age (Kim & Lipshultz, 1997).

(Feldman et al., 1994). The incidence of erectile dysfunction increases with age (as shown in Figure 15.1), although age itself does not cause erectile disorder. Diseases such as diabetes, high blood pressure, and cardiovascular problems that can accompany aging take their toll (Kim & Lipshultz, 1997). As "baby boomers" grow older, the numbers of men with erectile problems will increase. It is common for men to occasionally be unable to achieve or maintain an erection due to minor factors like fatigue, stress, or alcohol or drug use. Male erectile disorder is defined by urologists as the inability to have or maintain an erection sufficient for penetrative intercourse to the satisfaction of both partners for a period of 6–12 months (Nash, 1997). Erectile problems may be classified broadly into two types. The label *acquired erectile disorder* is applied to cases where the man has previously had erections with his partner(s), but finds himself presently unable to consistently experience a functional erection. Men with *lifelong erectile disorder* have, throughout their lives, attempted but never experienced maintained penetration.

Approximately 80% of erectile disorder cases involve some degree of organic impairment (Nactsheim, 1994), but it can be difficult to determine whether erectile problems are organic or psychological (Martins & Reis, 1997). Special procedures have been developed to evaluate physical factors in erection problems. Some techniques, based on the fact that erections normally occur during sleep, involve recording erection patterns during sleep. Unfortunately, these procedures are not completely reliable (Morales et al., 1990). Other instruments measure penile blood pressure and flow to determine whether erectile difficulties are caused by vascular problems (Melman, 1992). Injections of medications that produce erections can also be used to detect possible difficulties: If no erection occurs following an injection, then vascular impairment is likely (Lue, 1994).

Orgasm-Phase Difficulties

The problems we have been discussing are primarily ones of desire and excitement. Some other sexual difficulties specifically affect orgasmic response, and a variety of problems are reported by both women and men. Some of these difficulties are infrequency or total absence of orgasms. Others involve reaching orgasm too rapidly or too slowly. Sometimes a partner may fake orgasm to conceal its absence.

Female Orgasmic Disorder

The term *frigidity* has been used as a general, descriptive label for female sexual problems including lack of interest, arousal, or orgasm. It is both imprecise and pejorative, mistakenly implying that women with these difficulties are totally sexually unresponsive and emotionally cold or unloving. Many sex educators and therapists now use the word **anorgasmia** (AN-or-GAZ-mē-uh), meaning the absence of orgasm.

Anorgasmia
A sexual difficulty involving the absence of orgasm in women.

Some women who do not achieve orgasm experience arousal, lubrication, and enjoyment from sexual contact. However, their sexual response does not increase to the point of orgasm. Some may feel satisfied with their sexual experience without orgasm; others are highly disappointed and distressed. The lack of peak arousal and physical release from orgasm can result in experiences that are less and less enjoyable.

A woman who has *generalized, lifelong anorgasmia* has never experienced orgasm by masturbation or with a partner. A woman who has *situational anorgasmia* experiences orgasm rarely, or in some situations but not in others; for example, she may be orgasmic when masturbating but not from stimulation with a partner.

Surveys have indicated that approximately 5–10% of adult women in the United States have never experienced orgasm by any means of self- or partner stimulation (Spector & Carey, 1990). Table 15.4 shows incidence of orgasm in college students. There are some indications that the number of lifelong anorgasmic women has decreased, and some sex-therapy clinics are seeing a smaller percentage of women with this problem (LoPiccolo, 1985). This apparent decrease may be due to the accessibility of excellent self-help books and videos for women who want to learn to experience orgasm. Much of the self-help information in Chapter 16 comes from these sources.

Table 15.4 College Students Answer: Have You Ever Had an Orgasm?

	Female	*Male*
Yes	87%	94%
No	13%	6%

Source: Elliott & Brantley, 1997.

Female Orgasm During Intercourse

Most sex therapists believe that women who enjoy intercourse and experience orgasm in some way other than during coitus do not have a sexual problem (LoPiccolo, 1985). The absence of routine orgasm during coitus without additional manual–clitoral stimulation is a common and normal pattern for women. *The Hite Report* (1976) asked women if they routinely experienced orgasm during coitus without simultaneous manual stimulation of the clitoral area; only 30% responded that they did. As sex therapist pioneer Helen Kaplan stated, "There are millions of women who are sexually responsive, and often multiply orgasmic, but who cannot have an orgasm during intercourse unless they receive simultaneous clitoral stimulation" (1974, p. 397). For many women the indirect clitoral stimulation that occurs during coitus is simply less effective than direct manual or oral stimulation of the clitoral area.

Anorgasmia often reflects cultural perceptions. As we saw in Chapter 6, Freud's belief that clitoral orgasms were inferior to vaginal orgasms has lingered in popular mythology, contributing to misunderstanding among men and women, as the following account illustrates:

> I thought that there was something wrong with me because I did not have orgasm during penile–vaginal intercourse. Then I learned in my human sexuality class that I was not the only one that needs additional stimulation. But sometimes I am scared that when I get married my husband will get tired of having to do the extra work. I do not want him to think there is something wrong with me. (Authors' files)

Women who require direct clitoral stimulation to reach orgasm may be reluctant to ask for or engage in manual stimulation or to request noncoital stimulation after their partners ejaculate (Davidson & Moore, 1994). In fact, anorgasmic women report greater discomfort in communicating to a partner about their desires for direct clitoral stimulation than do women who experience orgasm during coitus (Kelly et al., 1990).

Sometimes anorgasmia has a physiological cause. Occasionally medications (particularly the Prozac family of antidepressants) or physical conditions can impair the vascular system or nerve supply of the genital area, causing an inhibited orgasmic response. Many women who have not experienced orgasm have not learned what is arousing to them or, for some reason, avoid becoming aroused enough to climax. Chapter 16 discusses approaches that can be helpful in treating anorgasmia.

Male Orgasmic Disorder

Male orgasmic disorder The inability of a man to ejaculate during sexual activity.

The term **male orgasmic disorder** generally refers to the inability of a man to ejaculate during sexual activity. Eight percent of men experience this difficulty (Laumann et al., 1994). Most men who are troubled by orgasmic disorder are able to reach orgasm through masturbation or manual or oral stimulation from their partners. In some cases, however, a man may not ejaculate at all during a sexual encounter, as revealed in the following account:

> I began a sexual relationship several months ago with a man who has a problem I've never before encountered. He has no difficulty getting an erection. In fact, he usually seems real excited when we make love. But he never comes. The first time I thought it was great—he seemed to be able to go on forever. But after a while it started getting to me. I've tried everything—going down on him, using my hand, stroking his scrotum when he is inside me—nothing works. He doesn't want to talk about it, but I sense he is as frustrated as I am, maybe more. Once I got him to admit he climaxes when he masturbates. Why can't he come with me? (Authors' files)

Chapter 16 addresses approaches to resolving male orgasmic disorder.

Premature Ejaculation

Premature ejaculation A sexual difficulty whereby a man ejaculates so rapidly as to impair his own or his partner's pleasure.

A common male orgasm difficulty is **premature ejaculation.** We define premature ejaculation as consistently reaching orgasm so quickly that it significantly diminishes a man's own enjoyment of the experience, impairs a partner's gratification, or both. This definition eliminates arbitrary time goals, takes into account the partner's pleasure, and views the person's own subjective needs as an important determinant of what constitutes reaching orgasm too fast.

The average duration of intercourse for American couples is between five and ten minutes. Taking this norm into account, some experts consider premature ejaculation on a continuum. First, the premature ejaculation label is not applied if neither the man nor his partner considers the rapidity of ejaculation a problem. Otherwise, ejaculation before penetration or after only a minute or two of intercourse, or needing to use intrusive and unpleasant techniques to delay ejaculation throughout the length of intercourse, is considered a problem (Schover et al., 1982).

Approximately 29% of men experience premature ejaculation (Laumann et al., 1994). Masters and Johnson stated that it was the most prevalent male sexual problem and estimated that millions were troubled by it. In anonymous surveys of students who enrolled in our human sexuality classes, consistently over 75% of the men have reported that premature ejaculation was at least sometimes a problem. And 25% of our male students have reported premature ejaculation to be an ongoing difficulty.

Premature ejaculation is usually not physiologically based. However, some men may have a particularly low threshold to physical stimulation and therefore may be physiologically predisposed to rapid ejaculation (Strassberg, 1994). Anxiety can also play a role in premature ejaculation by increasing muscle tension (myotonia), which tends to hasten orgasm. See Chapter 16 for a discussion of strategies for dealing with premature ejaculation.

Faking Orgasms

A final orgasmic difficulty we discuss is **faking orgasms**—pretending to experience orgasm without actually doing so. This kind of sexual deception is typically discussed in reference to women, and it happens quite often, as shown in Table 15.5.

What are your thoughts about why a person might fake orgasm?

Unlike some of the other difficulties discussed in this chapter, faking orgasm reflects a conscious decision. The most common reason given by women for pretending orgasm was to avoid disappointing or hurting their partners (Darling & Davidson, 1986). A person is often motivated to engage in such deception by real or imagined performance pressures. Some additional factors related to faking orgasm may include poor communication or limited knowledge of sexual techniques, a need for partner approval, little hope of changing the partner's behavior, and an attempt to hide a deteriorating relationship or to protect a partner's ego (Lauersen & Graves, 1984). The following comments, both by women, reveal some of these motivations:

Faking orgasms
A sexual difficulty whereby a person pretends to experience orgasm during sexual interaction.

He feels badly if I don't have an orgasm during intercourse, so I fake it, even though I have real ones from oral sex. (Authors' files)

I started our sexual relationship faking, and I don't know how to stop. (Authors' files)

Although some women may find faking orgasm to be an acceptable solution in their individual situations, others find that faking itself becomes troublesome, as revealed in the second of the preceding comments. The effects of faking orgasm can include increased resentment, guilt, anger, and fear of being discovered (Lauersen & Graves, 1984). At the least, faking orgasms creates emotional distance at a time of potential closeness and satisfaction (Masters & Johnson, 1976). One student who understands this states:

I want to know what feels good to him and I tell him what feels good to me. I am not a good liar. When it comes to sex, the last thing that I want to deal with is deceit. (Authors' files)

What other disadvantages do you think are associated with faking orgasm?

A vicious cycle is often involved in faking orgasms. The person's partner is likely not to know that his or her partner has pretended to climax. Consequently, the deceived partner continues to do what he or she has been led to believe is effective, and the other partner continues to fake to prevent discovery of the deception. This makes it more difficult for the couple to talk about and discover what is gratifying to both of them. Once established, a pattern of deception may be quite difficult to break.

How to best change this pattern of interaction is a matter of personal decision. Some people may not want to change because faking orgasm serves a purpose in a relationship. A person who does want to change might decide to discontinue faking orgasms without discussing the decision with her or his partner. Under such circumstances, some of the procedures for enhancing sexual pleasure outlined in Chapter 16 might prove helpful. Another alternative would be to inform one's partner of one's past deception and to

Table 15.5 College Students Answer: Have You Ever Faked an Orgasm?

	Female Heterosexual	*Lesbian or Bi*	*Male Heterosexual*	*Gay Male or Bi*
Yes	60%	71%	17%	27%
No	40%	29%	83%	73%

Source: Elliott & Brantley, 1997.

discuss the reasons why pretending to climax seemed necessary. Some of the communication strategies outlined in Chapter 8 may help in this process. Maybe some specific difficulties will surface as the motivation for deception, such as female orgasmic problems, or retarded ejaculation. It may be helpful, or perhaps necessary, to engage a counselor to help communicate with a partner. Seeing a counselor may also facilitate efforts to establish more rewarding sexual behaviors.

Dyspareunia

Dyspareunia
Pain or discomfort during intercourse.

The medical term for painful intercourse is **dyspareunia** (DIS-puh-ROO-nē-uh). Both men and women can experience coital pain, although it is more common for women to have this problem.

Dyspareunia in Men

Painful intercourse in men is unusual but does occur. If the foreskin of an uncircumcised male is too tight, he may experience pain during sexual arousal and have difficulty reaching orgasm. In such circumstances, minor surgery may be indicated. Inadequate hygiene of an uncircumcised penis can result in the accumulation of smegma or infections beneath the foreskin, causing irritation of the glans during sexual stimulation. This problem can be prevented by routinely pulling back the foreskin and washing the glans area with soap and water.

Peyronie's disease
Abnormal fibrous tissue and calcium deposits in the penis.

Another possible source of pain or discomfort for men is **Peyronie's disease** (PA-runeez) in which fibrous tissue and calcium deposits develop in the space above and between the cavernous bodies of the penis. This fibrosis results in pain and curvature of the penis with erection that, in severe cases, interferes with erection and even intercourse (Devine, 1997). Medical treatments can sometimes be effective in treating this condition (Weidner et al., 1997). Finally, problems and infections of the urethra, bladder, prostate gland, or seminal vesicles may induce burning, itching, or pain during or after ejaculation (Davis & Noble, 1991). Proper medical attention can generally alleviate this source of discomfort during coitus.

Dyspareunia in Women

Experiencing pain with intercourse is more common among women. At least 60% of women experience dyspareunia at some point in their lives (Jones et al., 1997). It is very likely to affect a woman's sexual arousal and interest (Jantos et al., 1997). Coital discomfort stems from a variety of causes, and for this reason it is important for the woman to determine specifically where the pain is (Forbes, 1998; Fry et al., 1997).

Discomfort at the vaginal entrance or inside the vaginal walls is commonly caused by inadequate arousal and lubrication. Physiological conditions such as insufficient hormones may also reduce lubrication. Using a lubricating jelly can provide a temporary solution so that intercourse can take place comfortably, but this may bring only short-term relief. A permanent solution is more likely if the woman discovers the cause of her discomfort and takes steps to remedy the situation.

A variety of other factors may cause vaginal discomfort during intercourse. Yeast, bacterial, and trichomoniasis infections cause inflammations of the vaginal walls and may result in painful intercourse. Such inflammations are often related to the problem just described: Intercourse with insufficient lubrication can irritate the vaginal walls and increases the possibility of vaginal infections. Foam, contraceptive cream or jelly, condoms, and diaphragms may irritate the vaginas of some women. Pain at the opening of the vagina may also be attributed to an intact or inadequately ruptured hymen, a

Bartholin's gland infection, or scar tissue at the opening (Brashear & Munsick, 1991). Inflammation of the bladder wall can cause moderate to severe pain during intercourse.

Severe pain at the entrance of the vagina may be caused by a condition known as *vulvar vestibulitis syndrome.* Typically, a small reddened area is very painful even with light pressure, but the area may be so small that it is even difficult for the health care practitioner to see (Koglin, 1996). Another area where there may be discomfort is the clitoral glans. Occasionally smegma collects under the clitoral hood and may cause distress when the hood is moved during sexual stimulation. Gentle washing of the clitoris and hood may help prevent this.

Pain deep in the pelvis during coital thrusting may be due to jarring of the ovaries or stretching of the uterine ligaments. A woman may experience this type of discomfort only in certain positions or at certain times in her menstrual cycle. Some women report that such pain only occurs around the time they are ovulating. Avoiding positions or movements that aggravate the pain is the first solution. If a woman has more control of pelvic movements during coitus, she may feel more secure about being able to avoid pain.

Another source of deep pelvic pain is *endometriosis,* a condition in which tissue that normally grows on the walls of the uterus implants on various parts of the abdominal cavity. This extra tissue can prevent internal organs from moving freely, resulting in pain during coitus. Birth control pills are sometimes prescribed to control the buildup of tissue during the monthly cycle (Reiter & Milburn, 1994). Gynecological surgeries for uterine and ovarian cancer can also cause dyspareunia.

Infections in the uterus, such as gonorrhea, may also result in painful intercourse. In fact, pelvic pain may often be the first physical symptom noticed by a woman who has gonorrhea. If the infection has caused considerable scar tissue to develop, surgery may be necessary. Childbirth and rape may tear the ligaments that hold the uterus in the pelvic cavity, which can result in pain during coitus. Surgery can relieve this difficulty partially or completely.

Psychological factors can also contribute to dyspareunia. Early influences that create negative and fearful feelings about intercourse or relationship problems that affect the sexual experience can result in painful intercourse. Most commonly, dyspareunia involves a combination of physical and psychological factors (Meana & Binik, 1994).

Vaginismus

Vaginismus (vaj-in-IZ-mus) is characterized by strong involuntary contractions of the muscles in the outer third of the vagina. The contraction can be so strong that attempts at inserting a penis into the vagina are very painful to the woman. A woman with vaginismus usually, but not always, experiences the same contracting spasm during a pelvic exam. Even the insertion of a finger into her vagina can cause great discomfort.

Vaginismus
A sexual difficulty in which a woman experiences involuntary spasmodic contractions of the muscles of the outer third of the vagina.

An estimated 2% of women have vaginismus (Renshaw, 1990). Some women who experience vaginismus are sexually responsive and orgasmic with manual and oral stimulation, but others are unable to experience desire and arousal (LoPiccolo, 1989). Because most couples regard coitus as a highly important component of their sexual relationship, vaginismus typically causes great concern, even if the couple is sexually involved in other ways.

Milder forms of vaginismus can produce minor unpleasant sensations that are chronically irritating—enough to have an inhibiting effect on a woman's sexual interest and arousal. It is important for women and their partners to know that intercourse, tampon use, and pelvic exams should not be uncomfortable. If they are, it is essential to investigate the cause of the discomfort.

The painful contractions of vaginismus are a conditioned, involuntary response to fearful, painful, or conflicted situations or feelings. Vaginismus often follows chronic painful intercourse, repeated erectile difficulties of a woman's partner, strong orthodox religious taboos about sex, a homosexual orientation, past physical or sexual assault, or feelings of hostility or fear toward a partner (Masters & Johnson, 1970; van de Weil et al., 1990). It is important to note that although a woman who experiences vaginismus can learn to prevent the contractions, she does not consciously will them to occur. In fact, the effort of deliberately trying to overcome the problem can have just the opposite effect, contributing to a vicious cycle. When a woman experiences physical pain from vaginismus, she will probably be anxious about pain occurring the next time she attempts intercourse. Her apprehensions will increase the likelihood of involuntary muscle contractions, and when her expectations are once again met, she will be even more anxious on subsequent occasions (Renshaw, 1995). Ways of dealing with vaginismus are considered in Chapter 16.

This chapter has outlined some of the reasons and ways people encounter dissatisfactions, problems, or discomfort in what can be an experience of great pleasure and joy. It remains for us to explore ways of preventing or overcoming these difficulties. This will be our focus in the next chapter.

Summary

Sexual problems in the general population appear to be common. The National Health and Social Life Survey found that many people reported problems in their sex lives.

ORIGINS OF SEXUAL DIFFICULTIES

Physiological conditions can be the primary causes of sexual problems or can combine with psychological factors to result in sexual dysfunction. It is important to rule out organic causes of sexual problems through medical examinations.

Chronic illnesses and their treatments can have great impact on sexuality. Diseases of the neurological, vascular, and endocrine systems can impair sexual functioning. Medications, pain, and fatigue can also interfere.

Diabetes causes damage to nerves and the circulatory system, impairing sexual arousal.

Arthritis does not directly impair sexual response, but chronic pain and fatigue may lessen a person's sexual interest.

Cancer and its therapies can impair the hormonal, vascular, and neurological functions necessary for normal sexual activity. Pain can also greatly interfere with sexual interest and arousal. Cancer of the reproductive organs—cervix, uterus, ovary, prostate, and testis—can greatly influence sexual response.

Multiple sclerosis is a neurological disease of the brain and spinal cord that can affect sexual interest, genital sensation, arousal, or capacity for orgasm.

Cerebrovascular accidents, or strokes, can reduce a person's frequency of interest, arousal, and sexual activity.

Although a spinal-cord injury does not necessarily impair sexual desire, a person with SCI may have impaired ability for arousal and orgasm; this varies according to the specific injury.

People with cerebral palsy, which is characterized by mild to severe lack of muscular control, may need help with preparation and positioning for sexual relations.

Blindness and deafness may cause depression, lowered self-esteem, and social withdrawal; however, in themselves, these conditions do not appear to physically impair sexual interest or response.

Individuals and couples can best cope with the sexual limitations of their illness or disability by accepting the limitations and developing the possible options remaining to them.

Medications that can impair sexual functioning include drugs used to treat high blood pressure, psychiatric disorders, depression, and cancer. Recreational drugs (including barbiturates, narcotics, and marijuana), alcohol abuse, and even tobacco smoking can interfere with sexual interest, arousal, and orgasm.

Erectile disorders are most likely to be caused by some degree of organic impairment.

Negative attitudes about sexuality and shameful feelings about one's genitals learned during childhood can be detrimental to adult acceptance of one's body and sexual feelings.

The sexual double standard prescribes opposite expectations of sexual behavior for males and females. Both sets of expectations can have negative effects on sexuality.

The cultural notion that sex equals coitus often limits the erotic potential of sexual interactions.

Goal orientation in sexual expression is a culturally acquired attitude that can increase performance anxiety and reduce pleasurable options in lovemaking.

Sexual difficulties can be related to personal factors such as limited or inaccurate sexual knowledge, problems of self-concept, or emotional difficulties.

Experiencing sexual abuse as a child or sexual assault as an adult often leads to sexual problems. Due to the abuse experiences, sexual activity is associated with negative, traumatic feelings.

Relationship problems, ineffective communication, and fear of pregnancy or sexually transmitted diseases can often inhibit sexual satisfaction.

A woman or man whose sexual orientation is homosexual will often have difficulty with sexual interest, arousal, and orgasm in a heterosexual sexual relationship.

DESIRE-PHASE DIFFICULTIES

Hypoactive sexual desire (HSD) is characterized by a lack of interest in sexual activity and fantasy. HSD most commonly reflects relationship problems but may also be caused by other physical or personal difficulties.

Dissatisfaction with frequency of sexual activity occurs when individual differences in sexual interest are significant and a couple is not able to compromise about their individual preferences.

Sexual aversion disorder is an extreme, irrational fear or dislike of sexual activity. Many individuals with sexual aversion experience physical symptoms of anxiety when they attempt to engage in sexual activity.

EXCITEMENT-PHASE DIFFICULTIES

Female sexual arousal disorder is an inhibition of the vasocongestive response. This inhibition may be caused by physiological or psychological factors. Reduced lubrication is a normal occurrence during breast-feeding and following menopause.

Male erectile disorder is more commonly caused by physical factors than other sexual problems, especially among older men. A variety of procedures can help evaluate physical factors in erection problems.

ORGASM-PHASE DIFFICULTIES

Female orgasmic disorder, or anorgasmia, can be lifelong or nonlifelong, generalized or situational.

Generalized, lifelong anorgasmia means that a woman has never experienced orgasm by any means of self- or partner stimulation.

Situational anorgasmia describes a condition in which a woman can experience orgasm in one situation but not another; for example, during masturbation but not with a partner.

Coitus provides mostly indirect clitoral stimulation and for many woman is not sufficient to result in orgasm.

Male orgasmic disorder is the inability of a man to ejaculate (usually during coitus).

This text defines premature ejaculation as reaching orgasm so quickly as to significantly reduce a man's enjoyment of the experience or to interfere with the partner's gratification. Premature ejaculation is a common problem.

Some men may ejaculate quickly due to a low threshold to sexual stimulation.

Both men and women fake orgasm, although it is more often women who do so. Pretending usually perpetuates ineffective patterns of relating and reduces the intimacy of the sexual experience.

DYSPAREUNIA

Dyspareunia, or pain during coitus, is very disruptive to sexual interest and arousal in both women and men. Numerous physical problems can cause painful intercourse.

Peyronie's disease, in which fibrous tissue and calcium deposits develop in the penis, can cause pain and curvature of the penis during erection.

Vaginismus is an involuntary contraction of the outer vaginal muscles that makes penetration of the vagina difficult and painful. Many women who have vaginismus are interested in and enjoy sexual activity.

Thought Provokers

1. How would your sexuality change if you incurred a spinal-cord injury in an accident?
2. What positive and negative effects do you think traditional gender roles can have on sexual functioning?
3. Describe a hypothetical example of an individual with a sexual problem stemming from a combination of cultural, personal, interpersonal, and organic factors.
4. Do you think men or women are more prone to sexual problems? Why?

Suggested Readings

Kroll, Ken; and Klein, Erica (1992). *Enabling Romance.* New York: Harmony Books. Written by a disabled husband and his wife, this book explores sexual alternatives for people with a wide array of disabilities.

Lieblum, Sandra; and Rosen, Raymond (1988). *Sexual Desire Disorders.* New York: Guilford Press. A comprehensive text by leading experts about the theories, research, and treatments for sexual desire problems.

Maltz, Wendy (1991). *The Sexual Healing Journey.* New York: HarperCollins. An excellent and sensitive book for adult survivors of sexual abuse and their partners. It explores the impact of sexual abuse on sexuality and explains the steps that survivors and their partners can take to reclaim their sexuality.

Ogden, Gina (1994). *Women Who Love Sex.* New York: Pocket Books. Personal portraits of women who find great meaning and pleasure in sexual expression.

Zilbergeld, Bernie (1992). *The New Male Sexuality: A Guide to Sexual Fulfillment.* New York: Bantam. An exceptionally well-written and informative treatment of male sexuality, including such topics as sexual functioning, self-awareness, and overcoming difficulties.

Suggested Videotape

Maltz, Wendy (1990). *Partners in Healing.* An excellent videotape of three couples discussing the effects of childhood sexual abuse on their intimate relationships and the steps they took to recover from their traumas. Available from Independent Video Services, 401 East 10th Ave., Suite 160, Eugene, OR 97401.

Web Resources

WWW.

Sexual Health Network
www.sexualhealth.com/
This Web site offers information on sexuality for people with disabilities or other health problems, and provides descriptions of other published or online sources for further reference.

Dyspareunia
www.sexualitydata.com/topics/dyspareunia.html
This page is a fact sheet about dyspareunia, provided on the Sexuality Database Web site.

Erectile Dysfunction
noah.cuny.edu/wellconn/impotence.html
Candid, detailed, and accessible information on male erectile dysfunction is provided free to visitors of this Web site. Beyond descriptions of various symptoms and treatments, recent research articles and Web links to related organizations are included.

16

Sex Therapy and Enhancement

Basics of Sexual Enhancement and Sex Therapy

How can individuals increase their sexual self-awareness?

What are the guidelines in sensate focus?

Specific Suggestions for Women

What are the steps for a woman who wants to learn to experience orgasm?

What is the process for resolving vaginismus?

Specific Suggestions for Men

How can a man learn to prolong his arousal before ejaculating?

What is the typical course of therapy for a man having difficulty with erections, and what medical options may be helpful?

Treating Hypoactive Sexual Desire

Why does HSD often require more intensive therapy than other sexual problems?

Seeking Professional Assistance

What are the four levels of therapy in the PLISSIT model?

How might someone select a sex therapist?

When I was 20, my girlfriend and I were in her room and decided to have sex. She told me to make it quick and to be quiet because her mom was in the next room. Getting an erection was no problem, but after having sex for a couple of minutes I lost it. I completely freaked out, thinking I had become impotent overnight. I was in a panic for days and wouldn't let her touch me. I was utterly humiliated. I began placing calls to doctors specializing in penile problems, but not one would answer me over the phone, and I was in no financial situation to afford a doctor visit. It wasn't until my girlfriend showed me a book from a human sexuality class she'd taken that I mellowed out about the whole ordeal and chalked my problem up to a bad situation. (Authors' files)

This chapter focuses on methods for increasing sexual satisfaction and various approaches in sex therapy. The activities we discuss may be pursued individually or by a couple; they range from expanding self-knowledge to sharing more effectively with a partner. Much of what follows embraces our belief that all of us have the potential for self-help. The "Suggested Readings" at the end of the chapter provide further self-help options.

The various suggestions offered here have proved helpful to many people. However, the same techniques do not work for everyone, and exercises often need to be individually modified. Furthermore, professional help may be called for in those cases where individual efforts, couple efforts, or both do not produce the desired results. Recognizing that therapy is sometimes necessary to promote change, we have included guidelines for seeking sex therapy in the last section of this chapter. In addition, it is important to consult a physician to rule out any physical causes for the sexual difficulty.

Basics of Sexual Enhancement and Sex Therapy

Many people's childhood sexual development is influenced by negative conditioning, limiting attitudes, and a lack of self-exploration—factors that can hinder later sexual enjoyment or functioning. As is discussed in the box "How Modern Sex Therapy Can Clash with Cultural Values," these influences may be part of a particular cultural subgroup's traditions. Increased self-knowledge is often an important step in modifying negative preconceptions and feelings. With this in mind, we briefly outline procedures for improving awareness and acceptance of your body, as well as activities that provide the most pleasurable stimulation. These "basics" can also be useful for individuals and couples whose sexual life is already satisfactory.

What do you think are the basic elements in a positive sexuality? 

Self-Awareness

People who know themselves—their sexual feelings, their needs, and how their bodies respond—are often better able to share this valuable information with a partner than are people who are unaware of their sexual needs and potentials. Physical and emotional self-awareness and self-expression are crucial elements in satisfying sexual experiences. In the book *Women Who Love Sex,* Gina Ogden found an overall message in the stories of women she interviewed. She concluded that

> sexual pleasure is good. . . . life enlarging, particularly as women become more adept at exploring the vast arena that pleasure *is.* . . . To celebrate the erotic, to feel motivated by satisfaction rather than by guilt and suffering, is a radical reframe for many women. It means women don't have to give up sex to be safe. . . . It means shifting from control—the ability to say "No"—to power—the ability to say "Yes." . . . It means sharing responsibility for initiating, for setting

goals, for enjoyment. With self-ownership comes voice. . . . There can be a closer meeting of minds and bodies, hearts and souls. (Ogden, 1994, p. 23)

A good way to increase self-awareness, as well as comfort with our sexuality, is to become well acquainted with our sexual anatomy. It is not unusual for women to report never having looked at their own vulvas. Men may be more familiar with their bodies, but many are not comfortable with their genitals. You may decide to become familiar with your genitals by looking and touching, so as to be more comfortable with your own body. It can be helpful to examine all areas of your anatomy, not just the genital region. Examine yourself visually and experiment with different touches, perhaps using a massage lotion to make the movements more pleasant.

Masturbation exercises are an effective way for both men and women to learn about and experience sexual response. These exercises can be enjoyed for themselves, and the knowledge they provide can be shared with a partner. Masturbation also can help older people who do not have a current partner to maintain sexual functioning (Lieblum & Bachmann, 1988). Further information about masturbation can be found later in this chapter in the section "Becoming Orgasmic."

Explorations of your own body may provide the motivation to take the same approach in exploring and examining your partner's body. Exchanging information can be immensely valuable in increasing both comfort with and knowledge about each other. A later section, "Sensate Focus," will elaborate on mutual exploration.

Sexuality and Diversity

How Modern Sex Therapy Can Clash with Cultural Values

Modern Western sex therapy is based on the assumption that the values of open communication, emotional intimacy, and physical pleasure for both partners guide treatment and are its goals. However, these principles are antithetical to many cultures' norms. Cultural beliefs influence sexual practices, the perception of sexual problems, and modes of treatment. In cultures where male superiority predominates, a woman is expected to be sexual as an obligation of marriage rather than for her own pleasure. Lack of orgasm and low sexual desire would not be viewed as a problem, but vaginismus would be, because it interferes with the man's sexual activity and the possibility of conception (Lavee, 1991).

A study conducted in Saudi Arabia, where the marital relationship is based primarily on the two dimensions of male sexual potency and couple fertility, found that the most common presenting problem to sex therapy was erectile disorder. This was likely caused by males becoming overanxious about their sexual performance. Females in Saudi Arabia, who are raised to inhibit their sexual desires, only came to sex therapy with problems of painful intercourse. Unlike in Western countries, lack of desire, arousal, or orgasm did not lead them to seek help. For both men and women, only when intercourse itself was impaired—not interest or pleasure—did couples seek treatment. Once again, we see that sociocultural factors affect even what kinds of sexual anxieties people experience (Osman & Al-Sawaf, 1995).

Many cultural traditions allow for little or no communication about sexual matters. Among Asians, it can be considered shameful to discuss sex, especially with someone outside the family (Greene, 1994). Muslims are taught to avoid talking to the other sex (including their spouses) about sexuality. Taking a sex history may be distressing for clients with these beliefs, especially when the husband and wife are interviewed together. In cultures where women are expected to be innocent about sex, the sex-education component of therapy conflicts with the prevailing values.

Specific sex therapy techniques often contradict cultural values. For example, masturbation exercises to treat anorgasmia, erectile difficulties, or premature ejaculation would conflict with religious prohibitions of orthodox Jews. Female-above intercourse position may pose a problem in cultures where male dominance is prevalent. The gender equality inherent in sensate focus exercises and avoidance of intercourse are also often objectionable to many ethnic groups.

Sex therapy needs to take into account the clients' cultural values and the implications they have for intimate behavior. Therapists should attempt to adjust therapy to their clients' well-integrated ethnic and religious perspectives. This is likely to be more helpful than attempting to impose the cultural norms inherent in Western sex therapy (Lavee, 1991).

Communication

When you first discussed the stop–start technique [discussed later in this chapter] in class, I was excited to try it out with my partner. However, I didn't know how to talk about it. It wasn't like he had never mentioned his problem before. He would say he was sorry he was so fast, and that maybe it would get better with time. Finally, I asked him to come to class with me the day you showed the film demonstrating the technique. Man, did we do a lot of talking after it was over. He was anxious to give it a try. At first we made some mistakes. In fact, it was only when we were really talking openly that things began to work well. He showed me how he liked to be stimulated, things he had never told me before. We shared a lot of feelings. He became much more aware of my needs and what I needed to be satisfied. We really started getting into a lot of variety in our lovemaking, instead of just kissing and intercourse. By the way, the technique did work in slowing him down, but I think the biggest benefit has been breaking down the communication barriers. It sure makes sex a whole lot better! (Authors' files)

This quotation from the authors' files illustrates not only how difficult it can sometimes be to talk constructively about sexual problems but also how important communication can be in solving them. Communication itself may not solve a sexual difficulty. Indeed, as we have seen, a number of problems have a physiological basis. Communication is, however, a very important element—not only in working out a specific problem but also in establishing and maintaining mutual understanding, which can make a relationship stronger. Couples who have better communication than other couples prior to sex therapy are more likely to be successful in treatment (Hawton et al., 1992).

We encourage you to review Chapter 8. Many people find it difficult to talk about the sexual aspects of their relationships, but failing to communicate needs and expectations can hinder the resolution of sexual problems and may even contribute to some difficulties (McCabe & Delaney, 1992). One of the primary benefits of sex therapy, whether the immediate goal is learning to have orgasms with partners, how to overcome premature ejaculation, or almost any other shared problem, is that couples participating together in the treatment process often develop more effective communication skills. The "Love Talk Exercise" box offers some suggestions.

Let's Talk About It

Love Talk Exercise

Developing skills in sexual communication is one of the biggest challenges couples face. The following sentence openers are tools to expand the all-important communication between sexual partners. If you decide to do the exercise, review the communication chapter for using "I" language and listening skills. Do the exercise at some time other than when you're being sexual. Be sure to agree beforehand that it's okay to skip any item either of you don't feel ready to discuss. Take turns being first to read and complete the sentence openers.

Sentence openers:

"Something I really like about our sexual connection is . . ."
"What really turns me on is . . ."
"What brings me to the most intense orgasm is . . ."
"What I like about your orgasm is . . ."
"Something you could do to really get me in the mood for sex is . . ."
"Something sexual I really don't like is . . ."
"Something I'm curious about is . . ."
"Something sexual I've always wanted to try is . . ."
"One thing I'd like from you sexually is . . ."
"The thing I most want to tell you that I haven't yet is . . ."
"Something I'd like to ask you is . . ."
"One of my sexual fantasies is . . ."
"One thing that worries me about our sexual relationship is . . ."
"When we have sex I feel . . ."
(Add your own sentence openers if there's something you'd like to address that is not covered here.)

Source: Adapted from Linda De Villers, *Love Skills* (1997).

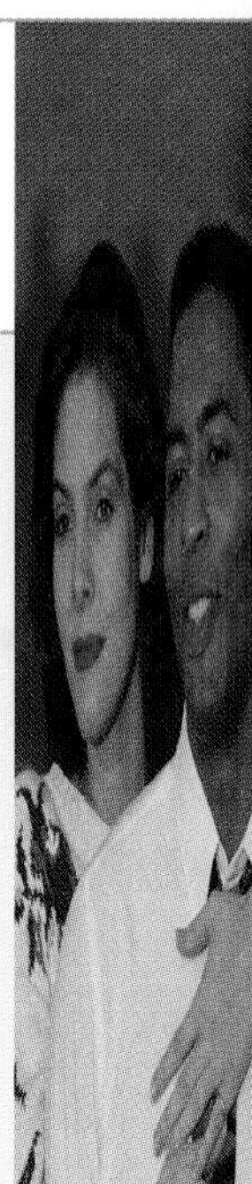

Such communication skills are not easy to develop. In his writing, psychologist David Schnarch notes that "intimacy during sex doesn't come 'naturally'—it's a learned ability and an acquired taste" (1993, p. 44). In this frame, adult eroticism depends more on emotional maturity than sexual technique. A solid sense of self is needed to risk expressing oneself as fully as is necessary for intense erotic experiences within a long-term committed marriage. It requires the ability to risk initiating sexual behaviors and to tolerate the possibility that the partner may not respond positively. Schnarch states, "The essence of sexual intimacy lies . . . in the ability to allow oneself to deeply know and to be deeply known by one's partner." He acknowledges that "to really see each other . . . during sex requires the courage, integrity and maturity to face oneself and, even more frightening, convey that self . . . to the partner" (1993, p. 43). Schnarch suggests that couples maintain eye contact during lovemaking; he considers the ability to experience an "eyes-open" orgasm as an important indicator that couples have learned to tolerate a high level of self-expression and sexual intimacy.

Sensate Focus

One of the most useful couple-oriented activities for enhancing mutual sexual enjoyment is a series of touching exercises called **sensate focus** (see Figure 16.1). Masters and Johnson labeled this technique and have used it as a basic step in treating sexual problems. It can be helpful in reducing anxiety caused by goal orientation and in increasing communication, pleasure, and closeness. This technique is by no means appropriate only for sex therapy, but can be used by all couples to enhance their sexual relationships. In the sensate focus touching exercises, partners take turns touching each other while following some essential guidelines. In the following descriptions, we assume that the one doing the touching is a woman and the one being touched is a man. Of course, homosexual as well as heterosexual couples can do these exercises, and in either case the partners periodically change roles.

Sensate focus
A process of touching and communication used to enhance sexual pleasure and to reduce performance pressure.

To start, the person who will be doing the touching takes some time to "set the scene" such that it is comfortable and pleasant for herself—for example, by unplugging the phone and arranging a warm, cozy place with relaxing music and lighting. The two people then undress, and the toucher begins to explore her partner's body, following this important guideline: She is *not* to touch to please or arouse her partner, but for her *own*

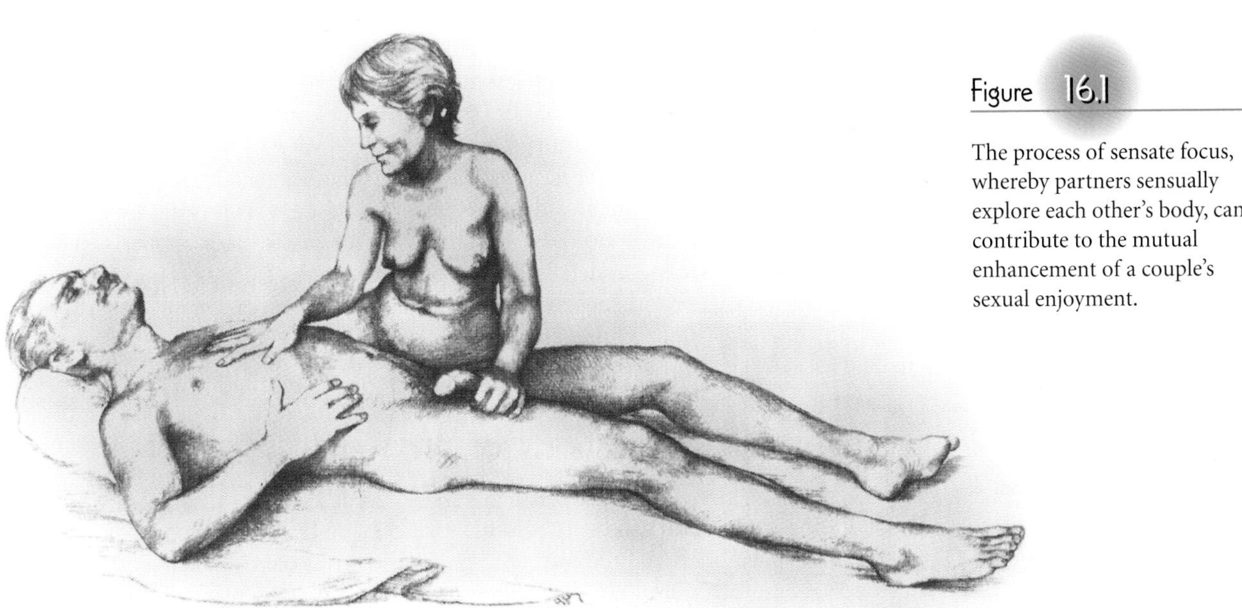

Figure 16.1

The process of sensate focus, whereby partners sensually explore each other's body, can contribute to the mutual enhancement of a couple's sexual enjoyment.

interest and pleasure. The goal is for the toucher to focus on her perception of textures, shapes, and temperatures. The nondemand quality of this kind of touching helps reduce or eliminate performance anxiety, which can inhibit arousal for both partners. The person being touched remains quiet except when any touch is uncomfortable. In that case, he describes the uncomfortable feeling and what the toucher could do to make it more comfortable; for example, "That feels ticklish—please touch the other side of my arm." This guideline helps the toucher attend fully to her own sensations and perceptions without worrying whether something she is doing is unpleasant to her partner.

In the next sensate focus exercise, the two people switch roles, following the same guidelines as before. In these first sensate focus experiences, intercourse and touching breasts and genitals are prohibited. Only after the partners have focused on touch perceptions and on communicating uncomfortable feelings do they include breasts and genitals as part of the exercise. Again, the toucher explores for her own interest and pleasure, not her partner's. After the inclusion of breasts and genitals, the partners progress to a simultaneous sensate focus experience. Now they touch one another at the same time and experience feelings from both touching and being touched.

Sensate focus is an excellent way to learn to respond erotically with all areas of the body. It is also a good exercise for learning the sensitive areas on your partner's body. In sex therapy, sensate focus exercises usually precede and form the foundation for specific techniques for resolving arousal and orgasm difficulties. These techniques are discussed later in this chapter.

Masturbation with a Partner Present

It can be particularly valuable for couples to let each other know what kind of touching they find arousing. Masturbating in the presence of a partner may be a way to share this kind of information. This activity can be particularly helpful for women learning to experience orgasm with a partner and for resolving premature ejaculation and erectile difficulties, as discussed further in the sections "Lasting Longer" and "Dealing with Erectile Difficulties."

Couples who feel comfortable incorporating self-stimulation into their sexual relationship open many options for themselves. When only one of them feels sexual, that person can masturbate with the other present, perhaps touching, perhaps kissing.

The experiences suggested in the preceding pages may all be helpful in increasing sexual satisfaction, whether an individual or couple have a specific difficulty or their goal is simply to find out more about themselves. Beyond these general exercises, though, specific exercises or techniques can sometimes aid in reducing or overcoming particular sexual difficulties that can be highly troublesome. We described some of these difficulties in Chapter 15, and in the remainder of this chapter we look at some strategies that have been used to deal with them. For purposes of clarity and easy reference, these strategies are organized according to whether they deal with primarily female or primarily male sexual problems, except treatment of hypoactive sexual desire, which is discussed later in the chapter. We should stress, however, that these discussions are not applicable to only one sex. Men can gain some understanding of both their female partners and themselves from reading the section on specific female strategies; women can gain similarly from reading the discussions of techniques for men.

Specific Suggestions for Women

The following paragraphs suggest procedures that may be helpful to women in learning to increase sexual arousal and to reach orgasm by themselves or with a partner. They also include suggestions for dealing with vaginismus. When origins of these problems are complex, self-help may not be sufficient to resolve them.

Becoming Orgasmic

Learning effective self-stimulation is often recommended for women who have never experienced orgasm. One advantage to self-stimulation is that a woman without a partner can learn to become orgasmic. For a woman with a sexual partner, becoming orgasmic first by masturbation may help develop a sense of sexual autonomy that can increase the likelihood of satisfaction with a partner.

Therapy programs for anorgasmia are based on progressive self-awareness activities that a woman does at home between therapy sessions. The step-by-step activities may be presented by a therapist in a small group of women who want to learn to experience orgasm; these same steps are also used in individual sex counseling. At the beginning of treatment, body exploration, genital self-exam, and Kegel exercises (see Chapter 4) are emphasized; then therapy and home exercises move progressively to self-stimulation exercises similar to those described in Chapter 9 (see "Self-Pleasuring Techniques").

Vibrators are sometimes used to help an anorgasmic woman experience orgasm for the first time so she knows that she can have this response. (A vibrator is often less tiring to use and supplies more intense stimulation than the fingers.) After she has experienced a few orgasms with the vibrator, it is helpful for her to return to manual stimulation, so she can learn to respond in this manner, too. This step is important because it is easier for a partner to replicate a woman's own touch than the stimulation of a vibrator.

Even in therapy, it may take considerable time for some women to learn to experience orgasm. However, counselors can facilitate the process by answering questions and providing personal assistance; they may also help a woman work through broader-based problems that contribute to anorgasmia. Information on the role of counselors in sex therapy, as well as guidelines for seeking help, appears later in this chapter.

Experiencing Orgasm with a Partner

Once a woman has learned to experience orgasm through self-stimulation, sharing her discoveries with her partner can help her partner to know what forms of stimulation are most pleasing to her. A woman's sexual assertiveness—initiating what is arousing to her and making her erotic wishes known is essential in improving her sexual experience (Apt, 1996).

After the couple is comfortable with the sensate focus exercises described earlier, they proceed to genital exploration. The exercise is called a *sexological exam*. Each partner takes turns visually exploring the other's genitals, locating all the parts discussed in Chapters 4 and 5. After looking thoroughly, they experiment with touch, noticing and sharing what different areas feel like.

The next step is for the woman to stimulate herself in her partner's presence. The woman can use self-stimulation methods that she has learned are effective and share her arousal with her partner, who can be holding and kissing her or lying beside her, as is shown in Figure 16.2. This step is often a difficult one. One woman describes how she dealt with her discomfort:

> When I wanted to share with my partner what I had learned about myself through masturbation, I felt anxious about how to do it. Finally, we decided that to begin with, I would be in the bedroom, and he would be in the living room, knowing I was masturbating. Then he would sit on the bed, not looking at me. The next step was for him to hold and kiss me while I was touching myself. Then I could be comfortable showing him how I touch myself. (Authors' files)

Next the partner begins nondemanding manual–genital pleasuring. The couple can do this in any position that suits them. Masters and Johnson (1970) recommended the position illustrated in Figure 16.3. (We are supposing in this discussion that the partner is a man.) The partner reclines against cushions or pillows; the woman sits between his legs with her back supported by his chest. The woman places her hand over her partner's

Figure 16.2

Masturbating in the presence of a partner can be an effective way for an individual to indicate what kind of touching she or he finds arousing.

Figure 16.3

The back-to-chest position for genital sensate focus.

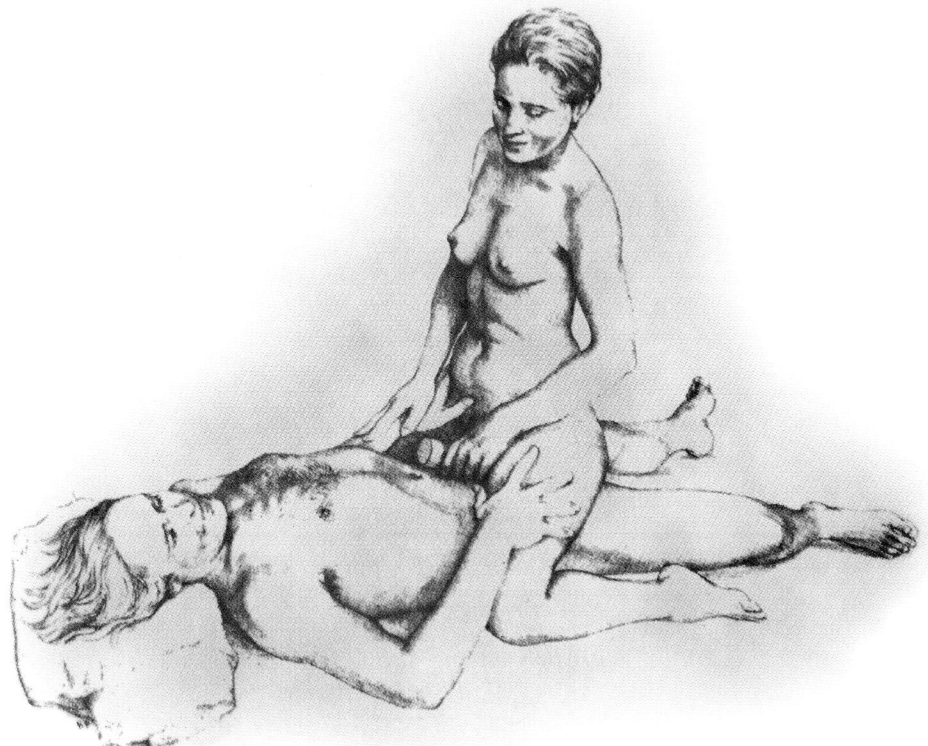

Figure 16.4

The use of an electric vibrator for clitoral stimulation during coitus.

hand on her genitals to guide the stimulation. They can use lubricants to increase sensation. The partner makes no assumptions about how to touch but rather is guided by the woman's words and hand. The purpose of initial sessions is for the partner to discover what is arousing to the woman, rather than to produce orgasm. If the woman thinks she is ready to experience orgasm, she indicates to her partner to continue the stimulation until she experiences climax. Orgasm will probably not occur until the couple has had several sessions.

Couples can use several specific techniques to increase a woman's arousal and the possibility of orgasm during intercourse. The first has to do with when to begin intercourse. Rather than beginning intercourse after a certain number of minutes of foreplay or when there is sufficient lubrication, a woman can be guided by her feeling of what might be called "readiness." Not all women experience this feeling of readiness, but for those who do, beginning intercourse at this time (and not before) may enhance the ensuing erotic sensations. Of course, her partner will have to cooperate by waiting for the woman to indicate when she is ready and by not attempting to begin intercourse before then.

A woman who wants increased stimulation during coitus may benefit from initiating movements herself:

> Orgasms during intercourse . . . usually seemed to result from a conscious attempt by the woman to center some kind of clitoral area contact for herself during intercourse, usually involving contact with the man's pubic area. . . . This is essentially the way men get stimulation during intercourse. They rub their penises against our vaginal walls so that the same area they stimulate during masturbation is being stimulated during intercourse. In other words, you have to get the stimulation centered where it feels good. (Hite, 1976, p. 276)

Even more direct stimulation of the clitoris can occur during intercourse. The woman can stimulate her clitoris manually during intercourse or use a vibrator, as shown in Figure 16.4. Some men report the vibrations transmitted to their penises as pleasurable. The woman can then guide her partner in touching her clitoris. One comfortable way for him to be able to touch her clitoris is to turn his hand slightly and use his thumb. (Side-lying and rear-entry coital positions also allow either of them to touch her clitoris easily.) The woman may also find it helpful to experiment with Kegel exercises during penetration.

After several sessions of the woman controlling the pelvic movements and incorporating manual stimulation, the man initiates nondemanding thrusting. The couple can also experiment with other coital positions. For women who wish to try experiencing orgasm without direct clitoral stimulation, Kaplan (1974) has suggested the *bridge maneuver*. In this, manual stimulation during intercourse is employed until the woman is very close to climaxing. Then manual stimulation is stopped, and she actively moves her pelvis to provide sufficient stimulation to induce orgasm.

The techniques just described are useful in exploring ways of relating sexually and may allow a woman to experience orgasm in some cases. A number of books are available for couples who want more information than we have had space to present here; some of these are listed in the "Suggested Readings" at the end of this chapter.

Dealing with Vaginismus

Treatment for vaginismus usually begins during a pelvic exam, with the physician demonstrating the vaginal spasm reaction to the woman or couple. Subsequent therapy starts with relaxation and self-awareness exercises, which the woman performs at home to reach a degree of comfort and control on her own (Plant & RachBeisel, 1998). These exercises typically begin with a soothing bath, general body exploration, and manual external genital pleasuring; then proceed to dealing with vaginismus as the woman learns to insert first a fingertip, then a finger, and eventually three fingers into her vagina without experiencing muscle contractions. At each stage, the woman practices relaxing and contracting the vaginal muscles, as with Kegel exercises (see Chapter 4). Dilators, which are cylindrical rods of graduated sizes, are sometimes used to accustom the vaginal walls to stretching. Concurrently with these "home-play" exercises, she meets with her therapist to discuss her reactions.

Once the woman has completed the preceding steps, her partner may begin to participate. Together, they follow the same steps she followed alone, starting with a visual examination of the vulva. Open communication is essential, and progress is very gradual. No attempt at penile–vaginal penetration is made until the man can insert three fingers without inducing a muscle spasm. When the penis is inserted into the vagina, the purpose is for the woman to become familiar with the sensations involved in vaginal containment of the penis, so the couple remain motionless. Pelvic movements and pleasure focusing are added later, only when both partners are comfortable with penetration. Research suggests that vaginismus can sometimes be difficult to treat successfully, especially when couples have never experienced penile–vaginal intercourse (LoPiccolo, 1982). More extensive therapy may be necessary to address vaginismus.

Specific Suggestions for Men

In the following paragraphs, we outline methods for dealing with the common difficulties of premature ejaculation and erectile disorder. We also discuss a way of treating the less common condition of orgasmic disorder. As in the preceding discussion of women's sexual difficulties, we caution that the origins of such problems are complex and that solutions are frequently not simple. Again, we refer readers who are interested in pursuing these topics to the "Suggested Readings" and also to the discussion under "Seeking Professional Assistance."

Lasting Longer

Although premature ejaculation is a common dissatisfaction, the prospects for positive change are good. Most professional sex therapists use a multiphased program that focuses on the stop–start technique, discussed shortly (McCarthy, 1994). The successful approaches to learning ejaculatory control are quite easy to implement, even, in some cases, without professional guidance. There are also simpler strategies for helping to delay ejaculation, and we discuss these first.

Some Helpful Strategies for Delaying Ejaculation

In some cases, men can gain considerable control over premature ejaculation by practicing a few simple strategies. Men for whom premature ejaculation is not a problem as well as women readers may find the following discussion valuable simply because they would sometimes like sexual intercourse to last longer.

• *Ejaculate more frequently.* Men with premature ejaculation problems sometimes find that they can delay ejaculation when they are having more frequent orgasms. If partner sex is not a viable option, frequent masturbation to orgasm can be helpful.

• *"Come again!"* Because of the limiting assumption that male orgasm is the end point of sexual interaction, few men or their partners consider or explore the potential for slowed responsiveness after a first climax. From our earlier discussion of the male refractory period (see Chapter 6), it is clear that sexual activity that follows an initial male orgasm is not typically characterized by rapid ejaculation. Many men might be pleased with the results of continued interaction. A couple can experiment with continuing sexual interaction following the man's ejaculation, then resume intercourse when his erection returns.

• *Change positions.* Excessive muscle tension is detrimental to a man who ejaculates rapidly. All things being equal, increased muscle tension is typically associated with a rapid sexual response cycle. For a man who wants to delay ejaculation, the man-above position is about the worst way to have intercourse. The muscle tension from supporting his own weight as he thrusts results in a more rapid ejaculation.

Many men gain a desirable amount of control by lying on their backs (see page 265 for variations of the woman-above position). Note that this position by itself is not sufficient; another requirement is relaxation. If a man attempts energetic pelvic movements in this position, he will be moving not only his own weight but that of his partner as well, increasing muscle tension to even higher levels.

Immediate results do not always follow position modification. Sometimes the novelty of the position will increase his arousal and temporarily hasten ejaculation. However, after some experience with this change in position, he often experiences the advantages of increased relaxation.

• *Talk with each other.* Communicating during coitus may help prolong the experience. To delay climax, it is often essential to slow down or completely cease movements. Without communication, a partner may find it difficult to anticipate the precise moment to reduce or stop stimulation. The man needs to become comfortable asking his partner for help.

Some men can maintain intercourse for very long periods of time if they allow sexual tension to rise and fall between plateau and excitement levels. Not uncommonly, men report that an added sense of control comes with repeated episodes of going to the brink, reducing stimulation, and then moving once again to the edge.

• *Consider alternatives.* In minimizing performance anxiety about rapid ejaculation (and most of the other problems discussed here), it is often useful to think of intercourse as just one of several options for sexual sharing. Many people have discovered that reaching orgasm during intercourse is not necessary for pleasure, particularly if other methods are used to produce orgasm. Occasionally, manual stimulation, oral–genital contact, or using a vibrator will reduce performance anxiety enough to considerably prolong arousal. It can be comforting to know that there are many options for obtaining and giving sexual pleasure. It is also important to realize that an activity may be very enjoyable even when it does not produce orgasm.

The Stop–Start Technique

James Semans, a urologist, hypothesized that premature ejaculation stemmed from a man's lack of awareness of the neuromuscular sensations that precede orgasm and ejaculation. A man who ejaculates rapidly, for whatever reasons, has not noticed this sensory feedback, yet such awareness is essential to bringing any reflex function under control.

Stop–start technique A treatment technique for premature ejaculation, consisting of stimulating the penis to the point of impending orgasm and then stopping until the preejaculatory sensations subside.

Working from this assumption, Semans developed a **stop–start technique.** This technique is designed to prolong the sensations prior to orgasm, enabling the man to become acquainted with, and ultimately to control, his ejaculatory reflex. The partner is instructed to stimulate the man's penis, either manually or orally, to the point of impending orgasm—at which time stimulation is stopped until the preejaculatory sensations subside (Semans, 1956).

With a less commonly used technique, the *squeeze technique,* the partner applies strong pressure with her thumb on the frenulum and her second and third fingers on the top side of the penis, one above and one below the corona, until the man loses the urge to ejaculate. Initially, the man with rapid ejaculation places his hand over his partner's to demonstrate how hard to squeeze.

Training sessions such as those just described generally last around 15–30 minutes and occur as often as once a day for several days or weeks. During each session, the couple repeats the stimulation and stop–start procedure several times; then allows ejaculation to occur on the last cycle. The couple should reach an agreement about sexual stimulation and orgasm for the man's partner. If this is desired, they can engage in noncoital activity.

A man working with the stop–start technique usually experiences immediately observable benefits. As his ejaculatory control improves appreciably, the couple progresses to intercourse. Heterosexual couples use the woman-above position shown on page 265, with the woman sitting astride. This position is especially well suited for this next stage because the man can relax his body. The first step is for the man to put his penis in the woman's vagina and lie quietly for several moments before beginning slow movements. When he begins to feel close to orgasm, they lie quietly again. This stop–start intercourse technique is continued as the man experiences progressively better ejaculatory control. In most cases, the man is able to prevent a too-hasty orgasm (Masters and Johnson reported a 98% success rate). A major advantage of the stop–start technique is the almost inevitable improvement of communication that results when two people treat the problem of premature ejaculation together.

A man can benefit from using this technique on himself during solo masturbation sessions (Zilbergeld, 1992). However, to gain the full returns of improved communication, we encourage couples to practice this technique together whenever practical.

Medical Treatments

Research has found that small doses of some medications usually prescribed for depression can help men who normally ejaculate quickly, to prolong intercourse for 20 minutes or longer. This research was conducted because one of the side effects of these medications when used at higher doses to treat depression is suppressed orgasm in men and women. Further research is needed to clarify the most effective dosages, to determine long-term usage and effects, and to ensure that side effects are as minimal as they appear to be (Kim & Seo, 1998; Petit, 1994).

Dealing with Erectile Difficulties

With the exception of organically caused erection difficulties, anxiety is the major stumbling block to erectile response. Therefore, all behaviorally focused approaches to this problem concentrate on reducing or eliminating anxiety. A major goal is to create an atmosphere in which the man is able to achieve some success in obtaining an erection, thus restoring his confidence and diminishing performance fear.

Initially, a couple will use the sensate focus exercises discussed earlier in this chapter. It is important that both partners understand that these exercises are not designed to produce an erect penis. The main point is that the time spent touching is *not* goal oriented. For this reason, therapists restrict coitus and ejaculation during these exercises. The following account shows how one man reacted to the regimen imposed by his therapist:

When I was told that intercourse was off limits, at least for the time being, I couldn't believe how relieved I felt. After years of trying to make my body get up for a performance, suddenly the doctor's advice eliminated this pressure. It was like being given permission to feel again. If I couldn't get hard, so what? After all, I was told not to use it even if it happened. Looking back, I think those first few times touching and getting touched by my wife were the first really worry-free pleasurable times I had experienced in years. Soon I was getting erections all over the place. (Authors' files)

Avoiding intercourse and ejaculation does not necessarily mean that a man's partner may not have an orgasm. If a couple wants to, they can agree in advance for the partner to have an orgasm at the close of a session by whatever mode of stimulation seems comfortable to both (self-stimulation, being touched by the partner, oral stimulation, or whatever). One key restriction is that such activity is noncoital and does not result in ejaculation by the man who has the erectile difficulty. When anxiety is reduced and the couple has progressed to a point where both feel comfortable with the pleasures of body exploration, it is time to move to the next phase. Although the man who has experienced psychologically based arousal difficulties will probably have begun to have spontaneous erections by this time, their occurrence is not essential to deciding to move forward. The critical condition is that both partners feel relaxed and positive about their mutually experienced sensuality. In the next phase, the two people direct their attention toward whatever kinds of genital stimulation are particularly arousing to the man—manual or oral pleasuring, or both. The intercourse ban is still in effect. If the man achieves a complete erection, his partner should stop whatever actions have aroused him.

Why do you think it is helpful to stop stimulation after the man with erection problems has an erection?

Sometimes people are perplexed at this suggestion, thinking that the logical next step would be to progress to penetration. However, in view of the past history of the vast majority of men troubled by erectile inhibition, it is crucial that the erection be allowed to subside at this point. Why? To alter the man's belief that once an erection is lost it will not return. When his partner stops providing optimal stimulation, the man allows his erection to subside. This may take several minutes of nonstimulation if the level of arousal is very high. This time can be spent holding each other close or exchanging nongenital caresses. When his erection has completely abated, the man's partner again resumes genital pleasuring. By experiencing that erections can be lost and regained, the fear diminishes that he has "had it" if he loses the first one.

The final phase of treatment, for heterosexual couples who desire intercourse, involves penetration and coitus. With the man on his back and the woman astride, the couple begins with sensate focus, then moves to genital stimulation. When the man has an erection, his partner lowers herself onto his penis, maintaining stimulation with gentle pelvic movements. It is important to allow the man to be "selfish," concentrating exclusively on his own pleasure (Kaplan, 1974). Worries such as "Is she going to come?" or "Am I doing well?" can intrude on his own sensual feelings. For this reason, couples may agree to consider her orgasm only after he has experienced his.

Occasionally a man loses his erection after penetration. If this happens, his partner can again provide the kind of oral or manual stimulation that originally produced his erection. If his response continues to be blocked, it is wise to stop genital contact, returning once again to the original nondemand pleasuring of sensate focus. Erection loss after penetration is not uncommon, and couples should not be overly anxious if it happens. A few successful coital encounters will generally alleviate psychologically caused erectile inhibition. Should the problem recur, the couple is now experienced in techniques they can use to avoid establishing a pattern of difficulty.

Medical Treatments

Some men who have impaired erectile functioning as the result of physiological problems make a very satisfactory sexual adjustment to the absence of erection by emphasizing and enjoying other ways of sexual sharing. For other men whose illness or injury has left them unable to have erections, several types of medical treatments are available (Guay, 1998, Hanash, 1997; Hawton, 1998). The most recent development, pills for erectile problems, is described in Table 16.1.

Because vascular impairment may be a factor in erectile difficulty, one avenue of treatment is injection of the same vasoactive medications used to diagnose vascular impairment in erectile disorder. These medications relax smooth muscle tissue in the spongy body of the penis, causing increased blood flow which in turn results in engorgement and erection. A physician teaches the man to inject the medication into the cavernous bodies of the penis; erection typically occurs within four to ten minutes after the almost painless injection and lasts from one to four hours (Althof, 1996). Complications may include transitory numbness of the glans, infection, tissue damage at the injection site, and prolonged erection. Long-term effects of these injections are not yet known. Medication inserted into the urethra in a suppository is also available (Padma-Nathan et al., 1997). Topical gel or a skin patch may be options in the future (Kim et al., 1995).

Yohimbine, a substance found in the bark of the yohimbine plant that is occasionally prescribed for hypotension, may help induce erection in some cases, but appears to be of limited value (Ernst & Pittler, 1998; Kim & Lipshultz, 1997).

Table 16.1 A Pill for Erectile Problems

The first oral medicine for erectile problems, Viagra, became available in 1998. It was the fastest-selling prescription drug in history (Handy, 1998). Painless and discreet, unlike injections, it does not cause erections without physical stimulation and begins working in about 20 minutes (Erdley, 1998). Viagra will be tested in women to determine if it will increase blood flow to the vulva and vagina during sexual stimulation (Mann, 1998). Other medications are also being developed.

Oral medication	*Description*	*Pros and Cons*	*Duration*
Viagra (sildenafil)	Relaxes smooth muscle cells, the first step in achieving an erection.	Can cause headaches, vision problems, and diarrhea.	Taken an hour before sex. Stimulation needed to get an erection.
*Spontane (apomorphine) in final trials by manufacturer**	Process is unclear, but drug may affect neural center that triggers erections.	Studies indicate it helps most mild cases—70% in one study.	Works only in response to physical stimulation.
*Vasomax (phentolamine) under FDA review**	Blocks adrenaline, relaxing smooth muscle tissue and dilating arteries.	Helped 60–80% of those tested. Fewer side effects than Viagra.	Taken 20 to 40 minutes before sex. Requires stimulation for erection.

*As of May 1998.

Source: (Becker et al., 1998; Leland, 1997)

Mechanical Devices

Devices that suction blood into the penis and hold it there during intercourse have also been available since the mid-1980s (Korenman & Viosca, 1992). Available by prescription, external vacuum constriction devices consist of a vacuum chamber, pump, and penile constriction bands. The vacuum chamber is placed over the flaccid penis. The pump creates a negative pressure within the chamber and draws blood into the penis. The elastic band is then placed onto the base of the penis to trap the blood, and the chamber is removed.

A new nonprescription product, called Rejoyn, is a penile support sleeve made from soft, medical quality rubber that fits over the penis to provide the support necessary for intercourse. A lubricated, open-ended condomlike cover fits over the sleeve. It can accommodate an erect as well as a flaccid penis.

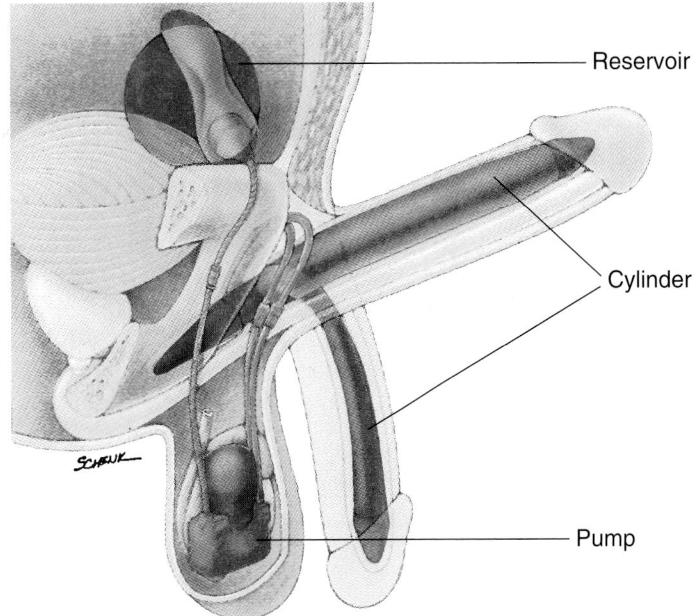

Figure 16.5

An inflatable penile prosthesis.

Surgical Treatments

A surgically implanted penile prosthesis is another available option. Because the surgery is expensive and involves risks, including infection, it is wise to evaluate this option carefully in comparison with others, and to include one's partner in pre- and postsurgical counseling (Wilson & Delk, 1995). There are two basic types of penile implants. One consists of a pair of semirigid rods placed inside the cavernous bodies of the penis. Although this type is easier to implant than the second type, a potential disadvantage is that the penis is always semierect. The second type of prosthesis is an inflatable device that enables the penis to be either flaccid or erect (see Figure 16.5). Two inflatable cylinders are implanted into the cavernous bodies of the penile shaft. They are connected to a fluid-filled reservoir located near the bladder and to a pump in the scrotal sac. When a man wants an erection, he squeezes the pump several times, and the fluid fills the collapsed cylinders, producing an erection. When an erection is no longer desired, a release valve causes the fluid to go back into the reservoir. Neither of these devices can restore sensation or the ability to ejaculate if these have been lost due to medical problems. They do, however, provide an alternative for men who want to mechanically restore their ability to have erections (Garber, 1997).

Although some studies have found a high degree of satisfaction with penile implants (Holloway & Farah, 1997), a few cautions should be noted. In general, men with inflatable prostheses have been more satisfied than men with semirigid rods (Mohr & Beutler, 1990). In both cases, dissatisfaction with the surgery may occur due to altered sensations during erection (Hrebinko et al., 1990). In addition, it is important for men considering penile implants to be aware that any ability to experience natural erection prior to surgery will be impaired by the surgery (Benet et al., 1994). Implants may need to be repaired or replaced in rare cases, or infection may occur. And finally, some prostheses are made of silicone and have been one of the targets (along with silicone breast implants) of immunodeficiency lawsuits.

Another surgical solution for erectile difficulties involves microsurgical vascular repairs (Kim & McVary, 1995). Done only at a few centers, for carefully selected patients, revascularization surgery can be helpful in restoring sexual functioning but not in the majority of people (Nash, 1997).

Reducing Male Orgasmic Disorder

A behavioral approach is generally used in treating male orgasmic disorder. In addition, psychotherapy aimed at reducing resentment in the relationship may be helpful when dislike or anger toward a partner contributes to a man's ejaculatory difficulty. The program outlined in the following paragraphs is suitable for either a heterosexual or a homosexual couple; however, for purposes of descriptive simplicity, we will assume a male–female pair.

Therapy usually begins with a few days of sensate focus, during which time the man should not attempt to have an ejaculation, either intravaginally or by some other form of stimulation. If his partner desires orgasm, this may be accomplished in whatever fashion is comfortable to both, excluding coitus. It is desirable for a man to maintain this consideration for his partner's needs throughout the program.

When they have become comfortable with the nondemand pleasuring of sensate focus, the couple may move on to the next phase of treatment. Now the man should experience ejaculation by whatever method is most likely to succeed. Ideally, this involves his partner so that he may begin to associate his orgasmic pleasure with her. Frequently, the man begins by masturbating himself to orgasm after first being stimulated to a highly aroused state by his partner. The essential idea is for him to begin connecting his partner's presence and activity with his own pleasure.

Once both partners feel comfortable with the man's self-stimulation in the woman's presence, the couple may move on to the next phase, where she attempts to bring him to orgasm with manual or oral stimulation. Communication is especially important at this time. The man can greatly heighten his pleasure and arousal by demonstrating or verbalizing what feels best to him. It may take several days or longer before his partner's stimulation produces an ejaculation; there is no need to rush or feel panicked if it does not happen immediately. Most therapists agree that once he can reach orgasm by her touch, an important step has been accomplished.

When the man is ejaculating consistently in response to partner stimulation, the couple may move on to the final phase of treatment, in which ejaculation takes place during vaginal penetration. The female partner sits astride the man, who is lying on his back, and stimulates him to the point where he signals that he is about to reach orgasm. She then inserts his penis and begins active pelvic thrusting. If he starts to ejaculate before

On the Edge

The Sexual Enhancement Potential of the Internet

Many students in our college human sexuality courses say, "I sure wish this class had been offered in my high school. I really could have used it then." We take this to mean that there remains a lack of useful, accurate, and comprehensive sexual health information, particularly for adolescents. The numbers of teens who have had formal sexual health education are tiny in comparison to the prevalence of sexual representations in the commercial media.

The Internet could provide a bridge between sexuality educators and therapists and teens. It provides professionals an unprecedented opportunity to speak directly to millions of people about sexuality in the privacy of their own homes. However, the difficulty for users lies in sorting out useful information from erroneous and "entertaining" materials. The Internet has more than its share of misinformation, along with exploitive and sexist sexual content. Using the keyword "sex" will turn up an overwhelming number of explicit pictures, movies, and chat rooms rather than educational information. In evaluating its usefulness, Net users need to consider who is providing the information.

The advantages of the Net as a resource for teens are great: Many are already comfortable and knowledgeable and skillful at using the Net. (Quite a few parents enlist their children's help in finding their way around cyberspace.) Information on the Net can be multidimensional—text, graphics, sound, video—and quickly updated. As authors who want you insertion is completed, this should not be a cause for concern. If he does not ejaculate shortly after penetration, she should withdraw and resume manual stimulation until he is again about to ejaculate, at which point she reinserts his penis. Once the man experiences a few intravaginal ejaculations, the mental block that is usually associated with ejaculatory disorder often disappears.

Treating Hypoactive Sexual Desire

Many therapists consider sexual desire problems the most complicated sexual difficulty to treat, requiring multifaceted interventions to help couples resolve their problems (Trudel et al., 1995). Many aspects of the treatment for hypoactive sexual desire (HSD) are similar to specific suggestions for resolving other sexual problems (Bass, 1996). These include (LoPiccolo & Friedman, 1988):

- Encouraging erotic responses through self-stimulation and arousing fantasies
- Reducing anxiety with appropriate information and sensate focus exercises
- Enhancing sexual experiences through improved communication and increased skills, both in initiating desired and in refusing undesired sexual activity
- Expanding the repertoire of affectionate and sexual activities

Therapeutic support to set aside more time for enjoyable couple activities and to prioritize a busy lifestyle (in order not to leave sex until last, when everyone is tired) can also be helpful.

HSD is likely to require more intensive therapy than problems such as rapid ejaculation, anorgasmia, or vaginismus, and the therapy is less likely to be effective (Assalian, 1996). The goal is to modify the person's pattern of inhibiting his or her erotic impulses. To achieve this, the therapist helps the client understand the underlying motivation to suppress sexual feelings and the reasons for refusing sexual intimacy. Most therapists combine suggestions for specific activities with insight therapy that may help the person understand and resolve unconscious conflicts about sexual pleasure and intimacy (see the discussion later in this chapter, "The PLISSIT Model of Sex Therapy").

HSD is often a symptom of unresolved relationship problems. In these situations, therapy focuses on the interactions between the couple that contribute to the lack of

On the Edge

to find the information about sexuality that you need, we describe a few of the better sites you might investigate.

Coalition for Positive Sexuality: Sex Ed for Teens, at *www.positive.org/cps/*, is an example of a site created by a volunteer sex-education organization to encourage positive attitudes about safe, consensual sexual activities. Using both clinical and street terminology, the basic informational text features comic-book-style drawings. A "Frequently Asked Questions" list has answers to common concerns such as "Is it OK to masturbate? How much is too much?" The site also has interactive capability on its "Let's Talk" page where teens can ask specific questions to which other teens respond.

Other sites offer teens the opportunity to email questions to sexuality educators. The educator selects several questions each week to answer publicly. Two examples are Australia's "Sexuality Bytes/The Sex Files" at *www.sexualitybytes.com.au/* and Columbia University Health Service's "Go Ask Alice!" at *www.columbia.edu/cu/healthwise/catl.html.* Dr. Ruth's Sexnet (*www.drruth.com*) also provides information. The need for independent problem solving and decision making—to think and act in the present based on future consequences—is far more difficult to provide than basic information. Creative skill-building activities, simulated role-plays, and real-time dialogues with sexual health educators may offer value beyond information (Roffman et al., 1997).

Because of the Internet's accessibility and anonymity, it is on its way to becoming a major source of information and attitudes about sexuality for young people. We hope that constructive educational options will continue to develop and that users will benefit from them.

sexual desire. A skilled therapist helps the couple resolve such issues as a power imbalance (where one person has most of the power and control in the relationship), fears about vulnerability and closeness, or poor sexual skills (LoPiccolo & Friedman, 1988). The therapist may also help each individual, as well as the couple together, develop a better balance between independence and interdependence (Lobitz & Lobitz, 1996).

Seeking Professional Assistance

After exploring the information and suggestions in this text and other readings, or on the Internet, as discussed in the "Sexual Enhancement Potential of the Internet" box, you may continue to experience considerable sexual dissatisfaction. Perhaps you find it difficult to progress beyond a particular stage in an exercise program. Although some people with sexual problems improve over time without therapy (De Amicis et al., 1984), you may decide to seek professional help. A skilled therapist can offer useful information, emotional support, a perspective other than your own, and specific problem-solving techniques, all of which may help you make the desired changes in your sex life. What are the basic assumptions behind sex therapy, and how do you go about seeking professional assistance? We explore these questions in the last section of this chapter.

The PLISSIT Model of Sex Therapy

There are many approaches to sex therapy, and most have several elements in common. One representative model, the PLISSIT model (Annon, 1974), specifies four levels of therapy; each provides treatment at an increasingly deeper level. PLISSIT is an acronym for these four levels: *permission, limited information, specific suggestions,* and *intensive therapy*.

At the first level, the therapist reassures clients that thoughts, feelings, fantasies, desires, and behaviors that enhance their satisfaction and do not have potentially negative consequences are normal. Giving individuals and couples permission to appreciate their unique patterns and desires, without comparing themselves to others, is sometimes all the help they need. At the same time, people are given permission *not* to engage in certain behaviors unless they choose to do so.

At the second level, limited information, therapists provide clients with information specific to their sexual concerns. Factual information about concerns with penis size, clitoral sensitivity, or the effects of aging or medications on sexual response can alleviate anxiety and problems related to lack of knowledge. Third, specific suggestions are the activities and "homework" exercises—for instance, masturbation techniques, sensate focus, or the stop–start technique—that therapists recommend to clients to help them reach a goal. Most of these behavioral approaches are designed to reduce anxiety, enhance communication, and teach new, arousal-enhancing behaviors (McCarthy, 1995).

In some cases, personal emotional difficulties or relationship problems may interfere with sexual expression such that the first three therapy levels are not adequate to resolve the difficulties. In these cases, intensive therapy may be required. In *insight-oriented therapy* or **psychosexual therapy,** the therapist provides interpretation and reflection to help clients gain awareness and understanding of unconscious feelings and thoughts that contribute to sexual difficulties (Kaplan, 1974). Insights gained in psychosexual therapy often pertain to patterns developed in childhood. Because intimate adult relationships can be greatly affected by the first significant relationships with parents, awareness and insights into these early patterns are sometimes necessary to resolve sexual difficulties.

Psychosexual therapy Treatment designed to help clients gain awareness of their unconscious thoughts and feelings that contribute to their sexual problems.

Systems therapy Treatment that focuses on interactions within a couple relationship and on the functions of the sexual problems in the relationship.

Systems therapy can be another element of intensive therapy (LoPiccolo, 1992). In contrast to psychosexual therapy, systems theory is based on the concept that the identified problems are serving important current functions in the relationship. For instance, one woman with hypoactive sexual desire was in a relationship that was so close that she was unconsciously responding to a need to keep some distance (Fish et al., 1984). *Post-*

modern sex therapy is the integration of systems, psychosexual, and behavioral approaches.

Some therapists are including a new and intriguing therapy method in their treatment of sexual disorders, sexual compulsions, and sexual abuse flashbacks that occur during sexual activity. The specific technique consists of the client thinking about the problem while moving his or her eyes back and forth, following the movements of the therapist's fingers. **EMDR, eye movement desensitization and reprocessing,** appears to stimulate rapid and helpful informational and emotional processing in the brain, similar to that which occurs during REM sleep. (During REM sleep, our eyes naturally move back and forth.) EMDR has been shown to be effective in alleviating persistent symptoms stemming from past trauma (Shapiro, 1995), and therapists are expanding its use to other problems, including sexual difficulties (Zangwill, 1996).

EMDR therapy
A therapy technique that combines eye movements with concentrating on the problem that may be helpful as a part of treatment for sexual difficulties.

What Happens in Therapy?

Many people are apprehensive about going to see a sex therapist, and it can be helpful to have some idea about what to expect. Sex therapists must adhere to strict codes of ethics (see the boxed discussion, "Sex Between Therapist and Client"). Each therapist works differently, but most follow certain steps. At the first interview, the therapist will help the person or couple to clarify the problems and their feelings about it and to identify their goals for the therapy. The therapist will usually ask questions about when the difficulty first began, how it has developed over time, what the person thinks has caused it, and how she or he has already tried to resolve the problem. The therapist will likely gather some information about medical history and current physical functioning and then make referrals, if necessary, for further physical screenings. Increasingly sophisticated and refined techniques for diagnosing vascular, neurological, and endocrine causes of sexual problems have been and continue to be developed.

Over the next few sessions, the therapist may gather more extensive sexual, personal, and relationship histories. During these sessions, the therapist will screen for major psychological problems that could interfere with therapy, explore whether the clients have a lifestyle conducive to a good emotional and sexual relationship, and determine whether they have problems with substance abuse or domestic violence (LoPiccolo, 1985).

Ethical/Legal Issues

Sex Between Therapist and Client

It is highly unethical for professional therapists to engage in sexual relationships with clients whom they have in treatment. Psychiatry, psychology, social work, and counseling professional associations have codes of ethics against sexual relations between psychotherapists and their clients. The American Association for Marriage and Family Therapy prohibits sexual contact for two years after therapy has ended, and many professionals believe that sex with a former client is unethical at any time. In addition, some states have criminalized sexual behavior with patients (Laury, 1992). However, research finds the rate of psychotherapists who *admit* to sexual contact with clients is as high as 30 percent (Sloan et al., 1998).

If a sexual relationship develops in the context of therapy, attention would likely be diverted from the client's original concerns, and the preexisting problems would not be resolved. In addition, the sexual involvement can have other negative effects on the client (Plaut, 1996). Research has indicated that women who experienced sexual contact with their therapists (including psychotherapists in general, not just sex therapists) felt greater mistrust of and anger toward men and therapists than did a control group of women. They also experienced more psychological and psychosomatic symptoms, including anger, shame, anxiety, and depression (Regehr & Glancy, 1995). If at any time your therapist makes verbal or physical sexual advances toward you, you have every right to leave immediately and terminate therapy. It would be helpful to others who may be victims of this abuse of professional power if you reported this incident to the state licensing board for the therapist's profession (Schoener, 1995).

Once the therapist and the individual or couple more fully realize the nature of the difficulty and have defined the therapy goals, the therapist helps the client(s) understand and overcome obstacles to meeting the goals as the sessions continue. Most therapy occurs in one-hour weekly sessions. The therapist often gives assignments such as masturbation or sensate focus exercises for the client(s) to do between therapy sessions. Successes and difficulties with the assignments are discussed at subsequent meetings. Therapy is terminated when the clients reach their goals. It is often helpful for client(s) to leave with a plan for continuing and maintaining progress. The therapist and client(s) may also plan one or more follow-up sessions.

Selecting a Therapist

Depending on your situation, you may wish to see a therapist alone or with your partner. Many women who want to learn to experience orgasm may not have an available partner or may decide they prefer to attain orgasm initially by self-stimulation; the same may be true for men with ejaculation or erection problems. Others may not have a partner, or their partner may not be willing to be involved in treatment. Individual therapy can be effective, but most therapists believe that a couple's sexual functioning, including difficulties one or the other may experience, is based on their interaction. Therefore, most counseling is done with both partners. Masters and Johnson have also promoted the use of female and male co-therapists to work with heterosexual couples, but research has not indicated that co-therapy is more effective than an individual therapist (Arentewicz & Schmidt, 1983).

To select a therapist, you might ask your sexuality course instructor or health care practitioner for referrals. Also, the American Association of Sex Educators, Counselors and Therapists (AASECT) can give you the names of therapists in your area who have qualified for AASECT certification (435 N. Michigan Ave., Suite 1717, Chicago, IL 60611-4067; [312] 644-0828). You may have a preference for a male or female therapist, or one with a particular therapeutic approach. Gays and lesbians should select a therapist who is knowledgeable about the dynamics of living in a society that is hostile to homosexuals. At times, the therapist must be more positive about homosexuality than the client who is struggling with internalized negative stereotypes.

After consulting some of these sources, you should have several potential therapists from which to choose. There are many factors to consider in making your selection. A basic criterion is training; professionals from a variety of backgrounds do sex therapy. The title "sex therapist" does not assure competence: There are few regulations on the use of that title. At this time, there are few advanced degree programs in sex therapy. Rather, a professional who has specialized in this area should have a minimum of a master's degree and credentials as a psychiatrist, psychologist, social worker, or counselor. To do sex therapy, he or she should also have participated in sex therapy training, supervision, and workshops. It is highly appropriate for you to inquire about the specific training and certification of a prospective therapist.

To help determine if a specific therapist will meet your needs, you may wish to cover the following topics at your first meeting:

1. What do you want from therapy? You and your therapist should reach an agreement on your and the therapist's goals. This agreement is sometimes referred to as the *therapy contract.*
2. What is the therapist's approach? You can ask about the general process in the therapy sessions (what the therapist will do) and what kind of participation is expected of you.
3. How do you feel about talking with the therapist? Therapy is not intended to be a light social interaction. It can be difficult. At times it may be quite uncomfortable for a client to discuss personal sexual concerns. However, for therapy to be useful, you will want to have the sense that the therapist is open and willing to understand you.
4. What is the therapist's fee for services, and how many sessions does she or he estimate will be needed? Fees vary considerably. Psychiatrists (who are medical doctors) are usu-

ally at the upper end, psychologists (who have Ph.D.s) are in the middle, and social workers and counselors (who have master's degrees) are usually at the lower end. A higher fee does not necessarily indicate better sex therapy skills. Some practitioners offer sliding fee schedules based on the client's income.

After the initial interview, you can decide to continue with this therapist or ask for a referral to another therapist more appropriate to your personality or needs. If you become dissatisfied once you begin therapy, discuss your concerns with your therapist. Decide jointly, if possible, whether to continue therapy or to seek another therapist. It is usually best to continue for several sessions before making a decision to change. Occasionally clients expect magic cures rather than the difficult but rewarding work that therapy often demands.

Sex therapy can be a useful tool for individuals and couples who want to resolve their sexual difficulties. The process of sex therapy may also have additional benefits. Clients often experience reduced anxiety as well as improved communication, marital adjustment, and satisfaction following sex therapy (Zilbergeld & Kilmann, 1984). Couples may be more assertive and emotionally expressive with each other (Tullman et al., 1981). Individuals and couples who have met their goals may experience increased self-confidence and emotional satisfaction (Clement & Pfäfflin, 1980). The combined efforts of the therapist and client(s) can replace doubt and anxiety with the joy of satisfying sexual intimacy.

Summary

BASICS OF SEXUAL ENHANCEMENT AND SEX THERAPY

Self-awareness is a good beginning for therapy. Exploring one's own body increases one's knowledge and comfort and may prepare one for exploring a partner's body.

Masturbation exercises are an effective way for an individual to learn about and experience sexual response. They can be enjoyed for themselves, and the acquired knowledge can be shared with a partner.

Good communication between partners is an important element of therapy. It can help work out specific problems and foster stronger relationships.

The experience of sensate focus, nondemand pleasuring shared by sexual partners, is an excellent vehicle for mutually enhancing sexual potentials.

Masturbating in each other's presence may be an excellent way for a couple to indicate to each other what kind of touching they find arousing.

SPECIFIC SUGGESTIONS FOR WOMEN

Therapy programs for anorgasmic women are based on progressive self-awareness activities.

Women who wish to become orgasmic during lovemaking with a partner may benefit from programs that commence with sensate focus, mutual genital exploration, masturbation, and nondemand genital pleasuring by the partner.

A couple may increase the probability of female orgasm during intercourse by incorporating knowledge acquired during sensate focus and nondemand pleasuring and by combining intercourse with manual stimulation of the woman's clitoris (by herself or her partner).

Treatment for vaginismus generally involves promoting increased self-awareness and relaxation. Insertion of a lubricated finger (first one's own and later the partner's) into the vagina is an important next step in overcoming this condition. Penile insertion is the final phase of treatment for vaginismus.

SPECIFIC SUGGESTIONS FOR MEN

A variety of approaches may help a man learn to delay his ejaculation. Potentially helpful suggestions include ejaculating more frequently, having a second orgasm, using a more relaxed intercourse position, and openly communicating a need to modulate movements and/or engage in noncoital activities to reduce stimulation.

If a couple has the time and inclination to work together in resolving premature ejaculation difficulties, the stop–start or squeeze technique is often effective.

A behavioral approach designed to reduce anxiety has proven quite successful in treating psychologically based erectile disorder. This treatment method has several phases: sensate focus, followed by genital stimulation, then penetration.

Vascular surgery, vasoactive injections, external vacuum constriction devices, and surgically implanted penile prostheses are options for men who have a permanent, physiologically caused inability to experience erections.

Pills to treat erectile disorder are the newest option to stimulate blood flow to the penis.

A behavioral approach for the treatment of male orgasmic disorder combines sensate focus with self- and partner manual stimulation, ultimately leading to intravaginal ejaculation.

TREATING HYPOACTIVE SEXUAL DESIRE

Problems with HSD often require more intensive therapy to help people understand and change their suppression and avoidance of sexual feelings.

SEEKING PROFESSIONAL ASSISTANCE

The PLISSIT model outlines four progressive levels of sex therapy: permission, limited information, specific suggestions, and intensive therapy.

Intensive therapy often combines specific behavioral techniques with insight-oriented psychosocial therapy or with a systems theory approach that focuses on the function of the problem within the relationship. The use of EMDR is also being explored.

Professional counseling is often helpful and sometimes necessary in overcoming sexual difficulties.

A skilled therapist can offer useful information, emotional support, a more objective perspective, problem-solving strategies, and specific sex therapy techniques.

A lack of regulations governing sex therapy suggests that one should be careful in selecting a therapist. Referrals may be given by sex educators, health care practitioners, or AASECT.

Thought Provokers

1. Why might someone be reluctant to seek professional assistance for a sexual difficulty?
2. How do you think the sensate focus experience challenges gender-role stereotyped behavior of men and women?
3. If you were a man and were not able to experience erection due to irreversible physical causes, would you get a penile prosthesis? Why or why not? Would you want your partner to get one?

Suggested Readings

Douglas, Marcia, and Douglass, Lisa (1997). *Are We Having Fun Yet?* New York: Hyperion. This book promotes women to be involved in sex on their own terms.

George, Stephen; and Caine, Winston (1998). *A Lifetime of Sex.* Emmaus, PA: Rodale Press. Frank and fresh information on sex for every stage of a man's life.

Heiman, Julia; and LoPiccolo, Joseph (1988). *Becoming Orgasmic: A Sexual and Personal Growth Program for Women.* Englewood Cliffs, NJ: Prentice Hall. An excellent guide for women who want to learn to experience orgasm and enhance their sexual pleasure by themselves or with a partner.

Renshaw, Domeena (1995). *Seven Weeks to Better Sex.* New York: Random House. This book provides questionnaires and experiences to enhance communication and sexual expression.

Schnarch, David (1997). *Passionate Marriage.* New York: W. W. Norton & Co. Illustrates the connection between personal development and enhancing sexual potential.

Yaffe, Maurice; and Fenwick, Elizabeth (1992). *Sexual Happiness for Men: A Practical Approach.* New York: Henry Holt.

Yaffe, Maurice; and Fenwick, Elizabeth (1992). *Sexual Happiness for Women: A Practical Approach.* New York: Henry Holt. Developed for readers who want to enhance their sexuality or resolve specific difficulties, these books offer step-by-step guidelines.

Resource

Impotence Anonymous is a self-help group for men and their partners. For more information about the over 100 chapters in the United States, send a stamped, self-addressed envelope to 119 S. Ruth Street, Maryville, TN 37801.

Web Resources

Go Ask Alice!
www.goaskalice.columbia.edu/Cat6.html
A refreshingly frank and lively Web site, sponsored by Columbia University, where questions posed about common and uncommon sexual concerns are answered with sensitivity and wit.

Dr. Ruth
www.drruth.com
Sexual problems are discussed frankly on this Web site sponsored by one of the most widely known sex therapists, Dr. Ruth Westheimer. Sex tips, online polls, and posted answers to visitors' questions are among the highlights of this site.

Viagra Information
www.fda.gov/cder/news/viagra.htm
On this site, the U. S. Food and Drug Administration provides information on Viagra for both the consumer and the medical professional. The in-depth research and reviews that were performed prior to the FDA approving Viagra are detailed here as well.

17

Sexually Transmitted Diseases

The possibility of getting a sexually transmitted disease has caused me to be extremely cautious and selective about who I choose to be sexual with. It also makes every decision in a sexual relationship so critical and has made me much more careful in the choices I make. (Authors' files)

Sexually transmitted diseases (STDs) Diseases that are transmitted by sexual contact.

In this chapter we discuss a variety of **sexually transmitted diseases (STDs)**—that is, diseases that can be transmitted through sexual interaction. Our purpose in including a chapter on STDs is not to discourage you from exploring the joys of sexuality. Rather, we wish to facilitate your process of making good decisions by presenting a realistic picture of what sexually transmitted diseases are, how to recognize them, what should be done to treat them, and what measures can be taken to avoid contracting or transmitting them. We believe that this information is especially relevant to our college-age readers in that (1) 86% of all STDs in the United States occur among 15- to 29-year-olds, (2) about one in five people has been treated for an STD by age 21, (3) approximately 50% of the U.S. population will acquire one or more STDs by ages 30 to 35 and (4) STDs are occurring at epidemic rates among young adults in the United States (Carson, 1997; Gilbert & Alexander, 1998; Sharts-Hopco, 1997). Consider the following startling statistics that apply to America's youth:

1. In the United States, it is estimated that three million adolescents—one of every six—are infected with an STD every year (Sieving et al., 1997).
2. Adolescents have the highest rate of STDs of any sexually active age group (Shafer, 1997), and it is estimated that one in four sexually active teenagers will be infected with an STD before graduation from high school (Miller et al., 1998).
3. The incidence of chlamydia, a potentially very damaging STD, is extremely high among 15- to 19-year-olds (Gunn et al., 1997; Shafer, 1997).
4. Female adolescents aged 15 to 19 have the highest rates of gonorrhea of any age group in the United States (Sieving et al., 1997).
5. The largest proportion of AIDS cases in the United States are people in their 20s and 30s who were infected with the AIDS virus (HIV) in their teens or 20s (Hu et al., 1994; Sieving et al., 1997). (The incubation time between HIV infection and the onset of severe symptoms of AIDS typically ranges from 8 to 11 years or more.)

You may wonder why our discussion of AIDS is postponed until the latter portion of this chapter. Certainly AIDS has received far more attention in the media in recent years than any of the other diseases discussed in this chapter. This emphasis on AIDS, while understandable in view of the continuing worldwide epidemic of this deadly disease, tends to obscure the fact that many other STDs are substantially more prevalent. Furthermore, many of these commonly occurring STDs, such as chlamydia and genital warts, pose major health risks that are escalating in proportion to the increasing incidence of many STDs.

What do you think are some of the factors that contribute to the rise in the incidence of STDs?

It is not entirely clear why the incidence of STDs is so high. Undoubtedly, a number of factors contribute to what many writers and health authorities have labeled an epidemic. Increasing sexual activity among young people has commonly been advanced as one prime reason for the accelerating rate of STDs. Related to this is an increasing tendency to have multiple sexual partners, particularly during adolescence and early adulthood, when the incidence of STDs is the highest. It is also believed that increased use of birth control pills has contributed by reducing the use of vaginal spermicides and the condom, contraceptive methods known to offer some protection against STDs.

The spread of STDs is facilitated by the unfortunate fact that many of these diseases do not produce obvious symptoms. In some cases, particularly among women, there may be no outward signs at all. Under these circumstances, people may unknowingly infect others. In addition, feelings of guilt and embarrassment that often accompany having an STD may prevent people from seeking adequate treatment or informing their sexual partners. The boxed discussion "Telling a Partner" explores why this action is important and suggests ways to more easily share such information.

The following sections focus on the most common STDs. There is also an expanded discussion of AIDS and the progress being made in treating this dreadful disease. Table 17.1 summarizes the STDs discussed in this chapter. If you want more information, we recommend contacting your county health service or STD clinic or calling the National STD Hotline.* These services will answer questions, send free literature, and most important, give you the name and phone number of a local physician or public clinic that will treat STDs free or at minimal cost.

Let's Talk About It

Telling a Partner

Most of us would find it difficult to discuss with our lover(s) the possibility that we have transmitted a disease to her or him during sexual activity. Due to the stigma often associated with STDs, it can be bad enough admitting to having one of these diseases ourselves. The need to tell others that they may have "caught" something from you may seem a formidable task. You might fear that such a revelation will jeopardize a valued relationship or worry that you will be considered "dirty." In relationships presumed to be monogamous, a person might fear that telling his or her partner about an STD will threaten mutual trust. At the same time, however, concealing a sex-related illness places a good deal more at risk in the long run.

Most important, not disclosing the existence of an STD risks the health of a partner. Many people may not have symptoms and thus may not become aware that they have contracted a disease until they discover it for themselves, perhaps only after they have developed serious complications. Furthermore, if a lover remains untreated, she or he may reinfect you even after you have been cured. Unlike some diseases (such as measles and chicken pox), STDs do not provide immunity against future infections. You can get one, give it to your lover, be cured, and then get it back again if he or she remains untreated.

The following suggestions provide some guidelines for telling a partner about your STD. Remember, these are only suggestions that have worked for some people; they may need to be modified to fit your particular circumstances. This is a sensitive issue that requires thoughtful consideration and planning.

1. Be honest. There is nothing to be gained by downplaying the potential risks associated with STDs. If you tell a partner, "I have this little drip, but it probably means nothing," you may regret it. Stick with the facts and be sure your partner understands the importance of obtaining a medical evaluation.
2. Even if you suspect that your partner may have been the source of your infection, there is little to be gained by blaming him or her. Instead, you may wish simply to acknowledge that you have the disease and are concerned that your partner gets proper medical attention.
3. Your attitude may have considerable impact on how your partner receives the news. If you display high levels of anxiety, guilt, fear, or disgust, your partner may reflect these feelings in her or his response. Try to present the facts in as clear and calm a fashion as you can manage.
4. Be sensitive to your partner's feelings. Be prepared for reactions of anger or resentment. These are understandable initial responses. Being supportive and demonstrating a willingness to listen without becoming defensive may be the best tactics for diffusing negative responses.
5. Engaging in sexual intimacies after you become aware of your condition and before you obtain medical assurances that you are no longer contagious is clearly inappropriate.
6. Medical examinations and treatments for STDs, when necessary, can be a financial burden. Offering to pay for some or all of these expenses may help to maintain (or reestablish) goodwill in your relationship.
7. In the case of herpes, where recurrences are unpredictable and the possibility of infecting a new partner is an ongoing concern, it is a good idea to discuss your herpes before sexual intimacies take place. You may wish to preface your first sexual interaction by saying, "There is something we should talk over first."

*The National Sexually Transmitted Disease Hotline can be dialed toll free from 8:00 A.M. to 8:00 P.M. weekdays and from 10:00 A.M. to 6:00 P.M. weekends, Pacific time. The number is (800) 227-8922 (in California, [800] 982-5883).

Table 17.1 Common Sexually Transmitted Diseases (STDs): Mode of Transmission, Symptoms, and Treatment

STD	*Transmission*	*Symptoms*	*Treatment*
Chlamydia infection	The *Chlamydia trachomatis* bacterium is transmitted primarily through sexual contact. It may also be spread by fingers from one body site to another.	In women, PID (pelvic inflammatory disease) caused by *Chlamydia* may include disrupted menstrual periods, pelvic pain, elevated temperature, nausea, vomiting, headache, infertility, and ectopic pregnancy. In men, chlamydia infection of the urethra may cause a discharge and burning during urination. *Chlamydia*-caused epididymitis may produce a sense of heaviness in the affected testicle(s), inflammation of the scrotal skin, and painful swelling at the bottom of the testicle.	Doxycycline, azithromycin, or ofloxacin
Gonorrhea ("clap")	The *Neisseria gonorrhoeae* bacterium ("gonococcus") is spread through genital, oral–genital, or genital–anal contact.	The most common symptoms in men are a cloudy discharge from the penis and burning sensations during urination. If disease is untreated, complications may include inflammation of scrotal skin and swelling at base of the testicle. In women, some green or yellowish discharge is produced but commonly remains undetected. Later, PID (pelvic inflammatory disease) may develop.	Dual therapy of a single dose of ceftriaxone, cefixime, ciprofloxacin, or ofloxacin plus doxycycline for seven days
Nongonococcal urethritis (NGU)	Primary causes are believed to be the bacteria *Chlamydia trachomatis* and *Ureaplasma urealyticum,* most commonly transmitted through coitus. Some NGU may result from allergic reactions or from *Trichomonas* infection.	Inflammation of the urethral tube. A man has a discharge from the penis and irritation during urination. A woman may have a mild discharge of pus from the vagina but often shows no symptoms.	A single dose of azithromycin or doxycycline for seven days
Syphilis	The *Treponema pallidum* bacterium is transmitted from open lesions during genital, oral–genital, or genital–anal contact.	*Primary stage:* A painless chancre appears at the site where the bacterium entered the body. *Secondary stage:* The chancre disappears and a generalized skin rash develops. *Latent stage:* There may be no visible symptoms. *Tertiary stage:* Heart failure, blindness, mental disturbance, and many other symptoms may occur. Death may result.	Benzathine penicillin G, doxycycline, tetracycline, or erythromycin
Chancroid	The *Haemophilus ducreyi* bacterium is usually transmitted by sexual interaction.	Small bumps (papules) in genital regions eventually rupture and form painful, soft, craterlike ulcers that emit a foul-smelling discharge.	Single doses of either ceftriaxone or azithromycin or seven days of erythromycin

Table 17.1 continued

STD	*Transmission*	*Symptoms*	*Treatment*
Herpes	The genital herpes virus (HSV-2) seems to be transmitted primarily by vaginal, anal, or oral-genital intercourse. The oral herpes virus (HSV-1) is transmitted primarily by kissing.	Small, painful red bumps (papules) appear in the genital region (genital herpes) or mouth (oral herpes). The papules become painful blisters that eventually rupture to form wet, open sores.	No known cure; a variety of treatments may reduce symptoms; oral or intravenous acyclovir (Zovirax) promotes healing and suppresses recurrent outbreaks.
Genital warts (condylomata acuminata)	The virus is spread primarily through vaginal, anal, or oral–genital sexual interaction.	Hard and yellow-gray on dry skin areas; soft, pinkish-red, and cauliflowerlike on moist areas.	Freezing, application of topical agents such as trichloroacetic acid or podofilox, cauterization, surgical removal, or vaporization by carbon dioxide laser
Viral hepatitis	The hepatitis B virus may be transmitted by blood, semen, vaginal secretions, and saliva. Manual, oral, or penile stimulation of the anus are strongly associated with the spread of this virus. Hepatitis A seems to be primarily spread via the fecal-oral route. Oral-anal sexual contact is a common mode for sexual transmission of hepatitis A.	Vary from nonexistent to mild, flulike symptoms to an incapacitating illness characterized by high fever, vomiting, and severe abdominal pain.	No specific therapy; treatment generally consists of bed rest and adequate fluid intake.
Bacterial vaginosis	The most common causative agent, the *Gardnerella vaginalis* bacterium, is sometimes transmitted through coitus.	In women, a fishy- or musty-smelling, thin discharge, like flour paste in consistency and usually gray. Most men are asymptomatic.	Metronidazole (Flagyl) by mouth or intravaginal applications of topical metronidazole gel or clindamycin cream
Candidiasis (yeast infection)	The *Candida albicans* fungus may accelerate growth when the chemical balance of the vagina is disturbed; it may also be transmitted through sexual interaction.	White, "cheesy" discharge; irritation of vaginal and vulval tissues.	Vaginal suppositories or topical cream, such as clotrimazole and miconazole, or oral fluconazole
Trichomoniasis	The protozoan parasite *Trichomonas vaginalis* is usually passed through genital sexual contact.	White or yellow vaginal discharge with an unpleasant odor; vulva is sore and irritated.	Metronidazole (Flagyl) for both women and men
Pubic lice ("crabs")	*Phthirus pubis*, the pubic louse, is spread easily through body contact or through shared clothing or bedding.	Persistent itching. Lice are visible and may often be located in pubic hair or other body hair.	1% permethrin cream for body areas and 1% Lindane shampoo for hair
Scabies	*Sarcoptes scabiei* is highly contagious and may be transmitted by close physical contact, sexual and nonsexual.	Small bumps and a red rash that itch intensely, especially at night.	5% permethrin lotion or cream
Acquired immunodeficiency syndrome (AIDS)	Blood and semen are the major vehicles for transmitting HIV, which attacks the immune system. It appears to be passed primarily through sexual contact, or needle sharing among injection drug users.	Vary with the type of cancer or opportunistic infections that afflict an infected person. Common symptoms include fevers, night sweats, weight loss, chronic fatigue, swollen lymph nodes, diarrhea and/or bloody stools, atypical bruising or bleeding, skin rashes, headache, chronic cough, and a whitish coating on the tongue or throat.	Commence treatment after seroconversion with a combination of three antiviral drugs ("triple drug therapy") plus other specific treatments, if necessary, of opportunistic infections and tumors.

Bacterial Infections

A variety of STDs are caused by bacterial agents. We begin this section with a discussion of chlamydia, one of the most prevalent and damaging of all STDs. Other bacterial infections to be described include gonorrhea, nongonococcal urethritis, syphilis, and chancroid. Bacterial vaginosis, a very common vaginal infection, will be discussed in a later section of this chapter.

Chlamydia Infection

Chlamydia infection
Urogenital infection caused by the bacterium *Chlamydia trachomatis.*

Chlamydia (clah-MID-e-a) **infection** is caused by *Chlamydia trachomatis,* a bacterial microorganism. Although classified as a bacterium, *Chlamydia trachomatis* is like a virus in that it grows within body cells. This organism is now recognized as the cause of a diverse group of genital infections. *Chlamydia trachomatis* also is involved in a number of infections of newborns and is a common cause of preventable blindness.

Incidence and Transmission

It is now widely recognized that chlamydia infections are among the most prevalent and most damaging of all STDs. Chlamydia infection is the most common bacterial STD in the United States and the most prevalent infectious disease reported to state health departments throughout the United States (Adair et al., 1998; Centers for Disease Control, 1997c; Howell et al., 1997). Furthermore, during the period of 1987–1995 the annual reported rate of chlamydia infections increased 281% (Centers for Disease Control, 1997c). An estimated four to five million American men, women, and infants develop a chlamydia infection each year (Howell et al., 1997; Moran, 1997a; Todd et al., 1997). Sexually active teenagers have higher infection rates than any other age group (Gunn et al., 1997; Shafer, 1997). Young women who use oral contraceptives seem to be at particularly high risk for developing chlamydia infection if they are exposed (Ivey, 1997).

Chlamydia disease is transmitted primarily through sexual contact. It may also be spread by fingers from one body site to another, such as from the genitals to the eyes.

Symptoms and Complications

There are two general types of genital chlamydia infections in females. The first of these, infection of the mucosa of the lower reproductive tract, commonly takes the form of *urethritis* (inflammation of the urethral tube) or *cervicitis* (infection of the cervix). In both cases, women may experience few or no symptoms. When symptoms do occur, they may include a mild irritation or itching of the genital tissues, burning during urination, and a slight vaginal discharge.

Pelvic inflammatory disease (PID)
An infection in the uterus and pelvic cavity.

The second type of genital chlamydia infection in women is invasive infection of the upper reproductive tract, expressed as **pelvic inflammatory disease (PID)** (Salzer, 1997; Shafer, 1997). PID typically occurs when *Chlamydia trachomatis,* gonococcus (the bacteria that causes gonorrhea), or other infectious organisms spread from the cervix upward, infecting the lining of the uterus *(endometritis),* the fallopian tubes *(salpingitis),* and possibly the ovaries and other adjacent abdominal structures. *Chlamydia trachomatis* may account for as many as half of the more than one million recognized cases of PID that occur annually in the United States (Howell et al., 1997; McCormack, 1994). Furthermore, chlamydia infection is probably the most common cause of PID in teenagers (Shafer, 1997). Experts estimate that approximately 70% of the women diagnosed with PID annually in the United States are younger than age 25 (Ivey, 1997).

PID resulting from invasion of the upper reproductive tract by *Chlamydia trachomatis* often produces a variety of symptoms, which may include disrupted menstrual periods, chronic pelvic pain, fever, nausea, vomiting, and headache. Chlamydia salpingitis is the primary preventable cause of female infertility and ectopic pregnancy (Hillis,

1994; Ivey, 1997). Even after PID has been effectively treated, residual scar tissue in the fallopian tubes leaves some women sterile (Hillis et al., 1997).

Are there any limitations on the kind of birth control that is appropriate for a woman who has had PID?

A woman who has had PID should be cautioned about the use of the IUD as a method of birth control. An IUD does not prevent fertilization (see Chapter 11 for an explanation of how the IUD prevents pregnancy); thus, a tiny sperm cell may negotiate a partially blocked area of a scarred fallopian tube and fertilize an ovum that, because of its larger size, subsequently becomes lodged in the scarred tube. The result is an ectopic pregnancy, a serious hazard to the woman. The CDC (Centers for Disease Control and Prevention) recently announced that the incidence of ectopic pregnancies in the United States has increased sixfold in the last two decades due largely to a dramatic escalation in the occurrence of chlamydia infections. Ectopic pregnancies account for about one out of every ten pregnancy-related deaths (Hillis et al., 1997).

In men, the *Chlamydia trachomatis* organism is estimated to be the cause of approximately half the cases of *epididymitis* (infection of the epididymis) and *nongonococcal urethritis (NGU)* (infection of the urethral tube not cause by gonorrhea). The symptoms of epididymitis may include a sensation of heaviness in the affected testicle(s), inflammation of the scrotal skin, and the formation of a small area of hard, painful swelling at the bottom of the testicle. Symptoms of NGU include a discharge from the penis and burning during urination (more details are provided in a later section on NGU).

One of the most disheartening aspects of chlamydia disease is that symptoms are either minimal or nonexistent in most women with lower-reproductive-tract chlamydia infections (Parks, 1997; Shafer, 1997). Most women and men with rectal chlamydia infections and approximately half of men with genital chlamydia infections also manifest few or no symptoms (Centers for Disease Control, 1997c). Laboratory diagnostic tests are necessary to confirm the presence of *Chlamydia trachomatis.* Cultures are typically not required for diagnosis, however, and the procedure is relatively simple and inexpensive. Recently introduced laboratory tests that can be performed on urine have made testing for chlamydia infection even easier (Moran, 1997a).

Trachoma
A chronic, contagious form of conjunctivitis caused by chlamydia infections.

Conjunctivitis
Inflammation of the mucous membrane that lines the inner surface of the eyelid and the exposed surface of the eyeball.

Another complication associated with *Chlamydia trachomatis* is **trachoma** (tra-KŌ-ma), a chronic, contagious form of **conjunctivitis** (kon-junk′-ti-VĪ-tis) (inflammation of the mucous membrane that lines the inner surface of the eyelid and the exposed surface of the eyeball). Trachoma is the world's leading cause of preventable blindness; it is particularly prevalent in Asia and Africa. *Chlamydia trachomatis* is also the most common cause of eye infections in newborns, who can become infected as they pass through the birth canal (Majeroni, 1994). Studies have variously estimated that 20–50% of infants born to infected mothers will develop conjunctivitis (Majeroni, 1994; Rivlin, 1992). In addition, many babies of infected mothers will develop chlamydia pneumonia during the first few months of their lives (Adair et al., 1998; Centers for Disease Control, 1998b). Chlamydia infection in pregnant women can also lead to premature delivery or fetal death (Sharts-Hopco, 1997; Todd et al., 1997).

Chlamydia conjunctivitis in a newborn acquired from an infected mother during birth.

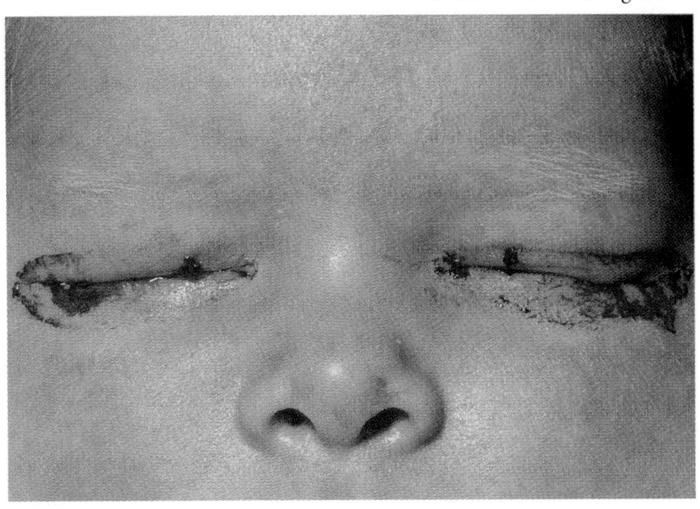

Treatment

Recent CDC guidelines suggest treating uncomplicated chlamydia infections with a seven-day regimen of doxycycline by mouth or a single 1-gram dose of azithromycin. Because chlamydia infection often coexists with gonorrhea, health practitioners frequently prescribe seven days of ofloxacin, a drug effective against both chlamydia and gonorrhea infections. For pregnant women and others who should not take doxycycline and ofloxacin, alternative drugs are erythromycin and azithromycin. All sexual partners exposed to *Chlamydia trachomatis* should be examined for STDs and treated if necessary.

To reduce the risk of an infant developing chlamydia conjunctivitis after passing through the birth canal of an infected mother, either erythromycin or tetracycline ointment is put into the eyes of exposed newborns as soon as possible after birth.

Gonorrhea

Gonorrhea A sexually transmitted disease that initially causes inflammation of mucous membranes.

Gonorrhea (gon-ō-RĒ-a), known in street language as "the clap," is an STD caused by the bacterium *Neisseria gonorrhoeae* (also called "gonococcus").

Incidence and Transmission

Gonorrhea is a very common communicable disease. Estimates of its prevalence in the U.S. population range from 600,000 to over a million new infections annually (Centers for Disease Control, 1998b; Weisfuse, 1998). The late 1970s witnessed the beginning of an intensified public health effort to curtail gonorrhea infections in the United States. These efforts resulted in a downward trend in the overall incidence of gonorrhea in the U.S. population, a decline that still continues. Unfortunately, this reduction has not been consistent throughout the population. Gonorrhea rates remain exceptionally high among teenagers and young adults, especially within lower socioeconomic ethnic minority communities.

The gonococcus bacterium thrives in the warm mucous membrane tissues of the genitals, anus, and throat. Its mode of transmission is by sexual contact—penile–vaginal, oral–genital, or genital–anal.

Symptoms and Complications

Early symptoms of gonorrhea infection are more likely to be evident in men than women. Most men who experience gonococcal urethritis will have some symptoms, ranging from mild to quite pronounced. However, it is not uncommon for men with this type of infection to have no symptoms and yet be potentially infectious (Schwebke, 1991a; Nicholas, 1998). The incidence of asymptomatic gonorrhea is considerably greater in women; as many as 80% will not detect the disease until it has progressed considerably (Braverman & Strasburger, 1994b; Nicholas, 1998).

EARLY SYMPTOMS IN THE MALE In men, early symptoms typically appear within one to five days after sexual contact with an infected person. However, symptoms may show up as late as two weeks after contact or, in a small number of cases, may not appear at all. The two most common signs of infection are a bad-smelling, cloudy discharge from the penis (see Figure 17.1) and burning sensations during urination. About 30–40% of infected men also have swollen and tender lymph glands in the groin. These early symptoms sometimes clear up on their own without treatment. However, this is no guarantee that the disease has been eradicated by the body's immune system. The bacteria may still be present, and a man may still be able to infect a partner.

COMPLICATIONS IN THE MALE If the infection continues without treatment for two to three weeks, it may spread up the genitourinary tract. Here it may involve the prostate, bladder, kidneys, and testicles. Most men who continue to harbor the gonococcus have only periodic flare-ups of the minor symptoms of discharge and burning during urination. In a small number of men, however, abscesses form in the prostate. These may result in fever, painful bowel movement, difficulty urinating, and general discomfort. In approximately one out of five men who remain untreated for longer than a month, the bacteria move down the vas deferens to infect one or both of the epididymal structures that lie along the back of each testicle. Generally, only one side is infected initially, usually the left. (Symptoms of epididymitis were described in the discussion of chlamydia infection.) Even after successful treatment, gonococcal epididymitis leaves scar tissue, which can block the flow of sperm from the affected testicle. Sterility does not usually result because this complication usually affects only one testicle. However, if treatment is still not carried out after epididymitis has occurred on one side, the infection may spread to the other testicle, causing permanent sterility.

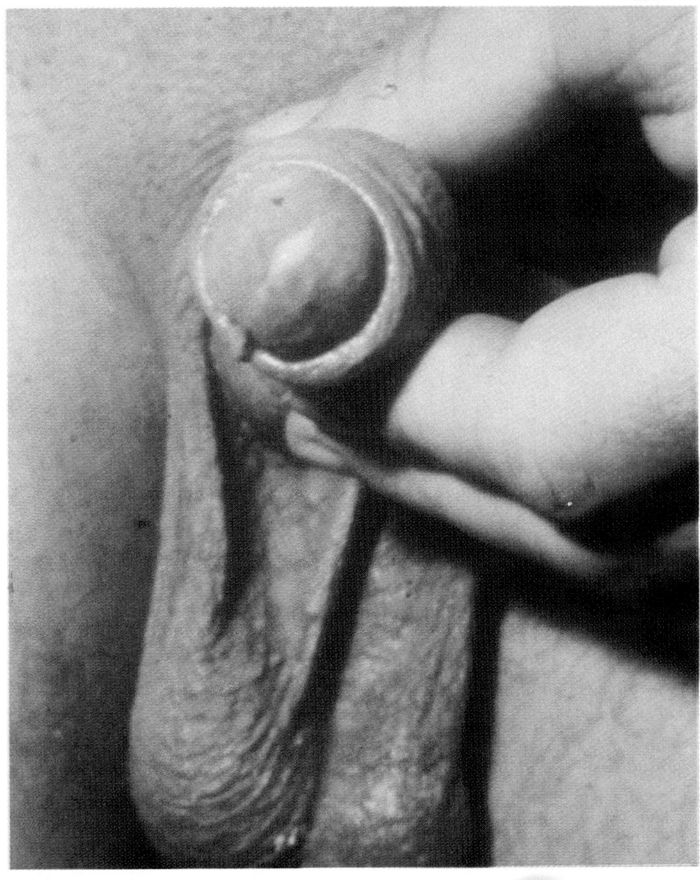

Figure 17.1

A cloudy discharge symptomatic of gonorrhea infection.

EARLY SYMPTOMS IN THE FEMALE As mentioned earlier, women are often unaware of the early signs of gonorrhea infection. The primary site of infection, the cervix, may become inflamed without producing any observable symptoms. A yellow-green discharge usually results, but because this is rarely heavy, it commonly goes unnoticed. A woman who is very aware of her vaginal secretions is more likely to note the infection during these early stages. Sometimes the discharge may be irritating to the vulval tissues. However, when a woman seeks medical attention for an irritating discharge, her physician may fail to consider gonorrhea because many other infectious organisms produce this symptom. Also, many women who have gonorrhea also have trichomoniasis (discussed later in this chapter), and this condition may mask the presence of gonorrhea. Consequently, it is essential for any woman who thinks she may have gonorrhea to make certain that she is tested for gonorrhea when she is examined. (A Pap smear is *not* a test for gonorrhea.)

COMPLICATIONS IN THE FEMALE The Bartholin's glands may be invaded by the gonococcus organism. When this happens, there are usually no symptoms. Far more serious complications result from the spread of this disease to the upper reproductive tract, where it often causes PID. The symptoms of PID, discussed in the section on chlamydia infection, are often more severe when the infecting organism is gonococcus rather than *Chlamydia trachomatis.* Sterility and ectopic pregnancy are very serious consequences occasionally associated with gonococcal PID. Another serious complication that may result from PID is the development of tough bands of scar-tissue adhesions that may link several pelvic cavity structures (fallopian tubes, ovaries, uterus, and so forth) to each other, to the abdominal walls, or to both. These adhesions can cause severe pain during coitus or when a woman is standing or walking.

OTHER COMPLICATIONS IN BOTH SEXES In about 1–3% of adult men and women with gonorrhea, the gonococci enter the bloodstream (a condition called *disseminated gonococcal infection*) and spread throughout the body to produce a variety of symptoms including chills, fever, loss of appetite, skin lesions, and arthritic pain in the joints (Braverman & Strasburger, 1994b; Moran, 1997a). If arthritic symptoms develop, quick treatment is essential to avoid permanent joint damage. In very rare cases, the gonococcus organism may invade the heart, liver, spinal cord, and brain.

An infant may develop a gonococcal eye infection, which may cause blindness, after passing through the birth canal of an infected woman (Sharts-Hopco, 1997). The use of silver nitrate eye drops or erythromycin or tetracycline ophthalmic ointment immediately

after birth averts this potential complication (Centers for Disease Control, 1998b). In a few rare cases, adults have transmitted the bacteria to their eyes by touching this region immediately after handling their genitals—one reason why it is important to wash with soap and water immediately after self-examination.

Oral contact with infected genitals may result in transmission of the gonococcal bacteria to the throat, causing pharyngeal gonorrhea (Barlow, 1997). Although this form of the disease may cause a sore throat, most people experience no symptoms. Rectal gonorrhea may be caused by anal intercourse or, in a woman, by transmission of the bacteria from the vagina to the anal opening via menstrual bleeding or vaginal discharge. This form of gonorrhea is often asymptomatic, particularly in females, but it may be accompanied by itching, rectal discharge, and bowel disorders.

Because infections of the throat or anus often do not produce observable symptoms, it is very important to examine laboratory cultures taken from the throats or anuses of people who have engaged in oral–genital or anal intercourse with those suspected of having gonorrhea (Barlow, 1997). Health practitioners often overlook these important tests unless a person requests them.

Treatment

Because gonorrhea is often confused with other ailments, it is important to make the correct diagnosis. Because coexisting chlamydia infections often accompany gonorrhea, health practitioners often use a treatment strategy that is effective against both (Centers for Disease Control, 1998b). Up to 1976, gonorrhea could be effectively treated by penicillin or tetracycline. Since then, however, antibiotic-resistant strains of gonococcal bacteria have emerged (Deguchi et al., 1997; Moran, 1997a). Consequently, treatment guidelines suggest the use of drugs effective against both resistant and nonresistant strains of *Neisseria gonorrhoeae.* The current CDC-recommended treatment regimen includes the dual therapy of a single dose of ceftriaxone, cefixime, ciprofloxacin, or ofloxacin plus doxycycline for seven days. This regimen is also effective for treating chlamydia infection, a coexisting condition in up to 40% of some populations (Bowie et al., 1994; Moran, 1997a).

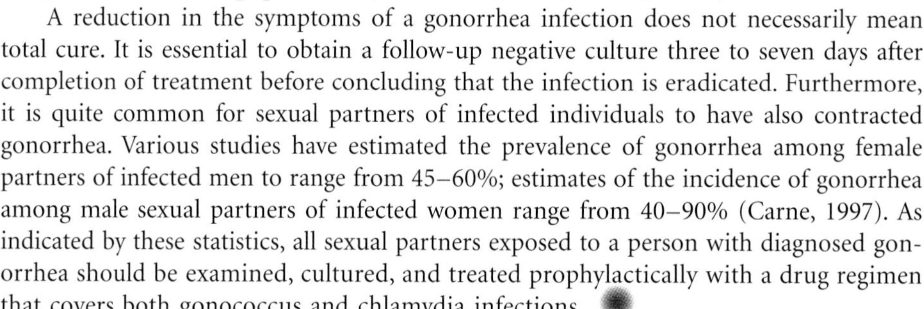

A reduction in the symptoms of a gonorrhea infection does not necessarily mean total cure. It is essential to obtain a follow-up negative culture three to seven days after completion of treatment before concluding that the infection is eradicated. Furthermore, it is quite common for sexual partners of infected individuals to have also contracted gonorrhea. Various studies have estimated the prevalence of gonorrhea among female partners of infected men to range from 45–60%; estimates of the incidence of gonorrhea among male sexual partners of infected women range from 40–90% (Carne, 1997). As indicated by these statistics, all sexual partners exposed to a person with diagnosed gonorrhea should be examined, cultured, and treated prophylactically with a drug regimen that covers both gonococcus and chlamydia infections.

Nongonococcal Urethritis

Any inflammation of the urethra that is not caused by gonorrhea is called **nongonococcal urethritis (NGU).** It is believed that two separate microscopic organisms, *Chlamydia trachomatis* and *Ureaplasma urealyticum* (a member of a group of bacteria called mycoplasmas) are primary causes of NGU (Centers for Disease Control, 1998b). NGU may also result from invasion by other infectious agents (such as trichomonas, fungi, or bacteria), allergic reactions to vaginal secretions, or irritation by soaps, vaginal contraceptives, or deodorant sprays.

Nongonococcal urethritis (NGU)
An inflammation of the male urethral tube caused by other than gonococcus organisms.

Incidence and Transmission

NGU is quite common among men: In the United States, it occurs much more frequently than gonococcal urethritis (Handsfield, 1992). Although NGU generally produces urinary tract symptoms only in men, there is evidence that women harbor the chlamydia or mycoplasma organisms. The most common forms of NGU, caused by these two organisms, are generally transmitted through coitus. That NGU rarely occurs in men who are not involved in sexual interaction supports this contention.

Recent research has demonstrated that oral sex (fellatio) is strongly associated with nonchlamydia NGU in both heterosexual and homosexual men (Lafferty et al., 1997). This finding suggests that oral bacteria or other oral factors can cause NGU.

Symptoms and Complications

Men who contract NGU often manifest symptoms similar to those of gonorrhea infection, including discharge from the penis and mild burning during urination. Often the discharge is less pronounced than with gonorrhea; it may be evident only in the morning before urinating.

Women infected with *Chlamydia trachomatis* or *Ureaplasma urealyticum* are generally unaware of the disease until they are informed that NGU has been diagnosed in a male partner. They frequently show no symptoms, although there may be some itching, burning during urination, and a mild discharge of pus from the vagina. (Cultures may reveal the presence of the causative organism.) A woman may have the infection for a long time, during which she may pass it to sexual partners.

The symptoms of NGU generally disappear after two to three months without treatment. However, the disease may still be present. If left untreated in women, it may result in cervical inflammation or PID; in men it may spread to the prostate, epididymis, or both. In rare cases, NGU can produce a form of arthritis.

Treatment

A single dose of azithromycin or doxycyline for seven days usually clears up the condition. All sexual partners of individuals diagnosed as having NGU should be examined for the presence of an STD and treated if necessary.

Syphilis

Syphilis (SIF-uh-lis) is an STD caused by a thin, corkscrewlike bacterium called *Treponema pallidum* (also commonly called a "spirochete").

Syphilis
A sexually transmitted disease caused by a spirochete called *Treponema pallidum.*

Incidence and Transmission

The incidence of syphilis in the United States has increased and decreased several times in recent decades. After rising steadily in the 1970s and early 1980s, syphilis cases declined in the mid-1980s, especially among male homosexuals—probably as a result of behavioral changes related to the AIDS epidemic (Schwebke, 1991b). This decline was short-lived, however, for incidence rose by roughly 75% in the closing years of the 1980s. Particularly disturbing was the increase in syphilis among the urban poor, especially within minority groups (Reyes & Akhras, 1995). Several studies have demonstrated a link between increasing rates of syphilis, gonorrhea, AIDS, and other STDs and the use of crack cocaine and the exchange of sex for drugs or money (Coles et al., 1995; Somlai et al., 1998).

Fortunately, syphilis rates have declined in the United States over the last five years (Farley, 1997). However, despite this decline, the disease has begun to reemerge in several poor inner-city areas, especially within Philadelphia, New Orleans, and Atlanta (Moran, 1997b). Furthermore, the actual incidence of syphilis is undoubtedly much higher than reported. In fact, for every case of syphilis that is reported, it is estimated, three are not (Sharts-Hopco, 1997). Regardless of its frequency, syphilis should not be taken lightly: Unlike most STDs, syphilis can result in death.

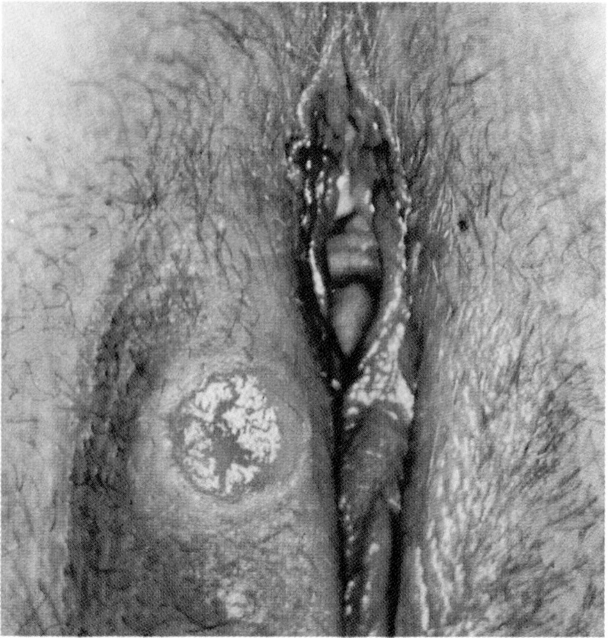

(a)

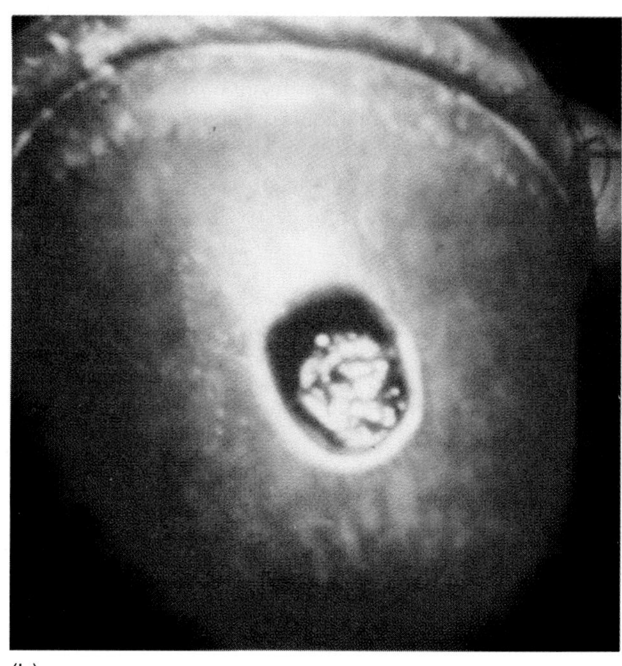

(b)

Figure 17.2

The first stage of syphilis. A syphilitic chancre as it appears on (a) the labia and (b) the penis.

Treponema pallidum requires a warm, moist environment for survival. It is transmitted almost exclusively from open lesions of infected individuals to the mucous membranes or skin abrasions of sexual partners through penile–vaginal, oral–genital, or genital–anal contacts. *Treponema pallidum* may also be transmitted from an infected pregnant woman to her unborn child through the placental blood system. The resulting *congenital syphilis* can cause death or extreme damage to infected newborns (Mobley et al., 1998; Rawstron et al., 1997). A resurgence of congenital syphilis in recent years has been linked to maternal illicit drug use, especially cocaine (Sison et al., 1997). If syphilis is successfully treated before the fourth month of pregnancy, the fetus will not be affected. Therefore, pregnant women should be tested for syphilis sometime during their first three months of pregnancy.

Symptoms and Complications

If untreated, syphilis can progress through the primary, secondary, latent, and tertiary phases of development. A brief description of each follows.

PRIMARY SYPHILIS In its initial or primary phase, syphilis is generally manifested in the form of a painless sore called a **chancre** (SHAN-ker), which appears about three weeks after initial infection at the site where the spirochete organism entered the body (see Figure 17.2). In women who have coitus with infected men, this sore most commonly appears on the inner vaginal walls or cervix. It may also appear on the external genitals, particularly the labia. In men, the chancre most often occurs on the glans of the penis, but it may also show up on the penile shaft or on the scrotum. Although 95% of chancres are genital, they may occur in the mouth or rectum or on the anus or breast. People who have had oral sex with an infected individual may develop a sore on the lips or tongue. Anal intercourse may result in chancres appearing in the rectum or around the anus. The following is an excellent description of the chancre:

Chancre
A raised, red, painless sore that is symptomatic of the primary phase of syphilis.

> When the chancre first develops, it is a dull red bump about the size of a pea. The surface of the bump soon breaks down and the chancre becomes a rounded, dull red, open sore which may be covered by a yellow or grey crusty scab. The chancre is painless and does not bleed easily. In about 50% of cases, the chancre is surrounded by a thin pink border. The edges of the chancre are often raised and hard, like the edges of a button. The hardness may spread to

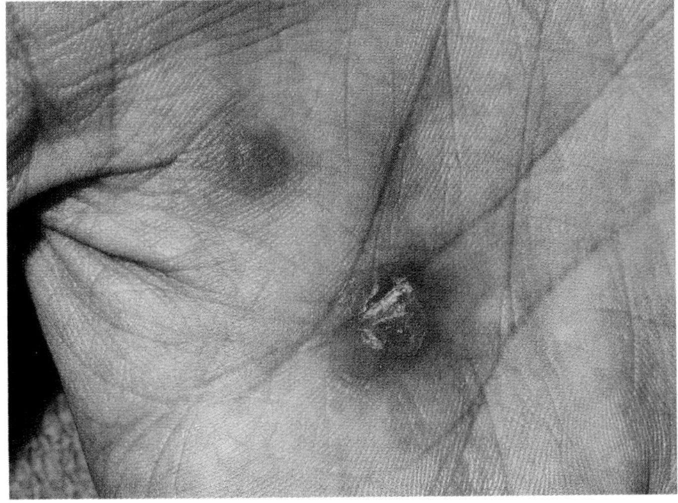

(a)

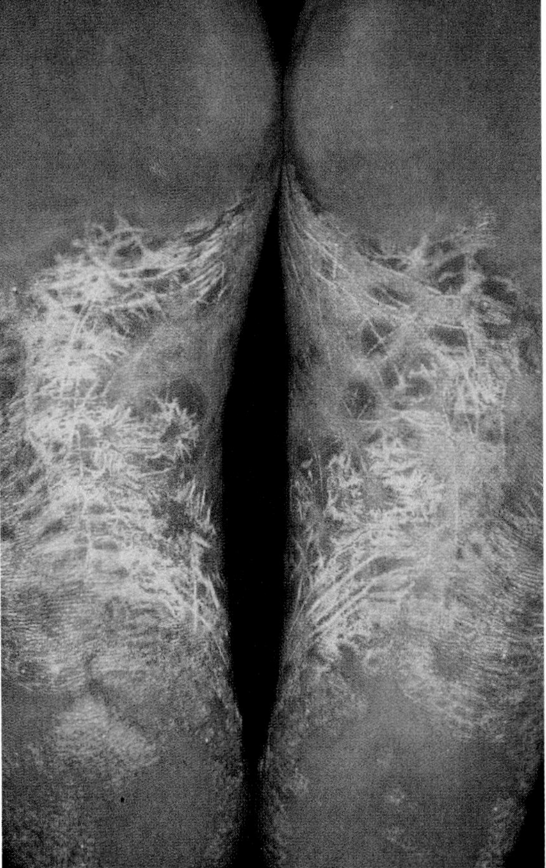

(b)

Figure 17.3

In the secondary phase of syphilis, a skin rash appears on the body, often on the palms (a) and the feet (b).

the base of the chancre and eventually to the surrounding tissue, making the whole area feel hard and rubbery. (Cherniak & Feingold, 1973, p. 30)

In view of the typically painless nature of the chancre, it often goes undiscovered when it occurs on internal structures such as the rectum, vagina, or cervix. (Occasionally, chancres may be painful, and they may occur in multiple sites.) Even when it is noticed, some people do not seek treatment. Unfortunately (from the long-term perspective), the chancre generally heals without treatment one to six weeks after it first appears. For the next few weeks, the person usually has no symptoms but may infect an unsuspecting partner. After about six weeks (although sometimes after as little as two weeks or as long as six months), the disease progresses to the secondary stage in about 50% of the people with untreated primary syphilis (Goens et al., 1994a).

SECONDARY SYPHILIS In the secondary phase, a skin rash appears on the body, often on the palms of the hands and soles of the feet (see Figure 17.3). The rash may vary from barely noticeable to severe, with raised bumps that have a rubbery, hard consistency. Although the rash may look terrible, it typically does not hurt or itch. If it is at all noticeable, it generally prompts a visit to a physician, if the earlier appearance of a chancre did not. Besides a generalized rash, a person may have flulike symptoms such as fever, swollen lymph glands, fatigue, weight loss, and joint or bone pain (Moran, 1997b). Even when not treated, these symptoms usually subside within a few weeks. Rather than being eliminated, however, the disease may enter the potentially more dangerous latent phase.

LATENT SYPHILIS The latent stage can last for several years, during which time there may be no observable symptoms (Moran, 1997b). Nevertheless, the infecting organisms may continue to multiply, preparing for the final stage of syphilitic infection. After one year of the latent stage, the infected individual is no longer contagious to sexual partners. However, a pregnant woman with syphilis in any stage can pass the infection to her fetus.

TERTIARY SYPHILIS Approximately one-third of those individuals who do not obtain effective treatment during the first three stages of syphilis enter the tertiary stage later in life (Goens et al., 1994a). The final manifestations of syphilis can be severe, often resulting in death. They occur anywhere from 3 to 40 years after initial infection and may include such conditions as heart failure, blindness, ruptured blood vessels, paralysis, skin ulcers, liver damage, and severe mental disturbance (Moran, 1997b). Depending on the extent of the damage, treatment even at this late stage may be beneficial.

Treatment

Primary, secondary, or latent syphilis of less than one year's duration may be effectively treated with intramuscular injections of benzathine penicillin G (Centers for Disease Control, 1998b). People who are allergic to penicillin may be treated with doxycycline, tetracycline, or erythromycin. Syphilis of more than one year's duration is treated with intramuscular injections of benzathine penicillin G once a week for three successive weeks.

All sex partners exposed to a person with infectious syphilis should be treated. *All* individuals who have been treated for this disease should have several diagnostic blood tests at 3, 6, and 12 months after treatment is completed to make certain that they are completely free of the *Treponema pallidum* organism (Moran, 1997b).

Chancroid

Chancroid
A sexually transmitted bacterial disease characterized by small bumps in the region of the genitals, perineum, or anus that eventually rupture and form painful ulcers with a foul discharge.

Chancroid (shang-kroyd) is an infection caused by the bacterium *Haemophilus ducreyi.*

Incidence and Transmission

Chancroid is widely prevalent in tropical and semitropical regions of the world, especially in Africa, where it is one of the most common causes of genital ulcers (Goens et al., 1994b). Although still relatively uncommon in the United States, the incidence of this disease has increased sharply in recent years (Moran, 1997b). This has been a cause of concern among health officials, since chancroid is associated with an increased prevalence of HIV infections (Bowie et al., 1994; Moran, 1997b). This disease is usually transmitted by sexual interaction.

Symptoms and Complications

Chancroid is characterized by the formation of small bumps or papules, usually in the region of the genitals, perineum, or anus, that occur four to five days after contact with an infected person. These lesions eventually rupture and form painful, soft, craterlike ulcers that emit a foul-smelling discharge. The softness and painfulness of the chancroid ulcers distinguish them from the hard, painless chancres of syphilis. Chancroid infection frequently is accompanied by swollen lymph nodes, which may also ulcerate. The extensive ulceration associated with chancroid infections is a worrisome complication in that HIV is able to gain easy access to the blood through these lesions.

Treatment

Current treatments of choice for chancroid are single doses of either ceftriaxone or azithromycin or seven days of oral erythromycin.

Viral Infections

Viruses are the cause of several common STDs. A virus is an organism that invades, reproduces, and lives within a cell, thereby disrupting normal cellular activity. Most viruses are transmitted through direct contact with infectious blood or other body fluids. We begin our discussion with herpes, the most common viral STD. Next we describe genital warts caused by several varieties of viruses that have reached epidemic proportions in the U.S.

population. We conclude with some information about viral hepatitis. AIDS, caused by the HIV virus, is described in detail later in this chapter.

Herpes

Herpes is caused by the *Herpes simplex* virus (HSV). Eight different herpes viruses infect humans, the most common being varicella-zoster virus (VZV) that causes chicken pox followed in frequency by *Herpes simplex* virus type 1 (HSV-1) and *Herpes simplex* virus type 2 (HSV-2) (Erlich, 1997; Levy, 1997a). In the following discussion we confine our attention to HSV, types 1 and 2, because these are the two herpes viruses that are widely transmitted through sexual contact. Type 1 typically manifests itself as lesions, or sores, of the type called "cold sores," or "fever blisters," in the mouth or on the lips (oral herpes). Type 2 generally causes lesions on and around the genital areas (genital herpes).

Herpes
A disease that is characterized by blisters on the skin in the regions of the genitals or mouth, and that is caused by a virus and easily transmitted by sexual contact.

Is it possible for a person to contract genital herpes from a cold sore on the mouth, and vice versa?

Although genital and oral herpes are generally associated with different herpes viruses, oral–genital transmission is possible. Type 1 may affect the genital area, and, conversely, type 2 may produce a sore in the mouth area (Hensleigh et al., 1997).

Incidence and Transmission

Current estimates indicate that over 100 million Americans are afflicted with oral herpes, and 45 million have genital herpes. A recent nationally representative survey of over 13,000 Americans revealed that "HSV-2 is now detectable in roughly one of five persons 12 years of age or older nationwide" (Fleming et al., 1997, p. 1105). This extraordinarily high incidence of HSV-2 has prompted some health authorities to observe that people "who have unprotected contact with multiple partners should know that unsuspected exposure to HSV is virtually guaranteed" (Arvin & Prober, 1997, p. 1158). Current estimates suggest that 300,000 to 500,000 new cases of genital herpes appear annually in the United States.

Genital herpes appears to be transmitted primarily by penile–vaginal, oral–genital, genital–anal, or oral–anal contact. Oral herpes may be transmitted by kissing. A person who receives oral sex from a partner who has a cold sore or fever blister in the mouth region may develop genital herpes of either the type 1 or type 2 variety.

When any herpes sores are present, the infected person is highly contagious. It is extremely important to avoid bringing the lesions into contact with someone else's body through touching, sexual interaction, or kissing.

Can HSV be transmitted when no sores or other symptoms are present?

Although it was once believed that herpes could only be transmitted when lesions were present, we now know that HSV may be transmitted even when there are no symptoms (Centers for Disease Control, 1998b; Erlich, 1997; Moran, 1997b). In fact, research strongly indicates that asymptomatic "viral shedding" (the emission of viable HSV onto body surfaces) likely occurs at least some of the time in many people infected with HSV. This asymptomatic viral shedding can result in transmission of the virus "despite the absence of signs or symptoms that suggest active infection" (Erlich, 1997, p. 211). However, viral shedding is considerably less common in the absence of symptoms. Various studies of HSV-infected persons during asymptomatic periods have found cultures positive for the virus between 1% and 7% of the days tested (Erlich, 1997).

Research has shown that HSV-2 will not pass through latex condoms. Thus, condoms may be effective in preventing transmission from a male whose only lesions occur on the glans or shaft of the penis. However, because condoms sometimes break or come off, many health officials recommend that men abstain from intercourse during active outbreaks. Condoms are helpful but less effective in preventing transmission from a female to a male because vaginal secretions containing the virus may wash over the male's scrotal area.

People may also spread the virus from one part of their bodies to another by touching a sore and then scratching or rubbing somewhere else, a process referred to as *autoinoculation.* However, self-infection appears to be possible only immediately after the initial appearance of infection. Soon the body produces antibodies that ward off infection at other sites. Nevertheless, it is good practice for people with herpes to wash their hands thoroughly with soap and water after touching a sore. It is better to avoid touching the sores if possible.

Symptoms and Complications

The symptoms associated with HSV-1 and HSV-2 infections are quite similar.

GENITAL HERPES (TYPE 2) SYMPTOMS The incubation period of genital herpes is 2–14 days, and the symptoms usually last about 20 days (Erlich, 1997). However, some individuals with genital herpes do not experience recognizable symptoms (Erlich, 1997). When symptoms are present, they consist of one or more small, painful red bumps, called *papules,* that usually appear in the genital region. In women, the areas most commonly infected are the labia. The mons veneris, clitoris, vaginal opening, inner vaginal walls, and cervix may also be affected (Hensleigh et al., 1997). In men, the infected site is typically the glans or shaft of the penis. Homosexual men and heterosexual women who have engaged in anal intercourse may develop eruptions in and around the anus.

Soon after their initial appearance, papules rapidly develop into tiny painful blisters filled with a clear fluid containing highly infectious virus particles (see Figure 17.4a). The body then attacks the virus with white blood cells, causing the blisters to fill with pus (see Figure 17.4b). Soon the blisters rupture to form wet, painful, open sores surrounded by a red ring (health practitioners refer to this as the period of "viral shedding"). A person is highly contagious during this time. About 10 days after the first appearance of the papule, the open sore forms a crust and begins to heal, a process that may take as long as 10 more days. Sores on the cervix may continue to produce infectious material for as long as 10 days after labial sores have completely healed. Consequently, it is wise to avoid coitus for a 10-day period after all external sores have healed.

Other symptoms may accompany genital herpes, including swollen lymph nodes in the groin, fever, muscle aches, and headaches. In addition, urination may be accompanied by a burning sensation, and women may experience increased vaginal discharge.

Figure 17.4

Genital herpes blisters as they appear on (a) the labia and (b) the penis.

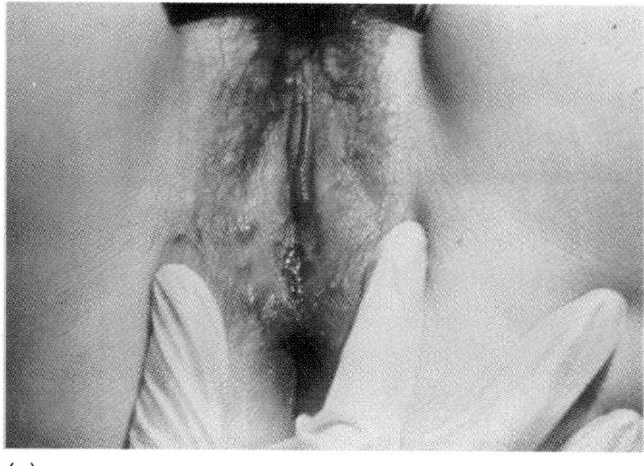

(a)

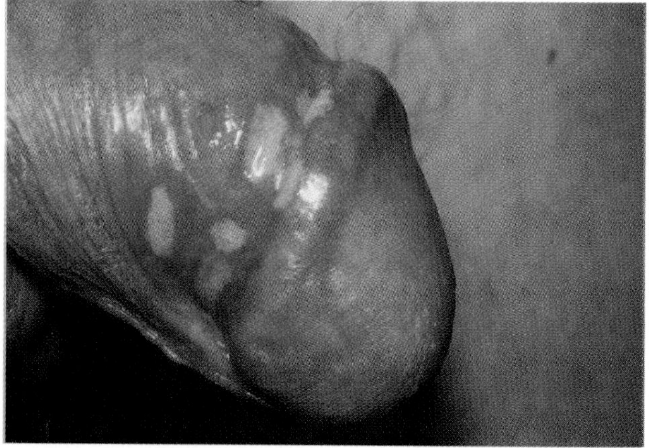

(b)

ORAL HERPES (TYPE 1) SYMPTOMS Oral herpes is characterized by the formation of papules on the lips and sometimes on the inside of the mouth, the tongue, and the throat. (HSV-1 only infrequently occurs within the mouth, and should not be confused with canker sores.) These blisters tend to crust over and heal within 10–16 days. Other symptoms may include fever, general muscle aches, swollen lymph nodes in the neck, flulike symptoms, increased salivation, and sometimes bleeding in the mouth.

RECURRENCE Even after complete healing, lesions may recur. Unfortunately, the herpes virus does not typically go away; instead, it retreats up the nerve fibers leading from the infected site (Erlich, 1997; Whitley et al., 1998). Ultimately, the genital herpes virus finds a resting place in nerve cells adjacent to the lower spinal column, whereas the oral herpes virus becomes lodged in nerve cells in the back of the neck (Arvin & Prober, 1997). The virus may remain dormant in these cells, without causing any apparent damage, perhaps for the person's entire lifetime. However, in many cases there will be periodic flare-ups as the virus retraces its path back down the nerve fibers leading to the genitals or lips.

Although some people never experience a recurrence of herpes following the initial or primary infection, research suggests that most people who have undergone a primary episode of genital herpes infection experience at least one recurrence (Centers for Disease Control, 1998b). Individuals who experience recurrences may do so frequently or only occasionally. Studies have shown that the more extensive the primary attack, the greater the chance of recurrence (Benedetti et al., 1994). Symptoms associated with recurrent attacks tend to be milder than primary episodes, and the disease tends to run its course more quickly (Hensleigh et al., 1997).

Most people prone to recurrent herpes outbreaks experience some type of **prodromal symptoms** that give advance warning of an impending eruption. These indications include itching, burning, throbbing, or "pins-and-needles" tingling at the sites commonly infected by herpes blisters and sometimes pain in the legs, thighs, groin, or buttocks. Many health authorities believe that a person's degree of infectiousness increases during this stage and that it further escalates when the lesions appear. Consequently, a person should be particularly careful to avoid direct contact from the time he or she first experiences prodromal symptoms until the sores have completely healed. Even during an outbreak, it is possible to continue sexual intimacies with a partner, as long as infected skin does not come in contact with healthy skin. During this time partners may wish to experiment with other kinds of sensual pleasuring, such as sensate focus (see Chapter 16), hugging, or manual stimulation.

Prodromal symptoms
Symptoms that give advance warning of an impending herpes eruption.

A variety of factors may trigger reactivation of the herpes virus, including emotional stress, anxiety, depression, acidic food, sunburn, cold, menstruation, poor nutrition, being overtired or run-down, and trauma to the skin region affected (Clark et al., 1995). One person noted:

> For several years, I have been having a herpes outbreak on my lips. It usually happens just once a year and coincides with the start of fishing season when I sit in a boat too long without protection from the sun. Now that I am aware of the pattern, I plan to take proper precautions in the future. (Authors' files)

Because triggering factors vary so widely, it is often difficult to associate a specific event with a recurrent herpes outbreak.

Some people may not experience a relapse of genital herpes until several years after the initial infection. Therefore, if you have been in what you believe is a sexually exclusive relationship and your partner shows symptoms or transmits the virus to you, it does not necessarily mean that she or he contracted the disease from someone else during the course of your relationship. Furthermore, as stated earlier, some people with HSV-2 infections are asymptomatic or have such mild symptoms that they are often unrecognizable. Thus, a first episode of symptomatic genital herpes may not be due to recent sexual contact with an infected person.

OTHER COMPLICATIONS Although the sores are painful and bothersome, it is very unlikely that men will experience major physical complications of herpes. Women, however, may face two very serious, although quite uncommon, complications: cancer of the cervix and infection of a newborn. Evidence suggests that the risk of developing cervical cancer is higher among women who have had genital herpes (Aral & Holmes, 1991). However, it remains unclear if genital herpes is causally linked to cervical cancer. "Some medical authorities have argued that genital herpes might only be a marker for high-risk sexual behaviors that could also transmit other STDs—perhaps even an unrecognized STD that was the true cause of cervical cancer" (Aral & Holmes, 1991, p. 66). Fortunately, the great majority of women infected with herpes will never develop cancer of the cervix. Nonetheless, it is advisable for all women, particularly those who have had genital herpes, to obtain an annual cervical Pap smear. Some authorities recommend that women with genital herpes should have this test every six months.

A newborn may be infected with genital herpes while passing through the birth canal (Hensleigh et al., 1997; Randolph et al., 1996). About half of newborns infected with herpes will die or be severely damaged (Overall, 1994; Schlesinger & Storch, 1994). It is believed that viral shedding from the cervix, vagina, or vulva plays the primary role in transmitting the disease from mother to infant. Most infected newborns develop typical skin sores (papules) which should be cultured to confirm a herpes diagnosis. Some health practitioners recommend treating exposed infants with acyclovir, a drug shown to be somewhat effective in suppressing herpes outbreaks. The presence of genital herpes sores when delivery is imminent poses a significant risk for transmission of HSV from an infected mother to her baby. To avert this possibility, a cesarean delivery may be performed (Randolph et al., 1996; Roberts et al., 1995).

One additional serious complication can occur when a person transfers the virus to an eye after touching a virus-shedding sore. This may lead to a severe eye infection known as ocular herpes, or *herpes keratitis* (usually caused by HSV-1). The best way to prevent this complication is to avoid touching herpes sores. If you cannot avoid contact, thoroughly wash your hands with hot water and soap immediately after touching the lesions. There are effective treatments for ocular herpes, but they must be started quickly to avoid eye damage.

Many people who have recurrent herpes outbreaks are troubled with mild to severe psychological distress (Hoon et al., 1991). In view of the physical discomfort associated with the disease, the unpredictability of recurrent outbreaks, and the lack of an effective cure (see next section), it is no small wonder that people who have herpes undergo considerable stress. We believe that becoming better informed about herpes may help to alleviate some of these emotional difficulties. In addition, talking with supportive partners may ease a person's psychological adjustment to recurrent genital herpes infections. Certainly, herpes is not the dread disease that some people believe it to be. In fact, many individuals have learned to cope quite effectively with it, as did the person in the following account:

> When I first discovered I had herpes several years ago, my first reaction was "Oh no, my sex life is destroyed!" I was really depressed and angry with the person who gave me the disease. However, with time I learned I could live with it, and I even began to gain some control over it. Now, on those infrequent occasions when I have an outbreak, I know what to do to hurry up the healing process. Most of the time things are just the same as before I got it, and my sex life is only occasionally disrupted. (Authors' files)

Treatment

The most common method of diagnosing herpes is direct observation by a health care practitioner. Clinical symptoms, together with a thorough patient history, usually yield an accurate diagnosis. In cases where the diagnosis is in question, a number of laboratory tests can detect herpes virus infections (Moran, 1997b).

At the time of this writing, no medical treatment has been proven effective in curing either oral or genital herpes. However, medical researchers are pursuing an effective treatment on many fronts, with mounting optimism. Current treatment strategies are designed to reduce discomfort and to speed healing during an outbreak.

An antiviral drug, acyclovir, sold under the trade name Zovirax, is often highly effective in the management of herpes. The drug is available in three forms: topical (ointment), oral, and injectable. Although the ointment has not proven to be particularly helpful, a number of studies have shown that acyclovir administered orally or intravenously significantly reduces the length and severity of initial herpes outbreaks (Erlich, 1997; Moran, 1997b). Oral acyclovir taken several times daily is by far the most common drug treatment for HSV. Intravenous (injected) acyclovir is generally employed only with very severe HSV infections.

In recent years two new antiviral agents, famciclovir and valacyclovir hydrochloride, taken orally, have been approved for the treatment of genital herpes (Erlich, 1997; Mertz et al., 1997). Both these new drugs are more bioavailable than acyclovir (in other words, are absorbed better and thus produce higher levels of blood serum antiviral activity). However, research to date has not shown either of these drugs to be superior to acyclovir as treatment for herpes. Therefore, oral acyclovir remains the treatment of choice for most HSV infections.

Oral acyclovir taken prophylactically, in the absence of symptoms, has been shown to both suppress and reduce the duration of recurrent episodes of herpes outbreaks (Centers for Disease Control, 1998b; Erlich, 1997; Moran, 1997b). Long-term suppressive acyclovir therapy is often used for people who experience six or more outbreaks per year, or those with exceptionally severe HSV recurrences (Erlich, 1997). Research indicates that daily suppressive therapy will reduce the frequency of recurrences by at least 75% "but will not totally eliminate symptomatic or asymptomatic viral shedding or the potential for transmission" (Moran, 1997b, p. 65).

A number of other measures can help provide relief from the discomfort associated with herpes. The following suggestions may be helpful. Because the effectiveness of these measures varies from person to person, we encourage people to experiment to find an approach that best meets their needs.

1. Keeping herpes blisters clean and dry will lessen the possibility of secondary infections, significantly shorten the period of viral shedding, and reduce the total time of lesion healing. Washing the area with warm water and soap two to three times daily is adequate for cleaning. After bathing, dry the area thoroughly by patting it gently with a soft cotton towel or by blowing it with a hair dryer set on cool. Because the moisture that occurs naturally in the genital area may slow the healing process, sprinkling the dried area liberally with cornstarch or baby powder can help. It is desirable to wear loose cotton clothing that does not trap in moisture (cotton underwear absorbs moisture, but nylon traps it).
2. Two aspirin every three to four hours may help to reduce the pain and itching. Application of a local anesthetic, such as lidocaine jelly, may also help to reduce soreness. Ice packs applied directly to the lesions may also provide temporary relief (but avoid wetting them as the ice melts). Keeping the area liberally powdered may also alleviate itching.
3. Some people have an intense burning sensation when they urinate if the urine comes into contact with herpes lesions. This discomfort may be reduced by pouring water over the genitals while voiding or by urinating in a bathtub filled with water. It may help to dilute the acid in the urine by drinking lots of fluids (but avoid liquids that make the urine more acidic, like cranberry juice).
4. Because stress has been implicated as a triggering event in recurrent herpes, it is a good idea to try to reduce this negative influence. A variety of approaches may help reduce stress. These include relaxation techniques, yoga or meditation, and counseling about ways to cope with daily pressures.

5. If you are prone to repeated relapses of herpes, try recording events that occur immediately before an outbreak (either after the fact or as part of an ongoing journal). You may be able to recognize common precipitating events like fatigue, stress, or excessive sunlight, which you can then avoid in the future.

Researchers are currently working on vaccines to protect people from herpes infections and a number of clinical trials with human subjects are currently in progress (Erlich, 1997; Rosenthal et al., 1997). Some experimental vaccines, tested on laboratory animals, show considerable promise for protecting animals from HSV infection. For example, in one recent study guinea pigs provided with a vaccine designed to prevent infection with HSV-2 demonstrated complete protection when inoculated with HSV-2 viruses. Furthermore, a reduction in recurrent disease symptoms were observed following therapeutic vaccination of animals already infected with HSV-2 (Boursnell et al., 1997). It is our hope that clinical trials with human subjects, currently being conducted, will yield an effective vaccine.

Genital Warts

Genital warts
Viral warts that appear on the genitals and are primarily transmitted sexually.

Genital warts, sometimes referred to as *condylomata acuminata,* are caused by a virus called the *human papillomavirus* (HPV). Application of recently developed technology has led to the identification of about 100 types of HPV, several of which cause genital infections (Iwasawa et al., 1997; Vernon, 1997). Of the various forms of HPV that cause genital/anal warts, types 6 and 11 are most often the causative varieties (Centers for Disease Control, 1998b; Friis et al., 1997; Monk & Burger, 1998).

Incidence and Transmission

The incidence of genital and anal warts has been increasing so rapidly in both sexes that the disease has reached epidemic proportions in recent years. At the present time, genital and anal HPV is an extremely common viral STD in the United States (Ho et al., 1998; Monk & Burger, 1998). It is estimated that approximately 40 million people in the United States are infected with HPV and that each year 750,000 to one million more are infected (Carson, 1997; Monk & Burger, 1998). HPV is primarily transmitted through vaginal, anal, or oral–genital sexual interaction.

Subclinical or asymptomatic infections with HPV are very common and viral shedding can occur during asymptomatic periods of infection (Strand et al., 1997; Vernon, 1997). In fact, research indicates that HPV is "most commonly transmitted from individuals without current symptoms" (Strand et al., 1997, p. 140).

Symptoms and Complications

Genital warts appear from three weeks to eight months after contact with an infected person, with an average incubation period of about three months (Vernon, 1997). In women, genital warts most commonly appear on the bottom part of the vaginal opening. They may also occur on the perineum, the labia, the inner walls of the vagina, and the cervix. In men, genital warts commonly occur on the glans, foreskin, or shaft of the penis (see Figure 17.5). In moist areas (such as the vaginal opening and under the foreskin), genital warts are pink or red and soft, with a cauliflowerlike appearance. On dry skin areas, they are generally hard and yellow-gray.

Genital warts are sometimes associated with serious complications. They may invade the urethra, causing urinary obstruction and bleeding. Research has also revealed a strong association between HPV infections and cancers of the cervix, vagina, vulva, urethra, penis, and anus (Friis et al., 1997; Kaufman et al., 1997; Spigener & Mayeaux, 1998). HPV types 6 and 11 are strongly linked to cancers of the genitals and anus, whereas types 16

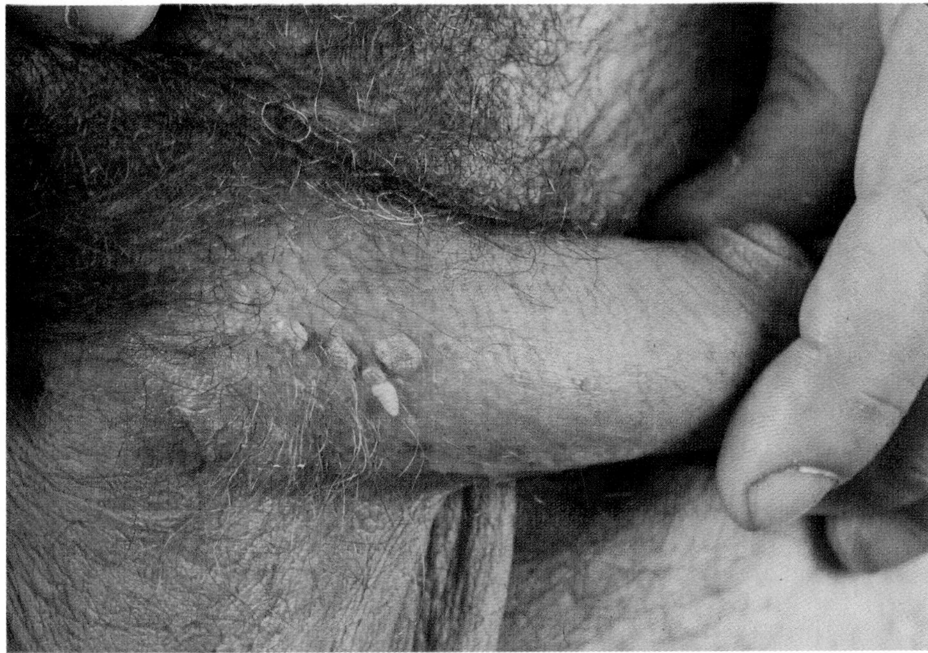

Figure 17.5

Genital warts on penis.

and 18 are most often associated with the development of cervical cancer (Friis et al., 1997; Vernon, 1997). It is not known if HPV acts alone to cause these cancers or if it acts in conjunction with cofactors such as other infections, smoking, immunosuppression, pregnancy, the use of oral contraceptives, and poor nutrition (Carson, 1997; Spigener & Mayeaux, 1998; Vernon, 1997).

Another rare but serious complication of HPV is that pregnant women infected with the virus may transmit it to their babies during birth (Carson, 1997; Morrison, 1994). Transmission of HPV from mother to infant at birth occurs in one to four deliveries per 100,000 births (Carson, 1997; Vernon, 1997). Infected infants may develop a condition known as *respiratory papillomatosis* that results from HPV infections of their upper respiratory tracts. Respiratory papillomatosis may have serious health consequences that produce lifelong distress and require multiple surgeries.

Treatment

No form of therapy has been shown to entirely eradicate HPV, nor has any single treatment been uniformly effective in removing warts or in preventing them from recurring (Abramowicz, 1994; Carson, 1997). Current CDC guidelines suggest several fairly conservative approaches to HPV management that focus on the removal of visible warts rather than eradication of the virus (Centers for Disease Control, 1998b). The most widely used treatments include cryotherapy (freezing) with liquid nitrogen or cryoprobe and topical applications of podofilox, imiquimod cream, or trichloroacetic acid (Carson, 1997; Centers for Disease Control, 1998b). The response rate to these forms of therapy is only about 60–70%, and at least 20–30% of people experience recurrence after treatment (Abramowicz, 1994). Consequently, a second or extended period of treatment with freezing or topical agents may be necessary. For large or persistent warts, cauterization by electric needle, vaporization by carbon dioxide laser, or surgical removal may be necessary. However, these more radical treatments can cause severe side effects.

There is increasing evidence that many people treated for visible genital warts also have asymptomatic or subclinical HPV infections that are extremely difficult or impossible to eradicate (Braverman & Strasburger, 1994b; Strand et al., 1997). Follow-up medical evaluations of these individuals, every four to six months, are recommended.

Viral Hepatitis

Viral hepatitis
A disease in which liver function is impaired by a viral infection.

Viral hepatitis (hep-a-TĪ-tis) is a disease in which liver function is impaired by a viral infection. There are three major types of viral hepatitis: hepatitis A (formerly called infectious hepatitis), hepatitis B (formerly called serum hepatitis), and non-A/non-B hepatitis (which is caused by at least three different viruses: types C, D, and E [Filips, 1995; Lemon & Thomas, 1997]). Each of these forms of viral hepatitis is caused by a different virus.

Incidence and Transmission

Hepatitis A is the most common form of viral hepatitis in the United States, followed in order of frequency by hepatitis B and non-A/non-B hepatitis. Estimates suggest that as many as 700,000 Americans are annually afflicted with acute hepatitis infections. Of this total, about 47% are hepatitis A infections and 34% are hepatitis B infections (Lemon & Thomas, 1997). Both the A and B types can be transmitted sexually, but sexual transmission of the non-A/non-B type is believed to be relatively uncommon (Lemon & Thomas, 1997; Thomas et al., 1995). It is believed that hepatitis B is transmitted more often through sexual activity than is hepatitis A (Hook et al., 1995; Sharfstein & Wise, 1997). However, hepatitis A is a relatively common infection of young homosexual men, especially those who have multiple sex partners and those who engage in anal intercourse (Katz et al., 1997). Furthermore, both A and B types are often transmitted via needle sharing among injection drug users (Katz et al., 1997; Sharfstein & Wise, 1997).

Hepatitis B may be transmitted via blood or blood products, semen, vaginal secretions, and saliva (Bertino et al., 1997). Manual, oral, or penile stimulation of the anus are practices strongly associated with the spread of this viral agent. Hepatitis A seems to be spread primarily via the fecal–oral route (Kools, 1992). Consequently, epidemics often occur when infected handlers of food do not wash their hands properly after using the bathroom. Oral–anal sexual contact seems to be a primary mode for sexual transmission of hepatitis A. However, in one recent study of 411 homosexual and bisexual men, of the 28% who tested positive for hepatitis A infection, very few reported participating in oral–anal intercourse. Instead, genital–anal intercourse was found to be significantly associated with infection, which led the researchers to speculate that "men touched their penis after withdrawal and subsequently touched their mouth" (Katz et al., 1997, p. 1228). These investigators also noted that a systematic underreporting of oral–anal sexual contact could explain the lack of association between this behavior and transmission of hepatitis A to the study participants.

Symptoms and Complications

Symptoms of viral hepatitis may vary from nonexistent to mild flulike symptoms (poor appetite, upset stomach, diarrhea, sore muscles, fatigue, headache) to an incapacitating illness characterized by high fever, vomiting, and severe abdominal pain. One of the most notable signs of viral hepatitis is a yellowing of the whites of the eyes; the skin of light-complexioned people may also take on a yellow, or jaundiced, look. Hospitalization is required only in severe cases. Some evidence suggests that people who have had hepatitis B are at increased risk for developing cancer of the liver. On rare occasions, severe medical complications associated with viral hepatitis infections result in death. An estimated 16,000 people die each year of chronic liver disease associated with persistent viral hepatitis infection (Lemon & Thomas, 1997). About 5000 of these deaths are caused by hepatitis B; however, the majority—about 11,000 deaths—result from non-A/non-B hepatitis (Lemon & Thomas, 1997; Sharfstein & Wise, 1997).

Treatment

At the present time, no specific therapy is known to be effective against the various types of viral hepatitis. Treatment generally consists of bed rest and adequate fluid intake to prevent dehydration. The disease generally runs its course in a few weeks, although complete recovery may take several months in cases of severe infection.

An effective and safe vaccine to prevent hepatitis B infection has been available since 1982, and in 1995 the federal Food and Drug Administration approved an effective and safe hepatitis A vaccine. Persons at high risk for contracting either of these vaccines should seriously consider getting immunized. These high-risk people include health care workers who are exposed to blood, injection drug users and their sex partners, homosexual and bisexual men, heterosexually active persons with multiple sexual partners, sexual partners or housemates of people infected with the hepatitis A or B virus, people with chronic liver disease, and military personnel working in field conditions (Filips, 1995; Sharfstein & Wise, 1997).

Common Vaginal Infections

Several kinds of vaginal infections can be transmitted through sexual interaction. The infections we discuss in this section are also frequently contracted through nonsexual means. *Vaginitis* and *leukorrhea* are general terms applied to a variety of vaginal infections characterized by a whitish discharge. The secretion may also be yellow or green because of the presence of pus cells, and it often has a disagreeable odor. Additional symptoms of vaginitis may include irritation and itching of the genital tissue, burning during urination, and pain around the vaginal opening during intercourse.

Vaginal infections are very common. Practically every woman experiences one or more of these infections during her life. In fact, vaginitis is one of the most common reasons women consult health care providers. Under typical circumstances, many of the organisms that cause vaginal infections are relatively harmless. In fact, some routinely live in the vagina and cause no trouble unless something alters the normal vaginal environment and allows them to overgrow. The vagina normally houses bacteria (lactobacilli) that help maintain a healthy vaginal environment (Priestly et al., 1997). The pH of the vagina is usually sufficiently acidic to ward off most infections. However, certain conditions may alter the pH toward the alkaline side, which may leave a woman vulnerable to infection. Some factors that increase the likelihood of vaginal infection include antibiotic therapy, use of contraceptive pills, menstruation, pregnancy, wearing pantyhose and nylon underwear, douching, and lowered resistance from stress or lack of sleep. Recent research also suggests that the alkaline nature of seminal fluid may also be a factor in altering vaginal pH, thus increasing susceptibility to infections (Priestly et al., 1997).

Most women with vaginitis have an infection caused by *Gardnerella, Candida,* or *Trichomonas,* either alone or in combination. Bacterial vaginosis is the most common of these infections.

Bacterial Vaginosis

Bacterial vaginosis (BV) is a vaginal infection typically caused by a bacterium known as *Gardnerella vaginalis* (Nilsson et al., 1997; Priestly et al., 1997).

Bacterial vaginosis
A vaginal infection, usually caused by a bacterium called *Gardnerella vaginalis,* that may be the most common form of vaginitis among American women.

Incidence and Transmission

Not long ago, the *Gardnerella vaginalis* bacterium was dismissed as a harmless organism in the normal vaginal flora. However, it is now recognized that although the presence of some *Gardnerella vaginalis* bacteria in the vaginal flora is normal, an increased growth of the organism together with a decrease in lactobacilli results in the development of bacterial vaginosis (MacDermott, 1995). There is evidence that overgrowth of *Gardnerella vaginalis* bacteria is perhaps the most common cause of vaginitis in American women (Easmon et al., 1992). A recent study of 956 women attending family planning clinics in

Sweden reported that 131 (13.7%) of the participants were diagnosed with BV (Nilsson et al., 1997). Many male partners of women with diagnosed bacterial vaginosis also harbor the *Gardnerella vaginalis* organism, usually without any clinical symptoms (Nilsson et al., 1997). Although the role of sexual transmission in BV is not fully understood, it is believed that coitus often provides a mode for transmission of the infection. However, BV is not necessarily sexually transmitted in that this infection has been diagnosed in women who are not sexually active (Nilsson et al., 1997; Priestly et al., 1997).

Symptoms and Complications

The most prominent symptom of bacterial vaginosis in women is a foul-smelling, thin discharge that resembles flour paste in consistency. The discharge is usually gray, but it may also be white, yellow, or green. The disagreeable odor, often noticed first by an infected woman's sexual partner, is typically described as fishy or musty. This smell may be particularly noticeable after coitus because the alkaline seminal fluid reacts with the bacteria, causing the release of the chemicals that produce the smell. A small number of infected women experience irritation of the genital tissues and mild burning during urination. Recent evidence suggests a link between bacterial vaginosis and both pelvic inflammatory disease and adverse pregnancy outcome, including premature rupture of the amniotic sac and preterm labor (Newton et al., 1997; Nilsson et al., 1997). As mentioned earlier, most men are asymptomatic. However, some males infected with *Gardnerella vaginalis* develop inflammation of the foreskin and glans of the penis, **urethritis** (inflammation of the urethral tube), and **cystitis** (bladder infection).

Urethritis
An inflammation of the urethral tube.

Cystitis
An inflammation of the urethra or bladder, characterized by discomfort during urination.

Treatment

For many years the treatment of choice for bacterial vaginosis has been metronidazole (Flagyl) by mouth for seven days. However, recent research indicates that intravaginal application of topical metronidazole gel or clindamycin cream are as effective as oral metronidazole (Atkins, 1997a; Centers for Disease Control, 1998b). Furthermore, women report more satisfaction with the topical intravaginal preparations than with the oral drug (Atkins, 1997a). Studies indicate that there is little or no proven benefit of treatment of sex partners of women diagnosed with BV (Centers for Disease Control, 1998b; Mead & Eschenbach, 1998). However, some health practitioners recommend treating partners in cases of recurrent BV infection (Braverman & Strasburger, 1994b).

Candidiasis

Candidiasis (kan-de-DI-a-sis), also commonly referred to as *moniliasis* or a *yeast infection,* is primarily caused by a yeastlike fungus called *Candida albicans.*

Candidiasis
An inflammatory infection of the vaginal tissues caused by the yeastlike fungus *Candida albicans.*

Incidence and Transmission

Candidiasis is the second most common vaginal infection in North America (Sobel et al., 1998) encountered by health practitioners. An estimated 13 million cases of vaginal candidiasis occur annually in the United States (Spinillo et al., 1997). The microscopic *Candida albicans* organism is normally present in the vagina of many women; it also inhabits the mouth and large intestine of large numbers of women and men. A disease state results only when certain conditions allow the yeast to overgrow other microorganisms in the vagina. This accelerated growth may result from pregnancy, use of birth control pills, or diabetes—conditions that increase the amount of sugar stored in vaginal cells (*Candida albicans* thrives in the presence of sugar). If a nonpregnant woman has repeated yeast infections, it may be advisable for her to be tested for diabetes or other blood sugar disorders. Another factor is the use of oral antibiotics, which reduce the number of lactobacilli (mentioned earlier as important for a healthy vaginal environment). This reduction permits *Candida albicans* to multiply rapidly.

Diet can play an important role in the incidence of candidiasis. Eating large amounts of dairy products, sugar, and artificial sweeteners leads to the excessive excretion of urine sugars that may promote *Candida albicans* overgrowth. Reducing the intake of these substances can dramatically reduce the frequency of yeast infections.

If the yeast organism is not already present in the woman's vagina, it may be transmitted to this area in a variety of ways. It can be conveyed from the anus by wiping back-to-front or on the surface of a menstrual pad, or it can be transmitted through sexual interaction because the organism may be harbored under the foreskin of an uncircumcised man. The organism can also be passed from a partner's mouth to a woman's vagina during oral sex (Greer, 1998).

Some health professionals maintain that candidiasis should not be considered an STD, because it can occur in women who are not sexually active (Braverman & Strasburger, 1994b; Greer, 1998).

Symptoms

A woman with a yeast infection may notice that she has a white, clumpy discharge that looks something like cottage cheese. In addition, candidiasis is often associated with intense itching and soreness of the vaginal and vulval tissues, which typically become red and dry. A woman who has a yeast infection may find coitus quite painful, and irritation from intercourse may worsen the infection.

Treatment

A variety of treatments may prove effective in combating yeast infections. Traditional treatment strategies consist of vaginal suppositories or topical creams such as clotrimazole, miconazole, butoconazole, or terconazole. Over-the-counter intravaginal preparations of clotrimazole and miconazole are now available for treatment of candidiasis; however, these are recommended only for women who have previously been medically diagnosed and treated and who have a recurrence of symptoms (Atkins, 1997b). Research indicates that many women incorrectly diagnose themselves as having vaginal candidiasis and thus commence a course of self-treatment with over-the-counter antifungal medications (Ferris et al., 1996; Mead & Eschenbach, 1998). Even though women who self-treat conditions mistaken for candidiasis may eventually realize their error and seek medical attention, this delay in treatment can have serious consequences (Atkins, 1997b).

A drug taken by mouth, fluconazole, has also proven to be effective in treating candidiasis (Greer, 1998). Because *Candida albicans* is a hardy organism, treatment should be continued for the prescribed length of time (usually several days to two weeks), even though the symptoms may disappear in two days.

Trichomoniasis

Trichomoniasis (trick-ō-mon-ī-ah-sis) is caused by a one-celled protozoan parasite called *Trichomonas vaginalis.*

Trichomoniasis
A form of vaginitis caused by a one-celled protozoan called *Trichomonas vaginalis.*

Incidence and Transmission

In females, trichomoniasis accounts for about one-fourth of all cases of vaginitis. An estimated 20% of women experience one or more trichomoniasis infections sometime during their reproductive years (Sharts-Hopco, 1997). Not all infected women have noticeable symptoms. Men may carry the infection too, but they generally have no observable symptoms. Nevertheless, some authorities believe that most male sex partners of infected women carry the *Trichomonas vaginalis* organism in their urethras and under the foreskin if they are uncircumcised. The primary mode of transmission of this infection is through sexual contact (Hook et al., 1995).

Symptoms and Complications

The most common symptom of trichomoniasis infection in women is an abundant, frothy, white or yellow-green vaginal discharge with an unpleasant odor. The discharge frequently irritates the tissues of the vagina and vulva, causing them to become inflamed, itchy, and sore. The infection is usually limited to the vagina and sometimes the cervix, but occasionally the organism may invade the urethra, bladder, or Bartholin's glands. Some health specialists believe that long-term trichomonal infection may damage the cells of the cervix and increase susceptibility to cervical cancer. However, prompt, effective treatment prevents permanent cervical damage.

Treatment

To avoid passing the disease back and forth, it is important that the male partner(s) of the infected woman be treated even if asymptomatic (Centers for Disease Control, 1998b). A cure rate of approximately 95% occurs when both sexual partners are treated simultaneously (Moran, 1997a). If a male partner is not treated, the couple should use condoms to prevent reinfection. The recommended drug regimen for both sexes is a single 2-gram dose of metronidazole (Flagyl) taken by mouth. Metronidazole is strongly contraindicated in the first trimester of pregnancy. Topical creams, such as clotrimazole, may provide symptomatic improvement and some cures in women unable to take metronidazole (Moran, 1997a).

Ectoparasitic Infections

Ectoparasites
Parasitic organisms that live on the outer skin surfaces.

Ectoparasites are parasitic organisms that live on the outer skin surfaces of humans and other animals (*ecto* means "outer"). *Trichomonas vaginalis,* discussed in the previous section, is an *endoparasite* (*endo* means "inner") that causes an infection within the vagina. Two relatively common STDs are caused by ectoparasites: pubic lice and scabies.

Pubic Lice

Pubic lice
Lice that primarily infest the pubic hair and are transmitted by sexual contact.

Pubic lice, more commonly called "crabs," belong to a group of parasitic insects called biting lice. They are known technically as *Phthirus pubis.* Although very tiny, adult lice are visible to the eye. They are yellowish-gray in appearance, and under magnification resemble a crab, as Figure 17.6 shows. A pubic louse generally grips a pubic hair with its claws and sticks its head into the skin, where it feeds on blood from tiny blood vessels.

Incidence and Transmission

Pubic lice are quite common and are seen frequently in public health clinics and by private physicians. They are often transmitted during sexual contact when two people bring their pubic areas together. Crabs may live away from the body for as long as one day, particularly if their stomachs are full of blood. They may drop off onto underclothes, bedsheets, sleeping bags, and so forth. Eggs deposited by the female louse on clothing or bedsheets may survive for several days. Thus, it is possible to get pubic lice by sleeping in someone else's bed or by wearing his or her clothes. Furthermore, a successfully treated person may be reinfected by being exposed to her or his own unwashed sheets or underclothes. Pubic lice do not necessarily limit themselves to the genital areas. They may be transmitted, usually by fingers, to the armpits or scalp.

Symptoms

Most people begin to suspect something is amiss when they start itching. Suspicions become stronger when scratching brings no relief. However, a few people seem to have

Figure 17.6

A pubic louse, or "crab."

great tolerance for the bite of a louse, experiencing very little if any discomfort. Self-diagnosis is possible simply by locating a louse on a pubic hair.

Treatment

The recommended regimen for treatment of pubic lice is 1% permethrin cream rinse applied to all affected areas and washed off after 10 minutes (Centers for Disease Control, 1998b). It is advisable to apply the cream to all areas where there are concentrations of body hair—the genitals, armpits, scalp, and even eyebrows. Scalp hair is treated with 1% Lindane shampoo applied for 4 minutes and then thoroughly washed off. These treatments should be repeated seven days later (eggs take seven days to hatch). Be sure to wash all clothes and sheets that were used prior to treatment.

Scabies

Scabies is caused by a tortoise-shaped parasitic mite with four stubby legs called *Sarcoptes scabiei.* Unlike pubic lice, mites are too tiny to be seen by the naked eye. Scabies infestations are initiated by the female mite; after mating, she burrows beneath the skin to lay her eggs, which hatch shortly thereafter. Each hatched egg becomes a full-grown adult in 10 to 20 days. The adult ectoparasitic mite forages for nourishment in its host's skin that is adjacent to the site of the original burrow. The average person with scabies is infested with 10 to 15 live adult female mites (Schleicher & Stewart, 1997).

Scabies
An ectoparasitic infestation of tiny mites.

Incidence and Transmission

Although scabies is not among those infectious diseases reported to health organizations in America and elsewhere, "it is safe to say it affects millions of people worldwide" (Schleicher & Stewart, 1997, p. 54). Scabies is a highly contagious condition that may be transmitted by close physical contact between people, both sexual and nonsexual. The mites may also be transferred on clothing or bedding, where they can remain viable for up to 48 hours (Schleicher & Stewart, 1997). In addition to sexually active people, schoolchildren, nursing home residents, and the indigent are especially at risk for scabies infestations.

Symptoms

Small vesicles or pimplelike bumps occur in the area where the female mite tunnels into the skin. A red rash around the primary lesion indicates the area where hatched adult mites are feeding. Areas of infestation itch intensely, especially at night. Favorite sites of infestation typically include the webs and sides of fingers, wrists, abdomen, genitals, buttocks, and female breasts.

Treatment

Scabies is treated with a topical scabicide that is applied from the neck down to the toes. The current scabicide of choice is one ounce (30 grams) of 5% permethrin lotion or cream applied at bed time and left on for 8 to 14 hours, then washed off with soap and water (Centers for Disease Control, 1998b). A single application is usually effective, although some physicians advocate a second treatment in one week. It is recommended that all household members and close contacts with an infested person, including asymptomatic ones, be treated simultaneously. In addition, all clothing and bedding used by treated people should be washed in hot water or dry cleaned.

Acquired Immunodeficiency Syndrome (AIDS)

Acquired immunodeficiency syndrome (AIDS)
A catastrophic illness in which a virus (HIV) invades and destroys the ability of the immune system to fight disease. HIV appears to be passed primarily through sexual contact, needle sharing among injection drug users, or less commonly, through administration of contaminated blood products.

Human immunodeficiency virus (HIV)
An immune-system-destroying virus that causes AIDS.

The **acquired immunodeficiency syndrome (AIDS)** epidemic, which constitutes a worldwide public health threat of rapidly increasing magnitude, is now recognized as the most serious disease epidemic of our time. In the United States, AIDS is the second leading cause of death, after accidents, among persons ages 25–44 years (Centers for Disease Control, 1997d). An all-out research assault on this deadly disease, unprecedented in scope and extent, is being conducted throughout the world, and new findings are surfacing with startling rapidity. Consequently, it is very likely that at least some of the information that follows will be obsolete by the time you read it.

AIDS results from infection with a virus called **human immunodeficiency virus (HIV).** HIV falls within a special category of viruses called *retroviruses,* so named because they reverse the usual order of reproduction within the cells they infect, a process called *reverse transcription.*

In recent years, it has become clear that more than one virus is linked with the development of AIDS. The first virus to be identified, and the one that causes the greatest number of AIDS cases, has been designated as human immunodeficiency virus type 1 (HIV-1). This virus appears to be the most virulent member of a growing family of AIDS and AIDS-related viruses. HIV is a formidable enemy in that it is constantly mutating and is present in multiple strains. To simplify our discussion of AIDS in the following pages, we refer to the infectious agent simply as HIV.

In spite of a great deal of speculation and theorizing, the origin of AIDS remains undetermined. It has been variously proposed that HIV came from residents of Africa or Haiti, mosquitoes, monkeys, and pigs. However, "precisely where, when, and why HIV began to spread in human populations cannot be determined. Although the first AIDS cases to be recognized and reported were in the United States in 1981, it is clear from retrospective studies that this syndrome has been occurring in several other areas of the world since the mid-1970s" (Chin & Mann, 1990, p. 128). A recent discovery of a version of HIV in a frozen blood sample collected in 1959 from an adult African male (Zhu et al., 1998) suggests that HIV had a human history long before it went global, perhaps as early as the late 1940s (Wain-Hobson, 1998).

HIV specifically targets and destroys the body's CD4 lymphocytes, also called T-helper cells or helper T-4 cells. In healthy people, these cells coordinate the immune system's response to disease. The impairment of the immune system resulting from HIV infection leaves the body vulnerable to a variety of cancers and opportunistic infections

(infections that take hold because of the reduced effectiveness of the immune system). Initially, HIV infection was diagnosed as AIDS only when the immune system became so seriously impaired that the person developed one or more severe, debilitating diseases, such as pneumonia or cancer. However, effective January 1, 1993, the CDC broadened this definition of AIDS to include anyone infected with HIV whose immune system is severely impaired. Now anyone who is HIV infected and has a CD4 count of 200 cells per cubic millimeter of blood or less is considered to have full-blown AIDS, regardless of other symptoms. (Normal CD4 cell counts in healthy people not infected with HIV range from 600 to 1200 per cubic millimeter of blood.)

This revised definition emerged as the result of intense criticism that the earlier definition was too restrictive. More specifically, it did not include manifestations of HIV disease common among women and injection drug users, such as invasive cervical cancer, bacterial pneumonia, and pulmonary tuberculosis. Furthermore, the new definition, "by using a marker of immune deficiency to define AIDS, avoids the problem of piecemeal addition of newly recognized manifestations of HIV infection" (Chang et al., 1992, p. 973). By moving the AIDS diagnostic label earlier into the disease continuum, the new definition has generally resulted in persons being diagnosed with AIDS one to two years earlier, on average, in their illness.

Incidence

By January 1998, almost 645,000 cumulative cases of AIDS had been reported in the United States, and almost 400,000 had died of the disease since it was first diagnosed in 1981. An estimated 650,000 to more than 1 million people in the United States are currently infected with HIV (Steinbrook, 1997). To date, about 31 million people worldwide are HIV infected. (For a perspective on the worldwide AIDS epidemic, see the boxed discussion, "A Global View of HIV/AIDS.") Figure 17.7 provides an overview of the worldwide incidence of HIV infection.

The number of new AIDS cases reported annually in the United States grew rapidly through the early 1980s, increasing by about 85% per year, reaching a peak growth rate in the middle of the decade. The rate of new AIDS diagnoses slowed in the late 1980s, and this more moderate rate has continued into the 1990s. Table 17.2 provides detailed information about people, aged 13 and older, diagnosed with AIDS in the period 1992

Table 17.2 Number and Percentage of Persons Aged 13 Years or Older Reported with AIDS, by Sex and Race/Ethnicity—United States, 1981–1996

	Year of report											
	1992		*1993**		*1994*		*1995*		*1996*		*1981–1996*	
Characteristic	*No.*	*%*	*No.*	*%*	*No.*	*%*	*No.*	*%*	*No.*	*%*	*No.*	*%*
Sex												
Male	40,330	86	87,945	84	64,730	82	59,285	81	54,653	80	488,300	85
Female	6,307	14	16,671	16	13,830	18	13,682	19	13,820	20	85,500	15
Race/Ethnicity												
White	22,320	48	47,468	45	32,677	42	29,402	40	26,229	38	267,487	47
Black	15,576	33	37,523	36	30,373	39	28,729	39	28,346	41	198,780	35
Hispanic	8,223	18	18,410	18	14,612	19	13,961	19	12,966	19	101,253	18
Other	518	1	1,215	1	898	1	875	1	932	1	6,280	1
Total	46,637		104,616		78,560		72,967		68,473		573,800	

*Year the expanded AIDS case definition was implemented

Source: Centers for Disease Control, 1997d.

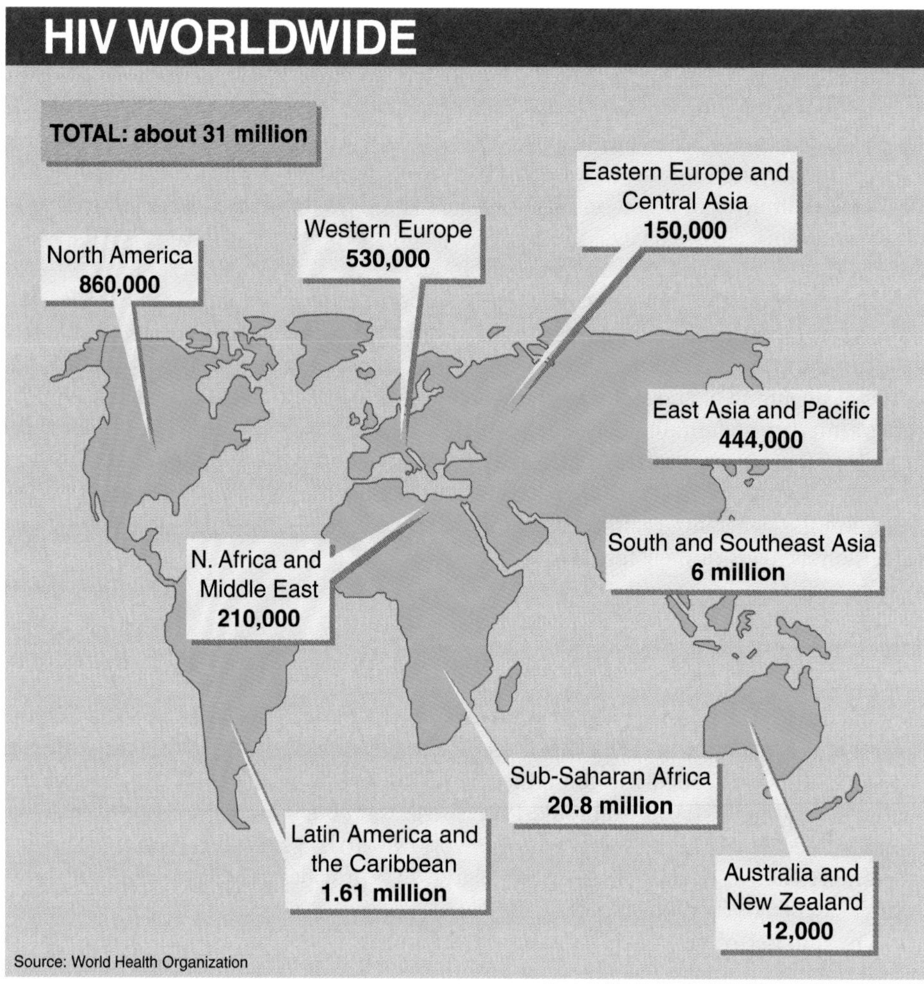

Figure 17.7

Worldwide distribution of HIV infections in 1997.

through 1996. The dramatic increase in total reported new AIDS cases in 1993 represents the one-time effect of the broadening of the AIDS definition at the beginning of 1993. A steady decline in reported AIDS cases from 1994 through 1996 is consistent with the belief that the AIDS epidemic in the United States has leveled off. However, it is indeed sobering to note that the 68,473 new AIDS cases reported during 1996 was substantially higher (47%) than the number reported during 1992.

You will also note in Table 17.2 that from 1992 through 1996 women, African Americans, and Hispanic Americans accounted for increasing proportions of reported AIDS cases. In 1996 women accounted for an all-time high of 20% of persons aged 13 and older reported with AIDS. Furthermore, ethnic/racial minority groups account for the greatest percentage of reported AIDS cases, approximately 62% in 1996. In 1996, 41% of reported AIDS cases were African Americans, exceeding for the first time the proportion who were white Americans (38%). The higher AIDS rates among ethnic/racial minority groups may reflect, among other factors, (1) reduced access to health care associated with disadvantaged socioeconomic status, (2) cultural or language barriers that limit access to information about strategies for preventing STDs, and (3) differences in HIV risk behavior, especially higher rates of injection drug use (Centers for Disease Control, 1997d; Searight & McClaren, 1997; Stone et al., 1997).

Since AIDS first appeared in the United States, most cases (more than 80%) have been directly or indirectly related to two risk-exposure categories: men who have sex with men (MSM) and injection drug use (IDU) (Graham, 1997). However, some significant shifting trends in exposure risk categories have begun to emerge in recent years. The proportion of reported AIDS cases among MSM has declined nearly 20%, from 64% during

1981–1987 to 45% during 1993–1995. However, during the same time period the cases attributable to IDU increased from 17% during 1981–1987 to 27% during 1993–1995. Furthermore, cases attributable to heterosexual transmission rose from 3 to 10% during the same time periods (see Table 17.3). During the first six months of 1996, reported cases attributable to heterosexual contact increased to 12%, a trend that reflects, among other factors, "transmission from the large population of IDUs with HIV/AIDS to their heterosexual partners" (Centers for Disease Control, 1997d, p. 171).

The pronounced rise in cases attributable to heterosexual contact is reflected in the rapid increase in cases reported among U.S. women over the past decade. The number of new AIDS cases among women in 1996 was more than double the 1992 rate. In fact, Table 17.2 shows that although the overall incidence of AIDS among men has actually declined slightly in the period 1992–1996, it has steadily increased among women. This data indicates that "a mini-epidemic is occurring among women that is uncomfortably similar to the early years of the epidemic among MSM" (Graham, 1997, p. 4). AIDS is now the third leading cause of death for all U.S. women ages 25–44 years (Stone et al., 1997).

Despite the fact that the largest percentage of HIV infections in the United States and other industrialized nations have been transmitted by MSM, sexual transmission of HIV is clearly not dependent on sexual orientation. As we have seen, in the United States the pattern of transmission is beginning to change, with an acceleration of the heterosexual AIDS epidemic occurring at the same time that rates are slowing among MSM (see Table 17.3). Furthermore, in developing countries, especially Africa, Asia, the Caribbean, and Latin America, heterosexual contact has always been the primary form of HIV transmission (Skurnick et al., 1998). In Africa, where the majority of worldwide HIV infections exist, it has been estimated that 80% of HIV infections are acquired through heterosexual transmission (Fiore et al., 1997).

Even though it has been speculated that the AIDS epidemic in the United States might plateau during the next five years, "it appears that a second-wave epidemic may be

Sexuality and Diversity

A Global View of HIV/AIDS

According to the World Health Organization (WHO), by late 1997 about 31 million people worldwide were infected with HIV, the vast majority of whom live in developing nations (see Figure 17.7). WHO predicts that this number will reach 40 million or more by the year 2000, with 90% of this total living in developing countries in Africa, Asia, Latin America, and the Caribbean. Furthermore, by the end of this century it is estimated that at least two million people worldwide will die each year of AIDS (Adler, 1997).

Nearly 70% of the world's HIV-infected people live in Africa. In some sub-Saharan African nations (countries below the Sahara Desert), such as South Africa, the number of HIV-infected persons is doubling every 5 to 12 months (Tyson, 1996), and AIDS is currently the leading cause of adult death in several of these countries. By the year 2000, it is estimated that at least 10% of Kenya's population will be infected with HIV. One out of six adults in Botswana, Zambia, and Zimbabwe is HIV positive (Stein & Susser, 1997). In Zambia, where STDs account for almost half of all visits to hospitals, over 50% of hospital-treated patients test positive for HIV (Faxelid & Ramstedt, 1997). In Uganda, one of the nations most devastated by AIDS, almost every family has been touched by this dread disease.

According to WHO, the rate of HIV infections is higher for women than men in most African nations. In several large cities in Africa, one out of three pregnant women are HIV infected (Bogert et al., 1995). A large percentage of these women are monogamous but nevertheless have been infected by husbands who, "according to longstanding African tradition, are not" (Bogert et al., 1995, p. 52). According to one expert on African cultural traditions, African women "who are conditioned to their husbands having other women, are not in a position to negotiate safe sex, with the result that they develop reproductive tract infections which, in turn, increase their risk of contracting HIV" (Haslegrave, 1997, p. s11). In one recent study almost 4000 men and women in Nigeria were interviewed regarding their attitudes about male sexual behavior. The majority of the respondents, both males and females, indicated that men are naturally nonmonogamous irrespective of their marital status (Orubuloye et al., 1997). The wide-

(continued on next page)

Table 17.3 Percentage of Adult and Adolescent AIDS Cases in the United States by Exposure Category During Three Time Periods

Exposure Category	*1981–1987*	*1988–1992*	*1993–1995*
Men who have sex with men	64.0%	54.6%	44.9%
Injection drug use	17.2%	24.2%	27.3%
Heterosexual contact	2.5%	6.1%	10.1%

Source: Graham, 1997.

gaining momentum outside the traditional exposure categories, population groups, and geographic areas hit hardest by the first wave" (Graham, 1997, p. 2). An escalation of AIDS in young age categories and those due to heterosexual contact represent relatively recent trends suggesting that "HIV infection is an endemic problem that will affect successive generations" (Graham, 1997, p. 2). The AIDS epidemic in the United States has also recently extended its geographic reach from first-wave concentrations in large metropolitan areas (populations in excess of 500,000 people) in the Northeast and West to second-wave smaller cities and rural areas in the Midwest and South. In fact, during the two-year period from 1993 to 1995, higher proportions of new reported cases occurred among people living in smaller cities and rural areas in the South and Midwest than in the West and the Northeast (Centers for Disease Control, 1995c). Nevertheless, the largest number of AIDS cases remain concentrated in large metropolitan areas where rates are two to three times higher than in smaller cities and about five times higher than rural areas. At the present time the four metropolitan areas with the highest annual rates of AIDS per 100,000 population are New York; Miami; Jersey City, N.J.; and San Francisco (Centers for Disease Control, 1997e).

Sexuality and Diversity

spread nature of these cultural beliefs in African nations is just one of many factors that impede efforts to slow the HIV/AIDS pandemic in this hardest-hit area of the world.

Africa is not alone in suffering the ravages of the HIV/AIDS pandemic. The continent of Asia now ranks second to Africa in the number of cases of HIV/AIDS, and many world health experts fear that in the near future Asia may surpass Africa, led by countries such as India and Thailand, where HIV/AIDS is fast becoming endemic in the population. HIV/AIDS is also rapidly expanding in Latin America. As in Africa, HIV is primarily transmitted by heterosexual activity in both Asia and Latin America, and women are often the hardest hit by this deadly epidemic.

Thailand is a country that has seen the epidemic sweep through its population with unprecedented speed since the first case of AIDS was reported in 1984 (Maticka-Tyndale et al., 1997). An estimated 700,000 to 1 million Thai citizens are already HIV infected (Gray et al., 1997). One of the primary reasons why the HIV epidemic is raging in Thailand is that a commercial sex industry flourishes in this country, where it is something of a cultural tradition for men to use the services of a prostitute. One recent study found that 50% of married men and 43% of single men had visited a female prostitute sometime in their lives, and that 13% of married men had done so within the previous year (Maticka-Tyndale et al., 1997). This is an especially troubling finding in light of other research indicating that over 50% of Thailand's female sex workers are HIV infected (Gray et al., 1997). Thai health officials, worried that the epidemic may be beyond control through traditional safer sex programs (condom distribution, etc.), are preparing to implement a more daring prevention plan in the near future—a large-scale human population study of an HIV vaccine (see discussion on page 529 of this chapter).

The infection of infants at birth or shortly thereafter is fast emerging as an especially tragic consequence of the global HIV/AIDS pandemic. WHO estimates that well over a million children worldwide are infected with HIV, the majority in sub-Saharan Africa. Babies often acquire HIV from their mothers through breast-feeding. As awareness of this mode of transmission increases, another dimension might be added to the horror of Africa's HIV/AIDS tragedy. Clearly, many African children, who live in conditions of poverty, would suffer from lack of proper nourishment if they could no longer be breast-fed.

Finally, one additional horrific aspect of Africa's struggle with HIV/AIDS is beginning to emerge. A recent report from the United Nations Program on HIV/AIDS estimates that there will be more than 10 million African children orphaned by the disease by the end of the century.

Many, probably the majority, of young people with AIDS were infected during their adolescent years. The growing problem of HIV infections among adolescents has been attributed to a number of factors, including the following:

- Many teenagers have multiple sexual partners, increasing their exposure to infection.
- Many adolescents engage in sexual activity without using condoms.
- Access to condoms is generally more difficult for adolescents than for other groups.
- Teenagers have very high rates of other STDs, which are often associated with HIV infection.
- Substance abuse, which often increases risky behavior, is relatively widespread among adolescents.
- Teenagers tend to be especially likely as a group to have feelings of invulnerability (see Chapter 13).

Transmission

HIV has been found in the semen, blood, vaginal secretions, saliva, urine, and breast milk of infected individuals. It also may occur in any other bodily fluids that contain blood, including cerebrospinal fluid, amniotic fluid, and so forth. Blood and semen are the two bodily fluids that most consistently contain high concentrations of the virus in infected people. Most commonly, HIV enters the body as bodily fluids are exchanged during unprotected anal or vaginal intercourse or oral–genital contact with an infected person. Transmission of HIV through sexual contact is estimated to be the cause of between 75% and 85% of the approximately 31 million HIV infections worldwide (Royce et al., 1997). HIV is also readily transmitted via blood-contaminated needles shared by injection drug users. The virus can also be passed perinatally from an infected woman to her fetus or infant before or during birth or after by breast feeding (Graham, 1997; Tess et al., 1998).

The likelihood of HIV being transmitted during sexual contact depends both on the viral dose and the routes of HIV exposure (Royce et al., 1997). Viral dose is a direct effect of the **viral load**—how much virus is present in an infected person's blood. In general, the greater the viral load the higher the chance of transmitting the infection. As common sense would suggest, when a person is in late stages of HIV/AIDS disease, with more advanced infection, and thus greater viral load, he or she is highly infectious. However, many of our readers might be surprised to hear that evidence strongly indicates that in the initial period between exposure to HIV and the appearance of HIV antibodies in the blood—a period called *primary infection* that usually lasts a few months—viral load may be very high, creating a state of heightened infectiousness (Koopman, 1996; Royce et al., 1997). This relatively brief peak in the transmissibility of HIV soon after a person is infected is especially troubling in that most infected people are likely to remain unaware during these few months that they have been invaded by HIV. Some experts believe that transmission during primary infection may account for a large portion of the HIV infections worldwide.

Viral load
How much HIV virus is present in an infected person's blood.

In reference to the routes of HIV exposure, the likelihood of infection is greater when HIV is transmitted directly into the blood (for example, through small tears in the rectal tissues or vaginal walls) than onto a mucous membrane. Despite a few reports of the virus being transmitted to the receptive partner during oral sex when HIV comes into contact with mucous membrane tissues in the mouth (Lafferty et al., 1997; Schacker et al., 1996), there has been a general tendency to view oral sex as a relatively safe practice (Cohen, 1997a). However, the results of a recent monkey study (Baba et al., 1997) cast serious doubts on just how "safe" oral sex is in the age of AIDS. In this study, researchers gently placed various concentrations of a simian version of the AIDS virus, called SIV, on the backs of the tongues of seven rhesus monkeys. Six of the monkeys became infected!

There are some important caveats to this animal study. The monkeys were exposed to cell-free SIV, whereas human oral exposure would more likely occur via HIV-infected cells, and this could make it harder to transfer an infection. Furthermore, there is some evidence that human saliva may render HIV less infectious (Cohen, 1997a; Malamud, 1997). (Even though HIV has been found in saliva, there is no documented evidence of saliva as a source of HIV infection [Lafferty et al., 1997; Malamud, 1997].) Nevertheless, this provocative study does provide strong indicators that semen from an HIV-infected man might result in transmission of the virus to another person if it comes into contact with mucosal tissues in that person's mouth. It is noteworthy that current CDC recommendations for preventing HIV transmission call for using a condom during mouth-to-penis contact. Furthermore, in light of the often substantial concentration of HIV in vaginal fluids, one might also be cautious about engaging in cunnilingus with a partner who has not tested negative for HIV.

In the early 1980s, before the federal government required screening of donated blood for HIV, contaminated blood and blood products infected an estimated 25,000 transfusion recipients and people with blood-clotting disorders (such as hemophilia) in the United States (Gilbert, 1991; Graham, 1997). However, since early 1985, donated blood and blood products have been screened with extensive laboratory testing for the presence of HIV antibodies. The recent transition from partially paid to all-volunteer donors has further enhanced the integrity of America's blood supply by eliminating persons who would donate primarily for monetary gain (Williams et al., 1997). (Health officials believe that blood donors may be less candid about their histories when offered incentives to give blood.) In addition, U.S. blood centers now use behavioral history-based screening procedures in a format of face-to-face oral interviews by trained staff. These developments have reduced the risk of transfusion-transmitted HIV to an estimated level of approximately two infections per 1 million blood units. This minuscule number of infections are due almost entirely to donations made in the early stage of primary infection before antibodies are present in the blood (Williams et al., 1997).

The late Arthur Ashe, tennis great, at a news conference with his wife announcing he had AIDS as a result of being transfused with HIV-tainted blood.

However, precautions designed to safeguard the nation's blood supply, while admirably effective, are not foolproof. One problem is that the blood test detects antibodies to HIV rather than the virus itself. And because HIV antibodies may take months, or even years in a few cases, to show up in the blood, contaminated units of blood have on rare occasions slipped by. There is, however, no danger of being infected as a result of donating blood. Blood banks, the Red Cross, and other blood-collection centers use sterile equipment and a new, disposable needle for each donor.

Recent research indicates that a small percentage of people appear to be resistant to HIV infection (Misrahi et al., 1998; Royce et al., 1997). There are documented cases of prostitutes and homosexual men who remain uninfected despite repeatedly engaging in unprotected sexual intercourse with HIV-infected partners (Dean et al., 1996; Fowke et al., 1996; Shearer & Clerici, 1995). Hopefully, research will soon unlock these mysteries of immunity and perhaps pave the way to development of better prevention/treatment strategies.

What degree of risk exists for HIV transmission through casual contact, as when sharing food, utensils, or clothing with a good friend or family member?

It is believed that the risk of transmitting HIV via saliva, tears, and urine is extremely low. Furthermore, no evidence indicates that the virus can be transmitted by casual contact such as hugging, shaking hands, cooking or eating together, or other forms of casual contact with an infected person (Courville et al., 1998). All of the research to date confirms that it is sexual contact with an infected person, or sharing contaminated needles, that places an individual at risk of HIV infection. Furthermore, certain high-risk behaviors increase the chance of infection. These behaviors include having multiple sexual partners, engaging in unprotected sex (sex without latex condoms and vaginal spermicides), sexual contact with people known to be at high risk (such as IDUs, prostitutes, and people with multiple sexual partners), and sharing drug injection equipment.

AIDS and Women

As we have seen, over the last few years the number of women infected with HIV has steadily increased in the United States and the incidence of AIDS is now increasing more rapidly among women than men. Furthermore, data from developing countries indicate that more women than men may be infected with HIV. Thus, in summary, the AIDS epidemic, which was first seen largely among men in the early years of its evolution, lately has expanded dramatically among women (Suligoi, 1997).

What explains this trend? Women are more likely than men to have sexual partners who are at risk as a result of having multiple partners, injecting drugs (there are many more male than female IDUs), or engaging in bisexual activity. In addition, research indicates that HIV is not as easily transmitted from women to men as it is from men to women (Suligoi, 1997). Thus, the risk of becoming infected through heterosexual intercourse appears to be much greater for a female with an HIV-infected male partner than for a male with an infected female partner. Some researchers note that "evidence suggests that male-to-female transmission of HIV may be at least 20 times as efficient as female-to-male transmission" (Billy et al., 1993, p. 52).

Can you think of a plausible reason why HIV is more easily transmitted from male to female than from female to male during intercourse?

One explanation for women's greater risk during heterosexual intercourse is that semen contains a much higher concentration of HIV than occurs in vaginal fluids (Forrest, 1991). In addition, a larger area of mucosal surface is exposed in the vulva and vagina than on the penis. Furthermore, some women experience unprotected anal intercourse, a high-risk behavior in that HIV transmission is thought to be five times as likely with anal intercourse as with vaginal intercourse (Seidman & Rieder, 1994). In fact, unprotected receptive anal intercourse by either sex has been shown to be associated with the highest risk of HIV infection via sexual activity (Silverman & Gross, 1997). Finally, adolescent women are particularly biologically vulnerable to HIV infection because the immature cervix is easily infected. In fact, teenage women are probably at considerably greater risk for HIV infection than adult women (Braverman & Strasburger, 1994b).

Symptoms and Complications

Like many viruses, HIV often causes a brief, flulike illness within a few weeks after initial infection (Royce et al., 1997). Symptoms may include fevers, muscle aches, skin rashes, loss of appetite, and swollen lymph glands. These initial reactions, which represent the body's defenses at work, tend to fade fairly rapidly. However, as the virus continues to deplete the immune system, other symptoms may occur, such as persistent or periodically repeating fevers, night sweats, weight loss, chronic fatigue, persistent diarrhea or bloody stools, easy bruising, persistent headaches, a chronic dry cough, and oral candidiasis (yeast). Oral candidiasis of the mouth and throat is the most common infection in HIV-infected people (Laguna et al., 1997). Many of these physical manifestations also may indicate common, everyday ailments that are by no means life-threatening. However, observing that you have one or more of these symptoms that are persistent can alert you to seek a medical diagnosis of your ailment.

HIV Antibody Tests

Within a few months of being infected with HIV, most people develop antibodies to the virus (a process called *seroconversion*). HIV infection may be detected by standard blood tests for blood serum antibodies to HIV (tests such as ELISA and Western blot). Although quite uncommon, "silent" HIV infections can be present in some individuals for three years or more before being detected by standard serum antibody tests. More costly and more labor-intensive tests for the virus itself, such as the polymerase chain reaction (PCR), may be performed to detect a silent or latent infection. Once infected with HIV, a person should be considered contagious and capable of infecting others indefinitely, regardless of whether clinical signs of disease are present. In fact, as we previously noted, the period of primary infection (sometimes also called the "window period"), that typically extends from the time of initial infection for several weeks or months forward to seroconversion, is often a period of very high infectiousness.

In the first few years after HIV antibody tests became available in 1985, many gay activist groups counseled people to avoid being tested, arguing that a positive result would cause a person to become a target of discrimination. What would be the point, they asked? The risks were great—possible discrimination, loss of job, housing, or insurance coverage—and the benefits were remote in that there was little to offer by way of effective treatments. However, recent development of better treatment strategies offer compelling reasons for those at risk to discover their HIV status as early as possible (Gostin & Webber, 1998). Current evidence favors an aggressive interventional strategy of treatment early in the course of HIV disease (Stryker & Coates, 1997). In light of dramatically improved treatment, most gay activists have changed their minds and, despite the persistence of HIV-based discrimination and stigmatization, now advocate, along with public health officials, routine HIV testing. Clearly, there are now compelling ethical and medical reasons to find and care for infected people. Furthermore, once people become aware of their

HIV/AIDS and the Law

Penny Simpson Brooke (1997), a health professional and attorney, recently published an excellent review of the literature pertaining to legal issues that involve both the people afflicted with HIV/AIDS and those involved in the management of this disease. She notes that between 1991 and 1996, over 300 cases were litigated in the courts in which HIV/AIDS was a central issue. Two of the key issues that the legal system and legislators have been contending with include (1) the confidentiality of a person's HIV status versus the need for disclosure and (2) mandatory versus voluntary HIV testing.

When a person becomes infected with HIV, who has the right to know? Does his or her HIV status have to be reported to health authorities or caregivers? What about the infected person's spouse or lover(s)—do they have a right to know? All 50 states require reporting of AIDS cases to either the CDC or state health departments, and patient consent is not required. Some states require the reporting of specific data, such as name, address, sex, and age; other states prohibit the disclosure of specific patient data. Furthermore, about three-fifths of the states also require the reporting of the names of all people who test positive for HIV, but not the ones (such as California and New York) with the largest numbers of infected persons (Steinbrook, 1997).

State confidentiality statutes generally prohibit medical personnel from disclosing a person's HIV status to anyone other than a health care provider, and several court cases have upheld these laws. Brooke provides one example of a controversial legal decision in which the staff of a mental health treatment facility in Washington, D.C., was prohibited from informing the husband of a patient that his wife had tested positive for HIV (*N.O.L. v. District of Columbia,* 674a.2d 498, [D.C. App. 1995]).

However, Brooke also notes that in recent years an increasing number of courts and state legislatures have allowed exceptions to strict confidentiality rules and permitted disclosure of a person's HIV status to people who have a "need to know." Just who falls into this category varies somewhat by state; however, most states do allow disclosure of a person's HIV status to his or

HIV status, they presumably will be much less likely to pass the infection on to others. The box "HIV/AIDS and the Law" discusses the legal issue of mandatory versus voluntary HIV testing.

Efforts to encourage testing have been focused most directly on people at higher-than-normal risk for HIV infection, including MSM, IDUs, clients at STD clinics, people who have unprotected sexual intercourse with multiple partners, and health care workers exposed to patients' blood. By 1997 more than 30 million U.S. residents had been tested for HIV, most while in the process of being screened as blood donors, applying for insurance benefits, or joining the military (Stryker & Coates, 1997). Unfortunately, an alarmingly high proportion of those at highest risk have not yet been tested (Graham, 1997; Stryker & Coates, 1997). This is especially true of men and women who engage in unprotected heterosexual intercourse with many partners (Merson et al., 1997), a very disturbing observation in light of the escalating epidemic of heterosexual transmission in North America. Clearly, when large numbers of infected people remain unaware of their infection, sometimes for many years, many will continue to pass the virus to their sexual or needle-sharing partners.

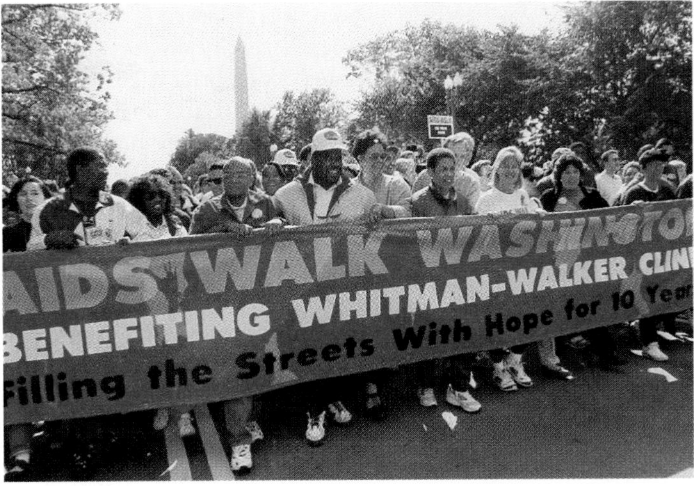

Activists rally in Washington, D.C., to dramatize the need for early and aggressive treatment of HIV/AIDS and better funding of AIDS therapy and research.

Two encouraging new developments in HIV diagnostic testing will hopefully result in more people being tested. The first breakthrough involves the recent development of an oral diagnostic testing procedure for detecting HIV antibodies in a mucosal transudate component of fluids collected from the mouth. This test, called OraSure, was approved for use by the Food and Drug Administration (FDA) in June 1996. Oral

On the Edge

her health care providers. Some states have recently taken an even more liberal approach and extended the right to know to all who are viewed as being at risk for infection. This broadening of the scope of disclosure may extend beyond a patient's primary caregivers to emergency medical personnel, morticians, and even the patient's spouse or significant other. However, although these more liberalized statutes permit a broadening of the "need to know" parameters, they do not mandate disclosure. Generally, the responsibility for decisions regarding disclosure is left up to the treating physician(s) or local health department officials. A recent and interesting departure from the trend to not mandate disclosure of a person's HIV status occurred in Florida in January 1998 when an Orlando judge ordered an HIV-infected man to obtain written consent from potential sex partners before engaging in sex with them and to file these consent forms with his probation officer (Reuters, 1998). (This man had previously been prosecuted for transmitting his HIV infection to a 16-year-old woman.)

In reference to the second issue of mandatory versus voluntary HIV testing, at the present time compulsory testing is generally prohibited by law with the exceptions of certain limited categories of people such as U.S. military personnel and inmates of federal prisons. However, some states have statutes that allow HIV testing without patient's consent in those exceptional circumstances in which health care personnel have been accidentally exposed to a person's blood.

The CDC and the U.S. Public Health Service do not support compulsory testing under any circumstances, including accidental exposure of health care providers. These federal entities argue that mandatory testing violates patients' rights to privacy, undermines the trust on which patient–provider relationships are based, and could discourage people who may be HIV-infected from seeking essential medical treatments. However, in July 1996 the powerful American Medical Association took a contrary position by endorsing mandatory testing of pregnant women and newborns. This organization based its recommendation on research evidence demonstrating that administering antiviral drugs prenatally to a pregnant HIV-infected woman and to her newborn significantly reduces the incidence of perinatal transmission of HIV (Centers for Disease Control, 1994; Frenkel et al., 1997). In February 1997, New York became the first state to require mandatory HIV testing of all newborns and the disclosure of test results to their mothers. Other states are likely to follow New York's lead in the near future.

specimens are tested for antibodies with modified ELISA and Western blot assay systems designed specifically for this purpose. Two recent studies found that OraSure demonstrated a degree of high accuracy equivalent to that achieved with tests performed on blood serum (Gallo et al., 1997; Malamud, 1997). Health experts are particularly enthusiastic about this new oral testing procedure for several reasons: (1) it eliminates the possibility of accidental HIV transmission to health care workers from puncture injuries that occur while testing for HIV; (2) it may prove to be more cost effective, because it does not require the services of a trained phlebotomist (blood drawer); and (3) it is easy to use and portable and thus available for use outside traditional medical settings. Furthermore, the noninvasiveness of the oral test may promote increased willingness to accept HIV testing, especially in those people who are needle shy.

The second development involves the marketing of self-test kits that provide people with a private, anonymous, and cost-effective way for learning their HIV status. The first generation of HIV self-tests, recently approved by the FDA, involve screening blood. The subject pricks a finger and puts a few drops of blood on a card that is mailed to a laboratory. The results are available, anonymously, by telephone within a few days. People who test positive for HIV receive counseling over the phone and referrals, if desired, to local health professionals. A recent study found that subject-collected dried blood samples yielded results as accurate as those collected by professional phlebotomists (Frank et al., 1997). Many health professionals and AIDS researchers are hopeful that these relatively new efforts to market home access, HIV self-test kits will reach people who might not otherwise seek testing. Furthermore, later versions of self-test kits may allow screening on samples of oral fluids or urine, a less invasive mode of testing that might yield even greater numbers of home HIV testers (Merson et al., 1997).*

Development of AIDS

As HIV continues to proliferate and invade healthy cells in an infected person's body, the immune system loses its capacity to defend itself against opportunistic infections. The incubation time for AIDS in adults (that is, the time between HIV infection and the onset of one or more severe, debilitating diseases associated with extreme impairment of the immune system) typically ranges from 8 to 11 years or more, with a median duration of about 10 years (Paul, 1997b). However, a small percentage of people infected with HIV remain symptom-free for much longer periods. Furthermore, as we shall see, the recent development of powerful new treatment strategies may also dramatically slow the progress of HIV/AIDS in those individuals who have access to these very costly treatments.

Patterns of disease progression have been studied extensively in adults infected with HIV. These patterns can be divided roughly into three groups (Paul, 1997b):

1. *People with rapidly progressive HIV/AIDS disease.* Research indicate that about 10% of HIV-infected adults progress to one or more of the severe diseases typical of full-blown AIDS within the first three years of infection.
2. *People with the usual pattern of progression.* These infected adults, which represent about 80–85% of infected people, demonstrate a typical pattern of progression to full-blown AIDS within approximately 10 years.
3. *People who are long-term nonprogressors.* Approximately 5–10% of HIV-infected adults are clinically asymptomatic after 7–10 years.

Viral load in the blood is an important indicator of the rate of HIV disease progression to AIDS and death (Chesebro & Everett, 1998; Louis et al., 1997; Rachlis & Zaroway, 1998). In adults who exhibit the usual pattern of progression, the initially high

*Two self-test kits have been FDA approved and marketed to date. One product called Confide, marketed by Johnson & Johnson, was recently withdrawn because of weak sales. The other product, Home Access, is currently available directly from the manufacturer (call 1-[800] HIV TEST) or from a variety of retail pharmacy outlets.

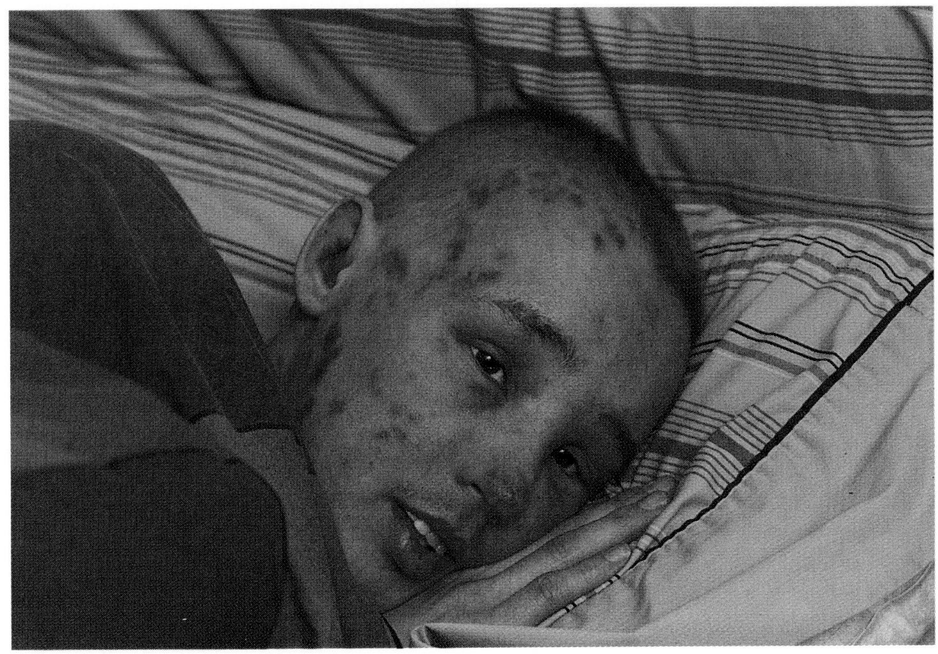

Kaposi's sarcoma, shown here with its distinctive skin lesions, is the most common cancer afflicting people with AIDS.

viral load present during the early weeks or months of primary infection begins to diminish as the anti-HIV immune response kicks in. However, rapid progressors have a high viral load that does not appreciably fall after the initial period of primary infection. Finally, and predictably, viral load is generally the lowest in adults who are nonprogressors (Paul, 1997b).

In the absence of definitive, clarifying data, explanations for nonprogression have relied primarily on two theories: (1) that mutant strains of HIV exist that are unable to reproduce as well as other strains or (2) that some infected individuals' immune systems mount a "super response" to HIV that wards off disease progression. Clearly, unraveling the mysteries of those who do not progress normally to AIDS would be a crucial breakthrough that could have a profound impact on the treatment of the large majority of people who do progress to AIDS.

As the disease progresses to full-blown AIDS, people may experience a range of serious, life-threatening complications. The most common severe infectious disease among HIV-infected people, and one that accounts for many AIDS deaths, is pneumocystic carinii pneumonia, caused by overgrowth of a microorganism that normally inhabits the lungs of healthy people (Turner et al., 1995). There are indications that HIV-infected people are at least 100 times more susceptible to developing pneumonia than people who are not HIV infected (Rodriguez-Barradas et al., 1997). Some other opportunistic infections associated with HIV include shingles and cytomegalovirus (caused by herpes viruses), encephalitis (viral infection of the brain), severe fungal infections that cause a type of meningitis, tuberculosis, and salmonella illnesses (bacterial diseases), and toxoplasmosis (caused by a protozoan). The body is also vulnerable to cancers such as lymphomas (cancers of the lymph system), cervical cancer, and Kaposi's sarcoma, the most common cancer in AIDS patients, which affects approximately 20% of these people (Foreman et al., 1997).

Once an AIDS patient develops life-threatening illnesses, such as pneumonia or cancer, the disease tends to run a fairly rapid course. Death usually occurs in one to two years for both men and women (Suligoi, 1997). Children with perinatally acquired HIV (passed from mother to fetus or infant) tend to progress more rapidly and have shorter survival times overall than HIV-infected adults (Paul, 1997b).

A majority of people (over 60%) who have developed AIDS since the beginning of the epidemic in the United States have already died. However, data released by the CDC indicated a significant recent decline in AIDS deaths in the United States—down 19% in the first nine months of 1996, the first year that deaths have declined since the onset of the epidemic. This reversal in death trends is largely due to dramatic improvement in combination drug therapies to be discussed in the following section. Unfortunately, no such reversal is occurring worldwide, especially in Africa and Asia, where HIV/AIDS is continuing to escalate both in numbers of infections and deaths. The high cost and difficulty of administering new and better therapies are barriers to their effective use in poor, undeveloped nations.

Treatment

At the time of writing this edition, there is still no cure for HIV/AIDS. However, thousands of scientists are involved in an unprecedented, worldwide effort to ultimately cure and/or prevent this horrific disease. These efforts are being waged on several fronts, including attempts to develop effective antiviral drugs that will kill or at least neutralize HIV, and efforts to create a vaccine effective against HIV. As we shall see, recent and dramatic improvements in drug therapy strategies have created a great deal of enthusiasm and optimism among AIDS specialists.

As described earlier, HIV is classified as a retrovirus because, after invading a living cell, it works backward, using an enzyme called *reverse transcriptase,* to make a DNA (deoxyribonucleic acid) copy called a provirus that directs further synthesis of its own RNA (ribonucleic acid). HIV also encodes another enzyme called a *protease* (protein-digesting) that is equally critical to its reproduction. Once HIV invades a host CD4 cell, it eventually takes over the host cell's genetic material and manufacturing capacity, producing additional viruses to infect other cells. During this process, HIV kills the host cell and injects copies of its own lethal RNA into the blood to invade other healthy cells.

To date, most treatment strategies have focused on drug intervention designed to block the proliferation and seeding of HIV throughout the immune system and other bodily tissues and organs. Until recently, the main class of drugs employed to combat HIV were drugs that inhibited the action of the reverse transcriptase enzyme. These reverse transcriptase inhibitor drugs, such as zidovudine (also known as AZT), were designed to prevent the virus from copying its own genetic material and making more viruses. Unfortunately, this early class of antiviral drugs provided only modest and transitory clinical benefits to HIV-infected people (Volberding, 1994). However, a number of studies have conclusively demonstrated that zidovudine taken during pregnancy can substantially reduce the risk of perinatal HIV transmission from an infected woman to her fetus (Centers for Disease Control, 1998c; Simonds et al., 1998).

A major breakthrough in antiviral drug therapy took place with the emergence of a new class of drugs that inhibit HIV's protease enzyme, which the virus uses to assemble new copies of itself. By early 1997 the FDA had approved four protease inhibitors for treatment of HIV/AIDS: ritonavir, nelfinavir, indinavir, and saquinavir.

Triple Drug Therapy

When a protease inhibitor is combined with two of the older reverse transcriptase inhibitors, the combination can, in many cases, reduce the viral load in blood plasma to minimal or undetectable levels (Louis et al., 1997; Montaner et al., 1998; Volberding, 1998). For example, in one study 18 of 21 patients who took the protease inhibitor indinavir plus zidovudine and lamivudine (both reverse transcriptase inhibitors) had undetectable or extremely low levels of HIV in the blood and lymph nodes after 68 weeks of treatment (Wong et al., 1997). In another study, which employed an identical three-drug regimen, 90% of 97 patients had undetectable levels of HIV in their blood after 48 weeks of therapy (Gulick et al., 1996).

The use of a combination of three antiviral drugs, which has come to be known in the literature as triple drug therapy, or in the popular media as the "AIDS cocktail," has led to a surge of optimism that this advance in antiviral drug therapy may not only delay HIV/AIDS progression but also ultimately eradicate the virus (Wong-Staal, 1997). Triple drug therapy has already provided dramatic increases in the longevity of some HIV-infected persons (Katzenstein, 1997; Laurence, 1998; Palella et al., 1998). Several studies have shown that hitting HIV infections hard with triple drug therapy regimens results in complete suppression of viral replication, as measured by tests of blood viral load, in more than 80% of treated patients (Katzenstein, 1997). It now appears that many different three-drug combinations are effective in treating patients as long as the mix contains one protease inhibitor and two reverse transcriptase inhibitors and is administered consistently according to an outlined drug regimen.

There are, however, good reasons to rein in some of the excessive optimism expressed in the popular media about triple drug therapy. Many researchers have expressed concern that these drugs may not successfully eradicate the virus from latent reservoirs in various bodily tissues or organs where the virus may reside, undetected and intact, even though tests of blood plasma viral loads demonstrate an absence of HIV (Cavert et al., 1997; Chun et al., 1997). Researchers and clinicians presently use viral load tests to measure the amount of HIV in the bloodstream. However, at the time of this writing there is no way to measure the virus in the brain, lymph nodes, intestines, and other tissues and organs without performing biopsies of these potential reservoirs for HIV. Virologists are currently conducting research to discover whether such organs and tissues can become a "sanctuary" for the virus during the times when viral load in blood plasma drops to minimal or undetectable levels. Research indicates that HIV infection can be sustained by relatively few infected cells that may reside outside the reach of viral load tests (Chun et al., 1997).

In 1991 Earvin (Magic) Johnson, Los Angeles Lakers basketball All-Star, announced that he had been infected with HIV through heterosexual contact. By April 1997, triple drug therapy had reduced HIV to undetectable levels in his body.

Another problem with triple drug therapy is the potential for adverse drug side effects, which may include anemia, nausea, insomnia, mouth ulcers, diarrhea, pancreatitis (inflammation of the pancreas), respiratory difficulties, and disorders of the nervous system (Heylen & Miller, 1997; Katzenstein, 1997). Some of these side effects may be so severe that affected people are unable to tolerate triple drug therapy.

A third area of difficulty posed by the new triple drug therapy is that to be effective, patients must strictly adhere to a very rigid and difficult regimen that requires taking as many as 20 pills daily at several different time intervals. In fact, some observers of this new triple drug therapy have noted that "the drug regimens involved are too complicated to be a practical option for many patients" (Day, 1997, p. 4). People undergoing triple drug therapy may have to take four protease inhibitor pills three times daily plus two lots of reverse transcriptase inhibitors three times a day, sometimes on an empty stomach. Furthermore, the different drug classes often have to be taken at separate times, such as an hour apart.

Unfortunately, patients often fail to appreciate the reasons for the complicated dosing schedule involved in triple drug therapy. Thus, although we have research demonstrating how powerful this new drug treatment strategy is in hammering down HIV, we must remember that taking the medications properly in a highly controlled research study is often a world apart from the everyday settings of patients' lives. Research indicates that in some cases where one or more

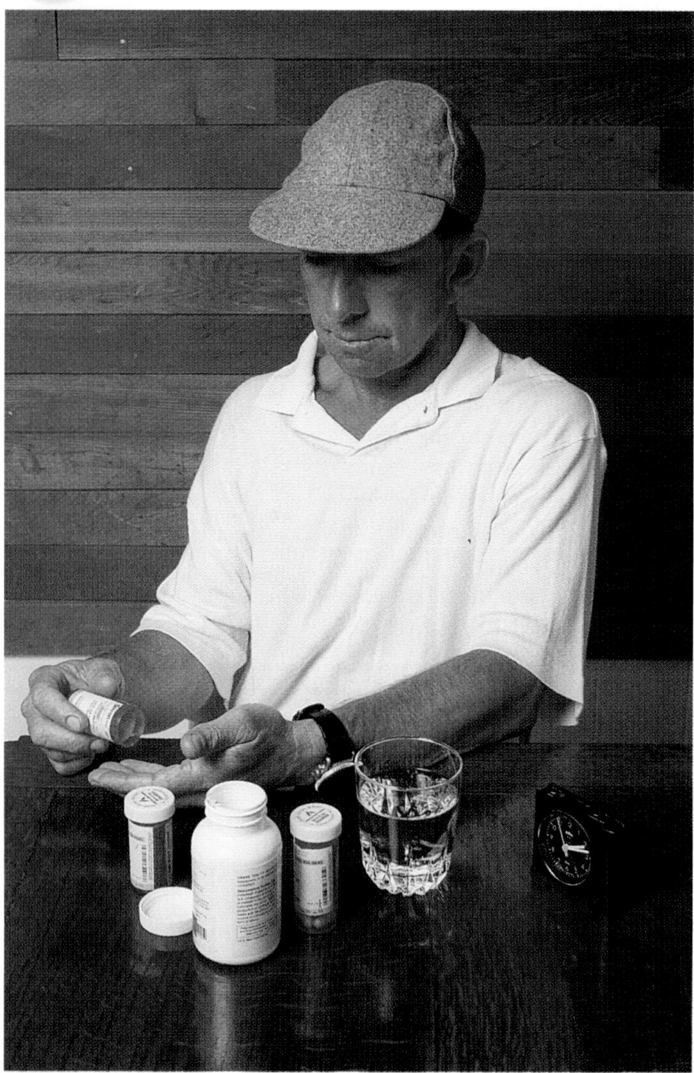

Patients undergoing triple drug therapy must strictly adhere to a very rigid and difficult regimen that involves taking large daily doses of drugs spaced at several different time intervals.

of the drugs in the triple drug regimen have been interrupted or stopped, there has been a rapid rebound of blood viral load (Katzenstein, 1997).

Another concern is the cost of triple drug therapy, which can be prohibitive. The total price tag, which is well over $10,000 per year, assuming no major problems with drug toxicity, includes the price of drugs, the cost of viral load testing to monitor the effects of drug therapy, and tests to monitor for potential adverse drug side effects (Deeks et al., 1997). Although at least some of these expenses are picked up by Medicaid or private insurers, many HIV-infected people fall outside the circle of insurance coverage (Haffner, 1998). For example, at the time of this writing, Medicaid benefits for low-income HIV-infected people do not apply until a person meets the definition of full-blown AIDS. In light of the demonstrated benefits of antiviral drug therapy early in the course of HIV disease, many AIDS activists are calling for government to expand the Medicaid program to cover people in the early stages of HIV disease.

Another issue regarding triple drug therapy is, when should this complex antiviral treatment commence? Even though research has demonstrated that triple antiviral drug treatment can suppress blood viral load in people in both early and late stage disease (Cameron et al., 1998), among researchers and clinicians a general consensus is emerging that early detection and treatment of HIV infection is important to optimal management of HIV disease (Volberding, 1998).

Finally, the development of resistance to antiviral drugs and the subsequent loss of drug effectiveness is of major concern to AIDS researchers and clinicians who treat HIV/AIDS patients. When people fail to take the recommended dosages, or when misinformed physicians reduce the dosage levels because of the patient's complaints about side effects, the door is flung open to mutations of HIV to drug-resistant strains. Adhering to the proper dosage is likely to minimize the development of drug resistance. However, resistance to antiviral drugs has been shown to occur in some patients even when standard drug doses are consistently employed (Deeks et al., 1997).

Unfortunately, data beginning to emerge at the time of this writing suggest that the lauded AIDS cocktail not uncommonly fails in real-world use (Kempf et al., 1998). The data previously presented pertaining to the efficacy of triple drug therapy were obtained from carefully controlled clinical trials, conducted largely with patients who were still relatively healthy at the onset of research, who had not had much if any drug therapy in the past, and who were highly motivated. Many HIV/AIDS experts have observed that these subjects are not the typical HIV patient. A recent study reported a 53% "failure" rate among 136 "real-world" patients who had commenced taking the AIDS cocktail, outside of a controlled clinical trial, at a large public AIDS clinic in San Francisco. Although most of the patients in this group had initially responded dramatically, with their viral levels dropping to undetectable levels, over half experienced a rebound to detectable viral levels within about a year of beginning treatment (Deeks, 1997). There are several possible explanations for such failures, including problems with compliance with the complex treatment regimen, beginning treatment too late in disease progression, or development of drug resistance. However, "most treatment failures seen in clinical practice do not represent failure of the drugs per se, but rather the inability of patients to follow their regimens exactly as prescribed" (Volberding, 1998, p. 101). Hopefully, future improvements in managing triple drug therapy, including commencement of treatment at an earlier stage of disease progression, will help to minimize such disheartening failures. Pharmaceutical companies are aware of the problems associated with complicated dosing schedules, and are currently in the process of developing a number of drug combinations that require less frequent dosing (Volberding, 1998). For the present, it is essential to emphasize that the HIV/AIDS epidemic is not over and that triple drug therapy is a *treatment* and not a *cure*.

The Search for a Vaccine

We close this section on treatment with an update on efforts to develop a vaccine(s) effective against HIV. There are two broad categories of vaccines: (1) those that prevent initial infection by HIV (prophylactic vaccines) and (2) those that delay or prevent progression of disease in those already infected (therapeutic vaccines). Although progress has been made in developing both categories of vaccines, many health officials believe we may be years away from discovering an effective HIV vaccine. Furthermore, we cannot predict with certainty that 100% effective HIV vaccines for humans will ever be developed. A number of problems confront vaccine researchers, including the facts that HIV is extremely complicated, that the virus is present in multiple strains, and that it can change rapidly due to genetic mutations. For the sake of the world's population, especially in developing countries where minuscule per capita health expenditures rule out costly drug therapies, we can only hope that effective vaccines are available soon.

By mid-1997, more than two dozen vaccines had been tested in small-scale human studies to evaluate their safety and effectiveness against HIV (Cohen, 1997b). None of these preliminary tests has yet to evolve into a full-scale efficacy trial, which would involve thousands of subjects and cost millions of dollars. In June 1994, plans were in place to commence two such large-scale human efficacy studies, each of which would study one of two varieties of a genetically engineered vaccine derived from gp120, a protein found on the surface of HIV. (Vaccine researchers often employ synthetic copies of fragments of a virus in an effort to trigger an effective immune response.) However, a panel convened by the National Institutes of Health (NIH) decided, at the 11th hour, that the probability of either of these vaccines being effective against HIV was too low to warrant government funding of these trials.

Other countries, facing an even more serious AIDS epidemic than the United States, may elect to conduct large-scale efficacy tests of these genetically engineered vaccines in the near future. In fact, Chiron Corporation recently developed a new gp120 vaccine made with HIV subtype E, a strain common in Thailand, where AIDS is endemic in the population. If all goes well in preliminary, small-scale tests, Chiron hopes to commence a large-scale efficacy trial in Thailand by the year 2000 (Cohen, 1997b).

We end this discussion of vaccines by noting a very recent positive event: In May 1997 President Clinton called for a new national goal for science to develop an HIV/AIDS vaccine within a decade. Whether or not this ambitious goal will be achieved remains to be seen. One nationally recognized AIDS authority, Anthony Fauci, recently expressed optimism about this quest by observing, "I'm convinced that we will have a vaccine and that we will have it in a reasonable period of time" (in Cohen, 1997b, p. 1196).

Prevention

The only certain way to avoid contracting HIV *sexually* is either to avoid all varieties of interpersonal sexual contact that place one at risk for infection, or to be involved in a monogamous, mutually faithful relationship with one uninfected partner. If neither of these conditions is applicable, a wise person will act in a way that significantly reduces his or her risk of becoming infected with HIV.

Safer sex practices that reduce the risk of contracting HIV/AIDS and other STDs are described in some detail in the last section of this chapter. Most of these preventive methods are directly applicable to HIV/AIDS. However, it is important to note that any strategies that reduce your risk of developing any of the other STDs previously discussed will also reduce your risk of HIV infection because of the known association between HIV/AIDS and other STDs. Research throughout the world has shown that the risk of contracting HIV is elevated in people who have other STDs such as genital herpes, gonorrhea, syphilis, chancroid, chlamydia infection, and trichomoniasis. STDs that cause genital ulcers, such as syphilis, chancroid, and herpes, have shown the highest association with HIV infection in North America and Africa (Morse et al., 1997; Royce et al., 1997), because genital ulcers allow HIV easy access to the bloodstream.

Beyond the obvious safer-sex strategies of consistently and correctly using latex condoms and avoiding sex with multiple partners or with individuals at high-risk for HIV, some suggestions particularly relevant to avoiding HIV infection follow. You will note that several of these suggestions, such as avoiding oral contact with semen and vaginal fluids, are less significant for two healthy people in a monogamous relationship who apply common sense in evaluating what is most likely to be risky for them.

1. If you use injected drugs, do not share needles or syringes (boiling does not guarantee sterility). If needle sharing continues, use bleach to clean and sterilize your needles and syringes. However, be aware that research has shown that bleach has only limited effectiveness for the disinfection of injection equipment (Lurie & Drucker, 1997).
2. Injection drug users may wish to check with local health departments to see if a needle or syringe-exchange program exists. These programs provide clean syringes or needles on an exchange basis.
3. Avoid oral, vaginal, or anal contact with semen.
4. Avoid anal intercourse, because this is one of the riskiest of all sexual behaviors associated with HIV transmission (Royce et al., 1997; Silverman & Gross, 1997). Anal intercourse has a greater HIV-infection risk for women than does vaginal intercourse, just as receptive anal intercourse carries a very high risk for males. The high risk associated with anal intercourse is due to the fact that anal penetration causes small abrasions in the rectal tissues, through which HIV can easily pass.
5. Do not engage in insertion of fingers or fists ("fisting") into the anus as an active or receptive partner. Fingernails can easily cause tears in the rectal tissues, thereby creating a route for HIV to penetrate the blood.
6. Avoid oral contact with the anus (a practice commonly referred to as "rimming").
7. Avoid oral contact with vaginal fluids.
8. Do not allow a partner's urine to enter your mouth, anus, vagina, eyes, or open cuts or sores.
9. Avoid sexual intercourse during menstruation. Research indicates that men who have intercourse with HIV-infected menstruating women are about three times as likely to become HIV infected as those who do not (Royce et al., 1997).
10. In view of the remote possibility that HIV may be transmitted via prolonged open-mouth, wet kissing, it might be wise to avoid this activity. The CDC continues to maintain there is no risk of HIV transmission through closed-mouth kissing.
11. Do not share razor blades, toothbrushes, or other implements that could become contaminated with blood.
12. Avoid sexual contact with prostitutes (male or female). Research has found that prostitutes have unusually high rates of HIV infection (Boles & Elifson, 1994; Mastro et al., 1994).

At the present time, the best hope for curtailing the epidemic spread of HIV/AIDS is through education and behavior changes. Because neither an effective vaccine nor a drug-based cure seems likely in the near future, the only viable available strategy for significantly curtailing this epidemic is preventing exposure through effective risk reduction education. Because HIV is transmitted almost exclusively through behaviors that individuals can modify, health and education officials are hopeful that educational programs aimed at encouraging people to engage in safer sexual practices will be effective in controlling HIV/AIDS.

A number of studies of populations of gay men have shown that fear of contracting AIDS has resulted in trends toward safer sexual behavior and away from HIV risk behavior (Kelaher et al., 1994; Lafferty et al., 1997; Morris & Dean, 1994). Many gay men have adopted safer modes of sexual expression, reduced their number of partners, or entered into monogamous relationships. However, several recent studies of gay men suggest an appreciable and disturbing relapse into HIV risk behavior (Heitz, 1997; Lafferty et al., 1997). One recent study found that 39% of a sample of 86 HIV-infected gay and bisexual men reported engaging in unprotected anal intercourse while aware of their HIV status (Kalichman et al., 1997). Other data recently released by the CDC (1997f) reveal that despite the overall decline in the rate of gonorrhea infections in the United States, the trend among MSM is reversing. This finding suggests that there has been a relapse of high-risk behavior among some MSM. Clearly, the frequency of unsafe sex among gay and bisexual men, especially those who are young, remains a concern.

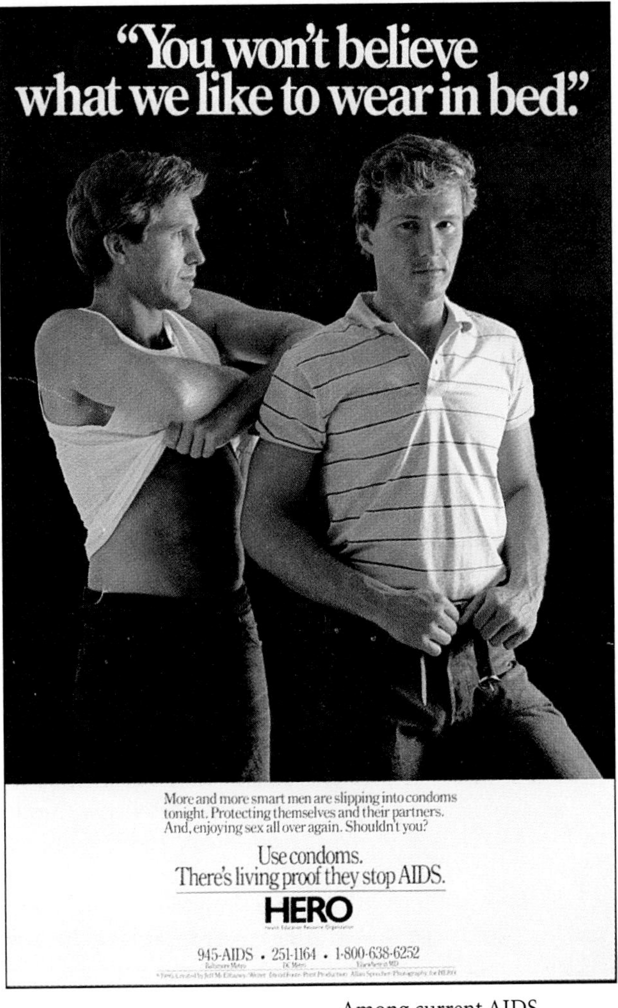

Among current AIDS educational efforts are those directed at younger gay men emphasizing the need to continue practicing safer sex and the importance of preventing a relapse of high-risk behaviors among all gay men.

Hopefully, further educational efforts targeted at young gay men, and at relapse prevention among all homosexual men, will maintain the trend toward safer behavior. Furthermore, we can only hope that educational efforts aimed at the general population will also reduce high-risk behaviors. A recent survey of a nationally representative population suggests that fear of contracting HIV/AIDS may influence at least some people in the broader population to engage in safer sex. Approximately 30% of the respondents in this study indicated making changes in their sexual behavior because of AIDS. Some of the reported changes included using condoms more often, limiting themselves to one sex partner, choosing partners more carefully, and abstaining from sex entirely (Feinlieb & Michael, 1995).

Preventing Sexually Transmitted Diseases

Many approaches to curtailing the spread of STDs have been advocated. These range from attempting to discourage sexual activity among young people to providing easy public access to information about the symptoms of STDs, along with free medical treatment. Unfortunately, the efforts of public health agencies have not been very successful in curbing the rapid spread of STDs. For this reason, it is doubly important to stress a variety of specific preventive measures that may be taken by an individual or couple.

Clearly, abstinence from partner sex is one virtually surefire way to avoid an STD infection. Being disease-free and monogamous yourself and having a partner who is also disease-free and monogamous is another way to prevent contracting an STD. However, it is often very difficult for people to assess the disease-risk status of prospective or current partners and, for that matter, how committed their partners are to being monogamous. For example, in one recent study of 119 couples dating in college, investigators found that most of the participants were generally unaware of their partner's past and concurrent sexual risk behavior in spite of their involvement together in a range of shared sexual activities (Seal, 1997).

Having a frank and open discussion prior to initial sexual interaction may seem difficult and embarrassing. However, in this era of epidemic health-damaging and/or life-threatening STDs, such discussions are essential to making sound judgments that may have profound ramifications for your physical and psychological well-being. Consequently, we address this issue early in our outline of prevention guidelines.

Prevention Guidelines

We discuss several methods of prevention—steps that can be taken before, during, or shortly after sexual contact to reduce the likelihood of contracting an STD. Many of these methods are effective against the transmission of a variety of diseases. Several are applicable to oral–genital and anal–genital contacts in addition to genital–genital interaction. None is 100% effective, but each acts to significantly reduce the chances of infection. Furthermore—and this cannot be overemphasized—the use of preventive measures may help curtail the booming spread of STDs. Because many infected people have sexual contact with one or more partners before realizing they have a disease and seeking treatment, improved prevention rather than better treatment seems to hold the key to reducing these unpleasant effects of sexual expression.

Assess Your and Your Partner's Risk Status

As a result of informed concern about acquiring an STD, you may understandably focus on assessing the risk status of a prospective sexual partner. However, in doing so you may overlook the equally important need to evaluate your own risk status. If you had previous sexual activity with others, is there any possibility you may have contracted an STD from them? Have you been tested for STDs in general, not one specific infectious agent? Remember, many of the STDs discussed in this chapter may produce little or no noticeable symptoms in an infected person. If you care enough to be sexually intimate with a new partner, is it not reasonable that you should also be open and willing to share information about your own physical sexual health?

Some experts maintain that one of the single most important STD-prevention messages to convey to people is to spend time, ideally several months or more, getting to know prospective sexual partners before engaging in genital sex. Take time to develop a warm, caring relationship in which mutual empathy and trust are key ingredients. Use this time to convey to the other person any relevant information from your sexual history regarding your risk status—and to inquire about his or her present or past behavior in the areas of sex and injection drug use. As discussed in Chapter 8, self-disclosure can be an effective strategy for getting a partner to open up. Thus, you might begin your dialogue about these matters by discussing why you think that such an information exchange is vitally important in the AIDS era, followed by information about your own sexual history.

Getting to know someone well enough to trust his or her answers to these important questions means taking the time to assess a person's honesty and integrity in a variety of situations. If you observe your prospective partner lying to friends, family members, or you about other matters, you may rightfully question the truthfulness of her or his responses to your risk-assessment queries.

Research suggests that we cannot always assume that potential sexual partners will accurately disclose their risk for STDs. One study found that a sizable percentage of both men and women said that they would not be fully honest when questioned about their past sexual and drug-use histories. Of over 400 sexually experienced southern California college students surveyed, 35% of the men and 10% of the women said that they had lied about such things as pregnancy risk and other sexual involvements in order to have sex. In addition, 47% of the men and 42% of the women said that they would report fewer previous sexual partners than they really had. Finally, 20% of the men and 4% of the women indicated that they would falsely claim that they had tested negative for HIV (Cochran & Mays, 1990). In another survey of 169 students at a large midwestern university, approximately 30% of the male respondents and 6% of the females admitted lying in order to have sex. In addition, close to half of the women and a third of the men believed they had been lied to in order to have sex (Stebleton & Rothenberger, 1993). In still another more recent study, researchers found that 40% of 203 HIV-infected men and women (40% IDUs, 20% homosexual or bisexual men, 39% heterosexually infected) had not disclosed their HIV status to all their sexual partners in the prior six months. Of the 40% nondisclosers, half had not disclosed to their one and only partner. Furthermore, among those who had not disclosed, only 42% used condoms consistently (Stein et al., 1998).

Obtain Prior Medical Examinations

Even when people are entirely candid about their own sexual histories, there is no way to assure that their previous sexual partners were honest with them—or, for that matter, that they even asked previous partners about STD risk status. In view of these concerns, we strongly encourage couples who want to begin a sexual relationship to abstain from any activity that puts them at risk for STDs until they both have medical examinations and laboratory testing designed to rule out STDs. It is encouraging that at least some couples currently seek testing for HIV and other STDs before starting a sexual relationship in a strategy that some health professionals have dubbed "negotiated safety" (Merson et al., 1997). Taking this step not only reduces one's chance of contracting a disease; it also contributes immeasurably to a sense of mutual trust and comfort with developing intimacy. If cost is an issue, contact your campus health service or public health clinics in your area, both of which may provide examinations and laboratory testing free of charge or on a sliding fee scale commensurate with your financial status.

If people in newly formed relationships do not obtain tests for STDs and are unwilling to delay the onset of sexual intercourse, health experts strongly encourage using condoms and spermicides consistently during all sexual episodes. This practice will offer some protection against many STDs whose symptoms might emerge during the initial weeks or months of a relationship or until a couple may become more comfortable with obtaining medical examinations and laboratory tests to rule out STDs.

Health departments often provide screening and treatment for STDs.

Use Condoms and Spermicides

It has been known for decades that condoms, when correctly used, help to prevent the transmission of many STDs. The condom is one of the great underrated aids to sexual interaction. Used in combination with vaginal spermicides, condoms are often effective in preventing both undesired conception and the transmission of many STDs, including HIV (Centers for Disease Control, 1997g; Royce et al., 1997). Some experts believe that "condoms offer the best defense against the growing international AIDS epidemic" (Pinkerton & Abramson, 1997, p. 364). The membranes of condoms made of latex do not have pores and thus offer greater protection against STDs than do natural-membrane ("skin") condoms. The use of condoms plus a spermicide (foams, creams, jellies) containing nonoxynol-9 (which kills a variety of infectious agents as well as sperm cells) offers more protection than condoms used alone. Nonoxynol-9 is incorporated in the lubricant of some condoms. Condoms plus spermicides should be used as a protection against STDs even if contraception is not needed. Spermicides containing nonoxynol-9 protect against transmission of bacterial infections, but their effect against HIV is uncertain (Royce et al., 1997). At the time of this writing, several trial studies of nonoxynol-9 formulations to prevent HIV infections are in progress, and preliminary data suggest that nonoxynol-9 may reduce the risk of HIV transmission (Wittkowski et al., 1998). We strongly encourage you to use spermicides with nonoxynol-9, because they are known to be effective killing agents against a wide range of infectious organisms and may well offer protection against HIV.

Condoms are most valuable in preventing sexual transmission of bacterial vaginosis, candidiasis, trichomoniasis, *Chlamydia trachomatis,* gonorrhea, NGU, syphilis, and HIV. They are less effective against the spread of herpes and genital warts and have no value in combating pubic lice and scabies. Chapter 11 contains a description of the proper way to put on a condom. A review of the proper use of condoms follow.

- Store condoms in a cool, dry place out of direct sunlight.
- Throw away condoms in damaged packages and any that are brittle, sticky, discolored, or show any other signs of age.
- Handle condoms with care so that they are not punctured.
- Put on a condom before any genital contact to prevent exposure to fluids that may contain infectious agents.
- Be sure the condom is adequately lubricated. If you need to add a lubricant, be sure to use only water-based products such as spermicides or K-Y jelly. Latex is weakened by petroleum- or oil-based lubricants (such as Vaseline, baby oil, cooking oils, shortening, and many body lotions).
- Do not blow up a condom like a balloon or fill it with water before using it to test for leaks. Such stretching weakens the latex and makes it more likely that the condom will break during use.
- Do not unroll the condom first and then pull it on like a sock; this also tends to weaken the latex, making it more likely that the condom will break during use. The proper way to put on a condom is to unroll it directly onto the erect penis (either while pinching the reservoir tip or while holding a twisted end to create a reservoir area).
- If a condom does break, replace it immediately.
- After ejaculation, take care that the condom does not slip off. Withdraw the condom-clad penis while the penis is still erect, holding the base of the condom firmly to prevent slippage.
- Never reuse a condom.

A final word on condoms as a preventive device: Using condoms **DOES NOT GUARANTEE** protection against STD infections. Some critics of condom campaigns assert that people too often are lulled into a sense of false complacency that as long as they use condoms, they are safe. However, more than 1 out of 10 women who use condoms as their only method of birth control become pregnant in one year's time (Post & Botkin, 1995). We can safely assume that the actual failure rate of condoms due to inconsistent or improper use, breakage, slippage, and other factors, must be considerably higher than indicated by pregnancy statistics. Conception can occur on only a few days each month, but an STD can be contracted any time sexual interaction with an infected person coincides with a failure of preventive methods. One major study using a technique called meta-analysis (a complex statistical procedure that collectively analyzes data from many studies) found that although condoms are 87% effective in preventing pregnancy, they may reduce the risk of HIV infection by only 69% (Weller, 1993). A recent survey of a nationally representative sample of young American men, aged 17–23, found that 23% of the respondents who used condoms reported experiencing one or more condom breakages during the previous year (Lindberg et al., 1997). Another study reported that condoms either broke or slipped off in 14.6% of uses during penile–vaginal intercourse (Trussell et al., 1992). In still another study that surveyed a national representative sample of French men and women, the rate of condom breakage or slippage at last penile–vaginal intercourse was about 5% (Messiah et al., 1997). Even among couples proficient in condom usage, however, some occasionally report intravaginal spillage of seminal fluid (Drew et al., 1990).

Correctly used condoms help prevent the transmission of many STDs including HIV.

Various surveys have indicated that rates of condom slippage and breakage may be considerably higher during anal intercourse than during vaginal intercourse (Silverman & Gross, 1997). Furthermore, condoms manufactured in the United States are generally labeled for vaginal use only, a manufacturer's caveat that reflects concern that condoms designed for use during vaginal intercourse may fail at unacceptably high rates when used during anal intercourse. This uncertainty about the protection against STDs offered by condoms during anal intercourse is especially troubling in light of the relatively high prevalence of this form of sexual interaction among heterosexual, bisexual, and homosexual people. Although some European manufacturers have marketed thicker or stronger condoms designed for anal intercourse, the efficacy of these specialty condoms has only been studied in limited fashion, and data on their effectiveness are scarce. Thus, until such time that specialty condoms known to be effective during anal intercourse are available, we urge readers who engage in anal intercourse to be especially cautious in their use of condoms during this variety of sexual interaction (for example, avoid rigorous thrusting, use adequate lubrication, take special care to avoid slippage, and so forth). To be effective as STD prophylactics, condoms must be used correctly EVERY TIME a person has sex. That may be difficult to do, particularly since logic has a tendency to shut down in the heat of passion. Thus, we strongly encourage you to incorporate into your sex life knowledge about both the nonfoolproof nature of condoms and how they may be used most effectively to prevent both disease transmission and conception.

Avoid Sexual Activity with Multiple Partners

You may wish to reevaluate the importance of sex with multiple partners in light of the clear and extensive evidence that having many sexual partners is one of the strongest predictors of becoming infected with HIV, HSV-2, *Chlamydia trachomatis,* HPV, and numerous other sexually transmitted infections. You may also elect not to have sex with individuals that you know or suspect have had multiple partners. People with multiple partners will probably know each partner less well and thus may be less successful in avoiding people who engage in high-risk behaviors.

Inspect Your Partner's Genitals

Examining your partner's genitals prior to coital, oral, or anal contact may reveal the symptoms of an STD. Herpes blisters, vaginal and urethral discharges, chancres and rashes associated with syphilis, genital warts, and gonorrhea may be seen. In most cases, symptoms will be more evident on a man. (If he is uncircumcised, be sure to retract the foreskin.) The presence of a discharge, unpleasant odor, sores, blisters, rash, warts, or anything else out of the ordinary should be viewed with some concern. "Milking" the penis is a particularly effective way to detect a suspicious discharge. This technique, sometimes called the "short-arm inspection," involves grasping the penis firmly and pulling the loose skin up and down the shaft several times, applying pressure on the base-to-head stroke. Then part the urinary opening to see if any cloudy discharge is present.

People frequently find it difficult to openly conduct such an inspection before sexual involvement. Sometimes the simple request "Let me undress you" will provide some opportunity to examine your partner's genitals. Sensate focus pleasuring, discussed in Chapter 16, could provide the opportunity for more detailed visual exploration. Some people suggest a shower before sex, with an eye toward examining a partner. This may be quite helpful for noting visible sores, blisters, and so forth, but soap and water may also remove the visual and olfactory cues associated with a discharge.

If you note signs of infection, you may justifiably and wisely elect not to have sexual relations. Your intended partner may or may not be aware of his or her symptoms. Therefore, it is important that you explain your concerns. Some people may decide to continue their sexual interaction after discovering possible symptoms of an STD; they would be wise, though, to restrict their activities to kissing, hugging, touching, and manual–genital stimulation.

Wash Your—and Your Partner's—Genitals Before and After Sexual Contact

There is some difference of opinion about the extent of benefits associated with soap-and-water washing of the genitals before sexual interaction. However, there can be little doubt that washing has some benefits. Washing the man's penis is generally more effective as a prophylactic measure, although washing the woman's vulva can also be helpful.

You may find it difficult to suggest that your partner wash (or allow you to wash) his or her genitals before having sex. However, you may accomplish this unobtrusively by including washing of the genitals in the sex play that occurs in the shower or bathtub. Or you may frankly announce that you are cleansing your partner's and your own genitals for your mutual protection.

After sexual contact, thorough washing of the genitals and surrounding areas with soap and water is highly recommended as a preventive procedure when the transmission of an infection is a possibility. We are not, however, suggesting that this procedure should always follow sexual activity. Many lovers with long-term, monogamous relationships would find this unnecessary and possibly even offensive, implying that a person is somehow unclean after sex.

Promptness is very important in postsex washing, probably as important as thoroughness. However, some people might object to jumping out of bed immediately to wash, as this may break the relaxed and intimate mood. For those who are uncomfortable letting their partners know that they are taking this precaution, perhaps simply announcing that you need to go to the bathroom (a not uncommon need after sex) will suffice. Both women and men can wash their genitals while sitting over the sink. First fill the sink with warm, soapy water, then turn your back to it and boost yourself up to straddle it. In this position it is relatively easy to thoroughly wash your exposed genitals with a soapy washcloth.

Urinating after coitus may have some limited prophylactic benefits, particularly for men. Many infectious organisms do not survive in the urethra in the acidic environment created by urine. Urinating may also help to flush out disease-causing organisms.

Obtain Routine Medical Evaluations

Many authorities recommend that sexually active people with multiple partners routinely visit their health practitioner or local STD clinic for periodic checkups, even when no symptoms of disease are evident. In view of the number of people, both women and men, who are symptomless carriers of STDs, this seems like very good advice. How often to have such examinations is a matter of opinion. Our advice to people who are sexually active with multiple partners is that they should have checkups preferably every three months and certainly no less often than twice a year.

Inform Your Partner(s) If You Have an STD

The high frequency of infections without symptoms makes it imperative for infected individuals to tell their sexual partner(s) once they are diagnosed as having an STD. However, we cannot assume that a previous sexual partner will be forthcoming about a newly diagnosed STD. For example, two studies revealed that very few past sexual partners of individuals diagnosed as HIV infected were informed of their risk by the infected person (Landis et al., 1992; Marks et al., 1992). Furthermore, one cannot assume that a partner who has been infected with a disease during sexual interaction will have symptoms or that she or he will understand the meaning of any symptoms that might occur and seek proper medical treatment. The box "Telling a Partner," which appears earlier in this chapter, offers some suggestions that may be helpful when telling a partner about an STD infection. In addition, the box "Sexual Deception and the Court System," provides some sobering information about possible consequences of not informing a partner about an STD.

Ethical/Legal Issues

Sexual Deception and the Court System

In recent years the American legal system has witnessed the emergence of a new kind of legal action based on sexual fraud. Perhaps the most noteworthy and visible are the cases in which people who have tested positive for HIV engage in unprotected sexual contact with partners who are uninformed about their HIV status. Such actions typically result in severe legal sanctions. Several such legal proceedings have occurred in the authors' home state of Oregon, including the first man in the United States convicted and sentenced to prison for attempted murder based on evidence that he had unprotected sexual relations with three women despite his knowledge that he was HIV-positive.

In addition to cases involving criminal prosecution, sexual-deceit civil lawsuits increasingly provide the basis for successful civil litigation in American courts. In these civil proceedings, it is alleged that a person has lied about an STD—either through failure to disclose the condition to a partner or by engaging in outright deception. In many states, most notably California, state appeals courts have given a green light for such legal actions, thus providing an impetus for monetary court judgments and out-of-court settlements ranging well into six figures.

Some legal experts are now calling for the formal adoption of a new legal theory for sexual-deception lawsuits that acknowledges their rightful place in the court system. One leading spokesperson, law professor Jane Larson, recently proposed that legal action would be for "sexual fraud," which she describes as "an act of intentional, harmful misrepresentation made for the purpose of gaining another's consent to sexual relations" (in Pollack, 1993, p. B1).

We will watch with interest as litigation involving sexual deception becomes more common in contemporary America. Certainly it is becoming abundantly clear that, aside from ethical and moral considerations, there are now good legal reasons for informing all prospective sexual partners of STD infections.

Summary

In the United States, the incidence of sexually transmitted diseases (STDs) is increasing, especially among young people aged 15–29 years.

A number of factors probably contribute to the high incidence of STDs, including increased sexual activity among young people, more people having sex with multiple partners, the increased use of birth control pills, and the fact that many of these diseases do not produce obvious symptoms, which results in people unknowingly infecting others.

BACTERIAL INFECTIONS

Chlamydia infections are among the most prevalent and the most damaging of all STDs. Chlamydia disease is transmitted primarily through sexual contact. It may also be spread by fingers from one body site to another, as from the genitals to the eyes.

There are two general types of genital chlamydia infections in females: infections of the lower reproductive tract, commonly manifested as urethritis or cervicitis, and invasive infections of the upper reproductive tract, expressed as PID (pelvic inflammatory disease).

Most women with lower reproductive tract chlamydia infections have few or no symptoms. Symptoms of PID caused by chlamydia infection include disrupted menstrual periods, pelvic pain, elevated temperature, nausea, vomiting, and headache.

Chlamydia salpingitis (infection of the fallopian tubes) is a major cause of infertility and ectopic pregnancy.

In men, chlamydia infections are a common cause of epididymitis and NGU. Possible symptoms of chlamydia infections in men are a discharge from the penis and burning during urination.

Chlamydia infection also causes trachoma, the world's leading cause of preventable blindness.

Recommended drugs for treating chlamydia infections include doxycycline, azithromycin, and ofloxacin.

Gonorrhea, a very common communicable disease in the United States, is a bacterial infection transmitted through sexual contact. The infecting organism is commonly called a gonococcus bacterium.

Early symptoms of gonorrhea infection are more likely to be manifested by men, who will probably have a discharge from the penis and burning during urination. The early sign in women, often not detectable, is a mild vaginal discharge that may be irritating to vulval tissues.

Complications of gonorrhea infection in men include prostate, bladder, and kidney involvement and, infrequently, gonococcal epididymitis, which may lead to sterility. In women, gonorrhea may lead to PID, sterility, and abdominal adhesions.

Recommended treatment for gonorrhea is the dual therapy of a single dose of ceftriaxone, cefixime, cipofloxacin, or ofloxacin plus doxycycline for seven days.

Nongonococcal urethritis (NGU) is a very common infection of the urethral passage, typically seen in men. It is primarily caused by infectious organisms transmitted during coitus.

Symptoms of NGU, most apparent in men, include penile discharge and slight burning during urination. Women may have a minor vaginal discharge and are thought to harbor the infecting organisms.

Doxycycline or azithromycin therapy usually clears up NGU.

Syphilis is less common but potentially more damaging than gonorrhea. It is almost always transmitted through sexual contact.

If untreated, syphilis may progress through four phases: primary, characterized by the appearance of chancre sores; secondary, distinguished by the occurrence of a generalized skin rash; latent, a several-year period of no overt symptoms; and tertiary, during which the disease may produce cardiovascular disease, blindness, paralysis, skin ulcers, liver damage, and severe mental pathology.

Syphilis may be treated with penicillin at any stage of its development. People allergic to penicillin may be treated with doxycycline, tetracycline, or erythromycin.

Although still relatively uncommon in the United States, the incidence of chancroid has increased sharply in recent years. Chancroid is transmitted by sexual interaction.

Chancroid infection produces small papules in the genital, perineal, or anal regions that eventually rupture and form painful, soft, craterlike ulcers that emit a foul-smelling discharge.

Chancroid may be treated via single doses of either ceftriaxone or azithromycin or seven days of oral erythromycin.

VIRAL INFECTIONS

Some of the most common herpes viruses are type 1, which generally produces cold sores on or in the mouth, and type 2, which generally infects the genital area. Type 1 may sometimes be found in the genital area and type 2 in the mouth area. Type 2 is transmitted primarily through sexual contact; type 1 may be passed by sexual contact, kissing, or by using the toilet articles or eating utensils of an infected person.

It has been estimated that over 100 million Americans are afflicted with oral herpes and that 45 million people in the United States have genital herpes.

The presence of painful sores is the primary symptom of herpes. A person is highly contagious during a herpes eruption, but evidence indicates that herpes may also be transmitted during asymptomatic periods.

Genital herpes may predispose a woman to cervical cancer. It may also infect her newborn child, producing severe damage or death of the infant.

Herpes has no known cure. Treatment is aimed at reducing pain and speeding the healing process. Acyclovir administered orally or intravenously is effective in promoting healing during first episodes and, if taken continuously, in suppressing recurrent outbreaks.

Genital and anal warts are an extremely common viral STD in the United States.

Genital warts are primarily transmitted through vaginal, anal, or oral–genital sexual interaction.

Research has revealed a strong association between genital warts and cancers of the cervix, vagina, vulva, urethra, penis, and anus.

Genital warts are treated by freezing, applications of topical agents, cauterization, surgical removal, or vaporization by a carbon dioxide laser.

Hepatitis A, hepatitis B, and non-A/non-B hepatitis are three major types of viral infections of the liver. Both the A and B types can be sexually transmitted.

Hepatitis B may be transmitted via blood or blood products, semen, vaginal secretions, and saliva. Manual, oral, or penile stimulation of the anus are practices strongly associated with the spread of this viral agent.

Oral–anal contact seems to be the primary mode of sexual transmission of hepatitis A.

The symptoms of viral hepatitis may vary from mild to incapacitating illness. No specific therapy is available to treat this disease. Most infected people recover in a few weeks with adequate bed rest.

COMMON VAGINAL INFECTIONS

Bacterial vaginosis, typically caused by a bacterium known as *Gardnerella vaginalis,* is perhaps the most common cause of vaginitis (vaginal infection) in American women. Male partners of infected women also harbor the *Gardnerella vaginalis* organism, usually without clinical symptoms. Coitus often provides a mode of transmission of this infection.

The most prominent symptom of bacterial vaginosis in women is a fishy- or musty-smelling, thin discharge that is like flour paste in consistency. Women may also experience irritation of the genital tissues. A small number of men may develop inflammation of the foreskin and glans, urethritis, or cystitis.

The treatment for bacterial vaginosis is metronidazole (Flagyl) by mouth or intravaginal applications of topical metronidazole gel or clindamycin cream.

Candidiasis is a yeast infection that affects many women. The *Candida albicans* organism is commonly present in the vagina but causes problems only when overgrowth occurs. Pregnancy, diabetes, the use of birth control pills or oral antibiotics, and the ingestion of large amounts of dairy products, sugar, and artificial sweeteners are conditions often associated with yeast infections. The organism can be transmitted via sexual or nonsexual means.

Symptoms of yeast infections include white, clumpy discharge and intense itching of the vaginal and vulval tissues.

Traditional treatment for candidiasis infection consists of vaginal suppositories or topical creams such as clotrimazole, miconazole, or butoconazole.

Trichomoniasis accounts for about one-fourth of all cases of vaginitis. Male partners of infected women are thought to carry the *Trichomonas vaginalis* organism in the urethra and under the foreskin if they are uncircumcised. The primary mode of transmission of this infection is through sexual contact.

Women infected with trichomoniasis and their male sexual partners may be successfully treated with the drug Flagyl.

ECTOPARASITIC INFECTIONS

Ectoparasites are parasitic organisms that live on the outer skin of humans and other animals. Pubic lice and scabies are two relatively common STDs caused by ectoparasites.

Pubic lice ("crabs") are tiny biting insects that feed on blood from small vessels in the pubic region. They may be transmitted through sexual contact or by using sheets or clothing contaminated by an infested individual.

The primary symptom of a pubic lice infestation is severe itching that is not relieved by scratching. Sometimes pubic lice can be seen.

Pubic lice are treated by application of 1% permethrin cream to affected body areas and 1% Lindane shampoo for hair.

Scabies is caused by a tiny parasitic mite that forages for nourishment in its host's skin. Scabies is a highly contagious condition that may be transmitted by close physical contact between people, both sexual and nonsexual.

The primary symptoms of scabies are small bumps and a red rash, which indicate areas of infestation that itch intensely, especially at night.

A single application of 5% permethrin lotion or cream, applied from the neck to the toes, is usually an effective treatment.

ACQUIRED IMMUNODEFICIENCY SYNDROME (AIDS)

AIDS is caused by infection with a virus (HIV) that destroys the immune system, leaving the body vulnerable to a variety of opportunistic infections and cancers.

In spite of a great deal of speculation and theorizing, the origin of HIV remains undetermined.

An estimated 650,000 to more than 1 million people in the United States and 31 million people worldwide are infected with HIV.

The number of new AIDS cases reported annually in the United States grew rapidly through the early 1980s, moderated in the late 1980s and early 1990s, and actually declined from 1994 through 1996.

In recent years women, African Americans, and Hispanic Americans have accounted for increasing proportions of reported AIDS cases.

Although most AIDS cases that have occurred in the United States since the beginning of the epidemic have involved men who have sex with men (MSM) and injection drug users (IDUs), cases attributable to heterosexual transmission have risen steadily.

The acceleration of heterosexually transmitted HIV in the United States, together with the known fact that heterosexual transmission of HIV has predominated worldwide, clearly demonstrates that it is sexual contact with an infected person (or sharing contaminated IDU equipment), rather than one's sexual orientation, that places one at risk for becoming infected with HIV.

HIV has been found in semen, blood, vaginal secretions, saliva, tears, urine, breast milk, and any other bodily fluids that may contain blood.

Blood and semen are the major vehicles for transmitting the virus, which appears to be passed primarily through sexual contact and through needle sharing among injection drug users.

HIV may be transmitted to the receptive partner during oral sex when HIV comes into contact with mucous membrane tissues in the mouth.

The present possibility of being infected with HIV via transfusion of contaminated blood is quiet remote. Furthermore, there is no danger of being infected as a result of donating blood.

A small percentage of people appear to be resistant to HIV infection.

The risk of transmitting HIV via saliva, tears, and urine appears to be very low. There is no evidence that HIV can be transmitted by casual contact.

High-risk behaviors that increase one's chances of becoming infected with HIV include engaging in unprotected sex, having multiple sexual partners, sexual contact with people known to be at high risk, and sharing injection equipment for drug use.

HIV is not as easily transmitted from women to men as it is from men to women.

HIV often causes a brief, flulike illness within a few weeks after initial infection that tends to fade fairly rapidly. However, as the virus continues to deplete the immune system, other subsequent symptoms may occur.

Most people develop antibodies to HIV within months of being infected, but some "silent" infections may go undetected for three years or more.

HIV infection may be detected by standard blood tests for blood serum antibodies to HIV. Two encouraging new developments in HIV diagnostic testing involve the recent availability of an oral diagnostic testing procedure and the marketing of self-test kits that provide people with a private and anonymous way for learning their HIV status.

The incubation time for AIDS—defined as the time between infection with HIV and the onset of one or more severe, debilitating diseases—is estimated to range between 8 and 11 years.

Three patterns of HIV/AIDS disease progression have been identified: rapid progression, usual patterns of progression, and long-term nonprogression.

It has been theorized that nonprogression may result when a person is (1) infected with a weak, mutant strain of HIV or (2) the immune system mounts a "superresponse" to HIV that wards off disease progression.

The symptoms of HIV/AIDS disease are many and varied, depending on the degree to which the immune system is compromised and the particular type of cancer or opportunistic infection(s) that afflict an infected person.

There is still no cure for HIV/AIDS. However, the recent emergence of a new type of drug therapy, that uses a combination of three antiviral drugs, has led to a surge of optimism that this so-called triple drug therapy may not only delay HIV/AIDS progression but also ultimately eradicate the virus.

Triple drug therapy has already provided dramatic increases in the longevity of HIV-infected persons. Triple drug therapy regimens have completely suppressed viral replication in more than 80% of treated patients.

However, triple drug therapy may not successfully eradicate HIV from latent reservoirs in various bodily tissues or organs. Furthermore, this drug therapy may cause adverse drug side effects, requires adherence to a very rigid and difficult regimen, is extremely expensive, and may fail in "real-world use."

Most researchers and clinicians believe that early detection and treatment of HIV infection, with triple drug therapy, is important to optimal management of HIV disease.

Although progress has been made in developing HIV vaccines, many health officials believe that we may be years away from having available an effective vaccine. Furthermore, we cannot predict with certainty that a 100% effective vaccine for humans will ever be developed.

The best hope for curtailing the HIV/AIDS epidemic is through education and behavioral change.

A person may significantly reduce her or his risk of becoming infected with HIV by following safer-sex strategies, which include, among others, using condoms and avoiding sex with multiple partners or with individuals who are at high risk for HIV infection.

PREVENTING SEXUALLY TRANSMITTED DISEASES

Taking the time to carefully assess your and your partner's risk status for transmitting STDs is perhaps the single most important preventive strategy.

Since it is often difficult to accurately assess risk status from conversations alone, couples are encouraged to undergo medical examinations and laboratory testing to rule out STDs prior to engaging in any sexual activity that puts them at risk for STDs.

Condoms, when used correctly in conjunction with spermicides containing nonoxynol-9, offer good, but not foolproof, protection against the transmission of many STDs.

Avoid sex with multiple partners or with individuals who likely have had multiple partners.

Inspecting a partner's genitals prior to sexual contact may be a way to detect symptoms of an STD.

Washing the genitals with soap and water both before and after sexual interaction offers additional protection against being infected with an STD.

Sexually active people with multiple partners should routinely visit their health practitioner or local STD clinic for periodic checkups, even when no symptoms of disease are present.

It is imperative for infected individuals to tell their sexual partner(s) once they are diagnosed as having an STD.

Thought Provokers

1. Do you think that the threat of contracting STDs such as AIDS, herpes, or *Chlamydia trachomatis* will alter or has already altered patterns of sexual interaction among college students and other young adults? Explain your answer.
2. Many individuals with herpes have very rare outbreaks of the disease. It is also true that some people afflicted with this disease have experienced rejection by prospective sexual partners when they explain their condition. In view of these facts, do you believe that people who carefully monitor their health and take proper precautions can justifiably enter into sexual relationships without revealing that they have herpes?
3. It has been suggested that all adolescents and adults should be required to undergo screening for the presence of HIV. Do you agree with this recommendation? How might the results of such testing be effectively employed to reduce the transmission of HIV? What problems might occur as a result of compulsory screening? Do you believe that such mandatory testing would be an unjustifiable violation of privacy rights?
4. Assume that you are in the preliminary stages of a sexual encounter when you notice one or more symptoms of an STD in your partner. What would you do? Would you make up an excuse for not continuing the sexual activity, or would you tell your companion the true reason for your concerns? Would your response be different with a new versus a familiar lover?

Suggested Readings

AIDS Education and Prevention. This interdisciplinary journal, which is the official journal of the International Society for AIDS Education, is available in many major library systems and contains excellent information regarding the prevention of AIDS. One of the best available sources of material on AIDS education.

Centers for Disease Control. *The MMWR (Morbidity and Mortality Weekly Report)* of the National Centers for Disease Control is available in most major library systems (particularly medical libraries) and frequently contains valuable information about the nature, transmission, prevention, and treatment of STDs. It is perhaps the single best source for keeping abreast of the latest developments regarding AIDS and other STDs.

Hatcher, Robert (Ed.) (1991). *Safely Sexual.* New York: Irvington Publishers. A sensible, accurate, sensitive, and very practical guide to a safer sexual life, including suggestions for ways to relate sexually while remaining protected from AIDS, other STDs, and unwanted pregnancies.

Shilts, Randy (1987). *And the Band Played On: Politics, People, and the AIDS Epidemic.* New York: St. Martin's Press. This compelling book, written by an investigative reporter, provides shocking information about how government incompetence and infighting among research groups in the scientific and medical communities hindered efforts to mobilize an effective campaign against the AIDS epidemic. This book also humanizes the AIDS crisis by telling personal stories of people who have lived with and died from AIDS.

Resources

CDC National HIV/AIDS Hotline: (800) 342-AIDS (English), (800) 344-7432 (Spanish), (800) 243-7889 (TTY service for hearing impaired). An informative recording with current information. Those who have specific questions not answered by the recording can call (800) 447-AIDS. Many cities have a local AIDS information hot line; check your local white pages for listings.

The Herpes Resource Center, a program of the American Social Health Association, provides excellent services including a quarterly journal complete with up-to-date information about herpes, access to local chapters (support groups), and a private telephone information, counseling, and referral service. For information about these services, call (800) 230-6039 or send $1 (postage and handling) to Herpes Resource Center, ASHA, Dept. PR46, P.O. Box 13827, Research Triangle Park, NC 27709. (No self-addressed, stamped envelope is required.)

Herpes Anonymous, P.O. Box 278, Westbury, NY 11590; (516) 334-5718. A nonprofit social organization comprised of people with herpes who wish to help others overcome the difficulties associated with this disease. Herpes Anonymous assists in developing companionable associations among people who have herpes. The organization also distributes a free newsletter containing up-to-date information about this disease.

Web Resources

American Social Health Association
sunsite.unc.edu/ASHA/
Included on this Web site are STD resources including a sexual health glossary, educational brochures, hotline numbers, links to support groups, a Herpes Resource Center, and an "STD News" bulletin.

JAMA HIV/AIDS Information Center
www.ama-assn.org/special/hiv/hivhome.htm
The Journal of the American Medical Association maintains this Web site with updates on the latest treatment strategies for people with HIV/AIDS, a reference library, and a resource center for patient and support group information.

Sexually Transmitted Diseases
h-devil-www.mc.duke.edu/h-devil/stds/stds.htm
This Web site, sponsored by the Student Health Service at Duke University, provides detailed information about preventing, identifying, and treating chlamydia, gonorrhea, syphilis, HPV, HIV/AIDS, and other STDs.

18

Atypical Sexual Behavior

My last sexual partner was very much into golden showers. Having spent a little of my time watching G. G. Allen movies, I was well acquainted with the existence of watersports, but somehow it never occurred to me that I would like to partake in them. When my partner revealed his desire to drink my urine, I was taken off guard. I have been known to try some things I would deem a little atypical, so I gave it a shot. I was very nervous about the actual art of the procedure, though. Thoughts such as "What if he was joking—he would think I'm nuts" and "What if I completely miss" entered my head. It was nerve-racking and made it especially hard to pee. Eventually, my anxiety subsided and I was able to participate. His reaction was amazing to me. He began to masturbate feverishly and lapped up my urine ecstatically. I had never seen him so turned on. More surprising though was how much I enjoyed it. Although I cannot imagine being on the other end, it was really an empowering and enjoyable experience. (Authors' files)

This description of a rather unusual sexual experience, recently provided by a student in a sexuality class, may strike our readers as reflecting an abnormal or perhaps even deviant form of sexual behavior. However, we believe it is more realistic to consider this anecdote to be an account of uncommon or atypical sexual behavior. One note of caution: Because HIV has been found in the urine of infected persons, it is prudent to avoid contact with a partner's urine unless he or she is known to be HIV negative and not infected with any other STDs. Now let us consider for a moment what constitutes atypical sexual behavior.

What Constitutes Atypical Sexual Behavior?

Paraphilia
Term used to describe uncommon types of sexual expression.

Atypical sexual behaviors
Behaviors not typically expressed by most people in our society.

In this chapter, we focus on a number of sexual behaviors that have been variously labeled as deviant, perverted, aberrant, or abnormal. More recently, the less-judgmental term **paraphilia** (pair-uh-FIL-e-uh) has been used to describe these somewhat uncommon types of sexual expression. Literally meaning "beyond usual or typical love," this term stresses that such behaviors are usually not based on an affectionate or loving relationship, but rather are expressions of psychosexually disordered behavior in which sexual arousal and/or response depends on some unusual, extraordinary, or even bizarre activity (American Psychiatric Association, 1994). The term *paraphilia* is used in much of the psychological and psychiatric literature. However, in our own experience in dealing with and discussing variant sexual behaviors, the one common characteristic that stands out is that each behavior in its fully developed form is not typically expressed by most people in our society. Therefore, we also categorize the behaviors discussed in this chapter as **atypical sexual behaviors.**

Several points should be noted about atypical sexual expression in general before we discuss specific behaviors. First, like many other sexual expressions discussed in this book, the behaviors singled out in this chapter represent extreme points on a continuum. Atypical sexual behaviors exist in many gradations, ranging from mild, infrequently expressed tendencies to full-blown, regularly manifested behaviors. Although these are *atypical* behaviors, many of us may recognize some degree of such behaviors or feelings within ourselves—perhaps manifest at some point in our lives, or mostly repressed, or emerging only in very private fantasies.

A second point has to do with the state of our knowledge about these behaviors. In most of the discussions that follow, the person who manifests the atypical behavior is assumed to be male, and evidence strongly indicates that in most reported cases of atypical or paraphilic behaviors, the agents of such acts are male (American Psychiatric Association, 1994; Money, 1988). However, the tendency to assume that males are predominantly involved may be influenced by the somewhat biased nature of differential reporting and prosecution. Female exhibitionism, for example, is far less likely to be reported than is similar behavior in a male. John Money (1981) has suggested that atypical sexual behavior may be decidedly more prevalent among males than females because male *erotosexual differentiation* (the development of sexual arousal in response to various kinds of images or stimuli) is more complex than that of the female and subject to more errors.

A third noteworthy point is that atypical behaviors often occur in clusters. That is, the occurrence of one paraphilia appears to increase the probability that others will also be manifested, simultaneously or sequentially (Bradford et al., 1992; Fedora et al., 1992). One hypothesis offered to account for this cluster effect is that engaging in one atypical behavior, such as exhibitionism, may reduce the participant's inhibitions to the point where engaging in another paraphilia, such as voyeurism, becomes more likely (Stanley, 1993).

A final consideration is the impact of atypical behaviors both on the person who exhibits them and on others to whom they may be directed. People who manifest atypical sexual behaviors often depend on these acts for sexual satisfaction. The behavior is frequently an end in itself. It is also possible that their unconventional behavior will alienate others. Consequently, these people often find it very difficult to establish satisfying sexual/intimate relationships with partners. Instead, their sexual expression may assume a solitary, driven, even compulsive quality. Some of these behaviors do involve other people whose personal space is violated in a coercive, invasive fashion. In the following section we consider the distinction between coercive and noncoercive paraphilias.

Noncoercive versus Coercive Paraphilias

A key distinguishing characteristic of paraphilias is whether or not they involve an element of coercion. Several of the paraphilias are strictly solo activities or involve the participation of consensual adults who agree to engage in, observe, or just put up with the particular variant behavior. Because coercion is not involved, and a person's basic rights are not violated, such so-called noncoercive atypical behaviors are considered by many to be relatively benign or harmless. Clearly, the chapter opening account falls into this category. However, as we shall see, these noncoercive behaviors may occasionally engender potentially adverse consequences for people drawn into their sphere of influence. We will consider eight varieties of noncoercive paraphilias.

Some paraphilias are definitely coercive or invasive in that they involve unwilling recipients of behavior such as peeping or exhibitionism. Furthermore, research suggests that such coercive acts may have harmful effects on the targets of such deeds, who may be psychologically traumatized by the experience. They may feel they have been violated or that they are vulnerable to physical abuse, and they may develop fears that such unpleasant episodes will recur. This is one reason many of these coercive paraphilias are illegal. On the other hand, many people who encounter such acts are not adversely affected. Because of this and because many of these coercive behaviors do not involve physical or sexual contact with another, many authorities view them as minor sex offenses (sometimes called "nuisance" offenses). However, evidence that some people progress from nuisance offenses to more serious forms of sexual abuse may lead to a reconsideration of whether these offenses are "minor" (Bradford et al., 1992; Fedora et al., 1992). We examine this issue in more detail later in this chapter and the next.

In our discussion of both types of paraphilias, coercive and noncoercive, we examine how each of these behaviors is expressed, some of the common characteristics of those exhibiting it, and the various factors thought to contribute to its development. More severe forms of sexual victimization, such as rape, incest, and child abuse, are discussed in Chapter 19.

Noncoercive Paraphilias

In this section we first discuss four fairly common types of noncoercive paraphilias: fetishism, transvestism, sexual sadism, and sexual masochism. We will also describe four less common varieties of noncoercive paraphilias.

Fetishism

Fetishism
Obtaining sexual excitement primarily or exclusively from an inanimate object or a particular part of the body.

Fetishism (FET-ish-iz-um) refers to sexual behavior in which an individual becomes sexually aroused by focusing on an inanimate object or a part of the human body. As with many other atypical behaviors, it is often difficult to draw the line between normal activities that may have fetishistic overtones and those that are genuinely paraphilic. Many people are erotically aroused by the sight of undergarments and certain specific body parts, such as feet, legs, buttocks, thighs, and breasts. Many men and some women may use articles of clothing and other paraphernalia as an accompaniment to masturbation or sexual activity with a partner. Only when a person becomes focused on these objects or body parts to the exclusion of everything else is the term *fetishism* truly applicable. In some instances, a person may be unable to experience sexual arousal and orgasm in the absence of the fetish object. In other situations where the attachment is not so strong, sexual response may occur in the absence of the object but often with diminished intensity. For some people, fetish objects serve as substitutes for human contact and are dispensed with if a partner becomes available. Some common fetish objects include women's lingerie, shoes (particularly high-heeled), boots (often affiliated with themes of domination), hair, stockings (especially black mesh hose), and a variety of leather, silk, and rubber goods (American Psychiatric Association, 1994; Davison & Neale, 1993).

Inanimate objects or a part of the human body, such as feet, may be sources of sexual arousal for some people.

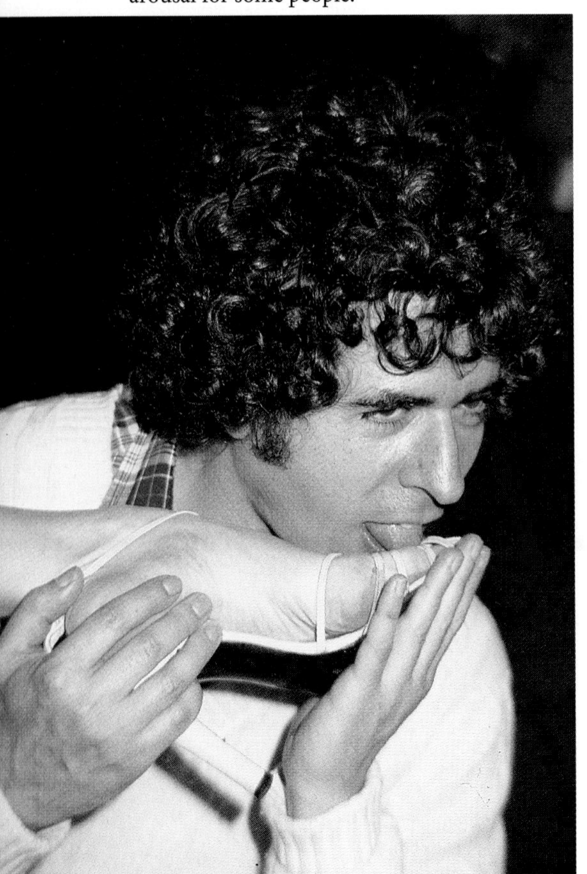

How does fetishism develop? One way is through incorporating the object or body part, often through fantasy, in a masturbation sequence where the reinforcement of orgasm strengthens the fetishistic association. This is a kind of classical conditioning in which some object or body part becomes associated with sexual arousal. This pattern of conditioning was demonstrated some years ago by Rachman (1966), who created a mild fetish among male subjects under laboratory conditions by repeatedly pairing a photograph of women's boots with erotic slides of nude females. The subjects soon began to show sexual response to the boots alone. This reaction also generalized to other types of women's shoes. Although some critics have suggested that Rachman's experiment was tainted by methodological problems (O'Donohue & Plaud, 1994), two additional studies provided further evidence for classical conditioning of fetishism (Langevin & Martin, 1975; Rachman & Hodgson, 1968).

Another possible explanation looks to childhood in explaining the origins of some cases of fetishism. Some children may learn to associate sexual arousal with objects (such as panties or shoes) which belong to an emotionally significant person, like the mother or older sister (Freund & Blanchard, 1993). The process by which this may occur is sometimes called *symbolic transformation.* Here, the object of the fetish becomes endowed with the power or essence of its owner, so that the child (usually a male) responds to this object as he might react to the actual person (Gebhard et al., 1965). If these patterns become sufficiently ingrained, the person will engage in little or no sexual interaction with others during the developmental years, and even as an adult may continue to substitute fetish objects for sexual contact with other humans.

Only rarely does fetishism develop into an offense that might harm someone. Occasionally, an individual may commit burglary to supply an object fetish, as in the following account:

Common fetish objects: women's lingerie, gloves, and shoes.

Some years ago we had a bra stealer loose in the neighborhood. You couldn't hang your brassiere outside on the clothesline without fear of losing it. He also took panties, but bras seemed to be his major thing. I talked to other women in the neighborhood who were having the same problem. This guy must have had a roomful. I never heard that he was caught. He must have decided to move on because the thefts suddenly stopped. (Authors' files)

Burglary is the most frequent serious offense associated with fetishism. Uncommonly, a person may do something bizarre such as cut hair from an unwilling person. In extremely rare cases, a man may murder and mutilate his victim, preserving certain body parts for fantasy–masturbation activities.

Transvestism

Transvestism
Deriving sexual arousal from wearing clothing of the other sex.

The term **transvestism** is applied to behaviors whereby an individual obtains sexual excitement from putting on the clothes of the other sex. In defining transvestism, it is important to emphasize the differences among people who cross-dress to experience sexual arousal, female impersonators (who cross-dress to entertain), male homosexuals who occasionally "go in drag," and transsexuals who, as we discussed in Chapter 3, cross-dress to obtain a partial sense of physical and emotional completeness rather than for sexual titillation.

Transvestism comprises a range of behaviors. Some people prefer to don the entire garb of the other sex. This is often a solitary activity, occurring privately in their homes. Occasionally a person may go out on the town while so attired, but this is unusual. Generally the cross-dressing is a momentary activity, producing sexual excitement that often culminates in gratification through masturbation or sex with a partner. In many cases of transvestism, a person becomes aroused by wearing only one garment, perhaps a pair of panties or a brassiere. This behavior has a strong element of fetishism, which has led many writers to link the two conditions. A distinguishing feature of transvestism is that the article is actually worn instead of just being viewed or fondled.

It would appear that in most cases it is men who are attracted to transvestism. This seems true of all contemporary societies for which we have data. However, a few isolated cases of female transvestism also appear in the clinical literature (Stoller, 1982). Some

Transvestism is usually a solitary activity expressed by a heterosexual male in the privacy of his own home.

writers contend that transvestism is more common among females than we are aware of because the opportunities for cross-dressing without detection are obviously much greater for women. Although this may be true, we know that males who cross-dress are not aroused by wearing ambiguous or unisex attire. Rather, they prefer feminine apparel that only women wear, such as panties, bras, or nylons. Consequently, we might expect women engaging in transvestism to become sexually aroused while wearing something strictly identified with males, such as a pair of men's briefs or a jock strap rather than jeans or a flannel work shirt, which are more unisex clothing. These behaviors among women are extremely rare in the clinical literature.

Several studies of both clinical and nonclinical populations suggest that transvestism occurs primarily among married men with predominantly heterosexual orientations (Brown, 1990; Talamini, 1982; Wise & Meyer, 1980). A recent national survey of 372 male cross-dressers reported that although a majority of these men were heterosexual, a significant portion (more than 30%) classified themselves as bisexual, homosexual, or not sexually active with another person (Bullough & Bullough, 1997).

Most married men who engage in transvestism do not tell their wives about their interest in cross-dressing prior to marriage, primarily because they believe the urge will disappear once they settle into married life. This usually does not happen, however, and most wives eventually find out. Data suggest that most wives only tolerate rather than support their husbands' cross-dressing (Brown & Collier, 1989; Bullough & Weinberg, 1988). Even if their initial reaction is not particularly negative, resentment and disgust may sometimes develop, as revealed in the following account:

The first time my husband asked if he could wear my panties I thought he was joking. When he put them on, I could see that he wasn't kidding around. Actually, we had a real good session that night, and I guess this kind of blunted my concern. After a while, it just started really bugging me. It seems like we can never just make love without his first putting on my underthings. Now I'm sick and tired of it. The whole thing seems weird. (Authors' files)

What do you think might be some of the factors associated with the development of transvestism? Could there be some similarity in how this condition and fetishism evolve?

Like fetishism and some other atypical behaviors, the development of transvestism often reveals a pattern of conditioning. Reinforcement, in the form of arousal and orgasm, may accompany cross-dressing activities at an early point in the development of sexual interest, as illustrated in the following anecdote:

When I was a kid, about 11 or 12, I was fascinated and excited by magazine pictures of women modeling undergarments. Masturbating while looking at these pictures was great. Later, I began to incorporate my mother's underthings in my little masturbation rituals, at first just touching them with my free hand, and later putting them on and parading before the mirror while I did my hand-job. Now, as an adult, I have numerous sexual encounters with women that are quite satisfying without the dress-up part. But I still occasionally do the dress-up when I'm alone, and I still find it quite exciting. (Authors' files)

Some males who engage in transvestism report having dressed up as girls during their childhood for a variety of reasons (Bullough et al., 1983). Occasionally parents initiated this behavior by dressing their young son in dainty girls' clothes because they thought it was "cute" or because they wanted a little girl rather than a boy. Often the case histories of men who engage in transvestism have revealed that as boys they were punished by being forced to dress in girls' clothes (American Psychiatric Association, 1994; Stoller, 1977). This attempt to punish by humiliation is sometimes the first step toward transvestism.

Occasionally transvestism is a behavior of the heterosexual male who is striving to explore the feminine side of his personality, an often difficult effort in a society that extols the "Marlboro Man" image. In essence, such men create two separate worlds—the one dominated by the masculine image they exhibit in public, and the private world of dress-up at home, where they can express their gentle, sensuous "feminine" selves.

Anthropologist Robert Munroe (1980) has noted that transvestism tends to appear most frequently in cultures where males shoulder a greater portion of the economic burden than their female counterparts. Munroe has speculated that in some instances transvestism may allow men in these cultures to temporarily unburden themselves from perceived pressures of responsibility by escaping into the female role, complete with feminine attire and behaviors.

Most people who engage in transvestism are not inclined to seek professional help (Brown, 1990). Even when therapy is undertaken, it is unlikely that the behavior will be appreciably altered (Wise & Meyer, 1980).

Sexual Sadism and Sexual Masochism

Sadism and masochism are often discussed under the common category **sadomasochistic** (SĀ-dō-MAS-ō-kiz-tic) **behavior** (also known as *SM*) because they are two variations of the same phenomenon, the association of sexual expression with pain. Furthermore, the dynamics of the two behaviors are similar and overlapping. Thus, in the discussion that follows, we will often refer to SM behavior or activities. However, a person who engages in one of these behaviors does not necessarily express the other, and thus sadism and masochism are actually distinct behavioral entities. The American Psychiatric Association's DSM-IV (1994) underlines this distinction by listing separate categories for each of these paraphilias: **sexual sadism** and **sexual masochism.**

Sadomasochistic behavior The association of sexual expression with pain.

Sexual sadism The act of obtaining sexual arousal through giving physical or psychological pain.

Sexual masochism The act of obtaining sexual arousal through receiving physical or psychological pain.

Labeling behavior as sexual sadism or sexual masochism is complicated because many people enjoy some form of aggressive interaction during sex play (such as "love bites") for which the label SM seems inappropriate. Alfred Kinsey and his colleagues found that 22% of the males and 12% of the females in his sample responded erotically to stories with SM themes. Furthermore, over 25% of both sexes reported erotic response to receiving love bites during sexual interaction. Hunt (1974) found that 10% of males and 8% of females in his sample (under age 35) reported obtaining sexual pleasure from SM activities during interaction with a partner. A more recent survey of 975 men and women found that 25% reported occasionally engaging in a form of SM activity with a partner (Rubin, 1990). Although sadomasochistic practices have the potential for being physically dangerous, most participants generally stay within mutually agreed-on limits, often confining their activities to mild or even symbolic SM acts with a trusted partner. In mild forms of sexual sadism, the pain inflicted may often be more symbolic than real. For example, a willing partner may be "beaten" with a feather or a soft object designed to resemble a club. Under these conditions, the receiving partner's mere feigning of suffering is sufficient to induce sexual arousal in the individual inflicting the symbolic pain.

People with masochistic inclinations may be aroused by such things as being whipped, cut, pierced with needles, bound, or spanked. The degree of pain one must experience to achieve sexual arousal varies from symbolic or very mild to, on rare occasions, severe beatings or mutilations. Sexual masochism is also reflected in individuals who achieve sexual arousal as a result of "being held in contempt, humiliated, and forced to do menial, filthy, or degrading service" (Money, 1981, p. 83). The common misconception that any kind of pain, physical or mental, will sexually arouse a person with masochistic inclinations is not true. The pain must be associated with a staged encounter whose express purpose is sexual gratification.

Bondage
Deriving sexual pleasure from being bound, tied up, or otherwise restricted.

In yet another version of masochism, some individuals derive sexual pleasure from being bound, tied up, or otherwise restricted. This behavior, called **bondage,** usually takes place with a cooperative partner who binds or restrains the individual and often administers *discipline,* such as spankings or whippings. One survey of 975 heterosexual women and men revealed that bondage may be a fairly common practice: One-fourth of respondents reported engaging in some form of bondage during some of their sexual encounters (Rubin, 1990).

Many individuals who engage in SM activities do not confine their participation to exclusive sadistic or masochistic behaviors. Some alternate between the two roles, often out of necessity, because it may be difficult to find a partner who prefers only to inflict or to receive pain. Most of these people seem to prefer one or the other role, but some may be equally comfortable in either (Moser & Levitt, 1987; Weinberg et al., 1984).

There are some indications that individuals with sexual sadistic tendencies are less common than their masochistic counterparts (Gebhard et al., 1965). This imbalance may reflect a general social script—certainly it is more virtuous to be punished than to carry out physical or mental aggression toward another. A person who needs severe pain as a prerequisite to sexual response may have difficulty finding a cooperative partner. Consequently, such individuals may resort to causing their own pain by burning, mutilating, or autoerotic asphyxia. Likewise, a person who needs to inflict intense pain in order to achieve sexual arousal may find it very difficult to find a willing partner, even for a price. We occasionally read of sadistic assaults against unwilling victims: The classic lust murder is often of this nature (Money, 1990). In these instances, orgasmic release may be produced by the homicidal violence itself.

Many people in contemporary Western societies view SM in a highly negative light. This is certainly understandable, particularly for those who regard sexual sharing as a loving, tender interaction between partners who wish to exchange pleasure. However, much of this negativity stems from a generalized perception of SM activities as perverse forms of sexual expression involving severe pain, suffering, and degradation. It is commonly assumed that individuals caught up in such activities are often victims rather than willing participants.

One group of researchers disputed these assumptions, suggesting that the traditional medical model of SM as a pathological condition is based on a limited sample of individuals who come to the attention of clinicians as a result of personality disorders or severe personality problems. As with some other atypical behaviors discussed in this chapter, these researchers argued that it is misleading to draw conclusions from such a sample. They conducted their own extensive fieldwork in nonclinical environments, interviewing a variety of SM participants and observing their behaviors in many different settings. Although some subjects' behaviors fit traditional perceptions, the researchers found that, for most participants, SM was simply a form of sexual enhancement involving elements of dominance and submission, role-playing, and consensuality "which they voluntarily and mutually chose to explore" (Weinberg et al., 1984, p. 388).

What factors might motivate a person to engage in SM activity?

Many people who engage in SM activities are motivated by a desire to experience dominance and/or submission rather than pain (Weinberg, 1987). This desire is reflected in the following account recently provided by a student in a sexuality class:

> I fantasize about sadomasochism sometimes. I want to have wild animalistic sex under the control of my husband. I want him to "force" me to do things. Domination and mild pain would seem to fulfill the moment. I have read books and talked to people about the subject, and I am terrified at some of the things, but in the bounds of my trusting relationship I would not be afraid. It seems like a silly game, but it is so damned exciting to think about. Maybe someday it will happen. (Authors' files)

Studies of sexual behavior in other species reveal that many nonhuman animals engage in what might be labeled combative or pain-inflicting behavior before coitus.

Some theorists have suggested that such activity has definite neurophysiological value, heightening accompaniments of sexual arousal such as blood pressure, muscle tension, and hyperventilation (Gebhard et al., 1965). For a variety of reasons (such as guilt, anxiety, or apathy), some people may need additional nonsexual stimuli to achieve sufficient arousal. It has also been suggested that resistance or tension between partners enhances sex and that SM is just a more extreme version of this common principle (Tripp, 1975).

SM may also provide participants with an escape from the rigidly controlled, restrictive role they must play in their everyday, public lives. This helps to explain why men who engage in SM activity are much more likely to play masochistic roles than are women (Baumeister, 1988). John Money describes the scenario in which "men who may be brokers of immense political, business or industrial power by day [become] submissive masochists begging for erotic punishment and humiliation at night" (1984, p. 169). Conversely, individuals who are normally meek may welcome the temporary opportunity to assume a powerful, dominant role within the carefully structured role-playing of SM. A related theory sees sexual masochism as an attempt to escape from high levels of self-awareness. Similar to some other behaviors (such as getting drunk) in which a person may attempt to "lose" himself or herself, masochistic activity blocks out unwanted thoughts and feelings, particularly those that may induce anxiety, guilt, or feelings of inadequacy or insecurity (Baumeister, 1988).

Clinical case studies of people who engage in SM sometimes reveal early experiences that may have established a connection between sex and pain. For example, being punished for engaging in sexual activities (such as masturbation) might result in a child or adolescent associating sex with pain. A child might even experience sexual arousal while being punished—for example, getting an erection or lubricating when one's pants are pulled down and a spanking is administered (spanking is a common SM activity). Paul Gebhard and his colleagues (1965) reported one unusual case in which a man developed a desire to engage in SM activities following an episode during his adolescence in which he experienced a great deal of pain while a fractured arm was set without the benefit of anesthesia. During the ordeal he was comforted by an attractive nurse, who caressed him and held his head against her breast in a way that created a strong conditioned association between sexual arousal and pain.

Many people, perhaps the majority, who participate in SM do not depend on these activities to achieve sexual arousal and orgasm. Those who practice it only occasionally may find that at least some of its excitement and erotic allure stems from the fact that it represents a marked departure from more conventional sexual practices. Other people who indulge in SM acts may have acquired strong negative feelings about sex, often believing it is sinful and immoral. For such people, masochistic behavior provides a guilt-relieving mechanism: Either they get their pleasure simultaneously with punishment, or they first endure the punishment to entitle them to the pleasure. Similarly, people who indulge in sadism may be punishing partners for engaging in anything so evil. Furthermore, people who have strong feelings of personal or sexual inadequacy may resort to sadistic acts of domination over their partners to temporarily alleviate these feelings.

Other Noncoercive Paraphilias

In this section we consider four additional varieties of noncoercive paraphilias that are generally uncommon or even rare. We begin our discussion by describing autoerotic asphyxia, a very dangerous form of variant sexual behavior. We then offer a few brief comments about three other uncommon noncoercive paraphilias: klismaphilia, coprophilia, and urophilia.

Autoerotic Asphyxia

Autoerotic asphyxia The enhancement of sexual excitement and orgasm by pressure-induced oxygen deprivation.

Autoerotic asphyxia (also called *hypoxyphilia* or *asphyxiophilia*) is an extraordinarily rare and life-threatening paraphilia in which an individual, almost always a male, seeks to reduce the supply of oxygen to the brain during a heightened state of sexual arousal (American Psychiatric Association, 1994; Stanley, 1993). The oxygen deprivation is usually accomplished by applying pressure to the neck with a chain, leather belt, ligature, or rope noose (via hanging). Occasionally a plastic bag or chest compression may be used as the asphyxiating device. A person may engage in these oxygen-depriving activities while alone or with a partner.

We can only theorize from limited data what motivational dynamics underlie such bizarre behavior. People who practice autoerotic asphyxia rarely disclose this activity to relatives, friends, or therapists, let alone discuss why they engage in such behavior (Garza-Leal & Landron, 1991; Saunders, 1989). For some, the goal seems to be to increase sexual arousal and to enhance the intensity of orgasm. In this situation, the item used to induce oxygen deprivation (such as a rope) is typically tightened around the neck to produce heightened arousal during masturbation and then released at the time of orgasm. Individuals often devise elaborate techniques that enable them to free themselves from the strangling device prior to losing consciousness.

The enhancement of sexual excitement by pressure-induced oxygen deprivation may bear some relationship to reports that orgasm may be intensified by inhaling amyl nitrate ("poppers"), a drug used to treat heart pain. This substance is known to temporarily reduce brain oxygenation through peripheral dilation of the arteries that supply the brain with blood.

It has also been suggested that autoerotic asphyxia may be a highly unusual variant of sexual masochism in which participants act out ritualized bondage themes (American Psychiatric Association, 1994; Cosgray et al., 1991). People who engage in this practice sometimes keep diaries of elaborate bondage fantasies and, in some cases, describe experiencing fantasies of being asphyxiated or harmed by others as they engage in this rare paraphilia.

One important fact about this seldom-seen paraphilia is quite clear: This is a very dangerous activity that often results in death (Blanchard & Hucker, 1991; Cosgray et al., 1991). Accidental deaths sometimes occur due to equipment malfunction or mistakes such as errors in the placement of the noose or ligature. Data from the United States, England, Australia, and Canada indicate that one to two deaths per million population are caused by autoerotic asphyxiation each year (American Psychiatric Association, 1994). The Federal Bureau of Investigation estimates that deaths in the United States resulting from this activity may run as high as 1000 per year.

Klismaphilia

Klismaphilia
A very unusual variant in sexual expression in which an individual obtains sexual pleasure from receiving enemas.

Klismaphilia (klis-ma-FIL-ē-uh) is a very unusual variant in sexual expression in which an individual obtains sexual pleasure from receiving enemas. Less commonly, the erotic arousal may be associated with giving enemas. The case histories of many individuals who express klismaphilia reveal that as infants or young children they were frequently administered enemas by concerned and affectionate mothers. This association of loving attention with anal stimulation may eroticize the experience for some people so that as adults they may manifest a need to receive an enema as a substitute for or necessary prerequisite to genital intercourse.

Coprophilia and Urophilia

Coprophilia
A sexual paraphilia in which a person obtains sexual arousal from contact with feces.

Urophilia
A sexual paraphilia in which a person obtains sexual arousal from contact with urine.

Coprophilia (cop-rō-FIL-ē-uh) and **urophilia** (yoo′-rō-FIL-ē-uh) refer to activities in which people obtain sexual arousal from contact with feces and urine, respectively. Individuals who exhibit coprophilia achieve high levels of sexual excitement from watching someone defecate or by defecating on someone. In rare instances, they may achieve arousal when someone defecates on them. Urophilia is expressed by urinating on someone or being urinated on. This activity, reflected in the chapter-opening anecdote, has been referred to as "water sports" and "golden showers." There is no consensus opinion as to the origins of these highly unusual paraphilias.

Coercive Paraphilias

In this section we first discuss three very common forms of coercive paraphilic behaviors: exhibitionism, obscene phone calls, and voyeurism. Three other varieties of coercive paraphilias—frotteurism, necrophilia, and zoophilia—will also be discussed.

Exhibitionism

Exhibitionism
The act of exposing one's genitals to an unwilling observer.

Exhibitionism, often called "indecent exposure," refers to behavior in which an individual (almost always male) exposes his genitals to an involuntary observer (usually an adult woman or female child) (American Psychiatric Association, 1994; Marshall et al., 1991). Typically, a man who has exposed himself obtains sexual gratification by masturbating shortly thereafter, using mental images of the observer's reaction to increase his arousal (Blair & Lanyon, 1981). Some men may, while having sex with a willing partner, fantasize about exposing themselves or replay mental images from previous episodes (Money, 1981). Still others may have orgasm triggered by the very act of exposure, and a few may masturbate while exhibiting themselves (American Psychiatric Association, 1994; Freund et al., 1988). The reinforcement of associating sexual arousal and orgasm with the actual act of exhibitionism, or with mental fantasies of exposing oneself, contributes significantly to the maintenance of exhibitionistic behavior (Blair & Lanyon, 1981). Exposure may occur in a variety of locations, most of which allow for easy escape. Subways, relatively deserted streets, parks, and cars with a door left open are common places for exhibitionism to occur. However, sometimes a private dwelling may be the scene of an exposure, as revealed in the following account:

One evening I was shocked to open the door of my apartment to a naked man. I looked long enough to see that he was underdressed for the occasion and then slammed the door in his face. He didn't come back. I'm sure my look of total horror was what he was after. But it is difficult to keep your composure when you open your door to a naked man. (Authors' files)

Certainly, many of us have exhibitionistic tendencies: We may go to nude beaches, parade before admiring lovers, or wear provocative clothes or scanty swimwear. However, such behavior is considered appropriate by a society that in many ways exploits and celebrates the erotically portrayed human body. The fact that legally defined exhibitionistic behavior involves generally unwilling observers sets it apart from these more acceptable variations of exhibitionism.

Our knowledge of who displays this behavior is based almost exclusively on studies of arrested offenders—a sample that may be unrepresentative. This sampling problem is common to many forms of atypical behavior that are defined as criminal. From the available data, however limited, it appears that most people who exhibit themselves are adult males in their 20s or 30s, and over half are married or have been. They are often very shy, nonassertive people who feel inadequate and insecure and suffer from problems with intimacy (Arndt, 1991; Marshall et al., 1991). They may function quite efficiently in their daily lives and be commonly characterized by others as "nice, but kind of shy." Their sexual relationships are likely to have been quite unsatisfactory. Many were reared in atmospheres characterized by puritanical and shame-inducing attitudes toward sexuality.

What influences a person to engage in exhibitionism? What do you think might motivate such behavior?

A number of factors may influence the development of exhibitionistic behavior. Many individuals may have such powerful feelings of personal inadequacy that they are afraid to reach out to another person out of fear of rejection (Minor & Dwyer, 1997). Their exhibitionism may thus be a limited attempt to somehow involve others, however

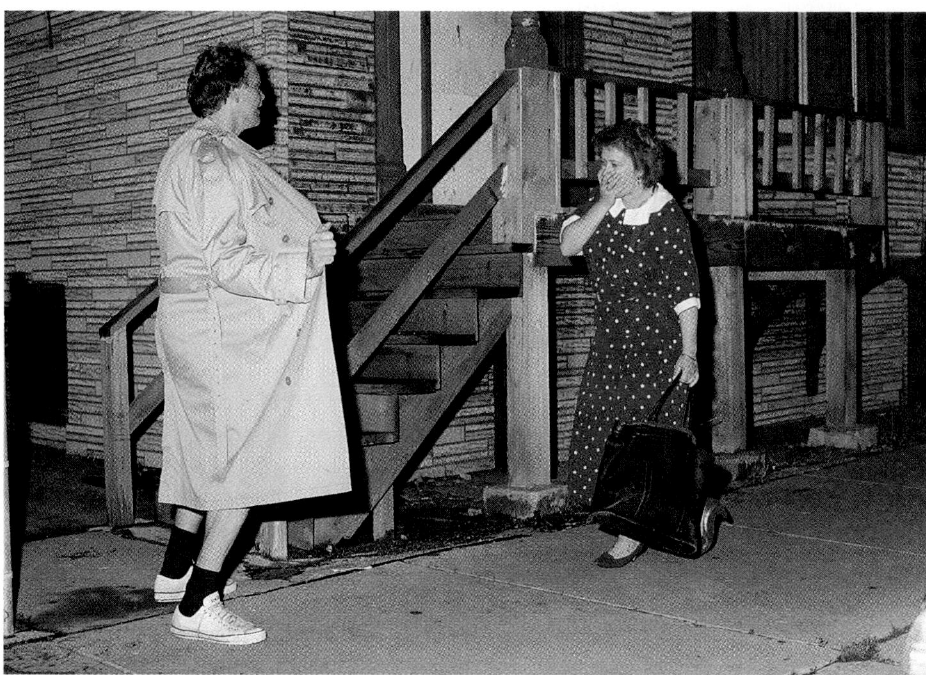

Exhibitionists often want to elicit reactions of shock, disgust, fear, or terror. The best response is to calmly ignore the person and casually go about your business.

fleetingly, in their sexual expression. Limiting contact to briefly opening a raincoat before dashing off minimizes the possibility of overt rejection. Some men who expose themselves may be looking for affirmation of their masculinity. Others, feeling isolated and unappreciated, may simply be seeking attention they desperately crave. A few may feel anger and hostility toward people, particularly women, who have failed to notice them or who they believe have caused them emotional pain. In these circumstances, exposure may be a form of reprisal, designed to shock or frighten the people they see as the source of their discomfort. In addition, exhibitionism is not uncommon in emotionally disturbed, intellectually disabled, or mentally disoriented individuals. In these cases, the behavior may reflect a limited awareness of what society defines as appropriate actions, a breakdown in personal ethical controls, or both.

In contrast to the public image of an exhibitionist as one who lurks about in the shadows, ready to grab hapless victims and drag them off to ravish them, most men who engage in exhibitionism limit this activity to exposing themselves (American Psychiatric Association, 1994; Davison & Neale, 1993). Yet the word *victim* is not entirely inappropriate, in that observers of such exhibitionistic episodes may be emotionally traumatized by the experience (Cox, 1988; Marshall et al., 1991). Some may feel that they are in danger of being raped or otherwise harmed. A few, particularly young children, may develop negative feelings about genital anatomy from such an experience.

Investigators have noted that some people who expose themselves, probably a small minority, may actually physically assault their victims. Furthermore, it also seems probable that some men who engage in exhibitionism progress from exposing themselves to more serious offenses such as rape and child molesting. In a one-of-a-kind study, Gene Abel (1981), a Columbia University researcher, conducted an in-depth investigation of the motives and behavior of 207 men who admitted to a variety of sexual offenses, including child molesting and rape. This research is unique in that all participants were men outside the legal system who voluntarily sought treatment after being guaranteed confidentiality. Abel found that 49% of the rapists in his sample had histories of other types of variant sexual behavior, generally preceding the onset of rape behavior. The most common of these were child molestation, exhibitionism, voyeurism, incest, and sadism. A more recent study of 274 Canadian sex offenders, all adult males, revealed that most had engaged in multiple types of variant sexual behavior, including paraphilias and more serious forms of sexual victimization, such as child molestation and rape. Collectively, these subjects admitted to 7677 total incidents of sexual offenses, an average of 28 incidents per offender. These findings suggest that "paraphiliacs tend to have multiple types of sexual aberrations as well as a high frequency of deviant acts per individual" (Bradford et al., 1992, p. 104). These findings do not imply that people who engage in such activities as exhibitionism and voyeurism will inevitably develop into child molesters and rapists. However, it seems clear that some people may progress beyond these relatively minor acts to far more severe patterns of sexual aggression.

Although perhaps all of us would like protection against being sexually used without our consent, it seems unnecessarily harsh and punitive to imprison people for exhibitionistic behavior, particularly first-time offenders. In recent years, at least in some locales, there has been some movement toward therapy as an alternative to incarceration. Later in this chapter, we will discuss a variety of therapeutic techniques used to treat exhibitionism and other paraphilias.

What is an appropriate response if someone exposes himself to you? It is important to keep in mind that most people who express exhibitionist behavior want to elicit reactions of shock, fear, disgust, or terror. Although it may be difficult not to react in any of these ways, a better response is to calmly ignore the exhibitionist act and go about your business. Of course, it is also important to immediately distance yourself from the offender and to report such acts to the police or campus security as soon as possible.

Obscene Phone Calls

People who make obscene phone calls share similar characteristics with those who engage in exhibitionism. Thus, obscene phone calling (sometimes called *telephone scatologia*) is viewed by some professionals as a subtype of exhibitionism. People who make obscene phone calls typically experience sexual arousal when their victims react in a horrified or shocked manner, and many masturbate during or immediately after a "successful" phone exchange. As one extensive study has indicated, these callers are typically male, and they often suffer from pervasive feelings of inadequacy and insecurity (Matek, 1988; Nadler, 1968). Obscene phone calls are frequently the only way they can find to have sexual exchanges. However, when relating to the other sex, they frequently show greater anxiety and hostility than do people inclined toward exhibitionism, as revealed in the following account:

> One night I received a phone call from a man who sounded quite normal until he started his barrage of filth. Just as I was about to slam the phone down, he announced, "Don't hang up. I know where you live (address followed) and that you have two little girls. If you don't want to find them all mangled up, you will hear what I have to say. Furthermore, I expect you to be available for calls every night at this time." It was a nightmare. He called night after night. Sometimes he made me listen while he masturbated. Finally I couldn't take it any longer, and I contacted the police. They were unable to catch him, but they sure scared him off in short order, thank heaven. I was about to go crazy. (Authors' files)

Fortunately, a caller rarely follows up his verbal assault with a physical attack on his victim.

A recent survey of a nationally representative sample of several hundred women found that 16% had received at least one obscene phone call during the previous six months. The majority of these calls appeared to not be random but rather targeted in some fashion, often on women less than 65 years of age who were neither married nor widowed. The study's author suggests that her findings indicate that obscene phone calls occur in patterns similar to that of the expression of rage and perhaps can be best explained as "displaced aggression against a vulnerable population" (Katz, 1994, p. 155).

What is the best way to handle obscene phone calls? Information about how to deal with obscene phone calls is available from most local phone company offices. Because they are commonly besieged by such queries, you may need to be persistent in your request. A few tips are worth knowing; they may even make it unnecessary to seek outside help.

First, quite often the caller has picked your name at random from a phone book or perhaps knows you from some other source and is just trying you out to see what kind of reaction he can get. Your initial response may be critical in determining his subsequent actions. He wants you to be horrified, shocked, or disgusted; thus, the best response is usually not to react overtly. Slamming down the phone may reveal your emotional state and provide reinforcement to the caller. Simply set it down gently and go about your business. If the phone rings again immediately, ignore it. Chances are that he will seek out other, more responsive victims.

Other tactics may also be helpful. One, used successfully by a former student, is to feign deafness. "What is that you said? You must speak up. I'm hard of hearing, you know!" Setting down the phone with the explanation that you are going to another extension (which you never arrive at) may be another practical solution. Finally, screening calls via an answering machine may also prove helpful. The caller is likely to hang up in the absence of an emotionally responding person.

If you are persistently bothered by obscene phone calls, you may need to take additional steps. Your telephone company should cooperate in changing your number to an unlisted one at no charge. It is probably not a good idea to heed the common advice to blow in the mouthpiece with a police whistle (which may be quite painful and even harmful to the caller's ear) because you may end up receiving the same treatment from your caller.

A relatively new service offered by many telephone companies, called *call trace* or call tracing, may assist you in dealing with repetitive obscene or threatening phone calls. After breaking connection with the caller, you enter a designated code, such as star 57. The telephone company then automatically traces the call. After a certain number of successful traces to the same number, a warning letter is sent to the offender indicating that he or she has been identified as engaging in unlawful behavior, which must stop. The offender is warned that police intervention or civil legal action may be an option if the behavior continues. Call trace is clearly not effective when calls are placed from a public pay phone, and calls made from cellular phones cannot be traced.

Voyeurism

Voyeurism
The act of obtaining sexual gratification by observing undressed or sexually interacting people without their consent.

Voyeurism (voi-YUR-iz-um) refers to deriving sexual pleasure from looking at the naked bodies or sexual activities of others, usually strangers, without their consent (American Psychiatric Association, 1994). Because a degree of voyeurism is socially acceptable (witness the popularity of R- and X-rated movies and magazines like *Playboy* and *Playgirl*), it is sometimes difficult to determine when voyeuristic behavior becomes a problem (Arndt, 1991; Forsyth, 1996). To qualify as atypical sexual behavior, voyeurism must be preferred to sexual relations with another or indulged in with some risk (or both). People who engage in this behavior are often most sexually aroused when the risk of discovery is high—which may explain why most are not attracted to such places as nudist camps and nude beaches, where looking is acceptable (Tollison & Adams, 1979).

As the common term *peeping Tom* implies, this behavior is typically, although not exclusively, expressed by males (Davison & Neale, 1993). Voyeurism includes peering in bedroom windows, stationing oneself by the entrance to women's bathrooms, and boring holes in the walls of public dressing rooms. Some men travel elaborate routes several nights a week for the occasional reward of a glimpse through a window of bare anatomy or, rarely, a scene of sexual interaction.

Again, people inclined toward voyeurism often share some characteristics with people who expose themselves (Arndt, 1991; Langevin et al., 1979). They may have poorly developed sociosexual skills, with strong feelings of inferiority and inadequacy, particularly as directed toward potential sexual partners. They tend to be very young men, usually in their early 20s (Davison & Neale, 1993; Dwyer, 1988). They rarely "peep" at someone they know, preferring strangers instead. Voyeurism is not typically associated with other antisocial behavior. Most individuals who engage in such activity are content merely to look, keeping their distance. However, in some instances, such individuals go on to more serious offenses such as burglary, arson, assault, and even rape (Abel, 1981; Langevin et al., 1985; MacNamara & Sagarin, 1977).

It is difficult to isolate specific influences that trigger voyeuristic behavior, particularly because so many of us demonstrate these tendencies in a somewhat more controlled fashion. The adolescent or young adult male who displays this behavior often feels great curiosity about sexual activity (as many of us do) but at the same time feels very inadequate or insecure. Peeping becomes a vicarious fulfillment because he may be unable to consummate sexual relationships with others without experiencing a great deal of anxiety. In some instances, voyeuristic behavior may also be reinforced by feelings of power and superiority over those who are secretly observed.

Frotteurism is a fairly common paraphilia practiced in crowded public places, such as buses, subways, or outdoor concerts.

Other Coercive Paraphilias

We conclude our discussion of coercive paraphilias with a few brief comments about three additional varieties of these coercive or invasive forms of paraphilias. The first two, frotteurism and zoophilia, are actually fairly common. The third variant form, necrophilia, is quite rare in addition to being an extremely aberrant form of sexual expression.

Frotteurism

Frotteurism (fro-TUR-izm) is a fairly common coercive paraphilia that goes largely unnoticed. It involves an individual, usually a male, who obtains sexual pleasure by pressing or rubbing against a fully clothed female in a crowded public place, such as an elevator, bus, subway, large sporting events, or an outdoor concert. The most common form of contact is between the man's clothed penis and a woman's buttocks or legs. Less commonly he may use his hands to touch a woman's thighs, pubic region, breasts, or buttocks. Often the contact seems to be inadvertent, and the woman who is touched may not notice or pay little heed to the seemingly casual contact. On the other hand, she may feel victimized and angry. In rare cases, she may reciprocate (Money, 1984).

Frotteurism
A fairly common paraphilia in which a person obtains sexual pleasure by pressing or rubbing against another in a crowded public place.

The man who engages in frotteurism may achieve arousal and orgasm during the act. More commonly, he incorporates the mental images of his actions into masturbation fantasies at a later time. Men who engage in this activity have many of the characteristics manifested by those who practice exhibitionism. They are frequently plagued with feelings of social and sexual inadequacy. Their brief, furtive contacts with strangers in crowded places allow them to include others in their sexual expression in a safe, nonthreatening manner.

As with other paraphilias, it is difficult to estimate just how common this variety of coercive paraphilias is. One study of a sample of reportedly typical or normal college men found that 21% of the respondents had engaged in one or more frotteuristic acts (Templeman & Sinnett, 1991).

Zoophilia

Zoophilia (ZŌ-Ō-FIL-ē-uh), sometimes called *bestiality,* involves sexual contact between humans and animals (American Psychiatric Association, 1994). You may wonder why we classify this as a coercive paraphilia because such behavior does not involve coercing other people into acts they would normally avoid. In many instances of zoophilia, it is reasonable to presume that the involved animals are also unwilling participants, and the performed acts are often both coercive and invasive. Consequently, assigning this paraphilia to the coercive category seems quite appropriate.

Zoophilia
A paraphilia in which a person has sexual contact with animals.

In Kinsey's sample populations, 8% of the males and almost 4% of the females reported having had sexual experience with animals at some point in their lives. The frequency of such behavior among males was highest for those raised on farms (17% of these men reported experiencing orgasm as a result of animal contact). The animals most frequently involved in sex with humans are calves, sheep, donkeys, large fowl (ducks and geese), dogs, and cats. Males are most likely to have contact with farm animals and to engage in penile–vaginal intercourse or to have their genitals orally stimulated by the animals (Hunt, 1974; Kinsey et al., 1948). Women are more likely to have contact with household pets, involving the animals licking their genitals or masturbating a male dog. Less commonly, some adult women have trained a dog to mount them and engage in coitus (Gendel & Bonner, 1988; Kinsey et al., 1953).

Sexual contact with animals is commonly only a transitory experience of young people to whom a human sexual partner is inaccessible or forbidden (Money, 1981). Most adolescent males and females who experiment with zoophilia make a transition to adult sexual relations with human partners. Occasionally an adult may engage in such behavior as a "sexual adventure" (Tollison & Adams, 1979). True or nontransitory zoophilia exists only when sexual contact with animals is preferred regardless of what other forms of sexual expression are available. Such behavior, which is quite rare, is generally only expressed by people with deep-rooted psychological problems or distorted images of the other sex. For example, a man who has a pathological hatred of women may be attempting to express his contempt for them by choosing animals in preference to women as sexual partners.

Necrophilia

Necrophilia
A rare sexual paraphilia in which a person obtains sexual gratification by viewing or having intercourse with a corpse.

Necrophilia (nek-rō-FIL-ē-uh) is an extremely rare sexual variation in which a person obtains sexual gratification by viewing or having intercourse with a corpse. This paraphilia appears to occur exclusively among males, who may be driven to remove freshly buried bodies from cemeteries or to seek employment in morgues or funeral homes (Tollison & Adams, 1979). However, the vast majority of people who work in these settings do not have tendencies toward necrophilia.

There are a few cases on record of men with necrophilic preferences who kill someone in order to gain access to a corpse. The notorious Jeffrey Dahmer, the Milwaukee man who murdered and mutilated his victims, is believed by some experts on criminal pathology to have been motivated by uncontrollable necrophilic urges. More commonly, the difficulties associated with gaining access to dead bodies lead some men with necrophilic preferences to limit their deviant behavior to contact with simulated corpses. Some prostitutes cater to this desire by powdering themselves to produce the pallor of death, dressing in a shroud, and lying very still during intercourse. Any movement on their part may inhibit their customers' sexual arousal.

Men who engage in necrophilia almost always manifest severe emotional disorders (Goldman, 1992). They may see themselves as sexually and socially inept and may both hate and fear women. Consequently, the only "safe" woman may be one whose lifelessness epitomizes a nonthreatening, totally subjugated sexual partner (Rosman & Resnick, 1989; Stoller, 1977).

Treatment of Coercive Paraphilias

In most instances noncoercive paraphilias, while clearly atypical, fall within the boundaries of acceptable modes of sexual expression. Furthermore, since they rarely cause personal anguish or harm to others, treatment is generally not called for. However, in view of the invasive nature of coercive paraphilias, which often harm others, treatment is appropriate and often necessary. Unfortunately, getting people who engage in these paraphilias to seek or accept therapeutic intervention is another matter. People who embrace one or more of the coercive paraphilias usually do not voluntarily seek treatment, nor do they acknowledge that they are in need of and/or will benefit from treatment. These individuals are thus more likely to become involved with the mental health system only after either being arrested and processed by the legal system, or because of pressure from family members who have discovered their paraphilic behavior(s).

The treatment difficulties attributable to the nonvoluntary nature of client referrals is further compounded by the fact that paraphilic behaviors are typically a source of immense pleasure. Consequently, most people are highly motivated to continue rather than give up these acts (Money, 1988; Money & Lamacz, 1990). Therapeutic treatment, regardless of the specific techniques or strategies employed, is often not very successful with clients who are resistant to change.

Finally, people who compulsively engage in one or more of the coercive paraphilias often claim they are unable to control their urges. This perceived lack of control runs counter to a basic tenet of most mental health therapies, which, simply stated, maintains that before we can constructively change our behavior we first must accept responsibility for our actions, no matter how driven or uncontrollable they may appear to be. Thus, a first step in a successful treatment program is to break through a client's belief that he is powerless to change his behavior.

A number of different approaches have been used in the treatment of coercive paraphilias with varied degrees of success. We will consider four of the more commonly used avenues of treatment: psychotherapy, behavior therapies, drug treatments, and social skills training.

Psychotherapy

Individual **psychotherapy**—in which a client talks with a psychologist, psychiatrist, or social worker for an hour or more each week—has generally not proven very effective in treating coercive paraphilias. It is difficult to overcome years of conditioning and the resultant powerful urges to continue paraphilic behavior, however problematic, in one or two hours a week of verbal interaction.

Limited success in treating paraphilias has been reported by psychologists who employ **cognitive therapies.** Cognitive therapies are based on the premise that most psychological disorders result from distortions in a person's cognitions or thoughts. Psychotherapists who operate within the cognitive framework attempt to demonstrate to their clients how their distorted or irrational thoughts have contributed to their difficulties, and they use a variety of techniques to help them change these cognitions to more appropriate ones (Johnston et al., 1997). Thus, although the goal of therapy is to change a person's maladaptive paraphilic behavior, the method in cognitive therapies is to first change what the person thinks.

Psychotherapy
A noninvasive procedure involving verbal interaction between a client and therapist designed to improve a person's adjustment to life.

Cognitive therapies
Approaches to therapy that are based on the premise that most psychological disorders result from distortions in cognitions or thoughts.

Unfortunately, it is often very difficult to modify the distorted ideas or cognitions that people use to justify their paraphilic behaviors. In addition to being highly invested in continuing these intensely pleasurable activities, most people who engage in coercive paraphilias believe that the problems associated with these acts result from society's intolerance of their variant behaviors, and not from the fundamental inappropriateness of such acts. Changing these distorted cognitions can be a real challenge.

Behavior Therapies

Traditional models of psychotherapy have emphasized the underlying causes of psychological disorders, which are viewed as distinct from those that mold so-called normal

Behavior therapy Therapy based on the assumption that maladaptive behavior has been learned and can therefore be unlearned.

behavior. **Behavior therapy** departs from this traditional conception. Its central thesis is that maladaptive behavior has been learned, and that it can be unlearned. Furthermore, the same principles that govern the learning of normal behavior also determine the acquisition of abnormal or atypical behaviors. Behavior therapy draws heavily on the extensive body of laboratory research on strategies for helping people to unlearn maladaptive behavior patterns. Behavior therapy focuses on the person's current behaviors that are creating problems. These maladaptive patterns are considered to be the problem, and behavior therapists are not interested in restructuring personalities or searching for repressed conflicts. To change these inappropriate behaviors, they enact appropriate changes in the interaction between the client and his or her environment. For example, a person who responds sexually while exposing himself might be treated through repeated exposures to an aversive stimulus paired with the situation/stimuli that elicits the inappropriate arousal pattern. This technique, called *aversive conditioning,* is one of several behavior therapy techniques outlined as follows.

Aversive Conditioning

Aversive conditioning A behavior therapy method that substitutes a negative response for positive responses to inappropriate stimuli.

The goal of **aversive conditioning** is to substitute a negative (aversive) response for a positive response to an inappropriate stimulus situation. For example, an undesired sexual behavior, such as masturbating while replaying mental images from previous episodes of exhibitionism, is paired repeatedly with an aversive stimulus such as a painful but not damaging electric shock, a nausea-inducing drug, or a very unpleasant odor. Similarly, an aversive stimulus may be administered to a person while he views photographs or color slides depicting the paraphilic behavior.

A recent study reported some success in the use of aversive conditioning to treat exhibitionism. A number of male offenders were instructed to carry smelling salts (a very unpleasant odor) and told to inhale deeply whenever they felt compelled to expose themselves. This approach helped some of the offenders to develop some control over their paraphilic behaviors by virtue of learning to associate the aversive odor with their deviant fantasies/urges (Marshall et al., 1991).

Aversive conditioning is not a pleasant experience, and you may wonder why anyone would undergo it voluntarily. The answer is that aversive conditioning as a treatment for coercive paraphilias is most commonly used with men required by the legal system to undergo treatment. However, in some cases family pressures or a personal dissatisfaction with the complications associated with paraphilic behavior have led some men to voluntarily seek this therapeutic intervention.

Systematic Desensitization

Systematic desensitization Behavior therapy technique that pairs slow, systematic exposure to anxiety-inducing situations with relaxation training.

One of the most widely used behavior therapy techniques is **systematic desensitization,** a strategy originally developed by Joseph Wolpe (1958 & 1985) to treat people who are excessively anxious in certain situations. This behavioral technique is based on the premise that people cannot be both relaxed and anxious at the same time. Therefore, if individuals can be trained to relax when confronted with anxiety-inducing stimuli, they will be able to overcome their anxiety.

People who engage in paraphilias frequently depend on these acts for sexual satisfaction, because they often find it very difficult to establish satisfying sexual relationships with partners, due to strong feelings of personal inadequacy and poorly developed interpersonal skills. Consequently, helping people to overcome their anxieties about relating to others by conditioning them to relax in sociosexual situations can help to replace inappropriate paraphilic behaviors with more healthy expressions of intimacy and sexuality. Furthermore, relaxation is also incompatible with sexual arousal. Therefore, systematic desensitization can also be used to break the link between sexual arousal and inappropriate paraphilic behavior by substituting relaxation for arousal.

The key to successful application of this therapeutic method is to proceed slowly and systematically. The first step is to construct a hierarchy of situations that trigger anxiety or inappropriate sexual arousal with the most intense anxiety-inducing or sexually arousing at the top of the list and the least at the bottom. The next phase is to teach the client to relax selected muscle groups in his body. In the final stage, muscle relaxation is paired repeatedly with each of a series of progressively more intense images. When the client is able to repeatedly imagine the mildly threatening or arousing situation at the bottom of the list without experiencing any anxiety or arousal, his attention is then directed to the next image in the hierarchy. Over the course of several sessions, relaxation gradually replaces anxiety or sexual arousal to each of the stimulus situations, even the most intense at the top of the hierarchical list.

Orgasmic Reconditioning

The goal of this version of behavior therapy is to increase sexual arousal and response to appropriate stimuli by pairing imagery/fantasies of socially normative or acceptable sexual behavior with the reinforcing pleasure of orgasm (Laws & Marshall, 1991; Walen & Roth, 1987). In **orgasmic reconditioning,** the client is instructed to masturbate to his usual paraphilic images or fantasies. However, when he feels orgasm is imminent, he switches to more socially appropriate imagery, on which he is told to focus during orgasm. Ideally, after practicing this technique several times, he will become accustomed to having orgasms in conjunction with more healthy imagery/fantasies. Once this is achieved, the client is encouraged to move these more appropriate images to a progressively earlier phase of his masturbation-produced sexual arousal and response. In this fashion he may gradually become conditioned to experiencing sexual arousal and orgasm in the context of socially acceptable behaviors.

Orgasmic reconditioning
A behavior therapy technique in which a client is instructed to switch from paraphilic to healthy fantasies at the moment of masturbatory orgasm.

Satiation Therapy

Another, related technique for treating coercive paraphilias in which masturbation plays a central role is called **satiation therapy.** In this approach to treatment the client masturbates to orgasm while fantasizing or imagining images of appropriate sexual situations. He is instructed to switch to his favorite paraphilic fantasy immediately after orgasm and to continue masturbating. The premise or theory behind this approach is that the low level of arousal and response accompanying the postorgasmic masturbation to paraphilic images will eventually result in these inappropriate stimuli becoming unarousing and perhaps even irritating (Abel et al., 1992; Laws & Marshall, 1991).

Satiation therapy
A technique for reducing arousal to inappropriate stimuli by first masturbating to orgasm while imagining appropriate stimuli and then continuing to masturbate while fantasizing about paraphilic images.

Drug Treatment

Antiandrogen drugs (see Chapter 6) that drastically lower testosterone levels have been used effectively in some instances to block the inappropriate sexual arousal patterns underlying coercive paraphilic behavior (Abel et al., 1992; Bradford, 1998; Rösler & Witztum, 1998). *Medroxyprogesterone acetate* (MPA, also known by its trade name, *Depo-Provera*) and *cyproterone acetate* (CPA) are two antiandrogen drugs most commonly used to treat sex offenders, including those whose paraphilic behaviors have brought them into contact with legal authorities.

Antiandrogen drugs
Drugs that may block inappropriate sexual arousal patterns by lowering testosterone levels.

Drug treatment of coercive paraphilias is most effective when combined with other therapeutic methods such as psychotherapy or behavior therapy (Abel et al., 1992; Bradford & Pawlak, 1993b). The major advantage of these drugs as adjuncts to other treatment techniques is that they markedly reduce the driven or compulsive nature of the paraphilia. This better enables the client to focus his efforts on other therapeutic procedures without being so strongly distracted by his paraphilic urges.

Social Skills Training

Social skills training Training designed to teach socially inept clients the skills necessary to initiate and maintain satisfying relationships.

Finally, people who engage in paraphilias often have great difficulty forming sociosexual relationships and thus may not have access to healthy forms of sexual expression. Consequently, these individuals may benefit from **social skills training** designed to teach them the skills necessary to initiate and maintain satisfying relationships with potential intimate/sexual partners. Such training, often conducted in conjunction with other therapeutic interventions, may involve practice in initiating social interaction with prospective companions, conversational skills, how to ask someone out on a date, and how to cope with perceived rejection.

Sexual Addiction: Fact, Fiction, or Misnomer?

In recent years, both the professional literature and the popular media have directed considerable attention to a condition commonly referred to as sexual addiction. The idea that people may become dominated by insatiable sexual needs has been around for a long time, exemplified by the terms *nymphomania,* applied to women, and *satyriasis* or *Don Juanism,* applied to men. Many professionals have traditionally reacted negatively to these labels, suggesting that they are disparaging terms likely to induce unnecessary guilt in individuals who enjoy an active sex life. Furthermore, it has been argued that one cannot assign a label implying excessive sexual activity when no clear criteria establish what constitutes "normal" levels of sexual involvement. The criteria often used to establish alleged subconditions of *hypersexuality*—nymphomania and satyriasis—are subjective and value laden. Therefore, these terms are typically defined moralistically rather than scientifically, a fact that has generated harsh criticism from a number of professionals (Klein, 1991; Levine & Troiden, 1988). Nevertheless, the concept of compulsive sexuality achieved a heightened legitimacy with the publication of Patrick Carnes's book, *The Sexual Addiction* (1983), later retitled *Out of the Shadows: Understanding Sexual Addiction* (1992, 2nd ed.).

According to Carnes, many people who engage in some of the atypical or paraphilic behaviors described in this chapter (as well as victimization behaviors, such as child molesting, described in Chapter 19) are manifesting the outward symptoms of a process of psychological addiction in which feelings of depression, anxiety, loneliness, and worthlessness are temporarily relieved through a sexual high not unlike the high achieved by mood-altering chemicals such as alcohol or cocaine. Carnes suggested that a typical addiction cycle progresses through four phases. Initially, the sex addict enters a trancelike state of *preoccupation* in which obsessive thoughts about a particular sex behavior, such as exposing oneself, create a consuming need to achieve expression of the behavior. This intense preoccupation induces certain *ritualistic* behaviors, such as running a regular route through a particular neighborhood where previous incidents of exposing have occurred. Their ritualistic behaviors tend to further intensify the sexual excitement that was initially aroused during the preoccupation phase. The next phase is the actual expression of the *sexual act,* in this case exposing oneself. This is followed by the final phase, one of *despair,* in which sex addicts are overwhelmed by feelings of worthlessness, depression, and anxiety. One way to minimize or anesthetize this despair is to start the cycle again. With each repetitive cycle, the addiction behavior becomes more intense and unmanageable, "thus confirming the basic feelings of unworthiness that are the core of the addict's belief system" (Carnes, 1986, p. 5).

Carnes's conception of the sexual addict has generated considerable attention within the professional community. However, many sexologists do not believe that sexual addiction should be a distinct diagnostic category, because it is both rare and lacking in distinction from other compulsive disorders, such as gambling and eating disorders, and

The 1977 film *Looking for Mr. Goodbar* featured Diane Keaton in the role of a woman who compulsively sought sex from strange men at bars (the other actor in this scene is Richard Gere).

because this label negates individual responsibility for "uncontrollable" sexual compulsions that victimize others (Barth & Kinder, 1987; Levine & Troiden, 1988; Peele & Brodsky, 1987). This position is reflected in a decision not to include a category encompassing hypersexuality in the most recent version of the *Diagnostic and Statistical Manual* (DSM-IV) of the American Psychiatric Association (1994) (the most widely accepted system for classifying psychological disorders).

A number of professionals acknowledge the validity of such arguments against the addiction concept but nevertheless recognize that some people may become involved in patterns of excessive sexual activity that reflect a lack of control. Noteworthy in this group is sexologist Eli Coleman (1990 & 1991), who prefers to describe these behaviors as symptomatic of sexual compulsion rather than addiction. According to Coleman, a person manifesting excessive sexual behaviors often suffers from feelings of shame, unworthiness, inadequacy, and loneliness. These negative feelings cause great psychological pain and this pain then causes the person to search for a "fix," or an agent that has pain-numbing qualities, such as alcohol, certain foods, gambling, or, in this instance, sex. Indulging oneself in this fix produces only a brief respite from the psychological pain that returns in full force, thus triggering a greater need to engage in these behaviors to obtain temporary relief. Unfortunately, these repetitive, compulsive acts soon tend to be self-defeating in that they compound feelings of shame and lead to intimacy dysfunction by interrupting the development of normal, healthy interpersonal functioning.

The topic of compulsive sexual behavior has been the subject of growing interest in both the professional community and the popular media (Black et al., 1997). We can expect that professionals within the field of sexuality will continue to debate for some time how to diagnose, describe, and explain problems of excessive or uncontrolled sexuality. Even as this discussion continues, professional treatment programs for compulsive or addictive sexual behaviors have emerged throughout the nation (over 2000 programs at last count), most modeled after Alcoholics Anonymous's twelve-step program. Data pertaining to treatment outcomes for these programs are still too limited to evaluate therapeutic effectiveness. Besides formal treatment programs, a number of community-based, self-help organizations have surfaced throughout the United States. Some of these groups are Sex Addicts Anonymous, Sexaholics Anonymous, Sexual Compulsives Anonymous, and Sex and Love Addicts Anonymous.

Summary

WHAT CONSTITUTES ATYPICAL SEXUAL BEHAVIOR?

Atypical, paraphilic sexual behavior involves a variety of sexual activities that in their fully developed form are statistically uncommon in the general population.

Such behaviors exist in many gradations, ranging from mild, infrequently expressed tendencies to full-blown, regularly manifested behaviors.

Paraphilias are usually expressed by males, sometimes harm others, may be preludes to more serious sexual offenses, and tend to occur in clusters.

NONCOERCIVE PARAPHILIAS

Noncoercive paraphilias are often solo activities or ones that involve the participation of consensual adults who agree to engage in, observe, or just put up with the particular variant behavior.

Fetishism, transvestism, sexual sadism, sexual masochism, klismaphilia, coprophilia, and urophilia are all varieties of noncoercive paraphilias.

Fetishism is a form of atypical sexual behavior wherein an individual obtains arousal by focusing on an inanimate object or a part of the human body.

Fetishism often is a product of conditioning, in which the fetish object becomes associated with sexual arousal through the reinforcement of masturbation-produced orgasm.

Transvestism involves obtaining sexual excitement by cross-dressing. It is usually a solitary activity, expressed by a heterosexual male in the privacy of his own home.

Some males who engage in transvestism were dressed up as girls by parents who thought it was cute or who wanted a girl, or perhaps as a form of punishment.

Transvestism may allow some men to unburden themselves from the pressures of responsibility by temporarily escaping into the female role.

Sadomasochism (SM) may be defined as obtaining sexual arousal through receiving or giving physical and/or mental pain.

The majority of participants in SM view it as a form of sexual enhancement that they voluntarily and mutually choose to explore.

People who engage in SM behavior may be seeking additional nonsexual stimuli to achieve sufficient arousal. They may also be acting out of deeply rooted beliefs that sexual activity is sinful and immoral.

For some participants, SM may act as an escape valve whereby they are able to temporarily step out of the rigid, restrictive roles they play in their everyday lives.

Individuals who engage in SM sometimes describe early experiences that may have established a connection between sex and pain.

Autoerotic asphyxia is a rare and life-threatening paraphilia in which an individual, almost always a male, seeks to enhance sexual excitement and orgasm by pressure-induced oxygen deprivation.

Klismaphilia is a paraphilia that involves achieving sexual pleasure from receiving enemas.

Coprophilia and urophilia are, respectively, obtaining sexual arousal from contact with feces or urine.

COERCIVE PARAPHILIAS

Coercive paraphilias are invasive in that they involve unwilling recipients of behavior such as voyeurism or exhibitionism. Coercive acts may have harmful effects on the targets of such deeds, who may be psychologically traumatized by the experience.

Exhibitionism, obscene phone calls, voyeurism, frotteurism, necrophilia, and zoophilia are all varieties of coercive paraphilias.

Exhibitionism is behavior in which an individual, almost always a male, exposes his genitals to an involuntary observer.

People who exhibit themselves are usually young, adult males who have strong feelings of inadequacy and insecurity. Sexual relationships with others, either past or present, are likely to be unsatisfactory.

Gratification is usually obtained when the reaction to exhibitionism is shock, disgust, or fear. Physical assault is generally not associated with such behavior.

The characteristics of individuals who make obscene phone calls are similar to those who engage in exhibitionism.

Although there may be an element of vicious verbal hostility in obscene phone calls, the caller rarely follows up his verbal assault with a physical attack on his victim.

Voyeurism is obtaining sexual pleasure from looking at the exposed bodies or sexual activities of others, usually strangers.

People inclined toward voyeurism, typically males, are often sociosexually underdeveloped, with strong feelings of inferiority and inadequacy.

Frotteurism involves obtaining sexual pleasure by pressing or rubbing against a person in a crowded public place.

Zoophilia involves sexual contact between humans and animals; it occurs most commonly as a transitory experience of young people to whom a sexual partner is inaccessible or forbidden.

Necrophilia involves obtaining sexual gratification by viewing or having intercourse with a corpse.

TREATMENT OF COERCIVE PARAPHILIAS

People who engage in coercive paraphilias usually do not voluntarily seek treatment, nor are they likely to acknowledge that they are in need of and/or will benefit from treatment.

Because paraphilic behaviors are typically a source of immense pleasure, most people are highly motivated to continue rather than give up these activities.

People who compulsively engage in one or more of the coercive paraphilias often claim they are unable to control their urges.

Psychotherapy has generally not proved very effective in the treatment of coercive paraphilias. Limited success has been reported by cognitive therapists who attempt to change a person's maladaptive paraphilic behaviors by changing what he thinks about these acts.

Behavior therapy is based on the assumption that maladaptive paraphilic behavior has been learned and can therefore be unlearned. Varieties of behavior therapies used to treat coercive paraphilias include aversive conditioning, systematic desensitization, orgasmic reconditioning, and satiation therapy.

Antiandrogen drugs have been used effectively in some instances to block the inappropriate sexual arousal patterns underlying paraphilic behavior. Drug treatment is most effective when combined with other therapeutic methods.

People who engage in paraphilias may benefit from social skills training designed to teach them the skills necessary to initiate and maintain satisfying relationships with potential intimate/sexual partners.

SEXUAL ADDICTION: FACT, FICTION, OR MISNOMER?

The concept of sexual addiction suggests that some people who engage in excessive sexual activity are manifesting the outward symptoms of a process of psychological addiction in which feelings of depression, anxiety, loneliness, and worthlessness are temporarily relieved through a sexual high.

Many sexologists do not believe that sexual addiction should be a distinct diagnostic category because it is both rare and lacking in distinction from other compulsive disorders, such as gambling and eating disorders, and because this label negates individual responsibility for "uncontrollable" sexual compulsions that victimize others.

Thought Provokers

1. Which of the atypical sexual behaviors discussed in this chapter do you find the most unacceptable? Why?
2. Do you think that social and cultural conditioning contributes to the much higher incidence of atypical sexual behavior among men than among women? Explain.
3. People typically are much less concerned about female exhibitionism than they are about male exhibitionism. For example, if a woman were seen observing a man undressing in front of a window, the man might be accused of being an exhibitionist. However, if the roles were reversed and the woman was undressing, the man would probably be labeled a voyeur. What do you think of this sex-based inconsistency in labeling these behaviors?

Suggested Readings

Arndt, William (1991). *Gender Disorders and the Paraphilias.* Madison, CT: International Universities Press. This informative book provides an excellent overview of the scientific literature on paraphilias as well as a comprehensive analysis of transsexualism.

Bullough, Vern; and Bullough, Bonnie (1993). *Cross-Dressing, Sex and Gender.* Philadelphia: University of Pennsylvania Press. This informative text provides excellent information about transvestism for an historical and cultural perspective and describes and interprets research findings regarding this paraphilia.

Money, John; and Lamacz, Margaret (1989). *Vandalized Lovemaps.* New York: Prometheus. These authors offer an intriguing theory about how the erotosexual experiences we have in childhood establish patterns in the brain, called "lovemaps," that determine the kinds of sexual stimuli and activities that become sexually arousing to each of us. The primary thesis of their book is that when these lovemaps become distorted or vandalized by traumatic childhood experiences, various paraphilias result.

Stoller, Robert (1977). "Sexual Deviations." In F. Beach (Ed.), *Human Sexuality in Four Perspectives.* Baltimore: Johns Hopkins University Press (also available in paperback from the same publisher, 1978). Provides a review of several common atypical sexual behaviors with accompanying case examples.

Weinberg, Thomas; and Kamel, G. W. Levi (Eds.) (1983). *Studies in Sadomasochism.* Buffalo, NY: Prometheus Books. A collection of 18 articles that provides a considerable amount of thought-provoking information about sadomasochism.

Wilson, Glenn (Ed.) (1986). *Variant Sexuality: Research and Theory.* Baltimore: Johns Hopkins University Press. An excellent sourcebook that contains a wealth of information about the varied theoretical explanations for why people engage in atypical sexual behavior.

Web Resources

WWW.

Paraphilias and Fetishes
www.umkc.edu/sites/hsw/issues/para.html
Visitors to this site, part of the Human Sexuality web site provided by the University of Missouri at Kansas City, can gain a better understanding of various paraphilias and fetishes.

The Paraphilias and Paraphilia-Related Disorders
www.mhsource.com/edu/psytimes/p960627.html
Explanations of common paraphilias and disorders related to paraphilias are described on this web site from the *Psychiatric Times* journal.

19

Sexual Victimization

Rape

What sociocultural factors help explain the high incidence of rape in our society?

What four motivational patterns are used to categorize types of rapes?

Sexual Abuse of Children

How prevalent is child sexual abuse in the United States? How does its incidence compare with that in other countries?

What can parents and other caregivers do to make children less vulnerable to abuse?

Sexual Harassment

What forms of sexual harassment occur in the workplace? in academia?

What strategies should a person use in dealing with sexual harassment in the workplace? in academic settings?

I was sexually abused by my stepbrother throughout a great part of my childhood. The abuse started the summer I was ten. He is three and a half years older than me, and he was my designated baby-sitter all summer. He usually wasn't violent. It was more coaxing and coercion, and threats of what would happen if I told. The strongest memories I have are of times when it was particularly physically painful. I put myself out of my body, and would just watch the ceiling fan go around and around. When I was 13 I saw a talk show on incest and then told a woman at my church what was happening to me, and it kind of all fell apart from there. As much as the thought of the whole experience is repulsive, what hurt the most is my parents calling it child's play and that was how it was reported to CPS [Child Protection Services]. My parents even had me believing at one point that I really had wanted it and was telling them about it for attention. Because of this reaction, I believed for a while that it was my fault and that I was dirty because of it. My stepbrother plea-bargained his case, and he was put on probation. I was taken out of the home and put in foster and group homes. I attempted suicide numerous times and was in four different psychiatric hospitals over about four years. I no longer have any contact with the "family." I am blessed to have been adopted into another loving family. My new dad is the one who saved me from hating all men forever. But I still have problems regarding sex. My boyfriend can't even hold me romantically. I have only stopped having flashbacks and nightmares fairly recently. I am in therapy for the umpteenth time, but this time it is really working. (Authors' files)

A person has been sexually victimized when she or he is deprived of free choice and coerced or forced to comply with sexual acts under duress. Victims of coercive sexual acts often suffer grievous consequences as revealed in the above account provided by a 19-year-old college student. In this chapter, we focus on three particularly abusive and exploitive forms of sexual victimization: rape, the sexual abuse of children, and sexual harassment. All these behaviors involve strong elements of coercion, sometimes even violence.

Rape

Rape
Sexual intercourse that occurs without consent as a result of actual or threatened force.

Statutory rape
Intercourse with a person under the legal age of consent.

Stranger rape
Rape of a person by an unknown assailant.

Acquaintance rape
Forced sexual assault by a friend, acquaintance, or date.

Date rape
Forced sexual assault by an acquaintance when on a date.

Rape, which is commonly thought of as sexual relations forced by a man on an unconsenting woman, has occurred throughout history. The legal definition of rape varies from state to state; however, most laws define rape as sexual intercourse that occurs under actual or threatened forcible compulsion that overcomes the earnest resistance of the victim. Within this broad category are several specific kinds of rape. **Statutory rape** is intercourse with a person who is under the age of consent. (The age of consent varies in different states—see Table 19.1.) Statutory rape is considered to have occurred regardless of the apparent willingness of the underage partner. **Stranger rape** is the rape of a person by an unknown assailant. **Acquaintance rape,** or **date rape,** is committed by someone who is known to the rape victim.

Unfortunately, it is exceedingly difficult to obtain accurate statistics on the number of rapes and rape victims in the United States, due to the reluctance of many people to report being assaulted. Estimates of the percentage of rapes that women victims report to police or other public agencies range from 8% (Koss, 1988) to 16% (National Victim Center, 1992). Some writers suggest that rape may be the most underreported crime in America (Lonsway & Fitzgerald, 1994).

What factors do you think deter women from reporting a rape?

As we will see later in this chapter, a large proportion of rapes are committed by an acquaintance of the victim. Under these circumstances, a woman's preconceived notion of a "real" rape—a violent, blitz-type attack by a stranger—may not match her experience of an acquaintance rape (Kahn et al., 1994b). Other reasons why rape victims may be reluctant to acknowledge to themselves or others that they have been raped include self-blame ("I shouldn't have had so much to drink"), concern for the rapist, and an attempt to block their recall of a traumatic experience (Parrot, 1991). Mistrust of the police or legal system, fear of reprisal by the offender or his family, and concern about unwanted publicity may also deter women from reporting stranger or acquaintance rapes.

With these limitations in mind, consider the following statistics, obtained from contemporary surveys that provide some indication of the numbers of American women who have experienced attempted or completed rape. The sample size and victim percentages from five of these studies are as follows: 19% of 3700 women (Crooks, 1991), 30% of 518 women (Ward et al., 1991), 24% of 500 women (DeVisto et al., 1984), 25% of 3187 women (Koss et al., 1987), and 25% of 404 women (Mims & Chang, 1984). If we add other forms of sexual abuse to the rape statistics, it becomes clear that an alarming number of American women are sexually victimized. In the following sections, we look at some of the false beliefs people hold about rape, the psychosocial bases of rape, and the aftermath of rape.

Table 19.1 Age of Consent by State

State	Age	State	Age
Alabama	16	*Montana*	16
Alaska	18	*Nebraska*	16
Arizona	18	*Nevada*	16
Arkansas	18	*New Hampshire*	16
California	18	*New Jersey*	16
Colorado	18	*New Mexico*	17
Connecticut	16	*New York*	17
Delaware	16	*North Carolina*	16
District of Columbia	16	*North Dakota*	18
Florida	18	*Ohio*	18
Georgia	16*	*Oklahoma*	18
Hawaii	14	*Oregon*	18
Idaho	18	*Pennsylvania*	16
Illinois	18	*Rhode Island*	16
Indiana	16	*South Carolina*	15
Iowa	16	*South Dakota*	16
Kansas	16	*Tennessee*	18
Kentucky	16	*Texas*	17
Louisiana	17	*Utah*	17
Maine	16	*Vermont*	16
Maryland	16	*Virginia*	16
Massachusetts	16	*Washington*	16
Michigan	16	*West Virginia*	16
Mississippi	18	*Wisconsin*	18
Missouri	17	*Wyoming*	16

*The age of consent in Georgia was 14 in June 1996; it was raised to 16 in October 1996.

Source: Adapted from Donovan, 1997.

False Beliefs About Rape

In explaining the high incidence of rape in our society, one important factor is the prevalence of misconceptions about this crime. False beliefs abound concerning rape, rapists, and rape victims (Hall & Barongan, 1997; Lonsway & Fitzgerald, 1994 & 1995). Many people believe that roughing up a woman is acceptable, that many women are sexually aroused by such activity, and that it is impossible to rape a healthy woman against her will (Gilbert et al., 1991; Malamuth et al., 1980). Unfortunately, the effect of such rape myths is often "to deny and justify male sexual aggression against women" (Lonsway & Fitzgerald, 1994, p. 133). Another frequent effect is to place the blame on the victim.

As we consider some of the more common misconceptions about rape in the following paragraphs, ask yourself whether you have ever voiced similar beliefs. What were the circumstances that led you to make these assumptions?

False Belief: "You Can't Thread a Moving Needle"

The belief that women can always successfully ("if they *really* want to") resist a rape attempt is false, for several important reasons. First, men are usually physically larger and stronger than women. Small stature is a physical reality, but the way women feel about and use their bodies is learned. Stereotypical female gender-role conditioning often trains a woman to be compliant, submissive, and passive—the recipient rather than the initiator. These elements of gender-role conditioning limit the options a woman believes she has in resisting a rape attack. It simply may not be in her repertoire of behavior to be offensive or aggressive or to resort to socially unacceptable behaviors to defend herself against the person attacking her.

Second, the man who rapes chooses the time and place. He has the element of surprise on his side. The fear and intimidation a woman usually experiences when attacked works to the assailant's advantage. His use of weapons, threats, or physical force further encourages her compliance. Furthermore, many rapes are perpetrated by two or more attackers.

False Belief: "Women Say No When They Mean Yes"

Some rapists have distorted perceptions of their interactions with the women they rape, both before and during the assault. They may believe that women want to be coerced into sexual activity, even to the extent of being sexually abused (Abel, 1981; Beal & Muehlenhard, 1987).

These distorted beliefs may help the rapist justify his behavior: His acts are not rape but rather "normal" sex play. Such a man might meet a woman in a bar, take her for a drive, park, and attempt intercourse—which he would force if she resisted. Even if he has to "slap her around" to convince her to have sex, he believes he is only acting in accordance with her hidden wishes and expectations. Afterward, he may have little or no guilt about his behavior because, in his own mind, it was not rape. Of 114 imprisoned rapists who were interviewed in one study, over 80% did not see themselves as rapists. Those who did not deny having sexual contact with their accusers used a variety of explanations to justify their actions, including such distorted perceptions as claiming that women say no when they mean yes, women are seducers who "lead you on," and most women eventually relax and enjoy it (Scully & Marolla, 1984). Unfortunately, there seems to be considerable support for such attitudes in the general population. Later in this chapter, we will examine some of the sociocultural factors that perpetuate such perceptions and also look at the importance of clear communication between men and women in dating situations.

False Belief: "Many Women 'Cry Rape'"

False accusations of rape are quite uncommon, and they are even less frequently carried as far as prosecution. Given the difficulties that exist in reporting and prosecuting a rape, few women (or men) could successfully proceed with an unfounded rape case. Available data suggest that, contrary to the myth that they falsely cry rape, "women are much more likely to suffer rape victimization and not report the crime to any authorities" (Lonsway & Fitzgerald, 1994, p. 136).

False Belief: "All Women Want to Be Raped"

Novels and films sometimes perpetuate the notion that women want to be raped. Typically, fictionalized rape scenes begin with a woman resisting her attacker, only to melt into passionate acceptance. In the rare cases where male-to-male rape is shown, as in the films *Deliverance* and *The Shawshank Redemption,* the violation and humiliation of rape are more likely to be realistically portrayed.

The fact that some women do occasionally have rape fantasies is sometimes used to support the idea that women want to be sexually assaulted. However, it is important to understand the distinction between an erotic fantasy and a conscious desire to lose one's free will to someone whose intent is to inflict harm. In a fantasy, a person still retains ultimate control. But a basic element in an actual rape is the terrifying powerlessness of the woman. A fantasy carries no threat of physical harm or death; a rape does.

An extremely negative consequence of the belief that women want to be raped is that many victims may believe that the rape was basically their fault. Even when they may have simply been in the wrong place at the wrong time, a pervasive sense of personal guilt may remain. Unfortunately, when a woman continues to feel self-blame following a rape, the man who raped her is still indirectly maintaining some control over her life. Rape self-help groups or personal counseling may help a woman resolve these feelings.

False Belief: "It Could Never Happen to Me"

Many women may think that, because they are too young, too old, too unattractive, married, "not that kind of girl," exceedingly cautious, or possess any of a variety of unique characteristics, they will not be raped. This belief may promote a false sense of security by denying the personal vulnerability of *all* women (Lonsway & Fitzgerald, 1994). It also tends, once again, to place blame for the rape on some characteristic or behavior of the woman herself. The truth is that any female is a potential victim.

Even women who are never raped live daily with the threat of a sexual attack (Hickman & Muhlenhard, 1997). The possibility of rape makes it more difficult for women to lead independent lives. Although rape can happen to virtually any woman, there are some things that can be done to reduce (but not eliminate) the likelihood of its occurrence. Some suggestions for prevention, and for coping with a rape if it cannot be prevented, appear in the box "Dealing with Rape," on pages 579–581.

Sexuality and Diversity

Marry Your Victim and Avoid Prosecution: An Ignoble Peruvian Rape Law

A recent editorial in *Ms.* magazine (March/April 1997) described efforts by women activists in Peru to repeal an abominable law based on Peruvian custom dating to antiquity. This law allows a rapist to avoid prosecution if he marries his victim. This practice stems from a viewpoint entrenched in Peruvian culture that the rape of a woman both markedly diminishes her marriageability and should be dealt with privately by her family. "Rather than risk a loss of honor, especially if a rape case is reported to authorities and thus becomes public knowledge, many families give their daughters to the men who raped them" (p. 16). Not all families take this stance when one of their own is raped. However, noncompliance with this loathsome custom may result in intense pressure. There have been cases in which a rapist repeatedly harasses and threatens the family until they finally agree to a marriage spawned by violence.

A small victory in the campaign to eliminate this repugnant law from the Peruvian legal system was achieved in 1991 when activists, led by a group of lawyers, called Defense of Women's Rights (DEMUS), succeeded in getting the law amended so that now when a woman is gang-raped, only the rapist who married her is precluded from prosecution. As difficult as it may be to believe, prior to this modification in the law, all men involved in a gang rape were exempted from prosecution if one of the perpetrators married the victim. In the spring of 1997, lawyers from DEMUS were actively representing 15 women who had been forced to marry their rapists.

Sadly, a number of prominent public leaders in Peru actively supported this detestable law. According to one legislator, "It is the custom among the indigenous people of our fatherland. Men wait for women in the countryside and take them by surprise, and rape is the beginning of a generally stable relationship" (p. 18). Fueled by such audacious statements justifying violence as a basis for marriage, a firestorm of publicity about and protests against Peru's rape laws have recently swept the country. At the time of this writing, Peru's Congress had yet to act to repeal this reprehensible law. Hopefully, change is in the wind and Peru's victimized women, many of whom are under age 14, will soon be able to see the perpetrators of these acts behind bars rather than in their marriage beds.

The Psychosocial Bases of Rape

Why do men rape women? Researchers have attempted to answer this question for many years. Until very recently, many of their efforts were hindered by both a narrow conceptualization of rape and inadequate research methods. Our awareness of the characteristics and motivations of men who rape has been based, until recently, largely on studies of men convicted of the crime, a sample group that probably represents fewer than 1% of all males who rape. We cannot say with certainty that men who rape without being prosecuted and convicted demonstrate traits similar to those of convicted rapists. In fact, there is good reason to believe that convicted rapists are less educated, are more inclined to commit other antisocial or criminal acts, and tend to be more alienated from society than are rapists who do not pass through the criminal justice system (Smithyman, 1979).

Many of the men incarcerated for rape offenses appear to have a strong proclivity toward violence that is often reflected in their acts of rape. This fact, along with certain assumptions about male–female relationships, has led a number of writers to argue that rape is not sexually motivated but is rather an act of power and domination (Brownmiller, 1975). This viewpoint prevailed for a number of years, during which time the sexual component of rape and other assaultive offenses was de-emphasized. However, recent research has made it clear that while power and domination are often involved in sexual coercion, such acts are also frequently motivated by a desire for sexual gratification. This view has been supported by several excellent recent studies of the incidence and nature of sexual coercion among nonincarcerated males. Particularly noteworthy in this regard is the growing body of data pertaining to acquaintance or date rape, which we discuss shortly.

It is becoming increasingly apparent that rape is more often a product of socialization processes that occur within the fabric of "normal" society than of severe pathology of the individual rapist (Allison & Wrightsman, 1993; Hall & Barongan, 1997). Strong support for the view that rape is in many ways a cultural phenomenon was provided by the research of Peggy Reeves Sanday (1981), an anthropologist who compared the incidence of rape in 95 societies. Sanday found that women in America are several hundred times more likely to be raped than are women in certain other societies.

What kinds of factors might account for such wide variation in rape statistics among different societies?

Sanday's research indicated that the incidence of rape in a given society is influenced by several important cultural factors. Prime among these were the nature of relations between the sexes, the status of women, and the attitudes that boys acquire during their developmental years. She found that "rape-prone" societies—those with a high incidence of rape—tolerate and even glorify masculine violence, encouraging boys to be aggressive and competitive and viewing physical force as natural and exemplary. Men in such societies generally have special gathering spots, such as men's clubs or corner taverns, and they frequently demean women. Men frequently have greater economic and political power, remaining aloof from "women's work" such as childrearing and household duties.

In contrast, relations between the sexes are very different in societies where there is virtually no rape. Women and men in "rape-free" societies share power and authority, and both contribute equally to the community welfare. In addition, children of both sexes in these societies are raised to value nurturance and to avoid aggression and violence. With this cultural framework in mind, let us take a closer look at some of the aspects of male socialization within our own culture that contribute to the occurrence of rape and other forms of sexual coercion.

Sociocultural Factors Associated with Rape

We are beginning to understand why the United States is among the societies identified as rape prone. (Statistics recently released by the International Criminal Police Organization [Interpol] reveal that the United States has the highest incidence of rapes among all Western nations [Contemporary Sexuality, 1996a].) One important factor has to do with stereotypical gender roles. Males in our society often learn that power, aggressiveness, and getting what one wants are all part of the proper male role. Furthermore, they frequently learn that they should seek sex and expect to be successful—often with few qualms about using unethical means. In one study of male college students, almost 80% of self-disclosed date rapists had attempted to get a female drunk to gain sexual access, while 86% had falsely expressed love for this purpose (Kanin, 1985). It is no surprise, then, that many American men view aggression as a legitimate means to achieve sexual access to women. "Sexual assault is a logical extension of a system in which men are taught to fight for what they want, whereas women are taught to be passive and yielding and to put men's needs above their own" (Muehlenhard et al., 1991, p. 161). Researcher Andrea Parrot notes a direct relationship between men's adherence to traditional gender roles and male sexual dominance and their likelihood to engage in sexual assault, verbal sexual coercion, and rape (Parrot, 1994).

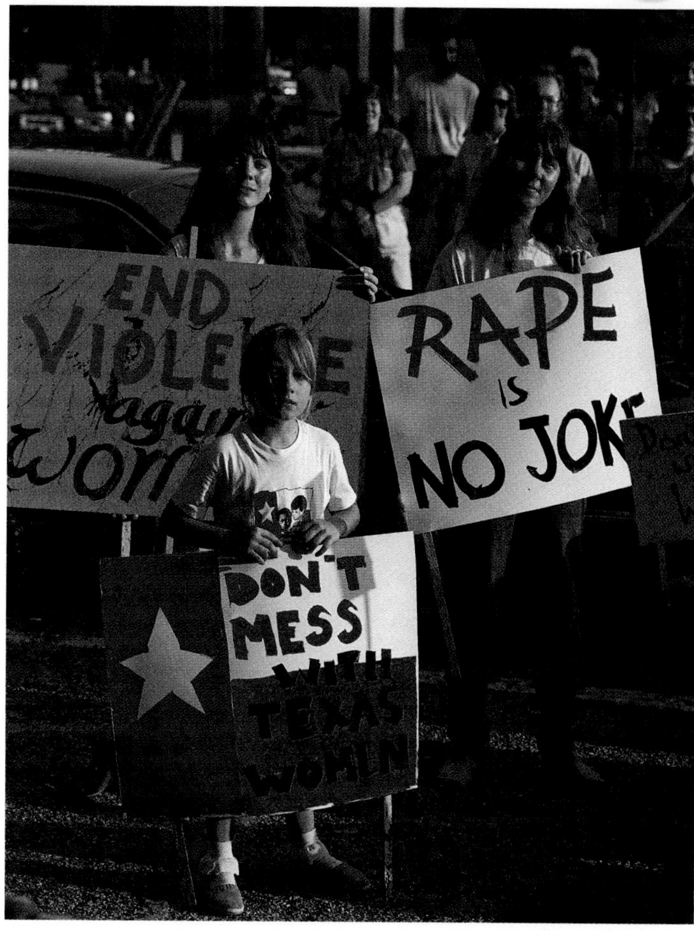

Women in Austin, Texas, protest against sexual assault. These women, and others like them, have helped challenge societal assumptions about rape.

Men whose peer groups openly legitimize and support these attitudes and behaviors are particularly likely to victimize women sexually (Sanday, 1996). In one study, the most predictive factor distinguishing men who had engaged in sexually aggressive behavior (defined as physically forced sexual activity carried to the point where the woman was crying, fighting, or screaming) was having male friends who were sexually aggressive (Adler, 1985). In another study comparing male college students who admitted to date rape with a control sample of nonrapists (also male college students), the rapists were much more likely to have friends who engaged in "rough sex" and labeled certain types of females as legitimate targets for rape. The rapists in this study also reported considerably more peer pressure to acquire sexual experience than did the nonrapists (Kanin, 1985). Similar findings have prompted UCLA researcher Neil Malamuth (1982 & 1986) to conclude that a man's perception of peer-group acceptance of rape was the best predictor of his inclination to engage in rape, followed by the presence of callous attitudes toward women.

The Impact of Sexually Violent and Degrading Media

A number of researchers have provided compelling evidence that sexually violent films, books, magazines, and videos may contribute to some rapists' assaultive behaviors (Boeringer, 1994; Hall, 1996; Linz et al., 1988 & 1992). Other evidence strongly suggests that exposure to degrading but nonviolent erotica may also have deleterious effects on men's attitudes toward sex and women, and may increase their inclinations to engage in coercive sex (Check & Guloien, 1989; Zillmann, 1989). In the discussion that follows, we will focus our attention primarily on the connection between sexually violent media and rape.

In one of the first major studies in this area, Neil Malamuth and James Check (1981) recruited 271 college men and divided them into two groups. Subjects in one group were shown nonviolent erotic movies. The other group viewed R-rated movies in which men committed sexual violence against women who eventually experienced a transformation from victim to willing erotic partner—a theme reinforcing the culturally perpetuated myth that women welcome violence. Several days after the film-viewing sessions, all subjects completed a questionnaire. The men who had viewed violent erotica were much more inclined to have an accepting attitude toward sexual violence than were subjects exposed to consensual, nonviolent erotic themes.

Research demonstrates that exposure to violent pornography can decrease men's sensitivity to the damaging impact of rape on the victim. It can also increase men's likelihood of condoning aggressive acts against females—and perhaps most alarming, increase their willingness to admit that they would commit a rape if they thought they could get away with it (Boeringer, 1992 & 1994; Boeringer et al., 1991; Linz et al., 1992). Repeated exposure to sexually explicit materials as well as films associating violence with sex may desensitize men to violence against women, decreasing their inclination to see rape as a crime (Donnerstein & Linz, 1984; Gray, 1984). One study found that both rapists and child molesters were more likely than nonoffenders to report having used sexually explicit materials during adolescence and adulthood (Marshall, 1988).

It is not pornography per se that is a key factor in increasing men's aggressiveness toward women, but violent, humiliating, and degrading pornography (Scott & Schwalm, 1988). One survey found that male college students who had used sexually violent pornography in the past year admitted more willingness to use sexual force against a woman than did those who had used only nonviolent pornography (Demaré et al., 1988). Another noteworthy survey of college students had similar results. Scot Boeringer (1994) found that while exposure to nonviolent pornography was not predictive of any form of sexual coercion or rape, the use of hard-core pornography depicting violent rape was strongly associated not only with judging oneself capable of sexual coercion and aggression but also with engaging in such acts. "It is probable," concludes Boeringer, "that, for some persons, violent pornography not only presents techniques for sexual assault, but it also provides justification for violence and rape" (p. 299). Furthermore, evidence strongly indicates that "exposure to media that combine arousing sexual images with violence may promote the development of deviant patterns of physiological sexual arousal" (Hall & Barongan, 1997, p. 5).

Is rape, then, a "sexualization" of violence? Some evidence suggests that it is. In three separate studies, the erectile responses of matched groups of rapists and nonrapists were measured as they listened to audiotape descriptions of rape and of mutually consenting sexual activity. In all three studies, rapists were more aroused by the sexual assault description than were nonrapists (Abel et al., 1977; Barbaree et al., 1979; Quinsey et al., 1984). However, some other research has failed to support this conclusion, finding little difference in the erectile responses of rapists and nonrapists in similar research designs (Eccles et al., 1994; Proulx et al., 1994; Wormith et al., 1988). Clearly, more research is needed to clarify these findings.

Characteristics of Men Who Rape

A number of characteristics have been linked to men who rape. Men who embrace traditional gender roles, particularly the element of male dominance, are more likely than men who do not accept these attitudes to commit rape (Harney & Muehlenhard, 1991; Muehlenhard & Falcon, 1990). Many rapists have self-centered personalities, which may render them insensitive to others' feelings (Dean & Malamuth, 1997; Marshall, 1993; Pithers, 1993). Furthermore, anger toward women in general is a prominent attitude among some men who sexually assault women (Hall & Barongan, 1997). Alcohol use may also contribute to rapists' behavior; rapists have often been drinking just prior to assaulting their victims (Ladouceur & Temple, 1985; Muehlenhard & Linton, 1987).

Some particularly illuminating evidence pertaining to the characteristics of men who rape was provided by Gene Abel (1981), a Columbia University researcher who developed an elaborate system of confidentiality that allowed over 200 New York men who had engaged in a variety of sexual victimization behaviors to participate in his research without being identified by the criminal justice system. Approximately half the rapists in Abel's sample had histories of other types of sexual offenses, most notably sexual abuse of children, exhibitionism, voyeurism, and sadism. This suggests that the behavior of at least some rapists may escalate through a series of progressively more violent sexual offenses.

Abel also found that some of the rapists in his sample had extensive histories of fantasizing about rape and violence long before becoming rapists. He described a pattern in which many of these men had begun masturbating frequently to the accompaniment of rape fantasies as early as their mid-teens. As this pattern continued, the deviant urge to rape became progressively stronger until ultimately their attempts to resist acting on this impulse failed, and they became rapists. A similar pattern was suggested by a recent British study. Thirteen rapists reported that they had often responded to unpleasant emotional states (such as anger, loneliness, and humiliation) by masturbating to deviant sexual fantasies. This pattern seemed to be a precursor to rape and other deviant sexual acts (McKibben et al., 1994).

Types of Rapes and Rapists

Just as no singular pattern characterizes the men who commit rape, a wide range of individual differences exists in the motivations underlying sexual assault and in how that assault is committed. From this perspective, we can identify four types of rape: anger rape, power rape, sadistic rape, and sexual gratification rape. The typology for the first three types of rape in this categorization was developed by Nicholas Groth and William Hobson (1983), based on over 16 years of extensive clinical experience with more than 1000 rapists in a variety of institutional and community settings.

Anger Rape

According to Groth and Hobson, "The anger rape is an unpremeditated, savage, physical attack prompted by feelings of hatred and resentment" (1983, p. 163). The assailant is motivated to vent his rage and contempt, and sexual gratification has little or nothing to do with his assaultive behavior. Anger rape is often characterized by the use of physical violence far in excess of the amount necessary to force sexual submission. Many anger rapists exhibit a pattern of long-term hostility toward women. They perceive the rape as an act of revenge in which they attempt to get even for the "put-downs," humiliation, and rejection they believe they have suffered at the hands of women.

The victim of anger rape is usually a total stranger to the perpetrator. She is often subjected to physical injury and extreme degradation. She may be forced to engage in acts such as fellatio and anal intercourse, and sometimes foreign objects are used to penetrate her vagina or anus. The anger rapist often has difficulty obtaining sufficient sexual arousal to achieve and sustain an erection, and he usually does not find the rape to be sexually gratifying.

An anger rape is not premeditated but rather occurs impulsively when some triggering event, like a conflict with a lover or spouse, causes a man to reach a breaking point under an accumulated load of anger and resentment. An anger rapist's assaults tend to occur irregularly, often separated by months or even years.

Power Rape

A power rape is motivated primarily by a desire to exert control over another human being. Sexual gratification may be an aspect of this type of rape, but it is secondary to the power rapist's desire to demonstrate that he can dominate and control his victim. Such an offender may rape women in an "effort to resolve disturbing doubts about his masculine identity and worth," or in an attempt "to combat deep-seated feelings of insecurity and vulnerability" (Groth & Hobson, 1983, p. 165). The power rapist is often overwhelmed by an increasing sense of failure. His psychological makeup, socioeconomic background, or both ill equip him to cope with the economic and social stresses in his life. He may feel powerless, hopeless, and unable to deal effectively with escalating stress. Rape may represent his attempt to regain some of the power that is absent from his life.

The power rapist usually employs only enough force to cause the woman to cooperate in a submissive fashion. His intention is not to physically injure her but rather to achieve control over her. Power rapes are typically premeditated and often highly repetitive, and they may exhibit a pattern of increasing frequency over time.

Sadistic Rape

"The sadistic rape is a preplanned, ritualistic assault, frequently involving bondage, torture, and sexual abuse, in which aggression and sexuality become inseparable" (Groth & Hobson, 1983, pp. 167–168). In this type of rape, aggression is an erotic experience. Power and anger or both may be eroticized. If power is the primary source of sexual arousal, the victim may be subjected to certain ritualistic acts such as bondage, being shaved, or being assaulted with an instrument. If the anger components of rape are sexualized, the victim is likely to be subjected to torture, such as having her breasts or genitals bitten, burned, or otherwise mutilated.

The motivational forces underlying sadistic rape are complex and more difficult to delineate than in anger and power rapes. Groth and Hobson have suggested that, for this type of assailant, rape may represent a perverse attempt to regain some sense of control and psychological equilibrium, while discharging pent-up frustration over unresolved conflicts. This type of rapist is likely to exhibit a particularly strong preoccupation with violent pornography. Explicit erotica without a component of violence is unlikely to hold the interest of a sadistic rapist.

Sexual Gratification Rape

The motivation propelling this type of rape is primarily sexual in nature. Here, the rapist is interested in obtaining sexual gratification and willing to use varying degrees of force to obtain it. Because sexual gratification is the primary goal, this type of rapist is likely to use no more force than necessary to accomplish this end. If it becomes clear that an excessive amount of force or violence is necessary to overcome the woman's resistance, the sexual gratification rapist may terminate his assaultive act.

It is likely that a majority of acquaintance rapes fit into this category. Many men who force an acquaintance or date to submit to unwanted sexual intercourse may be acting out some of the male themes common in our culture that were discussed earlier. These include glorifying the virtues of being a strong, virile, aggressive male who gets what he wants by taking it. The "caveman" mentality of dragging a woman off by her hair for sexual conquest is, unfortunately, all too prevalent in our rape-prone society. In light of statistics suggesting a high incidence of acquaintance rape and rape by family members and friends, it is possible, even probable, that sexual gratification rape is the most common kind of rape committed in American society.

It is important to note that these four types of rape are not necessarily mutually exclusive. Any act of rape may involve components from one or more of these four types of sexual assault. However, the characteristics and motivational dynamics of one type are frequently predominant in a given assault.

Acquaintance Rape and Sexual Coercion

Most rapes are committed by someone who is known to the raped woman, not (as in the popular stereotype) by a stranger lurking in the bushes (Harney & Muehlenhard, 1990; Koss, 1992; Small & Kerns, 1993). A significant number of these acquaintance rapes occur in dating situations—hence the term *date rape.* Acquaintance rapes are much less likely to be reported than stranger rapes (Kahn et al., 1994b; Muehlenhard et al., 1991).

In recent years, researchers have provided extensive evidence regarding the prevalence of sexual coercion in dating situations (Kalof, 1993; Small & Kerns, 1993). Thirty-five percent of 930 San Francisco women reported having been victims of either attempted or completed acquaintance rape, usually in dating situations (Russell, 1984). Twenty percent of 1149 teenage women reported experiencing forced intercourse or some other form of unwanted sexual contact during the previous year, most commonly in dating situations (Small & Kerns, 1993). A recent survey of almost 200 Canadian high school students found that 30% of the female respondents reported being forced into some type of sexual activity (Rhynard et al., 1997). In still another recent survey of 8th- through 12th-grade students in 79 public and private schools in Vermont, 30% of almost 4000 sexually active girls reported ever being forced or pressured to have sexual intercourse (Shrier et al., 1998).

Statistics pertaining to acquaintance rape may err on the low side, for reasons discussed earlier in this chapter. Many victims often have difficulty labeling this act as rape because the experience does not match their preconceived idea of a violent, forceful act by a stranger (Kahn et al., 1994b; Rickert & Wiemann, 1998). Some other research suggests a considerably higher incidence of acquaintance rape or sexual coercion. In a series of three surveys of college students, Charlene Muehlenhard and her associates found an alarmingly high proportion of women—between 79.7% and 97.5%—who reported being sexually coerced (Muehlenhard & Cook, 1988; Muehlenhard & Long, 1988; Muehlenhard et al., 1985). And in another survey of 275 university women, fully 95.3% reported having been coerced into one or more sexual behaviors (Christopher, 1988).

Women are not the only ones to experience sexual coercion. The Canadian study mentioned previously found that 22% of the male high-school-age respondents reported experiencing some form of forced sexual activity (Rhynard et al., 1997). In the survey of Vermont middle and high school students, 10% of about 4000 sexually active boys reported ever being forced or pressured to have sexual intercourse (Shrier et al., 1998). In Muehlenhard's three surveys of college students, she found that between 62.1% and 93.5% of men reported experiencing sexual coercion (Muehlenhard & Cook, 1988; Muehlenhard & Long, 1988; Muehlenhard et al., 1985). It is important to note that although many of the women in these studies were forced to engage in unwanted sex acts, physical force was rarely employed in the sexual coercion of male respondents. However, men are sometimes victims of forced sexual coercion and rape, as is discussed later in this chapter.

Why might people engage in unwanted sexual activity when force is not used? Do you think there are reasons that are common to both sexes? What explanations might apply to only one sex?

A number of factors help explain why people may engage in unwanted sexual acts even when physical force is not used. Many inducements are common to both sexes. They include enticement (being turned on by a partner's actions or touches and later regretting it); threats to end a relationship; a desire to be popular; peer pressure; a partner questioning one's sexuality; being intoxicated; and feeling obliged because of the time or money expended by a partner. An additional factor for men may be the societal stereotype that a "real man" should take advantage of any opportunity for sex (Muehlenhard & Schrag, 1991; Muehlenhard et al., 1991; Rhynard et al., 1997).

Acquaintance Rape: The Role of Perceptions and Communication

Earlier in this chapter we examined the relationship between sexual coercion and cultural expectations for males in our society. The socializing process that programs some men to be aggressive in order to get what they want is undoubtedly an important factor. Yet some experts argue that in at least some cases of acquaintance rape, the picture is more complicated.

Consider the issue of men's misinterpretation of women's signals. Men often consider women's actions such as cuddling or kissing as indicating a desire to engage in intercourse (Muehlenhard, 1988; Muehlenhard & Linton, 1987). However, a woman who feels like cuddling does *not* necessarily want to have sex, and she may express this to her date. But here again, some men misinterpret women's signals. Even if a woman clearly expresses her desire not to have sex, her date may read her actions as "token resistance," concluding that she really wants to have sex but does not want to appear "too easy" (Check & Malamuth, 1983; Muehlenhard & Hollabaugh, 1989).

This misreading may be entirely motivated by some men's exploitive self-interest. But unfortunately, some women *do* say no when they mean yes. One study of 610 female undergraduates revealed that 39.3% had engaged in token resistance to sex at least once. Reasons for saying no when they really meant yes included not wanting to appear promiscuous, uncertainty about a partner's feelings, undesirable surroundings, game-playing (wanting a partner to be more physically aggressive, to persuade her to have sex, etc.), and wanting to be in control (Muehlenhard & Hollabaugh, 1989). This kind of double message may actually promote rape by providing men with a rationale for ignoring sincere refusals. If a man has had the experience of ignoring a woman's protests, only to find that she actually did want to have sex, the researchers in this study concluded that "his belief that women's refusals are not to be taken seriously will be strengthened" (p. 878). He may thus proceed with his sexual advances despite further protests and genuine resistance from his date. Such a man may not even define his actions as rape. This cycle underscores the importance of building a foundation of clear communication, the topic of Chapter 8.

Even men who believe their partners when they say no may think it is defensible to use force to obtain sex if they feel that they have been "led on." A number of studies have found that many men regard rape as justifiable if a woman leads a man on by such actions as dressing "suggestively" or going to his apartment (Goodchilds & Zellman, 1984; Muehlenhard & Linton, 1987; Muehlenhard et al., 1991). The implications of these findings for acquaintance rape prevention are discussed in the box "Dealing with Rape."

The Date Rape Drug

In October 1996 President Clinton signed a bill that outlawed the drug Rohypnol (ro-HIP-nol) and added 20 years to rapists' prison sentences if the rapist used this drug to incapacitate victims. This marks the first time that using a drug as a weapon has been classified as a crime in the United States. Rohypnol, commonly known on the street as "roofies," is the brand name for flunitrazepam, a powerful tranquilizer with a sedative effect 7 to 10 times more potent than Valium. In addition to producing a sedative effect within 20 to 30 minutes that lasts for several hours, Rohypnol also causes muscle relaxation and mild to pronounced amnesia. When combined with alcohol, the drug effects are markedly enhanced, and may result in a dramatic "high," markedly reduced inhibitions, unconsciousness, and total amnesia for events that occur while a person is under its influence.

Reports are surfacing with increasing frequency of Rohypnol being used to facilitate sexual conquest or incapacitate victims who are then sexually molested or raped (O'Neill, 1997; Staten, 1997). Women have reported waking up naked in college fraternity houses, or in the homes of date companions or casual acquaintances, with no recall of the previous several hours. Many cases have emerged of women being raped after their "dates" have given them the drug, often without their awareness—hence the name "date rape drug." In the authors' home state of Oregon, a man was recently indicted on 12 counts of rape in which Rohypnol was reportedly used (Gregory, 1997). His victims were women he had provided with shots of tequila laced with the drug. (Rohypnol has no taste or odor when dissolved in drinks.) Over one hundred victims of the "date rape drug" have surfaced in Oregon, and elsewhere in the nation thousands of reports have emerged of the reprehensible use of Rohypnol as a facilitator of sexual assault.

Wartime Rape

Records of mass rapes of women during war abound from the time of ancient Greece to the more recent atrocities in the war-torn regions of the former Yugoslavia and Rwanda. Widespread media reports of mass rapes perpetrated by Serbian soldiers on an estimated 30,000 to 50,000 Muslim and Croatian women and girls increased the public's awareness and support for measures to stop mass rape as a crime of war. This awareness was further heightened by reports that 250,000 to 500,000 women and girls were raped during the 1994 war in Rwanda (Flanders, 1998). In 1996 the United Nations' International Criminal Tribunal for the Former Yugoslavia ruled that wartime rape is a crime punishable by severe criminal sanctions (marking the first time that sexual assault has been treated separately as a crime of war). Although it is gratifying to see this ruling, there is nothing unprecedented about rape as a strategy of war. It is common in the annals of wars fought throughout the world. In this century alone, hundreds of thousands of women have been victimized by wartime rape (Brownmiller, 1993; Carlson, 1997; Swiss & Giller, 1993).

When German troops invaded Belgium early in World War I, rape of Belgian women was so widespread that "the Rape of the Hun became a ruling metaphor" (Brownmiller, 1993, p. 37). Again in World War II, German soldiers carried out mass rape of Russian

Your Sexual Health

Dealing with Rape

Although rape is a societywide problem, it is the rape victim who experiences the direct, personal violation. The suggestions offered below present strategies for preventing stranger rape, followed by recommendations for reducing the risk of acquaintance rape. However, following these suggestions offers no guarantee of avoiding rape. Even a woman who leads an extremely cautious and restricted life may be raped.

Reducing the Risk of Stranger Rape

Rape prevention consists primarily of making it as difficult as possible for a rapist to make you his victim. Many of the following suggestions are commonsense measures against other crimes as well as rape.

1. Do not advertise that you are a woman living alone. Use initials on your mailbox and in the phone book; even add a fictitious name.
2. Install and use secure locks on doors and windows, changing door locks after losing keys or moving into a new residence. A peephole in your front door can be particularly helpful.
3. Do not open your door to strangers. If a repairman or public official is at your door, ask him to identify himself and call his office to verify he is a reputable person on legitimate business.
4. When you are in situations where strangers may be encountered, demonstrate self-confidence through your body language and speech to communicate that you will not be intimidated. Research reveals that rapists often tend to select as victims women who exhibit passivity and submissiveness (Richards et al., 1991).
5. Lock your car when it is parked and while you are driving.
6. Avoid dark and deserted areas and be aware of the surroundings where you are walking. This may help if you need an opportunity to escape. Should a driver ask for directions when you are a pedestrian, avoid approaching his car. Instead, call out your reply from a safe distance.

Many women take self-defense training to protect themselves from assault.

(continued on next page)

and Jewish women in occupied communities, a pattern that was reciprocated when the Soviet army marched through Germany. For many Chinese, reference to the "Rape of Nanking" raises painful memories of countless sexual atrocities committed by Japanese troops who occupied the wartime capital of China in 1937. During World War II, between 100,000 and 200,000 Asian women, mostly Korean, were abducted as sexual conscripts for the Japanese army and forced into sexual slavery (Swiss & Giller, 1993). In 1996 Japan began making financial restitution payments from a private fund to compensate Asian women forced into sexual slavery (Pollack, 1996). Estimates of the number of women raped by Pakistani soldiers during Bangladesh's 1971 war for independence range from 250,000 to 400,000 (Brownmiller, 1975). A recent report indicated that between April 1994 and April 1995, almost 16,000 women and girls were raped in the Central African nation of Rwanda (Contemporary Sexuality, 1996b). U.S. soldiers have also been guilty of wartime rape. Cases of gang rape appear in the records of courts-martial for American troops in Vietnam (Brownmiller, 1993).

Why is rape so common during war, and what are its roots? Wartime rape, in addition to being used as a means to dominate, humiliate, and control women, "can also be intended to disable an enemy by destroying the bonds of family and society" (Swiss & Giller, 1993, pp. 612–613). In wars instigated by ethnic conflict, as in the cases of the for-

Your Sexual Health

7. Have house or car keys in hand before coming to the door, and check the back seat before getting into your car.
8. Should your car break down, attach a white cloth to the antenna and lock yourself in. If someone other than a uniformed officer in an official car stops to offer help, ask this person to call the police or a garage but do not open your locked car door.
9. Wherever you go, it can be very helpful to carry a device for making a loud noise, like a whistle, or even better, a small pint-sized compressed-air horn available in many sporting goods and boat supply stores. Sound the noise alarm at the first sign of danger.

Many cities have crime-prevention bureaus that will provide further suggestions and home-safety inspections.

What to Do in Threatening Situations Involving Strangers
If you are approached by a man or men who may intend to rape you, you will have to decide what to do. *Each situation, assailant, and woman is unique: There are no absolute rules.*

1. Run away if you can.
2. Resist if you cannot run. Make it difficult for the rapist. On locating a potential victim, many men test her to see if she is easily intimidated. Resistance by the woman is responsible for many thwarted attempts (Fischhoff, 1992; Furby & Fischhoff, 1992; Siegel et al., 1989). Active and vociferous resistance—shouting, being rude, causing a scene, running away, fighting back—may deter the attack. This was the finding of a recent study of 150 rapes or attempted rapes: Women who used forceful verbal or physical resistance (screaming, hitting, kicking, biting, running, etc.) were more likely to avoid being raped than women who tried pleading, crying, or offering no resistance (Zoucha-Jensen & Coyne, 1993).
3. Ordinary rules of behavior do not apply. Vomiting, screaming, or acting crazy—whatever you are willing to try—can be appropriate responses to an attempted rape.
4. Talking can be a way to stall and give you a chance to devise an escape plan or another strategy. It can be helpful to get the attacker to start talking ("What has happened to make you so angry?"), to express some empathy ("It is really discouraging to lose a job"), or to negotiate ("Let's take time to talk about this"). Even when talking does not prevent an assault, it may reduce the degree of violence (Prentky et al., 1986).
5. Remain alert for an opportunity to escape. In some situations, it may be initially impossible to fight or elude an attacker. However, you may later have a chance to deter the attack and escape—for example, if the rapist becomes distracted or a passerby comes on the scene.

Self-defense classes are a resource for learning techniques of physical resistance that can injure the attacker(s) or distract them long enough for you to escape.

Reducing the Risk of Acquaintance Rape

1. When dating someone for the first time, seriously consider doing so in a group situation or meeting him at a public place. This will allow you to assess your date's behavior in a relatively safe environment.
2. Watch for inclinations that your date may be a controlling or dominating person who may try to control your behavior. A man who plans all activities and makes all decisions during a date may also be inclined to dominate in a private setting.
3. If the man drives and pays for all expenses, he may think he is justified in using force to get "what he paid for." If you cover some of the expenses, he may be less inclined to use

mer Yugoslavia and Rwanda, mass rape may be employed as a military strategy to terrorize a whole population, to destroy their cultural integrity, and sometimes to force entire communities to flee their houses, thereby achieving the goal of "ethnic cleansing" (Carlson, 1997; Post, 1993; Rojnik et al., 1995). Thus, although this aspect is often overlooked by people in noncombatant countries, rape is an act of war that assaults not only the individual woman, but her family and her community as well. "In one act of aggression," concludes Susan Brownmiller, "the collective spirit of women and of the nation is broken, leaving a reminder long after the troops depart" (1993, p. 37).

The Aftermath of Rape

Whether a person is raped by a stranger or an acquaintance, the experience is likely to be very traumatic for the victim and may often have long-term repercussions. In this section, we look at the emotional impact of rape on both the victim and her partner. Because most rape victims are females, our discussion draws primarily from studies of women who have been raped.

Your Sexual Health

this rationale to justify acting in a sexually coercive manner (Muehlenhard & Schrag, 1991; Muehlenhard et al., 1991).

4. Avoid using alcohol or other drugs when you definitely do not wish to be sexually intimate with your date. Consumption of alcohol and/or other drugs, by both victim and perpetrator, is commonly associated with acquaintance rape (Gross & Billingham, 1998; Synovitz & Byrne, 1998). Drug intoxication can both diminish your capacity to escape from an assault and reduce your date's reluctance to engage in assaultive behavior.
5. Avoid behavior that may be interpreted as "teasing." Clearly state what you do and do not wish to do in regard to sexual contact. For example, you might say, "I hope you do not misinterpret my inviting you back to my apartment. I *definitely* do not want to do anything more than relax, listen to some music, and talk." If you are interested in initiating an exploration of some kind of early physical contact, you might say, "Tonight I would like to hold you and kiss, but I would not be comfortable with anything else at this point in our relationship." Such direct communication can markedly reduce a man's inclinations to force unwanted sexual activity or to feel "led on" (Muehlenhard & Andrews, 1985; Muehlenhard et al., 1985).
6. If, despite direct communication about your intentions, your date behaves in a sexually coercive manner, you may use a "strategy of escalating forcefulness—direct refusal, vehement verbal refusal, and, if necessary, physical force" (Muehlenhard & Linton, 1987, p. 193). One recent study found that college students were most likely to label a scenario of date sex as rape if such activity was preceded by a clearly stated "no" (Sawyer et al., 1998). In another study, the response rated by men as most likely to get men to stop unwanted advances was the woman vehemently saying, "This is rape, and I'm calling the cops" (Beal & Muehlenhard, 1987). If verbal protests are ineffective, reinforce your refusal with physical force such as pushing, slapping, biting, kicking, or clawing your assailant. Men are more likely to perceive their actions as at least inappropriate, if not rape, when a woman protests not only verbally but also physically (Beal & Muehlenhard, 1987; Muehlenhard & Linton, 1987).

What to Do If You Have Been Raped

If you have been raped, you will have to decide whether to report the attack to the police.

1. It is advisable to report a rape, even an unsuccessful rape attempt. The information you provide may prevent another woman from being raped.
2. When you report a rape, any information you can remember about the attack will be helpful—the assaulter's physical characteristics, voice, clothes, car, even an unusual smell.
3. If you have been raped, you should call the police as soon as possible; do not bathe or change your clothes. Semen, hair, and material under fingernails or on your clothing all may be useful in identifying the rapist.
4. It may be very helpful to contact a rape crisis center, where qualified staff members may assist you in dealing with your trauma. Most large urban communities in the United States have such programs. If you are unable to make the contact yourself, have a friend, family member, or the police make the call.
5. Finally, it is important to remember that many women will mistakenly blame themselves for the rape. However, being raped is not a crime—the crime has been committed by the man who raped you.

Emotional Repercussions

Given the characteristics of rape—the physical violation and psychological trauma it inflicts and our societal attitudes about it—it is understandable that many rape survivors suffer long-lasting emotional effects. The emotional repercussions women experience following rape or attempted rape have been labeled **rape trauma syndrome** (Burgess & Holmstrom, 1974a, 1974b, & 1988).

Rape trauma syndrome
A two-phase reaction to rape that involves an initial acute phase of potentially intense emotions, that may last several weeks, followed by a long-term phase during which the survivor reorganizes her life.

Rape trauma usually consists of two phases. The first, known as the *acute phase,* begins immediately following the rape and may continue for hours, days, or often several weeks. During the first few hours after the attack, a woman will tend to react in either an expressive or controlled manner. In the expressive reaction, she will likely cry and be obviously upset. In the controlled reaction, she will appear subdued and matter-of-fact. She may, however, experience the expressive reaction at a later time. The feelings that many victims report during the acute phase cover a wide range, often including shame, anger, fear, nervousness, guilt, self-blame, lack of control, and a sense of powerlessness (Golding, 1994; Ruch et al., 1991). Physical symptoms such as nausea, headaches, gastrointestinal disorders, sleep disorders, and nightmares are also commonly associated with the emotional trauma (Leserman & Drossman, 1995; Walker, 1994). Some physical symptoms may be due to the assault itself (Beebe, 1991; Slaughter & Brown, 1992). In one recently reported study, medical practitioners found that 68% of 311 female victims of sexual assault experienced genital trauma at one or more sites of injury (Slaughter et al., 1997). Injuries such as bruises, abrasions, and vaginal or rectal tears take time to heal.

Fear and nervousness often continue during the second phase, called the *long-term reorganization phase,* which may last for several years (Sales et al., 1984). The woman may fear retaliation by the rapist, and she may change her place of residence frequently during this time. She may have fearful or negative feelings about sexual relations, particularly intercourse. In one long-term study of rape survivors, 40% refrained from sexual contact for six months to a year after the assault, and almost 75% reported that the frequency of their sexual activity remained below preassault levels for as long as four to six years. Many of these women reported problems of sexual desire and arousal; a smaller number experienced orgasmic difficulties, painful intercourse, and vaginismus (Burgess & Holmstrom, 1979). In another study, a large proportion of rape survivors reported fear of sex and lack of arousal and desire, whereas fewer reported orgasmic problems (Becker et al., 1984). These findings suggest that rape interferes less with the survivor's physiosexual response than with the psychological aspects of sexual activity. Rape survivors may associate sexual touches or sex talk with the trauma of their assault. As a result, these sexual stimuli may be more likely to induce anxiety rather than sexual desire or arousal.

In recent years there has been an increased tendency to describe rape survivors as suffering from the effects of *posttraumatic stress disorder (PTSD).* PTSD, an official diagnostic category of the American Psychiatric Association (1994), refers to long-term psychological distress that often develops after a person is subjected to a psychologically traumatic event (or events). People who experience a profoundly disturbing incident, such as sexual assault, wartime combat, or a horrendous accident, often exhibit a range of distressing symptoms as an aftermath of the occurrence. These symptoms include disturbing dreams, nightmares, depression, anxiety, and not feeling safe. In addition, just as Vietnam veterans may have flashbacks of traumatic war experiences, so too might a rape survivor have vivid flashbacks of the attack in which she reexperiences all the terror of the assault.

Women often find that supportive counseling, either individually or in groups, can help ease the trauma caused by rape (Burgess & Holmstrom, 1988; Roth et al., 1988). It is very important to begin counseling as soon as possible (Burgess & Holmstrom, 1988). Research has shown that women who receive help soon after an assault experience less severe emotional repercussions than women whose treatment is delayed (Duddle, 1991; Stewart et al., 1987). Most rape survivors find that they need to talk about their assault and the emotional upheaval they are experiencing. Often the process of reviewing the event allows them to gain control over their painful feelings and to begin the process of healing. The box "Helping a Partner or Friend Recover from Rape" provides some suggestions for ways to communicate and interact with a rape victim.

Sexual Assault and Rape of Males

Health professionals who work with rape survivors know that men are raped. Some writers estimate that 5–10% of rapes committed annually in the United States involve male victims (Scarce, 1997). However, statistics on the frequency of rapes of males are difficult to obtain for a variety of reasons, not the least of which is that men are probably less likely than women to report that they have been raped (Harney & Muehlenhard, 1990; Scarce, 1997). Furthermore, the sexual assault of men is rarely reported in the media or in the psychological and medical literature (Stermac et al., 1996). Only in the last decade have many states revised their criminal codes to include adult males within the definition of rape (Isley & Gehrenbeck-Shim, 1997).

Fortunately, a recent surge of interest in this often overlooked area of sexual victimization has resulted in the increased availability of research data. One of the most

Let's Talk About It

Helping a Partner or Friend Recover from Rape

The rape of a partner or friend can be a difficult experience for both partners and friends of rape survivors. To some degree partners and close friends are also victimized by the assault. They may feel a range of emotions including rage, disgust, and helplessness. They may also be confused and unsure about how to react to a lover or friend's victimization. This lack of direction may prove costly, because reactions of partners and friends can have a profound impact on a rape survivor's recovery. In the following material we offer suggestions for ways to communicate and interact with a rape victim to help her recover from this traumatic experience. Some of these suggestions are adapted from two excellent books: *Sexual Solutions* (1980) by Michael Castleman and *"Friends" Raping Friends: Could It Happen to You?* (1987) by Jean Hughes and Bernice Sandler. Although we will frequently refer to the victim as female, our recommendations are equally applicable to male rape survivors.

- *Listen.* Probably the most important thing a person can do to help a rape victim begin recovering is to listen to her. A person comforting a rape survivor might understandably try to divert her attention from the terrible event. However, professionals who work with survivors of sexual assault have found that many victims need to talk repeatedly about the assault to come to terms with it. A partner or friend can help by encouraging her to discuss the rape in any way that she can.
- *Express that you believe her account of what happened.* A rape survivor needs to be believed by people she loves or feels close to. Consequently, it is essential to accept her version of the assault without questioning any of the facts. A simple statement, such as "What you describe is an intolerable violation, and I am so sorry that you had to endure such a dreadful experience," will clearly convey both your acceptance of her account and your empathy with her pain.
- *Let her know that it was not her fault and that she is not to blame.* Many victims of rape may believe they were somehow responsible for the attack ("I should not have invited him to my home," "I should have tried to fight him," etc.). Such impressions can lead to profound feelings of guilt. Try to head off these damaging self-recriminations by stating clearly and calmly, "I know that you are in no way to blame for what happened," or "You are the victim here and absolutely not responsible in any way for what happened to you."
- *Control your own emotions.* The last thing a rape survivor needs is to have her judgment questioned ("Why did you park on a dark side street?"). Equally counterproductive is the response of the partner who gets sidetracked by focusing his attention on his own anger or imagined shortcomings ("I should have been along to protect you"). She has just been victimized by a violent man (or men), and being confronted with her own partner's or friends' outbursts will not help her regain control.
- *Give comfort.* A rape victim is urgently in need of comfort, especially from someone she loves or cares about. She may want to be held, and the nurturing comfort of being encircled by the arms of someone she loves may provide a powerful beginning to the process of healing. Words can also be quite nurturing. Simply being told "I love you very much

(continued on next page)

ambitious examples of this emerging research trend is a recent survey of hundreds of agencies across the United States that provide help for sexual assault victims (such as rape crisis centers, sexual assault units, etc.). These agencies provided information about the extent and nature of their contact with male sexual assault victims. The survey, conducted by Paul Isely and David Gehrenbeck-Shim (1997), defined adult male sexual assault as any nonconsensual sexual acts perpetrated against a man, 16 years or older, by a male or female. Fifty-one percent of the 336 agencies responding to the survey reported encountering male victims between the years 1972 and 1991. Some of the key findings of this study are as follows:

- A total of 3635 male victims were seen in the period 1972–1991.
- The majority of these victims were both Caucasian and heterosexual.
- Most of the assaults involved physical force, physical threat, or occurred while the victim was impaired by drugs or alcohol.
- Of the rapists, 93.7% were male and 6.3% were female.
- Fewer than 15% of the victims reported their assaults to the police.
- The majority of the victimized men reported experiencing a variety of adverse symptoms similar to those described previously in our discussion of rape trauma syndrome in female victims.

Let's Talk About It

and will be here for you in any way that is right for you" may offer a great deal of welcome comfort.

- *Allow the victim to make decisions.* A rape survivor may recover more quickly when she is able to decide for herself how to deal with the assault. Making her own decisions about what should be done after a rape is an important step in regaining control over her life after being stripped of control by her attacker(s). Asking some open-ended questions (see Chapter 8) may help to facilitate the process whereby she regains control. Some possible queries might include "What kind of living arrangements for the next few days or weeks would you be comfortable with?" or "What can I do for you now?" Sometimes suggesting alternatives can be helpful. For example, in the process of encouraging her to take some type of positive action, you might ask, "Would you like to call the police, go to a hospital, or call a rape hotline?" Remember, the decision is hers and one that needs to be respected and not questioned even if you do not agree with it.
- *Offer shelter.* If she does not already live with you, offer to stay with her at her home, have her stay with you, or assist in securing other living arrangements that she is comfortable with. Again, this will be her choice.
- *Continue to provide support.* In the days, weeks, and even months following the rape, partners and friends can continue to provide empathy, support, and reassurance to a rape survivor. They can encourage her to resume a normal life and support her when she feels particularly vulnerable, fearful, or angry. They can be there to listen, even if it means hearing the same things over and over again. In the event that her assailant is prosecuted, she is likely to be in need of support and understanding throughout the often arduous legal proceedings.
- *Be patient about resuming sexual activity.* Resuming sexual activity after a rape may present problems for both the victim and her partner. Rape may precipitate sexual difficulties for the woman; she may not want to be sexually intimate for quite a while. However, some women may desire relations very soon after the attack, perhaps for assurance that their lovers still care for them and do not consider them "tainted." Open-ended questions may help to fuel dialogue about resuming sexual sharing. Some examples of possibly helpful queries include "What are your thoughts and feelings about being sexual with me?" or "What kinds of concerns do you have about resuming our sexual activity?" Some women may prefer not to have intercourse for a while but instead just want closeness and affection. Deciding when and how to engage in intimate sharing is best left up to the woman. Her partner's support in this matter is very important. Even when sexual intimacy resumes, it may be some time before she is able to relax and respond the way she did before the rape. A patient, sensitive partner can help her reach the point where she is again able to experience satisfying sexual intimacy.
- *Consider counseling.* Sometimes a rape victim needs more help than lovers, friends, and families are able to provide, no matter how supportive they are. People close to her may recognize these needs and encourage her to seek professional help. Short- or long-term therapy may help a victim recover from the emotional trauma and reconstruct her life. Similarly, partners of sexually assaulted women may also need help coping with severe conflicts and deep feelings of rage and guilt.

Many, probably the majority, of rapes of males are perpetrated by heterosexual men who often commit their crime with one or more cohorts (Frazier, 1993; Isely & Gehrenbeck-Shim, 1997; Scarce, 1997). As in rape of women, violence and power are often associated with the sexual assault of men. The possibility of being raped is a very serious issue among male homosexuals because they are often the victims of such attacks. Although homosexual men are often raped by heterosexual men, the rapist is sometimes a homosexual man. This was revealed in a recent survey of 930 homosexual men, 27.6% of whom had been sexually assaulted at some point in their lives, one-third by men with a known homosexual orientation (Hickson et al., 1994).

Rape of inmates in penal institutions is a serious problem (Cotton & Groth, 1982; Wooden & Parker, 1982). Men who do the raping typically consider themselves to be heterosexual. When released, they usually resume sexual relations with women. The men who are raped often experience brutal gang assaults. Such a man may become the sexual partner of one particular dominant inmate for protection from others (Braen, 1980).

Only rarely do men report being sexually coerced by women who employ threats of bodily harm, and this type of assault is undoubtedly a very uncommon phenomenon. However, in recent years such cases have been reported with increasing frequency. It is very difficult to assess just how rare this offense is because most men would probably be intensely embarrassed to acknowledge that their presumed male prerogative to initiate and control sexual encounters had been usurped by one or more female assailants.

The idea that mature males can be raped by women has been widely rejected because it has been assumed that a man cannot function sexually in a state of extreme anxiety or terror. However, this common impression is not accurate. Alfred Kinsey and his associates were perhaps the earliest sex researchers to acknowledge that human males can function sexually in a variety of severe emotional states. They noted that "the physiologic mechanism of any emotional response (anger, fright, pain, etc.) may be the mechanism of sexual response" (Kinsey et al., 1948, p. 165). This finding, that males may respond sexually in situations involving intense fear and degradation, is paralleled by the observation that "most women lubricate and some women respond at orgasmic levels while they are being sexually molested" (Sarrel & Masters, 1982, p. 118). Sexual response during an assault, particularly if orgasm occurs, may be a source of great confusion and anxiety to both female and male rape survivors. In some instances they may find their sexual response to be more upsetting than the physical/psychological trauma and social humiliation produced by the assault.

Philip Sarrel and William Masters (1982) reported on 11 men who had been raped by women. None of the victims reported the assault, and none was able to talk about it until he became involved in therapy several years later. A common belief among the male victims was that something was drastically wrong with them because they had responded sexually in circumstances they thought would render any normal man incapable of erection. All these men experienced emotional distress, sexual performance anxieties, feelings of inadequacy, and impaired sexual functioning. A number of other studies have also reported that, like women, men who are sexually assaulted often experience long-term emotional consequences. Fears about one's sexuality is the most frequently cited negative consequence (Isely & Gehrenbeck-Shim, 1997). Postrape traumatic stress, depression, anxiety, anger, and hostility are other negative emotional states that are also common in sexually assaulted men, and these conditions may persist for years if untreated (Frazier, 1993; Isely & Gehrenbeck-Shim, 1997). Furthermore, victimized men who do not receive effective therapeutic intervention may also develop sexual difficulties that may include erectile or orgasmic disorders and sexual aversion (Isely & Gehrenbeck-Shim, 1997; Mezy & King, 1989).

Sexual assault of males also occurs during war. However, men as victims of wartime rape and sexual assault have received only scant media coverage and limited research attention. Among the few studies in this area are investigations of male sexual assault during wars in Greece (Lindholm et al., 1980), El Salvador (Agger & Jensen, 1994), and Croatia (Medical Center for Human Rights, 1995). The widespread belief that only females can be victimized by sexual assault has led many national and state legal systems to bury the issue of wartime male sexual assault under the more generalized categories of torture or abuse (Carlson, 1997). However, awareness that men also may be victimized was recently expanded when the International Criminal Tribunal for the Former Yugoslavia reported that many men were raped or otherwise sexually assaulted during the conflict in the former Yugoslavia (Carlson, 1997).

Sexual Abuse of Children

Child sexual abuse Sexual abuse involving contact between an adult and a child. A distinction is generally made between nonrelative child sexual abuse (called pedophilia or child molestation) and incest involving sexual contact between a child and adult who are relatives.

Child sexual abuse is defined as an adult engaging in sexual contact of any kind with a child (inappropriate touching, oral–genital stimulation, coitus, etc.). Such interaction is considered coercive and illegal in that the child victim is not considered mature enough to provide informed consent to sexual involvement. *Informed consent* implies the possession of adequate intellectual and emotional maturity to understand fully both the meaning and possible consequences of a particular action. One of the most reprehensible aspects of child sexual abuse is that the adult perpetrator obtains his or her sexual gratification by exploiting the naiveté, immaturity, and trust of a child. In recent years this

On the Edge
Pedophiles in Cyberspace

Recent events have alerted us to the serious dangers of pedophiles lurking in cyberspace. It is now all too clear that the Internet has generated on-line sites that serve as electronic support groups where pedophiles exchange child pornography, discuss their molestation experiences, and validate each others' deviant impulses. Worse yet, these cyberspace predators can explore the target-rich bulletin boards on such Internet servers as America Online and Compuserve and cruise chat rooms designed for children. These chat rooms provide fertile hunting grounds for sexual predators looking for unsuspecting kids in need of attention and/or with confused notions of sexuality (Petersen, 1995; Trebilcock, 1997).

A review of the available literature yields many examples of child sexual abuse in which the Internet was an unwitting accomplice. One particularly illuminating article (Trebilcock, 1997) described several of these cases in which a common theme or strategy is often exhibited. Typically, pedophiles first gain a child's trust by appearing to be genuinely empathic and interested in their problems/concerns. Then these cyberspace predators may try to get their intended victims to agree to e-mail, postal mail, or phone contacts. Next they may ply them with pornographic materials designed to suggest that adult–child sexual interaction is normal and appropriate. The final step is to arrange a meeting. One case in which this strategy was employed involved a 30-year-old Philadelphia engineer who pled guilty to having sexual relations in an Illinois motel room with a 13-year-old girl he had met over the Internet. In another case, a 29-year-old Oregon man was convicted of rape after he had sexual relations with a 14-year-old girl he had also met on-line. In still another case, a 46-year-old New Hampshire man, who had been previously incarcerated for molesting young boys, was apprehended by authorities after it was discovered he had engaged in graphic sexual conversations with boys he had met in chat rooms and had e-mailed pornographic photographs to some of these boys.

In one of the most shocking cases of cyberspace pedophilia to date, a 10-year-old girl was invited to a slumber party at the home of a friend in Greenfield, California, in April 1996. Unbeknownst to this child and her parents, the father of the host girl was Ronald Riva, a member of the Orchid Club, an on-line collection of male pedophiles who used Internet chat rooms to exchange child pornography and discuss their true-life experiences molesting children. Riva and a fellow club member, who was a house guest, woke the girl from sleep and proceeded to molest her while filming the abuse with a digital camera connected to a computer. These images were broadcast to other members of the club, who watched the live event on their computer monitors and responded interactively, using keystrokes to indicate what they would like to see next. This heinous crime was discovered and investigated by U.S. Customs and other agencies. This first known example of pedophiles using the Internet for real-life and real-time abuse of a child resulted in indictments of 16 members of the Orchid Club. By May 1997, 14 of the 16 had elected to plead guilty. Riva, described as the club leader, was sentenced to life in prison (Mintz, 1997).

Prior to the emergence of the Internet, pedophiles were largely isolated with fewer resources for exchanging informa-

exploitation of the naiveté of unsuspecting victims has become a serious problem for children who use the Internet, as described in the box "Pedophiles in Cyberspace."

Most researchers distinguish between nonrelative child sexual abuse, referred to as **pedophilia** or **child molestation,** and **incest,** which is sexual contact between two people who are related (one of whom is often a child). Both forms of child sexual abuse are illegal in every state. Incest includes sexual contact between siblings, as well as between children and their parents, grandparents, uncles, or aunts. Sexual contact between first cousins is a gray area; not all state legal codes contain laws against these unions. Although incest may occur between related adults, more commonly it involves a child victim and an adult relative (or older sibling) perpetrator. Although its definition may vary slightly from culture to culture, incest is one of the most widely prohibited sexual behaviors throughout the world.

Some gray areas exist in the definition of child molestation. For instance, if a 21-year-old male has sexual intercourse with a 15-year-old female, is he guilty of pedophilia, statutory rape, or simply bad judgment? The issue is often further complicated when his partner willingly participates and may, in fact, have been the initiator. Each state has its own legal codes that specify at what age sexual interaction between an adult and a younger person is considered child molestation (usually if the younger person is under

Pedophilia
Sexual contact between an adult and a child.

Child molestation
See Pedophilia.

Incest
Sexual interaction between close relatives other than husband and wife.

On the Edge

tion and receiving support from others with similar deviant impulses. Now, with several pedophile support groups on-line, child molesters may receive both validation for their abusive acts and materials, which serve to strengthen their unhealthy impulses. Furthermore, and perhaps most alarming, "The support group sites give pedophiles a real sense of power, and the impetus to go out and molest someone" (Hewitt in Trebilcock, 1997, p. 138).

What can be done to combat pedophiles in cyberspace? In September 1996 the U.S. Congress passed the Communications Decency Act (CDA), which prohibited distributing indecent materials to minors by computer. In July 1997 the Supreme Court overruled this congressional act on constitutional grounds, concluding that the CDA would seriously erode free speech and "threaten to torch a large segment of the Internet community" (Levy, 1997, p. 28). The busiest gateway to the Internet, America Online (AOL) has attempted to protect children from cyberspace predators by using "guards" to monitor kids-only chat rooms for inappropriate or suspicious dialogue (Trebilcock, 1997). Although this attempt to safeguard vulnerable children is commendable, these efforts are only minimally effective, because private messages cannot be screened. Knowledgeable cyberspace pedophiles are most likely to make conversations private before making inappropriate overtures. Furthermore, a recent lawsuit filed against AOL claimed that its "rules of the road" prohibiting customers from distributing pornographic or illegal materials were so poorly enforced that AOL has become "a home shopping network for pedophiles and child pornographers" (Hiassen, 1997, p. B1). This lawsuit, filed by a Florida woman in January 1997, accused AOL of allowing pornographic videotapes of her 13-year-old son to be distributed through its chat rooms. In June 1997 a judge ruled that AOL could not be held responsible for the actions of its customers, even those who used its chat rooms to peddle pornography.

Without effective laws or in-house procedures to curb cyberspace pedophilia, the responsibility for protecting children becomes largely a function for parents.* Parental involvement is the key. Just as most of us would not be comfortable with our children playing unsupervised in potentially dangerous places, we should not allow them unlimited opportunities to cruise cyberspace or spend hours in chat rooms without some supervision. One potentially helpful strategy is to keep computers in a central location where children can be easily monitored when they go on-line. It may be especially beneficial for parents to go on-line with a child and to instruct him or her how to identify inappropriate requests. Parents should stress that their children are never to give out personal information such as a phone number or home address without parental approval. Parents should also strongly stress that a child should never meet a cyberspace acquaintance in person without a parent or other responsible adult present. Finally, parents concerned about cyberspace pornography may wish to purchase Internet-filtering software—such as Cyber Patrol, SurfWatch, Net Nanny, and WebChaperone—designed to block children's access to Web sites with obscene pictures or vulgar words. Screening software may help to curtail children's surfing of porno sites, but unfortunately it offers little protection for children exposed to pedophiles in chat rooms.

*Parents and other concerned individuals can report cyberspace predators and other on-line abusers by calling CyberTipLine at (800) 843-5678.

age 12); statutory rape (generally 12 to 16 or 17); and a consenting sexual act. The age of consent in the United States generally ranges from 16 to 18 but can be as low as 14 or 15 (see Table 19.1). The legal codes may appear ludicrous at times, particularly in cases involving teenage interactions where one partner is technically an adult and the other technically a minor, though only one or two years separate their ages. Incest is illegal regardless of the ages of the participants. However, an incestuous relationship between consenting adult relatives is considerably less likely to precipitate legal action than one involving an adult and a child.

Incest occurs at all socioeconomic levels. However, it is reported to occur with greater frequency in families disrupted by a variety of problems including severe marital conflict, spouse abuse, alcoholism, unemployment, and emotional illness. It is commonly assumed that father–daughter incest is the most prevalent, but studies have shown that brother–sister and first-cousin contacts are more common (Canavan et al., 1992; Finkelhor, 1979). However, father–daughter sexual abuse is far more likely to be reported to authorities.

Sexual relations between brothers and sisters are seldom discovered, and when they are, they do not typically elicit the extreme reactions that father–daughter sexual contacts often do. Furthermore, it is not uncommon for participating siblings to look favorably on their shared experiences when no coercion was involved (Finkelhor, 1980). Coercive sibling sexual abuse and sexual abuse by a parent, however, often has a devastating impact on the child victim.

The incestuous involvement of a father (or stepfather) and his daughter often begins before the female child understands its significance. Frequently it starts as a kind of playful activity involving wrestling, tickling, kissing, and touching. Over time the father may gradually include touching of the genitals and breasts, perhaps followed by oral or manual stimulation of the genitals and intercourse. In most cases, the father does not need to use physical force but relies on his position of authority or the pair's emotional closeness to get what he wants. He may pressure his daughter into sexual activity by reassuring her that he is "teaching" her something important, by offering rewards or by exploiting her need for love. Later, when she discovers that the behavior is not appropriate or finds her father's demands to be unpleasant and traumatizing, it may be difficult for her to escape from an already well-established pattern. Occasionally a daughter may value the relationship for the special recognition or privileges it brings her. The incestuous involvement may come to public attention when she gets angry with her father, often for nonsexual reasons, and "tells on him." Sometimes a mother may discover, much to her horror, what has been transpiring between her husband and daughter. However, in some cases she may be aware of such behavior but allow it to continue for various reasons. These may include shame, fear of reprisals, concern about having her family disrupted if her husband is jailed, or the fact that the incestuous activity allows her to avoid her husband's sexual demands.

Once detected, a father who engages in sexual relations with his child may be prosecuted under state criminal codes. Sometimes an entire family may be disrupted, with the father imprisoned, the mother facing economic difficulties, and perhaps the victim and other siblings placed in foster homes. Separation or divorce may result. These potential consequences of revealing an incestuous relationship place tremendous pressures on the child. For these and other reasons, she may be extremely reluctant to tell anyone else in her family, let alone public authorities.

Prevalence of Child Sexual Abuse

It is difficult to estimate accurately the incidence of either incest or pedophilia. For reasons previously mentioned, a child victim of incest frequently does not reveal what is occurring at the time—and may in fact not utter a word about it until she reaches adulthood, if then. Furthermore, concealment by families and powerful social taboos against such activity significantly reduce the chances that incestuous behavior will come to public attention. Acts of child molestation are unlikely to be reported at the time they occur for several reasons. First, a child may not recognize that what has transpired is improper behavior. Second, he or she may be unable to distinguish between expressions of affection and illicit sexual contact; the fact that the offender is often a friend may further confuse the issue. A third reason for low reporting stems from the fact that even when a child does inform his or her parents of improper sexual advances, the parents may not believe the child or may be reluctant to expose the child to the stress of legal proceedings. This reluctance to prosecute may be compounded when the offender is a friend or acquaintance of the family.

How common is sexual abuse of children in American society? Are the perpetrators of such abuse more commonly strangers, or friends and relatives of the victims? And are the victims more commonly females or males?

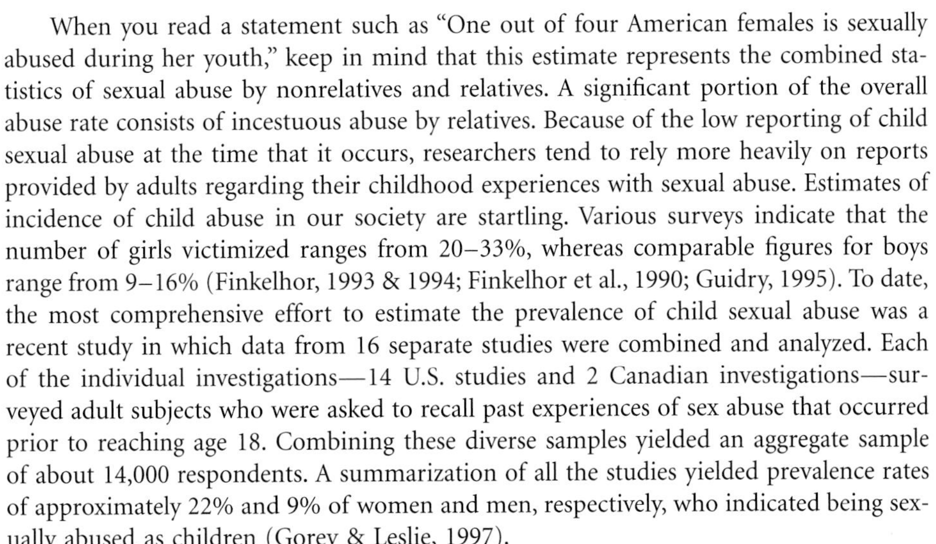

When you read a statement such as "One out of four American females is sexually abused during her youth," keep in mind that this estimate represents the combined statistics of sexual abuse by nonrelatives and relatives. A significant portion of the overall abuse rate consists of incestuous abuse by relatives. Because of the low reporting of child sexual abuse at the time that it occurs, researchers tend to rely more heavily on reports provided by adults regarding their childhood experiences with sexual abuse. Estimates of incidence of child abuse in our society are startling. Various surveys indicate that the number of girls victimized ranges from 20–33%, whereas comparable figures for boys range from 9–16% (Finkelhor, 1993 & 1994; Finkelhor et al., 1990; Guidry, 1995). To date, the most comprehensive effort to estimate the prevalence of child sexual abuse was a recent study in which data from 16 separate studies were combined and analyzed. Each of the individual investigations—14 U.S. studies and 2 Canadian investigations—surveyed adult subjects who were asked to recall past experiences of sex abuse that occurred prior to reaching age 18. Combining these diverse samples yielded an aggregate sample of about 14,000 respondents. A summarization of all the studies yielded prevalence rates of approximately 22% and 9% of women and men, respectively, who indicated being sexually abused as children (Gorey & Leslie, 1997).

Although clinical literature has indicated that more girls than boys are victims of sexual abuse, the number of young boys who are sexually molested in the United States may be substantially higher than previously estimated (Finkelhor, 1993; Hack et al., 1994; Lenderking et al., 1997). Furthermore, awareness is increasing among mental health professionals that while most child sexual abusers are male, some children are being sexually abused by women (Elliott, 1992; Guidry, 1995). The belief that women sometimes sexually victimize children has been slow to emerge, both because of the prevailing notion that child sexual abuse is a male activity and because "this subject is more of a taboo because female sexual abuse is more threatening—it undermines feelings about how women should relate to children" (Elliott, 1992, p. 12).

How do you think incidence rates of child sexual abuse in the United States compare with the prevalence of this activity in other countries?

The problem of child sexual abuse has received more attention from clinicians and the media in the United States than in any other nation. This disproportionate attention, together with America's dubious distinction as a hotbed of crime and violence, has influenced some observers to assume that sexual abuse of children is also considerably more common here than abroad. However, as revealed in Table 19.2, the incidence of child molestation is similarly high in most other countries for which statistics are available.

The Aftermath of Child Sexual Abuse

Child sexual abuse can be a severely traumatizing and emotionally damaging experience, with long-term negative consequences for the victim (Gorey & Leslie, 1997; Luster & Small, 1997). Clinical contact with adult survivors of child sexual abuse often reveals

Table 19.2 Prevalence Rates of Child Sexual Abuse in 20 Nations

	Prevalence per 100	
	Females	*Males*
Austria	36	19
South Africa	34	29
Netherlands	33	—
Costa Rica	32	13
New Zealand	32	—
Australia	28	9
United States	27	16
Spain	23	15
Norway	19	9
Belgium	19	—
Canada	18	8
Greece	16	6
Denmark	14	7
Great Britain	12	8
Switzerland	11	3
Germany	10	4
Sweden	9	3
France	8	5
Ireland	7	5
Finland	7	4

— = statistics not available

Source: Adapted from Finkelhor, 1994.

memories of a joyless youth filled with pain. Survivors speak of their loss of childhood innocence, the contamination and interruption of normal sexual development, and a profound sense of betrayal at the hands of a beloved family member or trusted friend.

A number of factors influence the severity of a child victim's response to sexual abuse. "In general, the more intrusive the abuse, the more violent the assault, the longer the sexual molestation has occurred, and the closer the relationship of the perpetrator to the victim, the worse the prognosis and the greater the need for long-term treatment" (Krugman et al., 1991). Feelings of powerlessness and betrayal may be especially pronounced when physical force is used to perpetrate an act of child sexual abuse or when the victim has a close relationship to the offender. These two factors—physical force and victim–offender relationship—probably show the strongest relationship to subsequent negative consequences for child sexual abuse survivors (Banyard & Williams, 1996; Rind & Tromovitch, 1997).

Many victims of child sexual abuse have difficulty forming intimate adult relationships (Collins, 1994; Felitti, 1991). When relationships are established, they often lack emotional and sexual fulfillment (Jackson et al., 1990; Meiselman, 1978). Sexual abuse is not uncommon in the histories of people who seek treatment for sexual difficulties (Kinzl et al., 1995; Sarwer & Durlak, 1996). Other common problems of sexual abuse survivors include low self-esteem, guilt, shame, depression, alienation, a lack of trust in others, revulsion at being touched, drug and alcohol abuse, obesity, elevated suicide rates, a predisposition to being repeatedly victimized in a variety of ways, and long-term medical problems such as chronic pelvic pain and gastrointestinal disorders (Garnefski & Diekstra, 1997; Goodman & Fallot, 1998; Luster & Small, 1997).

Recent research indicates that there may be some sex differences in the impact of childhood sex abuse. One study provided evidence indicating that such abuse may not be as likely to cause adult sexual dysfunctions in men as it is in women (Sarwer et al., 1997). Another recent investigation of about 1500 12-to-19-year-olds, half of whom had a history of abuse, found that sexually abused males had considerably more emotional and behavioral problems than their female counterparts (Garnefski & Diekstra, 1997). Some of the sex differences reported in this study include the following:

- Whereas "suicidality" (suicidal thoughts or suicide attempts) was reported almost 5 times more often by sexually abused females than by nonabused females, it was reported almost 11 times more often by sexually abused males than by their nonabused counterparts.
- Emotional problems, while 2.5 times more common in abused than nonabused girls, were a startling 6 times more common in sexually abused boys than their nonabused counterparts.
- Aggressive/criminal behaviors and addiction-risk behaviors were reported substantially more often by sexually abused boys than by sexually abused girls.
- Of the sexually abused boys, 65% reported problems in multiple problem-area categories, versus 38% of the sexually abused girls. (Categories included in this study included suicidality, emotional problems, and aggressive/criminal and addiction-risk behavior.)

Particularly troubling are cases of childhood sexual abuse so traumatic that they have been repressed or otherwise hidden from conscious memory by the victim, only to be remembered years later. In recent years a number of controversial lawsuits have centered around such cases. Are such recovered memories reliable? The boxed discussion on page 592 "Recovered Memories of Childhood Sexual Abuse: Real or Imagined?" investigates this question.

A variety of treatment approaches have recently emerged to help survivors of child sexual abuse resolve issues regarding these experiences and their emotional aftermath (Cahill et al., 1991; Courtois, 1997; Hack et al., 1994). These treatment strategies range from individual therapy to group and couples-oriented approaches. Most metropolitan areas in the United States also have self-help support organizations for sexual abuse survivors. (If you wish more information about how to seek professional therapeutic assistance, we suggest reviewing the guidelines outlined in Chapter 16.)

Characteristics of Child Sex Offenders

What kind of personality traits and behavioral characteristics would you expect to find in people who commit sexual offenses against children?

No "classic profile" of the pedophile offender has been identified, other than that most are male and are known to the victim (Gibbons & Vincent, 1994; Guidry, 1995). Child molesters represent the spectrum in terms of social class, educational achievement, intelligence, occupation, religion, and race. Some evidence suggests that many pedophile offenders, especially those who are prosecuted, tend to be shy, lonely, poorly informed about sexuality, and very moralistic or religious (Bauman et al., 1984). Many are likely to have poor interpersonal and sexual relations with other adults, and may feel socially inadequate and inferior (McKibben et al., 1994; Minor & Dwyer, 1997). However, it is not uncommon to encounter child sex offenders outside the legal system who are well educated, socially adept, civic-minded, and successful (Baur, 1995). Child victims are often family friends, neighbors, or acquaintances. Relating to these children sexually may represent a way of coping with powerful feelings of inadequacy that are likely to emerge in sociosexual relationships with other adults.

Alcoholism, severe marital problems, sexual difficulties, and poor emotional adjustment are frequently experienced by pedophiles (Johnston, 1987; McKibben et al., 1994). These offenders have often been sexually victimized themselves during their own childhoods (Gaffney et al., 1984; Seghorn et al., 1987).

Like pedophiles, incest offenders are primarily males who cannot be easily identified or categorized by a "classic profile." Rather, "they are a complex, heterogeneous group of individuals who look like everyone else" (Scheela & Stern, 1994, p. 91). However, the incest offender does tend to share some of the traits of the pedophile. He is often economically disadvantaged, a heavy drinker, unemployed, devoutly religious, and emotionally immature (Furniss, 1985; Rosenberg, 1988). His behavior may result from general tendencies toward pedophilia, severe feelings of inadequacy in adult sexual relations, or rejection by a hostile spouse; it may also be an accompaniment to alcoholism or other psychological disturbances (Rosenberg, 1988). Not uncommonly, the man who molests his own child comes from a family where patterns of incest were modeled for him by parents, siblings, or both (Delson & Clark, 1981; Scheela & Stern, 1994). He also frequently has certain distorted ideas about adult–child sex—for example, that a child who does not resist desires sexual contact, that adult–child sex is an effective way for children to learn about sex, that a father's relationship with his daughter is enhanced by having sexual contact with her, and that a child does not report contact because she enjoys it (Abel et al., 1984).

Preventing Child Sexual Abuse

Specialists in the field of child sexual abuse are attempting to develop more effective strategies for preventing the sexual victimization of children. This is essential because the available evidence indicates that most children do not reveal that they have been victimized, and when they do, families are often reluctant to seek outside help (Finkelhor, 1984a). The experiences of health professionals who work with victims suggest that many children could have avoided being victimized if they had been provided with some important messages concerning their right to say no, the difference between "okay" and "not-okay" touches, and strategies for coping with an adult's attempt to coerce them into inappropriate intimate contact.

Perhaps the best prospects for reducing the high levels of child sexual abuse in our society lie in developing effective programs to be implemented in the early stages of a child's public education. As indicated in Chapter 13, parents often avoid discussing sex with their children. Therefore, it is probably unrealistic to expect better parent–child communication to resolve the issue. Furthermore, parents themselves are often the abusers. The following list of suggestions, drawn from the writings of a number of child abuse specialists, offers some suggestions for preventing child sexual abuse that may be helpful to parents, educators, and other caregivers of children:

1. It is important to present prevention-oriented material to young children, because as many as 25% of child sexual abuse victims are younger than age seven (Finkelhor, 1984a). Be sure to include boys, because they too may be abused.
2. Educators and parents will be more effective if they avoid complicated discussions of ethics, social responsibility, and complex notions of appropriate sexual activity. A more realistic approach is to keep things simple and "to translate the notions of sex-

Ethical/Legal Issues

Recovered Memories of Childhood Sexual Abuse: Real or Imagined?

Can a person repress memories of sexual abuse that may have occurred years or decades earlier and then suddenly or gradually "recover" them after exposure to certain triggering stimuli? Or, can a "memory" be suggested and then remembered as true? These questions lie at the heart of an ongoing debate among practitioners of the law, clinicians, and researchers. From a legal perspective, this debate has become increasingly acrimonious as the American legal system responds to a flood of civil lawsuits and criminal prosecutions based on recovered memories of childhood sexual abuse.

Over the last decade the media has reported numerous cases in which alleged perpetrators of sex abuse have been accused and convicted based on the testimony of adult women who "recover" memories of their abuse, usually in the context of receiving psychotherapy for a variety of disorders. Skeptics of recovered memories lament that thousands of families and individual lives are being devastated by the widespread inclination to accept these claims at face value in the absence of validating evidence. These critics offer as evidence many cases in which falsely accused and convicted individuals are later exonerated, either by the legal system or by victim recantation.

In one famous legal case, a California man, accused of sexually molesting his daughter for 12 years after she "recovered" memories of abuse while undergoing psychotherapy as an adult, fought these accusations by suing her therapist. He won a judgment against the therapist in a landmark 1994 case described in detail in a book by journalist Moira Johnson (1997): *Spectral Evidence: The Ramona Case: Incest, Memory and Truth on Trial in Napa Valley.* Other court cases have also struck at the validity of recovered memory. Among these is a recent malpractice lawsuit in Oregon in which a woman and her family members received substantial financial settlements from two psychotherapists for damages allegedly caused by the implanting of false memories of ritualistic sexual/physical abuse while the plaintiff was undergoing therapy for depression (Hoover, 1997).

Clearly, the possibility of being falsely accused of such a heinous crime is the substance of nightmares. But just how likely is this prospect and what are the probabilities that recovered memories are imagined? To gain some perspective on this issue, let us briefly consider some of the available evidence.

Support for the legitimacy of recovered memories has been provided by several studies. In one investigation, 59% of 450 clients being treated for childhood sexual abuse reported that there had been varying time periods prior to age 18 when they could not remember their abuse (Briere & Conte, 1993). In another study, 129 adult women who had experienced childhood sexual abuse in the 1970s were identified and interviewed in the 1990s. Of this group, 38% did not recall the abuse that had been reported and documented 17 years earlier. The author of this investigation concluded that if having no recall of child sexual abuse is a common occurrence for adult women, as indicated by the study's results, "later recovery of child sexual abuse by some women should not be surprising" (Williams, 1994, p. 1174). In another study, 56% of 45 adult women survivors of childhood sexual abuse indicated ual abuse into concepts that make sense within the world of the child" (Finkelhor, 1984b, p. 3).

3. It is wise to avoid making a discussion of child sexual abuse unduly frightening. A child may develop so much fear that she or he will feel powerless and incapable of acting effectively in an abuse situation. It is important that children be sufficiently concerned that they will be on the lookout for potentially abusive adult behavior. However, they should also be confident in their ability to avoid such a situation should it occur.
4. Take time to carefully explain the differences between okay touches (pats, snuggles, and hugs) and not-okay touches that make a child feel uncomfortable or confused. Not-okay touches can be explained as touching under the panties or underpants or touching areas that bathing suits cover. In discussing touches that are not okay, be sure to indicate that a child does not have to touch an adult in these same areas even if the adult says it is all right. It is also a good idea to talk about not-okay kisses (prolonged lip contact or tongue in mouth).
5. Encourage children to believe that they have rights—the right to control their bodies and the right to say no when they are being touched in a way that makes them uncomfortable.

Ethical/Legal Issues

that they had been amnesic from their abuse for varied lengths of time, and 16% reported remembering their abuse in the context of receiving psychotherapy (Rodriguez et al., 1997b). Finally, a recent survey of several hundred university students found that 20% of 111 victims of childhood sexual abuse reported that they had recovered previously forgotten memories of abuse (Melchert & Parker, 1997).

On the other side of the debate, several research scientists express skepticism about recovered memories of childhood sexual abuse. Some have argued that "repressed memories" may be inadvertently planted in suggestible clients by overzealous or poorly trained psychotherapists who believe that most psychological problems stem from childhood sexual abuse (Dawes, 1994; Lindsay & Read, 1994; Yapko, 1994). Numerous studies have demonstrated the relative ease with which false "memories" of events that never occurred can be created in the research laboratory (Loftus, 1993; Loftus & Ketcham, 1994; Loftus et al., 1994). In one 11-week study, for instance, young children were asked at weekly intervals whether they had ever experienced five distinct events. Four of the events were real, while one—getting treated in the hospital for an injured finger—was fictitious. The children readily recognized the real events. However, more than a third also became gradually convinced over the course of the 11 weeks that one of their fingers had been injured. In some cases, they even "remembered" elaborate details about their injuries. Many continued to insist that these false memories were true even after being told otherwise (Ceci et al., 1994).

Clearly, the concept of client suggestibility has become central to the arguments offered by critics of recovered memories. However, results of a recent investigation call into question the suggestibility rationale for dismissing reports of recovered memories of childhood sexual abuse. In this study, a psychological scale was used to measure suggestibility in 44 women who had previously reported recovered memories of childhood sexual abuse and in a comparison group of 31 women without a history of sex abuse. Subjects without a history of abuse were more inclined to alter memory to suggestive prompts than were the recovered memory subjects (Leavitt, 1997).

So where are we now on this controversial issue? The American Psychological Association, American Psychiatric Association, and American Medical Association have all issued statements supporting the belief that forgotten memories can be recovered later in life. These same professional organizations also acknowledge that a "memory" may be suggested and then remembered as true. As the debate continues it is important to remember that, despite the media spotlight on defendants who claim they have been falsely accused, "the battle against child sexual abuse is no witch hunt" (Vachss, 1996, p. 5). Sexual predators do exist in alarming numbers in American society, and child sexual abuse is a fact, not a disputed issue. We must guard against the possibility that widespread repudiation of recovered memories might turn back the clock to a time when victims of sexual abuse were reluctant to report their traumatic experiences out of fear of being ridiculed or condemned for lying. In the same spirit, we must act responsibly to protect the innocent from wrongful accusations that stem from false memories. To this end, in April 1997 the U.S. Supreme Court recommended that all interviews with alleged victims of sex abuse be videotaped so that independent experts can evaluate the nature of the questioning and the veracity of answers. Recent research has demonstrated an effective interview protocol for video-recorded child sexual abuse investigations (Cheung, 1997), but at the time of this writing no state has adopted these guidelines.

6. Encourage children to tell someone right away if an adult has touched them in a way that is inappropriate or has made them do something about which they are uncomfortable. Emphasize that you will not be angry with them and that they will be okay when they tell, even if someone has told them that they will get in trouble. Stress that no matter what happened, it was not their fault, and they will not be blamed. Also, warn them that not all adults will believe them. Tell them to keep telling people until they find someone like you who will believe them.
7. Discuss with children some of the strategies that adults may use to gain compliance with their deviant sexual demands. For example, tell them to trust their own feelings when they think something is wrong, even if an adult who is a friend or relative says that it is okay and that they are "teaching" them something about which they need to learn. Given that many adults use the "this is our secret" strategy, it can be particularly helpful to explain the difference between a secret (something they are never to tell—a bad idea) and a surprise (a good idea because it is something they tell later to make someone happy).
8. Discuss strategies for getting away from uncomfortable or dangerous situations. Let them know that it is okay to scream, yell, run away, or get assistance from a friend or trusted adult.
9. Encourage children to state clearly to the adult who touches them inappropriately that they will tell a particular responsible adult about what went on. Interviews with child sexual abuse offenders have revealed that many would be deterred in their abusive actions by a child saying that she or he would tell a specific adult about the assault (Budin & Johnson, 1989; Daro, 1991).
10. Perhaps one of the most important things to incorporate in this prevention discussion, particularly for parents, is the message that private touching can be a very joyous and pleasurable experience, as they will discover when they grow older and meet someone they care for or love. Without some discussion of the positive aspects of sexuality, there is a risk that a child will develop a very negative view of any kind of sexual contact between people, regardless of the nature of their relationship.

What kinds of responses might be appropriate or helpful in the event you discovered that your child was involved in a sexual encounter with an adult? Consider this question in terms of what might be most beneficial for the emotional health of your child.

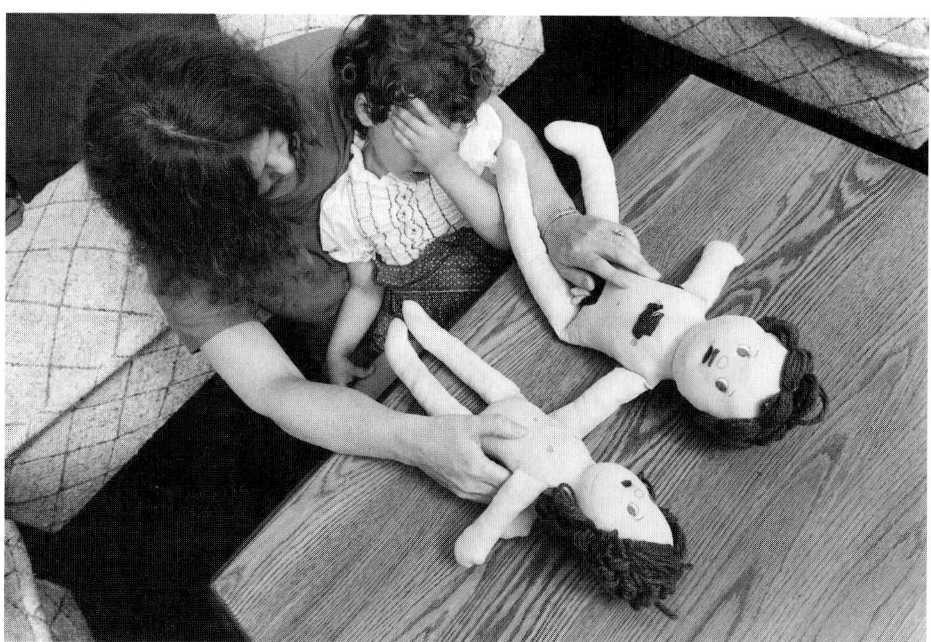

Specialists in the field of child sexual abuse sometimes use anatomically correct dolls to educate children about "okay" touches. These dolls may also be used in discussions with very young victims to clarify the nature of the abuse that has occurred.

The emotional trauma a child experiences as a result of a sexual encounter with an adult may be magnified by excessive parental reactions (Davies, 1995). When telling a parent what happened, children may merely be relaying a sense of discomfort over something they do not fully understand. If parents understandably react with extreme agitation, children are likely to respond with increased emotional negativity, developing a sense of being implicated in something terrible, and often feeling extremely guilty about having participated in such an event. Children may feel guilty about such experiences even without parental displays of distress because they sense the guilt of the person who molested them.

It is important that parents respond appropriately to instances of child abuse involving their children. Such acts should not be ignored! While remaining calm in the face of their child's revelation, parents should take great precautions to see that the child is not alone with the offending party again. In many instances, children are repeatedly molested by the same person, and they may come to feel a sense of obligation and guilt. It is essential to ensure that the child is protected from further experiences of this kind. Because it also is very likely that your child is not the offender's only victim, it is essential to report the offender to the police to protect other children.

Sexual Harassment

Sexual harassment in the workplace or an academic setting is widespread within U.S. society. In the following sections, we define and discuss this form of sexual victimization as it occurs both on the job and in educational environments.

Sexual harassment Unwanted attention of a sexual nature from someone at the workplace or in an academic setting.

Sexual Harassment in the Workplace

Many working people are subjected to sexual harassment on the job. This form of sexual victimization, while perhaps not as extreme as sexual abuse of children or rape, is nevertheless a major concern that is receiving increasing attention. Job-related sexual harassment gained unprecedented public attention in the early 1990s as a result of two incidents that received national media coverage: law professor Anita Hill's allegations that she had been sexually harassed by Supreme Court nominee Clarence Thomas, and the U.S. Navy's Tailhook scandal, in which Pentagon investigators concluded that many women had been sexually harassed or assaulted by drunken aviators. More recently, sexual harassment was again thrust before the public due to extensive media coverage of two significant events: Paula Jones's sexual harassment lawsuit against President Clinton and a sexual scandal that rocked the Army. Although the Clinton lawsuit has not been resolved by the time of this writing, the Army has moved forcefully to deal with sexual harassment and assault within the ranks, as described in the box "Scandal in the Army: Sexual Victimization in the Ranks."

Law professor Anita Hill, who testified during the confirmation hearings of Supreme Court Justice Clarence Thomas, triggered a national debate about the nature of sexual harassment in the workplace.

Sexual harassment in the workplace is prohibited by Title VII of the 1964 Civil Rights Act. Perhaps the best overall definition of this form of sexual victimization was provided in 1980 by the Equal Employment Opportunity

Commission (EEOC) when it issued guidelines on sexual harassment. These guidelines emphasize that both verbal and physical harassment are illegal:

> Unwelcome sexual advances, requests for sexual favors, and other verbal or physical conduct of a sexual nature constitute sexual harassment when 1) submission to such conduct is made either explicitly or implicitly a term or condition of an individual's employment, 2) submission to or rejection of such conduct by an individual is used as a basis for employment decisions affecting such individual, or 3) such conduct has the purpose or effect of unreasonably interfering with an individual's work performance or creating an intimidating, hostile, or offensive working environment. (Equal Employment Opportunity Commission, 1980, pp. 74676–74677)

These guidelines, written for employment settings but also applicable to academic environments, describe two kinds of sexual harassment. One form, commonly labeled "quid pro quo," is reflected in the first two situations described in the guidelines. This form of harassment is generally carried out by someone with power or authority. Here, compliance with unwanted sexual advances is made a condition for securing a job or education benefits, or for desirable treatment in employment or academic settings (such as receiving a promotion or high grades) (Pierce, 1994, p. 5). In the latter case, harassment is often evident in reprisals that follow refusals to comply (Charney & Russell, 1994).

A second form of sexual harassment, often referred to as a "hostile or offensive environment," is described in the third situation in the EEOC guidelines. This kind of sexual harassment is less clear but probably more common than the quid pro quo variety. Here,

On the Edge

Scandal in the Army: Sexual Victimization in the Ranks

In September 1996 several women trainees at the Army's Aberdeen Proving Ground in Maryland decided to take a stand against repeated incidences of sexual abuse by male drill instructors. One of these women, a 17-year-old recruit, charged that she had been a target of unwanted sexual advances from 10 different drill sergeants. Several of these women had attempted to report instances of sexual victimization long before the first formal charges were filed in September, but "according to a senior Army source, their complaints were 'deep sixed' at a low level" (Vistica, 1996, p. 31).

After weeks of internal investigation, the Army went public with this scandal in November 1996 and announced it had filed charges against three male officers and were investigating about 20 others. Anxious to avoid a repeat of the Navy's notorious Tailhook scandal in 1991—in which 26 women attending the Tailhook convention in Las Vegas were sexually assaulted by drunken Navy aviators, none of whom were convicted—the Army moved quickly to demonstrate a "zero tolerance" policy regarding sexual misconduct. A toll-free hotline set up by the Army logged about 7000 calls in the first 12 weeks of operation, including well over 1000 allegations of abuse that Army investigators considered legitimate enough for further evaluation (Shenon, 1997).

By spring 1997 over 50 women recruits had filed official complaints of sexual abuse against male officers at Aberdeen, 27 of them for rape. By the time of this writing the military justice system had convicted 18 male officers (6 from Aberdeen) for various sexual offenses, the most serious of which resulted in an Aberdeen staff sergeant drill instructor receiving a 25-year prison sentence after being convicted of 18 counts of rape against six women. In another case, involving an Army captain (the highest-ranking defendant in the Aberdeen sex-abuse scandal), the Army dropped charges of rape and forcible sodomy in return for guilty pleas to lesser offenses. His sentence: four months in jail followed by dismissal from the military. Pentagon officials announced in September 1997 that the former commander of the base, a two-star general, and several of his deputies have received career-ending letters of reprimand.

After the eruption of widespread media attention to the Aberdeen scandal, the Army commenced two separate but similar investigations of sexual misconduct in its ranks, one study headed by the inspector general of the Army and the other by a retired general. In September 1997 the Army announced the results of these almost year-long investigations, both of which found that "sexual harassment exists through-one or more supervisors, coworkers, teachers, or students engage in persistent, inappropriate behaviors that make the workplace or academic environment hostile, abusive, and generally unbearable. Unlike quid pro quo harassment, this second form does not necessarily involve power or authority differences.

What constitutes a hostile or offensive environment? This question is the topic of continuing debate. A number of recent court decisions have embraced a "reasonable person" position as a "litmus test." Essentially, a hostile environment is seen as one in which a reasonable person in the same or similar circumstances would find the conduct of the harasser(s) to be intimidating, hostile, or abusive.

The reasonable person interpretation is illustrated by a recent legal decision. The United States Supreme Court ruled unanimously that a Tennessee woman was subjected to sexual harassment in the form of a hostile environment "that would seriously affect a reasonable person's psychological well-being" (Justice Sandra Day O'Connor writing for the Court in *Harris* v. *Forklift Systems,* 92 U.S. 1168, 1993). In this case, the victim's male boss (the company president) (1) urged her to retrieve coins from his front pants pocket, (2) ridiculed the size of her buttocks, (3) described her as a "dumb-ass woman" in the presence of others, and (4) insinuated that she had won a large sales contract by providing sexual favors. His attorney tried to pass off these behaviors as merely joking without any hostile intent. This case is noteworthy in that it involved neither sexual blackmail or unwanted touching. Nevertheless, the Supreme Court ruled that a reasonable person would find the offensive sexual speech to be intimidating and abusive.

On the Edge

out the Army, crossing gender, rank and racial lines" (Shenon, 1997, p. A1). It is now painfully evident that tens of thousands of Army women are sexually harassed or assaulted every year. (Sexual victimization is also endemic in other branches of the military as revealed in Table 19.3.) An Army-wide survey conducted in conjunction with these investigations revealed that 47% of the women soldiers polled reported experiencing unwanted sexual attention, 15% had been subjected to sexual coercion, and 7% had been victimized by sexual assault. About half as many male troops also reported experiencing sexual harassment, with 30% indicating being targets of unwanted sexual attention, and 8% reporting sexual coercion. Only 12% of the soldiers who reported being sexually victimized had filed a formal complaint (Shenon, 1997).

During the period when the Army was investigating sexual abuse in the ranks, prompted by the Aberdeen scandal, it was further embarrassed when its highest-ranking enlisted soldier was accused of sexual misconduct. In May 1997 the Army charged Gene McKinney, the sergeant major of the Army and personal representative of 410,000 enlisted soldiers, with indecent assault and sexual misconduct involving several service women over nearly three years. McKinney, whose rank is equivalent to a three-star general, strongly denied the accusation. In October 1997 he was ordered to face a court-martial on 19 counts of misconduct stemming from accusations made by six women. A request by the prosecution that he be charged with rape was rejected. If convicted on all counts, McKinney could have been sentenced to a maximum prison sentence of 55 years. However, after a lengthy trial in early 1998, McKinney was exonerated on all charges of sexual misconduct and convicted of just one count of obstructing justice. The only penalty imposed by the Army was a reduction in rank of one grade. Subsequent to this ruling, a number of military analysts predicted that the McKinney trial verdict may discourage victims from coming forward and "would have a chilling effect on female soldiers who believe they have been the object of unwanted sexual advances by superiors" (Healy, 1998, p. A1).

In late 1997 the Army announced a plan to produce both better compliance with and enforcement of rules against sexual misconduct in the ranks. Furthermore, the Army pledged to revise its procedures for the selection and training of drill sergeants and other instructors whose positions of authority offer ample opportunities to coerce sex from young recruits. The Army does appear to be responding forcefully to curtail sexual misconduct in its ranks. Rape-prevention classes are now provided for new recruits, and basic training has been expanded by adding an additional week of instruction in ethics and values. Furthermore, drill sergeants are now exposed to additional education about sexual harassment. It is hoped that these efforts will significantly reduce the abysmally high numbers of soldiers sexually victimized during their military careers.

Varieties and Incidence of Sexual Harassment on the Job

Sexual harassment on the job can take many forms. Mild forms include such things as remarks of a sexual nature; sexist comments; unwelcome attention; violations of personal space; repeated unwelcome requests for a date; inappropriate, derogatory put-downs; leering and/or whistling; offensive and crude language; and displaying sexually oriented objects, materials, or pictures that create a hostile or offensive environment. Some of these "milder" behaviors occupy a gray area in that not all people would view them as genuine sexual harassment. However, they clearly become sexual harassment if they persist after the target of such acts has asked the offending person to stop.

At an intermediate level of severity, sexual harassment in the workplace may include inappropriate, graphic comments about a person's body or sexual competence; sexual propositions not directly linked to employment; verbal abuse of a sexual nature; and unwanted physical contact of a nonsexual nature. In its most severe manifestations, sexual harassment on the job may involve a boss or supervisor requiring sexual services from an employee as a condition for keeping a job or getting a promotion, unwanted physical contact or conduct of a sexual nature, and, less commonly, sexual assault.

How common is sexual harassment in the workplace? Do you think that it is confined largely to blue-collar occupations, or does it occur across the board?

The annual number of sexual harassment complaints filed with the EEOC more than doubled from 6,000 in 1990 to 15,300 in 1996 (Kaufman, 1997), and a number of surveys reveal that sexual harassment is all too common in the workplace. Perhaps the most reliable available data come from a national survey of more than 24,000 federal employees. This survey, which adhered closely to the EEOC definition of sexual harassment, had an 85% response rate. Of the more than 20,000 respondents, 42% of women and 15% of men reported experiencing sexual harassment (U.S. Merit Systems Protection Board, 1981). A later update of this survey found the same incidence of sexual harassment (U.S. Merit Systems Protection Board, 1988). Other surveys have found sexual harassment rates among working women ranging from 88% (Safran, 1976) to roughly 66% (MacKinnon, 1979) to 50% (Gutek, 1985; Loy & Stewart, 1984). (Safran's 88% estimate is probably high; it comes from a survey of *Redbook* respondents, admittedly not a representative sample of the general population.) A 1995 survey of 90,000 active-duty women service members found that half or more of the respondents in each branch of the military believed they had been sexually harassed (Vistica, 1996). The highest percentage of women reporting harassment (64%) were in the Marines. Table 19.3 summarizes the finding of this military study.

Sexual harassment creates anxiety and tension in the workplace.

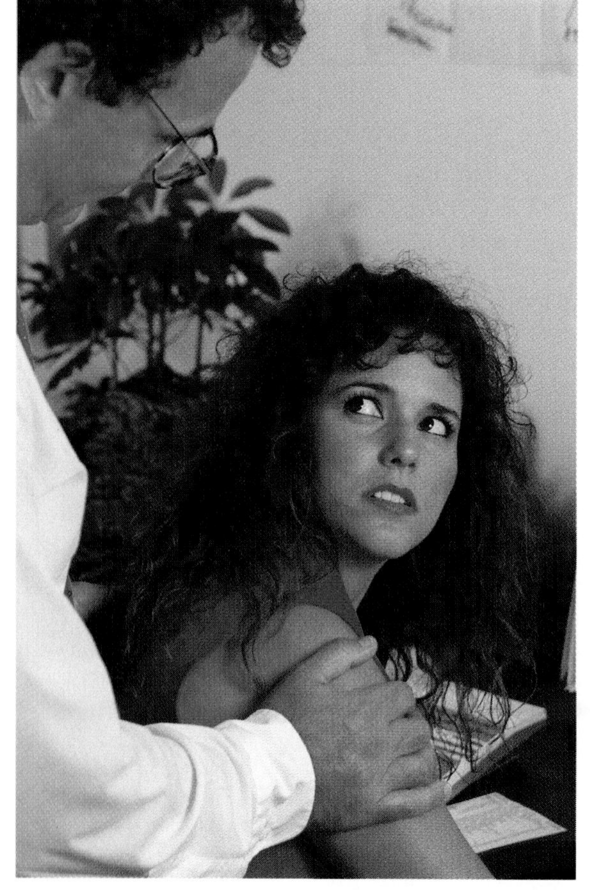

The incidence of sexual harassment is not limited to low-paying jobs, the military, or indeed to any particular segment of the employment force. Several studies have revealed high incidences of sexual harassment even in medical settings. In one survey of 133 physicians, 73% of the female respondents and 22% of the men reported experiencing sexual harassment during their residency training (Komaromy et al., 1993). Another survey of 496 nurses revealed that 82% had experienced sexual harassment on the job (Grieco, 1987). Finally, of 422 female physicians who responded to a survey investigating harassment of physicians by their patients, 77% reported they had been sexually harassed by patients, the vast majority of whom were male (Phillips & Schneider, 1993).

Table 19.3 Sexual Harassment of Women in the Military

Percentage of Women in Each Service Reporting Harassment	Marines 64%	Army 61%	Navy 53%	Air Force 49%
Types of Reported Harassment				
Teasing, Inappropriate Jokes	44%			
Looks, Gestures	37			
Touching, Cornering	29			
Whistles, Calls	23			
Pressure for Dates	22			
Letters, Phone Calls	12			
Pressure for Sexual Favors	11			
Actual or Attempted Rape	4			
Reported Perpetrators of Sexual Harassment				
Military Coworkers of Equal Rank	44%			
Higher-Ranking Personnel	43			
Other Military Persons	24			
Immediate Supervisors	18			
Military Subordinates	10			
When Harassment Was Reported, What Action Was Taken?				
Perpetrator Was Talked to	50%			
Complaint Not Taken Seriously	23			
Perpetrator Was Counseled	20			
No Action Was Taken	15			
Supervisor Was Hostile	12			
Victim Was Encouraged to Drop Complaint	10			

Source: 1995 Pentagon survey of 90,000 active duty female service members, as reported in Vistica, 1996.

Same-Sex Sexual Harassment in the Workplace

In recent years sexual harassment involving members of the same sex has become an increasing issue both in the workplace and America's courts. People who are victims of same-sex sexual harassment have generally found it difficult to obtain satisfactory legal judgments regardless of their own sexual orientation. This unfortunate situation is due both to the absence of a federal law specifically prohibiting sexual harassment and to the fact that many courts have narrowly interpreted Title VII as prohibiting sex discrimination only between people of different biological sex (Landau, 1997). To circumvent this loophole in Title VII, attorneys representing victims of same-sex harassment frequently find themselves in the position of needing to prove that accused same-sex harassers acted out of "sexual interest." This can be extremely difficult, because most defendants in these cases claim to be heterosexual. Furthermore, gay plaintiffs may be afraid of being "outed" or exposed and, if not gay, may fear being thought of as gay (Gover, 1996).

Lower courts have issued varied decisions about whether Title VII applies to same-sex sexual harassment. One federal appeals court ruled that it offers no protection to victims of same-sex harassment. Another federal court ruled that Title VII is applicable only if the perpetrator is homosexual. Still another regional federal court took a more expansive approach by ruling that Title VII applies regardless of the sexual orientation of either victim or perpetrator (Epstein, 1997c). In October 1996 the U.S. Supreme Court refused to hear three separate appeals cases that were all asking this body to declare that Title VII applies equally to both same- and other-sex sexual harassment. However, in March 1998 the Court reversed itself by ruling that workplace sexual harassment involving an offender and victim of the same sex is prohibited by Title VII. The Court's nine justices unanimously voted to reactivate a Louisiana lawsuit previously thrown out by a federal appeals court. In this case (*Oncale v. Sundowner Offshore Services*), an offshore oil rig worker has claimed that male coworkers taunted and touched him sexually. At the time of this writing, this revived lawsuit is pending on the docket of a lower court.

Effects of Workplace Sexual Harassment on the Victim

On-the-job sexual harassment can seriously erode a victim's financial status, job performance, career opportunities, psychological and physical health, and personal relationships (Charney & Russell, 1994; Rhode, 1997). The financial ramifications of refusing to endure sexual harassment may be devastating, especially for people in lower-level positions. Many victims, particularly if they are supporting families, cannot afford to be unemployed. Many find it exceedingly difficult to look for other jobs while maintaining their present employment. If they are fired for resisting harassment, they may be unable to obtain unemployment compensation—and even if they do obtain compensation, it will probably provide only half of their former income. Thus, a person who quits or is fired as a result of sexual harassment faces the prospect of severe financial difficulties.

Various surveys report that the great majority (between 75% and 90%) of harassed workers report adverse psychological effects, including crying spells, loss of self-esteem, and feeling angry, humiliated, ashamed, embarrassed, nervous, irritable, alienated, vulnerable, helpless, and unmotivated (Charney & Russell, 1994; Gutek, 1985; Hamilton et al., 1987). The sense of degradation and helplessness reported by many victims of sexual harassment is similar to that experienced by many rape victims (Safran, 1976).

Finally, many victims of sexual harassment report a variety of physical symptoms that stem directly from pressures associated with their victimization. These include headaches, stomach ailments, depressed appetite, weight loss, back and neck pain, decreased sleep, respiratory or urinary tract infections, and a variety of other stress-related symptoms (Charney & Russell, 1994; Loy & Stewart, 1984).

Dealing with Sexual Harassment on the Job

If you face sexual harassment at work, a number of options are available to you. The suggestions listed below provide guidelines for dealing with this exploitive abuse:

1. If the harassment includes actual or attempted rape or assault, you can file criminal charges against the perpetrator.
2. If the harassment has stopped short of attempted rape or assault, you may wish to confront the person who is harassing you. State in clear terms that what he or she is doing is clearly sexual harassment, that you will not tolerate it, and that if it continues you will file charges through appropriate channels. You may prefer to document what has occurred and your response to it in a letter directed to the harasser (keep a copy). In such a letter, you should include specific details of previous incidents of harassment, your unequivocal rejection of such inappropriate overtures, and your intent to take more serious action if they do not stop immediately.
3. If the offender does not stop the harassment after direct confrontation, it may be helpful to discuss your situation with your supervisor and/or the supervisor of the offender.
4. If neither the harasser nor the supervisors responds appropriately to your concern, you may want to gather support from your coworkers (you may not be the only victim in your company). Discussing the offense with other sympathetic women and men in your workplace may produce sufficient pressure to terminate the harassment. Be sure of your facts, though, because such actions could result in a slander lawsuit.

5. If your attempt to deal with this problem within your company does not work or if you are fired, demoted, or refused promotion because of your efforts to end harassment, you can file an official complaint with your city or state Human Rights Commission or Fair Employment Practices Agency (the names may vary locally). You can also ask that the local office of the federally funded Equal Employment Opportunity Commission investigate the situation.
6. Finally, you may wish to pursue legal action to resolve your problem with sexual harassment. Lawsuits can be filed in federal courts under the Civil Rights Act. They can also be filed under city or state laws prohibiting employment discrimination. One lawsuit can be filed in a number of jurisdictions. A person who has been a victim of such harassment is most likely to receive a favorable court judgment if she or he has first tried to resolve the problem within the company before going to court.

There is evidence that employers are becoming increasingly sensitive to the issue of sexual harassment in the workplace, motivated in part by a number of court decisions that have awarded large payments to victims. It is estimated that the cost of sexual harassment averages at least $6 million a year for a Fortune 500 company (Rhode, 1997). One particularly noteworthy 1994 court decision awarded $7.1 million (later reduced to $3.5 million) in punitive damages to a woman who had been sexually harassed by a male partner at the world's largest law firm, Chicago-based Baker & McKenzie. In another 1994 court decision a jury awarded a female former employee of a Wal-Mart store in Warsaw, Missouri, $50 million in punitive damages for sexual harassment suffered in a hostile job environment. Even though later reduced to $5 million, it was a record verdict for an individual plaintiff in a sexual harassment case (Kaufman, 1997). These staggering judgments are sending a wake-up call to America's business community. The fact that Title VII imposes liability on companies for sexual harassment perpetrated by their employees, unless the company takes immediate and appropriate action to quell the harassment, has been a major impetus behind the establishment of many corporate programs designed to sensitize employees to the issue of sexual harassment.

Sexual Harassment in Academic Settings

Sexual harassment occurs in educational settings. College students too often find themselves in the unpleasant situation of experiencing unwanted sexual advances from their professors or supervisors. Both sexes are vulnerable to this form of harassment. However, most commonly male professors or instructors harass female students. Sexual harassment also occurs all too frequently in high schools and middle schools. In 1992 the U.S. Supreme Court ruled that school districts are liable for hostile sexual environments created by school employees and can be sued for damages. However, the Supreme Court has yet to extend this liability to sexual harassment perpetrated by peers. Nevertheless, many district courts have allowed students to litigate in cases of peer harassment under Title IX, a 1972 civil rights law that prohibits federally funded schools from denying students opportunities based on their sex (Scher, 1997). Furthermore, the U.S. Department of Education recently published a manual outlining peer sexual harassment guidelines in which it clearly stated that schools that do not take measures to remedy this form of harassment could lose federal funds (Scher, 1997).

Academic sexual harassment differs somewhat from that which occurs in the workplace. For one thing, a student who is faced with unwanted sexual advances often has the option of selecting a different instructor or adviser. In contrast, workers in an employment setting tend to have fewer alternatives for avoiding or escaping the harassment while still keeping their jobs. However, students may experience coercive compliance pressures associated with the need to obtain a good grade, a letter of recommendation, or a desirable work or research opportunity (Riger, 1991). Students also tend to be more naive than workers about the implications of becoming sexually involved with someone who is in a position to give or withhold aid that may be very important to their successful pursuit of a career. There is a very real potential for inappropriate exploitation of youthful naiveté and awe regarding prestige and power. Furthermore, evidence has suggested that sexual harassment in the classroom can negatively affect a student victim who "might wonder whether her academic success has been due to her ability or her professor's sexual interest in her" (Satterfield & Muehlenhard, 1990, p. 1).

A growing number of colleges and universities have policies prohibiting faculty from dating students in their classrooms. The growing debate over professor–student romances, together with decisions to ban such relationships, is fueled largely by the belief that many relationships between faculty and students seem consensual on the surface but actually are not. Rather, the power of professors and/or advisers to determine students' futures, via grades and recommendations, often creates pressure for students to comply in order to protect their classroom standing or future prospects (Begley, 1993).

Just how common is sexual harassment in academia? At the precollege academic level, a survey of California high schools found that approximately 50% of the women respondents reported experiencing sexual harassment (Roscoe et al., 1994). Another recent survey of over 1000 Canadian adolescent women in grades 7 through 12 reported that over 23% of the respondents indicated experiencing at least one event of sexual harassment in the last six months (Bagley et al., 1997). In surveys of college and university populations, 20–30% of undergraduate women and 30–50% of graduate women report having been the target in one or more incidents of sexual harassment in an academic setting (Roscoe et al., 1987; Rubin & Borgers, 1990; Sundt, 1994). Because most studies of college populations have included only female students, we have less information about harassment of male students. However, men may also be victimized in this fashion, and available data indicate that between 9–20% of male undergraduates report having been sexually harassed (Mazer & Percival, 1989; Sundt, 1994). Several surveys of medical students reveal that anywhere from a third to over half report experiencing sexual harassment while in school, with females reporting substantially higher incidence rates (Baldwin et al., 1991; Richman et al., 1992; Wolf et al., 1991).

A recent study examined one population within the college community that has been largely overlooked: women faculty. Using a nationally representative sample of female faculty at 270 colleges and universities, Eric Dey and his associates (1994) found that 24% of full professors, 20% of associate professors, 13% of assistant professors, and 9% of instructors reported being sexually harassed. The survey did not ask respondents to indicate the nature of the sexual harassment they encountered.

Dealing with Sexual Harassment on Campus

What should you do if you are a victim of sexual harassment on campus? Some students elect to avoid or escape the harassment by dropping a class, finding another faculty adviser, or even leaving school. However, we would advise someone who feels that she or he is being harassed to report it, if for no other reason than to curtail these inappropriate actions and reduce the likelihood that other students may be victimized by the same professor (it is common for people who harass students to have multiple targets). You may wish to speak to the chairperson or dean who supervises the offending individual. If you are not satisfied with that person's response, contact the campus officer or department that handles matters dealing with civil rights or affirmative action. Understandably you may be concerned about grade discrimination or loss of position. Federal affirmative action guidelines forbid these forms of discrimination against people who, in good conscience, file legitimate claims of sexual harassment. Furthermore, a professor guilty of such action is not likely to continue to behave in a harassing or discriminatory fashion toward you because he or she will likely be closely monitored (repeat infractions may result in termination of employment).

Recently, a state agency in California issued an unprecedented ruling that universities can be held legally responsible for on-campus sexual harassment. This decision, made by the Fair Employment and Housing Commission, encompasses harassment involving two students, two professors, or a professor and a student. "By opening up a new avenue of redress for sex harassment cases on campus, this ruling could expose universities to an onslaught of costly claims" (Chiang, 1993). Now student harassment victims in California are able to file claims under California's Unruh Civil Rights Act, an easier and less costly avenue for seeking redress. We hope this California ruling will be duplicated in other states, and university officials, mindful of their financial exposure, will have additional incentive to take steps to lessen sexual harassment on campus.

Summary

RAPE

The legal definition of rape varies from state to state, but most laws define rape as sexual intercourse that occurs under actual or threatened forcible compulsion that overcomes the earnest resistance of the victim.

Although evidence strongly suggests that rape is widespread, it is exceedingly difficult to obtain accurate statistics on the actual number of rapes and rape victims in the United States.

Many false beliefs about rape tend to hold the victim responsible for the crime and excuse the attacker.

Significant changes are occurring in rape laws regarding legal definitions and prosecution proceedings.

Rape is often a product of socialization processes that occur within certain rape-prone societies that glorify masculine violence, teach boys to be aggressive, and demean the role of women in the economic and political aspects of life.

Males in our society often acquire callous attitudes toward women that, when combined with a belief that "might makes right," provide a cultural foundation for rape and other acts of sexual coercion.

Exposure to sexually violent media may contribute to more accepting attitudes toward rape, decrease one's sensitivity to the tragedy of rape, and perhaps even increase men's inclinations to be sexually aggressive toward women.

Rapists frequently reveal extensive histories of sexual offenses, rape and violence fantasies, and being sexually abused in their childhoods. They also may exhibit displaced anger toward women and distorted perceptions of their rape behavior.

No singular pattern characterizes the violent act of rape, and a wide range of individual differences exist among rapists. From the perspective of motivational intent, rapes can be categorized as anger rapes, power rapes, sadistic rapes, or sexual gratification rapes.

The majority of rapes are acquaintance rapes, where the perpetrator is known to the victim.

Sexual coercion in dating situations is quite prevalent. Both sexes experience sexual coercion, but women are more likely than men to be physically forced into unwanted sexual activity.

Rape survivors often suffer severe emotional difficulties that are manifested in the two phases of the rape trauma syndrome, the acute phase and the long-term reorganization phase.

Women often find that supportive counseling, either individually or in groups, can help ease the trauma caused by rape.

A rape survivor's recovery may be facilitated by a partner or friend who listens and provides support and encouragement.

Some rape-prevention tactics may help reduce the chances of a woman being raped.

Men are also raped and many, probably the majority of male rapes, are perpetrated by heterosexual men.

Men who are sexually assaulted often experience long-term adverse consequences similar to those reported by females who are sexually victimized.

SEXUAL ABUSE OF CHILDREN

Child sexual abuse is sexual contact between an adult and a child.

A distinction is generally made between nonrelative child sexual abuse, called pedophilia or child molestation, and incest involving sexual contact between an adult and a child relative.

It is difficult to obtain accurate estimates of the frequency of incest and pedophilia in American society. Estimates of the number of girls sexually victimized range from 20 to 33%, whereas comparable estimates for boys range from 9 to 16%.

The majority of child sexual abusers are male relatives, friends, or neighbors of their victims.

Recent research suggests that the number of boys who are sexually molested in the United States may be substantially higher than has been reported.

Child sexual abuse can be a traumatic and emotionally damaging experience with long-term negative consequences for the child.

Survivors often experience a loss of childhood innocence, a disruption of their normal sexual development, and a profound sense of betrayal. Other damaging consequences include low self-esteem and difficulty establishing satisfying sexual and emotional relationships as adults.

There are a number of treatment programs for survivors of child sexual abuse, ranging from individual therapy to group and couples-oriented approaches.

Although no "classic profile" of the pedophile exists other than that most are male and known to the victim, there are indications that prosecuted offenders tend to be shy, lonely, conservative, and often very moralistic or religious. They frequently have poor social and sexual relations with other adults and may feel inadequate and inferior.

Incest offenders are often economically disadvantaged, heavy drinkers, unemployed, religious, and very conservative.

Not uncommonly, pedophiles were sexually victimized themselves during their childhoods, while men who engage in incest often grew up in families where patterns of incest were modeled.

It is important to talk to children about protecting themselves from sexual abuse. Things children need to know include the difference between okay and not-okay touches, the fact that they have rights, that they can report abuse without fear of blame, and strategies for getting away from uncomfortable situations.

SEXUAL HARASSMENT

Sexual harassment is any unwanted attention of a sexual nature from someone on the job that creates discomfort and/or interferes with the job.

Guidelines provided by the Equal Employment Opportunity Commission essentially describe two kinds of sexual harassment. In the "quid pro quo" variety, a worker or student believes that failure to comply with sexual advances will result in job or education detriment. In the second form, the actions of supervisors, coworkers, professors, or students make the workplace or academic setting a "hostile or offensive environment."

Title VII of the 1964 Civil Rights Act prohibits sexual harassment. A company can be liable for such coercive actions by its employees.

Estimates of the percentage of women sexually harassed on the job range from 42 to 88%. A comparable estimate for men is approximately 15%.

In spite of increased attention to the issue of same-sex sexual harassment, victims of this form of harassment have generally found it difficult to obtain legal satisfaction in America's courts.

Victims of sexual harassment may experience a variety of negative financial, emotional, and physical effects.

Sexual harassment also occurs in educational settings. Most commonly, perpetrators are male professors or instructors who harass female students.

Surveys indicate that 20–30% of undergraduate women, 30–50% of graduate women, and 9–20% of male undergraduates report having been sexually harassed.

Thought Provokers

1. How do false beliefs about rape perpetuate the belief that the victim is responsible, rather than the attacker? In your opinion, what effect does this belief have on the prosecution of rape? On its incidence? On the survivor?
2. Many people perceive a woman who wears "suggestive clothing" and is then raped as somehow responsible for her own rape. In contrast, a man who dons an expensive suit, carries lots of cash, and wears a Rolex watch is seldom, if ever, held responsible for being robbed on the street. What are your thoughts about this inconsistency in assigning the label "victim precipitation" to these two events? Is it ever appropriate to label a victim responsible for her or his own victimization?
3. If your child were a victim of sexual abuse, what would you do to reduce the potentially adverse effects of such an experience? What steps would you take to prevent the recurrent victimization of your child?
4. Do you believe that sexual harassment by professors is a significant problem on your campus? What experience, if any, have you or your friends had with this form of sexual victimization? How might a student effectively deal with instances of sexual harassment by a professor?

Suggested Readings

Bart, Pauline; and O'Brien, Patricia (1985). *Stopping Rape: Successful Survival Strategies.* New York: Pergamon Press. An excellent and very helpful overview of various strategies for reducing the risk of becoming a victim of sexual assault.

Bass, Ellen; and Davis, Laura (1988). *The Courage to Heal.* New York: Harper & Row. This powerful, moving book is aimed at assisting women survivors of child sexual abuse to recover from the emotional aftermath of being sexually victimized.

Brady, Katherine (1979). *Father's Days.* New York: Dell. A courageous and powerful true story of a woman's sexual victimization by her father.

Brownmiller, Susan (1975). *Against Our Will: Men, Women, and Rape.* New York: Simon & Schuster. Offers a powerful, illuminating examination of rape from the feminist perspective that rape is an act of power and domination.

Colao, Flora; and Hosansky, Tamar (1983). *Your Children Should Know.* New York: Bobbs-Merrill. This very fine book, written in an engaging style, provides a wealth of information about preventing child sexual abuse and strategies for coping with such occurrences. Children, parents, educators, and health professionals all might profit from reading this excellent text.

Francke, Linda Bird (1997). *Ground Zero: The Gender Wars in the Military.* New York: Simon & Schuster. A sobering account of the extent to which women in the military are consistently subjected to demeaning and disparaging treatment, including sexual harassment and sexual assault.

Grauerholz, Elizabeth; and Koralewski, Mary (Eds.) (1990). *Sexual Coercion: A Sourcebook on Its Nature, Causes, and Prevention.* Lexington, MA: Lexington Books. This valuable collection of articles provides several illuminating perspectives on the nature of sexual coercion in its various forms, together with insights into how it may be prevented.

Groth, A. Nicholas (1979). *Men Who Rape.* New York: Plenum. Written by the director of a sex-offender program in Connecticut, this book provides important insights into the character and motivation patterns of rapists.

Maltz, Wendy (1991). *The Sexual Healing Journey: A Guide for Survivors of Sexual Abuse.* New York: HarperCollins. This excellent book helps sexual abuse survivors and their partners understand and recover from the effects of sexual abuse.

Parrot, Andrea; and Bechhofer, Laurie (Eds.) (1991). *Acquaintance Rape: The Hidden Crime.* New York: Wiley. This very fine book provides in-depth analysis of the nature and extent of acquaintance rape, together with excellent suggestions for its treatment and prevention.

Sanday, Peggy Reeves (1996). *A Woman Scorned: Acquaintance Rape on Trial.* New York: Doubleday. This first-rate text, written by an eminent anthropologist who has conducted extensive cross-cultural research on rape, analyzes several recent rape trials (such as that of boxer Mike Tyson) and describes the cultural traditions that have made the United States a "rape-prone" society.

Resources

Rape crisis centers are listed in the phone books of many cities.

Web Resources

Rape Abuse and Incest National Network (RAINN)
www.rainn.org
A nonprofit organization, the Rape Abuse and Incest National Network provides on this site news, hotlines, a list of local crisis centers, and statistics on the incidence of rape and incest.

Sexual Assault Information Page
www.cs.utk.edu/~bartley/saInfoPage.html
This web site includes an extensive listing of resources dealing with sexual assault and abuse and help for survivors. Among the topics covered is rohypnol—one of the so-called date rape drugs.

Sexual Assault Throughout the United States
www.ama-assn.org/public/releases/assault/guide.htm
This site features the American Medical Association's guide about sexual assault, strategies and guidelines for prevention and treatment, and explanations of the mental health effects of sexual violence.

20

Sex for Sale

Pornography

How is pornography defined?

What are four legal issues related to pornography?

What problems are created by sexually explicit materials available through the Internet?

How did the 1986 U.S. Attorney General's Commission on Pornography react to erotica that was not violent or degrading?

Prostitution

When did prostitution begin?

What is the age and marital status of most customers of prostitutes?

What are the different types of female and male prostitutes?

Who profits financially from prostitution?

I view porn as dirty smut magazines and movies that old perverted men look at. I really don't appreciate pornography, it does nothing for me. I love naked women in person and in bed, but seeing magazines or movies is a pointless turn-on. Pornography is really degrading toward women, and it gives young people the wrong ideas about women. (Authors' files)

I have found that when my partner and I watch pornos I get extremely aroused and let myself go wild with my sexuality. One time I got so turned on that I took control of the evening by making him do everything I wanted, like being rough, domineering, or sensitive. We also tried different areas in the room, like the coffee table, recliner, and couch. It wore us out so bad that we fell asleep naked in the middle of the floor tangled in each other's embrace. I feel that my partner and I have really benefited from including pornos in our sex. We have become so comfortable, close, and in love knowing that sex is a good thing. (Authors' files)

Throughout this text we have explored many aspects of sexuality, from biology and behavior to sexual and social problems and their treatment. One topic we have not yet investigated is sex as business—the exchange of money for sexual stimulation. A great deal of controversy surrounds sex in the marketplace and what the consequences are of "sex for sale," as we will see in this chapter. In the following pages, we will examine pornography and prostitution, as well as some of the social and legal issues surrounding these activities. We look first at pornography.

Pornography

Pictorial and written representations of sexuality are not modern inventions. Prehistoric cave drawings depict sexual activity. Ancient Greek and Roman societies used sexual themes to decorate housewares and public architecture. The ancient Indian love manual Kama Sutra, dating from about A.D. 400, summarized philosophies of sexuality and spirituality in its descriptions of specific sexual techniques. Graphic representations of coitus in Japanese *schunga* paintings and woodcuts from the 1600s and 1700s were regarded as art masterpieces.

Are these examples of pornography? If not, what sets them apart from pornography?

Individual opinions vary greatly about what is or is not pornographic. Indeed, the U.S. judicial system has not been able to establish a consistent definition (Jones, 1998). Generally speaking, pornography might include any written, visual, or spoken material depicting or describing sexual conduct or genital exposure that is arousing to the viewer. This definition is broad, however. Taken literally, it could include anything from the ancient works just described, to the suggestive advertisements that commonly appear on billboards and in magazines, to explicit video portrayals of sexual interaction and sexually oriented violence. (Table 20.1 indicates the high demand for pornographic videos.) Newer forms of high-tech pornography include "900" lines for phone sex, cable and satellite television adult programs. Various forms of "cybersex"—adults-only software, including interactive CD-ROMs, and adult-oriented bulletin boards with interactive adult games, personal ads, and libraries of X-rated pictures to view or download off websites are available. Porn sites on the Internet are generating revenue in the millions. Almost 99% of its consumers are men (Elmer-Dewitt, 1995). For the purposes of this chapter's discussions of legal issues related to **pornography,** we define the term as visual and written materials of a sexual nature used for the purpose of sexual arousal.

Pornography
Visual and written materials of a sexual nature that are used for purposes of sexual arousal.

Obscene
A term that implies a personal or societal judgment that something is offensive.

Pornography itself is not illegal in the United States, but materials considered obscene are. Thus, many of the controversies that surround pornography center on what is to be legally defined as **obscene,** a term that implies a personal or societal judgment that something is offensive. This category usually includes pornography that is violent and aggressive or degrading and dehumanizing. Central to both violent and degrading pornography is the depiction of an unequal balance of power for the purpose of sexual stimulation and entertainment. *Violent pornography* involves aggression and brutality; the violence may take the form of rape, beatings, dismemberment, and even murder. *Degrading pornography* objectifies and denigrates its subjects (Donnerstein et al., 1987). Racial stereotypes presented in interracial pornography are another form of degradation found in pornography (Cowan & Campbell, 1994).

Erotic sculpture on Hindu temple built around 1000 A.D.

Many observers consider a third category of sexually explicit material, *erotica,* not to be pornography. Erotica consists of "depictions of sexuality which display mutuality, respect, affection, and a balance of power" (Stock, 1985, p. 13). As feminist Gloria Steinem points out, erotica offers "a spontaneous sense of people who are there because they want to be, out of shared pleasure" (1980, p. 37). Contrary to the notion that women find romance sexy and men find explicit sex most exciting, a study of college students 21 years old and older found a similar, rather than different, pattern to what each sex found most arousing. Researchers selected four video segments, each of which represented different combinations of high versus low expressions of love and affection in conjunction with high versus moderate sexual explicitness ("hard core" versus "soft core" X-rated material). The study found that men and women subjects responded similarly to displays of love and affection in highly sexually explicit videos: Both male and female subjects rated most arousing the video that was both highly romantic and highly explicit. The researchers speculated that these results may indicate, at least for college-educated men, a greater integration of love and affection into sexual arousal (Quackenbush et al., 1995).

Table 20.1 New Video Releases in 1997

Hollywood	*Pornographic Film Industry*
471	7,852

Source: Lapham, 1997.

The various categories previously described are useful as a working model to conceptualize different types of sexually explicit material, but we should stress that in real life, distinctions are not always neat. What is erotica to one person may be offensive pornography to another. And what may be harmless in one context (for instance, a couple using an erotic video to explore different ways of making love) may be potentially damaging in another (such as a child gaining access to sexually explicit material on the Internet). For reasons like these, pornography is surrounded by complex legal issues. In this section, we will look at four questions that have been particularly troublesome from a legal standpoint: What constitutes obscenity? Should freedom of speech protect obscene materials? How should the dissemination of pornography be regulated? Does pornography discriminate against women?

What Constitutes Obscenity?

We saw earlier that the term *obscenity* implies a judgment that something is offensive. Such a determination is difficult to establish legally. Over the years, the courts have attempted to refine the definition, with incomplete success. Early U.S. courts considered material to be obscene if it depraved and corrupted the user. (The courts then faced the problem of establishing that a person had been depraved by the materials.) Since 1957, three criteria established by the U.S. Supreme Court have been used for evaluating obscenity.

PRURIENT-OBSESSIVE INTEREST IN SEX

1. The dominant theme of the work as a whole must appeal to *prurient* interest in sex.
2. The work must be patently offensive to contemporary community standards.

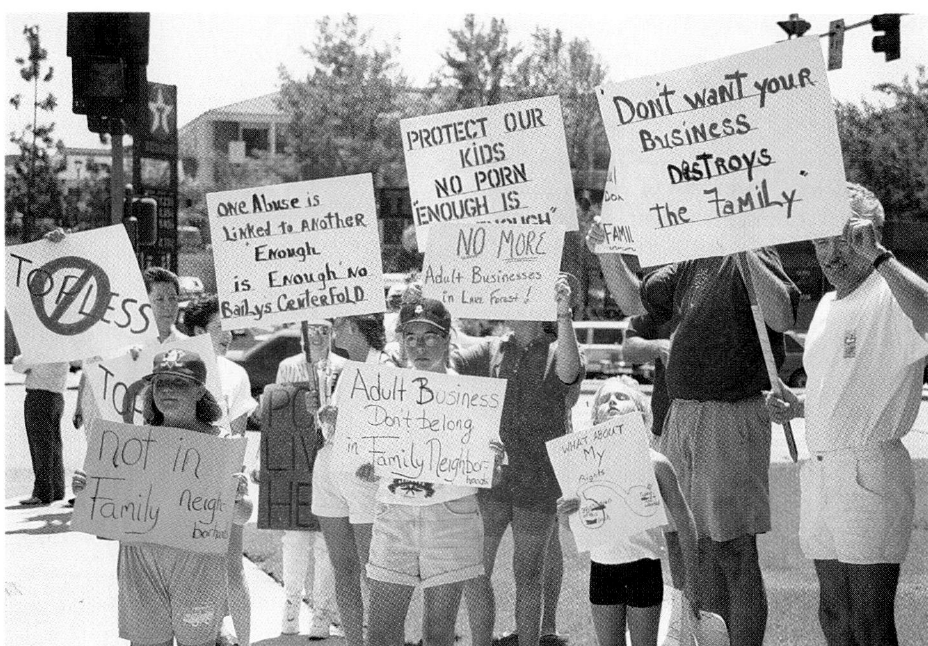

Local citizens protest the presence of an adult business in their neighborhood.

3. Third, it must be without serious literary, artistic, political, or scientific value (*Miller* v. *California,* 413 U.S. 15, 1973; *Roth* v. *United States,* 354 U.S. 476, 1957).

Critics point out that these criteria are still highly subjective (Penley, 1996). After all, *prurience* (an obsessive interest in sex) is in the mind of the beholder, as is the judgment of whether a work has serious artistic or other value. And community standards of obscenity vary dramatically. In many large cities, all manner of explicit sexual films is openly advertised and shown. But in other areas, especially in small, rural communities, books and magazines such as *Playboy* have been banned. The subjectivity of these criteria is perhaps best reflected in Supreme Court Justice Potter Stewart's comment regarding obscenity: It is difficult to define intelligently, "but I know it when I see it" (*Jacobelis* v. *Ohio,* 379 U.S. 197, 1965). Courts, communities, and pornographic entrepreneurs still struggle with the legal definition of obscenity.

Should Freedom of Speech Protect Obscene Materials?

A second legal question regarding pornography concerns its standing under the U.S. Constitution's First Amendment guarantee of freedom of speech and of the press. Do these constitutional protections apply to obscene materials? In a 1957 decision, the Supreme Court declared that the Constitution's First Amendment guarantees did not apply categorically to obscene materials. Vigorous arguments against this position have been presented by civil libertarians as well as by some of the justices of the Supreme Court.

Does pornography have a damaging effect on the people who use it? Should some types of obscene material be exempted from free speech protection? If so, where should the line be drawn between protected and unprotected materials?

The Commissions on Obscenity and Pornography

If you find it difficult to answer the preceding questions, you are not alone. Two presidential commissions have been appointed to study pornography in the past few decades, and they have come to very different conclusions. In the late 1960s, President Lyndon Johnson appointed a Commission on Obscenity and Pornography to study the effects of sexually explicit materials. Its report was published in 1970. This commission studied the effects of legalization of pornography in Denmark (which had occurred in 1967). It also analyzed the findings of various studies in the United States and offered recommendations.

In its study of Denmark, the commission found not only that sales of pornography to Danes decreased in the years after legalization (although sales to foreign tourists increased) but also that the increased availability of pornography after legalization did *not* result in an increase in sex offenses. (Critics point out that a cause-and-effect relationship is difficult to establish. For example, legalization may have had the effect of increasing tolerance of lesser offenses such as exhibitionism, which could have reduced the number of cases resulting in prosecution.) U.S. studies have also not found a link between pornography laws and rape and sex offense reports (Winick & Evans, 1996).

The 1970 commission also analyzed current research and found that imprisoned sex offenders had not had more exposure to pornography than had other prison inmates or nonprison populations. In its summary of research on the effects of sexually explicit materials, the commission concluded that no significant, long-lasting changes in behavior were evident in college-student volunteer research subjects after being exposed to pornography. On the basis of this information, this commission recommended repealing all laws prohibiting access to pornography for adults. However, both President Nixon and the U.S. Senate rejected these recommendations.

The Meese Commission

In 1986, President Ronald Reagan appointed another commission to study pornography. The U.S. Attorney General's Commission on Pornography (sometimes called the Meese Commission, after then-Attorney General Edwin Meese) reached drastically different conclusions and made radically different recommendations from the 1970 commission. The Meese Commission Report concluded that violent pornography caused sexually aggressive behavior toward women. It also found that degrading pornography fostered accepting attitudes toward rape and had some causal relationship to sexual violence. As noted in Chapter 19, these conclusions have been supported by considerable research.

The Meese Commission went further, however. Some members also viewed nonviolent, nondegrading erotica as destructive to the moral environment of society because it promotes promiscuity and sex outside of marriage. The commission recommended:

- vigorous law enforcement and prosecution of pornography
- citizen filing of complaints, pressuring the legal system, and monitoring and boycotting businesses that sell sexually explicit materials
- prohibiting obscene cable television programming
- prohibiting "Dial-a-Porn" telephone services (examples in Table 20.2)
- making possession of child pornography a felony

Many of the Meese Commission's findings were just as controversial as those of the 1970 commission. One criticism concerns the commission's conclusions about violent pornography. Most researchers in this area have found that the violent nature of material, whether it is sexual or not, is

Table 20.2 X-Rated Phone Services

The Meese Commission recommended prohibiting "Dial-a-Porn" telephone services such as the following:

Adults Only!! (Very Explicit)	
Hot Gay Action:	1-809-XXX-8044
Submissive 19 Yr. Olds:	1-800-XXX-0069
2 Horny Girls & You:	1-800-XXX-3825
Lesbo Action:	011-592-XXX-879X
Local Swingers:	1-800-XXX-2428(CHAT)
Asians, Fresh Off The Boat:	1-800-XXX-6661
Gay Paradise:	1-268-XXX-4441
Unfulfilled Gay Men:	011-XXX-1057
Dominant Mistresses:	1-800-XXX-4321
Busty Girls:	1-800-XXX-3301
Horny H.S. Seniors:	1-800-XXX-5243
Horny Black Girls:	1-800-XXX-4188
Cheatin' Young Wives:	1-800-XXX-2878
Horny Oriental Bimbos:	1-800-XXX-7548
Horny Wives at home:	1-800-XXX-0100
Horny Old Women:	1-800-XXX-5565

associated with aggressive tendencies in men (Scott & Schwalm, 1988). Leading researchers criticized the Meese Commission report because it ignored the "inescapable conclusion that it is violence, whether or not it is accompanied by sex, that has the most damaging effect. . . . [A]ll violent material, whether sexually explicit or not, . . . promotes violence against women" (Donnerstein & Linz, 1986, p. 5). One survey's findings suggest that the public's response to these distinctions between violent and nonviolent sexual material varies. A random phone survey found that about 75% support censorship of sexually violent media, half support censorship of violent media, and about one-third support censorship of nonviolent sexually explicit media (Fisher et al., 1994).

Vigorous arguments continue as to whether or not obscene materials should be protected by freedom of speech. In favor of First Amendment guarantees, civil libertarians have supported the unrestricted availability of pornography to adults, arguing that any censorship is unconstitutional. In response to the Meese Commission's report, the American Civil Liberties Union (ACLU) has argued that many of its restrictions "strike not only the First Amendment directly, but intrude upon civil liberties values like due process, privacy, and choice" (American Civil Liberties Union, 1986, p. 4). More graphically stated by the owner of *Hustler* magazine, Larry Flynt, "If the First Amendment will protect a scumbag like me, then it will protect all of you" (Alter, 1996).

Some countries do not concern themselves with the question of freedom of speech in general or specific to sexual materials. For example, in China almost all written, audio, and visual materials describing any kind of sexual behavior have been banned since 1989. The government maintains that exposure to such materials creates sexual offenders. Punishment is harsh for those violating the ban: Publishers have been arrested, and at least 20 people have been put to death for selling sexually explicit materials (Pan, 1993).

How Should the Dissemination of Pornography Be Regulated?

A third difficult question regards the dissemination of pornography. How can this be regulated so that individuals who have a right to use pornography have access to it, while those who may be harmed by it will be protected from it?

Possession Versus Dissemination of Pornography

The distinction between possession and dissemination of pornography is a long-standing legal issue. In 1969 the U.S. Supreme Court ruled that private possession of pornography in the home was not a crime, nor was it subject to government regulation (*Stanley* v. *Georgia,* 394 U.S. 557). However, the dissemination of pornography is regulated. Federal laws prohibit broadcasting, mailing, importation, and interstate transport of obscene materials, although by the 1990s very little was held to be outright obscene.

Most of these pornography dissemination statutes stem from the Comstock Act of 1873 (mentioned in Chapter 11), which made it a felony to deposit any materials of "indecent character" in the U.S. mail. During the first eight years of his involvement in the New York Society for the Suppression of Vice, self-appointed censor Anthony Comstock supervised the destruction of 27,584 pounds of books; the confiscation of 1,376,939 "obscene" songs, poems, pamphlets, and catalogs; and the recording of 976,125 names and addresses of people on mailing lists for pornography (Kilpatrick, 1960). Federal mailing laws have also been invoked in contemporary times in the prosecution of purveyors of obscene materials, and the 1986 Attorney General's Commission on Pornography recommended increasing funds for enforcing these laws.

The dissemination of pornography is regulated in other ways as well. Many cities limit the areas where adult bookstores and movie houses can be located. Containment of such bookstores and movie houses by zoning and land-use regulations attempts to protect nonusers of pornography from being visually assaulted by offensive material on the basis of the right to freedom from involuntary exposure to pornography. Because of zoning ordinances, high concentrations of pornographic establishments have arisen in some cities. The "Combat Zone" in Boston and North Beach and the Tenderloin District in San Francisco are examples of such areas. In other states, laws prohibit zoning limitations for nude bars and adult video stores (Bates, 1995).

Pornography in Cyberspace

The regulation of X-rated computer materials has been a hot censorship issue in the 1990s, and will continue to be so into the next millennium. States, cities, and countries vary in their definitions of obscenity, yet cyberspace does not have borders. The community standards criteria for obscenity has been blurred by X-rated networks that are available anywhere in the world. Owners in California of an adult bulletin board were convicted of transporting obscene material across state lines when X-rated pictures were downloaded and judged obscene in Tennessee. Unsolicited junk e-mail, or "spam," for X-rated materials has become an unwelcome feature of on-line life for many people. An e-mail address may bring you ads such as "JOIN US AT PINK PUSSY CLUB—THE HOTTEST SITE FOR XXX LIVE GIRLS SEX SHOWS!!!! CLICK HERE TO ENTER." On-line services are attempting to protect subscribers and their children from unwanted junk mail, but there's no absolute way to prevent the problem (Lemonick, 1997).

Child pornography is distributed over the Internet and has been targeted for prosecution by the Attorney General's office. Children and minors being exposed to sexually oriented communications or being exploited via computer are of concern. A case in which a 51-year-old man communicated on-line with an eighth-grade girl and arranged to meet at her school and photograph her alarmed many who seek to protect children. Such abuses may result in an increase in prosecution and legislation regarding on-line sexual content and limits of computer privacy. Software that blocks sexually explicit material from being transmitted to a particular computer has been developed and will help parents shield their children from "adult" materials (Levy, 1997b). Internet sting operations where federal agents pose as bookstore owners have brought arrests of child pornographers.

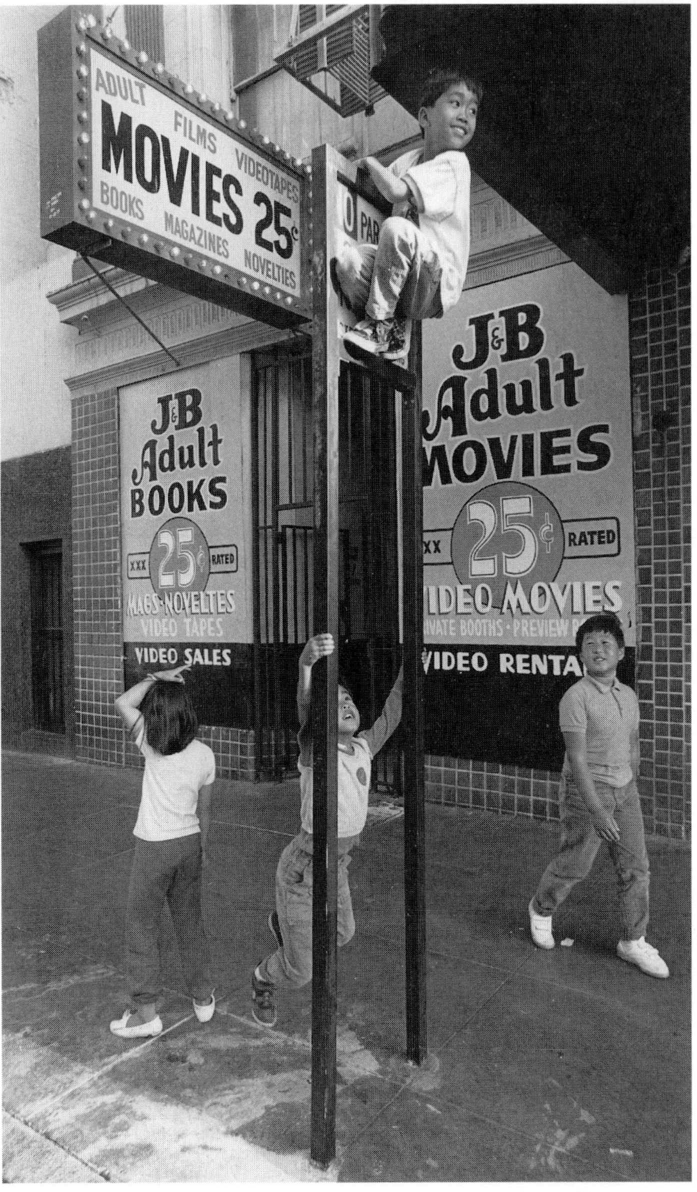

Due to zoning ordinances, high concentrations of pornographic shops and "adult" entertainments have arisen in some cities.

Does Pornography Discriminate Against Women?

In this chapter's discussion and in Chapter 19, we have seen that pornography is most often directed toward male fantasies. Women are frequently portrayed as sexual playthings, eager to accommodate every sexual urge of men (Zillman & Bryant, 1982). Sexual depictions that degrade, debase, and dehumanize women are a common pornographic theme. For example, *Hustler,* the largest distributed hard-core pornographic magazine in the world, has portrayed women hung on meat hooks with objects shoved up their genitals, being tortured, and even murdered; or a man forcing his wife to sit spread-legged while her genitals are invaded by cockroaches (Schroeder, 1995; Steinem, 1997). The violent and abusive nature of many of the fantasies acted out in chat rooms with titles such as "Torture Females" or "daughter blows dad" raise concerns about whether people will act on these fantasies in real life (Michals, 1997). Not surprisingly, research has shown that exposure to pornography can increase acceptance of male dominance and female servitude (Zillman & Bryant, 1988a).

A number of communities across the United States have considered laws establishing pornography as a form of sexual discrimination. These laws would be similar to those that allow people to file complaints against discrimination in employment: Individuals could press civil suits against the makers, distributors, or exhibitors of sexually explicit depictions of the subordination of women. Proponents of such laws and ordinances maintain that pornography harms a woman's opportunities for equal rights because it fosters exploitation and subordination based on sex.

Opponents of this type of legislation believe that such laws would infringe on freedom of personal choice by giving the courts power to interpret and rule on a wide variety of sexual images. For example, in 1992 in Canada an antipornography organization persuaded the Canadian supreme court to include sexual expression that is "degrading" and "dehumanizing" to women within their definition of criminal obscenity. Since then books have been confiscated by customs officials from over half of all Canadian feminist bookstores. Canada's lesbian and gay bookstores were persistently harassed, reflecting the homophobia that considers all homoerotic expression "degrading" (Strossen, 1995). What has occurred in Canada with this particular law demonstrates the inherent danger of censorship laws: Censorship inevitably rebounds against women, especially those who challenge their traditional roles. Censorship is applied at the discretion of those with the most political power. The use of federal antiobscenity laws of the early twentieth century that were used to prosecute Margaret Sanger for printing information about contraception is an example (McElroy, 1995). There are also concerns about antisexual bias: Sexual explicitness is singled out as the target of these proposed laws and defined as degrading to women, rather than sexist images in general (Gillespie, 1994). Some opponents also maintain that eliminating pornography would not alleviate discrimination toward women. Historically, women have been oppressed even when pornography was not a significant part of the culture (Duggan et al., 1985). One research study actually found that the political, economic, and legal status of women is higher in states with higher circulation rates of nonviolent, soft-core pornography. According to the researchers, their results indicated a political tolerance where gender equality and pornography flourish (Baron, 1990). A professor of a course on pornography in a film studies program argues that throughout history pornography has had the role of challenging political authority and the social norms and hypocrisy of organized religion and the middle, professional, and upper classes. She maintains that contemporary pornography is a vital source of countercultural ideas about sexuality and sexual roles. She sees the pervasive theme of popular pornography to be men's "utopian desire for a world where women aren't socially required to say and believe that they don't like sex as much as men do" (Penley, 1996).

If pornography in general portrays women as subservient, how do you think it affects intimate relationships between men and women?

Several observers have expressed concerns about the impact of pornography on intimate relationships between women and men. One criticism of pornography is that it contributes to unrealistic expectations about sexuality. Pornography often stresses performance and conquest rather than pleasure. It perpetuates myths that a real man is always ready for sex, and that sex can be obtained without regard for the other person or the complex nature of the man himself (Zilbergeld, 1978). In addition, women are often portrayed in pornography as intensely responsive to just about any stimulation from men. When women do not react in such a manner in real life, men may feel cheated, and both women and men may doubt the normality of their own sexuality. One study of undergraduate students and the general population found that after repeated exposure to pornography, men and women became less satisfied with the physical appeal and sexual performance of their partners (Zillman & Bryant, 1988b).

Prostitution

Prostitution is the exchange of sexual services for money. It is illegal in every state of the United States except Nevada. Prostitution is typically thought of in terms of a woman selling sexual services to a man, although transactions between two males are also common. Payment for a man's services to a woman is less usual. Nude dancers, phone and Internet sex workers, and X-rated video performers are also part of the sex industry.

Prostitution
The exchange of sexual services for money.

Prostitution's History

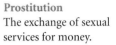

Prostitution has existed throughout history and has been called "the oldest profession." However, its significance and meaning have varied in different times and societies. In ancient Greece the practice was tolerated. During some periods of Greek history, certain types of prostitutes were valued for their intellectual, social, and sexual companionship. Prostitution was part of revered religious rituals in other ancient societies. Sexual relations between prostitutes and men often took place within temples and were seen as sacred acts; in some cultures the man in this transaction was considered to be a representative of the deity. In medieval Europe prostitution was tolerated, and the public baths provided opportunities for contacts between customers and prostitutes. In England during the Victorian era, prostitution was viewed as a scandalous but necessary sexual and social outlet for men: It was a lesser evil for a man to have sexual relations with a prostitute than with another man's wife or daughter (Taylor, 1970).

Prostitutes and Their Customers

Who do you think is a prostitute's typical customer, or "john"? What types of individuals become prostitutes?

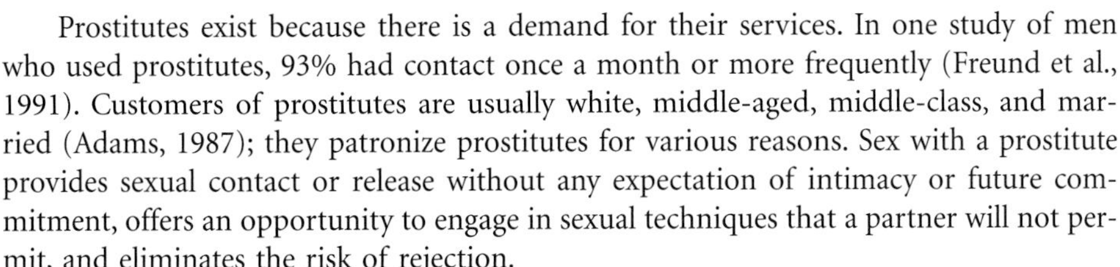

Prostitutes exist because there is a demand for their services. In one study of men who used prostitutes, 93% had contact once a month or more frequently (Freund et al., 1991). Customers of prostitutes are usually white, middle-aged, middle-class, and married (Adams, 1987); they patronize prostitutes for various reasons. Sex with a prostitute provides sexual contact or release without any expectation of intimacy or future commitment, offers an opportunity to engage in sexual techniques that a partner will not permit, and eliminates the risk of rejection.

No single theory can explain the motivation for being a prostitute. A combination of psychological, social, environmental, and economic factors is involved. Economic incentive is usually the primary motivation for becoming a prostitute (McElroy, 1995). Studies have also reported a high incidence of childhood sexual abuse in the history of female prostitutes; one researcher found that prostitutes have a 46–60% incidence of childhood sexual abuse (Bachmann et al., 1988).

Some prostitutes work on a part-time basis and otherwise pursue conventional school, work, or social lifestyles. Prostitutes may be delinquent school dropouts and runaways or well-educated adults. "Prostitutes have exceedingly diverse life histories, aspirations, and present life conditions" (de Zalduardo, 1991, p. 241). People who work as prostitutes on a temporary, part-time basis and have other occupational skills can more easily leave prostitution. Many of the women and men have not identified themselves as prostitutes, or "professionals." The full-time prostitute, who is alienated from traditional values and has identified herself or himself as part of the subculture (being arrested facilitates this identification), typically has little education and few marketable skills. These people usually find it very difficult to become successfully independent of prostitution. Legal problems, health hazards, and fear of personal injury are serious concerns of prostitutes. However, according to one study, 70% of the 46 street prostitutes interviewed reported enjoying intercourse with customers at least some of the time (Savitz & Rosen, 1988).

Prostitution and the Law

The legal status of prostitution has been debated for some time in the United States. There are several arguments for maintaining its status as a criminal offense. One view is that if prostitution were not a punishable offense, many women would take it up and it would be more difficult to enforce any restrictions on prostitution activities. Another argument is that it is the responsibility of government to regulate public morals, and the absence of laws against prostitution signifies government tolerance of commercialized vice (United Nations Study on Traffic in Persons and Prostitution, 1959).

Arguments against the criminal status of prostitution center on the difficulty of effective prosecution. Prostitution flourishes despite criminal sanctions against it, as it has throughout history in most societies where it has been prohibited. Other arguments are concerned with the possible negative results of outlawing prostitution. For instance, its criminal status may encourage connections with organized crime and hamper the rehabilitation of prostitutes (who may find it difficult to find other kinds of work once they have a criminal record) (Weiner, 1996). There are also arguments that center on discrimination in applying penalties. Customers and prostitutes are equally responsible in the vast majority of cases, but it is the prostitute, not the customer, who is arrested, jailed, and prosecuted. The On the Edge box below discusses using a police web site to serve as a deterrent to customers.

There are at least two alternatives to the criminal status of prostitution. One is its *legalization;* the other is *decriminalization.* If legalized, prostitution could be regulated, licensed, and taxed by the government. Prostitutes would be registered and required to follow certain procedures such as periodic STD checks to maintain their licenses, as in Nevada. If prostitution were decriminalized, criminal penalties for engaging in prostitution would be removed; however, prostitutes would be neither licensed nor regulated. Laws concerning solicitation and laws against the involvement of minors would remain, even if prostitution were legalized or decriminalized. (McElroy, 1995).

The rationale for legalization or decriminalization is based on several factors. Prostitution is usually considered a "victimless crime," an act that does not harm the people engaged in it. (However, prostitution may not be victimless in all senses because the pros-

On the Edge

Police Department Posts Photos of "Johns" on Its Web Site

The St. Paul police department has taken a high-tech approach to prevention of prostitution. It posts on its web site the names and photographs of people who have been arrested for engaging in prostitution. It posts both prostitutes and customers, but proponents of the electronic mug shot practice hope that public exposure of customers, or "johns," will help the most to discourage the activity in St. Paul. The city council president wrote, "The Internet is the newest form of information access, and there's no reason in the world why the Internet should not become a vehicle for passing along information about the status of crime in the community. . . . Men who seek sexual relief publicly are indeed sick individuals. . . . I believe these jokers have forfeited their privacy." Mug shots are considered public information under the state's Data Privacy Act, so the postings are legal. What do you think the pros and cons are of web site exposure of prostitutes and johns?

titute is often the victim of abuse from customers and pimps and of discriminatory laws and social stigmas.) Decriminalizing or legalizing prostitution would perhaps allow the criminal justice system to expend more efforts combating crimes that harm people or property. Also, if prostitution were legal, its association with organized crime might be weakened. And the victimization of prostitutes by pimps, customers, the judicial system, and others who profit at their expense would perhaps also be reduced (*The Economist,* 1998).

Some prostitutes have organized for political change and mutual support. The prostitutes' union, COYOTE (Call Off Your Old Tired Ethics), acts as a collective voice for the prostitutes' concerns; what ultimate impact this organization will have on U.S. laws pertaining to prostitution remains to be seen.

Prostitution and HIV

AIDS is also a concern with prostitution. In parts of Africa, sex with prostitutes is a primary mode of transmission of the HIV virus. One study found that 85% of 1000 prostitutes tested in Nairobi, Kenya, were infected with the HIV virus (Lambert, 1988). HIV-infection rates among prostitutes in the United States are generally lower and vary greatly from one geographic area to another. Because prostitution is illegal, it is very difficult to obtain reliable statistics. Prostitutes in county-licensed brothels in Nevada are required by law to be tested monthly for HIV antibodies and to use condoms to prevent HIV infection (Albert et al., 1998). Prostitutes of low socioeconomic status are much more likely to be infected with HIV than are high-priced prostitutes, and HIV rates were 35% in the New York study of streetwalkers in Table 20.3. The greatest risk factor for prostitutes becoming HIV infected is injected drug use or having sex partners who are injected drug users. Male prostitutes who service other men are at great risk of becoming infected with and transmitting HIV (Calhoun & Weaver, 1996).

Teenage Prostitution

There are many teenage prostitutes in the United States. Teenagers often become prostitutes as a means of survival after they have run away from home (Carnes, 1991). Other options for earning money are limited or nonexistent. As one adolescent prostitute has stated:

> There's no doors opened to us. . . . How are you going to be able to hold down a job if you have no high school diploma, if you're not able to take a shower every day, if you don't have clean clothes to wear to work? And let's say you came out here because of "certain circumstances" at home. You're scared out here. (Hersch, 1988, p. 35)

Most teenage prostitutes come from unstable, problem-ridden families (McCaghy & Hou, 1994): Approximately 95% have been victims of sexual abuse, and most have been abandoned by their families (Rio, 1991). Most teenage prostitutes did not perform well in school and have poor self-images. Over 80% of girls and 60% of boys in prostitution have seriously contemplated or attempted suicide (Carnes, 1991). One study of adolescent male prostitutes found two dominant themes in their earlier lives: They were likely to have had an unstructured and unsupervised home life, and they also felt rejected by peers at school and had few friends (Price et al., 1984).

The children who become prostitutes are often seeking adult attention and affection, and they believe at first that prostitution is a life of glamour and adventure. However, in reality they must cope with the extreme dangers of street life, including serious risks of contracting HIV, through either sexual contact or shared needles (many adolescent prostitutes are injected drug users).

Children involved in prostitution often suffer emotional distress and have poor life adjustment. Many develop a concept of themselves as objects to be sold. They frequently have problems with employment because of the stigma of their past and their dissatisfaction with the lower pay of a regular job. They may have difficulty establishing meaningful relationships and are likely to become involved in crime (Burgess et al., 1984).

Female Prostitutes

There are various types of female prostitutes who service male customers. The variations relate to such characteristics as the public visibility of the woman, the amount of money she charges, and her social class. We look at a few different categories, defined roughly in terms of the method a woman uses to contact customers. These include *streetwalkers,* women who work in brothels or massage parlors, and *call girls.*

Streetwalkers can be seen on the streets of most large cities. They solicit customers on the street or in bars. They are often from lower socioeconomic backgrounds, charge less than do other types of prostitutes for their services, and must share a large portion of their earnings with their pimps (discussed later in this chapter). Streetwalkers are at the bottom of the hierarchy of prostitution. The prostitutes in this group are most likely to have histories of traumatic family backgrounds (Rio, 1991). Because of their visibility, streetwalkers are easily subject to arrest. Most streetwalkers repeat the cycle of arrest, short jail sentences, and release many times throughout their careers. Even in the few cities where laws inflict penalties on the customer as well as the prostitute, the male customers of streetwalkers and other prostitutes are rarely arrested. Some characteristics of streetwalkers are outlined in Table 20.3.

Brothel
A house in which a group of prostitutes works.

A **brothel** is a house in which a group of prostitutes work. Brothels were common in earlier American history and remain so in some other countries. They are legal in some areas of Nevada today; the best known one is the Mustang Ranch south of Reno (Maxwell, 1996). Brothels range from expensive establishments to run-down, seedy places. They are usually managed by a "madam" who acts as the hostess and business manager of the house. Prostitutes who work in brothels in areas where prostitution is illegal are somewhat more protected from arrest than are streetwalkers because they are less visible to the police. Prostitutes are also less vulnerable to physical assault from their customers within the brothel setting.

Massage parlors are often seen as a modern "quick service" version of brothels. Manual stimulation (a "local" or "hand finishing") or oral stimulation to orgasm is often

Streetwalkers are at high risk for abuse by customers and pimps.

arranged for a fee once the customer is in the massage room. The customer also can often dictate in what state of dress or undress he would like his masseuse to be. Intercourse may or may not occur as part of the "massage." Most of the massage parlor customers in one study were white-collar businessmen over the age of 35 (Velarde & Warlick, 1973). Zoning and business-license laws are sometimes used to attempt to control the location or existence of massage parlors.

Call girls generally earn more than other kinds of prostitutes. They often come from middle-class backgrounds. Call girls frequently offer social companionship as well as sexual services for their customers. Their customer contacts are usually made by personal referral, or through "escort services," and they often have several regular customers (Blackmun, 1996b). Their public visibility is minimal, and their risk of arrest is much less than that of the streetwalker. The Hollywood madam, Heidi Fleiss, arrested in 1993 in a sting operation, had an exclusive and star-studded clientele (Maxwell, 1996). Call girls charge more for their services and provide themselves with attractive wardrobes and apartments—all part of their business expenses. They are also more likely than other types of prostitutes to be given goods such as clothing or living accommodations by regular customers.

Table 20.3 Characteristics of Streetwalker Prostitutes in New York City

Race
Black = 52%
White = 21%
Hispanic = 27%
Most likely to:
Abuse alcohol = blacks
Be homeless = blacks
Use IV heroin = whites
Have HIV = Hispanics
Positive for HIV = 35%
Never use condoms = 50%
Education:
Didn't complete high school = 50%
Completed high school = 33%
Had education beyond high school = 17%
Children:
Have at least one child = 69%
Average number of children = 2.25
Living situation of children:
With mothers = 20%
With family or friends = 70%
Foster care = 10%

This research was done by a mobile outreach van that provides HIV testing and counseling, condoms, and needle-cleaning kits. Two thousand female streetwalker prostitutes participated in the study (Weiner, 1996).

Male Prostitutes

In contrast to female prostitutes, most male prostitutes work independently without a pimp (Calhoun & Weaver, 1996). Men who provide sexual services for women in exchange for money and gifts are called **gigolos.** The role of a gigolo is most similar to that of a call girl, because he usually acts as a social companion as well as a sexual partner. His customers are usually wealthy middle-aged women seeking the attentions of attractive young men. There is often a pretense, on the gigolo's part, of romantic interest in the woman. The exchange of money for services is less explicit than in most interactions between female prostitutes and male customers. It is unknown how common this type of male prostitution is, but it is probably far less common than female prostitution.

Male prostitutes who cater to homosexual men have not been studied as extensively as female prostitutes. Like female prostitutes, they can be classified into different groups. Street *hustlers* make contact with customers on the streets, in gay bars or bath houses, or in public parks or toilets. Most hustlers come from chaotic family backgrounds and live in a social milieu of drug abuse and unstable personal relationships (Calhoun & Weaver, 1996). One study found that male street hustlers lack knowledge about sexually transmitted diseases and do not take adequate precautions. As one young hustler said, "I always look them over, if they look clean like me, . . . then they are all right" (Calhoun & Weaver, 1996, p. 232). *Call boys* work similarly to call girls. They have regular customers and are often social companions as well as sexual partners. Call boys find their customers through advertisements (often in gay newspapers) or through personal referrals. *Kept boys* are partially or fully supported by an older male. *Peer-delinquent prostitutes* often work in small groups and use homosexual prostitution as a vehicle for assault and robbery. Most peer-delinquent prostitutes are between 14 and 17 years old. Their usual modus operandi is for one or more of them to solicit a customer who is willing to pay to perform fellatio on them; they then rob and physically assault the customer. Peer-delinquent prostitutes

Gigolos
Men who provide social companionship and sexual services to women for financial gain.

often define their contacts with customers as a demonstration of their masculinity and heterosexuality to their peers. However, beneath this facade many have strong homosexual feelings (Allen, 1980).

Economics and Profit from Prostitution

For many men and women who sell sexual services, prostitution is a way of earning a living; most view their work as an economic opportunity. Recognizing the connection between prostitution and economic disadvantage, the 1959 United Nations Commission study of prostitution concluded that creating other economic opportunities for women is important for its prevention.

Sexuality and Diversity

Worldwide Exploitation of Children and Women in Prostitution

The exploitation of children and women through prostitution has become a multimillion-dollar global growth industry. Each year an estimated one million children are drawn into child prostitution. Poverty, political instability, and wars leave women and children vulnerable to exploitation. After the fall of the iron curtain and communism in the mid-1990s, many women fled from the poverty of their home countries to western Europe only to be forced into prostitution. Children whose families have been killed in the ethnic and tribal wars of eastern Europe and Africa are highly vulnerable to exploitation. Parents in developing countries who have died from AIDS will have created 10 million orphans, 90% in Africa, by the year 2000. Children who are abandoned or turn to the streets to escape abusive families frequently turn to prostitution as their last resort for survival (Rios, 1996).

The growing "sex tourism" industry with its "clients" from industrialized countries profits from the desperation of the urban and rural poor of developing countries. The industry is strongest in the Asian countries of Thailand, the Philippines, India, Sri Lanka, Vietnam, and Cambodia, and in the South American country of Brazil. Most tours bring Japanese, German, Scandinavian, Arab, and U.S. men to these countries. Advertising builds on the stereotype of Asian women as "docile and adoring." An economics professor from Thailand estimates that the sex trade earns four to five times more than the agricultural industry (Budhous, 1997).

Women and girls from poor villages are lured to the cities with promises of a better life. Younger and younger children are sought for prostitution because customers regard them to be more likely free of HIV. Each year thousands of women and girls are smuggled from Nepal into India with promises of jobs, to be sold into brothels where they are repeatedly beaten and raped into submission by brothel guards. Many return to their homeland after they have become ill with AIDS, locally known as "Bombay disease." Adding to the tragedy of this is the fact that children are particularly vulnerable to the deadly virus; their vaginas and anuses are easily torn, creating wounds that are easily infected (Kristof, 1996).

Children are bought from parents as indentured sexual servants. For example, an 11-year-old Cambodian girl, Sriy, was sold to a Cambodian brothel by her stepfather after her mother became ill. The brothel owner claims to prospective customers that the now 13-year-old Sriy has just lost her virginity and is "clean." The truth is that Sriy has serviced about 10 customers a night for the last two years. She is considered the brothel owner's property and will be locked up, beaten, and starved if she tries to escape. Other children are just kidnapped, which almost happened to four Cambodian girls who helped a woman who appeared to be ill. As a thank you for their help, the woman gave each of the girls a drugged cookie, causing the girls to pass out. The women then hired a taxi to take them to a brothel. When she went into the brothel to negotiate a sale, the taxi driver realized what was about to happen, and drove off with the girls and returned them home (Kristof, 1996).

Most sex workers in developing countries lack the education or skills to make a different life for themselves. Many women's organizations and other human rights groups have consistently advocated for women's educational and economic empowerment to eradicate the connection between poverty and sexual exploitation. Unfortunately, efforts to elicit meaningful aid from governments and corporations have been met with limited success (Budhous, 1997).

Although women and men usually become prostitutes to earn money for themselves, the practice also profits many other parties. In fact, it may not be as lucrative for the prostitute as it is for the other people involved, either directly or indirectly, a fact dramatically highlighted in the box entitled "Worldwide Exploitation of Women and Children in Prostitution." Pimps, the criminal justice system, referral agents, and hotel operators all benefit financially from prostitution (Usry, 1995). *Pimps* are men who "protect" prostitutes (usually streetwalkers) and live off their earnings. (Women are more likely than men to have pimps.) The illegality of prostitution contributes to the prostitutes' need for a pimp. Pimps bail the women in their "stables" out of jail when they are arrested. They may offer companionship, a place to live, clothing, food, and in some cases, drugs. They often assume a highly controlling, authoritarian, sometimes abusive relationship with their prostitutes while being supported by the women's earnings. Pimps keep much of the streetwalkers' earnings, which they often invest in ostentatious clothing and cars that represent the pimp's status and his prostitutes' earning power.

Because prostitution is illegal, police officers, attorneys, judges, bail bondsmen, and jailers spend part of their work time attempting to control, litigate, or process prostitutes through the judicial bureaucracy. In this way, prostitution provides some of the business for the criminal justice system. (Some people argue that the time and money spent in actions against prostitution impede the judicial system's effectiveness in working with more serious crimes.)

Referral agents also make money from prostitution. Cabdrivers, hotel desk clerks, and bartenders get cash tips from customers as well as from prostitutes for helping establish the contact. Prostitutes who work out of their apartments may have to give doormen, hotel proprietors, and elevator operators an ongoing supply of tips, high rental fees, or sexual services (or any combination thereof) so that they will not report them to the authorities.

Summary

PORNOGRAPHY

A clear definition of pornography and obscenity has yet to be established by the judicial system. The criteria established by the Supreme Court in attempting to decide what is obscene are that the dominant theme of the work as a whole must appeal to prurient interest, be offensive to contemporary community standards, and be without serious literary, artistic, political, or scientific value.

Characteristics of erotica include mutual affection, respect, and pleasure. Unlike violent and degrading pornography, erotica has no known significant negative effects.

The U.S. Constitution's First Amendment guarantee of freedom of speech and of the press does not apply categorically to obscene materials. Legal regulation of pornography occurs through mailing laws and zoning of pornography outlets.

The increased availability and legalization of pornography in Denmark were not followed by an increase in reported sex offenses.

There are conflicting data on the effects of pornography. The 1970 Commission on Obscenity and Pornography reported that pornography did not have significant, long-lasting effects. However, more recent research has suggested that sexually violent and degrading materials could have a significant impact on attitudes toward women and could promote the myth that women want to be raped. The controversial 1986 Attorney General's Commission on Pornography Report maintained that sexually violent and degrading pornography caused sexual aggression toward women.

Research has found that nonsexual violence in media materials was associated with aggressive tendencies in men. However, the Meese Commission Report ignored research in this area.

Computer access to sexually explicit materials raises many issues related to censorship and the protection of children.

Some communities have considered laws establishing pornography as a form of sexual discrimination.

Considerable debate exists about whether pornography fosters subordination of women or provides a forum for challenging constrictive sexual roles.

PROSTITUTION

Prostitution refers to the exchange of sexual services for money. Many prostitutes have a childhood history of sexual abuse. However, sex workers have diverse backgrounds and working conditions. Streetwalkers, women in brothels or massage parlors, and call girls are general categories of female prostitutes.

Two alternatives to the criminal status of prostitution are legalization and decriminalization.

Prostitutes most at risk of contracting or transmitting HIV are injected drug users, have sexual partners who are injected drug users, or do not use condoms consistently during sexual encounters.

Male prostitutes who service women are called gigolos. Male prostitutes who service homosexual men may be categorized as hustlers, call boys, kept boys, or peer-delinquent prostitutes.

Women or men who turn to prostitution do so, in part, for economic opportunity. However, pimps, the criminal justice system, referral agents, and hotel operators also profit from prostitution.

Thought Provokers

1. When did you first encounter pornographic material? How did it affect you?
2. What effects, if any, do you think violent and degrading pornography have on intimate relationships between men and women? What do you think is the effect of mutual, affectionate, and explicit erotica?
3. What do you think could, and should, be done about unsolicited X-rated material sent to people via e-mail?
4. What kinds of laws about prostitution make sense to you? How do you justify your point of view?

Suggested Readings

American Civil Liberties Union (1986). *Polluting the Censorship Debate.* Washington, DC: American Civil Liberties Union. A summary and critique of the Final Report of the Attorney General's Commission on Pornography.

Butler, Anne (1985). *Daughters of Joy, Sisters of Mercy.* Urbana: University of Illinois Press. A detailed book about the lives and the socioeconomic impact of prostitutes in the American West in the late 1800s.

Delacoste, Frederique; and Alexander, Priscilla (1987). *Sex Work: Writings by Women in the Sex Industry.* Pittsburgh: Cleis Press. This edited book is written by women in the sex industry—prostitutes, nude dancers, porn movie actresses, and workers in massage parlors—who speak out about their work.

Green, Richard (1992). *Sexual Science and the Law.* Cambridge, MA: Harvard University Press. A lawyer and sex researcher illustrates sexuality in a legal context related to sexual privacy, prostitution, pornography, homosexuality, and abortion.

McElroy, Wendy (1995). *A Woman's Right to Pornography.* New York: St. Martin's Press. The author emphasizes the importance to women of sexual free speech.

Web Resources

Prostitutes' Education Network
www.bayswan.org/penet.html
The Prostitutes' Education Network sponsors this site, devoted to providing information about legislative, health, and cultural issues as they affect prostitutes and other sex workers. The point of view is decidedly sympathetic to prostitution.

Online Free Speech
www.eff.org/blueribbon.html
Sponsored by the Electronic Frontier Foundation (EFF), this site is devoted to the Blue Ribbon Campaign for Online Free Speech, a movement that vigorously opposes censorship on the Internet.

Glossary

Acquaintance rape Forced sexual assault by a friend, acquaintance, or date.

Acquired immunodeficiency syndrome (AIDS) A catastrophic illness in which a virus (HIV) invades and destroys the ability of the immune system to fight disease. HIV appears to be passed primarily through sexual contact, needle sharing among injection users, or less commonly, through administration of contaminated blood products.

Afterbirth The placenta and amniotic sac following their expulsion through the vagina after childbirth.

Amenorrhea The absence of menstruation.

Amniocentesis A procedure in which amniotic fluid is removed from the uterus and tested to determine if certain fetal birth defects exist.

Amniotic fluid The fluid inside the amniotic sac surrounding the fetus during pregnancy.

Androgen insensitivity syndrome (AIS) A condition resulting from a genetic defect that causes chromosomally normal males to be insensitive to the action of testosterone and other androgens. These individuals develop female external genitals of normal appearance.

Androgens A class of hormones that promote the development of male genitals and secondary sex characteristics and influence sexual motivation in both sexes. These hormones are produced by the adrenal glands in males and females and by the testes in males.

Androgyny A blending of typical male and female behaviors in one individual.

Anorgasmia A sexual difficulty involving the absence of orgasm in women.

Antiandrogen drugs Drugs that may block inappropriate sexual arousal patterns by lowering testosterone levels.

Areola The darkened circular area surrounding the nipple of the breast.

Artificial insemination A medical procedure whereby semen is placed in a woman's vagina, cervix, or uterus.

Atypical sexual behaviors Behaviors not typically expressed by most people in our society.

Autoerotic asphyxia The enhancement of sexual excitement and orgasm by pressure-induced oxygen deprivation.

Autosomes The 22 pairs of human chromosomes that do not significantly influence sex differentiation.

Aversive conditioning A behavior therapy method that substitutes a negative response for positive responses to inappropriate stimuli.

Backup methods Using a second contraceptive method simultaneously with a first.

Bacterial vaginosis A vaginal infection, usually caused by a bacterium called *Gardnerella vaginalis,* that may be the most common form of vaginitis among American women.

Bartholin's glands Two small glands slightly inside the vaginal opening that secrete a few drops of fluid during sexual arousal.

Basal body temperature A method of birth control based on body temperature changes before and after ovulation.

Behavior therapy Therapy based on the assumption that maladaptive behavior has been learned and can therefore be unlearned.

Bisexuality Attraction to both same- and other-sex partners.

Blastocyst Multicellular descendant of the united sperm and ovum that implants on the wall of the uterus.

Body temperature A method of birth control based on body temperature changes before and after ovulation.

Bondage Deriving sexual pleasure from being bound, tied up, or otherwise restricted.

Brothel A house in which a group of prostitutes works.

Calendar method A method of birth control based on abstinence from intercourse during calendar-estimated fertile days.

Candidiasis An inflammatory infection of the vaginal tissues caused by the yeastlike fungus *Candida albicans.*

Case study Examines either a single subject or a small group of subjects, each studied individually and in depth.

Castration Surgical removal of the testes.

Cavernous bodies The structures in the shaft of the clitoris that engorge with blood during sexual arousal.

Celibacy Historically defined as the state of being unmarried; currently defined as not engaging in sexual behavior.

Cervical cap A plastic or rubber cover for the cervix that provides a contraceptive barrier to sperm.

Cervix The small end of the uterus, located at the back of the vagina.

Cesarean section A childbirth procedure in which the infant is removed through an incision in the abdomen and uterus.

Chancre A raised, red, painless sore that is symptomatic of the primary phase of syphilis.

Chancroid A sexually transmitted bacterial disease characterized by small bumps in the region of the genitals, perineum, or anus that eventually rupture and form painful ulcers with a foul discharge.

Child molestation See Pedophilia.

Child sexual abuse Sexual abuse involving contact between an adult and a child. A distinction is generally made between nonrelative child sexual abuse (called pedophilia or child molestation) and incest involving sexual contact between a child and adult who are relatives.

Chlamydia infection Urogenital infection caused by the bacterium *Chlamydia trachomatis*.

Chorionic villus sampling (CVS) A prenatal test that detects some birth defects.

Climacteric Physiological changes that occur during the transition period from fertility to infertility in both sexes.

Clitoris A highly sensitive structure of the female external genitals, the only function of which is sexual pleasure.

Cognitive therapies Approaches to therapy that are based on the premise that most psychological disorders result from distortions in cognitions or thoughts.

Cohabitation Living together and having a sexual relationship without being married.

Colostrum A thin fluid secreted by the breasts during later stages of pregnancy and the first few days following delivery.

Coming out The process of becoming aware of and disclosing one's homosexual identity.

Commitment The thinking component of Steinberg's triangular love theory.

Companionate love A type of love characterized by friendly affection and deep attachment based on extensive familiarity with the loved one.

Complete celibacy Engaging neither in masturbation nor in interpersonal sexual contact.

Condom A sheath that fits over the penis and is used for protection against unwanted pregnancy and sexually transmitted diseases.

Conjunctivitis Inflammation of the mucous membrane that lines the inner surface of the eyelid and the exposed surface of the eyeball.

Consensual extramarital relationship A sexual relationship that occurs outside the marriage bond with the consent of one's spouse.

Constant-dose combination pills Birth control pills that contain a constant daily dose of estrogen and progestin.

Coprophilia A sexual paraphilia in which a person obtains sexual arousal from contact with feces.

Corpus luteum A yellowish body that forms on the ovary at the site of the ruptured follicle and secretes progesterone.

Crura The innermost tips of the cavernous bodies that connect to the pubic bones.

Cunnilingus Oral stimulation of the vulva.

Cystitis An inflammation of the urethra or bladder, characterized by discomfort during urination.

Date rape Forced sexual assault by an acquaintance when on a date.

Demographic bias A kind of sampling bias in which certain segments of society (such as Caucasian, middle-class, white-collar workers) are disproportionately represented in a study population.

Dependent variable In an experimental research design, the outcome or resulting behavior that the experimenter observes and records but does not control.

DHT-deficient male Chromosomally normal (XY) male who develops external genitalia resembling those of a female as a result of a genetic defect that prevents the prenatal conversion of testosterone into DHT.

Diaphragm A birth control device consisting of a latex dome on a flexible spring rim. The diaphragm is inserted into the vagina with contraceptive cream or jelly and covers the cervix.

Dilation and evacuation (D and E) An abortion procedure in which a curette and suction equipment are used.

Direct observation A method of research in which subjects are observed as they go about their activities.

Domestic partnership Unmarried couples living in the same household in committed relationships.

Douching Rinsing out the vagina with plain water or a variety of solutions. It is usually unnecessary for hygiene, and too-frequent douching can result in vaginal irritation.

Dysmenorrhea Pain or discomfort before or during menstruation.

Dyspareunia Pain or discomfort during intercourse.

Ectoparasites Parasitic organisms that live on the outer skin surfaces.

Effacement Flattening and thinning of the cervix that occurs before and during childbirth.

Either/or question A question that allows statement of a preference.

Elective abortion Medical procedure performed to terminate pregnancy.

EMDR therapy A therapy technique that combines eye movements with concentrating on the problem that may be helpful as a part of treatment for sexual difficulties.

Endometriosis A condition in which uterine tissue grows on various parts of the abdominal cavity.

Endometrium The tissue that lines the inside of the uterine walls.

Episiotomy An incision in the perineum that is sometimes made during childbirth.

Estrogens A class of hormones that produce female secondary sex characteristics and affect the menstrual cycle.

Exhibitionism The act of exposing one's genitals to an unwilling observer.

Experimental research Research conducted in precisely controlled laboratory conditions so subjects' reactions can be reliably measured.

Extramarital relationship Sexual interaction by a married person with someone other than his or her spouse.

Failure rate The number of women out of 100 who become pregnant by the end of one year of using a particular contraceptive.

Faking orgasms A sexual difficulty whereby a person pretends to experience orgasm during sexual interaction.

Fallopian tubes Two tubes in which the egg and sperm travel, extending from the sides of the uterus.

Fellatio Oral stimulation of the penis.

Fetal alcohol syndrome (FAS) Syndrome caused by heavy maternal prenatal alcohol use; characterized by congenital heart defects, damage to the brain and nervous system, numerous physical malformations of the fetus, and below-normal IQ.

Fetally androgenized female Chromosomally normal (XX) female who, as a result of excessive exposure to androgens during prenatal sex differentiation, develops external genitalia resembling those of a male.

Fetishism Obtaining sexual excitement primarily or exclusively from an inanimate object or a particular part of the body.

Fimbriae Fringelike ends of the fallopian tubes into which the released ovum enters.

First-stage labor The initial stage of childbirth, in which regular contractions begin and the cervix dilates.

Follicle-stimulating hormone (FSH) A pituitary hormone. Secreted by a female during the secretory phase of the menstrual cycle, FSH stimulates the development of ovarian follicles. In males, it stimulates sperm production.

Frotteurism A fairly common paraphilia in which a person obtains sexual pleasure by pressing or rubbing against another in a crowded public place.

Gamete intrafallopian transfer (GIFT) Procedure in which the sperm and ova are placed directly in the fallopian tube.

Gay A homosexual, particularly a homosexual man.

Gender The psychological and sociocultural characteristics associated with our sex.

Gender assumptions Assumptions about how people are likely to behave based on their maleness or femaleness.

Gender dysphoria See Transsexual.

Gender identity How one psychologically perceives oneself as either male or female.

Gender nonconformity A lack of conformity to stereotypic masculine and feminine behaviors.

Gender role A collection of attitudes and behaviors that are considered normal and appropriate in a specific culture for people of a particular sex.

Genital warts Viral warts that appear on the genitals and are primarily transmitted sexually.

Gigolos Men who provide social companionship and sexual services to women for financial gain.

Giving permission Providing reassurance to one's partner that it is okay to talk about certain specific feelings or needs.

Glans The head of the clitoris; richly endowed with nerve endings.

Gonadotropins Pituitary hormones that stimulate activity in the gonads (testes and ovaries).

Gonads The male and female sex glands—ovaries and testes.

Gonorrhea A sexually transmitted disease that initially causes inflammation of mucous membranes.

Grafenberg spot Glands and ducts located in the anterior wall of the vagina. Some women may experience sexual pleasure, arousal, orgasm, and an ejaculation of fluids from stimulation of the Grafenberg spot.

Gynecology The medical practice specializing in women's health and in diseases of the female reproductive and sexual organs.

Herpes A disease that is characterized by blisters on the skin in the regions of the genitals or mouth, and that is caused by a virus and easily transmitted by sexual contact.

Homophobia Irrational fears of homosexuality, the fear of the possibility of homosexuality in oneself, or self-loathing toward one's own homosexuality.

Homosexual A person whose primary erotic, psychological, emotional, and social orientation is toward members of the same sex.

Hormone-replacement therapy (HRT) The use of supplemental hormones during and after menopause.

Human chorionic gonadotropin (HCG) A hormone that is detectable in the urine of a pregnant woman within one month after conception.

Human immunodeficiency virus (HIV) An immune-system-destroying virus that causes AIDS.

Hymen Tissue that partially covers the vaginal opening.

Hypoactive sexual desire disorder (HSD) Lack of interest in sexual activity.

In vitro fertilization (IVF) Procedure in which mature eggs are removed from a woman's ovary and fertilized by sperm in a laboratory dish.

Incest Sexual interaction between close relatives other than husband and wife.

Independent variable In an experimental research design, a condition or component that is under the control of the researcher who manipulates or determines its value.

Intimacy The emotional component of Steinberg's triangular love theory.

Intracytoplasmic sperm injection (ICSI) Procedure in which a sperm is injected into an egg.

Intrauterine device (IUD) A small, plastic device that is inserted into the uterus for contraception.

Introitus The opening to the vagina.

Intromission Insertion of the penis into the vagina.

Kegel exercises A series of exercises that strengthen the muscles underlying the external female or male genitals.

Klinefelter's syndrome A condition, characterized by the presence of two X chromosomes and one Y (XXY), in which affected individuals have undersized external male genitals.

Klismaphilia A very unusual variant in sexual expression in which an individual obtains sexual pleasure from receiving enemas.

Labia majora The outer lips of the vulva.

Labia minora The inner lips of the vulva, one on each side of the vaginal opening.

Lamaze A method of childbirth preparation using breathing and relaxation.

Lesbian A female homosexual.

Lochia A reddish uterine discharge that occurs following childbirth.

Luteinizing hormone (LH) The hormone secreted by the pituitary gland that stimulates ovulation in the female. In males it is called interstitial cell hormone (ISCH) and stimulates production of androgens by the testes.

Male erectile disorder Persistent lack of erection sufficiently rigid for penetrative intercourse.

Male orgasmic disorder The inability of a man to ejaculate during sexual activity.

Mammary glands Milk glands in the female breast.

Mammography A highly sensitive X-ray test for the detection of breast cancer.

Mastectomy Surgical removal of the breast(s).

Masturbation Stimulation of one's own genitals to create sexual pleasure.

Menarche The initial onset of menstrual periods in a young woman.

Menopause Cessation of menstruation due to the aging process or surgical removal of the ovaries.

Menstrual phase The phase of the menstrual cycle when menstruation occurs.

Menstrual synchrony Simultaneous menstrual cycles that sometimes occur among women who live in close proximity.

Menstruation The sloughing off of the built-up uterine lining that takes place if conception has not occurred.

Mere exposure effect The phenomenon by which repeated exposure to novel stimuli tends to increase an individual's liking for such stimuli.

Mons veneris A triangular mound over the pubic bone above the vulva.

Mucosa Collective term for the mucous membranes; moist tissue that lines certain body areas such as the penile urethra, vagina, and mouth.

Mucus method A birth control method based on determining the time of ovulation by means of the cyclical changes of the cervical mucus.

Multiphasic pills Birth control pills that vary the dosages of estrogen and progestin during the cycle.

Mutual empathy The underlying knowledge that each partner in a relationship cares for the other and knows that the care is reciprocated.

Myometrium The smooth muscle layer of the uterine wall.

Necrophilia A rare sexual paraphilia in which a person obtains sexual gratification by viewing or having intercourse with a corpse.

Nipple The central pigmented area of the breast, which contains numerous nerve endings and milk ducts.

Nocturnal orgasm Involuntary orgasm during sleep.

Nonconsensual extramarital sex Engaging in an outside sexual relationship without the consent (or presumably the knowledge) of one's spouse.

Nongonococcal urethritis (NGU) An inflammation of the male urethral tube caused by other than gonococcus organisms.

Nonresponse The refusal to participate in a research study.

Obscene A term that implies a personal or societal judgment that something is offensive.

Open marriage A marriage in which spouses, with each other's permission, have intimate relationships with other people as well as the marital partner.

Open-ended question A question that allows a respondent to share any feelings or information she or he thinks is relevant.

Orgasmic reconditioning A behavior therapy technique in which a client is instructed to switch from paraphilic to healthy fantasies at the moment of masturbatory orgasm.

Os The opening in the cervix that leads to the interior of the uterus.

Outercourse Noncoital forms of sexual intimacy.

Ovaries Female gonads that produce ova and sex hormones.

Ovulation The release of a mature ovum from the ovary.

Ovum The female reproductive cell.

Pap smear A screening test for cancer of cells from the cervix.

Paraphilia Term used to describe uncommon types of sexual expression.

Paraphrasing A listener summarizing the speaker's message in his or her own words.

Partial celibacy Not engaging in interpersonal sexual contact but continuing to engage in masturbation.

Passing Appearing to be heterosexual and avoiding presenting oneself as homosexual.

Passion The motivational component of Steinberg's triangular love theory.

Passionate love State of extreme absorption in another person. Also known as romantic love.

Pedophilia Sexual contact between an adult and a child.

Pelvic inflammatory disease (PID) An infection in the uterus and pelvic cavity.

Perimetrium The thin membrane covering the outside of the uterus.

Perineum The area between the vagina and anus of the female and the scrotum and anus of the male.

Petting Physical contact including kissing, touching, and manual or oral–genital stimulation but excluding coitus.

Peyronie's disease Abnormal fibrous tissue and calcium deposits in the penis.

Physical attractiveness Physical beauty is a powerful factor in attracting lovers to each other.

Placenta A disk-shaped organ attached to the uterine wall and connected to the fetus by the umbilical cord. Nutrients, oxygen, and waste products pass between mother and fetus through its cell walls.

Placenta previa A birth complication in which the placenta is between the cervical opening and the infant.

Pornography Visual and written materials of a sexual nature that are used for purposes of sexual arousal.

Postpartum period The first several weeks following childbirth.

Premature ejaculation A sexual difficulty whereby a man ejaculates so rapidly as to impair his own or his partner's pleasure.

Premenstrual syndrome (PMS) Symptoms of physical discomfort and emotional irritability, also called premenstrual tension, that occur 2 to 12 days prior to menstruation.

Prepared childbirth Birth following an education process that can involve information, exercises, breathing, and working with a labor coach.

Prepuce The foreskin or fold of skin over the clitoris.

Prodromal symptoms Symptoms that give advance warning of an impending herpes eruption.

Progestational compounds A class of hormones, including progesterone, that are produced by the ovaries.

Progestin-only pills Contraceptive pills that contain a small dose of progestin and no estrogen.

Proliferative phase The phase of the menstrual cycle in which the ovarian follicles mature.

Prostaglandins Hormones that are used to induce uterine contractions and fetal expulsion for second-trimester abortions.

Prostitution The exchange of sexual services for money.

Proximity The geographical nearness of one person to another, which is an important factor in interpersonal attraction.

Pseudohermaphrodites Individuals whose gonads match their chromosomal sex, but whose internal and external reproductive anatomy has a mixture of male and female structures or structures that are incompletely male or female.

Psychosexual therapy Treatment designed to help clients gain awareness of their unconscious thoughts and feelings that contribute to their sexual problems.

Psychosocial Refers to a combination of psychological and social factors.

Psychotherapy A noninvasive procedure involving verbal interaction between a client and therapist designed to improve a person's adjustment to life.

Puberty A period of rapid physical changes in early adolescence during which the reproductive organs mature.

Pubic lice Lice that primarily infest the pubic hair and are transmitted by sexual contact.

Random sample A randomly chosen subset of a population.

Rape Sexual intercourse that occurs without consent as a result of actual or threatened force.

Rape trauma syndrome A two-phase reaction to rape that involves an initial acute phase of potentially intense emotions, that may last several weeks, followed by a long-term phase during which the survivor reorganizes her life.

Reciprocity The principle that when we are recipients of expressions of liking or loving, we tend to respond in kind.

Representative sample A type of limited research sample that provides an accurate representation of a larger target population of interest.

Rugae The folds of tissue in the vagina.

Sadomasochistic behavior The association of sexual expression with pain.

Satiation therapy A technique for reducing arousal to inappropriate stimuli by first masturbating to orgasm while imagining appropriate stimuli and then continuing to masturbate while fantasizing about paraphilic images.

Scabies An ectoparasitic infestation of tiny mites.

Second-stage labor The middle stage of labor, in which the infant descends through the vaginal canal.

Secondary sex characteristics The physical characteristics other than genitals that indicate sexual maturity, such as body hair, breasts, and deepened voice.

Secretory phase The phase of the menstrual cycle in which the corpus luteum develops and secretes progesterone.

Self-selection The bias introduced into research study results due to participants' willingness to respond.

Sensate focus A process of touching and communication used to enhance sexual pleasure and to reduce performance pressure.

Sex Biological maleness and femaleness.

Sex chromosomes A single set of chromosomes that influences biological sex determination.

Sexology The study of sexuality.

Sexual aversion Extreme and irrational fear of sexual activity.

Sexual harassment Unwanted attention of a sexual nature from someone at the workplace or in an academic setting.

Sexual masochism The act of obtaining sexual arousal through receiving physical or psychological pain.

Sexual orientation Sexual attraction to one's own sex (homosexual) or the other sex (heterosexual).

Sexual sadism The act of obtaining sexual arousal through giving physical or psychological pain.

Sexually transmitted diseases (STDs) Diseases that are transmitted by sexual contact.

Shaft The length of the clitoris between the glans and the body.

Similarity Similarity of beliefs, interests, and values is a factor attracting people to one another.

Smegma A cheesy substance of glandular secretions and skin cells that sometimes accumulates under the hood of the clitoris.

Social skills training Training designed to teach socially inept clients the skills necessary to initiate and maintain satisfying relationships.

Socialization The process whereby our society conveys behavioral expectations to the individual.

Sodomy An ill-defined legal category for noncoital genital contacts such as oral–genital and anal intercourse.

Speculum An instrument with two blades used to open the vaginal walls during a gynecological exam.

Sperm The male reproductive cell.

Spontaneous abortion or miscarriage The spontaneous expulsion of the fetus from the uterus early in pregnancy, before it can survive on its own.

Statutory rape Intercourse with a person under the legal age of consent.

Stereotype A generalized notion of what a person is like that is based only on that person's sex, race, religion, ethnic background, or similar criterion.

Stop–start technique A treatment technique for premature ejaculation, consisting of stimulating the penis to the point of impending orgasm and then stopping until the preejaculatory sensations subside.

Stranger rape Rape of a person by an unknown assailant.

Suction curettage A procedure in which the cervical os is dilated by graduated metal dilators or by a laminaria; then a small plastic tube, attached to a vacuum aspirator, is inserted into the uterus, drawing the fetal tissue, placenta, and built-up uterine lining out of the uterus.

Surrogate mother A woman who is artificially inseminated by the male partner in a childless couple, carries the pregnancy to term, delivers the child, and gives it to the couple for adoption.

Survey A research method in which a sample of people are questioned about their behaviors and/or attitudes.

Swinging The exchange of marital partners for sexual interaction.

Syphilis A sexually transmitted disease caused by a spirochete called *Treponema pallidum.*

Systematic desensitization Behavior therapy technique that pairs slow, systematic exposure to anxiety-inducing situations with relaxation training.

Systems therapy Treatment that focuses on interactions within a couple relationship and on the functions of the sexual problems in the relationship.

Testes Male gonads inside the scrotum that produce sperm and sex hormones.

Third-stage labor The last stage of childbirth, in which the placenta separates from the uterine wall and comes out of the vagina.

Toxemia A dangerous condition during pregnancy in which high blood pressure occurs.

Toxic shock syndrome (TSS) A disease that may cause a person to go into shock, occurring most commonly in menstruating women.

Trachoma A chronic, contagious form of conjunctivitis caused by chlamydia infections.

Transsexual A person whose gender identity is opposite to his or her biological sex.

Transvestism Deriving sexual arousal from wearing clothing of the other sex.

Trichomoniasis A form of vaginitis caused by a one-celled protozoan called *Trichomonas vaginalis.*

True hermaphrodites Exceedingly rare individuals who have both ovarian and testicular tissue in their bodies; their external genitals are often a mixture of male and female structures.

Tubal sterilization Female sterilization accomplished by severing or tying the fallopian tubes.

Turner's syndrome A relatively rare condition, characterized by the presence of one unmatched X chromosome (XO), in which affected individuals have normal female external genitals, but their internal reproductive structures do not develop fully.

Urethra The tube through which urine passes from the bladder to outside the body.

Urethritis An inflammation of the urethral tube.

Urophilia A sexual paraphilia in which a person obtains sexual arousal from contact with urine.

Uterus A pear-shaped organ inside the female pelvis, within which the fetus develops.

Vagina A stretchable canal in the female that opens at the vulva and extends about four inches into the pelvis.

Vaginal spermicides Foam, cream, jelly, suppositories, and film that contain a chemical that kills sperm.

Vaginismus A sexual difficulty in which a woman experiences involuntary spasmodic contractions of the muscles of the outer third of the vagina.

Vaginitis Inflammation of the vaginal walls caused by a variety of vaginal infections.

Validating The process of indicating that a partner's point of view is reasonable, given some assumptions that one may not share with one's partner.

Varicocele A damaged or enlarged vein in the testis or vas deferens.

Vasectomy Male sterilization procedure that involves removing a section from each vas deferens.

Vasocongestion The engorgement of blood vessels in particular body parts in response to sexual arousal.

Vernix caseosa A waxy, protective substance on the fetus's skin.

Vestibular bulbs Two bulbs, one on each side of the vaginal opening, that engorge with blood during sexual arousal.

Vestibule The area of the vulva inside the labia minora.

Viral hepatitis A disease in which liver function is impaired by a viral infection.

Viral load How much HIV virus is present in an infected person's blood.

Voyeurism The act of obtaining sexual gratification by observing undressed or sexually interacting people without their consent.

Vulva The external genitals of the female, including the mons veneris, labia majora, labia minora, clitoris, and urinary and vaginal openings.

Yes-or-no question A question that asks for a one-word answer and thus provides little opportunity for discussing an issue.

Zoophilia A paraphilia in which a person has sexual contact with animals.

Zygote The single cell resulting from the union of sperm and egg cells.

Zygote intrafallopian transfer (ZIFT) Procedure in which the egg is fertilized in the laboratory and then placed in the fallopian tube.

Bibliography

AAUW (American Association of University Women) (1992). *Shortchanging Girls, Shortchanging America*. Washington, DC: Author.

Abel, G. (1981). The evaluation and treatment of sexual offenders and their victims. Paper presented at St. Vincent Hospital and Medical Center, Portland, OR, October 15.

Abel, G., Barlow, D., Blanchard, E., & Guild, D. (1977). The components of rapists' sexual arousal. *Archives of General Psychiatry*, 34, 895–903.

Abel, G., Becker, J., & Cunningham-Ratder, J. (1984). Complications, consent, and cognitions in sex between children and adults. *International Journal of Law and Psychiatry*, 7, 89–103.

Abel, G., Osborn, C., Anthony, D., & Gardos, P. (1992). Current treatment of paraphiliacs. *Annual Review of Sex Research*, 3, 255–290.

Abrahams, J. (1982). Azoospermia before puberty. *Medical Aspects of Human Sexuality*, 1, 13.

Abramowicz, M. (Ed.) (1994). Drugs for sexually transmitted diseases. *The Medical Letter*, 36, 1–6.

Absi-Semaan, N., Crombie, G., & Freeman, C. (1993). Masculinity and femininity in middle childhood: Developmental and factor analysis. *Sex Roles*, 28, 187–202.

Abusharaf, R. (1998). Unmasking tradition. *The Sciences*, March/April, 22–27.

Acker, M., & Davis, M. (1992). Intimacy, passion and commitment in adult romantic relationships: A test of the triangular theory of love. *Journal of Social and Personal Relationships*, 9, 21–50.

Ackerman, M., Montague, D., & Morganstern, S. (1994). Impotence: Help for erectile dysfunction. *Patient Care*, March, 22–56.

ACSF Investigators (1992). AIDS and sexual behavior in France. *Nature*, 360, 407–409.

Adair, C., Gunter, M., Stovall, T., McElroy, G., Veille, J., & Ernst, J. (1998). Chlamydia in pregnancy: A randomized trial of azithromycin and erythromycin. *Obstetrics & Gynecology*, 91, 165–168.

Adams, D. (1990). Identifying the assaultive husband in court: You be the judge. *Response to the Victimization of Women and Children*, 13, 13–16.

Adams, F. (1987). The role of prostitution in AIDS and other STDs. *Medical Aspects of Human Sexuality*, 21, 27–33.

Adams, S., Jr., Dubbert, P., Chupurdia, K., Jones, A., Jr., Lofland, K., & Leermakers, E. (1996). Assessment of sexual beliefs and information in aging couples with sexual dysfunction. *Archives of Sexual Behavior*, 25, 249–260.

Addiego, F., Belzer, E., Comolli, J., Moger, W., Perry, J., & Whipple, B. (1981). Female ejaculation: A case study. *Journal of Sex Research*, 17, 13–21.

Adducci, C., & Ross, L. (1991). Common urethral injuries in men. *Medical Aspects of Human Sexuality*, October, 32–44.

Adler, C. (1985). An exploration of self-reported sexually aggressive behavior. *Crime and Delinquency*, 31, 306–331.

Adler, M. (1997). HIV: The other dimension. *The Lancet*, 349, 498–500.

Adler, N., Hendrick, S., & Hendrick, C. (1989). Male sexual preference and attitudes toward love and sexuality. *Journal of Sex Education and Therapy*, 12, 27–30.

Advocate Report (1997). Washington. *The Advocate*, November 11, 16.

Aganoff, J., & Boyle, G. (1994). Aerobic exercise, mood states and menstrual cycle symptoms. *Journal of Psychosomatic Research*, 38, 183–192.

Agger, I., & Jensen, S. (1994). Sexuality as a tool of political repression. In H. Riquelme (Ed.), *Era in Twilight: Psychocultural Situation Under State Terrorism in Latin America*. Bilbao, Spain: Instituto Horizonte.

Aguillaume, C., & Tyrer, L. (1995). Current status and future projections on use of RU-486. *Contemporary Ob/Gyn*, June, 23–40.

Ahluwalia, I., Grummer-Strawn, L., & Scanlon, K. (1997). Exposure to environmental tobacco smoke and birth outcome: Increased effects on pregnant women aged 30 years or older. *American Journal of Epidemiology*, 146, 42–47.

Alan Guttmacher Institute (1998). *Facts in Brief: Teen Sex and Pregnancy*. New York: Alan Guttmacher Institute.

Albert, A., Warner, D., & Hatcher, R. (1998). Facilitating condom use with clients during commercial sex in Nevada's legal brothels. *American Journal of Public Health*, 88(4), 64.

Albertsen, P., Aaronson, N., Muller, M., Keller, S., & Ware, J. (1997). Health-related quality of life among patients with metastatic prostate cancer. *Urology*, 49, 207–217.

Aldous, P. (1994). A booster for contraceptive vaccines. *Science*, 266, 1484–1486.

Alexander, C., Sipski, M., & Findley, T. (1994). Sexual activities, desire, and satisfaction in males pre- and post-spinal cord injury. *Archives of Sexual Behavior*, 22, 217–228.

Allen, J., Philliber, S., & Hoggson, N. (1990). School-based prevention of teenage pregnancy and school dropout: Process evaluation of the national replication of Teen Outreach Program. *American Journal of Community Psychology*, 18, 505–524.

Allen, K., & Demo, D. (1995). The families of lesbians and gay men: a new frontier in family research. *Journal of Marriage and the Family*, 57, 111–127.

Allen, D. (1980). Young male prostitutes: A psychosocial study. *Archives of Sexual Behavior*, 9, 399–426.

Allen, L., & Gorski, R. (1990). Sex difference in the bed nucleus of the stria terminalis of the human brain. *Journal of Comparative Neurology*, 302, 697–706.

Allen, L., Hines, M., Shryne, J., & Gorski, R. (1989). Two sexually dimorphic cell groups. *Journal of Neurosciences*, 9, 497–506.

Allgeier, E. (1981). The influence of androgynous identification on heterosexual relations. *Sex Roles*, 7, 321–330.

Allison, J., & Wrightsman, L. (1993). *Rape: The Misunderstood Crime.* Newbury Park, CA: Sage.

Alter, J. (1989). Sexuality education for parents. In C. Cassell & P. Wilson (Eds.), *Sexuality Education: A Resource Book.* New York: Garland.

Alter, J. (1996). The right to be wrong. *Newsweek*, December 23, 64.

Althof, S. (1996). Choosing among contemporary alternatives: Self-injection versus vacuum pump therapy. Paper presented at the 21st annual meeting of the Society for Sex Therapy and Research, Miami, March.

Alzate, H., & Londono, M. (1984). Vaginal erotic sensitivity. *Journal of Sex and Marital Therapy*, 10, 49–56.

American Civil Liberties Union (1986). *Polluting the Censorship Debate.* Washington, DC: American Civil Liberties Union.

American Psychiatric Association (1994). *Diagnostic and Statistical Manual of Mental Disorders* (4th ed.). Washington, DC: American Psychiatric Association.

American Psychological Association (1990). Ethical principles of psychologists. *American Psychologist*, 45, 390–395.

American Society for Reproductive Medicine's Ethics Committee (1997). *Ethical Considerations of Assisted Reproductive Technologies*, 67(5), 1S–9S.

Anand, M. (1989). *The art of sexual ecstasy.* Los Angeles: Tarcher.

Andersen, B., Anderson, B., & deProsse, C. (1989). Controlled prospective longitudinal study of women with cancer: I. Sexual functioning outcomes. *Journal of Consulting and Clinical Psychology*, 57, 683–691.

Andersen, B., Woods, X., & Copeland, L. (1997). Sexual self-schema and sexual morbidity among gynecologic cancer survivors. *Journal of Consulting and Clinical Psychology*, 65(2), 221–229.

Anderson, A. (1998). Strengths of gay male youth: An untold story. *Child and Adolescent Social Work Journal*, 15(1), 55–69.

Andolsek, K. (1990). *Obstetric Care: Standards of Prenatal, Intrapartum, and Postpartum Management.* Philadelphia: Lea & Febiger.

Andrews, A., & Patterson, E. (1995). Searching for solutions to alcohol and other drug abuse during pregnancy: Ethics, values, and constitutional principles. *Journal of the National Association of Social Workers*, 40, 55–63.

Andrews, W. (1995). The transitional years and beyond. *Obstetrics & Gynecology*, 85, 1–5.

Anez, B. (1997). Montana Supreme Court strikes down ban on gay sex. *The Oregonian*, July 6, A22.

Angier, N. (1994). Mother's milk found to be potent cocktail of hormones. *The New York Times*, May 24, B5–B6.

Annon, J. (1974). *The Behavioral Treatment of Sexual Problems*, Vol. 1. Honolulu: Enabling Systems.

Apt, C. (1996). Outcome research on the treatment of female sexual disorders. Paper presented at the 21st annual meeting of the Society for Sex Therapy and Research, Miami, March.

Apt, C., Hurlbert, D., & Powell, D. (1993). Men with hypoactive sexual desire disorder: The role of interpersonal dependency and assertiveness. *Journal of Sex Education and Therapy*, 19(2), 108–116.

Aral, S., & Holmes, K. (1991). Sexually transmitted diseases in the AIDS era. *Scientific American*, 264, 62–69.

Arentewicz, B., & Schmidt, G. (Eds.) (1983). *The Treatment of Sexual Disorders.* New York: Basic Books.

Arndt, W. (1991). *Gender Disorders and the Paraphilias.* Madison, CT: International Universities Press.

Aronson, A. (1998). Arabesque: A new twist on the romance novel. *Ms.*, March/April, 77–78.

Arvin, A., & Prober, C. (1997). Herpes simplex virus type 2—A persistent problem. *New England Journal of Medicine*, 337, 1158–1159.

Assalian, P. (1996). Research outcome in sex therapy. Paper presented at the 21st annual meeting of the Society for Sex Therapy and Research, Miami, March.

Athanasiou, R., Shaver, P., & Tavris, C. (1970). Sex. *Psychology Today*, July, 39–52.

Atkins, H. (1997a). More choices for bacterial vaginosis. *Emergency Medicine*, January, 103.

Atkins, H. (1997b). Self-treatment of vulvovaginal candidiasis. *Emergency Medicine*, February, 57.

Atwood, J., & Seifer, M. (1997). Extramarital affairs and constructed meanings: A social constructionist therapeutic approach. *American Journal of Family Therapy*, 25, 55–75.

Austin, R., & McLendon, W. (1997). The Papanicolaou smear. *Journal of the American Medical Association*, 277(9), 754–755.

Baba, T., Trichel, A., An, L., Liska, V., Martin, L., Murphey-Corb, M., & Ruprecht, R. (1997). Infection and AIDS in adult macaques after nontraumatic oral exposure to cell-free SIV. *Science*, 272, 1486–1489.

Bachmann, G. (1991). Sexual dysfunction in the older woman. *Medical Aspects of Human Sexuality*, February, 42–45.

Bachmann, G. (1992). Using androgens to increase libido. *Medical Aspects of Human Sexuality*, 26, 6.

Bachrach, C. (1984). Contraceptive practice among American women, 1973–1982. *Family Planning Perspectives*, 16, 253–259.

Bagley, C., Bolitho, F., & Bertrand, L. (1997). Sexual assault in school, mental health and suicidal behaviors in adolescent women in Canada. *Adolescence*, 32, 361–366.

Bahamondes, L., Lavin, P., Ojeda, G., Petta, C., Diaz, J., Maradiegue, E., & Monteiro, I. (1997). Return of fertility after discontinuation of the once-a-month injectable contraceptive cyclofem. *Contraception*, 55, 307–310.

Bailey, J., Gaulin, S., Agyei, Y., & Gladue, B. (1994). Effects of gender and sexual orientation on evolutionarily relevant aspects of human mating psychology. *Journal of Personality and Social Psychology*, 66, 1081–1093.

Bailey, J. M., Bobrow, D., Wolfe, M. & Mikach, S. (1995). Sexual orientation of adult sons of gay fathers. *Developmental Psychology*, 31, 124–129.

Bailey, J. M., & Pillard, R. (1991). A genetic study of male sexual orientation. *Archives of General Psychiatry*, 48, 1089–1096.

Bailey, J. M., & Pillard, R. (1994). The innateness of homosexuality. *The Harvard Mental Health Letter*, 10, 4–6.

Bailey, J. M., Pillard, R., Neale, M., & Agyei, Y. (1993). Heritable factors influence sexual orientation in women. *Archives of General Psychiatry*, 50, 217–223.

Bailey, J. M., & Zucker, K. (1995). Childhood sex-typed behavior and sexual orientation: A conceptual analysis and quantitative review. *Developmental Psychology*, 31, 43–55.

Baird, D., Weinberg, C., Voigt, L., & Daling, J. (1996). Vaginal douching and reduced fertility. *American Journal of Public Health*, 86, 844–850.

Baird, P., Sadovnick, A., & Yee, I. (1991). Maternal age and birth defects: A population study. *The Lancet*, 337, 527.

Baker, J. (1990). Lesbians: Portrait of a community. *Newsweek*, March 12, 24.

Baker, N. (1994). In defense of her daughters. *The Oregonian*, February 7, C1–C10.

Baker, S., Thalberg, S., & Morrison, D. (1988). Parents' behavioral norms as predictors of adolescent sexual activity and contraceptive use. *Adolescence*, 23, 278–281.

Baldwin, D., Daugherty, S., & Eckenfels, E. (1991). Student perceptions of mistreatment and harassment during medical school: A survey of ten United States schools. *Western Journal of Medicine*, 155, 140–145.

Baldwin, J., Whiteley, S., & Baldwin, J. (1992). The effect of ethnic group on sexual activities related to contraception and STDs. *Journal of Sex Research*, 29, 189–205.

Bancroft, J. (1984). Hormones and human sexual behavior. *Journal of Sex and Marital Therapy*, 10, 3–21.

Bancroft, J., Sherwin, B., Alexander, G., Davidson, D., & Walker, A. (1991). Oral contraceptives, androgens, and the sexuality of young women: II. The role of androgens. *Archives of Sexual Behavior*, 20, 121–135.

Bangs, L. (1985). Aging and positive sexuality: A descriptive approach. Doctoral dissertation, U.S. International University.

Banmen, J., & Vogel, N. (1985). The relationship between marital quality and interpersonal sexual communication. *Family Therapy*, 12, 45–58.

Banyard, V., & Williams, L. (1996). Characteristics of child sexual abuse as correlates of women's adjustment: A prospective study. *Journal of Marriage and the Family*, 58, 853–865.

Barbach, L. (1982). *For Each Other: Sharing Intimacy.* New York: Anchor Press/Doubleday.

Barbaree, H., Marshall, W., & Lanthier, R. (1979). Deviant sexual arousal in rapists. *Behavior Research and Therapy*, 17, 215–222.

Bardoni, B., Zanaria, E., Guioli, S., Floridia, G., Worley, K., Tonini, G., Ferrante, E., Chiumello, G., McCabe, E., Fraccaro, M., Zuffardi, O., & Camerino, G. (1994). A dosage sensitive locus at chromosome Xp21 is involved in male to female sex reversal. *Nature Genetics*, 7, 497–501.

Barfield, R., Wilson, C., & Mcdonald, P. (1975). Sexual behavior: Extreme reduction of postejaculatory refractory period by midbrain lesions in male rats. *Science*, 189, 147–149.

Barile, L. (1997). Theories of menopause. Brief comparative synopsis. *Journal of Psychosocial Nursing*, 35, 36–39.

Barker, R. (1987). *The Green-Eyed Marriage: Surviving Jealous Relationships.* New York: Free Press.

Barkley, B., & Mosher, E. (1995). Sexuality and Hispanic culture: Counseling with children and their parents. *Journal of Sex Education & Therapy*, 21, 255–267.

Barlow, D. (1997). The diagnosis of oropharyngeal gonorrhoea. *Genitourinary Medicine*, 73, 16–17.

Barlow, D., Cardozo, L., Francis, R., Griffin, M., Hart, D., Stephens, E., & Sturdee, D. (1997). Urogenital ageing and its effect on sexual health in older British women. *British Journal of Obstetrics and Gynaecology*, 104, 87–91.

Barnhart, K., Coutinho, E., Furman, I., Devoto, L., & Pommer, R. (1997). Changes in the menstrual bleeding of users of a subdermal contraceptive implant of nomegestrol acetate (Uniplant) do not influence sexual frequency, sexual desire, or sexual enjoyment. *Fertility and Sterility*, 67(2), 244–249.

Barnhart, K., Furman, I., & Devoto, L. (1995). Attitudes and practice of couples regarding sexual relations during the menses and spotting. *Contraception*, 51, 93–98.

Baron, L. (1990). Pornography and gender equality: An empirical analysis. *Journal of Sex Research*, 27, 363–380.

Barone, N., & Wiederman, M. (1998). Young women's sexuality as a function of perceptions of maternal sexual communication during childhood. *Journal of Sex Education and Therapy*, 22(3), 33–38.

Barrett, J. (1997). School's out. *The Advocate*, September 16, 34–42.

Barth, R., & Kinder, B. (1987). The mislabeling of sexual impulsivity. *Journal of Sex and Marital Therapy*, 13, 15–23.

Basade, M., & Gulati, S. (1998). High-dose chemotherapy in metastatic breast cancer. *The Lancet*, 351, 386–387.

Basoff, E., & Glass, G. (1982). The relationship between sex roles and mental health: A meta-analysis of twenty-six studies. *Counseling Psychologist*, 10, 105–112.

Basow, S. (1992). *Gender: Stereotypes and Roles* (3rd ed.). Pacific Grove, CA: Brooks/Cole.

Bass, B. (1996). Short-term cognitive-behavioral treatment of hypoactive sexual desire in an individual with a history of childhood sexual abuse. *Journal of Sex and Marital Therapy*, 22, 284–289.

Batchelor, E. (Ed.) (1980). *Homosexuality and Ethics.* New York: Pilgrim.

Bates, T. (1995). Oregon XXX-rated. *The Oregonian*, May 7, D1–D4.

Bauman, R., Kasper, C., & Alford, J. (1984). The child sex abusers. *Corrective and Social Psychiatry*, 30, 76–81.

Baumeister, R. (1988). Masochism as escape from self. *Journal of Sex Research*, 25, 28–59.

Baumeister, R., Wotman, S., & Stillwell, A. (1993). Unrequited love: On heartbreak, anger, guilt, scriptlessness, and humiliation. *Journal of Personality and Social Psychology*, 64, 377–394.

Baur, K. (1995). Socioeconomic and personality traits of nonadjudicated child sex offenders in a clinical practice. Unpublished research.

Bawer, B. (1998). Last word. *The Advocate*, February 3, 64.

Beach, F. (Ed.). (1978). *Human Sexuality in Four Perspectives.* Baltimore: Johns Hopkins University Press.

Beal, G., & Muehlenhard, C. (1987). Getting sexually aggressive men to stop their advances: Information for rape prevention programs. Paper presented at the Annual Meeting of the Association for Advancement of Behavior Therapy, Boston, November.

Becerra, R. (1988). The Mexican American family. In C. Mindel, R. Habenstein, & R. Wright (Eds.), *Ethnic Families in America* (3rd ed.). New York: Elsevier.

Beck, J. G., Bozman, A., & Qualtrough, T. (1991). The experience of sexual desire: Psychological correlates in a college sample. *Journal of Sex Research*, 28, 443–456.

Beck, M. (1989). Baby blues, the sequel. *Newsweek*, July 3, 62.

Beck, M., Katel, P., & Annin, P. (1994). Propaganda made me do it. *Newsweek*, February 28, 34.

Beck, M., Wickelgren, I., Quade, V., & Wingert, P. (1988). Miscarriages. *Newsweek*, August 15, 46–49.

Becker, A., Stief, C., Machtens, S., Schultheiss, D., Hartmann, U., Truss, M., & Jonas, U. (1998). Oral phentolamine as treatment for erectile dysfunction. *Journal of Urology*, 159, 1214–1216.

Becker, E. (1978). *Female Sexuality Following Spinal Cord Injury.* Bloomington, IL: Accent Special Publications.

Becker, H., & Maraist, F. (1987). Immediate breast reconstruction after mastectomy using a permanent tissue expander. *Southern Medical Journal,* 80, 154–160.

Becker, J., Skinner, L., Abel, G., Axelrod, R., & Chicon, J. (1984). Sexual problems of sexual assault survivors. *Women and Health,* 9, 5–20.

Becker, J., Skinner, L., Abel, G., Axelrod, R. (1986). Level of postassault sexual functioning in rape and incest victims. *Archives of Sexual Behavior,* 15, 37–49.

Beebe, D. (1991). Emergency management of the adult female rape victim. *American Family Physician,* 43, 2041–2046.

Begany, T. (1997). Current approaches to endometriosis. *Patient Care,* January 15, 34–44.

Begley, S. (1993). Hands off Mr. Chips! *Newsweek,* May 3, 58.

Begley, S. (1995). The baby myth. *Newsweek,* September 4, 38–47.

Begley, S. (1996). The trials of silicone. *Newsweek,* December 16, 56–58.

Begley, S., & Rosenberg, D. (1995). Abortion by prescription. *Newsweek,* September 11, 76.

Begley, S., & Springen, K. (1997). A clear signal on estrogen. *Newsweek,* June 30, 60–61.

Behnke, M., Eyler, F., Conlon, M., Casanova, O., & Woods, N. (1997). How fetal cocaine exposure increases neonatal hospital costs. *Pediatrics,* 99, 204–208.

Bell, A., & Weinberg, M. (1978). *Homosexualities: A Study of Diversity Among Men and Women.* New York: Simon & Schuster.

Bell, A., Weinberg, M., & Hammersmith, S. (1981). *Sexual Preference: Its Development in Men and Women.* Bloomington: Indiana University Press.

Bellerose, S., & Binik, Y. (1993). Body image and sexuality in oophorectomized women. *Archives of Sexual Behavior,* 22, 435–459.

Bellizzi, J., & Milner, L. (1991). Gender positioning of a traditionally male-dominant product. *Journal of Advertising Research,* 31, 72–79.

Belsey, E., & Pinol, A. (1997). Menstrual bleeding patterns in untreated women. *Contraception,* 55, 57–65.

Belzer, E., Whipple, B., & Moger, W. (1984). A female ejaculation. *Journal of Sex Research,* 20, 403–406.

Bem, D. (1996). Exotic becomes erotic: A developmental theory of sexual orientation. *Psychological Review,* 103, 320–335.

Bem, S. (1974). The measurement of psychological androgyny. *Journal of Consulting and Clinical Psychology,* 42, 155–162.

Bem, S. (1975). Sex role adaptability: One consequence of psychological androgyny. *Journal of Personality and Social Psychology,* 31, 634–643.

Bem, S., Martyna, W., & Watson, C. (1976). Sex-typing and androgyny: Further explorations of the expressive domain. *Journal of Personality and Social Psychology,* 34, 1016–1023.

Benagiano, G., & Cottingham, J. (1997). Contraceptive methods: Potential for abuse. *International Journal of Gynecology & Obstetrics,* 56, 39–46.

Benedetti, J., Corey, L., & Ashley, R. (1994). Recurrence rates in genital herpes after symptomatic first-episode infection. *Annals of Internal Medicine,* 121, 847–854.

Benet, A., Sharaby, J., & Melman, A. (1994). Male erectile dysfunction assessment and treatment options. *Comprehensive Therapy,* 20(12), 669–673.

Bennett, W. (1996). Leave marriage alone. *Newsweek,* June 3, 27.

Benson, R. (1985). Vacuum cleaner injury to penis: A common urologic problem? *Urology,* 25, 41–44.

Berard, E. (1989). The sexuality of spinal cord injured women: Physiology and pathophysiology. *Paraplegia,* 27, 99–112.

Berenson, A., & Wiemann, C. (1995). Use of levonorgestrel implants versus oral contraceptives in adolescence: A case-control study. *American Journal of Obstetrics and Gynecology,* 172, 1128–1137.

Berenson, A., Wiemann, C., Rickerr, V.,& McCombs, S. (1997). Contraceptive outcomes among adolescents prescribed Norplant implants versus oral contraceptives after one year of use. *American Journal of Obstetrics and Gynecology,* 176, 586–592.

Beresford, S., Weiss, N., Voigt, L., & McKnight, B. (1997). Risk of endometrial cancer in relation to use of oestrogen combined with cyclic progestagen therapy in postmenopausal women. *The Lancet,* 349, 458–461.

Berga, S. (1998). Understanding premenstrual syndrome. *The Lancet,* 351, 465.

Berger, R. (1982). *Gay and Gray.* Urbana: University of Illinois Press.

Berger, R. (1990). Passing: Impact on the quality of same-sex couple relationships. *Social Work,* 35, 328–332.

Berkman, C., & Zinberg, G. (1997). Homophobia and heterosexism in social workers. *Journal of the National Association of Social Workers,* 42(4), 319–332.

Berliner, D., Monti-Bloch, L., Jennings-White, C., & Diaz-Sanchez, V. (1996). The functionality of the human vomeronasal organ (VNO): Evidence for steroid receptors. *Steroid Biochemistry & Molecular Biology,* 58, 259–265.

Bernhard, L. (1994). Laser endometrial ablation: An alternative to hysterectomy. *Health Care for Women International,* 15, 123–133.

Bertino, J., Tirrell, P., Greenberg, R., Keyserling, H., Poland, G., Gump, D., Kumar, M., & Ramsey, K. (1997). A comparative trial of standard or high-dose S subunit recombinant hepatitis B vaccine versus a vaccine containing S subunit, pre-S, and pre-S2 particles for revaccination of healthy adult nonresponders. *Journal of Infectious Diseases,* 175, 678–681.

Best, D., & Davis, S. (1997). Testicular cancer education: Differences in approaches. *American Journal of Health Behavior,* 21, 83–87.

Best, D., Davis, S., Vaz, R., & Kaiser, M. (1996). Testicular cancer education: A comparison of teaching methods. *American Journal of Health Behavior,* 20, 229–241.

Bidwell, R., & Deisher, R. (1991). Adolescent sexuality: Current issues. *Pediatric Annals,* 20, 293–302.

Bieber, I., Dain, H., Dince, P., Drellich, M., Grand, H., Gundlach, R., Kremer, M., Rifkin, A., Wilbur, C., & Bieber, T. (1962). *Homosexuality.* New York: Vintage Books.

Bihrle, R., Foster, R., Sanghvi, N., Donohue, J., & Hood, P. (1994). High intensity focused ultrasound for the treatment of benign prostatic hyperplasia: Early United States clinical experience. *Journal of Urology,* 151, 1271–1275.

Biley, A. (1995). Making sense of . . . diagnosing and treating endometriosis. *Nursing Times,* 91(9), 33–34.

Billhorn, D. (1994). Sexuality and the chronically ill older adult. *Geriatric Nursing,* 15, 106–108.

Billy, J., Tanfer, K., Grady, W., & Klepinger, D. (1993). The sexual behavior of men in the United States. *Family Planning Perspectives,* 25, 52–60.

Birchard, K. (1998). China plans to change policy on one-child limit to families. *The Lancet,* 351, 890.

Bishop, T. (1997). Female genital mutilation. *Journal of the National Medical Association,* 89(4), 233–236.

Black, A. (1994). Perverting the diagnosis: The lesbian and the scientific basis of stigma. *Historical Reflections,* 20, 201–216.

Black, D., Kehrberg, L., Flumerfelt, D., & Schlosser, S. (1997). Characteristics of 36 subjects reporting compulsive sexual behavior. *American Journal of Psychiatry*, 154, 243–249.

Blackmun, M. (1996a). The tie that binds knots later in life. *The Oregonian*, March 13, A9.

Blackmun, M. (1996b). Escort services: Look all you want but don't touch. *The Oregonian*, June 16, D1, D4.

Blair, C., & Lanyon, R. (1981). Exhibitionism: Etiology and treatment. *Psychological Bulletin*, 89, 439–463.

Blakeslee, S. (1993). Cryptic sensory system gains attention. *The Oregonian*, September 15, B10 & B11.

Blanchard, R., & Hucker, S. (1991). Age, transvestism, bondage, and concurrent paraphilic activities in 117 fatal cases of autoerotic asphyxia. *British Journal of Psychiatry*, 159, 371–377.

Blanchard, R., Legault, S., & Lindsay, W. (1987). Vaginoplasty outcome in male-to-female transsexuals. *Journal of Sex and Marital Therapy*, 13, 265–275.

Blanchard, R., Steiner, B., & Clemmensen, L. (1985). Gender dysphoria, gender reorientation, and the clinical management of transsexualism. *Journal of Consulting and Clinical Psychology*, 53, 295–304.

Blee, K., & Tickamyer, A. (1995). Racial differences in men's attitudes about women's gender roles. *Journal of Marriage and the Family*, 57, 21–30.

Blumstein, P., & Schwartz, P. (1983). *American Couples*. New York: Morrow.

Blumstein, P., & Schwartz, P. (1990). Intimate relationships and the creation of sexuality. In D. McWhirter, S. Sanders, & J. Reinisch (Eds.), *Homosexuality/Heterosexuality: Concepts of Sexual Orientation*. New York: Oxford University Press.

Boeringer, S. (1992). Sexual coercion among college males: Assessing three theoretical models of coercive sexual behavior. Unpublished doctoral dissertation.

Boeringer, S. (1994). Pornography and sexual aggression: Association of violent and nonviolent depictions with rape and rape proclivity. *Deviant Behavior*, 15, 289–304.

Boeringer, S., Shehan, C., & Akers, R. (1991). Social contexts and social learning in sexual coercion and aggression: Assessing the contribution of fraternity membership. *Family Relations*, 40, 58–64.

Bogaert, A. (1996). Volunteer bias in human sexuality research: Evidence for both sexuality and personality differences in males. *Archives of Sexual Behavior*, 25, 125–140.

Bogert, C., & Wehrfritz, G. (1996). Rethinking family values. *Newsweek*, January 22, 44–45.

Bogert, C., Chubbuck, K., & Hammer, J. (1995). Making men listen. *Newsweek*, September 25, 52.

Bogren, L. (1991). Changes in sexuality in women and men during pregnancy. *Archives of Sexual Behavior*, 20, 35–46.

Boles, J., & Elifson, K. (1994). Sexual identity and HIV: The male prostitute. *Journal of Sex Research*, 31, 39–46.

Bollen, N., Tournaye, H., Camus, M., Devroey, P., Staessen, C., & Van Steirteghem, A. (1991). The incidence of multiple pregnancy after in vitro fertilization and embryo transfer, gamete, or zygote intrafallopian transfer. *Fertility and Sterility*, 55, 314–319.

Bolton, F., & MacEachron, A. (1988). Adolescent male sexuality: A developmental perspective. *Journal of Adolescent Research*, 3, 259–273.

Bolus, J. (1994). Teaching teens about condoms. *Registered Nurse*, March, 44–47.

Bond, T. (1997). Emergency contraceptive methods revisited. *Journal of the National Medical Association*, 89, 165–167.

Booth, A., & Johnson, D. (1988). Premarital cohabitation and marital success. *Journal of Family Issues*, 9, 255–272.

Booth, W. (1989). WHO seeks global data on sexual practices. *Science*, 244, 418–419.

Boring, C., Squires, T., Tong, T., & Montgomery, S. (1994). Cancer statistics. *Ca-A Cancer Journal for Clinicians*, 44, 7–26.

Boswell, J. (1980). *Christianity, Social Tolerance, and Homosexuality*. Chicago: University of Chicago Press.

Boursnell, M., Entwisle, C., Blakely, D., Roberts, C., Duncan, I., Chisholm, S., Martin, G., Jennings, R., Nichallonair, D., Sobek, I., Inglis, S., & Mclean, C. (1997). A genetically inactivated herpes simplex virus type 2 (HSV-2) vaccine provides effective protection against primary and recurrent HSV-2 disease. *Journal of Infectious Diseases*, 175, 16–25.

Bowie, W., Hammerschlag, M., & Martin, D. (1994). STDs in '94: The new CDC guidelines. *Patient Care*, 28, 29–53.

Boyd, M. (1997). Male bonding. *The Advocate*, June 24, 11.

Boyers, S., & Gilbert, W. (1998). Elective repeat caesarean section versus trial of labour: The neonatologist's view. *The Lancet*, 351, 155.

Bradford, J. (1998). Treatment of men with paraphilia. *New England Journal of Medicine*, 338, 464–465.

Bradford, J., Boulet, J., & Pawlak, A. (1992). The paraphilias: A multiplicity of deviant behaviors. *Canadian Journal of Psychiatry*, 37, 104–107.

Bradford, J., & Pawlak, A. (1993a). Effects of cyproterone acetate on sexual arousal patterns of pedophiles. *Archives of Sexual Behavior*, 22, 629–641.

Bradford, J., & Pawlak, A. (1993b). Double-blind placebo crossover study of cyproterone acetate in the treatment of paraphilias. *Archives of Sexual Behavior*, 22, 383–402.

Bradshaw, C. (1994). Asia and Asian American women: Historical and political considerations in psychotherapy. In L. Comas-Diaz & B. Greene (Eds.), *Women of Color*. New York: Guilford.

Braen, G. (1980). Examination of the accused: The heterosexual and homosexual rapist. In C. Warner (Ed.), *Rape and Sexual Assault*. Germantown, MD: Aspen Systems.

Brahams, D. (1995). Warning about natural reversal of vasectomy. *The Lancet*, 345, 444.

Brashear, D., & Munsick, R. (1991). Hymenal dyspareunia. *Journal of Sex Education & Therapy*, 17, 27–31.

Braverman, P., & Strasburger, V. (1994a). The practitioner's role. *Clinical Pediatrics*, 33, 100–109.

Braverman, P., & Strasburger, V. (1994b). Sexually transmitted diseases. *Clinical Pediatrics*, January, 26–37.

Brawer, M. (1997). Editorial: Prostate cancer. *Journal of Urology*, 157, 207–208.

Brecher, E. (1984). *Love, Sex and Aging*. Boston: Little, Brown.

Breedlove, S. (1995). Another important organ. *Nature*, 378, 15–16.

Bremer, J. (1959). *Asexualization*. New York: Macmillan.

Brenner, P. (1988). The menopausal syndrome. *Obstetrics & Gynecology*, 72, 6S–11S.

Breslau, K. (1997). Climbing Mt. Rushmore. *Newsweek*, May 26, 33.

Bretl, D., & Cantor, J. (1988). The portrayal of men and women in U.S. television commercials: A recent content analysis and trends over 15 years. *Sex Roles*, 18, 595–610.

Bretschneider, J., & McCoy, N. (1988). Sexual interest and behavior in healthy 80-to-102-year-olds. *Archives of Sexual Behavior*, 17, 109.

Brewster, K. (1994). Race differences in sexual activity among adolescent women: The role of neighborhood characteristics. *American Sociological Review*, 59, 408–424.

Briddell, D., & Wilson, G. (1976). Effects of alcohol and expectancy set on male sexual arousal. *Journal of Abnormal Psychology,* 85, 225–234.

Briere, J., & Conte, J. (1993). Self-reported amnesia for abuse in adults molested as children. *Journal of Traumatic Stress,* 6, 21–31.

Briggs, D. (1997). Bishops urge parents of gays to put love first. *The Oregonian,* October 1, A9–10.

Bright, P. (1987). Adolescent pregnancy and loss. *Maternal–Child Nursing Journal,* 16, 1–12.

Brinton, L., & Schairer, C. (1997). Postmenopausal hormone-replacement therapy—time for a reappraisal? *New England Journal of Medicine,* 336(25), 1821–1822.

Britton, G., & Lumpkin, M. (1984). Battle to imprint for the 21st century. *Reading Teacher,* 37, 724–733.

Britton, T. (1988). Personal communication.

Brooke, P. (1997). HIV and the law. *RN,* May, 59–64.

Brooks, J., & Watkins, M. (1989). Recognition memory and the mere exposure effect. *Journal of Experimental Psychology: Learning, Memory, and Cognition,* 15, 968–976.

Brown, E. (1988). Affairs: The hidden meanings have major impact on therapeutic approach. *Behavior Today,* October 24, 3–4.

Brown, G. (1990). The transvestite husband. *Medical Aspects of Human Sexuality,* June, 35–42.

Brown, G., & Collier, L. (1989). Transvestites' women revisited: A nonpatient sample. *Archives of Sexual Behavior,* 18, 73–83.

Brown, J., & Hart, D. (1977). Correlates of females' sexual fantasies. *Perceptual and Motor Skills,* 45, 819–825.

Brown, L. (1997a). Hot chat: Case commentary 2. *Networker,* May/June, 73–76.

Brown, L. (1997b). Introduction. In L. Brown (Ed.), *Two Spirit People.* New York: Harrington Park Press.

Brown, M. (1994). Marital discord during pregnancy: A family systems approach. *Family Systems Medicine,* 12, 221–234.

Brown, M., & Zimmer, P. (1986). Personal and family impact of premenstrual symptoms. *Journal of Obstetrical, Gynecological and Neonatal Nurses,* 15, 31–38.

Browne, J., & Minichiello, V. (1994). The condom: Why more people don't put it on. *Sociology of Health & Illness,* 16(2), 229–249.

Brownmiller, S. (1975). Against Our Will: Men, Women, and Rape. New York: Simon & Schuster.

Brownmiller, S. (1993). Making female bodies the battlefield. *Newsweek,* January 4, 37.

Bruce, K., & Tarant, S. (1997). Characteristics of female college students attending the NAMES project AIDS memorial quilt. *Journal of Sex Education and Therapy,* 22(2), 31–36.

Bryant, S., & Demian, N. (1998). Terms of same-sex endearment. *Siecus Report,* 26(4), 10–13.

Bryjak, G., & Soroka, M. (1994). *Sociology: Cultural Diversity in a Changing World,* (2nd ed.). Boston: Allyn and Bacon.

Budhos, M. (1997). Putting the heat on sex tourism. *Ms.,* March/April, 12–16.

Budin, L., & Johnson, C. (1989). Sex abuse prevention programs: Offenders' attitudes about their efficacy. *Child Abuse and Neglect,* 13, 77–87.

Budoff, P. (1987). Cyclic estrogen progesterone therapy. In M. Walsh (Ed.), *The Psychology of Women.* New Haven, CT: Yale University Press.

Bulcroft, R., Carmady, D., & Bulcroft, K. (1996). Patterns of parental independence giving to adolescents: Variations by race, age, and gender of child. *Journal of Marriage and the Family,* 58, 866–883.

Bull, C. (1997). A clean sweep. *The Advocate,* July 22, 35–36.

Bullough, B., & Bullough, V. (1997). Are transvestites necessarily heterosexual? *Archives of Sexual Behavior,* 26, 1–12.

Bullough, V., & Weinberg, T. (1988). Women married to transvestites: Problems and adjustments. *Journal of Psychology and Human Sexuality,* 1, 83–104.

Bullough, V., Bullough, B., & Smith, R. (1983). Comparative study of male transvestites, male-to-female transsexuals, and male homosexuals. *Journal of Sex Research,* 19, 238–257.

Bumpass, L., & Sweet, J. (1989). National estimates of cohabitation. *Demography,* 26, 615–625.

Burcky, W., Reuterman, N., & Kopsky, S. (1988). Dating violence among high school students. *School Counselor,* 35, 353–358.

Burgess, A., Hartman, C., McCausland, M., & Powers, P. (1984). Response patterns in children and adolescents exploited through sex rings and pornography. *American Journal of Psychiatry,* 141, 656–662.

Burgess, A., & Holmstrom, L. (1974a). Rape trauma syndrome. *American Journal of Psychiatry,* 131, 981–986.

Burgess, A., & Holmstrom, L. (1974b). *Rape: Victims of Crisis.* Bowie, MD: Robert J. Brady.

Burgess, A., & Holmstrom, L. (1979). Rape: Sexual disruption and recovery. *American Journal of Orthopsychiatry,* 49, 648–657.

Burgess, A., & Holmstrom, L. (1988). Treating the adult rape victim. *Medical Aspects of Human Sexuality,* January, 36–43.

Burke, W., Daly, M., Garber, J., Botkin, J., Kahn, M., Lynch, P., McTiernan, A., Offit, K., Perlman, J., Petersen, G., Thomson, E., & Varricchio, C. (1997). Recommendations for follow-up care of individuals with an inherited predisposition to cancer. *Journal of the American Medical Association,* 277(12), 997–1003.

Burkman, R., Jr. (1995). Oral contraceptives: An update. *Hospital Practice,* 30, 85–97.

Burn, S., O'Neil, A., & Nederend, S. (1996). Childhood tomboyism and adult androgyny. *Sex Roles,* 34, 419–428.

Burr, C. (1996a). *A Separate Creation.* New York: Hyperion.

Burr, C. (1996b). Gimme Shelter. *The Advocate,* July 23, 37–38.

Burt, K. (1995). The effects of cancer on the body image and sexuality. *Nursing Times,* 91(7), 36–37.

Bush, C., Bush, J., & Jennings, J. (1988). Effects of jealousy threats on relationship perceptions and emotions. *Journal of Social and Personal Relationships,* 5, 285–303.

Buss, D. (1994). *The Evolution of Desire: Strategies of Human Mating.* New York: Basic Books.

Buss, D., Larsen, R., & Semmelroth, J. (1992). Sex differences in jealousy: Evolution, physiology, and psychology. *Psychological Science,* 3, 251–255.

Buss, D., Larsen, R., & Westen, D. (1996). Sex differences: Not gone, not forgotten, and not explained by alternative hypotheses. *Psychological Science,* 7, 373–375.

Buttenweiser, S. (1997). Over time. *Ms.,* November/December, 49–51.

Buttermore, S., & Nolan, C. (1993). Six years of clinical experience using postcoital contraception in college women. *College Health,* 42, 61–63.

Butts, J. (1981). Adolescent sexuality and teenage pregnancy from a black perspective. In T. Ooms (Ed.), *Teenage Pregnancy in a Family Context.* Philadelphia: Temple University Press.

Buunk, B., & Bringle, R. (1987). Jealousy in love relationships. In D. Perlman & S. Duck (Eds.), *Intimate Relationships.* Newbury Park, CA: Sage.

Buunk, B., Angleitner, A., Oubaid, V., & Buss, D. (1996). Sex differences in jealousy in evolutionary and cultural perspective: Tests from the Netherlands, Germany, and the United States. *Psychological Science*, 6, 359–363.

Byar, D. (1973). The Veterans Administration Cooperative Research Group's studies of cancer of the prostate. *Cancer*, 32, 1126–1130.

Byrne, C., Schairer, C., Wolfe, J., Parekh, N., Salane, M., Brinton, L., Hoover, R., & Haile, R. (1995). Mammographic features and breast cancer risk: Effects with time, age, and menopause status. *Journal of the National Cancer Institute*, 87, 1622–1629.

Byrne, D., Clore, G., & Smeaton, G. (1986). The attraction hypothesis: Do similar attitudes affect anything? *Journal of Personality and Social Psychology*, 51, 1167–1170.

Byrne, D., & Murnen, S. (1988). Maintaining loving relationships. In R. Sternberg & M. Barnes (Eds.), *The Psychology of Loving.* New Haven, CT: Yale University Press.

Byrne, J. (1996). How silicone ended up in women's breasts. *Ms.*, March/April, 46–50.

Cado, S., & Leitenberg, H. (1990). Guilt reactions to sexual fantasies during intercourse. *Archives of Sexual Behavior*, 19, 49–71.

Caggiula, A. (1970). Analysis of the copulation–reward properties of posterior hypothalamic stimulation in male rats. *Journal of Comparative and Physiological Psychology,* 70, 399–412.

Caggiula, A., & Hoebel, B. (1966). Copulation–reward site in the posterior hypothalamus. *Science,* 153, 1284–1285.

Cagle, J. (1995). America sees shades of gay. *Entertainment Weekly,* September 8, 20–31.

Cahill, C., Llewelyn, S., & Pearson, C. (1991). Treatment of sexual abuse which occurred in childhood: A review. *British Journal of Clinical Psychology,* 30, 1–12.

Cain, R. (1991). Relational contexts and information management among gay men. *Families in Society,* June, 344–352.

Calamidas, E. (1997). Promoting healthy sexuality among older adults: Educational challenges for health professionals. *Journal of Sex Education and Therapy*, 22(2), 45–49.

Calderone, M. (1983). Fetal erection and its message to us. *SIECUS Report,* 11, 9–10.

Calderone, M., & Johnson, E. (1989). *The Family Book About Sexuality,* (rev. ed.). New York: Harper & Row.

Caldwell, J., Orubuloye, I., & Caldwell, P. (1997). Male and female circumcision in Africa from a regional to a specific Nigerian examination. *Social Science Medicine*, 44(8), 1181–1193.

Calhoun, T., & Weaver, G. (1996). Rational decision-making among male street prostitutes. *Deviant Behavior: An Interdisciplinary Journal*, 17, 209–227.

Cameron, D., Heath-Chiozzi, M., Danner, S., Cohen, C., Kravcik, S., Maurath, C., Sun, E., Henry, D., Rode, R., Potthoff, A., & Leonard, J. (1998). Randomized placebo-controlled trial of ritonavir in advanced HIV-1 disease. *The Lancet*, 351, 543–549.

Campion, M. (1992). The adequate cervical smear: A modern dilemma. *Journal of Family Practice*, 34, 273–275.

Canavan, M., Meyer, W., & Higgs, D. (1992). The female experience of sibling incest. *Journal of Marital and Family Therapy,* 18, 129–142.

Cantor, S., Mitchell, M., Tortolero-Luna, G., Bratka, C., Bodurka, D., & Richards-Kortum, R. (1998). Cost-effectiveness analysis of diagnosis and management of cervical squamous intraepithelial lesions. *Obstetrics & Gynecology*, 91(2), 270–277.

Capewell, A., McIntyre, M., & Elton, R. (1992). Post-menopausal atrophy in elderly women: Is a vaginal smear necessary for diagnosis? *Age and Aging*, 21, 117–120.

Caplan, L. (1994). "Don't ask, don't tell"—Marine style. *Newsweek,* June 13, 28.

Carlson, E. (1997). Sexual assault on men in war. *The Lancet*, 349, 129.

Carne, C. (1997). Epidemiological treatment and tests of cure in gonococcal infection: Evidence for value. *Genitourinary Medicine*, 73, 12–15.

Carnes, P. (1983). *Out of the Shadows: Understanding Sexual Addiction.* Minneapolis: Compcare Publication.

Carnes, P. (1986). Progress in sexual addiction: An addictive perspective. *SIECUS Report,* July, 4, 6.

Carnes, P. (1991). *Don't Call It Love.* New York: Bantam Books.

Carr, B., & Ory, H. (1997). Estrogen and progestin components of oral contraceptives: Relationship to vascular disease. *Contraception*, 55, 267–272.

Carson, S. (1997). Human papillamatous virus infection update: Impact on women's health. *The Nurse Practitioner*, 22, 24–37.

Carswell, R. (1969). Historical analysis of religion and sex. *Journal of School Health,* 39, 673–683.

Carter, M., Hollander, M., & Lipshultz, L. (1994). Drug clues to male infertility. *Contemporary Ob/Gyn,* October 15, 30–44.

Castleman, M. (1980). *Sexual Solutions.* New York: Simon & Schuster.

Castleman, M. (1981). Men, lovemaking and cramps. *Medical Self-Care,* Spring, 21.

Catalona, W., Partin, A., Slawin, K., Brawer, M., Flanigan, R., Patel, A., Richie, J., deKernion, J., Walsh, P., Scardino, P., Lange, P., Subong, E., Parson, R., Gasior, G., Loveland, K., & Southwick, P. (1998). Use of percentage of free prostate-specific antigen to enhance differentiation of prostate cancer from benign prostate disease: A prospective multicenter clinical trial. *Journal of the American Medical Association,* 279, 1542–1547.

Catania, J., Gibson, D., Marin, B., Coates, T., & Greenblatt, R. (1990). Response bias in assessing sexual behaviors relevant to HIV transmission. *Evaluation and Program Planning,* 13, 19–29.

Catanzarite, V., Deutchman, M., Johnson, C., & Scherger, J. (1995). Pregnancy after 35: What's the real risk? *Patient Care,* January 15, 41–51.

Cates, W. (1991). Teenagers and sexual risk taking: The best of times and the worst of times. *Journal of Adolescent Health,* 12, 84–94.

Cates, W., & Stone, K. (1992). Family planning, sexually transmitted diseases and contraceptive choice: A literature update: Part I. *Family Planning Perspectives,* 24, 75–84.

Caufriez, A. (1997). The pubertal spurt: Effects of sex steroid on growth hormone and insulin-like growth factor I. *European Journal of Obstetrics & Gynecology and Biology*, 71, 215–217.

Cavert, W., Notermans, D., Staskus, K., Wietgrefe, S., Zupancic, M., Gebhard, K., Henry, K., Zhang, Z., Mills, R., McDade, H., Goudsmit, J., Danner, S., & Haase, A. (1997). Kinetics of response in lymphoid tissues to antiretroviral therapy of HIV-1 infection. *Science*, 276, 960–962.

Ceci, S., Loftus, E., Leichtman, M., & Bruck, M. (1994). The role of source misattributions in the creation of false beliefs among preschoolers. *International Journal of Clinical and Experimental Hypnosis,* 42, 304–320.

Centers for Disease Control (1992). Sexual behavior among high school students. *Morbidity and Mortality Weekly Report,* 40, 885–888.

Centers for Disease Control (1994). Recommendation of the U.S. Public Health Service Task Force on the use of zidovudine to reduce perinatal transmission of human immunodeficiency virus. *Morbidity and Mortality Weekly Report*, 43 (RR-11), 1.

Centers for Disease Control (1995a). Disease summary tables. *Morbidity and Mortality Weekly Report,* 44, 9–11.

Centers for Disease Control (1995b). Trends in sexual risk behavior among high school students—United States, 1990, 1991, and 1993. *Morbidity and Mortality Weekly Report,* 44, 124–132.

Centers for Disease Control (1995c). First 500,000 AIDS cases—United States. *Morbidity and Mortality Weekly Report,* 44, 849–853.

Centers for Disease Control (1995d). Update: Acquired immunodeficiency syndrome—United States, 1994. *Morbidity and Mortality Weekly Report,* 44, 64–67.

Centers for Disease Control (1996). Youth risk behavior surveillance—United States, 1995. *Morbidity and Mortality Weekly Report,* 45 (SS-4), 1–84.

Centers for Disease Control (1997a). Alcohol consumption among pregnant and childbearing-aged women—United States, 1991 and 1995. *Morbidity and Mortality Weekly Report,* April 25, 46, 346–350.

Centers for Disease Control (1997b). Total and primary cesarean rates. *Monthly Vital Statistics Report,* 45(11–3), July 16.

Centers for Disease Control (1997c). *Chlamydia trachomatis* genital infections—United States, 1995. *Morbidity and Mortality Weekly Report,* 46, 193–199.

Centers for Disease Control (1997d). Update: Trends in AIDS incidence, deaths, and prevalence—United States, 1996. *Morbidity and Mortality Weekly Report,* 46, 165–173.

Centers for Disease Control (1997e). AIDS rates. *Morbidity and Mortality Weekly Report,* 46, 333–334.

Centers for Disease Control (1997f). Gonorrhea among men who have sex with men—selected sexually transmitted diseases clinics, 1993–1996. *Morbidity and Mortality Weekly Report,* 46, 889–892.

Centers for Disease Control (1997g). Contraceptive practices before and after an intervention promoting condom use to prevent HIV infection and other sexually transmitted diseases among women—selected U.S. sites, 1993–1995. *Morbidity and Mortality Weekly Report,* 46, 373–377.

Centers for Disease Control (1998a). Births, marriages, divorces, and deaths for August 1997. *Monthly Vital Statistics Report,* 40(8), April 13.

Centers for Disease Control (1998b). 1998 guidelines for treatment of sexually transmitted diseases. *Morbidity and Mortality Weekly Report,* 47, 1–116.

Centers for Disease Control (1998c). Public Health Service Task Force recommendations for the use of antiretroviral drugs in pregnant women infected with HIV-1 for maternal health and for reducing perinatal HIV-1 transmission in the United States. *Morbidity and Mortality Weekly Report,* 47, 1–29.

Chan, C. (1995). Issues of sexual identity in an ethinic minority: The case of Chinese American lesbians, gay men and bisexual people. In A. D'Augelli & C. Patterson (Eds.), *Lesbian, Gay, and Bisexual Identities Over the Lifespan.* New York: Oxford University Press.

Chandra, A., & Stephen, E. (1998). Impaired fecundity in the United States: 1982–1995. *Family Planning Perspectives,* 30(1), 34–42.

Chang, H., & Holt, G. (1991). The concept of *yuan* and Chinese interpersonal relationships. In S. Ting-Toomey & F. Korzenny (Eds.), *Cross-Cultural Interpersonal Communication.* Newbury Park, CA: Sage.

Chang, S., Katz, M., & Hernandez, S. (1992). The new AIDS case definition. *Journal of the American Medical Association,* 267, 273–275.

Chapman, J. (1984). Sexual anhedonia: Disorders of sexual desire. *Journal of the American Osteopathic Association,* 82, 709–714.

Chapman, L. (1991). Expectant fathers' roles during labor and birth. *Journal of Obstetrics, Gynecology & Neonatal Nurses,* 21(2), 114–120.

Chapman, S. (1997). Making "I do" stick. *The Oregonian,* July 17, C8.

Chara, P., & Kuennen, L. (1994). Diverging gender attitudes regarding casual sex: A cross-sectional study. *Psychological Reports,* 74, 57–58.

Charlton, A. (1994). Children and passive smoking: A review. *Journal of Family Practice,* 38(3), 267–277.

Charney, D., & Russell, R. (1994). An overview of sexual harassment. *American Journal of Psychiatry,* 151, 10–17.

Chasan-Taber, L., & Stampfer, M. (1998). Epidemiology of oral contraceptives and cardiovascular disease. *Annals of Internal Medicine,* 128, 467–477.

Chauncey, S. (1994). Emotional concerns and treatment of male partners of female sexual abuse survivors. *Social Work,* 39, 669–676.

Chaze, W., Hawkins, S., & Lord, M. (1987). Fear of AIDS chills sex industry. *U.S. News and World Report,* February 16, 25.

Check, J., & Guloien, T. (1989). Reported proclivity for coercive sex following repeated exposure to sexually violent pornography, nonviolent dehumanizing pornography, and erotica. In D. Zillman & J. Bryant (Eds.), *Pornography: Research Advances and Policy Considerations.* Hillsdale, NJ: Erlbaum.

Check, J., & Malamuth, N. (1983). Sex role stereotyping and reactions to depictions of stranger versus acquaintance rape. *Journal of Personality and Social Psychology,* 45, 344–356.

Chen, F., Lee, N., Wang, C., Cherng, W., & Soong, Y. (1998). Effects of hormone replacement therapy on cardiovascular risk factors in postmenopausal women. *Fertility and Sterility,* 69(2), 267–273.

Cherfas, J. (1991). Sex and the single gene. *Science,* 252, 782.

Cherlin, A. (1981). *Marriage, Divorce, Remarriage.* Cambridge, MA: Harvard University Press.

Cherniak, D., & Feingold, A. (1973). *VD Handbook.* Montreal: Montreal Press.

Chesebro, M., & Everett, W. (1998). Understanding the guidelines for treating HIV disease. *American Family Physician,* 57, 315–322.

Cheung, K. (1997). Developing the interview protocol for video-recorded child sexual abuse investigations: A training experience with police officers, social workers, and clinical psychologists in Hong Kong. *Child Abuse & Neglect,* 21, 273–284.

Chevarley, F., & White, E. (1997). Recent trends in breast cancer mortality among white and black US women. *American Journal of Public Health,* 87, 775–781.

Chiang, H. (1993). Universities liable in sex harassment. *San Francisco Chronicle,* December 7, A1–A2.

Chin, J., & Mann, J. (1990). HIV infections and AIDS in the 1990s. *Annual Review of Public Health,* 11, 127–142.

China rediscovers the joy of sex. (1997). *Economist,* 344, 47.

Chiriboga, D., & Thurnher, M. (1980). *Journal of Divorce,* 3, 379–390.

Choo, V. (1994). Maternal transmission of HIV. *The Lancet,* 343, 533.

Chrisler, J., Johnston, I., Champagne, N., & Preston, K. (1994). Menstrual joy. *Psychology of Women Quarterly,* 18, 375–387.

Chrisler, J., & Levy, K. (1990). The media construct a menstrual monster: A content analysis of PMS articles in the popular press. *Women & Health,* 16(2), 89–104.

Christopher, F. (1988). An initial investigation into a continuum of premarital sexual pressure. *Journal of Sex Research,* 25, 255–266.

Chu, K., Tarone, R., Kessler, L., et al. (1996). Recent trends in U.S. breast cancer incidence, survival, and mortality rates. *Journal of the National Cancer Institute,* 88, 1571–1579.

Chun, T., Carruth, L., Finzi, D., Shen, X., DiGuiseppe, J., Taylor, H., Hermankova, M., Chadwick, K., Margolick, J., Quinn, T., Kuo, Y., Brookmeyer, R., Zeiger, M., Barditch-Crovo, P., & Siliciano, R. (1997). Quantification of latent tissue reservoirs and total body viral load in HIV-1 infection. *Nature*, 387, 183–188.

Chung, W., & Choi, H. (1990). Erotic erection versus nocturnal erection. *Journal of Urology,* 143, 294–297.

Clanton, G., & Smith, L. (1977). *Jealousy.* Englewood Cliffs, NJ: Prentice Hall.

Clark, J., Smith, E., & Davidson, J. (1984). Enhancement of sexual motivation in male rats by yohimbine. *Science,* 225, 847–849.

Clark, J., Tatum, N., & Noble, S. (1995). Management of genital herpes. *American Family Physician,* 51, 175–182.

Clark, L., Brasseux, C., Richmond, D., Getson, P., & D'Angelo, L. (1998). Effect of HIV counseling and testing on sexually transmitted diseases and condom use in an urban adolescent population. *Archives of Pediatric and Adolescent Medicine*, 152, 269–273.

Clark, P. (1997). Male order problems. *Nursing Times*, 93, 32–33.

Clark, R., & Hatfield, E. (1989). Gender differences in receptivity to sexual offers. *Journal of Psychology and Human Differences,* 2, 39–55.

Clark, W., & Serovich, J. (1997). Twenty years and still in the dark? Content analysis of articles pertaining to gay, lesbian, and bisexual issues in marriage and family therapy journals. *Journal of Marital and Family Therapy*, 23(3), 239–253.

Clarke, G. (1985). In the middle of a war. *Time,* August 12, 46.

Clarnette, T., Sugita, Y., & Hutson, J. (1997). Genital anomalies in human and animal models reveal the mechanisms and hormones governing testicular descent. *British Journal of Urology*, 79, 99–112.

Cleek, M., & Pearson, T. (1985). Perceived causes of divorce: An analysis of interrelationships. *Journal of Marriage and the Family,* 47, 179–183.

Clement, U. (1990). Surveys of heterosexual behavior. *Annual Review of Sex Research,* 1, 45–74.

Clement, U., & Pfäfflin, F. (1980). Changes in personality scores among couples subsequent to sex therapy. *Archives of Sexual Behavior*, 9, 235–244.

Clements, M. (1992). Should abortion remain legal? *Parade,* May 17, 4–5.

Clements, M. (1994). Sex in America today. *Parade,* August 7, 4–6.

Clements, M. (1996). Sex after 65. *Parade,* March 17, 4–6.

Cochran, S., & Mays, V. (1990). Sex, lies, and HIV. *New England Journal of Medicine,* 322, 774.

Cochran, S., & Mays, V. (1994). Depressive distress among homosexually active African American men and women. *American Journal of Psychiatry,* 151, 524–529.

Cochran, S., Mays, V., & Leung, L. (1991). Sexual practices of heterosexual Asian American young adults: Implications for risk of HIV infection. *Archives of Sexual Behavior*, 20, 381–392.

Cocores, J., & Gold, M. (1989). Substance abuse and sexual dysfunction. *Medical Aspects of Human Sexuality.* February, 22–31.

Coetzee, L., Layfield, Hars, V., & Paulson, D. (1997). Proliferative index determination in prostatic carcinoma tissue: Is there any additional prognostic value greater than that of the Gleason score, ploidy and pathological stage? *Journal of Urology*, 157, 214–218.

Cogen, R., & Steinman, W. (1990). Sexual function and practice in elderly men of lower socioeconomic status. *Journal of Family Practice,* 32, 162–166.

Cohen, B. (1991). The reproductive cycle. In *Management of infertility: A clinician's manual* (2nd ed). Durant, OK: Essential Medical Information Systems.

Cohen, J. (1997a). SIV data raise concern on oral-sex risk. *Science,* 272, 1421–1422.

Cohen, J. (1997b). AIDS vaccine: Looking for leads in HIV's battle with the immune system. *Science*, 276, 1196–1197.

Cohen-Kettenis, P., & van Goozen, S. (1997). Sex reassignment of adolescent transsexuals: A follow-up study. *Journal of the American Academy of Child and Adolescence Psychiatry*, 36, 263–271.

Cohn, B. (1992). Discrimination: The limits of the law. *Newsweek,* September 14, 38–39.

Cohn, B. (1994). In search of human skin pheromones. *Archives of Dermatology*, 130, 1048–1051.

Coker, A., Hulka, B., McCann, M., & Walton, L. (1992). Barrier methods of contraception and cervical intraepithelial neoplasia. *Contraception,* 45, 1.

Cole, C., O'Boyle, M., Emory, L., & Meyer, W. (1997). Comorbidity of gender dysphoria and other major psychiatric diagnoses. *Archives of Sexual Behavior*, 26, 13–26.

Cole, D. (1987). It might have been: Mourning the unborn. *Psychology Today,* July, 64–65.

Coleman, B. (1997). Study raises questions about early puberty in girls. *The Oregonian*, April 8, A9.

Coleman, E. (1990). The obsessive-compulsive model for describing compulsive sexual behavior. *American Journal of Preventive Psychiatry and Neurology,* 2, 9–14.

Coleman, E. (1991). Compulsive sexual behavior: New concepts and treatments. *Journal of Psychology and Human Sexuality,* 4, 37–51.

Coleman, M., & Ganong, L. (1985). Love and sex role stereotypes: Do macho men and feminine women make better lovers? *Journal of Personality and Social Psychology,* 49, 170–176.

Coles, F., Hipp, S., Silberstein, G., & Chen, J. (1995). Congenital syphilis surveillance in upstate New York, 1989–1992: Implications for prevention and clinical management. *Journal of Infectious Diseases,* 171, 732–735.

Coles, R., & Stokes, G. (1985). *Sex and the American Teenager.* New York: Harper & Row.

Coley, C., Barry, M., Fleming, C., & Mulley, A. (1997a). Early detection of prostate cancer. Part I: Prior probability and effectiveness of tests. *Annals of Internal Medicine*, 126, 394–406.

Coley, C., Barry, M., Fleming, C., Fahs, M., & Mulley, A. (1997b). Early detection of prostate cancer. Part II: Estimating the risks, benefits, and costs. *Annals of Internal Medicine*, 126, 468–479.

Colino, S. (1991). Sex and the expectant mother. *Parenting,* February, 111.

Collaer, M., & Hines, M. (1995). Human behavioral sex differences: A role for gonadal hormones during early development. *Psychological Bulletin*, 118, 55–107.

Collier, M. (1991). Conflict competence within African, Mexican and Anglo American friendships. In S. Ting-Toomey & F. Korzenny (Eds.), *Cross-Cultural Interpersonal Communication.* Newbury Park, CA: Sage.

Collins, S. (1994). The long-term effects of contact and noncontact forms of child sexual abuse in a sample of university men. *Child Abuse & Neglect,* 19, 1–6.

Comas-Diaz, L. (1987). Feminist therapy with mainland Puerto Rican women. *Psychology of Women Quarterly,* 11, 461–474.

Comas-Diaz, L., & Greene B. (Eds.) (1994). *Women of Color.* New York: Guilford.

Comfort, A. (1972). *The Joy of Sex.* New York: Crown.

Condon, L. (1997). Executive order: Enough hate already. *The Advocate,* October 14, 29–30.

Connell, E. (1991). Contraceptive options for the woman over 40. *Medical Aspects of Human Sexuality,* April, 20–24.

Connell, E. (1994). The female condom—a new contraceptive option. *Contemporary Ob/Gyn,* October 15, 20–27.

Connell, J. (1992). Seeking common ground. *The Oregonian,* April 5, B1–B4.

Contemporary Sexuality (1996a). U.S. has most rapes in the Western world. Author, 30, 5.

Contemporary Sexuality (1996b). Rape rampant in Rwanda. Author, 30, 8.

Cook, L., Kamb, M., & Weiss, N. (1997). Perineal powder exposure and the risk of ovarian cancer. *American Journal of Epidemiology,* 145, 459–465.

Cook, L., Koutsky, L., & Holmes, K. (1994). Circumcision and sexually transmitted diseases. *American Journal of Public Health,* 84, 197–201.

Cora-Bramble, D., Bradshaw, M., & Sklarew, B. (1992). The sex education practicum: Medical students in the elementary school classroom. *Journal of School Health,* 62, 32–34.

Coreil, J., & Parcel, G. (1983). Sociocultural determinants of parental involvement in sex education. *Journal of Sex Education and Therapy,* 9, 22–25.

Corliss, R. (1996). The final frontier. *Time,* March 11, 66–68.

Cosgray, R., Hanna, V., Fawley, R., & Money, M. (1991). Death from auto-erotic asphyxiation in long-term psychiatric setting. *Perspectives in Psychiatric Care,* 27, 21–24.

Cotton, D., & Groth, A. (1982). Inmate rape: Prevention and intervention. *Journal of Prison and Jail Health,* 2, 45–57.

Courtois, C. (1997). Healing the incest wound: A treatment update with attention to recovered memory issues. *American Journal of Psychotherapy,* 51, 464–496.

Courville, T., Caldwell, B., & Brunell, P. (1998). Lack of evidence of transmission of HIV-1 to family contacts of HIV-1 infected children. *Clinical Pediatrics,* 37, 175–178.

Cowan, G., & Campbell, R. (1994). Racism and sexism in interracial pornography. *Psychology of Women Quarterly,* 18, 323–338.

Cowan, P., & Cowan C. (1992). *When Partners Become Parents.* New York: HarperCollins.

Cowden, C., & Koch, P. (1995). Attitudes related to sexual concerns: Gender and orientation comparisons. *Journal of Sex Education and Therapy,* 21(2), 78–87.

Cowley, G. (1995). Silicone: Juries vs. science. *Newsweek,* November 13, 75.

Cowley, G., & Rosenberg, D. (1992). A needle instead of a knife. *Newsweek,* April 13, 62.

Cowley, G., & Springen, K. (1997). Multiplying the risks. *Newsweek,* December 1, 66.

Cowley, G., Laris, M., & Hager, M. (1996). From freedom to fear: When AIDS hits China. *Newsweek,* April 1, 49.

Cowley, J., & Brooksbank, B. (1991). Human exposure to putative pheromones and changes in aspects of social behavior. *Journal of Steroid Biochemistry and Molecular Biology,* 39, 647–659.

Cox, D. (1988). Incidence and nature of male genital exposure behavior as reported by college women. *Journal of Sex Research,* 24, 227–234.

Cramer, D., Xu, H., & Harlow, B. (1995). Does "incessant" ovulation increase risk for early menopause? *American Journal Obstetrics & Gynecology,* 172, 568–573.

Creinin, M., Vittinghoff, E., Schaff, E., Klaisle, C., Darney, P., & Dean, C. (1997). Medical abortion with oral methotrexate and vaginal misoprostol. *Obstetrical and Gynecological Survey,* 90, 611–616.

Crenshaw, T. (1996). *The Alchemy of Love and Lust.* New York: Putnam.

Crenshaw, T., & Goldberg, J. (1996). *Sexual Pharmacology: Drugs That Affect Sexual Function.* New York: Norton.

Crews, D. (1994). Animal sexuality. *Scientific American,* January, 109–114.

Critelli, J., & Suire, D. (1998). Obstacles to condom use: The combination of other forms of birth control and short-term monogamy. *Journal of American College Health,* 46, 215–221.

Crohan, S. (1996). Marital quality and conflict across the transition to parenthood in African American and white couples. *Journal of Marriage and the Family,* 58, 933–944.

Cromer, B., & Harel, Z. (1997). Prescribing long-acting progestin-only contraceptives for adolescents. *Comtemporary Ob/Gyn,* March, 145–154.

Cromer, B., McClean, C., & Heald, F. (1992). A critical review of comprehensive health screening in adolescents. *Journal of Adolescent Health,* 13, 15S–65S.

Crooks, R. (1991). Incidence of rape victimization among female college students enrolled in human sexuality courses. Unpublished research.

Cunningham, G., Cordero, E., & Thornby, J. (1989). Testosterone replacement with transdermal therapeutic systems. *Journal of the American Medical Association,* 261, 2525–2531.

Curtis, K., Savitz, D., & Arbuckle, T. (1997). Effects of cigarette smoking, caffeine consumption, and alcohol intake on fecundability. *American Journal of Epidemiology,* 146, 32–41.

Curtis, R., & Miller, K. (1988). Believing another likes or dislikes you: Behavior making the beliefs come true. *Journal of Personality and Social Psychology,* 51, 284–290.

Cutler, W., Preti, G., Krieger, A., Huggins, G., Garcia, C., & Lawley, H. (1986). Human axillary secretions influence women's menstrual cycles: The role of donor extract from men. *Hormones and Behavior,* 20, 463–473.

D'Augelli, A., & Hershberger, S. (1993). Lesbian, gay, and bisexual youth in community settings: Personal challenges and mental health problems. *American Journal of Community Psychology,* 21(4), 421–447.

D'Emilio, J., & Freedman, E. (1988). *Intimate Matters.* New York: Harper & Row.

D'Epiro, P. (1997a). Complicated UTI. *Patient Care,* April 15, 196–208.

D'Epiro, P. (1997b). Breast cancer update. Progress and conflict. *Patient Care,* June, 110–142.

Dagg, P. (1991). The psychological sequelae of therapeutic abortion denied and completed. *American Journal of Psychiatry,* 148, 578–585.

Dahir, M. (1997). Heaven, hell, and heresy. *The Advocate,* July 22, 41–45.

Daly, M., Wilson, M., & Weghorst, S. (1982). Male sexual jealousy. *Ethology and Sociobiology,* 3, 11–27.

Darling, C., & Davidson, J. (1986). Enhancing relationships: Understanding the feminine mystique of pretending orgasm. *Journal of Sex and Marital Therapy,* 12, 182–196.

Darling, C., Davidson, J., & Conway-Welch, C. (1990). Female ejaculation: Perceived origins, the Grafenberg spot/area, and sexual responsiveness. *Archives of Sexual Behavior,* 19, 29–47.

Darling, C., Davidson, J., & Passarello, L. (1992). The mystique of first intercourse among college youth: The role of partners, contraceptive practices, and psychological reactions. *Journal of Youth and Adolescence,* 21, 97–117.

Darling, L. (1997). Dear Ravager, I've never done this before. *Esquire,* July, 40–101.

Daro, D. (1991). Child sexual abuse prevention: Separating fact from fiction. *Child Abuse & Neglect,* 15, 1–4.

Datey, S., Gaur, L., & Saxena, B. (1995). Vaginal bleeding patterns of women using different contraceptive methods (implants, injectables, IUDs, oral pills)—an Indian experience. *Contraception,* 51, 155–165.

Davidson, J., & Moore, N. (1994). Guilt and lack of orgasm during sexual intercourse: Myth versus reality among college women. *Journal of Sex Education & Therapy,* 20(3), 153–174.

Davidson, J., & Rosen, R. (1992). Hormonal determinants of erectile function. In R. Rosen & S. Leiblum (Eds.), *Erectile Disorders: Assessment and Treatment.* New York: Guilford.

Davidson, K., Darling, C., & Conway-Welch, C. (1989). The role of the Grafenberg spot and female ejaculation in the female orgasmic response: An empirical analysis. *Journal of Sex and Marital Therapy,* 15, 102–119.

Davies, M. (1995). Parental distress and ability to cope following disclosure of extra-familial sexual abuse. *Child Abuse & Neglect,* 19, 399–408.

Davis, B., & Noble, M. (1991). Putting an end to chronic testicular pain. *Medical Aspects of Human Sexuality,* April, 26–34.

Davis, K. (1985). Near and dear: Friendship and love compared. *Psychology Today,* February, 22–30.

Davis, K., & Latty-Mann, H. (1987). Love styles and relationship quality: A contribution to validation. *Journal of Social and Personal Relationships,* 4, 409–428.

Davison, G., & Neale, J. (1993). *Abnormal Psychology* (6th ed.). New York: Wiley.

Dawes, R. (1994). *House of Cards: Psychology and Psychotherapy Built of Myth.* New York: Free Press.

Day, M. (1997). Don't believe the AIDS cure hype. *New Scientist,* February, 4.

Day, N., & Schoenrade, P. (1997). Staying in the closet versus coming out: Relationships between communication about sexual orientation and work attitudes. *Personnel Psychology,* 50, 147–163.

Day, R. (1992). The transition to first intercourse among socially and culturally diverse youth. *Journal of Marriage and the Family,* 54, 749–762.

De Amicis, L., Goldberg, D., LoPiccolo, J., Friedman, J., & Davies, L. (1984). Three-year follow-up of couples evaluated for sexual dysfunction. *Journal of Sex and Marital Therapy,* 10, 215–228.

De Bro, S., Campbell, S., & Peplau, L. (1994). Influencing a partner to use a condom. *Psychology of Women Quarterly,* 18, 165–182.

De Bruyn, M. (1992). Women and AIDS in developing countries. *Social Sciences and Medicine,* 34, 249–262.

De Knijff, D., Vrijhof, H., Arends, J., & Janknegt, R. (1997). Persistence or reappearance of nonmotile sperm after vasectomy: Does it have clinical consequences? *Fertility and Sterility,* 67, 332–335.

De Villers, L. (1996). *Love Skills.* San Luis Obispo, CA: Impact Publishers.

de Zalduardo, B. (1991). Prostitution viewed cross-culturally: Toward recontextualizing sex work in AIDS intervention research. *Journal of Sex Research,* 28, 223–248.

Dean, K., & Malamuth, N. (1997). Characteristics of men who aggress sexually and men who imagine aggressing: Risk and moderating variables. *Journal of Personality and Social Psychology,* 72, 449–455.

Dean, M., Carrington, M., & Winkler, C. (1996). Genetic restriction of HIV-1 infection and progression to AIDS by a deletion allele of the CKR5 structural gene. *Science,* 273, 1856–1862.

DeCaro, F. (1997). Finally out, and suddenly in. *Newsweek,* May 12, 83.

Deckers, P., & Ricci, A., Jr. (1992). Pain and lumps in the female breast. *Hospital Practice,* February 28, 67–94.

Deeks, S. (1997). Paper presented at the 37th Interscience Conference on Antimicrobial Agents and Chemotherapy, Toronto, September 29.

Deeks, S., Smith, M., Holodniy, M., & Kahn, J. (1997). HIV-1 protease inhibitors. *Journal of the American Medical Association,* 277, 145–153.

DeGarmo, D., & Kitson, G. (1996). Identity relevance and disruption as predictors of psychological distress for widowed and divorced women. *Journal of Marriage and the Family,* 58, 983–997.

Degler, C. (1980). *At Odds: Women and the Family in America from the Revolution to the Present.* Oxford: Oxford University Press.

Deguchi, T., Saito, I., Tanaka, M., Sato, K., Deguchi, K., Yasuda, M., Nakano, M., Nishino, Y., Kanematsu, E., Ozek, S., & Kawada, Y. (1997). Fluoroquinolone treatment failure in gonorrhea. *Sexually Transmitted Diseases,* 24, 247–250.

Deitch, C. (1983). Ideology and opposition to abortion: Trends in public opinion, 1972–1980. *Alternative Lifestyles,* 6, 6–26.

Dekker, J., Everaerd, W., & Verhelst, N. (1985). Attending to stimuli or to images of sexual feelings: Effects on sexual arousal. *Behavior Research and Therapy,* 23, 139–149.

Del Carmen, R. (1990). Assessment of Asian-Americans for family therapy. In F. Serafica, A. Schwebel, R. Russell, P. Isaac, & L. Myers (Eds.), *Mental Health of Ethnic Minorities.* New York: Praeger.

Delaney, J., Lupton, M., & Toth, E. (1976). *The Curse, A Cultural History of Menstruation.* New York: Dutton.

Delson, N., & Clark, M. (1981). Group therapy with sexually molested children. *Child Welfare,* 50, 161–174.

Démare, D., Briere, J., & Lips, H. (1988). Violent pornography and self-reported likelihood of sexual aggression. *Journal of Research in Personality,* 22, 140–153.

DeMartino, M. (1970). How women want men to make love. *Sexology,* October, 4–7.

Dempsey, C. (1994). Health and social issues of gay, lesbian, and bisexual adolescents. *Families in Society: The Journal of Contemporary Human Services,* March, 160–167.

Dennerstein, L., Burrows, G., Wood, C., & Hyman, G. (1980). Hormones and sexuality: The effects of estrogen and progestogen. *Obstetrics & Gynecology,* 56, 316–322.

Dennerstein, L., Gotts, G., Brown, J., Morse, C. Farley, T., & Pinol, A. (1994). The relationship between the menstrual cycle and female sexual interest in women with PMS complaints and volunteers. *Psychoneuroendochrinology,* 19, 293–304.

Denny, N., Field, J., & Quadagno, D. (1984). Sex differences in sexual needs and desires. *Archives of Sexual Behavior,* 13, 233–245.

Derlego, V., Metts, S., Petronia, S., & Margulis, S. (1993). *Self-Disclosure.* Newbury Park, CA: Sage.

Desiderato, L., & Crawford, H. (1995). Risky sexual behavior in college students: Relationships between number of sexual partners, disclosure of previous risk behavior, and alcohol use. *Journal of Youth and Adolescence,* 24, 55–68.

Deutchman, M., Leaman, D., & Thomason, J. (1994). Vaginitis: Diagnosis is the key. *Patient Care,* 28, 39–57.

Developments in contraceptive methods for men (1996). *Contemporary Sexuality*, 30(12), 1–2.

Devi, K. (1977). *The Eastern Way of Love: Tantric Sex and Erotic Mysticism.* New York: Simon & Schuster.

Devine, C., Jr. (1997). Peyronie's disease. *Journal of Urology*, 157, 272–275.

Devisto, P., Kaufman, A., Rosner, L., Jackson, R., Christy, J., Pearson, S., & Burgett, T. (1984). The prevalence of sexually stressful events among females in the general population. *Archives of Sexual Behavior*, 13, 59–67.

Dew, M. (1985). The effect of attitudes on inferences of homosexuality and perceived physical attractiveness in women. *Sex Roles,* 12, 143–155.

Dey, E., Sax, L., & Korn, J. (1994). Betrayal by the academy: The sexual harassment of women college faculty. Paper presented at the annual meeting of the American Educational Research Association, New Orleans, April 8.

Diamond, M. (1991). Hormonal effects on the development of cerebral lateralization. *Psychoneuroendocrinology,* 16, 121–29.

Diamond, M., & Sigmundson, H. (1997). Sex reassignment at birth: Long-term review and clinical implications. *Archives of Pediatric and Adolescent Medicine*, 151, 298–304.

Dickinson, R. (1949). *Atlas of Human Sex Anatomy.* Baltimore: Williams & Wilkins.

Dion, K. L., & Dion, K. K. (1987). Belief in a just world and physical attractiveness stereotyping. *Journal of Personality and Social Psychology,* 52, 775–780.

Dipierri, D. (1994). RU 486, Mifepristone: A review of a controversial drug. *Nurse Practitioner,* June, 59–61.

Djerassi, C., & Leibo S. (1994). A new look at male contraception. *Nature,* 370, 11–12.

Dobosz, A. (1997). Thicker thighs by Thanksgiving. *Ms.*, November/December, 89–91.

Dobosz, A., Mitchell, K., Papazian, E., Sepah, T., & Smith, S. (1997a). Abortion laws. *Ms.*, September/October, 25.

Dobosz, A., Mitchell, K., Papazian, E., Sepah, T., & Smith, S. (1997b). Politics. *Ms.*, September/October, 27.

Dodson, B. (1974). *Liberating Masturbation.* New York: Betty Dodson.

Donnelly, S. (1997). The postpartum prosecutor. *Time*, December 15, 4.

Donnerstein, E., & Linz, D. (1984). Sexual violence in the media: A warning. *Psychology Today,* January, 14–15.

Donnerstein, E., & Linz, D. (1986). The question of pornography. *Psychology Today.* December, 56–59.

Donnerstein, E., Linz, D., & Penrod, S. (1987). *The Question of Pornography.* New York: Free Press.

Donovan, P. (1997). Can statutory rape laws be effective in preventing adolescent pregnancy? *Family Planning Perspectives*, 29, 30–35.

Dotinga, R. (1998). Holy matrimony. *The Advocate*, April 14, 56–57.

Douglass, F., & Douglass, R. (1993). The validity of the Myers-Briggs Type Indicator for predicting expressed marital problems. *Family Relations,* 42, 422–426.

Dow, M., Hart, D., & Forrest, C. (1983). Hormonal treatments of unresponsiveness in post-menopausal women: A comparative study. *British Journal of Obstetrics and Gynecology,* 90, 361–366.

Dowd, M. (1997). We must correct the eros of our ways. *The Oregonian*, June 22, D3.

Doyle, J. (1991). *The Male Experience* (2nd ed.). Dubuque, IA: Brown and Benchmark.

Doyle, J., & Paludi, M. (1991). *Sex and Gender* (2nd ed.). Dubuque, IA: Brown and Benchmark.

Dranov, P. (1995). Making sense of scents. *Cosmopolitan*, August, 204–207.

Drew, W., Blair, M., Minor, R., & Conant, M. (1990). Evaluation of the virus permeability of a new condom for women. *Sexually Transmitted Diseases,* 17, 110–112.

Druzin, P., Shrier, I., Yacowar, M., & Rossignol, M. (1998). Discrimination against gay, lesbian and bisexual family physicians by patients. *Canadian Medical Association Journal*, 158(5), 593–597.

Dubovsky, S. (1991). When sexual dysfunction masks anxiety and depression. *Medical Aspects of Human Sexuality,* October, 22–30.

Duckworth, J., & Levitt, E. (1985). Personality analysis of a swingers' club. *Lifestyles: A Journal of Changing Patterns,* 8, 35–45.

Duda, R. (1995). Risk factors for the development of breast cancer. *Comprehensive Therapy,* 21, 29–34.

Duddle, M., (1991). Emotional sequelae of sexual assault. *Journal of the Royal Society of Medicine,* 84, 26–28.

Duggan, L., Hunter, N., & Vance, C. (1985). False promises: New antipornography legislation in the U.S. *SIECUS Report,* 13, 1–5.

Dunn, J., Bretherton, I., & Munn, P. (1987). Conversations about feeling states between mothers and their children. *Developmental Psychology*, 23, 132–139.

Dunn, M., & Trost, J. (1989). Male multiple orgasms: A descriptive study. *Archives of Sexual Behavior*, 18, 377–388.

Dunsmuir, W., & Emberton, M. (1997). Surgery, drugs, and the male orgasm. *British Medical Journal*, 314, 319–320.

Durden-Smith, J., & Ashmore, R. (1995). Gender is determined biologically. In D. Bender & B. Leone (Eds.), *Human Sexuality: Opposing Viewpoints.* San Diego, CA: Greenhaven Press.

Durden-Smith, J., & deSimone, D. (1995). Gender is determined biologically. In D. Bender & B. Leone (Eds.), *Human Sexuality: Opposing Viewpoints.* San Diego, CA: Greenhaven Press.

Dwyer, M. (1988). Exhibitionism/voyeurism. *Journal of Social Work and Human Sexuality,* 7, 101–112.

Earl, D., & David, D. (1994). Depo-Provera: An injectable contraceptive. *American Family Physician,* 49(4), 891–894.

Easmon, C., Hay, P., & Ison, C. (1992). Bacterial vaginosis: A diagnostic approach. *Genitourinary Medicine,* 68, 134–138.

Easterday, C., Grimes, D., & Riggs, J. (1983). Hysterectomy in the United States. *Obstetrics and Gynecology,* 62, 203–212.

Ebong, R. (1997). Female circumcision and its health implications: A study of the Uruan local government area of Akwa Ibom State, Nigeria. *Journal of the Royal Society of Health*, 117(2), 95–99.

Eccles, A., Marshall, W., & Barbaree, H. (1994). Differentiating rapists and non-rapists using the rape index. *Behaviour Research and Therapy,* 32, 539–546.

Eccles, J., & Midgley, C. (1990). Changes in academic motivation and self-perception during adolescence. In R. Montemayor, G. Adams, & T. Gullotta (Eds.), *From Childhood to Adolescence: A Transitional Period?* Newbury Park, CA: Sage.

Edgerton, M. (1984). The role of surgery in the treatment of transsexualism. *Annals of Plastic Surgery,* 13, 473–476.

Edwards, W. (1996). Operating within the mainstream: Coping and adjustment among a sample of homosexual youths. *Deviant Behavior: An Interdisciplinary Journal*, 17, 229–251.

Eggert, A., & Muller, J. (1989). Mating success of pheromone-emitting necrophorus males: Do attracted females discriminate against resource owners? *Behaviour,* 110, 248–257.

Ehrenreich, B. (1998). Where have all the babies gone? *Life*, January, 69–76.

Eicher, E. (1994). Sex and trinucleotide repeats. *Nature Genetics*, 6, 221–223.

Eisenberg, V., & Schenker, J. (1997). Pregnancy in the older woman: Scientific and ethical aspects. *International Journal of Gynecology & Obstetrics*, 56, 163–169.

Eisenman, R. (1994). Conservative sexual values: Effects of an abstinence program on student attitudes. *Journal of Sex Education and Therapy*, 20(12), 75–78.

Eisner, T., Conner, J., & Carrel, J. (1990). Systemic retention of ingested cantharidin by frogs. *Chemoecology*, 1, 57–62.

Eitzen, D., & Zinn, M. (1994). *Social Problems* (6th ed.). Boston: Allyn and Bacon.

El Hadi, A. (1997). A step forward for opponents of female genital mutilation in Egypt. *The Lancet*, 349, 129–130.

Elder, J. (1988). The undescended testis: Hormonal and surgical management. *Surgery Clinics of North America*, 68, 983–1005.

Elias, J., & Gebhard, P. (1969). Sexuality and sexual learning in childhood. *Phi Delta Kappan*, 50, 401–405.

Eliason, M., & Morgan, K. (1998). Lesbians define themselves: Diversity in lesbian identification. *Journal of Gay, Lesbian, and Bisexual Identity*, 3(1), 47–63.

Eliasson, R., & Lindholmer, C. (1976). Functions of male accessory genital organs. In E. Hafez (Ed.), *Human Semen and Fertility Regulations in Men*. St. Louis: Mosby.

Elkind, D. (1967). Egocentrism in adolescence. *Child Development*, 38, 1025–1034.

Elliott, L., & Brantley, C. (1997). *Sex on Campus*. New York: Random House.

Elliott, M. (1992). Tip of the iceberg? *Social Work Today*, March, 12–13.

Ellis, L., Burke, D., & Ames, M. (1987). Sexual orientation as a continuous variable: A comparison between the sexes. *Archives of Sexual Behavior*, 16, 523.

Emery, R., & Tuer, M. (1993). Parenting and the marital relationship. In T. Luster & L. Okagaki (Eds.), *Parenting: An Ecological Perspective*. Hillsdale, NJ: Erlbaum.

Epp, S. (1997). The diagnosis and treatment of athletic amenorrhea. *Physician Assistant*, March, 129–144.

Epstein, A. (1997a). Foreword. In L. B. Brown (Ed.), *Two Spirit People*. New York: Harrington Park Press.

Epstein, A. (1997b). Rights activists worry as courts give fetuses protection. *The Oregonian*, August 4, B6.

Epstein, A. (1997c). Justices will rule on issue of same-sex harassment. *The Oregonian*, June 10, A1.

Equal Employment Opportunities Commission (1980). Guidelines on discrimination because of sex. *Federal Register*, 45, 74676–74677.

Erdley, I. (1998). New oral therapies for the treatment of erectile dysfunction. *British Journal of Urology*, 81, 122–127.

Erikson, E. (1965). Youth and the life cycle. In D. Hamachek (Ed.), *The Self in Growth, Teaching and Learning*. Englewood Cliffs, NJ: Prentice Hall.

Erlich, K. (1997). Management of herpes simplex and varicella-zoster virus infections. *Western Journal of Medicine*, 166, 211–215.

Ernst, E., & Pittler, M. (1998). Yohimbine for erectile dysfunction: A systematic review and meta-analysis of randomized clinical trials. *Journal of Urology*, 159, 433–436.

Ernst, F., et al. (1991). Condemnation of homosexuality in the black community: A gender-specific phenomenon? *Archives of Sexual Behavior*, 20, 579–585.

Eskeland, B., Thom, E., & Svendsen, K. (1997). Sexual desire in men: Effects of oral ingestion of a product derived from fertilized eggs. *Journal of International Medical Research*, 25, 62–70.

Espin, O. (1987). Issues of identity in the psychology of Latina lesbians. In Boston Lesbian Psychologies Collective, *Lesbian Psychologies*. Urbana: University of Illinois Press.

Espin, O. (1992). Cultural and historical influences on sexuality in Hispanic/Latin women. In M. Andersen & P. Collins (Eds.), *Race, Class, and Gender*. Belmont, CA: Wadsworth.

Essoyan, S. (1997). Hawaii law adds rights for couples. *The Oregonian*, April 30.

Esterberg, K. (1990). From illness to action: Conceptions of homosexuality in *The Ladder, 1956–1965*. *Journal of Sex Research*, 27, 65–80.

Ethics Committee of the American Society for Reproductive Medicine (1997). *Ethical Considerations of Assisted Reproductive Medicine*, 67(5), 15–95.

Etzioni, A. (1997). Marriage with no easy outs. *The New York Times*, August 13.

Everitt, B. (1990). Sexual motivation: A neural and behavioural analysis of the mechanisms underlying appetive and copulatory responses of male rats. *Neuroscience and Biobehavioral Reviews*, 14, 217–232.

Everitt, B., & Bancroft, J. (1991). Of rats and men: The comparative approach to male sexuality. *Annual Review of Sex Research*, 2, 77–118.

Eyler, F., Behnke, M., Conlon, M., Woods, N., & Wobie, K. (1998). Birth outcome from a prospective, matched study of prenatal crack cocaine use: I. Interactive and dose effects on health and growth. *Pediatrics*, 101(2), 229–237.

Faderman, L. (1997). Last word. It's not just a movie. *The Advocate*, July 22, 72.

Faerman, M., Kahila, G., & Smith, P. (1997). DNA analysis reveals the sex of infanticide victims. *Nature*, 385, 212.

Fair, W., Fuks, Z., & Scher, H. (1993). Cancer of the urethra and penis. In V. DeVita, S. Hellman, & S. Rosenberg (Eds.), *Cancer: Principles and Practice of Oncology*, Vol. 1 (4th ed.). Philadelphia: Lippincott.

Faison, S. (1997). One-child limitation eases in China. *The Oregonian*, August 17, A8.

Falk, G., & Falk, U. (1980). Sexuality and the aged. *Nursing Outlook*, 28, 51–55.

Fallon, B., Miller, R., & Gerber, W. (1981). Nonmicroscopic vasovasostomy. *Journal of Urology*, 126, 361.

Famighetti, R. (Ed.) (1995). *The World Almanac and Book of Facts 1995*. New York: St. Martin's Press.

Farber, N. (1992). Sexual standards and activity: Adolescents' perceptions. *Child and Adolescent Social Work*, 9, 53–76.

Farley, T. (1997). Approaches to screening and antibiotic use for syphilis prevention. *Sexually Transmitted Diseases*, 24, 227–228.

Fausto-Sterling, A. (1985). *Myths of Gender: Biological Theories About Women and Men*. New York: Basic Books.

Faux, M. (1984). *Childless by Choice*. New York: Anchor.

Faxelid, E., & Ramstedt, K. (1997). Partner notification in context: Swedish and Zambian experiences. *Social Science and Medicine*, 44, 1239–1243.

Fedora, O., Reddon, J., Morrison, J., & Fedora, S. (1992). Sadism and other paraphilias in normal controls and aggressive and nonagressive sex offenders. *Archives of Sexual Behavior*, 21, 1–15.

Feingold, A. (1992). Good-looking people are not what we think. *Psychological Bulletin,* 111, 304–341.

Feinleib, J., & Michael, R. (1995). Paper presented at the Annual Meeting of the American Association for the Advancement of Science, Atlanta, February 17.

Feldblum, P., Morrison, C., & Cates, W. (1995). The effectiveness of barrier methods of contraception in preventing the spread of HIV. *AIDS,* 9, 585–593.

Feldman, H., Goldstein, I. Hatzichristou, D., Krane, R., & McKinlay, J. (1994). Impotence and its medical and psychosocial correlates: Results of the Massachusetts male aging study. *Journal of Urology,* 151, 54–61.

Felitti, V. (1991). Long-term medical consequences of incest, rape, and molestation. *Southern Medical Journal,* 84, 328–331.

Felsman, D., Brannigan, G., & Yellin, P. (1987). Control theory in dealing with adolescent sexuality and pregnancy. *Journal of Sex Education and Therapy,* 13, 15–16.

Fergusson, D., Lawton, J., & Shannon, F. (1988). Neonatal circumcision and penile problems: An 8-year longitudinal study. *Pediatrics,* 81, 537–540.

Ferris, D., Litaker, M., & Dekle, C. (1996). Women's use of over-the-counter antifungal medications for gynecologic symptoms. *Journal of Family Practice,* 42, 595–600.

Festinger, L., Schachter, S., & Black, K. (1950). *Social Pressures in Informal Groups: A Study of Human Factors in Housing.* New York: Harper & Row.

Fielo, S., & Warren, S. (1997). Sexual expression in a very old man: A nursing approach to care. *Geriatric Nursing,* 18, 61–64.

Fihn, S., Boyko, E., Chen, C., Normand, E., Yarbro, P., & Scholes, D. (1998). Use of spermicide-coated condoms and other risk factors for urinary tract infection caused by *Staphylococcus saprophyticus. Archives of Internal Medicine,* 158, 281–287.

Filips, J. (1995). Hex on hepatitis. *The Oregonian,* April 13, C9 & C10.

Findlay, J., Place, V., & Snyder, P. (1989). Treatment of primary hypogonadism in men by the transdermal administration of testosterone. *Journal of Clinical Endocrinology and Metabolism,* 68, 369–373.

Fineman, H. (1993). Marching to the mainstream. *Newsweek,* May 3, 42–45.

Finger, W., Lund, M., & Slagle, M. (1997). Medications that may contribute to sexual disorders. *Journal of Family Practice,* 44, 33–43.

Finkelhor, D. (1979). *Sexually Victimized Children.* New York: Free Press.

Finkelhor, D. (1980). Sex among siblings: A survey on prevalence, variety, and effects. *Archives of Sexual Behavior,* 9, 171–194.

Finkelhor, D. (1984a). *Child Sexual Abuse: Theory and Research.* New York: Free Press.

Finkelhor, D. (1984b). The prevention of child sexual abuse: An overview of needs and problems. *SIECUS Report,* 13, 1–5.

Finkelhor, D. (1993). Epidemiological factors in the clinical identification of child sexual abuse. *Child Abuse and Neglect,* 17, 67–70.

Finkelhor, D. (1994). The international epidemiology of child sexual abuse. *Child Abuse and Neglect,* 18, 409–417.

Finkelhor, D., Hotaling, G., Lewis, I., & Smith, C. (1990). Sexual abuse in a national sample of adult men and women: Prevalence, characteristics, and risk factors. *Child Abuse and Neglect,* 14, 19–28.

Fiore, J., Zhang, Y., Bjorndal, A., Di Stefano, M., Angarano, G., Pastore, G., & Fenyo, E. (1997). Biological correlates of HIV-1 heterosexual transmission. *AIDS,* 11, 1089–1094.

Fiorica, J., Schorr, S., & Sickles, E. (1998). Benign breast disorders: First rule out cancer. *Contemporary Ob/Gyn,* A3, 154–172.

Firestone, W. (1994). The content and context of sexuality education: An exploratory study in one state. *Family Planning Perspectives,* 26, 125–131.

Fischhoff, B. (1992). Giving advice: Decision theory perspectives on sexual assault. *American Psychologist,* 47, 577–588.

Fish, L., Fish, R., & Sprenkle, D. (1984). Treating inhibited sexual desire: A marital therapy approach. *American Journal of Family Therapy,* 12, 3–12.

Fisher, H. (1992). *Anatomy of Love: The Natural History of Monogamy, Adultery, and Divorce.* New York: Norton.

Fisher, R., Cook, I., & Shirkey, E. (1994). Correlates of support for censorship of sexual, sexually violent, and violent media. *Journal of Sex Research,* 31, 229–240.

Fisher, T. (1987). Family communication and the sexual behavior and attitudes of college students. *Journal of Youth and Adolescence,* 16, 481–495.

Fisher, W. (1983). Gender, gender role identification, and response to erotica. In E. Allgeier & N. McCormick (Eds.), *Changing Boundaries: Gender Roles and Sexual Behavior.* Mountain View, CA: Mayfield.

Fisher, W., Branscombe, N., & Lemery, C. (1983). The bigger the better? Arousal and attributional responses to erotic stimuli that depict different size penises. *Journal of Sex Research,* 19, 377–396.

Fisher, W., & Gray, J. (1988). Erotophobia erotophilia and sexual behavior during pregnancy and postpartum. *Journal of Sex Research,* 25, 379–396.

Fisher-Thompson, D. (1990). Adult sex typing of children's toys. *Sex Roles,* 23, 291–303.

Flanders, L. (1998). Rwanda's living casualties. *Ms.,* March/April, 27–30.

Fleming, C., Wasson, J., Albertsen, P., Barry, M., & Wennberg, J. (1993). A decision analysis of alternative treatment strategies for clinically localized prostate cancer. *Journal of the American Medical Association,* 269(20), 2650–2658.

Fleming, D., McQuillan, G., Johnson, R., Nahmias, A., Aral, S., Lee, F., & St. Louis, M. (1997). Herpes simplex virus type 2 in the United States, 1976 to 1994. *New England Journal of Medicine,* 337, 1105–1111.

Foa, U., Anderson, B., Converse, J., & Urbanski, W. (1987). Gender-related sexual attitudes: Some cross-cultural similarities and differences. *Sex Roles,* 16, 511–519.

Foley, D. (1998). Sodomy laws and you. *The Advocate,* March 17, 9.

Foley, D., & Nechas, L. (1995). *Before You Hit the Pillow, Talk.*

Follingstad, D., & Kimbrell, D. (1986). Sex fantasies revisited: An expansion and further clarification of variables affecting sex fantasy production. *Archives of Sexual Behavior,* 15, 475–486.

Fong, R., Spickard, P., & Ewalt, P. (1995). A multiracial reality: Issues for social work. *Journal of the National Association of Social Workers,* 40(6), 725–728.

Fontaine, K., & Seal, A. (1997). Optimism, social support, and premenstrual dysphoria. *Journal of Clinical Psychology,* 53(3), 243–247.

Fontana, A., & Badawy, S. (1997). Perceptual and coping processes across the menstrual cycle: An investigation in a premenstrual syndrome clinic and a community sample. *Behavioral Medicine,* 22, 152–159.

Foote, D. (1998). And baby makes one. *Newsweek,* February 2, 68, 70.

Forbes, G. (1992). Body size and composition of perimenarchal girls. *American Journal of Diseases in Children,* 146, 63–66.

Forbes, P. (1998). Diagnosis and treatment of chronic pelvic pain. *The Practitioner,* 242, 120–125.

Ford, C., & Beach, F. (1951). *Patterns of Sexual Behavior.* New York: Harper & Row.

Foreman, K., Friborg, J., Kong, W., Woffendin, C., Polverini, P., Nickoloff, B., & Nabel, G. (1997). Propagation of a human herpesvirus from AIDS-associated Kaposi's cancer. *New England Journal of Medicine*, 336, 163–171.

Forrest, B. (1991). Women, HIV, and mucosal immunity. *The Lancet*, 337, 835–837.

Forrest, J., & Singh, S. (1990). The sexual and reproductive behavior of American women, 1982–1988. *Family Planning Perspectives*, 22, 206–214.

Forsyth, C. (1996). The structuring of vicarious sex. *Deviant Behavior: An Interdisciplinary Journal*, 17, 279–295.

Forward, S., & Buck, C. (1992). *Obsessive Love: When It Hurts Too Much to Let Go*. New York: Bantam Books.

Foster, M. (1992). Aberrant puberty. *Obstetrics and Gynecology Clinics of North America*, 19, 59–70.

Fowke, K., Nagelkerke, N., Kiman, J., Simonsen, J., Anzala, A., Bwayo, J., MacDonald, K., Nguigi, E., & Plummer, F. (1996). Resistance to HIV-1 infection among persistently seronegative prostitutes in Nairobi, Kenya. *The Lancet*, 348, 1347–1351.

Fox, B., & Joyce, C. (1991). Americans compete for control over sex. *New Scientist*, January 12, 23.

Fox, M. (1994). Vasectomy reversal—Microsurgery for best results. *British Journal of Urology*, 73, 449–53.

Fox, R. (1990). Bisexuality and sexual orientation self-disclosure. Paper presented at The Society for the Scientific Study of Sex Annual Western Region Conference, San Diego, April 25.

Francis, M. (1997). Intimate Internet. *The Oregonian*, October 12, L1, L8.

Frank, A., Wandell, M., Headings, M., Conant, M., Woody, G., & Michel, C. (1997). Anonymous HIV testing using home collection and telemedicine counseling. *Archives of Internal Medicine*, 157, 309–314.

Frank, M., et al. (1993). One year experience with subdermal contraceptive implants in the United States. *Contraception*, 48, 229–243.

Frank, P., et al. (1993). The effect of induced abortion on subsequent fertility. *British Journal of Obstetrics and Gynecology*, 100, 575–580.

Frayser, S. (1985). *Varieties of Sexual Experience: An Anthropological Perspective on Human Sexuality.* New Haven, CT: Human Relations Area Files Press.

Frayser, S. (1994). Defining normal childhood sexuality: An anthropological approach. *Annual Review of Sex Research*, 5, 173–217.

Frazier, P. (1993). A comparative study of male and female victims seen at hospital-based rape crises programs. *Journal of Interpersonal Violence*, 8, 65–79.

Freda, M. (1994). Childbearing, reproductive control, aging women, and health care: The projected ethical debates. *Journal of Obstetrical, Gynecological and Neonatal Nurses*, 23, 144–151.

Freedman, L. (1997). Hot chat. *Networker*, May/June, 69–71.

Freeman, E., Rickels, K., Huggins, G., Celso-Ramon, G., & Polin, G. (1980). Emotional distress patterns among women having first or repeat abortions. *Obstetrics & Gynecology*, 55, 630–636.

Frenkel, L., Cowles, M., Shapiro, D., Melvin, A., Watts, D., McLellan, C., Mohan, K., Murante, B., Burchett, S., Bryson, Y., O'Sullivan, M., Mitchell, C., & Landers, D. (1997). Analysis of the maternal components of the AIDS clinical trial group 076 zidovudine regimen in the prevention of mother-to-infant transmission of human immunodeficiency virus type 1. *Journal of Infectious Diseases*, 175, 971–974.

Freund, K., & Blanchard, R. (1993). Erotic target location errors in male gender dysphorics, paedophiles, and fetishists. *British Journal of Psychiatry*, 162, 558–563.

Freund, K., Watson, R., & Rienzo, D. (1988). The value of self-reports in the study of voyeurism and exhibitionism. *Annals of Sex Research*, 1, 243–262.

Freund, M., Lee, N., & Leonard, T. (1991). Sexual behavior of clients with street prostitutes in Camden, N.J. *Journal of Sex Research*, 28, 579–591.

Friday, N. (1980). *Men in Love.* New York: Delacorte.

Friedan, B. (1994). *The Fountain of Age.* New York: Simon & Schuster.

Friedman, R., Hurt, S., Arnoff, M., & Clarkin, J. (1980). Behavior and the menstrual cycle. *Signs*, 5, 719–738.

Friedman, S. (1994). *Secret Lives: Women With Two Lives.* New York: Crown.

Friedrich, W., Grambsch, P., Broughton, D., Kuiper, J., & Beilke, R. (1991). Normative sexual behavior in children. *Pediatrics*, 88, 456–464.

Friess, S. (1998). A place where no one knows your name. *The Advocate*, February 3, 24–31.

Friis, S., Kjaer, S., Frisch, M., Mellemkjaer, L., & Olsen, J. (1997). Cervical intraepithelial neoplasia, anogenital cancer, and other cancer types in women after hospitalization for condylomata acuminata. *Journal of Infectious Diseases*, 175, 743–748.

Frisch, R. (1988). Fatness and fertility. *Scientific American*, March, 88–95.

Frisch, R., & McArthur, J. (1974). Menstrual cycles: Fatness as a determinant of minimum weight for height necessary for their maintenance or onset. *Science*, 185, 949–951.

Frizzell, J. (1998). The PSA test. *American Journal of Nursing*, 98, 14–15.

Fromm, E. (1965). *The Ability to Love.* New York: Farrar, Straus & Giroux.

Fry, R., Crisp, A., & Beard, R. (1997). Sociopsychological factors in chronic pelvic pain: A review. *Journal of Psychosomatic Research*, 42, 1–15.

Fullerton, D. (1997). A review of approaches to teenage pregnancy. *Nursing Times*, 93, 48–49.

Furberg, H., Newman, B., Moorman, P., & Millikan, R. (1997). Lactation and breast cancer risk. Abstract of the 30th Annual Meeting of Society for Epidemiologic Research, Edmonton, Alberta, Canada, 297.

Furby, L., & Fischhoff, B. (1992). Rape self-defense strategies: A review of their effectiveness. *Victimology.*

Furniss, T. (1985). Conflict-avoiding and conflict-regulating patterns in incest and child sexual abuse. *Acta Paedopsychiatrica*, 50, 299–313.

Furuhjelm, M., Karlgren, E., & Carstrom, K. (1984). The effect of estrogen therapy on somatic and psychical symptoms in postmenopausal women. *Acta Obstetricia et Gynecologica Scandinavica*, 63, 655–661.

Gaffney, G., Luries, S., & Berlin, F. (1984). Is there familiar transmission of pedophilia? *Journal of Nervous and Mental Disease*, 172, 546–548.

Gagnon, J. (1977). *Human Sexualities.* Glenview, IL: Scott, Foresman.

Gagnon, J., & Simon, W. (1987). The sexual scripting of oral genital contacts. *Archives of Sexual Behavior*, 16, 1–25.

Gallagher, J. (1994). Is God gay? *The Advocate*, December 13, 40–46.

Gallagher, J. (1997a). Blacks and gays: The unexpected divide. *The Advocate*, December 9, 37–41.

Gallagher, J. (1997b). Marriage compromised. *The Advocate*, May 27, 71.

Gallagher, J. (1997c). Special report. *The Advocate*, September 30, 20–25.

Gallagher, J., & Moss, J. (1997). Penalty phase. *The Advocate*, June 24, 78–83.

Gallo, D., George, J., Fitchen, J., Goldstein, A., & Hindahl, M. (1997). Evolution of a system using oral mucosal transudate for HIV-1 antibody screening and confirmatory testing. *Journal of the American Medical Association*, 277, 254–258.

Galvin, P. (1997). All about in & out. *The Advocate*, September 16, 28–30.

Gambert, S. (1997). The crucial prostate exam. *Emergency Medicine*, January, 45–52.

Ganong, L., & Coleman, M. (1987). Sex, sex roles, and family love. *Journal of Genetic Psychology*, 148, 45–52.

Ganong, L., & Coleman, M. (1989). Preparing for remarriage: Anticipating the issues, seeking solutions. *Family Relations*, 38, 28–33.

Garber, B. (1997). Outpatient inflatable penile prosthesis insertion. *Urology*, 49(4), 600–603.

Garcia, A. (1996). Foreword. In J. Longres (Ed.), *Men of Color*. New York: Harrington Park Press.

Garcia, L. (1982). Sex-role orientation and stereotypes about male female sexuality. *Sex Roles*, 8, 863–876.

Gardner, J. (1992). Descriptive study of genital variation in healthy, nonabused premenarchal girls. *Journal Pediatrics*, 120, 251–257.

Garnefski, N., & Diekstra, R. (1997). Child sexual abuse and emotional and behavioral problems in adolescence: Gender differences. *Journal of the Academy of Child and Adolescent Psychiatry*, 36, 323–329.

Garner, C. (1997). Endometriosis: What you need to know. *RN*, January, 27–31.

Garnick, M. (1994). The dilemmas of prostate cancer. *Scientific American*, April, 73–81.

Garza-Leal, J., & Landron, F. (1991). Autoerotic asphyxial death initially misinterpreted as suicide and review of the literature. *Journal of Forensic Science*, 36, 1753–1759.

Gavzer, B. (1987). Why more older women are marrying younger men. *Parade*, May 24, 12–13.

Gaylin, N. (1991). An intergenerational perspective of marriage: Love and trust in cultural context. *Marriage and Family Review*, 16, 143–159.

Gburek, B., Kollmorgen, T., Qian, J. D'Souza-Gburek, S., Lieber, M., & Jenkins, R. (1997). Chromosomal anomalies in stage D1 prostate adenocarcinoma primary tumors and lymph node metastases detected by fluorescence in situ hybridization. *Journal of Urology*, 157, 223–227.

Geary, D. (1989). A model for representing gender differences in the pattern of cognitive abilities. *American Psychologist*, 44, 1155–1156.

Geasler, M., Dannison, L., & Edlund, C. (1995). Sexuality education of young children: Parental concerns. *Family Relations*, 44, 184–188.

Gebhard, P. (1965). Situational factors affecting human sexual behavior. In F. Beach (Ed.), *Sex and Behavior*. New York: Wiley.

Gebhard, P. (1966). Factors in marital orgasm. *Journal of Social Issues*, 22, 88–95.

Gebhard, P. (1971). Human sexual behavior: A summary statement. In D. Marshall & R. Suggs (Eds.), *Human Sexual Behavior: Variations in the Ethnographic Spectrum*. Englewood Cliffs, NJ: Prentice Hall.

Gebhard, P. (1977). The acquisition of basic sex information. *Journal of Sex Research*, 13, 148–169.

Geller, A. (1991). Sexual problems of the recovering alcoholic. *Medical Aspects of Human Sexuality*, March, 56–59.

Gelman, D., et al. (1993). Tune in, come out. *Newsweek*, November 8, 70–71.

Gendel, E., & Bonner, E. (1988). Gender identity disorders and paraphilias. In H. Goldman (Ed.), *Review of General Psychiatry*. Norwalk, CT: Appleton & Lange.

Genevie, L., & Margolies, E. (1987). *The Motherhood Report: How Women Feel About Being Mothers*. New York: Macmillan.

Genuis, S., & Genuis, S. (1995). Adolescent sexual involvement: Time for primary prevention. *The Lancet*, 345, 240–241.

Gerdes, C. (1997). Psychophysiologic and laboratory testing. In M. Sipski & C. Alexander (Eds.), *Sexual Function in People with Disability and Chronic Illness*. Gaithersburg, MD: Aspen Publishers.

Gerrard, M. (1987). Sex, sex guilt, and contraceptive use revisited: The 1980s. *Journal of Personality and Social Psychology*, 52, 975–980.

Geschwind, N., & Behan, P. (1984). Laterality, hormones, and immunity. In N. Geschwind & A. Galaburda (Eds.), *Cerebral Dominance: The Biological Foundations*. Cambridge, MA: Harvard University Press.

Ghalwash, M. (1997). Egyptian court upholds female circumcision ban. *The Oregonian*, December 29, A5.

Gibbons, M., & Vincent, C. (1994). Childhood sexual abuse. *American Family Physician*, 49, 125–137.

Gibbs, E. (1989). Psychosocial development of children raised by lesbian mothers: A review of research. *Women and Therapy*, 8, 65–75.

Gideonse, T. (1997a). Are we an endangered species? *The Advocate*, May 27, 28–30.

Gideonse, T. (1997b). The sexual blur. *The Advocate*, June 24, 28–43.

Gideonse, T. (1998). Hot copy. *The Advocate*, January 20, 84–87.

Gilbert, B., Heesacker, M., & Gannon, L. (1991). Changing the sexual aggression-supportive attitudes of men: A psychoeducational intervention. *Journal of Counseling Psychology*, 38, 197–203.

Gilbert, H. (1991). Bad blood. *Northwest Magazine*, February 17, 8–13.

Gilbert, L., & Alexander, L. (1998). A profile of sexual health behaviors among college women. *Psychological Reports*, 82, 107–116.

Gillespie, M. (1994). Where do we stand on pornography? *Ms.*, January/February, 32–45.

Gillespie, M. (1997). Holding on to our stuff. *Ms.*, March/April 1.

Gilmartin, B. (1977). Swinging: Who gets involved and how? In R. Libby & R. Whitehurst (Eds.), *Marriage and Alternatives: Exploring Intimate Relationships*. Glenview, IL: Scott, Foresman.

Ginsburg, E., Mello, N., Mendelson, J., Barbieri, R., Teoh, S., Rothman, M., Gao, X., & Sholar, J. (1996). Effects of alcohol ingestion on estrogens in postmenopausal women. *Journal of the American Medical Association*, 276, 1747–1751.

Ginsburg, K. (1995). Some practical approaches to treating PMS. *Contemporary Ob/Gyn*, May, 24–48.

Ginsburg, K., Wolf, N., & Fidel, P. (1997). Potential effects of midcycle cervical mucus on mediators of immune reactivity. *Fertility and Sterility*, 67, 46–56.

Giovannuccci, E., Ascherio, A., Rimm, E., Colditz, G., Stampfer, M., & Willett, W. (1993). A prospective cohort study of vasectomy and prostate cancer in U.S. men. *Journal of the American Medical Association*, 269, 873–877.

Gittleson, N. (1980). Marriage: What women expect and what they get. *McCall's*, January, 87–89.

Gladstone, J., Levy, M., Nulman, I., & Koren, G. (1997). Characteristics of pregnant women who engage in binge alcohol consumption. *Canadian Medical Association Journal*, 156(6), 789–794.

Glasser, M., Dennis, J., Orthoefer, J., Carter, S., & Hollander, E. (1989). Characteristics of males at a public health department contraceptive service. *Journal of Adolescent Health Care*, 10, 115–118.

Gluckman, G., Stoller, M., Jacobs, M., & Kogan, B. (1995). Newborn penile glans amputation during circumcision and successful reattachment. *Journal of Urology*, 153, 778–779.

Glynn, M., & Butterfield (1997). World's oldest mom. *National Enquirer*, May 13, 24–27.

Gober, P. (1997). The role of access in explaining state abortion rates. *Social Science Medicine*, 44, 1003–1016.

Gochros, H. (1992). The sexuality of gay men with HIV infection. *Social Work*, 37, 105–109.

Goens, J., Janniger, C., & De Wolf, K. (1994a). Dermatologic and systematic manifestations of syphilis. *American Family Physician*, 50, 1013–1020.

Goens, J., Schwartz, R., De Wolf, K. (1994b). Mucocutaneous manifestations of chancroid, lymphogranuloma venereum and granuloma inguinale. *American Family Physician*, 49, 415–425.

Gold, D., Balzano, B., & Stamey, R. (1991). Two studies of females' sexual force fantasies. *Journal of Sex Education & Therapy*, 17, 15–26.

Gold, M., Schein, A., & Coupey, S. (1997). Emergency contraception: A national survey of adolescent health experts. *Family Planning Perspectives*, 29, 15–19 & 24.

Golden, K. (1998). Ellen DeGeneres. *Ms.*, January/February, 54–55.

Golding, J. (1994). Sexual assault history and physical health in randomly selected Los Angeles women. *Health Psychology*, 13, 130–138.

Goldman, H. (1992). *Review of General Psychiatry.* Norwalk, CT: Appleton & Lange.

Goldman, R., & Goldman, J. (1982). *Children's Sexual Thinking: A Comparative Study of Children Aged 5 to 15 Years in Australia, North America, Britain, and Sweden.* London: Routledge & Kegan Paul.

Golombok, S., & Fivush, R. (1995). Gender is determined biologically and socially. In D. Bender & B. Leone (Eds.), *Human Sexuality: Opposing Viewpoints.* San Diego, CA: Greenhaven Press.

Golombok, S., & Tasker, F. (1996). Do parents influence the sexual orientation of their children? Findings from a longitudinal study of lesbian families. *Developmental Psychology*, 32, 3–11.

Goluboff, E., Saidi, J., Mazer, S., Bagiella, E., Heitjan, D., Benson, M., & Olsson, C. (1998). Urinary continence after radical prostatectomy: The Columbia experience. *Journal of Urology*, 159, 1276–1280.

Gomez, J. (1997). Race: The growing chasm. *The Advocate*, October 14, 101.

Goodchilds, J., & Zellman, G. (1984). Sexual signaling and sexual aggression in adolescent relationships. In N. Malamuth & E. Donnerstein (Eds.), *Pornography and Sexual Aggression.* Orlando, FL: Academic Press.

Goodman, E. (1995). Nation can't avoid debate on abortion. *The Oregonian*, January 22, B3.

Goodman, L., & Fallot, R. (1998). HIV risk-behavior in poor urban women with serious mental disorders: Association with childhood physical and sexual abuse. *American Journal of Orthopsychiatry*, 68, 73–83.

Goolsby, M., (1998). Screening, diagnosis, and management of prostate cancer: Improving primary care outcomes. *The Nurse Practitioner*, 23, 11–35.

Gordon, S., & Gordon, J. (1989). *Raising a Child Conservatively in a Sexually Permissive World.* New York: Simon & Schuster.

Gordon, S., Brenden, J., Wyble, J., & Ivey, C. (1997). When the Dx is penile cancer. *RN*, March, 41–44.

Gore, A. (1998). The genetic moral code. *The Advocate*, March 31, 9.

Gorey, K., & Leslie, D. (1997). The prevalence of child sexual abuse: Integrative review adjustment for potential response and measurement biases. *Child Abuse & Neglect*, 21, 391–398.

Gorney, C. (1998). *Articles of Faith.* New York: Simon & Schuster.

Gostin, L., & Webber, D. (1998). HIV infection and AIDS in the public health and health care systems: The role of law and litigation. *Journal of the American Medical Association*, 279, 1108–1113.

Gottman, J. (1991). Predicting the longitudinal course of marriages. *Journal of Marital and Family Therapy*, 17, 3–7.

Gottman, J. (1993). *What Predicts Divorce.* Hillsdale, NJ: Lawrence Erlbaum.

Gottman, J. (1994a). Why marriages fail. *Networker*, May/June, 41–48.

Gottman, J. (1994b). *Why Marriages Succeed or Fail.* New York: Simon & Schuster.

Gottman, J., Coan, J., Carrere, S., & Swanson, C. (1998). Predicting marital happiness and stability from newlywed interactions. *Journal of Marriage and the Family*, 60, 5–22.

Gottman, J., Notarius, C., Gonso, J., & Markman, H. (1976). *A Couple's Guide to Communication.* Champaign, IL: Research Press.

Gover, T. (1996). Occupational hazards. *The Advocate*, November 26, 36–38.

Gower, D., & Ruparelia, B. (1993). Olfaction in humans with special reference to odorous 16-androstenes: Their occurrence, perception and possible social, psychological and sexual impact. *Journal of Endocrinology*, 137, 167–187.

Grady, W., Klepinger, D., Billy, J., & Tanfer, K. (1993). Condom characteristics: The perceptions and preferences of men in the United States. *Family Planning Perspectives*, 25, 67–73.

Grafenberg, E. (1950). The role of urethra in female orgasm. *International Journal of Sexology*, 3, 145–148.

Graham, N. (1997). Epidemiology of acquired immunodeficiency syndrome: Advancing to an endemic era. *American Journal of Medicine*, 102 (Supplement 4A), 2–8.

Gram, I., Austin, H., & Stalsberg, H. (1992). Cigarette smoking and the incidence of cervical intraepithelial neoplasia, grade III, and the cancer of the cervix uteri. *American Journal of Epidemiology*, 135, 341–346.

Granberg, D., & Granberg, B. (1980). Abortion attitudes, 1965–1980: Trends and determinants. *Family Planning Perspectives*, 12, 250–261.

Grant, L. (1994). The timid crusade. *The NPG Forum*, January, 1–12.

Gravholt, C., Juul, S., Naeraa, R., & Hansen, J. (1998). Morbidity in Turner syndrome. *Journal of Clinical Epidemiology*, 51, 147–158.

Gray, C. (1984). Pornography and violent entertainment: Exposing the symptoms. *Canadian Medical Association Journal*, 130, 769–772.

Gray, J., Dore, G., Li, Y., Supawitkul, S., Effler, P., & Kaldor, J. (1997). HIV-1 infection among female commercial sex workers in rural Thailand. *AIDS*, 11, 89–94.

Gray, J., & Wolfe, L. (1992). An anthropological look at human sexuality. In W. Masters, V. Johnson, & R. Kolodny, *Human Sexuality* (4th ed.). New York: HarperCollins.

Gray, P. (1993). What is love? *Time*, February 15, 47–49.

Green, A. (1997). Senate approves ban on gay marriages. *The Oregonian*, May 23, A18.

Green, G., & Clunis, D. (1989). Married lesbians. *Women and Therapy*, 8, 41–49.

Green, R. (1974). *Sexual Identity Conflict in Children and Adults*. New York: Basic Books.

Green, R. (1987). *The "Sissy Boy" Syndrome and the Development of Homosexuality*. New Haven, CT: Yale University Press.

Green, R. (1992). *Sexual Science and the Law*. Cambridge, MA: Harvard University Press.

Green, R., & Fleming, D. (1990). Transsexual surgery follow-up: Status in the 1990s. *Annual Review of Sex Research*, 1, 163–174.

Greenberg, B., & Russelle, R. (1996). Soap operas and sexual activity: A decade later. *Journal of Communication*, 46(4), 153–161.

Greenburg, D. (1986). *Dan Greenburg's Confessions of a Pregnant Father*. New York: Macmillan.

Greene, B. (1994). African-American woman. In L. Comas-Diaz & B. Greene (Eds.), *Women of Color*. New York: Guilford.

Greene, B. (1994). Ethnic-minority lesbians and gay men: Mental health and treatment issues. *Journal of Consulting and Clinical Psychology*, 62, 243–251.

Greene, R., & Field, S. (1989). Social support coverage and the well-being of elderly widows and married women. *Journal of Family Issues*, 10, 33–51.

Greenhouse, L. (1994). High court hears anti-abortion appeal. *San Francisco Chronicle*, April 29, A2.

Greenstein, A., Plymate, S., & Katz, G. (1995). Visually stimulated erection in castrated men. *Journal of Urology*, 153, 650–652.

Greenwald, E., & Leitenberg, H. (1989). Long-term effects of sexual experiences with siblings and nonsiblings during childhood. *Archives of Sexual Behavior*, 18, 389–400.

Greenwood, S. (1989). No more UTI misery. *Medical Self Care*, January/February, 18–64.

Greer, P. (1998). Vaginal thrush: Diagnosis and treatment options. *Nursing Times*, 94, 50–52.

Gregory, G. (1997). Sex-assault suspect known as "Tequila Man." *The Oregonian*, February 26, B7.

Gregory, K., Henry, O., Gellens, A., Hobel, C. & Platt, L. (1994). Repeat cesareans: How many are elective? *Obstetrics & Gynecology*, 84, 574–578.

Grieco, A. (1987). Scope and nature of sexual harassment in nursing. *Journal of Sex Research*, 23, 261–266.

Grimes, D. (1997). Medical abortion in early pregnancy: A review of the evidence. *Obstetrics & Gynecology*, 89, 790–796.

Grisell, T. (1988). Brief report. *Indiana Medical Journal*, 81, 252.

Grodstein, F., Stampfer, M., Colditz, G., Willett, W., Manson, J., Joffe, M., Rosner, B., Fuchs, C., Hankinson, S., Hunter, D., Hennekens, C., & Speizer, F. (1997). Postmenopausal hormone therapy and mortality. *New England Journal of Medicine*, 336, 1769–1775.

Gross, W., & Billingham, R. (1998). Alcohol consumption and sexual victimization among college women. *Psychological Reports*, 82, 80–82.

Grossman, J. (1971). Evaluation of computer acquired patient histories. *Journal of the American Medical Association*, 215, 1286–1289.

Groth, N., & Hobson, W. (1983). The dynamics of sexual assault. In L. Schlesinger & E. Revitch (Eds.), *Sexual Dynamics of Anti-Social Behavior*. Springfield, IL: Thomas.

Gudykunst, W., Matsumoto, Y., Ting-Toomey, S., Nishida, T., Kim, K., & Keyman, S. (1996). The influence of cultural individualism-collectivism, self construals, and individual values on communication styles across cultures. *Human Communication Research*, 22, 510–543.

Guerrero Pavich, E. (1986). A Chicano perspective on Mexican culture and sexuality. In L. Lister (Ed.), *Human Sexuality, Ethnoculture, and Social Work*. New York: Haworth Press.

Guidry, H. (1995). Childhood sexual abuse: Role of the family physician. *American Family Physician*, 51, 407–414.

Gulick, R., Mellors, J., Havlir, D., Eron, J., Gonzalez, C., McMahon, D., & Richman, D. (1996). Potent and sustained activity of indinavir, zidovudine, and lamivudine. Paper presented at the 11th International Conference on AIDS, Vancouver, BC, July.

Gunn, R., Veinbergs, E., & Friedman, L. (1997). Adolescent health care providers. *Sexually Transmitted Diseases*, 24, 90–93.

Gur, R., Mozley, L., Mozley, P., Resnick, S., Karp, J., Alavi, A., Arnold, S., & Gur, R. (1995). Sex differences in regional cerebral glucose metabolism during a resting state. *Science*, 267, 528–531.

Gurian, B. (1988). Loss of father's libido after childbirth. *Medical Aspects of Human Sexuality*, 22, 102–116.

Gutek, B. (1985). *Sex and the Workplace*. San Francisco: Jossey-Bass.

Guthmann, E. (1997). In like Clint. *The Advocate*, November 11, 25–35.

Guttmacher, S., Lieberman, L., Ward, D., Freudenberg, N., Radosh, A., & Des Jarlais, D. (1997). Condom availability in New York City public high schools: Relationships to condom use and sexual behavior. *American Journal of Public Health*, 87, 1427–1433.

Haas, G. (1994). Promising therapy for infertility—IUI and superovulation. *Contemporary Ob/Gyn*, March, 55–68.

Hack, T., Osachuk, T., De Luca, R. (1994). Group treatment for sexually abused preadolescent boys. *Families in Society*, April, 217–228.

Hackenbruck, P. (1987). Adolescent sexuality: Differential development. Paper presented at Sexual Identity Issues of Adolescence, National Association of Social Workers, Vancouver, March.

Hadi, A. (1997). A step forward for opponents of female genital mutilation in Egypt. *The Lancet*, 349, 129–131.

Haffner, D. (1993). Toward a new paradigm of adolescent sexual health. *Siecus Report*, 21, 26–30.

Haffner, D. (1994). Sexuality and aging: The family physician's role as educator. *Geriatrics*, 49(9), 26.

Haffner, D. (1997). The really good news: What the Bible says about sex. *Siecus Report*, 26(1), 3–8.

Haffner, D. (1998). The HIV pandemic still deserves the best from us. *Siecus Report*, 26, 3–4.

Haffner, D., & Portelli, C. (1998). On the brink of abolishing discrimination against lesbians and gays. *Siecus Report*, 26(4), 3–4.

Hagan, P., & Knott, P. (1998) Diagnosing and treating polycystic ovary syndrome. *The Practitioner*, 242, 98–106.

Hage, M., Helms, M., Hammond, W., & Hammond, C. (1988). Changing rates of cesarean delivery: The Duke experience, 1978–86. *Obstetrics & Gynecology*, 72, 99–101.

Hager, M., & Miller, S. (1997). Mammogram war. *Newsweek*, February 24, 55–58.

Hakim, L., & Goldstein, I. (1996). Diabetic sexual dysfunction. *Endocrinology and Metabolism Clinics of North America*, 25(2), 379.

Halberstadt, A. (1985). Race, socioeconomic status, and nonverbal behavior. In A. Siegman & S. Feldstein (Eds.), *Multichannel Integration of Nonverbal Behavior*. Hillsdale, NJ: Erlbaum.

Hales, D. (1994). *An Invitation to Health* (6th ed.). Redwood City, CA: Benjamin/Cummings.

Hales, D. (1996). Sex after 65. *Parade Magazine*, March 17, 4–6.

Hall, G. (1996). *Theory-Based Assessment, Treatment, and Prevention of Sexual Aggression*. New York: Oxford University Press.

Hall, G., & Barongan, C. (1997). Prevention of sexual aggression: Sociocultural risk and protective factors. *American Psychologist*, 52, 5–14.

Hally, C., & Pollack, R. (1993). The effects of self-esteem, variety of sexual experience, and erotophilia on sexual satisfaction in sexually active heterosexuals. *Journal of Sex Education & Therapy*, 19(3), 183–192.

Halpern, D. (1992). *Sex Differences in Cognitive Abilities* (2nd ed.). Hillsdale, NJ: Erlbaum.

Hamer, D., Hu, S., Magnuson, V., Hu, N., & Pattatucci, A. (1993). A linkage between DNA markers on the X chromosome and male sexual orientation. *Science*, 261, 321–327.

Hamilton, E. (1978). *Sex, with Love*. Boston: Beacon Press.

Hamilton, J., Alagna, S., King, L., & Lloyd, C. (1987). The emotional consequences of gender-based abuse in the workplace: New counseling programs for sex discrimination. *Women and Therapy*, 6, 155–182.

Hamilton, K., & Miller, S. (1997). Internet U—No ivy, no walls, no keg parties. *Newsweek*, March 10, 12.

Hanash, K. (1997). Comparative results of goal oriented therapy for erectile dysfunction. *Journal of Urology*, 157, 2135–2138.

Handsfield, H. (1992). Recent developments in STDs: II. Viral and other syndromes. *Hospital Practice*, January 15, 175–200.

Handy, B. (1998). The Viagra craze. *Time*, May 4, 49–57.

Handyside, A., Penketh, R., Winston, R., Pattinson, J., Delhanty, J., & Tuddenham, E. (1989). Biopsy of human preimplantation embryos and sexing by DNA amplification. *The Lancet*, February 18, 347–349.

Haney, D. (1994). Study strongly ties environment to birth defects. *San Francisco Examiner*, July 7, A7.

Hanna, G. (1988). Gender differences in mathematical achievement among eighth graders: Results from twenty countries. Paper presented at the annual meeting of the American Association for the Advancement of Science, Boston, February.

Hanrahan, S. (1994). Historical review of menstrual toxic shock syndrome. *Women & Health*, 21, 141–157.

Hansen, T., & Lundvall, F. (1997). Factors influencing the reliability of oral contraceptives. *Acta Obstetricia et Gynecologica Scandinavica*, 76, 61–64.

Hanson, V. (1997). How to provide postcoital contraception. *Patient Care*, April 15, 81–85.

Hanukoglu, A., Hanukoglu, D., Danielli, L., Katzir, Z., & Gorenstein, A. (1995). Serious complications of routine ritual circumcision in a neonate. *European Journal of Pediatrics*, 154, 314–315.

Hardesty, C., Wenk, D., & Morgan, C. (1995). Paternal involvement and the development of gender expectations in sons and daughters. *Youth & Society*, 26, 283–297.

Hardie, A. (1997). Estrogen may be key to old age. *Monterey Herald*, September 5, D1–D2.

Hargreaves, D., & Plail, R. (1994). Fracture of the penis causing a corporo-urethral fistula. *British Journal of Urology*, 73, 97.

Harley, V., Jackson, D., Hextall, P., Hawkins, J., Berkovitz, G., Sockanathan, S., Lovell-Badge, R., & Goodfellow, P. (1992). DNA binding activity of recombinant SRY from normal males and XY females. *Science*, 255, 453–456.

Harlow, H., & Harlow, M. (1962). The effects of rearing conditions on behavior. *Bulletin of the Menninger Clinic*, 26, 13–24.

Harlow, S., & Matanoski, G. (1991). The association between weight, physical activity, and stress and variation in the length of the menstrual cycle. *American Journal of Epidemiology*, 133, 38–49.

Harney, P., & Muehlenhard, C. (1990). Rape. In E. Grauerholz & M. Korlewski (Eds.), *Sexual Coercion: A Sourcebook on Its Nature, Causes, and Prevention*. Lexington, MA: Lexington Books.

Harney, P., & Muehlenhard, C. (1991). Rape. In E. Grauerholz & M. Koralewski (Eds.), *Sexual Coercion: A Sourcebook on Its Nature, Causes, and Prevention*. Lexington, MA: Lexington Books.

Harris, C., & Christenfeld, N. (1996). Gender, jealousy, and reason. *Psychological Science*, 7, 364–366.

Hart, R., & Magos, A. (1998). How long should a woman take HRT? *The Practitioner*, 242, 114–119.

Hartman, W., & Fithian, M. (1984). Any man can: Multiple orgasmic response in males. Paper presented at the Regional Conference of the American Association of Sex Educators, Counselors, and Therapists, Las Vegas, October.

Hartmann, B., & Huber, J. (1997). Mythology of hormone replacement therapy. *British Journal of Obstetrics and Gynaecology*, 104, 163–168.

Harvey, S. (1987). Female sexual behavior: Fluctuations during the menstrual cycle. *Journal of Psychosomatic Research*, 31, 101–110.

Haslegrove, M. (1997). What she wants. *The Lancet*, 349, s11–s12.

Hass, A. (1979). *Teenage Sexuality*. New York: Macmillan.

Hasset, J. (1978). Sex and smell. *Psychology Today*, March, 40–45.

Hatcher, R. (1988). *Contraceptive Technology 1988–1989*. New York: Irvington.

Hatcher, R., Trussell, J., Stewart, F., Stewart, G., Kowal, D., Guest, F., Cates, W., & Policar, M. (1994). *Contraceptive Technology* (16th ed.). New York: Irvington.

Hatfield, E. (1993). *Love, Sex, and Intimacy: Their Psychology, Biology, and History*. New York: HarperCollins College.

Hatfield, E., & Rapson, R. (1987). Passionate love/sexual desire: Can the same paradigm explain both? *Archives of Sexual Behavior*, 16, 259–278.

Hatfield, E., & Rapson, R. (1993). *Love, Sex, & Intimacy: Their Psychology, Biology, and History*. New York: HarperCollins.

Hatfield, E., & Sprecher, S. (1986a). Measuring passionate love in intimate relationships. *Journal of Adolescence*, 9, 383–410.

Hatfield, E., & Sprecher, S. (1986b). *Mirror, Mirror . . . The Importance of Looks in Everyday Life*. Albany: State University of New York Press.

Hatfield, R. (1994). Touch and sexuality. In V. Bullough & B. Bullough (Eds.), *Human Sexuality: An Encyclopedia*. New York: Garland.

Hawton, K. (1998). Integration of treatments for male erectile dysfunction. *The Lancet*, 351, 7–8.

Hawton, K., Catalan, J., & Fagg, J. (1992). Sex therapy for erectile dysfunction: Characteristics of couples, treatment outcome, and prognostic factors. *Archives of Sexual Behavior*, 21, 161–175.

Healy, D., Trounson, A., & Andersen, A. (1994). Female infertility: Causes and treatment. *The Lancet*, 343, 1539–1544.

Healy, M. (1998). McKinney ruling may discourage future claims. *The Oregonian*, March 15, A1 & A12.

Heath, D. (1984). An investigation into the origins of a copious vaginal discharge during intercourse "enough to wet the bed" that is not urine. *Journal of Sex Research*, 20, 194–215.

Heath, R. (1972). Pleasure and brain activity in man. *Journal of Nervous and Mental Disease*, 154, 3–18.

Heaton, J., & Varrin, S. (1991). The impact of alcohol ingestion on erections in rats as measured by a novel bio-assay. *Journal of Urology,* 145, 192–194.

Hecht, M., Ribeau, S., & Collier, M. (1993). *African American Communication: Ethnic Identity and Cultural Interpretation.* Thousand Oaks, CA: Sage.

Hecht, M., Ribeau, S., & Sedano, M. (1990). A Mexican American perspective on interethnic communication. *International Journal of Intercultural Relations*, 14, 31–55.

Heck, K., & Pamuk, E. (1997). Explaining the relation between education and postmenopausal breast cancer. *American Journal of Epidemiology*, 145(4), 366–372.

Heidrich, F., Berg, A., & Bergman, J. (1984). Clothing factors and vaginitis. *Journal of Family Practice,* 19, 491–494.

Heim, N. (1981). Sexual behavior of castrated sex offenders. *Archives of Sexual Behavior*, 10, 11–19.

Heimer, L., & Larsson, K. (1964). Drastic changes in the mating behavior of male rats following lesions in the junction of diencephalon and mesencephalon. *Experientia,* 20, 460–461.

Heinlein, R. (1961). *Stranger in a Strange Land.* New York: Putnam.

Heitz, D. (1997). Men behaving badly. *The Advocate*, July 8, 26–34.

Helstrom, L., Sorbom, D., & Backstrom, T. (1995). Influence of partner relationship on sexuality after subtotal hysterectomy. *Acta Obstetricia et Gynecologica Scandinavica,* 74, 142–146.

Hendrick, C., & Hendrick, S. (1993). *Romantic Love.* Newbury Park, CA: Sage.

Hendrick, C., Hendrick, S., & Adler, N. (1988). Romantic relationships: Love, satisfaction, and staying together. *Journal of Personality and Social Psychology,* 54, 980–988.

Hendrick, S., & Hendrick, C. (1992). *Liking, Loving, and Relating,* 2nd ed. Pacific Grove, CA: Brooks/Cole.

Henley, J. (1993). The significance of social context: The case of adolescent childbearing in the African American community. *Journal of Black Psychology*, 19, 461–477.

Henley, N. (1977). *Body Politics: Power, Sex, and Nonverbal Communication.* Englewood Cliffs, NJ: Prentice Hall.

Henshaw, S., & Kost, K. (1996). Abortion patients in 1994–1995: Characteristics and contraceptive use. *Family Planning Perspectives*, 28, 140–147 & 158.

Hensleigh, P., Andrews, W., Brown, Z., Greenspoon, J., Yasukawa, L., & Prober, C. (1997). Genital herpes during pregnancy: Inability to distinguish primary and recurrent infections clinically. *Obstetrics and Gynecology*, 89, 891–895.

Herdt, G. (1992). Coming out as a rite of passage: A Chicago study. In G. Herdt (Ed.), *Gay Culture in America.* Boston: Beacon Press.

Herek, G., Kimmel, D., Amaro, H., & Melton, G. (1991). Avoiding heterosexist bias in psychological research. *American Psychologist,* 46, 957–963.

Herman-Giddens, M., Slora, E., Wasserman, R., Bourdony, C., Bhapkar, M., Koch, G., & Hesemeier, C. (1997). Secondary sexual characteristics and menses in young girls seen in office practice: A study from the pediatric research office settings network. *Pediatrics*, 99, 505–512.

Herrell, R. (1992). The symbolic strategies of Chicago's Gay and Lesbian Pride Day Parade. In G. Herdt (Ed.), *Gay Culture in America,* Boston: Beacon Press.

Hersch, P. (1988). Coming of age on city streets. *Psychology Today,* January, 28–37.

Hersch, P. (1991). Secret lives. *Networker,* January/February, 37–40.

Herschel, M., Khoshnood, B., Ellmam, C., Maydew, N., & Mittendorf, R. (1998). Neonatal circumcision. *Archives of Pediatric and Adolescent Medicine*, 152, 279–284.

Hershberger, S., & D'Augelli, A. (1995). The impact of victimization on the mental health and suicidality of lesbian, gay, and bisexual youths. *Developmental Psychology,* 31, 65–74.

Herzog, L. (1989). Urinary tract infections and circumcision. *American Journal of Diseases of Children,* 143, 348–350.

Heyl, P. (1997). Multiplying the risks. *Newsweek*, December 1, 66.

Heylen, R., & Miller, R. (1997). Adverse effects and drug interactions of medications commonly used in the treatment of adult HIV positive patients. *Genitourinary Medicine*, 73, 5–11.

Hiaasen, S. (1997). American Online not liable for customers. *The Palm Beach Post*, June 14, B1.

Hickman, S., & Muehlenhard, C. (1997). College women's fears and precautionary behavior relating to acquaintance rape and stranger rape. *Psychology of Women Quarterly*, 21, 527–547.

Hickson, F., Davies, P., Hunt, A., Weatherburn, P., McManus, T., & Coxon, A. (1994). Gay men as victims of nonconsensual sex. *Archives of Sexual Behavior*, 23, 281–294.

Hiedemann, B., Suhomlinova, O., & O'Rand, A. (1998). Economic independence, economic status, and empty nest in midlife marital disruption. *Journal of Marriage and the Family*, 60, 219–231.

Higginbotham, A. (1996). Teen mags: How to get a guy, drop 20 pounds, and lose your self-esteem. *Ms.*, March/April, 82–87.

Higgins, C. (1997). Screening for cervical cancer. *Nursing Times*, 84, 34–36.

Hillis, S. (1994). PID prevention: Clinical and societal stakes. *Hospital Practice*, 29, 121–130.

Hillis, S., Owens, L., Marchbanks, P., Amsterdam, L., & Mackenzie, W. (1997). Recurrent chlamydial infections increase the risks of hospitalization for ecotopic pregnancy and pelvic inflammatory disease. *American Journal of Obstetrics and Gynecology*, 176, 103–107.

Himelein, M., Vogel, R., & Wachowiak, D. (1994). Non-consensual sexual experiences in precollege women: Prevalence and risk factors. *Journal of Counseling and Development*, 72, 411–415.

Hiratsuka, J. (1993). Outsiders: Gay teens, straight world. *National Association of Social Workers,* April, 3.

Hirschkowitz, M., Karacan, I., Howell, J., Arcasoy, M., & Williams, R. (1992). Nocturnal penile tumesence in cigarette smokers with erectile dysfunction. *Urology*, 39, 101–107.

Hitchcock, J. (1995). The witch within me. *Newsweek,* March 27, 16.

Hite, S. (1976). *The Hite Report: A Nationwide Study of Female Sexuality.* New York: Dell Books.

Hite, S. (1981). *The Hite Report on Male Sexuality.* New York: Knopf.

Hitt, J., Hendericks, S., Ginsberg, S., & Lewis, J. (1970). Disruption of male but not female sexual behavior in rats by medial forebrain bundle lesions. *Journal of Comparative and Physiological Psychology,* 73, 377–384.

Ho, G., Bierman, R., Beardsley, L., Chang, C., & Burk, R. (1998). Natural history of cervicovaginal papillomavirus infection in young women. *New England Journal of Medicine*, 338, 423–428.

Ho, M. (1987). *Family Therapy with Ethnic Minorities.* Newbury Park, CA: Sage.

Hoffner, C. (1996). Children's wishful identification and parasocial interaction with favorite television characters. *Journal of Broadcasting and Electronic Media*, 40, 389–402.

Holden, C. (1992). Twin study links genes to homosexuality. *Research News,* January, 33.

Holland, B. (1998). The long good-bye. *Smithsonian*, March, 87–93.

Holloway, F., & Farah, R. (1997). Intermediate term assessment of the reliability, function and patient satisfaction with the AMS700 Ultrex Penile Prosthesis. *Journal of Urology*, 157, 1687–1691.

Holman, T., & Daoli, B. (1997). Premarital factors influencing perceived readiness for marriage. *Journal of Family Issues*, 18(2), 124–144.

Hook, E. (1981). Rates of chromosome abnormalities at different maternal ages. *Obstetrics and Gynecology*, 282–284.

Hook, E., Sondheimer, S., & Zenilman, J. (1995). Today's treatment for STDs. *Patient Care*, 29, 40–56.

Hooker, E. (1957). The adjustment of the male overt homosexual. *Journal of Projective Techniques*, 21, 18–31.

Hoon, E., Hoon, P., Rand, K., Johnson, J., Hall, N., & Edwards, N. (1991). A psycho-behavioral model of genital herpes recurrence. *Journal of Psychosomatic Research*, 35, 25–36.

Hooton, T. (1996). A simplified approach to urinary tract infection. *Hospital Practice*, February 15, 23–30.

Hooton, T., Hillier, S., Johnson, C., Roberts, P., & Stamm, W. (1991). *Escherichia coli* bacteriuria and contraceptive method. *Journal of the American Medical Association*, 265, 64–69.

Hoover, E. (1997). Memory therapy turns woman's life into nightmare. *The Oregonian*, April 13, A1 & A12.

Horner, R., Kolasa, K., Irons, T., & Wilson, K. (1994). Racial differences in rural adults' attitudes toward issues of adolescent sexuality. *American Journal of Public Health*, 84, 456–459.

Horta, B., Victora, C., Menezes, A., & Barros, F. (1997). Environmental tobacco smoke and breastfeeding duration. *American Journal of Epidemiology*, 146(2), 128–133.

Horwitz, A., White, H., & Howell-White, S. (1996). Becoming married and mental health: A longitudinal study of a cohort of young adults. *Journal of Marriage and the Family*, 58, 895–907.

Howards, S. (1994). Vasectomy and prostate cancer. *Western Journal of Medicine*, 160, 166–167.

Howards, S., & Peterson, H. (1993). Vasectomy and prostate cancer: Chance, bias, or a casual relationship? *Journal of the American Medical Association*, 269, 913–914.

Howell, R., Kassler, W., & Haddix, A. (1997). Partner notification to prevent pelvic inflammatory disease in women: Cost effectiveness of two strategies. *Sexually Transmitted Diseases*, 24, 287–292.

Hrebinko, R., Bahnson, R., Schwentker, F., & O'Donnell, W. (1990). Early experience with the DuraPhase penile prosthesis. *Journal of Urology*, 143, 60–61.

Hu, D., Fleming, P., Mays, M., & Ward, J. (1994). The expanding regional diversity of the acquired immunodeficiency syndrome epidemic in the United States. *Archives of Internal Medicine*, 154, 654–659.

Hudson, W., Harrison, D., & Crosscup, P. (1981). A short form scale to measure sexual discord in dyadic relationships. *Journal of Sex Research*, 17, 157–174.

Hughes, C., Jr., Wall, L. L., & Creasman, W. (1991). Reproductive hormone levels in gynecologic oncology patients undergoing surgical castration after spontaneous menopause. *Gynecologic Oncology*, 40, 42–45.

Hughes, J., & Sandler, B. (1987). *"Friends" Raping Friends: Could It Happen to You?* Washington, DC: Association of American Colleges.

Hulter, B., & Lundberg, P. (1994). Sexual function in women with hypothalamo-pituitary disorders. *Archives of Sexual Behavior*, 23, 171–183.

Hummel, W., & Kettel, L. (1997). Assisted reproductive technology: The state of the ART. *Annals of Medicine*, 29, 207–214.

Humphrey, F. (1987). Treating extramarital sexual relationships in sex and couples therapy. In G. Weeks & L. Hof (Eds.), *Integrating Sex and Marital Therapy: A Clinical Guide.* New York: Brunner/Mazel.

Hunt, M. (1974). *Sexual Behavior in the 1970s.* Chicago: Playboy Press.

Hunt, M., & Hunt, B. (1977). *The Divorce Experience.* New York: Signet.

Hunter, E. (1991). For want of a child. *The Oregonian*, October 20, L1.

Hunter, J. (1990). Violence against lesbian and gay male youths. *Journal of Interpersonal Violence*, 5, 295–300.

Hurlbert, D., & Whittaker, K. (1991). The role of masturbation in marital and sexual satisfaction: A comparative study of female masturbators and nonmasturbators. *Journal of Sex Education & Therapy*, 17, 272–282.

Huston, R., Martin, L., & Foulds, M. (1990). Effect of a program to facilitate parent–child communication about sex. *Clinical Pediatrics*, 29, 626–630.

Hutchinson, K. (1995). Androgens and sexuality. *American Journal of Medicine*, 98 (Supplement 1A), 1115–1155.

Hwang, K. (1997). Living with a disability: A woman's perspective. In M. Sipski & C. Alexander (Eds.), *Sexual Function in People with Disability and Chronic Illness.* Gaithersburg, MD: Aspen Publishers.

Hwang, S., & Saenz, R. (1997). Fertility of Chinese immigrants in the U.S.: Testing a fertility emancipation hypothesis. *Journal of Marriage and the Family*, 59, 50–61.

Hyde, J. (1996). *Half the Human Experience: The Psychology of Women* (5th ed.). Boston: Houghton Mifflin.

Hyde, J., Fenneman, E., & Lamon, S. (1990). Gender differences in mathematics performance: A meta-analysis. *Psychological Bulletin*, 107, 139–155.

Hyde, J., Krajnik, M., & Skuldt-Niederberger, K. (1991). Androgyny across the life span: A replication and longitudinal follow-up. *Developmental Psychology*, 27, 516–19.

Hyde, J., & Plant, A. (1995). Magnitude of psychological gender differences. *American Psychologist*, 50, 159–61.

Icard, L. (1996). Assessing the psychosocial well-being of African American gays: A multidimensional perspective. In J. Longres (Ed.), *Men of Color.* New York: Harrington Park Press.

Icard, L., Longres, J., & Williams, J. (1996). An applied research agenda for homosexually active men of color. In J. Longres (Ed.), *Men of Color.* New York: Harrington Park Press.

Imperato-McGinley, J., Peterson, R., Gautier, T., & Sturla, E. (1979). Androgens and the evolution of male-gender identity among male pseudohermaphrodites with 5-alpha-reductase deficiency. *New England Journal of Medicine*, 300, 1233–1237.

Iovine, V. (1997a). *The Girlfriends' Guide to Pregnancy.* New York: Perigee.

Iovine, V. (1997b). *The Girlfriends' Guide to Surviving the First Year of Motherhood.* New York: Perigee.

Irvine, J. (1990). *Disorders of Desire, Sex, and Gender in Modern American Sexology.* Philadelphia: Temple University Press.

Isay, R. (1989). *Being Homosexual: Gay Men and Their Development.* New York: Farrar, Straus, & Giroux.

Isely, P., & Gehrenbeck-Shim, D. (1997). Sexual assault of men in the community. *Journal of Community Psychology*, 25, 159–166.

Isensee, R. (1996). *Love Between Men.* Englewood Cliffs, NJ: Prentice Hall.

Isherwood, C. (1997). Breaking out of the celluloid closet. *The Advocate*, September 30, 44–48.

Ivey, J. (1997). The adolescent with pelvic inflammatory disease: Assessment and management. *The Nurse Practitioner*, February, 78–91.

Iwasawa, A., Hiltunen-Bock, E., Reunala, T., Nieminen, P., & Paavonen, J. (1997). Human papillomavirus DNA in urine speciments of men with condyloma acuminatum. *Sexually Transmitted Diseases,* 24, 165–168.

Jacklin, C., Dipietro, J., & Maccoby, E. (1984). Sex-typing behavior and sex-typing pressure in child–parent interaction. *Archives of Sexual Behavior,* 13, 413–425.

Jackson, J., Calhoun, K., Amick, A., Maddever, H., & Habif, V. (1990). Young adult women who report childhood intrafamilial sexual abuse: Subsequent adjustment. *Archives of Sexual Behavior,* 19, 211–221.

Jackson, M. (1984). Sex research and the construction of sexuality: A tool of male supremacy? *Women's Studies International Forum,* 7, 43–51.

Jacobs, C., & Wolf, E. (1995). School sexuality education and adolescent risk-taking behavior. *Journal of School Health,* 65, 91–95.

Jacques, J., & Chason, K. (1979). Cohabitation: Its impact on marital success. *Family Coordinator,* 28, 35–39.

Jamison, L. (1996). Denise Bilezikjian interview. *Ms.,* March/April 48.

Jamison, P., & Gebhard, P. (1988). Penis size increase between flaccid and erect states: An analysis of the Kinsey data. *Journal of Sex Research,* 24, 177–183.

Jancin, B. (1989). Prenatal gender selection appears to be gaining acceptance. *Obstetrical and Gynecological News,* 23, 30.

Jankowiak, W., & Fischer, E. (1992). Cross-cultural perspective on romantic love. *Ethnology,* 31, 149–155.

Janoff-Bulman, R., & Golden, D. (1984). Attributions and adjustment to abortion. Paper presented at a meeting of the American Psychological Association, Toronto, August 24.

Jantos, M., & White, G. (1997). The vestibulitis syndrome. *Journal of Reproductive Medicine,* 42(3), 145–151.

Janus, S., & Janus, C. (1993). *The Janus Report on Sexual Behavior.* New York: Wiley.

Jarow, J., Goluboff, E., Chang, T., & Marshall, F. (1994). Relationship between antisperm antibodies and testicular histologic changes in humans after vasectomy. *Urology,* 43, 521–526.

Jenny, C., Roesler, T., & Poyer, K. (1994). Are children at risk for sexual abuse by homosexuals? *Pediatrics,* 94, 41–44.

Jewkes, R., Wood, K., & Maforah, N. (1997). Backstreet abortion in South Africa. *Southern Africa Medical Journal,* 87, 417–418.

John, E., Savitz, D., & Sandler, D. (1991). Prenatal exposure to parents' smoking and childhood cancer. *American Journal of Epidemiology,* 133, 123–132.

Johnson, A., Wadsworth, J., Wellings, K., Bradshaw, S., & Field, J. (1992). Sexual lifestyles and HIV risk. *Nature,* 360, 410–412.

Johnson, C. A. (1991). Making sense of dysfunctional uterine bleeding. *American Family Physician,* 44, 149–157.

Johnson, D. (1994). Colorado's anti-gay amendment invalidated. *San Francisco Chronicle,* October 12, A3.

Johnson, E., & Huston, T. (1998). The perils of love, or why wives adapt to husbands during the transition to parenthood. *Journal of Marriage and the Family,* 60, 195–204.

Johnston, L., Ward, T., & Hudson, S. (1997). Deviant sexual thoughts: Mental control and the treatment of sexual offenders. *Journal of Sex Research,* 34, 121–130.

Johnston, S. (1987). The mind of the molester. *Psychology Today,* February, 60–63.

Jones, E., & Forrest, J. (1992). Contraceptive failure rates based on the 1988 NSFG. *Family Planning Perspectives,* 24, 12–19.

Jones, E., Forrest, J., Goldman, N., Henshaw, S., Lincoln, R., Rosoff, J., Westoff, C., & Wulf, D. (1985). Teenage pregnancy in developed countries: Determinants and policy implications. *Family Planning Perspectives,* 17, 53–63.

Jones, F., & Koshes, R. (1995). Homosexuality and the military. *American Journal of Psychiatry,* 152, 16–21.

Jones, K., Lehr, S., & Hewell, S. (1997). Dyspareunia: Three case reports. *Journal of Obstetrical, Gynecological and Neonatal Nurses,* 26, 19–23.

Jones, M. (1992). The management of the mildly abnormal smear. *Maternal and Child Health,* February, 52–56.

Jones, M. (1998). Can art photography be kiddie porn? *Newsweek,* March 9, 58.

Jones, W., Chernovetz, M., & Hansson, R. (1978). The enigma of androgyny: Differential implications for males and females. *Journal of Consulting and Clinical Psychology,* 46, 298–313.

Josefson, D. (1998). FDA approves genetic test for women with breast cancer. *British Medical Journal,* 316, 168.

Joseph, R. (1991). A case analysis in human sexuality: Counseling to a man with severe cerebral palsy. *Sexuality and Disability,* 9(2), 149–59.

Josselson, R. (1992). *The Space Between Us: Exploring Dimensions of Human Relationships.* San Francisco: Jossey-Bass.

Jouriles, E., Bourg, W., & Farris, A. (1991). Marital adjustment and child conduct problems: A comparison of the correlation across subsamples. *Journal of Consulting and Clinical Psychology,* 59, 354–357.

Jouzaitis, C. (1994). Study of mifepristone to begin amid volatile social climate in U.S. *The Oregonian,* October 27, A12.

Jow, W., & Goldstein, M. (1994). No-scalpel vasectomy offers minimal invasiveness. *Contemporary Ob/Gyn,* May, 83–96.

Kahn, A., Groswasser, J., Sottiaux, M., Kelmanson, I., Rebuffat, E., Franco, P., Dramaix, M., & Wayenberg, J. (1994a). Prenatal exposure to cigarettes in infants with obstructive sleep apneas. *Pediatrics,* 93(5), 778–783.

Kahn, A., Mathie, V., & Torgler, C. (1994b). Rape scripts and rape acknowledgment. *Psychology of Women Quarterly,* 18, 53–66.

Kaiser, C. (1994). Life before Stonewall. *Newsweek,* July 4, 78–79.

Kalash, S., & Young, J. (1984). Fracture of the penis: Controversy of surgical versus conservative treatment. *Urology,* 24, 21–24.

Kalb, C. (1997). How old is too old? *Newsweek,* May 5, 64.

Kalichman, S., Kelly, J., & Rompa, D. (1997). Continued high-risk sex among HIV seropositive gay and bisexual men seeking HIV prevention services. *Health Psychology,* 16, 369–373.

Kallen, D., & Stephenson, J. (1982). Talking about sex revisited. *Journal of Youth and Adolescence,* 11, 11–23.

Kallen, K. (1997). Maternal smoking during pregnancy and limb reduction malformations in Sweden. *American Journal of Public Health,* 87, 29–32.

Kalof, L. (1993). Rape-supportive attitudes and sexual victimization experiences of sorority and nonsorority women. *Sex Roles,* 29, 767–780.

Kanin, E. (1985). Date rapists: Differential sexual socialization and relative deprivation. *Archives of Sexual Behavior,* 14, 219–231.

Kantrowitz, B. (1992). Sexism in the schoolhouse. *Newsweek,* February 24, 62–70.

Kantrowitz, B. (1996). Parents come out. *Newsweek,* November 4, 51–57.

Kantrowitz, B. (1997). A bitter new battle over partial-birth abortions. *Newsweek*, March 17, 66.

Kantrowitz, B., & Wingert, P. (1993) The Norplant debate. *Newsweek*, February 15, 37–41.

Kaplan, D., & Klaidman, D. (1996). A battle, not the war. *Newsweek*, June 3, 22–30.

Kaplan, H. (1974). *The New Sex Therapy: Active Treatment of Sexual Dysfunction.* New York: Brunner/Mazel.

Kaplan, H. (1979). *Disorders of Sexual Desire.* New York: Brunner/Mazel.

Karlberg, J., Mattsson, L., & Wiklund, I. (1995). A quality of life perspective on who benefits from estradiol replacement therapy. *Acta Obstetricia et Gynecologica Scandinavica, 74*, 367–372.

Karlen, A. (1988). *Threesomes: Studies in Sex, Power, and Intimacy.* New York: Beech Tree/Morrow.

Katz, J. (1976). *Gay American History.* New York: Avon Books.

Katz, J. (1995). *The Invention of Heterosexuality*. New York: Dutton.

Katz, J. (1994). Empirical and theoretical dimensions of obscene phone calls to women in the United States. *Human Communication Research*, 21, 155–182.

Katz, M., Hsu, L., Wong, E., Liska, S., Anderson, L., & Janssen, R. (1997). Seroprevalence of and risk factors for hepatitis A infection among young homosexual and bisexual men. *Journal of Infectious Diseases*, 175,1225–1229.

Katz, P., & Ksansnak, K. (1994). Developmental aspects of gender role flexibility and traditionality in middle childhood and adolescence. *Developmental Psychology,* 30, 272–282.

Katzenstein, D. (1997). Antiretroviral therapy for human immunodeficiency virus infection in 1997. *Western Journal of Medicine*, 166, 319–325.

Kaufman, L. (1997). A report from the front: Why it has gotten easier to sue for sexual harassment. *Newsweek*, January 13, 32.

Kaufman, R., Adam, E., Icenogle, J., Lawson, H., Lee, N., Reeves, K., Irwin, J., Simon, T., Press, M., Uhler, R., Entman, C., & Reeves, W. (1997). Relevance of human papillomavirus screening in management of cervical intraepithelial neoplasia. *American Journal of Obstetrics and Gynecology,* 176, 87–92.

Kaunitz, A. (1994). Long-acting injectible contraception with depot medroxyprogesterone acetate. *American Journal of Obstetrics & Gynecology,* 170, 1543–1549.

Kauntiz, A., & Jordan, C. (1997). Two long-acting hormonal contraceptive options. *Contemporary Ob/Gyn*, February, 27–50.

Keen, S. (1991). *Fire in the Belly.* New York: Bantam Books.

Kelaher, M., Ross, M., Rohrsheim, R., Drury, M., & Clarkson, A. (1994). Dominant situational determinants of sexual risk behavior in gay men. *AIDS,* 8, 101–105.

Keller, B. (1994). Zimbabwe takes a lead in use of contraceptives. *The New York Times,* September 4, Y7.

Kelley, K. (1985). Sex, sex guilt, and authoritarianism: Differences in responses to explicit heterosexual and masturbatory slides. *Journal of Sex Research,* 21, 68–85.

Kelly, J. (1982). Divorce: The adult perspective. In B. Wolman & G. Stricker (Eds.), *Handbook of Developmental Psychology.* Englewood Cliffs, NJ: Prentice Hall.

Kelly, J., & Rice, S. (1986). The aged. In H. Gochros, J. Gochros, & J. Fisher (Eds.), *Helping the Sexually Oppressed.* Englewood Cliffs, NJ: Prentice Hall.

Kelly, M. (1998). View from the field out in education: Where the personal and political collide. *Siecus Report*, 26(4), 14–15.

Kelly, M., Strassberg, D., & Kircher, J. (1990). Attitudinal and experiental correlates of anorgasmia. *Archives of Sexual Behavior*, 19, 165–181.

Kempf, D., Rode, R., Sun, E., Health-Chiozzi, M., Valdes, J., Japour, A., Danner, S., Boucher, C., Molla, A., & Leonard, J. (1998). The duration of viral suppression during protease inhibitor therapy for HIV-1 infection is predicted by plasma HIV-1 RNA at the nadir. *AIDS*, 12, F9–F14.

Kendrick, J., Atrash, H., Strauss, L., Gargiullo, P., & Ahn, Y. (1997). Vaginal douching and the risk of ectopic pregnancy among black women. *American Journal of Obstetrics & Gynecology*, 176, 991–997.

Kenemans, P. (1997). State of the art of practical HRT. Risks and benefits of long-term HRT: A calculated risk? *European Journal of Obstetrics & Gynecology and Reproductive Biology*, 71, 187.

Kenemans, P., Scheele, F., & Burger, C. (1997). Hormone replacement therapy and breast cancer morbidity, mortality and recurrence. *European Journal of Obstetrics & Gynecology and Reproductive Biology*, 71, 199–203.

Kennedy, S. (1997). Primary dysmenorrhoea. *The Lancet*, 349, 1116.

Kent, C. (1994). Eleven states refuse to comply with Medicaid abortion rule. *Faulkner and Gray's Medicine and Health,* 48(19), 2.

Kettl, P., Zarefoss, S., Jacoby, K., Garman, C., Hulse, C., Rowley, F., Corey, R., Sredy, M., Bixler, E., & Tyson, K. (1991). Female sexuality after spinal cord injury. *Sexuality and Disability,* 9(4), 287–295.

Kilkku, P. (1983). Supravaginal uterine amputation vs. hysterectomy: Effects on coital frequency and dyspareunia. *Acta Obstetricia et Gynecologica Scandinavica,* 62, 141–145.

Kilpatrick, J. (1960). *The Smut Peddlers.* Garden City, NY: Doubleday.

Kim, E., & Lipshultz, L. (1997). Advances in the treatment of organic erectile dysfunction. *Hospital Practice*, April 15, 101–120.

Kim, E., & McVary, K. (1995). Long-term results with penile vein ligation for venogenic impotence. *Journal of Urology,* 153, 655–658.

Kim, E., El-Rashidy, R., & McVary, K. (1995). Papaverine topical gel for treatment of erectile dysfunction. *Journal of Urology,* 153, 361–365.

Kim, S., & Seo, K. (1998). Efficacy and safety of fluoxetine, sertraline and clomipramine in patients with premature ejaculation: A double-blind, placebo controlled study. *Journal of Urology*, 159, 425–427.

Kimble, D. (1996). *Biological Psychology* (3rd ed.). Fort Worth, TX: Harcourt Brace Jovanovich.

Kimlicka, T., Cross, H., & Tarnai, J. (1983). A comparison of androgynous, feminine, masculine, and undifferentiated women on self-esteem, body satisfaction, and sexual satisfaction. *Psychology of Women Quarterly,* 1, 291–294.

Kimmel, D. (1978). Adult development and aging: A gay perspective. *Journal of Social Issues,* 34, 113–130.

Kinard, E., & Reinherz, H. (1987). School aptitude and achievement in children of adolescent mothers. *Journal of Youth and Adolescence,* 16, 69–78.

Kinsey, A., Pomeroy, W., & Martin, C. (1948). *Sexual Behavior in the Human Male.* Philadelphia: Saunders.

Kinsey, A., Pomeroy, W., Martin, C., & Gebhard, P. (1953). *Sexual Behavior in the Human Female.* Philadelphia: Saunders.

Kinzl, J., Traweger, C., & Biebl, W. (1995). Sexual dysfunctions: Relationship to childhood sexual abuse and early family experiences in a nonclinical sample. *Child Abuse & Neglect*, 19, 785–792.

Kirby, R. (1994). Impotence: Diagnosis and management of male erectile dysfunction. *British Medical Journal,* 308, 957–960.

Kirchmeyer, C. (1996). Gender roles in decision-making in demographically diverse groups: A case for reviving androgyny. *Sex Roles*, 34, 649–663.

Kirk, M., & Madsen, H. (1989). *After the Ball.* New York: Doubleday.

Kirk-Smith, M., Booth, D., Carroll, D., & Davies, P. (1978). Human social attitudes affected by androstenal. *Research Communications in Psychology, Psychiatry, and Behavior,* 3, 379–384.

Kissinger, P., Trim, S., Williams, E., Mielke, E., Koporc, K., & Brown, R. (1997). An evaluation of initiatives to improve family planning use by African-American adolescents. *Journal of the National Medical Association*, 89, 110–114.

Kitano, H. (1988). The Japanese-American family. In C. Mindel, R. Habenstein, & R. Wright (Eds.), *Ethnic Families in America,* 3rd ed. New York: Elsevier.

Kite, M., Deaux, K., & Miele, M. (1991). Stereotypes of young and old: Does age outweigh gender? *Psychology and Aging,* 6, 19–27.

Kitzinger, C., & Wilkinson, S. (1995). Transitions from heterosexuality to lesbianism: The discursive production of lesbian identities. *Developmental Psychology,* 31, 95–104.

Klagsbrun, G. (1985). *Married People: Staying Together in the Age of Divorce.* New York: Bantam Books.

Klaich, D. (1974). *Woman Plus Woman: Attitudes Towards Lesbianism.* New York: Simon & Schuster.

Klein, M. (1991). Why there's no such thing as sexual addiction and why it really matters. In R. Francoeur (Ed.). *Taking Sides: Clashing Views of Controversial Issues in Human Sexuality* (3rd ed.). Guilford, CT: Dushkin.

Klitsch, M. (1988). FDA approval ends cervical cap's marathon. *Family Planning Perspectives,* 20, 137–138.

Kluwer, E., Heesink, J., & Van de Vliert, E. (1996). Marital conflict about the division of household labor and paid work. *Journal of Marriage and the Family*, 58, 958–969.

Knafo, D., & Jaffe, Y. (1984). Sexual fantasizing in males and females. *Journal of Research in Personality,* 19, 451–462.

Knoll, L., & Abrams, J. (1998). Evaluation of penile ultrasonic velocitometry versus penile duplex ultrasonography to assess penile arterial hemodynamics. *Urology*, 51, 89–93.

Koch-Straube, U. (1982). Attitude toward sexuality in old age. *Zeitschrift für Gerontologie,* 15, 220–227.

Koff, E., Rierdan, J., & Stubbs, M. (1990). Conceptions and misconceptions of the menstrual cycle. *Women & Health,* 16, 119–135.

Koff, W., & Scaletscky, R. (1990). Malformations of the epididymis in undescended testis. *Journal of Urology,* 143, 340–343.

Koglin, O. (1996). A woman's pain. *The Oregonian*, June 20, A20.

Koglin, O. (1998). Tamoxifen prevents breast cancer. *The Oregonian*, April 7, A1 & A7.

Kohlberg, L. (1966). A cognitive-developmental analysis of children's sex-role concepts and attitudes. In E. Maccoby (Ed.), *The Development of Sex Differences.* Stanford, CA: Stanford University Press.

Kolasa, K., & Weismiller, D. (1997). Nutrition during pregnancy. *American Family Physician*, 56, 205–212.

Kolasa, K., Horner, R., Wilson, K., Irons, T., Black, C., & Causby, V. (1995). Community perceptions of adolescent health and sexuality. *Archives of Pediatric Adolescent Medicine,* 149, 611–614.

Kolata, G. (1997a). Ethicists debate propriety of old-age motherhood. *Monterey County Herald*, April 27, A8.

Kolata, G. (1997b). Requests for dead men's sperm increasing. *Monterey County Herald*, May 30, A9.

Kolodny, R. (1980). Adolescent sexuality. Paper presented at the Michigan Personnel and Guidance Association Annual Convention, Detroit, November.

Kolodny, R., Masters, W., & Johnson, V. (1979). *Textbook of Sexual Medicine.* Boston: Little, Brown.

Komaromy, M., Bindman, A., Haber, R., & Sande, M. (1993). Sexual harassment in medical training. *New England Journal of Medicine,* 328, 322–326.

Kools, A. (1992). Hepatitis A, B, C, D, and E: Update on testing and treatment. *Postgraduate Medicine,* 91, 109–114.

Koopman, J. (1996). Emerging objectives and methods in epidemiology. *American Journal of Public Health*, 86, 630–632.

Kopenec, S. (1997). Southern Baptists boycott Disney over "gay-friendly" policies. *Monterey County Herald*, June 19, A6.

Koppelman, A. (1988). A feminist model of women's sexual health. Paper presented at the Association for Women in Psychology, Bethesda, Maryland.

Korenman, S., & Viosca, S. (1992). Use of a vacuum tumescence device in the management of impotence in men with a history of penile implant or severe pelvic disease. *Journal of the American Geriatric Society,* 40, 61–64.

Kornblum, J. (1997). Gay and gray. *The Advocate*, July 8, 46–48.

Kortenhaus, C., & Demarest, J. (1993). Gender role stereotyping in children's literature: An update. *Sex Roles,* 28, 219–232.

Kosnik, A., Carroll, W., Cunningham, A., Modras, R., & Schulte, J. (1977). *Human Sexuality: New Directions in American Catholic Thought.* New York: Paulist Press.

Koss, L., Gidycz, C., & Seibel, C. (1988). Stranger and acquaintance rape. *Psychology of Women Quarterly,* 12, 1–24.

Koss, L., Gidycz, C., & Wisniewski, N. (1987). The scope of rape: Incidence and prevalence of sexual aggression and victimization in a national sample of higher education students. *Journal of Consulting and Clinical Psychology,* 55, 162–170.

Koss, M. (1988). Hidden rape: Sexual aggression and victimization in a national sample of students in higher education. In A. Burgess (Ed.), *Rape and Sexual Assault II.* New York: Garland.

Koss, M. (1992). The underdetection of rape: Methodological choices influence incidence estimates. *Journal of Social Issues,* 48, 61–75.

Koukounas, E., & McCabe, M. (1997). Sexual and emotional variables influencing sexual response to erotica. *Behavior Research & Therapy*, 35, 221–231.

Kristof, N. (1996). The youngest prostitutes. *The Oregonian*, June 12, A12.

Kroll, K., & Klein E. (1992). *Enabling Romance.* New York: Harmony Books.

Krugman, R., Bays, J., Chadwick, D., Levitt, C., McHugh, M., & Whitworth, J. (1991). Guidelines for the evaluation of sexual abuse of children. *Pediatrics,* 87, 254–260.

Kruse, R., Guttenbach, M., Schartmann, B., Schubert, R., van der Ven, H., Schmid, M., & Propping, P. (1998). Genetic counseling in a patient with XXY/XXXY/XY mosaic Klinefelter's syndrome: Estimates of sex chromosome aberrations in sperm before intracytoplasmic sperm injection. *Fertility and Sterility*, 69, 482–485.

Krystal, H. (1982). Alexithymia and the effectiveness of psychoanalytic treatment. *International Journal of Psychoanalytical Psychotherapy*, 9, 353–378.

Ku, L., Sonenstein, F., & Pleck, J. (1993). Young men's risk behaviors for HIV infection and sexually transmitted diseases, 1988 through 1991. *American Journal of Public Health,* 83, 1609–1615.

Kuffel, G. (1997). A lesson in coming out. *The Advocate*, September 16, 9.

Kulin, H. (1991). Hypothalamic-pituitary changes of puberty. In R. Lerner, A. Petersen, & J. Brooks-Gunn (Eds.), *Encyclopedia of Adolescence.* New York: Garland.

Kumar, S. (1994). Legislation on prenatal sex-determination in India. *The Lancet,* 344, 399.

Kurdek, L. (1988). Relationship quality of gay and lesbian cohabitating couples. *Journal of Homosexuality*, 15, 93–118.

Kurdek, L. (1995). Developmental changes in relationship quality in gay and lesbian cohabiting couples. *Developmental Psychology,* 31, 86–94.

Kusseling, F., Wenger, N., & Shapiro, M. (1995). Inconsistent contraceptive use among female college students: Implications for intervention. *Journal of American College Health,* 43, 191–195.

Kyes, K. & Tumbelaka, L. (1994). Comparison of Indonesian and American college students' attitudes toward homosexuality. *Psychological Reports,* 74, 227–237.

Ladas, A. (1989). False information about female anatomy causes great unhappiness. *Contemporary Sexuality,* 21, 5 & 11.

Ladouceur, P., & Temple, M. (1985). Substance use among rapists: A comparison with other serious felons. *Crime and Delinquency,* 31, 269–294.

Lafferty, W., Hiltunen-Back, E., Reuwala, T., Niemen, P., & Paavonen, J. (1997). Sexually transmitted diseases in men who have sex with men. *Sexually Transmitted Diseases*, 24, 272–278.

Lagrew, D., Jr. (1996). Physician "report cards" cut c-section rates. *American Journal of Obstetrics and Gynecology*, 174, 184–191.

Laguna, F., Rodriquez-Tudela, J., Martinez-Suarez, J., Polo, R., Valencia, E., Diaz-Guerra, T., Dronda, F., & Pulido, F. (1997). Patterns of fluconazole susceptibility in isolates from human immunodeficiency virus-infected patients with oropharyngeal candidiasis due to *Candida albicans. Clinical Infectious Diseases*, 24, 124–130.

Lai, T. (1992). Asian-American women: Not for sale. In M. Andersen & P. Collins (Eds.), *Race, Class, and Gender.* Belmont, CA: Wadsworth.

Lamb, M. (1981). The development of father–infant relationships. In M. Lamb (Ed.), *The Role of the Father in Child Development.* New York: Wiley.

Lamb, M., Hopps, K., & Elster, A. (1987). Strange situation behavior of infants with adolescent mothers. *Infant Behavior and Development,* 10, 39–48.

Lambert, B. (1988). AIDS among prostitutes not as prevalent as believed, studies show. *The New York Times,* September 20, B1.

Lammer, E., Chen, D., Hoar, R., Agnish, N., Benke, P., Braun, J., Curry, C., Fernhoff, P., Grix, A., Lott, I., Richard, J., & Sun, S. (1985). Retinoic acid embryopathy. *New England Journal of Medicine,* 313, 837–841.

Lancaster, J. (1997). Egypt will permit female circumcision. *The Oregonian*, June 25, A3.

Landau, J. (1997). Out of order: How same-sex harassers beat the rap. *The New Republic*, 216, 9–10.

Landen, M., Walinder, J., & Lundstrom, B. (1998). Clinical characteristics of a total cohort of female and male applicants for sex reassignment: A descriptive study. *Acta Psychiatrica Scandinavica*, 97, 189–194.

Landers, A. (1997). Gay youth needs supportive counseling. *The Oregonian*, May 25, L4.

Landis, S., Schoenbach, V., Weber, D., Mittal, M., Krishan, B., Lewis, K., & Koch, G. (1992). Results of a randomized trial of partner notification in cases of HIV infection in North Carolina. *New England Journal of Medicine,* 326, 101–106.

Landry, D., & Forrest, J. (1995). How old are U.S. fathers? *Family Planning Perspectives*, 27, 159–161 & 165.

Landsberg, M. (1996). Gays, lesbians gain U.S. asylum. *The Oregonian*, December 8, A14.

Landsberg, M. (1997). Breast cancer conference: Clean the earth, save lives. *Ms.*, November/December, 12–17.

Lange, P. (1995). New information about prostate-specific antigen and the paradoxes of prostate cancer. *Journal of the American Medical Association,* 273, 336–337.

Langevin, R., & Martin, M. (1975). Can erotic response be classically conditioned? *Behavior Therapy,* 6, 350–355.

Langevin, R., Paitich, D., & Ramsay, G. (1979). Experimental studies of the etiology of genital exhibitionism. *Archives of Sexual Behavior*, 8, 307–331.

Langlois, J., Roggman, L., & Rieser-Danner, L. (1990). Infants' differential social responses to attractive and unattractive faces. *Developmental Psychology*, 26, 153–159.

Langlois, J., Roggman, L., Casey, R., Ritter, J., Rieser-Danner, L., & Jenkins, Y. (1987). Infants' preferences for attractive faces: Rudiments of a stereotype? *Developmental Psychology*, 23, 363–369.

Lapham, L. (1997). In the garden of tabloid delight. *Harper's Magazine*, August, 35–39, 42,43.

Larimore, W. (1995). Family-centered birthing: History, philosophy, and need. *Family Medicine,* 27(2), 132–137.

Larsen, K., & Long, E. (1988). Attitudes toward sex roles: Traditional or egalitarian? *Sex Roles,* 19, 1–12.

Larson, M. (1996). Sex roles and soap operas: What adolescents learn about single motherhood. *Sex Roles*, 35, 97–110.

Lauer, J., & Lauer, R. (1985). Marriages made to last. *Psychology Today,* June, 22–26.

Lauersen, N., & Graves, Z. (1984). Pretended orgasm. *Medical Aspects of Human Sexuality,* 18, 74–81.

Laumann, E., Gagnon, J., Michael, R., & Michaels, S. (1994). *The Social Organization of Sexuality: Sexual Practices in the United States.* Chicago: University of Chicago Press.

Laumann, E., Masi, C., & Zuckerman, E. (1997). Circumcision in the United States: Prevalence, prophylactic effects, and sexual practice. *Journal of the American Medical Association*, 277, 1052–1057.

Laurence, J. (1998). HIV prevention strategies: Quo vadis? *AIDS Patient Care and STDs*, 12, 165–166.

Laurent, S., Garrison, C., Thompson, S., Moore, E., & Addy, C. (1992). An epidemiologic study of smoking and primary infertility in women. *Fertility and Sterility,* 57, 565–572.

Laury, G. (1992). When women sexually abuse male psychiatric patients under their care. *Journal of Sex Education & Therapy,* 18, 11–16.

Lavee, Y., Sharlin, S., & Katz, R. (1996). The effect of parenting stress on marital quality. *Journal of Family Issues*, 17, 114–135.

Lavee,Y. (1991). Western and non-western human sexuality: Implications for clinical practice. *Journal of Sex and Marital Therapy,* 17, 203–213.

Laws, D., & Marshall, W. (1991). Masturbatory reconditioning with sexual deviates: An evaluative review. *Advances in Behavior Research and Therapy*, 13, 13–25.

Leadbeater, B., & Way, N. (1995). *Urban Adolescent Girls: Resisting Stereotypes.* New York: University Press.

Leaper, C., Anderson, K., & Sanders, P. (1998). Moderators of gender effects on parents' talk to their children: A meta-analysis. *Developmental Psychology*, 34, 3–27.

Leavitt, F. (1997). False attribution of suggestibility to explain recovered memory of childhood sexual abuse following extended amnesia. *Child Abuse & Neglect*, 21, 265–272.

Leavitt, F., & Berger, J. (1990). Clinical patterns among male transsexual candidates with erotic interest in males. *Archives of Sexual Behavior*, 19, 491–505.

Lebow, J. (1997). Is couples therapy obsolete? *Networker*, September/October, 81–88.

Lee, A., & Scheurer, V. (1983). Psychological androgyny and aspects of self-image in women and men. *Sex Roles*, 9, 289–306.

Lee, J. (1988). Love-styles. In R. Sternberg & M. Barnes (Eds.), *The Psychology of Love*. New Haven, CT: Yale University Press.

Lee, M., Donahoe, P., Silverman, B., Hasegawa, T., Hasegawa, Y., Gustafson, M., Chang, Y., & MacLaughlin, D. (1997). Measurements of serum mullerian inhibitory substance in the evaluation of children with nonpalpable gonads. *New England Journal of Medicine*, 336, 1480–1486.

Lee, N., Rubin, G., & Borucki, R. (1988). The intrauterine device and pelvic inflammatory disease revisited: New results from the women's health study. *Obstetrics & Gynecology*, 72, 1–6.

Lefebvre, K. A. (1997). Performing a sexual evaluation on the person with disability or illness. In M. Sipski & C. Alexander (Eds.), *Sexual Function in People with Disability and Chronic Illness*. Gaithersburg, MD: Aspen Publishers.

Leiblum, S., & Bachmann, G. (1988). The sexuality of the climacteric woman. In B. Eskin (Ed.), *The Menopause: Comprehensive Management*. New York: Yearbook Medical Publications.

Leigh, B. (1989). Reasons for having and avoiding sex: Gender, sexual orientation, and relationship to sexual behavior. *Journal of Sex Research*, 26, 199–208.

Leiner, S. (1997). Urinary tract infections in otherwise healthy nonpregnant adult women. *Physician Assistant*, May, 36–68.

Leitenberg, H., & Henning, K. (1995). Sexual fantasy. *Psychological Bulletin*, 117(3), 469–496.

Leitenberg, H., Detzer, M., & Srebnik, D. (1993). Gender differences in masturbation and the relation of masturbation experience in preadolescence and/or early adolescence to sexual behavior and sexual adjustment in young adulthood. *Archives of Sexual Behavior*, 22, 87–98.

Leland, J. (1994). Homophobia. *Newsweek*, February 14, 42–47.

Leland, J. (1995). Bisexuality. *Newsweek*, July 17, 44–50.

Leland, J. (1997). A pill for impotence? *Newsweek*, November 17, 62–65.

Leland, J., & Beals, G. (1997). In living color. *Newsweek*, May 5, 58–60.

Lemon, B. (1997). Mr. USA is gay! *The Advocate*, July 22, 26–30.

Lemon, S., & Thomas, D. (1997). Vaccines to prevent viral hepatitis. *New England Journal of Medicine*, 336, 196–203.

Lemonick, M. (1997). America Online's little problem. *Time*, December 15, 76.

Lenderking, W., World, C., Mayer, K., Goldstein, R., Losina, E., & Seage, G. (1997). Childhood sexual abuse among homosexual men. *Journal of General Internal Medicine*, 12, 250–253.

Lerner, R., Petersen, A., & Brooks-Gunn, J. (1991). *Encyclopedia of Adolescence*. New York: Garland.

Leserman, J., & Drossman, D. (1995). *General Hospital Psychiatry*, 17, 71–74.

Letourneau, E., Schewe, P., & Frueh, B. (1997). Preliminary evaluation of sexual problems in combat veterans with PTSD. *Journal of Traumatic Stress*, 10, 125–132

Levant, R. (1997). *Men and Emotions: A Psychoeducational Approach*. New York: Newbridge Communications.

LeVay, S. (1991). A difference in hypothalamic structure between heterosexual and homosexual men. *Science*, 253, 1034–1037.

Lever, J. (1994). Sexual revelations. *The Advocate*, August 23, 17–24.

Lever, J. (1995). Lesbian sex survey. *The Advocate*, August 22, 21–30.

Levin, R., & Levin, A. (1975). The Redbook report on premarital and extramarital sex. *Redbook*, October, 51.

Levine, M., & Troiden, R. (1988). The myth of sexual compulsivity. *Journal of Sex Research*, 25, 347–363.

Levine, S. (1992). Intrapsychic and interpersonal aspects of impotence: Psychogenic erectile dysfunction. In R. Rosen & S. Leiblum (Eds.), *Erectile Disorders*. New York: Guilford.

Levine, S., & Althof, S. (1991). The pathogenesis of psychogenic erectile dysfunction. *Journal of Sex Education & Therapy*, 4, 251–266.

Levinson, R. (1995). Reproductive and contraceptive knowledge, contraceptive self-efficacy, and contraceptive behavior among teenage women. *Adolescence*, 30, 65–85.

Levitan, M., & Montagu, A. (1977). *A Textbook of Human Genetics* (2nd ed.). New York: Oxford University Press.

Levy, D. (1994). Amnesty International to fight persecution of homosexuals. *San Francisco Chronicle*, February 9, A4.

Levy, J. (1997a). Three new human herpes viruses (HHV6, 7, and 8). *The Lancet*, 349, 558–562.

Levy, S. (1997b). On the Net, anything goes. *Newsweek*, July 7, 28–30.

Lewes, K. (1988). *The Psychoanalytic Theory of Male Homosexuality*. New York: Simon & Schuster.

Lewis, K., & Moon, S. (1997). Always single and single again women: A qualitative study. *Journal of Marital and Family Therapy*, 23(2), 115–134.

Lidster, C., & Horsburgh, M. (1994). Masturbation—Beyond myth and taboo. *Nursing Forum*, 29(3), 18–26.

Lieberman, A. (1987). *Giving Birth*. New York: St. Martin's Press.

Lieblich, J., & Rios, D. (1995). A ritual of oppression. *The Oregonian*, September 17, E1–E8.

Lieblum, S. (1997). Sex and the net: Clinical implications. *Journal of Sex Education and Therapy*, 22(1), 21–28.

Lieblum, S., & Bachmann, G. (1988). The sexuality of the climacteric woman. In B. Eskin (Ed.), *The Menopause Comprehensive Management*. New York: Yearbook Medical Publications.

Liebowitz, M. (1983). *The Chemistry of Love*. Boston: Little, Brown.

Lief, H., & Hubschman, L. (1993). Orgasm in the postoperative transsexual. *Archives of Sexual Behavior*, 22, 145–155.

Lindberg, C. (1997). Emergency contraception: The nurse's role providing postcoital options. *Journal of Obstetrical & Gynecological Neonatal Nurses*, March/April, 145–151.

Lindberg, L., Sonenstein, F., Ku, L., & Levine, G. (1997). Young men's experience with condom breakage. *Family Planning Perspectives*, 29, 128–131 & 140.

Lindholm, J., Lunde, I., Rasmussen, O., & Wagner, G. (1980). Gonadal and sexual functions in tortured Greek men. *Danish Medical Bulletin*, 27, 243–245.

Lindsay, M., Carmichael, S., Peterson, H., Risby, J., Williams, H., & Klein, L. (1997). Correlation between self-reported cocaine use and urine toxicology in an inner-city prenatal population. *Journal of the National Medical Association*, 89, 57–60.

Lindsay, S., & Read, D. (1994). Psychotherapy and memories of childhood sexual abuse: A cognitive perspective. *Applied Cognitive Psychology*, 8, 281–338.

Lindsey, K. (1977). Sexual harassment on the job. *Ms.*, November, 47.

Linz, D., Donnerstein, E., & Penrod, S. (1988). Effects of long-term exposure to violent and sexually degrading depictions of women. *Journal of Personality and Social Psychology,* 55, 758–768.

Linz, D., Wilson, B., & Donnerstein, E. (1992). Sexual violence in the mass media: Legal solutions, warnings, and mitigation through education. *Journal of Social Issues,* 48, 145–171.

Lips, H. (1997). *Sex and Gender* (3rd ed.). Mountain View, CA: Mayfield.

Lisk, R. (1966). Increased sexual behavior in the male rat following lesions in the mammillary region. *Journal of Experimental Zoology,* 161, 129–136.

Lively, V., & Lively, E. (1991). *Sexual Development of Young Children.* Albany, NY: Delmar.

Livingston, L. (1997). Personal communication.

Livson, F. (1983). Gender identity: A life-span view of sex-role development. In R. Weg (Ed.), *Sexuality in the Later Years: Roles and Behavior.* New York: Academic Press.

Lobitz, W., & Lobitz, G. (1996). Resolving the sexual intimacy paradox: A developmental model for the treatment of sexual desire disorders. *Journal of Sex and Marital Therapy,* 22, 71–84.

LoCicero, A. (1993). Explaining excessive rates of cesareans and other childbirth interventions: Contributions from contemporary theories of gender and psychosocial development. *Social Science Medicine,* 37(10), 1261–1269.

Loftus, E. (1993). The reality of repressed memories. *American Psychologist,* 48, 518–537.

Loftus, E., & Ketcham, K. (1994). *The Myth of Repressed Memory.* New York: St. Martin's Press.

Loftus, E., Polonsky, S., & Fullilove, M. (1994). Memories of childhood sexual abuse: Remembering and repressing. *Psychology of Women Quarterly,* 18, 67–84.

Longres, J. (1996). Preface. In J. Longres (Ed.), *Men of Color.* New York: Harrington Park Press.

Lonsway, K., & Fitzgerald, L. (1994). Rape myths. *Psychology of Women Quarterly,* 18, 133–164.

Lonsway, K., & Fitzgerald, L. (1995). Attitudinal antecedents of rape myth acceptance: A theoretical and empirical reexamination. *Journal of Personality and Social Psychology,* 68, 704–711,

LoPiccolo, J. (1982). Personal communication, July.

LoPiccolo, J. (1985). Advances in diagnosis and treatment of sexual dysfunction. Paper presented at the Twenty-Eighth Annual Meeting of the Society for the Scientific Study of Sex, San Diego, September 19–22.

LoPiccolo, J. (1989). Sexual dysfunctions: Advances in diagnosis and treatment. Workshop for Oregon Division of The American Association for Marriage and Family Therapy, Portland, Oregon, April.

LoPiccolo, J. (1991). Counseling and therapy for sexual problems in the elderly. *Clinics in Geriatric Medicine,* 7, 161–179.

LoPiccolo, J. (1992). Postmodern sex therapy for erectile failure. In R. Rosen & S. Leiblum (Eds.), *Erectile Disorders.* New York: Guilford.

LoPiccolo, J., & Friedman, J. (1988). Broad-spectrum treatment of low sexual desire: Integration of cognitive, behavioral, and systemic therapy. In S. Leiblum & R. Rosen (Eds.), *Sexual Desire Disorders.* New York: Guilford.

LoPiccolo, J., & Heiman, J. (1978). The role of cultural values in the prevention and treatment of sexual problems. In C. Qualls, J. Wincze, & D. Barlow (Eds.), *The Prevention of Sexual Disorders.* New York: Plenum.

LoPresto, C., Sherman, M., & Sherman, N. (1985). The effects of a masturbation seminar on high school males' attitudes, false beliefs, guilt, and behavior. *Journal of Sex Research,* 21, 142–156.

Lorber, J. (1995). Gender is determined by social practices. In D. Bender & B. Leone (Eds.), *Human Sexuality: Opposing Viewpoints.* San Diego, CA: Greenhaven Press.

Lothstein, L. (1984). Psychological testing with transsexuals: A 30-year review. *Journal of Personality Assessment,* 48, 500–507.

Louderback, L., & Whitley, B., Jr. (1997). Perceived erotic value of homosexuality and sex-role attitudes as mediators of sex differences in heterosexual college students' attitudes toward lesbians and gay men. *Journal of Sex Research,* 34(2), 175–182.

Louis, M., Wasserheit, J., & Gayle, H. (1997). Editorial: Janus considers the HIV pandemic—harnessing recent advances to enhance AIDS prevention. *American Journal of Public Health,* 87, 10–12.

Loulan, J. (1984). *Lesbian Sex.* San Francisco: Spinsters Ink.

Lovdal, L. (1989). Sex role messages in television commercials: An update. *Sex Roles,* 21, 715–724.

Love, S. (1997). A surgeon's challenge. *Newsweek,* February 24, 60.

Lowie, R. (1935). *The Crow Indians.* New York: Farrar and Rinehart.

Lown, J., & Dolan, E. (1988). Financial challenges in remarriage. *Lifestyles: Family and Economic Issues,* 9, 73–88.

Lown, J., McFadden, J., & Crossman, S. (1989). Family life education for remarriage focus on financial management. *Family Relations,* 38, 40–45.

Loy, P., & Stewart, L. (1984). The extent and effects of the sexual harassment of working women. *Sociological Focus,* 17, 31–43.

Lu-Yao, G., Potosky, A., Albertsen, P., Wasson, J., Barry, M., & Wennberg, J. (1996). Follow-up prostate cancer treatments after radical prostatectomy: A population-based study. *Journal of the National Cancer Institute,* 88, 166–173.

Lue, T. (1994). Editorial: Erectile dysfunction associated with cavernous and neurological disorders. *Journal of Urology,* 151, 890–891.

Luey, H., Glass, L., & Elliott, H. (1995). Hard-of-hearing or deaf: Issues of ears, language, culture, and identity. *Journal of the National Association of Social Workers,* 40, 177–182.

Luker, K. (1975). *Taking Chances: Abortion and the Decision Not to Contracept.* Berkeley: University of California Press.

Lukes, C., & Land, H. (1990). Biculturality and homosexuality. *Social Work,* 35, 155–161.

Lundstrom, B., Pauly, I., & Walinder, J. (1984). Outcome of sex reassignment surgery. *Acta Psychiatrica Scandinavica,* 70, 289–294.

Lurie, P., & Drucker, E. (1997). An opportunity lost: HIV infections associated with lack of a national needle-exchange programme in the U.S.A. *The Lancet,* 349, 604–608.

Luster, T., & Small, S. (1994). Factors associated with sexual risk-taking behaviors among adolescents. *Journal of Marriage and the Family,* 56, 622–632.

Luster, T., & Small, S. (1997). Sexual abuse history and problems in adolescence: Exploring the effects of moderating variables. *Journal of Marriage and the Family,* 59, 131–142.

Lynch, C., Sinnott, J., Holt, D., & Herold, A. (1991). Use of antibiotics during pregnancy. *American Family Physician,* 43, 1365–1368.

Lynch, F. (1992). Nonghetto gays: An ethnography of suburban homosexuals. In G. Herdt (Ed.), *Gay Culture in America.* Boston: Beacon Press.

Lynch, H., & Casey, M. (1997). The role of prophylactic surgery for hereditary breast and ovarian cancer. *Contemporary Ob/Gyn,* July, 41–58.

Lynxwiler, J., & Gay, D. (1994). Reconsidering race differences in abortion attitudes. *Social Science Quarterly,* 75, 67–84.

Lytton, H., & Romney, D. (1991). Parents' differential socialization of boys and girls: A meta-analysis. *Psychological Bulletin,* 109, 267–296.

Maccoby, E. (1988). Gender as a social category. *Developmental Psychology,* 26, 755–765.

Maccoby, E. (1990). Gender and relationships: A developmental account. *American Psychologist,* 45, 513–520.

Maccoby, E., & Jacklin, C. (1974). *The Psychology of Sex Differences.* Palo Alto, CA: Stanford University Press.

Maccoby, E., & Jacklin, C. (1987). Gender segregation in childhood. *Advances in Child Development and Behavior,* 20, 239–287.

MacDermott, R. (1995). Bacterial vaginosis. *British Journal of Obstetrics and Gynaecology,* 102, 92–94.

MacDonald, A., Jr. (1981). Bisexuality: Some comments on research and theory. *Journal of Homosexuality,* 6, 21–35.

MacFarlane, A., & McPherson, A. (1992). Sex and teenagers. *Health Visitor,* 65, 18–19.

Mackey, R., & O'Brien, B. (1998). Marital conflict management: Gender and ethnic differences. *Journal of the National Association of Social Workers,* 43(2), 128–141.

MacKinnon, C. (1979). *Sexual Harassment of Working Women.* New Haven, CT: Yale University Press.

MacKinnon, C. (1986). Pornography: Not a moral issue. *Women's Studies International Forum,* 9, 63–78.

MacNamara, D., & Sagarin, E. (1977). *Sex, Crime, and the Law.* New York: Free Press.

Madore, C., Hawes, W., Many, F., & Hexter, A. (1981). A study on the effects of induced abortion on subsequent pregnancy outcome. *American Journal of Obstetrics and Gynecology,* 139, 516–521.

Maher, L. (1997). Uterine fibroids: Treat—or ignore? *Patient Care,* January 15, 48–55.

Mahmoodian, S. (1997). Cervical and breast cancer screening rates in Sioux Indian women. *Southern Medical Journal,* 90(3), 316–320.

Maier, J., & Maloni, J. (1997). Nurse advocacy for selective versus routine episiotomy. *Journal of Obstetrical, Gynecological & Neonatal Nurses,* 26, 155–161.

Mainous, A., & Hueston, W. (1994). The effect of smoking cessation during pregnancy on preterm delivery and low birthweight. *Journal of Family Practice,* 38(3), 262–266.

Majeroni, B. (1994). Chlamydial cervicitis: Complications and new treatment options. *American Family Physician,* 49, 1825–1829.

Malamud, D. (1997). Oral diagnostic testing for detecting human immunodeficiency virus-1 antibodies: A technology whose time has come. *American Journal of Medicine,* 102 (Suppl. 4A), 9–14.

Malamuth, N. (1982). Aggression against women: Cultural and individual causes. In N. Malamuth & E. Donnerstein (Eds.), *Pornography and Sexual Aggression.* New York: Academic Press.

Malamuth, N. (1986). Predictors of naturalistic sexual aggression. *Journal of Personality and Social Psychology,* 50, 953–962.

Malamuth, N., & Check, J. (1981). The effects of mass media exposure on acceptance of violence against women: A field experiment. *Journal of Research in Personality,* 15, 436–446.

Malamuth, N., Haber, S., & Feshback, S. (1980). Testing hypotheses regarding rape: Exposure to sexual violence, sex differences, and the normality of rapists. *Journal of Research in Personality,* 14, 121–137.

Malatesta, C., Culver, C., Tesman, J., & Shephard, B. (1989). The development of emotion expression during the first two years of life. *Monographs of the Society for Research in Child Development,* 50 (1–2, Serial No. 219).

Males, M., & Chew, K. (1996). The ages of fathers in California adolescent births, 1993. *American Journal of Public Health,* 86, 565–568.

Malina, R. (1991). Adolescent growth spurt. In R. Lerner, A. Petersen, & J. Brooks-Gunn (Eds.), *Encyclopedia of Adolescence.* New York: Garland.

Mallon, G. (1996). Don't ask, don't tell: Gay and lesbian adolescents in residential treatment. *Treatment Today,* Spring, 19–20.

Malloy, K., & Patterson, M. (1992). *Birth or Abortion? Private Struggles in a Political World.* New York: Plenum Press.

Maltz, W. (1995a). The Maltz hierarchy of sexual interaction. *Sexual Addiction and Compulsivity,* 2(1).

Maltz, W. (1995b). Personal communication.

Maltz, W. (1991). *The Sexual Healing Journey.* New York: HarperCollins.

Maltz, W. (1996). *Passionate Hearts.* Novato, CA: New World Library.

Maltz, W., & Boss, S. (1997). *In the Garden of Desire.* New York: Broadway Books.

Maltz, W., & Holman, B. (1987). *Incest and Sexuality: A Guide to Understanding and Healing.* Lexington, MA: Lexington Books.

Mandel, M. (1997). Virtual Valentines. *The Oregonian,* February 13, N1–6.

Mandoki, M., Sumner, G., Hoffman, R., & Riconda, D. (1991). A review of Klinefelter's syndrome in children and adolescents. *Journal of the American Academy of Child and Adolescence Psychiatry,* 30, 167–172.

Mangan, S., Legano, L., Rosen, C., McHugh, M., Fierman, A., Dreyer, B., Palusci, V., & Winkler, B. (1997). Increased prevalence of abnormal Papanicolaou smears in urban adolescents. *Archives of Pediatric and Adolescent Medicine,* 151, 481.

Mann, A. (1998). Cross-gender sex pill. *Time,* April 6, 62.

Mann, K., Klingler, T., Noe, S., Roeschke, J., Mueller, S., & Benkert, O. (1996). Effects of yohimbine on sexual experiences and nocturnal tumescence and rigidity in erectile dysfunction. *Archives of Sexual Behavior,* 25, 1–16.

Mannino, D., Klevens, R., & Flanders, W. (1994). Cigarette smoking: An independent risk factor for impotence? *American Journal of Epidemiology,* 140, 1003–1008.

Mannion, K. (1981). Psychology and the lesbian: A critical view of the research. In S. Cox (Ed.), *Female Psychology: The Emerging Self,* 2nd ed. New York: St. Martin's Press.

Mansfield, P., Voda, A., & Koch, P. (1995). Predictors of sexual response changes in heterosexual midlife women. *Health Values,* 19, 10–19.

Marcus, E. (1993). Ignorance is not bliss. *Newsweek,* July 5, 10.

Marin, R., & Miller, S. (1997). Ellen steps out. *Newsweek,* April 14, 65–67.

Markos, A., Wade, A., & Walzman, M. (1992). Oral sex and recurrent vulvo-vaginal candidiasis. *Genitourinary Medicine,* 68, 61–62.

Marks, G., Richardson, J., Ruiz, M., & Maldonado, N. (1992). HIV-infected men's practices in notifying past sexual partners of infection risk. *Public Health Reports,* 107, 100–109.

Marks, N. (1996). Flying solo at midlife: Gender, marital status, and psychological well-being. *Journal of Marriage and the Family,* 58, 917–932.

Marshall, D. (1971). Sexual behavior on Mangaia. In D. Marshall & R. Suggs (Eds.), *Human Sexual Behavior: Variations in the Ethnographic Spectrum.* Englewood Cliffs, NJ: Prentice Hall.

Marshall, W. (1988). The use of sexually explicit stimuli by rapists, child molesters, and nonoffenders. *Journal of Sex Research,* 25, 267–288.

Marshall, W. (1993). A revised approach to the treatment of men who sexually assault adult females. In G. Hall, R. Hirschman, J. Graham, & M. Zaragoza (Eds.), *Sexual Aggression: Issues in Etiology, Assessment, and Treatment.* Washington, DC: Taylor & Francis.

Marshall, W., Eccles, A., & Barbaree, H. (1991). The treatment of exhibitionists: A focus on sexual deviance versus cognitive and relationship features. *Behaviour Research and Therapy,* 29, 129–135.

Marsiglio, W. (1993). Adolescent males' orientation toward paternity and contraception. *Family Planning Perspectives,* 25, 22–31.

Martin, C. (1990). Attitudes and expectations about children with nontraditional and traditional gender roles. *Sex Roles,* 22, 151–165.

Martin, D., & Lyon, P. (1972). *Lesbian-Woman.* New York: Bantam Books.

Martins, F., & Reis, J. (1997). Visual erotic stimulation test for initial screening of psychogenic erectile dysfunction: A reliable noninvasive alternative? *Journal of Urology,* 157, 134–139.

Martinson, F. (1980). Childhood sexuality. In B. Wolman & J. Money (Eds.), *Handbook of Human Sexuality.* Englewood Cliffs, NJ: Prentice Hall.

Martinson, F. (1994). *The Sexual Life of Children.* Westport, CT: Bergin & Garvey.

Massad, L., Meyer, P., & Hobbs, J. (1997). Knowledge of cervical cancer screening among women attending urban colposcopy clinics. *Cancer Detection and Prevention,* 21(1), 103–109.

Masters, W., & Johnson, V. (1961). Orgasm, anatomy of the female. In A. Ellis & A. Abarbonel (Eds.), *Encyclopedia of Sexual Behavior,* Vol. 2. New York: Hawthorn.

Masters, W., & Johnson, V. (1966). *Human Sexual Response.* Boston: Little, Brown.

Masters, W., & Johnson, V. (1970). *Human Sexual Inadequacy.* Boston: Little, Brown.

Masters, W., & Johnson, V. (1976). *The Pleasure Bond.* New York: Bantam Books.

Masters, W., Johnson, V., & Kolodny, R. (1994). *Heterosexuality.* New York: HarperCollins.

Mastro, T., Satten, G., Nopkesorn, T., Sangkhoromya, I., & Longini, I. (1994). Probability of female-to-male transmission of HIV-1 in Thailand. *The Lancet,* 343, 204–207.

Mastroianni, L., & Robinson, J. C. (1995). Hassle-free methods of contraception. *Patient Care,* March 15, 46–58.

Matek, O. (1988). Obscene phone callers. *Journal of Social Work and Human Sexuality,* 7, 113–30.

Mathes, E., & Verstrate, C. (1993). Jealous aggression: Who is the target, the beloved or the rival? *Psychological Reports,* 72, 1071–1074.

Maticka-Tyndale, E., Elkins, D., Haswell-Elkins, M., Rujkorakorn, D., Kuyyakanand, T., & Stam, K. (1997). Contexts and patterns of men's commercial sexual partnerships in Northeastern Thailand: Implications for AIDS prevention. *Social Science and Medicine,* 44, 199–213.

Matteo, S., & Rissman, E. (1984). Increased sexual activity during the midcycle portion of the human menstrual cycle. *Hormones and Behavior,* 18, 249–255.

Matteson, D. (1997). Bisexual and homosexual behavior and HIV risk among Chinese-, Filipino-, and Korean-American men. *Journal of Sex Research,* 34, 93–104.

Matthews, G., McGee, K., & Goldstein, M. (1997). Microsurgical reconstruction following failed vasectomy reversal. *Journal of Urology,* 157, 844–846.

Maxwell, K. (1996). *A Sexual Odyssey: From Forbidden Fruit to Cybersex.* New York: Plenum Press.

May, R. (1969). *Love and Will.* New York: Norton.

Mazer, D., & Percival, E. (1989). Students' experiences of sexual harassment at a small university. *Sex Roles,* 20, 1–22.

McAninch, C., Milich, R., Crumb, G., & Funtowicz, M. (1996). Children's perception of gender-role–congruent and –incongruent behavior in peers: Fisher-Price meets Price Waterhouse. *Sex Roles,* 35, 619–638.

McBride, G. (1992). U.S. Supreme Court will decide women's right to abortion. *British Medical Journal,* 304, 271–272.

McBride, W. (1991). Spontaneous abortion. *American Family Physician,* 43, 175–182.

McCabe, M., & Delaney, S. (1992). An evaluation of therapeutic programs for the treatment of secondary inorgasmia in women. *Archives of Sexual Behavior,* 21, 69–87.

McCaghy, C., & Hou, C. (1994). Family affiliation and prostitution in a cultural context: Career onsets of Taiwanese prostitutes. *Archives of Sexual Behavior,* 23, 251–265.

McCarthy, B. (1994). Etiology and treatment of early ejaculation. *Journal of Sex Education and Therapy,* 20(1), 5–6.

McCarthy, B. (1995). Bridges to sexual desire. *Journal of Sex Education and Therapy,* 21(2), 132–141.

McCarthy, B. (1997). Chronic sexual dysfunction: Assessment, intervention, and realistic expectations. *Journal of Sex Education and Therapy,* 22(2), 51–56.

McCarthy, S. (1998). The hard facts. *Ms.,* May/June, 96.

McCauley, A., Robey B., Blanc, A., & Geller, J. (1994). Family planning saves lives. *Population Reports,* 22, 4–9.

McCleary, P. (1994). Female genital mutilation and childbirth: A case report. *Birth,* 21(4), December, 221–223.

McClure, D. (1988). Men with one testicle. *Medical Aspects of Human Sexuality,* May, 22–32.

McConville, B. (1998). A bloody tradition. *Nursing Times,* 94(3), 34–36.

McCormack, W. (1994). Pelvic inflammatory disease. *New England Journal of Medicine,* 330, 115–119.

McCormick, C., Witelson, S., & Kingstone, E. (1990). Left-handedness in homosexual men and women: Neuroendocrine implications. *Psychoneuroendocrinology,* 15, 69–76.

McCoy, N., & Matyas, J. (1996). Oral contraceptives and sexuality in university women. *Archives of Sexual Behavior,* 25, 73–89.

McCoy, N., Cutler, W., & Davidson, J. (1985). Relationships among sexual behavior, hot flashes, and hormone levels in perimenopausal women. *Archives of Sexual Behavior,* 14, 385–394.

McCulloch, D., Young, R., Prescott, R., Campbell, I., & Clarke, B. (1984). The natural history of impotence in diabetic men. *Diabetologia,* 26, 437–440.

McElroy, W. (1995). *A Woman's Right to Pornography.* New York: St. Martin's Press.

McFarlane, J., Martin, C., & Williams, T. (1988). Mood fluctuations: Women versus men and menstrual versus other cycles. *Psychology of Women Quarterly,* 12, 201–224.

McFarlane, J., & Williams, T. (1994). Placing premenstrual syndrome in perspective. *Psychology of Women Quarterly,* 18, 339–373.

McGee, C. (1997). Secondary amenorrhea leading to osteoporosis: Incidence and prevention. *Nurse Practitioner*, 22(5), 38–63.

McGonigle, K. (1997). How progestins reduce endometrial cancer risk in ERT users. *Contemporary Ob/Gyn*, February, 96–108.

McGrath, J., & Strasburger, U. (1995). Preventing AIDS in teenagers in the 1990s. *Clinical Pediatrics*, 34, 46–48.

McGrew, M., & Shore, W. (1991). The problem of teenage pregnancy. *Journal of Family Practice*, 32, 17–25.

McHale, S., Bartko, W., Crouter, A., & Perry-Jenkins, M. (1990). Children's housework and psychosocial functioning: The mediating effect of parents' sex-role behaviors and attitudes. *Child Development*, 61, 1413–1426.

McKennett, M., & Fullerton, J. (1995). Vaginal bleeding in pregnancy. *American Family Physician*, 51, 639–646.

McKeon, V. (1997). The breast cancer prevention trial: Evaluating tamoxifen's efficacy in preventing breast cancer. *Journal of Obstetrical, Gynecological & Neonatal Nurses*, 26, 79–89.

McKibben, A., Proulx, J., & Lusignan, R. (1994). Relationships between conflict, affect, and deviant sexual behaviors in rapists and pedophiles. *Behavior Research and Therapy*, 32, 571–575.

McKirnan, D., Stokes, J., Doll, L., & Burzette, R. (1995). Bisexually active men: Social Characteristics and Sexual Behavior. *Journal of Sex Research*, 32, 65–76.

McLaren, A. (1990). *A History of Contraception: From Antiquity to the Present Day.* Cambridge, MA: Basil Blackwell.

McLaren, N., & Neiburg, P. (1988). Fetal tobacco syndrome and other problems caused by smoking during pregnancy. *Medical Aspects of Human Sexuality*, August, 69–75.

McNaught, B. (1991). Personal communication.

McNeil, E., & Rubin, Z. (1977). *The Psychology of Being Human.* San Francisco: Canfield Press.

McNeill, K., Rienzi, B., & Kposowa, A. (1998). Families and parenting: A comparison of lesbian and heterosexual mothers. *Psychological Reports*, 82, 59–62.

McNew, J. & Abell, N. (1995). Survivors of childhood sexual abuse. *Social Work*, 40, 115–126.

McNiven, P., Hodnett, E., & O'Brien-Pallas, L. (1992). Supporting women in labor: A work sampling study of the activities of labor and delivery nurses. *Birth*, 19, 3–8.

McQuaide, S. (1998). Women at midlife. *Journal of the National Association of Social Workers*, 43, 21–31.

Mead, M. (1963). *Sex and Temperament in Three Primitive Societies.* New York: Morrow.

Mead, P., & Eschenbach, D. (1998). Vaginitis 1998: Update and guidelines. *Contemporary OB/GYN*, January, 116–132.

Meana, M., & Binik, Y. (1994). Painful coitus: A review of female dyspareunia. *Journal of Nervous and Mental Disease*, 182, 264–272.

Media Report to Women (1993a). Depiction of women in mainstream TV shows still stereotypical, sexual. *Media Report to Women*, 21, 4.

Media Report to Women (1993b). Muppet gender gap. *Media Report to Women*, 21, 8.

Medical Center for Human Rights (1995). *Characteristics of Sexual Abuse of Men During War in the Republic of Croatia and Bosnia.* Zagreb, Croatia: Medical Center for Human Rights.

Medical Research Council: Prostate Cancer Working Party Investigations Group (1997). Immediate versus deferred treatment for advanced prostatic cancer: Initial results of the Medical Research Council trial. *British Journal of Urology*, 79, 235–246.

Meers, E. (1996). Web of intrigue. *The Advocate*, February 6, 34–38.

Meiselman, K. (1978). *Incest.* San Francisco, Jossey-Bass.

Melchert, T., & Parker, R. (1997). Different forms of childhood abuse and memory. *Child Abuse & Neglect*, 21, 125–135.

Melman, A. (1992). Neural and vascular control of erection. In R. Rosen & S. Leiblum (Eds.), *Erectile Disorders.* New York: Guilford.

Menon, M. (1997). Editorial: Predicting biological aggressiveness in prostate cancer—desperately seeking a marker. *Journal of Urology*, 157, 228–229.

Merson, M., Feldman, E., Bayer, R., & Stryker, J. (1997). Rapid self testing for HIV infection. *The Lancet*, 348, 352–353.

Mertz, G., Loveless, M., Levin, M., Kraus, S., Fowler, S., Goade, D., & Tyring, S. (1997). Oral famciclovir for suppression of recurrent genital herpes simplex virus infection in women. *Archives of Internal Medicine*, 157, 343–349.

Messenger, J. (1971). Sex and repression in an Irish folk community. In D. Marshall & R. Suggs (Eds.), *Human Sexual Behavior: Variations in the Ethnographic Spectrum.* Englewood Cliffs, NJ: Prentice Hall.

Messiah, A., Dart, T., Spencer, B., Warszawski, J., and the French National Survey on Sexual Behavior Group (1997). *American Journal of Public Health*, 87, 421–424.

Mestel, R. (1997). A safer estrogen. *Health*, November/December, 73–75.

Meston, C., Gorzalka, B., & Wright, J. (1997). Inhibition of subjective and physiological sexual arousal in women by clonidine. *Psychosomatic Medicine*, 59, 399–407.

Meuwissen, I., & Over, R. (1991). Multidimensionality of the content of female sexual fantasy. *Behavior Research and Therapy*, 29, 179–189.

Meyer, J., & Dupkin, C. (1985). Gender disturbance in children. *Bulletin of the Menninger Clinic*, 49, 236–269.

Meyer, V. (1991). A critique of adolescent pregnancy prevention research: The invisible white male. *Adolescence*, 26, 217–222.

Meyer, W., Webb, A., Stuart, C., Finkelstein, J., Lawrence, B., & Walker, P. (1986). Physical and hormonal evaluation of transsexual patients: A longitudinal study. *Archives of Sexual Behavior*, 15, 121–138.

Meyer-Bahlburg, H., Ehrhardt, A., Rosen, L., Gruen, R., Veridiano, N., Vann, F., & Neuwalder, H. (1995). Prenatal estrogens and the development of homosexual orientation. *Developmental Psychology*, 31, 12–21.

Mezey, G., & King, M. (1989). The effects of sexual assault on men: A survey of 22 victims. *Psychological Medicine*, 19, 205–209.

Michael, R., Bonsall, R., & Warner, P. (1974). Human vaginal secretions: Volatile fatty acid content. *Science*, 186, 1217–1219.

Michael, R., Gagnon, J., Laumann, E., & Kolata, G. (1994). *Sex in America.* Boston: Little, Brown.

Michael, R., Keverne, E., & Bonsall, R. (1971). Pheromones: Isolation of male sex attractants from a female primate. *Science*, 172, 964–966.

Michals, D. (1997). Cyber-rape: How virtual is it? *Ms.*, March/April, 68–72.

Middleman, A., & Emans, S. (1995). Adolescent sexuality and reproductive health. *Pediatrics*, 21, 127–134.

Middleton, R. (1997). Prostate cancer: Are we screening and treating too much? *Annals of Internal Medicine*, 126, 465–467.

Mifflin, M. (1997). Women and the art of tattooing. *Ms.*, July/August, 69–71.

Milan, R., & Kilmann, P. (1987). Interpersonal factors in premarital conception. *Journal of Sex Research*, 23, 289–321.

Miller, B., Norton, M., Fan, X., & Christopherson, C. (1998). Pubertal development, parental communication, and sexual values in relation to adolescent sexual behaviors. *Journal of Early Adolescence*, 18, 27–52.

Miller, C. (1995). Medications and sexual functioning in older adults. *Geriatric Nursing*, 16, 94–95.

Millstein, S., & Irwin, C. (1983). Acceptability of computer-acquired sexual histories in adolescent girls. *Journal of Pediatrics*, 103, 815–819.

Milow, V. (1983). Menstrual education: Past, present and future. In S. Golub (Ed.), *Menarche.* Lexington, MA: Lexington Books.

Mims, F., & Chang, A. (1984). Unwanted sexual experiences of young women. *Psychosocial Nursing*, 22, 7–14.

Minor, M., & Dwyer, S. (1997). The psychosocial development of sex offenders: Differences between exhibitionists, child molesters, and incest offenders. *International Journal of Offenders Therapy and Comparative Criminology*, 41, 36–44.

Mintz, H. (1997). Most alleged members of Internet child pornography ring plead guilty. *Knight-Ridder/Tribune News Service*, May 12.

Miracle-McMahill, H., Calle, E., Kosinski, A., Rodriguez, C., Wingo, P., Thun, M., & Heath, C., Jr. (1997). Tubal ligation and fatal ovarian cancer in a large prospective cohort study. *American Journal of Epidemiology*, 145(4), 349–357.

Misrahi, M., Teglas, J., N'Go, N., Burgard, M., Mayaux, M., Rouzioux, C., Delfraissy, J., & Blanche, S. (1998). CCR5 chemokine receptor variant in HIV-1 mother-to-child transmission and disease progression in children. *Journal of the American Medical Association*, 279, 277–280.

Mita, T., Dermer, M., & Knight, J. (1977). Reversed facial images and the mere-exposure hypothesis. *Journal of Personality & Social Psychology*, 35, 597–601.

Mittwoch, U., & Burgess, A. (1991). How do you get sex? *Journal of Endocrinology*, 128, 329–331.

Mobley, J., McKeown, R., Jackson, K., Sy, F., Parham, J., & Brenner, E. (1998). Risk factors for congenital syphilis in infants of women with syphilis in South Carolina. *American Journal of Public Health*, 88, 597–602.

Mohr, D., & Beutler, L. (1990). Erectile dysfunction: A review of diagnostic and treatment procedures. *Clinical Psychology Review*, 10, 123–150.

Moller, L., Hymel, S., & Rubin, K. (1992). Sex typing in play and popularity in middle childhood. *Sex Roles*, 26, 331–335.

Monaghan, J. (1992). Norplant insertion and removal. *Patient Care*, March 15, 231–237.

Money, J. (1961). Sex hormones and other variables in human eroticism. In W. Young (Ed.), *Sex and Internal Secretions* (3rd ed.). Baltimore: Williams & Wilkins.

Money, J. (1963). Cytogenetic and psychosexual incongruities with a note on space-form blindness. *American Journal of Psychiatry*, 119, 820–827.

Money, J. (1975). Ablatio penis: Normal male infant sex-reassigned as a girl. *Archives of Sexual Behavior*, 4, 65–72.

Money, J. (1980). *Love and Lovesickness.* Baltimore: Johns Hopkins University Press.

Money, J. (1981). Paraphilias: Phyletic origins of erotosexual dysfunction. *International Journal of Mental Health*, 10, 75–109.

Money, J. (1983). Food, fitness, and vital fluids: Sexual pleasure from Graham Crackers to Kellogg's Cornflakes. Paper presented at the Sixth World Congress of Sexology, May 27.

Money, J. (1984). Paraphilias: Phenomenology and classification. *American Journal of Psychotherapy*, 38, 164–179.

Money, J. (1988). *Gay, Straight, and In-Between: The Sexology of Erotic Orientation.* New York: Oxford University Press.

Money, J. (1994a). *Sex Errors of the Body and Related Syndromes: A Guide to Counseling Children, Adolescents, and Their Families* (2nd ed.). Baltimore, MD: Brookes.

Money, J. (1994b). The concept of gender identity disorder in childhood and adolescence after 39 years. *Journal of Sex and Marital Therapy*, 20, 163–177.

Money, J., & Ehrhardt, A. (1972). Prenatal hormonal exposure: Possible effects on behavior in man. In R. Michael (Ed.), *Endocrinology and Human Behavior.* London: Oxford University Press.

Money, J., & Lamacz, M. (1990). *Vandalized Lovemaps.* Buffalo, NY: Prometheus Press.

Money, J., & Primrose, C. (1968). Sexual dimorphism and dissociation in the psychology of male transsexuals. *Journal of Nervous and Mental Disorders*, 147, 472–486.

Money, J., & Walker, P. (1977). Counseling the transsexual. In J. Money & H. Musaph (Eds.), *Handbook of Sexology.* Amsterdam: Elsevier/North-Holland Biomedical Press.

Money, J., Hampson, J., & Hampson, J. (1955). An examination of some basic sexual concepts: The evidence of human hermaphroditism. *Bulletin of Johns Hopkins Hospital*, 97, 301–319.

Monga, T., & Kerrigan, A. (1997). Cerebrovascular accidents. In M. Sipski & C. Alexander (Eds.), *Sexual Function in People with Disability and Chronic Illness.* Gaithersburg, MD: Aspen Publishers.

Monk, B., & Burger, R. (1998). New therapies for genital condyloma in women. *Contemporary OB/GYN*, February, 81–96.

Monroe, I. (1997). A garden of homophobia. *The Advocate*, December 9, 9.

Montagu, A., & Matson, F. (1979). *The Human Connection.* New York: McGraw-Hill.

Montaner, J., Reiss, P., Cooper, D., Vella, S., Harris, M., Conway, B., Wainberg, M., Smith, D., Robinson, P., Hall, D., Myers, M., & Lange, J. (1998). A randomized, double-blind trial comparing combinations of nevirapine, didanosine, and zidovudine for HIV-infected patients. *Journal of the American Medical Association*, 279, 930–937.

Montauk, S., & Clasen, M. (1989). Sex education in primary care: Infancy to puberty. *Medical Aspects of Human Sexuality*, January, 22–36.

Montgomery, M., & Sorell, G. (1997). Differences in love attitudes across family life stages. *Family Relations*, 46, 55–61.

Monti-Bloch, L., Jennings-White, C., Dolberg, D., & Berliner, D. (1994). The human vomeronasal system. *Psychoneuroendocrinology*, 19, 673–686.

Mooney, T., Cole, T., & Chilgren, R. (1975). *Sexual Options for Paraplegics and Quadraplegics.* Boston: Little, Brown.

Morales, A., Condra, M., & Reid, K. (1990). The role of nocturnal penile tumescence monitoring in the diagnosis of impotence: A review. *Journal of Urology*, 143, 141–145.

Morales, A., Johnston, B., Heaton, J., & Lundie, M. (1997). Testosterone supplementation for hypogonadal impotence: Assessment of biochemical and therapeutic outcomes. *Journal of Urology*, 157, 849–854.

Morales, E. (1992). Latino gays and Latina lesbians. In S. Dworkin & F. Gutierrez (Eds.), *Counseling Gay Men and Lesbians: Journey to the End of the Rainbow.* Alexandria, VA: American Association for Counseling and Development.

Moran, G. (1997a). Diagnosing and treating STDs Part 2: Lesionless disorders. *Emergency Medicine*, February, 20–31.

Moran, G. (1997b). Diagnosing STDs Part 1: Ulcerating diseases. *Emergency Medicine*, January, 63–72.

Moran, M. (1992). Effects of sexual orientation similarity and counselor experience level on gay men's and lesbians' perceptions of counselors. *Journal of Counseling Psychology*, 39, 247–251.

Moran, N. (1996). Lesbian health care needs. *Canadian Family Physician*, 42, 879–884.

Moreland, R., & Zajonc, R. (1982). Exposure effects in person perceptions: Familiarity, similarity, and attraction. *Journal of Experimental Social Psychology*, 18, 395–415.

Morgan, E. (1978). The Puritans and sex. In M. Gordon (Ed.), *The American Family in Social-Historical Perspective*. New York: St. Martin's Press.

Morganthau, T. (1997). Baptists vs. Mickey. *Newsweek*, June 30, 51.

Morin, J. (1981). *Anal Pleasure and Health*. Burlingame, CA: Down There Press.

Morokoff, P. (1986). Volunteer bias in the psychophysiological study of female sexuality. *Journal of Sex Research*, 22, 35–51.

Morrell, M., Dixen, J., Carter, C., & Davidson, J. (1984). The influence of age and cycling status on sexual arousability in women. *American Journal of Obstetrics and Gynecology*, 148, 66–71.

Morris, M., & Dean, L. (1994). Effect of sexual behavior change on long-term human immunodeficiency virus prevalence among homosexual men. *American Journal of Epidemiology*, 140, 217–232.

Morris, N., & Udry, J. (1978). Pheromonal influences on human sexual behavior: An experiential search. *Journal of Biosocial Science*, 10, 147–159.

Morrison, E. (1994). Natural history of cervical infection with human papillomaviruses. *Clinical Infectious Diseases*, 18, 172–180.

Morrow, D. (1993). Social work with gay and lesbian adolescents. *Journal of the National Association of Social Workers*, 38, 655–660.

Morse, S., Trees, D., Htun, Y., Radebe, F., Orle, K., Dangor, Y., Beck-Sague, C., Schmid, S., Fehler, G., Weiss, J., & Ballard, R. (1997). Comparison of clinical diagnosis and standard laboratory and molecular methods for the diagnosis of genital ulcer disease in Lesotho: Association with human immunodeficiency virus infection. *Journal of Infectious Diseases*, 175, 583–589.

Mortola, J. (1998). Premenstrual syndrome: Pathophysiologic considerations. *New England Journal of Medicine*, 338(4), 256–257.

Moseley, D., Fellingstad, D., Harley, H., & Heckel, R. (1981). Psychological factors that predict reaction to abortion. *Journal of Clinical Psychology*, 37, 276–279.

Mosgaard, B., Lidegaard, O., & Andersen, A. (1997). The impact of parity, infertility and treatment with fertility drugs on the risk of ovarian cancer. *Acta Obstetricia et Gynecologica Scandinavica*, 76, 89–95.

Mosher, C., & Levitt, E. (1987). An exploratory-descriptive study of a sadomasochistically oriented sample. *Journal of Sex Research*, 23, 322–337.

Mosher, C., & Tomkins, S. (1988). Scripting the macho man: Hypermasculine socialization and enculturation. *Journal of Sex Research*, 25, 60–84.

Mosher, D., & MacIan, P. (1994). College men and women respond to X-rated videos intended for male or female audiences: Gender and sexual scripts. *Journal of Sex Research*, 31, 99–113.

Moss, J. (1996). Barbara Jordan: The other life. *The Advocate*, March 5, 39–43.

Mott, F., & Haurin, R. (1988). Linkages between sexual activity and alcohol and drug use among American adolescents. *Family Planning Perspectives*, 20, 128–137.

Moul, J., & Belman, B. (1988). A review of surgical treatment of undescended testes with emphasis on anatomical position. *Journal of Urology*, 140, 125–128.

Ms. (1997). Peruvian women challenge an ugly rape law. Author, March/April, 18.

Muehlenhard, C. (1988). Misinterpreting dating behaviors and the risk of date rape. *Journal of Social and Clinical Psychology*, 6, 20–37.

Muehlenhard, C., & Andrews, S. (1985). Open communication about sex: Will it reduce risk factors related to rape? Paper presented at the Annual Meeting of the Association for Advancement of Behavior Therapy, Houston, November.

Muehlenhard, C., & Cook, S. (1988). Men's self-reports of unwanted sexual activity. *Journal of Sex Research*, 24, 58–72.

Muehlenhard, C., & Falcon, P. (1990). Men's heterosexual skill and attitudes toward women as predictors of verbal sexual coercion and forceful rape. *Sex Roles*, 23, 241–259.

Muehlenhard, C., Felts, A., & Andrews, S. (1985). Men's attitudes toward the justifiability of date rape: Intervening variables and possible solutions. Paper presented at the Midcontinent Meeting of the Society for the Scientific Study of Sex, Chicago, June.

Muehlenhard, C., Goggins, M., Jones, J., & Satterfield, A. (1991). Sexual violence and coercion in close relationships. In K. McKinney & S. Sprecher (Eds.), *Sexuality in Close Relationships*. Hillsdale, NJ: Erlbaum.

Muehlenhard, C., & Hollabaugh, L. (1989). Do women sometimes say no when they mean yes? The prevalence and correlates of women's token resistance to sex. *Journal of Personality and Social Psychology*, 54, 872–879.

Muehlenhard, C., & Linton, M. (1987). Date rape and sexual aggression in dating situations: Incidence and risk factors. *Journal of Consulting Psychology*, 34, 186–196.

Muehlenhard, C., & Long, P. (1988). Men's versus women's reports of pressure to engage in unwanted sexual intercourse. Paper presented at the Western Region Meeting of the Society for the Scientific Study of Sex, Dallas, May.

Muehlenhard, C., & Schrag, J. (1991). Nonviolent sexual coercion. In A. Parrot & L. Bechhofer (Eds.), *Acquaintance Rape: The Hidden Crime*. New York: Wiley.

Muldoon, K. (1997a). Doctors urge routine mammograms. *The Oregonian*, March 28, B1–B3.

Muldoon, K. (1997b). Kitzhaber joins trend of older moms. *The Oregonian*, June 22, C3.

Mulligan, T., & Palguta, R., Jr. (1991). Sexual interest, activity, and satisfaction among male nursing home residents. *Archives of Sexual Behavior*, 20, 199–204.

Mullins, L., Lynch, J., Orten, J., Youll, L., Verschraegen-Spae, A., Dypere, H., Speleman, F., Dhoult, M., & DePaepe, A. (1991). Developing a program to assist Turner's syndrome patients and families. *Social Work in Health Care*, 16, 69–79.

Munger, K. (1995). Host–viral gene interactions in cervical cancer. *Contemporary Ob/Gyn*, April, 27–37.

Munroe, R. (1980). Male transvestism and the couvade: A psychocultural analysis. *Ethos*, 8, 49–59.

Murray, L. (1992). Love and Longevity. *Longevity*, August, 64.

Murray, L. (1995). Marital "boot camps" help predict success. *The Oregonian*, October 29.

Murray, L. (1995). The therapist can see you now: Just press "enter" to continue. *The Oregonian,* June 7, C3.

Murrey, G., Bolen, J., Miller, N., Simensted, K., Robbins, M. & Truskowski, F. (1993). History of childhood sexual abuse in women with depressive and anxiety disorders: A comparative study. *Journal of Sex Education & Therapy,* 19(1), 13–19.

Murry, V. (1996). An ecological analysis of coital timing among middle-class African American adolescent females. *Journal of Adolescent Research,* 11, 261–279.

Murstein, B., & Mercy, T. (1994). Sex, drugs, relationships, contraception, and fears of disease on a college campus over 17 years. *Adolescence,* 29, 303–22.

Mwamwenda, T., & Monyooe, L. (1998). Do African husbands own their wives? *Psychological Reports,* 82, 25–26.

Myers, L., Dixen, J., Morrissette, D., Carmichael, M., & Davidson, J. (1990). Effects of estrogen, androgen, and progestin on sexual psychophysiology and behavior in postmenopausal women. *Journal of Clinical Endocrinology and Metabolism,* 70, 1124–1131.

Nachtigall, R. (1991). Assessing fecundity after age 40. *Contemporary Ob/Gyn,* March, 11–33.

Nachtigall, R., Becker, G., & Wozny, M. (1992). The effects of gender-specific diagnosis on men's and women's response to infertility. *Fertility and Sterility,* 57, 113–121.

Nachtsheim, D. (1994). Treating impotence. *Western Journal of Medicine,* 160, 168–69.

Nadler, R. (1968). Approach to psychodynamics of obscene telephone calls. *New York Journal of Medicine,* 68, 521–526.

Nadler, S. (1997). Arthritis and other connective tissue diseases. In M. Sipski & C. Alexander (Eds.), *Sexual Function in People with Disability and Chronic Illness.* Gaithersburg, MD: Aspen Publishers.

Nanson, J. (1997). Binge drinking during pregnancy: Who are the women at risk? *Canadian Medical Association Journal,* 156(6), 807–808.

Napolitane, C. (1997). *Living and Loving After Divorce.* New York: Signet.

Nash, J. (1997). Personal communication.

National Center for Health Statistics (1992). *Monthly Vital Statistics Report,* 40, No. 12.

National Center of Health Statistics (1995). Annual summary of births, marriages, divorces, and deaths: United States, 1994. *Monthly Vital Statistics Report,* 43, 1–7.

National Victim Center (1992). *Rape in America: A Report to the Nation.* Report prepared by the Crime Victims Research and Treatment Center. Charleston: Medical University of South Carolina.

Nelson, J. (1980). Gayness and homosexuality: Issues for the church. In E. Batchelor, Jr. (Ed.), *Homosexuality and Ethics.* New York: Pilgrim Press.

Nelson, J. (1985). Male sexuality and masculine spirituality. *SIECUS Report,* 13, 1–4.

Nelson, J. (1997). Gay, lesbian, and bisexual adolescents: Providing esteem-enhancing care to a battered population. *Nurse Practitioner,* 22(2), 94–109.

Nevid, J. (1984). Sex differences in factors of romantic attraction. *Sex Roles,* 11, 401–411.

Newcomb, M., & Bentler, P. (1980). Assessment of personality and demographic aspects of cohabitation and marital success. *Journal of Personality Development,* 4, 11–24.

Newcomer, S., & Udry, J. (1985). Oral sex in an adolescent population. *Archives of Sexual Behavior,* 14, 41–46.

Newcomer, S., & Udry, J. (1988). Adolescents' honesty in a survey of sexual behavior. *Journal of Adolescent Research,* 3, 419–423.

Newton, E., Piper, J., & Peairs, W. (1997). Bacterial vaginosis and intraamniotic infection. *American Journal of Gynecology,* 176, 672–677.

Nicholas, H. (1998). Gonorrhoea: Symptoms and treatment. *Nursing Times,* 94, 52–54.

Nichols, M. (1989). Sex therapy with lesbians, gay men and bisexuals. In S. Lieblum & R. Rosen (Eds.), *Principles and Practice of Sex Therapy.* New York: Guilford.

Nickel, J. (1998). Placebo therapy of benign prostatic hyperplasia: A 25-month study. *British Journal of Urology,* 81, 383–387.

Nielsen, J., & Wohlert, M. (1991). Chromosome abnormalities found among 34,910 newborn children: Results from a 13-year incidence study in Arhus, Denmark. *Human Genetics,* 87, 81–83.

Nilsson, L., Bergh, C., Bryman, I., & Thorburn, J. (1994). How do we treat unexplained infertility? *ACTA Obstetrica et Gynecologica Scandinavia.* 73, 174–175.

Nilsson, U., Hellberg, D., Shoubnikova, M., Nilsson, S., & Mardh, P. (1997). Sexual behavior risk factors associated with bacterial vaginosis and chlamydial trachomatis infection. *Sexually Transmitted Diseases,* 241–246.

Nimmons, D. (1994). Sex and the brain. *Discover,* March, 64–71.

Nock, S. (1995). A comparison of marriages and cohabiting relationships. *Journal of Family Issues,* 16, 53–76.

Norris, J. (1988). *Serial Killers: The Growing Menace.* New York: Doubleday.

Nuttin, J. (1987). Affective consequences of mere ownership: The name letter effect in twelve European languages. *European Journal of Social Psychology,* 17, 381–402.

O'Connor, A. (1998). Marriages that cross racial line increase in U.S. *The Oregonian,* May 3, A20.

Odden, T., & Fick, D. (1998). Identifying and managing exercise-induced amenorrhea. *Journal of the American Academy of Physician Assistants,* 11(3), 59–80.

Odoi, A., Brody, S., & Elkins, T. (1997). Female genital mutilation in rural Ghana, West Africa. *International Journal of Gynecology & Obstetrics,* 56, 179–180.

O'Donohue, W., & Plaud, J. (1994). The conditioning of human sexual arousal. *Archives of Sexual Behavior,* 23, 321–344.

Office of Technological Assessment, U.S. Congress (1988). *Infertility: Medical and Social Choices.* Washington, DC: Government Printing Office.

Ogden, G. (1994). *Women Who Have Sex.* New York: Pocket Books.

O'Hanlan, K. (1995). In the family way: Insemination 101. *The Advocate,* June 27, 49–50.

O'Hare, T., Williams, C., & Ezoviski, A. (1996). Fear of AIDS and homophobia: Implications for direct practice and advocacy. *Journal of the National Association of Social Workers,* 41, 51–55.

O'Hare, M., Schlechte, J., Lewis, D., & Wright, E. (1991). Prospective study of postpartum blues. *Archives of General Psychiatry,* 48, 801–806.

O'Keefe, M. (1995). The times are trying politicians' souls. *The Oregonian,* April 20, A1.

Olds, D., Henderson, C., & Tatelbaum, R. (1994). Intellectual impairment in children of women who smoke cigarettes during pregnancy. *Pediatrics,* 93(2), 221–227.

Olds, J. (1956). Pleasure centers in the brain. *Scientific American,* 193, 105–116.

O'Leary, T., Tellado, M., Buckner, S., Ali, I., Stevens, A., & Ollayos, C. (1998). PAPNET-assisted rescreening of cervical smears. *Journal of the American Medical Association*, 279(3), 235–237.

Olivera, A. (1994). Sexual dysfunction due to Clomipramine and Sertraline: Nonpharmacological resolution. *Journal of Sex Education and Therapy*, 20(2) 119–122.

Olson, D., Fournier, D., & Druckman, J. (1987). *Counselors Manual for PREPARE/ENRICH* (rev. ed.). Minneapolis, Minn: PREPARE/ENRICH.

O'Neill, N., & O'Neill, G. (1972). *Open Marriage*. New York: Evans.

O'Neill, P. (1997). Date-rape drug may be in Oregon. *The Oregonian*, February 26, B1 & B7.

O'Neill, P. (1988). Prenatal neglect poses future health costs for society. *The Oregonian*, December 4, A1.

Ono, A. (1994). Personal communication.

Orr, D., Langefeld, C., Katz, B., Caine, V., Dias, P., Blythe, M., & Jones, R. (1992). Factors associated with condom use among sexually active female adolescents. *Journal of Pediatrics*, 120, 311–317.

Ortiz, E. (1998). Female genital mutilation and public health: Lessons from the British experience. *Health Care for Women International*, 19, 119–129.

Orubuloye, I., Caldwell, J., & Caldwell, P. (1997). Perceived male sexual needs and male sexual behaviour in southwest Nigeria. *Social Science and Medicine*, 44, 1195–1207.

Osman, A., & Al-Sawaf, M. (1995). Cross-cultural aspects of sexual anxieties and the associated dysfunction. *Journal of Sex Education and Therapy*, 21, 174–181.

Otis, J. (1994). For Cuba's gays, repression is past. *San Francisco Chronicle*, October 21, A1.

Overall, J. (1994). Herpes simplex virus infection of the fetus and newborn. *Pediatric Annals*, 23, 131–136.

Owen, L. (1993). *Her Blood Is Gold*. San Francisco: HarperCollins.

Padawer, J., Fagan, C., Janoff-Bulman, R., Strickland, B., & Chorowski, M. (1988). Women's psychological adjustment following emergency cesarean versus vaginal delivery. *Psychology of Women Quarterly*, 12, 25–34.

Padawer, R. (1998). The Advocate Report Front Page. *The Advocate*, February 3, 13.

Padma-Nathan, H., Hellstrom, W., Kaiser, F., Labasky, R., Lue, T., Nolten, W., Norwood, P., Peterson, C., Shabsigh, R., Tam, P., Place, V., & Gesundheit, N. (1997). Treatment of men with erectile dysfunction with transurethral alprostadil. *New England Journal of Medicine*, 336, 1–7.

Page, D., Mosher, R., Simpson, E., Fisher, E., Mardon, G., Pollack, J., McGillivray, B., Chapelle, A., & Brown, L. (1987). The sex-determining region of the human Y chromosome encodes a finger protein. *Cell*, 51, 1091–1104.

Palella, F., Delany, K., Moorman, A., Loveless, M., Fuhrer, J., Satten, G., Aschman, D., & Holmberg, S. (1998). Declining morbidity and mortality among patients with advanced immunodeficiency virus infection. *New England Journal of Medicine*, 338, 853–860.

Paluska, S. (1997). Vacuum-assisted vaginal delivery. *American Family Physician*, 55, 2197–2203.

Pam, A., Plutchik, R., & Conte, H. (1975). Love, a psychometric approach. *Psychological Reports*, 37, 83–88.

Pan, S. (1993). China: Acceptability and effect of three kinds of sexual publication. *Archives of Sexual Behavior*, 22, 59–71.

Paperny, D. (1997). Computerized health assessment and education for adolescent HIV and STD prevention in health care settings and schools. *Health Education and Behavior*, 24, 54–70.

Paperny, D., Aono, J., & Lehman, R. (1990). Computer-assisted detection and intervention in adolescent high-risk behaviors. *Journal of Pediatrics*, 116, 456–462.

Papini, D., Farmer, F., Clark, S., & Snell, W. (1988). An evaluation of adolescent patterns of sexual self-disclosure to parents and friends. *Journal of Adolescent Research*, 3, 387–401.

Paradis, B. (1997). Multicultural identity and gay men in the era of AIDS. *American Journal of Orthopsychiatry*, 67(2), 300–307.

Parker, L. (1998). Ambiguous genitalia: Etiology, treatment, and nursing implications. *Journal of Obstetrics, Gynecology, and Neonatal Nursing*, 27, 15–22.

Parker, P. (1994). Premenstrual syndrome. *American Family Physician*, November 1, 1309–1317.

Parks, K., Dixon, P., Richey, C., & Hook, E. (1997). Spontaneous clearance of chlamydia trachomatis infection in untreated patients. *Sexually Transmitted Diseases*, 24, 229–235.

Parrot, A. (1991). Institutionalized response: How can acquaintance rape be prevented? In A. Parrot & L. Bechhofer (Eds.), *Acquaintance Rape: The Hidden Crime*. New York: Wiley.

Parrott, T. (1989). Summary of annual meeting of the section on pediatric urology. *Pediatrics*, 83, 591–596.

Parsons, J. (1983). Sexual socialization and gender roles in childhood. In E. Allgeier & N. McCormick (Eds.), *Changing Boundaries: Gender Roles and Sexual Behavior*. Palo Alto, CA: Mayfield.

Pasquale, S. (1994). Helping patients make informed contraceptive decisions. *Contemporary Ob/Gyn*, June 15, 9–25.

Patterson, C. (1995). Sexual orientation and human development: An overview. *Developmental Psychology*, 31, 3–11.

Patterson, J., & Kim, P. (1991). *The Day America Told the Truth*. Englewood Cliffs, NJ: Prentice Hall.

Paul, J. (1984). The bisexual identity: An idea without social recognition. *Journal of Homosexuality*, 9, 45–63.

Paul, L., & Galloway, J. (1994). Sexual jealousy: Gender differences in response to partner and rival. *Aggressive Behavior*, 20, 203–211.

Paul, M. (1997a). Occupational reproductive hazards. *The Lancet*, 349, 1385–1388.

Paul, M. (1997b). The immune system in vertical HIV infection: The immune response and disease progression. *AIDS Research and Human Retroviruses*, 13, 1–4.

Pauly, I. (1974). Female transsexualism: Part II. *Archives of Sexual Behavior*, 3, 509–526.

Pauly, I. (1990). Gender identity disorders: Evaluation and treatment. *Journal of Sex Education and Therapy*, 16, 2–24.

Pavlovich, C., & Schlegel, P. (1997). Fertility options after vasectomy: A cost-effectiveness analysis. *Fertility and Sterility*, 67, 133–141.

Pearce, J., Hawton, K., Blake, F., Barlow, D., Rees, M., Fagg, J., & Keenan, J. (1997). Psychological effects of continuation versus discontinuation of hormone replacement therapy by estrogen implants: A placebo-controlled study. *Journal of Psychosomatic Research*, 42(2), 177–186.

Pearson, L. (1992). The stigma of infertility. *Nursing Times*, 88(1), 36–38.

Peele, S., & Brodsky, A. (1987). *Love and Addiction*. New York: NAL/Dutton.

Pela, R. (1998). Gays of our lives. *The Advocate*, January 20, 93.

Penley, C. (1996). From NASA to the 700 Club (with a detour through Hollywood). Cultural studies in the public sphere. In C. Nelson & D. Gaonkar (Eds.), *Disciplinarity and Dissent in Cultural Studies*. New York: Routledge.

Pepe, M., & Byrne, T. J. (1991). Women's perceptions of immediate and long-term effects of failed infertility treatment on marital and sexual satisfaction. *Family Relations,* 40, 303–309.

Peplau, L. (1981). What homosexuals want in relationships. *Psychology Today,* 15(3), 28–38.

Peplau, L., & Conrad, E. (1984). Beyond nonsexist research: The perils of feminist methods in psychology. *Psychology of Women Quarterly*, 13, 381–402.

Peplau, L., Garnets, L., Spalding, L., Conley, T., & Veniegas, R. (1998). A critique of Bem's "exotic becomes erotic" theory of sexual orientation. *Psychological Review*, 128, 140–156.

Perelson, A., Newmann, A., Markowitz, M., Leonard, J., & Ho, D. (1996). HIV-1 dynamics in vivo: Virion clearance rate, infected cell life-span, and viral generation. *Science*, 27, 582–586.

Perez, A., Labbok, M., & Queenan, J. (1992). Clinical study of the lactational amenorrhoea method for family planning. *The Lancet,* 339, 968–970.

Perry, J., & Whipple, B. (1981). Pelvic muscle strength of female ejaculators: Evidence in support of a new theory of orgasm. *Journal of Sex Research,* 17, 22–39.

Petersen, J. (1995). On-line pedophiles. *Playboy*, 42, 39.

Peterson, H., Xia, Z., Hughes, J., Wilcox, L., Tylor, L., & Trussell, J. (1997). The risk of ectopic pregnancy after tubal sterilization. *New England Journal of Medicine*, 336, 762–767.

Peterson, J., Kretchmer, A., Nellis, B., Lever, J., & Hertz, R. (1983). The *Playboy* readers' sex survey, Part 2. *Playboy,* March, 90–92; 178–184.

Peterson, L., Oakley, D., Potter, L., & Darroch, J. (1998). Women's efforts to prevent pregnancy: Consistency of oral contraceptive use. *Family Planning Perspectives*, 30(1), 19–23.

Petit, C. (1994). Treatment found for premature ejaculation. *San Francisco Chronicle,* May 17, A4.

Petitti, D., & Reingold, A. (1988). Tampon characteristics and menstrual toxic shock syndrome. *Journal of the American Medical Association,* 259, 686–687.

Peyser, M. (1997a). The life of the party. *Newsweek*, June 23, 76.

Peyser, M. (1997b). A deadly dance. *Newsweek*, September 29, 76–77.

Phillips, G., & Over, R. (1995). Differences between heterosexual, bisexual, and lesbian women in recalled childhood experiences. *Archives of Sexual Behavior*, 24, 1–20.

Phillips, S., & Schneider, M. (1993). Sexual harassment of female doctors by patients. *New England Journal of Medicine,* 329, 1936–1939.

Piccinino, L., & Mosher, W. (1998). Trends in contraceptive use in the United States: 1982–1995. *Family Planning Perspectives,* 30(1), 4–10 & 46.

Pienta, K., Ying Kau, T., Demers, R., Montie, J., Hoff, M., & Severson, R. (1995). Effect of age and race on the survival of men with prostate cancer in the Metropolitan Detroit Tricounty Area, 1973 to 1987. *Urology,* 45, 93–98.

Pierce, P. (1994). Sexual harassment: Frankly, what is it? *Journal of Intergroup Relations,* 20, 3–12.

Pietropinto, A., & Simenauer, J. (1990). *Not Tonight Dear: How to Reawaken Your Sexual Desire.* New York: Doubleday.

Pinhas, V. (1985). Personal communication, June.

Pinhas, V. (1989). Treatment of sexual problems in chemically dependent women. *The Female Patient,* 20, 27–30.

Pinkerton, S., & Abramson, P. (1997). Condoms and the prevention of AIDS. *American Scientist*, 85, 364–373.

Pinkowish, M. (1997). More optimism about PSA testing, please. *Patient Care,* January 30, 19.

Pistella, C., & Bonati, F. (1998). Communication about sexual behavior among adolescent women, their family, and peers. *Families in Society: The Journal of Contemporary Human Services*, 79, 206–211.

Pithers, W. (1993). Treatment of rapists: Reinterpretation of early outcome date and exploratory constructs to enhance therapeutic efficacy. In G. Hall, R. Hirschman, J. Graham, & M. Zaragoza (Eds.), *Sexual Aggression: Issues in Etiology, Assessment, and Treatment.* Washington, DC: Taylor & Francis.

Plaut, S. (1995). Informed consent for sex between health professional and patient or client. *Journal of Sex Education and Therapy*, 21(2), 129–131.

Plaut, S. (1996). *Sexual Exploitation by Health Professionals: The Victim's Perspective.* Paper presented at the 21st Annual Meeting of the Society of Sex Therapy and Research, Miami, March.

Plaut, S., & RachBeisel, J. (1998). Use of anxiolytic medication in the treatment of vaginismus and severe aversion to penetration: Case report. *Journal of Sex Education and Therapy*, 22(3), 43–46.

Pleck, J., Sonenstein, F., & Ku, L. (1993). Changes in adolescent males' use of and attitudes toward condoms, 1988–1991. *Family Planning Perspectives,* 25, 106–109 & 117.

Pogrebin, L. (1998). Ovarian cancer: Women break the silence. *Ms.*, March/April, 34–36.

Poindexter, C. (1997). Sociopolitical antecedents to Stonewall: Analysis of the origins of the gay rights movement in the United States. *Journal of the National Association of Social Workers*, 42, 607–616.

Pokorny, S. (1997). Pediatric & adolescent gynecology. *Comprehensive Therapy*, 23(5), 337–344.

Polinsky, M. (1995). Functional status of long-term breast cancer survivors: Demonstrating chronicity. *Health & Social Work,* 19(3), 165–173.

Polit-O'Hara, D., & Kahn, J. (1985). Communication and adolescent contraceptive practices in adolescent couples. *Adolescence*, 20, 33–43.

Pollack, A. (1996). Japan gives money to army sex slaves. *The Oregonian*, August 15, A8.

Pollack, A., & Girvin, S. (1992). When should an IUD be removed and replaced? *Medical Aspects of Human Sexuality,* 26(2), 46–58.

Pollis, C. (1988). An assessment of the impacts of feminism on sexual science. *Journal of Sex Research*, 25, 85–105.

Pollock, E. (1993). As remedy for certain broken promises, professor proposes "sexual fraud" suits. *The Wall Street Journal,* June 11, B1 & B5.

Polonsky, D. (1998). What do you do when they won't do it? The therapeutic dilemma of low desire. *Journal of Sex Education and Therapy*, 22(3), 5–12.

Pomeroy, W. (1965). Why we tolerate lesbians. *Sexology,* May, 652–54.

Poppen, P. (1994). Adolescent contraceptive use and communication: Changes over a decade. *Adolescence,* 29, 503–514.

Post, S., & Botkin, J. (1995). Adolescents and HIV prevention. *Clinical Pediatrics,* 34, 41–45.

Post, T. (1993). A pattern of rape. *Newsweek,* January 4, 32–36.

Potts, M. (1997). Social support and depression among older adults living alone: The importance of friends within and outside of a retirement community. *Journal of the National Association of Social Workers*, 42(3) 348–362.

Poussaint, A. (1990). An honest look at black gays and lesbians. *Ebony*, September, 124, 126, 130–131.

Power, C. (1998). The new Islam. *Newsweek,* March 16, 35–38.

Power, T. (1985). Mother-and-father-infant play: A developmental analysis. *Child Development,* 56, 1514–1524.

Powlishta, K., Serbin, L., & Moller, L. (1993). The stability of individual differences in gender typing: Implication for understanding gender segregation. *Sex Roles,* 29, 723–737.

Pratt, C., & Schmall, V. (1989). College students' attitudes toward elderly sexual behavior: Implications for family life education. *Family Relations,* 38, 137–141.

Prentky, R., Burgess, A., & Carter, D. (1986). Victim responses by rapist type: An empirical and clinical analysis. *Journal of Interpersonal Violence,* 1, 73–98.

Prescott, J. (1975). Body pleasure and the origins of violence. *The Futurist,* April, 64–74.

Prescott, J. (1986). The abortion of "The Silent Scream." *The Humanist,* 46, 10–17.

Prescott, J. (1989). Affectional bonding for the prevention of violent behaviors: Neurological, psychological and religious/spiritual determinants. In L. Hertzberg (Ed.), *Violent Behavior.* Vol. 1: *Assessment and Intervention.* New York: PMA Publishing.

Price, V., Scanlon, B., & Janus, M. (1984). Social characteristics of adolescent male prostitution. *Victimology,* 9, 211–221.

Priestly, C., Jones, B., Dhar, J., & Goodwin, L. (1997). What is normal vaginal flora? *Genitourinary Medicine,* 73, 23–28.

Prior, J., & Vigna, Y. (1991). Ovulation disturbances and exercise training. *Clinical Obstetrics and Gynecology,* 34, 180–190.

Prisant, L., Carr, A., Bottini, P., Solursh, D., & Solursh, L. (1994). Sexual dysfunction with antihypertensive drugs. *Archives of Internal Medicine,* 154, 730–736.

Pritchard, K. (1997). Breast cancer: The real challenge. *The Lancet,* 349, 124–125.

Proctor, C., & Groze, V. (1994). Risk factors for suicide among gay, lesbian, and bisexual youths. *Social Work,* 39, 504–513.

Proctor, F., Wagner, N., & Butler, J. (1974). The differentiation of male and female orgasm: An experimental study. In N. Wagner (Ed.), *Perspectives on Human Sexuality.* New York: Behavioral Publications.

Proulx, J., Aubut, J., McKibben, A., & Cote, M. (1994). Penile responses of rapists and nonrapists to rape stimuli involving physical violence or humiliation. *Archives of Sexual Behavior,* 23, 295–310.

Pryor, J., & Reeder, G. (Eds.). (1993). *The Social Psychology of HIV Infection.* Hillsdale, NJ: Erlbaum.

Prysak, M., Lorenz, R., & Kisly, A. (1995). Pregnancy outcome in nulliparous women 35 years and older. *Obstetrics & Gynecology,* 85, 65–70.

Purcell, P., & Stewart, L. (1990). Dick and Jane in 1989. *Sex Roles,* 22, 177–185.

Purcell, S. (1985). Relation between religious orthodoxy and marital sexual functioning. Paper presented at a meeting of the American Psychological Association, Los Angeles, August 25.

Quackenbush, D., Strassberg, D., & Turner, C. (1995). Gender effects of romantic themes in erotica. *Archives of Sexual Behavior,* 24, 21–35.

Quadagno, D., & Sprague, J. (1991). Reasons for having sex. *Medical Aspects of Human Sexuality,* June, 52.

Quimby, C. (1994). Women and the family of the future. *Journal of Obstetrical, Gynecological and Neonatal Nurses,* 23, 113–123.

Quimby, E., & Friedman, S. (1989). Dynamics of black mobilization against AIDS in New York City. *Social Problems,* 36, 403–415.

Quinn, D. (1997). Hate. *The Advocate,* June 10, 50–52.

Quinsey, V., Chaplin, T., & Upfold, D. (1984). Sexual arousal to nonsexual violence and sadomasochistic themes among rapists and non sex-offenders. *Journal of Consulting and Clinical Psychology,* 52, 4, 651–657.

Rabin, D. (1998). Understanding why women won't take HRT. *Contemporary Ob/Gyn,* January, 133–141.

Rabock, J., Mellon, J., & Starka, L. (1979). Klinefelter's syndrome: Sexual development and activity. *Archives of Sexual Behavior,* 8, 333–340.

Rachlis, A., & Zarowny, D. (1998). Guidelines for antiviral therapy for HIV infection. *Canadian Medical Association Journal,* 158, 496–505.

Rachman, S. (1966). Sexual fetishism: An experimental analogue. *Psychological Record,* 16, 293–296.

Rachman, S., & Hodgson, R. (1968). Experimentally-induced "sexual fetishism": Replication and development. *Psychological Research,* 18, 25–27.

Radlove, S. (1983). Sexual response and gender roles. In E. Allgeier & N. McCormick (Eds.), *Changing Boundaries: Gender Roles and Sexual Behavior.* Mountain View, CA: Mayfield.

Rajfer, J. (1996). Nitric oxide and penile erection. Lecture presented at American Urological Association 91st Annual Meeting, May 5.

Rakic, Z., Starcevic, V., Maric, J., & Kelin, K. (1996). The outcome of sex reassignment surgery in Belgrade: 32 patients of both sexes. *Archives of Sexual Behavior,* 25, 515–525.

Rako, S. (1996). *The Hormone of Desire.* New York: Harmony Books.

Randolph, A., Hartshorn, R., & Washington, A. (1996). Acyclovir prophylaxis in late pregnancy to prevent neonatal herpes: A cost-effectiveness analysis. *Obstetrics and Gynecology,* 88, 603–610.

Rankin-Esquer, L., Burnett, C., Baucom, D., & Epstein, N. (1997). Autonomy and relatedness in marital functioning. *Journal of Marital and Family Therapy,* 23(2), 175–190.

Rankow, E. (1997). Primary medical care of the gay or lesbian patient. *North Carolina Medical* Journal, 58(2), 92–97.

Rao, M., Wilkinson, J., & Benton, D. (1991). Screening for undescended testes. *Archives of Disease in Children,* 66, 934–937.

Raphael, S., & Robinson, M. (1980). *Alternative Lifestyles,* 3, 207–229.

Rasheed, A., White, C., & Shaikh, N. (1997). The incidence of post-vasectomy chronic testicular pain and the role of nerve stripping (denervation) of the spermatic cord in its management. *British Journal of Urology,* 79, 269–270.

Rasmussen, L., Lee, T., Roelofs, W., Zhang, A., & Daves, G. (1996). Insect pheromone in elephants. *Nature,* 379, 684.

Rawstron, S., Vetrano, J., Tannis, G., & Bramberg, K. (1997). Congenital syphilis: Detection of *Treponema pallidum* in stillborns. *Clinical Infectious Diseases,* 24, 24–27.

Reamy, K., & Reamy, E. (1991). The climacteric: Sexual myths and realities. *Medical Aspects of Human Sexuality,* September, 20–26.

Recer, P. (1997). Pill, childbirth may reduce ovarian cancer. *Monterey Herald,* July 2, A1–A10.

Redei, E. & Freeman, E. (1995). Daily plasma estradiol and progesterone levels over the menstrual cycle and their relation to premenstrual symptoms. *Psychoneuroendocrinology,* 20(3), 259–267.

Reeder, H. (1996). The subjective experience of love through adult life. *International Journal of Aging and Human Development,* 43, 325–340.

Rees, H., Katzenellenbogen, J., Shabodien, R., Jewkes, R., Fawcus, S., McIntyre, J., Lombard, C., & Truter, H. (1997). The epidemiology of incomplete abortion in South Africa. *South Africa Medical Journal,* 87, 432–433.

Regehr, C., & Glancy, G. (1995). Sexual exploitation of patients: Issues for colleagues. *American Journal Orthopsychiatric,* 65(2), 194–202.

Reibstein, L. (1998). Arguing at fever pitch. *Newsweek*, January 26, 66–67.

Reid, P., & Comas-Diaz, L. (1990). Gender and ethnicity: Perspectives on dual status. *Sex Roles*, 22, 397–408.

Reifsnider, E. (1997). On the horizon: New options for contraception. *Journal of Obstetrical, Gynecological, & Neonatal Nurses*, January/February, 91–99.

Reiner, W. (1997). To be male or female—that is the question. *Archives of Pediatric and Adolescent Medicine*, 151, 224–225.

Reinisch, J., & Beasley, R. (1990). *The Kinsey Institute's New Report on Sex.* New York: St. Martin's Press.

Reinisch, J., Sanders, S., & Ziemba-Davis, M. (1988). The study of sexual behavior in relation to the transmission of human immunodeficiency virus: Caveats and recommendations. *American Psychologist*, 43, 921–927.

Reinisch, J., Ziemba-Davis, M., & Sanders, S. (1991). Hormonal contributions to sexually dimorphic behavioral development in humans. *Psychoneuroendocrinology*, 16, 213–278.

Reiter, R., & Milburn, A. (1994). Exploring effective treatment for chronic pelvic pain. *Contemporary Ob/Gyn*, March, 84–103.

Remafedi, G. (1994). *Death by Denial: Studies of Suicide in Gay and Lesbian Teenagers.* Boston: Alyson Publications.

Renshaw, D. (1987). Painful intercourse associated with cerebral palsy. *Journal of the American Medical Association*, 257, 2086.

Renshaw, D. (1990). Short-term therapy for sexual dysfunction: Brief counseling to manage vaginismus. *Clinical Practice in Sexuality*, 6(5), 23–29.

Renshaw, D. (1991). Female wet dreams. *Medical Aspects of Human Sexuality*, January, 63.

Renshaw, D. (1995). *Seven Weeks to Better Sex.* New York: Random House.

Renzetti, C., & Curran, D. (1992). *Women, Men, and Society* (2nd ed.). Boston: Allyn and Bacon.

Resnick, M., Bearman, P., Blum, R., Bauman, K., Harris, K., Jones, J., Tabor, J., Beuhring, T., Sieving, R., Shew, M., Ireland, M., Bearinger, L., & Udry, J. (1997). Protecting adolescents from harm: Findings from the National Longitudinal Study on Adolescent Health. *Journal of the American Medical Association*, 278, 823–832.

Reuters (1998). Florida man with HIV needs sex "yes" in writing. *CNN Custom News* (on the Internet), January 22.

Reyes, M., & Akhras, J. (1995). Dealing with maternal and congenital syphilis. *Contemporary Obstetrics & Gynecology*, June, 52–62.

Rhode, D. (1997). Harassment is alive and well and living at the water cooler. *Ms.*, November/December, 28–29.

Rhynard, J., Krebs, M., & Glover, J. (1997). Sexual assault in dating relationships. *Journal of School Health*, 67, 89–93.

Ribadeneira, D. (1998). More women step up to pulpit, but they still take a back pew. *The Oregonian*, April 19, G3.

Rich, A. (1976). *Of Woman Born.* New York: Norton.

Richards, L., Rollerson, B., & Phillips, J. (1991). Perceptions of submissiveness: Implications for victimization. *Journal of Psychology*, 125, 407–411.

Richardson, J., & Lazur, A. (1995). Sexuality in the nursing home patient. *American Family Physician*, 51, 121–124.

Richman, J., Flaherty, J., Rospenda, K., & Christensen, M. (1992). Mental health consequences and correlates of reported medical student abuse. *Journal of the American Medical Association*, 267, 692–694.

Rickert, V., & Wiemann, C. (1998). Date rape: Office-based solutions. *Contemporary OB/GYN*, 43, 133–153.

Riger, S. (1991). Gender dilemmas in sexual harassment policies and procedures. *American Psychologist*, 46, 497–505.

Rind, B., & Tromovitch, P. (1997). A meta-analytic review of findings from national samples of psychological correlates of child sexual abuse. *Journal of Sex Research*, 34, 237–255.

Ringler, G. (1996). Dissecting room. In G. Centola & K. Ginsburg (Eds.), *Evaluation and Treatment of the Infertile Male.* Cambridge, England: Cambridge University Press.

Rio, L. (1991). Psychological and sociological research and the decriminalization or legalization of prostitution. *Archives of Sexual Behavior*, 20, 205–217.

Rios, D. (1996). The gone girls. *The Oregonian*, November 17, E1–E3.

Ritter, T. (1919). The people's home medical book. In R. Barnum (Ed.), *The People's Home Library.* Cleveland: Barnum.

Rivlin, M. (1992). Chlamydia in pregnancy: Who should be tested? *Medical Aspects of Human Sexuality*, 26, 27–31.

Roan, A. (1998). A bad precedent. *Ms.*, March/April, 30.

Robbins, M., & Jensen, G. (1978). Multiple orgasm in males. *Journal of Sex Research*, 14, 21–26.

Roberto, L. (1983). Issues in diagnosis and treatment of transsexualism. *Archives of Sexual Behavior*, 12, 445–473.

Roberts, R., Lieber, M., Bostwick, D., & Jacobsen, S. (1997). A review of clinical and pathological prostatitis syndromes. *Urology*, 49, 809–821,

Roberts, S., Cox, S., Dax, J., Wendel, G., & Leveno, K. (1995). Genital herpes during pregnancy: No lesion, no cesarean. *Obstetrics and Gynecology*, 85, 261–264.

Robey, B., Ross, J., & Bhushan, I. (1996). Meeting unmet need: New strategies. *Population Reports*, Series J, No. 43, September.

Robey, B., Rutstein, S., Morris, L., et al. (1992). The reproductive revolution: New survey findings. *Population Reports*, M11.

Robinson, G., Garner, C., Gare, D., & Crawford, B. (1987). Psychological adaptation to pregnancy in childless women more than 35 years of age. *American Journal of Obstetrics and Gynecology*, 156, 323–328.

Robinson, J. (1993). Cervical cancer: Occupational risks. *The Lancet*, 2, 1496–1497.

Robinson, J., & Godbey, G. (1998). No sex, please. We're college graduates. *American Demographics*, 20(2), 18–23.

Robinson, R., & Frank, D. (1994). *Adolescence*, 29, 27–35.

Rodgers, C. (1987). Sex roles in education. In D. Hargraves & A. Colley (Eds.), *The Psychology of Sex Roles.* New York: Hemisphere.

Rodman, H., Sarvis, G., & Bonar, J. (1987). *The Abortion Question.* New York: Columbia University Press.

Rodriguez, C., Tatham, L., Thun, M., Calle, E., & Heath, C. (1997a). Smoking and fatal prostate cancer in a large cohort of adult men. *American Journal of Epidemiology*, 145, 466–475.

Rodriguez, N., Ryan, S., Vande Kemp, H., & Foy, D. (1997b). Posttraumatic stress disorder in adult female survivors of childhood sexual abuse: A comparison study. *Journal of Consulting and Clinical Psychology*, 65, 53–59.

Rodriquez-Barradas, M., Tharopel, R., Groover, J., Giron, K., Lacke, C., Houston, E., Hamill, R., Steinhoff, M., & Musher, D. (1997). Colonization by *Streptococcus pneumoniae* among human immunodeficiency virus-infected adults: Prevalence of antibiotic resistance, impact of immunization, and characterization by polymerase chain reaction with BOX primers of isolates from persistent *S. pneumoniae* carriers. *Journal of Infectious Diseases*, 175, 590–597.

Roelofs, W. (1995). Chemistry of sex attraction. *Proceedings of the National Academy of Sciences U.S.A*, 92, 44–49.

Roffman, D., Shannon, D., & Dwyer, C. (1997). Adolescents, sexual health, and the Internet: Possibilities, prospects, and challenges for educators. *Journal of Sex Education and Therapy*, 22, 49–55.

Rogel, J. (1978). A critical evaluation of the possibility of higher primate reproductive and sexual pheromones. *Psychological Bulletin*, 85, 810–830.

Rogers, C. (1951). *Client-Centered Therapy: Its Current Practice, Implications, and Theory.* Boston: Houghton Mifflin.

Rojnik, B., Andolsek-Jeras, L., & Obersnel-Kveder, D. (1995). Women in difficult circumstances: War victims and refugees. *International Journal of Gynecology & Obstetrics*, 48, 311–315.

Romer, D., Hornik, R., Stanton, B., Black, M., Li, X., Ricardo, I., & Feigelman, S. (1997). "Talking" computers: A reliable and private method to conduct interviews on sensitive topics with children. *Journal of Sex Research*, 34, 3–9.

Roosmalen, J. (1997). Previous caesarean birth "always a scar." *European Journal of Obstetrics & Gynecology and Reproductive Biology*, 72, 119–120.

Roscoe, B., Goodwin, M., Repp. S., & Rose, M. (1987). Sexual harassment of university students and student employees: Findings and implications. *College Student Journal*, 12, 254–273.

Roscoe, B., Strouse, J., & Goodwin, M. (1994). Sexual harassment: Early adolescents' self-reports of experiences and acceptance. *Adolescence*, 115, 515–523.

Roscoe, W. (1994). Beyond sexual dimorphism in culture and history. In G. Herdt (Ed.), *Third Sex Third Gender.* New York: Zone Books.

Rose, A., & Montemayor, R. (1994). The relationship between gender role orientation and perceived self-competency in male and female adolescents. *Sex Roles*, 31, 579–595.

Rosen, R. (1991). Alcohol and drug effects on sexual response: Human experimental and clinical studies. *Annual Review of Sex Research*, 2, 119–179.

Rosen, R., & Ashton, A. (1993). Prosexual drugs: Empirical status of the "new aphrodisiacs." *Archives of Sexual Behavior*, 22, 521–541.

Rosen, R., & Beck, J. (1988). *Patterns of Sexual Arousal.* New York: Guilford.

Rosenberg, M. (1988). Adult behaviors that reflect childhood incest. *Medical Aspects of Human Sexuality*, May, 114–124.

Rosenberg, M., Waugh, M., & Meehan, T. (1995). Use and misuse of oral contraceptives: Risk indicators for poor pill taking and discontinuation. *Contraception*, 51, 283–288.

Rosenthal, S., Starberry, L., Biro, F., Slaoui, M., Francotte, M., Koutsoukas, M., Hayes, M., & Bernstein. D. (1997). Seroprevalence of herpes simplex virus types 1 and 2 and cytomegalovirus in adolescents. *Clinical Infectious Diseases*, 24, 135–139.

Rosenzweig, J., & Daily, D. (1989). Dyadic adjustment/sexual satisfaction in women and men as a function of psychological sex role self-perception. *Journal of Sex and Marital Therapy*, 15, 42–56.

Rosler, A., & Witztum, E. (1998). Treatment of men with paraphilia with a long-acting analogue of gonadotropin-releasing hornome. *New England Journal of Medicine*, 338, 416–422.

Rosman, J., & Resnick, P. (1989). Sexual attraction to corpses: A psychiatric review of necrophilia. *Bulletin of the American Academy of Psychiatry and the Law*, 17, 153–163.

Ross, M., & Arrindell, W. (1988). Perceived parental rearing patterns of homosexual and heterosexual men. *Journal of Sex Research*, 24, 275–281.

Rosser, S. (1994). *Women's Health—Missing from U.S. Medicine.* Bloomington: Indiana University Press.

Rotello, G. (1995). The inning of outing. *The Advocate*, April 18, 80.

Rotello, G. (1996). Trickle-down liberation. *The Advocate*, February 20, 72.

Roth, S., Dye, E., & Lebowitz, L. (1988). Group therapy for sexual-assault victims. *Psychotherapy*, 25, 82–93.

Rothbaum, B., & Jackson, J. (1990). Religious influence on menstrual attitudes and symptoms. *Women & Health*, 16(1), 63–77.

Rotheram, M., & Weiner, N. (1983). Androgyny, stress, and satisfaction. *Sex Roles*, 9, 151–158.

Rovner, J. (1998). Republicans continue U.S. wrangling over abortion. *The Lancet*, 351, 46.

Rowland, D., Cooper, S., & Slob, A. (1996). Genital and psychoaffective response to erotic stimulation in sexually functional and dysfunctional Men. *Journal of Abnormal Psychology*, 105(2), 194–203.

Rowland, D., Kallan, K., & Slob, A. (1997a). Yohimbine, erectile capacity, and sexual response in men. *Archives of Sexual Behavior*, 26, 49–62.

Rowland, D., Cooper, S., Slob, A., & Houtsmuller, E. (1997b). The study of ejaculatory response in men in the psychophysiological laboratory. *Journal of Sex Research*, 34(2), 161–166.

Roy, R., & Roy, D. (1973). Is monogamy outdated? In E. Morrison & V. Borosage (Eds.). *Human Sexuality: Contemporary Perspectives.* Palo Alto, CA: National Press Books.

Royce, R., Sena, A., Cates, W., & Cohen, M. (1997). Sexual transmission of HIV. *New England Journal of Medicine*, 336, 1072–1078.

Roye, C., & Balk, S. (1997). Evaluation of an intergenerational program for pregnant and parenting adolescents. *Maternal-Child Nursing Journal*, 24, 32–36.

Ruan, F. (1991). *Sex in China.* New York: Plenum.

Ruben, D. (1992). Saying no to nursing. *Parenting*, March, 21.

Rubenstein, C. (1994). The 1994 infidelity report. *New Woman*, March, 65–69.

Rubin, J., Provenzano, F., & Luria, Z. (1974). The eye of the beholder: Parents' views on sex of newborns. *American Journal of Orthopsychiatry*, 44, 512–519.

Rubin, L. (1990). *Erotic Wars.* New York: Farrar, Straus & Giroux.

Rubin, L., & Borgers, S. (1990). Sexual harassment in the universities during the 1980s. *Sex Roles*, 23, 397–411.

Rubin, Z. (1970). Measurement of romantic love. *Journal of Personality and Social Psychology*, 16, 265–273.

Rubin, Z. (1973). *Liking and Loving.* New York: Holt, Rinehart & Winston.

Rubinsky, H., Eckerman, D., Rubinsky, E., & Hoover, C. (1987). Early-phase physiological response patterns to psychosexual stimuli: Comparisons of male and female patterns. *Archives of Sexual Behavior*, 16, 45–55.

Ruch, L., Amedeo, S., Gartrell, J., & Coyne, B. (1991). The sexual assault symptom scale: Measuring self-reported sexual assault trauma in the emergency room. *Psychological Assessment: A Journal of Consulting and Clinical Psychology*, 3, 3–8.

Russell, D. (1984). *Sexual Exploitation: Rape, Child Sexual Abuse, and Workplace Harassment.* Beverly Hills, CA: Sage.

Ryan, R., Longres, J., & Roffman, R. (1996). Sexual identity, social support and social networks among African-, Latino-, and European-American men in an HIV prevention program. In J. Longres (Ed.), *Men of Color*. New York: Harrington Park Press.

Saario, T., Jacklin, C., & Tittle, C. (1973). Sex role stereotyping in public schools. *Harvard Educational Review,* 43, 386–416.

Sacks, M. (1998). Sex survey's results raise eyebrows. *The Oregonian,* February 22, L10.

Sadker, M., & Sadker, D. (1985). Sexism in the schoolroom of the 80s. *Psychology Today,* 19, 54, 57.

Sadker, M., & Sadker, D. (1990). Confronting sexism in the college classroom. In S. Gabriel & I. Smithson (Eds.), *Gender in the Classroom: Power and Pedagogy.* Chicago: University of Illinois Press.

Sadker, M., & Sadker, D. (1994). *Failing at Fairness: How America's Schools Cheat Girls.* New York: Scribners.

Safran, C. (1976). What men do to women on the job: A shocking look at sexual harassment. *Redbook,* November, 148.

Saghir, M., & Robins, E. (1973). *Male and Female Homosexuality: A Comprehensive Investigation.* Baltimore: Williams & Wilkins.

Sakala, C. (1993). Medically unnecessary cesarean section births: Introduction to a symposium. *Social Science Medicine,* 37(10), 1177–1198.

Salazar, M., Wilkinson, W., DeRoos, R., et al. (1994). Breast cancer behaviors following participation in a cancer risk appraisal. *Health Values,* 18(3), 41–49.

Sales, E., Baum, M., & Shore, B. (1984). Victim readjustment following assault. *Journal of Social Issues,* 40, 117–136.

Salholz, E. (1990). The future of gay America. *Newsweek,* March 12, 20–25.

Salisbury, N. (1991). Personal communication.

Salzer, E. (1997). Pelvic inflammatory disease. *Physician Assistant,* April, 36–48.

Sampson, E. (1985). The decentralization of identity: Toward a revised concept of personal and social order. *American Psychologist,* 40, 1203–1211.

Samuels, H. (1997). The relationships among selected demographics and conventional and unconventional sexual behaviors among black and white heterosexual men. *Journal of Sex Research,* 34, 85–92.

Sanchez-Ayendez, M. (1988). The Puerto Rican American family. In C. Mindel, R. Habenstein, & R. Wright (Eds.), *Ethnic Families in America* (3rd ed.). New York: Elsevier.

Sanday, P. (1981). The socio-cultural context of rape: A cross-cultural study. *Journal of Social Issues,* 37, 5–27.

Sanday, P. (1996). *A Woman Scorned: Acquaintance Rape on Trial.* New York: Doubleday.

Sandelowski, M. (1994). Separate, but less unequal: Fetal ultrasonography and the transformation of expectant mother/fatherhood. *Gender & Society,* 8, 230–245.

Sanders, G. (1982). Social comparison as a basis for evaluating others. *Journal of Research in Personality,* 16, 21–31.

Sanders, G., & Mullis, R. (1988). Family influences on sexual attitudes and knowledge as reported by college students. *Adolescence,* 23, 837–845.

Sanger, C. (1998). *Roe v. Wade. Ms.,* January/February, 75.

Sarrell, P. (1988). Sex and menopause. Paper presented at the Twenty-First Annual Meeting of the American Association of Sex Educators, Counselors, and Therapists, San Francisco, April.

Sarrell, P., & Masters, W. (1982). Sexual molestation of men by women. *Archives of Sexual Behavior,* 11, 117–131.

Sarwer, D., & Durlak, J. (1996). Childhood sexual abuse as a predictor of adult female sexual dysfunction: A study of couples seeking sex therapy. *Child Abuse & Neglect,* 20, 963–972.

Sarwer, D., Crawford, I., & Durlak, J. (1997). The relationship between childhood sexual abuse and adult male sexual dysfunction. *Child Abuse & Neglect,* 21, 649–655.

Satterfield, A., & Muehlenhard, C. (1990). Flirtation in the classroom: Negative consequences on women's perceptions of their ability. Paper presented at the annual meeting of the Society for the Scientific Study of Sex, Minneapolis, November.

Saunders, C. (1998). Women and diabetes: Special health concerns. *Patient Care,* February 15, 112–135.

Saunders, C., Guay, A., Levine, S., & Montague, D. (1998). New treatments for erectile dysfunction. *Patient Care,* 34, 30–52.

Saunders, E. (1989). Life-threatening autoerotic behavior: A challenge for sex educators and therapists. *Journal of Sex Education and Therapy,* 15, 77–81.

Saunders, N. (1997). Pregnancy in the 21st century: Back to nature with a little assistance. *The Lancet,* 349, s17–s19.

Savin-Williams, R., & Dube, E. (1998). Parental reactions to their child's disclosure of a gay/lesbian identity. *Family Relations,* 47, 7–13.

Savitz, L., & Rosen, L. (1988). The sexuality of prostitutes: Sexual enjoyment reported by streetwalkers. *Journal of Sex Research,* 24, 200–208.

Sawyer, C. (1960). Reproductive behavior. In J. Field (Ed.), *Handbook of Physiology. Section I: Neurophysiology.* Washington, DC: American Physiological Society.

Sawyer, R., Pinciaro, P., & Jessell, J. (1998). Effects of coercion and verbal consent on university students' perception of date rape. *American Journal of Health Behavior,* 22, 46–53.

Scarce, M. (1997). Same-sex rape of male college students. *Journal of American College Health,* 45, 171–173.

Schachter, M., & Shoham, Z. (1994). Amenorrhea during the reproductive years. *Fertility and Sterility,* 62, 1–16.

Schacker, T., Collier, A., Hughes, J., Shea, T., & Corey, L. (1996). The clinical and epidemiological presentation of primary HIV infection. *Annals of Internal Medicine,* 125, 257–264.

Schaeffer, A. (1990). Editorial comment. *Journal of Urology,* 143, 226.

Schaff, E., Penmetsa, U., Eisinger, S., & Franks, P. (1997b). Methotrexate a single agent for early abortion. *Journal of Reproductive Medicine,* 42, 56–60.

Schaff, E., Stadalius, L., Eisinger, S., & Franks, P. (1997a). Vaginal misoprostol administered at home after mifepristone (RU486) for abortion. *Journal of Family Practice,* 44, 353–360.

Scheela, R., & Stern, P. (1994). Falling apart: A process integral to the remodeling of male incest offenders. *Archives of Psychiatric Nursing,* 8, 91–100.

Scher, H. (1997). The drive to stop harassment in schools. *Ms.,* March/April, 22.

Schifeling, D., & Hamblin, J. (1991). Early diagnosis of breast cancer. *Postgraduate Medicine,* 89(3), 55–61.

Schlegel, P. (1991). New treatment options for the infertile man. *Medical Aspects of Human Sexuality,* June, 22–31.

Schleicher, S., & Stewart, P. (1997). Scabies: The mite that roars. *Emergency Medicine,* June, 54–58.

Schlesinger, Y., & Storch, G. (1994). Herpes simplex meningitis in infancy. *Pediatric Infectious Diseases Journal,* 13, 141–144.

Schmaltz, J. (1993). Survey finds U.S. divided over gays. *The Oregonian,* March 5, A17.

Schmetzer, U. (1995). China decides it can't afford disabled children. *The Oregonian,* January 22, A8.

Schmetzer, U. (1997). Fundamentalist Muslims impose code on Malaysia. *The Oregonian*, November 16, A6.

Schmidt, P., Nieman, L., Danaceau, M., Adams, L., & Rubinow, D. (1998). Differential behavioral effects of gonadal steroids in women with and in those without premenstrual syndrome. *New England Journal of Medicine*, 338(4), 209–216.

Schmitt, E. (1994). "Don't ask" rule backfires against gays in military. *San Francisco Chronicle,* May 9, A3.

Schnarch, D. (1991). *Constructing the Sexual Crucible.* New York: Norton.

Schnarch, D. (1993). Inside the sexual crucible. *Networker,* March/April, 40–48.

Schnarch, D. (1997). Sex, intimacy and the Internet. *Journal of Sex Education and Therapy*, 22(1), 15–20.

Schoener, G. (1995). Assessment of professionals who have engaged in boundary violations. *Psychiatric Annals,* 25(2), 95–99.

Schoofs, M. (1997). Berlin. *The Advocate*, June 24, 115–116.

Schover, L., Friedman, J., Weiler, S., Heiman, J., & LoPiccolo, J. (1982). Multiaxial problem-oriented system for sexual dysfunctions. *Archives of General Psychiatry,* 39, 614–619.

Schover, L., & Jensell, S. (1988). *Sexuality and Chronic Illness.* New York: Guilford.

Schover, L., Thomas, A., Lakin, M., Montague, D., & Fischer, J. (1988). Orgasm phase dysfunction in multiple sclerosis. *Journal of Sex Research,* 25, 548–554.

Schrag, D., Kuntz, K., Garber, J., & Weeks, J. (1997). Decision analysis—Effects of prophylactic mastectomy and oophorectomy on life expectancy among women with BRCA1 or BRCA2 mutations. *New England Journal of Medicine*, 336, 1465–1471.

Schreiner-Engle, P., Schiavi, R., Veitorisz, D., and Smith, H. (1987). The differential impact of diabetes type on female sexuality. *Journal of Psychosomatic Research,* 31, 23–33.

Schrinsky, D. (1988). Personal communication, January.

Schroder, F. (1995). Detection of prostate cancer. *British Medical Journal,* 310, 140–141.

Schroder, M., & Carroll, R. (1996). New women: Sexological outcomes of gender reassignment surgery. Paper presented at the annual meeting of the Society for Sex Therapy and Research, Miami, Florida, March 14–17.

Schroeder, J. (1995). Offensive attack. *The Advocate*, August 22, 34–38.

Schulberg, P. (1995). TV sitcoms: Bastions of sexism? *The Oregonian*, September 20, E1 & E10.

Schwartz, J., & Kaplan, D. (1992). They're only trying to help. *Newsweek,* January 27, 47.

Schwartz, P. (1990). The future is the past: Gay custody decisions. Paper presented at The Society for the Scientific Study of Sex Annual Western Region Conference, San Diego, April 25.

Schwebke, J. (1991a). Gonorrhea in the 90s. *Medical Aspects of Human Sexuality,* March, 43–46.

Schwebke, J. (1991b). Syphilis in the 90s. *Medical Aspects of Human Sexuality,* April, 44–49.

Schweiger, U. (1991). Menstrual function and luteal-phase deficiency in relation to weight changes and dieting. *Clinical Obstetrics and Gynecology,* 34, 191–197.

Scott, J., & Schwalm, L. (1988). Rape rates and the circulation rates of adult magazines. *Journal of Sex Research,* 24, 241–250.

Scott, P. (1998). Assessing nipple discharge in nonlactating women. *Journal of the American Academy of Physician Assistants*, 11(3), 33–41.

Scott-Jones, D., & White, A. (1990). Correlates of sexual activity in early adolescence. *Journal of Early Adolescence,* 10, 221–238.

Scully, D., & Marolla, J. (1984). Convicted rapists' vocabulary of motives, excuses, and justifications. *Social Problems,* 31, 530–544.

Seal, D. (1977). Interpartner concordance of self-reported sexual behavior among college dating couples. *Journal of Sex Research*, 34, 39–55.

Seaman, B., & Seaman, G. (1978). *Women and the Crisis in Sex Hormones.* New York: Bantam Books.

Searight, H., & McClaren, A. (1997). Behavioral and psychiatric aspects of HIV infection. *American Family Physician*, March, 1227–1237.

Seccombe, K., & Ishii-Kuntz, M. (1994). Gender and social relationships among the never-married. *Sex Roles,* 30, 585–603.

Secker-Walker, R., Vacek, P., Flynn, B., & Mead, P. (1997). Smoking in pregnancy, exhaled carbon monoxide, and birth weight. *Obstetrics & Gynecology*, 89, 648–653.

Sedney, M. (1987). Development of androgyny: Parental influences. *Psychology of Women Quarterly,* 11, 311–326.

Seghorn, T., Prentky, R., & Boucher, R. (1987). Childhood sexual abuse in the lives of sexually aggressive offenders. *Journal of the American Academy of Child and Adolescent Psychiatry,* 26, 262–267.

Segraves, R., & Segraves, K. (1995). Human sexuality and aging. *Journal of Sex Education and Therapy*, 21(2), 88–102.

Seidman, S., & Rieder, R. (1994). A review of sexual behavior in the United States. *American Journal of Psychiatry,* 151, 330–341.

Seligmann, J. (1992). A condom for women moves one step closer to reality. *Newsweek,* February 10, 45.

Seligmann, J., & Springen, K. (1996). Fewer bundles of pain. *Newsweek*, March 4, 63.

Sem-Jacobsen, C. (1968). *Depth-Electrographic Stimulation of the Human Brain and Behavior.* Springfield, IL: Thomas.

Semans, J. (1956). Premature ejaculation, a new approach. *Southern Medical Journal,* 49, 353–358.

Serbin, L. (1980). The Pinks and the Blues. In *Nova,* Boston: WGBH Transcripts.

Service, R. (1997). New vaccines may ward off urinary tract infections. *Science*, 276, 533–610.

Shafer, M. (1997). Lower abdominal pain and the adolescent girl. *Emergency Medicine*, February, 91–99.

Shain, R., Miller, W., Holden, A., & Rosenthal, M. (1991). Impact of tubal sterilization and vasectomy on female marital sexuality: Results of a controlled longitudinal study. *American Journal of Obstetrics and Gynecology,* 164, 763–771.

Shainess, N., & Greenwald, H. (1971). Debate: Are fantasies during sexual relations a sign of difficulty? *Sexual Behavior,* 1, 38–54.

Shapiro, F. (1995). Opening ceremony. International EMDR Conference, June 23–25, Santa Monica, California.

Shapiro, J. (1987). The expectant father. *Psychology Today,* January, 36–42.

Shapiro, L. (1998). A long road to freedom. *Newsweek*, March 16, 57.

Sharfstein, J., & Wise, P. (1997). Inadequate hepatitis B vaccination of adolescents and adults at an urban community health center. *Journal of the National Medical Association*, 89, 86–92.

Sharpsteen, D. (1995). Sex, attachment, and infidelity: The context of jealousy. Paper presented at the annual meeting of the Southwestern Psychological Association, Austin, Texas, April.

Sharpsteen, D., & Kirkpatrick, L. (1997). Romantic jealousy and adult romantic attachment. *Journal of Personality and Social Psychology*, 72, 627–640.

Sharts-Hopco, N. (1997). STDs in women: What you need to know. *American Journal of Nursing*, 97, 46–54.

Shaul, S., Bogle, J., Hale-Harbaugh, J., & Norman, A. (1978). *Toward Intimacy: Family Planning and Sexuality Concerns of Physically Disabled Women.* New York: Human Sciences Press.

Shaw, C. (1997). The perimenopausal hot flash: Epidemiology, physiology, and treatment. *Nurse Practitioner*, 22(3), 55–66.

Shaw, J. (1994). Aging and sexual potential. *Journal of Sex Education and Therapy,* 20(2), 134–139.

Shaw, J. (1997b). Treatment rationale for Internet infidelity. *Journal of Sex Education and Therapy*, 22(1), 21–28.

Shaywitz, B., Shaywitz, S., Pugh, K., Constable, R., Skudlarski, P., Fulbright, R., Bronen, R., Fletcher, J., Shankweiler, D., Katz, L., & Gore, J. (1995). Sex differences in the functional organization of the brain for language. *Nature,* 373, 607–609.

Shearer, G., & Clerici, M. (1995). Protective immunity against HIV infection: Has nature done the experiment for us? *Immunology Today*, 17, 21–24.

Sheehy, G. (1993). What smart women ask about menopause. *Ladies Home Journal,* May, 116–120.

Sheehy, G. (1997). Beyond virility, a new vision. *Newsweek*, November 17, 69.

Sheeran, P. (1987). *Women, Society, the State and Abortion: A Structuralist Analysis.* New York: Praeger.

Sheinberg, M., & Penn, P. (1991). Gender dilemmas, gender questions, and the gender mantra. *Journal of Marital and Family Therapy,* 17, 33–44.

Shenon, P. (1997). Army cites its leaders in sexual harassment. *The Oregonian*, September 12, A1 & A22.

Sherfey, M. (1972). *The Nature and Evolution of Female Sexuality.* New York: Random House.

Sherman, R., & Jones, J. (1994). A response to the article on "The validity of the Myers-Briggs Type Indicator for predicting marital problems." *Family Relations,* 43, 94–95.

Shernoff, M. (1998). Coming out in therapy. *Networker*, March/April, 23–24.

Sherwen, L. (1987). *Psychosocial Dimensions of the Pregnant Family.* New York: Springer.

Sherwin, B., & Gelfand, M. (1987). The role of androgen in the maintenance of sexual functioning in oophorectomized women. *Psychosomatic Medicine,* 49, 397–409.

Sherwin, B., Gelfand, M., & Brender, W. (1985). Androgen enhances sexual motivation in females: A prospective crossover study of sex steroid administration in the surgical menopause. *Psychosomatic Medicine,* 47, 339–351.

Sheynkin, Y., & Schlegel, P. (1997). Sperm retrieval for assisted reproductive technologies. *Contemporary Ob/Gyn*, April 15, 113–129.

Shilts, R. (1993). *Conduct Unbecoming, Gays & Lesbians in the U.S. Military.* New York: St. Martin's Press.

Shoham, Z., Zosmer, A., & Insler, V. (1991). Early miscarriage and fetal malformations after induction of ovulation (by clomiphene citrate and/or human menotropins), in vitro fertilization, and gamete intrafallopian transfer. *Fertility and Sterility,* 55, 1–11.

Shostak, A. (1979). Abortion as fatherhood lost: Problems and reforms. *Family Coordinator,* 28, 569–574.

Shostak, A., McLouth, G., & Seng, L. (1984). *Men and Abortions: Lessons, Losses and Love.* New York: Praeger.

Shrier, L., Pierce, J., Emans, S., & DuRant, R. (1998). Gender differences in risk behaviors associated with forced or pressured sex. *Archives of Pediatric and Adolescent Medicine*, 152, 57–63.

Shurpin, K. (1997). Ovarian cancer. *American Journal Nursing*, 97(4), 34.

Siecus Report (1998). Fact sheet: Teenage pregnancy. *Author*, 26, 21–22.

Siegal, M. (1987). Are sons and daughters treated more differently by fathers than by mothers? *Developmental Review,* 7, 183–209.

Siegel, J., Sorenson, S., Golding, J., Burnam, M., & Stein, J. (1989). Resistance to sexual assault: Who resists and what happens? *American Journal of Public Health,* 79, 27–31.

Sieving, R., Resnick, M., Bearinger, L., Remafedi, G., Taylor, B., & Harmon, B. (1997). Cognitive and behavioral predictors of sexually transmitted disease risk behavior among sexually active adolescents. *Archives of Pediatric and Adolescent Medicine*, 151, 243–252.

Signorielli, N., McLeod, D., & Healy, E. (1994). Gender stereotypes in MTV commercials. *Journal of Broadcasting and Electronic Media*, 38, 333–337.

Signorile, M. (1995). *Outing Yourself.* New York: Fireside.

Silver, R., Straus, F., Vogelzang, N., Kellman, H., & Chodak, G. (1991). Response to orchidectomy following Zoladex therapy for metastatic prostate carcinoma. *Urology,* 37, 17–21.

Silverman, B., & Gross, T. (1997). Use and effectiveness of condoms during anal intercourse. *Sexually Transmitted Diseases*, 24, 11–17.

Simenauer, J., & Carroll, D. (1982). *Singles: The New Americans.* New York: Simon & Schuster.

Simonds, R., Steketee, R., Nesheim, S., Matheson, P., Palumbo, P., Alger, L., Abrams, E., Orloff, S., Lindsay, M., Bardequez, A., Vink, P., Byers, R., & Rogers, M. (1998). Impact of zidovudine use on risk and risk factors for perinatal transmission of HIV. *AIDS*, 12, 301–308.

Singer, J., & Singer, I. (1972). Types of female orgasms. *Journal of Sex Research,* 8, 255–267.

Singh, M., Saxena, B., Raghubanshi, R., Ledger, W., Harman, S., & Leonard, R. (1997). Biodegradable norethindrone (NET: cholesterol) contraceptive implants: Phase II-A: A clinical study in women. *Contraception*, 55, 23–33.

Sinnott, J. (1986). *Sex Roles and Aging: Theory and Research from a Systems Perspective.* Basel, Switzerland: Karger.

Sipe, A. (1990). *A Secret World, Sexuality and the Search for Celibacy.* New York: Brunner/Mazel.

Sipski, M. (1997a). Performing the medical sexual history and physical. In M. Sipski & C. Alexander (Eds.), *Sexual Function in People with Disability and Chronic Illness.* Gaithersburg, MD: Aspen Publishers.

Sipski, M. (1997b). Spinal cord injury and sexual function: An educational model. In M. Sipski & C. Alexander (Eds.), *Sexual Function in People with Disability and Chronic Illness.* Gaithersburg, MD: Aspen Publishers.

Sipski, M., & Alexander, C. (1997). Impact of disability or chronic illness on sexual function. In M. Sipski & C. Alexander (Eds.), *Sexual Function in People with Disability and Chronic Illness.* Gaithersburg, MD: Aspen Publishers.

Sison, C., Ostrea, E., Reyes, M., & Salari, V. (1997). The resurgence of congenital syphilis: A cocaine-related problem. *Journal of Pediatrics*, 130, 289–292.

Skene, A. (1980). Two important glands of the urethra. *American Journal of Obstetrics,* 265, 265–270.

Skolnick, A. (1992). *The Intimate Environment: Exploring Marriage and the Family*. New York: HarperCollins.

Skolnick, A. (1992). Ultrasound may help detect breast implant leaks. *Journal of the American Medical Association,* 267, 786.

Skurnick, J., Kennedy, C., Perez, G., Abrams, J., Vermund, S., Denny, T., Wright, T., Quinones, M., & Louria, D. (1998). Behavioral and demographic risk factors for transmission of human immunodeficiency virus Type 1 in heterosexual couples: Report from the heterosexual HIV transmission study. *Clinical Infectious Diseases*, 26, 855–864.

Slaughter, L., & Brown, C. (1992). Colposcopy to establish physical findings in rape victims. *American Journal of Obstetrics and Gynecology*, 166, 83–86.

Slaughter, L., Brown, C., Crowley, S., & Peck, R. (1997). Patterns of genital injury in female sexual assault victims. *American Journal of Obstetrics &Gynecology*, 176, 609–616.

Slaven, L., & Lee, C. (1997). Mood and symptom reporting among middle-aged women: The relationship between menopausal status, hormone replacement therapy, and exercise participation. *Health Psychology*, 16(3), 203–208.

Sloan, L., Edmond, T., Rubin, A., & Doughty, M. (1998). Social workers' knowledge of and experience with sexual exploitation by psychotherapists. *Journal of the National Association of Social Workers*, 43(1), 43–53.

Sloane, E. (1985). *Biology of Women* (2nd ed.). New York: Wiley.

Sluzki, C. (1982). The Latin lover revisited. In M. McGoldrick & J. Giordano (Eds.), *Ethnicity and Family Therapy*. New York: Guilford Press.

Small, S., & Kerns, D. (1993). Unwanted sexual activity among peers during early and middle adolescence: Incidence and risk factors. *Journal of Marriage and the Family*, 55, 941–952.

Smeltzer, S., & Kelley, C. (1997). Multiple sclerosis. In M. Sipski & C. Alexander (Eds.), *Sexual Function in People with Disability and Chronic Illness*. Gaithersburg, MD: Aspen Publishers.

Smith, A., & Hughes, P. (1998). The estrogen dilemma. *American Journal of Nursing*, 98(4), 17–20.

Smith, D. (1995). The dynamics of culture. *Treatment Today*, Spring, 15.

Smith, D., & Over, R. (1987). Correlates of fantasy-induced and film-induced male sexual arousal. *Archives of Sexual Behavior*, 16, 395–409.

Smith, J., Scardino, P., Resnick, M., Hernandez, A., Rose, S., & Egger, M. (1997). Transrectal ultrasound versus digital rectal examination for the staging of carcinoma of the prostate: Results of a prospective, multi-institutional trial. *Journal of Urology*, 157, 902–906.

Smith, L. (1994). A content analysis of gender differences in children's advertising. *Journal of Broadcasting & Electronic Media*, 38, 333–337.

Smith, R. (1985). Abortion, right and wrong. *Newsweek*, March 25, 16.

Smith, S. (1997). Breast cancer facts and statistics. *Ms.*, November/December, 16.

Smith, T. (1991). Adult sexual behavior in 1989: Number of partners, frequency of intercourse and risk of AIDS. *Family Planning Perspectives*, 23, 102–107.

Smithyman, S. (1979). Characteristics of undetected rapists. In W. Parsonage (Ed.), *Perspectives on Victimology*. Beverly Hills, CA: Sage.

Snyder, H. (1991). To circumcise or not. *Hospital Practice*, January 15, 201–207.

Sobel, J., Faro, S., Force, R., Foxman, B., Ledger, W., Nyirjesy, P., Reed, B., & Summers, P. (1998). Vulvovaginal candidiasis: Epidemiologic, diagnostic, and therapeutic considerations. *American Journal of Obstetrics and Gynecology*, 178, 203–211.

Sobieraj, S. (1997). Clinton addresses gay-rights group. *The Oregonian*, November 9, A9.

Solimini, C. (1991). Cures for yeast infections. *New Woman*, May, 129.

Solomon, R. (1981). The love lost in cliches. *Psychology Today*, October, 83–94.

Somlai, A., Kelly, J., Wagstaff, D., & Whitson, D. (1998). Patterns, predictors, and situational contexts of HIV risk behaviors among homeless men and women. *Social Work*, 43, 7–18.

Sonenstein, F. (1986). Risking paternity: Sex and contraception among adolescent males. In A. Elster & M. Lamb (Eds.), *Adolescent Fatherhood*. Hillsdale, NJ: Erlbaum.

Sonenstein, F., Pleck, J., & Ku, L. (1991). Levels of sexual activity among adolescent males in the United States. *Family Planning Perspectives*, 23, 162–167.

Sontag, D. (1997). Partial birth abortions. *The Oregonian*, March 22, A8.

Sontag, S. (1972). The double standard of aging. *Saturday Review*, September 23, 29–38.

Sorenson, R. (1973). *Adolescent Sexuality in Contemporary America*. New York: World.

Southerland, D. (1990). Limited "sexual revolution" seen in China: Nationwide survey shows more liberal attitudes developing in conservative society. *Washington Post*, May 27.

Soutter, W., De Barros Lopes, A., Fletcher, A., Monaghan, J., Duncan, I., Paraskevaidis, E., & Kitchener, H. (1997). Invasive cervical cancer after conservative therapy for cervical intraepithelial neoplasia. *The Lancet*, 349, 978–980.

Space, L. (1981). The computer as psychometrician. *Behavioral Research Methods, Instruments and Computers*, 13, 595.

Speckens, A., Hengeveld, M., Nijeholt, G., Van Hemert, A. & Hawton, K. (1995). Psychosexual functioning of partners of men with presumed non-organic erectile dysfunction: Cause or consequence of the disorder? *Archives of Sexual Behavior*, 24, 157–174.

Spector, I., & Carey, M. (1990). Incidence and prevalence of the sexual dysfunctions: A critical review of the empirical literature. *Archives of Sexual Behavior*, 19, 389–408.

Spence, J., & Helmreich, R. (1978). *Masculinity and Femininity*. Austin: University of Texas Press.

Speroff, L., Blas, R., & Kase, N. (1989). *Clinical Gynecologic Endocrinology and Infertility*. Baltimore: Williams & Wilkins.

Spigener, S., & Mayeaux, E. (1998). Patient education and issues of HPV infection. *Hospital Practice*, January 15, 133–135.

Spinillo, A., Capuzzo, E., Gulminetti, R., Marone, P., Colonna, L., & Piazzi, G. (1997). Prevalence of and risk factors for fungal vaginitis caused by non-*albicans* species. *Americal Journal of Obstetrics and Gynecology*, 176, 138–141.

Spinnato, J., II. (1997). Mechanism of action of intrauterine contraceptive devices and its relation to informed consent. *American Journal of Obstetrics and Gynecology*, 176, 503–506.

Sponaugle, G. (1989). Attitudes toward extramarital relations. In K. McKinney & S. Sprecher (Eds.), *Human Sexuality: The Societal and Interpersonal Context*. Norwood, NJ: Ablex.

Sprauve, M., Lindsay, M., Herbert, S., & Graves, W. (1997). Adverse perinatal outcome in parturients who use crack cocaine. *Obstetrics & Gynecology*, 89, 674–678.

Sprecher, S. (1989). Premarital sexual standards for different categories of individuals. *Journal of Sex Research*, 26, 232–248.

Sprecher, S., & McKinney, K. (1993). *Sexuality*. Newbury Park, CA: Sage.

Spring-Mills, E., & Hafez, E. (1980). Male accessory sexual organs. In E. Hafez (Ed.), *Human Reproduction*, New York: Harper & Row.

Spruyt, A., Steiner, M., Joanis, C., Glover, L., Piedrahita, C., Alvarado, G., Ramos, R., Maglaya, C., & Cordero, M. (1998). Identifying condom users at risk for breakage and slippage: Findings from three international sites. *American Journal of Public Health*, 88(2), 62.

Stack, P. (1997). Pap smears. *Postgraduate Medicine*, 101(4), 207–214.

Stack, S., & Gundlach, J. (1992). Divorce and sex. *Archives of Sexual Behavior*, 21, 359–368.

Stall, R., & Catania, J. (1994). AIDS risk behaviors among late middle-aged and elderly Americans. *Archives of Internal Medicine*, 154, 57–63.

Stammer, L. (1994). Poll finds dissent among priests, nuns on sex-related edicts. *San Francisco Chronicle*, February 21, A5.

Stanford, J., Lemaire, J., & Thurman, P. (1998). Women's interest in natural family planning. *Journal of Family Practice*, 46, 65–71.

Stanley, D. (1993). To what extent is the practice of autoerotic asphyxia related to other paraphilias? In K. Haas & A. Haas (Eds.), *Understanding Sexuality*. St. Louis: Mosby.

Staropoli, C., Flaws, J., Bush, T., & Moulton, A. (1997). Cigarette smoking and frequency of menopausal hot flashes. Abstract of the 30th Annual Meeting of Society for Epidemiologic Research, Edmonton, Alberta, Canada, 71.

Starr, B., & Weiner, M. (1981). *The Starr Weiner Report on Sex and Sexuality in the Mature Years*. New York: Stein & Day.

Starr, C. (1997). Beyond the birds and the bees: Talking to teens about sex. *Patient Care*, April 15, 103–129.

Staten, C. (1997). "Roofies," the new "date rape" drug of choice. *Emergency Net News*, October 21.

Stattin, P., Damber, J., Karlsburg, L., & Bergh, A. (1997). Cell proliferation assessed by K1–67 immunoreactivity on formalin fixed tissues is a predictive factor for survival in prostate cancer. *Journal of Urology*, 157, 219–222.

Stebleton, M., & Rothenberger, J. (1993). Truth or consequences: Dishonesty in dating and HIV/AIDS-related issues in a college-age population. *Journal of American College Health*, 42, 51–54.

Stein, E. (1994). The relevance of scientific research about sexual orientation to lesbian and gay rights. In T. Murphy (Ed.), *Gay Ethics: Controversies in Outing, Civil Rights, and Sexual Science*. New York: Haworth.

Stein, J., & Reiser, L. (1994). A study of white middle-class adolescent boys' responses to "semenarche" (the first ejaculation). *Journal of Youth and Adolescence*, 23, 373–384.

Stein, M., Freedberg, K., Sullivan, L., Savetsky, J., Levenson, S., Hingson, R., & Samet, J. (1998). Discosure of HIV-positive status to partners. *Archives of Internal Medicine*, 158, 253–257.

Stein, S. (1995). The belief that children suffer in divorce enters mainstream. *The Oregonian*, January 12, D1 & D2.

Stein, Z., & Susser, M. (1997). Editorial—An update on the global dynamics. *American Journal of Public Health*, 87, 901.

Steinberg, M., Juliano, M., & Wise, L. (1985). Psychological outcome of lumpectomy versus mastectomy in the treatment of breast cancer. *American Journal of Psychiatry*, 142, 34–39.

Steinbrook, R. (1997). Battling HIV on many fronts. *New England Journal of Medicine*, 337, 779–780.

Steinem, G. (1980). Erotica and pornography: A clear and present difference. In L. Lederer (Ed.). *Take Back the Night: Women on Pornography*. New York: Morrow.

Steinem, G. (1997). What's wrong with this picture? *Ms.*, March/April, 76.

Stenager, E., Stenager, E. N., Jensen, K., & Boldsen, J. (1990). Multiple sclerosis: Sexual dysfunctions. *Journal of Sex Education & Therapy*, 16, 262–269.

Stephen, T., & Harrison, T. (1985). A longitudinal comparison of couples with sex-typical and non-sex-typical orientation to intimacy. *Sex Roles*, 12, 195–206.

Stermac, L., Sheridan, P., Davidson, A., & Dunn, S. (1996). Sexual assault of adult males. *Journal of Interpersonal Violence*, 11, 52–64.

Stern, E. (1987). Sex during pregnancy. *American Baby*, March, 71–79.

Stern, K., & McClintock, M. (1998). Regulation of ovulation by human pheromones. *Nature*, 392, 177–179.

Sternberg, R. (1986). A triangular theory of love. *Psychological Review*, 93, 119–135.

Sternberg, R. (1988). Triangulating love. In R. Sternberg & M. Barnes (Eds.), *The Psychology of Love*. New Haven, CT: Yale University Press.

Stets, J., & Pirog-Good, M. (1987). Violence in dating relationships. *Social Psychology Quarterly*, 50, 237–246.

Stevens-Simon, C., & White, M. (1991). Adolescent pregnancy. *Pediatric Annals*, 20, 322–331.

Stevens-Simon, C., & Reichert, S. (1994). Sexual abuse, adolescent pregnancy, and child abuse. *Archives of Pediatric Adolescent Medicine*, 148, 23–27.

Stevens-Simon, C., Kelly, L., & Singer, D. (1996). Absence of negative attitudes toward childrearing among pregnant teenagers: A risk factor for repeat pregnancy. *Archives of Pediatric and Adolescent Medicine*, 150, 1037–1043.

Stevenson, M. (1990). Tolerance for homosexuality and interest in sexuality education. *Journal of Sex Educaton & Therapy*, 16, 194–197.

Stewart, B., Hughes, C., Frank, E., Anderson, B., Kendall, K., & West, D. (1987). The aftermath of rape. Profiles of immediate and delayed treatment seekers. *Journal of Nervous and Mental Disorders*, 175, 90–94.

Stewart, F., Giest, F., Stewart, G., & Hatcher, R. (1987). *Understanding Your Body*. New York: Bantam.

Stewart, R. (1997). Female circumcision: Implications for North American nurses. *Journal of Psychosocial Nursing*, 35, 35–39.

Stier, D., Leventhal, J., Berg, A., Johnson, L., & Mezger, J. (1993). Are children born to young mothers at increased risk of maltreatment? *Pediatrics*, 91, 642–648.

Stimson, A., Wase, J., & Stimson, J. (1981). Sexuality and self-esteem among the aged. *Research in Aging*, 3, 228–239.

Stock, W. (1985). The effect of pornography on women. Paper presented at a hearing of the Attorney General's Commission on Pornography, Houston, September 11–12.

Stockwell, A. (1997). Family feud. *The Advocate*, September 16, 51–52.

Stockwell, A. (1998). Yep, she rules. *The Advocate*, January 20, 92.

Stoller, R. (1972). Etiological factors in female transsexualism: A first approximation. *Archives of Sexual Behavior*, 2, 47–64.

Stoller, R. (1977). Sexual deviations. In F. Beach (Ed.), *Human Sexuality in Four Perspectives*. Baltimore: Johns Hopkins University Press.

Stoller, R. (1982). Transvestism in women. *Archives of Sexual Behavior*, 11, 99–115.

Stoller, R. *Sex & Gender*. (1968). New York: Science House.

Stoller, R., & Herdt, G. (1985). Theories of origins of male homosexuality. *Archives of General Psychiatry*, 42, 399–404.

Stone, M. (1976). *When God Was a Woman*. New York: Dial Press.

Stone, R., & Waszak, C. (1992). Adolescent knowledge and attitudes about abortion. *Family Planning Perspectives*, 24, 52–58.

Stone, V., Mauch, M., Steger, K., Janas, S., & Craven, D. (1997). Race, gender, drug use, and participation in AIDS clinical trials. *Journal of General Internal Medicine*, 12, 150–157.

Storms, M. (1980). Theories of sexual orientation. *Journal of Personality and Social Psychology*, 38, 783–792.

Stott-Kendall, N. (1997). *Torn Illusions*. Fort Lauderdale: Debcar.

Stout, R. (1981). New approaches to the design of computerized interviewing and testing situations. *Behavioral Research, Instruments and Computers*, 13, 436.

Stranc, L., Evans, J., & Hamerton, J. (1997). Chorionic villus sampling and amniocentesis for prenatal diagnosis. *The Lancet*, 349, 711–714.

Strand, A., Wilander, E., Zehbe, I., & Rylander, E. (1997). High risk HPV persists after treatment of genital papillomavirus infection but not after treatment of cervical intraepithelial neoplasia. *Acta Obstetricia et Gynecologica Scandinavica*, 76, 140–144.

Strassberg, D. (1994). A physiologically based model of early ejaculation: A solution or a problem? *Journal of Sex Education & Therapy*, 20(3), 215–217.

Strassberg, D., & Mahoney, J. (1988). Correlates of contraceptive behavior of adolescents/young adults. *Journal of Sex Research*, 25, 531–536.

Strickler, J. (1992). The new reproductive technology: Problem or solution? *Sociology of Health & Illness*, 14(1), 111–132.

Strossen, N. (1995). Big Sister is watching you. *The Advocate*, November 14, 62.

Stryker, J., & Coates, T. (1997). Home access HIV testing: What took so long. *Archives of Internal Medicine*, 157, 261–262.

Stuart, F., Hammond, C., & Pett, M. (1988). Inhibited sexual desire in women. *Archives of Sexual Behavior*, 16, 91–106.

Stuart, J. (1997). Tickled pink. *The Advocate*, September 30, 55–56.

Stubblefield, P., & Grimes, D. (1994). Septic abortion. *New England Journal of Medicine*, 331, 310–313.

Stulberg, I., & Smith, M. (1988). Psychosocial impact of the AIDS epidemic on the lives of gay men. *Social Work*, 33, 277–81.

Stump, J. (1985). *What's the Difference? How Men and Women Compare*. New York: Morrow.

Stutts, M., Patterson, L., & Hunnicutt, G. (1997). Females' perception of risks associated with alcohol consumption during pregnancy. *American Journal Health Behavior*, 21(2), 137–146.

Sue, D. (1979). Erotic fantasies of college students during coitus. *Journal of Sex Research*, 15, 299–305.

Suggs, D., & Miracle, A. (Eds.) (1993). *Culture and Human Sexuality*. Pacific Groves, CA: Brooks/Cole.

Suggs, R. (1962). *The Hidden Worlds of Polynesia*. New York: Harcourt, Brace & World.

Suligoi, B. (1997). The natural history of human immunodeficiency virus infection among women as compared with men. *Sexually Transmitted Diseases*, 24, 77–83.

Sullivan, A. (1996). Let gays marry. *Newsweek*, June 3, 26.

Sullivan, A. (1997). Winning the religious war. *The Advocate*, October 14, 91–93.

Sullivan, A. (1998a). The marriage moment. *The Advocate*, January 20, 59–67.

Sullivan, A. (1998b). Do we need these laws? *The Advocate*, April 14, 41–43.

Sullivan, K., & Bradbury, T. (1997). Are premarital prevention programs reaching couples at risk for marital dysfunction? *Journal of Consulting and Clinical Psychology*, 65, 24–30.

Suman, V., Van Winter, J., Evans, M., Simmons, P., Jacobsen, S., & Manolis, A. (1998). Levonorgestrel contraceptive implants in female patients 14 to 21 years old. *Mayo Clinic Proceedings*, 73, 10–16.

Sundt, M. (1994). Identifying the attitudes and beliefs that accompany sexual harassment. Unpublished doctoral dissertation, UCLA.

Superville, D. (1996). Genital mutilation ruled persecution. *The Oregonian*, June 15, A8.

Surra, C., & Hughes, D. (1997). Commitment processes in accounts of the development of permarital relationships. *Journal of Marriage and the Family*, 59, 5–21.

Swaab, D., & Fliers, E. (1985). A sexually dimorphic nucleus in the human brain. *Science*, 228, 1112–1115.

Swain, A., Narvaez, V., Burgoyne, P., Camerino, G., & Lovell-Badge, R. (1998). *Dax 1* antagonizes *Sry* action in mammalian sex determination. *Nature*, 391, 761–766.

Swartz, J. (1998). Surveyor of cybersex. *San Francisco Chronicle*, April 16, D3.

Swedish Institute (1997). Personal communication.

Swiss, S., & Giller, J. (1993). Rape as a crime of war. *Journal of the American Medical Association*, 270, 612–615.

Synovitz, L., & Byrne, J. (1998). Antecedents of sexual victimization: Factors discriminating victims from nonvictims. *Journal of American College Health*, 46, 151–158.

Takami, S., Getchell, M., Chen, Y., Monti-Bloch, L., Berliner, D., Stensaus, L., & Getchell, T. (1993). Vomeronasal epithelial cells of the adult human express neuron-specific molecules. *Neuroreport*, 4, 375–378.

Taddio, A., Stevens, B., Craig, K., Rastogi, P., Ben-David, S., Shennan, A., Mulligan, P., & Koren, G. (1997a). Efficacy and safety of lidocaine-prilocaine cream for pain during circumcision. *New England Journal of Medicine*, 336, 1197–1201.

Taddio, A., Katz, J., Ilevsich, A., & Koren, G. (1997b). Effects of neonatal circumcision on pain response during subsequent routine vaccination. *The Lancet*, 349, 599–603.

Tafel, R. (1998). A dead girl or a live boy. *The Advocate*, April 28, 9.

Talamini, J. (1982). *Boys Will Be Girls: The Hidden World of the Heterosexual Male Transvestite.* Washington, DC: University Press of America.

Tanenbaum, L. (1997). Can sperm affect fetal health? *Ms.*, March/April, 31.

Tang, C., & Chung, T. (1997). Psychosexual adjustment following sterilization: A prospective study on Chinese women. *Journal of Psychosomatic Research*, 42(2), 187–196.

Tannen, D. (1990). *You Just Don't Understand: Women and Men in Conversation.* New York: Ballantine Books (paperback edition, 1991).

Tasker, F., & Golombok, S. (1995). Adults raised as children in lesbian families. *American Journal of Orthopsychiatric*, 65(2) 203–215.

Tate-O'Brien, J. (1981). *Love in Deed: Manual for Engaged Couples*. St. Paul, MN: International Marriage Encounter.

Taub, G. (1997). The breast-screening brawl. *Science*, 275, 1056–1059.

Tavris, C., & Sadd, S. (1977). *The Redbook Report on Female Sexuality.* New York: Delacorte.

Taylor, J. (1971). In R. Haber & C. Eden (Eds.), *Holy Living* (rev. ed.). New York: Adler.

Taylor, M., & Hall, J. (1982). Psychological androgyny: Theories, methods, and conclusions. *Psychological Bulletin*, 92, 347–366.

Taylor, R. (1970). *Sex in History.* New York: Harper & Row.

Tchetgen, M., Song, J., Strawderman, M., Jacobsen, S., & Oesterling, J. (1996). Ejaculation increases the serum prostate-specific antigen concentration. *Urology*, 47, 511–516.

Telljohann, S., Price, J., Poureslami, M., & Easton, A. (1995). Teaching about sexual orientation by secondary health teachers. *Journal of School Health*, 65(1), 18–22.

Templeman, T., & Sinnett, R. (1991). Patterns of sexual arousal and history in a "normal" sample of young men. *Archives of Sexual Behavior*, 20, 137–150.

Tepper, M. (1997). Living with a disability: A man's perspective. In M. Sipski & C. Alexander (Eds.), *Sexual Function in People with Disability and Chronic Illness.* Gaithersburg, MD: Aspen Publishers.

Terry, J. (1990). Lesbians under the medical gaze: Scientists search for remarkable differences. *Journal of Sex Research*, 27, 317–339.

Tess, B., Rodrigues, L., Newell, M., Dunn, D., & Lago, T. (1998). Breastfeeding, genetic, obstetric and other risk factors associated with mother-to-child transmission of HIV-1 in San Paulo State, Brazil. *AIDS*, 12, 513–520.

Tessler, A., & Krahn, H. (1966). Varicocele and testicular temperature. *Fertility and Sterility*, 17, 201–203.

Testa, R., Kinder, B., & Aronson, G. (1987). Heterosexual bias in the perception of loving relationships of gay males and lesbians. *Journal of Sex Research*, 23, 163–172.

Tharaux-Deneux, C., Bouyer, J., Job-Spira, N., Coste, J., & Spira, A. (1998). Risk of ectopic pregnancy and previous induced abortion. *American Journal of Public Health*, 88(3), 401–405.

The Advocate Report (1996). Clinton growls at hate crimes. *The Advocate*, July 22, 20.

The Economist (1998). The sex business. *The Economist*, February 14, 17–18.

Thomas, A., Jr., & LeMelle, S. (1995). The Norplant system: Where are we in 1995? *Journal of Family Practice*, 40(2), 125–127.

Thomas, B. (1997). Shifting lines. *Newsweek*, June 16, 32–35.

Thomas, E. (1995). Endometriosis, 1995—Confusion or sense? *International Journal of Gynecology & Obstetrics*, 48, 149–155.

Thomas, K. (1998). FGM watch. *Ms.*, March/April, 28.

Thomas, L. E. (1991). Correlates of sexual interest among elderly men. *Psychological Reports*, 68, 620–622.

Thomas, L., Fox, S., Leake, B., & Roetzheim, R. (1996). The effects of health beliefs on screening mammography utilization among a diverse sample of older women. *Women & Health*, 24(3), 77–94.

Thomas, R., Cahill, J., & Santilli, L. (1997). Using an interactive computer game to increase skill and self-efficacy regarding safer sex negotiation: Field test results. *Health Education & Behavior*, 24, 71–86.

Thompson, I. (1997). Editorial: Prostate cancer. *Journal of Urology*, 157, 919–920.

Thompson, R. (1990). Is routine circumcision indicated in the newborn? An opposing view. *Journal of Family Practice*, 31, 189–196.

Thornburg, H. (1981). Adolescent sources of information about sex. *Journal of School Health*, 51, 274–277.

Thune, I., Brenn, T., Lund, E., & Gaard, M. (1997). Physical activity and the risk of breast cancer. *New England Journal of Medicine*, 336, 1269–1275.

Tilton, M. (1997). Diabetes and amputation. In M. Sipski & C. Alexander (Eds.), *Sexual Function in People with Disability and Chronic Illness.* Gaithersburg, MD: Aspen Publishers.

Ting-Toomey, S. & Korzenny, F. (Eds.) (1991). *Cross-Cultural Interpersonal Communication.* Newbury Park, CA: Sage.

Todd, C., Jones, R., Golichowski, A., & Arno, J. (1997). *Chlamydia trachomatis* and febrile complications of postpartum tubal ligation. *American Journal of Obstretrics and Gynecology*, 176, 100–102.

Tollison, C., & Adams, H. (1979). *Sexual Disorders: Treatment, Theory, Research.* New York: Gardner.

Torres, J. (1998). Masculinity and gender roles among Puerto Rican men: Machismo on the U.S. mainland. *American Journal of Orthopsychiatry*, 68, 16–26.

Toufexis, A. (1993). The right chemistry. *Time*, February 15, 49–51.

Toussie-Weingarten, C., & Jacobwitz, J. (1987). Alternatives in childbearing: Choices and challenges. In L. Sherwen (Ed.), *Psychosocial Dimensions of the Pregnant Family.* New York: Springer.

Townsend, J. (1995). Sex without emotional involvement: An evolutionary interpretation of sex differences. *Archives of Sexual Behavior*, 24, 173–182.

Townsend, J., & Levy, G. (1990). Effects of potential partners' physical attractiveness and socioeconomic status on sexuality and partner selection. *Archives of Sexual Behavior*, 19, 149–164.

Toyfexis, A. (1989). Too many mouths. *Newsweek*, January 2, 48–50.

Trafimow, D., Triandis, H., & Goto, S. (1991). Some tests of the distinction between the private self and the collective self. *Journal of Personality and Social Psychology*, 60, 649–655.

Tran, T. (1988). The Vietnamese American family. In C. Mindel, R. Habenstein, & R. Wright (Eds.), *Ethnic Families in America,* 3rd ed. New York: Elsevier.

Treadway, D. (1997). Hot chat: Case commentary 1. *Networker*, May/June, 71–73.

Trebilcock, B. (1997). Child molesters on the Internet: Are they in your home? *Redbook*, April, 100–103, 136–138.

Treiman, K., Liskin, L., Kols, A., & Rinehart, W. (1995). IUDs—an update. *Population Reports*, Series B, No. 6, December.

Tripp, C. (1975). *The Homosexual Matrix.* New York: McGraw-Hill.

Troiden, R. (1988). *Gay and Lesbian Identity: A Sociological Analysis.* New York: General Hall.

Trudel, G., Aubin, S., & Matte, B. (1995). Sexual behaviors and pleasure in couples with hypoactive sexual desire. *Journal of Sex Education and Therapy*, 21, 210–216.

Trudel, G., Boulos, L., & Matte, B. (1994). Dyadic adjustment in couples with hypoactive sexual desire. *Journal of Sex Education & Therapy,* 19(1), 31–36.

Trussell, J. (1988). Teenage pregnancy in the United States. *Family Planning Perspectives,* 20, 262–273.

Trussell, J., Koenig, J., Ellertson, C., & Stewart, F. (1997). Preventing unintended pregnancy: The cost-effectiveness of three methods of emergency contraception. *American Journal of Public Health*, 87, 932–933.

Trussell, J., Sturgen, K., Strickler, J., & Dominik, R. (1994). Comparative contraceptive efficacy of the female condom and other barrier methods. *Family Planning Perspectives,* 26, 66–72.

Trussell, J., Warner, D., & Hatcher, R. (1992). Condom slippage and breakage rates. *Family Planning Perspectives,* 24, 20–23.

Tucker, V., & Cho, C. (1991). AIDS and adolescents. *Postgraduate Medicine,* 89, 49–53.

Tudge, C. (1991). Can we end rhino poaching? *New Scientist*, 132, 34–35.

Tullman, G., Gilner, F., Kolodny, R., Dornbush, R., & Tullman, G. (1981). The pre- and post-therapy measurement of communication skills of couples undergoing sex therapy at the Masters & Johnson Institute. *Archives of Sexual Behavior*, 10, 95–99.

Turek, P., Cha, I., & Ljung, B. (1997). Systematic fine-needle aspiration of the testis: Correlation to biopsy and results of organ "mapping" for mature sperm in azoospermic men. *Urology*, 49, 743–748.

Turner, B., Eppes, S., McKee, L., Cosler, L., & Markson, L. (1995). A population-based comparison of the clinical course of children and adults with AIDS. *AIDS*, 9, 65–72.

Tyler, J., Jackman-Wheitner, L., Strader, S., & Lenox, R. (1997). A change-model approach to raising awareness of gay, lesbian, and bisexual issues among graduate students in counseling. *Journal of Sex Education and Therapy*, 22(2), 37–43.

Tyson, R. (1996). Worst may be yet to come in Africa's AIDS epidemic. *The Oregonian*, May 26, A9.

U.S. Attorney General's Commission on Pornography (1986). *Final Report of the Attorney General's Commission on Pornography.* Washington, DC: U.S. Justice Department.

U.S. Bureau of the Census (1978). *Statistical Abstract of the United States: 1978*, 99th ed. Washington, DC: U.S. Department of Commerce.

U.S. Bureau of the Census (1985). *Statistical Abstract of the United States: 1985*, 105th ed. Washington, DC: U.S. Department of Commerce.

U.S. Bureau of the Census (1993). *Statistical Abstract of the United States 1993.* Washington, DC: Government Printing Office.

U.S. Bureau of the Census (1997). *Statistical Abstract of the United States 1997.* Washington, DC: Government Printing Office.

U.S. Merit Systems Protection Board (1981). *Sexual Harassment in the Federal Workplace: Is It a Problem?* Washington, DC: Government Printing Office.

U.S. Merit Systems Protection Board (1988). *Sexual Harassment in the Federal Workplace: An Update.* Washington, DC: Government Printing Office.

Ubell, E. (1984). Sex in America today. *Parade*, October 28, 11–13.

Uehling, D., Hopkins, W., Balish, E., Xing, Y., & Heisey, D. (1997). Vaginal mucosal immunization for recurrent urinary tract infection: Phase II clinical trial. *Journal of Urology*, 157, 2049–2052.

Unger, R., & Crawford, M. (1992). *Women and Gender: A Feminist Psychology*. New York: McGraw-Hill.

United Nations Commission (1959). Study on traffic in persons and prostitution. ST/JOA/5D/8.

University of California at San Francisco Researchers (1996). Latino gender role-beliefs impede condom use. Study results presented at the 11th International Conference on AIDS, Vancouver, July 7–12.

Unkila-Kallio, L., Leminen, A., Titinen, A., Lehtovirta, P., Wahlstrom, T., & Ylikorkala, O. (1997). Malignant tumors of the ovary of the breast in association with infertility: A report of thirteen cases. *Acta Obstetricia et Gynecologica Scandinavica*, 76, 177–181.

Unlu, C., Gultan, S., & Aytac, R. (1997). A true hermaphrodite with an inguinal uterus and testis. *International Journal of Gynecology & Obstetrics*, 56, 63–64.

Uno, M., Deguchi, T., Ehara, H., Ishihara, S., & Kobayashi, S. (1998). Prostatic cancer 30 years after bilateral orchidectomy. *British Journal of Urology*, 81, 506–507.

Urassa, M., Todd, J., Boerma, J., Hayes, R., & Isingo, R. (1997). Male circumcision and susceptibility to HIV infection among men in Tanzania. *AIDS*, 11, 73–80.

Usry, B. (1995). *Sisterhood of the night: A true story.* Far Hills, NJ: New Horizon Press.

Utian, W., & Schiff, I. (1994). NAMS-Gallup survey on women's knowledge, information sources, and attitudes to menopause and hormone replacement therapy. *Menopause*, 1, 39–59.

Vachss, A. (1996). If we really want to protect children. *Parade*, November 3, 4–5.

Van de Ven, P. (1995). Talking with juvenile offenders about gay males and lesbians: Implications for combating homophobia. *Adolescence*, 30(117), 19–42.

Van de Wiel, H., Jaspers, J., Weijmar-Schultz, W., & Gal, J. (1990). Treatment of vaginismus: A review of concepts and treatment modalities. *Journal of Psychosomatic Obstetrics & Gynecology*, 11, 1–18.

Van den Bossche, F., & Rubinson, L. (1997). Contraceptive self-efficacy in adolescents: A comparative study of male and female contraceptive practices. *Journal of Sex Education and Therapy*, 22(2), 23–29.

Van Dis, H., & Larsson, K. (1971). Induction of sexual arousal in the castrated male rat by intracranial stimulation. *Physiological Behavior*, 6, 85–86.

Van Howe, R. (1998). Circumcision and infectious diseases revisited. *Pediatric Infectious Diseases Journal*, 17, 1–6.

Van Roosmalen, J. (1997). Previous caesarean birth "always a scar." *European Journal of Obstetrics & Gynecology and Reproductive Biology*, 72, 119–120.

Van Rooyen, M. (1997). Benign prostatic hyperplasia: Diagnosis and watchful waiting as management. *Physician Assistant*, January, 40–61.

Van Wyk, P. (1984). Psychosocial development of heterosexual, bisexual, and homosexual behavior. *Archives of Sexual Behavior*, 13, 505–544.

Vashi, A., & Oesterling, J. (1997). Percent free prostate-specific antigen: Entering a new era in the detection of prostate cancer. *Mayo Clinic Proceedings*, 72, 337–344.

Vasquez, M. (1994). Latinas. In L. Comas-Diaz & B. Greene (Eds.), *Women of Color.* New York: Guilford.

Vaughn, E., & Fisher, A. (1962). Male sexual behavior induced by intracranial electrical stimulation. *Science*, 137, 758–760.

Veith, J., Buck, M., Getzlaf, S., Van Dalfsen, P., & Slade, S. (1983). Exposure to men influences the occurrence of ovulation in women. Paper presented at the Ninety-First Convention of the American Psychological Association, Anaheim, California, August 27.

Velarde, A., & Warlick, M. (1973). Massage parlors: The sensuality business. *Society*, 11, 63–74.

Vernon, M. (1997). Issues in the management of human papillomavirus genital disease. *American Family Physician*, 55, 1813–1820.

Vines, G. (1994). Time to throw away your old contraceptives? *New Scientist*, April 30, 36–40.

Vinson, R., & Epperly, T. (1991). Counseling patients on proper use of condoms. *American Family Physician*, 43, 2081–2085.

Vistica, G. (1996). Rape in the ranks. *Newsweek*, November 25, 28–32.

Vistica, G., & Thomas, E. (1998). Backlash in the ranks. *Newsweek*, April 20, 27.

Vlajinac, H., Petrovic, R., Marinkovic, J., Sipetic, S., & Adanja, B. (1997). Effect of caffeine intake during pregnancy on birth weight. *American Journal of Epidemiology*, 145, 335–338.

Voeller, B. (1991). AIDS and heterosexual anal intercourse. *Archives of Sexual Behavior*, 20, 233–269.

Vohra, S., & Morgentaler, A. (1997). Congenital anomalies of the vas deferens, epididymis, and seminal vesicles. *Urology*, 49(3), 313–321.

Volberding, P. (1994). Treatment dilemmas in HIV infections. *Hospital Practice*, 29, 49–60.

Volberding, P. (1998). An aggressive approach to HIV antiviral therapy. *Hospital Practice*, January 15, 81–104.

Volm, L. (1997). Personal communication.

Von Schoultz, B. (1997). HRT and breast cancer risk, what to advise? *European Journal of Obstetrics & Gynecology and Reproductive Biology*, 71, 205–208.

Vonk, R., & Ashmore, R. (1993). The multifaceted self: Androgyny reassessed by open-ended self-description. *Social Psychology Quarterly*, 56, 278–287.

Wagner, G., Serafini, J., Rabkin, J., Remien, R., & Williams, J. (1994). Integration of one's religion and homosexuality: A weapon against internalized homophobia? *Journal of Homosexuality*, 26(4), 91–109.

Wain-Hobson, S. (1998). 1959 and all that. *Nature*, 391, 531–532.

Walbrecker, J. (1995). Start talking about testicular cancer. *RN*, 58, 34–35.

Walbroehl, G. (1984). Sexuality during pregnancy. *American Family Physician*, 29, 273–275.

Waldman, T., & Eliasof, B. (1997). Cancer. In M. Sipski & C. Alexander (Eds.), *Sexual Function in People with Disability and Chronic Illness.* Gaithersburg, MD: Aspen Publishers.

Walen, S., & Roth, D. (1987). A cognitive approach. In J. Geer & W. O'Donohue (Eds.), *Theories of Human Sexuality.* New York: Plenum.

Walfish, S., & Myerson, M. (1980). Sex role identity and attitudes toward sexuality. *Archives of Sexual Behavior*, 9, 199–203.

Walker, A. (1996). Couples watching television: Gender, power, and the remote control. *Journal of Marriage and the Family*, 58, 813–823.

Wallerstein, J., & Blakeslee, S. (1995). *The Good Marriage.* New York: Houghton Mifflin.

Wallick, M. (1997). Homophobia and heterosexism. Out of the medical school closet. *NCMJ*, 58(2), 123–125.

Walsh, A. (1991). *The Science of Love: Understanding Love and Its Effects on Mind and Body.* Buffalo, NY: Prometheus.

Walsh, R. (1989). Premarital sex among teenagers and young adults. In K. McKinney & S. Sprecher (Eds.), *Human Sexuality: The Societal and Interpersonal Context.* Norwood, NJ: Ablex.

Walster, E., & Walster, G. (1978). *A New Look at Love.* Reading, MA: Addison-Wesley.

Walters, A. (1994). Using visual media to reduce homophobia: A classroom demonstration. *Journal of Sex Education and Therapy*, 20(2), 92–100.

Walters, K. (1997). Urban lesbian and gay American Indian identity: Implications for mental health service delivery. In L. Brown (Ed.), *Two Spirit People.* New York: Harrington Park Press.

Wang, C., Vittinghoff, E., Hua, L., Yun, W., & Rong, Z. (1998). Reducing pregnancy and induced abortion rates in China: Family planning with husband participation. *American Journal of Public Health*, 88(4), 646–648.

Ward, L., & Wyatt, G. (1994). The effects of childhood sexual messages on African-American and white women's adolescent sexual behavior. *Psychology of Women Quarterly*, 18, 183–201.

Ward, S., Chapman, K., Cohn, E., White, S., & Williams, K. (1991). Acquaintance rape and the college social scene. *Family Relations*, 40, 65–71.

Warren, M. (1982). Onset of puberty later in athletic girls. *Medical Aspects of Human Sexuality*, 4, 77–78.

Warren, P. (1997). Down and out. *The Advocate*, August 19, 5.

Washburn, J. (1996). Reality check: Can 400,000 women be wrong? *Ms.*, March/April, 51–57.

Watson, P., Marcus, J., & Lynch, H. Prognosis of BRCA1 hereditary breast cancer. *The Lancet*, 351, 304–305.

Watson, R., & DeMeo, P. (1987). Premarital cohabitation vs. traditional courtship and subsequent marital adjustment: A replication and follow-up. *Family Relations*, 36, 193–97.

Wegner, D., Lane, J., & Dimitri, S. (1994). The allure of secret relationships. *Journal of Personality and Social Psychology*, 66, 287–300.

Wehrfritz, G. (1996). Joining the party. *Newsweek*, April 1, 46, 48.

Wehrle, K. (1994). The Norplant system: Easy to insert, easy to remove. *Nurse Practitioner*, April, 47–54.

Weidner, W., Schroeder-Printzen, I., Weiske, W., & Vosshenrich, R. (1997). Sexual dysfunction in Peyronie's disease: An analysis of 222 patients without previous local plaque therapy. *Journal of Urology*, 157, 325–328.

Weinberg, G. (1973). *Society and the Healthy Homosexual.* New York: Anchor.

Weinberg, M., Williams, C., & Moser, C. (1984). The social constituents of sadomasochism. *Social Problems*, 31, 379–389.

Weinberg, M., Williams, C., & Pryor, D. (1994). *Dual Attraction: Understanding Bisexuality.* New York: Oxford University Press.

Weinberg, T. (1987). Sadomasochism in the United States: A review of recent sociological literature. *Journal of Sex Research*, 23, 50–69.

Weiner, A. (1996). Understanding the social needs of streetwalking prostitutes. *Journal of the National Association of Social Workers*, 41, 97–105.

Weiner, D., & Rosen, R. (1997). Medications and their impact. In M. Sipski & C. Alexander (Eds.), *Sexual Function in People with Disability and Chronic Illness.* Gaithersburg, MD: Aspen Publishers.

Weinrich, J. (1990). Does childhood gender nonconformity predict adult high-risk behavior? Paper presented at The Society for the Scientific Study of Sex Annual Western Region Conference, San Diego, April 25.

Weinrich, J. (1997). Strange bedfellows: Homosexuality, gay liberation, and the Internet. *Journal of Sex Education and Therapy*, 22, 58–66.

Weinstein, E., & Rosen, E. (1991). The development of adolescent sexual intimacy: Implications for counseling. *Adolescence*, 26, 331–339.

Weis, D. (1983). Affective reactions of women to their initial experience of coitus. *Journal of Sex Research*, 19, 209–237.

Weisfuse, I. (1998). Gonorrhea control and antimicrobial resistance. *The Lancet*, 351, 928.

Weisman, C., Plichta, S., Nathanson, C., Ensminger, M., & Robinson, J. (1991). Consistency of condom use for disease prevention among adolescent users of oral contraceptives. *Family Planning Perspectives*, 23, 71–74.

Weisner, T., Garnier, H., & Loucky, J. (1994). Domestic tasks, gender egalitarian values and children's gender typing in conventional and nonconventional families. *Sex Roles*, 30, 23–54.

Weller, A. (1998). Communication through body odour. *Nature*, 392, 126–127.

Weller, L., & Weller, A. (1997). Menstrual variability and the measurement of menstrual synchrony. *Psychoneuroendocrinology*, 22(2), 115–128.

Weller, S. (1993). A meta-analysis of condom effectiveness in reducing sexually transmitted HIV. *Social Science of Medicine*, 36, 1635–1644.

Wells, B. (1983). Nocturnal orgasms: Females' perceptions of a "normal" sexual experience. *Journal of Sex Education and Therapy*, 9, 32–38.

Wells, J. (1991). The effects of homophobia and sexism on heterosexual sexual relationships. *Journal of Sex Education & Therapy*, 17, 185–195.

Wells, R., McCann, J., Adams, J., Voris, J., & Ensign, J. (1995). Emotional, behavioral, and physical symptoms reported by parents of sexually abused, nonabused, and allegedly abused prepubescent females. *Child Abuse & Neglect,* 19, 155–163.

Welner, S. (1997). Gynecologic care and sexuality issues for women with disabilities. *Sexuality and Disability*, 15, 33–39.

Werner, E. (1997). The cult of virginity. *Ms.*, March/April, 40–43.

Westall, J. (1997). Twins may protect against breast cancer. *British Medical Journal*, 314, 845.

Wheeler, M. (1991). Physical changes of puberty. *Endocrinology and Metabolism Clinics of North America,* 20, 1–14.

Whipple, B., & Komisaruk, B. (1988). Analgesia produced in women by genital self-stimulation. *Journal of Sex Research,* 24, 130–140.

Whipple, B., Ogden, G., & Komisaruk, B. (1992). Physiological correlates of imagery-induced orgasm in women. *Archives of Sexual Behavior*, 21, 121–133.

Whitam, F. (1980). The prehomosexual male child in three societies: The United States, Guatemala, Brazil. *Archives of Sexual Behavior*, 9, 87–99.

White, D. (1981). Pursuit of the ultimate aphrodisiac. *Psychology Today,* September, 9–11.

White, E. (1997). Elton John. *Rolling Stone*, July 10–24, 92.

White, G. (1981). Relative involvement, inadequacy, and jealousy: A test of a causal model. *Alternative Lifestyles*, 4, 291–309.

White, G., & Helbick, R. (1988). Understanding and treating jealousy. In R. Brown & J. Fields (Eds.), *Treatment of Sexual Problems in Individuals and Couples Therapy*. Boston: PMA Publishing.

White, S., & DeBlassie, R. (1992). Adolescent sexual behavior. *Adolescence,* 27, 183–191.

Whitehead, B. (1994). The failure of sex education. *Atlantic Monthly,* October, 55–80.

Whitley, R. Kimberlin, D., & Roizman, B. (1998). Herpes simplex viruses. *Clinical Infectious Diseases*, 26, 541–555.

Whittle, M. (1998). Commentary. Early amniocentesis: Time for a rethink. *The Lancet*, 351, 226–227.

Wiederman, M. (1993). Demographic and sexual characteristics of nonresponders to sexual experience items in a national survey. *Journal of Sex Research*, 30, 27–35.

Wiederman, M. (1997). Extramarital sex: Prevalence and correlates in a national survey. *Journal of Sex Research*, 34(2), 167–174.

Wiederman, M., & Allgeier, E. (1992). Gender differences in mate selection criteria: Sociobiological or socioeconomic explanations? *Ethology and Sociobiology,* 13, 115–124.

Wiederman, M., & Allgeier, E. (1993). Gender differences in sexual jealousy: Adaptionist or social learning explanation. *Ethology and Sociobiology*, 14, 115–140.

Wiederman, M., Weis, D., & Allgeier, E. (1994). The effect of question preface on response rates to a telephone survey of sexual experience. *Archives of Sexual Behavior*, 23, 203–216.

Wiest, W. (1977). Semantic differential profiles of orgasm and other experiences among men and women. *Sex Roles,* 3, 399–403.

Wiest, W., Harrison, J., Johanson, C., Laubsch, B., & Whitley, A. (1995). Paper presented at the Oregon Academy of Sciences meeting, February 25, Reed College, Portland.

Wilcox, A., Weinberg, C., & Baird, D. (1995). Timing of sexual intercourse in relation to ovulation. Effects on the probability of conception, survival of the pregnancy, and sex of the baby. *New England Journal of Medicine*, 333, 1517–1521.

Wilcox, L., Koonin, L., Pokras, R., Strauss, L., Xia, Z., & Peterson, H. (1994). Hysterectomy in the United States, 1988–1990. *Obstetrics & Gynecology,* April, 549–555.

Wiley, D., James, G., Furney, S., & Jordan-Belver, C. (1997). Using the youth risk behavior survey to compare risk behavior of Texas high school and college students. *Journal of School Health*, 67, 45–49.

Williams, A., Thomson, R., Schreiber, G., Watanabe, K., Bethel, J., Lo, A., Kleinman, S., Hollingsworth, C., & Nemo, G. (1997). Estimates of infectious disease risk factors in U.S. blood donors. *Journal of the American Medical Association*, 277, 967–972.

Williams, E., & Ellison, F. (1996). Culturally informed social work practice with American Indian clients: Guidelines for non-Indian social workers. *Journal of the National Association of Social Workers*, 41(2), 147–151.

Williams, L. (1994). Recall of childhood trauma: A prospective study of women's memories of child sexual abuse. *Journal of Consulting and Clinical Psychology,* 62, 1167–1176.

Williams, M. (1996). Developments in contraceptive methods for men. *Contemporary Sexuality*, December, 1–2.

Williams, P., & Smith, M. (1979). Interview in *The First Question*. London: British Broadcasting System Science and Features Department film.

Williamson, M. (1997). Circumcision anesthesia: A study of nursing implication for dorsal penile nerve block. *Pediatric Nursing*, 23, 59–63.

Willke, R., Glick, H., McCarron, T., Erder, M., Althof, S., & Linet, O. (1997). Quality of life effects of alprostadil therapy for erectile dysfunction. *Journal of Urology*, 157, 2124–2128.

Willson, J., & Carrington, E., & Ledger, W. (1983). *Obstetrics & Gynecology.* St. Louis: Mosby.

Wilson, B., & Lawson, D. (1976). Effects of alcohol on sexual arousal in women. *Journal of Abnormal Psychology,* 85, 489–497.

Wilson, C., Turner, C., & Keye, W., Jr. (1991). Firstborn adolescent daughters and mothers with and without premenstrual syndrome: A comparison. *Journal of Adolescent Health,* 12, 130–137.

Wilson, E. (1975). *Sociobiology: The New Synthesis.* Cambridge, MA: Harvard University Press.

Wilson, M. (1984). Female homosexuals' need for dominance and endurance. *Psychological Reports,* 55, 79–82.

Wilson, R. (1998). Randomised trial to assess safety and fetal outcome of early and midtrimester amniocentesis. *The Lancet*, 351, 242–247.

Wilson, S., & Delk, J., II. (1994). A new treatment for Peyronie's disease: Modeling the penis over an inflatable penile prosthesis. *Journal of Urology,* 152, 1121–1123.

Wincze, J., Albert A., & Bansal, S. (1993). Sexual arousal in diabetic females: Physiological and self-report measures. *Archives of Sexual Behavior*, 22, 587–600.

Wineberg, H. (1994). Marital reconciliation in the United States: Which couples are successful? *Journal of Marriage and the Family,* 56, 80–88.

Wingert, P., (1998). The battle over falling birthrates. *Newsweek*, May 11, 40.

Winick, C., & Evans, J. (1996). The relationship between nonenforcement of state pornography laws and rates of sex crime arrests. *Archives of Sexual Behavior*, 25(5), 439–453.

Winks, C., & Semans, A. (1994). *The Good Vibrations Guide to Sex.* Pittsburgh, PA: Cleis Press.

Wise, J. (1997). No risk of breast cancer with abortions. *British Medical Journal*, 314, 169.

Wise, T., & Meyer, J. (1980). Transvestism: Previous findings and new areas for inquiry. *Journal of Sex and Marital Therapy*, 6, 116–128.

Wiswell, T. (1997). Circumcision circumspection. *New England Journal of Medicine*, 336, 1244–1245.

Witelson, S. (1988). Neuroanatomical sex differences: Of no consequence for cognition? *Behavioral and Brain Sciences*, 11, 215–217.

Witelson, S. (1991). Neural sexual mosaicism: Sexual differentiation of the human temporo-parietal region for functional asymmetry. *Psychoneuroendocrinology*, 16, 131–153.

Witt, S. (1997). Parental influence on children's socialization to gender roles. *Adolescence*, 32, 253–258.

Wittkowski, K., Susser, E., & Dietz, K. (1998). The protective effect of condoms and nonoxynol-9 against HIV infection. *American Journal of Public Health*, 88, 590–596.

Wohl, R., & Kane, W. (1997). Teachers' beliefs concerning teaching about testicular cancer and testicular self-examination. *Journal of School Health*, 67, 106–111.

Wold, A., & Adlerberth, I. (1998). Does breastfeeding affect the infant's immune responsiveness? *Acta Paediatrica*, 87, 19–22.

Wolfe, A. (1998). Shut up about sex. *The Advocate*, April 14, 43–45.

Wolfe, L. (1981). *The Cosmo Report*. New York: Arbor House.

Wolpe, J. (1958). *Psychotherapy by Reciprocal Inhibition*. Stanford, CA: Stanford University Press.

Wolpe, J. (1985). *The Practice of Behavior Therapy* (3rd ed.). New York: Pergamon Press.

Women on Words & Images (1972). *Dick and Jane as Victims*. Princeton, NJ: Women on Words & Images.

Wong, J., Gunthard, H., Havlir, D., Haase, A., Zhang, Z., & Kwok, S. (1997). Reduction of HIV in blood and lymph nodes after potent antiretroviral therapy. Paper presented at the 4th Conference on Retroviruses and Other Opportunistic Infections, Washington, DC, January.

Wong, M. (1988). The Chinese American family. In C. Mindel, R. Habenstein, & R. Wright (Eds.), *Ethnic Families in America* (3rd ed.). New York: Elsevier.

Wong-Staal, F. (1997). Highlights from the University of California San Diego Center for AIDS Research. *AIDS Research and Human Retroviruses*, 13, 117–120.

Wood, G., & Ruddock, E. (1918). *Vitalogy*. Chicago: Vitalogy Association.

Wood, J. (1994). *Gendered Lives: Communication, Gender and Culture*. Belmont, CA: Wadsworth.

Wood, S., Thomas, D., Droppleman, L., & Meighan, R. (1997). Postpartum depression rates. *Maternal Child Nursing*, 22, 308–316.

Wooden, W., & Parker, J. (1982). *Men Behind Bars: Sexual Exploitation in Prison*. New York: Plenum.

Woodrum, D., Brawer, M., Partin, A., Catalona, W., & Southwick, P. (1998). Interpretation of free prostate specific antigen clinical research studies for the detection of prostate cancer. *Journal of Urology*, 159, 5–12.

Woods, N. (1986). Socialization and social context: Influences on perimenstrual symptoms, disability, and menstrual attitudes. In V. Olesen & N. Woods (Eds.), *Culture, Society, and Menstruation*. Washington, DC: Hemisphere.

Woods, N., Lentz, M., Mitchell, E., Lee, K., Taylor, D., & Allen-Barash, N. (1987). Women's health: The menstrual cycle/premenstrual symptoms: Another look. *Public Health Reports*, 106–112.

Woodward, K., & Underwood, A. (1997). A house divided. *Newsweek*, July 14, 62–63.

Woog, D. (1997). Our parents. *The Advocate*, October 28, 24–31.

Woog, D. (1998). Adopting a family. *The Advocate*, January 20, 69–71.

Woolard, D., & Edwards, R. (1997). Female circumcision: An emerging concern in college healthcare. *Journal of American College Health*, 45, 230–232.

Wormith, J., Bradford, J., Pawlak, A., Borzecki, M., & Zohar, A. (1988). The assessment of deviant sexual arousal as a function of intelligence, instructional set and alcohol ingestion. *Canadian Journal of Psychiatry*, 33, 800–808.

Wray, M., & Newitz, A. (Eds.). (1996). *White Trash*. New York: Routledge.

Xiao, E., & Ferin, M. (1997). Stress-related disturbances of the menstrual cycle. *Finnish Medical Society DUODECIM, Annals of Medicine*, 29, 215–219.

Yaffe, E. (1994). The truth about women and sex. *Health*, July/August, 53–60.

Yaffe, K., Sawaya, G., Lieberburg, I., & Grady, D. (1998). Estrogen therapy in postmenopausal women. *Journal of the American Medical Association*, 279(9), 688–695.

Yalcin, O., Hassa, H., Ozalp, S., Yildirim, A., & Sener, T. (1998). Results of the anti-incontinence operations and Kegel exercises in patients with Type II anotomic stress incontinence. *Acta Obstetricia et Gynecologica Scandinavica*, 77, 341–346.

Yapko, M. (1994). *Suggestions of Abuse: True and False Memories of Childhood Sexual Trauma*. New York: Simon & Schuster.

Yates, A., & Wolman, W. (1991). Aphrodisiacs: Myth and reality. *Medical Aspects of Human Sexuality*, December, 58–64.

Yen, S., & Jaffe, R. (Eds.) (1991). *Reproductive Endocrinology*. Philadelphia: Saunders.

Yoon, T., Lee, C., Sung, H., Cha, K., & Cha, S. (1997). Fertility outcome after laparoscopic microsurgical tubal anastomosis. *Fertility and Sterility*, 67, 19–22.

Youth at Risk. (1997). *The Advocate*, October 14, 15.

Zabin, L., Hirsch, M., Smith, E., & Hardy, J. (1984). Adolescent sexual attitudes and behavior: Are they consistent? *Family Planning Perspectives*, 16, 181–185.

Zak, A., & McDonald, C. (1997). Satisfaction and trust in intimate relationships: Do lesbians and heterosexual women differ? *Psychological Reports*, 80, 904–906.

Zambrana, R., & Scrimshaw, S. (1997). Maternal psychosocial factors associated with substance use in Mexican-origin and African American low-income pregnant women. *Pediatric Nursing*, 23(3), 253–254.

Zamora-Hernandez, C., & Patterson, D. (1996). Homosexually active Latino men: Issues for social work practice. In J. Longres (Ed.), *Men of Color*. New York: Harrington Park Press.

Zangwill, W. (1996). Eye movement desensitization and reprocessing in the treatment of sexual disorders. Paper presented at the 21st Annual Meeting of the Society of Sex Therapy and Research, Miami, March.

Zaviacic, M., & Whipple, B. (1993). Update on the female prostate and the phenomenon of female ejaculation. *Journal of Sex Research*, 30, 148–151.

Zaviacic, M., Zaviacicova, A., Holoman, I., Molcan, J., Dolezalova, S., Holoman, K., Mikulecky, M., & Bradil, V. (1988). Concentrations of fructose in female ejaculate and urine: A comparative biochemical study. *Journal of Sex Research*, 24, 319–325.

Zelkowitz, P., & Milet, T. (1995). Screening for post-partum depression in a community sample. *Canadian Journal of Psychiatry,* 40, 80–85.

Zelnick, M., & Kantner, J. (1977). Sexual and contraceptive experiences of young unmarried women in the United States, 1976 and 1971. *Family Planning Perspectives,* 9, 55–71.

Zhou, J., Hofman, M., Gooren, L., & Swaab, D. (1995). A sex difference in the human brain and its relation to transsexuality. *Nature,* 378, 68–70.

Zhu, T., Korber, B., Nahmias, A., Hooper, E., Sharp, P., & Ho, D. (1998). An African HIV-1 sequence from 1959 and implications for the origin of the epidemic. *Nature,* 391, 594–597.

Ziebe, S., Andersen, A., Andersen, A., Mikkelsen, A., & Lindenberg, S. (1997). Results of intracytoplasmic sperm injection in relation to indication. *Acta Obstetricia et Gynecologica Scandinavica,* 76, 335–339.

Zilbergeld, B. (1978). *Male Sexuality: A Guide to Sexual Fulfillment.* Boston: Little, Brown.

Zilbergeld, B. (1992). *The New Male Sexuality.* New York: Bantam Books.

Zilbergeld, B., & Kilmann, P. (1984). The scope and effectiveness of sex therapy. *Psychotherapy,* 21, 319–326.

Zillmann, D. (1989). Effects of prolonged consumption of pornography. In D. Zillman & J. Bryant (Eds.), *Pornography: Research Advances and Policy Considerations.* Hillsdale, NJ: Erlbaum.

Zillmann, D., & Bryant, J. (1982). Pornography, sexual callousness, and the trivialization of rape. *Journal of Communication,* Autumn, 10–21.

Zillmann, D., & Bryant, J. (1988a). Effects of prolonged consumption of pornography on family values. *Journal of Family Issues,* 9, 518–544.

Zillmann, D., & Bryant, J. (1988b). Pornography's impact on sexual satisfaction. *Journal of Applied Social Psychology,* 18, 438–453.

Zini, D., Carani, C., Baldini, A., Ghizzani, A., & Marrama, P. (1990). Sexual behavior of men with isolated hypogonadotropic hypogonadism or prepubertal anterior panhypopituitarism. *Hormones and Behavior,* 24, 174–185.

Zoldbrod, A. (1993). *Men, Women and Infertility.* New York: Norton.

Zoucha-Jensen, J., & Coyne, A. (1993). The effects of resistance strategies on rape. *American Journal of Public Health,* 83, 1633–1634.

Zuger, B. (1984). Early effeminate behavior in boys: Outcomes and significance for homosexuality. *Journal of Nervous and Mental Disorders,* 172, 90–97.

Zuger, B. (1989). Homosexuality in families of boys with early effeminate behavior: An epidemiological study. *Archives of Sexual Behavior,* 18, 155–165.

Author Index

Subject Index

Page numbers in *italics* followed by a "*t*" indicate a table
Page numbers in **bold** font indicate an **illustration,** including photos, sketches, and graphs

Credits

PHOTO CREDITS

Images for Let's Talk About It, On the Edge, and Sexuality and Diversity boxes from PhotoDisc.

Page 1: Adobe Image Library/background: PhotoDisc; **5:** Jim Sulley/The Image Works; **7:** "Adam and Eve in the Garden," Painting by Lucas Cranach. The Elder. 1472–1553. BPA2#6109. Burstein Collection/Corbis-Bettmann; **8:** Kalacakra, Supreme Buddha, "Wheel of Time," in yab-yum with Visvamata, "Mother of All"/Werner Forman Archive/ Philip Goldman Collection, London/Art Resource, NY; **9:** A. K. G., Berlin/SuperStock, Inc.; **10:** North Wind Picture Archive; **11:** Corbis-Bettmann; **12, left:** J. Schreibman/Photo Researchers; **12, right:** D. Wells/The Image Works; **13:** Mark Antman/The Image Works; **15:** John K. Hillers/Corbis-Bettmann; **19:** Digital Stock/background: PhotoDisc; **25:** Michael Newman/PhotoEdit; **27:** Brian Smith/Stock, Boston; **30:** Wallace Kirkland/Life Magazine © 1948 Time Inc.; **31:** Bruce Powell; **32:** P. Watson/The Image Works; **33, left, center:** Courtesy of Farrall Instruments, Inc.; **33, right:** Courtesy SRS Self Regulation Systems, Inc.; **41:** PhotoDisc; **44:** Custom Medical Stock Photo; **52:** "Man-Woman/Boy-Girl," 1972/John Money & Enke Erhardt, Baltimore/Johns Hopkins University Press; **55, left:** Art Phaneuf; **55, right:** David Young-Wolff/PhotoEdit; **59, both:** Courtesy Dr. D. Laub, Gender Dysphoria Program, Dept. of Plastic & Reconstructive Surgery, Stanford University; **64, left:** Erika Stone/Photo Researchers; **64, right:** Spencer Grant/Photo Researchers; **65:** Tom Rosenthal/SuperStock, Inc.; **67:** Barbara Filet/Tony Stone Images; **75:** PhotoDisc; **77:** Dion Ogust/The Image Works; **78, all:** Tee Corinne; **79, both:** © Judy Chicago, 1979/photos by © Donald Woodman; **82:** Courtesy The National Committee for Struggle Against the Practice of Excision, Burkina Faso; **89:** Prof. P. Motta/Department of Anatomy/University "La Sapienza," Rome/ SPL/Photo Researchers; **94, left:** Biophoto Associates/Science Source/Photo Researchers; **94, left center:** SIU Biomed Com/Custom Medical Stock Photo; **94, right center, right:** Custom Medical Stock Photo; **95:** Francoise Sauze/SPL/Photo Researchers; **98:** Nancy Fried, "Portrait of Grief," 1994/Courtesy of DC Moore Gallery; **99, left:** Amelia Davis; **99, right:** James P. Anthony M.D., UCSF Stanford; **101:** Corbis-Bettmann; **115:** PhotoDisc; **122:** Joel Gordon; **123:** Biophoto Associates/Photo Researchers; **125:** David M. Phillips/Photo Researchers; **129:** "Faun with staff of Aesculapius," Erotic scene. Fresco from Pompeii/Museo Archeologico Nazionale, Naples, Italy/Erich Lessing/Art Resource, NY; **130, all:** Justine Hill; **141:** PhotoDisc; **148, (1):** Thomas S. England/Photo Researchers; **148, (2):** Alain Eurard/Photo Researchers; **148, (3):** M. Salaber/The Image Works; **148, (4):** Bill Bachmann/PhotoEdit; **148, (5):** Robert Fried/Stock Boston; **148, (6):** Francois Gohier/Photo Researchers; **150:** Deborah Egan-Chin/Impact Visuals; **152:** Courtesy Erox Corp.; **179:** PhotoDisc; **180:** Culver Pictures, Inc.; **182:** Frank Siteman/Stock Boston; **187:** Ken Fisher/Tony Stone Images; **189, both:** Globe Photos; **193:** Lee Page/Tony Stone Images; **198:** John Huet/Leo de Wys Inc.; **201:** Bob Daemmrich/Stock, Boston; **204:** Bill Aron/Tony Stone Images; **205:** Mark E. Gibson/Photo 20–20; **211:** PhotoDisc; **215:** SuperStock, Inc.; **217:** Esbin-Anderson/The Image Works; **221:** Bruce Ayres/Tony Stone Images; **222:** Zigy Kaluzny/Tony Stone Images; **228:** Lee F. Snyder/Photo Researchers; **232:** Bob Daemmrich/Stock Boston; **235, top:** David Hanover/Tony Stone Images; **235, bottom:** Bob Daemmrich/Stock, Boston; **236:** Robert Brenner/PhotoEdit; **241:** Digital Vision/background: PhotoDisc; **243:** Jacques Chenet/Newsweek Magazine; **254, left:** Mark Antman/The Image Works; **254, right:** Kathleen Olson; **257:** Robert Llewellyn/SuperStock, Inc.; **269:** Gazelle Technologies/background: PhotoDisc; **275:** Bob Strong/The Image Works; **283:** Lisa Rose/Globe Photos Inc.; **284:** Donna Lynn Brophy; **287:** L. Mark /UPI/Corbis-Bettmann; **291:** Esbin-Anderson/Photo 20–20; **292:** David Rentas/NYP/Globe Photos, Inc.; **295, top:** Mick Hicks; **295, bottom:** Michael Willhoite; **301:** PhotoDisc; **303:** UPI/Bettmann; **304;** Richard Lord/The Image Works; **305:** Planned Parenthood of Eastern Oklahoma and Western Arkansas, Inc.; **307:** Jan Staller; **312:** Tony Freeman/PhotoEdit; **314:** Corbis-Bettmann; **315, both:** Hattie Young/SPL/Photo Researchers, Inc.; **317:** Rick Gerharter/Impact Visuals; **318, 319, 320:** Joel Gordon; **321:** Gary Parker/SPL/Photo Researchers; **323:** Joel Gordon; **325, both, 326:** Joel Gordon; **328:** Office of Population Research, Princeton University; **339:** PhotoDisc; **341:** Owen Franken/Stock Boston; **342:** David Scharf/Perter Arnold, Inc.; **347:** Marty Katz; **354:** UPI/Bettmann; **358:** Junebug Clark/Photo Researchers; **360:** Howard Sochurek/The Stock Market; **361:** Annie Leibovitz/Contact Press Images; **362, both:** © Lennart Nilsson, "A Child Is Born," Dell Publishing Company; **363:** Julie Marcotte/Tony Stone Images; **366:** National Enquirer; **368:** Joseph Nettis/Stock Boston; **369, all:** Beth Elkin; **374:** Erika Stone/Photo Researchers; **379:** PhotoDisc; **381:** Michael Newman/PhotoEdit; **383:** Jo Browne/Mick Smee/Tony Stone Images; **384:** Fredrik D. Bodin/Stock Boston; **391:** Richard Hutchings/PhotoEdit; **396, 403:** Will & Deni McIntyre/Photo Researchers; **404, left:** D. Wray/The Image Works; **404, right:** David Young-Wolff/PhotoEdit; **405:** Myrleen Ferguson/PhotoEdit; **409:** PhotoDisc; **411:** Frank Siteman/ New England Stock Photo; **413:** Rafael Macia/Photo Researchers, Inc.; **418:** Bruce Ayers/Tony Stone Images; **426:** Bill Feig/AP/Wide World Photos, Inc.; **427:** Art Phaneuf/New England Stock Photo; **430:** Barbara Alper/Stock Boston; **431, top:** Bruce Ayers/Tony Stone Images; **431, bottom:** Ken Fisher/Tony Stone Images; **432, left:** Dennis Macdonald/Unicorn Stock Photos; **432, right:** Alain McLaughlin/Impact Visuals; **433:** Joel Gordon; **435:** Frank Siteman/Tony Stone Images; **439:** PhotoDisc; **444:** David W. Hamilton/The Image Bank; **447:** Judy Gelles/Stock Boston; **454:** Carol Ford/Tony Stone Images; **465:** PhotoDisc; **487:** PhotoDisc; **491:** Western Ophthalmic Hospital/Science Photo Library/Custom Medical Stock Photo; **492:** Courtesy STD Training Center, Harborview Medical Center, Seattle, Wash.;

496, left: Centers for Disease Control and Prevention; **496, right:** Science Visuals Unlimited/Visuals Unlimited; **497, left:** SIU Biomedical Communications/Photo Researchers, Inc.; **497, right:** Biophoto Associates/Photo Researchers, Inc.; **500, both:** Courtesy of Centers for Disease Control, Atlanta, Ga.; **505:** Science Visuals Unlimited/ Visuals Unlimited; **511:** E. Gray/SPL/Photo Researchers; **520:** Henny Abrams/UPI/Corbis-Bettmann; **523:** J. Scott Applewhite/AP/ Wide World Photos, Inc.; **525:** A. Reininger/Woodfin Camp & Associates; **527:** Stephen Dunn/Allsport; **528:** Felicia Martinez/PhotoEdit; **531:** Jacques M. Chenet/Woodfin Camp & Associates; **533, 535:** Michael Newman/PhotoEdit; **543:** Carl Miller Estate/ background: PhotoDisc; **546:** C. Gatewood/The Image Works; **547:** Grunnitus/ Monkmeyer; **548:** Liselott Nissen/Gamma Liaison; **554:** L. Steinmark/Custom Medical Stock Photo; **557:** Michael Dwyer/Stock, Boston; **563:** The Kobal Collection; **567:** Digital Stock/background: PhotoDisc; **573:** Bob Daemmrich/The Image Works; **579:** Spencer Grant/Stock, Boston; **594:** Mary Ellen Mark Library; **595:** Paul Conklin/PhotoEdit; **598:** Willie Hill/The Image Works; **607:** PhotoDisc; **609:** Helen Marcus/Photo Researchers; **610:** Myrleen Ferguson/PhotoEdit; **613:** Nita Winter/The Image Works; **618:** Joel Gordon.

OTHER CREDITS

Page 100: poem reprinted from *Collected Poems 1930–1933* by May Sarton, with the permission of W. W. Norton & Company, Inc. Copyright © 1974, 1980, 1984, 1988, 1993 by May Sarton. **288:** DOONESBURY © 1997 G. B. Trudeau. Reprinted with permission of Universal Press Syndicate. All rights reserved. **414:** CATHY © 1997 Universal Press Syndicate. Reprinted with permission. All rights reserved. **416:** BLISS by Stephen Hersh. © 1998 Univeral Press Syndicate. Reprinted with permission. All rights reserved. **428:** STONE SOUP by Jan Eliot. © 1997 Universal Press Syndicate. Reprinted with permission. All rights reserved. **468:** From *Love Skills* by L. DeVillers. Copyright © 1997 Linda DeVillers. Reprinted by permission of the author.